PHILIP'S
WORLD REFERENCE
ATLAS

PICTURE ACKNOWLEDGEMENTS:

Page 9 (centre left) – NASA: Olympus Mons, *The Universe Revealed*, page 47 (top).
Page 10 – Science Photo Library/National Optical Astronomy Observationaries: Sun's corona (blue) *The Universe Revealed*, page 21.
Page 12 – Royal Greenwich Observatory, Herstmonceaux: Sun maximum, *Joy of Knowledge Science and Technology* (c 1976 pic), page 221.
Page 13 – NASA: UV shot of prominences *Joy of Knowledge Science and Technology*, page 223 (c 1976).
Page 14 – NASA: Mercury from Mariner. *The Universe Revealed*, page 25.
Page 15 – NASA: Venus (Octopus Publishing Group Ltd).
Page 16 (centre) – NASA: *Joy of Knowledge Science and Technology*, page 192.
Page 16 (bottom) – NASA: *The Universe Revealed*, page 35.
Page 17 – NASA: *The Universe Revealed*, page 47 (bottom).
Page 18 – NASA: Jupiter and Io (Octopus Publishing Group Ltd).
Page 19 – NASA: Saturn (Octopus Publishing Group Ltd).
Page 20 – NASA/Science Photo Library: Uranus.
Page 21 (centre) – NASA: Triton, moon of Neptune. *The Universe Revealed*, page 74.
Page 21 (bottom) – Space Telescope Science Institute/NASA/Science Photo Library: Hubble computer images of Pluto hemispheres.
Page 23 – NASA: comet Hale-Bopp. *The Universe Revealed*, page 78.
Page 24 – NASA: asteroid Ida. *The Universe Revealed*, page 80.

The Solar System and the Physical Earth compiled by Richard Widdows.

PHILIP'S

WORLD REFERENCE

ATLAS

Bounty Books

This 2000 edition published
by Chancellor Press, an imprint of Bounty Books,
a division of Octopus Publishing Group Ltd,
2-4 Heron Quays, London E14 4JP.

Reprinted 2002, 2003, 2004

Cartography by Philips

ISBN 0-75370-906-6

A CIP catalogue record for this book is available from the British Library

Produced by Toppan (HK) Ltd
Printed in Hong Kong

Contents

The Solar System

The Physical Earth

The Map Section

INDEX

SOLAR SYSTEM: EVOLUTION

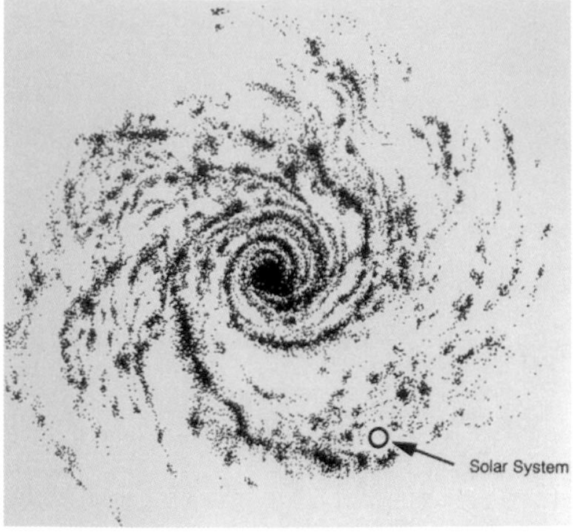

ABOVE Our Solar System is located in one of the home galaxy's spiral arms, a little under 28,000 light-years away from the galactic centre and orbiting around it in a period of about some 200 million years. There are at least 100 million other galaxies in the Universe.

ABOUT 15 BILLION years ago, time and space began with the most colossal explosion in cosmic history: the "Big Bang" that initiated the Universe. According to current theory, in the first millionth of a second of its existence it expanded from a dimensionless point of infinite mass and density into a fireball about 30 billion km (18.6 billion miles) across – and has been expanding at a phenomenal rate ever since.

It took almost a million years for the primal fireball to cool enough for atoms to form. They were mostly hydrogen, still the most abundant material in the Universe. But the new matter was not evenly distributed around the young Universe, and a few billion years later atoms in relatively dense regions began to cling together under the influence of gravity, forming distinct masses of gas separated by vast expanses of empty space.

At the beginning these first proto-galaxies were dark places – the Universe had cooled – but gravitational attraction continued its work, condensing matter into coherent lumps inside the galactic gas clouds. About three billion years later, some of these masses had contracted so much that internal pressure produced the high temperatures necessary to cause nuclear fusion: the first stars were born.

There were several generations of stars, each feeding on the wreckage of its extinct predecessors as well as the original galactic gas swirls. With each new generation, progressively larger atoms were forged in stellar furnaces and the galaxy's range of elements, once restricted to hydrogen, grew larger. About ten billion years after the Big Bang, a star formed on the outskirts of our galaxy with enough matter left over to create a retinue of planets. Some 4.6 billion years after that, a few planetary atoms had evolved into structures of complex molecules that lived, breathed and, eventually, pointed telescopes at the sky.

These early astronomers found that their Sun was just one of more than 100 billion stars in our home galaxy alone – the number of grains of rice it would take to fill a cathedral. Our galaxy, in turn, forms part of a local group of 25 or so similar structures, some much larger than ours. The most distant galaxy so far observed lies about 13.1 billion light-years away – and one light-year is some 9,461 million km (5,879 million miles).

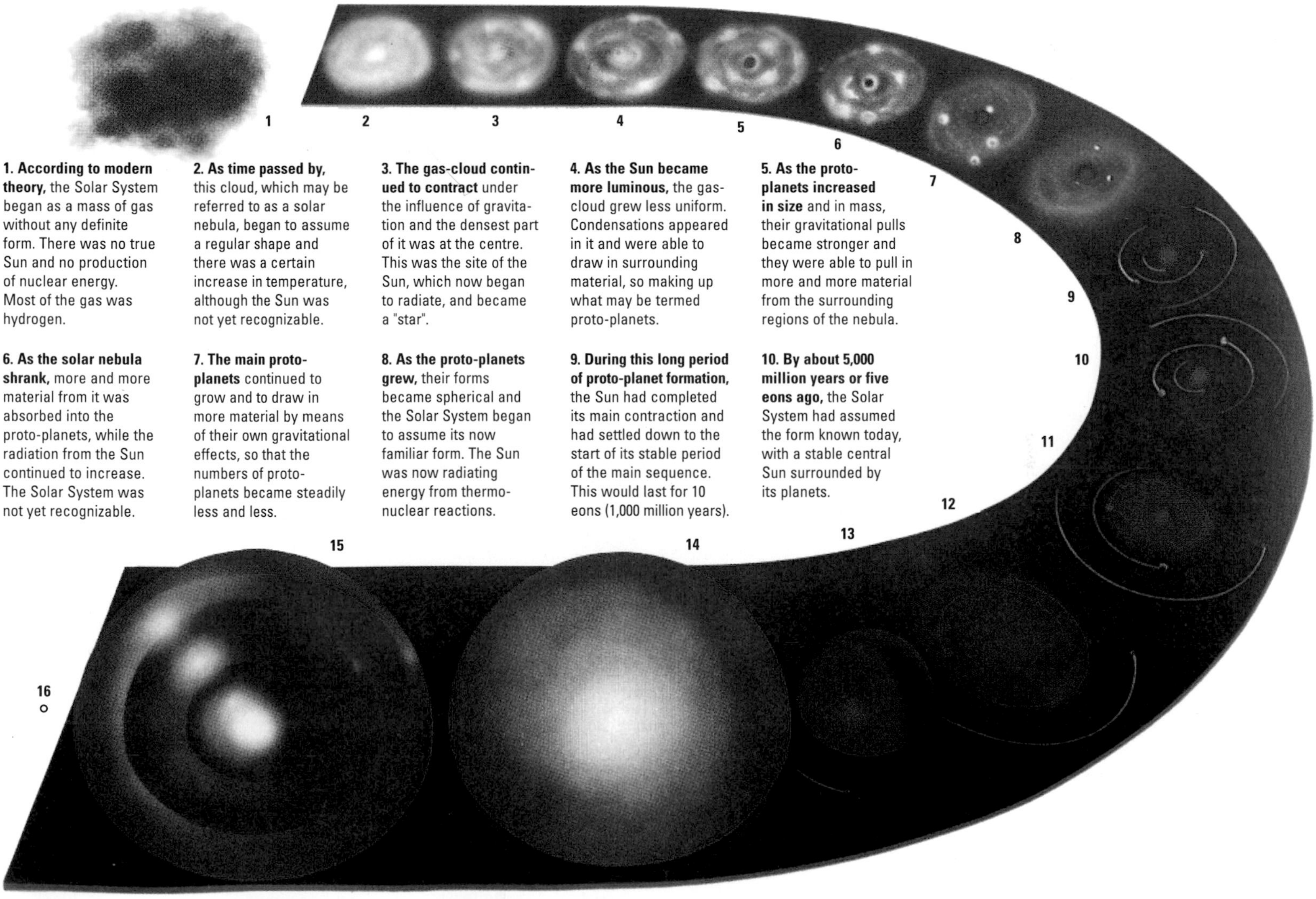

1. According to modern theory, the Solar System began as a mass of gas without any definite form. There was no true Sun and no production of nuclear energy. Most of the gas was hydrogen.

2. As time passed by, this cloud, which may be referred to as a solar nebula, began to assume a regular shape and there was a certain increase in temperature, although the Sun was not yet recognizable.

3. The gas-cloud continued to contract under the influence of gravitation and the densest part of it was at the centre. This was the site of the Sun, which now began to radiate, and became a "star".

4. As the Sun became more luminous, the gas-cloud grew less uniform. Condensations appeared in it and were able to draw in surrounding material, so making up what may be termed proto-planets.

5. As the proto-planets increased in size and in mass, their gravitational pulls became stronger and they were able to pull in more and more material from the surrounding regions of the nebula.

6. As the solar nebula shrank, more and more material from it was absorbed into the proto-planets, while the radiation from the Sun continued to increase. The Solar System was not yet recognizable.

7. The main proto-planets continued to grow and to draw in more material by means of their own gravitational effects, so that the numbers of proto-planets became steadily less and less.

8. As the proto-planets grew, their forms became spherical and the Solar System began to assume its now familiar form. The Sun was now radiating energy from thermonuclear reactions.

9. During this long period of proto-planet formation, the Sun had completed its main contraction and had settled down to the start of its stable period of the main sequence. This would last for 10 eons (1,000 million years).

10. By about 5,000 million years or five eons ago, the Solar System had assumed the form known today, with a stable central Sun surrounded by its planets.

11. In perhaps 5,000 million years from now the Sun will have exhausted its supply of available hydrogen and its structure will change. The core will shrink and the surface expand considerably, with a lower surface temperature.

12. The next stage of solar evolution will be expansion to the red giant stage, with luminosity increased by 100 times. The size of the globe will increase with the overall increase in energy output, and the inner planets will be destroyed.

13. With a further rise in core temperature, the Sun will begin to burn its helium, causing a rapid rise in temperature and increase in size. The Earth can hardly hope to survive this phase of evolution as the Sun expands to 50 times its size.

14. By now the Sun will be at its most unstable, with an intensely hot core and a rarefied atmosphere. The helium burning helium will give the so-called "helium flash". After a temporary contraction the Sun will be 400 times its present size.

15. Different kinds of reactions inside the Sun will lead to an even greater increase of core temperature. The system of planets will no longer exist in the form we know today, but the supply of nuclear energy will be almost exhausted.

16. When all the nuclear energy is used up, the Sun (as all stars eventually do) will collapse, very rapidly on the cosmic scale, into a small dense and very feeble white dwarf. It will continue to shine because it will still be contracting gravitationally.

Formation of the planets

The planets and larger satellites can be divided into two distinct classes. Mercury, Venus, Earth and Mars are all rocky "terrestrials", while Jupiter, Saturn, Uranus and Neptune are the large gaseous Jovian planets. Pluto can be classified, along with the large icy moons of the gas giants, as a third type. The terrestrial planets are closer to the Sun, have smaller masses and radii, and are more dense than the Jovian planets. These are big, low in density and have extensive satellite systems and rings.

The basic difference between the two families arose as a consequence of the temperature difference within the proto-solar cloud. This allowed icy material to condense well beyond the asteroid belt, producing cold proto-planets which effectively collected vast amounts of gas. The inner planets were too small and too hot to retain large amounts of original atmosphere in the face of the strong winds from the Sun.

Beyond the Solar System

Far beyond the gas giants, and outside the erratic orbit of Neptune, lie two regions of space that have intrigued astronomers since their discovery in the last half of the 20th century.

The Kuiper belt, named after one of the scientists who predicted its existence, is a disc of debris lying between about 35 and 100 astronomical units from the Sun; an astronomical unit (AU) is the average distance from the Earth to the Sun – 149,597,870km (92,958,350 miles). The first object was located there in 1992, so dim it was 10 million times fainter than the faintest stars seen by eye. It is now estimated that this belt may contain up to a billion comets, with a total mass just 1% of Earth.

Astronomers have now found over 60 Kuiper belt objects orbiting farther from the Sun than Neptune and Pluto, taking between 160 and 720 years to orbit the Sun. The smallest object seen is roughly 100km (60 miles) across, while the largest is 500 km (300 miles) in diameter, slightly smaller than Neptune's moon Triton. Indeed, Triton could be a body captured from the Kuiper belt, and Pluto and its moon Charon could be among its members.

Much further out in space is the Oort cloud, named in 1950 after the Dutch astronomer who identified it as a source of long-period comets. This is a rough sphere of rocky and icy debris left over from the solar nebula from which the Solar System formed. A vast size, it lies between 30,000 and 100,000AU from the Sun, a distance where gravity from passing stars could perurb it, sending comets in towards the Sun.

Future of the Solar System

We now know that dramatic consequences are in store for these terrestrial planets as a result of the dramatic changes that will happen to the Sun. Astronomers calculate that our star will be hot enough in 3 billion years to boil Earth's oceans away, leaving the planet a burned-out cinder, a dead and sterile place. Four billion years on, the Sun will balloon into a giant star, engulfing Mercury and becoming 2,000 times brighter than it is now. Its light will be intense enough to melt Earth's surface and turn the icy moons of the giant planets into globes of liquid.

Such events are in the almost inconceivably distant future, of course. For the present the Sun continues to provide us with an up-close laboratory of stellar astrophysics and evolution.

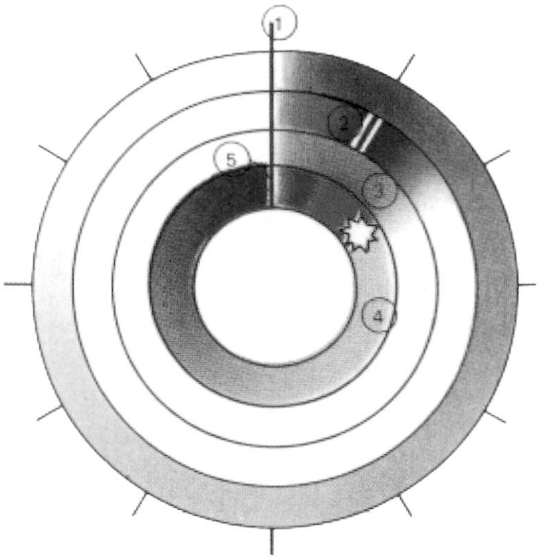

ABOVE The timescale of the Solar System can be represented on a 12-hour clock, tracing the lifespan of the Sun, the inner planets, Earth and the outer planets from the inner circle outwards. At the 12 o'clock position [1] the Solar System is created; after 4,000 million years, conditions on Earth are favourable for life [2]; as a red giant the Sun engulfs the inner planets [3] before collapsing as a white dwarf [4] and, possibly, end its long life as a brown dwarf [5].

BELOW The distance of the outermost planets – Jupiter, Saturn, Uranus, Neptune and Pluto – will save them from the Sun's helium burn, and each will continue its orbit. More precise predictions for their future are not possible.

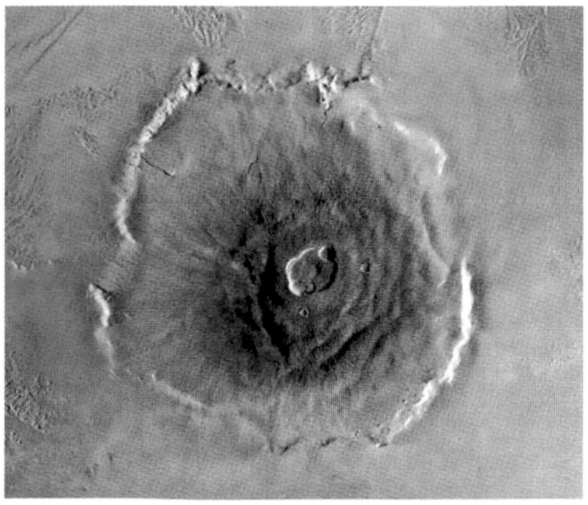

LEFT Olympus Mons is the largest volcano in the Solar System. Its peak rises to a staggering 27km (16.8 miles) above the mean surface level of Mars. More than three times as high as Earth's Mount Everest, it has a diameter of some 520km (323 miles). Olympus Mons is surrounded by a huge cliff up to 6km (3.7 miles) high, where the lower flanks appear to have fallen away in a gigantic landslide.

This collapse may have generated the peculiar blocky terrain of ridges separated by flat areas, the Olympus Mons aureole, that extends from the base of the cliff up to 1,000km (600 miles) from the volcano's summit. This contains a nested set of volcanic craters, the largest of them 80km (50 miles) across.

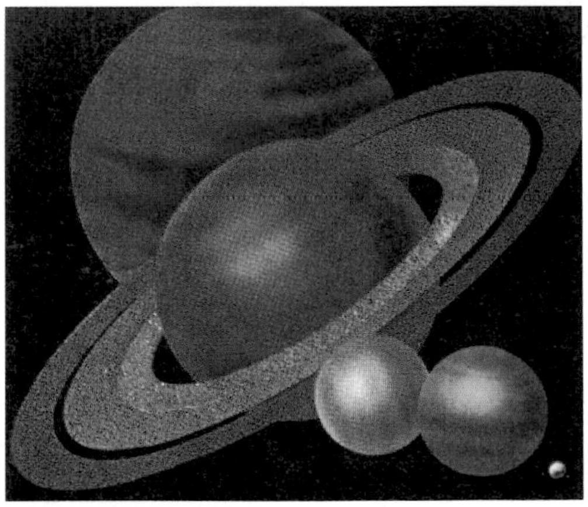

BELOW The lifespan of the Earth started from the material of the solar nebula [A] which at first had no regular form. When it reached its present size [B] the original hydrogen atmosphere had already been lost and replaced by a new one, caused by gases sent out from the interior. Life could begin and today the Earth is moving in a settled orbit round a stable star, so that it is habitable [C]. But this state of affairs will not persist indefinitely: long before the Sun enters the red giant stage, most scientists believe, the Earth will be overheated, the oceans will boil, and the atmosphere will be driven off [D]. Finally, the only planet known to have had life will be completely destroyed [E].

A

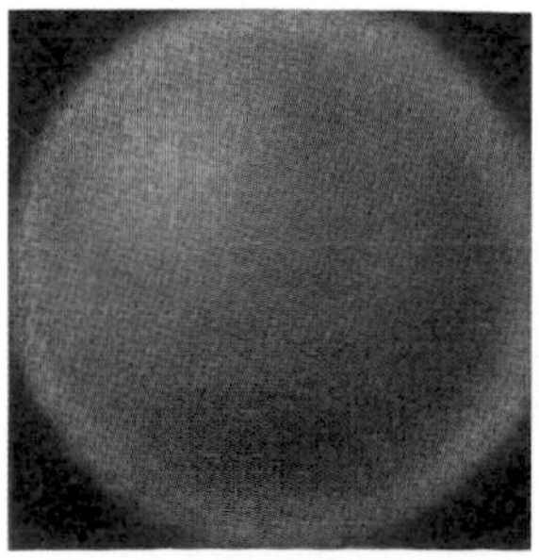

B

C

D

E

SOLAR SYSTEM: PROFILE

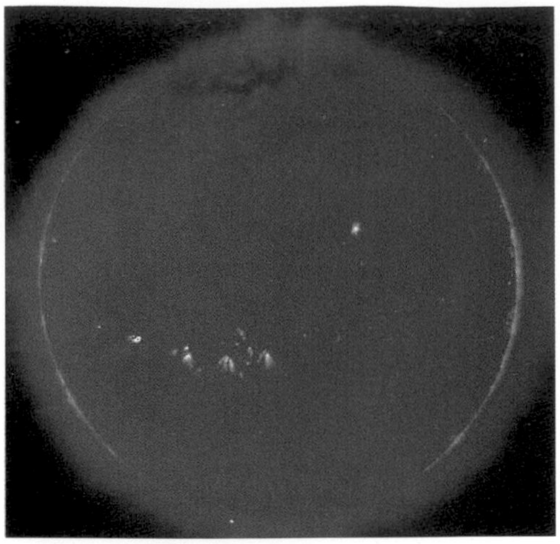

ABOVE The Sun's outer corona in ultraviolet light. The bright regions are areas of intense magnetism. This part of the corona is at a temperature of around 1,000,000°C. All the components of the Solar System are tethered by the immense gravitational pull of the Sun, the star whose thermonuclear furnaces provide them with virtually all their heat and light.

A TINY PART of one of the millions of galaxies (collections of stars) that make up the known Universe, the Solar System orbits at a mean distance of 29,700 light-years from the centre of our own galaxy, the "Milky Way". The present distance is 27,700 light-years, and it will reach the minimum distance of 27,600 in around 15 million years' time. It comprises one star, which we call the Sun, nine principal planets, and various bodies of lesser importance, including the satellites that attend some of the planets and a range of cosmic debris, notably asteroids, meteors and comets.

The system is entirely dependent on the Sun, which is by far the most massive body and the only one to be self-luminous: the remaining members of the Solar System shine by reflected sunlight and appear so brilliant in our skies that it is not always easy to remember that in universal terms they are nowhere near as large or important as they appear.

The inner planets

The planets are divided into two well-defined groups. First come the four relatively small planets of Mercury, Venus, Earth and Mars, with diameters ranging from 12,756km (7,926 miles) for Earth down to only 4,878km (3,031 miles) for Mercury. These planets have various factors in common. All, for example, have solid surfaces and are presumably made up of similar materials, although Earth and Mercury are more dense than Mars and Venus.

Although their orbits do not in general depart much from the circular, the paths of Mercury and Mars are considerably more eccentric than those of Earth and Venus. Mercury and Venus are known as the "inferior planets" because their orbits lie inside that of Earth; they show lunar-type phases from new to full and remain in the same region of the sky as the Sun. While Mercury and Venus are unattended by any satellites, Earth has one satellite (our familiar Moon) and Mars has two, Phobos and Deimos, both of which are very small and different in nature from the Moon.

Beyond Mars comes a wide gap, in which move thousands of small worlds known as the asteroids, or minor planets. Even Ceres, the largest, is only about 913km (567 miles) in diameter. This is much larger than was once thought, but still small by planetary standards. It is not therefore surprising that the asteroids remained hidden until relatively recent times, with Ceres discovered only in 1801. Just one of this new multitude, Vesta, is ever visible from Earth without the aid of a telescope.

The outer planets

Far beyond the main asteroid belt come the four giant planets of Jupiter, Saturn, Uranus and Neptune. These worlds are quite different from the terrestrial planets: they are fluid (that is, gas or liquid) rather than solid bodies with very dense atmospheres. Their masses are so great that they have been able to retain much of their original hydrogen; the escape velocity of Jupiter, for instance, is 60km (37 miles) per second as against

BELOW The planets of the Solar System shown to the same scale. On the right is a segment of the Sun [1]; from its surface rises a huge prominence [2]. Then come the inner planets: Mercury [3], Venus [4], Earth [5] with its Moon [6], and Mars [7]. Mars has two dwarf satellites Phobos [8] and Deimos [9], exaggerated here – if shown to the correct scale, they would be too small to be seen without a microscope. Then come the asteroids [10], of which even the largest is only about 913 (567 miles) in diameter. Beyond lie the giant planets: Jupiter [11], with its four largest satellites Io [12], Europa [13], Ganymede [14] and Callisto [15]; Saturn [16] with its retinue of satellites, of which the largest is Titan [17]; Uranus [18] with its many satellites; Neptune [19] with its large satellite Triton [20]; and finally misfit Pluto [21].

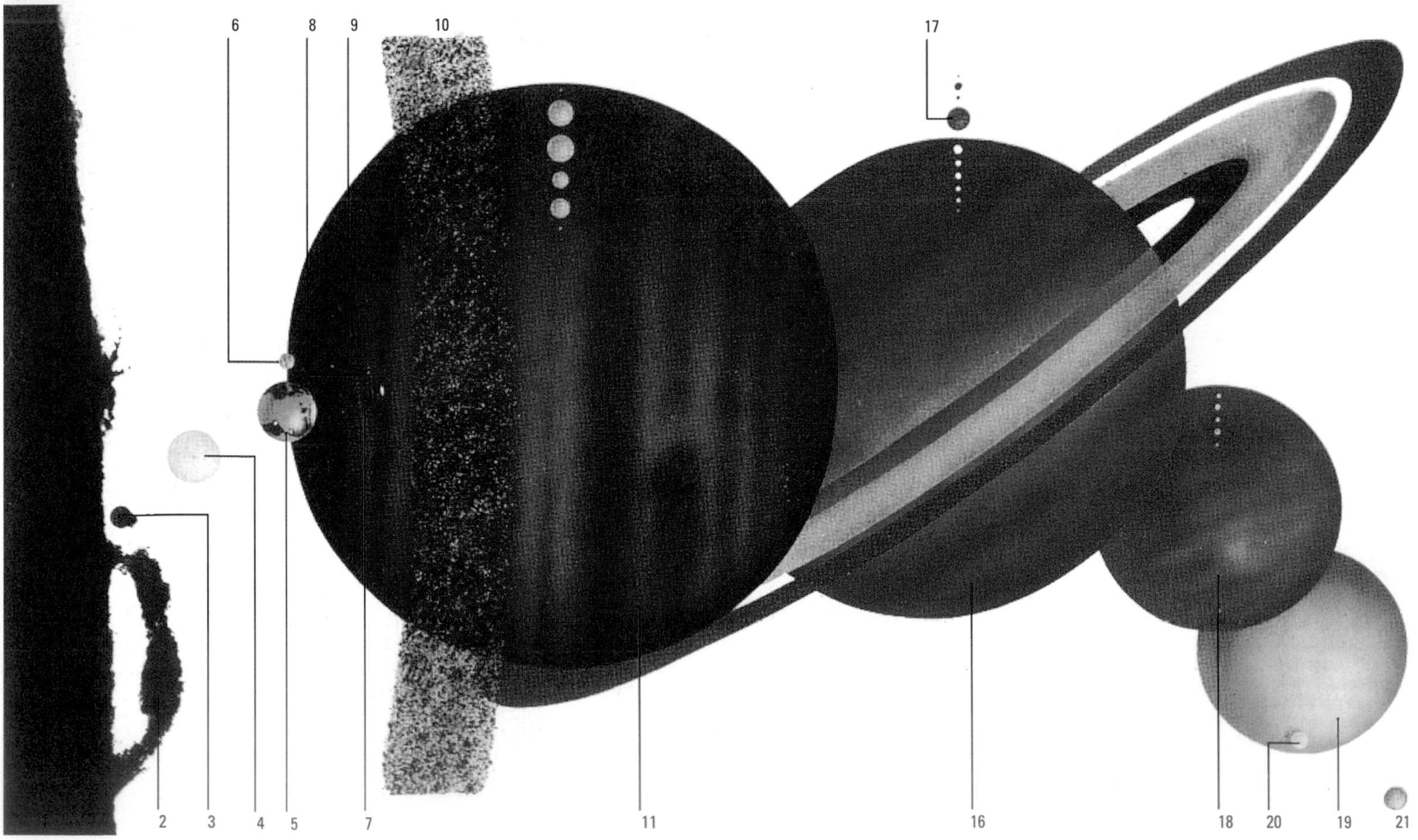

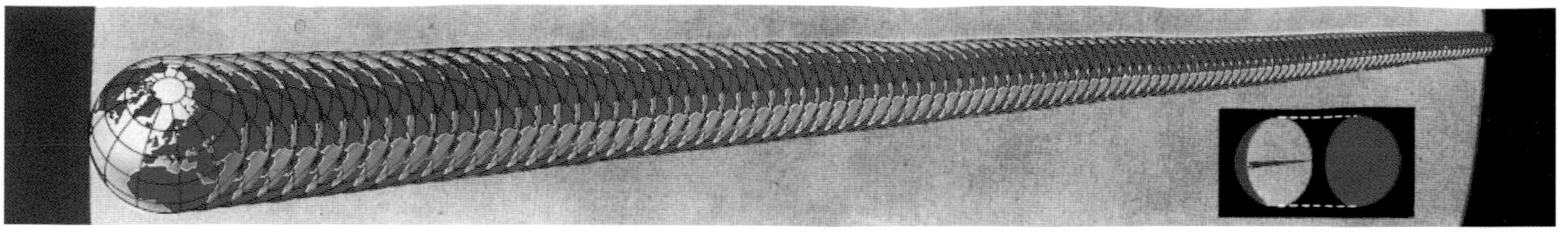

only 11.2km (7 miles) per second for Earth. Their mean distances from the Sun range from 778 million km (483 million miles) for Jupiter out to 4,497 million km (2,794 million miles) for Neptune. Conventional diagrams of the Solar System tend to be misleading as far as scale is concerned; it is tempting, for example, to assume that Saturn and Uranus are lying next to each other when in fact the distance of Uranus from the Earth's orbit is about twice that of Saturn.

The giant planets have various points in common, but differ markedly in detail. Their densities are comparatively low and the density of Saturn is actually less than that of water. Although Jupiter is seen solely by reflected sunlight, the planet does generate some heat of its own. However, even though the core temperature must be high, it is not nearly high enough for nuclear reactions to begin, so that Jupiter, though massive, cannot be compared to a star like the Sun.

Planetary discoveries

Five of the planets – Mercury, Venus, Mars, Jupiter and Saturn – have been known from ancient times, since all are prominent naked-eye objects. Uranus, just visible with the naked eye, was discovered fortuitously in 1781 by William Herschel and Neptune was added to the list of known planets in 1846 as a result of mathematical investigations carried out concerning movements of Uranus. All the giants are attended by satellites; Jupiter has 16 moons, Saturn 20, Uranus 15 and Neptune eight. Several of these are of planetary size, with diameters almost equal to Mercury's.

The outermost known planet is Pluto, discovered in 1930 by astronomers at the Lowell Observatory, Flagstaff, Arizona. It is far from another giant, being smaller than the Earth, and is usually ranked as a terrestrial-type planet, even though little is known about it.

Pluto's origin was long a mystery because of its size, rocky composition and highly unusual orbit. In recent years, however, it has become apparent that Pluto orbits within a "swarm" of tens of thousands of still smaller worlds orbiting well beyond the region of Neptune.

ABOVE Shown here in cross-section, the Sun has an equatorial diameter of 1,392,000km (865,000 miles), 109 times that of Earth. Despite the fact that its volume is more than a million times that of Earth, its mass is only 333,000 times greater because the density is lower: the mean specific gravity, on a scale where water = 1, is only 1.4.

LEFT While the Sun is the body on which the entire Solar System depends, and is more massive than all the planets combined, it is an ordinary main sequence star with a magnitude of +5 – small when compared with a giant star. The diagram shows the Sun alongside a segment of the red supergiant Betelgeuse, which marks Orion's right shoulder. Betelgeuse is of spectral class M2 – a very cool star – but has an absolute magnitude of –5.5. Its diameter is 300 to 400 times that of the Sun, and its globe is large enough to contain Earth's orbit. In 5 million years' time the Sun's life cycle will make it a modest red giant in its own right, and the solid inner planets of the Solar System will be destroyed by the heat and light that results from its phenomenal expansion.

RIGHT The ecosphere is the region around the Sun in which a planet can be at a suitable temperature for life as we conceive it to exist – assuming that the planet is of Earth "type". The inner yellow zone [1] is way too hot, and beyond the ecosphere [orange, 2], temperatures will become too low [3]. Earth [4] lies in the middle of the ecosphere, enjoying a near-perfect set of balanced conditions for life. Inhospitable Venus [5] orbits at the very inner limit and barren Mars [6] at the outer, but recent probes have proved that neither has the prerequisites for evolution. The best hope of finding life as we know it seems now to rest with a similar ecosphere – in one of the billions of other solar systems in the Universe.

THE SUN

ABOVE The "solar maximum" of 1958, pictured here, was the most energetic phase of the solar cycle ever recorded, and sunspots are clearly visible. Occurring where there is a local strengthening of the Sun's magnetic field, sunspots are regions in the photosphere that are cooler than their surroundings and therefore appear darker. Varying in size from 1,000 to 50,000km (600 to 30,000 miles) and occasionally up to 200,000km (125,000 miles), they comprise a dark central region called the umbra, and a grey outer region, the penumbra. Their duration varies from a few hours to several weeks, or months for the biggest ones.

The number of spots visible depends on the stage of the solar cycle. This is fairly regular and lasts around 11 years and is part of a longer 22-year solar cycle, but at the intervening "spot minima" the disc may remain featureless for several days or even weeks. The exact cause of sunspots is not fully understood – and no theory has been able to explain their disappearance between 1645 and 1715.

Sunspots are seen to move across the face of the Sun as it rotates. Most appear in pairs, but often complex groups emerge. They can be seen if you project an image of the Sun onto a piece of white paper or card.

THE SUN is a star, one of 100,000 million stars in our galaxy. In the Universe as a whole it is insignificant – classed as a yellow dwarf star with a spectrum of type G – but in our planetary system it is the all-important controlling body.

Immensely larger than Earth, the Sun has a diameter of 1,392,000km (865,000 miles). Though big enough to contain more than a million bodies the volume of Earth, its mass is only 1.99 x 10^{30} kg – approximately 333,000 times that of Earth. The reason why it is not as massive as might be expected is that its density is lower than that of an Earth-type planet. The mean value for the specific gravity is 1.409 (that is, 1.409 times an equal volume of water), but the Sun is not homogenous and density, pressure and temperature all increase rapidly beneath the brilliant outer surface towards the centre. It consists of about 70% hydrogen (by weight) and some 28% helium, with the remainder mostly oxygen and carbon.

The Sun lies some 32,000 light-years from the centre of our galaxy and takes approximately 200 million years to complete one journey round the galactic nucleus. It has an axial rotation period of 25.4 days at its equator, but because the Sun does not rotate in the manner of a solid body, this period is considerably longer near the solar poles.

In ordinary light the Sun appears to have a clear edge. This is because only a 500-km (300-mile) layer of its atmosphere, the photosphere, is at the correct temperature to emit light at visible wavelengths – a very small layer in comparison to the star's vast diameter.

The Sun's magnetic field

Overall, the Sun's magnetic field is roughly the same strength as Earth's, but the mechanism is entirely different. The Sun is not a solid body but a plasma created by heat removing the electrons of hydrogen atoms to leave negatively charged electrons and, possibly, positively charged ions. Magnetic fields can be created by the motion of electrically charged particles, and the Sun's turbulence and rotation create localized fields.

As the Sun rotates, the magnetic field lines get "trapped" and move around with the rotation. As the top layers bubble with convection the field lines become twisted up, and this squashing together increases the strength of the magnetic field in those areas. These intense pockets cause many of the phenomena seen on the Sun, notably sunspots.

Prominences and flares

The part of the solar atmosphere lying immediately above the photosphere is called the chromosphere ("colour sphere") because it has a characteristically reddish appearance. This is also the region of the large and brilliant prominences. To observe the prominences, instruments based on the principle of the spectroscope are used. There are two main types of prominences: eruptive and quiescent. Eruptive prominences are in violent motion and have been observed extending to more than 50,000km (312,500 miles) above the Sun's surface; quiescent prominences are much more stable and may hang in the chromosphere for days before breaking up. Both are most common near the peak of the solar cycle of activity.

Prominences are often associated with major spot-groups. Active groups also produce "flares", which are not usually visible, although a few have been seen. The flares are short-lived and emit streams of particles as well as short-wave radiation. These emissions have marked effects on Earth, producing magnetic storms or disturbances of Earth's magnetic field that affect radio communications and compasses. They also produce the beautiful solar lights or aurorae.

The solar wind

Less dense areas of the corona, the outer layer of the Sun, called coronal holes by astronomers, appear where the Sun's magnetic field opens to interplanetary space rather than looping back down. These areas are believed to be the major source of the solar wind, where charged particles, mainly protons and electrons, stream out into the interplanetary medium.

It is this emission that has a strong effect on the tails of comets, forcing them to point away from the Sun. Even when it reaches Earth, the wind's velocity exceeds 950km (590 miles) per second.

BELOW The structure of the Sun cannot be drawn to an accurate scale, and attempts at full cross-sections are misleading. In the core, about 400,000km (250,000 miles) across, continual nuclear transformations create energy and the temperature is perhaps 15 million °C (27 million °F). Further out in the solar interior, the radiative zone [1] , about 300,000km (200,000 miles) wide, diffuses radiation randomly, and temperatures range from 15 million to 1 million °C. In the convective layer [2] heat travels outward for 200,000km (125,000 miles) on convection currents, cooling from a million to 6,000°C (11,000°F). The relatively rarefied photosphere [3], the fairly well-defined "sphere of light" from which energy is radiated into space and where temperatures average 5,500°C (10,000°F), is surprisingly narrow – only 500km (300 miles) wide; because it is the layer of the Sun that radiates in visible wavelengths, this is the part of the Sun that we see, including the sunspots [4].

RIGHT Like all stars the Sun's energy is generated by nuclear reactions taking place under extreme conditions in the core. Here the Sun is continually converting four hydrogen atoms into one helium atom. The amount of energy produced in each individual reaction is tiny, but the Sun is converting 600,000 million kg (1,325,000 million lb) of hydrogen into helium every single second. The Sun's total power output, its luminosity, is 3.9 x 10^{26} watts (the equivalent of a million, million, million, million 100-watt light bulbs).

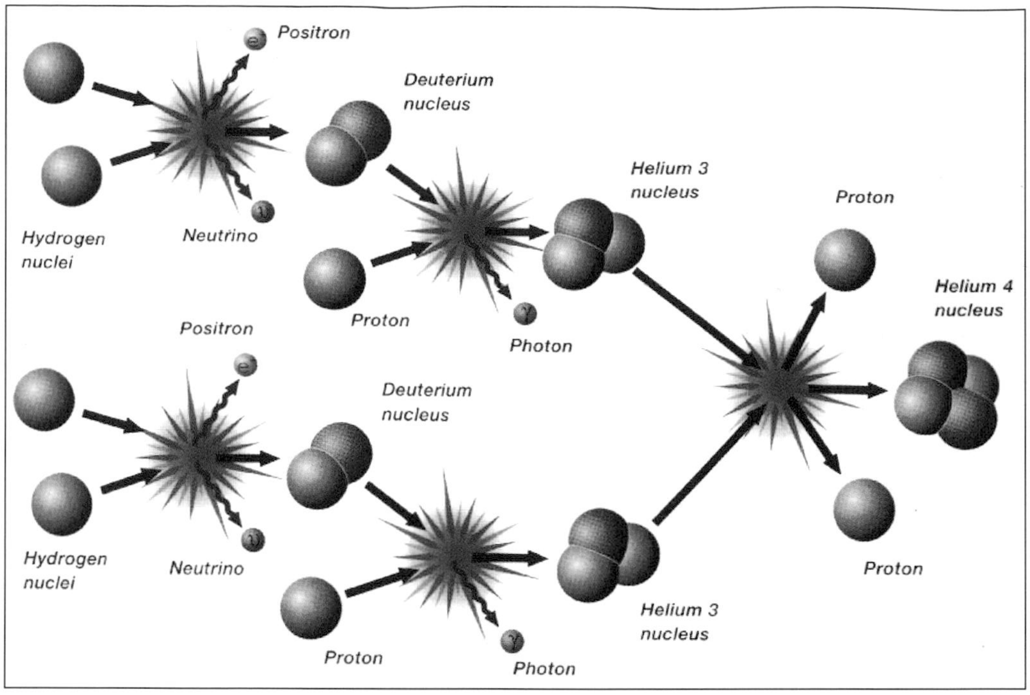
Positron
Deuterium nucleus
Helium 3 nucleus
Proton
Helium 4 nucleus
Hydrogen nuclei
Neutrino
Proton
Photon
Positron
Deuterium nucleus
Hydrogen nuclei
Neutrino
Proton
Photon
Helium 3 nucleus
Proton

Powerhouse of a star

It is a mistake to think of the Sun burning in the same way that a fire burns. A star made up entirely of coal, and radiating as fiercely as the Sun does, would not last long on the cosmic scale, and astronomers believe that the Sun is at least 5,000 million years old.

The source of solar energy is to be found in nuclear transformations. Hydrogen is the main constituent and near the core, where the temperatures and pressures are so extreme that the second lightest element, helium, is formed from hydrogen nuclei by nuclear fusion. It takes four hydrogen nuclei to make one nucleus of helium; in the process a little mass is lost, being converted into a large amount of energy. The energy produced keeps the Sun radiating: the loss of mass amounts to four million tonnes per second. This may seem significant, but it is negligible compared with the total mass of the Sun – and there is enough hydrogen available to keep the Sun shining in its present form for at least another 5,000 million years.

Eventually the hydrogen will start to become exhausted and the Sun will change its structure drastically. According to current theory, it will pass through a red giant stage, when it will have a luminosity at least 100 times as great as it does today. Once all its nuclear fuel has been used up, it will start to collapse into a small dense star of the type known as a white dwarf. Earth will have long gone: it will not survive the heat of the Sun's red giant stage, and along with the other inner planets will be totally destroyed.

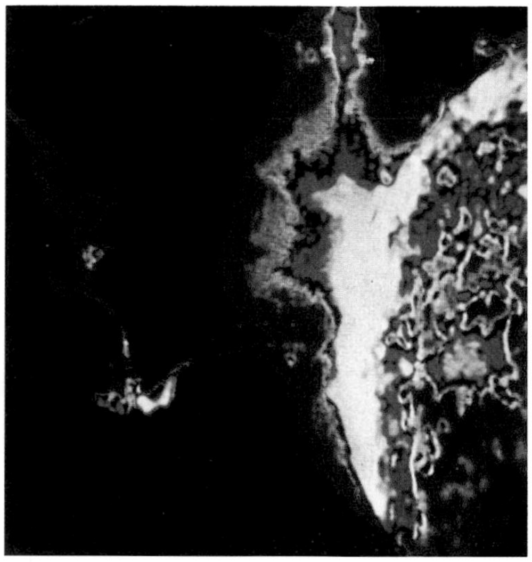

LEFT A solar prominence photographed by astronauts on board Skylab. In this extreme ultraviolet shot the colours are false: they represent the degree of radiation intensity from red, through yellow and blue, to purple and white, where the activity is most intense. This picture could only be taken with equipment carried above the layers of the Earth's atmosphere.

When viewed face-on against the bright photosphere, prominences are known as filaments. Narrow jets of gas called spicules can also be observed at the limb of the Sun. They move at around 20–30km (12–18 miles) a second from the lower chromosphere into the inner corona, and fall back or fade away after a few minutes. Flares, intense outpourings of energy, occur in complex sunspot groups, and can cause auroral activity and storms on Earth.

Above the photosphere lies the chromosphere [5], meaning "sphere of colour", and so-called because of its rosy tint when seen during a total solar eclipse. This is the region of flares and prominences [6], where the temperature rises from 6,000 to 50,000°C; temperature here is purely a measure of the speeds at which the atomic particles are moving and does not necessarily indicate extra "heat". In the chromosphere there are spicules [7], masses of high-temperature gases shooting up into the immensely rarefied corona [8], where temperatures can reach 1 million °C (1,800,000°F) – possibly due to the action of the Sun's magnetic field. Streamers [9] issue from the corona, which has no definite boundary and extends millions of kilometres out into space, eventually thinning to become the radiation we call the "solar wind". Together with the Sun's magnetic field, the solar wind dominates a vast indeterminate region of space called the heliosphere.

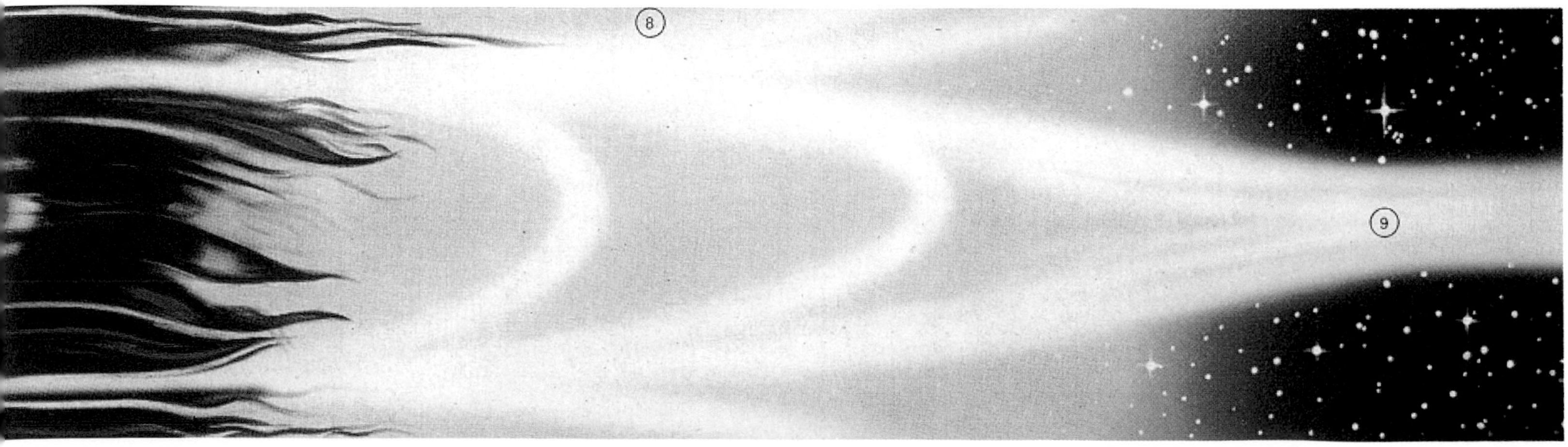
8
9

Mercury

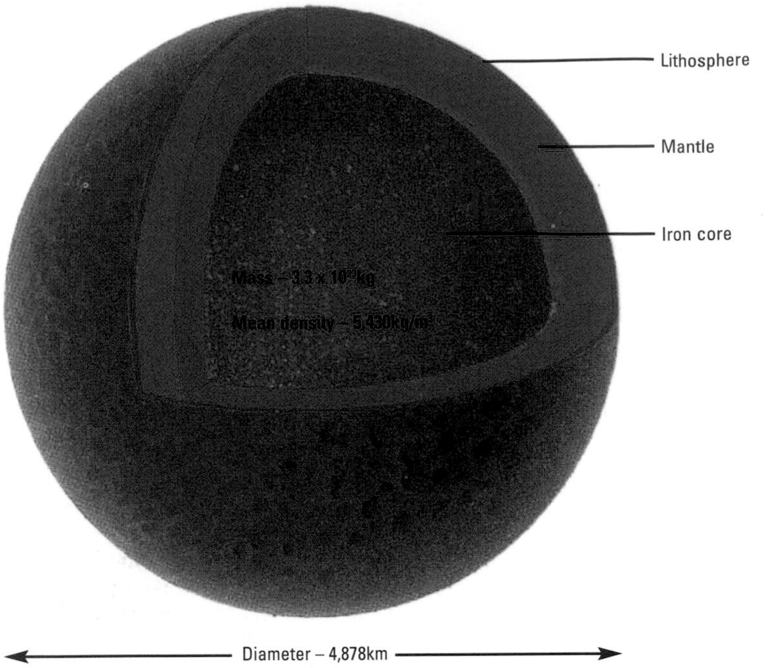
Lithosphere
Mantle
Iron core
Diameter – 4,878km

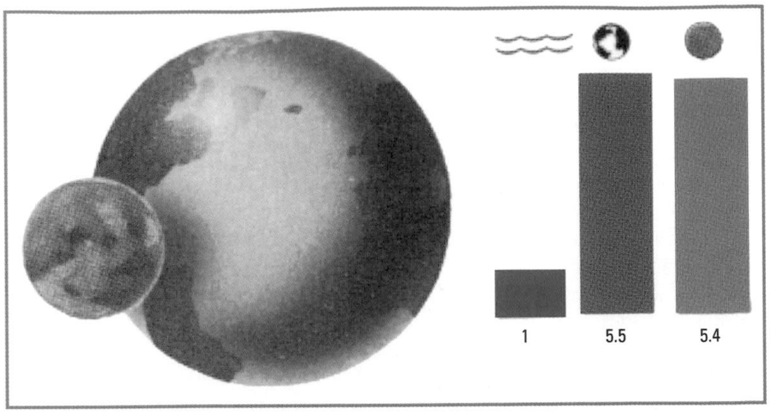
1
5.5
5.4

ABOVE **With a diameter of 4,878km (3,031miles), Mercury is dwarfed by Earth and is the Solar System's smallest planet after Pluto. However, its mean density (5.4 times that of water) is similar to Earth's. A small planet must contain a lot of iron to have so high a density, and astronomers believe that Mercury has twice as much, by proportion, as any other planet. Its iron core, thought to extend out to three-quarters of its entire radius, is surrounded by a mantle of rock and a thick hard crust. Mercury has a very tenuous and thin atmosphere, mostly hydrogen and helium, with a ground pressure only two-trillionths that of Earth.**

THE "FASTEST" planet, Mercury takes just 88 Earth days to orbit its massive close neighbour, the Sun – probably the reason the Romans named it after the fleet-footed messenger of the gods. It is the closest planet to the Sun and suffers the widest extremes of temperature: at noon, when the Sun is directly overhead, the temperature can soar to as high as 470°C (880°F), while during the long Mercurian night it can plunge to below –175°C (–283°F).

Mercury's orbit is elliptical: its aphelion (farthest point from the Sun) is 69,800,000km (43,400,000 miles), and its perihelion (closest point to the Sun) is 46,000,000km (28,600,000 miles).

The elusive planet

Although its existence has been known since the dawn of history, and it can appear to be brighter than the brightest star, Mercury is notoriously difficult to observe. This is because it is always too close to the Sun in the sky. The angle between Mercury and the Sun can never exceed 28°; this means that Mercury is lost in the Sun's glare because it sets no more than two hours after the Sun and rises no more than two hours before it. Once or twice a year, you may be able to see Mercury shining like a bright star close to the western horizon after sunset, or close to the eastern horizon before sunrise.

Mercury orbits the Sun in only 88 Earth days and undertakes the Earth at intervals of, on average, 115.88 days. On these occasions, Mercury lies between the Sun and Earth, but because of the tilt of its orbit (7°), usually passes above or below the Sun when viewed from Earth. Occasionally, when the alignment is right, Mercury passes directly in front of the Sun and can be seen as a small dot moving slowly across its face: such an event is called a transit. The alignments that allow transits of Mercury to take place occur only in the months of May or November, and the dates of early 21st-century transits are 7 May 2003, 8 November 2006, 9 May 2016, and 11 November 2019.

Until the 1960s, most astronomers believed that Mercury took exactly the same time to rotate on its axis as it took to orbit the Sun: one hemisphere would always face toward the Sun and constantly suffer its boiling heat, while the other was in constant darkness. However, radar measurements carried out since then have shown that this is not the case: Mercury rotates every 58.65 Earth days, precisely two-thirds of its orbital period or year.

Mercury's magnetic puzzle

The strength of the magnetic field at Mercury's surface is very low: only about 1% that of the Earth's. This is only just strong enough to deflect most of the incoming solar wind and to form a magnetosphere around the planet. Nevertheless, Mariner 10's discovery of the magnetic field came as a surprise to most astronomers. According to conventional theory, a planet can only sustain a magnetic field if it has an electrically conductive liquid interior and rotates rapidly on its axis.

Although Mercury has a large iron core, this should in theory have cooled and solidified by now because of the planet's small size. The presence of a magnetic field suggests that at least part of the deep interior must still be liquid – but even if this is the case, Mercury's slow rotation still makes the presence of a magnetic field puzzling.

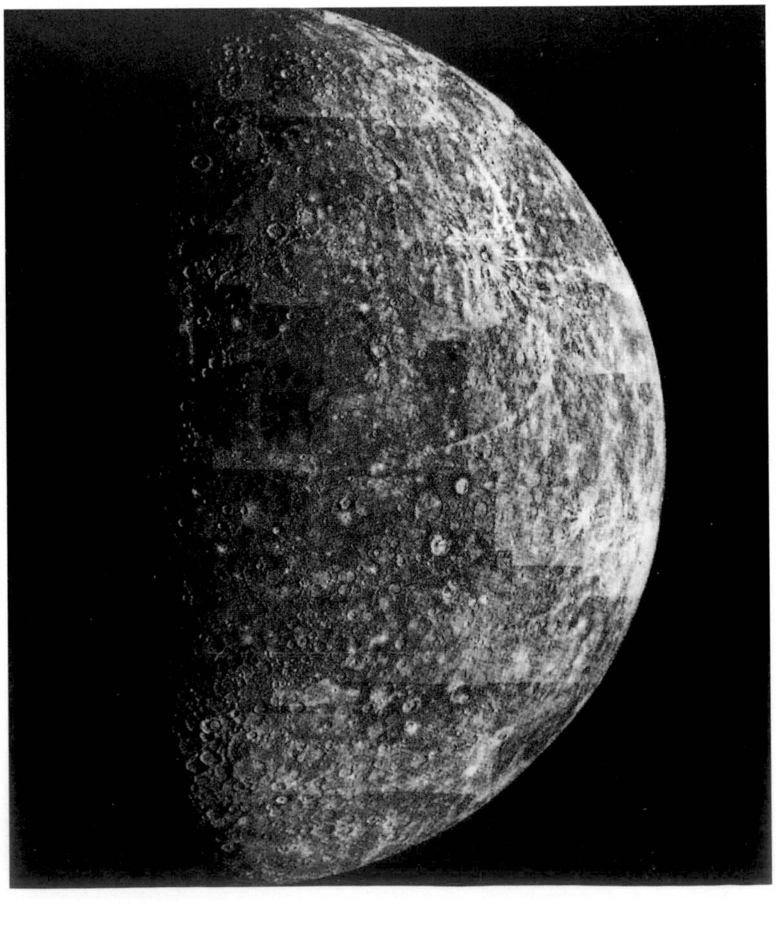

RIGHT **A mosaic of Mercury created from images taken by Mariner 10, the first two-planet probe, on its outward journey in March 1974. The craft flew within 703km (437 miles) of the planet, and in three encounters during 1974–75 took more than 12,000 images covering over half its surface. Images returned by Mariner 10 revealed that most of Mercury's surface is heavily cratered from impacts by meteorites, asteroids and comets, with many over 200km (125 miles) wide. As on the Moon, some are surrounded by lighter-coloured ejecta – material splashed out by the impacts. The largest feature pictured by the probe was the Caloris Basin, measuring 1,300km (800 miles) across.**

VENUS

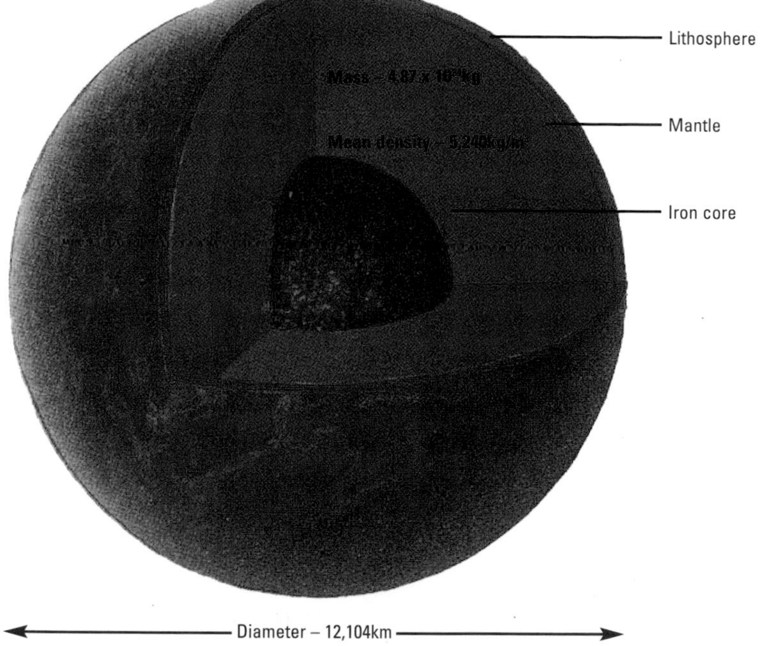
Lithosphere
Mantle
Iron core
Diameter – 12,104km

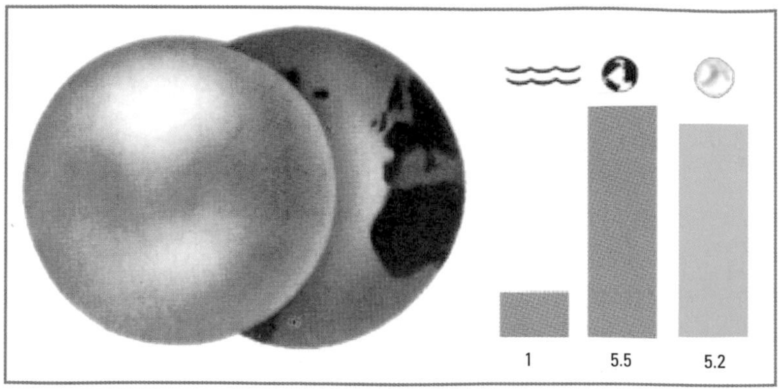
1
5.5
5.2

ABOVE The similarity in size, mass and density led to astronomers regarding Venus and Earth as "sister planets", formed at much the same time and part of space, but incredible heat and pressure make Venus an inhospitable body. Its internal structure, however, is probably much the same, with a nickel-iron core surrounded by a silicate mantle. The Mariner 2 probe of 1962 discovered it has a much weaker magnetic field than Earth, suggesting it may not have a liquid outer core. The lack of a strong magnetic field may also be a result of the planet's slow rotation of 243 days. Venus also rotates "backwards" (retrograde) as compared to other planets, but the reason remains a mystery.

TO THE NAKED EYE Venus is a splendid object and, as the evening and morning "star", is far brighter than any celestial object except the Sun and Moon – the reason it was named after the goddess of beauty. Telescopically, however, it has always been a disappointment, shrouded in cloud and, until very recently, mystery.

The orbit of Venus is nearer to circular than any planet, and the mean distance from the Sun – an average of 108,200,000km (67,200,000 miles) varies little. This revolution period is 224.7 Earth days, while the rotation takes 243 days.

Analysis of the sunlight reflected from the Venusian clouds revealed that the atmosphere was chiefly composed of carbon dioxide, and radio measurements suggested the surface was extremely hot. Space probe soundings of the atmosphere and surface later revealed a world completely devoid of all forms of water and confirmed searing surface temperatures that reached 480°C (895°F).

As if this were not enough, the dense atmosphere crushes down on the planet with a pressure 90 times that at the Earth's surface; a human being standing unprotected on the rock-strewn landscape of Venus would be simultaneously roasted, crushed and asphyxiated.

A dead planet

Liquid water is an essential ingredient for life as we know it, and without any water source it is extremely unlikely that any form of life ever existed on the planet. Venus's proximity to the Sun means that it probably started out with less water than the Earth – any water there would probably have existed as vapour rather than as liquid.

Even after the planets formed, the more intense solar radiation on Venus would have driven what little water remained from its atmosphere by breaking up the water molecules into their constituent parts of hydrogen and oxygen. Hydrogen is a very light gas and would have escaped off into space, while the oxygen would have been absorbed by the planet's surface. Even the rain of watery, icy comets that must have impacted Venus during its history was apparently insufficient to prevent the planet drying out.

The Venusian atmosphere

When the interiors of both Venus and Earth heated up from radioactivity, a great deal of volcanic activity occurred, causing vast amounts of carbon dioxide to be released. On Earth, the oceans dissolved some of this gas and carbonate rocks were formed, but on Venus there were no oceans and the carbon dioxide stayed in the atmosphere.

Findings in 1978 from the US Pioneer Venus 2 spacecraft, which parachuted through the atmosphere, established that Venus has sulphuric acid clouds concentrated in a layer at heights of 48–58km (30–36 miles) above the surface. Drops of the acid develop just like drops of water in our own clouds and when they are large enough, they fall as acid rain. However, this corrosive rain never reaches Venus' surface because the temperature difference, 13.3°C (56°F) at the top of the clouds and an oven-like 220°C (430°F) underneath them, causes them to evaporate at about 31km above the ground. Below this level, the Venera and Pioneer probes revealed that the atmosphere is remarkably clear, though the surface, subject to a fierce greenhouse effect, lies under a permanent overcast.

RIGHT This view of Venus was taken from 760,000km (450,000 miles) by Mariner 10's television cameras in 1974, en route to Mercury. Individual TV frames were computer-enhanced using invisible ultraviolet light: the blue appearance of the planet does not represent true colour, but is the result of darkroom processing of the images to enhance the UV markings on the clouds. It is this cloud cover that accounts for the brilliance of Venus. The picture is viewed with the predominant swirl at the South Pole. The clouds rotate 60 times faster than the planet's slow 243 days, taking only four days to go around Venus once, a rapid motion driven by the heating of the atmosphere by the nearby Sun.

EARTH

THE "THIRD rock from the Sun" is the heaviest of the stony planets and the most dense of all planets. The difference in size and mass between Earth and Venus is slight but Mars is much smaller

What makes Earth unique, however, is the fact that it has the perfect physical and chemical credentials for the evolution of life; slightly closer to the Sun, or slightly farther away, and life could not have developed. The "ecosphere", or the region in which solar radiation will produce tolerable conditions for terrestrial-type life, extends from just inside the orbit of Venus out to that of Mars. Until about 1960, it was thought that such life might exist throughout the region, but spaceprobes have shown both Venus and Mars to be incapable of creating and sustaining any form of life.

Approximately equal in density as well as size and mass, Venus absorbs about the same amount of solar energy as Earth because of the high reflecting power of its cloud. It was not until 1967, when the surface temperature of Venus was shown to register up to 480°C (895°F), that it was commonly accepted that advanced terrestrial life could develop only within a very limited zone.

Temperature depends not only on the distance of the planet from the Sun or the composition of its atmosphere; there is also the axial rotation period to be taken into account. Earth spins round once in approximately 24 hours, and the rotation period of Mars is only 37 minutes longer, but Mercury and Venus are very different – the periods are 58.7 days and 243 days respectively, leading to very peculiar "calendars". Were Earth a slow spinner, the climatic conditions would be both unfamiliar and hostile.

An atmosphere must not only enable living creatures to breathe, but also protect the planet from lethal short-wave radiations from space. There is no danger on the surface of Earth because the radiations are blocked out by layers in the upper atmosphere; had Earth been more massive, it might have been able to retain at least some of its original hydrogen (as the giants Jupiter and Saturn have done) and the resulting atmosphere might have been unsuitable for life.

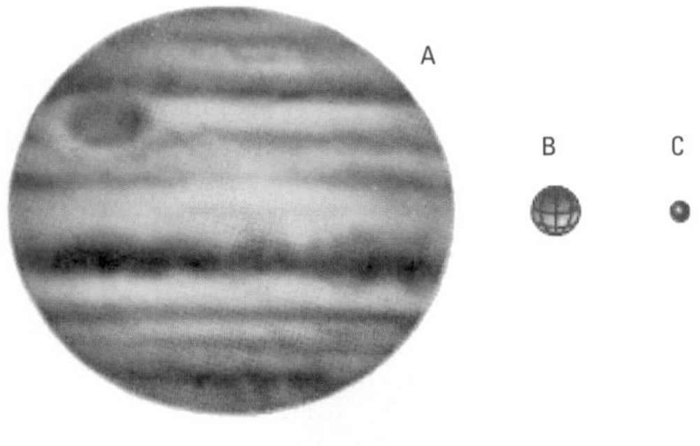

ABOVE The relative sizes of Jupiter [A], Earth [B] and Mercury [C]. Jupiter is the largest planet, Mercury the smallest (excluding the extraordinary misfit Pluto), and while Earth is intermediate in size, it is more nearly comparable with Mercury in the context of the Solar System. Earth is the largest of the so-called terrestrial planets – Mercury, Venus, Earth, Mars, Pluto – but far inferior in size even to the smallest of the four "gas giants", Neptune.

ABOVE Seen from space, Earth will show phases – just as the Moon does to us. These five photographs shown were taken from a satellite over a period of 12 hours.

RIGHT Earth as captured above the Moon's surface from an Apollo spacecraft. The contrast between the barren landscape of the Moon and the near-perfect balance of land, cloud and ocean on Earth is startling. Our planet is the only home of known life in the Solar System, though spheres in the same section of their ecospheres may well exist in the Universe.

Earth is unique in having a surface that is largely covered with water; thus although it is the largest of the four inner planets its land surface is much less than that of Venus and equal to that of Mars. There can be no oceans or even lakes on Mars, because of the low atmospheric pressure, and none on the Moon or Mercury, which are to all intents and purposes without atmosphere. On Venus the surface temperature is certainly too high for liquid water to exist, so that the old, intriguing picture of a "carboniferous" Venus, with luxuriant vegetation flourishing in a swampy and moist environment, has had to be given up.

Because Earth is so exceptional, it has been suggested that it was formed in a manner different from that of the other planets, but this is almost certainly not the case. The age of Earth, as measured by radioactive methods, is approximately 4,600 million years (4.6 eons) and studies of the lunar rocks show that the age of the Moon is the same; there is no reason to doubt that the Earth and all other members of the Solar System originated by the same process, and at about the same time, from the primeval solar nebula.

[For detailed profile of Earth, see pages 28–29; for Earth statistics, see page 54]

MARS

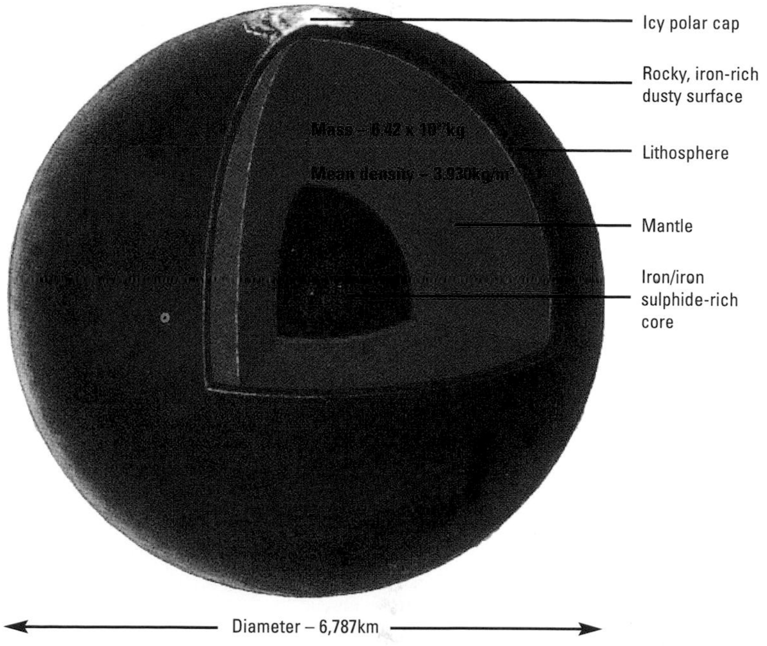
Icy polar cap
Rocky, iron-rich dusty surface
Lithosphere
Mantle
Iron/iron sulphide-rich core
Diameter – 6,787km

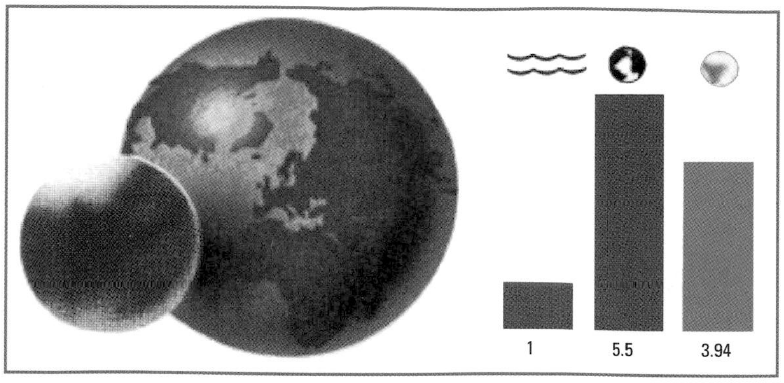
1
5.5
3.94

ABOVE **The surface area of Mars is 28% that of Earth. Its diameter of 6,787km (4,217 miles) is a just over half that of Earth, and about twice that of the Moon. It has only a tenth of Earth's mass. Observations suggest that Mars contains an iron-rich core, about 1,700km (1,050 miles) in diameter. The low density of Mars compared to the other terrestrial planets hints that this core may also contain a significant amount of sulphur. Apparently, this core is not convecting enough to create as strong a magnetic field as Earth: indeed, it was not until 1997 that Mars Global Surveyor detected its weak and patchy magnetic field.**

LIKE EARTH, Mars experiences seasons. Varying between 207 million km and 249 million km (129 and 158 million) miles from the Sun, its orbit is not circular and it is much closer to the Sun during the southern summer than in the northern summer, so that southern Martian summers are warmer than northern ones. But because the planet moves faster when it is closer to the Sun they are shorter and southern winters longer and colder than those in the north; one result is that the southern residual cap retains some frozen carbon dioxide (which melts at a lower temperature) as well as water.

In the late 1960s the Mariner 4, 6 and 7 spacecraft confirmed that the surface resides under only a thin atmosphere of carbon dioxide, with a pressure of only one hundredth of that at the Earth's surface at most, and in places even lower. They also revealed that Mars is cold, with mean annual temperatures ranging from –58°C (–72°F) at the equator to –123°C (–189°F) at the poles. At these temperatures and low pressures liquid water cannot currently exist on the Martian surface, although the Mariner and subsequent Viking pictures revealed evidence for the ancient action of flowing water.

RIGHT **A mosaic image of the Schiaparelli hemisphere created from images taken by the Viking orbiter in 1980. Mars was once considered the likeliest of planets to share Earth's cargo of life, the seasonal expansion of dark patches strongly suggesting vegetation and the icecaps indicating the presence of water.**

However, close inspection by spacecraft brought disappointment: some combination of chemical reactions, erosion and dark dust deposited by strong winds account for the "vegetation", and the "icecaps", though comprising a permanent layer of water ice, are covered from autumn to spring by a cover of carbon dioxide frost. Whatever oxygen the planet once possessed is now locked up in the iron-bearing rock that covers its cratered surface and gives it its characteristic red colour. The large crater near the centre is Schiaparelli, about 500km (370 miles) in diameter.

Mars is smaller and less "massive" than Earth or Venus, and so has a lower surface gravity and cannot hold on to a dense atmosphere. Mars' lower volume means that it could not generate and retain the same amount of internal heat as Venus or Earth, and does not maintain the same level of volcanic activity.

The core is surrounded by a molten rocky mantle denser and perhaps three times as rich in iron oxide as that of the Earth, overlain by a thin crust. The lack of plate tectonics and absence of current volcanic activity implies this mantle is also non-convecting – though one massive feature, the 4,500-km (2,800-mile) long Valles Marineris, may be a fracture in the crust caused by internal stresses.

Mars has two small moons, Phobos and Deimos, two potato-shape asteroids that were once captured by the planet's gravity.

JUPITER

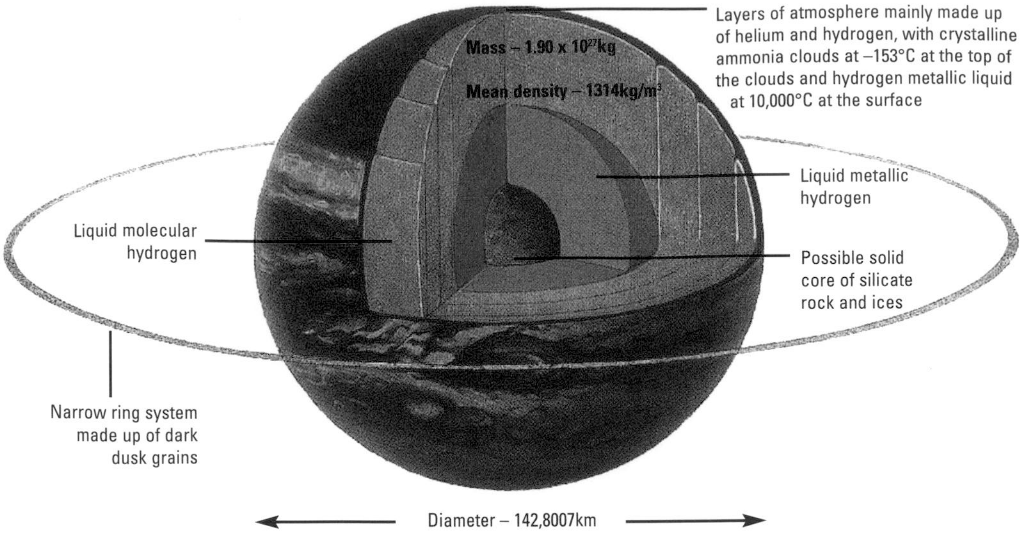

Mass – 1.90 x 10^27kg
Mean density – 1314kg/m^3
Layers of atmosphere mainly made up of helium and hydrogen, with crystalline ammonia clouds at –153°C at the top of the clouds and hydrogen metallic liquid at 10,000°C at the surface
Liquid metallic hydrogen
Liquid molecular hydrogen
Possible solid core of silicate rock and ices
Narrow ring system made up of dark dusk grains
Diameter – 142,8007km

Jupiter's mean density is only 1.3 times that of water *(right)*, but the outer layers are tenuous and the core is far denser. The Earth's axis is tilted at an angle of 23½° from the perpendicular to the plane of orbit, but Jupiter's is only just over 3° *(below)*.

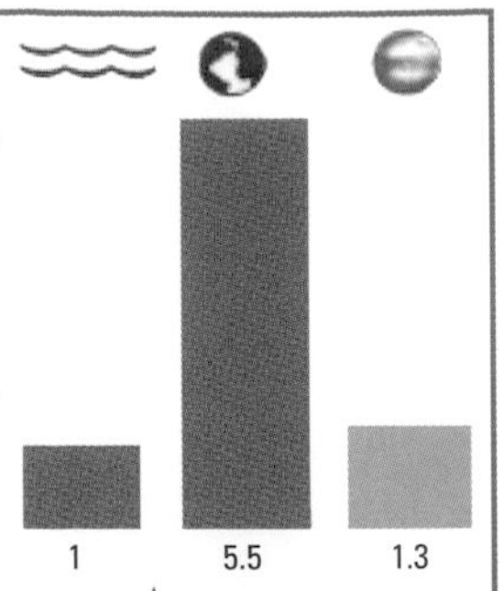

1
5.5
1.3

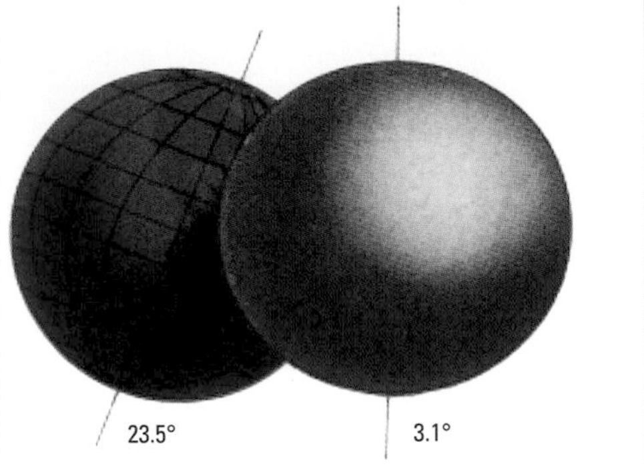

23.5°
3.1°

FAR BEYOND the main asteroid belt, at a mean distance of 778,300,000km (483,600,000 miles) from the Sun, lies Jupiter, the largest of the planets. This huge globe could swallow up 1,300 bodies the volume of Earth but its mass – despite being nearly three times as much as the other planets combined – is only 318 times that Earth because Jupiter is much less dense.

The planet is mostly gas, under intense pressure in its lower atmosphere above a core of fiercely compressed hydrogen and helium. The upper layers form strikingly coloured rotating belts, outward signs of the intense storms created by its rapid rotation of less than ten hours. This also means that the equator tends to bulge, and like Saturn the planet is clearly flattened at the poles: Jupiter's equatorial diameter is 143,000km (89,000 miles), whereas the polar diameter is less than 135,000km (84,000 miles).

When viewing the planet, you can only see the outermost part of its very deep atmosphere, which has several layers of cloud of different composition and colour. Jupiter rotates so fast that it spins the clouds into bands in which various spots, waves and other dynamic weather systems occur. The banded patterns in Jupiter's clouds arise because of the existence of convection cells in the atmosphere. The giant spots between, and sometimes within, the bands are giant eddies, or rotating masses of cloudy air, similar to enormous versions of our earthly hurricanes. Other weather systems, often of contrasting colour, appear embedded in the layers.

The Great Red Spot

While most of Jupiter's spots are short-lived, the Great Red Spot, by far the largest, is the notable exception. Under observation for over 300 years, it sometimes disappears but always returns, and has been prominent this time around since the mid-1960s. Occurring at a latitude of around 23° south, it is a huge, complex, cloudy vortex – variable in size but always far larger than the diameter of Earth – rotating in an anti-clockwise direction.

The "GRS" is believed to be a two-dimensional vortex which spirals outwards away from areas of high pressure, so although it appears like a hurricane it is a high- rather than low-pressure phenomenon. The reasons for its constant position and its characteristic colour, however, remain unclear.

Jupiter's rings

Recent investigations by spaceprobes have shown an orbiting ring system and discovered several previously unknown moons, and Jupiter has at least 16. The ring system is composed of three major components. The main ring is some 7,000km (4,350 miles) wide and has an average radius of about 126,000km (80,000 miles). At its inner edge this merges into the halo, a faint doughnut-shaped ring about 20,000km (12,400 miles) across, which extends over half the distance to the planet itself. Just outside the main ring is a faint gossamer ring made of fine material, extending out past the orbit of the innermost satellite Amalthea. These rings are not only more tenuous than Saturn's but are also darker, probably comprising dust rather than ice.

The magnetic field

Jupiter has a strong magnetic field, caused by the planet still cooling from its time of formation and constantly collapsing in on itself under its own gravitational pull. This gives off heat, producing dynamic convection movements in the fluid metallic interior. Coupled with the spin of Jupiter's rapid rotation, it produces an extensive magnetic field about 20,000 times stronger than that of the Earth – one which constantly alters size and shape in response to changes in the solar wind.

LEFT Voyager 1 took this photo of Jupiter and the innermost of its four Galilean satellites, Io, in 1979, with Io about 420,600km (260,000 miles) above Jupiter's Great Red Spot. The picture was taken about 20 million km (12,400,000 miles) from the planet. Slightly larger than our Moon, Io is the densest large object in the outer Solar System and most volcanically active, spewing material up to 300km (200 miles) into the air; in 1996, when Galileo detected an iron core and magnetic field, it found the moon's surface features had changed radically since the satellite was imaged by Voyager just 17 years before.

Jupiter's main moons are group-named after Galileo because it was his identification of their orbiting the planet that eventually led him to support Copernicus's revolutionary views that Earth revolved round the Sun. They are Europa, Callisto and Ganymede, the largest satellite in the Solar System and bigger than Mercury and Pluto, orbiting Jupiter at a distance of just over 1 million km (620,000 miles).

SATURN

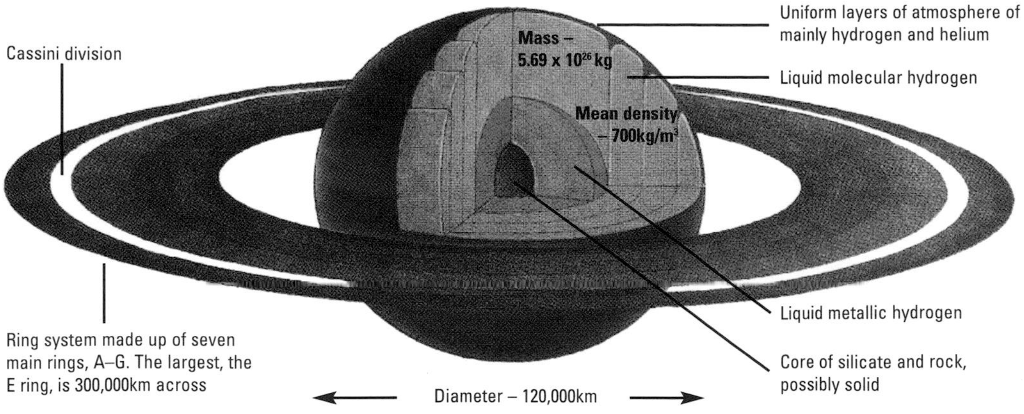

Cassini division
Mass – 5.69 x 10[26] kg
Mean density – 700kg/m[3]
Uniform layers of atmosphere of mainly hydrogen and helium
Liquid molecular hydrogen
Liquid metallic hydrogen
Core of silicate and rock, possibly solid
Ring system made up of seven main rings, A–G. The largest, the E ring, is 300,000km across
Diameter – 120,000km

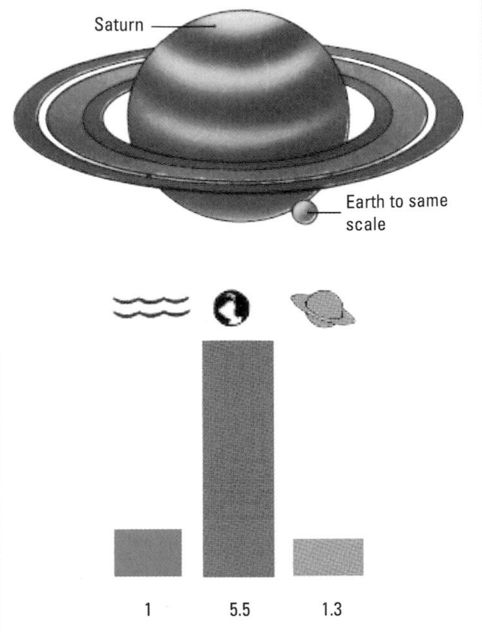

Saturn
Earth to same scale
1
5.5
1.3

ABOVE Though not as large as Jupiter, Saturn's globe is of impressive size – its volume is 1,000 times that of Earth. The mean density of Saturn is only 0.7 that of water, far less than any other planet, and it would float if it were dropped into an ocean. The low density is due to the preponderance of hydrogen.

OUTERMOST OF the planets known to ancient man and named after the Roman god of agriculture, Saturn lies at a mean distance of 1,427 million km (88 million miles) from the Sun and has a revolution period of 29.46 years. The second largest planet in the Solar System, its polar diameter of 120,000km (75,000 miles) is considerably less than its equatorial diameter.

Astronomers believe the temperatures in the core of Saturn exceed 11,700°C (21,000°F), and the atmosphere must be deeply convective since this is the only plausible way to transport the interior heat to levels where it can be radiated to space. Like its neighbours Jupiter and Uranus, Saturn radiates more energy into space than it receives from the Sun. The atmosphere of Saturn broadly resembles that of Jupiter: it has 80–90% hydrogen, 10–20% helium and less than 1% traces of other gases, including methane and ammonia detected by Earth-based and Voyager spectroscopy. Because the cloud layers are cooler than those of Jupiter, they tend to be thicker and more uniform in shape, forming deeper in the atmosphere. Saturn's distinctive hazy yellow hue, plus the deeper orange-yellow of Titan, largest of its 18 moons, are thought to be caused by deep haze layers of condensed hydrocarbons.

Saturn's magnetosphere is smaller than that of Jupiter, though it still extends well beyond the orbits of the outer moons, while the field is about 30 times weaker than that of its huge neighbour.

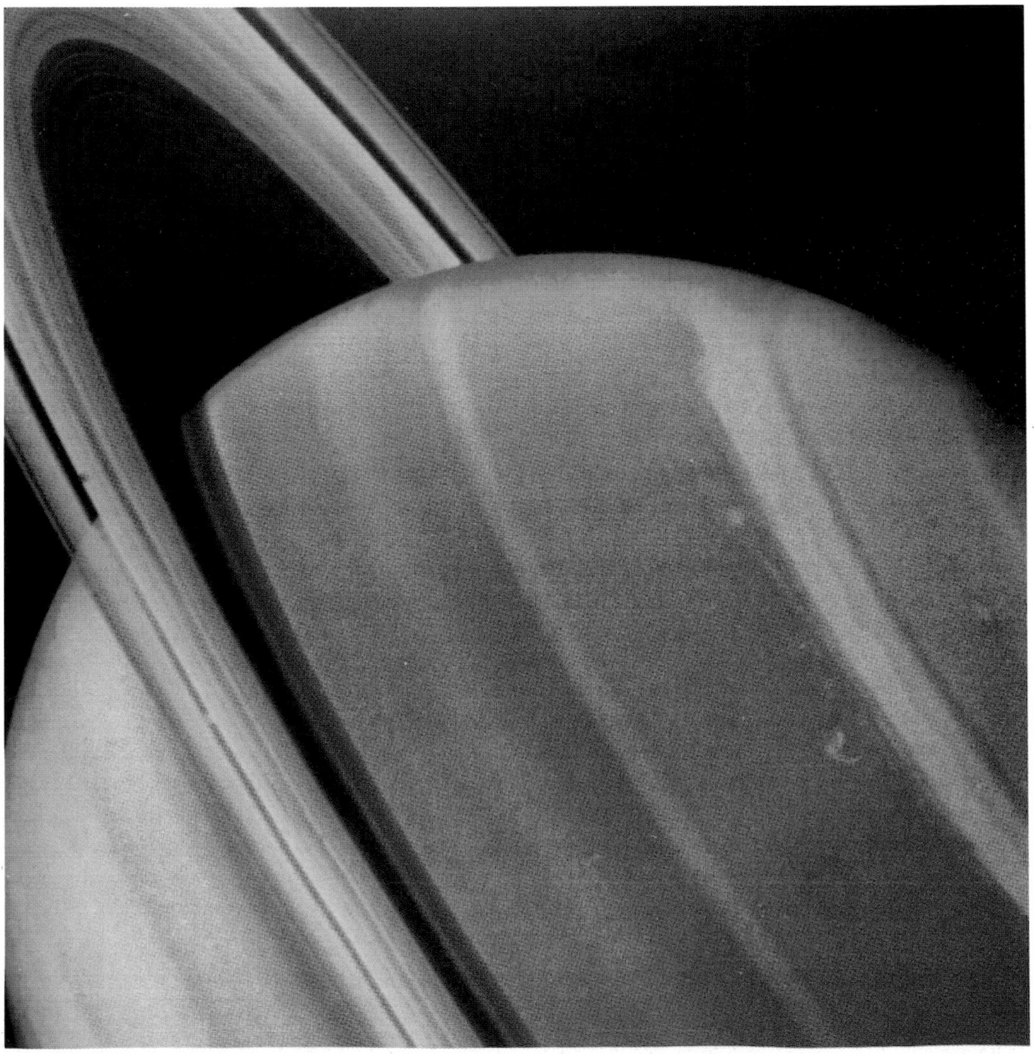

RIGHT Voyager 2 returned this view of Saturn in 1981, when the spacecraft was approaching the large, gaseous planet at about 1 million km (620,000 miles) a day.

The so-called "ribbon-like" feature in the white cloud band marks a high-speed jet at about 47° north; there, the westerly wind speeds are about 530km/h (330mph). Although less pronounced than on Jupiter, the bands, storms, ovals and eddies are all evident here, too, caused by the same combination of rapid rotation (just under 10 hours and 14 minutes) and convective atmosphere.

Saturn's stunning ring system – hundreds or even thousands of narrow ringlets – are grouped, giving the impression of broad bands, each of which has been designated a letter. Brighter than those of other outer planets and no more than 1.5km thick, they comprise millions of small objects ranging in size from tiny stones to rocks several metres long, and are composed at least in part of water ice, possibly plus rocky particles with icy coatings.

The bright A and B rings and the fainter C ring are visible from Earth through a telescope. The space between the A and B rings is called the Cassini division, while the much narrower Encke division splits the A ring. The complex structure is due to the gravitational effects of the satellites, which orbit close to and within the rings.

Saturn has 18 named satellites, six of them icy (resembling the three outer moons of Jupiter) and the others small and rocky. The unique atmosphere of Titan, second largest moon in the Solar System after Ganymede, make it the odd one out. About every 15 years we see Saturn's rings edge-on because of the orbital geometry between Saturn and Earth.

URANUS

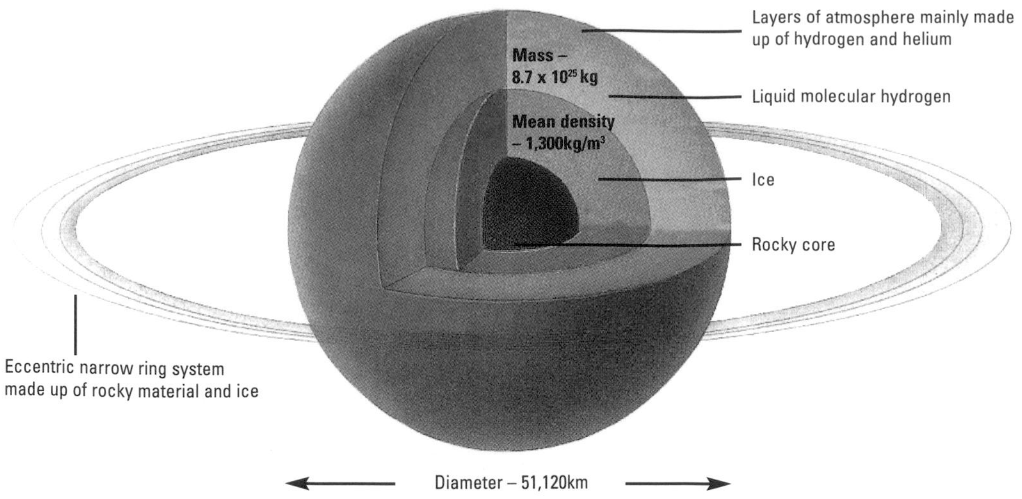
Layers of atmosphere mainly made up of hydrogen and helium
Mass – 8.7 x 10^{25} kg
Liquid molecular hydrogen
Mean density – 1,300kg/m^3
Ice
Rocky core
Eccentric narrow ring system made up of rocky material and ice
Diameter – 51,120km

DISCOVERED BY William Herschel in 1781, Uranus appears as a smooth, aqua-coloured sphere with very subtle hints of bands, but this calm facade gives no hint of a history fraught with spectacular catastrophe: at some stage a mighty collision wrenched the young planet off its axis. As a result the planet is tipped over on its side so that its rotation axis lies almost in the plane of the planet's orbit, giving rise to the most striking seasonal changes. Another collision may have been responsible for the fantastic geology of its moon Miranda.

Uranus has a mean distance from the Sun of 2,869,600,000km (1,783 million miles) and a revolution period of just over 84 years. Its basic composition is the same as the other giant planets and similar to that of the Sun – predominantly hydrogen (about 80%) with some helium (15%), the remainder of the atmosphere being methane, hydrocarbons (molecular mixtures of carbon, nitrogen, hydrogen and oxygen) and other trace elements.

RIGHT The tilt of Uranus's axis [A] compared to Earth [B] is 98°, unique in the Solar System. Its density is 1.2 times that of water, more than Jupiter and Saturn but far less than Earth.

Uranus' colour is caused by the small amount of methane – probably less than 3% – that preferentially absorbs red light, meaning the reflected sunlight we see is greenish-blue.

Temperatures at the outer layers of the atmosphere are very cold, about –200°C (330°F), but pressures and temperatures rise with depth and the hydrogen and helium transform from gas to a liquid state. At still greater depth, a transition occurs to a thick, viscous, partly solidified layer of highly compressed liquid water, which may have traces of ammonia and methane. Deep within the centre of Uranus, at extremely high pressure, a core of rocky material is thought to exist, with a mass almost five times that of Earth.

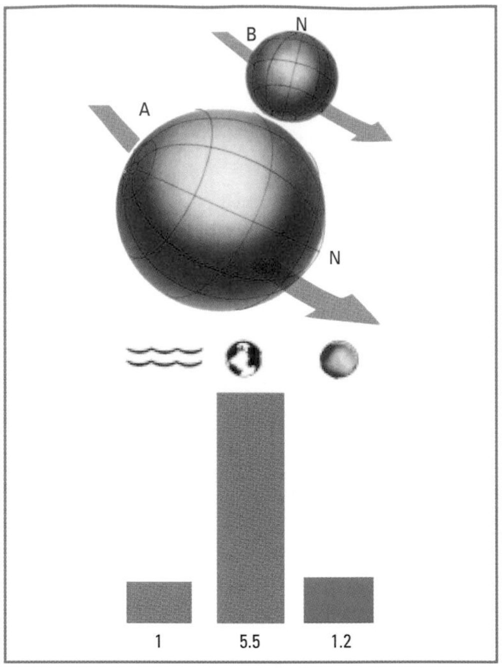
B
N
A
N
1
5.5
1.2

BELOW A composite image of Uranus, the striking but featureless blue planet, and five of its 15 moons, made from photographs taken by Voyager 2 in 1986. The moons (clockwise from top left) are Umbriel, Oberon, Titania, Miranda and Ariel. While an unexplained jumble of huge geological features dominates Miranda, tectonic activity has given Ariel the youngest surface of the moons. Voyager 2's discovery of 10 moons tripled Uranus's known total, while in 1997 two unnamed satellites, probably captured asteroids, were found by the Palomar Observatory. In 1977, astronomers discovered that Uranus has a ring system: there are nine well-defined rings, plus a fainter one and a wider fuzzy ring.

NEPTUNE

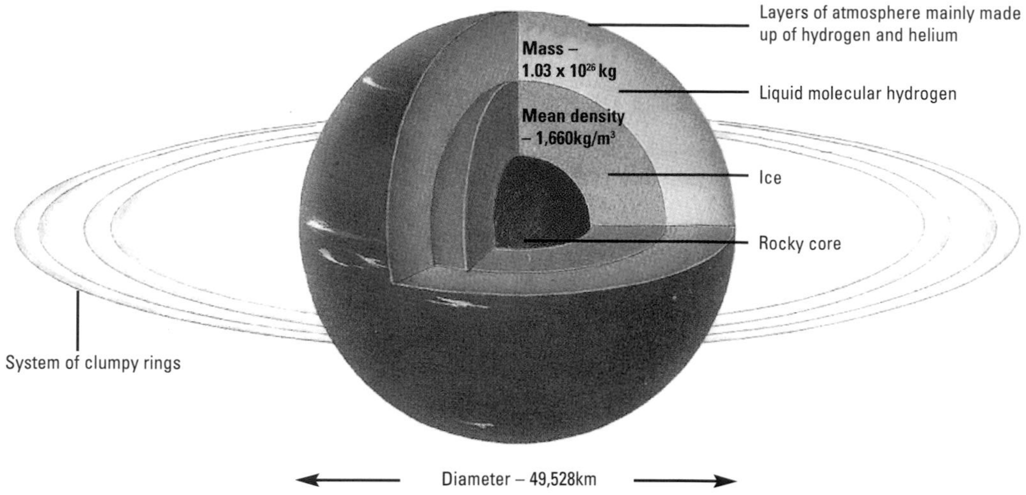
Layers of atmosphere mainly made up of hydrogen and helium
Mass – 1.03 x 10^26 kg
Liquid molecular hydrogen
Mean density – 1,660kg/m³
Ice
Rocky core
System of clumpy rings
Diameter – 49,528km

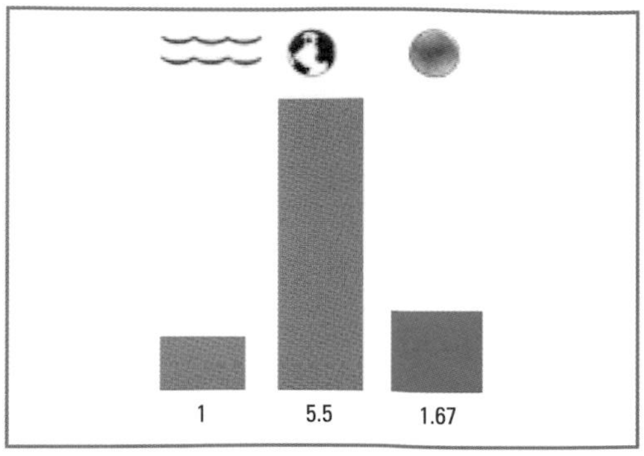
1
5.5
1.67

ABOVE Densest of the four main outer planets, Neptune's mass is 17.1 times that of Earth. Its almost circular orbit is always more than 4 billion km (2.5 billion miles) from Earth. Its rotation period is just over 16 hours.

A NEAR TWIN to Uranus in size, Neptune has a similar atmospheric make-up and internal structure, though its magnetic field is 60% weaker. A gas giant surrounded by clumpy rings and eight moons, it takes 164.8 years to orbit the Sun.

Unlike Uranus, which has no detectable internal heat source, Neptune has the strongest internal heat source of all the giant planets. It radiates almost three times more heat than equilibrium conditions would predict, as opposed to Jupiter and Saturn, which radiate about twice as much energy as expected.

Clouds and storms are the main features of Neptune's dynamic atmosphere. Dominating all is the Great Dark Spot, a hurricane-like storm in the southern hemisphere about half the size of Earth. Like all Neptune's weather conditions, it is constantly and rapidly changing. Neptune's winds are among the fastest in the Solar System, dwarfed only by Saturn's high-speed equatorial jet.

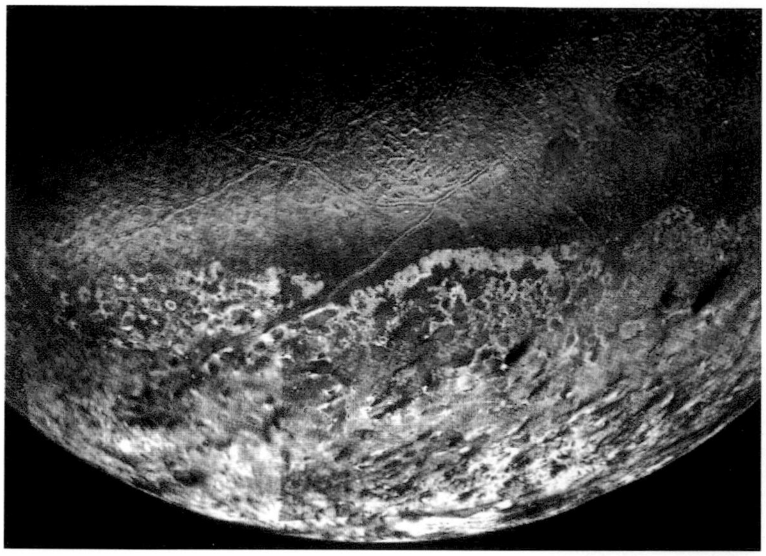

LEFT The southern hemisphere of Triton, largest of Neptune's eight moons, pictured from Voyager 2 in 1989. The large, lighter-coloured area is the polar icecap, probably nitrogen. Because of its retrograde and highly inclined orbit, it is thought Triton was captured by the gravitational pull of Neptune. Tiny Nereid was also known before 1989, when Voyager discovered six more satellites.

PLUTO

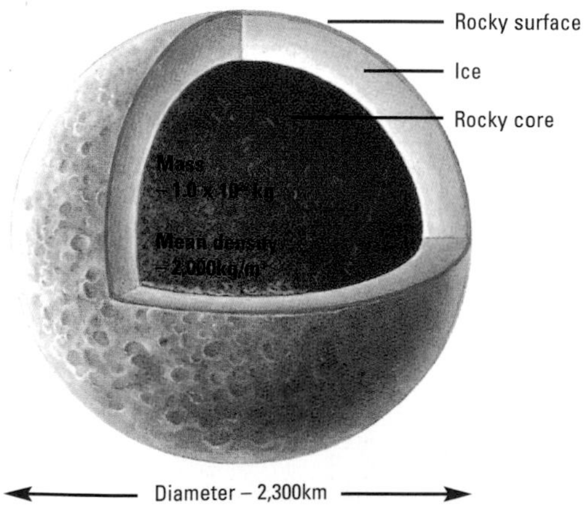
Rocky surface
Ice
Rocky core
Diameter – 2,300km

ABOVE Pluto has an average density about twice that of water ice, implying its interior is composed of rock; about 30% of its volume is thought to be water ice. Like Earth, Pluto's atmosphere is primarily nitrogen gas, but the changing surface pressure never exceeds about 10 millibars – around one hundred thousandth of the pressure on Earth at sea level.

FARTHEST PLANET from the Sun, Pluto's tiny size (smaller than Mercury) and rocky composition (like the terrestrial planets of the inner system) make it a real misfit among the gas giants of the outer system. In both size and surface constituents it is similar to Triton, a moon of Neptune, and many astronomers believe it is a former satellite of Neptune somehow separated from its parent.

Pluto has a long, elliptical and tilted orbit that takes over 248 Earth years to complete, of which about 20 years are inside the orbit of Neptune, the last occasion being from 1979 to 1999. Discovered only in 1930, its size and distance from Earth make it difficult to study, despite its high reflectivity: in our sky it is less than one 36,000th of a degree across – the equivalent of a walnut at a range of 50km (30 miles). It is thought that the surface of Pluto is largely nitrogen ice, with methane and carbon monoxide ices as impurities. At nearly half its size, the mysterious Charon (discovered in 1978) is the Solar System's largest moon in relation to its parent planet. Pluto did not form in isolation: it is simply the largest relic in space past Neptune left over from the formation of the Solar System.

RIGHT Hubble Space Telescope (HST) images from 1994 showing two hemispheres of Pluto. The two main images have been computer processed to show rotation and bring out the differences in brightness on the surface; the original "raw" images are at the top left of each panel. Twelve bright regions have been identified, including a large north polar cap.

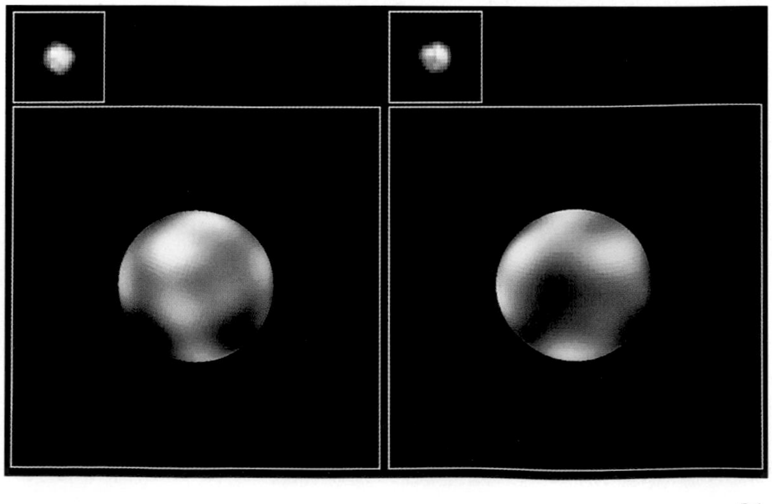

THE MOON

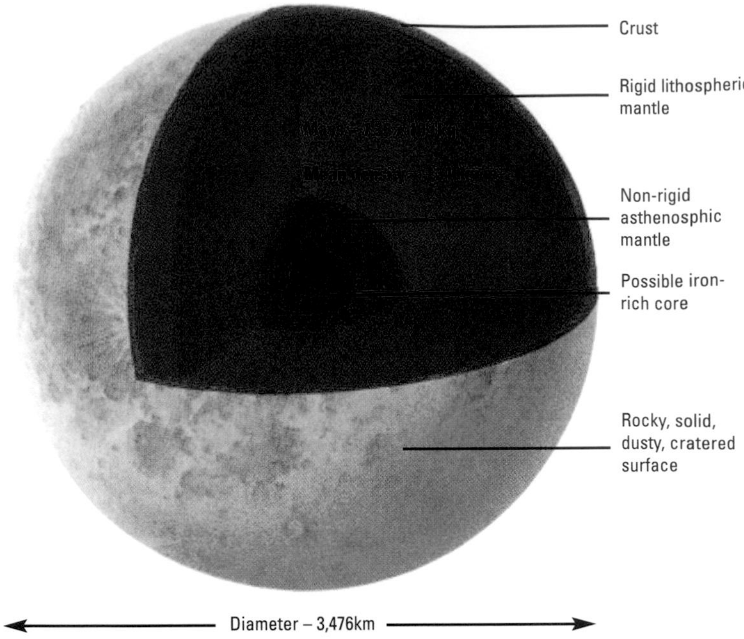
Crust
Rigid lithospheric mantle
Non-rigid asthenosphic mantle
Possible iron-rich core
Rocky, solid, dusty, cratered surface
Diameter – 3,476km

The average diameter of the Moon is 3,475km (2,159 miles), 0.27 times Earth. It has a mass of about 1/81 that of Earth, its surface gravity is one-sixth of Earth, and its density is 3.344 times that of water. It orbits the Earth at a mean distance of 384,199 km (238,731 miles) at an average speed of 3,683km/h (2,289mph) in relation to the Earth. It orbits its parent in 27.3 days.

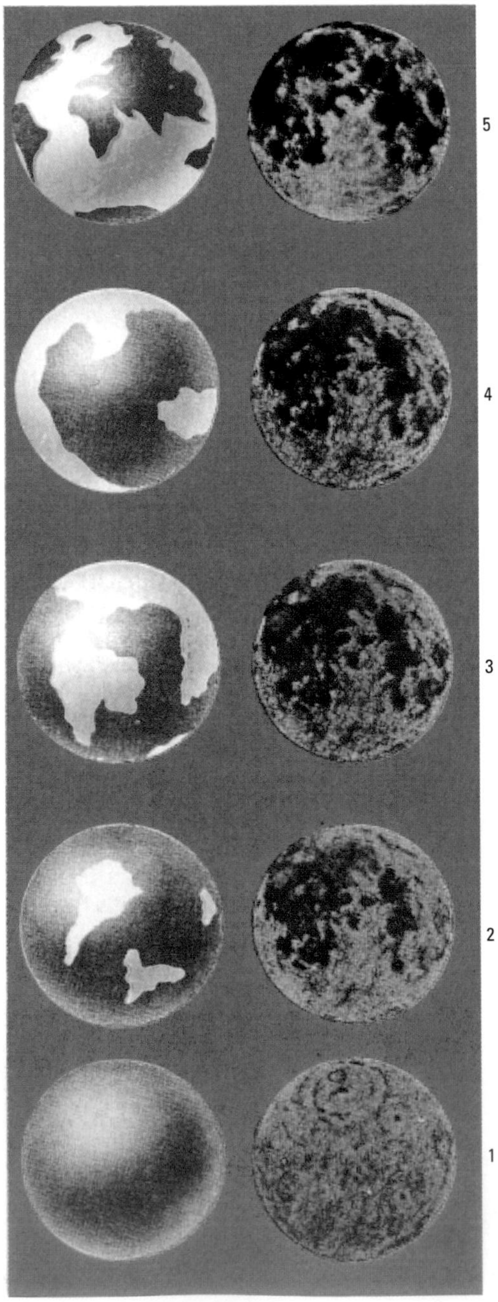
5
4
3
2
1

BECAUSE THE Moon is about 400 times smaller than the Sun, but about 400 times closer to Earth, humans have always seen them as roughly the same size. While the Moon is tiny in cosmic terms, however, its diameter is more than a quarter that of Earth, considerably more than Pluto and well over 70% that of Mercury. Despite its bright appearance it is a dark body, illuminated only by light reflected from the Sun.

Analysis of lunar samples suggests that the Moon was formed from the remnant of a Mars-sized body that collided with the juvenile planet Earth in a giant impact some 4,500 billion years ago. Any iron-rich core this body may have had appears to have been absorbed into the Earth's core, while the Moon grew out of the mostly rocky debris thrown into space by the crash. The lack of a large, fluid core explains the almost total lack of a magnetic field, which registers only one ten millionth of the strength of Earth's.

The Moon's characteristic dark patches – the face of the "Man in the Moon" – are low-lying regions once flooded by outpourings of basaltic lava, which scientists have dated as between 3 and 4 billion years ago. Known as the lunar seas (Latin *maria,* singular *mare*), they have appeared never to have contained any water, nor indeed any liquid.

Only about 59% of the Moon's surface is directly visible from Earth. Reflected light takes 1.25 seconds to reach us – compared to 8 minutes 27.3 seconds for light from the Sun. With the Sun overhead the temperature on the lunar equator can reach 117.2°C (243°F), and at night it can sink to –162.7°C (–261°C). An astronaut has only a sixth of his normal weight on the Moon, though his mass is unaltered. There is no local surface colour and the lunar sky is black, even when the Sun is above the horizon. There is no air or water – and there has never been any form of life.

LEFT The lunar "seas" were formed, either by internal accretion or by impact, at an early stage development of Moon and Earth surfaces around 4,000 million years ago [1]. The general aspect of the Moon then must have been similar to that of today, although the basins were not filled. The surface of both the Earth and the Moon then remained the same for a considerable period. Some 2,000 million years ago the basins on the Moon were filled in; 1,000 million years later [4] lunar activity was almost over, while Earth has since seen fabulous change.

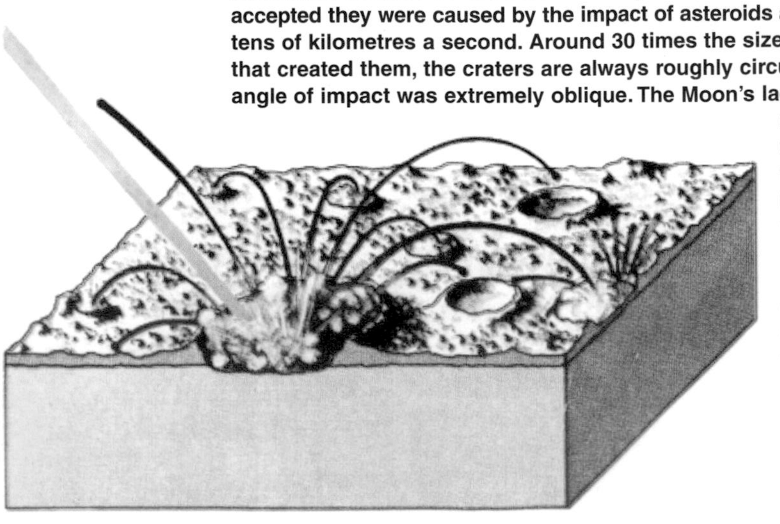

BELOW After the dark patches of the lunar seas, huge craters are the most noticeable features on the Moon. Once presumed volcanic in origin, it is now accepted they were caused by the impact of asteroids and comets travelling at tens of kilometres a second. Around 30 times the size of the foreign bodies that created them, the craters are always roughly circular unless, rarely, the angle of impact was extremely oblique. The Moon's lack of any atmosphere means that its surface remains unprotected from any form of impactors – an atmospheric layer, as on Earth, helps to burn up any encroaching objects – and this, combined with the fact that it has no geological processes, means that no crater is ever worn away or changed . . . except by the arrival of another foreign body.

COMETS

A GREAT COMET, with a brilliant head and a tail stretching way across the sky, is a spectacular object – and it is easy to understand they caused such terror in ancient times. Comets have always been regarded as unlucky and fear of them is still not dead in some primitive societies.

Yet a comet is not nearly as important as it may look: it is made up of small rock and ice particles and tenuous gas. On several occasions Earth passed through a comet's tail without suffering the slightest damage. Since Edmund Halley first calculated the paths of several comets in 1695 – including Halley's, whose period is 76 years and which last appeared in 1986 – astronomers have found over 600 such bodies orbiting the Sun.

Analysis of a comet

At the heart of every comet is the nucleus, a solid mass of ice that also contains small solid particles of rock called "dust". Most nuclei are between 1 and 10km (0.6 and 6 miles) across, though they can reach 100km (60 miles). The dark thin crust of icy dust that covers them reflects only 4% of sunlight, making them difficult to detect when distant from the Sun. Over 80% of the ice is simple water ice – the nucleus of Halley's comet contains more than 300,000 tonnes of it – and another 10% or more is frozen carbon dioxide and carbon monoxide. The coma and tails appear only when the comet approaches the Sun, which can be from any angle; as the comet recedes the tail disappears.

Because a comet nucleus shrinks every time it passes the Sun – Halley's by perhaps about a metre (3ft) on each orbit – no comet can have been in its present orbit since the birth of the Solar System. It is now believed that while some comets come from the Kuiper belt beyond Pluto, far more spend most of their time in the Oort cloud much farther out in space. Collisions occur, too: in 1994 at least 21 fragments of Shoemaker-Levy 9 exploded in Jupiter's upper atrmosphere, and Jupuiter may well have swept up many comets from farther out in the Solar System in the past.

RIGHT There are three main classes of comet. The faint short-period comets [A] often have their aphelia (furthest points from the Sun) at approximately the distance of Jupiter's orbit [1], and their periods amount to a few years. Long-period comets [B] have aphelia near or beyond Neptune's orbit [2], though Halley's is the only conspicuous member of the class. Comets with very long periods [C] have such great orbital eccentricities that the paths are almost parabolic. Apart from Halley's, all the really brilliant comets are of this type. Half the known comets orbit almost entirely within the paths of Jupiter and Saturn, taking 20 or so years; the quickest, Encke, takes just 3.3 years. At the other extreme there are comets with huge orbits: Hyakutake, last seen in 1996, will not be near the Sun again for another 14,000 years.

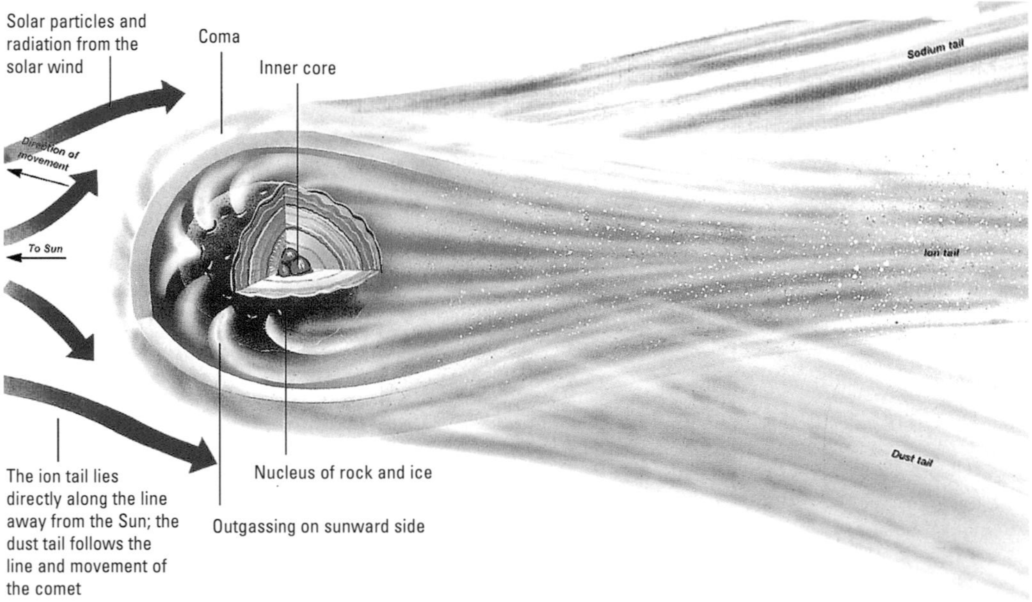

Solar particles and radiation from the solar wind
Coma
Inner core
Sodium tail
Direction of movement
To Sun
Ion tail
Dust tail
The ion tail lies directly along the line away from the Sun; the dust tail follows the line and movement of the comet
Nucleus of rock and ice
Outgassing on sunward side

ABOVE A comet has an irregular nucleus of rock and ice. As it nears the Sun, the ice vaporizes and combines with dust to produce the coma or head, hiding the nucleus from our view. The gas or ion tail, often blue and comprising charged electrons (ions) caught up in the solar wind, streams away from the direction of the Sun for up to 100 million km (60 million miles); the dust tail, often white in reflected sunlight, comprises tiny grains of rock and can stretch for up to 10 million km (6 million miles) behind the comet. When observing comet Hale-Bopp in 1997 astronomers also discovered a new type, the sodium tail, which accelerates a straight neutral gas tail up to 10 million km (6 million miles) behind the comet.

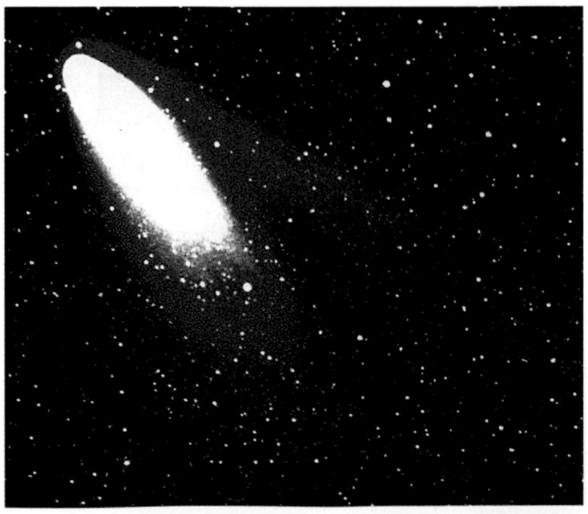

LEFT Hale-Bopp had its perihelion (closest approach to the Sun) in 1997, and it was easily seen with the naked eye from much of Earth for several days. Spectroscopy revealed 38 types of gas present in the comet's coma.

BELOW Following its visit in 1910, Halley's comet last returned to perihelion in 1986. Although not as bright as the great "non-periodical" comets, the increase and decline of the tail is clearly shown. As it approached perihelion the tail developed enormously; after the closest approach to the Sun the tail contracted, so that when the comet was last seen the tail had disappeared altogether. The seventh picture shows the tail shortly before perihelion.

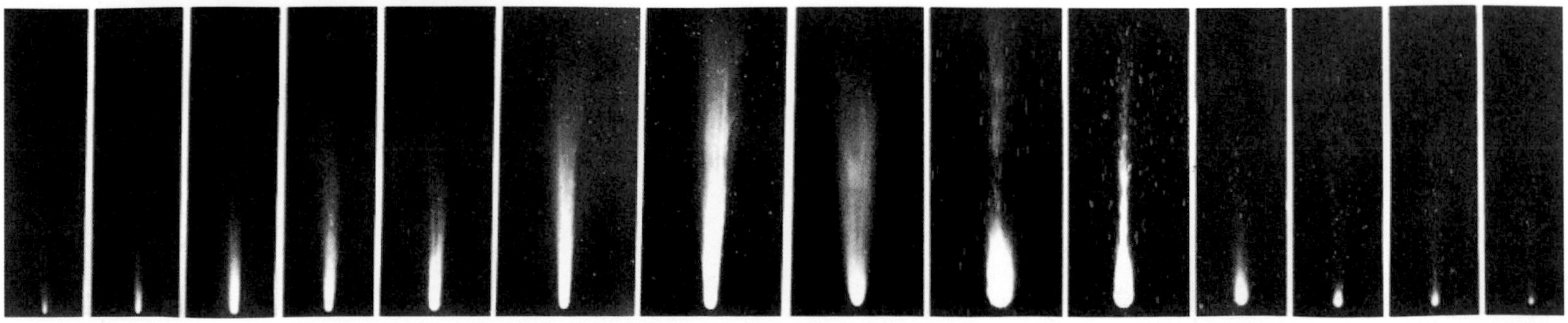

Asteroids and Meteoroids

SINCE THE BEGINNING of the 19th century, astronomers have catalogued more than 8,000 asteroids orbiting our Sun, and at least 10,000 more have been observed. It is estimated that there are at least a million of these rocky bodies with diameters of over 1km (0.6 miles), their numbers making nonsense of their previous description the "minor planets". Along with comets and meteoroids, they are better described as "space debris", though 95% are found in the main asteroid belt between Mars and Jupiter. Some tiny examples find their way to Earth as meterorites, but our knowledge of their formation and composition remains limited.

Asteroid orbits

The main belt asteroids are not smoothly distributed in cloud between Mars and Jupiter. There are gaps in the main belt where very few asteroids exist. These were discovered by an American astronomer, Daniel Kirkwood, and are known as the Kirkwood gaps and mark places where the orbital period would be a simple fraction of Jupiter's. For example, an asteroid orbiting the Sun at a distance of 375 million km (233 million miles) would complete exactly three orbits while Jupiter orbited the Sun once. It would feel a gravitational tug from Jupiter, away from the Sun, every orbit, and quickly be moved out of that position.

However, in some places more asteroids are seen than expected: one such place is Jupiter's orbit. A swarm of a few hundred asteroids is found 60° ahead of and behind Jupiter in the same orbit. Known as the Trojans, they orbit the Sun at the same rate as Jupiter, but hardly ever come close enough to the planet for their orbits to be disturbed.

Swarms can also be found within the main belt of asteroids. These are known as asteroid families, and are formed when two larger asteroids collide. Astronomers then see the resulting fragments as many smaller asteroids sharing similar orbits around the Sun.

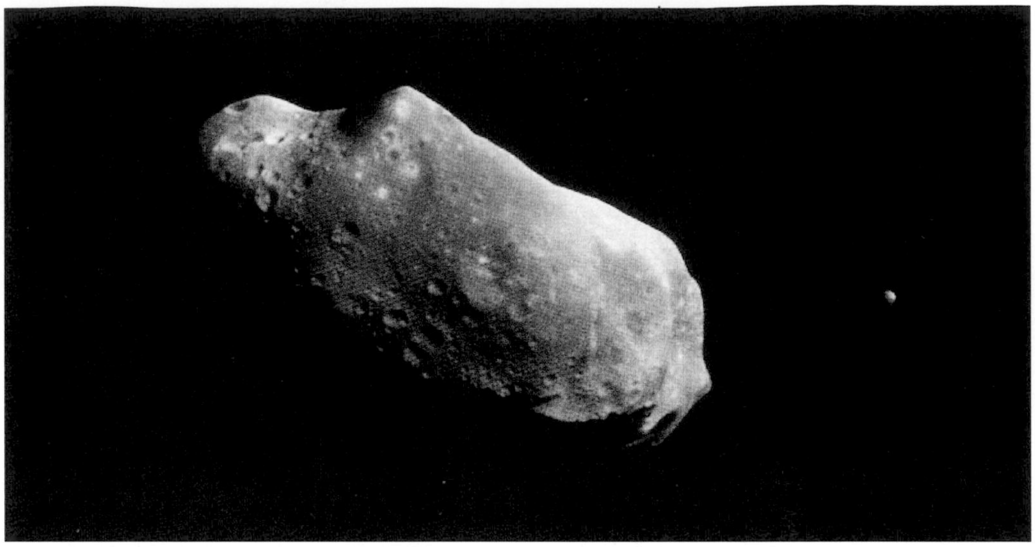

ABOVE The asteroid Ida as photographed by the Galileo spacecraft on its way to Jupiter in 1993. Galileo discovered a small moon, seen here on the right, orbiting at about 100km (60 miles); named Dactyl by surprised scientists, this irregularly shaped satellite measures only 1.7 cu. km (0.4 cu. miles). Galileo also passed the asteroids Gaspra and Mathilde, like Ida heavily cratered by small asteroids and meteorites: one crater on Mathilde was estimated at about 10km (6 miles) deep, huge in relation to the body's size.

Formation and composition of asteroids

For some time it was thought that the asteroids were the debris of a collision that destroyed a "missing" planet, but it now seems unlikely that a large planet ever formed between Mars and Jupiter – mainly because of the latter's gravitational field. Most of the mass present in that region during the early days of the Solar System was probably rotating in elliptical orbits and ended up colliding with the planets, their satellites or even the Sun.

No asteroid has ever been shown to have an atmosphere, so the light we see must be sunlight reflected from the surface. An asteroid's composition depends on its distance from the Sun. In the inner main belt nearest Mars, they are made of silicate rocks (minerals containing silicon and oxygen) similar to those found on Earth. These are called "S-type" asteroids. In the middle of the belt are mostly "C-type": these appear to have rocks containing carbon, similar to some types of meteorites landing on Earth.

The outer belt has asteroids that are so dark they only reflect 5% of the sunlight that reaches them, and are very red. Our best assumption about these "D-type" asteroids is that there is a large amount of ices such as water ice and frozen carbon monoxide

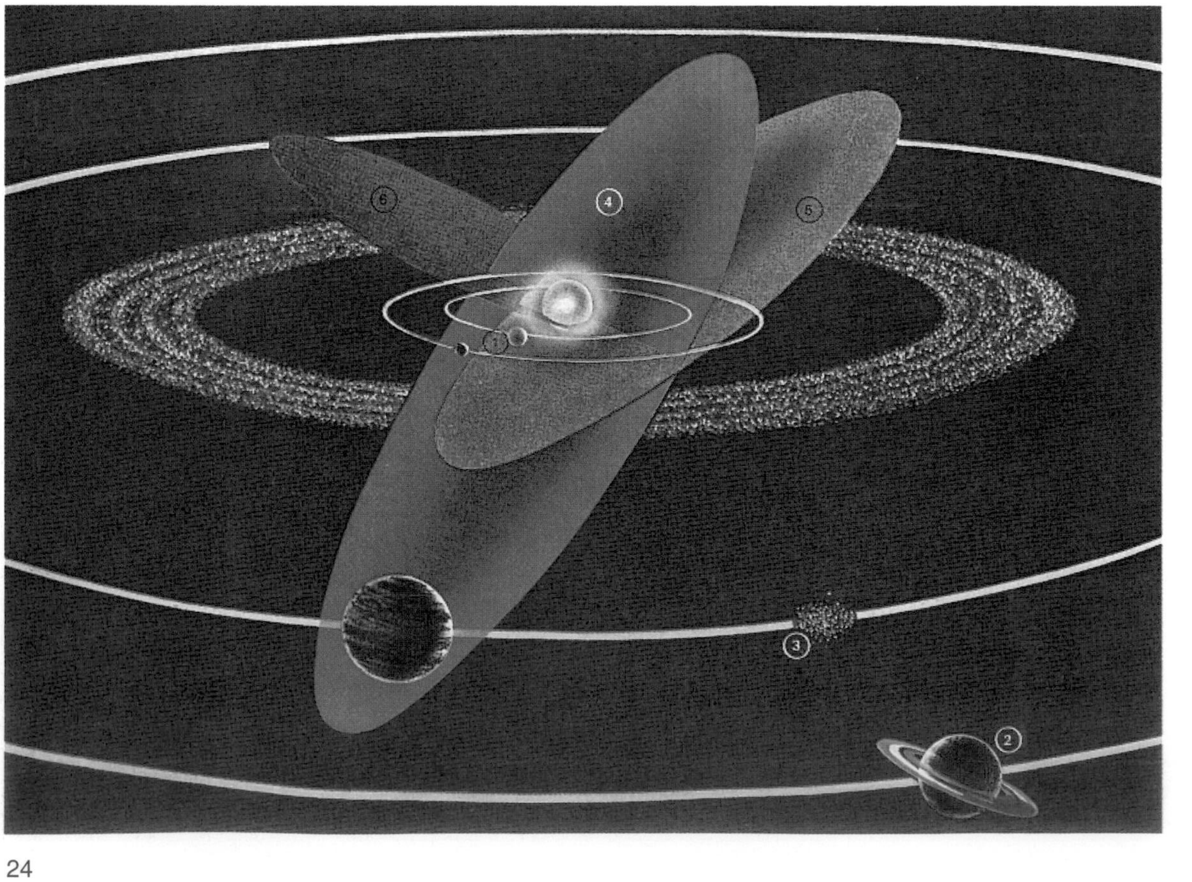

LEFT The orbits of the planets from Earth [1] out to Saturn [2], together with some notable asteroids (the illustration is not to scale). While most asteroids move in the region between the orbits of Mars and Jupiter, the so-called Trojan asteroids [3] move in the same orbit as Jupiter. They keep their distance, however, and collisions are unlikely to occur: one group moves 60° ahead of the planet and the other group 60° behind, though they move round for some distance to either side of their mean positions.

Hidalgo [4] has a path which is highly inclined and so eccentric – much like a comet – that its aphelion (farthest point from the Sun) is not far from the orbit of Saturn. Amor [5] and Apollo [6] belong to the so-called "Earth-grazing" asteroid group. All the Earth-grazers are very small: Amor has a diameter of 8km (5 miles) and Apollo only about 2km (1.25 miles). Both satellites of Mars, Phobos and Deimos, are asteroids captured by the gravitational pull of the planet.

mixed in with the rock, and that charged particles from the solar wind hitting them have created chemical reactions to form the dark red colour.

This change in asteroid make-up is logical if they were formed at the beginning of the Solar System, as this change in composition fits in with theories about how the planets formed. In addition, since their formation, asteroids nearer the Sun have been heated more than those farther out; this means that, over time, more ice melted and escaped. Farther away, lower temperatures mean that less of the ice has melted.

Asteroids undergo some of the most violent temperature changes in the Solar System. One asteroid, Icarus, actually approaches closer to the the Sun than the baked planet Mercury. At its perihelion (closest point), only 28 million km (17 million miles), its surface can reach more than 900°C (500°F); just 200 Earth days later it has reached its aphelion (farthest point), 295 million km (183 million miles) from the warmth of the Sun in the cool space beyond Mars.

Asteroids and Earth

In 1937 Hermes, a mere 1km (0.6 miles) in diameter, passed just 780,000km (485,000 miles) from Earth, less than twice the distance of the Moon. What would happen if such an object hit Earth? Besides the tremendous heat, enough rock and dust would be deposited in the atmosphere to change the climate all over the Earth, while if it landed near water, huge tsunamis would devastate cities on the edge of the ocean all over the globe. Indeed, it is now widely thought that the impact of an asteroid or comet 65 million years ago, producing a crater 180km (112 miles) wide in the Yucatan Peninsula of Mexico assisted in the extinction of the dinosaurs. Luckily for us, it's estimated that such devastating impacts are likely to happen only once every 100 million years or so.

Meteors

Commonly known as shooting stars, meteors are flashes of light caused by particles of rock entering the Earth's atmosphere at altitudes of around 100km (60 miles), most of them only the size of a grain of sand. As they travel at between 10 and 30km (6 to 18 miles) per second, friction with the air molecules rapidly heats them to thousands of degrees, and they vaporize in a flash of heat. Larger and therefore brighter meteors are known as fireballs, and can be anything from the size of a small pebble up to a large boulder. Before the rocks enter our atmosphere, they are following their own orbit about the Sun.

A "meteor shower" occurs when Earth passes through one of the meteor streams, belts of dust particles sharing their orbits with comets but too heavy to be swept out of the Solar System. For example, the Leonid shower shares the orbit of comet Temple-Tuttle. The best showers occur on 12 August and 13 December each year. They are called the Perseid meteor shower and the Geminid meteor shower because their radiant points appear to be in the constellations of Perseus and Gemini.

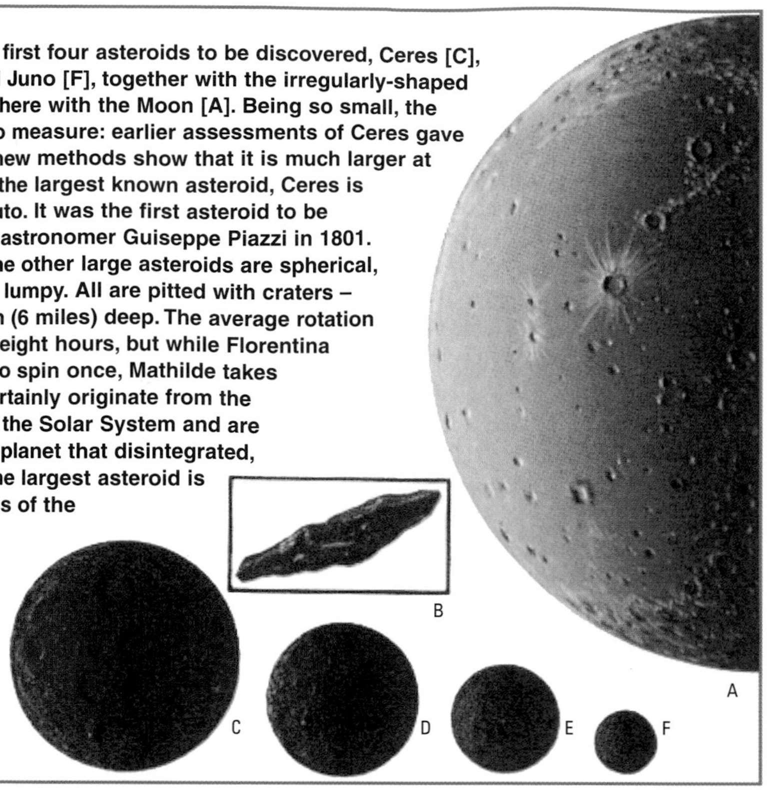

RIGHT The sizes of the first four asteroids to be discovered, Ceres [C], Vesta [D], Pallas [E] and Juno [F], together with the irregularly-shaped Eros [B], are compared here with the Moon [A]. Being so small, the diameters are difficult to measure: earlier assessments of Ceres gave 685km (426 miles), but new methods show that it is much larger at 913km (567 miles). Still the largest known asteroid, Ceres is two-fifths the size of Pluto. It was the first asteroid to be identified, by the Italian astronomer Guiseppe Piazzi in 1801.

While Ceres and some other large asteroids are spherical, most are elongated and lumpy. All are pitted with craters – one on Mathilde is 10km (6 miles) deep. The average rotation period of an asteroid is eight hours, but while Florentina takes only three hours to spin once, Mathilde takes 17 days. They almost certainly originate from the time of the formation of the Solar System and are not remnants of a large planet that disintegrated, as was once thought. The largest asteroid is less than 1% of the mass of the Moon, and the known asteroids combined are less than 10% of Earth's mass. The first encounter by a space probe was made by the Galileo mission in 1989.

Meteorites

While meteoroids usually burn up in the atmosphere, some are big enough to make it through the atmosphere without being completely vaporized and reach the ground; they are then called meteorites. Scientists estimate that about 300,000 meteorites reach the surface of the Earth every year, though many fall in the oceans or remote forests, deserts and mountains. Even those that fall near towns and cities can remain undiscovered, since many look like ordinary rocks to the untrained eye. Some meteorites are tiny particles, while others weigh up to 200 tonnes. Meteoroids weighing more than about 100 tonnes that don't break up are not decelerated as much as lighter bodies, and produce impressive impact craters.

When chemically analysed, there are many different types of meteorite. The most common finds are called chondrites, and appear to be the same type of iron- and silicon-bearing rock that S-type asteroids are made from. Much rarer are the carbonaceous chondrites, which have large amounts of carbon and appear to have come from the middle of the asteroid belt. Finally, about 10% of meteorites are the heavier stony-iron and iron-nickel type.

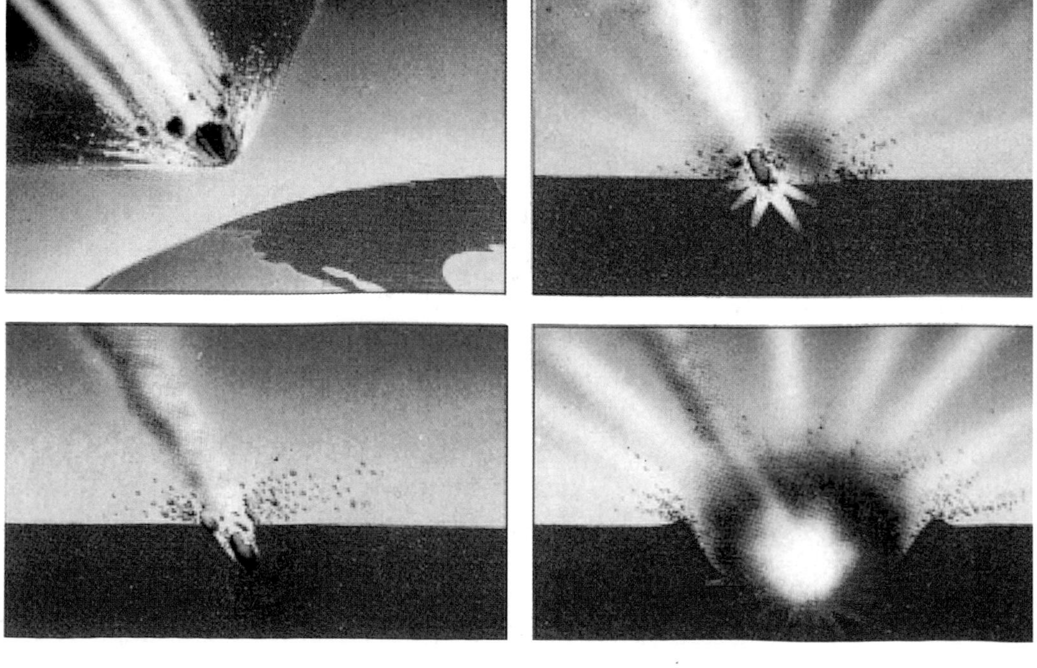

RIGHT Research suggests that craters such as the Barringer in Arizona, 1.6km (1 mile) wide and 180m (600ft) deep, was formed by nickel-iron meteorites up to about 50,000 years ago. Burning up as they plunged through the atmosphere, they shattered the Earth's outer layer of rock on impact (*top right*). Because of their high speed they burrowed into the ground, causing friction, heat, compression and shockwaves, culminating in a violent explosion that left the huge crater. More than 130 craters have so far been identified, though many more were created before being subsequently destroyed by geological activity and erosion.

Time and Motion

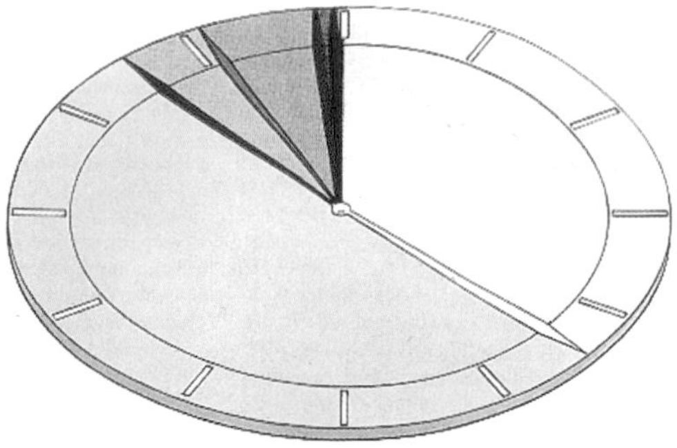

ABOVE A "clock" of the Earth's history, with 12 hours representing the 4,600 million years the world has been in existence. The first 2 hours and 52 minutes are still obscure, but the earliest rocks are then formed – though the planet remains a lifeless desert until 04.20, when bacterial organisms first appear.

Eons of time drag by until just after 10.30, when there is an explosion of invertebrate life in the oceans. Dinosaurs wander the land by 11.36, only to die out and replaced by birds and mammals 25 minutes later. Hominids arrive about 30 seconds before noon – and the last tenth of a second covers human civilization.

The oldest rocks of the great Precambrian shields of North America, Africa and Australia convey dates of up to about 3,500 million years ago. Only the past 570 million years show an abundance of plant and animal life. The most widely found fossil remains from any period are called index fossils and are used to correlate various rock formations of the same age.

THE BASIC unit of time measurement is the day, one rotation of the Earth on its axis. The subdivision of the day into hours, minutes and seconds is simply for our convenience. The present Western calendar is based on the "solar year", the 365.24 days the Earth takes to orbit the Sun.

Calendars based on the movements of the Sun and Moon, however, have been used since ancient times. The average length of the year, fixed by the Julian Calendar introduced by Julius Caesar, was about 11 minutes too long, and the cumulative error was eventually rectified in 1582 by the Gregorian Calendar. Pope Gregory XIII decreed that the day following 4 October that year was in fact 15 October, and that century years do not count as leap years unless they are divisible by 400. Britain did not adopt the reformed calendar until 1752 – by which stage it was lagging 11 days behind the continent; the Gregorian Calendar was imposed on all its possessions, including the American colonies, with all dates preceding 2 September marked O.S., for Old Style.

The seasons are generated by a combination of the Earth's revolution around the Sun and the tilt of its axis of 23½°. The solstices (from the Greek *sol*, sun, and *stitium*, standing) are the two times in the year when the Sun is overhead at one of the Tropics of Cancer and Capricorn, 23½° North and South, furthest from the Equator. The equinoxes (from the Greek *aequus*, equal, and *nox*, night) are the two times in the year when day and night are of equal length due to the Sun being overhead at the Equator. The longest and shortest days in each hemisphere fall on or around the solstices, and are opposites in each hemisphere.

The Earth's axis is inclined at 23.5° to the perpendicular to the orbital plane. This angle accounts for the complex seasonal variations in climate, notably in mid-latitudes. The varying distance of the Earth from the Sun has only a minor effect.

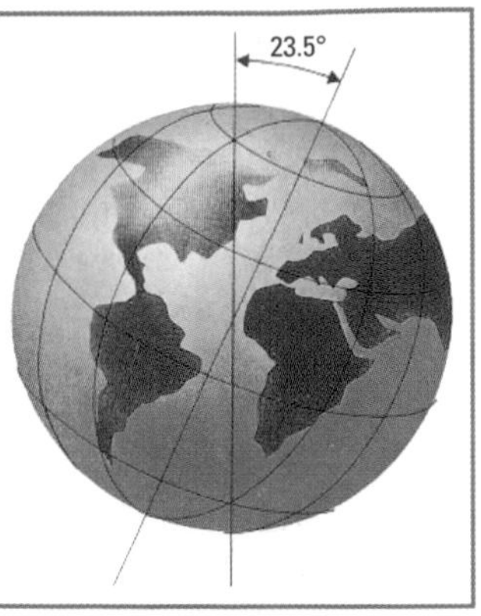

23.5°

Definitions of Time

Year: The time taken by the Earth to revolve around the Sun, or 365.24 days.

Month: The approximate time taken by the Moon to revolve around the Earth. The 12 months of the year in fact vary from 28 days (29 in a Leap Year – once every 4 years to offset the difference between the calendar and the solar year) to 31 days.

Week: An artificial period of 7 days. Unlike days, months and years – but like minutes and seconds – it is not based on astronomical time.

Day: The time taken by the Earth to complete one rotation (spin) on its axis.

Hour: A day comprises 24 hours, divided into hours a.m. (*ante meridiem*, before noon) and p.m. (*post meridiem*, after noon) – though timetables use the 24-hour system from midnight.

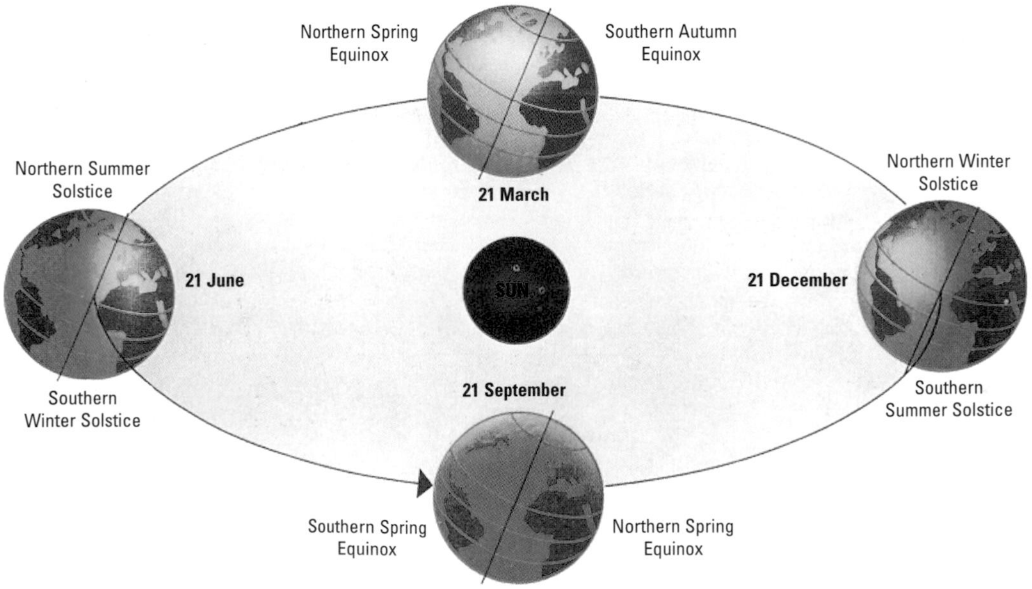

Northern Spring Equinox
Southern Autumn Equinox
21 March
Northern Summer Solstice
21 June
SUN
21 December
Northern Winter Solstice
Southern Summer Solstice
Southern Winter Solstice
21 September
Southern Spring Equinox
Northern Spring Equinox

LEFT Seasons occur because the Earth's axis is tilted at a constant angle of 23½° as it spins. When the Northern Hemisphere is tilted to a maximum extent towards the Sun, on 21 June, the Sun is overhead at noon at the Tropic of Cancer (23½° North): this is midsummer, or the summer solstice, in this hemisphere.

On 22 or 23 September the Sun is overhead at the Equator, and day and night are of equal length throughout the world: this is the autumn or fall equinox in the Northern Hemisphere. On 21 or 22 December, the Sun is overhead at the Tropic of Capricorn (23½° South), the winter solstice in the Northern Hemisphere. The overhead Sun then tracks north, until on 21 March it is overhead at the Equator: this is the spring equinox in the Northern Hemisphere.

In the Southern Hemisphere the seasons are the reverse of those in the Northern Hemisphere: autumn corresponds to spring and winter to summer.

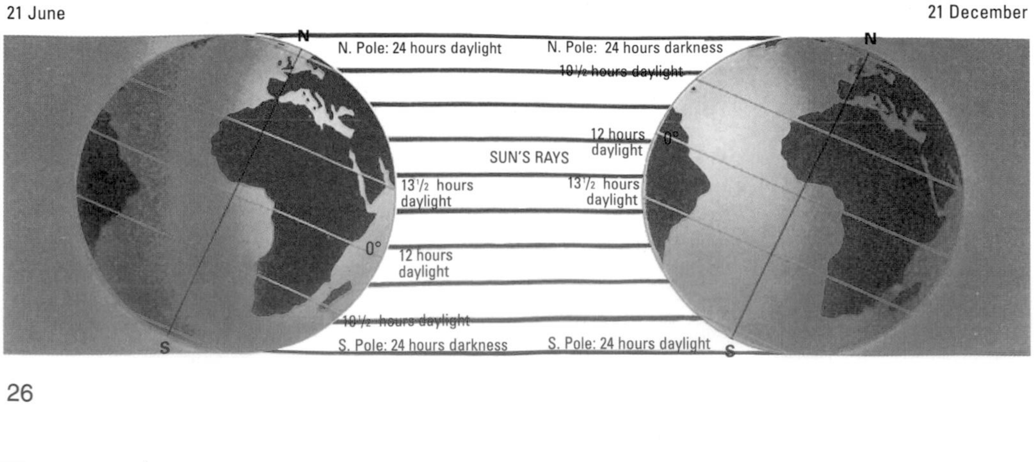

21 June
21 December
N
N. Pole: 24 hours daylight
N. Pole: 24 hours darkness
10½ hours daylight
12 hours daylight
SUN'S RAYS
0°
13½ hours daylight
13½ hours daylight
0°
12 hours daylight
10½ hours daylight
S. Pole: 24 hours darkness
S. Pole: 24 hours daylight
S

LEFT The Sun appears to "rise" in the east, reach its highest point at noon, and then "set" in the west, to be followed by night. In reality it is not the Sun that is moving but the Earth, rotating ("spinning" on its axis) from west to east. At the summer solstice in the Northern Hemisphere (21 June), the area inside the Arctic Circle has total daylight and the area inside the Antarctic Circle has total darkness. The opposite occurs at the winter solstice on 21 or 22 December. At the Equator, the length of day and night are almost equal all year round, with seasonal variations in between.

RIGHT The Moon rotates more slowly than the Earth, making one complete turn on its axis in just over 27 days. Since this corresponds to its period of revolution around the Earth, the Moon always presents the same hemisphere or face to us, and we never see its "dark side".

The interval between one full Moon and the next (and thus also between two new Moons) is about 29½ days – a lunar month. The apparent changes in the shape of the Moon are caused by its changing position in relation to the Earth; like the planets, the Moon produces no light of its own and shines only by reflecting the rays of the Sun.

BELOW The Earth rotates through 360° in 24 hours, and therefore moves 15° every hour. The world is divided into 24 standard time zones, each centred on lines of longitude at 15° intervals, 7½° on either side of its central meridian.

The prime or Greenwich meridian, based on the Royal Observatory in London, lies at the centre of the first zone. All places to the west of Greenwich are one hour behind for every 15° of longitude; places to the east are ahead by one hour for every 15°.

When it is 12 noon at the Greenwich meridian, at 180° east it is midnight of the same day – while at 180° west the day is only just beginning. To overcome this problem the International Dateline was established, approximately following the 180° meridian. If you travelled from Japan (140° east) to Samoa (170° west) you would pass from the night into the morning of the same day.

While some countries cope with several time zones (Russia experiences no fewer than 11), others "bend" the meridians to incorporate their territory in certain zones, and China, despite crossing five, follows just one. Others, including Iran and India, employ differences of half an hour.

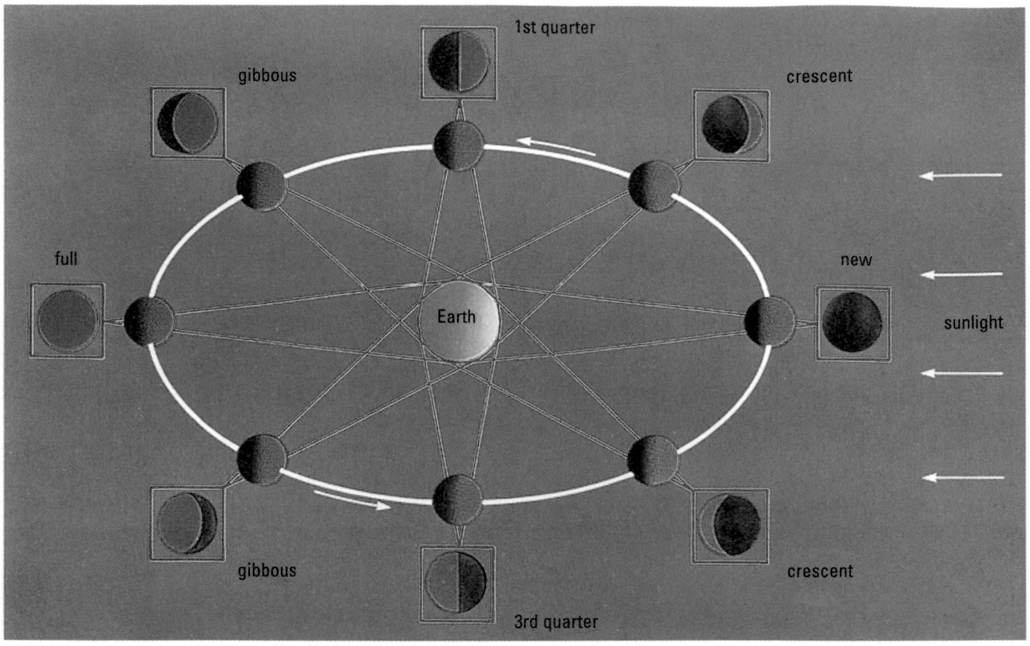

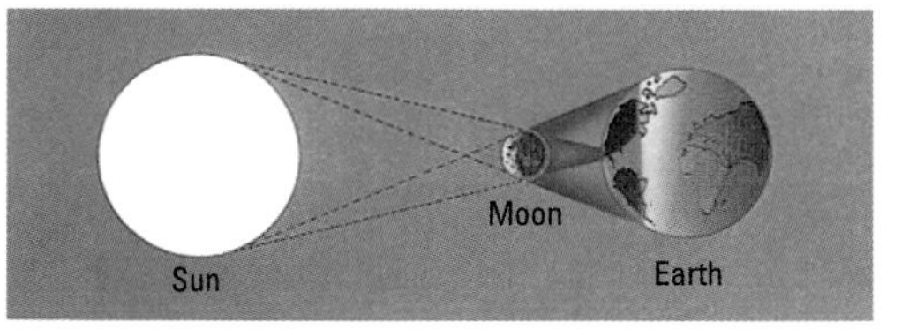

LEFT A solar eclipse occurs when the Moon passes between the Sun and the Earth. It will cause a partial eclipse of the Sun if the Earth passes through the Moon's outer shadow, or a total eclipse if the inner cone shadow crosses the Earth's surface. A total eclipse was visible in much of the Northern Hemisphere in 1999.

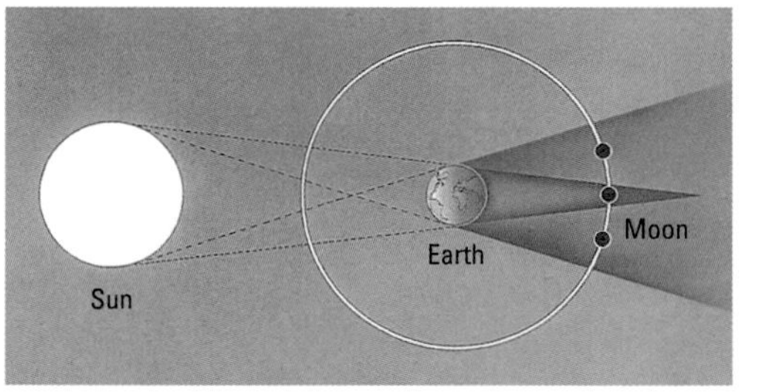

LEFT In a lunar eclipse the Earth's shadow crosses the Moon and, as with the solar version, provides either a partial or total eclipse. Eclipses do not occur every month because of the 5° difference between the plane of the Moon's orbit and the plane in which the Earth moves. In the 1990s, for example, only 14 eclipses were possible – seven partial and seven total – and each was visible only from certain and variable parts of the world.

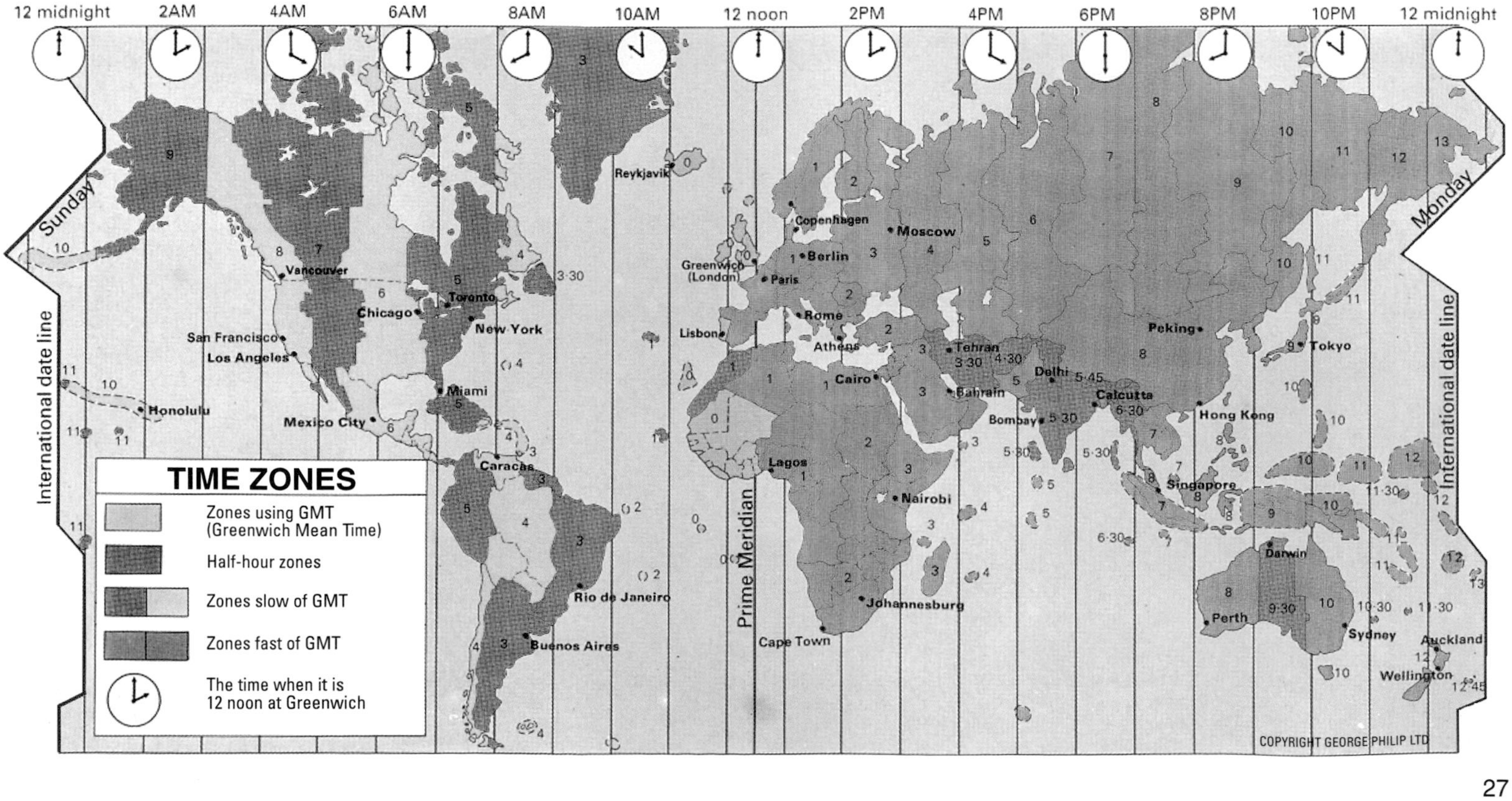

ANATOMY OF THE EARTH

THE EARTH is made up of several concentric shells, like the bulb of an onion. Each shell has its own particular chemical composition and physical properties. These layers are grouped into three main regions: the outermost is called the crust, which surrounds the mantle, and the innermost is the core. The solid, low-density crust on which we live is no thicker in relation to the Earth than an eggshell, taking up only 1.5% of the planet's volume. While the chemical distinction between crust and mantle is important, as far as physical processes go they behave as a single unit termed the lithosphere. It is a common fallacy that if you could drill through the Earth's crust you would find a molten mass: even well below the brittle outer shell that forms part of the lithosphere, the convecting part of the the mantle is still essentially solid, and pockets of liquid rock (magma) are relatively rare.

While the chemical composition of the crust and upper mantle is well known, little is absolutely certain about the layers beneath.

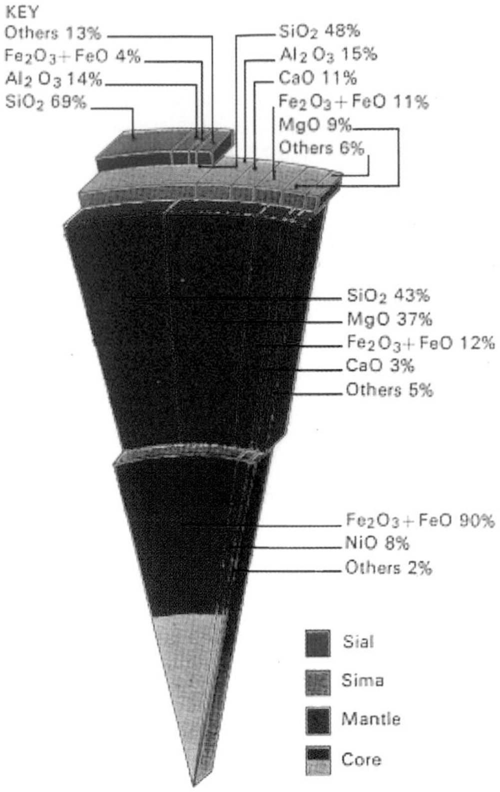

KEY
Others 13%
Fe_2O_3+FeO 4%
Al_2O_3 14%
SiO_2 69%
SiO_2 48%
Al_2O_3 15%
CaO 11%
Fe_2O_3+FeO 11%
MgO 9%
Others 6%
SiO_2 43%
MgO 37%
Fe_2O_3+FeO 12%
CaO 3%
Others 5%
Fe_2O_3+FeO 90%
NiO 8%
Others 2%
Sial
Sima
Mantle
Core

BELOW The Earth's crust varies in thickness from 40km (25 miles) under the continents to 5km (3 miles) under the seafloor. With the top of the mantle it forms the rigid lithosphere [1], which overlies a "plastic" layer, the asthenosphere [2], on which it may move. The upper mantle [3] goes down to about 700km (430 miles), where it overlies the lower mantle [4].

From the surface the temperature inside the Earth increases by 30°C for every kilometre (85°F for every mile), so that the asthenosphere is close to melting point. At 50km (30 miles), in the upper mantle, it reaches 800°C (1,480°F). After around 100km (60 miles) the rate of increase slows dramatically, and scientists now estimate the temperature to be 2,500°C (4,600°F) at the boundary of the lower mantle and core [5] – a depth of 2,900km (1,800 miles).

The mantle is separated from the outer core [6], which seismic observations suggest is in a liquid state. The density jumps from 5.5g/cm for the lower mantle to 10g/cm for the outer core, where it increases downwards to 12 or 13g/cm. The liquid outer core gives way to a solid inner core [7] at around 5,150km (3,200 miles] from the surface. Although the core is only around 16% of the Earth by volume, it represents 32% of its mass; it is thought to consist mostly of iron and some nickel, a hypothesis that fits the data and is inspired by iron-nickel meteorites which are probably the remnants of another planet. The temperature at the centre of the Earth (8) is estimated at least 3,000°C (5,400°F), and could be as high as 5,000°C (9,000°F).

ABOVE The Earth is composed of three main but unequal layers – the crust, mantle and core. The crust is subdivided into continental and oceanic material. The upper continental crust is mostly granite, abundant in silicon and aluminium – hence the term sial; over oceanic areas, and underlytng the continental sial, is a lighter material, essentially basalt and rich in silicon and magnesium – hence the term sima. The mantle comprises rock, rich in magnesium and iron silicates, and the dense core probably consists mainly of iron and nickel oxides, almost certainly in a molten condition. Heat is transferred to the surface by convection and conduction: in the solid layers it is probably transferred by conduction, and in the liquid layers it moves by convection.

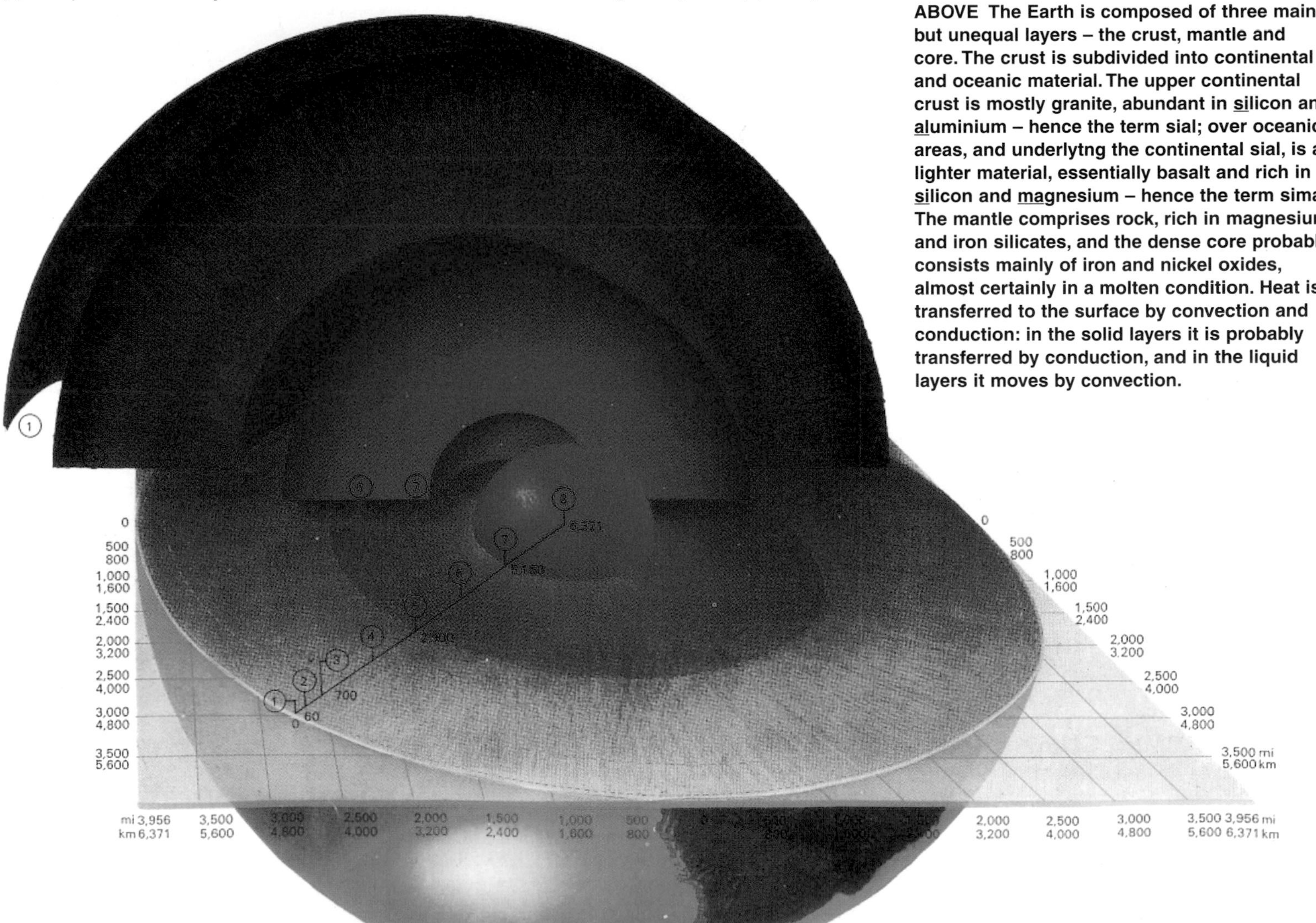

1
2
3
4
5
6
7
8
0
60
700
2,900
5,150
6,371
0
500
800
1,000
1,600
1,500
2,400
2,000
3,200
2,500
4,000
3,000
4,800
3,500
5,600
3,500 mi
5,600 km
mi 3,956
km 6,371
3,500 3,956 mi
5,600 6,371 km

The pressure at the Earth's inner core is 3.6 million times greater than that on the surface.

The Earth's mantle is separated from the core by a sudden change of density which shows up as a reflecting plane for the shear waves of earthquakes.

The Magnetic Earth

As the Earth spins on its axis, the fluid layer of the outer core allows the mantle and solid crust to rotate relatively faster than the inner core. As a result, electrons in the core move relative to those in the mantle and crust. It is this electron movement that constitutes a natural dynamo and produces a magnetic field similar to that produced by an electric coil.

The Earth's magnetic axis is inclined to its geographical axis by about 11°, and the magnetic poles don't coincide with the geographic north and south poles. The Earth's magnetic axis is continually changing its angle in relation to the geographic axis, but over a long time – some tens of thousands of years – an average relative position is established.

A compass needle points to a position some distance away from the geographical north and south poles. The difference (the declination), varies from one geographical location to the next, with small-scale variations in the Earth's magnetism. The magnetosphere is the volume of space in which the Earth's magnetic field predominates.

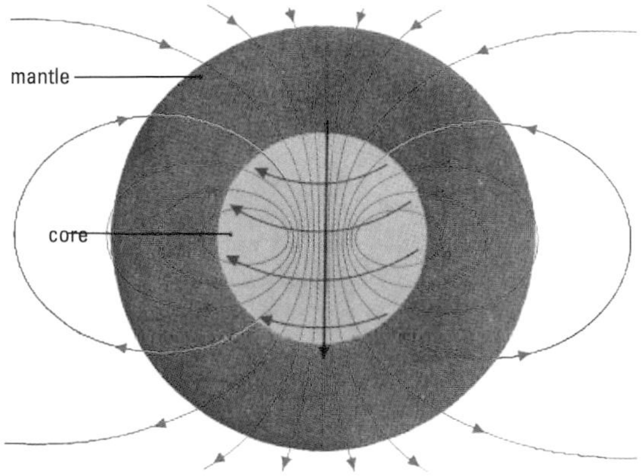

ABOVE The magnetic field originating inside the Earth makes up about 90% of the field observed at ground level: the remainder is due to currents of charged particles coming from the Sun and to the magnetism of rocks in the crust. The difference in rotation speed between the liquid outer core and the mantle creates a dynamo effect.

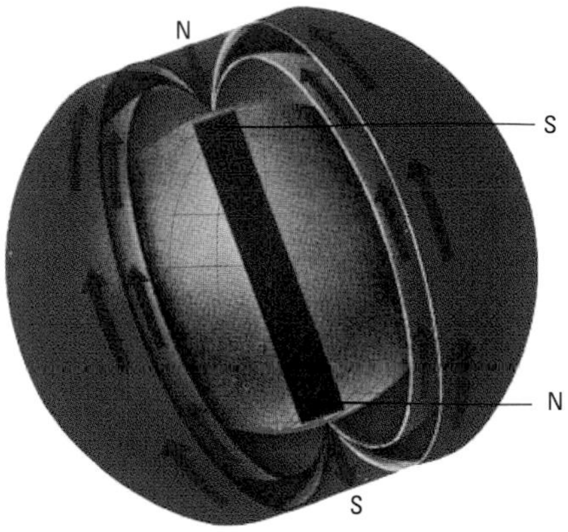

ABOVE The Earth's magnetic field is like that of a giant natural bar magnet placed inside the Earth, with its magnetic axis inclined at a small angle to the geographical axis. The poles of a compass needle are attracted by the magnetic poles of the Earth so that one end points to the north magnetic pole and the other to the south magnetic pole.

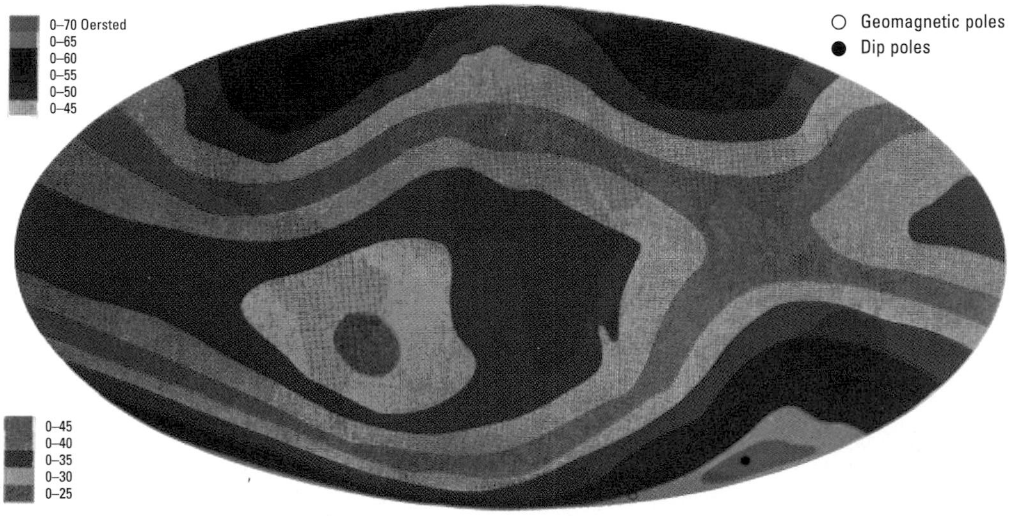

LEFT The intensity of the Earth's magnetic field is strongest at the poles and weakest in the equatorial regions. If the field were purely that of a bar magnet in the centre of the Earth and parallel to the spin axis, the lines of equal intensity would follow the lines of latitude and the magnetic poles would coincide with the geographic poles. In reality, however, the "bar magnet" field is inclined at about 11° to the spin axis and so are its geomagnetic poles.

Neither is the real field purely that of a bar magnet. The "dip poles", where the field direction is vertical (downwards at the north pole and upwards at the south dip pole), are themselves offset in respect to the geomagnetic poles – each by a different amount so that the south dip pole is not exactly opposite the north dip pole. Oersted is a traditional unit of magnetic field strength.

BELOW Until recent times taking account of the difference between the magnetic and geographic poles was crucial in navigation. The needle of a ship's magnetic compass, for example, swings to a position where its ends point to north and south along a line of force of the Earth's magnetic field. In navigation today, the magnetic compass is often replaced by the motor-driven gyrocompass, which indicates true north.

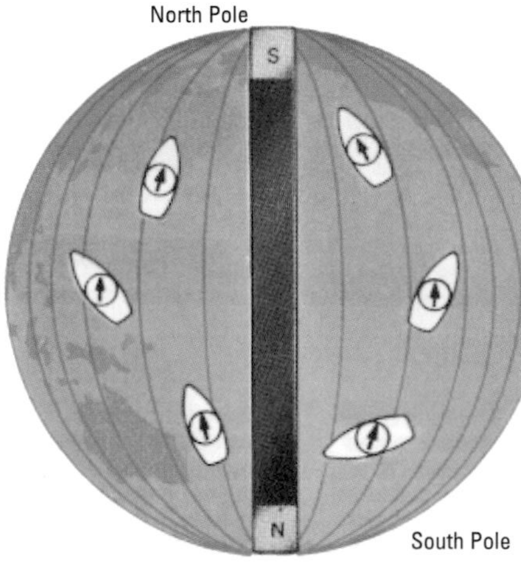

RIGHT The magnetosphere is the region in which the Earth's magnetic field can be detected. It would be symmetrical were it not for the "solar wind", electrically-charged particles from the Sun [A], which distort it to a teardrop shape. The particles meet the Earth's magnetic field at the shock front [1]. Behind this is a region of turbulence and inside the turbulent region is the magnetopause [2], the boundary of the magnetic field. The Van Allen belts [3] are two zones of high radiation in the magnetopause. The inner belt consists of high-energy particles produced by cosmic rays, the outer comprises solar electrons.

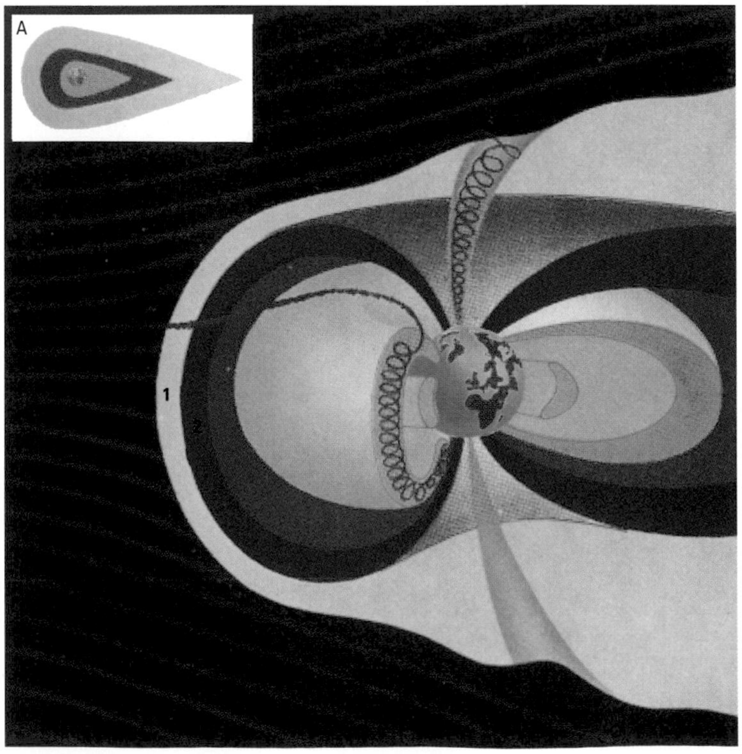

THE RESTLESS EARTH

THE THEORY of plate tectonics was advanced in the late 1960s and has had a revolutionary effect on the earth sciences. It is a unifying, all-embracing theory, offering a plausible and logical explanation for many of the Earth's varied structural phenomena, ranging from continental drift to earthquakes and mountain building.

The crust of the Earth, which together with the upper mantle forms the lithosphere, consists of rigid slabs called plates that are slowly but constantly moving their position in relation to each other. The plates are bounded by oceanic ridges, trenches and transform faults. Oceanic ridges are formed where two plates are moving apart, leaving a gap which is continuously filled by magma (molten rock) rising from the asthenosphere, on which the plates "float". As the magma cools, new crust is created on the ridges and becomes part of the oceanic plates.

This is the phenomenon known as seafloor spreading. Spreading rates, though slow, are not negligible: the North Atlantic is opening up by 4cm (1.6 in) a year, and the fastest rate is found at the East Pacific Rise, which creates 10cm (4 in) of new crust every year – 1,000km (620 miles) in the relatively short geological time of 10 million years.

Trenches as well as mountain ranges are formed where two plates converge. One of the plates slides steeply under the other and enters the mantle: the world's deepest trench, the Mariana, was formed when the Pacific plate was forced under the far smaller Philippine plate. Since the volume of the Earth does not change, the amount of crust created at the ridges is balanced by that destroyed at the trenches in an endless cycle of movement.

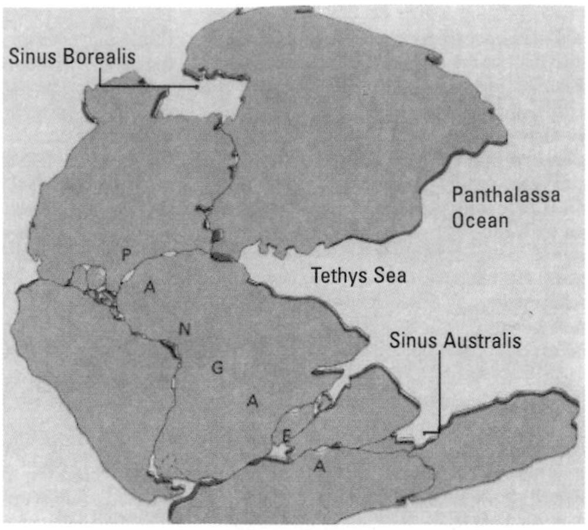

ABOVE First put forward by the German meteorologist Alfred Wegener in 1912, the theory of continental drift suggests the continents once formed a single land mass, Pangaea. The initial break-up created a northern mass, Laurasia, and a southern one, Gondwanaland, named after a province in India.

135 million years ago

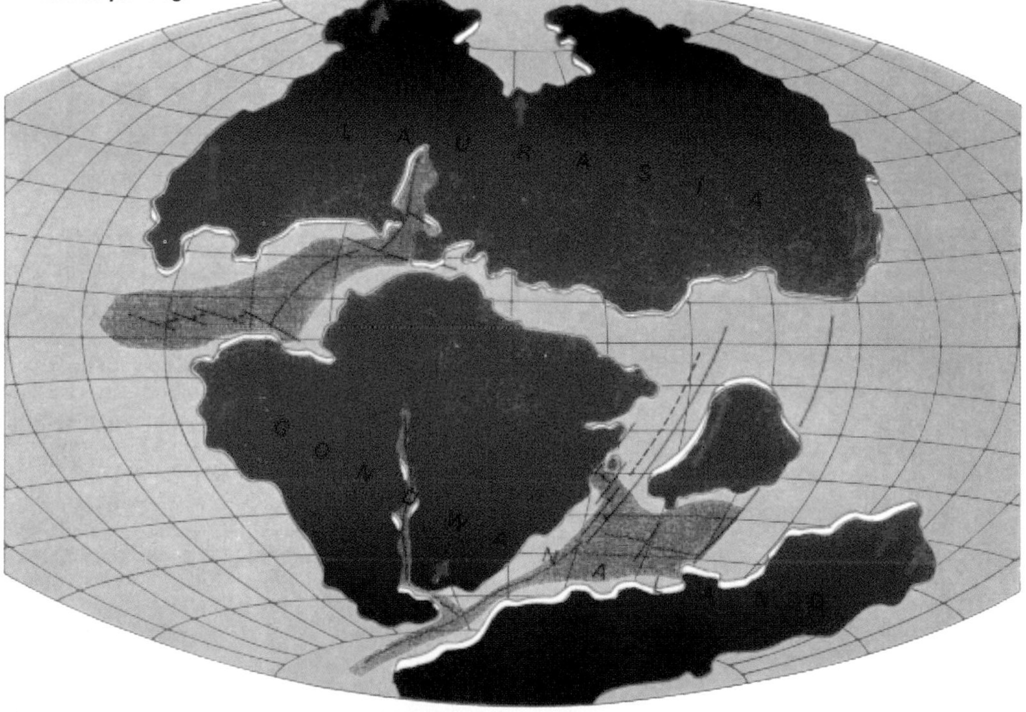

LEFT A map of Pangaea cannot be accurately constructed. The most suitable fit of the land masses is obtained by matching points midway down the continental slope, at about 200m (650ft). The easiest areas to fit together are the continents of Africa and South America, and while the linking of the northern lands is possible with a certain degree of accuracy, much remains to be learned of the complex fit of India, Antarctica and Australia with Africa and South America. The break-up of Pangaea began about 200 million years ago, and by the end of the Jurassic period, about 135 million years ago, the North Atlantic and Indian Oceans had become firmly established. The Tethys Sea was being diminished by the Asian land mass rotating in an anti-clockwise direction, and South America had begun to move away from Africa to form the South Atlantic.

65 million years ago

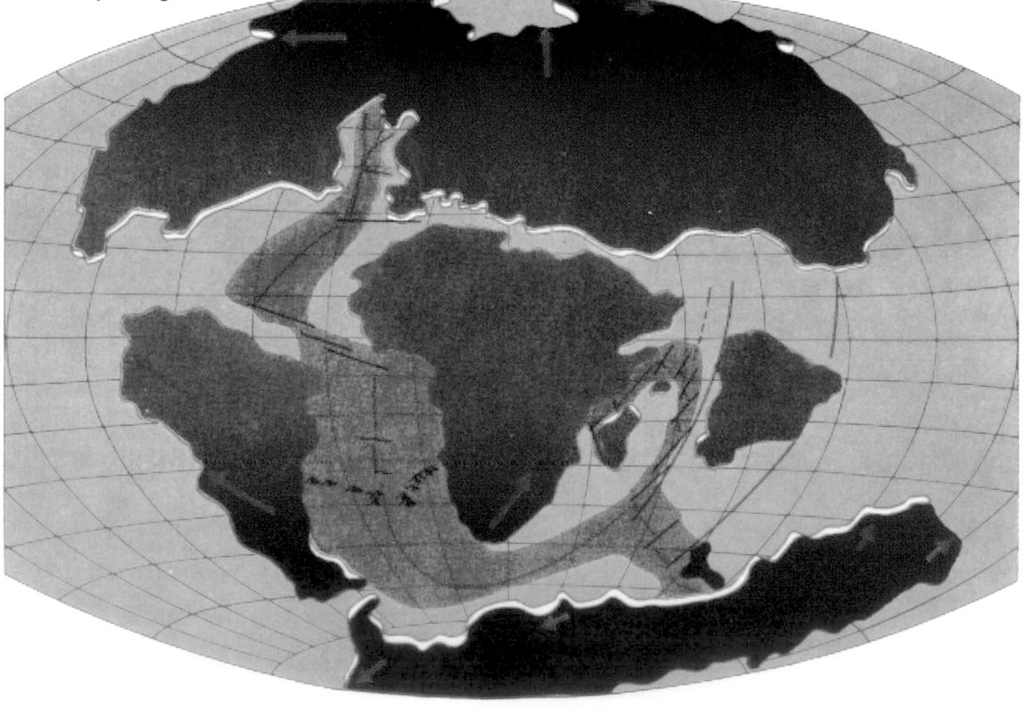

LEFT By the end of the Cretaceous period, about 65 million years ago, the South Atlantic had grown, Madagascar had parted from Africa and India had continued northwards. Antarctica was moving away from the central land mass, though still linked with Australia. The North Atlantic rift forked at the north, starting to form the island of Greenland.

Geological evidence that the continents were once linked is provided by distinctive rock formations that can be assembled into continuous belts when South America and Africa are juxtaposed; by the processes of mountain building, notably India grinding into Asia and crumpling up sediments to form the Himalayas; and by the dovetailed distribution of many plants and animals.

Perhaps the most important impetus to the theory of continental drift came from the twin theories of plate tectonics and seafloor spreading, which developed rapidly from the 1960s. One of the weakest points in Wegener's argument centred on the tremendous forces needed to drive the continents apart. The new plate theories, which have been substantially proven, provide an explanation of the source of the necessary power. Even so, much has still to be learned about the original continent.

RIGHT The debate about continental drift was followed by a more radical idea: plate tectonics. The basic theory proposes that the Earth's crust comprises a series of rigid plates that "float" on a softer layer of the mantle, and are moved about by continental convection currents within the Earth's interior. These plates slowly converge and diverge along margins marked by seismic (earthquake) activity.

Converging plates form either trenches (where the oceanic plate sinks below the lighter continental rock), or mountain ranges. The theory not only supports the notion of continental drift: it also explains the paradox that while there have always been oceans, none of the present seabeds contain sediments more than 150 million years old.

The six major mobile plates (the American, Eurasian, African, Indo-Australian, Pacific and Antarctic) contain smaller plates such as the Arabian and West Indian plates which "absorb" the geometrical discrepancies between major plates by creating or destroying compensating amounts of crustal material.

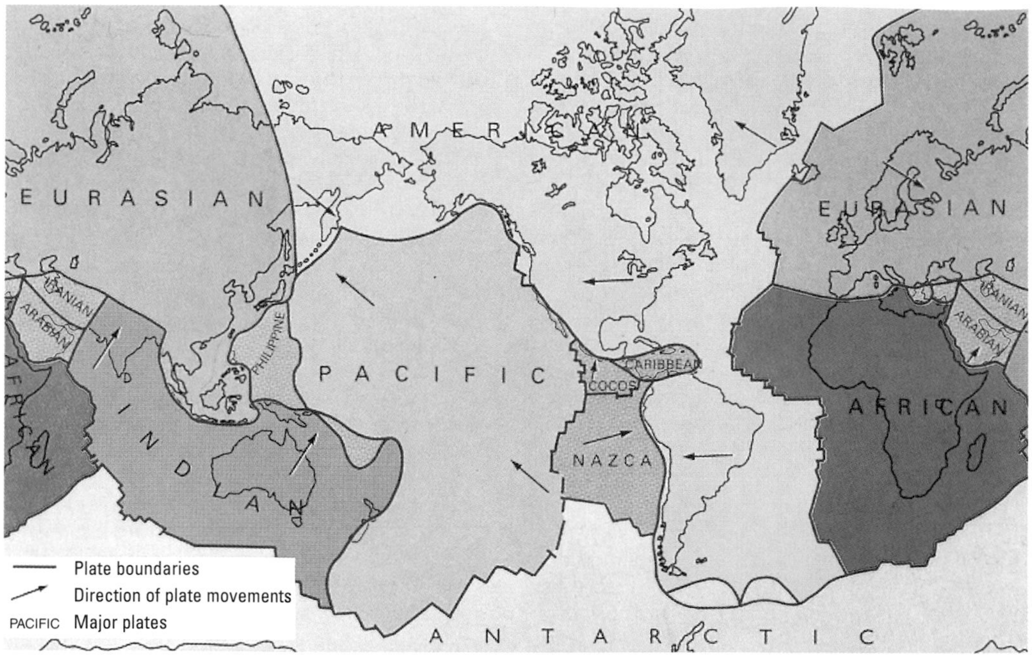

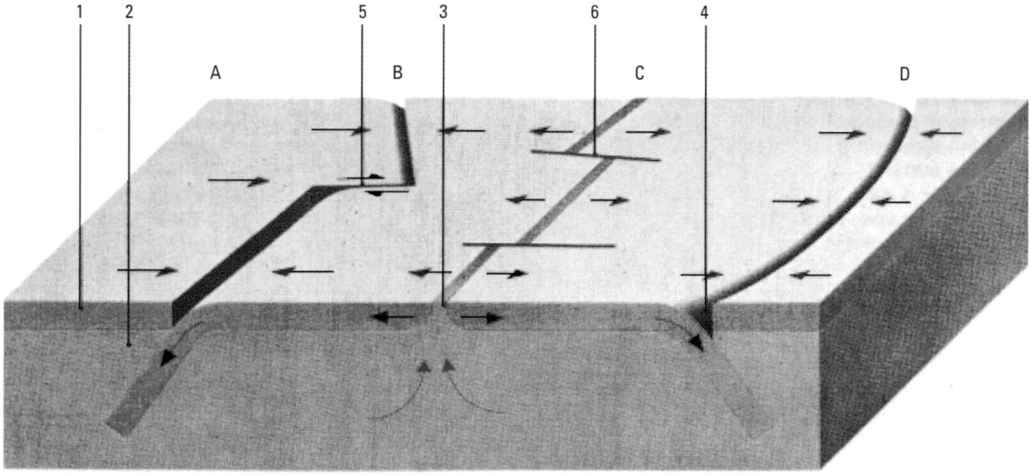

ABOVE The plate tectonics theory sees the Earth's lithosphere [1] as a series of rigid but mobile slabs called plates [A,B,C,D]. The lithosphere floats on a "plastic" layer called the asthenosphere [2]. There are three types of boundaries. At the mid-oceanic ridges [3], upwelling of mantle material occurs and new seafloor is formed. A trench [4] is formed where one plate of oceanic crust slides beneath the other, which may be oceanic or continental. The third type of boundary is where two plates slide past one another, creating a transform fault [5,6]. These link two segments of the same ridge [6], two ocean trenches [5] or a ridge to a trench. Plates move from ridges and travel like conveyor belts towards the trenches.

BELOW Collision zones are where two plates, each carrying a continental mass, meet. When one of the plates is forced beneath the other, the buoyant continental material is pushed upwards in a series of high overthrusts and folds, producing great mountain ranges. The Himalayas, formed when the northward-moving Indian plate crunched up against the Eurasian plate, were the result of such forces – as were other leading fold mountains such as the Alps in Europe (African/Eurasian plates), the Andes in South America (Nazca/American) and the western Rockies (Pacific/American).

50 million years ahead

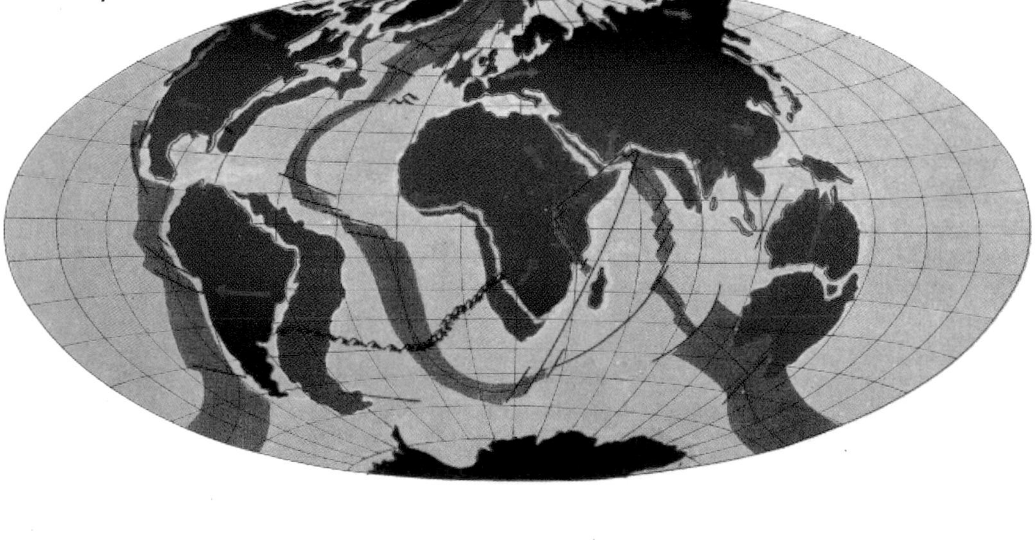

LEFT The continents are still drifting, and there is no reason to expect them to stop. This is how the world may look 50 million years from now if drift is maintained as predicted. The most striking changes in this "new world" are the joining of the Atlantic and Pacific Oceans; the splitting away from the USA of Baja California and the area west of the San Andreas fault line; the northward drift of Africa; the breaking away of that part of the African continent east of the present-day Great Rift Valley; and Australia's continued journey north towards Asia. The majority of the great continent of Antarctica, however, remains in its present southerly position. Plant fossils found in Antarctica's coal seams – remnants of its tropical past hundreds of millions of years ago – are among many examples of evidence supporting the tectonic theory of continent drift.

EARTHQUAKES

AN EARTHQUAKE is the sudden release of energy in the form of vibrations and tremors caused by compressed or stretched rock snapping along a fault in the Earth's surface. Rising lava under a volcano can also produce small tremors. It has been estimated that about a million earthquakes occur each year, but most of these are so minor that they pass unnoticed. While really violent earthquakes occur about once every two weeks, fortunately most of these take place under the oceans, and only rarely do they produce tsunamis.

Slippage along a fault is initially prevented by friction along the fault plane. This causes energy, which generates movement, to be stored up as elastic strain, similar to the effect created when a bow is drawn. Eventually the strain reaches a critical point, the friction is overcome and the rocks snap past each other, releasing the stored-up energy in the form of earthquakes by vibrating back and forth. Earthquakes can also occur when rock folds that can no longer support the elastic strain break to form a fault.

Shockwaves

Seismic or shockwaves spread outwards in all directions from the focus of an earthquake, much as sound waves do when a gun is fired. There are two main types of seismic wave: compressional and shear. Compressional waves cause the rock particles through which they pass to shake back and forth in the direction of the wave, and can be transmitted through both solids and liquids; they are therefore able to travel through the Earth's core. Shear waves make the particles vibrate at right-angles to the direction of their passage, and can travel only through solids; at the boundary of lower mantle and liquid outer core, they are reflected back to the Earth's surface. Neither type of seismic wave physically moves the particles – it merely travels through them.

Compressional waves, which travel 1.7 times faster than shear waves, are the first ones to be distinguished at an earthquake recording station. Consequently seismologists refer to them as primary (P) waves and to the shear waves as secondary (S) waves. A third wave type is recognized by seismologists – the long (L) wave which travels slowly along the Earth's surface, vertically or horizontally. It is L waves that produce the most violent shocks.

Measuring earthquakes

The magnitude of earthquakes is usually rated according to either the Richter or the Modified Mercalli scales, both formulated in the 1930s. Developed by the US geologist Charles Richter, the Richter scale measures the total energy released by a quake with mathematical precision, each upward step representing a tenfold increase in shockwave power. A magnitude of 2 is hardly felt, while a magnitude of 7 is the lower limit of an earthquake that has a devastating effect over a large area. Theoretically there is no upper limit, but the largest measured have been rated at between 8.8 and 8.9. The 12-point Mercalli scale, named after the Italian seismologist Guiseppe Mercalli, is based on damage done and thus varies in different places. It ranges from I (noticed only by seismographs) to XII (total destruction); intermediate points include VII (collapse of substandard buildings) and IX (conspicuous cracks in the ground).

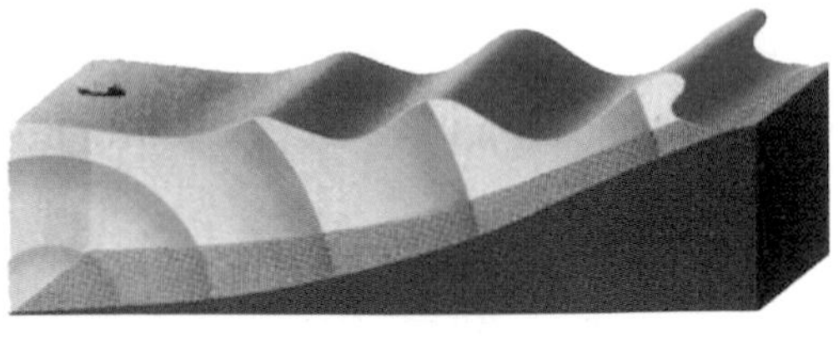

ABOVE The long wave length of tsunamis gives them tremendous speed. An earthquake in the Aleutian Trench in the far northern Pacific in 1946 triggered off a tsunami that devastated Honolulu; it took 4 hours 34 minutes to reach Hawaii, a distance of 3,220km (2,000 miles) – a speed of about 700km/h (440mph).

Tsunamis

Tsunami is the Japanese word for a seismic sea wave; they are often called tidal waves, though they have no connection with tides. Tsunamis are caused mainly by seismic disburbances below the seafloor (oceanic earthquakes), but also by submarine landslides and volcanic eruptions. Other tidal waves can be due to the surge of water when the barometric pressure is exceptionally low, such as in a hurricane. At sea, the height of the wave is seldom more than 60–90cm (2–3ft), but the wave length may be as long as 200km (120 miles), generating speeds of up to 750km/h (450mph).

Although the height of the crest is low out to sea, tsunamis have immense energy, which, as they lose speed in more shallow water, is converted into an increase in height. The waves, on reaching the shore, may be 40m (125ft) or more high. The most destructive tsunamis occur in the northern Pacific.

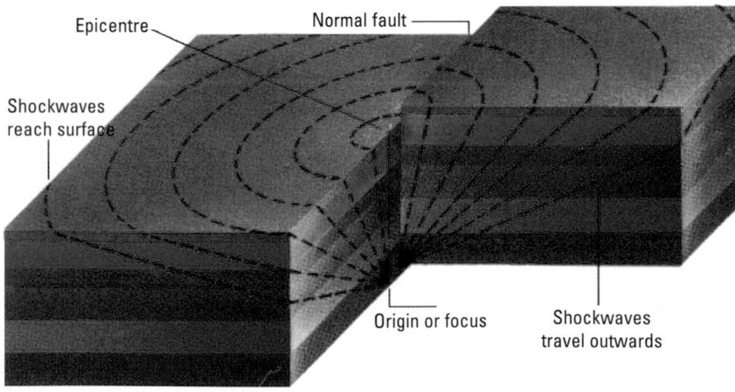
Epicentre
Normal fault
Shockwaves reach surface
Origin or focus
Shockwaves travel outwards

LEFT An earthquake takes place when two parts of the Earth's surface move suddenly in relation to each other along a crack called a fault. The point from which this movement originates is called the focus, usually located at depths between 8 and 30km (5 to 18 miles), and the point on the surface directly above this is called the epicentre. Shockwaves move outwards from the focus in a curved pattern; while speed varies with the density of rock, intensity decreases the farther the waves travel.

BELOW Earthquakes occur in geologically sensitive areas of the world such as mid-oceanic ridges and mountain-building regions, and can be classified according to the depth of their focus. Deep focus quakes occur at depths of between 300 and 650km (185-400 miles), intermediate focus quakes from 55 to 240km (35-150 miles), and shallow focus quakes from the surface down to a depth of 55km (35 miles).

EARTHQUAKE ZONES

Major earthquake zones
Areas experiencing frequent earthquakes

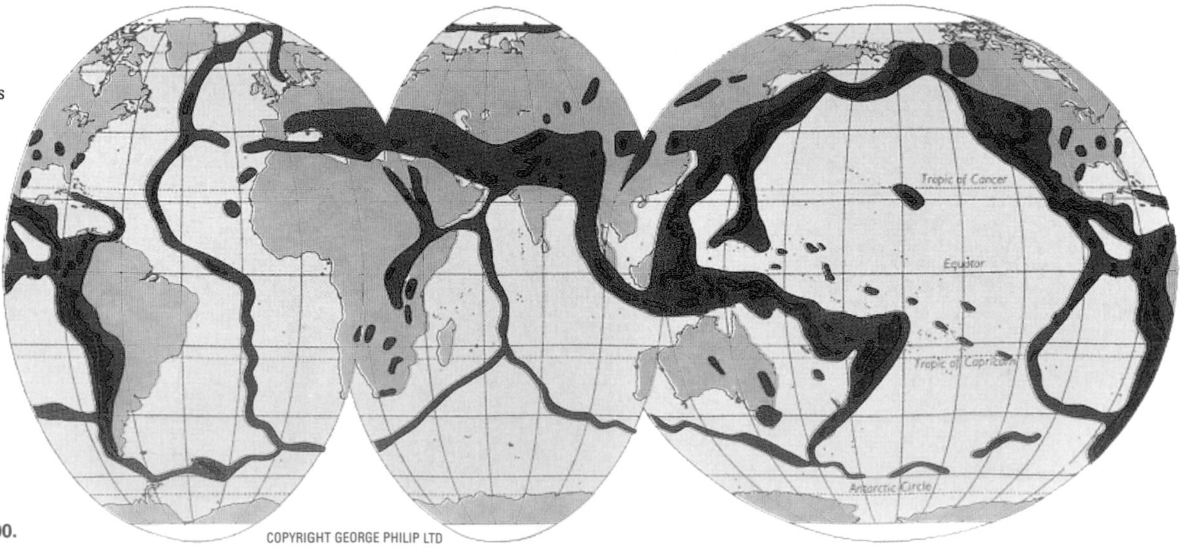
Tropic of Cancer
Equator
Tropic of Capricorn
Antarctic Circle
COPYRIGHT GEORGE PHILIP LTD

The highest magnitude recorded on the Richter scale is 8.9, for a quake that killed 2,990 people in Japan on 2 March 1933. The most devastating earthquake ever affected three provinces of central China on 2 February 1556, when it is believed that about 830,000 people perished. The highest toll in modern times was at Tangshan, eastern China, on 28 July 1976: the original figure of over 655,000 deaths has since been twice revised by the Chinese government to stand at 242,000.

VOLCANOES

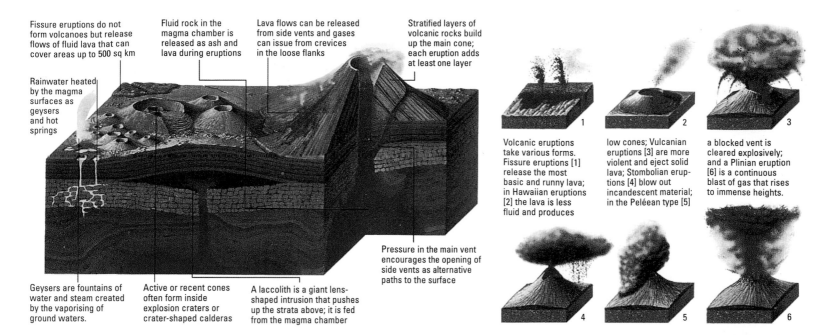

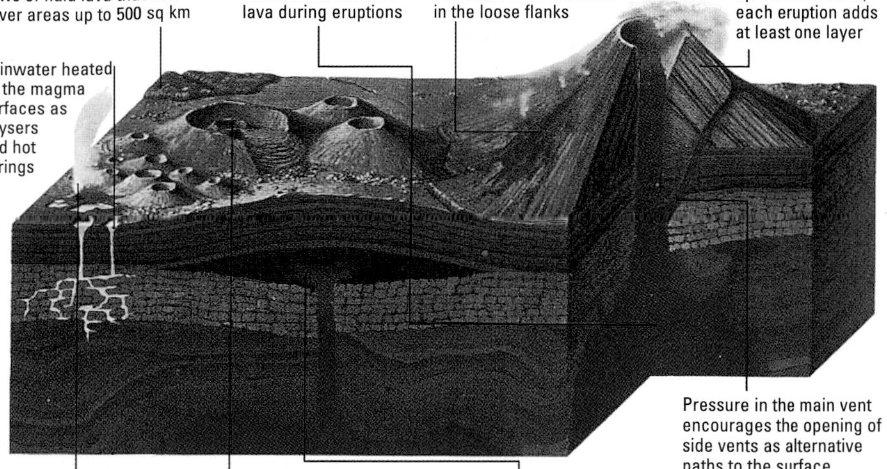

Fissure eruptions do not form volcanoes but release flows of fluid lava that can cover areas up to 500 sq km
Fluid rock in the magma chamber is released as ash and lava during eruptions
Lava flows can be released from side vents and gases can issue from crevices in the loose flanks
Stratified layers of volcanic rocks build up the main cone; each eruption adds at least one layer
Rainwater heated by the magma surfaces as geysers and hot springs
Pressure in the main vent encourages the opening of side vents as alternative paths to the surface
Geysers are fountains of water and steam created by the vaporising of ground waters.
Active or recent cones often form inside explosion craters or crater-shaped calderas
A laccolith is a giant lens-shaped intrusion that pushes up the strata above; it is fed from the magma chamber

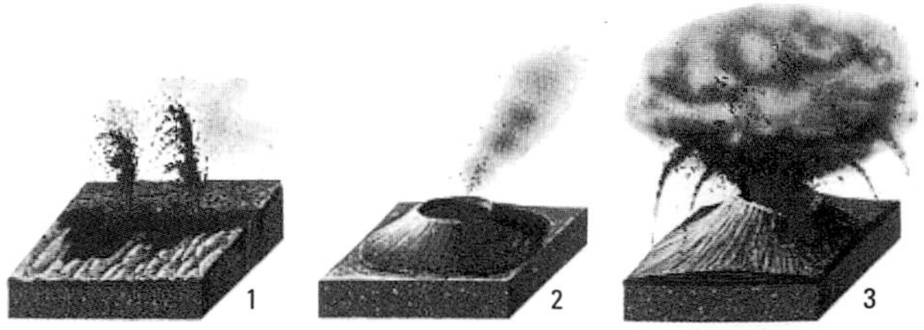

1
2
3

Volcanic eruptions take various forms. Fissure eruptions [1] release the most basic and runny lava; in Hawaiian eruptions [2] the lava is less fluid and produces low cones; Vulcanian eruptions [3] are more violent and eject solid lava; Stombolian eruptions [4] blow out incandescent material; in the Peléean type [5] a blocked vent is cleared explosively; and a Plinian eruption [6] is a continuous blast of gas that rises to immense heights.

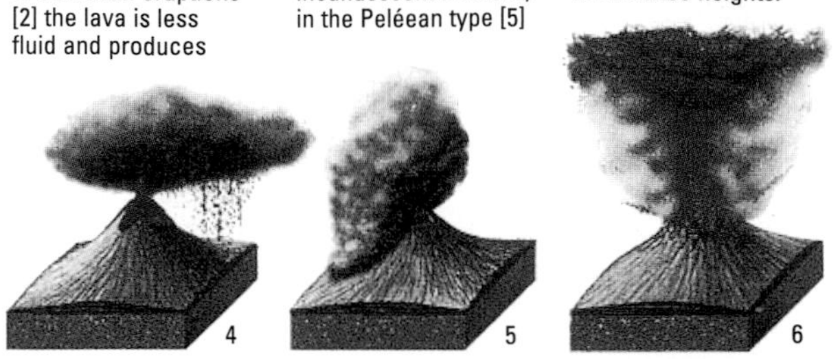

4
5
6

THE WORLD'S most spectacular natural displays of energy, volcanoes are responsible for forming large parts of the Earth's crust. Volcanoes occur when hot liquefied rock beneath the crust is pushed up by pressure to the surface as molten lava. They are found in places where the crust is weak – the mid-ocean ridges and their continental continuations, and along the collision edges of crustal plates. Some volcanoes erupt in an explosive way, throwing out rocks and ash, while others are effusive and lava flows out of the vent. Some, such as Mount Fuji in Japan, are both.

An accumulation of lava and cinders creates cones of various sizes and shapes. As a result of many eruptions over centuries Mount Etna in Sicily has a circumference of more than 120km (75 miles). Craters at rest are often filled by a lake – and the mudflow caused by an eruption can be as destructive as a lava flow and, because of its speed, even more lethal.

Despite the increasingly sophisticated technology available to geologists to monitor volcanoes, like earthquakes they remain both dramatic and unpredictable. For example, in 1991 Mount Pinatubo, located 100km (60 miles) north of the Philippines capital Manila, suddenly burst into life without any warning after lying dormant for over six centuries.

Most of the world's active volcanoes are located in a belt round the Pacific Ocean, on the edge of the Pacific crustal plate, called the "Ring of Fire" – a circle of fear that threatens over 400 million people. However, the soils formed by the weathering of volcanic rocks are usually exceptionally fertile, and despite the dangers large numbers of people have always lived in the shadows of volcanoes.

Climatologists believe that volcanic ash, if ejected high into the atmosphere, can influence temperature and weather conditions generally over a massive area and for several years afterwards. It has been estimated that the 1991 eruption of Mount Pinatubo in the Philippines threw up more than 20 million tonnes of dust and ash over 30km (18 miles) into the atmosphere, and it is widely believed that this accelerated the depletion of the ozone layer over large parts of the globe.

There are far more volcanoes on the seafloor than on the land, however. These "seamounts" exist because the oceanic crust is newer and thinner than continental crust and easily pierced by the underlying magma.The Pacific Ocean alone is thought to have more than 10,000 underwater volcanoes over 3,000m (9,850ft) high.

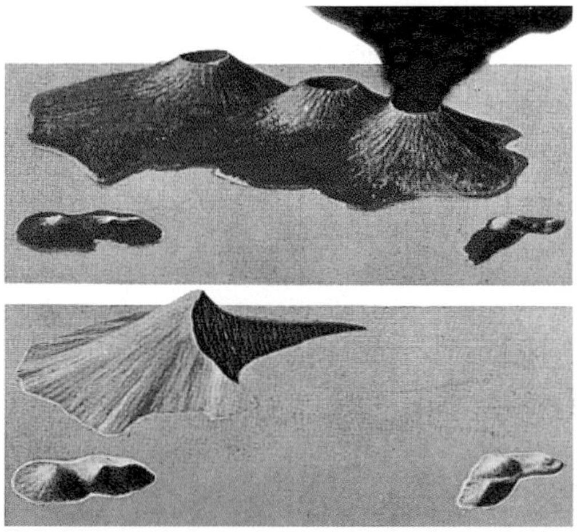

ABOVE Situated in the Sunda Strait of Indonesia, Krakatau was a small volcanic island inactive for over 200 years when, in August 1883, two-thirds of it was destroyed by a violent erruption. It was so powerful that the resulting tidal wave killed 36,000 people. Indonesia has the greatest concentration of volcanoes with 90, 12 of which are active.

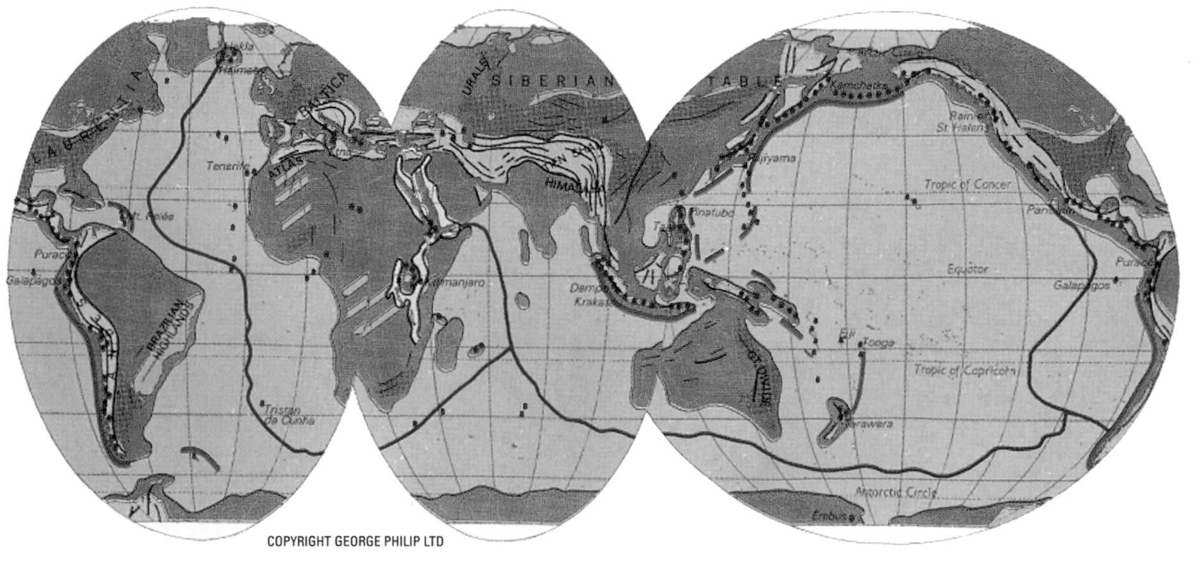

SIBERIAN
TABLE
HIMALAYA
Kamchatka
Rainier
St Helens
Fujiyama
Pinatubo
Tenerife
Kilimanjaro
Krakatau
Galapagos
Tristan da Cunha
Erebus
Tropic of Cancer
Equator
Tropic of Capricorn
Antarctic Circle
COPYRIGHT GEORGE PHILIP LTD

VOLCANIC ZONES

- Volcanoes
- Seafloor spreading centre
- Ocean trench
- Continental shelf

Structure

- Pre-Cambrian
- Caledonian folding
- Hercynian folding
- Tertiary folding
- Great Rift Valley
- Main trend lines

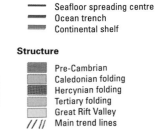

Of the 850 volcanoes to produce recorded eruptions, nearly three-quarters lie in the "Ring of Fire" that surrounds the Pacific Ocean on the edge of the Pacific plate.

SHAPING THE LANDSCAPE

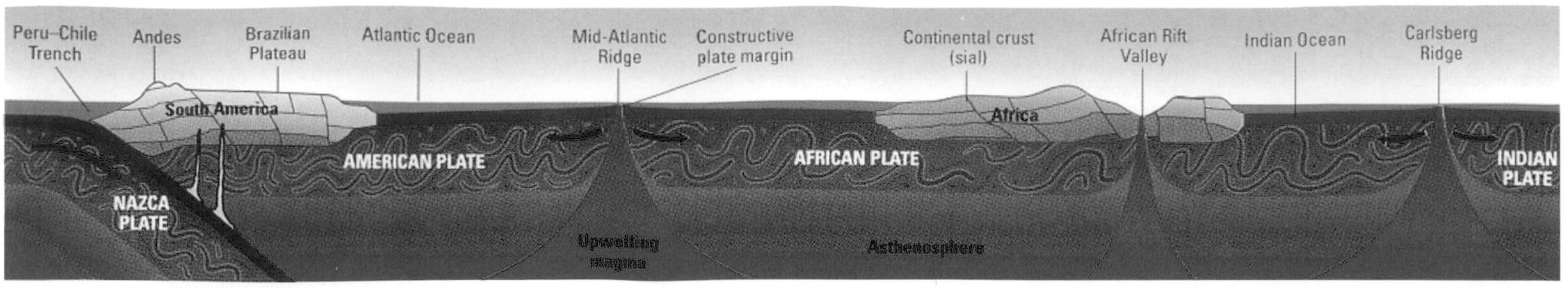
Peru–Chile Trench
Andes
Brazilian Plateau
Atlantic Ocean
Mid-Atlantic Ridge
Constructive plate margin
Continental crust (sial)
African Rift Valley
Indian Ocean
Carlsberg Ridge
South America
Africa
AMERICAN PLATE
AFRICAN PLATE
INDIAN PLATE
NAZCA PLATE
Upwelling magma
Asthenosphere

ABOVE A view of seafloor spreading along the Equator from the west coast of South America to the centre of the Indian Ocean. On the left, the Nazca plate has been subducted beneath the American plate to push up the Andes.

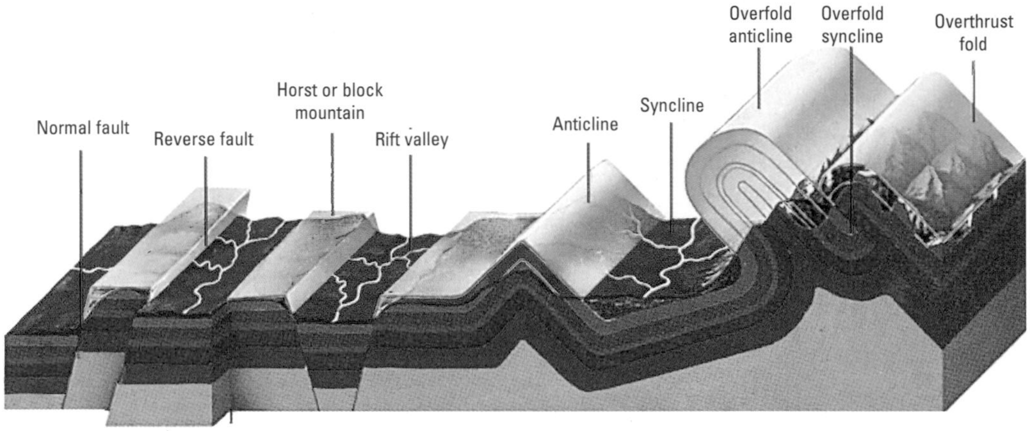
Normal fault
Reverse fault
Horst or block mountain
Rift valley
Anticline
Syncline
Overfold anticline
Overfold syncline
Overthrust fold

RIGHT A normal fault results when vertical movement causes the surface to break apart, while compression leads to a reverse fault. Horizontal movement causes shearing, known as a tear or strike-slip fault. When the rock breaks in two places, the central block may be pushed up in a "horst", or sink in a rift valley. Folds occur when rock strata are squeezed and compressed. Layers bending up form an anticline, those bending down form a syncline.

THE VAST ridges that divide the Earth beneath the world's oceans mark the boundaries between tectonic plates that are gradually moving in opposite directions. As the plates shift apart, molten magma rises from the mantle to seal the rift and the seafloor spreads towards the land masses. The rate of spreading has been calculated at about 40mm (1.6in) a year in the North Atlantic Ocean.

Near the ocean shore, underwater volcanoes mark the lines where the continental rise begins. As the plates meet, much of the denser oceanic crust dips beneath the continental plate at the "subduction zone" and falls back to the magma.

Mountains are formed when pressures on the Earth's crust caused by continental drift become so intense that the surface buckles or cracks. This happens where oceanic crust is subducted by continental crust, or where two tectonic plates collide: the Rockies, Andes, Alps, Urals and Himalayas all resulted from such impacts. These are known as fold mountains because they were formed by the compression of the sedimentary rocks, forcing the surface to bend and fold like a crumpled rug.

The other main mountain-building process occurs when the crust is being stretched or compressed so violently that the rock strata breaks to create faults, allowing rock to be forced upwards in large blocks; or when the pressure of magma inside the crust forces the surface to bulge into a dome, or erupts to form a volcano. Large and more complex mountain ranges may well reveal a combination of these features.

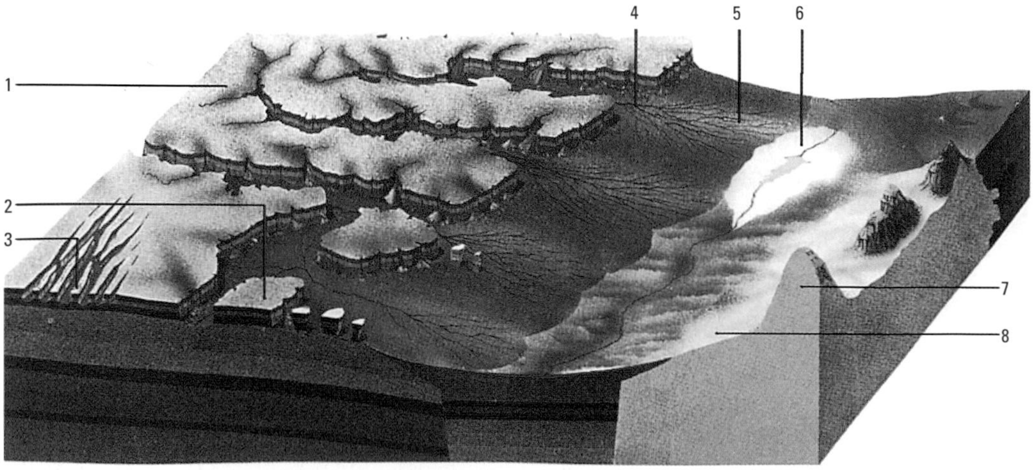
1
2
3
4
5
6
7
8

ABOVE The topography of a desert is characterized by the relative absence of the chemical weathering associated with water, and most erosion takes place mechanically through wind abrasion and the effect of heat – and cold.

Mesas [1] are large flat-topped areas with steep sides, while the butte [2] is a flat isolated hill, also with steep sides. Elongated in the direction of the prevailing wind, yardangs [3] comprise tabular masses of resistant rock resting on undercut pillars of softer material. Alluvial fans [5] are pebble-mounds deposited in desert deltas by flash floods, usually at the end of a wadi [4]. A saltpan [6] is a temporary lake of brackish water, also formed by flash floods. An inselberg [7] is an isolated hill rising from the plain, and a pediment [8] is a gently inclining rock surface.

AGENTS OF EROSION

Destruction of the landscape, however, begins as soon as it is formed. Wind, ice, water and sea, the main agents of erosion, maintain a constant assault that even the hardest rocks cannot withstand. Mountain peaks may dwindle by only a few millimetres a year, but if they are not uplifted by further movements of the Earth's crust they will eventually disappear. Over millions of years, even great mountain ranges can be reduced to a low, rugged landscape.

Water is the most powerful destroyer: it has been estimated that 100 billion tonnes of rock are washed into the oceans each year. Three Asian rivers alone account for a fifth of this total – the Hwang Ho in China, and the Ganges and the Brahmaputra in Bangladesh.

When water freezes, its volume increases by about 9%, and no rock is strong enough to resist this pressure. Where water has penetrated fissures or seeped into softer rock, a freeze followed by a thaw may result in rockfalls or earthslides, creating major destruction in minutes.

Over much longer periods, acidity in rain water breaks down the chemical composition of porous rocks such as limestone, eating away the rock to form deep caves and tunnels. Chemical decomposition also occurs in river beds and glacier valleys, hastening the process of mechanical erosion.

Like the sea, rivers and glaciers generate much of their effect through abrasion, pounding or tearing the land with the debris they carry. Yet as well as destroying existing landforms they also create new ones, many of them spectacular. Prominent examples include the Grand Canyon, the vast deltas of the Mississippi and the Nile, the rock arches and stacks off the south coast of Australia, and the deep fjords cut by glaciers in British Columbia, Norway and New Zealand.

While landscapes evolve from a "young" mountainous stage, through a "mature" hilly stage to an "old age" of lowland plain, this long-term cycle of erosion is subject to interruption by a number of crucial factors, including the pronounced effects of plate tectonics and climate change.

Shaping forces: ice

Many of the world's most dramatic landscapes have been carved by icesheets and glaciers. During the Ice Ages of the Pleistocene epoch (over 10,000 years ago) up to a third of the land surface was glaciated; even today a tenth is still covered in ice – the vast majority locked up in the huge icesheets of Antarctica and Greenland.

Valley glaciers are found in mountainous regions throughout the world, except Australia. In the relatively short geological time scale of the recent Ice Ages, glaciers accomplished far more carving of the topography than rivers and wind.

They are formed from compressed snow, called névé, accumulating in a valley head or cirque. Slowly the glacier moves downhill, moving at rates of between a few millimetres and several metres a day, scraping away debris from the mountains and valleys through which it passes. The debris, or moraine, adds to the abrasive power of the ice. The sediments are transported by the ice to the edge of the glacier, where they are deposited or carried away by meltwater streams.

Shaping forces: rivers

From their origins as small upland rills and streams channelling rainfall, or as springs releasing water that has seeped into the ground, all rivers are incessantly at work cutting and shaping the landscape on their way to the sea.

In highland regions flow may be rapid and turbulent, pounding rocks to cut deep gorges and V-shaped valleys through softer rocks, or tumbling as waterfalls over harder ones.

As they reach more gentle slopes, rivers release some of the pebbles and heavier sediments they have carried downstream, flow more slowly and broaden out. Levées or ridges are raised along their banks by the deposition of mud and sand during floods. In lowland plains the river drifts into meanders, depositing layers of sediment, especially on the inside of bends where the flow is weakest. As the river reaches the sea it deposits its remaining load, and estuaries are formed where the tidal currents are strong enough to remove them; if not, the debris creates a delta.

Shaping forces: the sea

Under the constant assault from tides and currents, wind and waves, coastlines change faster than most landscape features, both by erosion and by the building up of sand and pebbles carried by the sea. In severe storms, giant waves pound the shoreline with rocks and boulders; but even in much quieter conditions, the sea steadily erodes cliffs and headlands, creating new features in the form of sand dunes, spits and salt marshes. Beaches, where sand and shingle have been deposited, form a buffer zone between the erosive power of the waves and the coast. Because it is composed of loose materials, a beach can rapidly adapt its shape to changes in wave energy.

Where the coastline is formed from soft rocks such as sandstones, debris may fall evenly and be carried away by currents from shelving beaches. In areas with harder rock, the waves may cut steep cliffs and wave-cut platforms; eroded debris is deposited as a terrace. Bays and smaller coves are formed when sections of soft rock are carved away between headlands of harder rock. These are then battered by waves from both sides, until the headlands are eventually reduced to rock arches, which as stacks are later separated from the mainland.

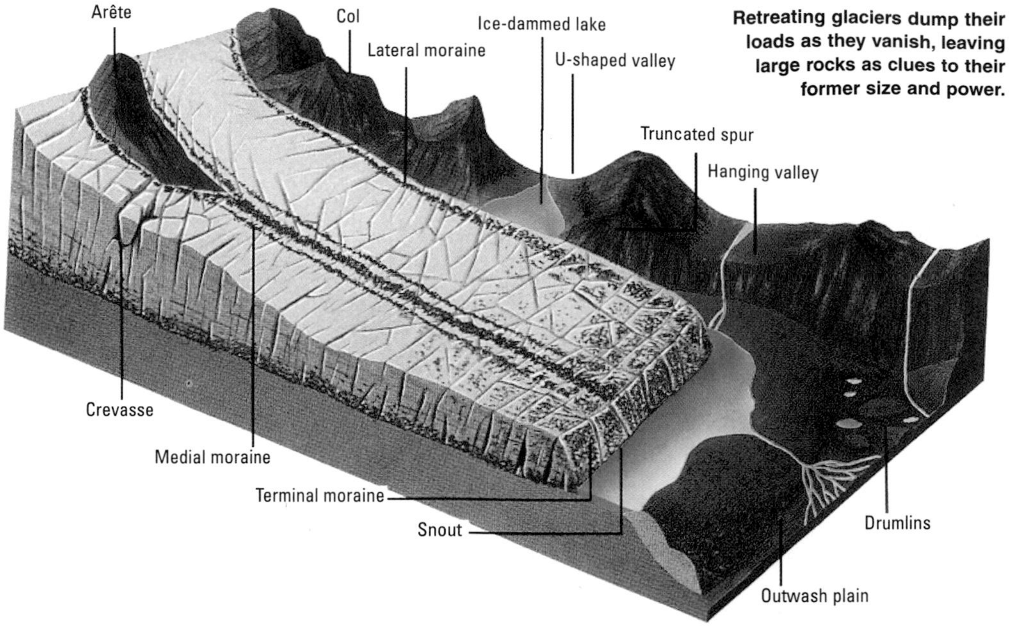

Retreating glaciers dump their loads as they vanish, leaving large rocks as clues to their former size and power.

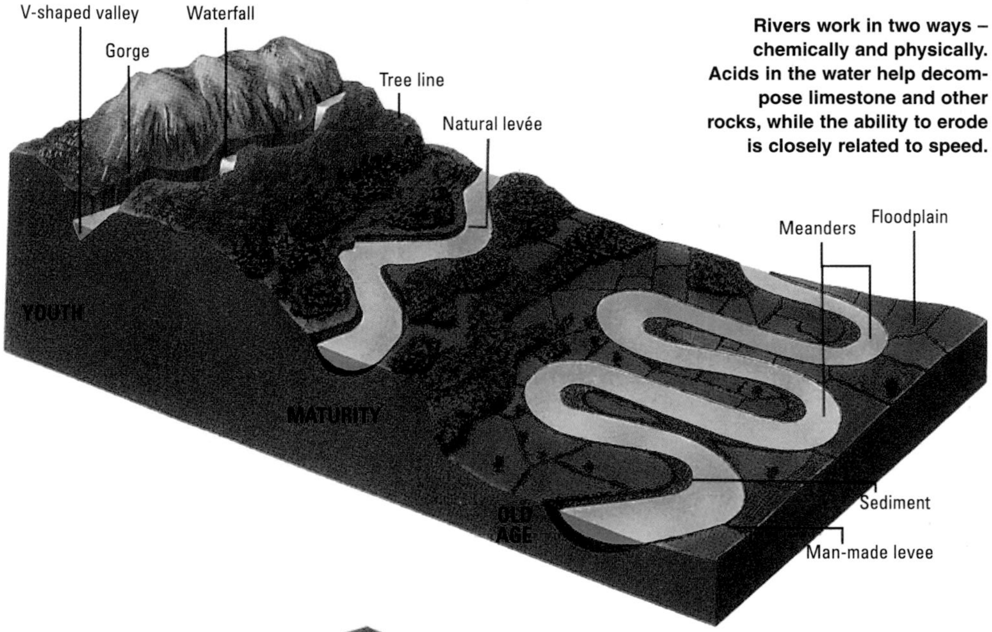

Rivers work in two ways – chemically and physically. Acids in the water help decompose limestone and other rocks, while the ability to erode is closely related to speed.

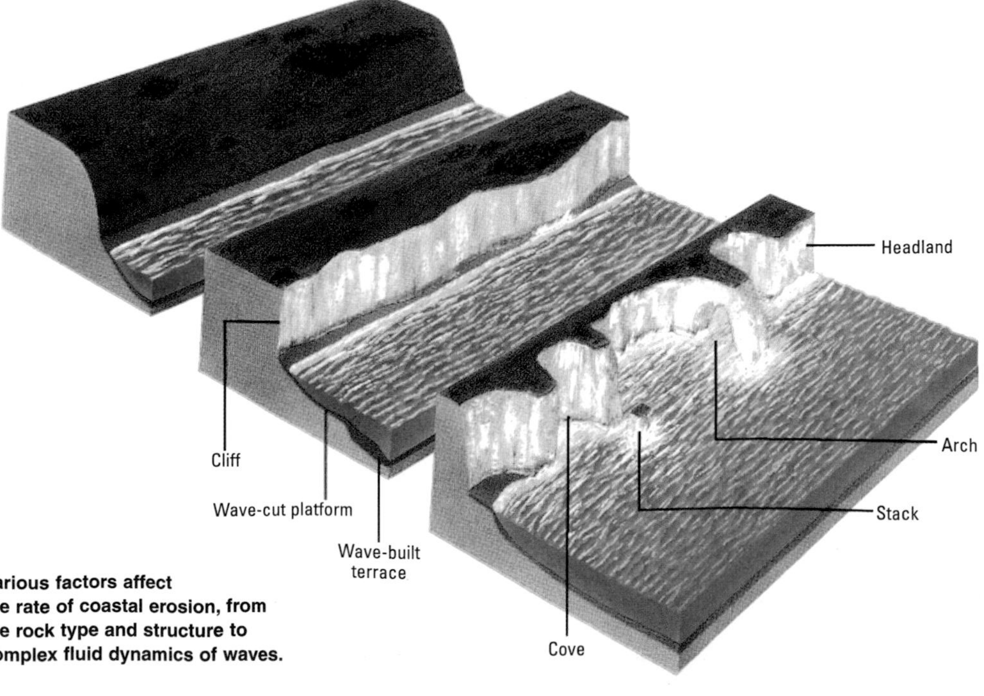

Various factors affect the rate of coastal erosion, from the rock type and structure to complex fluid dynamics of waves.

OCEANS: SEAWATER

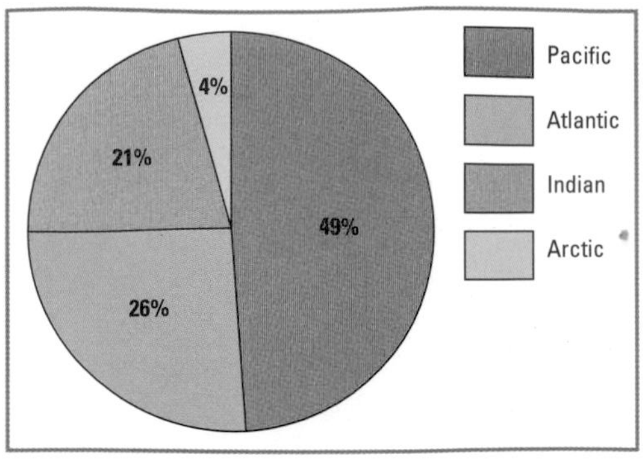
Pacific
Atlantic
Indian
Arctic
4%
21%
49%
26%

ABOVE In the strictest geographical sense the Earth has only three oceans – Atlantic, Indian and Pacific. The legendary "Seven Seas" would require these to be divided at the Equator and the addition of the smaller Arctic Ocean. Geographers do not recognize the Antarctic Ocean (much less the "Southern Ocean") as a separate entity.

The Earth is a watery planet: almost 71% of its surface is covered by its oceans and seas. This great liquid cloak gives our planet its characteristic and beautiful blue appearance from space, and is one of the two obvious differences between the Earth and its two near-neighbours, Venus and Mars. The other difference is the presence of life – and the two are closely linked.

50 m
100 m
150 m
200 m

ABOVE When sunlight strikes the surface of the ocean between 3% and 30% of it is immediately reflected. The amount reflected depends on the angle at which the light strikes – the smaller the angle the greater the reflection – which varies with latitude and the seasons.

Penetration of sunlight is selectively reduced according to wavelength. Radiation at the red or long-wave end of the visible spectrum is absorbed near the surface of the water, while the shorter blue wavelengths are scattered, giving the sea its characteristic blue colour.

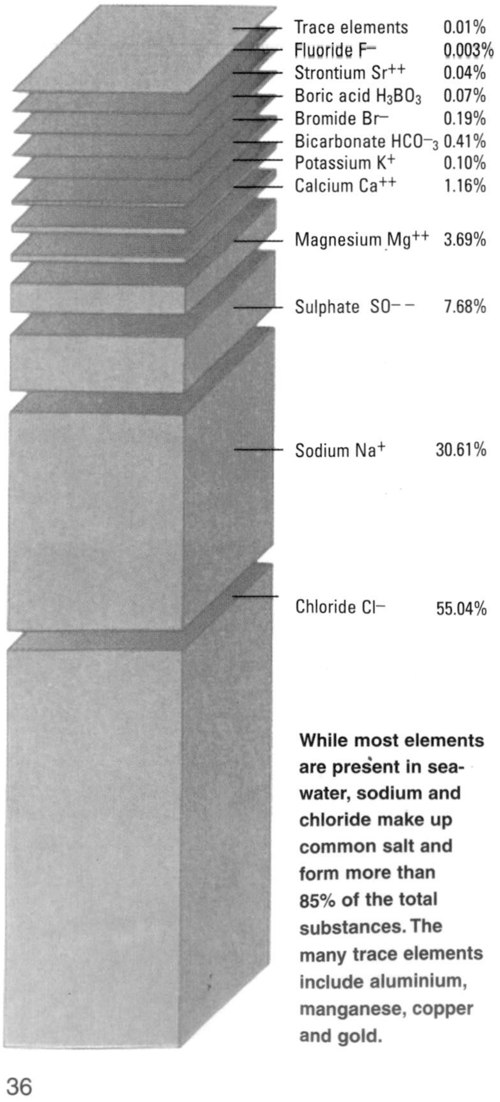
Trace elements 0.01%
Fluoride F^- 0.003%
Strontium Sr^{++} 0.04%
Boric acid H_3BO_3 0.07%
Bromide Br^- 0.19%
Bicarbonate HCO_3^- 0.41%
Potassium K^+ 0.10%
Calcium Ca^{++} 1.16%
Magnesium Mg^{++} 3.69%
Sulphate SO^{--} 7.68%
Sodium Na^+ 30.61%
Chloride Cl^- 55.04%

While most elements are present in seawater, sodium and chloride make up common salt and form more than 85% of the total substances. The many trace elements include aluminium, manganese, copper and gold.

EARTH IS something of a misnomer for our planet; "Ocean" would be a more suitable name, since the oceans and seas cover 70.8% of its total surface area. The oceans are not separate areas of water but form one continuous oceanic mass, and (as with some continental divisions) the boundaries between them are arbitrary lines drawn for convenience. The vast areas of interconnected oceans contain 97.2% of the world's total water supply.

The study of oceans, including their biology, chemistry, geology and physics, has now become a matter of urgency, because the future of humans on Earth may well depend on our knowledge of the ocean's potential resources not only of minerals and power but also of food.

Composition of seawater

The most obvious resource of the oceans is the water itself. But seawater is salty, containing sodium chloride (common salt), which makes it unsuitable for drinking or farming. One kilogramme (2.2lb) of seawater contains about 35g (1.2oz) of dissolved materials, of which chloride and sodium together make up nearly 30g (1oz) or about 85%.

Seawater is a highly complex substance in which 73 of the 93 natural chemical elements are present in measurable or detectable amounts. Apart from chloride and sodium it contains appreciable amounts of sulphate, magnesium, potassium and calcium, which together add up to over 13% of the total. The remainder, less than 1%, is made up of bicarbonate, bromide, boric acid, strontium, fluoride, silicon and various trace elements. Because the volume of the oceans is so great, there are substantial amounts of some trace elements: seawater contains more gold, for example, than there is on land, even though it's in a very low concentration of four-millionths of one part per million.

Also present in seawater are dissolved gases from the atmosphere, including nitrogen, oxygen and carbon dioxide. Of these, oxygen is vital to marine organisms. The amount of oxygen in seawater varies according to temperature. Cold water can contain more oxygen than warm water, but cold water in the ocean depths, which has been out of contact with the atmosphere for a long period, usually contains a much smaller amount of oxygen than surface water.

Other chemicals in seawater that are important to marine life include calcium, silicon and phosphates, all of which are used by marine creatures to form shells and skeletons. For building cells and tissue, marine organisms extract phosphates, certain nitrogen compounds, iron and silicon. The chief constituents of seawater – chloride, sodium, magnesium and sulphur – are hardly used by marine organisms.

Density, light and sound

The density of seawater is an important factor in causing ocean currents and is related to the interaction of salinity and temperature. The temperature of surface water varies between –2°C and 29°C (28°F and 85°F); ice will begin to form if the temperature drops below –2°C (28°F).

The properties of light passing through seawater determine the colour of the oceans. Radiation at the red or long-wave end of the spectrum is absorbed near the surface of the water, while the shorter blue wavelengths are scattered, giving the sea its characteristic colour.

The depth to which light can penetrate is important to marine life. In clear water light may reach to 110m (360ft), whereas in muddy coastal waters it may penetrate to only 15m (50ft). Below about 1,000m (3,300ft) there is virtually no light at all.

The most active zone in the oceans is the sunlit upper layer, falling to about 200m (650ft) at the edge of the continental shelf, where the water is moved around by windblown currents. This is the

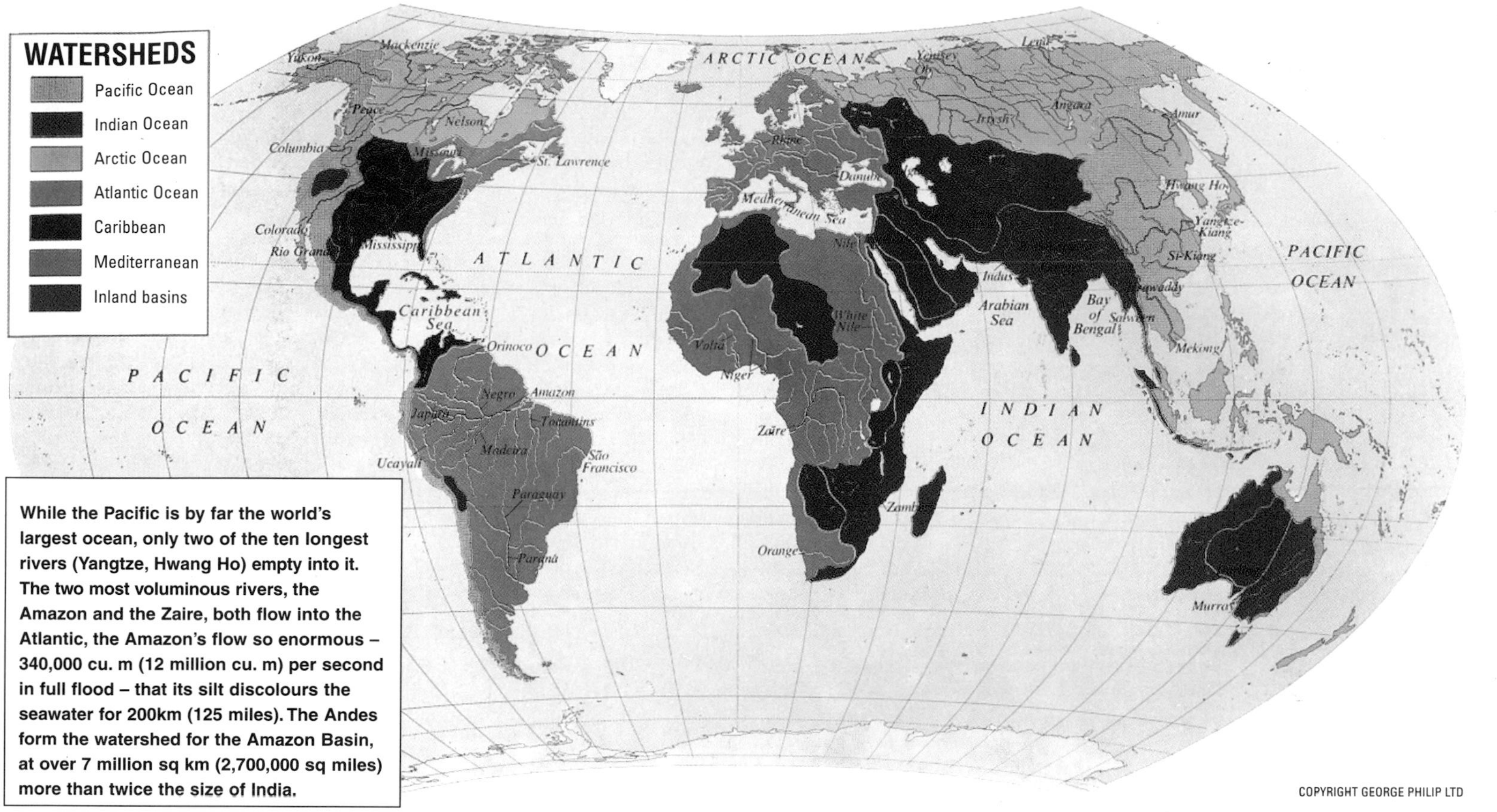

While the Pacific is by far the world's largest ocean, only two of the ten longest rivers (Yangtze, Hwang Ho) empty into it. The two most voluminous rivers, the Amazon and the Zaire, both flow into the Atlantic, the Amazon's flow so enormous – 340,000 cu. m (12 million cu. m) per second in full flood – that its silt discolours the seawater for 200km (125 miles). The Andes form the watershed for the Amazon Basin, at over 7 million sq km (2,700,000 sq miles) more than twice the size of India.

home of most sealife and acts as a membrane through which the ocean breathes, absorbing great quantities of carbon dioxide and partly exchanging it for oxygen.

As the depth increases light fades and temperatures fall until just before around 950m (3,000ft), when there is a marked temperature change at the thermocline, the boundary between the warm surface zones and the cold deep zones.

Water is a good conductor of sound, which travels at about 1,507m (4,954ft) per second through seawater, compared with 331m (1,087ft) per second through air. Echo-sounding is based on the measurement of the time taken for sound to travel from a ship to the seafloor and back again. However, temperature and pressure both affect the speed of sound, causing the speed to vary by about 100m (330ft) per second.

The salinity of the oceans

The volume of dissolved salts in seawater is called the salinity. The average salinity of seawater ranges between 33 and 37 parts of dissolved material per 1,000 parts of water. Oceanographers express these figures as 33 parts per thousand (33‰) to 37‰.

The salinity of ocean water varies with local conditions. Large rivers or melting ice reduce salinity, for example, whereas it is increased in areas with little rainfall and high evaporation.

To produce fresh water from seawater the dissolved salts must be separated out. This desalination can be carried out by electrical, chemical and change of phase processes. Change of phase processes involve changing the water into steam and distilling it, or changing it into ice, a process that also expels the salt. Eskimos have used sea ice as a source of fresh water for centuries, while primitive coastal tribes still take salt from the sea by damming water in pools and letting it evaporate in the Sun.

RIGHT The average salinity of seawater ranges between 33 and 37 parts of dissolved material per 1,000 parts of water. While the most saline water is generally found in semi-enclosed seas in temperate and tropical areas such as the Gulf of Mexico, Mediterranean and the Red Sea (where high rates of evaporation can produce a figure of 41 parts per thousand), the Baltic Sea, which receives large quantities of freshwater from rivers and melting snow, has a remarkably low salinity of 7.2‰.

In the oceans themselves, the least saline waters occur in areas of high freshwater discharge such as the edge of the Antarctic icecap and the mouths of large rivers. The most pronounced regional example of this is Southeast Asia, where a string of massive rivers – including the Ganges, Brahmaputra, Irrawaddy, Salween, Mekong, Si Kiang, Yangtze and Hwang Ho – flow into the coastal area from the Bay of Bengal to the Yellow Sea.

If the salt in the oceans were precipitated, it would cover the Earth's land areas with a layer more than 150m (500ft) thick.

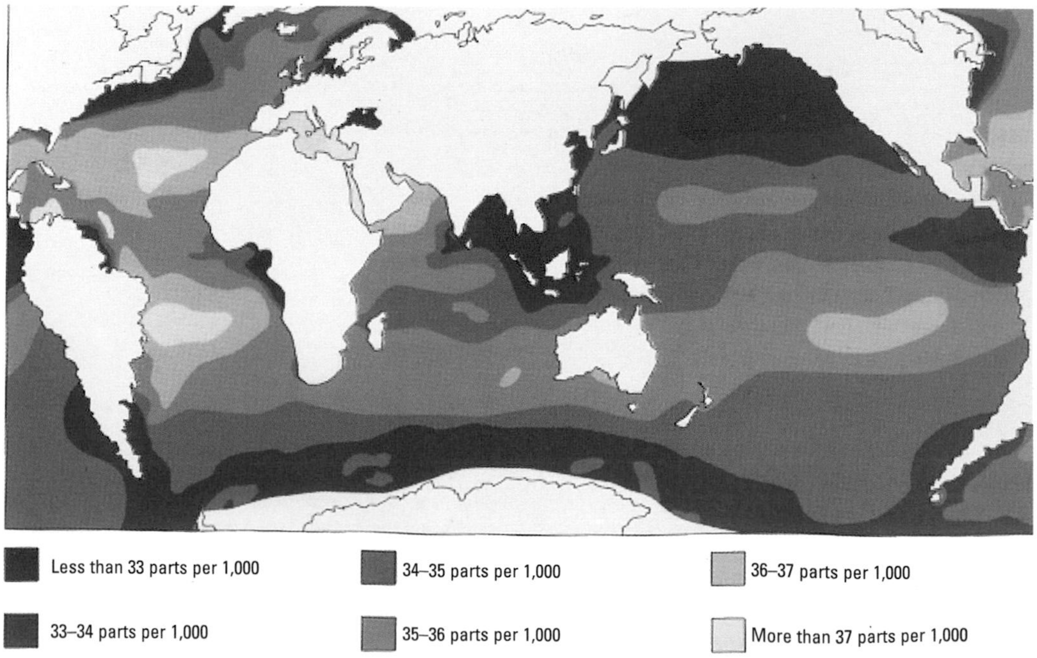

THE OCEANS: CURRENTS

NO PART of the ocean is completely still – although, in the ocean depths, the movement of water is often extremely slow. Exploration of the deeper parts of the oceans has revealed the existence of marine life. If the water were not in motion, the oxygen on which all lifeforms depend would soon be used up and not replaced. No life would therefore be possible.

Prevailing winds sweep surface water along to form drift currents. These surface currents do not conform precisely with the direction of the prevailing wind because of the Coriolis effect caused by the rotation of the Earth. This effect, which increases away from the Equator, makes currents in the Northern Hemisphere veer to the right of the wind direction and currents in the Southern Hemisphere veer to the left. The result is a general clockwise circulation of water in the Northern Hemisphere and an anticlockwise circulation in the Southern.

Other factors affecting currents are the configuration of the ocean bed and the shapes of land masses. For example, in the Atlantic Ocean the North Equatorial Current flows towards the West Indies. Most of this current is channelled into the Gulf of Mexico where it veers northeastwards, bursting into the Atlantic between Florida and Cuba as the Gulf Stream.

OCEAN CURRENTS

Winter in Northern Hemisphere

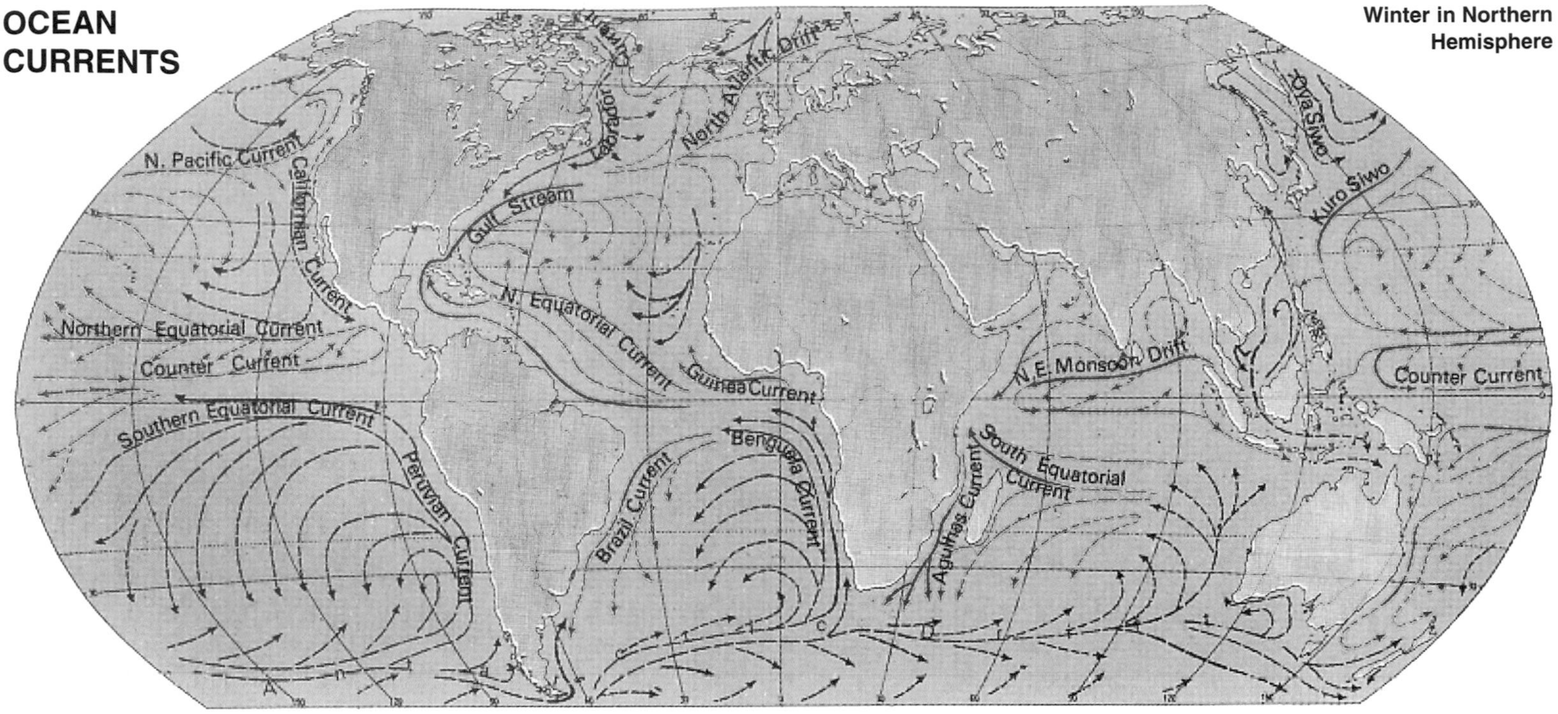

(cold currents are shown in blue, warm currents in red)

Summer in Northern Hemisphere

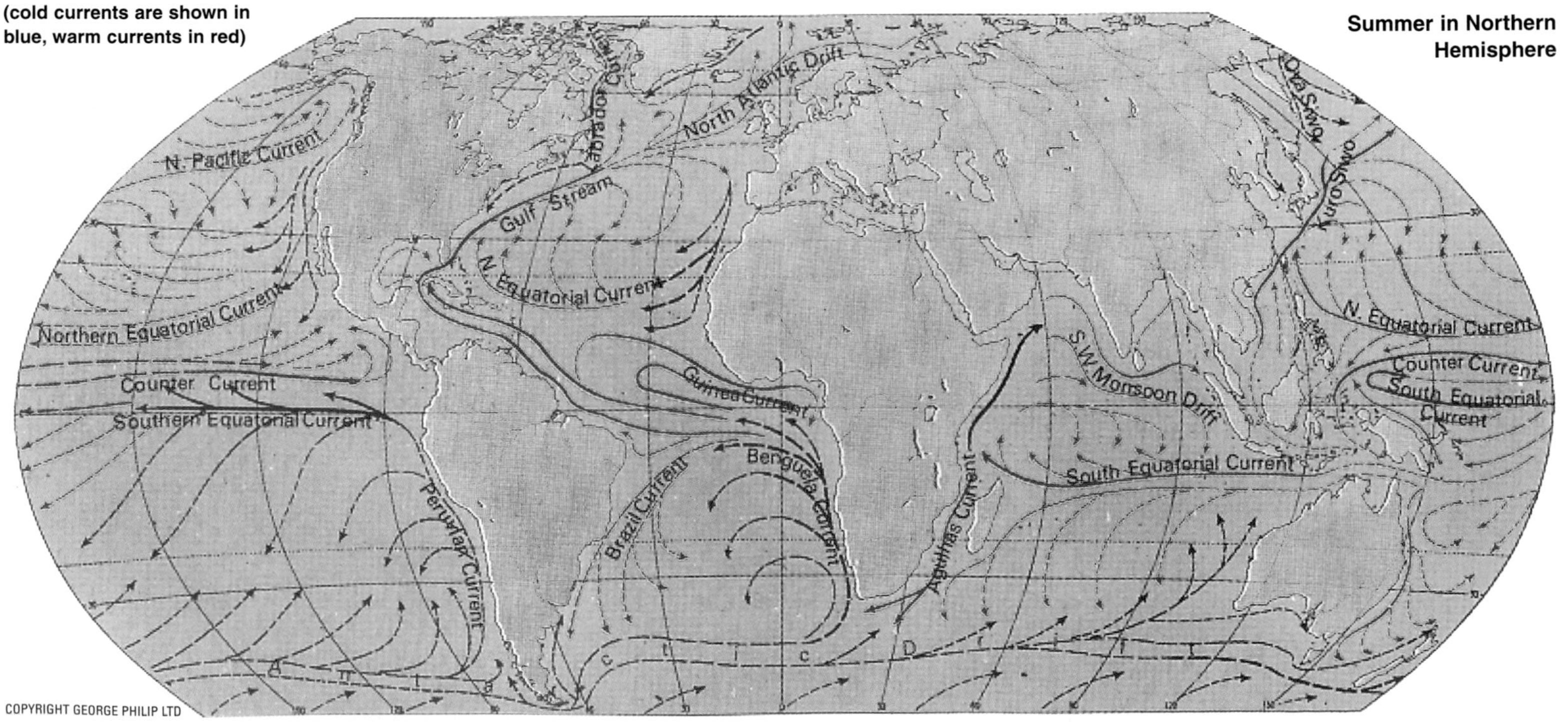

ABOVE The world's surface currents circulate in a clockwise direction in the Northern Hemisphere and in an anticlockwise direction in the Southern Hemisphere. These circulatory systems are called gyres. There are two large clockwise gyres in the Northern Hemisphere (North Atlantic and North Pacific) and three anticlockwise gyres in the Southern (South Atlantic, South Pacific and Indian Ocean).

Beneath the surface are undercurrents whose direction may be opposite to those at the surface. Under the Gulf Stream off the eastern USA lies a large, cold current flowing south from the Arctic. The Gulf Stream finally splits: while the North Atlantic Drift branches past eastern Greenland and western Europe, part of the current returns southwards to complete the gyre. Surface cold currents in the Northern Hemisphere generally flow southwards. In the Southern Hemisphere, cold water circulates around Antarctica, while offshoots flow northwards. The warm currents are very strong in tropical and subtropical regions, and include the various Equatorial currents.

The causes of currents that are not powered by winds are related to the density of ocean water, which varies according to temperature and salinity. Heating at the Equator causes the water to become less dense, while cooling round the poles has the opposite effect. Salinity is affected by the inflow of fresh water from rivers, melting ice and rainfall, and by evaporation. A high rate of evaporation increases the salinity and therefore the density.

Effects of ocean currents

One of the most important effects of ocean currents is that they mix ocean water and so affect directly the fertility of the sea. Mixing is especially important when subsurface water is mixed with surface water. The upwelling of subsurface water may be caused by strong coastal winds that push the surface water outwards, allowing subsurface water to rise up. Such upwelling occurs off the coasts of Peru, California and Mauritania, where subsurface water rich in nutrients (notably phosphorus and silicon) rises to the surface, stimulating the growth of plankton which provides food for great shoals of fish, such as Peruvian anchovies.

Water has a high heat capacity and can retain heat two and a half times as readily as land. The heat of the Sun absorbed by water around the Equator is transported north and south by currents. Part of the North Atlantic Drift flows past Norway, warming offshore winds and giving northwest Europe a winter temperature that is 11°C (20°F) above the average for those latitudes. The northward-flowing Peru and Benguela currents have a reverse effect, bringing cooler weather to the western coasts of South America and southern Africa.

In such ways, currents have a profound effect on climate. Currents from polar regions can also create hazards for shipping: the Labrador and East Greenland currents carry icebergs and pack ice into shipping lanes, and fog often occurs where cold and warm currents meet, most persistently off the coast of Newfoundland.

RIGHT Surface currents are caused largely by prevailing winds. The Coriolis effect caused by the rotation of the Earth results in the deflection of currents to the right of the wind direction in the Northern Hemisphere. In the same manner, the surface motion drags the subsurface layer at an angle to it, and so on.

Each layer moves at a slower speed than the one above it and at a greater angle from the wind. The spiral created has the overall effect of moving the water mass above the depth of frictional resistance at an angle of about 90° from the wind direction, while surface currents move at around 45°. The same effect reverses the direction of draining water from a bath in the Northern and Southern hemispheres.

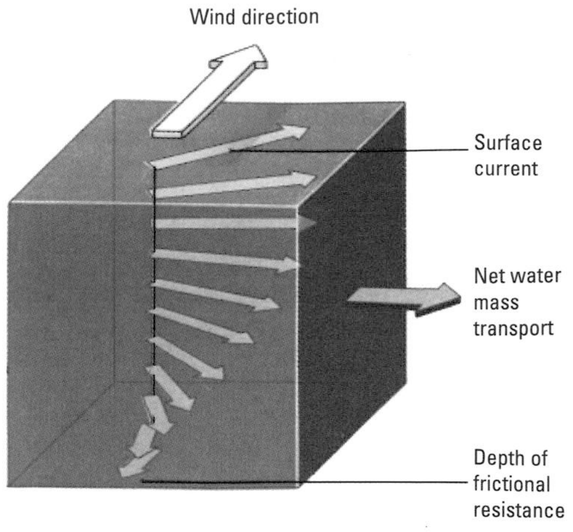

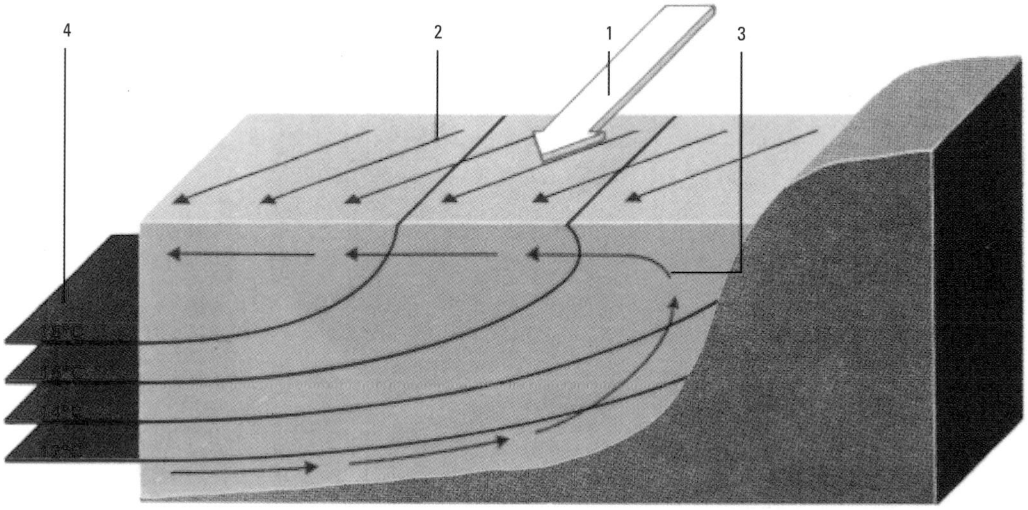

ABOVE Upwelling occurs when a longshore wind [1] pushes surface water away from a coast at an angle [2], allowing deeper water to rise [3]. The deeper water is not only colder [4] but usually rich in nutrients, and areas where upwelling occurs are often exceptional fishing grounds. A good example are the waters off the west coast of South America, the most productive in the world before the upwelling was suppressed by successive years of El Niño.

El Niño

El Niño is the most dramatic and influential of current reversals, producing devastating effects. Its 1997–98 visit was the most damaging yet, triggering (among other things) floods and landslides in northwest South America, storms in California, drought in southern Africa, monsoon failure in India and widespread rainforest fires in Southeast Asia. Estimates put the cost of the property damage alone as high as US$33 billion.

As the previous worst case in 1982–83 showed, the commercial cost is colossal and far-reaching. This includes declining fish stocks in the eastern Pacific (the anchovy catch dropped by over 90%), frost-wrecked orange groves in Florida, crop losses in Africa and brush fires in Australia.

While El Niño is unpredictable in both power and frequency – it used to appear every 2 to 7 years – the phenomenon now occurs more often, including five consecutive seasons from 1990 to 1994. It usually lasts about three months but can be far longer. The name was originally given by Peruvian fishermen to the warm but weak current that flowed south for a few weeks each year around Christmas – hence the name, which means "Christ child". Now the term is applied to a complex if irregular series of remarkable natural happenings.

The El Niño sequence begins in the western Pacific. The mass of warm water (white in centre), 8°C higher than in the east and generally kept in check by the prevailing westerly trade winds, breaks free of its moorings as these winds subside and moves in an equatorial swell towards South America. There it raises both sea temperatures and sea levels, suppressing the normal upwelling of the cold and nutrient-rich Peruvian current. Meanwhile, the western Pacific waters cool (purple) as the warm water is displaced.

The movement of such vast amounts of warm water results in chaotic changes to wind patterns, in turn creating freak weather conditions well outside the Pacific tropics. The passage of El Niño's warm water is also tracked by rainfall, leading to droughts in Southeast Asia and Australia and excessive levels of precipitation in South America.

This sequence traces El Niño's passage from March 1997 *(above left)* to October 1998 *(below right)*, when normal oceanic conditions were finally resumed – until the next time. In 1983, 1987 and 1995 El Niño was followed by the cool current La Niña ("the little girl").

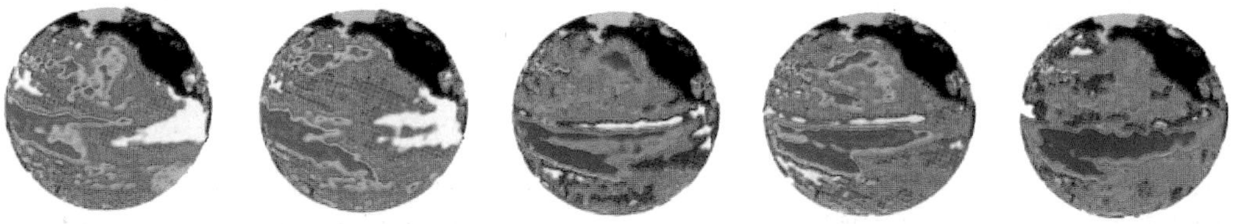

OCEANS: WAVES AND TIDES

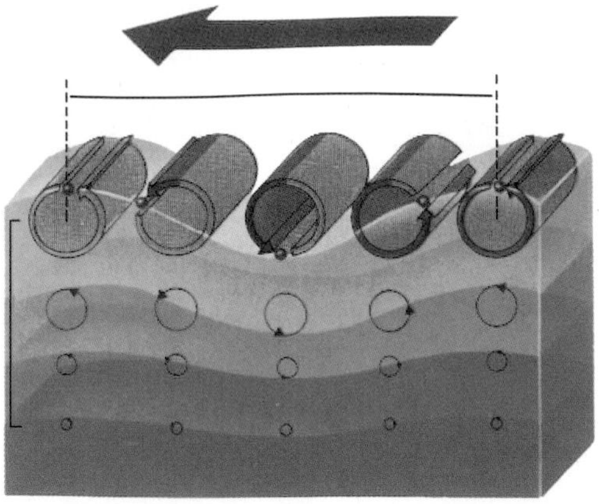

ABOVE Most waves are generated by the wind. As a wave travels in deep water, however, the water particles don't move up and down but rotate in circular orbits. As depth increases, the rotations of the water particles diminish rapidly – the reason why submarines escape the effects of severe storms at sea.

BECAUSE THEY affect coastal areas, waves and tides are the most familiar features of oceans and seas for most of us, but sometimes the energies of waves, tides and high winds combine with devastating effect. In January 1953 a high spring tide, storm waves and winds of 185km/h (115mph) combined to raise the level of the North Sea by 3m (10ft) higher than usual. This "surge" caused extensive flooding in eastern England, but in the Netherlands over 4% of the country was inundated: 1,800 people died and about 30,000 houses were destroyed or damaged by the seawater.

The motion of waves

While some wave motion occurs at great depth along the boundary of two opposing currents, most waves are caused by the wind blowing over an open stretch of water. This area where the wind blows is known as the "fetch". Waves there are confused and irregular and are referred to as a "sea". As they propagate beyond the fetch they combine into more orderly waves to form a "swell", which travels for long distances beyond the fetch. Waves are movements of oscillation – that is, the shape of the wave moves across the water, but the water particles rotate in a circular orbit with hardly any lateral movement. As a result, if there is no wind or current, a corked bottle bobs up and down in the waves, but is more or less stationary.

At sea, waves seldom exceed 12m (40ft) in height, although one 34m (115ft) high was accurately measured in the Pacific Ocean in 1933. Such a wave requires a long fetch measuring thousands of kilometres and high-speed winds.

Waves that break along a seashore may have been generated by storms in mid-ocean or by local winds. As a wave approaches shallow water, which is defined as a depth of half a wave length, it "feels" the bottom, gradually slowing down, and the crests tend to crowd together. When the water in front of a wave is insufficient to fill the wave form, the rotating orbit – and hence the wave – breaks. There are two main kinds of breakers: spilling breakers occur on gently sloping beaches, when the crests spill over to form a mass of surf, while plunging breakers occur on steeper slopes.

BELOW Waves have dimensions of both length and height. The wave length [14] is the distance between one crest [5] and another – in this case a peaking wave [4] – and between two crests is a trough [11]. The wave height [6] is the distance between the crest and the trough. If wave action ceased, the water would settle at the "still water level" [8]. Wave action extends to the wave base [7], where rotation becomes negligible. Wave distortion is caused by frictional drag on the seabed: if waves pass over a sandbar [10], a spilling breaker [9] may form. Sometimes, waves in shallow water move the whole body of the water forward in translation waves [2] towards the shore [1].

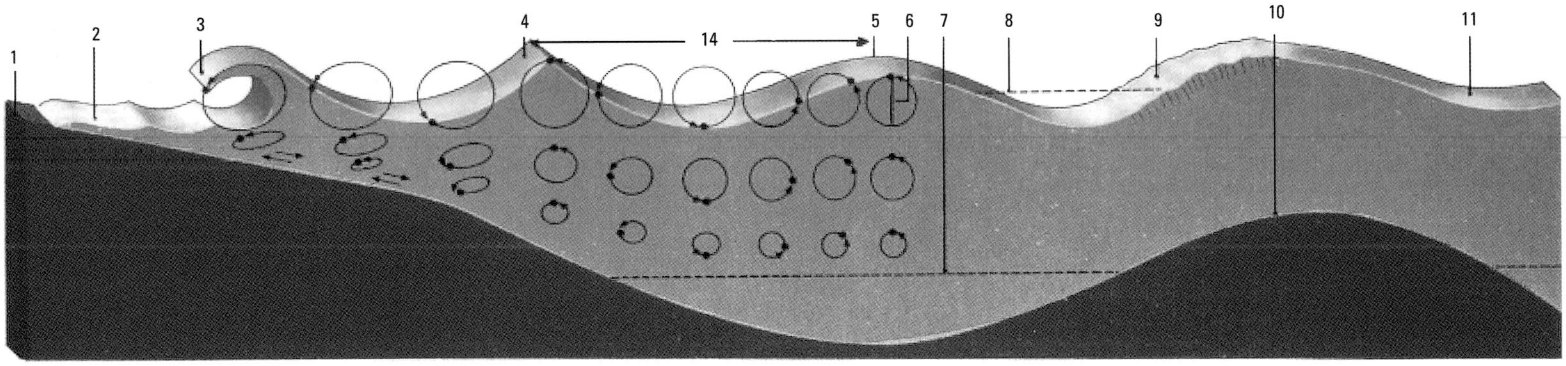
1
2
3
4
14
5
6
7
8
9
10
11

RIGHT Tides are the alternate rises and falls of the sea's surface level, caused by the gravitational pull of the Moon and the Sun. Although the Moon is much smaller than the Sun, it is much closer to Earth and its effect on the oceans is more than twice that of the Sun. The configurations of coasts and seafloors can accentuate these forces, while barometric pressure and wind effects can also superimpose an added "surge" element.

In the open sea the tidal range is small and in enclosed basins, such as the Mediterranean, it is little more than 30cm (12in). However, in shallow seas it may be more than 6m (20ft) and in tidal estuaries 12–15m (40–50ft). The highest tidal range recorded is about 16m (53ft) in the Bay of Fundy, which divides the peninsula of Nova Scotia from the Canadian mainland of New Brunswick.

In some 60 estuaries, such as Hangchow Bay in China and the Severn in England, tidal bores occur. These are bodies of water with a wall-like front that surge up rivers, formed because the estuaries act as funnels, leading to a rise in the height of the water. At spring tides the Hangchow bore attains heights of 7.5m (25ft) and speeds of 27km/h (17mph).

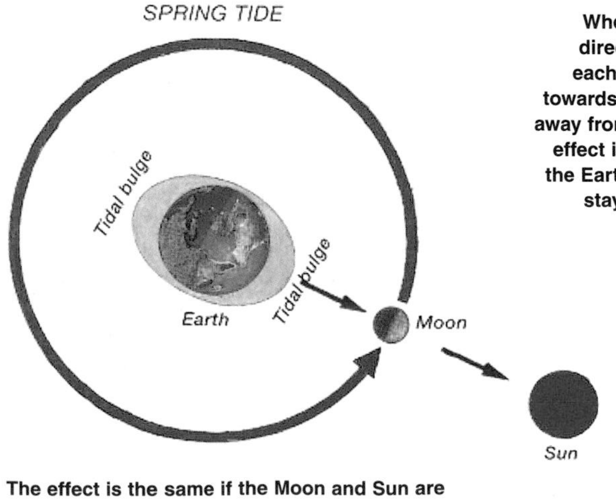
SPRING TIDE
Tidal bulge
Tidal bulge
Earth
Moon
Sun

When the Moon and Sun are roughly in the same direction (around the time of the new Moon), they each pull the oceans on the near side of the Earth towards them. They also pull the Earth towards them, away from the oceans on the far side of the Earth. The effect is to produce two bulges on opposite sides of the Earth. These will not rotate with the Earth but will stay with the forces that produced them, causing two high tides and two low tides a day.

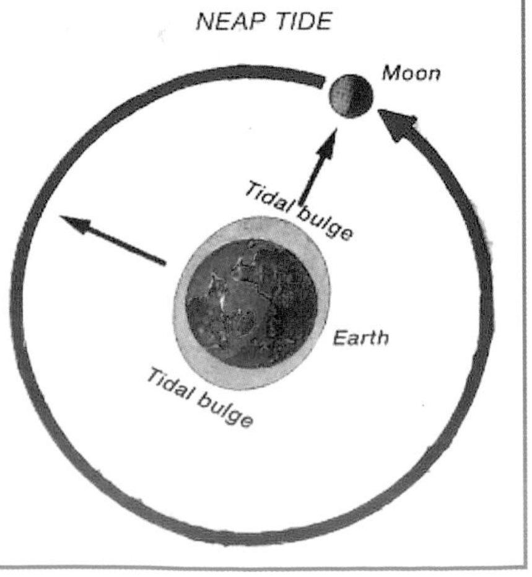
NEAP TIDE
Moon
Tidal bulge
Earth
Tidal bulge

The effect is the same if the Moon and Sun are aligned on opposite sides of the Earth (at the time of full Moon). Thus the tides are greatest at the time of new Moon and full Moon (spring tides). Tides are less pronounced when the Sun, Moon and Earth are not aligned, and are least strong when the three are at right-angles to each other (near the Moon's first and third quarters). In this situation solar and lunar forces compete: the lunar tide wins, but the difference between high and low tides is much less (neap tides).

OCEANS: THE SEAFLOOR

THE DEEP ocean floor was once thought to be flat, but maps compiled from readings made by sonar equipment show that it's no more uniform than the surface of the continents. Here are not just the deepest trench – the Challenger Deep of the Pacific's Mariana Trench plunges 11,022m (36,161ft) – but also the Earth's longest mountain chains and its tallest peaks.

The vast underwater world starts in the shallows of the seaside. Surrounding the land masses is the shallow continental shelf, composed of rocks that less dense than the underlying oceanic crust. The shelf drops gently to around 200m (650ft), where the seafloor suddenly falls away at an angle of 3° to 6° via the continental slope. Submarine canyons such as the 1.5km (5,000ft) gorge off Monterey, California are found on the continental slopes. They can be caused either by river erosion before the land was submerged by the sea, or by turbidity currents – underwater avalanches that carry mud, pebbles and sand far out to sea, scouring gorges out of both slope rock and sediment.

The third stage, the continental rise, made up of sediments washed down from the shelves, is more gradual, with gradients varying from 1 in 100 to 1 in 700. At an average depth of 5,000m (9,000ft) there begins the aptly named abyssal plain, massive submarine depths where sunlight fails to penetrate and only creatures specially adapted to deal with the darkness and the pressure can survive.

Underwater highlands

While the abyss contains large plains it is broken by hills, volcanic seamounts and mid-ocean ridges. Here new rock is being continually formed as magma rises through the Earth's crust, pushing the tectonic plates on each side apart towards the continents in the process called seafloor spreading.

Taken from base to top, many of the seamounts which rise from these plains rival and even surpass the biggest of continental mountains in height. Mauna Kea, Hawaii's highest peak, reaches 10,203m (33,475ft), some 1,355m (4,380ft) more than Mount Everest, though only 4,205m (13,795ft) is above sea level. Nearby is Mauna Loa, the world's biggest active volcano, over 84% of which is hidden from view.

Life in the ocean depths

Manned submersibles have now established that life exists even in the deepest trenches, where the pressure reaches 1,000 "atmospheres" – the equivalent of the force of a tonne bearing down on every sq cm (6.5 tons per sq in).

Further exploration in the pitch-black environment of the oceanic ridges has revealed extraordinary forms of marine life around the scalding hot vents: creatures include giant tubeworms, blind shrimps, and bacteria, some of which are genetically different from any other known lifeforms.

In 1996 an analysis of one micro-organism revealed that at least half its 1,700 or so genes were hitherto unknown. Based on chemicals, not sunlight, this alien environment may well resemble the places where life on Earth first began.

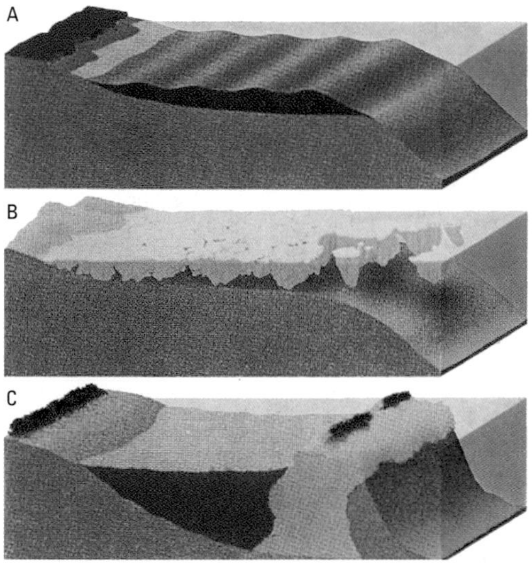
A
B
C

ABOVE Continental shelves are the regions immediately off the land masses, and there are several different types. Off Europe and North America the shelf has a gentle relief, often with sandy ridges and barriers [A]. In high latitudes, floating ice wears the shelf smooth [B], and in clear tropical seas a smooth shelf may be rimmed with a coral barrier such as the Great Barrier Reef off eastern Australia, leaving an inner lagoon area "dammed" by the reef [C].

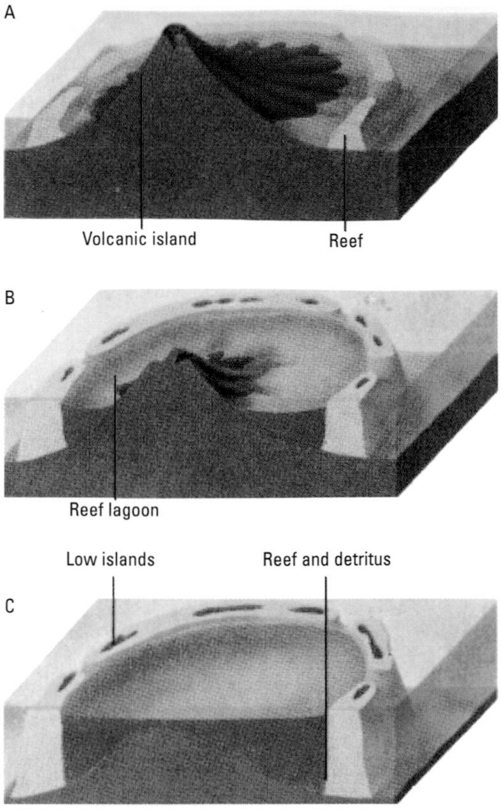
A
Volcanic island
Reef
B
Reef lagoon
Low islands
Reef and detritus
C

ABOVE The most intriguing of coral features, an atoll is a ring or horseshoe-shaped group of coral islands. Organisms with skeletons of calcium carbonate, corals grow in warm, fairly shallow water to depths of about 90m (300ft), but the depth of coral in many atolls is much greater than this.

The prevailing theory is that the coral began to form as a reef in the shallows of a volcanic island [A]. While the sea level began to rise and the island slowly sank [B], the coral growth kept pace with these gradual changes, leaving an atoll of hard limestone around its remnant [C]. In this way, coral can reach depths of up to 1,600m (5,250ft).

The world's largest atoll is Kwajalein in the Marshall Islands, in the central Pacific. Its slender 283-km (176-mile) coral reef encloses a lagoon of 2,850 sq km (1,100 sq miles).

RIGHT The seafloor consists of different zones, the most shallow being the continental shelf that lies between the coast and the 200m (650ft) depth contour. The shelf area occupies 7.5% of the seafloor and corresponds to the submerged portion of the continental crust. Beyond, the downward slope increases abruptly to form the continental slope (8.5%), an area that may be dissected by submarine canyons. The continental slope meets the abyssal basins at a more gentle incline (the continental rise). The basins lie at depths of 4,000m (13,200 ft) and feature mountain ranges and hills.

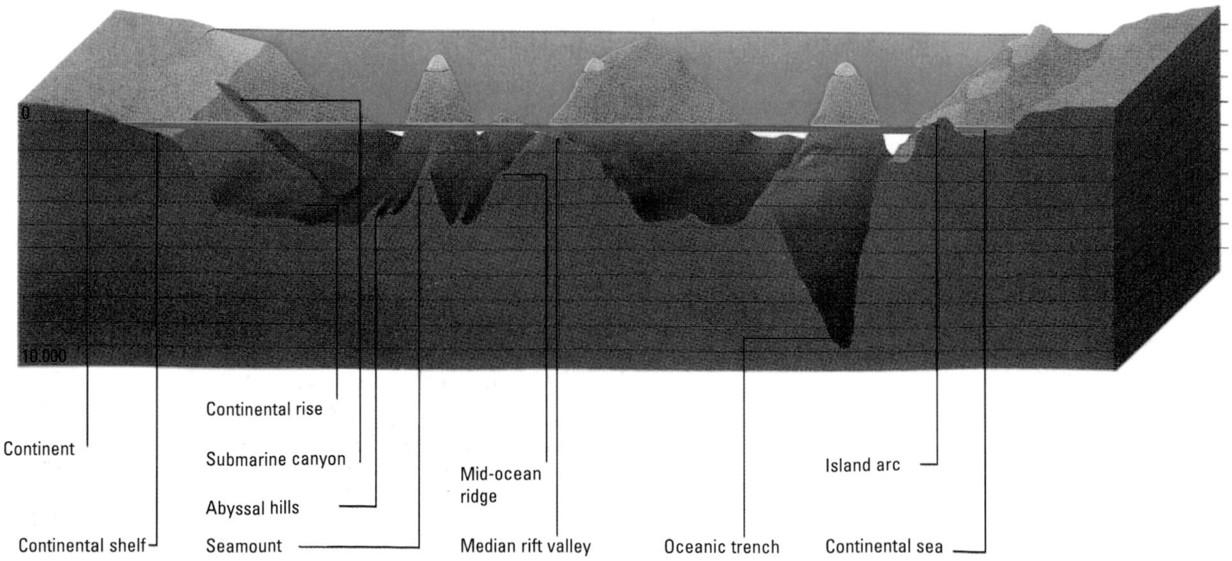
0
10,000
Continent
Continental shelf
Continental rise
Submarine canyon
Abyssal hills
Seamount
Mid-ocean ridge
Median rift valley
Oceanic trench
Island arc
Continental sea

THE ATMOSPHERE AND CLOUDS

THE ORIGIN of the atmosphere was closely associated with the origin of the Earth. When the Earth was still a molten ball, it was probably surrounded by a large atmosphere of cosmic gases, including hydrogen, that were gradually lost into space. As the Earth began to develop a solid crust over a molten core, gases such as carbon dioxide, nitrogen and water vapour were slowly released to form an atmosphere with a composition not unlike the present emissions from volcanoes. Further cooling probably led to massive precipitation of water vapour – so that today it occupies less than 4% by volume of the atmosphere. At a much later stage, the oxygen content of the atmosphere was created by green plants releasing oxygen.

Extending from the Earth's surface far into space, the atmosphere is a meteor shield, a radiation deflector, a thermal blanket and a source of chemical energy for the Earth's diverse lifeforms. Five-sixths of its total mass is located in the first 15 km (9 miles), the troposphere, which is no thicker in relative terms than the skin of an onion. Almost all the phenomena we call the weather occur in this narrow layer.

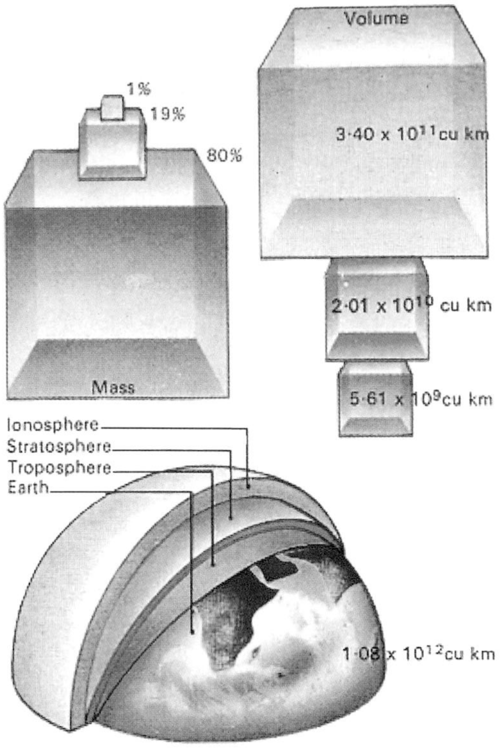

RIGHT Because air is easily compressed, the atmosphere becomes "squashed" by gravity. Thus the bulk of the atmosphere lies in the troposphere, occupying a volume of about 6 billion cu. km (1,560 million cu. miles). As air density decreases with altitude, the very much smaller amounts of air present in the stratosphere (19%) and the ionosphere and above (1%) occupy an increasingly greater volume.

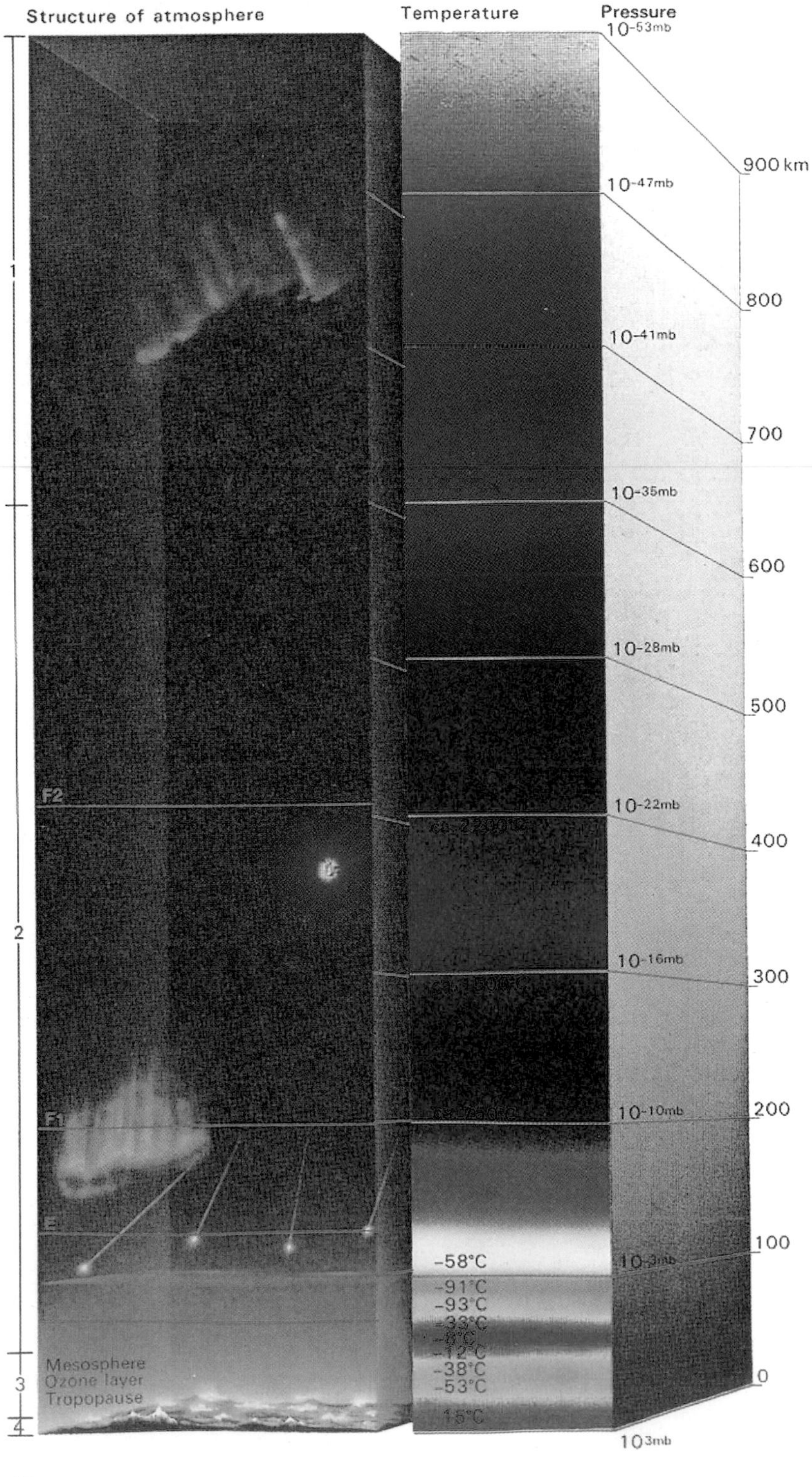

LEFT The discovery by British scientists of the hole in the ozone layer over Antarctica in 1985 triggered a growing interest in the structure of the atmosphere.

LAYERS OF THE ATMOSPHERE

1. EXOSHERE

The atmosphere's upper layer has no clear outer boundary, merging imperceptibly with interplanetary space. Its lower boundary, at an altitude of around 400km (250 miles), is almost equally vague. The exosphere is mainly composed of hydrogen and helium in changing proportions: helium vanishes with increasing altitude, and above 2,400km (1,500 miles) it is almost entirely hydrogen.

2. IONOSPHERE

Gas molecules in the ionosphere, mainly helium, oxygen and nitrogen, are ionized – electrically charged – by the Sun's radiation. Within the ionosphere's range of 50 to 400km (30 to 250 miles) they group themselves into four layers, known conventionally as D, E, F1 and F2, all of which can reflect radio waves of differing frequencies. The high energy of ionospheric gas gives it a notional temperature of more than 2000°C (3,600°F), although its density is negligible. The auroras – *aurora borealis* and its southern counterpart, *aurora australis* – occur in the ionosphere when charged particles from the Sun interact with the Earth's magnetic fields, at their strongest near the poles.

3. STRATOSPHERE

Separated at its upper and lower limits by the distinct thresholds of the stratopause and the tropopause, the stratosphere is a remarkably stable layer between about 15km and 50km (9 and 30 miles). Its temperature rises from –55°C (–67°F) at its lower extent to approximately 0°C (32°F) near the stratopause, where a thin layer of ozone – increasingly depleted with the acceleration in pollution by CFCs since the 1970s – absorbs ultraviolet radiation believed to cause skin cancer, cataracts and damage to the immune system in humans. Stratospheric air contains enough ozone to make it poisonous, although it is far too rarified to breathe. Overall, the stratopshere comprises 80% nitrogen, 18% oxygen, 1% argon and 1% ozone. "Mother-of-pearl" or nacreous cloud occurs at about 25km (15 miles).

4. TROPOSPHERE

The narrowest of all the atmospheric layers, the troposphere extends up to 15km (9 miles) at the Equator but only 8km (5 miles) at the poles. Since this thin region contains about 85% of the atmosphere's total mass and almost all of its water vapour, it is also the realm of the Earth's weather. Temperatures fall steadily with increasing height by about 1°C for every 100 metres (1.5°F for every 300 feet) above sea level. The main constituents are nitrogen (78%), oxygen (21%) and argon (1%).

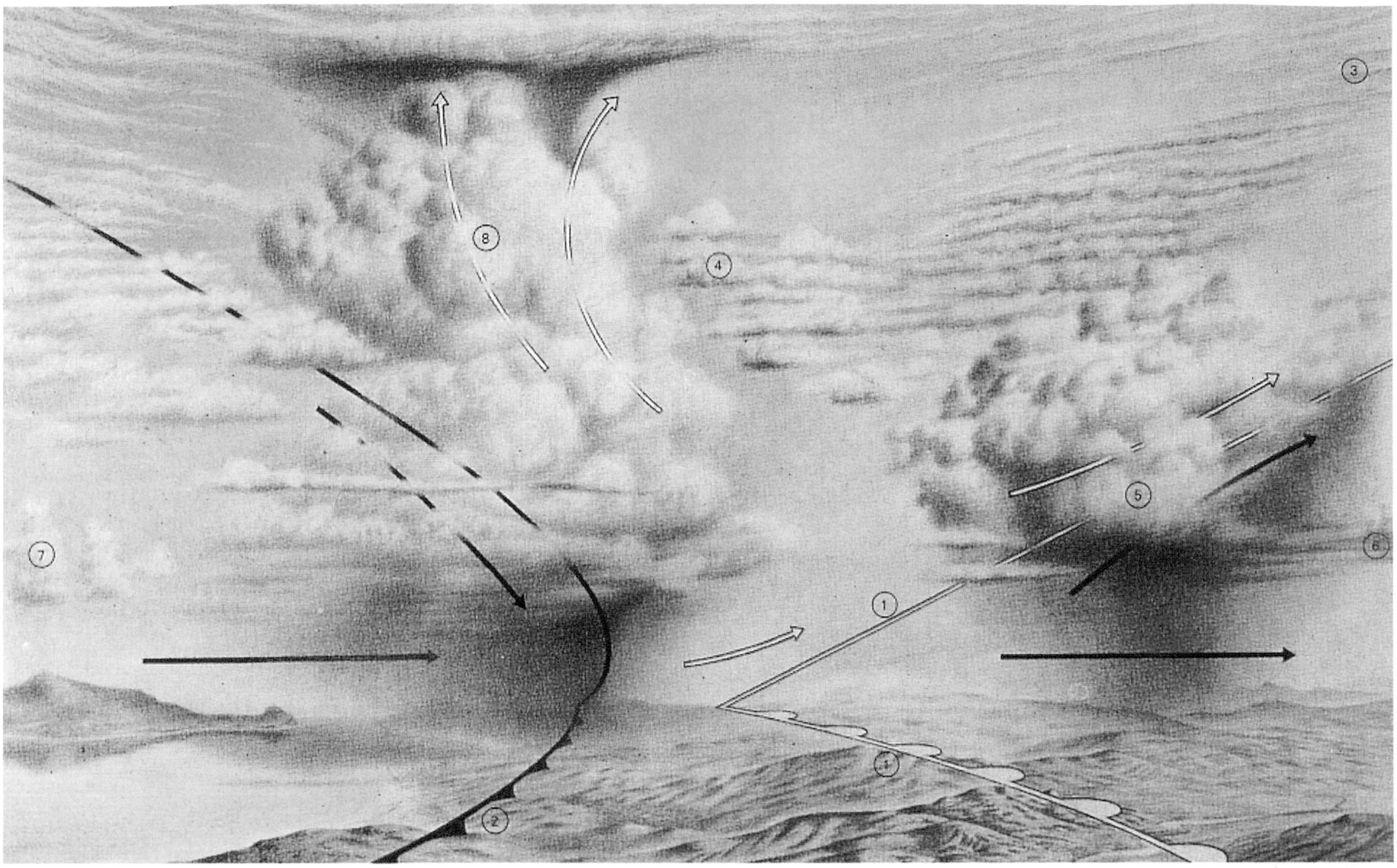

ABOVE The different cloud types are best illustrated within the context of the familiar mid-latitude frontal depression. Here a schematic, generalized Northern Hemisphere depression is viewed from the south as it moves eastwards, with both warm [1] and cold [2] fronts clearly visible. Over the warm front the air rises massively and slowly over the great depth of the atmosphere. This results in a fairly complete suite of layer-type clouds ranging from ice-crystal cirrus [3] and fluffy altocumulus [4] to grey-based nimbostratus [5].

The precipitation area often associated with such cloud types, and especially with nimbostratus, usually lies ahead of the surface warm front and roughly parallel to it [6]. Turbulence may cause some clouds to rise and produce heavy convective rainfall, as well as the generally lighter and more widespread classical warm front rainfall. Stratus often occupies the warm sector, but a marked change occurs at the cold front. Here the wind veers (blowing in a more clockwise direction) and cumulus clouds [7], brilliant white in sunlight, are often found in the cold air behind the front.

At the front itself the atmosphere is often unstable and cumulus clouds grow into dramatic cumulonimbus formations [8]. The canopy of cirrus clouds – of all types – may extend over the whole depression and is often juxtaposed with the anvil shape of the nimbus. These cloud changes are accompanied by changes in pressure, wind temperature and humidity as the fronts pass.

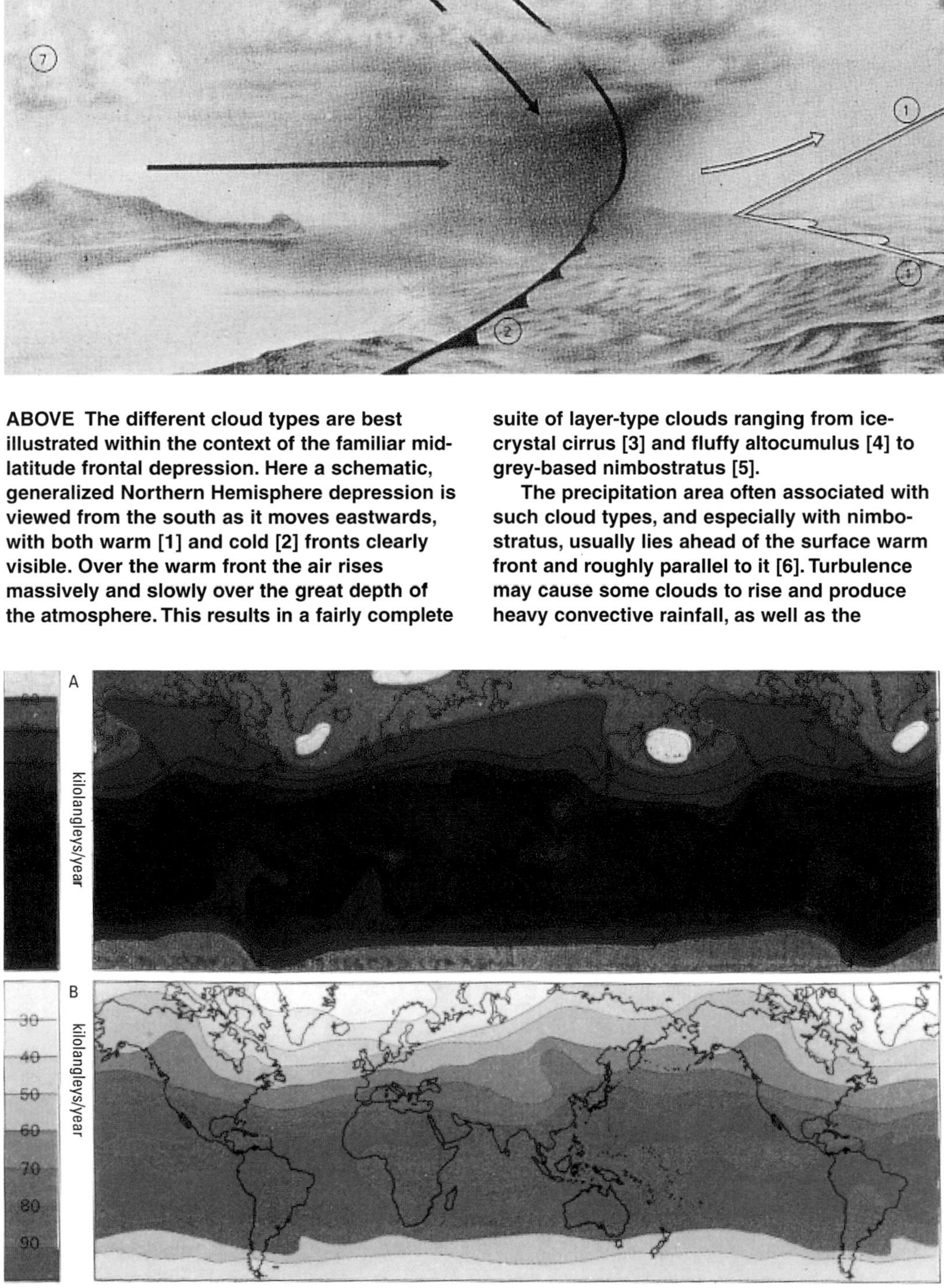

LEFT Temperatures in the atmosphere and on Earth result mainly from a balance of radiation inputs and outputs. Average annual solar radiation reaching the Earth, measured in kilolangleys – one calorie absorbed per sq cm (0.15 sq in) is highest in hot desert areas [A].

Comparison with the average annual long-wave radiation back from the Earth's surface [B] shows an overall surplus radiation for nearly all latitudes, but this is absorbed in the atmosphere and then lost in space, ensuring an overall balance. The extreme imbalance of incoming radiation between equatorial and polar latitudes is somewhat equalized through heat transfers by atmosphere and oceans. This balancing transfer between surplus and deficit radiation is greatest in mid-latitudes, where most cyclones and anticyclones occur.

WINDS AND THE WEATHER

WIND IS the movement of air, and large-scale air movements, both horizontal and vertical, are crucial in shaping weather and climate. The chief forces affecting horizontal air movements are pressure gradients and the Coriolis effect.

Pressure gradients are caused by the unequal heating of the atmosphere by the Sun. Warm equatorial air is lighter and therefore has a lower pressure than cold, dense, polar air. The strength of air movement from areas of high to low pressure – known as the pressure gradient – is proportional to the difference in pressure.

Along the Equator is a region called the doldrums, where the Sun's heat warms the rising air. This air eventually spreads out and flows north and south away from the Equator. It finally sinks at about 30°N and 30°S, creating subtropical high-pressure belts (the horse latitudes), from which trade winds flow back towards the Equator and westerlies flow towards the mid-latitudes.

The Coriolis effect is the deflection of winds caused by the Earth's rotation, to the right in the Northern Hemisphere and to the left in the Southern. As a result, winds don't flow directly from the point of highest pressure to the lowest; those approaching a low-pressure system are deflected round it rather than flowing directly into it. This creates air systems, with high or low pressure, in which winds circulate round the centre. Horizontal air movements are important around cyclonic (low-pressure) and anticyclonic (high-pressure) systems. Horizontal and vertical movements combine to create a pattern of prevailing global winds.

Weather and depressions

To most of us "weather" means rain and sunshine, heat and cold, clouds and wind. Humidity and visibility might be added to the list. If not precise in terminology, this layman's catalogue comprises the six main elements which also comprise weather for meteorologists: in their language they are precipitation, air temperature, cloud cover, wind velocity, humidity and barometric pressure.

Depressions occur when warm air flows into waves in a polar front while cold air flows in behind it, creating rotating air systems that bring changeable weather. Along the warm front (the boundary on the ground between the warm and cold air), the warm air flows upwards over the cold air, producing a sequence of clouds that help forecasters predict a depression's advance.

Along the cold front the advancing cold air forces warm air to rise steeply, and towering cumulonimbus clouds form in the rising air. When the cold front overtakes the warm front, the warm air is pushed up to form an occluded front. Cloud and rain persist along occlusions until temperatures equalize, the air mixes, and the depression dies out.

BELOW The world's zones of high and low pressure are both areas of comparative calm, but between them lie the belts of prevailing winds. West of Africa, wind patterns are remarkably constant between summer and winter, but in much of the east variations are caused by monsoons (reversals of wind flows) stemming in part from the unequal heating of land masses and the sea.

WINDS AND PRESSURE

January

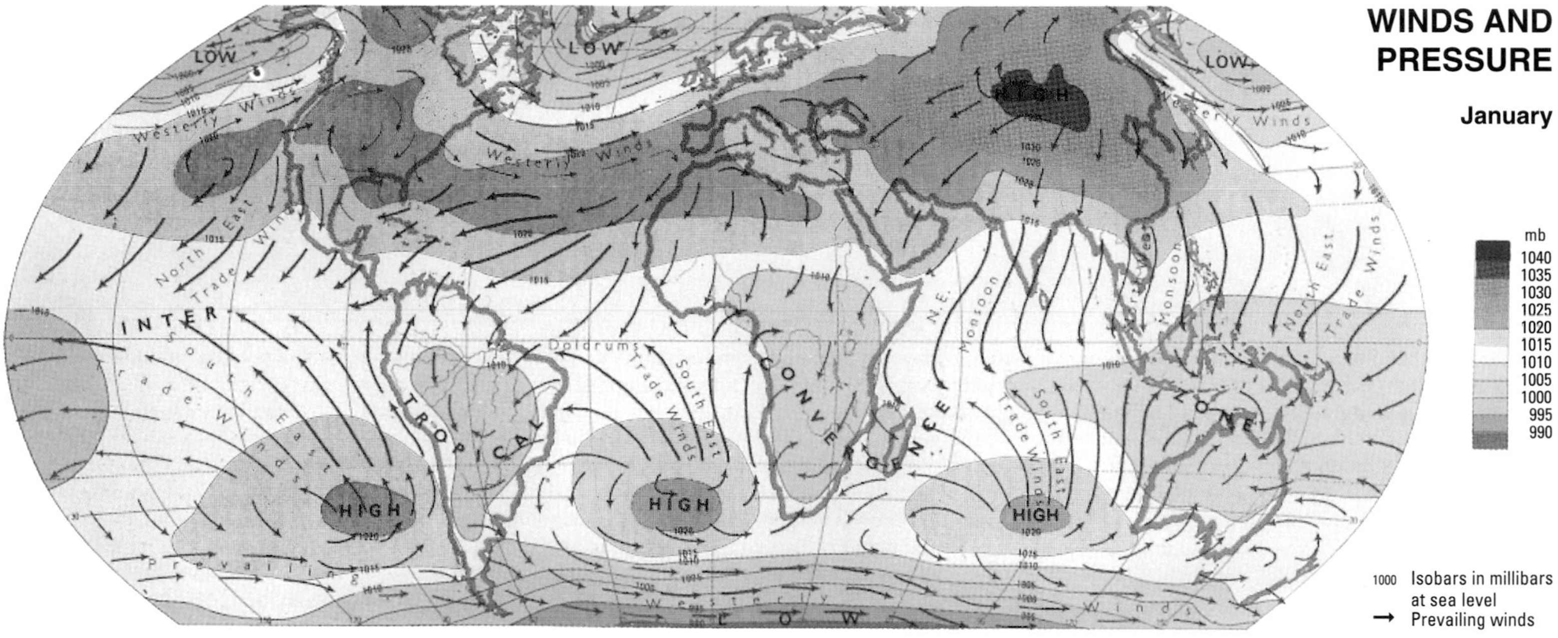

July

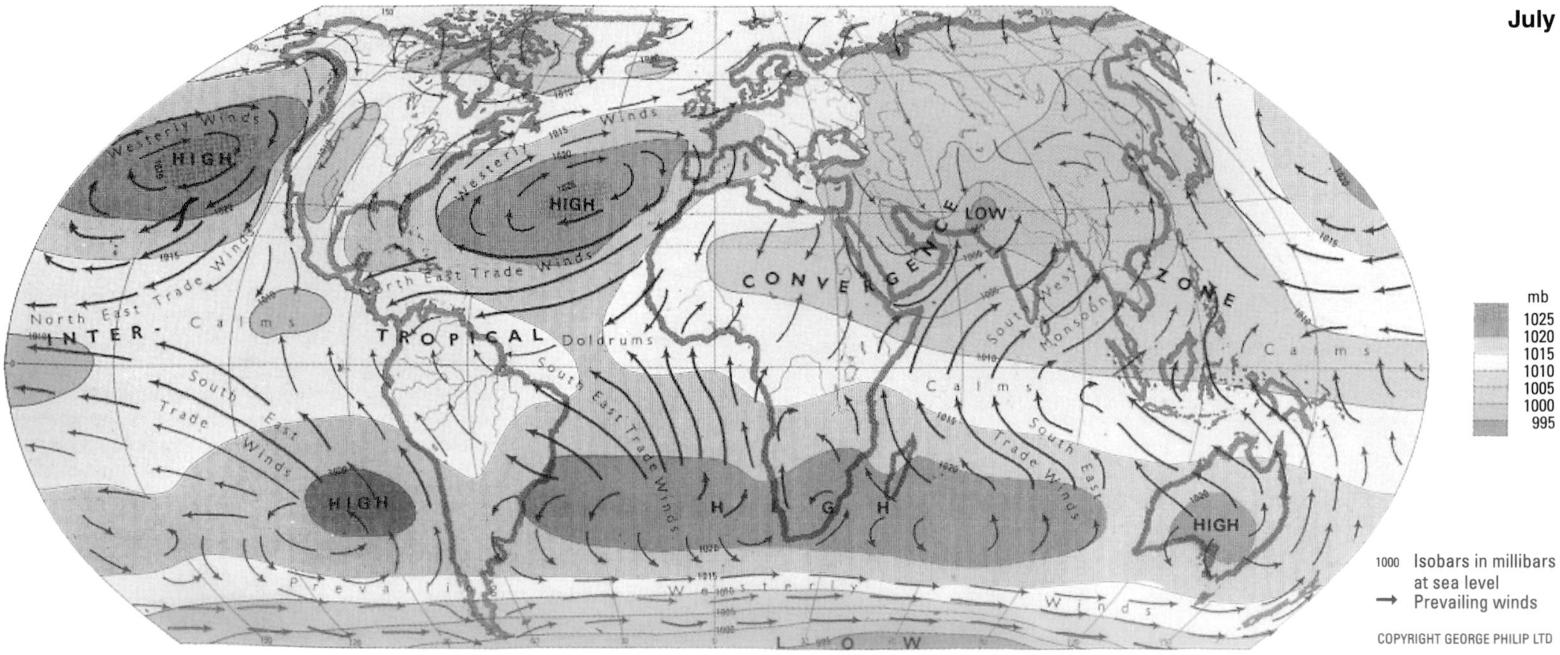

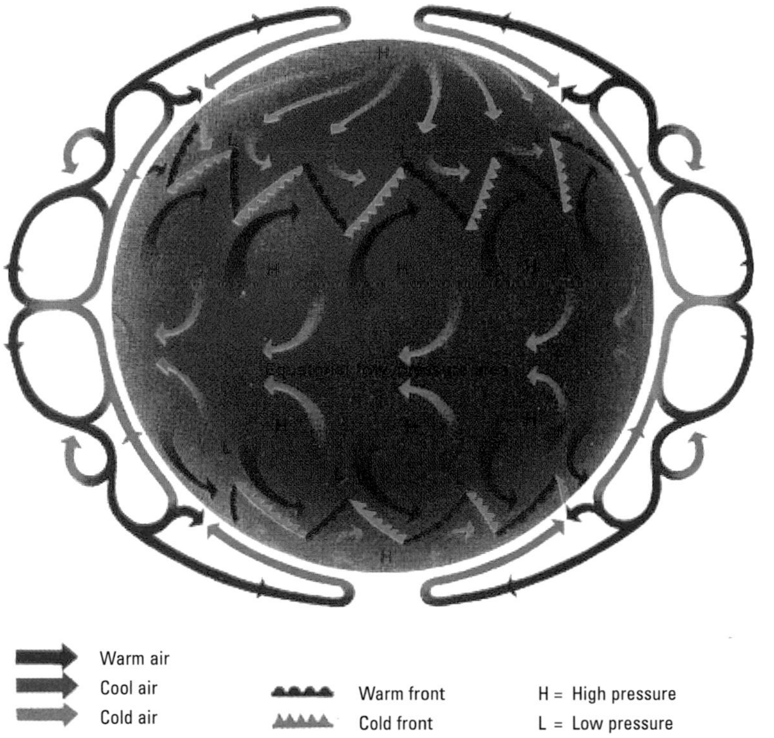
Warm air
Cool air
Cold air
Warm front
Cold front
H = High pressure
L = Low pressure

ABOVE The Earth's atmosphere acts as a giant heat engine. The temperature differences between the poles and the Equator provide the thermal energy to drive atmospheric circulation, both horizontal and vertical. In general, warm air at the Equator rises and moves towards the poles at high levels and cold polar air moves towards the Equator at low levels to replace it. Air also flows north and south from the high-pressure belts called the horse latitudes, and these airflows meet up with cold, dense air flowing from the poles along the polar front.

The basic global pattern of prevailing winds is complicated by the rotation of the Earth (which causes the Coriolis effect), by cells of high-pressure and low-pressure systems (depressions) and by the distribution and configuration of land and sea.

Climate Records

Highest barometric pressure: Agata, Siberia [at altitude of 262m (862ft)] 1,083.8 millibars, 31 December 1968.

Lowest barometric pressure: Typhoon Tip, 480km (300 miles) west of Guam, Pacific Ocean, 870 millibars, 12 October 1979.

Highest recorded wind speed: Mt Washington, New Hampshire, USA, 371km/h (231 mph), 12 April 1934; this is three times as strong as hurricane force on the Beaufort scale.

Worst recorded storm: Bangladesh (then East Pakistan) cyclone, 13 November 1970 – over 300,000 dead or missing; the 1991 cyclone in Bangladesh killed an estimated 138,000 people.

Worst recorded tornado: Missouri/Illinois/Indiana, USA, 18 March 1925 – 792 deaths; the tornado was only 275m (900ft) across.

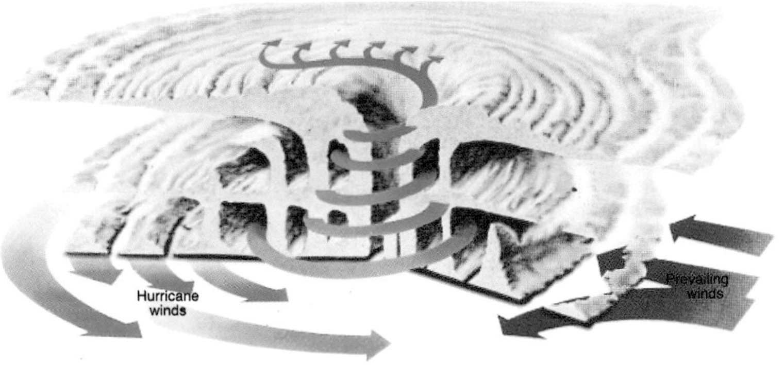
Hurricane winds
Prevailing winds

ABOVE Hurricanes consist of a huge swirl of clouds rotating round a calm centre – the "eye" – where warm air is sucked down. Hurricanes may be 400km (250 miles) in diameter and they extend through the troposphere, which is about 15-20km (9-12 miles) thick. Clouds, mainly cumulonimbus, are arranged in bands round the eye, the tallest forming the wall of the eye. Cirrus clouds usually cap the hurricane.

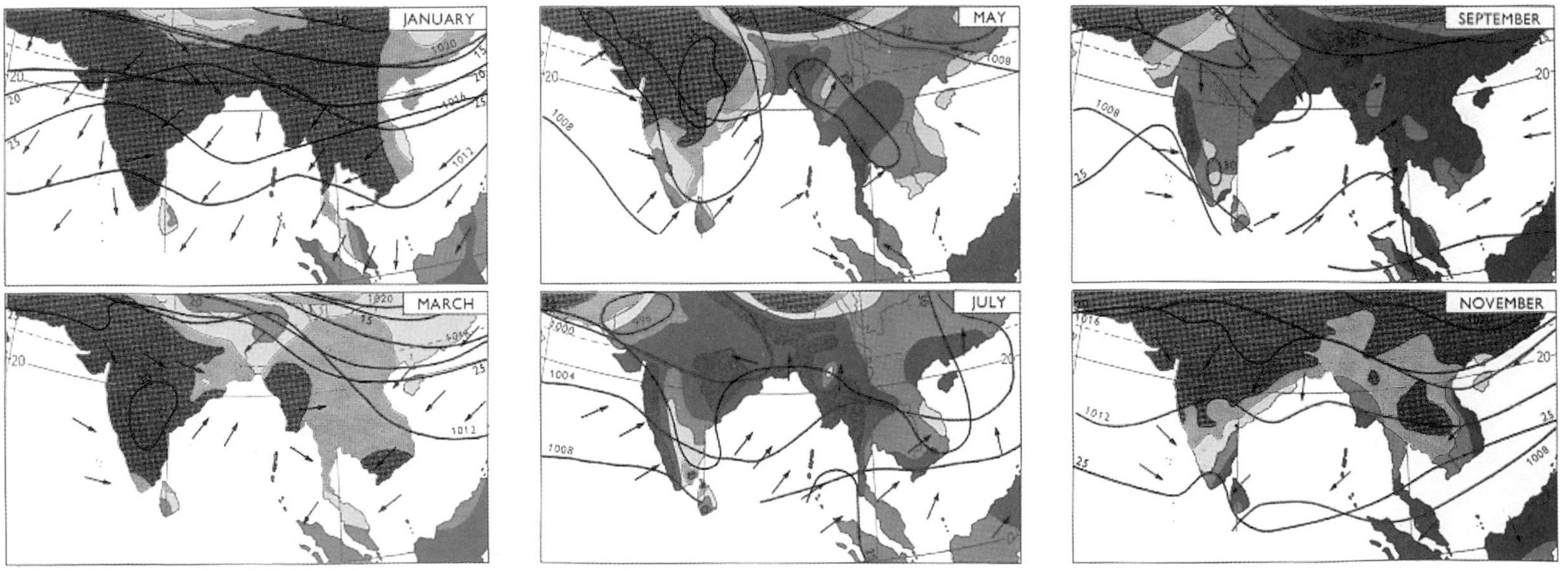
JANUARY
MAY
SEPTEMBER
MARCH
JULY
NOVEMBER

ABOVE "Monsoon" is the term given to the seasonal reversal of wind direction, most noticeably in South and Southeast Asia, where it results in very heavy rains. In January a weak anticylone in northern India gives the clear skies brought by northeasterly winds; in March temperatures increase and the anticyclone subsides, sea breezes bringing rain to coastal areas; by May the north is hot and a low pressure area begins to form, while the south is cooler with some rain; in July the low-pressure system over India caused by high temperatures brings the Southwest Monsoon from the high-pressure area in the south Indian Ocean; in September the Southwest Monsoon – with its strong winds, cloud cover, rain and cool temperatures – begins to retreat from the northwest; by the end of the cycle in November the subcontinent is cool and dry, though still wet in the southeast.

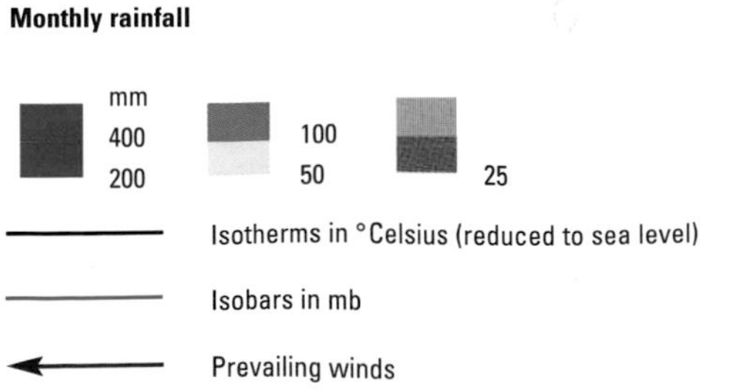
Monthly rainfall
mm
400
200
100
50
25
Isotherms in °Celsius (reduced to sea level)
Isobars in mb
Prevailing winds

WORLD CLIMATE

CLIMATE IS weather in the longer term, the seasonal pattern of hot and cold, wet and dry, averaged over time. Its passage is marked by a ceaseless churning of the atmosphere and the oceans, further agitated by the Earth's rotation and the motion it imparts to moving air and water.

There are many classifications of world climate, but most are based on a system developed in the early 19th century by the Russian meteorologist Vladimir Köppen. Basing his divisions on two main features, temperature and precipitation, and using a code of letters, he identified five main climatic types: tropical (A), dry (B), warm temperate (C), cool temperate (D) and cold (E). Each of these main regions was then further subdivided. (A highland mountain category was added later to account for the variety of climatic zones found in mountainous areas due to changes caused by altitude.)

Although latitude is a major factor in determining climate, other factors add to the complexity. These include the influence of ocean currents, different rates of heating and cooling of land and ocean, distance from the sea, and the effect of mountains on winds. New York, Naples and the Gobi Desert all share the same latitude, for example, but their climates are very different.

Climates are not stable indefinitely. Our planet regularly passes through cool periods – Ice Ages probably caused by the recurring long-term oscillations in the Earth's orbital path from almost circular to elliptical every 95,000 years, variations in the Earth's tilt from 21½° to 24½° every 42,000 years, and perhaps even fluctuations in the Sun's energy output. In the present era, the Earth is closest to the Sun in the middle of winter in the Northern Hemisphere and furthest away in summer; 12,000 years ago, at the height of the last Ice Age, northern winter fell with the Sun at its most distant.

Studies of these cycles suggest that we are now

CLIMATIC ZONES

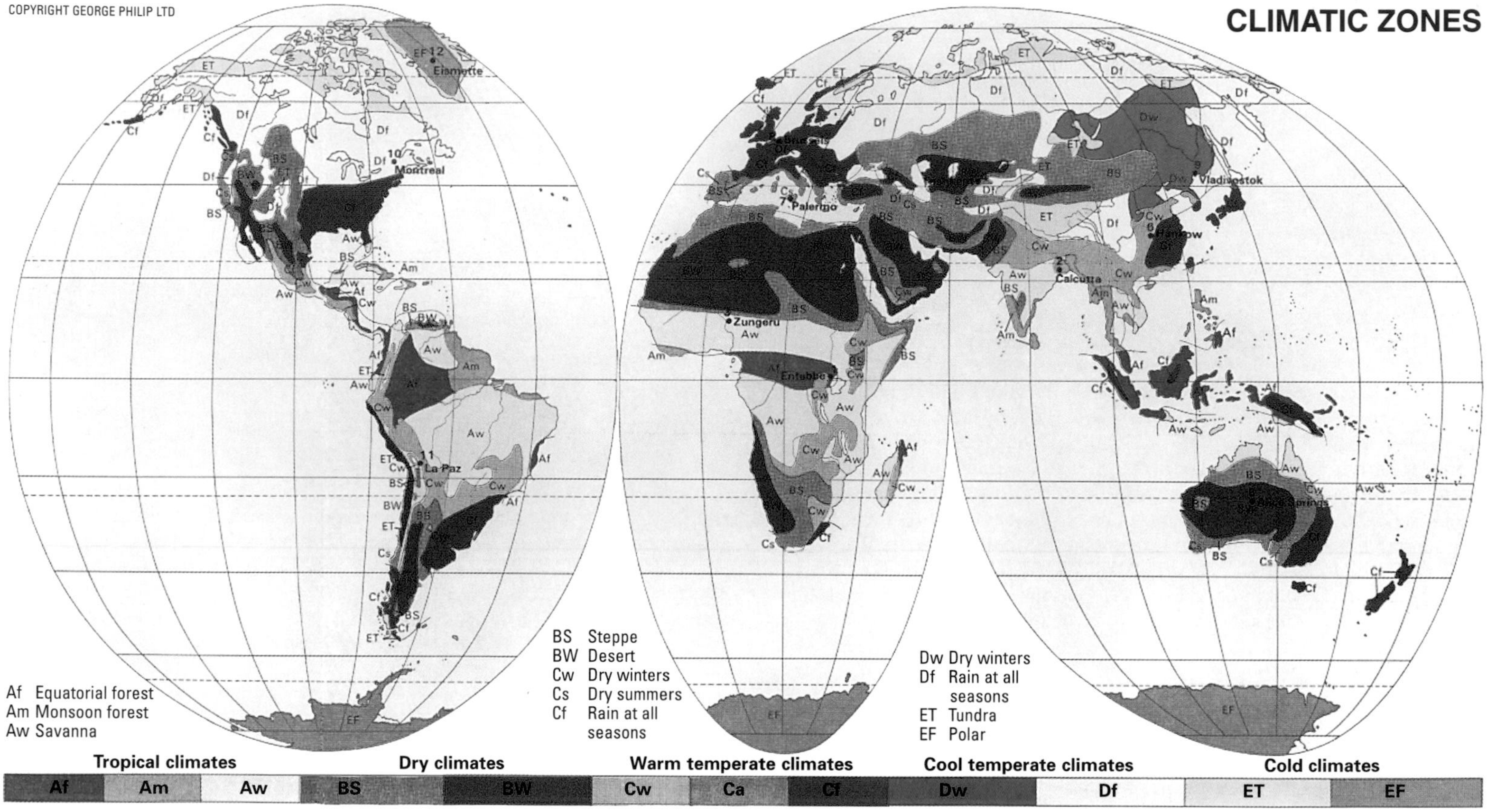
Af Equatorial forest
Am Monsoon forest
Aw Savanna
BS Steppe
BW Desert
Cw Dry winters
Cs Dry summers
Cf Rain at all seasons
Dw Dry winters
Df Rain at all seasons
ET Tundra
EF Polar
Tropical climates
Dry climates
Warm temperate climates
Cool temperate climates
Cold climates
Af Am Aw BS BW Cw Ca Cf Dw Df ET EF
Eismitte
Montreal
Palermo
Zungeru
Entebbe
La Paz
Tashkent
Calcutta
Vladivostok
Alice Springs

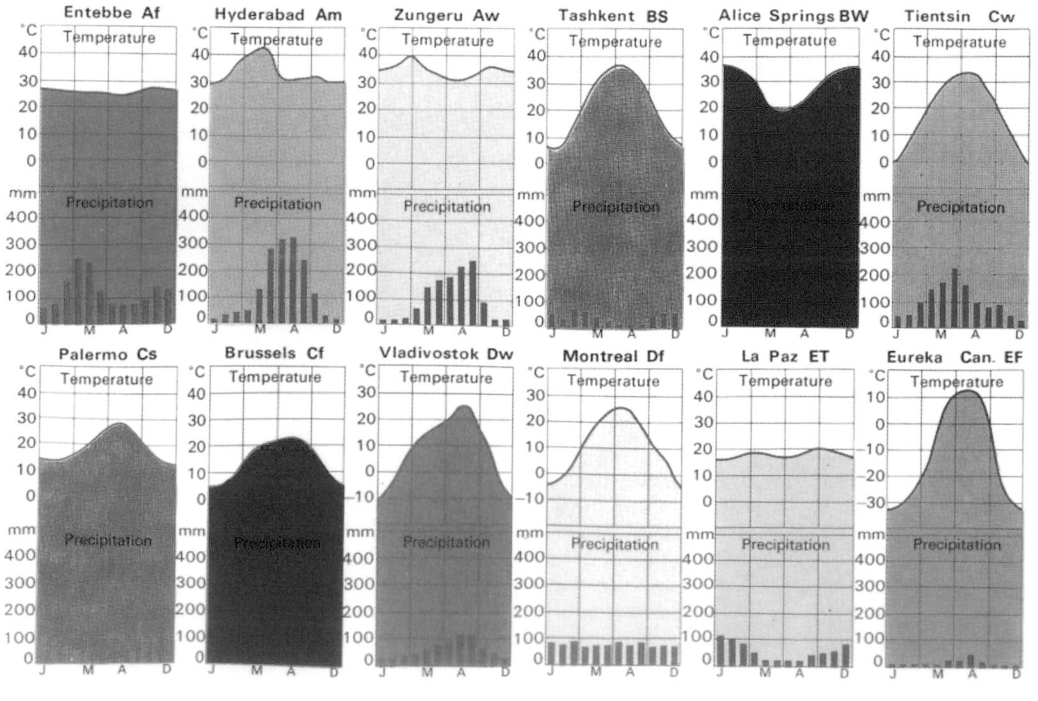
Entebbe Af
Hyderabad Am
Zungeru Aw
Tashkent BS
Alice Springs BW
Tientsin Cw
Palermo Cs
Brussels Cf
Vladivostok Dw
Montreal Df
La Paz ET
Eureka Can. EF
Temperature
Precipitation
°C
mm
J M A D

CLIMATE TERMS

Cyclone: Violent storm called a hurricane in N. America and a typhoon in the Far East.
Depression: Area of low pressure.
Frost: Dew when the air temperature falls below freezing point.
Hail: Frozen rain.
Humidity: Amount of moisture in the air.
Isobar: Line on a map connecting places of equal atmospheric pressure.
Isotherm: Line on a map connecting places of equal temperatutre.
Precipitation: Measurable amounts of rain, snow, sleet or hail.
Rain: Precipitation of liquid particles with diameter larger than 0.5mm (0.02 in); under this size is classified as drizzle.
Sleet: Partially melted snow.
Snow: Crystals formed when water vapour condenses below freezing point.
Tornado: Severe funnel-shaped storm that twists as hot air spins vertically; called a waterspout at sea.

in an interglacial period, but with a new glacial period on the way. For the forseeable future, however, the planet is likely to continue heating up because of global warming, caused largely by the burning of fossil fuels and deforestation. Figures show that average temperatures rose 1.7°C (0.9°F) in the 20th century, with most of that increase coming after about 1970, and despite attempts to stabilize the situation it's likely that the trend will continue. Such changes would not redraw Köppen's divisions, but they would make a significant difference to many local climates, with a dramatic effect on everything from agriculture to architecture.

Climate Records

TEMPERATURE

Highest recorded shade temperature: Al Aziziyah, Libya, 58°C (136.4°F), 13 Sep. 1922.

Highest mean annual temperature: Dallol, Ethiopia, 34.4°C (94°F), 1960-66.

Longest heatwave: Marble Bar, Western Australia, 162 days over 37.8°C (100°F), 23 October 1923 to 7 April 1924.

Lowest recorded temperature: Vostock Station, Eastern Antarctica, 21 July 1985, –89.2°C (–128.6°F)

(Lowest recorded temperature (outside poles): Verkhoyansk, Siberia, –68°C (–90°F), 6 February 1933.

Lowest mean annual temperature: Plateau Station, Antarctica, –56.6°C (–72.0°F).

PRECIPITATION

Longest drought: Calama, N. Chile – no recorded rainfall in 400 years to 1971.

Wettest place (12 months): Cherrapunji, Meghalaya, NE. India, 26,470mm (1,040 in), August 1860 to August 1861; Cherrapunji also holds the record for the most rainfall in a month: 2,930mm (115 in), July 1861.

Wettest place (average): Tututendo, Colombia, mean annual rainfall of 11,770mm (463.4 in).

Wettest place (24 hours): Cilaos, Réunion, Indian Ocean, 1,870mm (73.6 in), 15-16 March 1952.

Heaviest hailstones: Gopalganj, Bangladesh, up to 1.02kg (2.25lb), 14 April 1986 (92 people were killed).

Heaviest snowfall (continuous): Bessans, Savoie, France, 1,730mm (68 in) in 19 hours, 5-6 April 1969.

Heaviest snowfalls (season/year): Paradise Ranger Station, Mt Rainier, Washington, USA, 31,102mm (1,224.5 in), 19 February 1971 to 18 February 1972.

Conversions
°C = (°F -32) x 5/9; °F = (°C x 9/5) + 32; 0°C = 32°F
1 mm = 0.0394 in (100 mm = 3.94 in); 1 in = 25.4 mm

TEMPERATURE

Average temperature in January

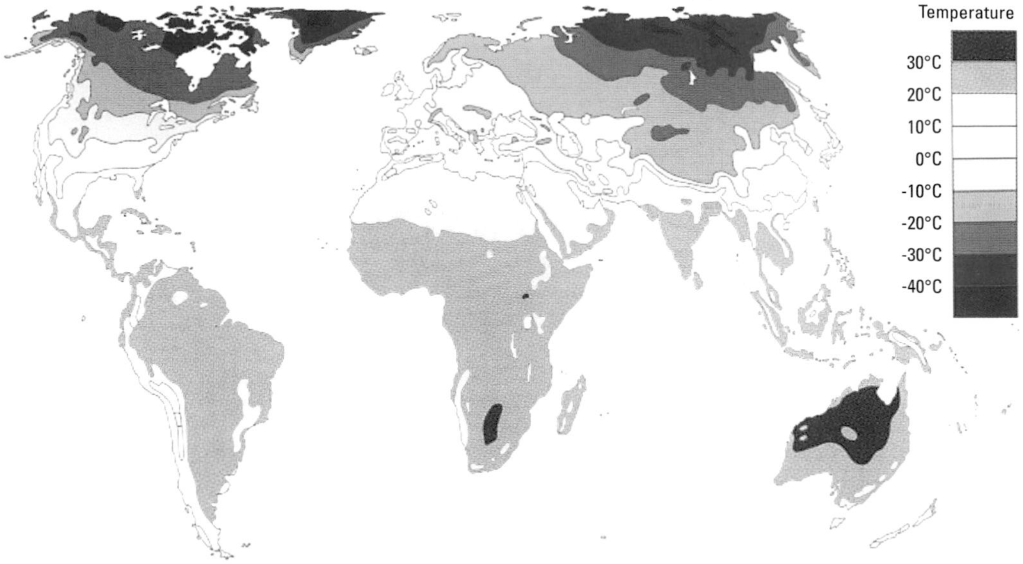
Temperature
30°C
20°C
10°C
0°C
-10°C
-20°C
-30°C
-40°C

Average temperature in July

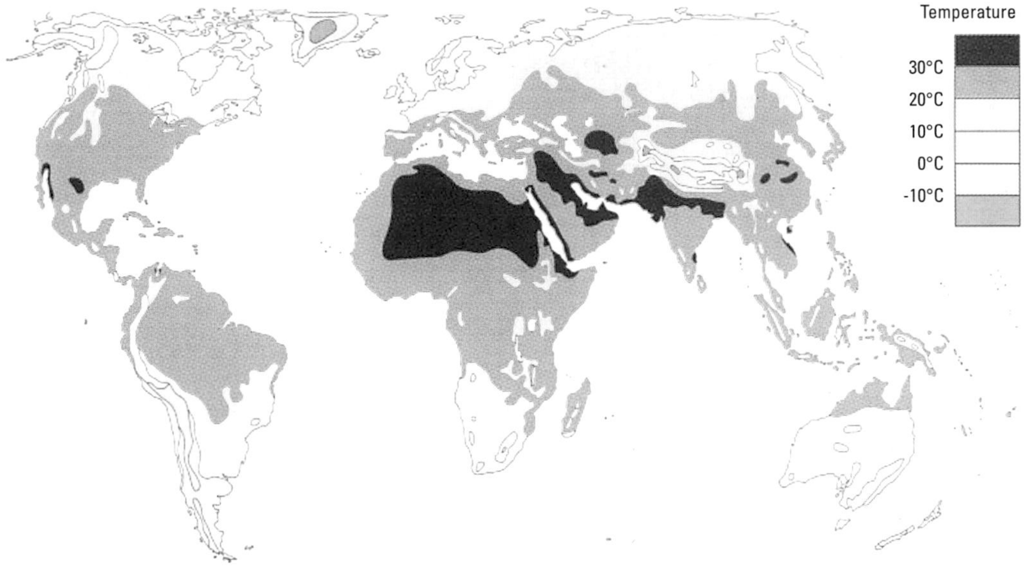
Temperature
30°C
20°C
10°C
0°C
-10°C

RAINFALL

Average annual precipitation

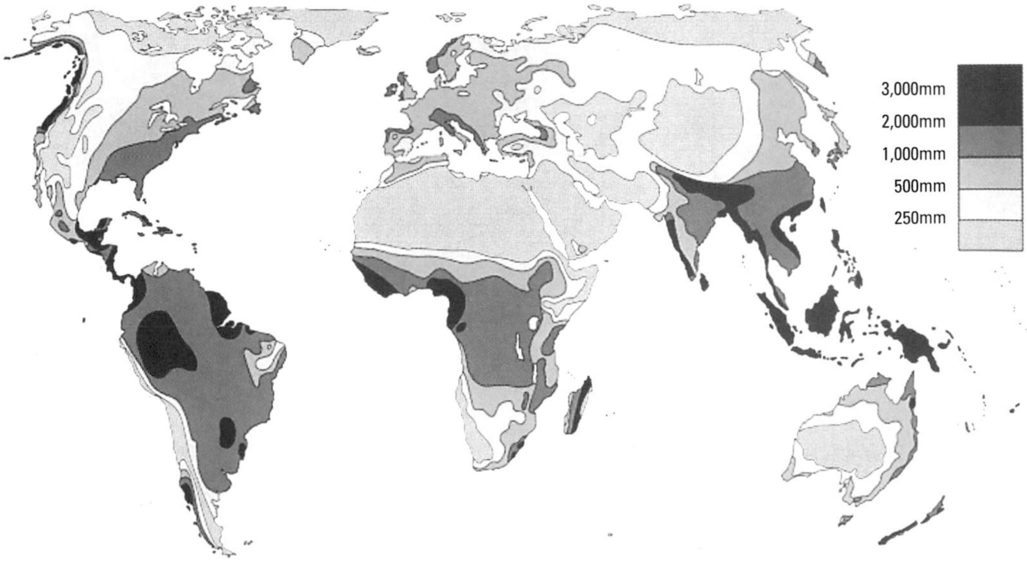
3,000mm
2,000mm
1,000mm
500mm
250mm

THE WORLD'S WATER

FRESH WATER is essential to all life on Earth, from the humblest bacterium to the most advanced technological society. Yet freshwater resources form a minute fraction of our 1.36 billion cu. km (326 million cu. miles) of water: most human needs must be met from the 2,000 cu. km (480 cu. miles) circulating in rivers.

Agriculture accounts for huge quantities: without large-scale irrigation, most of the world's people would starve. Since fresh water is just as essential for most industrial processes, the combination of growing population and advancing industry has put supplies under increasing strain.

Fortunately water is seldom used up: the planet's water cycle circulates it efficiently, at least on a global scale. More locally, however, human activity can cause severe shortages: water for industry and agriculture is being withdrawn from many river basins and underground aquifers faster than natural recirculation can replace it – a process exacerbated by global warming.

The demand for water has led to tensions between an increasing number of nations as supplies are diverted or hoarded. Both Iraq and Syria, for example, have protested at Turkey's dam-building programme, which they claim drastically reduces the flow of Tigris and Euphrates water to their land.

RIGHT Over 97% of the world's water is accounted for by the oceans. Of the total water on land more than 75% is frozen in icesheets and glaciers. Most of the rest, about 22%, is water collected below the Earth's surface (ground water). Relatively small quantities are in lakes and rivers (0.017% of the total), while water vapour represents only 0.001%. Without this, however, there would be no life on land.

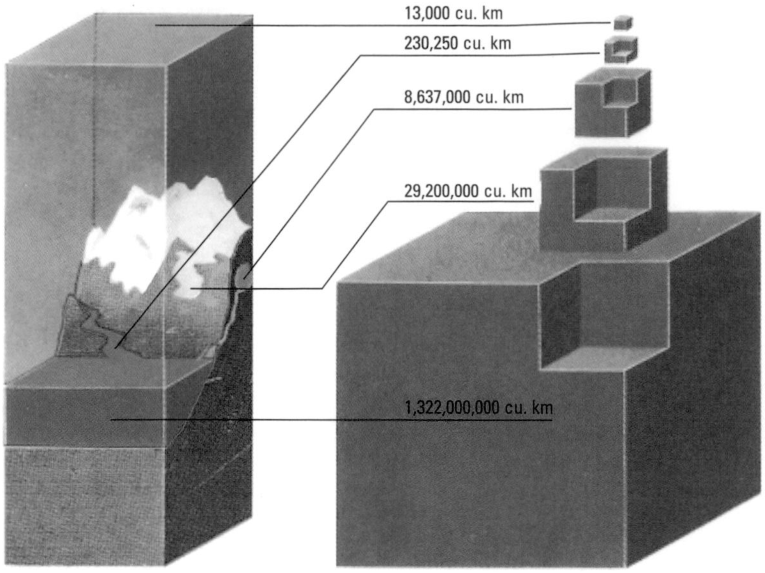

13,000 cu. km
230,250 cu. km
8,637,000 cu. km
29,200,000 cu. km
1,322,000,000 cu. km

The water cycle

Oceanic water is salty and unsuitable for drinking or farming. In some desert regions, where fresh sources are in short supply, seawater is desalinated to make fresh water, but most of the world is constantly supplied with fresh water by the natural process of the water or hydrological cycle, which relies on the action of two factors: gravity and the Sun's heat.

Over the oceans, which cover almost 71% of the Earth's surface, the Sun's heat causes evaporation, and water vapour rises on air currents and winds. Some of this vapour condenses and returns directly to the oceans as rain, but because of the circulation of the atmosphere, air bearing large amounts is carried over land, where it falls as rain or snow.

Much of this precipitation is quickly re-evaporated by the Sun. Some soaks into the soil, where it is absorbed by plants and partly returned to the air through transpiration; some flows over the land surface as run-off, which flows into streams and rivers; and some rain and melted snow seeps through the soil into the rocks beneath to form ground water.

In polar and high mountainous regions most precipitation is in the form of snow. There it is compacted into ice, forming icesheets and glaciers. The force of gravity causes these bodies of ice to move downwards and outwards, and they may eventually return to the oceans where chunks of ice break off at the coastline to form icebergs. Thus all the water that does not return directly to the atmosphere gradually returns to the sea to complete the water cycle. This continual movement of water and ice plays a major part in the erosion of land areas.

Of the total water on land, more than 75% is frozen in icesheets and glaciers, and two-thirds of all the Earth's fresh water is held in Antarctica. Twice the size of Australia, this frozen continent contains ice to depths of 3,500m (11,500ft) and land is covered in ice to an average depth of more than 2,000m (6,500ft). However, Antarctica receives very little precipitation, not even in the form of snow. It is, effectively, a polar desert.

Most of the rest of the water on land (about 22%) is collected below the Earth's surface and is called ground water; comparatively small but crucially important quantities are in lakes, rivers and in the soil. Water that is held in the soil and that nourishes plant growth is called capillary water: it is retained in the upper few metres by molecular attraction between the water and soil particles.

BELOW The water or hydrological cycle is the process whereby water, in its various forms, circulates from the oceans to land areas and back again. Fresh water is present on the Earth as water vapour in the atmosphere, as ice, and as liquid water.

The elements of the cycle are precipitation as rain [3], surface run-off [4], evaporation of rain in falling [5], ground water flow to rivers and streams [6], ground water flow to the oceans [7], transpiration from plants [8], evaporation from lakes and ponds [9], evaporation from the soil [10], evaporation from rivers and streams [11], evaporation from the oceans [13], flow of rivers and streams to the oceans [12], ground water flow from the oceans to arid land [16], intense evaporation from arid land [17], movement of moist air from and to the oceans [14,15], precipitation as snow [2], and ice-flow into the seas and oceans [1].

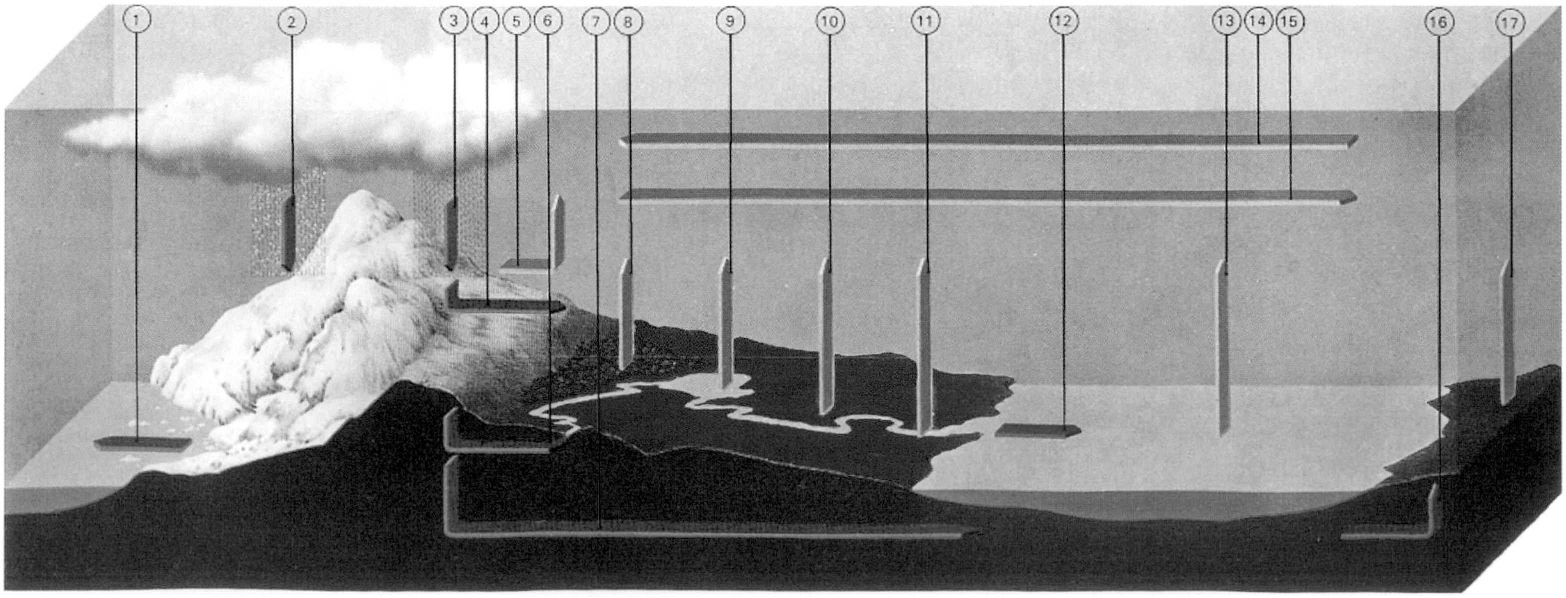

1
2
3
4
5
6
7
8
9
10
11
12
13
14
15
16
17

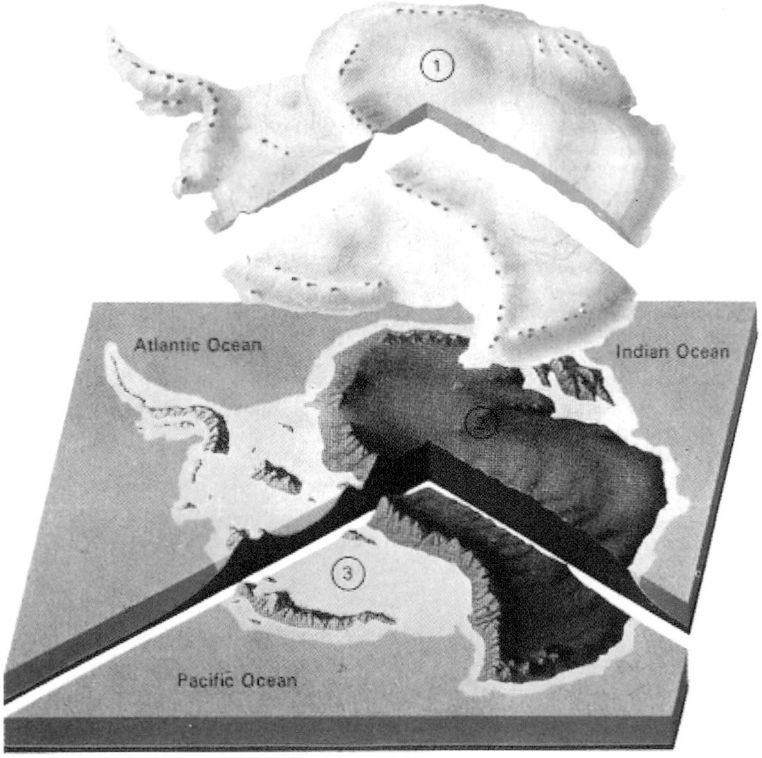
1
Atlantic Ocean
Indian Ocean
2
3
Pacific Ocean

ABOVE While 75% of the world's fresh water is frozen, continental ice-sheets are now found only in Antarctica and Greenland. In Antarctica the ice [1] covers the land [2] but also permanently frozen sea [3]. Beneath the ice the terrain is rugged and variable in height, but because of the weight of the ice, about 40% of the land is depressed below sea level.

BELOW Almost all our water supply is 3 billion years old, and all of it cycles endlessly through the hydrosphere, though at very different rates. Water vapour circulates over days, even hours, and deep ocean water over millennia, while icecap water remains solid for millions of years.

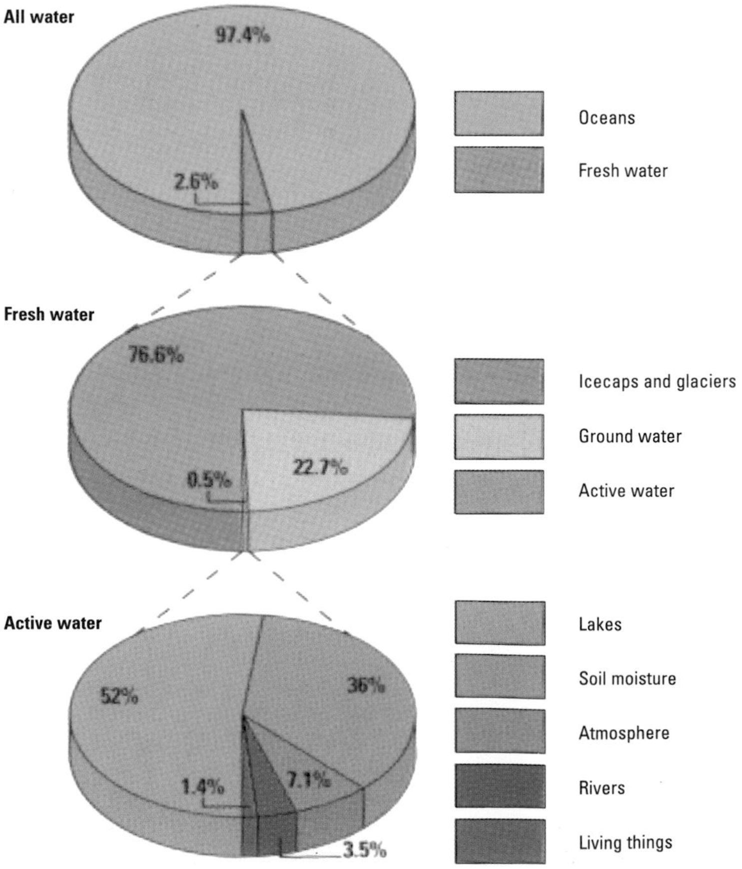
All water
97.4%
2.6%
Oceans
Fresh water
Fresh water
76.6%
0.5%
22.7%
Icecaps and glaciers
Ground water
Active water
Active water
52%
36%
1.4%
7.1%
3.5%
Lakes
Soil moisture
Atmosphere
Rivers
Living things

BELOW Ice in the form of icesheets and glaciers now covers 10% of the world's land area, but during the last glacial period, between about 110,000 and 10,000 years ago, icesheets covered up to 30% of the land. At periods of maximum glaciation, sea levels were 180m (600ft) lower than at the present time because of the large amount of water frozen in the ice. Many of today's islands were joined to adjacent continental masses: the British Isles, for example, would have been part of Europe.

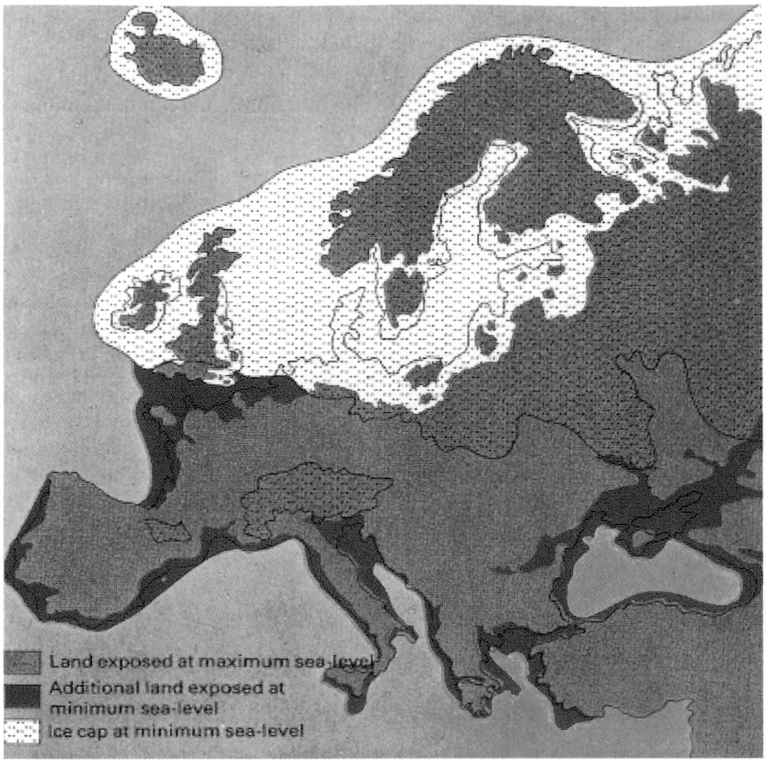
Land exposed at maximum sea-level
Additional land exposed at minimum sea-level
Ice cap at minimum sea-level

BELOW Rivers are the most visible part of the water cycle. The drainage pattern of a river and its tributaries is related primarily to the type of rocks on which it formed or flows. On rocks of equal or similar resistance (A), a dendritic pattern develops; in areas of alternating hard and soft rock (B), the water follows the softer rock to form a trellis pattern; and a radial pattern (C), forms on and around and rock domes and volcanoes.

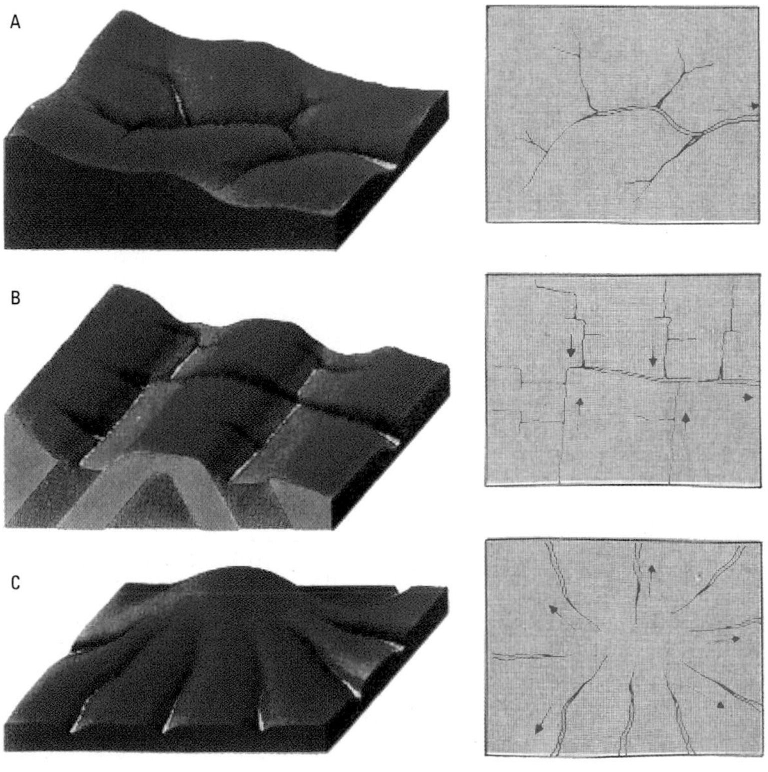
A
B
C

UNDERGROUND WATER

BELOW Gushes or seepages of water, springs are found where the water table or an aquifer appears at the surface, or where the aquifer is blocked by an impermeable rock such as a volcanic dyke. Spring water is usually fresh and clean because it passes through porous rocks.

Springs can occur where a fault brings an aquifer into contact with an impermeable layer [A]; where water pressure creates artesian springs at points of weakness [B]; where water seeps through jointed limestone until it emerges above an impermeable layer [C]; or where permeable strata overlay impermeable rock. An impermeable barrier may lead to the formation of a spring line [E].

GROUND WATER enters permeable rocks through what is called the zone of intermittent saturation, a layer that may retain water after continued rain but which soon dries up. Beneath this lies a rock zone where the pores or crevices are filled with water. Called the zone of saturation, this usually begins within 30m (100ft) of the surface, extending downwards until it reaches impermeable rock, through which it cannot percolate, lying below the water-holding layer (aquifer). The top of the saturated zone is the water table which, despite its name, is not level. It is often arched under hills, while beneath the softer rocks of plains it generally lies closer to the surface. The water table also varies in level during the year, depending on the amount of rainfall. In some places the water table intersects the surface, forming features such as oases in desert hollows, lakes, swamps and springs. Some springs

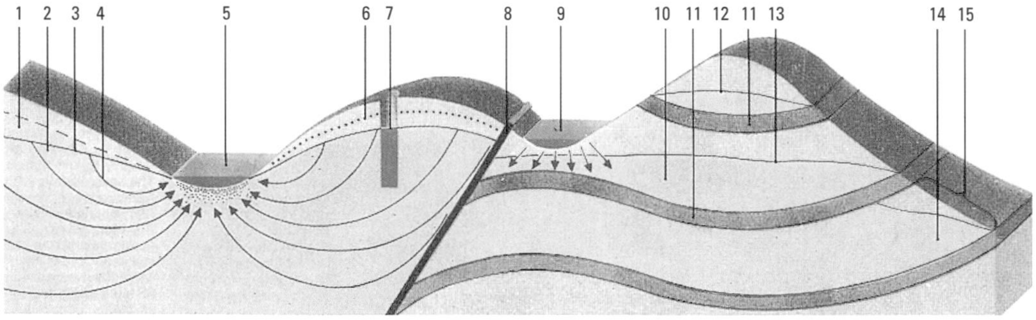

ABOVE Ground water seeps through the zone of intermittent saturation [1] until it reaches an impermeable layer, above which it forms the zone of saturation or aquifer [2,10]. The upper surface of the aquifer forms the water table [3,13], above which is the capillary fringe [6]. Because the capillary fringe is not saturated, wells [7] must be sunk to the water table.

Impermeable dikes [8] block the flow of ground water. In uniform material the water follows paths [4] that curve down and up again towards the nearest stream. If an aquifer is part of a series of strata including several impermeable layers [11], a "perched" water table [12] may result; if it lies between two impermeable strata it is said to be "confined" [14].

The recharge area [15] of the water table is where water enters the confined aquifer. A stream below the water table is called a gaining stream [5], while a stream flowing above it is known as a losing stream [9] because it loses water by seepage.

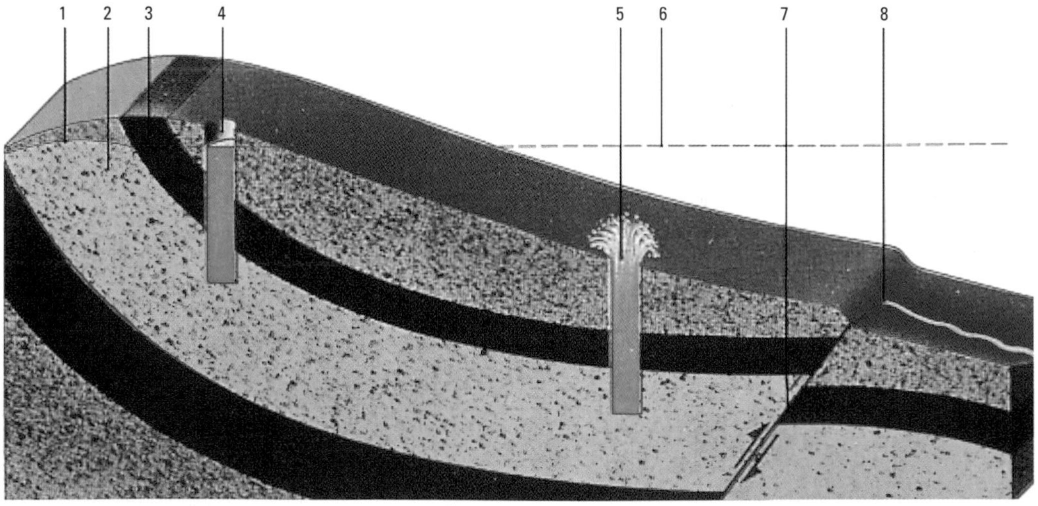

ABOVE The lowest level of the water table, reached at the driest time of the year, is called the permanent water table, and wells must be drilled to this depth if they are to guarantee a supply of water throughout the seasons.

Artesian springs and wells are found where ground water is under pressure, and in artesian wells water is forced to the surface by hydrostatic pressure. The water table [1] in the confined aquifer [2] lies near the top of the dipping layers. A well [4] drilled through the top impervious layer [3] is not an artesian well because the head of hydrostatic pressure [6] is not sufficient to force water to the surface; in such wells the water must be pumped or drawn to the surface.

The top of an artesian well [5] lies below the level of the head of hydrostatic pressure and so water gushes to the surface. Artesian springs [8] may occur along joints or faults [7] where the head of hydrostatic pressure is sufficient to force the water up along the fault.

Areas with artesian wells are called artesian basins. Artesian water is obtained from porous sandstone aquifers that underlie the Great Basin of Australia, which are supplied with water from rain that falls on the Eastern Highlands of Queensland and New South Wales. In the London and Paris artesian basins the water has been so heavily tapped in recent centuries that the water level has dropped below the level of the well-heads.

contain so much mineral substance in solution that their water is used for medicinal purposes and spa towns have grown up around them.

While sandstone is a highly porous rock through which water percolates easily, limestone is a permeable but non-porous rock. Ground water can seep through its maze of joints, fissures and caves, with apertures enlarged by the chemical action of rainwater containing dissolved carbon dioxide.

Rain coming off the Atlantic Ocean and Mediterreanean Sea and falling on the Atlas Mountains of Morocco and Algeria then drains into porous rocks underlying the northern parts of the Sahara Desert. The water seeps through these rocks which, wherever they come to the surface, give rise to fertile oases.

BELOW As rain falls, it dissolves carbon dioxide from the atmosphere and becomes a weak carbonic acid that attacks carbonate rock (limestone and dolomite) by transforming it into the soluble bicarbonate. Carbonate rocks are criss-crossed by vertical cracks and horizontal breaks along bedding planes [A]. Some geologists believe the caves were formed when the rock was saturated by water; others reckon they formed gradually by solution [B] into a major cave network [C]. Limestone caves contain many features formed from calcium carbonate.

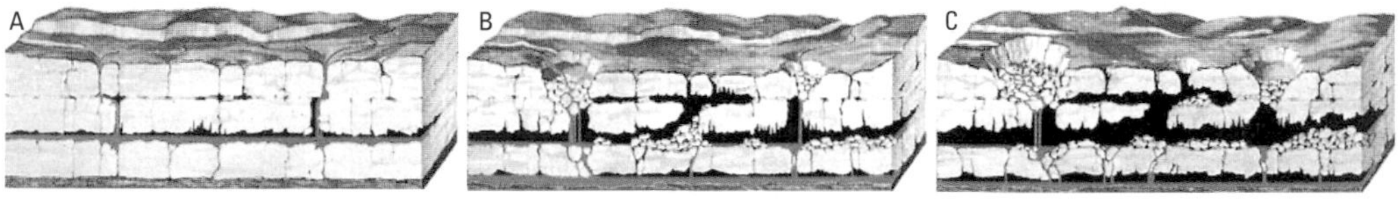

BELOW Limestone surfaces are often eroded into blocks called clints [1]. Surface streams flow into dissolved sink-holes [2] that lead to a deep chimney [3]; pot-holes [7] are dry chimneys. Gours [4] are ridges formed as carbonate is precipitated from turbulent water. Streams flow at the lowest level of the galleries [17], and abandoned galleries [13] are common. A siphon [12] occurs where the roof is below water level. Streams reappear at resurgences [20], and abandoned resurgences [19] may provide entrances to caves.

Stalactites [5] include macaroni stalactites [6], curtain stalactites or drapes [11] and "eccentric" stalactites [16], formed by water being blown sideways; stalagmites [14] sometimes have a fir-cone shape [15] caused by splashing, or resemble stacked plates [8]. Stalactites and stalagmites may also merge to form columns [10]. Signs of ancient humans [18] have been found in many caves, and they still harbour a variety of animal life adapted to the environment, including colourless shrimps and sightless newts – often called blind fish – which live in the dark pools [9].

VEGETATION AND SOIL

THE DISTRIBUTION of natural resources over the Earth's surface is far from even. The whereabouts of mineral deposits depends on random events in a remote geological past, while patches of fertile soil depend on more recent events such as the flow of rivers or the movement of ice.

For agriculture, the activity that has been basic to the survival of humanity and our huge increase in population, about a fifth of the Earth's surface is barred by ice or perennially frozen soil; a fifth is arid or desert; and another fifth is composed of highlands too cold, rugged or barren for the cultivation of crops. Between 5% and 10% of the remainder has no soil, either because it has been scraped by ice or because it is permanently wet or flooded. This leaves only 30% to 35% of the land surface where food production is even possible.

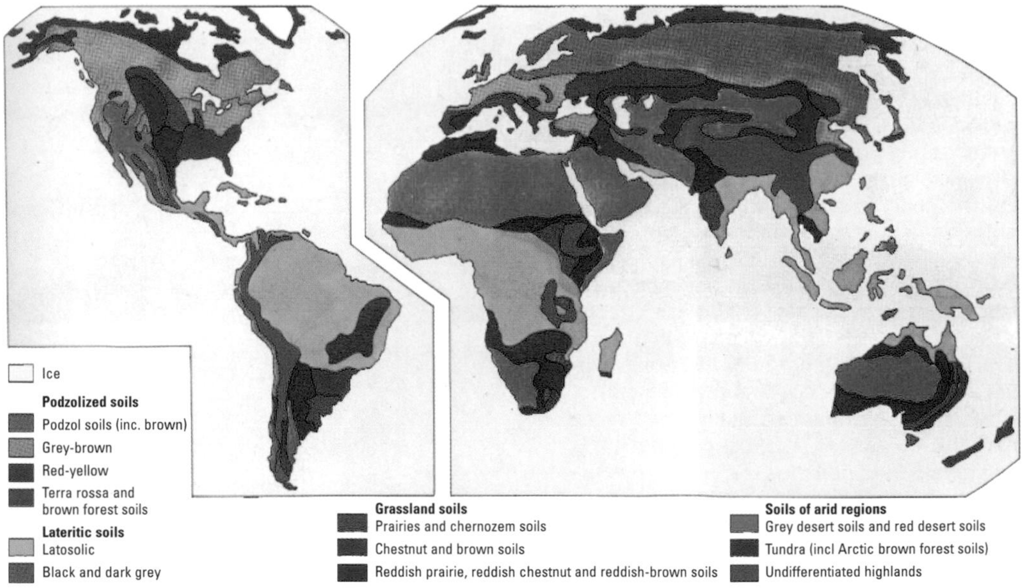
Ice
Podzolized soils
Podzol soils (inc. brown)
Grey-brown
Red-yellow
Terra rossa and brown forest soils
Lateritic soils
Latosolic
Black and dark grey
Grassland soils
Prairies and chernozem soils
Chestnut and brown soils
Reddish prairie, reddish chestnut and reddish-brown soils
Soils of arid regions
Grey desert soils and red desert soils
Tundra (incl Arctic brown forest soils)
Undifferentiated highlands

The importance of soil

The whole structure of life on Earth, with its enormous diversity of plant and animal types, is dependent on a mantle of soil which is rich in moisture and nutrients.

Soil is a result of all the processes of physical and chemical weathering on the barren, underlying rock mass of the Earth that it covers, and varies in depth from a few centimetres to several metres. The depth of soil is measured either by the distance to which plants send down their roots, or by the depth of soil directly influencing their systems. In some places only a very thin layer is necessary to support life.

Soil remains an unconsolidated mass of inorganic particles until it acquires a minimum organic content and plants take root and deposit their "litter". As the organic matter accumulates, fine humus builds up in the upper soil horizons, enriching them chemically and providing an environment for a wide variety of lifeforms. In the course of time plants, fungi, bacteria, worms, insects and burrowing animals such as rodents and moles reproduce in the soil and thrive in the complex ecosystem of a mature soil.

Formation of soil is the result of the complex interaction of five major elements – the parent rock (the source of the vast bulk of soil material), land topography, time, climate and decay. However, by far the most single important factor in the development of soil is climate, with water essential to all chemical and biological change. As it percolates through, water both leaches the surface layers and deposits material in the subsoil.

BELOW The map illustrates the natural "climax" vegetation of a region, as dictated by its climate and topography. In the vast majority of cases, however, human agricultural activity has drastically altered the pattern of vegetation. Western Europe, for example, lost most of its broadleaf forest many centuries ago, and in many areas irrigation has gradually turned natural semi-desert into productive land.

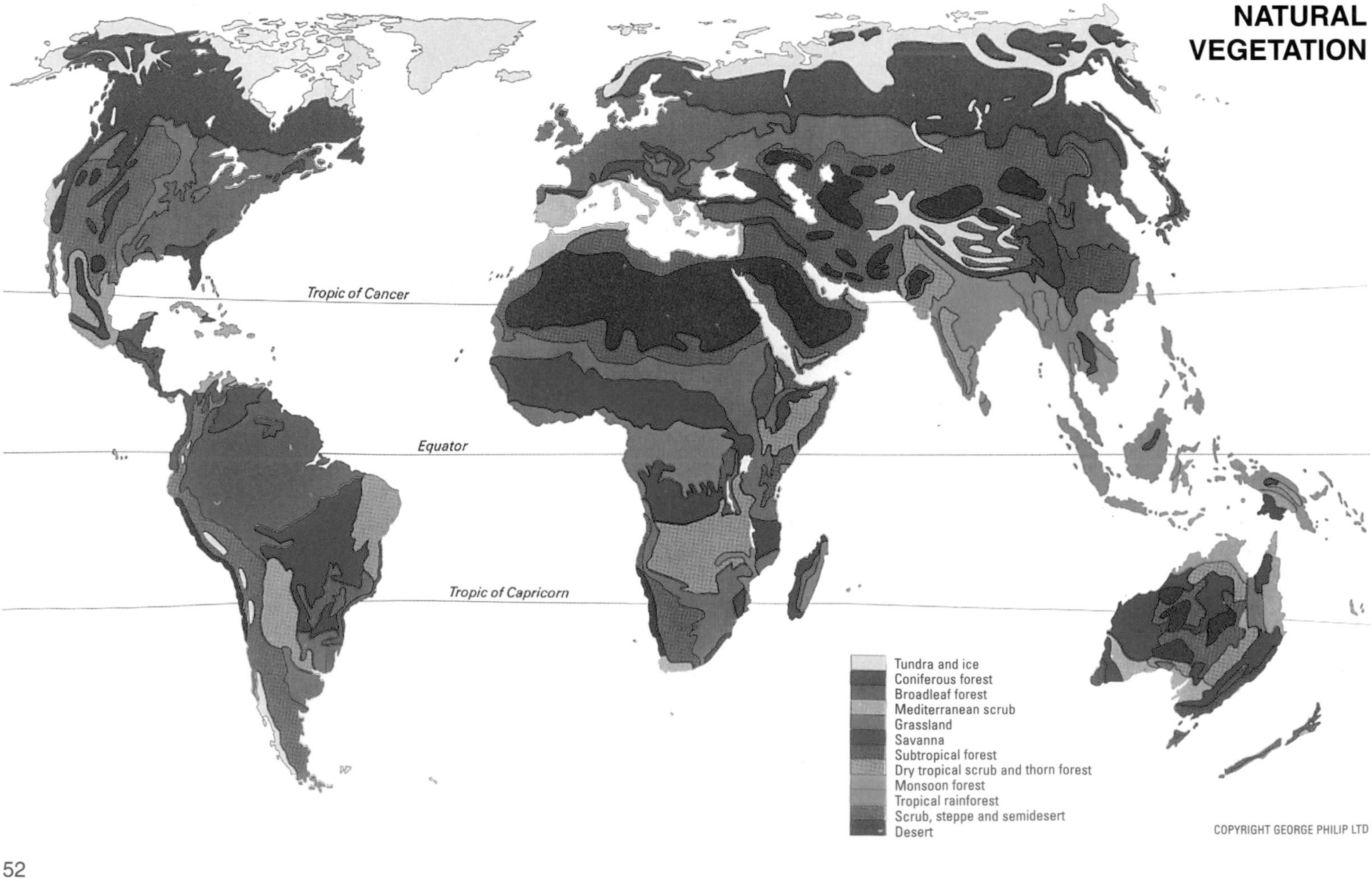
NATURAL VEGETATION
Tropic of Cancer
Equator
Tropic of Capricorn
Tundra and ice
Coniferous forest
Broadleaf forest
Mediterranean scrub
Grassland
Savanna
Subtropical forest
Dry tropical scrub and thorn forest
Monsoon forest
Tropical rainforest
Scrub, steppe and semidesert
Desert

RIGHT Some legume crops, such as clover, can obtain nitrogen from the air by the process known as fixation, but most plants need additional inorganic nitrogen and this element is the one most widely used in fertilizers.

Nitrogen undergoes a natural cycle. Together with its compounds it is involved in five basic processes: fixation of nitrogen from the air by micro-organisms and by lightning; use by plants of nitrates in the soil to make proteins; ammonium compound production in decaying plant and animal matter; nitrification of these to nitrites and then to nitrates; and denitrification of ammonium compounds back to nitrogen gas.

Nitrogen is removed from the soil whenever we consume food, but is replaced by the artificial addition of nitrogenous fertilizers to the soil by farmers. In its many forms nitrogen accounts for almost half of the world consumption of fertilizers: phosphoros makes up another 30% and potassium, the remaining primary nutrient, accounts for most of the balance.

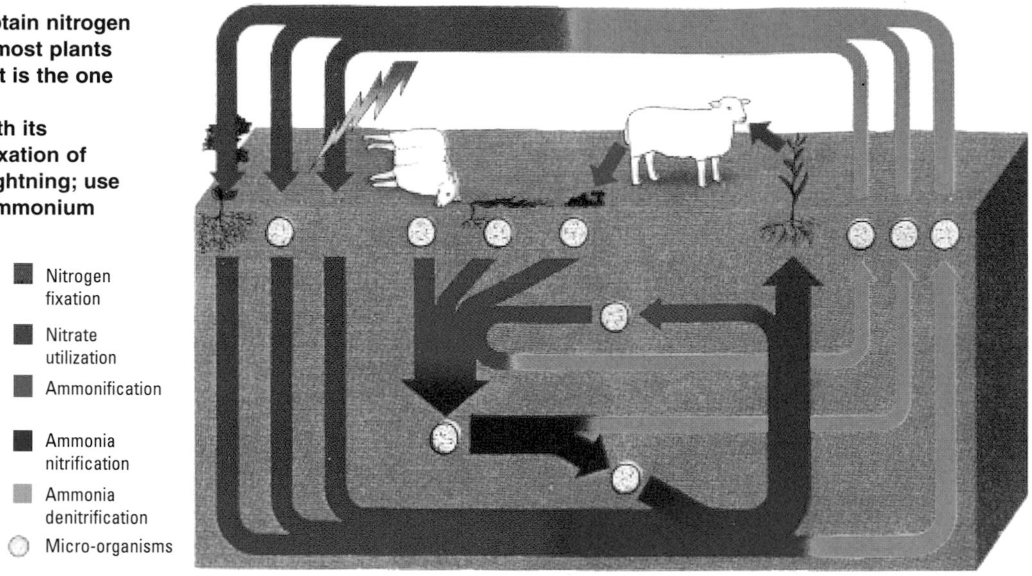

Nitrogen fixation
Nitrate utilization
Ammonification
Ammonia nitrification
Ammonia denitrification
Micro-organisms

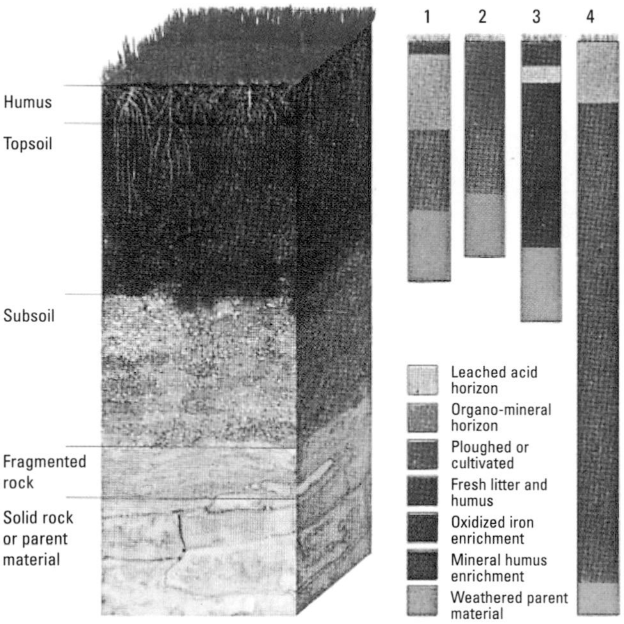

Humus
Topsoil
Subsoil
Fragmented rock
Solid rock or parent material
1
2
3
4
Leached acid horizon
Organo-mineral horizon
Ploughed or cultivated
Fresh litter and humus
Oxidized iron enrichment
Mineral humus enrichment
Weathered parent material

RIGHT Soil is identified by composition and colour. The tundra soil [1] has a dark, peaty surface. Light-coloured desert soil [2] is coarse and poor in organic matter. Chestnut-brown soil [3] and chernozem [4] – Russian for "black earth" – are humus-rich grassland soils typical of the central Asian steppes and prairies of North America. The reddish, leached latosol [5] of tropical savannas has a very thin but rich humus layer. Podzolic soils are typical of northern climates where rainfall is heavy but evaporation is slow: they include the organically rich brown forest podzol [6], the grey-brown podzol [8], and the grey-stony podzol [9] that supports mixed growths of conifers and hardwoods. All are relatively acid. The red-yellow podzol [9] is quite highly leached.

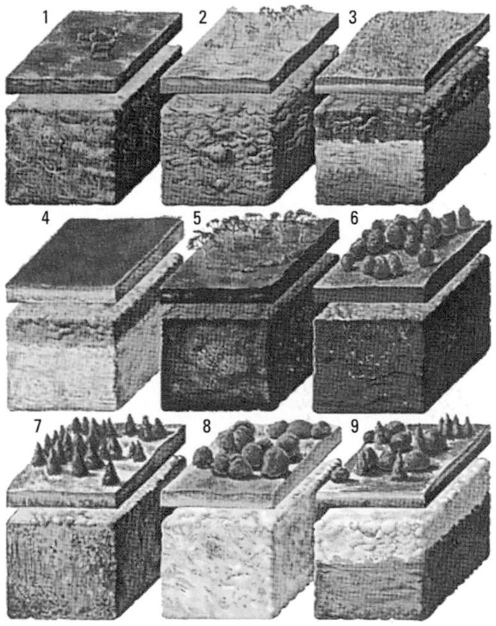

1
2
3
4
5
6
7
8
9

ABOVE Profile 1 is of acid brown earth found in temperate climates – this one on sandy rock – and 2 is a cultivated brown earth of the same region. Grey leached podzol [3] is typical of wet, cool climates such as the taiga in Russia – while oxisol [4], a thick red soil containing iron compounds, is found in humid, tropical lands with high chemical and biological activity.

BELOW The soil is a complex ecosystem. A cubic metre of fertile soil teems with more than 1,000 million individual forms of life, from microscopic organisms through insects and earthworms to large animals such as burrowing rodents. In the steppes, for example, these include marmots, susliks, hamsters and mole rats. All play an important part in helping to aerate the soil and to accelerate the processes of decay and humus formation.

The role of soil bacteria is perhaps the most crucial: they not only "fix" nitrogen from the air in a form that plants can use, but also promote the essential processes of decay. As they decay, plants provide the fine organic humus litter vital to healthy soil life.

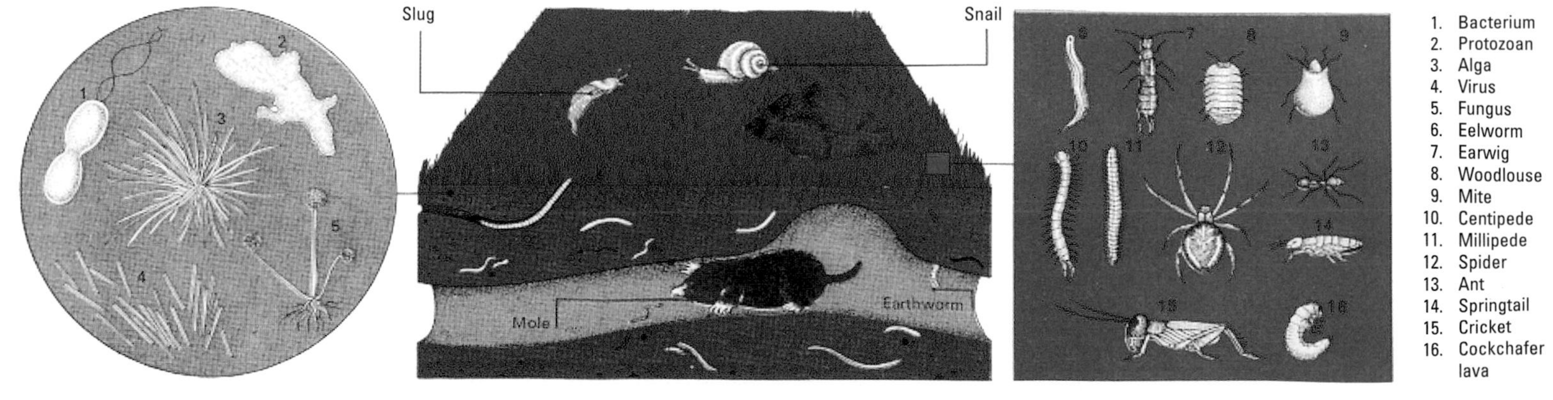

Slug
Snail
Mole
Earthworm
1. Bacterium
2. Protozoan
3. Alga
4. Virus
5. Fungus
6. Eelworm
7. Earwig
8. Woodlouse
9. Mite
10. Centipede
11. Millipede
12. Spider
13. Ant
14. Springtail
15. Cricket
16. Cockchafer lava

The Earth in Figures

PLANET EARTH

Mean distance from the Sun	149,500,000km (92,860,000 miles)
Average speed around the Sun	108,000km/h (66,600mph)
Age	approx. 4,500,000,000 years
Mass	5,975 million million million tonnes
Density	5,515 times that of water
Volume	1,083,207,000,000cu. km (260,000,000,000 cu. miles)
Area	509,450,000sq km (196,672,000sq miles)
Land surface	149,450,000sq km (57,688,000sq mi) – 29.3% of total
Water surface area	360,000,000sq km (138,984,000sq mi) – 70.7% of total
Equatorial circumference	40,075km (24,902 miles)
Polar circumference	40,008km (24,860 miles)
Equatorial diameter	12,756km (7,926 miles)
Polar diameter	12,714km (7,900 miles)

INSIDE THE EARTH

	Density (g/cm)	Temperature		State	Thickness	
Sial	2.8	≮ 500°C	(930°F)	Solid	0-30km	(0-18miles)
Sima	2.9	≮ 650°C	(1,200°F)	Solid	20-80km	(12-50miles)
Upper mantle	4.3	≮ 800°C	(1,480°F)	Molten	*c.* 700km	(435miles)
Lower mantle	5.5	≮ 2,500°C	(4,600°F)	Solid	*c.* 1,700km	(1,050miles)
Outer core	10.0	≮ 3,000°C	(5,400°F)	Molten	*c.* 2,100km	(1,305miles)
Inner core	13.5	≮ 5,000°C	(9,000°F)	Solid	*c.* 1,370km	(850miles)

SELECTED EARTH RECORDS

Greatest tides	Bay of Fundy, Nova Scotia, Canada, 16.3m (53.5ft)
Deepest gorge	Colca River, Peru, 3,205m (10,515ft)
Longest gorge	Grand Canyon, Arizona, USA, 350km (217 miles)
Deepest lake	Lake Baikal, Siberia, Russia, 1,620m (5,315ft)
Highest navigable lake	Lake Titicaca, Peru/Bolivia, 3,812m (12,506ft)
Deepest cave	Réseau Jean Bernard, Haute-Savoie, France, 1,602m (5,256ft)
Longest cave system	Mammoth Cave, Kentucky, USA, 560km (348 miles)
Deepest valley	Kali Gandaki, Nepal, 5,883m (19,300ft)
Longest glacier	Lambert-Fisher Ice Passage, Antarctica, 515km (320 miles)
Deepest depression	Dead Sea, Israel/Jordan, 395m (1,296ft)

The area of the Earth covered by sea is estimated at over 70% of the total. Occupying almost a hemisphere, the Pacific Ocean accounts for nearly half the oceans if adjacent seas are included, and 35.5% of the surface area of the world. The average depth of the hydrosphere is calculated at 3,554m (11,660ft), almost five times the figure for average height of land.

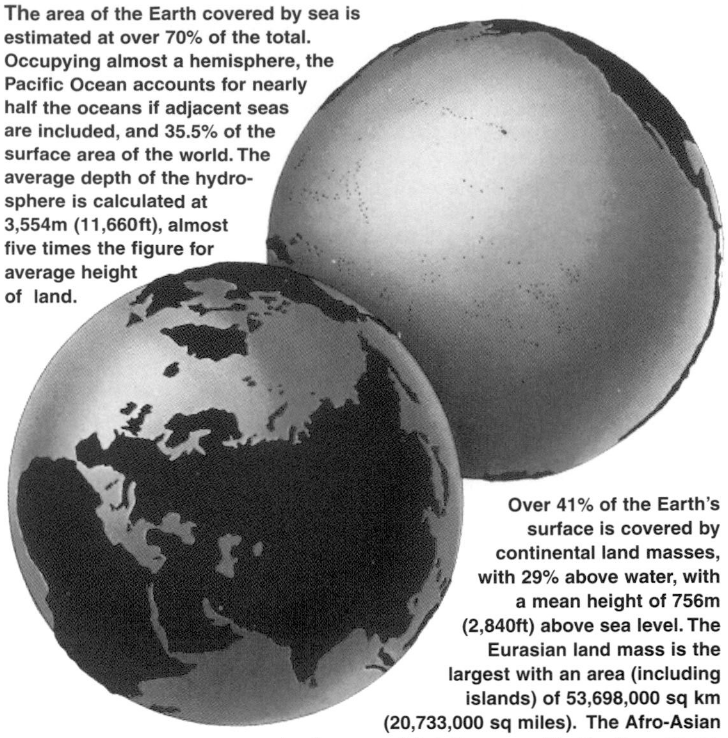

Over 41% of the Earth's surface is covered by continental land masses, with 29% above water, with a mean height of 756m (2,840ft) above sea level. The Eurasian land mass is the largest with an area (including islands) of 53,698,000 sq km (20,733,000 sq miles). The Afro-Asian land mass, artificially severed by the Suez Canal, covers 84,702,000 sq km (32,704,000 sq miles) – or 57.2% of the Earth's land mass.

LARGEST ISLANDS

	sq km	sq miles
Europe		
Great Britain [8]	229,880	88,700
Iceland	103,000	39,800
Ireland	84,400	32,600
Novaya Zemlya (N)	48,200	18,600
Sicily	25,500	9,800
Corsica	8,700	3,400
Asia		
Borneo [3]	744,360	287,400
Sumatra [6]	473,600	182,860
Honshu [7]	230,500	88,980
Celebes	189,000	73,000
Java	126,700	48,900
Luzon	104,700	40,400
Mindanao	95,000	36,700
Hokkaido	78,400	30,300
Sakhalin	76,400	29,500
Sri Lanka	65,600	25,300
Africa		
Madagascar [4]	587,040	226,660
Socotra	3,600	1,400
Réunion	2,500	965
North America		
Greenland [1]*	2,175,600	839,800
Baffin Island [5]	508,000	196,100
Victoria Island [9]	212,200	81,900
Ellesmere Island [10]	212,000	81,800
Cuba	110,860	42,800
Newfoundland	96,000	37,100
Hispaniola	76,200	29,400
Jamaica	11,400	4,400
Puerto Rico	8,900	3,400
South America		
Tierra del Fuego	47,000	18,100
Falkland Island (E)	6,800	2,600
Oceania		
New Guinea [2]	821,030	317,000
New Zealand (S)	150,500	58,100
New Zealand (N)	114,700	44,300
Tasmania	67,800	26,200
Hawaii	10,450	4,000

** Geographers consider Australia to be a continental land mass*

LARGEST INLAND LAKES AND SEAS

	Location	sq km	sq mi
Europe			
Lake Ladoga	Russia	17,700	6,800
Lake Onega	Russia	9,700	3,700
Saimaa system	Finland	8,000	3,100
Vänern	Sweden	6,500	2,100
Asia			
Caspian Sea [1]	W. Central Asia	371,800	143,550
Aral Sea* [6]	Kazakhstan/ Uzbekistan	33,640	13,000
Lake Baikal [9]	Russia	30,500	11,780
Tonlé Sap	Cambodia	20,000	7,700
Lake Balkhash	Kazakhstan	18,500	7,100
Africa			
Lake Victoria [3]	East Africa	68,000	26,000
Lake Tanganyika [7]	Central Africa	33,000	13,000
Lake Malawi [10]	East Africa	29,600	11,430
Lake Chad*	Central Africa	25,000	9,700
Lake Turkana	Ethiopia/Kenya	8,500	3,300
Lake Volta†	Ghana	8,480	3,250
North America			
Lake Superior [2]	Canada/USA	82,350	31,800
Lake Huron [4]	Canada/USA	59,600	23,010
Lake Michigan [5]	USA	58,000	22,400
Great Bear Lake [8]	Canada	31,800	12,280
Great Slave Lake	Canada	28,500	11,000
Lake Erie	Canada/USA	25,700	9,900
Lake Winnipeg	Canada	24,400	9,400
Lake Ontario	Canada/USA	19,500	7,500
Lake Nicaragua	Nicaragua	8,200	3,200
South America			
Lake Titicaca‡	Bolivia/Peru	8,300	3,200
Lake Poopó	Peru	2,800	1,100
Australia			
Lake Eyre§	Australia	8,900	3,400
Lake Torrens§	Australia	5,800	2,200
Lake Gairdner§	Australia	4,800	1,900

** Shrinking in area due to environmental factors; until the 1980s it was the world's 4th largest*
† Artificial lake created by Akosombo Dam (1966)
‡ Lake Maracaibo, in Venezuela, is far larger at 13,260 sq km (5,120 sq miles), but is linked to the Caribbean by a narrow channel and therefore not an "inland" lake
§ Salt lakes that vary in size with rainfall

BEAUFORT WIND SCALE

Named after the 19th-century British naval officer who devised it, the Beaufort Scale assesses wind speed according to its effects. Originally designed in 1806 as an aid for sailors, it has since been adapted for use on land and was internationally recognised in 1874.

Scale	Wind speed km/h	Wind speed mph	Name
0	0-1	0-1	Calm
1	1-5	1-3	Light air
2	6-11	4-7	Light breeze
3	12-19	8-12	Gentle breeze
4	20-28	13-18	Moderate
5	29-38	19-24	Fresh
6	39-49	25-31	Strong
7	50-61	32-38	Near gale
8	62.74	39-46	Gale
9	75-88	47-54	Strong gale
10	89-102	55-63	Storm
11	103-117	64-72	Violent storm
12	118+	73+	Hurricane

WINDCHILL FACTORS

A combination of cold and wind makes the human body feel cooler than the actual air temperature. The charts below give approximate equivalents for combinations of wind speed and temperature. In sub-zero temperatures even moderate winds will significantly reduce effective temperatures: if human skin was exposed to winds of 48km/h (30mph) in a temperature of –34°C (–30°F) it would freeze solid in 30 seconds.

Temp. °C	Wind speed (km/h) 16	32	48	64*	Temp. °F	Wind speed (mph) 10	20	30	40*
15	11	9	8	6	30	16	4	–2	–5
10	6	3	2	–1	20	3	–10	–18	–21
5	1	4	–5	–8	10	–9	–24	–33	–37
0	–8	–14	–17	–19	0	–2	–39	–49	–53
–5	–14	–21	–25	–27	–10	–34	–53	–6	–69
–10	–20	–28	–33	–35	–20	–46	–67	–79	–84
–15	–26	–36	–40	–43	–30	–58	–81	–93	–100
–20	–32	–42	–48	–51	–40	–71	–95	–109	–115

** Wind speeds of more than about 64km/h (40mph) have only a marginal cooling effect*

THE CONTINENTS

Continent	Area			Highest point above sea level			Lowest point below sea level		
	sq km	sq miles	%		metres	feet		metres	feet
Asia	44,500,000	17,179,000	29.8	Mt Everest (China/Nepal)	8,848	29,029	Dead Sea, Israel/Jordan	–396	–1,302
Africa	30,302,000	11,697,000	20.3	Mt Kilimanjaro, Tanzania	5,895	19,340	Lake Assal, Djibouti	–153	–502
North America	24,454,000	9,442,000	16.2	Mt McKinley, Alaska	6,194	20,321	Death Valley, California, USA	–86	–282
South America	17,793,000	6,868,000	11.9	Mt Aconcagua, Argentina	6,960	22,834	Peninsular Valdés, Argentina	–40	–131
Antarctica	14,100,000	5,443,000	9.4	Vinson Massif	4,897	16,066	*		
Europe	9,957,000	3,843.000	6.7	Mt Elbrus, Russia	5,633	18,481	Caspian Sea, W. Central Asia	–28	–92
Oceania	8,945,000	3,454,000	5.7	Puncak Jaya (Ngga Pulu), Indonesia	5,029	16,499	Lake Eyre (N), South Australia	–15	–50

**The Bentley trench (–2,540m/–8,333ft) is englacial and therefore not a surface point*

THE OCEANS

Ocean	Area			Average depth		Greatest known depth		
	sq km	sq miles	%	metres	feet		metres	feet
Pacific	179,679,000	69,356,000	49.9	4,300	14,100	Mariana Trench	11,022	36,161
Atlantic	92,373,000	35,657,000	25.7	3,700	12,100	Puerto Rico Deep*	9,200	30,138
Indian	73,917,000	28,532,000	20.5	3,900	12,800	Java Trench	7,450	24,442
Arctic	14,090,000	5,439,000	3.9	1,330	4,300	Molloy Deep	5,608	18,399

**7th deepest trench in the world; 8 of the deepest 10, including 1-6, are in the Pacific Ocean*

HIGHEST MOUNTAINS

	Location	metres	feet
Europe			
Elbrus*	Russia	5,642	18,510
Mont Blanc† ‡	France/Italy	4,807	15,771
Monte Rosa‡	Italy/Switzerland	4,634	15,203
Also			
Matterhorn (Cervino)‡	Italy/Switzerland	4,478	14,691
Jungfrau	Switzerland	4,158	13,642
Grossglockner	Austria	3,797	12,457
Mulhacen	Spain	3,478	11,411
Etna	Italy (Sicily)	3,340	10,958
Zugspitze	Germany	2,962	9,718
Olympus	Greece	2,917	9,570
Galdhopiggen	Norway	2,468	8,100
Ben Nevis	UK (Scotland)	1,343	4,406
Asia§			
Everest	China/Nepal	8,848	29,029
K2 (Godwin Austen)	China/Kashmir	8,611	28,251
Kanchenjunga‡	India/Nepal	8,598	28,208
Lhotse‡	China/Nepal	8,516	27,939
Makalu‡	China/Nepal	8,481	27,824
Cho Oyu	China/Nepal	8,201	26,906
Dhaulagiri‡	Nepal	8,172	26,811
Manaslu (Kutang)‡	Nepal	8,156	26,758
Nanga Parbat	Kashmir	8,126	26,660
Annapurna‡	Nepal	8,078	26,502
Also			
Pik Kommunizma	Tajikistan	7,495	24,590
Ararat	Turkey	5,165	16,945
Gunong Kinabalu	Malaysia (Borneo)	4.101	13,455
Fuji-san (Fujiyama)	Japan	3,776	12,388
Africa			
Kilimanjaro	Tanzania	5,895	19,340
Mt Kenya	Kenya	5,199	17,057
Ruwenzori	Uganda/Zaire	5,109	16,762
North America			
Mt McKinley (Denali)‡	USA (Alaska)	6,194	20,321
Mt Logan	Canada	5,959	19,551
Citlaltépetl (Orizaba)	Mexico	5,700	18,701
Mt St Elias	USA/Canada	5,489	18,008
Popocatépetl	Mexico	5,452	17,887
Also			
Mt Whitney	USA	4,418	14,495
Tajumulco	Guatemala	4,220	13,845
Chirripo Grande	Costa Rica	3,837	12,589
Pico Duarte	Dominican Rep.	3,175	10,417
South America			
Aconcagua#	Argentina	6,960	22,834
Ojos del Salado	Argentina/Chile	6,863	22,516
Pissis	Argentina	6,779	22,241
Mercedario	Argentina/Chile	6,770	22,211
Huascarán‡	Peru	6,768	22,204
Oceania			
Puncak Jaya	Indonesia (W Irian)	5,029	16,499
Puncak Trikora	Indonesia (W Irian)	4,750	15,584
Puncak Mandala	Indonesia (W Irian)	4,702	15,427
Mt Wilhelm	Papua New Guinea	4,508	14,790
Also			
Mauna Kea	USA (Hawaii)	4 205	13 796
Mauna Loa	USA (Hawaii)	4,170	13,681
Mt Cook (Aorangi)	New Zealand	3,753	12,313
Mt Kosciusko	Australia	2,237	7,339
Antarctica			
Vinson Massif	—	4,897	16,066
Mt Tyree	—	4,965	16,289

** The Caucasus Mountains include 14 other peaks higher than Mont Blanc, the highest point in non-Russian Europe*
† The highest point is in France; the highest point wholly in Italian territory is 4,760m (15,616ft)
‡ Many mountains, especially in Asia, have two or more significant peaks; only the highest ones are listed here
§ The ranges of Central Asia have more than 100 peaks over 7,315m (24,000ft); thus the first 10 listed here constitute the world's 10 highest mountains # Highest mountain outside Asia

HIGHEST WATERFALLS

Name	Total height		Location	River	Highest fall	
	m	ft			m	ft
Angel	979	3,212	Venezuela	Carrao	807	2,648
Tugela	947	3,110	Natal, South Africa	Tugela	410	1,350
Utigård	800	2,625	Nesdale, Norway	Jostedal Glacier	600	1,970
Mongefoseen	774	2,540	Mongebekk, Norway	Monge	—	—
Yosemite	739	2,425	California, USA	Yosemite Creek	739	2,425
Østre Mardøla Foss	656	2,154	Eikisdal, Norway	Mardals	296	974
Tyssestrengane	646	2,120	Hardanger, Norway	Tysso	289	948
Cuquenán	610	2,000	Venezuela	Arabopó	—	—
Sutherland	580	1,904	Otago, New Zealand	Arthur	248	815
Takkakaw	502	1,650	British Columbia, Canada	Daly Glacier	365	1,200
Ribbon	491	1,612	California, USA	Ribbon Fall Stream	491	1,612

The greatest falls by volume are the Boyoma (formerly Stanley) Falls on the Zaïre (formerly Congo), with a mean annual flow of 17,000 cu m/sec (600,000 cu ft/sec). The Niagara Falls come 4th and the Victoria Falls 9th in terms of volume, though both are relatively modest in height.

LONGEST RIVERS

	Outflow	km	miles
Europe			
Volga	Caspian Sea	3,700	2,300
Danube	Black Sea	2,850	1,770
Ural*	Caspian Sea	2,535	1,575
Asia			
Yangtze [3]	Pacific Ocean	6,380	3,960
Yenisey-Angara [5]	Arctic Ocean	5,550	3,445
Hwang Ho [6]	Pacific Ocean	5,464	3,395
Ob-Irtysh [7]	Arctic Ocean	5,410	3,360
Mekong [9]	Pacific Ocean	4,500	2,795
Amur [10]	Pacific Ocean	4,400	2,730
Africa			
Nile [1]	Mediterranean	6,620	4,140
Zaire (Congo) [8]	Atlantic Ocean	4,670	2,900
Niger	Atlantic Ocean	4,180	2,595
Zambezi	Indian Ocean	3,540	2,200
North America			
Mississippi-Missouri[4]	Gulf of Mexico	6,020	3,740
Mackenzie	Arctic Ocean	4,240	2,630
Mississippi	Gulf of Mexico	3,780	2,350
Missouri	Mississippi	3,780	2,350
Yukon	Pacific Ocean	3,185	1,980
Rio Grande	Gulf of Mexico	3,030	1,880
Arkansas	Mississippi	2,840	1,450
Colorado	Pacific Ocean	2,330	1,445
South America			
Amazon [2]	Atlantic Ocean	6,450	4,010
Paraná-Plate	Atlantic Ocean	4,500	2,800
Purus	Amazon	3,350	2,080
Madeira	Amazon	3,200	1,990
Sao Francisco	Atlantic Ocean	2,900	1,800
Australia			
Murray-Darling	Southern Ocean	3,750	2,830
Darling	Murray	3,070	1,905
Murray	Southern Ocean	2,575	1,600
Murrumbidgee	Murray	1,690	1,050

** Flows through Europe and Asia*

NOTABLE EARTHQUAKES*

Year	Location	Magnitude†	Deaths
1906	San Francisco, USA	8.3	503
1908	Messina, Italy	7.5	83,000
1920	Gansu (Kansu), China	8.6	180,000
1923	Yokohama, Japan	8.3	143,000
1927	Nan Xian, China	8.3	200,000
1932	Gansu (Kansu), China	7.6	70,000
1933	Sanriku, Japan	8.9 ‡	2,990
1935	Quetta, India §	7.5	60,000
1939	Chillan, Chile	8.3	28,000
1963	Skopje, Yugoslavia #	6.0	1,000
1964	Anchorage, Alaska	8.4	131
1970	N. Peru	7.7	86,794
1976	Guatemala	7.5	22,778
1976	Tangshan, China	8.2	242,000
1985	Mexico City, Mexico	8.1	4,200
1988	NW. Armenia	6.8	55,000
1990	N. Iran	7.7	36,000
1993	Maharastra, India	6.4	30,000
1995	Kobe, Japan	7.2	5,000
1995	Sakhalin Island, Russia	7.5	2,000
1997	NE Iran	7.1	2,400
1998	Takhar, Afghanistan	6.1	4,200
1999	NW Turkey	8.2	22,000
1999	Taiwan	7.6	4,600

** Since 1900 † On the Richter scale ‡ Highest ever recorded § Now Pakistan # Now Macedonia*

UNDERSTANDING MAPS

Mapmaking

While small areas can be mapped by plane (flat) surveying, larger areas must be done by geodesy, which takes into account the Earth's curvature. A variety of instruments and techniques is used to determine the position, height and extent of features – data essential to the cartographic process. Instruments such as graduated metal rods, chains, tapes and portable radar or radio transmitters are used for measuring distances, and the theodolite is used for angles. With measured distances and angles, further distances and angles as well as heights are calculated by triangulation.

Latitude and longitude

Accurate positioning of points on the Earth's surface is made possible by reference to latitude and longitude. Parallels of latitude are drawn west-east around the globe and numbered by degrees north and south of the Equator (0° of latitude). Meridians of longitude are drawn north-south and numbered by degrees east and west and the prime meridian (0° of longitude) which passes through the Royal Observatory at Greenwich in southeast London. Latitude and longitude are indicated by blue lines on the maps, and are straight or slightly curved according to the projection used.

Representing relief

Height and gradient can be represented on a map in many ways. Hachuring, in which fine lines follow the direction of the greatest slope, can give an excellent impression of the landscape but the lines may obscure other information. Hill shading, the representation of a landscape illuminated from one direction, is used alone or with colours. Contours can also be separated by colour and intermediate heights given as spot heights. These techniques are now often used in conjunction with sophisticated computerized technology, including digitalization.

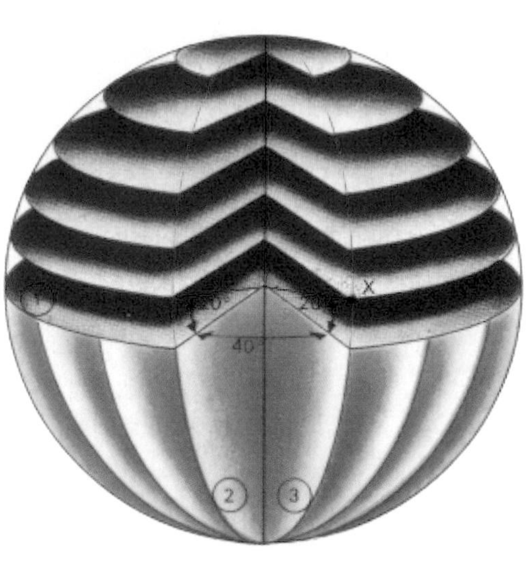

ABOVE Any point on the Earth's surface can be located in terms of longitude and latitude – in degrees, minutes and seconds east or west of the prime meridian for longitude, and north or south of the Equator for latitude. The latitude of X (the angle between X, the centre of the Earth and the plane of the Equator [1]) equals 20°, while its longitude (the angle between between the plane of the prime meridian [2] and that passing through X and the North and South Poles [3]) equals 40°.

RIGHT Reference to lines of longitude and latitude is the easiest and most common way of determining the relative positions of places on different maps, and for plotting compass directions.

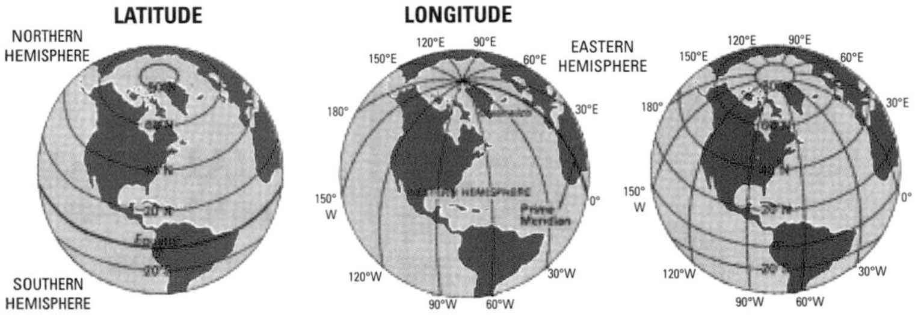

Projections

A map projection is the systematic depiction on a plane surface of the imaginary lines of latitude or longitude from a globe of the Earth. This network of lines is called the graticule and forms the framework on which an accurate depiction of the world is made. The basis of any map, the graticule, is constructed sometimes by graphical means but often by using mathematical formulas to give the intersections plotted as x and y co-ordinates.

The choice of projection is governed by the properties the cartographer wishes the map to possess, the map scale and also the extent of the area to be mapped. Since the globe is three-dimensional, it is not possible to depict its surface on a two-dimensional plane without distortion. Preservation of one of the basic properties involved – area, distance or shape – can only be secured at the expense of the others, and the choice of projection is often a compromise solution.

Map projections are constructions designed to maintain certain selected relationships of the Earth's surface. Most of the projections used for large-scale atlases, selected primarily to minimize distortion of size and distance, fall into one of three categories – conic [A], cylindrical [B] or azimuthal [C]. Each involves plotting the forms of the Earth's surface on a grid of lines of latitude and longitude, which may be shown as parallels, curved lines or radiating spokes *(see below)*.

Conical projections use the projection of the graticule from the globe onto a cone which is tangential to a line of latitude (termed the standard parallel). This line is always an arc and scale is always true along it. Because of its method of construction it is used mainly for maps depicting the temperate latitudes around the standard parallel – that is, where there is least distortion.

Cylindrical projections are constructed by the projection of the graticule from the globe onto a cylinder tangential to the globe, and permit the whole of the Earth's surface to be depicted on one map. Though they can depict all the land masses, there is colossal exaggeration of area and shape towards the poles at the expense of equatorial regions: Greenland, for example, grows to almost the size of Africa. However, the best known example, named after the pioneering 16th-century cartographer Gerardus Mercator, has been invaluable to navigators because any straight line drawn on it is a line of constant bearing.

Azimuthal projections, sometimes called zenithal, are constructed by the projection of part of the graticule from the globe onto a plane tangential to any single point on it. This plane may be tangential to the equator (equatorial case), the poles (polar case) or any other point (oblique case). Any straight line drawn from the point where the plane touches the globe is the shortest distance from that point and is known as a great circle.

ABOVE Recording a three-dimensional shape on a flat surface can be achieved by contour scaling. Here the cross-sections of a hill at heights of 50, 100, and 150 metres (or feet) are projected onto a map of the hill. The topography of the hill can be visualized fairly well from such a map when graduated colour is employed – the closer the gradations the steeper the slope – though the crudeness of the contour intervals loses some finer detail.

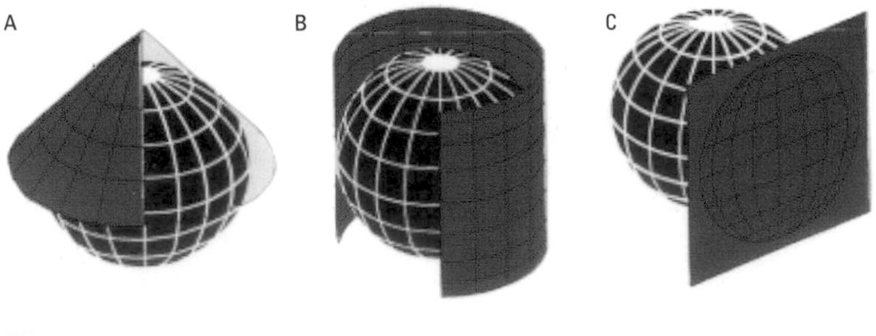

LEFT Most of the projections used for large-scale atlases, selected primarily to minimize distortion of size and distance, fall into one of three principal categories – conic [A], cylindrical [B] or azimuthal [C].

WORLD MAPS

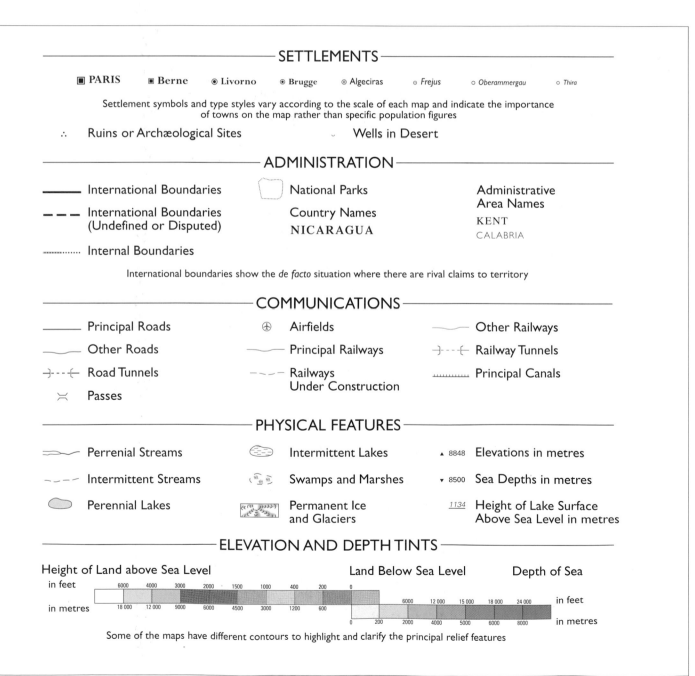

SETTLEMENTS

▣ PARIS ▪ Berne ⦿ Livorno ⦿ Brugge ◎ Algeciras ○ *Frejus* ○ *Oberammergau* ○ *Thira*

Settlement symbols and type styles vary according to the scale of each map and indicate the importance of towns on the map rather than specific population figures

∴ Ruins or Archæological Sites

Wells in Desert

ADMINISTRATION

International Boundaries

International Boundaries (Undefined or Disputed)

Internal Boundaries

National Parks

Country Names

NICARAGUA

Administrative Area Names

KENT

CALABRIA

International boundaries show the *de facto* situation where there are rival claims to territory

COMMUNICATIONS

Principal Roads

Other Roads

Road Tunnels

Passes

Airfields

Principal Railways

Railways Under Construction

Other Railways

Railway Tunnels

Principal Canals

PHYSICAL FEATURES

Perrenial Streams

Intermittent Streams

Perennial Lakes

Intermittent Lakes

Swamps and Marshes

Permanent Ice and Glaciers

▲ 8848 Elevations in metres

▼ 8500 Sea Depths in metres

1134 Height of Lake Surface Above Sea Level in metres

ELEVATION AND DEPTH TINTS

Height of Land above Sea Level

in feet	6000	4000	3000	2000	1500	1000	400	200	0
in metres	18 000	12 000	9000	6000	4500	3000	1200	600	

Land Below Sea Level

Depth of Sea

in feet	0	200	6000	12 000	15 000	18 000	24 000
in metres	0	200	2000	4000	5000	6000	8000

Some of the maps have different contours to highlight and clarify the principal relief features

THE WORLD : Political

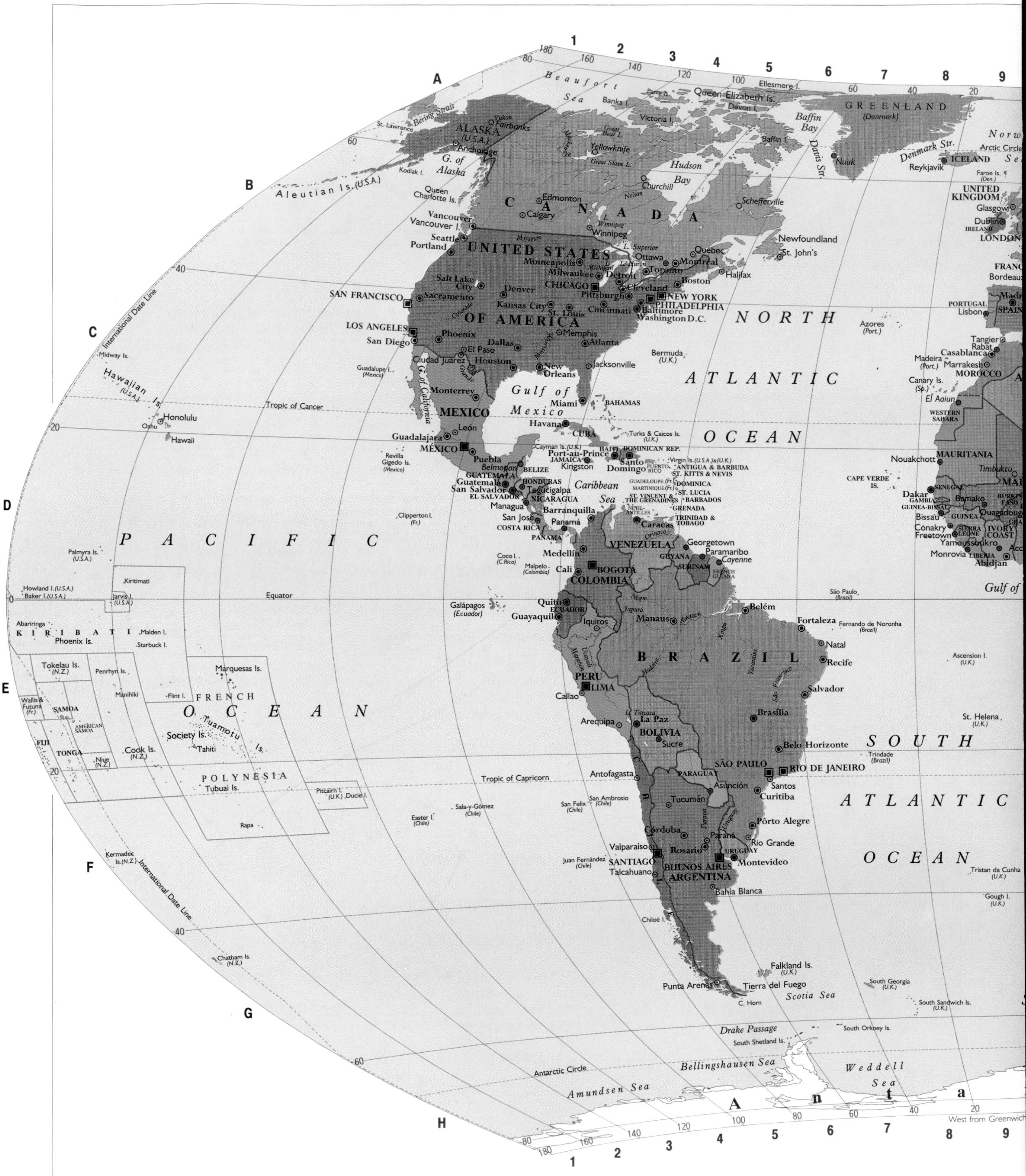

Projection: *Hammer Equal Area*

ARCTIC OCEAN
Svalbard (Norw.)
Barents Sea
Novaya Zemlya
Kara Sea
Severnaya Zemlya
Laptev Sea
New Siberian Is.
East Siberian Sea
Wrangel I.
Arctic Circle
Murmansk
Arkhangelsk
Norilsk
Salekhard
Verkhoyansk
Yakutsk
Magadan
Okhotsk
Sea of Okhotsk
Bering Sea
Petropavlovsk-Kamchatskiy
International Date Line
Sakhalin
Komsomolsk
Khabarovsk
Kuril Is.
RUSSIA
NORWAY
SWEDEN
FINLAND
Oslo
Helsinki
Stockholm
EST.
LATVIA
LITH.
ST. PETERSBURG
MOSCOW
Copenhagen
Minsk
BELARUS
POLAND
Berlin
Prague
Warsaw
Kiev
Brussels
GERMANY
CZECH
Vienna
AUSTRIA
PARIS
UKRAINE
Odessa
Budapest
ROMANIA
Bucharest
Belgrade
BULGARIA
Sofia
Milan
ITALY
Rome
Naples
Sardinia
Sicily
MALTA
Tunis
TUNISIA
Algiers
Mediterranean Sea
GREECE
Athens
Crete
CYPRUS
ISTANBUL
Ankara
TURKEY
Izmir
Black Sea
GEORGIA
Tbilisi
Yerevan
ARM.
AZER.
Baku
Caspian Sea
Astrakhan
Volgograd
Saratov
Samara
Kazan
Perm
Yekaterinburg
Chelyabinsk
Omsk
Novosibirsk
Tomsk
Krasnoyarsk
Barnaul
Irkutsk
L. Baikal
Ulan Ude
Astana
Qaraghandy
KAZAKSTAN
Aral Sea
L. Balkhash
UZBEKISTAN
TURKMENISTAN
Ashkhabad
Tashkent
Samarkand
Dushanbe
TAJIKISTAN
Bishkek
KYRGYZSTAN
Almaty
Ürümqi
Ulan Bator
MONGOLIA
Harbin
Changchun
Vladivostok
Sapporo
SHENYANG
BEIJING
TIANJIN
Dalian
NORTH KOREA
P'yŏngyang
SEOUL
SOUTH KOREA
JAPAN
TŌKYŌ
Ōsaka
Kitakyushu
CHINA
Lanzhou
Taiyuan
Xi'an
Nanjing
SHANGHAI
Wuhan
Chengdu
CHONGQING
Lhasa
TIBET
Kunming
GUANGZHOU
Fuzhou
Taipei
TAIWAN
HONG KONG
East China Sea
Ryukyu Is.
PACIFIC OCEAN
Bonin Is. (Japan)
Volcano Is. (Japan)
Marcus I. (Japan)
Tropic of Cancer
Wake I. (U.S.A.)
NORTHERN MARIANAS (U.S.A.)
GUAM (U.S.A.)
MARSHALL IS.
FEDERATED STATES OF MICRONESIA
Caroline Is.
Truk
Pohnpei
Yap
PALAU
Gilbert Is.
NAURU
KIRIBATI
TUVALU
SOLOMON IS.
Santa Cruz I.
VANUATU
FIJI
Suva
NEW CALEDONIA (Fr.)
Tabriz
TEHRAN
Mashhad
Esfahān
Shīrāz
IRAN
IRAQ
Baghdād
SYRIA
Damascus
Beirut
LEB.
ISR.
Jerusalem
JORDAN
Ammān
Alexandria
CAIRO
EGYPT
Aswân
KUWAIT
BAHRAIN
QATAR
The Gulf
Riyadh
SAUDI ARABIA
Mecca
U.A.E.
Abu Dhabi
Muscat
OMAN
Red Sea
YEMEN
Sana
Aden
G. of Aden
Socotra (Yemen)
AFGHANISTAN
Kābul
Islamabad
Lahore
PAKISTAN
KARACHI
DELHI
New Delhi
NEPAL
Katmandu
BHU.
Kanpur
INDIA
Ahmadabad
KOLKATA (Calcutta)
BANGLADESH
DACCA
Nagpur
MUMBAI (Bombay)
Arabian Sea
Bay of Bengal
Hyderabad
CHENNAI (Madras)
Bangalore
Lakshadweep Is. (India)
SRI LANKA
Colombo
MALDIVES
Andaman Is. (India)
Nicobar Is. (India)
BURMA MYANMAR
Rangoon
Hanoi
Hainan
LAOS
Vientiane
THAILAND
BANGKOK
CAMBODIA
Phnom Penh
VIETNAM
Ho Chi Minh City
South China Sea
MANILA
PHILIPPINES
MALAYSIA
Kuala Lumpur
PEN. MALAYSIA
SINGAPORE
SABAH
BRUNEI
SARAWAK
Borneo
Medan
Sumatra
Palembang
Banjarmasin
INDONESIA
Ujung Pandang
JAKARTA
Bandung
Java
Surabaya
EAST TIMOR
Timor
IRIAN JAYA
PAPUA NEW GUINEA
Port Moresby
New Ireland
New Britain
Arafura Sea
C. York
Darwin
Cairns
Townsville
Port Hedland
Alice Springs
AUSTRALIA
Rockhampton
Brisbane
Geraldton
Perth
Fremantle
Kalgoorlie-Boulder
Darling
Great Australian Bight
Adelaide
Newcastle
Sydney
Canberra
Melbourne
Tasmania
Hobart
Tasman Sea
Lord Howe I. (Austral.)
Norfolk I. (Austral.)
Auckland
North I.
NEW ZEALAND
Wellington
Christchurch
South I.
Stewart I.
Dunedin
Bounty Is. (N.Z.)
Antipodes Is.
Auckland Is. (N.Z.)
Campbell I. (N.Z.)
Macquarie Is. (Austral.)
LIBYA
Tripoli
Benghazi
NIGER
Niamey
CHAD
L. Chad
Ndjamena
Kano
NIGERIA
Abuja
Ibadan
Lagos
SUDAN
Omdurmân
Khartoum
White Nile
Blue Nile
Asmara
ERITREA
DJIBOUTI
Addis Ababa
ETHIOPIA
SOMALI REP.
Mogadishu
CAMEROON
Douala
Yaoundé
CENTRAL AFRICAN REP.
Bangui
EQUATORIAL GUINEA
SÃO TOMÉ & PRINCIPE
Libreville
GABON
CONGO
Brazzaville
Kinshasa
DEM. REP. OF THE CONGO
(Zaïre)
Kisangani
UGANDA
Kampala
L. Victoria
L. Turkana
KENYA
Nairobi
Kigali
RWANDA
BURUNDI
Bujumbura
Dodoma
Mombasa
Zanzibar
Dar es Salaam
TANZANIA
Tanganyika
Kananga
CABINDA (Angola)
Luanda
ANGOLA
Benguela
Lubumbashi
ZAMBIA
Lusaka
L. Malawi
Lilongwe
MALAWI
Harare
ZIMBABWE
MOZAMBIQUE
Mozambique Channel
Bulawayo
NAMIBIA
Windhoek
BOTSWANA
Gaborone
Pretoria
Johannesburg
Maputo
SWAZILAND
SOUTH AFRICA
LESOTHO
Durban
Cape Town
C. of Good Hope
Port Elizabeth
SEYCHELLES
Amirante Is.
Aldabra Is.
COMOROS
Mayotte (Fr.)
Agalega Is.
MADAGASCAR
Antananarivo
Cargados Carajos
Rodriguez
MAURITIUS
RÉUNION (Fr.)
Chagos Arch. (U.K.)
Diego Garcia
INDIAN OCEAN
Equator
Cocos Is. (Austral.)
Christmas I. (Austral.)
Tropic of Capricorn
Amsterdam I. (Fr.)
St. Paul (Fr.)
Prince Edward Is. (S.Africa)
Crozet Is. (Fr.)
Kerguelen (Fr.)
McDonald Is. (Austral.)
Heard I. (Austral.)
Bouvet I. (Norw.)
SOUTHERN OCEAN
Antarctic Circle
Antarctica
Ross Sea
East from Greenwich
10
11
12
13
14
15
16
17
18
A
B
C
D
E
F
G
H

Hanoi ● Capital Cities

COPYRIGHT GEORGE PHILIP LTD.

ARCTIC OCEAN 1:35 000 000

COPYRIGHT GEORGE PHILIP LTD

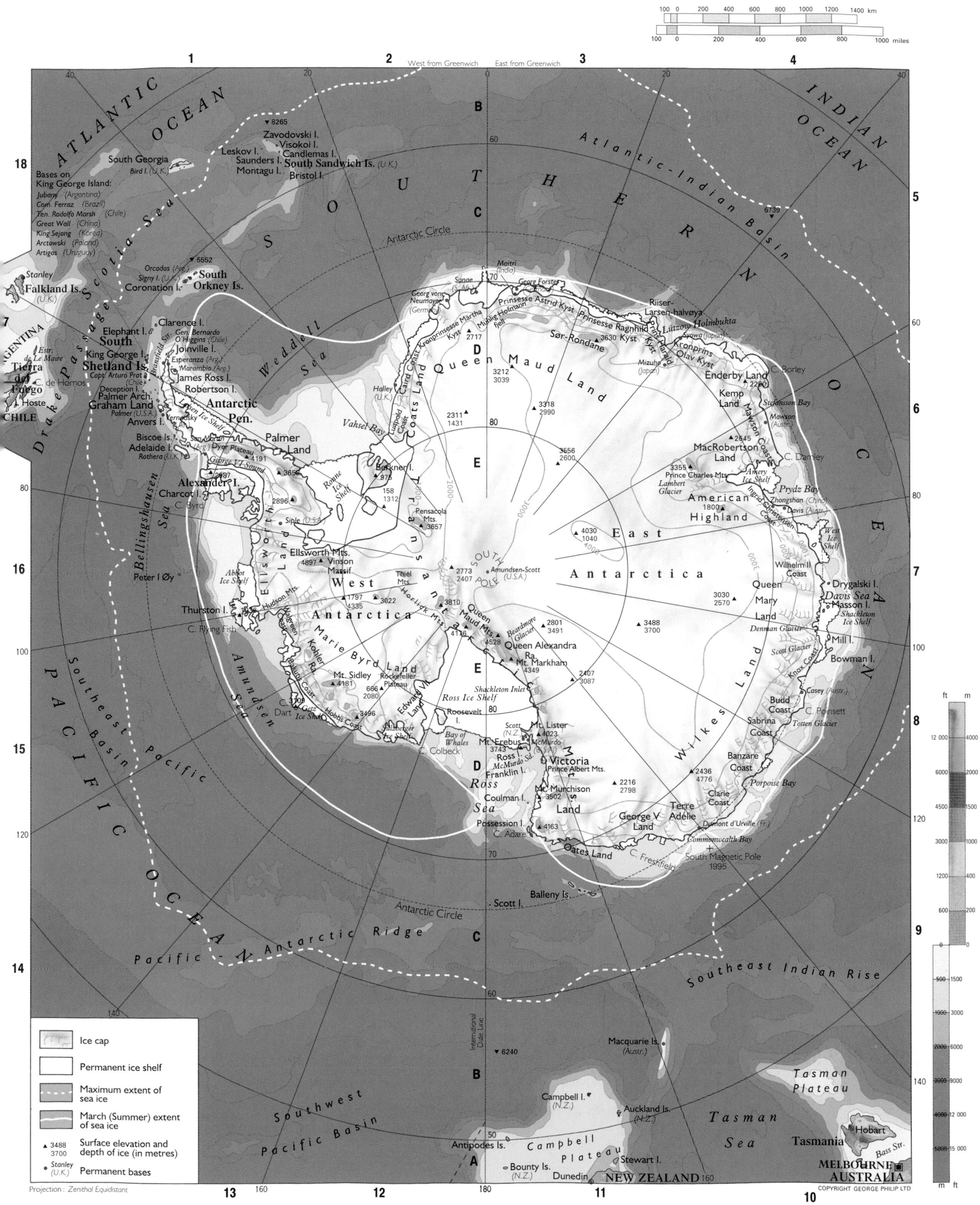

The Antarctic Treaty was signed in Washington in 1959 so that scientific and technical research could continue unhampered by international politics.

All territorial claims covering land areas south of latitude 60°S have been suspended. Those claims were:

Norwegian claim	45°E - 20°W
Australian claims	45°E - 136°E
	142°E - 160°E
French claim	136°E - 142°E
New Zealand claim	160°E - 150°W
Chilean claim	90°W - 53°W
British claim	80°W - 20°W
Argentine claim	74°W - 53°W

6 EUROPE : Physical 1:20 000 000

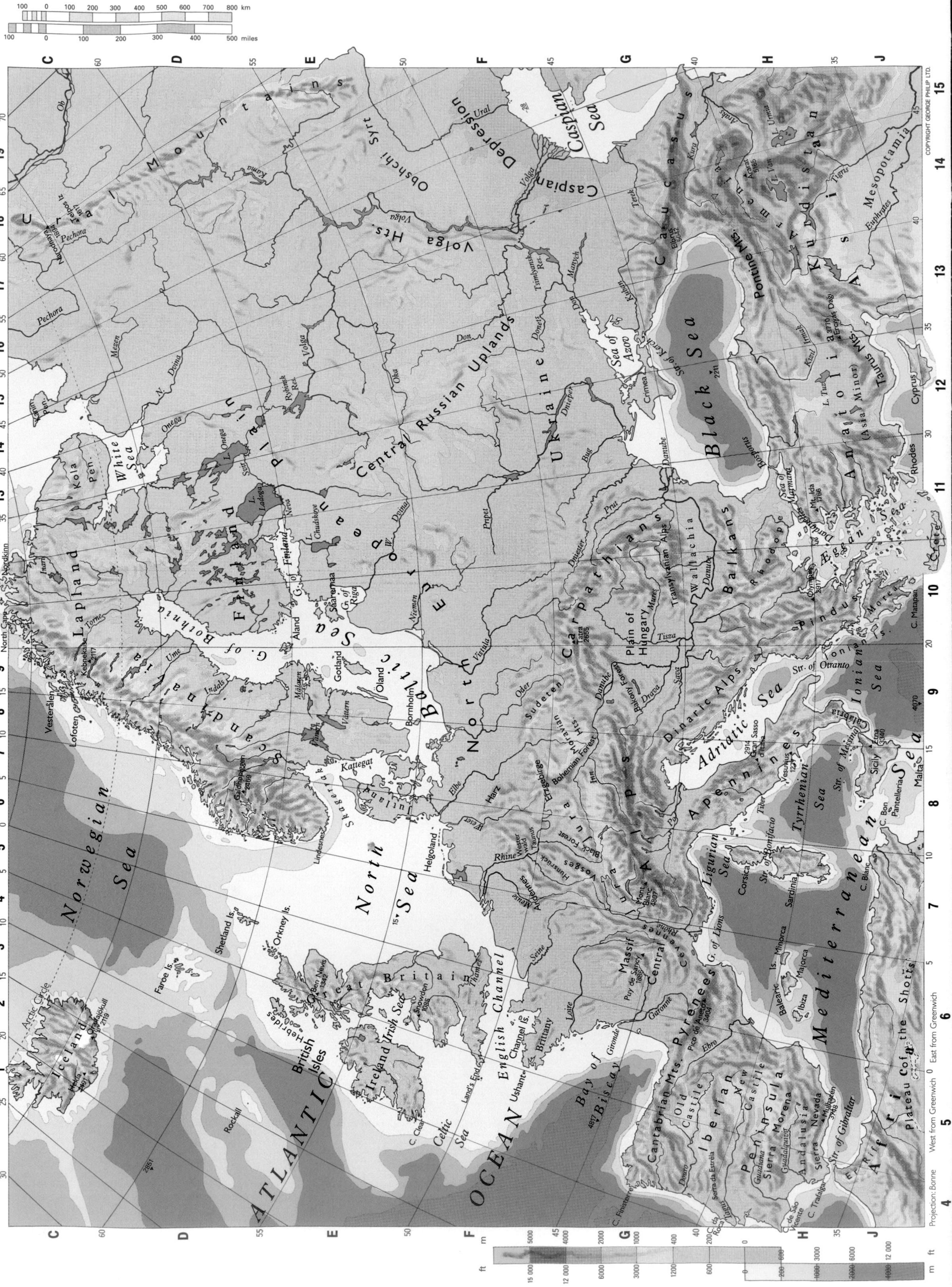
100 0 100 200 300 400 500 600 700 800 km
100 0 100 200 300 400 500 miles
Norwegian Sea
North Sea
Baltic Sea
Black Sea
Caspian Sea
Adriatic Sea
Tyrrhenian Sea
Ionian Sea
Mediterranean Sea
Ligurian Sea
Irish Sea
Celtic Sea
White Sea
Sea of Azov
Bay of Biscay
ATLANTIC OCEAN
English Channel
G. of Bothnia
G. of Finland
G. of Riga
Kattegat
Skagerrak
Alps
Pyrenees
Carpathians
Balkans
Apennines
Dinaric Alps
Transylvanian Alps
Ural Mountains
Caucasus
Pontine Mts.
Taurus Mts.
Central Russian Uplands
Volga Hts.
Obshchi Syrt
Caspian Depression
North European Plain
Plain of Hungary
Massif Central
Cevennes
Sierra Morena
Sierra Nevada
Cantabrian Mts.
Iberian Peninsula
Old Castile
New Castile
Andalusia
Scandinavia
Lapland
Finland
Ukraine
Kola Pen.
Jutland
Great Britain
British Isles
Ireland
Iceland
Faroe Is.
Shetland Is.
Orkney Is.
Hebrides
Channel Is.
Brittany
Corsica
Sardinia
Sicily
Malta
Crete
Cyprus
Rhodes
Majorca
Minorca
Ibiza
Balearic Is.
Crimea
Anatolia (Asia Minor)
Armenia
Kurdistan
Mesopotamia
Africa
Plateau of the Shotts
Wallachia
Rhodope
Pindus
Morea
Str. of Gibraltar
Str. of Otranto
Str. of Messina
Str. of Bonifacio
Str. of Kerch
Bosporus
Dardanelles
Sea of Marmara
Danube
Rhine
Volga
Don
Dnieper
Dniester
Elbe
Oder
Vistula
Loire
Seine
Garonne
Rhône
Po
Tiber
Ebro
Tagus
Douro
Guadalquivir
Euphrates
Tigris
Arctic Circle
COPYRIGHT GEORGE PHILIP LTD.
Projection: Bonne
West from Greenwich 0 East from Greenwich

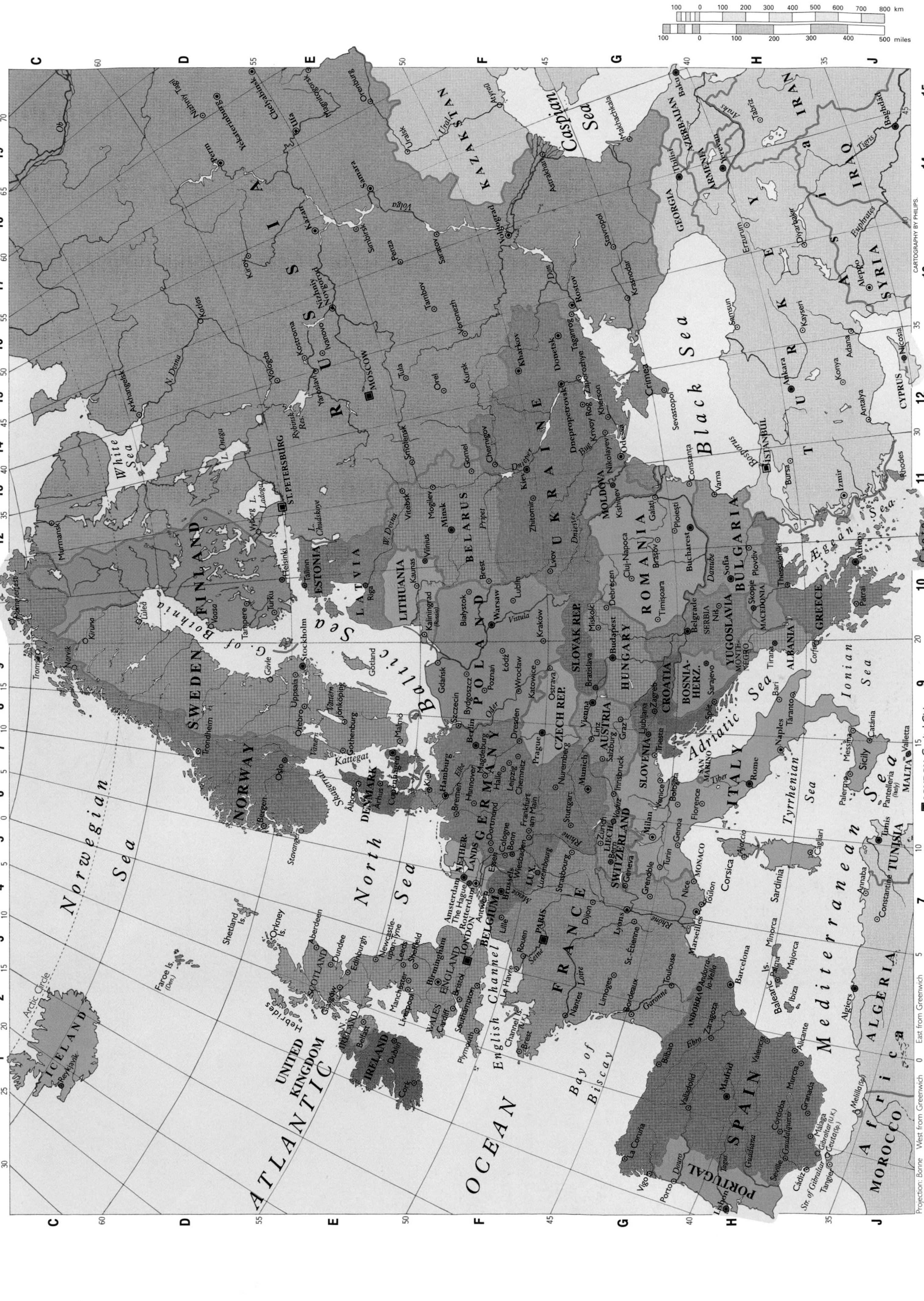
100 0 100 200 300 400 500 600 700 800 km
100 0 100 200 300 400 500 miles
RUSSIA
KAZAKSTAN
Caspian Sea
GEORGIA
ARMENIA
AZERBAIJAN
IRAN
IRAQ
SYRIA
TURKEY
CYPRUS
Black Sea
UKRAINE
MOLDOVA
BELARUS
LITHUANIA
LATVIA
ESTONIA
FINLAND
SWEDEN
NORWAY
DENMARK
POLAND
GERMANY
CZECH REP.
SLOVAK REP.
HUNGARY
ROMANIA
BULGARIA
YUGOSLAVIA
BOSNIA-HERZ.
CROATIA
SLOVENIA
AUSTRIA
SWITZERLAND
ALBANIA
MACEDONIA
GREECE
ITALY
FRANCE
BELGIUM
NETHER-LANDS
LUX.
UNITED KINGDOM
IRELAND
ICELAND
SPAIN
PORTUGAL
ANDORRA
MONACO
MALTA
ALGERIA
TUNISIA
MOROCCO
Africa
White Sea
Baltic Sea
G. of Bothnia
North Sea
Norwegian Sea
ATLANTIC OCEAN
Bay of Biscay
English Channel
Mediterranean Sea
Tyrrhenian Sea
Adriatic Sea
Ionian Sea
Ægean Sea
MOSCOW
ST. PETERSBURG
LONDON
PARIS
LONDON Capital Cities
Projection: Bonne
West from Greenwich
East from Greenwich
CARTOGRAPHY BY PHILIPS.

SCANDINAVIA 1:5 000 000

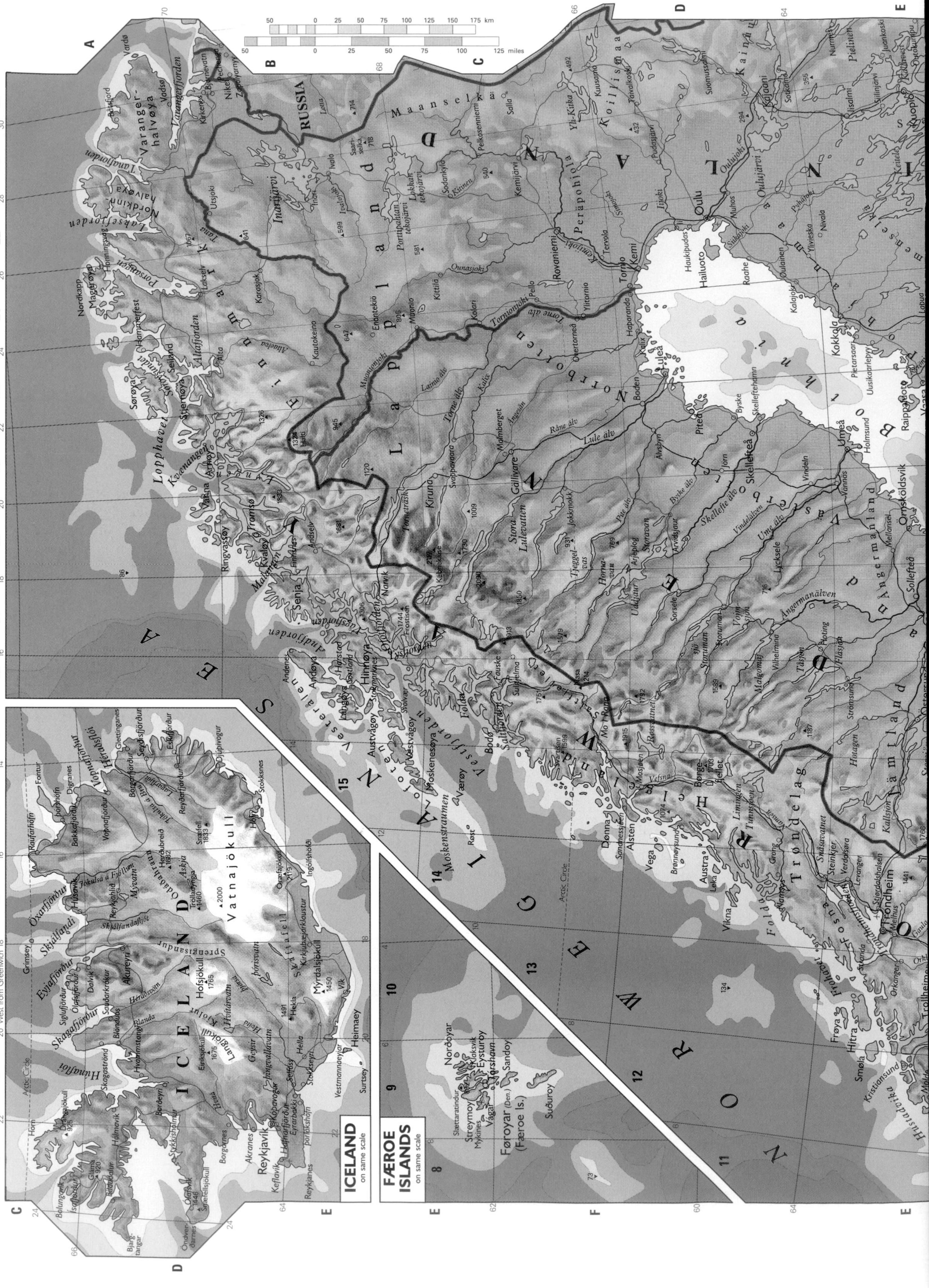

50 0 25 50 75 100 125 150 175 km
50 0 25 50 75 100 125 miles
RUSSIA
Varanger-halvøya
Vardø
Vadsø
Kirkenes
Nordkapp
Hammerfest
Alta
Karasjok
Kautokeino
Loppahavet
Tromsø
Narvik
Kiruna
Gällivare
Lappland
Norrbotten
Rovaniemi
Kemi
Tornio
Oulu
Luleå
Piteå
Skellefteå
Umeå
Kokkola
Raahe
Kajaani
Bodø
Trondheim
Trøndelag
Lofoten
Vesterålen
Arctic Circle
NORWEGIAN SEA
ICELAND
Vatnajökull
Hofsjökull
Langjökull
Akureyri
Reykjavík
Heimaey
ICELAND on same scale
FÆROE ISLANDS on same scale
Føroyar (Færoe Is.)
Streymoy
Sandoy
Suðuroy

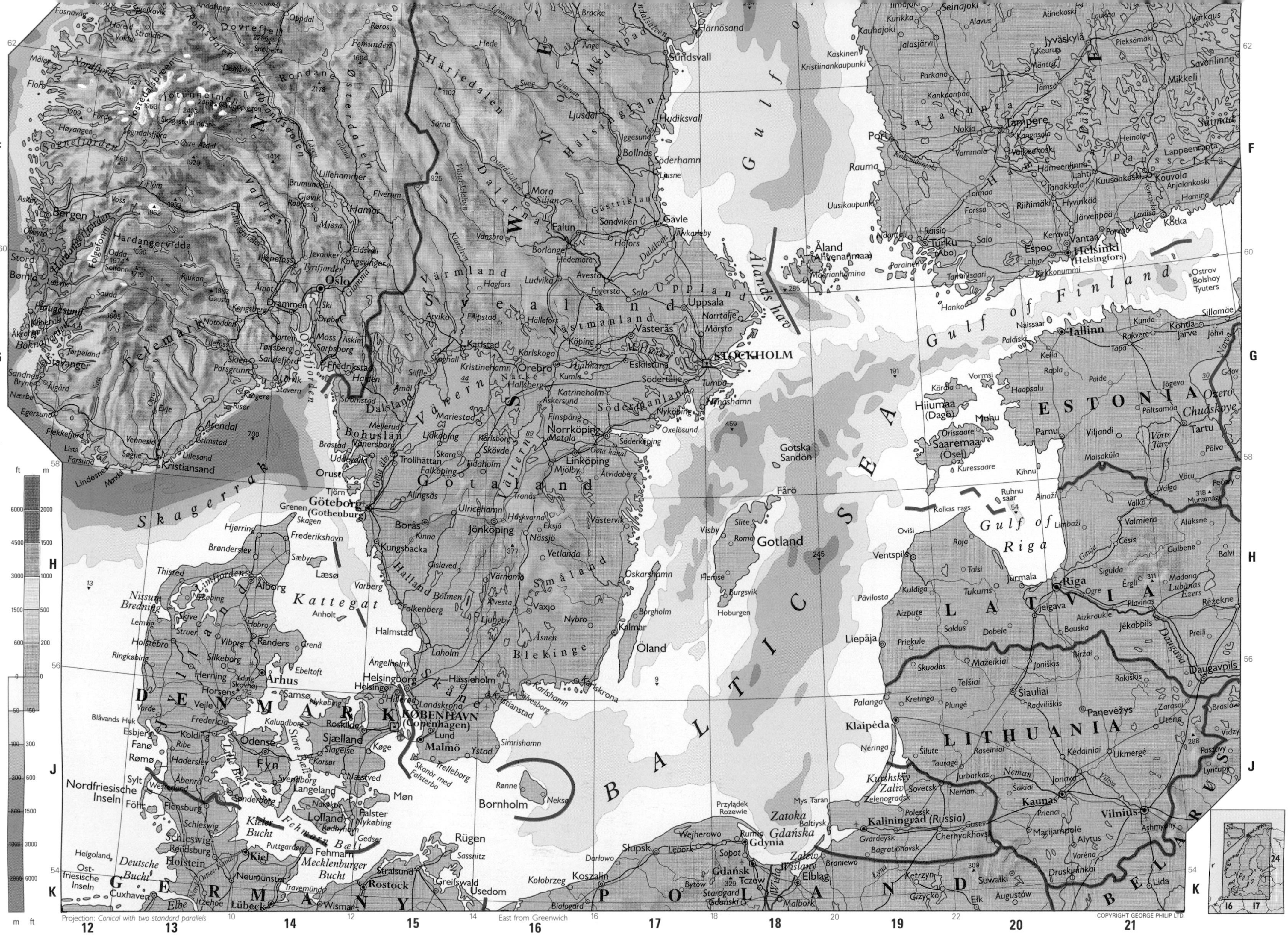

STOCKHOLM
KØBENHAVN (Copenhagen)
Oslo
Helsinki (Helsingfors)
Tallinn
Riga
Vilnius
ESTONIA
LATVIA
LITHUANIA
DENMARK
GERMANY
POLAND
BELARUS
NORWAY
SWEDEN
FINLAND
BALTIC SEA
Gulf of Bothnia
Gulf of Finland
Gulf of Riga
Ålands hav
Skagerrak
Kattegat
Bornholm
Gotland
Öland
Saaremaa (Ösel)
Hiiumaa (Dagö)
Åland (Ahvenanmaa)
Göteborg (Gothenburg)
Bergen
Stavanger
Kristiansand
Turku (Åbo)
Tampere
Uppsala
Västerås
Örebro
Norrköping
Linköping
Jönköping
Malmö
Helsingborg
Århus
Odense
Aalborg
Kaliningrad (Russia)
Gdańsk
Gdynia
Klaipėda
Kaunas
Šiauliai
Daugavpils
Liepāja
Ventspils
Tartu
Pärnu
Kiel
Lübeck
Rostock
Flensburg
Rügen
Sjælland
Fyn
Lolland
Falster
Jylland
Götaland
Svealand
Norrland
Dalarna
Värmland
Småland
Skåne
Telemark
Jotunheimen
Hardangervidda
Vänern
Vättern
Zatoka Gdańska
Kurshskiy Zaliv
Deutsche Bucht
Nordfriesische Inseln
Ostfriesische Inseln
Kieler Bucht
Mecklenburger Bucht
Fehmarn Bælt
Store Bælt
Lille Bælt
Oslofjorden
Projection: Conical with two standard parallels
East from Greenwich
COPYRIGHT GEORGE PHILIP LTD.

ENGLAND AND WALES 1:2 000 000

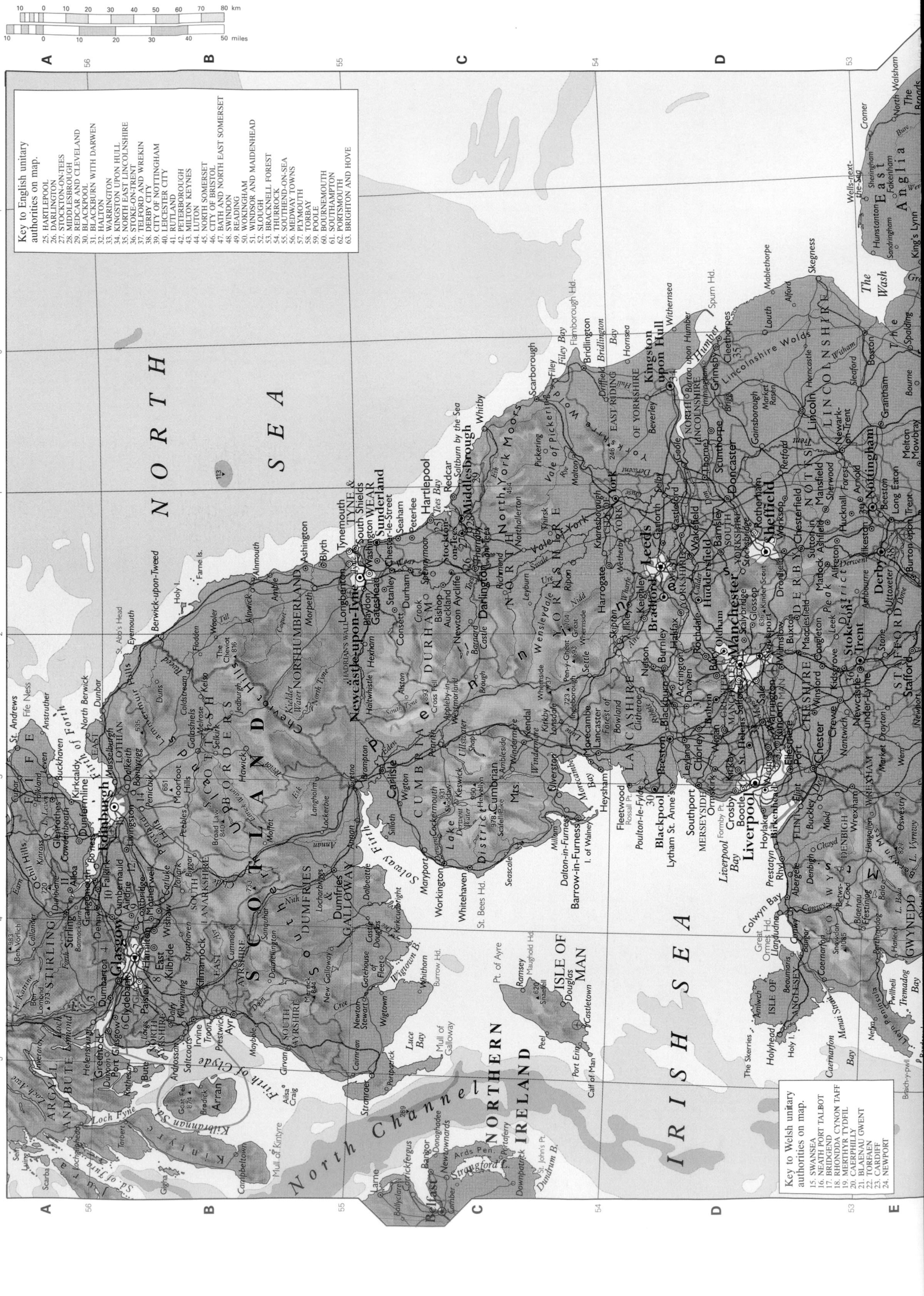
10 0 10 20 30 40 50 60 70 80 km
10 0 10 20 30 40 50 miles
Key to English unitary authorities on map.
25. HARTLEPOOL
26. DARLINGTON
27. STOCKTON-ON-TEES
28. MIDDLESBROUGH
29. REDCAR AND CLEVELAND
30. BLACKPOOL
31. BLACKBURN WITH DARWEN
32. HALTON
33. WARRINGTON
34. KINGSTON UPON HULL
35. NORTH EAST LINCOLNSHIRE
36. STOKE-ON-TRENT
37. TELFORD AND WREKIN
38. DERBY CITY
39. CITY OF NOTTINGHAM
40. LEICESTER CITY
41. RUTLAND
42. PETERBOROUGH
43. MILTON KEYNES
44. LUTON
45. NORTH SOMERSET
46. CITY OF BRISTOL
47. BATH AND NORTH EAST SOMERSET
48. SWINDON
49. READING
50. WOKINGHAM
51. WINDSOR AND MAIDENHEAD
52. SLOUGH
53. BRACKNELL FOREST
54. THURROCK
55. SOUTHEND-ON-SEA
56. MEDWAY TOWNS
57. PLYMOUTH
58. TORBAY
59. POOLE
60. BOURNEMOUTH
61. SOUTHAMPTON
62. PORTSMOUTH
63. BRIGHTON AND HOVE
Key to Welsh unitary authorities on map.
15. SWANSEA
16. NEATH PORT TALBOT
17. BRIDGEND
18. RHONDDA CYNON TAFF
19. MERTHYR TYDFIL
20. CAERPHILLY
21. BLAENAU GWENT
22. TORFAEN
23. CARDIFF
24. NEWPORT
NORTH SEA
IRISH SEA
North Channel
SCOTLAND
NORTHERN IRELAND
ISLE OF MAN
Edinburgh
Glasgow
Newcastle-upon-Tyne
Sunderland
Middlesbrough
Leeds
Bradford
Manchester
Liverpool
Sheffield
Kingston upon Hull
Nottingham
Stoke-on-Trent
Derby
Belfast

WALES
ENGLAND
FRANCE
ENGLISH CHANNEL
Bristol Channel
Cardigan Bay
Strait of Dover
Thames Estuary
Lyme Bay
Baie de la Seine
Baie de la Somme
CHANNEL ISLANDS (U.K.)
Alderney
Guernsey
Jersey
Sark
Herm
St. Peter Port
St. Helier
LONDON
BIRMINGHAM
Bristol
Cardiff
Southampton
Portsmouth
Plymouth
Brighton
Bournemouth
Le Havre
Rouen
Caen
Cherbourg
Calais
Dieppe
ISLE OF WIGHT
HAUTE-NORMANDIE
SEINE-MARITIME
CALVADOS
MANCHE
Isles of Scilly
On same scale
Projection : Lambert's Conformal Conic
West from Greenwich
East from Greenwich
COPYRIGHT GEORGE PHILIP LTD.

10 0 10 20 30 40 50 60 70 80 km
10 0 10 20 30 40 50 miles
Key to Scottish unitary authorities on map
1. CITY OF ABERDEEN
2. DUNDEE CITY
3. WEST DUNBARTONSHIRE
4. EAST DUNBARTONSHIRE
5. CITY OF GLASGOW
6. INVERCLYDE
7. RENFREWSHIRE
8. EAST RENFREWSHIRE
9. NORTH LANARKSHIRE
10. FALKIRK
11. CLACKMANNANSHIRE
12. WEST LOTHIAN
13. CITY OF EDINBURGH
14. MIDLOTHIAN
ORKNEY IS.
On same scale
SHETLAND IS.
On same scale
SCOTLAND
NORTH SEA
ATLANTIC OCEAN
ENGLAND
NORTHERN IRELAND
WESTERN ISLES
HIGHLAND
MORAY
ABERDEENSHIRE
ANGUS
PERTH AND KINROSS
FIFE
STIRLING
ARGYLL AND BUTE
EAST LOTHIAN
SCOTTISH BORDERS
DUMFRIES & GALLOWAY
SOUTH LANARKSHIRE
NORTH AYRSHIRE
EAST AYRSHIRE
SOUTH AYRSHIRE
NORTHUMBERLAND
CUMBRIA
DURHAM
Outer Hebrides
Inner Hebrides
North Minch
Little Minch
North West Highlands
Grampian Mountains
Cairngorm Mts.
Monadhliath Mts.
Southern Uplands
Cheviot Hills
Pentland Firth
Moray Firth
Firth of Forth
Firth of Tay
Firth of Clyde
Firth of Lorn
Solway Firth
North Channel
Edinburgh
Glasgow
Aberdeen
Dundee
Inverness
Perth
Stirling
Fort William
Oban
Stornoway
Kirkwall
Lerwick
Wick
Thurso
Ayr
Dumfries
Carlisle
Newcastle-upon-Tyne
Belfast
Ben Nevis 1342
Ben Macdhui 1309
Cairn Gorm 1245
Ben Lawers 1214
Lewis
Harris
North Uist
South Uist
Benbecula
Barra
Skye
Rhum
Mull
Islay
Jura
Arran
Tiree
Coll
Loch Ness
Loch Lomond
Projection : Lambert's Conformal Conic
West from Greenwich
COPYRIGHT GEORGE PHILIP LTD.

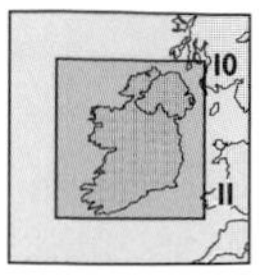

Projection : Lambert's Conformal Conic

West from Greenwich

BRITISH ISLES 1:5 000 000

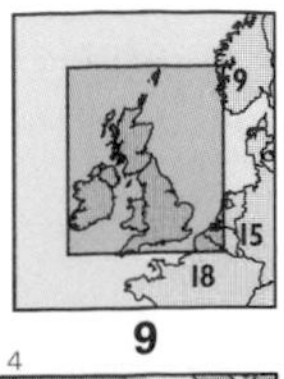

ATLANTIC OCEAN
NORTH SEA
CELTIC SEA
IRISH SEA
SCOTLAND
UNITED KINGDOM
IRELAND
ENGLAND
WALES
NORTHERN IRELAND
NORWAY
NETHERLANDS
BELGIUM
FRANCE
Shetland Is.
Orkney Is.
Outer Hebrides
Inner Hebrides
Grampian Mts.
North West Highlands
Southern Uplands
Pennines
Cambrian Mts.
Wicklow Mts.
English Channel
Bristol Channel
St. George's Channel
North Channel
North Minch
Pentland Firth
Moray Firth
Firth of Clyde
Cardigan Bay
Str. of Dover
The Wash
Edinburgh
Glasgow
Aberdeen
Dundee
Inverness
Belfast
Dublin
Cork
Limerick
Galway
Waterford
Newcastle-upon-Tyne
Sunderland
Middlesbrough
Leeds
Bradford
Manchester
Liverpool
Sheffield
Kingston upon Hull
Nottingham
Leicester
Birmingham
Coventry
Bristol
Cardiff
Swansea
Southampton
Plymouth
London
Brighton
Norwich
Dunkerque
Le Havre
Cherbourg
Channel Is. (U.K.)
Bergen
Stavanger
Projection: Conical with two standard parallels
East from Greenwich
West from Greenwich
COPYRIGHT GEORGE PHILIP LTD.

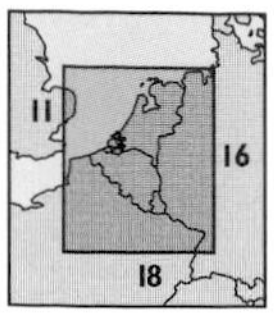
11
16
18

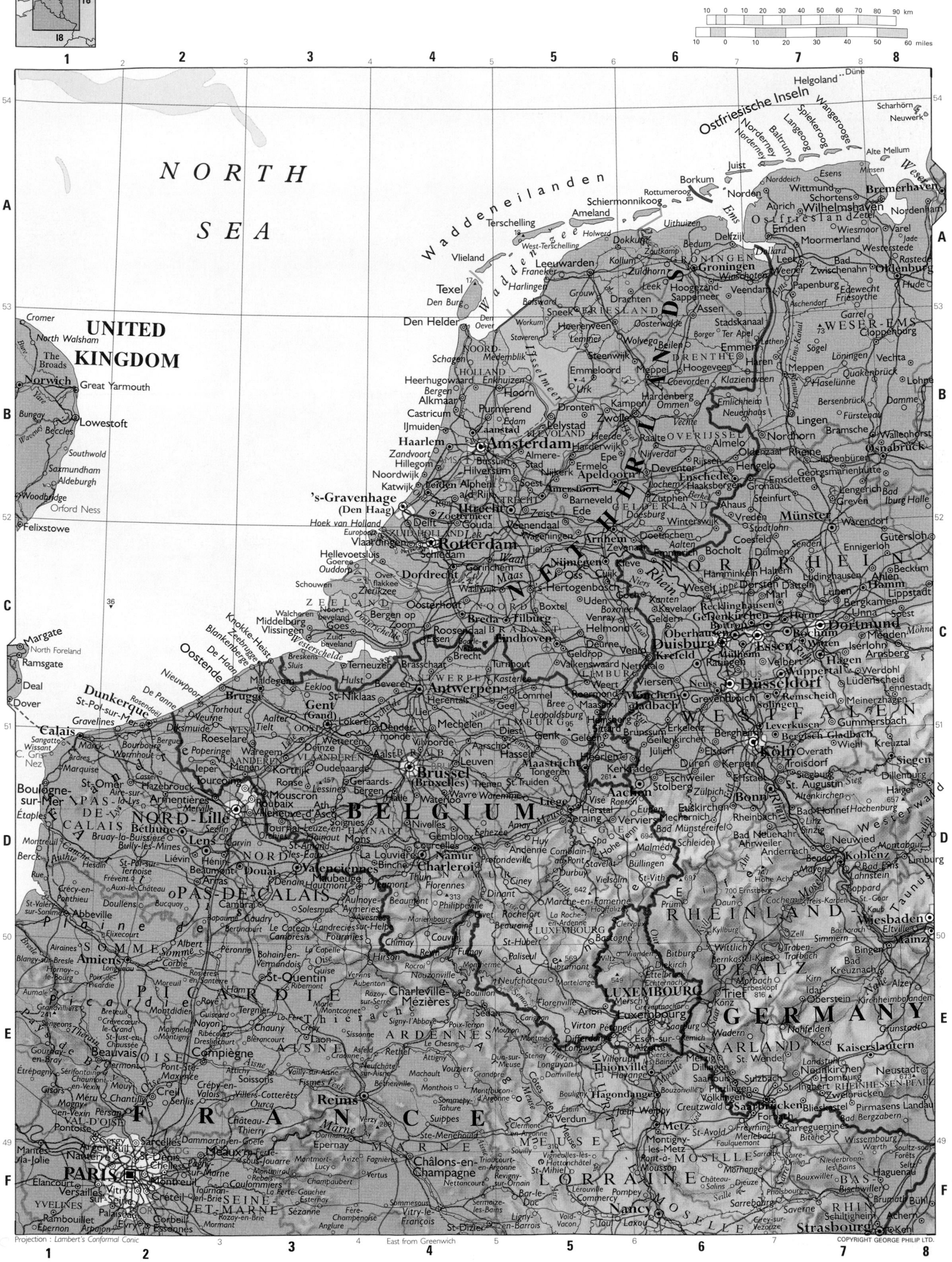
10 0 10 20 30 40 50 60 70 80 90 km
10 0 10 20 30 40 50 60 miles
NORTH SEA
UNITED KINGDOM
NETHERLANDS
BELGIUM
LUXEMBOURG
GERMANY
FRANCE
Waddeneilanden
Ostfriesische Inseln
Waddenzee
IJsselmeer
Amsterdam
Rotterdam
's-Gravenhage (Den Haag)
Utrecht
Antwerpen
Brussel (Bruxelles)
Luxembourg
Köln
Düsseldorf
Essen
Dortmund
Lille
Reims
Metz
Nancy
Strasbourg
PARIS
NORDRHEIN-WESTFALEN
RHEINLAND-PFALZ
SAARLAND
LORRAINE
PICARDIE
ARDENNES
Projection : Lambert's Conformal Conic
East from Greenwich
COPYRIGHT GEORGE PHILIP LTD.

ft m
1500 500
600 200
0 0
50
m ft

Underlined towns give their name to the administrative area in which they stand.

MIDDLE EUROPE 1:5 000 000

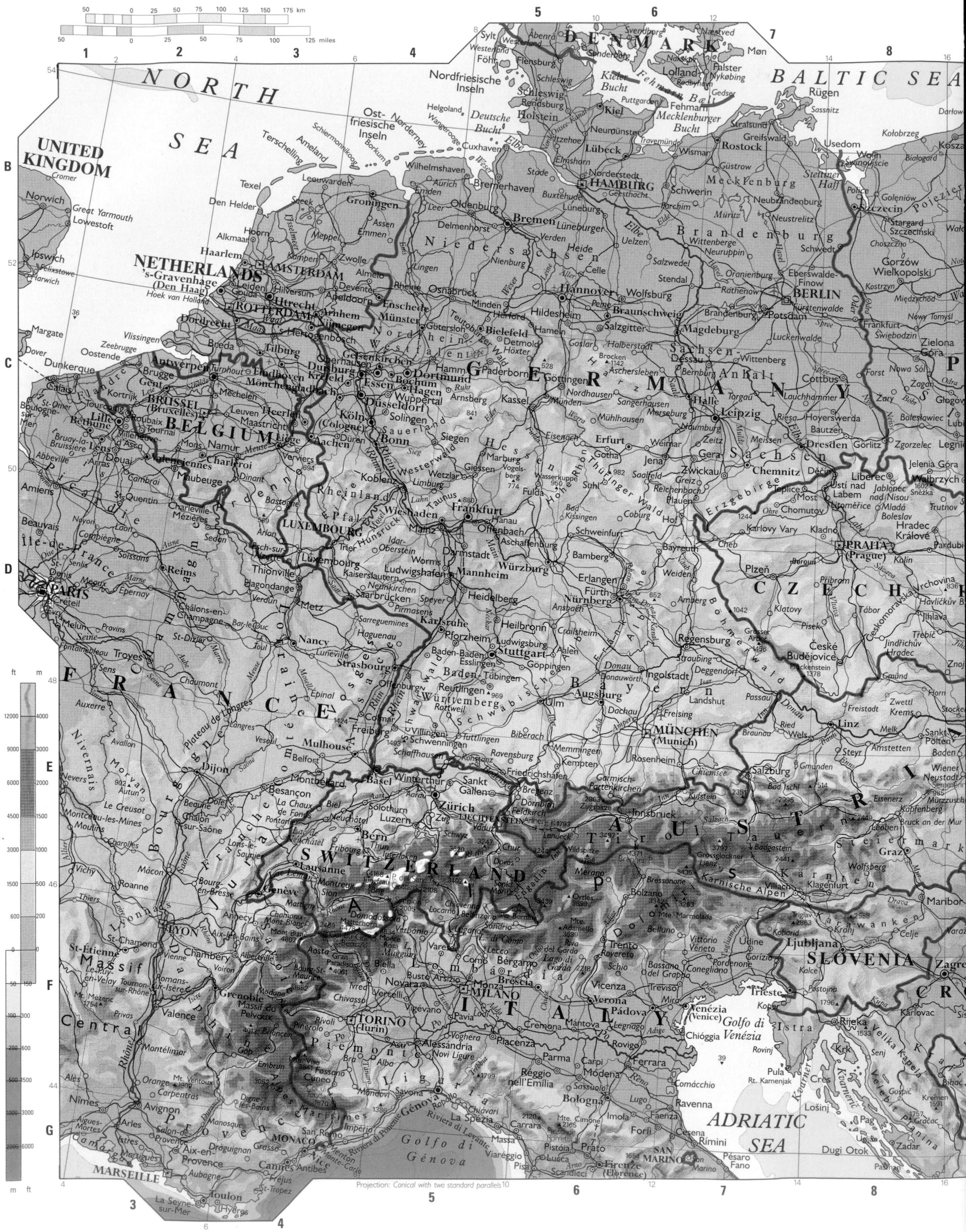

NORTH SEA
UNITED KINGDOM
NETHERLANDS
BELGIUM
LUXEMBOURG
FRANCE
GERMANY
DENMARK
BALTIC SEA
CZECH
AUSTRIA
SWITZERLAND
LIECHTENSTEIN
ITALY
SLOVENIA
MONACO
SAN MARINO
ADRIATIC SEA
Golfo di Venézia
Golfo di Génova
Kieler Bucht
Mecklenburger Bucht
Deutsche Bucht
Nordfriesische Inseln
Ostfriesische Inseln
AMSTERDAM
BRUSSEL (Bruxelles)
LUXEMBOURG
PARIS
BERLIN
PRAHA (Prague)
MÜNCHEN (Munich)
MILANO
TORINO (Turin)
HAMBURG
MARSEILLE
Projection: Conical with two standard parallels
50 0 25 50 75 100 125 150 175 km
50 0 25 50 75 100 125 miles
ft m
12000 4000
9000 3000
6000 2000
4500 1500
3000 1000
1500 500
600 200
m ft

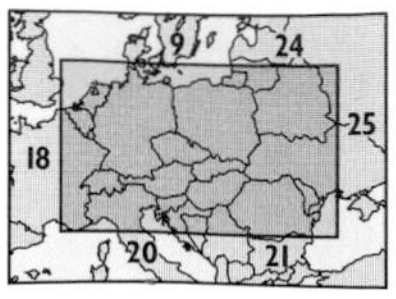
9
24
25
18
20
21

9 10 11 12 13 14 15 16
18 20 22 24 26 28 30
54 52 50 48 46 44
B C D E F G
Zatoka Gdańska
Baltiysk
Kaliningrad (Russia)
Polessk
Gusev
Chernyakhovsk
Gvardeysk
Bagrationovsk
Wejherowo
Rumia
Gdynia
Lębork
Sopot
Gdańsk
Tczew
Zalew Wiślany
Braniewo
Elbląg
Bytów
Starogard Gdański
Malbork
Kwidzyn
Pojezierze Mazurskie
Olsztyn
Ostróda
Iława
Szczytno
Chojnice
Szczecinek
Świecie
Grudziądz
Brodnica
Działdowo
Chełmno
Bydgoszcz
Toruń
Rypin
Mława
Ciechanów
Ostrołęka
Łomża
Ostrów Mazowiecka
Białystok
Hajnówka
Bielsk Podlaski
Kętrzyn
Giżycko
Suwałki
Ełk
Augustów
Sokółka
Inowrocław
Włocławek
Płock
Pułtusk
Sokołów Podlaski
Gniezno
Września
Poznań
Legionowo
Mińsk Mazowiecki
WARSZAWA (Warsaw)
Pruszków
Otwock
Siedlce
Biała Podlaska
Kutno
Koło
Łęczyca
Łowicz
Żyrardów
Skierniewice
Konin
Turek
Śrem
Kościan
Leszno
Krotoszyn
Kalisz
Zduńska Wola
Łódź
Pabianice
Sieradz
Ostrów Wielkopolski
Grójec
Tomaszów Mazowiecki
Radom
Puławy
Lublin
Chełm
Świdnik
Kraśnik
Łuków
Międzyrzec Podlaski
Włodawa
Piotrków Trybunalski
Wieluń
Oleśnica
Wrocław
Oława
Kluczbork
Radomsko
Końskie
Skarżysko-Kamienna
Starachowice
Kielce
Ostrowiec-Świętokrzyski
Częstochowa
Opole
Myszków
Zawiercie
Jędrzejów
Pińczów
Sandomierz
Stalowa Wola
Zamość
Tarnobrzeg
Mielec
Świdnica
Dzierżoniów
Kłodzko
Nysa
Tarnowskie Góry
Bytom
Zabrze
Sosnowiec
Gliwice
Katowice
Chorzów
Tychy
Racibórz
Oświęcim
Kraków
Tarnów
Rzeszów
Dębica
Jarosław
Przemyśl
Bochnia
Jasło
Krosno
Sanok
Nowy Sącz
Bielsko-Biała
Żywiec
Nowy Targ
Zakopane
Karviná
Havířov
Ostrava
Opava
Šumperk
Frýdek-Místek
Cieszyn
Přerov
Zlín
Brno
Západné Beskydy
Východné Beskydy
Dukelský Průsmyk
Tatry
Považská Bystrica
Žilina
Ružomberok
Poprad
Bardejov
Prešov
Humenné
Michalovce
Martin
Nízké Tatry
Banská Bystrica
Trenčín
Prievidza
Bielé Karpaty
SLOVAK REP.
Zvolen
Slovenské Rudohorie
Košice
Uzhhorod
Chop
Trnava
Nitra
Topoľčany
Malé Karpaty
Bratislava
Lučenec
Levice
Sátoraljaújhely
Nové Zámky
Komárno
Ózd
Miskolc
Salgótarján
Gyöngyös
Eger
Mezőkövesd
Vác
Hatvan
Esztergom
Dunakeszi
Jászberény
Hajdúböszörmény
Nyíregyháza
Debrecen
Győr
Mosonmagyaróvár
Sopron
Tatabánya
Pápa
Érd
BUDAPEST
Székesfehérvár
Cegléd
Szombathely
Ajka
Veszprém
Bakony
Balaton
Dunaújváros
Siófok
Szolnok
Mezőtúr
Nagykőrös
Kecskemét
Karcag
HUNGARY
Zalaegerszeg
Kiskunfélegyháza
Csongrád
Szentes
Békéscsaba
Gyula
Orosháza
Hódmezővásárhely
Nagykanizsa
Kalocsa
Kiskőrös
Kiskunhalas
Szekszárd
Kaposvár
Szeged
Makó
Pécs
Mohács
Baja
Subotica
Drava
Virovitica
Osijek
Vukovar
Vinkovci
Slavonski Brod
Novska
Bosanska Gradiška
Sava
Banja Luka
Doboj
Brčko
Bijeljina
Tuzla
Zenica
Travnik
Zepče
BOSNIA-HERZEGOVINA
Sarajevo
Han Pijesak
Višegrad
Cincar
Srebrenica
Sombor
Senta
Kikinda
Bečej
Vojvodina
Novi Sad
Zrenjanin
Petrovaradin
Sremska Mitrovica
Šabac
BEOGRAD (Belgrade)
Pančevo
Smederevo
Požarevac
Vršac
Bela Crkva
YUGOSLAVIA
Valjevo
Kragujevac
Jagodina
Čačak
Užice
Kraljevo
Zaječar
Negotin
Bor
Timok
Morava
Dunav
Prienai
Marijampolė
LITHUANIA
Vilnius
Varėna
Druskininkai
Hrodna
Lida
BELARUS
Ashmyany
Smarhon
Vileyka
Maladzyechna
Valozhyn
Zhodzina
Barysaw
Krupki
MINSK
Dzyarzhynsk
Cherven
Mahilyow
Shklow
Krychaw
Mstsislaw
Cherykaw
Slawharad
Bykhaw
Navahrudak
Nyoman
Masty
Dzyatlava
Vawkavysk
Slonim
Stowbtsy
Nyasvizh
Baranavichy
Slutsk
Asipovichy
Babruysk
Rahachow
Zhlobin
Svislach
Lyakhavichy
Klyetsk
Hantsavichy
Salihorsk
Glusk
Aktsyabrski
Svyetlahorsk
Homyel
Dobrush
Rechytsa
Ivatsevichy
Byarezina
Pruzhany
Bereza
Tsyelyakhany
Luninyets
Pripyats
Vasilevichi
Kalinkavichy
Zhabinka
Kobryn
Dragichyn
Yaselda
Ivanava
Pinsk
Davyd Haradok
Mazyr
Khoyniki
Loyew
Brest
Malaryta
Stolin
Pripet Marshes
Yelsk
Ubort
Pripyat
Chornobyl
Ovruch
Dubrovytsya
Kamin-Kashyrskyy
Olevsk
Belokorovichi
Korosten
Kyyivske Vdskh.
Dymer
Oster
Desna
Lyuboml
Kovel
Staryy Chartoriysk
Kostopil
Sluch
Novohrad-Volynskyy
Malyn
Irpin
KYYIV (Kiev)
Rozhyshche
Kivertsi
Volodymyr-Volynskyy
Lutsk
Oleksandriya
Rivne
Zdolbuniv
Korets
Radomyshl
Teterev
Novovolynsk
Horokhiv
Dubno
Ostroh
Zhytomyr
Korostyshev
Vasylkiv
Fastiv
Sokal
Chervonohrad
Berestechko
Radekhiv
Kremenets
Slavuta
Pershotravensk
Shepetivka
Polonne
Berdychiv
Bila Tserkva
Rava-Ruska
Kamyanka-Buzka
Brody
Izyaslav
Kozyatyn
Skvyra
Tarashcha
Nesterov
Yavoriv
Mostyska
Horodok
Lviv (Lvov)
Zolochiv
Zbarazh
Ternopil
Starokonstyantyniv
Khmelnik
UKRAINE
Tetiyev
Lipovets
Zhashkiv
Sambir
Drohobych
Boryslav
Truskavets
Skole
Stryy
Kalush
Khodoriv
Rogatyn
Berezhany
Terebovlya
Skalat
Hrymayliv
Kopychyntsi
Horodok
Khmelnytskyy
Podilska
Vinnytsya
Bar
Zhmerynka
Haysyn
Uman
Buchach
Chortkiv
Skala-Podilska
Kamyanets-Podilskyy
Tulchyn
Vapnyarka
Buh
Hayvoron
Bolekhiv
Ivano-Frankivsk
Horodenka
Dnister
Zalishchyky
Mohyliv-Podilskyy
Bershad
Balta
Volovets
Nadvirna
Pechenizhyn
Kolomyya
Khotyn
Novoselytsya
Lipcani
Ocnița
Yampil
Mukacheve
Berehove
Khust
Yaremcha
Chernivtsi
Hlyboka
Storozhynets
Edineț
Drochia
Soroca
Florești
Rîbnița
Ananyiv
Kotovsk
Yasinya
Rakhiv
Tyachiv
Vynohradiv
Dorohoi
Bălți
Fălești
Dubăsari Vdkhr.
Cornești
Orhei
Dubăsari
MOLDOVA
Chișinău
Tiraspol
Ungheni
Tighina
Rozdilna
Nistru
Dnister
Satu Mare
Carei
Sighetu-Marmatiei
Baia Mare
Borșa
Pietrosul
Rădăuți
Siret
Suceava
Botoșani
Fălticeni
Pașcani
Iași
Vatra-Dornei
Bistrița
Roman
Huși
Leova
Cimișlia
Basarabeasca
Bilhorod-Dnistrovskyy
Oradea
Zalău
Dej
Reghin
Piatra Neamț
Vaslui
Bacău
Comrat
Artsyz
Cluj-Napoca
Salonta
Turda
Târgu Mureș
Mureș
Munții Bihor
Abrud
Odorheiu Secuiesc
Miercurea Ciuc
Onești
Bârlad
Ciadâr-Lunga
Cahul
Tatarbunary
Ozero Sasyk
Aiud
Târnăveni
Sighișoara
Sfântu Gheorghe
Tecuci
Vulcanești
Bolhrad
Kiliya
Vylkove
Arad
Transilvania
Brad
Alba-Iulia
Mediaș
Focșani
Galați
Reni
Izmayil
Sânnicolau Mare
Deva
Sibiu
Făgăraș
Brașov
Săcele
Râmnicu Sărat
Brăila
Sulina
ROMANIA
Timișoara
Lugoj
Hunedoara
Simeria
Carpații Meridionali
Moldoveanu
Câmpina
Buzău
Tulcea
Babadag
Caransebeș
Reșița
Vf. Peleaga
Petroșani
Vulcan
Parângul Mare
Câmpulung
Vf. Omul
Curtea de Argeș
Târgoviște
Ploiești
Dunărea (Danube)
Lacul Razelm
Porta Orientalis
Târgu-Jiu
Râmnicu Vâlcea
Pitești
Slobozia
Fetești
Ialomița
Portile de Fier
Orșova
Drobeta-Turnu-Severin
Drăgășani
Wallachia
BUCUREȘTI (Bucharest)
Argeș
Dâmbovița
Medgidia
Năvodari
Constanța
Slatina
Craiova
Roșiori-de-Vede
Călărași
Oltenița
Silistra
Dobruja
Mangalia
Băilești
Caracal
Alexandria
Vedea
Olt
Giurgiu
Tutrakan
Turnu Măgurele
Zimnicea
Corabia
Vidin
Lom
Oryakhova
Ruse
Razgrad
Dobrich
Balchik
Nos Kaliakra
Varna
BULGARIA
East from Greenwich
COPYRIGHT GEORGE PHILIP LTD.

FRANCE 1:5 000 000

FRANCE
UNITED KINGDOM
BELGIUM
LUXEMBOURG
GERMANY
SWITZERLAND
ITALY
ANDORRA
MONACO
AUSTRIA
Corse (Corsica)
MEDITERRANEAN SEA
Bay of Biscay
English Channel
Golfe du Lion
Golfe de Gascogne
Channel Is. (U.K.)
PARIS
MARSEILLE
LYON
Bordeaux
Toulouse
Nantes
Lille
Strasbourg
Nice
Massif Central
Pyrénées
Alpes
Bassin Aquitain
Projection: Conical with two standard parallels
West from Greenwich
East from Greenwich
COPYRIGHT GEORGE PHILIP LTD

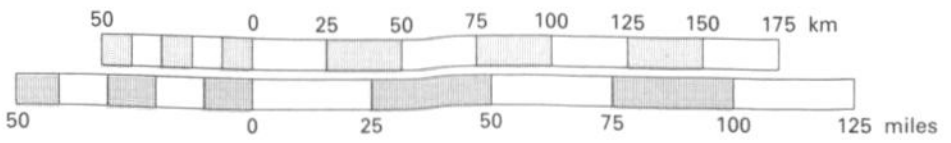

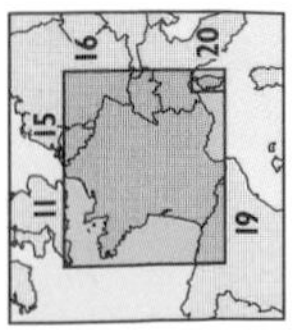

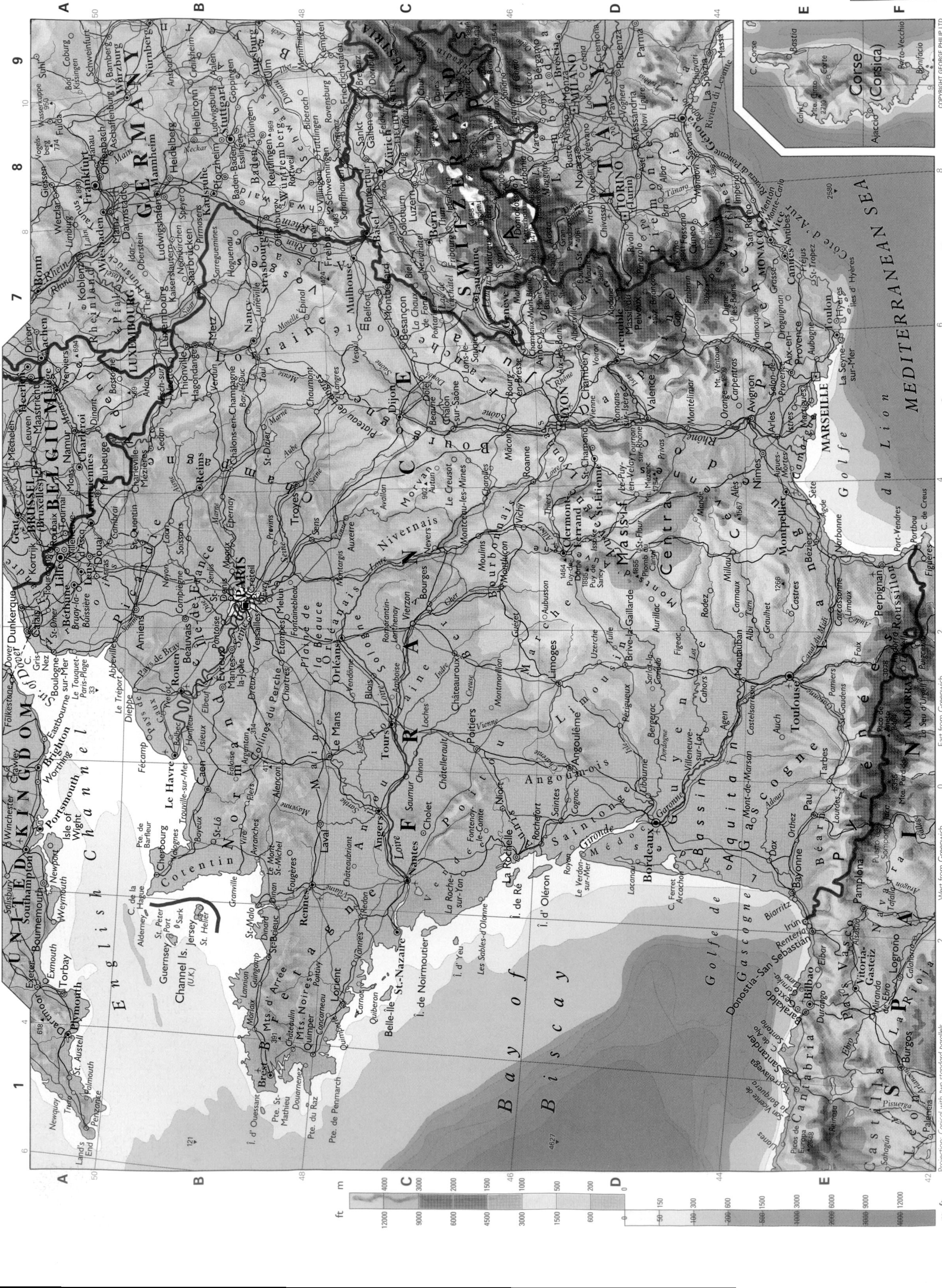

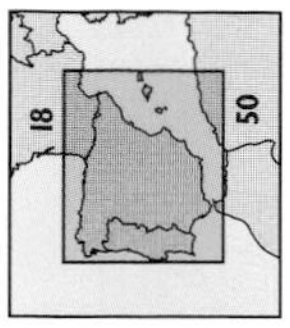

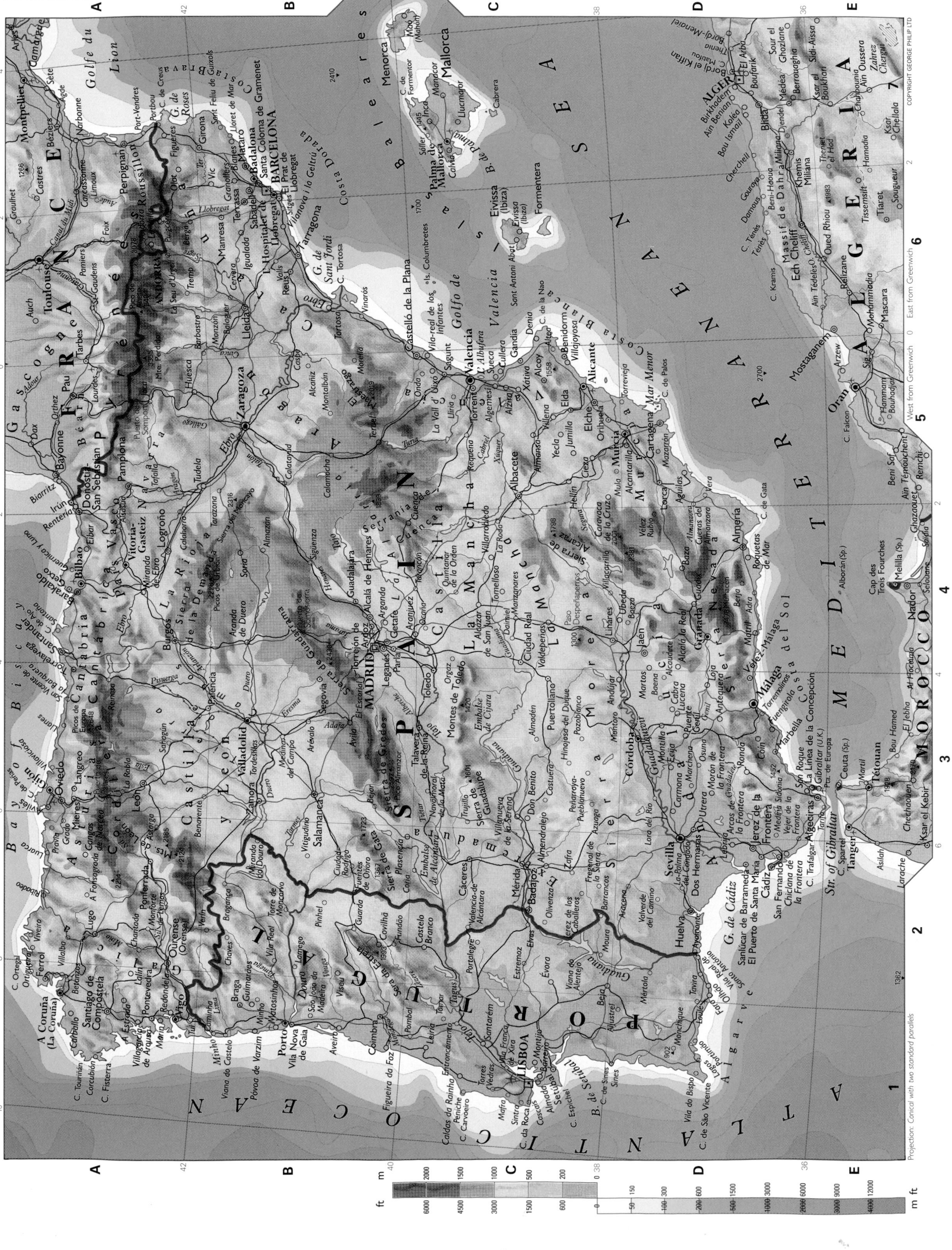

MADRID
LISBOA
BARCELONA
Valencia
Sevilla
Zaragoza
Málaga
Bilbao
Porto
Granada
Córdoba
Murcia
Alicante
Valladolid
Palma de Mallorca
Mallorca
Menorca
ALGER
Oran
Toulouse
Montpellier
Perpignan
Golfe du Lion
Golfo de Valencia
G. de Cádiz
Str. of Gibraltar
Gibraltar (U.K.)
Ceuta (Sp.)
Melilla (Sp.)
Tanger
Tétouan
COPYRIGHT GEORGE PHILIP LTD
Projection: Conical with two standard parallels
West from Greenwich
East from Greenwich

SWITZERLAND
AUSTRIA
SLOVENIA
CROATIA
FRANCE
ALGERIA
TUNISIA
MALTA
MONACO
SAN MARINO
VATICAN CITY
LIGURIAN SEA
TYRRHENIAN SEA
ADRIATIC SEA
MEDITER
Golfo di Génova
Golfo di Venézia
Golfo di Táranto
Golfe de Tunis
Golfe de Hammamet
G. di Oristano
G. di Cágliari
G. di Pálmas
Golfo dell' Asinara
Bouches de Bonifacio
Str. di Messina
Alpi
Dolomiti
Appennini
Alpes Maritimes
Karnische Alpen
Karawanken
Dauphiné
Provence
Liguria
Piemonte
Lombardia
Toscana
Lazio
Campania
Sicilia
Calabria
Istra
Corse
Sardegna
Elba
Íscole Eólie
Ísole Égadi
Ísole Pelagie (Italy)
Ísole Ponziane
Pantelleria (Italy)
Ústica (Italy)
Gozo
Roma
Milano
Torino (Turin)
Venézia (Venice)
Firenze (Florence)
Génova
Nápoli
Palermo
Bologna
Bari
Catánia
Messina
Cágliari
Sássari
Ancona
Pescara
Perúgia
Trieste
Ljubljana
Zagreb
Rijeka
Split
Zadar
Tunis
Annaba
Constantine
Bizerte
Sousse
Valletta
Lyon
Grenoble
Marseille
Toulon
Nice
Cannes
Avignon
Ajaccio
Bastia
Graz
Klagenfurt
Villach
Maribor
Verona
Pádova
Brescia
Bergamo
Parma
Módena
Réggio nell'Emilia
Ravenna
Rímini
Livorno
Pisa
Lucca
Siena
Arezzo
Terni
L'Àquila
Latina
Foggia
Táranto
Potenza
Salerno
Cosenza
Catanzaro
Crotone
Réggio di Calábria
Siracusa
Trápani
Marsala
Agrigento
Projection: Conical with two standard parallels

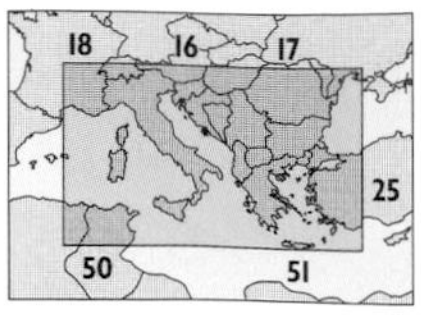
18
16
17
25
50
51

HUNGARY
ROMANIA
UKRAINE
YUGOSLAVIA
BOSNIA-HERZEGOVINA
SERBIA
MONTENEGRO
ALBANIA
MACEDONIA
BULGARIA
GREECE
TURKEY
BLACK SEA
IONIAN SEA
MEDITERRANEAN SEA
AEGEAN SEA
Marmara Denizi (Sea of Marmara)
BUCUREŞTI (Bucharest)
BEOGRAD (Belgrade)
SOFIYA
ATHÍNAI (Athens)
İSTANBUL
İZMIR (Smyrna)
Thessaloníki
Constanţa
Varna
Burgas
Tiranë
Skopje
Sarajevo
Pelopónnisos
Kríti
Kikládhes
Dhodhekánisos
Rhodopi Planina
Stara Planina
Carpaţii Meridionali
Transilvania
Valahia
Dobruja
Makedhonía
Thrace
Mysia
Lydia
Caria
Str. of Otranto
East from Greenwich
COPYRIGHT GEORGE PHILIP LTD.

THE BALEARICS, THE CANARIES AND MADEIRA

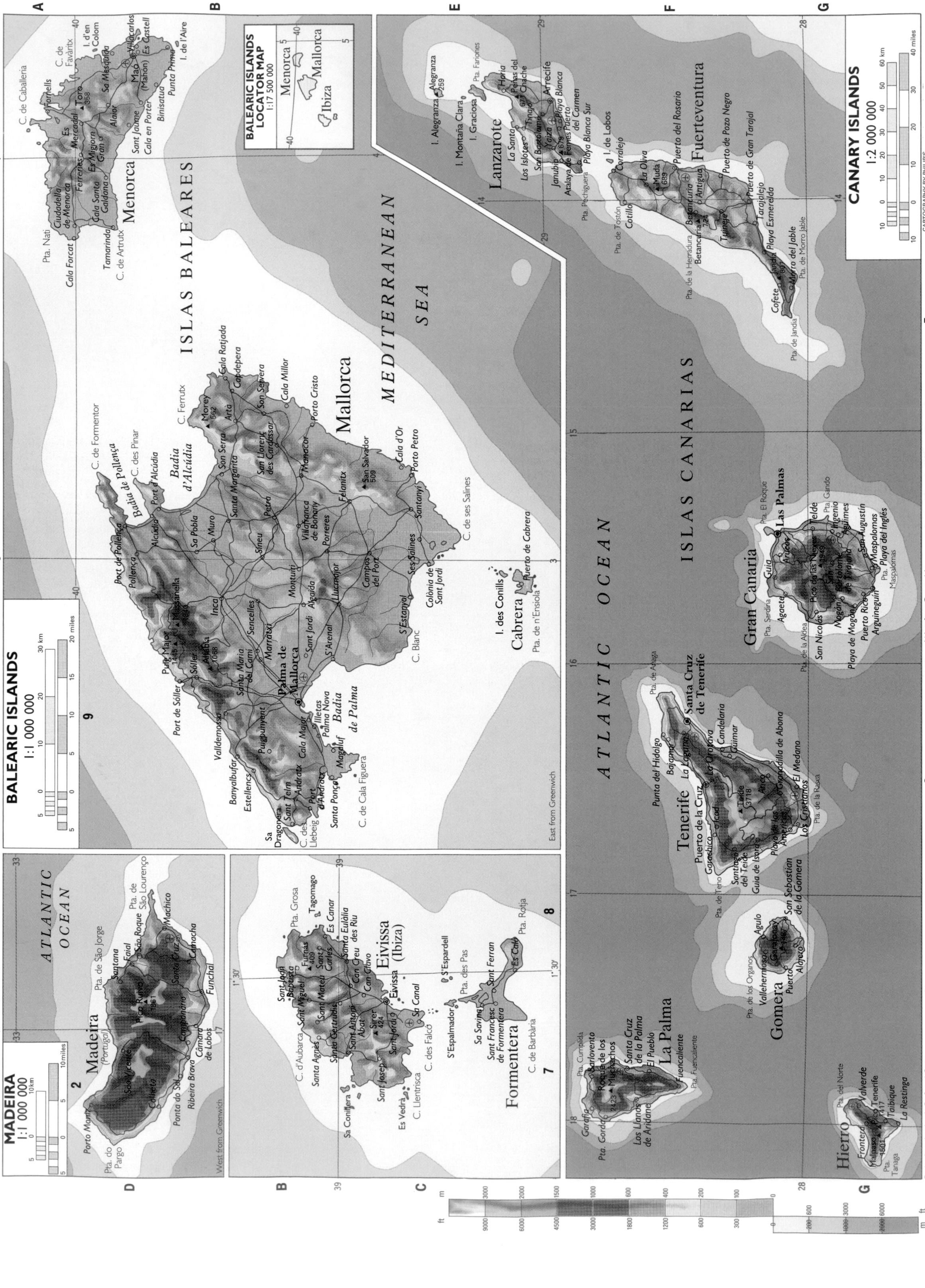

1:1 000 000
(Portugal)
Funchal
Pico Ruivo
ATLANTIC OCEAN
BALEARIC ISLANDS
1:1 000 000
BALEARIC ISLANDS LOCATOR MAP
1:17 500 000
ISLAS BALEARES
Mallorca
Palma de Mallorca
Badia de Palma
Badia d'Alcúdia
Badia de Pollença
Menorca
Eivissa (Ibiza)
Formentera
Cabrera
MEDITERRANEAN SEA
ATLANTIC OCEAN
ISLAS CANARIAS
La Palma
Tenerife
Santa Cruz de Tenerife
Gomera
Hierro
Gran Canaria
Las Palmas
Lanzarote
Arrecife
Fuerteventura
CANARY ISLANDS
1:2 000 000
East from Greenwich
West from Greenwich
Projection : Lambert's Conformal Conic
CARTOGRAPHY BY PHILIP'S.

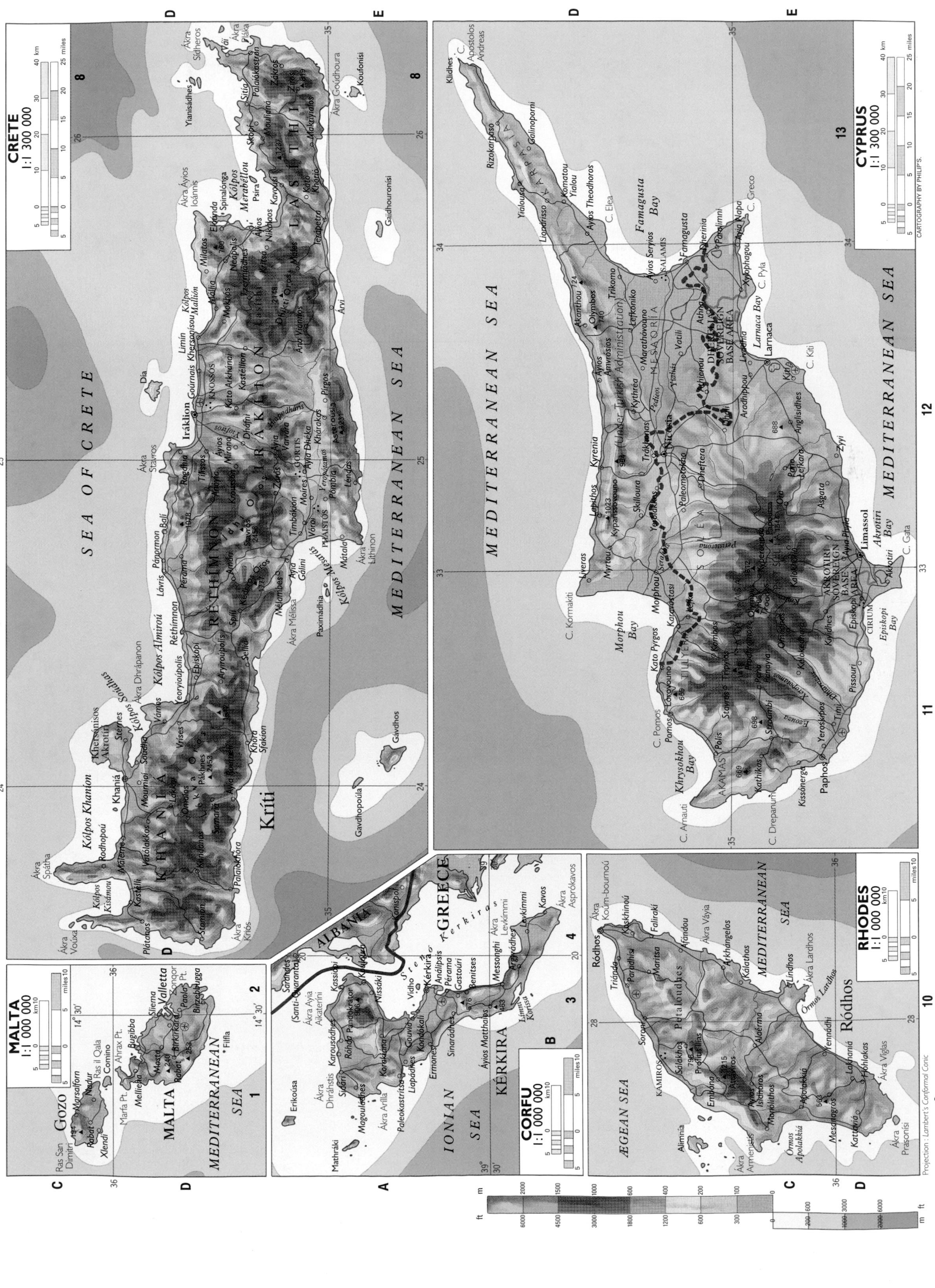
CRETE
1:1 300 000
CYPRUS
1:1 300 000
MALTA
1:1 000 000
CORFU
1:1 000 000
RHODES
1:1 000 000
SEA OF CRETE
MEDITERRANEAN SEA
IONIAN SEA
AEGEAN SEA
Kríti
Ródhos
Kérkira
Famagusta Bay
Morphou Bay
Larnaca Bay
Nicosia
Limassol
Iráklion
Khaniá
Valletta
Projection: Lambert's Conformal Conic
CARTOGRAPHY BY PHILIP'S

EASTERN EUROPE AND TURKEY 1:10 000 000

50 0 100 200 300 400 km
50 0 50 100 150 200 250 miles
B
C
BARENTS SEA
Beloye More
BALTIC SEA
Gulf of Bothnia
Gulf of Finland
Gulf of Riga
R U S S I A
FINLAND
SWEDEN
NORWAY
ESTONIA
LATVIA
LITHUANIA
BELARUS
POLAND
KARELIA
KOMI
UDMURTIA
TATARSTAN
BASHKORTOSTAN
CHUVASHIA
MORDVINIA
MARI EL
Lappland
Kolskiy Poluostrov
Poluostrov Kanin
Ostrov Kolguyev
Uralskie Gory
Timanskiy Kryazh
Severnyye Uvaly
Ladozhskoye Ozero
Onezhskoye Ozero
MOSKVA
SANKT-PETERBURG
Helsinki
Tallinn
Riga
MINSK
Vilnius
WARSZAWA
Arkhangelsk
Murmansk
NIZHNIY NOVGOROD
KAZAN
SAMARA
PERM
UFA
Volga
Pechora
Severnaya Dvina
Kama

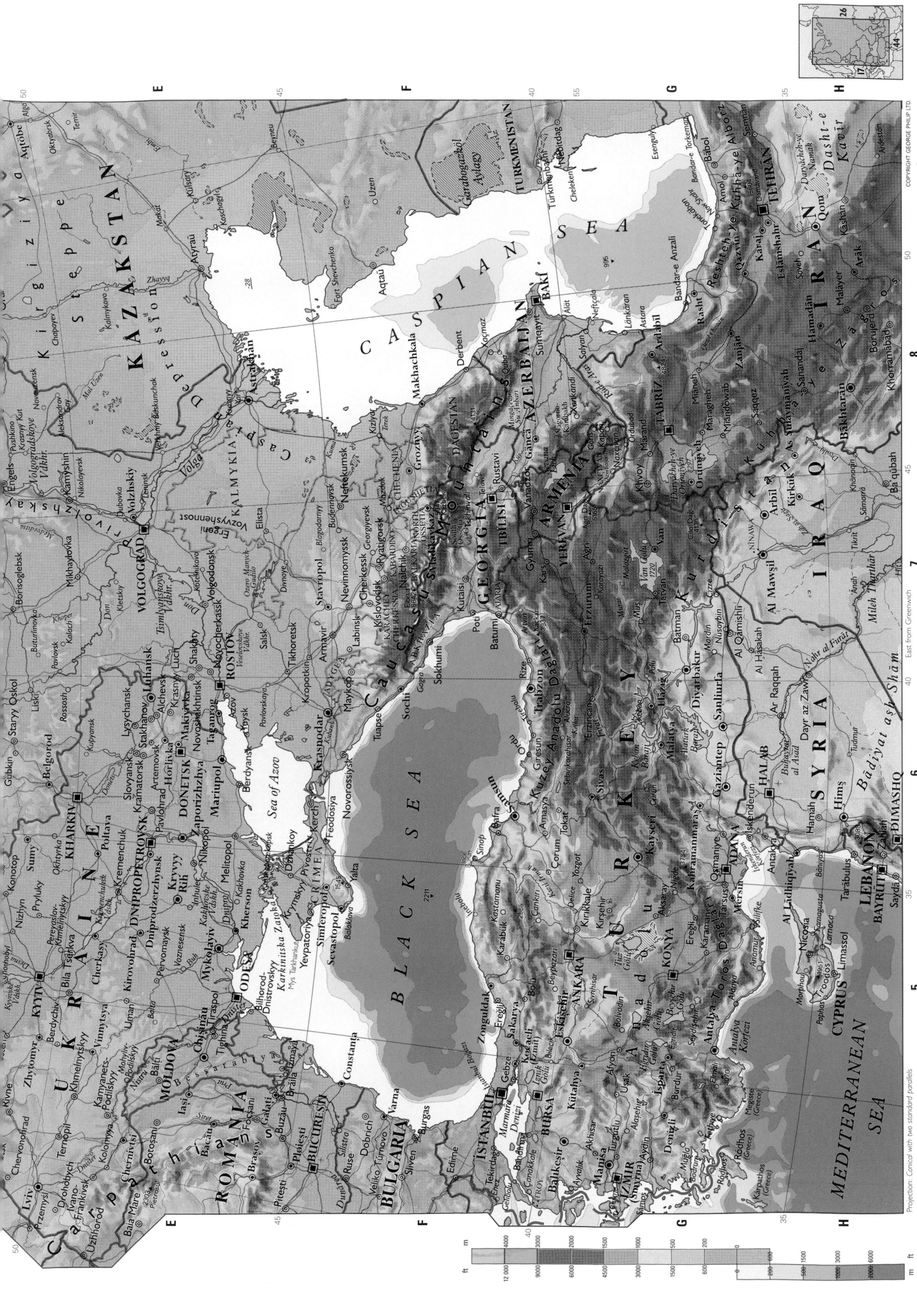
BLACK SEA
CASPIAN SEA
Sea of Azov
MEDITERRANEAN SEA
KAZAKSTAN
UKRAINE
TURKEY
IRAN
IRAQ
SYRIA
GEORGIA
ARMENIA
AZERBAIJAN
ROMANIA
BULGARIA
MOLDOVA
CYPRUS
LEBANON
TURKMENISTAN
KALMYKIA
CRIMEA
DAGESTAN
Caucasus Mountains
Anadolu Dağları
Kuzey Anadolu Dağları
Toros Dağları
Kurdistan
Zāgros
Caspian Depression
Kirgiziya Steppe
Privolzhskaya Vozvyshennost
Ergeni Vozvyshennost
Bādiyat ash Shām
Dasht-e Kavīr
Reshteh-ye Kūhhā-ye Alborz
KYYIV
ODESA
KHARKIV
DNIPROPETROVSK
DONETSK
VOLGOGRAD
ROSTOV
İSTANBUL
ANKARA
İZMIR
BURSA
ADANA
KONYA
TEHRAN
TABRIZ
BAKI
TBILISI
YEREVAN
BUCUREŞTI
CHIŞINĂU
HALAB
DIMASHQ
BAYRŪT
Astrakhan
Krasnodar
Stavropol
Sevastopol
Simferopol
Trabzon
Samsun
Erzurum
Kayseri
Gaziantep
Al Mawşil
Kirkūk
Arbīl
Qom
Hamadān
Rasht
Makhachkala
Groznyy
Nal'chik
Sochi
Batumi
Constanţa
Varna
Burgas
Nicosia
Mariupol
Zaporizhzhya
Kherson
Mykolayiv
Luhansk
Atyraū
Aqtaū
Beyneu
Türkmenbashi
E
F
G
H
4
5
6
7
8
9
East from Greenwich
Projection: Conical with two standard parallels
COPYRIGHT GEORGE PHILIP LTD.
m
ft
12 000
9000
6000
4500
3000
1500
600
0
4000
3000
2000
1500
1000
500
200
0
200
1500
3000
6000
600
5000
10 000
20 000

RUSSIA AND CENTRAL ASIA 1:20 000 000

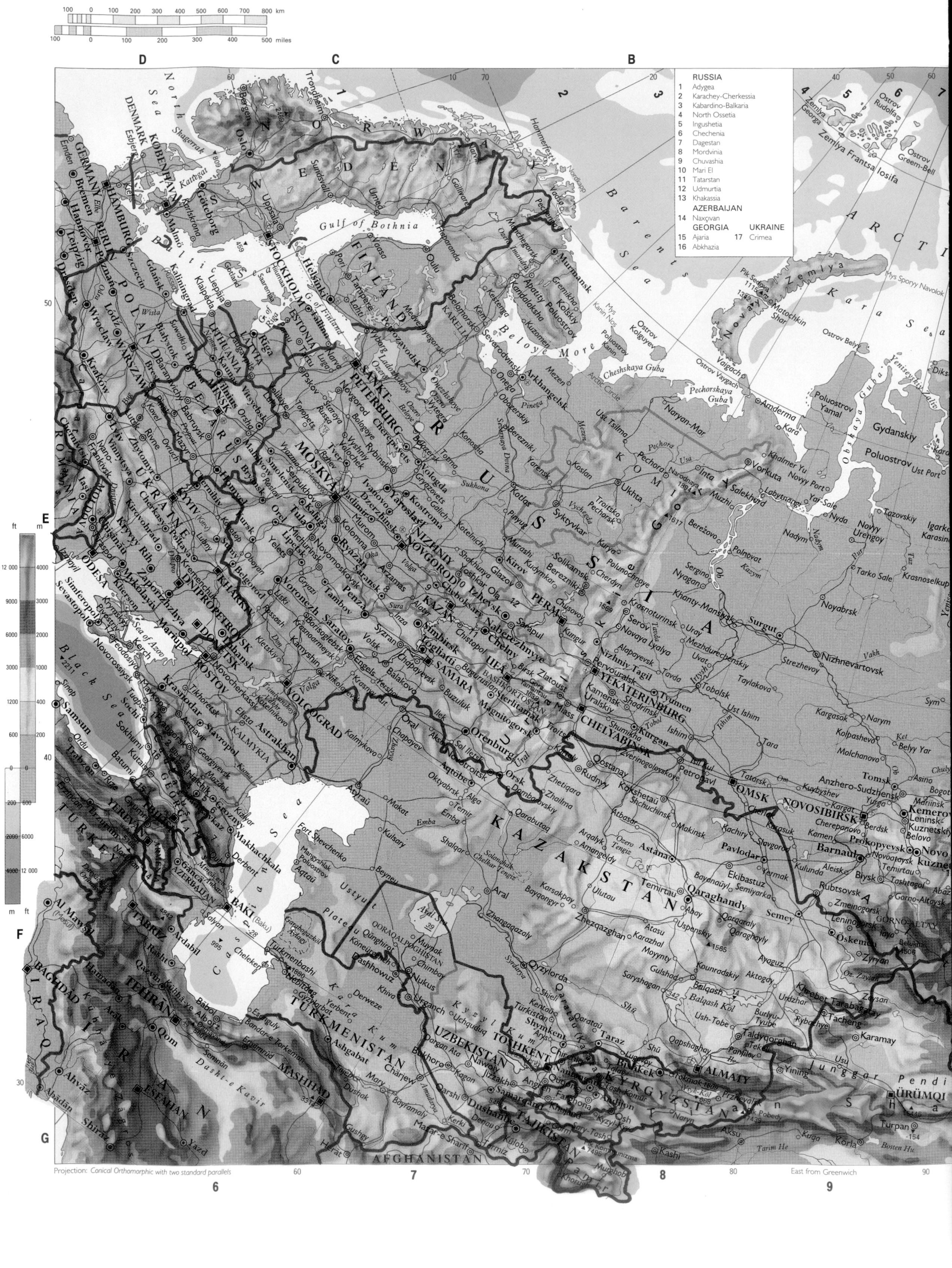
100 0 100 200 300 400 500 600 700 800 km
100 0 100 200 300 400 500 miles
RUSSIA
1 Adygea
2 Karachey-Cherkessia
3 Kabardino-Balkaria
4 North Ossetia
5 Ingushetia
6 Chechenia
7 Dagestan
8 Mordvinia
9 Chuvashia
10 Mari El
11 Tatarstan
12 Udmurtia
13 Khakassia
AZERBAIJAN
14 Naxçıvan
GEORGIA
15 Ajaria
16 Abkhazia
UKRAINE
17 Crimea
ft m
12 000 4000
9000 3000
6000 2000
3000 1000
1200 400
600 200
0 0
200 600
2000 6000
4000 12 000
m ft
Projection: Conical Orthomorphic with two standard parallels
East from Greenwich

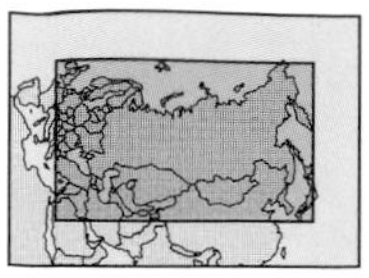

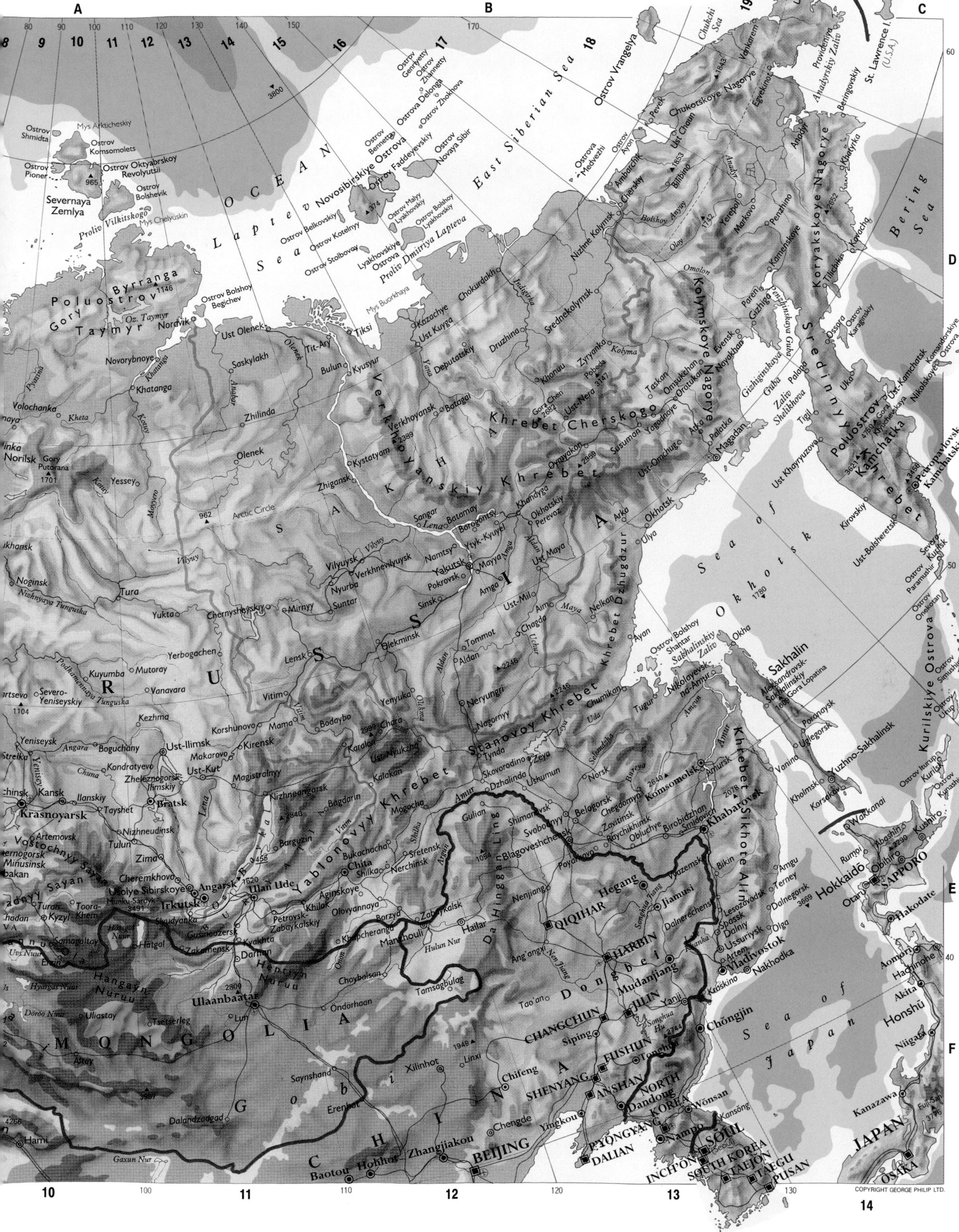
A
B
C
D
E
F
8
9
10
11
12
13
14
15
16
17
18
19
ARCTIC OCEAN
Lapte v Sea
East Siberian Sea
Chukchi Sea
Bering Sea
Sea of Okhotsk
Sea of Japan
Ostrov Shmidta
Mys Arkticheskiy
Ostrov Komsomolets
Ostrov Pioner
Ostrov Oktyabrskoy Revolyutsii
965
Ostrov Bolshevik
Severnaya Zemlya
Proliv Vilkitskogo
Mys Chelyuskin
Poluostrov Taymyr
Byrranga Gory
1146
Oz. Taymyr
Ostrov Bolshoy Begichev
Nordvik
Novosibirskiye Ostrova
Ostrov Bennetta
Ostrov Genriyetty
Ostrov Zhannetty
Ostrova Delonga
Ostrov Zhokhova
Ostrov Faddeyevskiy
Ostrov Novaya Sibir
Ostrov Belkovskiy
Ostrov Kotelnyy
Ostrov Stolbovoy
Lyakhovskiye Ostrova
Ostrov Malyy Lyakhovskiy
Ostrov Bolshoy Lyakhovskiy
Proliv Dmitriya Lapteva
374
3800
Ostrov Vrangelya
Ostrova Medvezhi
Ostrov Ayon
Mys Dezhneva (East C.)
Uelen
St. Lawrence I. (U.S.A.)
Provideniya
Anadyrskiy Zaliv
Beringovskiy
Chukotskoye Nagorye
1843
Vankarem
Egvekinot
Pevek
Ust Chaun
Bilibino
1853
Cherskiy
Ambarchik
Anadyr
Nizhne Kolymsk
Bolshoy Anyuy
Olay
Yerepol
Markovo
Penzhino
Koryakskoye Nagorye
2562
Khatyrka
Kamenskoye
Tilichiki
Korf
Korvacha
Mys Buorkhaya
Tiksi
Ust Olenek
Tit-Ary
Olenek
Saskylakh
Khatanga
Novorybnoye
Pyasina
Volochanka
Kheta
Norilsk
Gory Putorana
1701
Yessey
Kotuy
Zhilinda
Olenek
Anabar
Bulun
Kyusyur
Kazachye
Ust Kuyga
Chokurdakh
Indigirka
Srednekolymsk
Deputatskiy
Druzhina
Yana
Batagai
Verkhoyansk
Verkhoyanskiy Khrebet
2389
Kystatyam
Zhigansk
Arctic Circle
962
Khrebet Cherskogo
Gora Chen
2682
Ust-Nera
Pobeda
3147
Zyryanka
Khonuu
Kolyma
Kolymskoye Nagorye
Omolon
Evensk
Nayakhan
Omsukchan
Orotukan
Taskan
Yagodnoye
Susuman
Atka
Palatka
Magadan
Ust-Omchug
Oymyakon
2959
Khandyga
Batamay
Songar
Lena
Borogontsy
Ytyk-Kyuyel
Okhotskiy Perevoz
Arka
Okhotsk
Ulya
Ust Maya
Mayya
Yakutsk
Amga
Namtsy
Pokrovsk
Vilyuysk
Verkhnevilyuysk
Vilyuy
Nyurba
Suntar
Mirnyy
Sinsk
Ust-Mil
Aim
Maya
Nelkan
Chernyshevskiy
Yukta
Tura
Noginsk
Nizhnyaya Tunguska
Yerbogachen
Lensk
Olekminsk
Tommot
Chagda
Uchur
Aldan
Aldan
2246
Khrebet Dzhugdzur
Ayan
Ostrov Bolshoy Shantar
Sakhalinskiy Zaliv
Okha
Sakhalin
Aleksandrovsk-Sakhalinskiy
1609
Gora Lopatina
Poronaysk
Uglegorsk
Yuzhno-Sakhalinsk
Kholmsk
Korsakov
Vanino
Nikolayevsk-na-Amur
Tugur
Chumikan
Uda
Stanovoy Khrebet
Neryungri
Nagornyy
Yenyuka
Chara
2999
Olekma
Vitim
Mama
Bodaybo
Kodar
Kalar
Kalakan
Tynda
Skovorodino
Zeya
Ushumun
Dzhalinda
Amur
Norsk
Selemdzha
Bureya
Komsomolsk
Amursk
2640
Khrebet Sikhote Alin
Khabarovsk
2078
Birobidzhan
Smidovich
Obluchye
Raychikhinsk
Zavitinsk
Belogorsk
Chegdomyn
Blagoveshchensk
Svobodnyy
Shimanovsk
Gulian
Poyarkovo
Bikin
Lesozavodsk
Dalnerechensk
Spassk Dalniy
Ussuriysk
Artem
Vladivostok
Nakhodka
Kraskino
Amgu
Terney
Olga
Dalnegorsk
Kuyumba
Mutoray
Vanavara
Podkamennaya Tunguska
Severo-Yeniseyskiy
1104
Kezhma
Korshunovo
Kirensk
Ust-Ilimsk
Ust-Kut
Makarovo
Magistralnyy
Boguchany
Kondratyevo
Angara
Yeniseysk
Zheleznogorsk-Ilimskiy
Chuna
Bratsk
Kansk
Ilanskiy
Tayshet
Krasnoyarsk
Nizhneudinsk
Tulun
Zima
Artemovsk
Abakan
Minusinsk
Vostochnyy Sayan
Zapadnyy Sayan
Cheremkhovo
Usolye Sibirskoye
Angarsk
Irkutsk
Munku-Sardyk
3491
Slyudyanka
Kyzyl
Turan
Toora-Khem
Ulan Ude
1620
Nizhneangarsk
2840
Barguzin
Bagdarin
Baykal
Yablonovyy Khrebet
Mogocha
Chita
Bukachacha
Sretensk
Nerchinsk
Shilka
Aginskoye
Petrovsk-Zabaykalskiy
Khilok
Olovyannaya
Borzya
Zabaykalsk
Gusinoozersk
Kyakhta
Zakamensk
Darhan
Hatgal
Hövsgöl Nuur
Uvs Nuur
Hangayn Nuruu
Hentiyn Nuruu
2800
Ulaanbaatar
Choybalsan
Tamsagbulag
Öndörhaan
Uliastay
Tsetserleg
Altay
MONGOLIA
Saynshand
Gobi
Dalandzadgad
3957
Erenhot
Hami
4266
Gaxun Nur
Baotou
Hohhot
Zhangjiakou
BEIJING
Chengde
Chifeng
Linxi
Xilinhot
1949
CHINA
Manzhouli
Hailar
Hulun Nur
Da Hinggan Ling
1054
Nenjiang
QIQIHAR
Hegang
Jiamusi
HARBIN
Mudanjiang
Dongbei
Ang'angxi
Nen Jiang
Tao'an
CHANGCHUN
JILIN
Yanji
Siping
FUSHUN
Tonghua
SHENYANG
ANSHAN
Dandong
Yingkou
DALIAN
NORTH KOREA
PYONGYANG
Nampo
Chongjin
Wonsan
Kansong
SOUL
INCH'ON
SOUTH KOREA
TAEJON
TAEGU
PUSAN
2744
Poluostrov Kamchatka
Sredinnyy Khrebet
Ust-Kamchatsk
Klyuchevskaya
4750
Petropavlovsk-Kamchatskiy
3621
3456
Komandorskiye Ostrova
Nikolskoye
Ossora
Ostrov Karaginskiy
Palana
Tigil
Zaliv Shelikhova
Gizhiginskaya Guba
Penzhinskaya Guba
Gizhiga
Paren
Ust Khayryuzovo
Kirovskiy
Ust-Bolsheretsk
1750
Severo-Kurilsk
Ostrov Paramushir
Ostrov Onekotan
Ostrov Simushir
Ostrov Urup
Kurilskiye Ostrova
Ostrov Iturup
Kurilsk
Ostrov Kunashir
Wakkanai
Rumoi
Asahikawa
2290
Abashiri
Kushiro
Obihiro
Otaru
SAPPORO
Hokkaidō
Hakodate
3669
Aomori
Hachinohe
Akita
Honshū
Niigata
Kanazawa
Fuji-San
3776
JAPAN
OSAKA
40
50
60
80
90
100
110
120
130
140
150
170

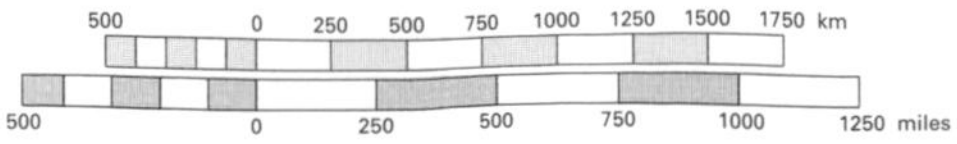
500 0 250 500 750 1000 1250 1500 1750 km
500 0 250 500 750 1000 1250 miles

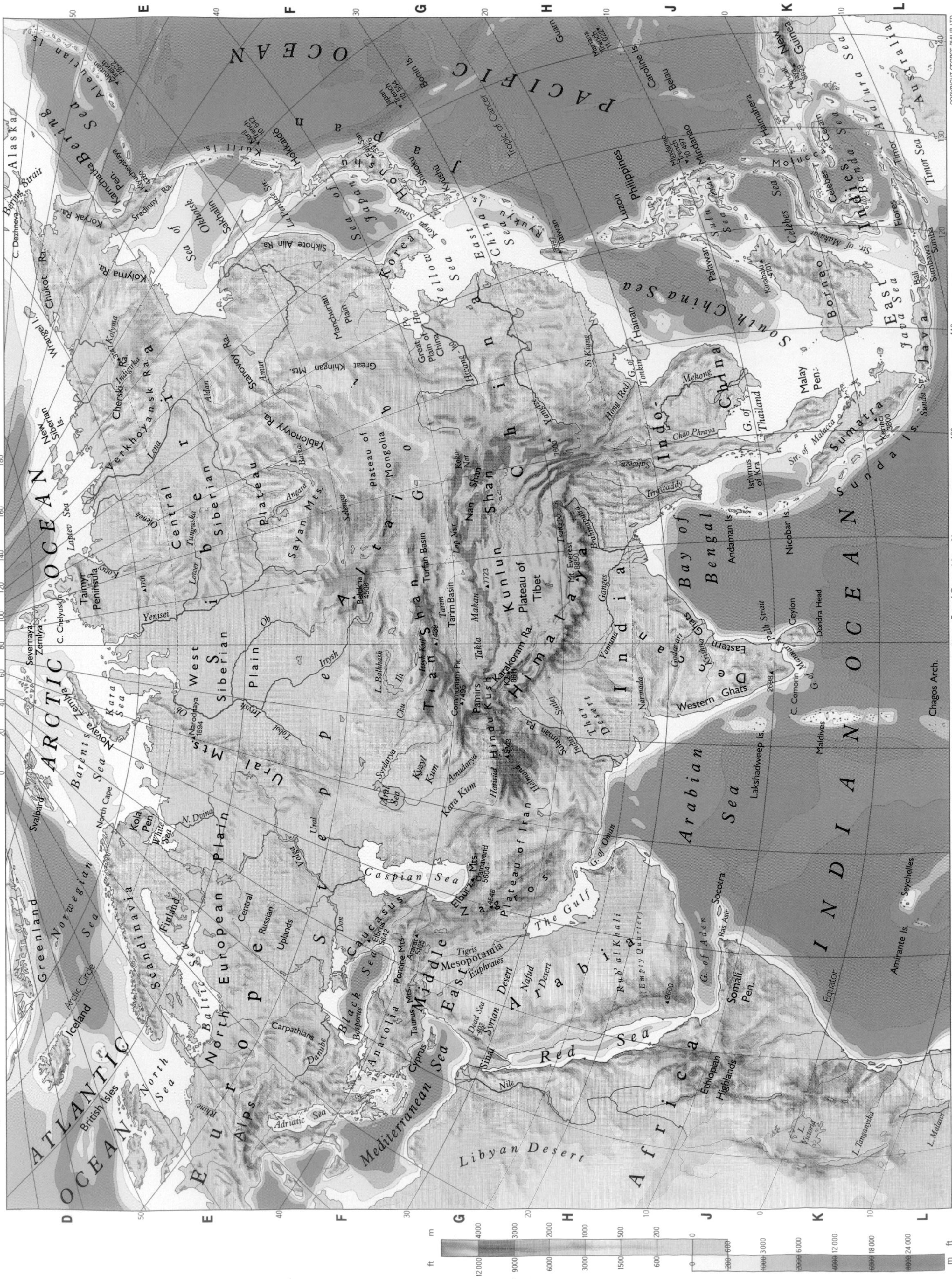
ARCTIC OCEAN
PACIFIC OCEAN
INDIAN OCEAN
ATLANTIC OCEAN
Bering Sea
Bering Strait
Sea of Okhotsk
Sea of Japan
Yellow Sea
East China Sea
South China Sea
Bay of Bengal
Arabian Sea
Caspian Sea
Black Sea
Mediterranean Sea
Red Sea
The Gulf
Aral Sea
Barents Sea
Kara Sea
Laptev Sea
Norwegian Sea
North Sea
Baltic Sea
White Sea
Java Sea
Banda Sea
Arafura Sea
Timor Sea
Celebes Sea
Sulu Sea
Molucca Sea
Alaska
Aleutian Is.
Kamchatka Pen.
Kuril Is.
Sakhalin
Hokkaido
Honshu
Kyushu
Shikoku
Japan
Korea
Taiwan
Hainan
Luzon
Philippines
Mindanao
Borneo
Celebes
Sumatra
Java
East Indies
New Guinea
Australia
Malay Pen.
Indo-China
Ceylon
Andaman Is.
Nicobar Is.
Maldives
Lakshadweep Is.
Chagos Arch.
Seychelles
Amirante Is.
Socotra
Somali Pen.
Ethiopian Highlands
Africa
Libyan Desert
Arabia
Syrian Desert
Nafud Desert
Rub' al Khali (Empty Quarter)
Middle East
Mesopotamia
Anatolia
Caucasus
Elburz Mts.
Plateau of Iran
Hindu Kush
Pamirs
Karakoram Ra.
Himalaya
Mt. Everest 8850
Plateau of Tibet
Kunlun Shan
Nan Shan
Tian Shan
Tarim Basin
Takla Makan
Turfan Basin
Gobi
Plateau of Mongolia
Altai
Sayan Mts.
Central Siberian Plateau
West Siberian Plain
Ural Mts.
Steppes
Siberia
Verkhoyansk Ra.
Cherski Ra.
Kolyma Ra.
Chukot Ra.
Koryak Ra.
Sredinnyy Ra.
Stanovoy Ra.
Yablonovyy Ra.
Great Khingan Mts.
Sikhote Alin Ra.
Manchurian Plain
Great Plain of China
China
India
Thar Desert
Western Ghats
Eastern Ghats
Deccan
Kara Kum
Kyzyl Kum
Europe
North European Plain
Central Russian Uplands
Scandinavia
Finland
Kola Pen.
Alps
Carpathians
British Isles
Iceland
Greenland
Svalbard
Novaya Zemlya
Severnaya Zemlya
Taimyr Peninsula
New Siberian Is.
Wrangel I.
C. Chelyuskin
C. Dezhneva
C. Comorin
Ob
Irtysh
Yenisei
Lena
Amur
Hwang Ho
Yangtze
Mekong
Ganges
Indus
Brahmaputra
Irrawaddy
Salween
Tigris
Euphrates
Nile
Volga
Ural
Don
Danube
L. Baikal
L. Balkhash
Cyprus
Sinai
Dead Sea
Arctic Circle
Tropic of Cancer
Equator
Projection: Bonne
East of Greenwich
COPYRIGHT GEORGE PHILIP LTD.

m 4000 3000 2000 1000 500 200 0 200 1000 2000 4000 6000 8000 m
ft 12 000 9000 6000 3000 1500 600 0 600 3000 6000 12 000 18 000 24 000 ft

500 0 250 500 750 1000 1250 1500 1750 km

500 0 250 500 750 1000 1250 miles

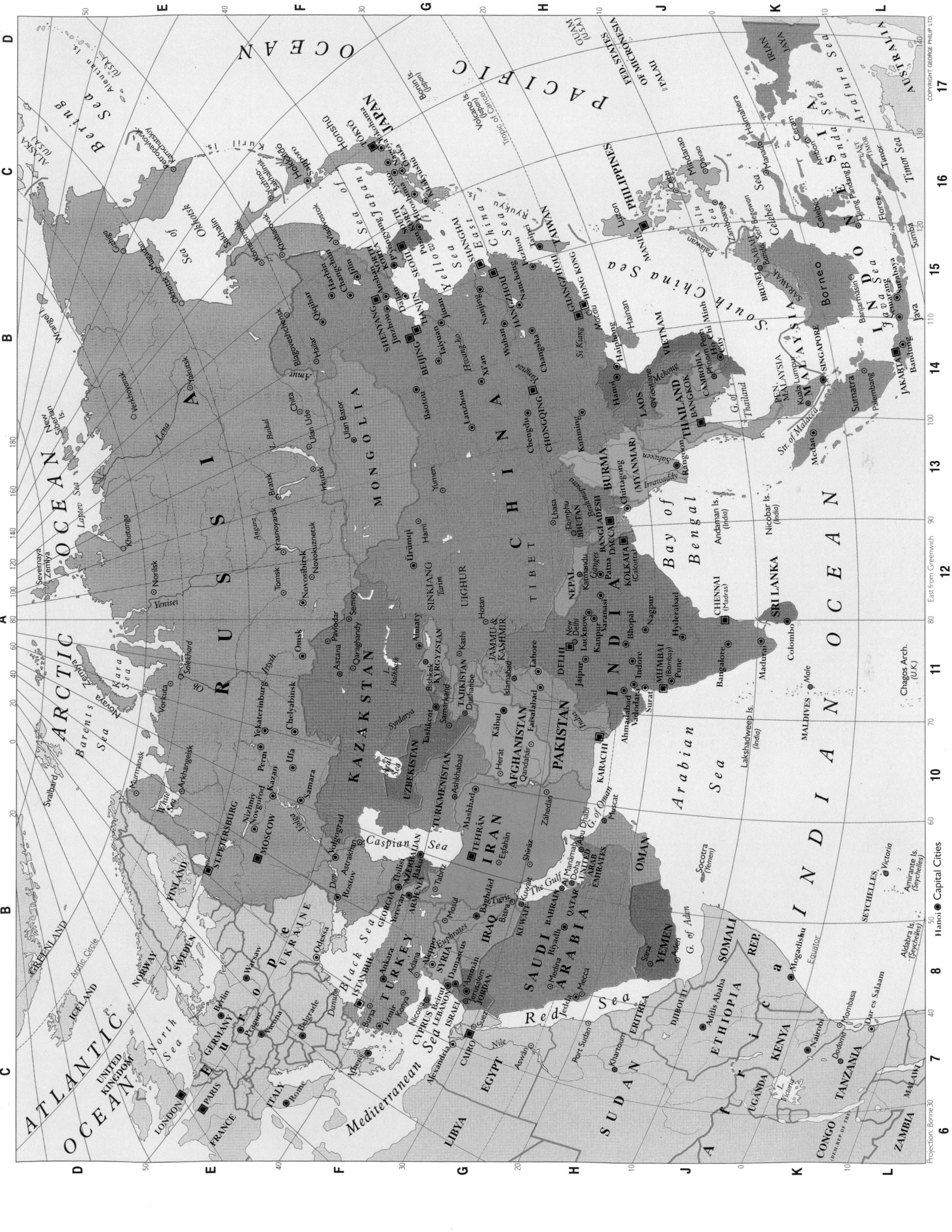

JAPAN 1:5 000 000

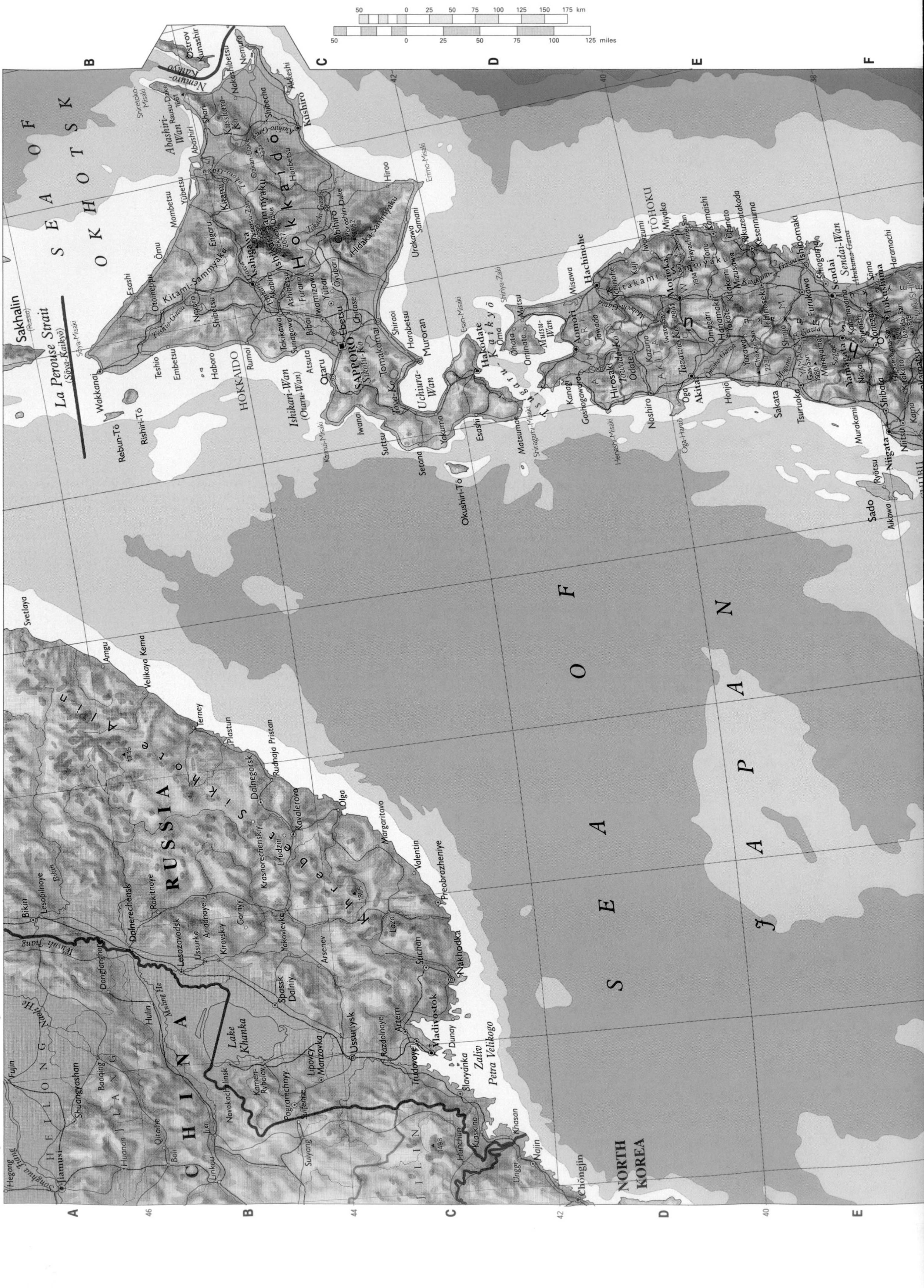
50 0 25 50 75 100 125 150 175 km
50 0 25 50 75 100 125 miles
SEA OF OKHOTSK
SEA OF JAPAN
Sakhalin (Russia)
La Perouse Strait (Sōya-Kaikyō)
Hokkaidō
HOKKAIDO
SAPPORO
Asahikawa
Kushiro
Obihiro
Hakodate
Otaru
Muroran
Tomakomai
Wakkanai
Abashiri
Nemuro
Rebun-Tō
Rishiri-Tō
Okushiri-Tō
Tsugaru-Kaikyō
TŌHOKU
Aomori
Hachinohe
Hirosaki
Morioka
Akita
Sendai
Sendai-Wan
Yamagata
Fukushima
Niigata
Sado
RUSSIA
CHINA
NORTH KOREA
Vladivostok
Nakhodka
Ussuriysk
Lake Khanka
Zaliv Petra Velikogo
Khasan
Chŏngjin
Jiamusi
Dalnerechensk
Olga
Terney
Svetlaya
Kunashir
Nemuro-Kaikyō

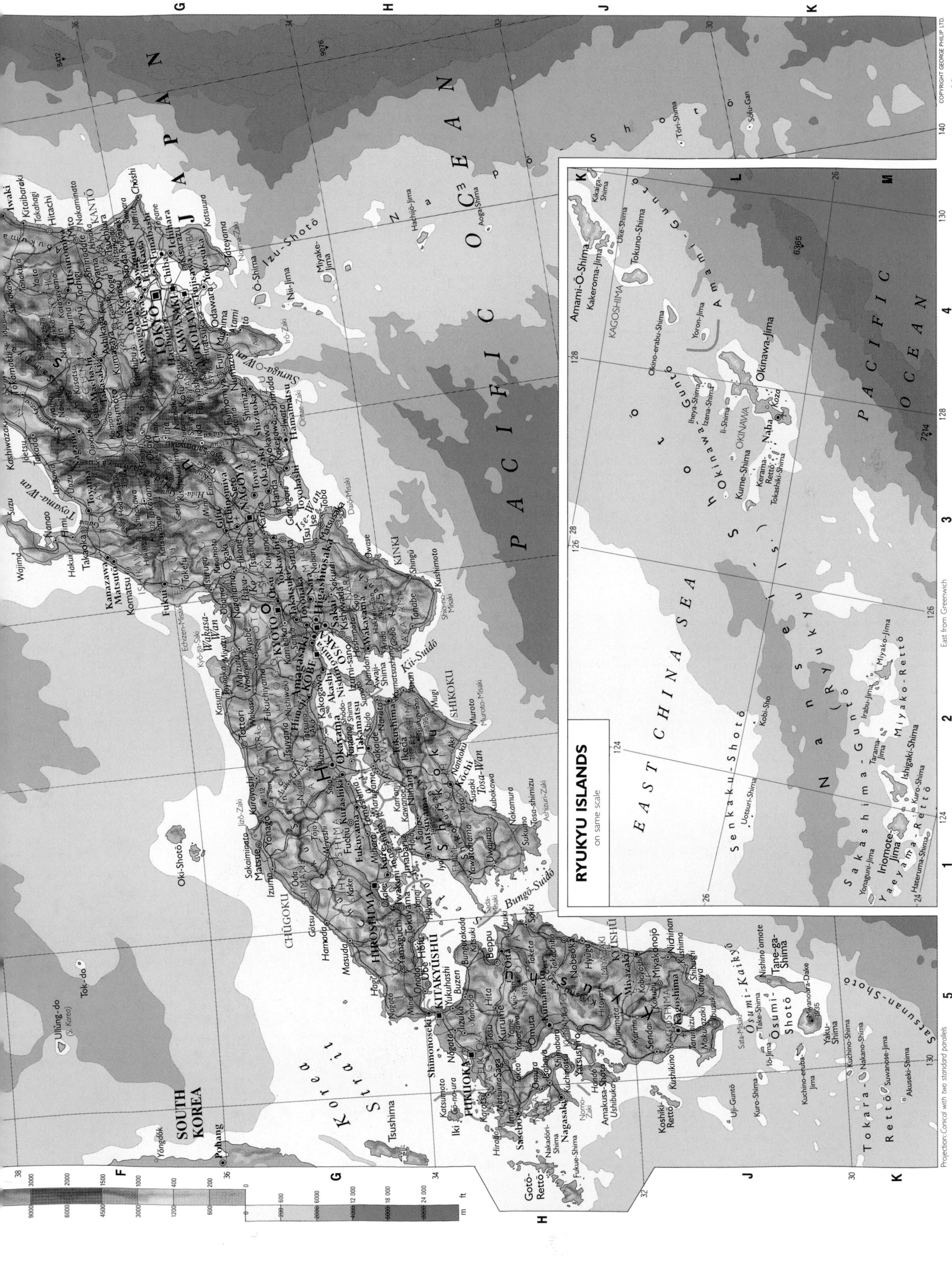

SOUTH KOREA
Korea Strait
PACIFIC OCEAN
EAST CHINA SEA
RYUKYU ISLANDS
on same scale
TOKYO
KYOTO
OSAKA
NAGOYA
KOBE
HIROSHIMA
KITAKYŪSHŪ
FUKUOKA
SHIKOKU
KYŪSHŪ
CHŪGOKU
KINKI
KANTŌ
Okinawa-Jima
Amami-Ō-Shima
Miyako-Rettō
Nansei-Shotō (Ryukyu-Rettō)
Projection: Conical with two standard parallels
East from Greenwich
COPYRIGHT GEORGE PHILIP LTD.

100 0 100 200 300 400 500 600 km
100 0 100 200 300 400 miles
KAZAKSTAN
RUSSIA
MONGOLIA
KYRGYZSTAN
Qaraghandy
Balqash Köl
Taldyqorghan
Bishkek
ALMATY
Ysyk-Köl
Tian Shan
Pik Pobedy 7439
Junggar Pendi
ÜRÜMQI
Turpan
Hami
Kuruktag
Tarim Pendi
XINJIANG UYGUR ZIZHIQU (SINKIANG)
Taklamakan Shamo
Kashi
Hotan
Lop Nur
Altun Shan
Aerhtai Shan (Altai)
Tannu Ola
Hangayn Nuruu
Ulaanbaatar
Qilian Shan
Qaidam Pendi
Kunlun Shan
QINGHAI
Xining
LANZHOU
Hoh Xil Shan
Bayan Har Shan
XIZANG ZIZHIQU (TIBET)
Tanggula (Dangla) Shan
Nyainqentanglha Shan
Lhasa
Aksai Chin
JAMMU & KASHMIR
Srinagar
Karakoram
K2
Zaskar Mts.
Great Himalaya
NEPAL
Katmandu
Mt. Everest 8850
BHUTAN
Thimphu
ARUNACHAL PRADESH
ASSAM
Brahmaputra
DELHI
New Delhi
Agra
KANPUR
LUCKNOW
UTTAR PRADESH
UTTARANCHAL
PATNA
VARANASI
BIHAR
INDIA
JHARKHAND
WEST BENGAL
KOLKATA (CALCUTTA)
BANGLADESH
DHAKA
CHITTAGONG
MEGHALAYA
Khasi Hills
Tropic of Cancer
MADHYA PRADESH
CHHATTISGARH
NAGPUR
ORISSA
Cuttack
BAY OF BENGAL
VISHAKHAPATNAM
BURMA (MYANMAR)
Mandalay
Kachin
Shan
THAILAND (SIAM)
LAOS
VIETNAM
HANOI
Haiphong
G. of Tonkin
KUNMING
CHENGDU
SICHUAN
GUIZHOU
GUIYANG
Zhaotong
Xiaguan
Dali
Lijiang
Panzhihua
NINGXIA HUIZU ZIZHIQU
Yinchuan
Wuhai
Hanzhong
Nanning
Projection: Bonne
East from Greenwich
1 2 3 4 5
B C D E

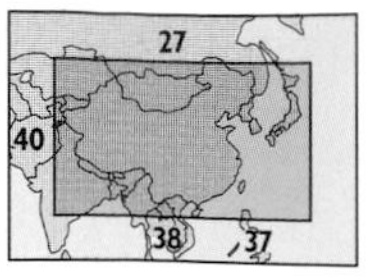
27
40
38
37

6
7
8
9
B
C
D
E
50
40
30
20
110
120
130
140
Oz. Baykal
Ulan Ude
Bukachacha
Chita
Sretensk
Nerchinsk
Olovyannaya
Borzya
Priargunsk
Manzhouli
Hulun Nur
Hailar
Buir Nur
Choybalsan
Kerulen
Tamsagbulag
Arxan
Solon
Gulian
Yilehuli Shan
Oroqen Zizhiqi
Shimanovsk
Svobodnyy
Chegdomyn
Amur
Komsomolsk
Aleksandrovsk-Sakhalinskiy
Blagoveshchensk
Aihui
Bureya
Ozero Bolon'
Birobidzhan
Khabarovsk
Obluchye
Nenjiang
Bei'an
Xiao Hinggan Ling
HEILONGJIANG
Yichun
Hegang
Jiamusi
Shuangyashan
Qianjin
Bikin
Khrebet Sikhote Alin
Vanino
Tartarskiy Proliv
Poronaysk
Mys Terpeniya
Sakhalin
Yuzhno-Sakhalinsk
Kholmsk
La Perouse Str.
Wakkanai
Kitami
Asahigawa
2290
Hokkaidō
Otaru
SAPPORO
Kushiro
Muroran
Erimo-misaki
Hakodate
Tsugaru-Kaikyō
Aomori
Hachinohe
Morioka
Akita
Ishinomaki
Sakata
Yamagata
Sendai
Sado
Niigata
Fukushima
Kōriyama
Jōetsu
Utsunomiya
Wajima
Mito
Toyama
Takaoka
Kanazawa
TŌKYŌ
KAWASAKI
YOKOHAMA
Komatsu
NAGOYA
Fuji-San
3776
Shizuoka
Hamamatsu
KYŌTO
ŌSAKA
KŌBE
Sakai
Wakayama
Okayama
HIROSHIMA
Shikoku
Kōchi
Matsuyama
Matsue
Shimonoseki
Kure
KITAKYUSHU
FUKUOKA
Sasebo
Nagasaki
Kumamoto
Kyūshū
Miyazaki
Kagoshima
Tane-ga-Shima
Yaku-Shima
Nampō-Shotō
Honshū
JAPAN
SEA OF JAPAN
Qiqihar
Daqing
Anda
Suihua
HARBIN
Jixi
Mishan
Hulin
L. Khanka
Horqin Youyi Qianqi
Shuangcheng
Baicheng
Tao'an
Fuyu
Mudanjiang
Ussuriysk
1855
Partizansk
Artem
Nakhodka
Vladivostok
Huolin Gol
Dongbei (Manchuria)
JILIN
CHANGCHUN
Shuangliao
Dunhua
Songhua Hu
Yanji
Hunchun
Saynshand
Xilinhot
1949
Linxi
Borhoyn Tal
Erenhot
Sonid Youqi
Tongliao
Siping
Liaoyuan
Changbei Shan
Baihe
Chŏngjin
Kimchaek
Duolun
Chifeng
Fuxin
Tieling
FUSHUN
SHENYANG
Benxi
Tonghua
Sayan Obo
MONGGOL ZIZHIQU (INNER MONGOLIA)
Hohhot
Jining
Zhangjiakou
Chengde
Chaoyang
Jinzhou
Liaoyang
ANSHAN
LIAONING
Yingkou
Dandong
Yalu Jiang
NORTH KOREA
Hamhung
Hŭngnam
Wŏnsan
Baotou
Datong
Xuanhua
BEIJING (PEKING)
BEIJING SHI
Qinhuangdao
Liaodong Wan
Liaodong Bandao
Korea Bay
P'YŎNGYANG
Nampo
TANGSHAN
TIANJIN SHI
TIANJIN
Anci
Baoding
3058
Yuanping
HEBEI
DALIAN
Haeju
Kaesŏng
Ch'unch'ŏn
Kangnŭng
SŎUL (SEOUL)
SOUTH KOREA
INCH'ŎN
TAIYUAN
SHIJIAZHUANG
Cangzhou
Bo Hai
Yangquan
Yantai
Weihai
Shandong Bandao
Dezhou
Ye Xian
Weifang
Fenyang
Yuci
JINAN
Huang He
ZIBO
SHANDONG
QINGDAO
YELLOW SEA
TAEJŎN
TAEGU
PUSAN
Kunsan
Chŏnju
KWANGJU
Masan
Mokp'o
1915
Handan
Anyang
Tai'an
Changzhi
Linfen
Rizhao
Jining
Jincheng
Xinxiang
Tsushima
Korea Strait
Cheju-do
1950
Tongchuan
Luoyang
Kaifeng
Zaozhuang
Lianyungang
Sanmenxia
ZHENGZHOU
Shangqiu
Grand Canal
Xuzhou
Qingjiang
Yancheng
XI'AN
HENAN
Huaibei
Pingdingshan
Shangshui
Fuyang
Bengbu
Taizhou
Nanyang
Han Shui
Zhumadian
Huainan
Huai He
Yangzhou
NANJING
Changzhou
Nantong
JIANGSU
Shiyan
Xinyang
HEFEI
Wuxi
Suzhou
SHANGHAI SHI
SHANGHAI
Ankang
Xiangfan
Dabie Shan
ANHUI
Ma'anshan
Wuhu
Zhongxiang
Tongling
Wuxing
Jiaxing
HANGZHOU
Hangzhou Wan
HUBEI
WUHAN
Yichang
Huangshi
Anqing
Chang Jiang (Yangtse)
Shaoxing
NINGBO
Enshi
Shashi
Tunxi
ZHEJIANG
EAST CHINA SEA
Yueyang
Jiujiang
Jingdezhen
Jinhua
LINHAI
Changde
Dongting Hu
Poyang Hu
Quzhou
NANCHANG
Shangrao
Wenzhou
Yiyang
CHANGSHA
JIANGXI
Wuyi Shan
2120
HUNAN
Xiangtan
Pingxiang
Linchuan
Shaoyang
Ji'an
Nanping
Hengyang
Min Jiang
Hongjiang
Sanming
FUZHOU
Ganzhou
Yong'an
FUJIAN
Xing'an
Ruijin
Putian
Quanzhou
Longyan
Zhangzhou
Nan Ling
Shaoguan
Guilin
Mei Xian
Xiamen
Chaozhou
Shantou
GUANGDONG
Wuzhou
GUANGZHOU (CANTON)
Foshan
Huizhou
Zhaoqing
Jiangmen
HONG KONG
Macau
Yangjiang
Maoming
Zhanjiang
Qiongzhou Haixia
Haikou
Hainan Dao
1879
HAINAN
Yacheng
Taiwan Strait
Chilung
T'AIPEI
Hsinchu
T'aichung
Changhua
Chiai
Yu Shan
3997
TAIWAN (FORMOSA)
T'ainan
T'aitung
P'ingtung
KAOHSIUNG
Batan Is.
PHILIPPINES
Babuyan Is.
SOUTH CHINA SEA
Amami-Ō-Shima
Tokuno-Shima
Ryūkyū-rettō
Okinawa-Jima
Naha
7507
Sakishima-Guntō
Miyako-Jima
Ishigaki-Shima
Iriomote-Jima
Tropic of Cancer
PACIFIC OCEAN

NORTHERN CHINA AND KOREA 1:6 000 000

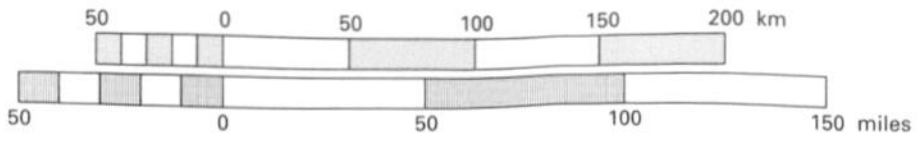

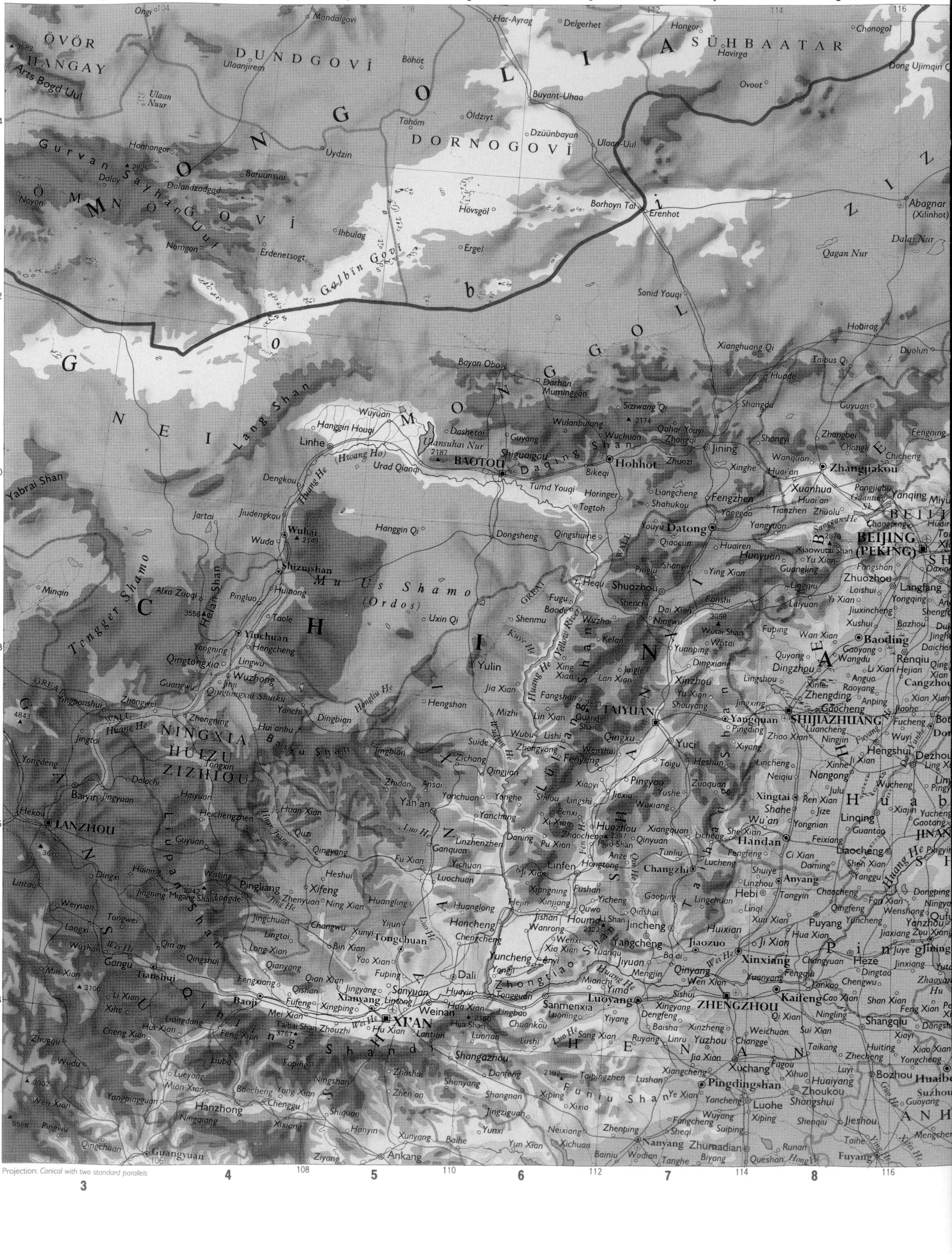

Projection: Conical with two standard parallels

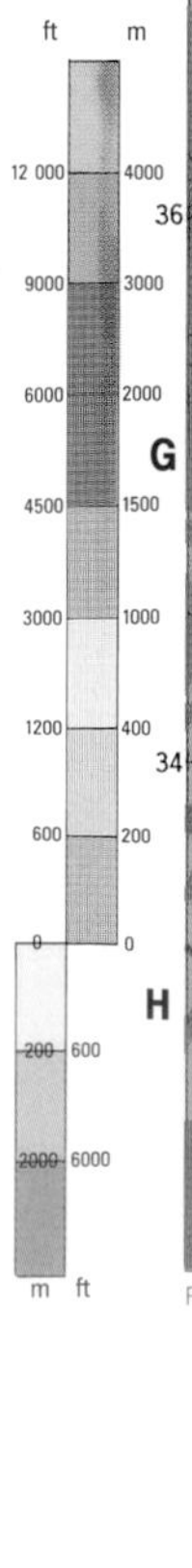

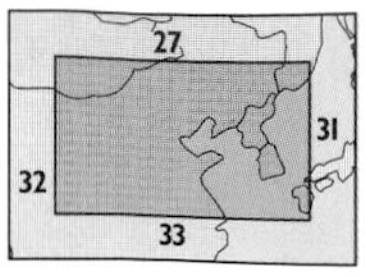
27
31
32
33

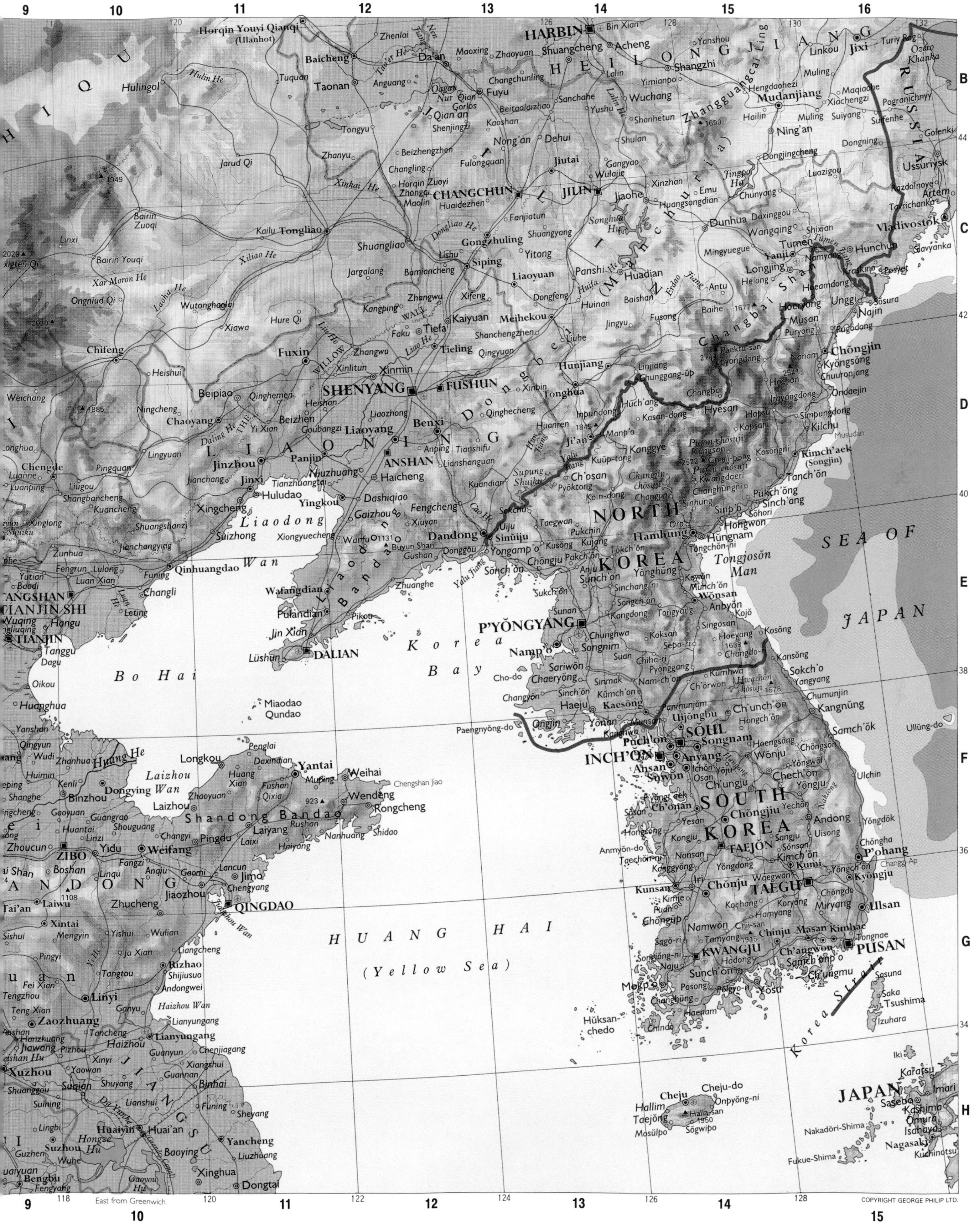
9
10
11
12
13
14
15
16
B
C
D
E
F
G
H
44
42
40
38
36
34
118
120
122
124
126
128
130
132
East from Greenwich
COPYRIGHT GEORGE PHILIP LTD.
HARBIN
Bin Xian
Acheng
Shuangcheng
Zhaoyuan
Maoxing
Zhenlai
Da'an
Baicheng
Horqin Youyi Qianqi
(Ulanhot)
Tuquan
Taonan
Anguang
Hulingol
Huolin He
Qagan Nur
Qian Gorlos
Fuyu
Qian'an
Shenjingzi
Tongyu
Changchunling
Sanchahe
Beitaalaizhao
Kaoshan
Nong'an
Dehui
Fulongquan
Jiutai
Beizhengzhen
Zhanyu
Changling
Jarud Qi
Horqin Zuoyi Zhongqi
Maolin
Huaidezhen
CHANGCHUN
JILIN
Xinkai He
Bairin Zuoqi
Kailu
Tongliao
Linxi
Bairin Youqi
Xiliao He
Xar Moron He
Ongniud Qi
Lauha He
Wutonghaolai
Xiawa
Hure Qi
Chifeng
Heishui
Fuxin
Beipiao
Qinghemen
Weichang
Ningcheng
Chaoyang
Dalinghe
Yi Xian
Beizhen
Goubangzi
Heishan
SHENYANG
FUSHUN
Xinmin
Xinlitun
Zhangwu
Tieling
Kaiyuan
Tiefa
Faku
Liao He
Zhangwu
Kangping
Shuangliao
Jargalang
Bamiancheng
Lishu
Siping
Gongzhuling
Fanjiatun
Shuangyang
Yitong
Liaoyuan
Dongfeng
Xifeng
Meihekou
Shanchengzhen
Qingyuan
Liuhe
Hunjiang
Tonghua
Xinbin
Qinghecheng
Huanren
Benxi
Liaoyang
Liaozhong
ANSHAN
Anping
Tianshifu
Lianshanguan
Haicheng
Niuzhuang
Panjin
Jinzhou
Lingyuan
Chengde
Luanne
Luanping
Pingquan
Liugou
Shangbancheng
Kuancheng
Jianchang
Jinxi
Tianzhuangtai
Huludao
Xingcheng
Yingkou
Dashiqiao
Gaizhou
Xiuyan
Fengcheng
Kuandian
Supung Shuiku
Dandong
Sinŭiju
Uiju
Yongamp'o
Wanfu
Buyun Shan
Gushan
Donggou
Zhuanghe
Pikou
Wafangdian
Pulandian
Jin Xian
Lüshun
DALIAN
Suizhong
Xiongyuecheng
Jianchangying
Shuangshanzi
Xinglong
Zunhua
Fengrun
Lulong
Funing
Qinhuangdao
Changli
Leting
Luan Xian
Yutian
Baodi
TANGSHAN
TIANJIN SHI
Wuqing
Hangu
TIANJIN
Tanggu
Dagu
Oikou
Huanghua
Yanshan
Qingyun
Wudi
Zhanhua
Huimin
Kenli
Binzhou
Dongying
Gaoyuan
Guangrao
Huantai
Linzi
Shouguang
ZIBO
Zhoucun
Yidu
Weifang
Changyi
Pingdu
Laixi
Boshan
Linqu
Anqiu
Gaomi
Jimo
Chengyang
Jiaozhou
Laiwu
Zhucheng
QINGDAO
Jiaozhou Wan
Xintai
Mengyin
Yishui
Wulian
Ju Xian
Rizhao
Liangcheng
Tangtou
Shijiusuo
Andongwei
Linyi
Fei Xian
Tengzhou
Teng Xian
Zaozhuang
Ganyu
Haizhou Wan
Lianyungang
Haizhou
Tancheng
Pizhou
Xuzhou
Xinyi
Yaowan
Guanyun
Guannan
Chenjiagang
Xiangshui
Binhai
Suqian
Shuyang
Shuanggou
Suining
Lianshui
Funing
Sheyang
Lingbi
Huaiyin
Huai'an
Hongze Hu
Suzhou
Wuhe
Baoying
Yancheng
Liuzhuang
Xinghua
Guzhen
Bengbu
Fengyang
Gaoyou Hu
Dongtai
Huang He
Laizhou Wan
Laizhou
Zhaoyuan
Huang Xian
Longkou
Penglai
Daxindian
Yantai
Muping
Weihai
Chengshan Jiao
Fushan
Qixia
Wendeng
Rongcheng
Laiyang
Rushan
Haiyang
Nanhuang
Shidao
Shandong Bandao
Miaodao Qundao
Bo Hai
Liaodong Wan
Liaodong Bandao
Korea Bay
HUANG HAI
(Yellow Sea)
HEILONGJIANG
JILIN
LIAONING
Dongbei
Manchuria
Zhangguangcai Ling
Changbai Shan
Yanshou
Shangzhi
Linkou
Jixi
Turiy Rog
Ozero Khanka
Lalin
Yimianpo
Hengdaohezi
Mudanjiang
Muling
Maqiaohe
Xiachengzi
Pogranichnyy
Wuchang
Yushu
Shanhetun
Shulan
Hailin
Ning'an
Muling
Suiyang
Suifenhe
Golenki
Dongning
Dongjingcheng
Ussuriysk
Gangyao
Wulajie
Jingpo Hu
Luozigou
Razdolnoye
Artem
Tavrichanka
Xinzhan
Jiaohe
Emu
Huangsongdian
Chunyang
Songhua Hu
Dunhua
Daxinggou
Wangqing
Shixian
Vladivostok
Slavyanka
Tumen
Yanji
Namyang
Mingyuegue
Longjing
Helong
Hunchun
Kraskino
Posyet
Panshi
Huadian
Erdao Jiang
Antu
Huifa He
Huinan
Baishan
Sosura
Hoeamdong
Unggi
Najin
Hoeryong
Musan
Puryong
Rajin
Baihe
Jingyu
Fusong
Paektu-san
2744
Sinpyongdong
Nanam
Chŏngjin
Kyŏngsŏng
Chuuronjang
Linjiang
Chunggang-ŭp
Changbai
Hyesan
Hoechon
Irhyangdong
Ondaejin
Hapsu
Simpungdong
Kilchu
Huch'ang
Kapsan
Kasan-dong
Inpundong
Manp'o
Ji'an
Kanggye
Pujon-chosuji
Chosan
Kimch'aek
(Songjin)
Kosŏngni
Tanch'ŏn
Changjin-chosuji
Kwangdaeri
Pyŏktong
Kuup-tong
Koin-dong
Chongjin
Changhungni
Pukch'ŏng
Sinch'ang
Sinhung
Sinp'o
Sohori
Hongwon
Hamhung
Hungnam
Tongchon-ni
NORTH KOREA
Oro
Pukchin
Taegwan
Sakchu
Kusong
Kujang
Tokch'ŏn
Chongju
Pakch'ŏn
Anju
Yŏnghung
Sunch'on
Sinchang-ni
Kowŏn
Munch'ŏn
Wŏnsan
Anbyŏn
Kojŏ
Tongjosŏn Man
Sŏnch'ŏn
Sukch'ŏn
Songch'ŏn
Kangdong
Tongyang
Sunan
P'YŎNGYANG
Chunghwa
Songnim
Koksan
Sepo-ri
Singosan
Hoeyang
Kosŏng
Changdo-ri
Kansŏng
Sokch'o
Yangyang
Nampo
Suan
Chiha-ri
Pyonggang
Kumhwa
Hwacheon-chosuji
Sariwŏn
Chaeryŏng
Cho-do
Sinmak
Nam-ch'ŏn
Ch'orwon
Sinch'ŏn
Kumch'on
Changyon
Haeju
Kaesŏng
Panmunjom
Uijŏngbu
Ch'unch'ŏn
Hongch'ŏn
Chumunjin
Kangnŭng
Samch'ŏk
Ullŭng-do
Paengnyŏng-do
Ongjin
Yonan
Kanghwa
Munsan
SOUL
Songnam
Inch'ŏn
Puch'ŏn
INCH'ON
Ansan
Suwon
Anyang
Ich'on
Yoju
Osan
Heongsŏng
Wŏnju
Chongson
Yongwol
Chech'on
Yongju
Ulchin
Ch'ungju
P'yongt'aek
Ch'ŏnan
SOUTH KOREA
Chongju
Yechon
Andong
Yongdok
Sosan
Yesan
Kongju
TAEJŎN
Sangju
Uisong
Chongha
P'ohang
Changgi-Ap
Hongsong
Anmyon-do
Taech'ŏn-ni
Nonsan
Kanggyong
Kimch'ŏn
Kumi
Yongch'ŏn
Kyongju
Iri
Chŏnju
Kunsan
Kimje
Waegwan
TAEGU
Chongdo
Miryang
Ulsan
Puan
Chongup
Namwon
Kochang
Koryong
Hamyang
Chiri-san
1915
Chinju
Masan
Kimhae
Tongnae
PUSAN
Songjong-ni
KWANGJU
Naju
Hadong
Ch'angwon
Samch'onp'o
Ch'ungmu
Sunch'on
Mokp'o
Posong
Polgyo-ri
Yosu
Changhung
Haenam
Chindo
Huksan-chedo
Korea Strait
Sasuna
Saka
Tsushima
Izuhara
Iki
Karatsu
Imari
Sasebo
Kashima
Omura
Isahaya
Nagasaki
Kuchinotsu
Nakadori-Shima
Fukue-Shima
JAPAN
Cheju
Cheju-do
Onpyong-ni
Hallim
Halla-san
1950
Taejŏng
Mosulpo
Sŏgwipo
SEA OF JAPAN
RUSSIA
1949
2029
2020
1885
1845
1690
1677
2522
1131
1108
923
1638
1578
Xigten Qi
Chengde
Tangshan
Luan He
Dalling He
Yalu Jiang
Tumen Jiang
Liao He
Liu He
Ji'an
Hun Jiang
Yellow Sea

INDONESIA AND THE PHILIPPINES 1:12 500 000

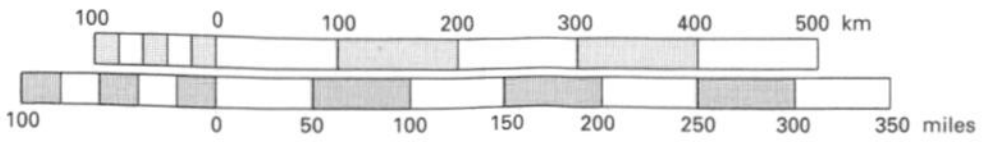

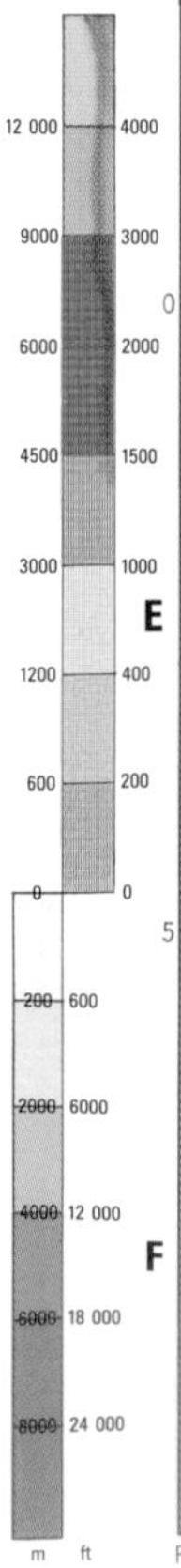

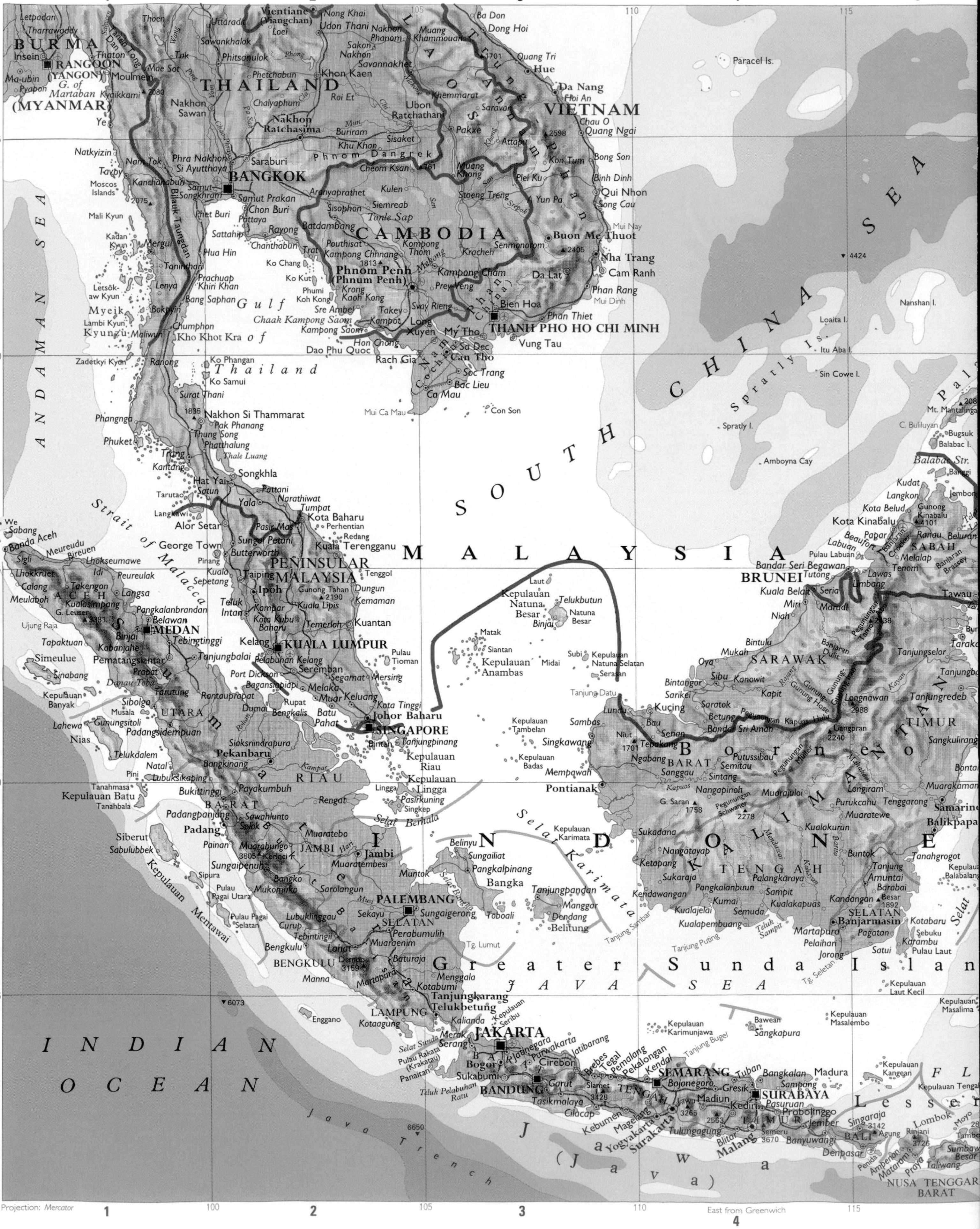

BURMA (MYANMAR)
RANGOON (YANGON)
THAILAND
BANGKOK
LAOS
VIETNAM
CAMBODIA
Phnom Penh (Phnum Penh)
THANH PHO HO CHI MINH
Vientiane (Viangchan)
Hue
Da Nang
Gulf of Thailand
SOUTH CHINA SEA
ANDAMAN SEA
Strait of Malacca
MALAYSIA
PENINSULAR MALAYSIA
KUALA LUMPUR
SINGAPORE
BRUNEI
Bandar Seri Begawan
SARAWAK
SABAH
Kota Kinabalu
Paracel Is.
Spratly Is.
Borneo
KALIMANTAN
Sumatera
MEDAN
Padang
PALEMBANG
JAKARTA
BANDUNG
SEMARANG
SURABAYA
JAVA SEA
Jawa (Java)
Java Trench
INDIAN OCEAN
Greater Sunda Islands
Lesser
Pontianak
Banjarmasin
Balikpapan
Projection: Mercator
East from Greenwich

JAVA AND MADURA
1 : 7 500 000
50 0 50 100 150 200 250 300 km
50 0 50 100 150 200 miles
JAKARTA
Bogor
BANDUNG
SEMARANG
Yogyakarta
SURABAYA
Surakarta
Malang
Madura
Kepulauan Karimunjawa
Bawean
Sangkapura
Bali
Nusa Barung
Selat Sunda
Selat Madura
BARAT
TENGAH
TIMUR
PACIFIC
OCEAN
FEDERATED STATES OF MICRONESIA
Ulithi Atoll
Yap
Ngulu Atoll
Sorol Atoll
Caroline Islands
PALAU
Babelthuap
Koror
Angaur
Sonsorol Islands
Pulo-Anna
Merir
Tobi
Helen Atoll
Equator
Mindanao Trench
PHILIPPINES
Luzon
QUEZON CITY
MANILA
Mindoro
Sibuyan Sea
Visayan Sea
Samar
Leyte
Tacloban
Panay
Iloilo
Negros
Cebu
Bohol
Bohol Sea
Mindanao
Davao
Zamboanga
Cagayan de Oro
Cotabato
General Santos
SULU SEA
Sulu Arch.
Jolo
CELEBES SEA
MOLUCCA SEA
Manado
Halmahera
Morotai
Ternate
Sulawesi (Celebes)
UTARA
TENGAH
SELATAN
TENGGARA
Teluk Tomini
Teluk Tolo
Teluk Bone
Makasar
Ujung Pandang
Kendari
Buton
Buru
Seram (Ceram)
Ambon
SERAM SEA
BANDA SEA
Kepulauan Banda
Kepulauan Kai
Kepulauan Aru
Kepulauan Tanimbar
Yamdena
Jazirah Doberai
Manokwari
Biak
Teluk Cenderawasih
IRIAN JAYA
Pegunungan Maoke
Pegunungan Van Rees
Jayapura
Puncak Jaya
Puncak Mandala
PAPUA NEW GUINEA
Merauke
Pulau Dolak
ARAFURA SEA
FLORES SEA
Flores
Sunda Is.
Sumba
Sawu Sea
Timor
Dili
EAST TIMOR
Kupang
Roti
Sawu
NUSA TENGGARA TIMUR
Wetar
Alor
COPYRIGHT GEORGE PHILIP LTD.

50 0 50 100 150 200 km
50 0 50 100 150 miles
G. of Tonkin
HAINAN
THAILAND
LAOS
CAMBODIA
BURMA (MYANMAR)
CHINA
YUNNAN
GUANGXI ZHUANGZU ZIZHIQU
GUANGDONG
Hanoi
Haiphong
Vientiane (Viangchan)
Luang Prabang
BANGKOK
Mandalay
RANGOON (YANGON)
Moulmein
Da Nang
Hue
Nakhon Ratchasima
Chiang Mai
Mekong
Salween
Phnom Dangrek
Dawna Range
TENASSERIM
Cao Nguyen Khorat
Tran Ninh
Boloven

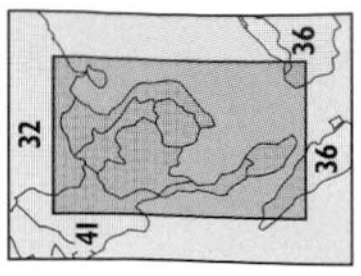

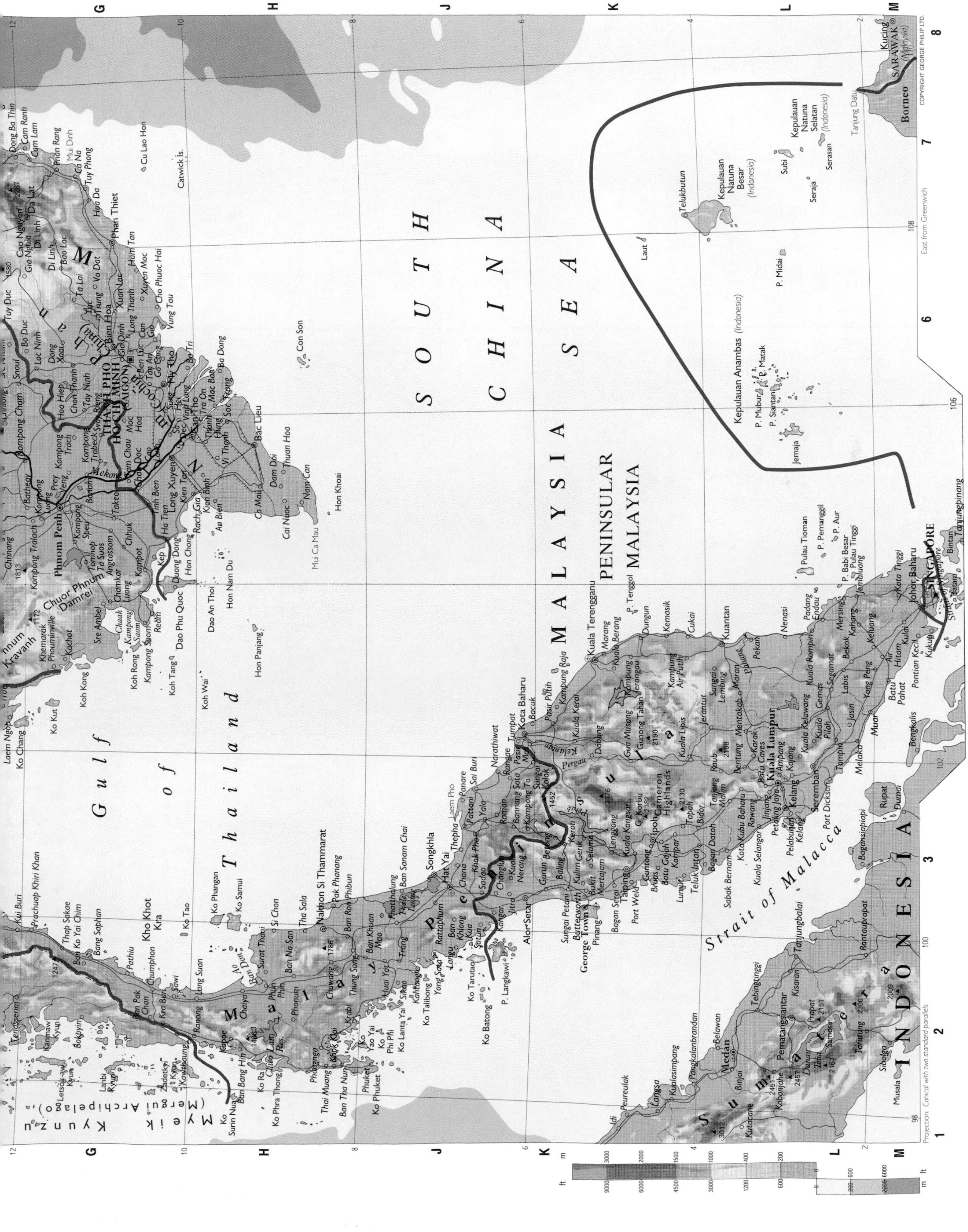

SOUTH CHINA SEA
Gulf of Thailand
MALAYSIA
PENINSULAR MALAYSIA
INDONESIA
Strait of Malacca
THANH PHO HO CHI MINH (SAIGON)
Phnom Penh
Kuala Lumpur
SINGAPORE
Kota Baharu
Kuala Terengganu
Kuantan
Johor Baharu
Songkhla
Hat Yai
Nakhon Si Thammarat
Medan
George Town
Alor Setar
Ipoh
Melaka
Seremban
Kepulauan Anambas (Indonesia)
Kepulauan Natuna Besar (Indonesia)
Kepulauan Natuna Selatan (Indonesia)
Borneo
SARAWAK (Malaysia)
Kucing
Con Son
Phan Thiet
Bac Lieu
Ca Mau
Sumatera
Projection: Conical with two standard parallels
East from Greenwich
COPYRIGHT GEORGE PHILIP LTD.

SOUTH ASIA 1:10 000 000

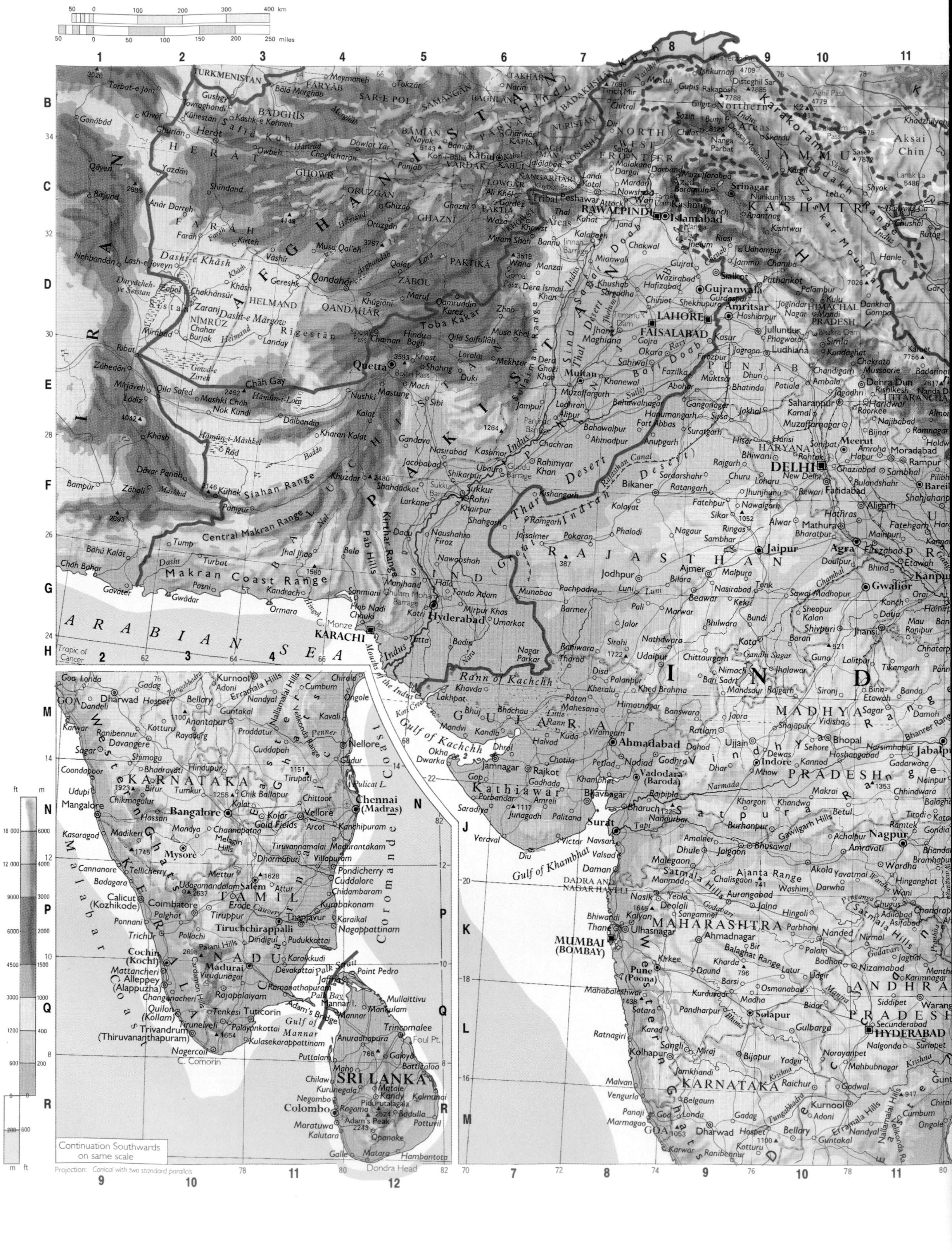

TURKMENISTAN
AFGHANISTAN
PAKISTAN
IRAN
INDIA
SRI LANKA
ARABIAN SEA
Hindu Kush
Karakoram
JAMMU & KASHMIR
Aksai Chin
NORTH WEST FRONTIER
Tribal Areas
PUNJAB
HARYANA
HIMACHAL PRADESH
UTTARANCHAL
RAJASTHAN
GUJARAT
MADHYA PRADESH
MAHARASHTRA
ANDHRA PRADESH
KARNATAKA
GOA
KERALA
TAMIL NADU
SIND
BALUCHISTAN
Thar or Great Indian Desert
Makran Coast Range
Central Makran Range
Siahan Range
Kirthar Range
Sulaiman Range
Toba Kakar
Safid Kuh
Dasht-e Khash
Dasht-e Margow
Rigestan
Rann of Kachchh
Gulf of Kachchh
Gulf of Khambhat
Kathiawar
Satpura Range
Vindhya Range
Ajanta Range
Western Ghats
Eastern Ghats
Malabar Coast
Coromandel Coast
Palk Strait
Gulf of Mannar
Adam's Bridge
Mouths of the Indus
Indus
Kabul
Islamabad
RAWALPINDI
Peshawar
LAHORE
FAISALABAD
Gujranwala
Multan
Quetta
Hyderabad
KARACHI
Srinagar
Amritsar
DELHI
Jaipur
Agra
Gwalior
Ahmadabad
Surat
Vadodara (Baroda)
Indore
Bhopal
Nagpur
MUMBAI (BOMBAY)
Pune (Poona)
Solapur
HYDERABAD
Bangalore
Mysore
Chennai (Madras)
Madurai
Cochin (Kochi)
Trivandrum (Thiruvananthapuram)
Colombo
Kandy
Jaffna
Herat
Qandahar
Zahedan
Tropic of Cancer
Dondra Head
Continuation Southwards on same scale
Projection: Conical with two standard parallels
50 0 100 200 300 400 km
50 0 50 100 150 200 250 miles

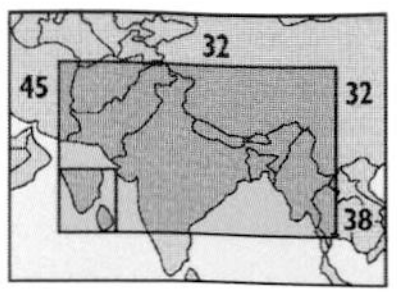
45
32
32
38

C H I N A
X I Z A N G
Z I Z H I Q U
(T I B E T)
Q I N G H A I
Huh Xil Shan
Bayan Har Shan
Tanggula (Dangla) Shan
Nyainqentanglha Shan
Kangri
Tanggula Shankou
Dogai Coring
Siling Co
Nam Co
Gyaring Co
Gyaring Hu
Ngoring Hu
Yushu
Dainkog
Nangqen
Garzê
Gamtog
Baiyü
Qamdo
Xinlong
Baqên
Dêngqên
Nagqu
Ombu
Coqên
Xainza
Lhari
Lhorong
Zhaxizê
Nu Jiang
S I C H U A N
Yajiang
Yidun
Litang
Lhünzhub
Gongbo'gyamda
Ningjing
Gogên
Lhasa
Riga
Muli Zangzu Zizhixian
Zhongba
Saga
Xigazê
Gyangzê
Lhazê
Nang Xian
Maquan He (Tsangpo)
Yarlung Zangbo Jiang
Mainkung
Zhongdian
Mustang
Gamba
Comai
Cona
Lhünzê
Nizamghat
Minutang
Dinggyê
Weixi
Lijiang
Mt. Everest
N E P A L
Nepalganj
Nuwakot
Gurkha
Nawakot
Katmandu
Bhaktapur
Dhaulagiri
Jumla
Simikot
Mugu
Jarwa
Nautanwa
Siwalik Range
Kanchenjunga
SIKKIM
Thimphu
Gangtok
Punakha
B H U T A N
Tongsa Dzong
Taga Dzong
Darjiling
Jaigaon
ARUNACHAL PRADESH
Tinsukia
Dibrugarh
North Lakhimpur
Sibsagar
Putao
Kawngtim
Konglu
Jianchuan
Bumhpa Bum
Patkai Bum
Hukawng Valley
KACHIN
Maingkwan
Yunlong
Dergaon
Jorhat
Tezpur
Rangia
Barpeta
Mairabari
Gauhati
Nowgong
Silghat
A S S A M
Brahmaputra
Kohima
NAGALAND
Mokokchung
Singkaling Hkamti
Myitkyina
Mogaung
Sadon
Baoshan
Y U N N A N
Tengchong
Longling
Changning
Lucknow
Faizabad
Gonda
Basti
Gorakhpur
Deoria
Bettiah
Raxaul
Birganj
Motihari
Darbhanga
Muzaffarpur
Siwan
Chhapra
Bankipore
Patna
Munger
Bhagalpur
Purnia
Kishanganj
Saidpur
Dhuburi
Kurigram
Rangpur
Shillong
MEGHALAYA
Cherrapunji
Tura
Barail Range
Haflong
Silchar
Sylhet
Ukhrul
Imphal
MANIPUR
Homalin
Chindwin
Allahabad
Varanasi
Ghazipur
Arrah
Jaunpur
Azamgarh
Sultanpur
Mirzapur
Sasaram
Gaya
Bihar
Jamalpur
Jehanabad
Aurangabad
Deoghar
Dinajpur
Ingraj Bazar
Bogra
Sirajganj
Mymensingh
SYLHET
Churachandpur
Thaungdut
Tamu
Indaw
Katha
Shwegu
Bhamo
Tropic of Cancer
Man Na
Kunlong
Hsenwi
Pang-Long
Rajshahi
Pabna
DHAKA
East Bengal
B A N G L A D E S H
TRIPURA
Agartala
Comilla
Chandpur
Kushtia
Jessore
Khulna
Barisal
Bhola
Madaripur
Narayanganj
Hatia
Lala Ghat
Kolasib
Aizawl
Sairang
MIZORAM
Lunglei
Dighinala
Tiddim
Falam
Kalewa
SAGAING
Mawlaik
Kyunhla
Wuntho
Tigyaing
Bawdwin
Namtu
Lashio
Mogok
Mingin
Shwebo
Budalin
Alon
Monywa
Madaya
Gokteik
Mandalay
Hsipaw
Mong Yai
Kawng
Pang-Yang
Mong Hsu
Jharkhand
JHARKHAND
Hazaribag
Giridih
Dhanbad
Gomoh
Ranchi
Ramgarh
Lohardaga
Asansol
Raniganj
Durgapur
Bankura
Barddhaman
WEST BENGAL
Purulia
Jamshedpur
Shrirampur
Bhatpara
Barakpur
Haora
KOLKATA
Diamond Harbour
Port Canning
Sundarbans
Chittagong
Karnaphuli Res.
Dohazari
Cox's Bazar
Chakradharpur
Chaibasa
Kharagpur
Medinipur
Haldia
Contai
Baleshwar
Mouths of the Ganges
Raurkela
Gua
Badampahar
Jharsuguda
Sambalpur
Keonjhargarh
Bhadrakh
Talcher
Dhenkanal
Cuttack
Kendrapara
Paradip
Bhubaneshwar
Puri
Chilka L.
Brahmapur
Chatrapur
Ichchapuram
Russellkonda
Bhawanipatna
Titlagarh
O R I S S A
Mahanadi
CHHATTISGARH
Raipur
Durg
Bilaspur
Raigarh
Sarangarh
Hirakud Dam
Dhamtari
Kanker
Bastar
Jagdalpur
Rayagada
Jeypore
Parvatipuram
Bobbili
Salur
Tekkali
Srikakulam
Vizianagaram
Anakapalle
Vishakhapatnam
Northern Circars
Pithapuram
Godavari Point
Kakinada
Vijayawada
Narasapur
Machilipatnam
Rajahmundry
B U R M A
(M Y A N M A R)
Paletwa
Kanpetlet
Mt. Victoria
CHIN
Gangaw
Yinmabin
Pakokku
Pauk
Myingyan
Meiktila
Sagaing
Kyaukse
Mong Kung
S H A N
Keng Tung
Keng Tawng
Mong Nai
Mong Ton
Mong Pan
Heho
Taunggyi
Thazi
Yamethin
Inle L.
Kyaukpadaung
Yenangyaung
Magwe
MAGWE
Minbu
Taungdwingyi
Pyinmana
Loi-kaw
Mawk Mai
KAYAH
Mae Hong Son
Chiang Mai
T H A I L A N D
Lamphun
Lampang
Muang
Chiang Rai
Thayetmyo
Bawlake
Toungoo
Sittwe (Akyab)
ARAKAN
Kyaukpyu
Ramree I.
Letpan
Taungup
Cheduba I.
Sandoway
Arakan Coast
Arakan Yoma
Pegu Yoma
Irrawaddy
Pye
Pyu
Myanaung
Letpadan
Henzada
Tharrawaddy
Madauk
Gwa
Kyonpyaw
Yandoon
Pegu
PEGU
Thaton
Pa-an
Martaban
RANGOON (YANGON)
Moulmein
MON
Bassein
Insein
Ma-ubin
Pyapon
IRRAWADDY
Myaungmya
G. of Martaban
Mouths of the Irrawaddy
Maudin Sun
Tak
Sangkhla Buri
Kalegauk Kyun
Lamaing
Ye
Natkyizin
Nam Tok
Yebyu
Tavoy
Moscos Is.
Maungmagan Kyunzu
Launglon Bok
B A Y O F B E N G A L
I N D I A N O C E A N
Preparis North Channel
Pariparit Kyun (Burma)
Preparis South Channel
Koko Kyunzu (Burma)
East from Greenwich
B
C
D
E
F
G
H
J
K
L
M
12
13
14
15
16
17
18
19
20
21
22

COPYRIGHT GEORGE PHILIP LTD.

THE INDO-GANGETIC PLAIN 1:6 000 000

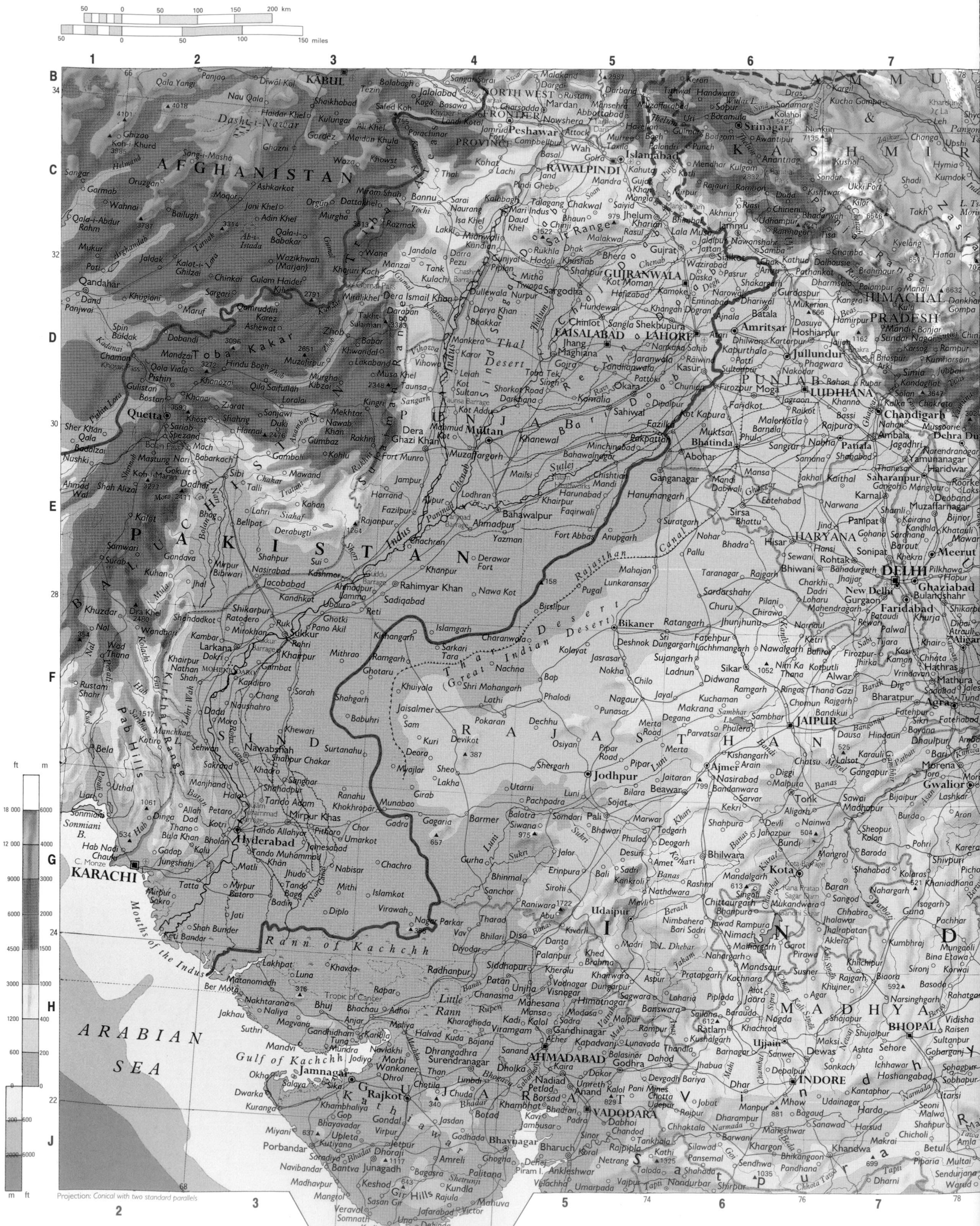

50 0 50 100 150 200 km
50 0 50 100 150 miles
AFGHANISTAN
PAKISTAN
INDIA
JAMMU & KASHMIR
HIMACHAL PRADESH
PUNJAB
HARYANA
RAJASTHAN
MADHYA PRADESH
GUJARAT
SIND
BALUCHISTAN
NORTH WEST FRONTIER PROVINCE
KABUL
Kandahar
Quetta
Peshawar
Islamabad
RAWALPINDI
Srinagar
Jammu
GUJRANWALA
FAISALABAD
LAHORE
Amritsar
Jullundur
LUDHIANA
Chandigarh
Multan
Bahawalpur
Sukkur
Hyderabad
KARACHI
Bikaner
DELHI
New Delhi
Agra
Meerut
JAIPUR
Jodhpur
Ajmer
Kota
Udaipur
Gwalior
AHMADABAD
VADODARA
Rajkot
Jamnagar
Bhavnagar
INDORE
Ujjain
BHOPAL
Thar Desert
(Great Indian Desert)
Rann of Kachchh
Gulf of Kachchh
ARABIAN SEA
Mouths of the Indus
Tropic of Cancer
Indus
Chenab
Sutlej
Thal Desert
Sulaiman Range
Kirthar Range
Salt Range
Toba Kakar
Gir Hills
Projection: Conical with two standard parallels

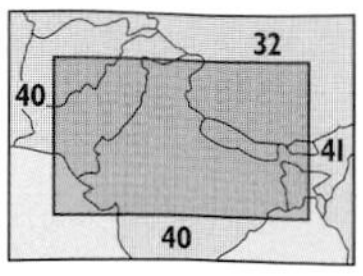
32
40
41
40

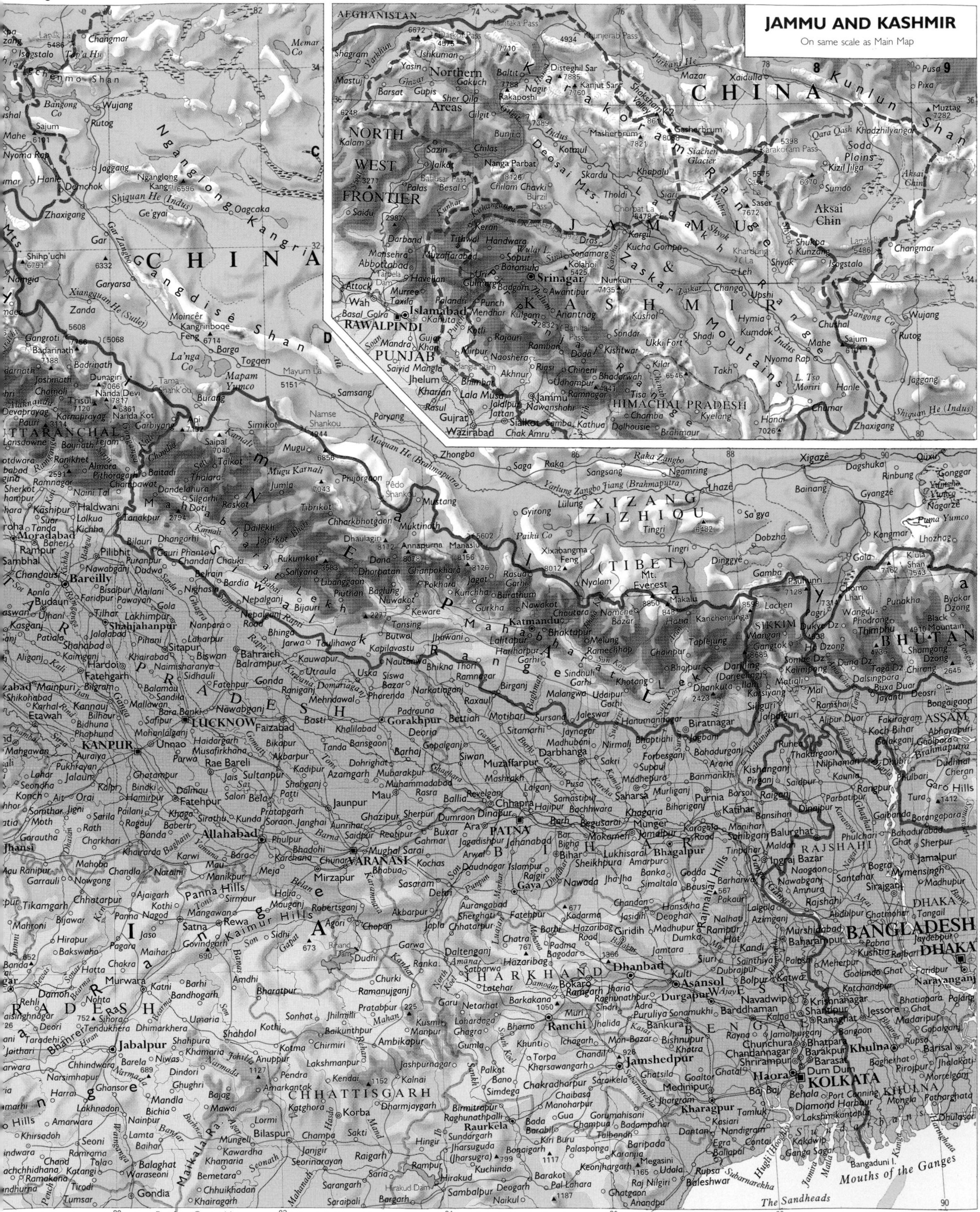
JAMMU AND KASHMIR
On same scale as Main Map
CHINA
AFGHANISTAN
NORTH WEST FRONTIER
Northern Areas
PUNJAB
RAWALPINDI
Islamabad
Srinagar
JAMMU
KASHMIR
HIMACHAL PRADESH
Karakoram Range
Ladakh Range
Zaskar Mountains
Kunlun Shan
Aksai Chin
Soda Plains
Siachen Glacier
Gasherbrum
Nanga Parbat
Deosai Mts.
Leh
Kargil
Gilgit
Skardu
Jhelum
Sialkot
Wazirabad
Gujrat
Mt. Everest
8850
XIZANG ZIZHIQU
(TIBET)
NEPAL
Katmandu
Mahabharat Lekh
Siwalik
SIKKIM
BHUTAN
Thimphu
ASSAM
BANGLADESH
DHAKA
RAJSHAHI
KHULNA
Khulna
KOLKATA
Haora
Mouths of the Ganges
The Sandheads
LUCKNOW
KANPUR
Allahabad
VARANASI
PATNA
BIHAR
JHARKHAND
CHHATTISGARH
BENGAL
UTTAR PRADESH
UTTARANCHAL
MADHYA PRADESH
Jabalpur
Jamshedpur
Ranchi
Dhanbad
Asansol
Durgapur
Gaya
Bareilly
Shahjahanpur
Moradabad
Gorakhpur
Darjeeling
Kanchenjunga
Makalu
Annapurna
Dhaulagiri
Manaslu
Kaimur Hills
Panna Hills
Rajmahal Hills
Garo Hills
Maikala Ra.
Nganglong Kangri
Gangdisê Shan
Yarlung Zangbo Jiang (Brahmaputra)
Brahmaputra
Ganga (Ganges)
Narmada
Son
Kali
Gandak
Kosi
Shiquan He (Indus)
Indus
East from Greenwich
COPYRIGHT GEORGE PHILIP LTD.

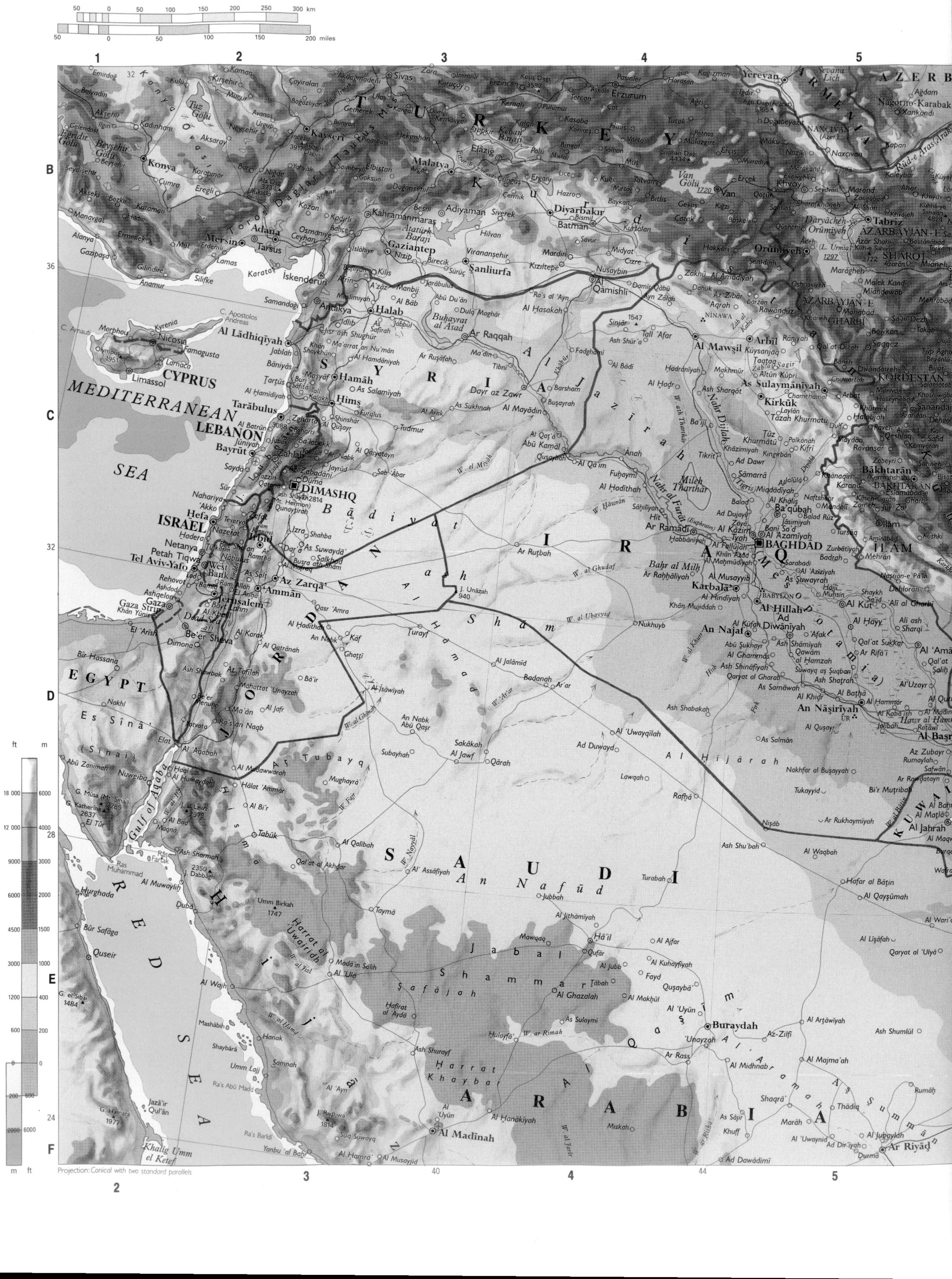

Projection: Conical with two standard parallels

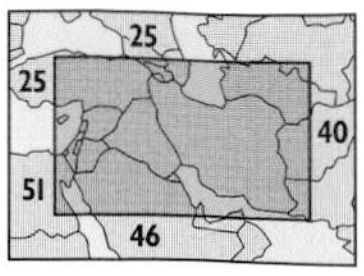
25
25
40
51
46

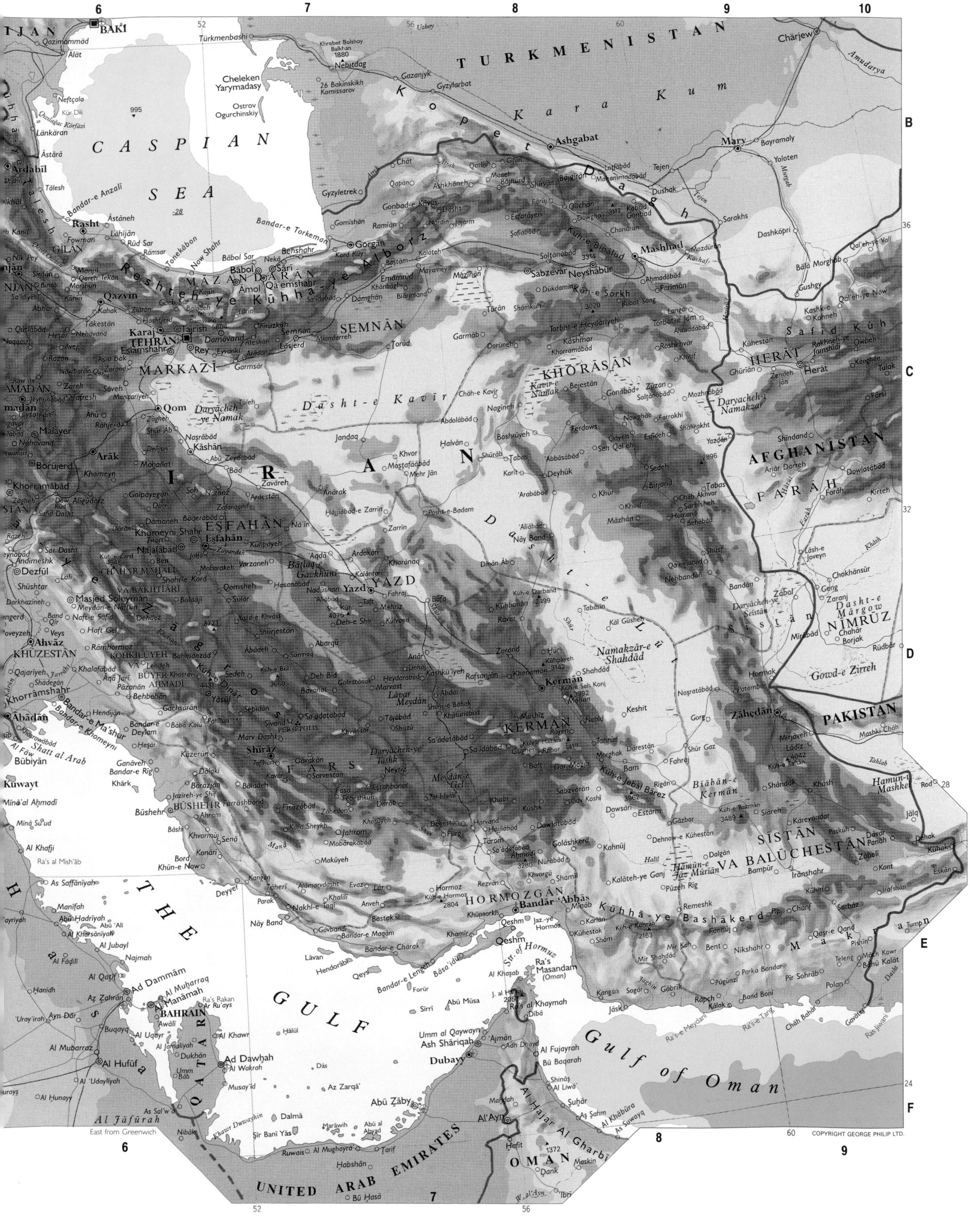
6
7
8
9
10
B
C
D
E
F
36
32
28
24
52
56
60
TURKMENISTAN
Kara Kum
Kopet Dagh
CASPIAN SEA
-28
995
BAKI
Qazimammäd
Älät
Neftçala
Länkäran
Ästärä
Ardabil
Tälesh
Bandar-e Anzali
Rasht
Ästäneh
Lähijän
Fowman
Rüd Sar
Rämsar
Tonekäbon
Now Shahr
GĪLĀN
Türkmenbashi
Cheleken Yarymadasy
Ostrov Ogurchinskiy
Khrebet Bolshoy Balkhan 1880
Nebitdag
26 Bakinskikh Komissarov
Gazanjyk
Gyzylarbat
Ashgabat
Gyzyletrek
Chat
Bandar-e Torkeman
Gorgan
Gonbad-e Kāvūs
Behshahr
Sārī
Bābol
Bābol Sar
Amol
Qā'emshahr
MĀZANDARĀN
Reshteh-ye Kūhhā-ye Alborz
Qazvin
Takestān
Karaj
Tajrish
TEHRĀN
Rey
Eslamshahr
Damāvand
Semnān
SEMNĀN
Dāmghān
Shāhrūd
Sabzevār
Neyshābūr
Mashhad
Kūh-e Bīnālūd
Qūchān
Bojnūrd
Shirvān
Esfarāyen
Kūh-e Sorkh
Torbat-e Heydarīyeh
Torbat-e Jām
Kāshmar
KHORĀSĀN
Chārjew
Amudarya
Mary
Bayramaly
Yoloten
Tejen
Dushak
Sarakhs
Dashköpri
Bālā Morghāb
Qal'eh-ye Now
Herāt
HERĀT
Safīd Kūh
Shindand
AFGHANISTAN
FARĀH
Farāh
NĪMRŪZ
Dasht-e Mārgow
Gowd-e Zirreh
Zābol
Daryācheh-ye Sīstān
Sīstān
Zāhedān
PAKISTAN
MARKAZĪ
Qom
Daryācheh-ye Namak
Dasht-e Kavīr
Kāshān
Arāk
Malāyer
Borūjerd
Khorramābād
IRAN
ESFAHĀN
Esfahān
Najafābād
Khomeynī Shahr
Nā'īn
Ardestān
Yazd
YAZD
Ardakān
Bāfq
Dasht-e Lūt
Namakzār-e Shahdād
Kermān
KERMĀN
Rafsanjān
Sīrjān
Bam
Bīābān-e Kermān
Ahvāz
KHUZESTĀN
Dezfūl
Shūshtar
Masjed Soleymān
Ābādān
Khorramshahr
Bandar-e Māhshahr
Bandar-e Khomeynī
Shatt al Arab
KOHKĪLŪYEH VA BŪYER AHMADĪ
CHAHĀR MAHĀL VA BAKHTIĀRĪ
Kūh-e Dīnār 4431
Zāgros
Shīrāz
FĀRS
Persepolis
Būshehr
BŪSHEHR
Kāzerūn
Daryācheh-ye Tashk
Kuwayt
Mīnā' al Ahmadī
Al Khafji
Ra's al Mish'āb
As Saffānīyah
Ad Dammām
Al Manāmah
BAHRAIN
Al Hufūf
QATAR
Ad Dawhah
THE GULF
Hormuz
HORMOZGĀN
Bandar 'Abbās
Qeshm
Str. of Hormuz
Ra's Masandam (Oman)
Ra's al Khaymah
Dubayy
Abū Zabī
UNITED ARAB EMIRATES
Al 'Ayn
OMAN
Al Hajar al Gharbī
Gulf of Oman
Jāsk
Chāh Bahār
SĪSTĀN VA BALŪCHESTĀN
Kūhhā-ye Bashākerd
Īrānshahr
Makran
Al Jāfūrah
East from Greenwich
COPYRIGHT GEORGE PHILIP LTD.

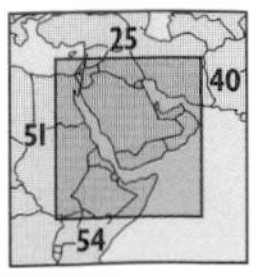
25
40
51
54

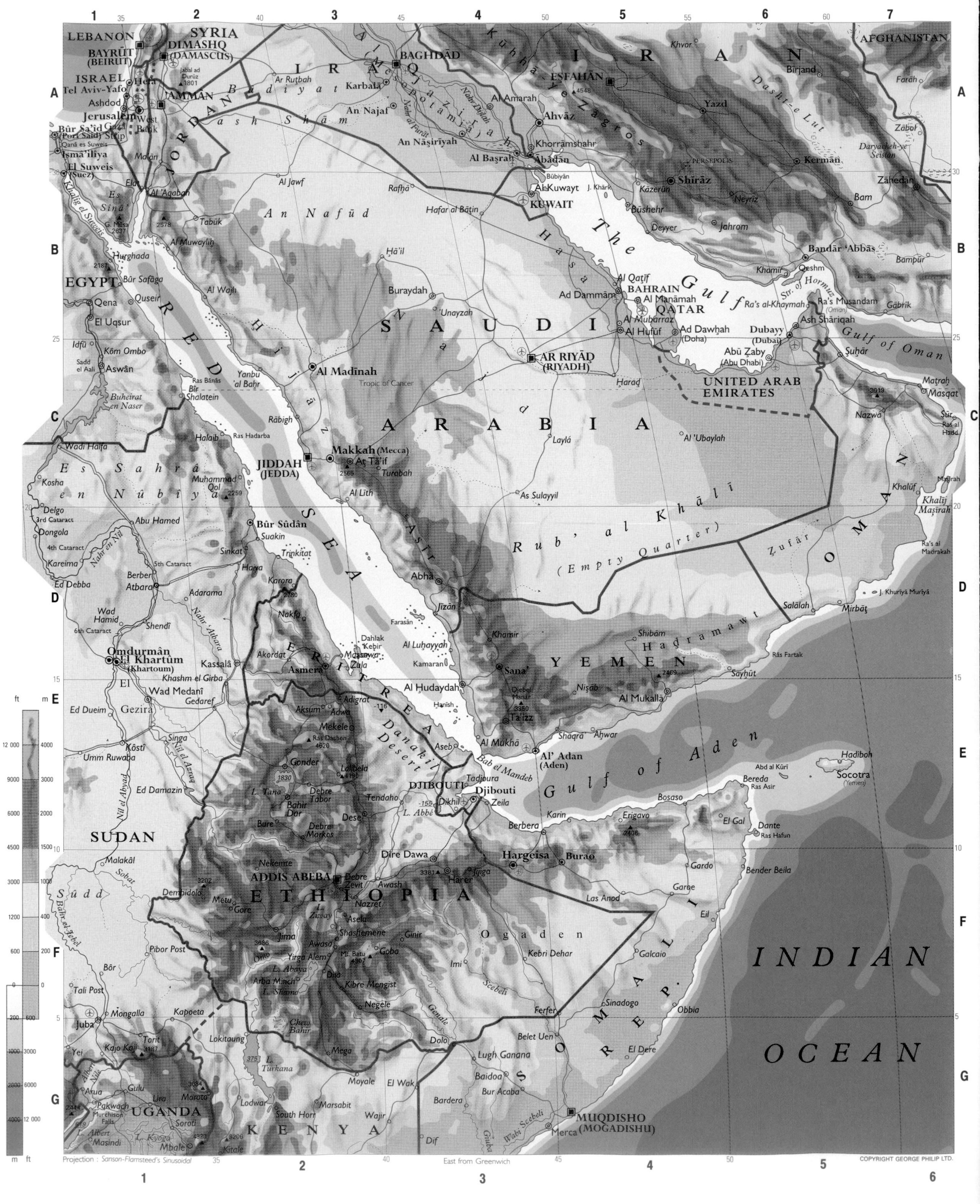
100 0 100 200 300 400 500 600 km
100 0 100 200 300 400 miles
LEBANON
SYRIA
DIMASHQ (DAMASCUS)
BAYRŪT (BEIRUT)
ISRAEL
Tel Aviv-Yafo
Ashdod
Jerusalem
West Bank
Gaza Strip
Bûr Sa'îd (Port Said)
Ismâ'ilîya
El Suweis (Suez)
'AMMĀN
JORDAN
Elat
Al 'Aqabah
G. Mûsa 2637
Tabūk
BAGHDĀD
IRAQ
Ar Ruṭbah
Karbalā
An Najaf
An Nāṣirīyah
Al Baṣrah
Al 'Amarah
Bādiyat ash Shām
Al Jawf
Rafḥā
Hafar al Bāṭin
AL KUWAYT
KUWAIT
IRAN
EŞFAHĀN
Ahvāz
Ābādān
Khorramshahr
Kūhhā-ye Zāgros
Shīrāz
Kermān
Yazd
Dasht-e Lut
Bīrjand
Khvor
Zāhedān
Bam
Jahrom
Būshehr
Bandar 'Abbās
Qeshm
AFGHANISTAN
Farāh
Zābol
Daryācheh-ye Sīstan
An Nafūd
Ḥā'il
Buraydah
'Unayzah
SAUDI ARABIA
AR RIYĀD (RIYADH)
Al Madīnah
Makkah (Mecca)
JIDDAH (JEDDA)
At Ṭā'if
Al Qaṭīf
Ad Dammām
Al Hufūf
BAHRAIN
Al Manāmah
QATAR
Ad Dawḥah (Doha)
The Gulf
Str. of Hormuz
Dubayy (Dubai)
Abū Ẓaby (Abu Dhabi)
UNITED ARAB EMIRATES
Ash Shāriqah
Ra's Musandam
Gulf of Oman
Ṣuḥār
Masqat
OMAN
Rub' al Khālī (Empty Quarter)
As Sulayyil
Laylā
Al 'Ubaylah
Ḥaraḍ
Tropic of Cancer
Abhā
Jīzān
YEMEN
Ṣana'
Ta'izz
Al Ḥudaydah
Al Mukallā
Ḥaḍramawt
Ẓufār
Şalālah
Mirbāṭ
Sayḥūt
Rās Fartak
Al' Adan (Aden)
Gulf of Aden
Bab el Mandeb
Socotra
Hadiboh
EGYPT
Hurghada
Bûr Safâga
Quseir
Qena
El Uqsur
Aswân
Kôm Ombo
Idfu
RED SEA
Buheirat en Naser
Wadi Halfa
Es Sahrâ en Nûbîya
Abu Hamed
Bûr Sûdân
Suakin
Berber
Atbara
Shendî
Omdurmân
El Khartûm (Khartoum)
Kassalâ
Wad Medanî
Gedaref
Kôstî
SUDAN
Malakâl
Sudd
Bahr el Jebel
Juba
ERITREA
Asmera
Massawa
Akordat
Dahlak Kebir
Danakil Desert
Aseb
DJIBOUTI
Djibouti
Tadjoura
Zeila
ETHIOPIA
ADDIS ABEBA
Gonder
L. Tana
Ras Dashen 4620
Aksum
Adigrat
Mekele
Dese
Dire Dawa
Harer
Jijiga
Nazret
Awasa
Jima
Gore
Nekemte
Debre Markos
Bahir Dar
Ogaden
Imi
Gode
Kebri Dehar
Hargeisa
Burao
Berbera
Bosaso
Erigavo
Las Anod
Gardo
Garoe
Galcaio
Bender Beila
Eil
Obbia
SOMALI REP.
Belet Uen
Ferfer
Lugh Ganana
Baidoa
Bur Acaba
MUQDISHO (MOGADISHU)
Merca
Kismaayo
INDIAN OCEAN
KENYA
Lodwar
Moyale
Marsabit
Wajir
L. Turkana
UGANDA
Gulu
Kitale
Mbale
Soroti
L. Kyoga
L. Albert
Masindi
Projection : Sanson-Flamsteed's Sinusoidal
East from Greenwich
COPYRIGHT GEORGE PHILIP LTD.

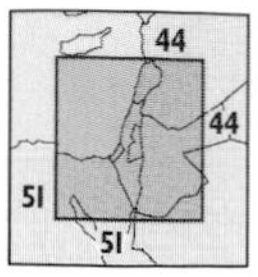
44
44
51
51

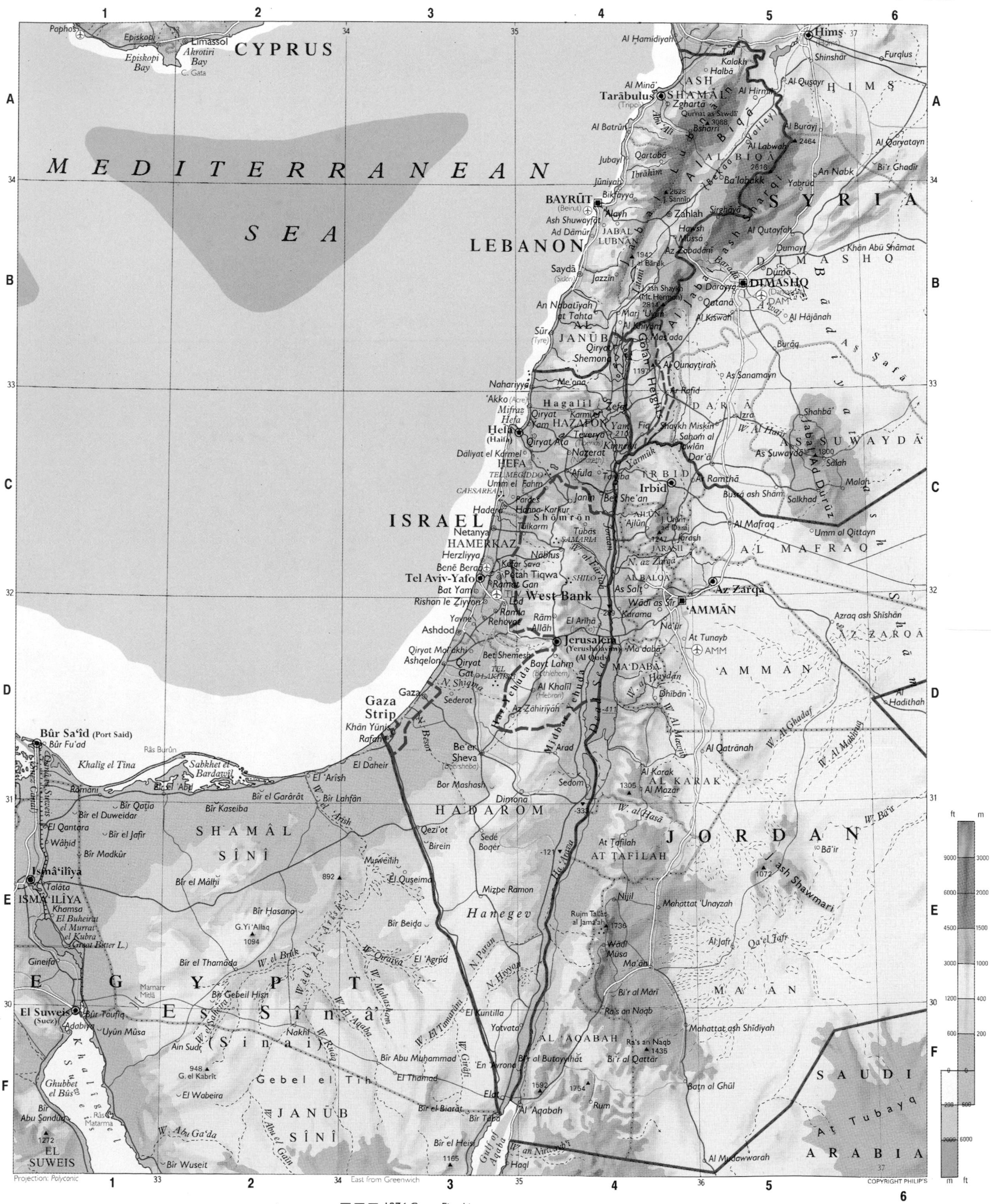
CYPRUS
Paphos
Episkopi
Limassol
Episkopi Bay
Akrotiri Bay
C. Gata
MEDITERRANEAN
SEA
LEBANON
SYRIA
ISRAEL
JORDAN
EGYPT
SAUDI ARABIA
West Bank
Gaza Strip
Hims
Shinshar
Furqlus
Al Hamidiyah
Tall Kalakh
Halba
Al Mina'
Tarabulus (Tripoli)
Zgharta
Qurnat as Sawda' 3088
Bsharri
Al Hirmil
Al Qusayr
Al Batrun
Al Burayj
Al Labwah
2464
Al Qaryatayn
Jubayl
Qartaba
Ibrahim
An Nabk
Bi'r Ghadir
Juniyah
Ba'labakk
Yabrud
Bikfayya
2628 J. Sannin
BAYRUT (Beirut)
Ash Shuwayfat
Alayh
Zahlah
Sirghaya
Ad Damur
JABAL LUBNAN
Hawsh Musa
Al Qutayfah
Khan Abu Shamat
Az Zabadani
Dumayr
Dumo
DIMASHQ
Sayda (Sidon)
Jazzin
1942 J. al Barak
J. ash Shaykh (Mt. Hermon) 2814
Darayya
Qatana
Al Kiswah
Al Hajanah
An Nabatiyah at Tahta
AL JANUB
Marj 'Uyun
Al Khiyam
Mas'ada
Sur (Tyre)
Qiryat Shemona
1197
Al Qunaytirah
Buraq
Golan Heights
Nahariyya
Me'ona
As Sanamayn
'Akko (Acre)
Hagalil
Zefat
Ar Rafid
Mifraz Hefa
Qiryat Yam
Karmi'el
HAZAFON
Hefa (Haifa)
Qiryat Ata
Teverya (Tiberias)
Yam Kinneret
Fiq
Shaykh Miskin
Sahm al Jawlan
Izra
W. Al Harir
Shahba'
As Suwayda'
AS SUWAYDA'
Jabal Ad Duruz
1800
Salah
Daliyat el Karmel
Nazerat (Nazareth)
Dar'a
HEFA
TEL MEGIDDO
Afula
Tayiba
Yarmuk
IRBID
Irbid
Ar Ramtha
Malah
CAESAREA
Umm el Fahm
Jenin
Bet She'an
Busra ash Sham
Salkhad
Hadera
Pardes Hanna-Karkur
Shomron
AJLUN
'Ajlun
J. Umm ad Daraj 1247
Al Mafraq
Umm al Qittayn
Netanya
Tulkarm
Tubas
SAMARIA
JARASH
Jarash
AL MAFRAQ
HAMERKAZ
Herzliyya
Benei Beraq
Kefar Sava
Petah Tiqwa
Ramat Gan
Nablus
W. al Far'ah
SHILO
N. az Zarqa
AL BALQA
Az Zarqa
Tel Aviv-Yafo
Bat Yam
Rishon le Ziyyon
Lod
Ramla
Rehovot
Yavne
Ashdod
As Salt
Wadi as Sir
AMMAN
Karama
Ram Allah
El Ariha (Jericho)
Jerusalem (Yerushalayim) (Al Quds)
Na'ur
Azraq ash Shishan
AZ ZARQA
Qiryat Mal'akhi
Ashqelon
Bet Shemesh
Qiryat Gat
TEL LAKHISH
Bayt Lahm (Bethlehem)
Ma'daba
MA'DABA
At Tunayb
AMM
AMMAN
Gaza
N. Shiqma
Sederot
Al Khalil (Hebron)
Adh Dhahiriyah
Har Yehuda
Dead Sea
Dhiban
W. al Haydan
Al Hadithah
Khan Yunis
Rafah
N. Besor
Arad
Midbar Yehuda
W. Al Mawjib
Al Qatranah
W. Al Ghadaf
W. Al Mahfuz
Bur Sa'id (Port Said)
Bur Fu'ad
Ras Burun
Sabkhet el Bardawil
Khalig el Tina
El 'Arish
El Daheir
Be'er Sheva (Beersheba)
Bor Mashash
Sedom
AL KARAK
Al Karak
Al Mazar
1305
Romani
Bir el Abd
Bir Lahfan
Bir el Garârât
Bîr Qatia
Bîr Kaseiba
Dimona
HADAROM
-335
W. al Hasa
W. Ba'ir
Bîr el Duweidar
El Qantara
Bîr el Jafir
Wâhid
Bîr Madkûr
SHAMÂL SÎNÎ
W. el 'Arish
Qezi'ot
Birein
Sede Boqer
-121
At Tafilah
AT TAFILAH
Ba'ir
Ismâ'ilîya
Talâta
ISMÂ'ILÎYA
Khamsa
El Buheirat el Murrat el Kubra (Great Bitter L.)
Muweilih
El Quseima
Mizpe Ramon
892
Bîr el Mâlhi
J. ash Shawmari
1072
Bîr Hasana
G. Yi'Allaq 1094
Bîr Beida
Hanegev
Nijil
Mahattat 'Unayzah
Rujm Tal'at al Jama'ah 1736
Al Jafr
Qa'el Jafr
Wadi Musa
Ma'an
Gineifa
Bîr el Thamâda
W. el Bruk
W. el 'Arish
W. Qiraiya
El 'Agrûd
N. Paran
N. Hiyyon
Ha 'Arava
Bi'r al Mari
MA'AN
Mamarr Mitla
Bîr Gebeil Hisn
W. Mahash
Sînâ' (Sinai)
El Suweis (Suez)
Bûr Taufiq
Adabiya
'Uyûn Mûsa
W. el Sahara
Nakhl
W. el 'Aqaba
W. el Rugâg
W. el Tamad
El Kuntilla
W. Girafi
Yotvata
Ra's an Naqb
Mahattat ash Shidiyah
AL 'AQABAH
Ra's an Naqb 1435
Bi'r al Qattar
'Ain Sudr
948 G. el Kabrît
Gebel el Tîh
Bîr Abu Muhammad
El Thamad
'En Avrona
Bîr al Butayyihat
Batn al Ghul
Ghubbet el Bûs
El Wabeira
1592
1754
Rum
Elat
Al 'Aqabah
Bîr Taba
Bîr el Biarât
Khalîg el Suweis
Bîr Abu Sandûq
Râs Matarma
JANÛB SÎNÎ
W. Abu Ga'da
W. Abu el Gain
Bîr el Heisi
Gulf of Aqaba
W. an Nu'aym
Al Mudawwarah
At Tubayq
1272
EL SUWEIS
Bîr Wuseit
1165
Haql
Projection: Polyconic
East from Greenwich
COPYRIGHT PHILIP'S
ft
m
9000
3000
6000
2000
4500
1500
3000
1000
1200
400
600
200
0
0
200
600
2000
6000
10 0 10 20 30 40 50 60 70 80 100 km
10 0 10 20 30 40 50 60 miles
1 2 3 4 5 6
A B C D E F
33 34 35 36 37
30 31 32 33 34

1974 Cease Fire Lines

AFRICA : Physical 1:42 000 000

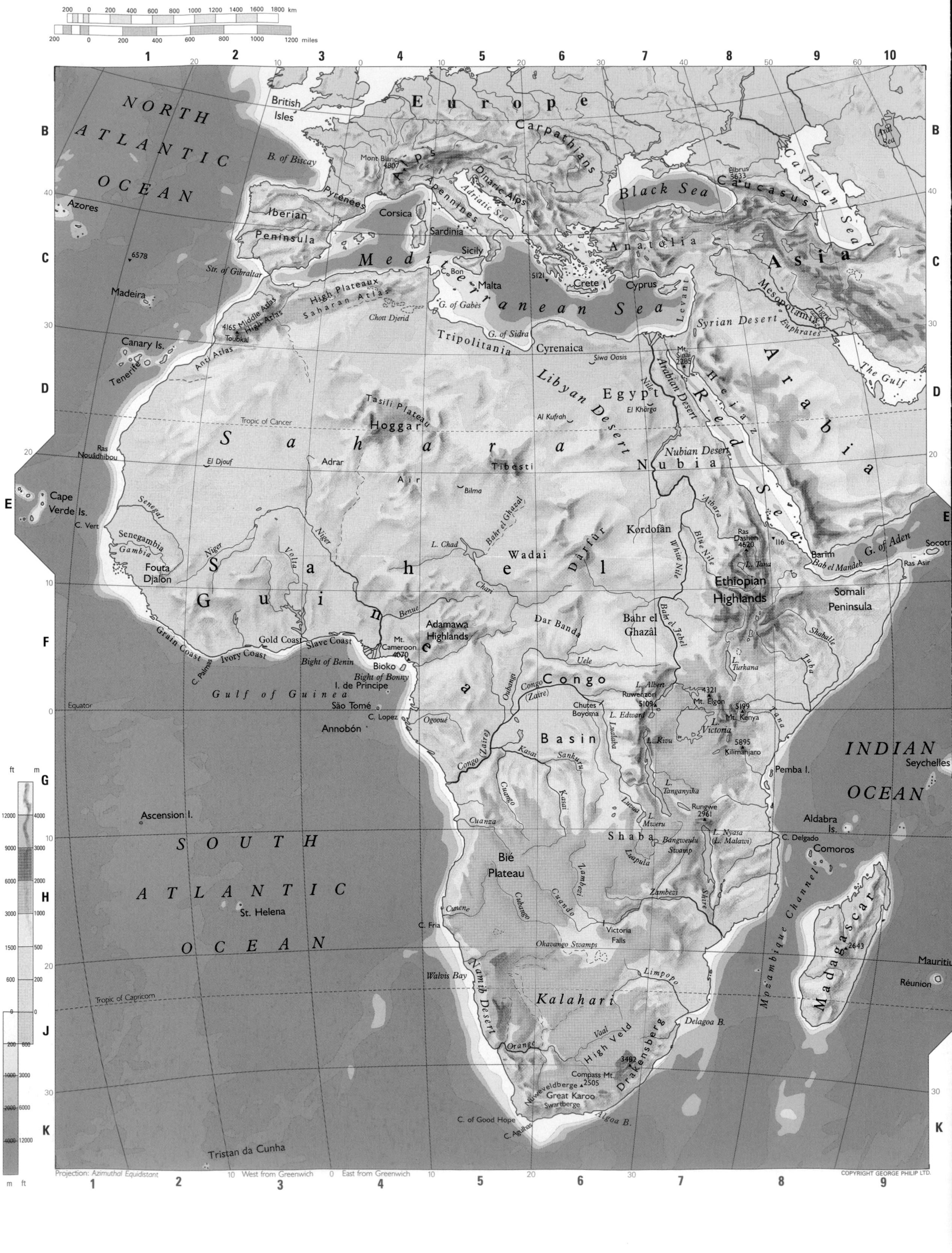

km
miles
NORTH ATLANTIC OCEAN
Azores
Madeira
Canary Is.
Tenerife
Cape Verde Is.
C. Vert
British Isles
B. of Biscay
Europe
Carpathians
Mont Blanc 4807
Alps
Pyrénées
Iberian Peninsula
Corsica
Sardinia
Apennines
Adriatic Sea
Dinaric Alps
Sicily
Malta
C. Bon
Str. of Gibraltar
Black Sea
Elbrus 5633
Caucasus
Caspian Sea
Aral Sea
Anatolia
Crete
5121
Cyprus
Levant
Asia
Mesopotamia
Tigris
Euphrates
Syrian Desert
The Gulf
Arabia
Mediterranean Sea
G. of Gabès
G. of Sidra
Tripolitania
Cyrenaica
Siwa Oasis
High Plateaux
Saharan Atlas
Chott Djerid
Middle Atlas
High Atlas
Anti Atlas
4165 Toubkal
Mt. Sinai 2285
Arabian Desert
Nile
Hejaz
Red Sea
Libyan Desert
Egypt
El Khârga
Al Kufrah
Tropic of Cancer
Tasili Plateau
Hoggar
Sahara
Ras Nouâdhibou
El Djouf
Adrar
Tibesti
Aïr
Bilma
Nubian Desert
Nubia
Senegal
Senegambia
Gambia
Fouta Djalon
Niger
Volta
Sahel
L. Chad
Bahr el Ghazal
Wadai
Dârfûr
Kordofân
Atbara
Blue Nile
White Nile
Ras Dashen 4620
L. Tana
116
Barim
Bab el Mandeb
G. of Aden
Socotra
Ras Asir
Ethiopian Highlands
Somali Peninsula
Shaballe
Juba
Guinea
Chari
Benue
Grain Coast
C. Palmas
Ivory Coast
Gold Coast
Slave Coast
Bight of Benin
Bight of Bonny
Mt. Cameroon 4070
Adamawa Highlands
Dar Banda
Bahr el Ghazâl
Bahr el Jebel
L. Turkana
Bioko
I. de Principe
Gulf of Guinea
São Tomé
C. Lopez
Annobón
Equator
Ogooué
Oubangui
Uele
Congo (Zaïre)
Congo
Basin
Chutes Boyoma
L. Albert
Ruwenzori 5109
L. Edward
L. Kivu
4321 Mt. Elgon
5199 Mt. Kenya
L. Victoria
5895 Kilimanjaro
Tana
INDIAN OCEAN
Seychelles
Pemba I.
Kasai
Sankuru
Lualaba
Cuango
L. Tanganyika
Rungwe 2961
Luvua
L. Mweru
Aldabra Is.
Ascension I.
Cuanza
Shaba
Bangweulu Swamp
Luapula
L. Nyasa (L. Malawi)
C. Delgado
Comoros
SOUTH ATLANTIC OCEAN
Bié Plateau
Lungwebungu
Zambezi
Shire
Cuando
Cubango
Cunene
C. Fria
St. Helena
Victoria Falls
Okavango Swamps
Mozambique Channel
Madagascar
2643
Mauritius
Réunion
Walvis Bay
Namib Desert
Limpopo
Kalahari
Tropic of Capricorn
Delagoa B.
Vaal
High Veld
Drakensberg
Orange
3482
Compass Mt. 2505
Nuweveldberge
Great Karoo
Swartberge
Algoa B.
C. of Good Hope
C. Agulhas
Tristan da Cunha
ft
m
Projection: Azimuthal Equidistant
West from Greenwich
East from Greenwich
COPYRIGHT GEORGE PHILIP LTD.

NORTH ATLANTIC OCEAN
SOUTH ATLANTIC OCEAN
INDIAN OCEAN
Mediterranean Sea
Red Sea
Black Sea
Caspian Sea
Gulf of Guinea
Bight of Benin
B. of Biscay
Mozambique Channel
G. of Aden
Sahara
UNITED KINGDOM
London
NETH.
BELG.
GERMANY
POLAND
Warsaw
RUSSIA
KAZAKSTAN
UKRAINE
Kiev
Volgograd
FRANCE
Paris
SWITZ.
AUSTRIA
Vienna
CZECH REP.
Prague
SLOVAK REP.
HUNGARY
ROMANIA
Odessa
CROATIA
BOS.-HERZ.
YUG.
BULGARIA
MAC.
ALB.
GREECE
Athens
Crete
ITALY
Rome
Corsica
Sardinia
Sicily
MALTA
SPAIN
Madrid
PORTUGAL
Lisbon
Azores (Port.)
Madeira (Port.)
Canary Is. (Sp.)
TURKEY
Ankara
GEORGIA
ARM.
AZER.
Baku
TURKMEN.
CYPRUS
SYRIA
Aleppo
Damascus
LEB.
ISRAEL
Tel Aviv-Jaffa
Jerusalem
JORDAN
IRAQ
Baghdad
Mosul
Basra
IRAN
Tehrān
Esfahān
KUWAIT
BAHRAIN
QATAR
The Gulf
SAUDI ARABIA
Riyadh
Medina
Jedda
Mecca
YEMEN
Socotra (Yemen)
Syrian Desert
MOROCCO
Rabat
Casablanca
Fès
Marrakesh
Tétouan
ALGERIA
Algiers
Annaba
Constantine
In Salah
TUNISIA
Tunis
Sfax
Chott Djerid
LIBYA
Tripoli
Misrātah
Benghazi
Marzūq
Al Jawf
EGYPT
Cairo
Alexandria
Port Said
Suez
El Faiyûm
Asyût
Aswân
WESTERN SAHARA
El Aaiún
Dakhla
Fdérik
MAURITANIA
Nouakchott
Ras Nouâdhibou
CAPE VERDE IS.
Praia
SENEGAL
Dakar
St-Louis
C. Vert
GAMBIA
Banjul
GUINEA-BISSAU
Bissau
GUINEA
Conakry
SIERRA LEONE
Freetown
LIBERIA
Monrovia
IVORY COAST
Yamoussoukro
Bouaké
Abidjan
MALI
Bamako
Tombouctou
BURKINA FASO
Ouagadougou
Bobo-Dioulasso
GHANA
Kumasi
Accra
Sekondi-Takoradi
TOGO
Lomé
BENIN
Porto Novo
NIGER
Niamey
Agadès
NIGERIA
Abuja
Lagos
Ibadan
Kano
Maiduguri
Enugu
Port Harcourt
CHAD
Ndjamena
L. Chad
Abéché
SUDAN
Khartoum
Omdurmân
Port Sudan
Wadi Halfa
Atbara
Wad Medanî
El Fâsher
El Obeid
Malakâl
Wau
ERITREA
Asmera
Mesewa
DJIBOUTI
Djibouti
ETHIOPIA
Addis Ababa
Harer
L. Tana
SOMALI REP.
Mogadishu
Berbera
Ras Asir
Kismayu
CAMEROON
Douala
Yaoundé
Malabo
EQUATORIAL GUINEA
SÃO TOMÉ & PRINCIPE
Annobón
GABON
Libreville
C. Lopez
CENTRAL AFRICAN REP.
Bangui
CONGO
Brazzaville
Pointe-Noire
CONGO (DEM. REP. OF THE)
Kinshasa
Kisangani
Mbandaka
Kananga
Lubumbashi
Likasi
Matadi
CABINDA (Angola)
UGANDA
Kampala
L. Albert
L. Edward
KENYA
Nairobi
Kisumu
Mombasa
L. Turkana
L. Victoria
RWANDA
Kigali
BURUNDI
Bujumbura
L. Kivu
TANZANIA
Dodoma
Dar es Salaam
Zanzibar
L. Tanganyika
L. Mweru
L. Malawi
SEYCHELLES
Aldabra Is.
ANGOLA
Luanda
Lobito
Huambo
Namibe
C. Fria
ZAMBIA
Lusaka
Ndola
MALAWI
Lilongwe
Blantyre
MOZAMBIQUE
Maputo
Beira
Moçambique
C. Delgado
COMOROS
Moroni
Mayotte (Fr.)
Mamoudzou
MADAGASCAR
Antananarivo
Antsiranana
Mahajanga
Toamasina
Fianarantsoa
MAURITIUS
Port Louis
Réunion (Fr.)
St-Denis
ZIMBABWE
Harare
Bulawayo
Livingstone
NAMIBIA
Windhoek
BOTSWANA
Gaborone
SOUTH AFRICA
Pretoria
Johannesburg
Kimberley
Cape Town
C. of Good Hope
C. Agulhas
Port Elizabeth
East London
Durban
SWAZ.
Mbabane
LESOTHO
Maseru
Ascension I. (U.K.)
St. Helena (U.K.)
Tristan da Cunha (U.K.)
Nile
Niger
Congo (Zaire)
Zambezi
Limpopo
Orange
Vaal
Tropic of Cancer
Equator
Tropic of Capricorn
Projection: Azimuthal Equidistant
West from Greenwich
East from Greenwich
Dakar Capital Cities
COPYRIGHT GEORGE PHILIP LTD.
200 0 200 400 600 800 1000 1200 1400 1600 1800 km
200 0 200 400 600 800 1000 1200 miles

1:15 000 000

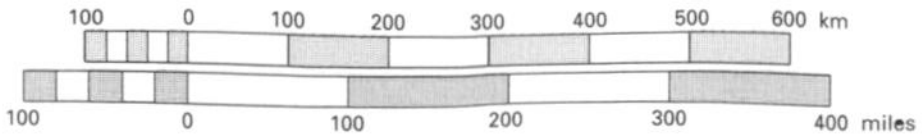
100 0 100 200 300 400 500 600 km
100 0 100 200 300 400 miles

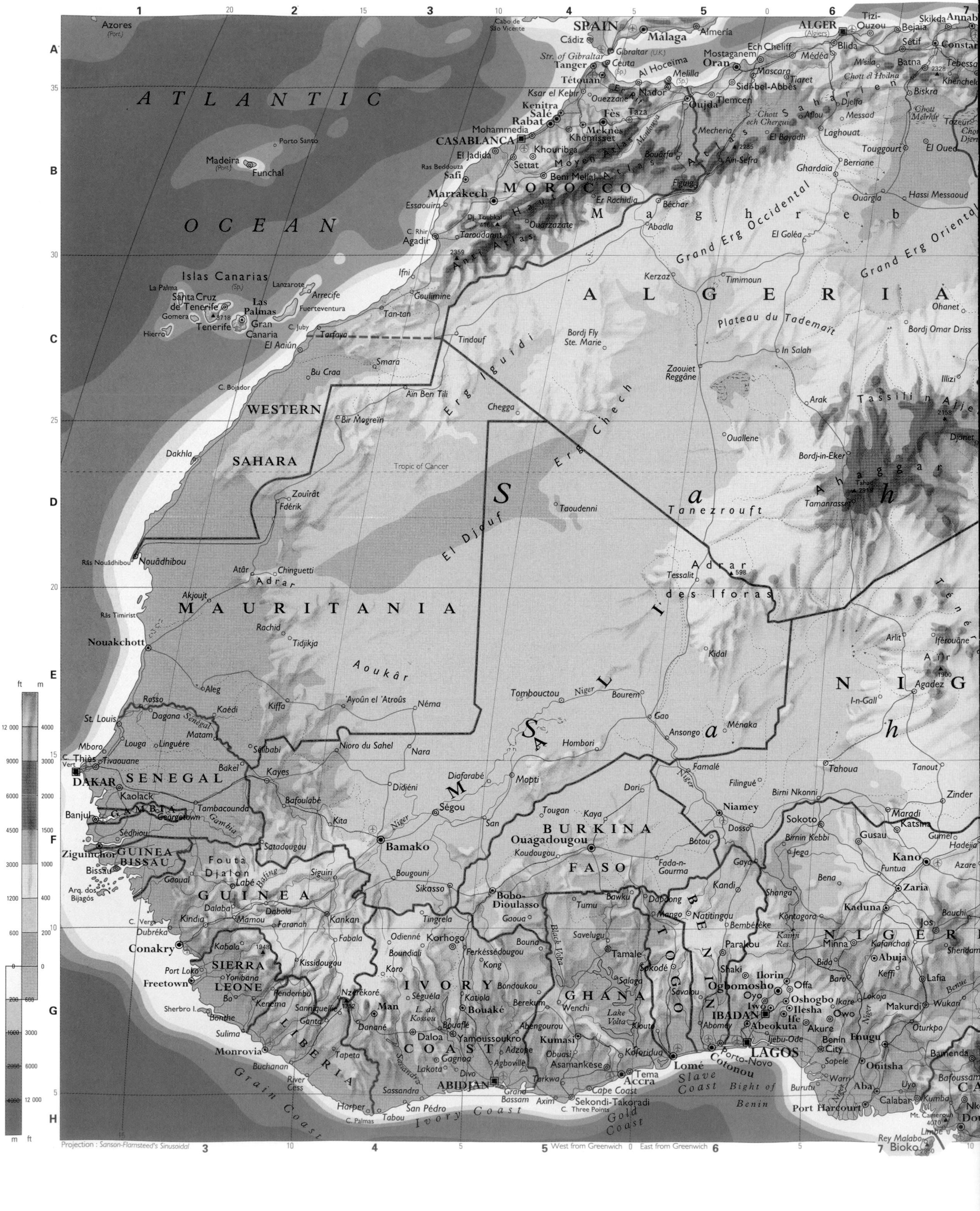
ATLANTIC OCEAN
Azores (Port.)
Madeira (Port.)
Porto Santo
Funchal
Islas Canarias (Sp.)
La Palma
Santa Cruz de Tenerife
Gomera
Tenerife
Hierro
Las Palmas
Gran Canaria
Lanzarote
Arrecife
Fuerteventura
C. Juby
SPAIN
Cádiz
Málaga
Almería
Str. of Gibraltar
Gibraltar (U.K.)
Ceuta (Sp.)
Melilla (Sp.)
Tanger
Tétouan
Al Hoceima
Nador
Ksar el Kebir
Ouezzane
Kenitra
Salé
Rabat
Fès
Taza
Meknès
Khemisset
Mohammedia
CASABLANCA
El Jadida
Khouribga
Settat
Beni Mellal
Ras Beddouza
Safi
Marrakech
Essaouira
MOROCCO
Dj. Toubkal 4165
Ouarzazate
Er Rachidia
Taroudannt
C. Rhir
Agadir
Ifni
Goulimine
Tan-tan
Tarfaya
El Aaiún
Smara
Bu Craa
C. Bojador
WESTERN SAHARA
Dakhla
Aïn Ben Tili
Bir Mogreïn
Tropic of Cancer
Zouîrât
Fdérik
Rås Nouâdhibou
Nouâdhibou
Atâr
Chinguetti
Adrar
Akjoujt
MAURITANIA
Rås Timirist
Nouakchott
Rachid
Tidjikja
Aoukâr
Aleg
Kiffa
'Ayoûn el 'Atroûs
Néma
Rosso
Kaédi
St. Louis
Dagana
Matam
Louga
Linguére
Mboro
Thiès
Tivaouane
C. Vert
DAKAR
SENEGAL
Bakel
Kaolack
Banjul
GAMBIA
Georgetown
Tambacounda
Sédhiou
Ziguinchor
GUINEA-BISSAU
Bissau
Arq. dos Bijagós
Gaoual
Fouta Djalon
Labé
GUINEA
Dalaba
Mamou
Dabola
Faranah
Kindia
Dubréka
Conakry
Kabala
1848
SIERRA LEONE
Port Loko
Yonibana
Freetown
Bo
Kenema
Sherbro I.
Bonthe
Sulima
Monrovia
LIBERIA
Buchanan
River Cess
Harper
C. Palmas
Grain Coast
Sélibabi
Kayes
Nioro du Sahel
Nara
Diafarabé
Mopti
Didiéni
Bafoulabé
Kita
Ségou
San
Bamako
Satadougou
Siguiri
Bougouni
Sikasso
Kankan
Fabala
Kissidougou
Nzérékoré
Tingrela
Odienné
Korhogo
Boundiali
Ferkéssédougou
Kong
Bouna
Koro
Man
IVORY COAST
Séguéla
Katiola
Bondoukou
Bouaké
L. de Kossou
Danané
Tapeta
Daloa
Bouaflé
Yamoussoukro
Gagnoa
Lakota
Divo
Sassandra
Abidjan
Grand Bassam
San Pédro
Tabou
Ivory Coast
Agboville
Adzopé
Abengourou
Berekum
Wenchi
GHANA
Kumasi
Obuasi
Asamankese
Tarkwa
Axim
Sekondi-Takoradi
C. Three Points
Cape Coast
Accra
Tema
Gold Coast
Lake Volta
Black Volta
Savelugu
Tamale
Salaga
Tumu
Bawku
Bobo-Dioulasso
Gaoua
BURKINA FASO
Ouagadougou
Koudougou
Tougan
Kaya
Dori
Fada-n-Gourma
Dapaong
Mango
Natitingou
TOGO
Sokodé
Savalou
Kpalimé
Lomé
BENIN
Kandi
Bembéréké
Parakou
Abomey
Porto-Novo
Cotonou
Slave Coast
Bight of Benin
Kaesong
MALI
Tombouctou
Niger
Bourem
Gao
Ansongo
Ménaka
Hombori
Kidal
Tessalit
Adrar des Iforas
598
Taoudenni
El Djouf
Erg Iguidi
Erg Chech
Chegga
Tindouf
Tanezrouft
SAHARA
ALGERIA
ALGER (Algiers)
Tizi-Ouzou
Blida
Médéa
Ech Cheliff
Mostaganem
Oran
Mascara
Tiaret
Sidi-bel-Abbès
Tlemcen
Oujda
Saharien Atlas
Chott ech Chergui
Aflou
Mecheria
2285
Aïn-Sefra
El Bayadh
Laghouat
Messad
Bouârfa
Figuig
Béchar
Haut Atlas
Moyen Atlas
Anti Atlas
Maghreb
Abadla
Ghardaïa
Berriane
Ouargla
Hassi Messaoud
El Goléa
Grand Erg Occidental
Grand Erg Oriental
Kerzaz
Timimoun
Bordj Fly Ste. Marie
Plateau du Tademaït
In Salah
Zaouiet Reggâne
Ouallene
Arak
Tassili n'Ajjer
2158
Djanet
Illizi
Bordj-in-Eker
Ahaggar
Tahat 2918
Tamanrasset
Ohanet
Bordj Omar Driss
Touggourt
El Oued
Biskra
Chott Melrhir
Tozeur
Batna
Sétif
Bejaïa
Skikda
Annaba
Constantine
M'sila
Chott el Hodna
2328
Tebessa
Khenchela
Arlit
Iférouâne
Aïr
Agadez
I-n-Gall
NIGER
Tahoua
Tanout
Zinder
Filingué
Birni Nkonni
Niamey
Dosso
Famalé
Maradi
Katsina
Sokoto
Birnin Kebbi
Gusau
Jega
Kano
Gumel
Hadejia
Azare
Funtua
Zaria
Bena
Shanga
Kontagora
Kaduna
Bauchi
Jos
Kainji Res.
NIGERIA
Minna
Kafanchan
Shendam
Abuja
Keffi
Lafia
Bida
Baro
Ilorin
Offa
Ogbomosho
Oyo
Oshogbo
Iwo
Ilesha
Ikare
Lokoja
Makurdi
Wukari
Ibadan
Ife
Owo
Abeokuta
Akure
Ijebu-Ode
Benin City
Enugu
Oturkpo
Lagos
Sapele
Warri
Onitsha
Aba
Uyo
Burutu
Port Harcourt
Calabar
Kumba
Bamenda
Bafoussam
Mt. Cameroun 4070
Limbe
Rey Malabo
Bioko
Gaya
Botou
Shaki
Projection: Sanson-Flamsteed's Sinusoidal
West from Greenwich 0 East from Greenwich
ft m
12 000 4000
9000 3000
6000 2000
4500 1500
3000 1000
1200 400
600 200
0 0
200 600
1000 3000
2000 6000
4000 12 000
m ft

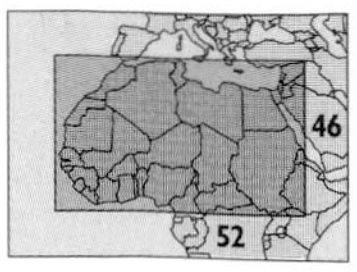
46
52

MEDITERRANEAN SEA
GREECE
TURKEY
CYPRUS
SYRIA
LEBANON
ISRAEL
JORDAN
IRAQ
SAUDI ARABIA
RED SEA
LIBYA
EGYPT
SUDAN
CHAD
ERITREA
ETHIOPIA
CENTRAL AFRICAN REPUBLIC
MALTA
Valletta
Sicilia
TUNIS
Bizerte
Sousse
Nabeul
Mahdia
Sfax
Golfe de Gabès
Île de Djerba
Gabès
Zarzis
Médenine
Tarābulus (Tripoli)
Al Khums
Az Zāwiyah
Gharyān
Misrātah
Mizdah
Tripolitania
Surt
Khalij Surt
Banghāzī
Al Marj
Darnah
Tubruq
Bardīyah
Salûm
Ajdābiyā
Suluq
Cyrenaica
Al Jaghbūb
Awjilah
Hūn
Zillah
Idehan Awbārī
Brach
Sabhah
Awbārī
Marzūq
Fezzan
Wāw al Kabīr
Al Qaṭrūn
Ghat
Ghudāmis
Daraj
Ṣaḥrā' Rebiana
Al Kufrah
Al Jawf
Sahrâ' Lîbîya
Antalya
ADANA
Antakya
ḤALAB
Rōdhos
Kríti
Iráklion
Al Lādhiqīyah
Nicosia
Tarābulus
Ḥimṣ
BAYRŪT (Beirut)
DIMASHQ (Damascus)
Jabal ad Durūz 1801
Haifa
Tel Aviv-Yafo
Ashdod
Jerusalem
West Bank
'AMMĀN
Ar Ruṭbah
Bādiyat ash Shām
Ma'ān
Al 'Aqabah
Elat
Al Jawf
Tabūk
Al Muwaylih
Al Wajh
Ḥijāz
Yanbu 'al Baḥr
Rābigh
EL ISKANDARÎYA (Alexandria)
El Mahalla el Kubra
Damanhûr
Dumyât
Bûr Sa'îd
El Mansûra
Tanta
Zagazig
Ismâ'ilîya
EL GÎZA
EL QAHIRA (Cairo)
El Suweis
Helwân
El Faiyûm
Beni Suef
Maghâgha
El Minyâ
Mallawi
Manfalût
Asyût
Tahta
Sohâg
Girga
Qena
THEBES
KARNAK
El Uqsur
Idfû
Kom Ombo
Aswân
Sadd el Aali
Buheirat en Nasr
ABU SIMBEL
Marsâ Matrûh
El Alamein
Munkhafed el Qattâra
-133
Siwa
Qasr Farâfra
Mût
El Wâhât el-Dakhla
El Khârga
El Wâhât el-Khârga
Es Sahrâ Esh Sharqîya
Sînâ
G. Mûsa 2637
Hurghada
Bûr Safâga
Quseir
Ras Banâs
Bîr Shalatein
Halaib
Ras Hadarba
Muhammad Qol
Bûr Sûdân
Suakin
Trinkitat
Karora
Nakfa
Akordat
Kassalâ
Wadi Halfa
Es Sahrâ en Nûbîya
El Wâhât el Selîma
Kosha
Delgo
3rd Cataract
Dongola
Abu Hamed
Kareima
4th Cataract
5th Cataract
Berber
Atbara
Ed Debba
Nahr en Nil
Bir 'Atrun
Adarama
Shendi
Wad Hamid
6th Cataract
Omdurmân
El Khartûm (Khartoum)
Nahr Atbara
El Wuz
Khashm el Girba
Wâd Medanî
Gedaref
El Gezira
Sodiri
Ed Dueim
El Obeid
Kôstî
Singa
Nîl el Azraq
Umm Ruwaba
Er Rahad
En Nahud
Abû Zabad
El Odaiya
Kordofân
Kâdugli
Ed Damazin
Nîl el Abyad
Gonder
L. Tana
Bahir Dar
Debre Markos
Burē
Nekemte
Dembidolo
Metu
Gorē
Jima
Omo
L. Abaya
Arba Minch
L. Shamo
Chew Bahir
L. Turkana
Lokitaung
Kapoeta
Torit
Juba
Mongalla
Tali Post
Bôr
Pibor Post
Malakâl
Sobat
Sudd
Bahr el Jebel
Bahr el Ghazâl
Gogriâl
Wâw
Tonj
Rumbêk
Toinya
Amadi
El Istiwa'iya
Yambio
Yei
Kajo Kaji
Faradje
Dungu
Uele
Ango
Bondo
Bomu
Obo
Bakouma
Bangassou
Mobaye
Mobayi
Ubangi
Zongo
Bosobolo
Libenge
Bangui
Mbaïki
Berbérati
Bossembélé
Carnot
Batouri
Bertoua
Abong-Mbang
Nanga-Eboko
Yaoundé
Sanaga
Bouar
Bozoum
Bossangoa
Baboua
Bétaré Oya
Yoko
Foumban
Massif de l'Adamaoua
Ngaoundéré
Banyo
Gashaka
Baïbokoum
Paoua
Kaga Bandoro
Yalinga
Ippy
Bambari
Sibut
Ndélé
Sa'id Bundas
Raga
Bahr el Ghazâl
Bahr el Arab
Songo
Birao
1326
Moundou
Doba
Koumra
Sarh
Lai
Logone
Pala
Garoua
Guider
Mubi
Maroua
Bongor
Chari
Massenya
Kousséri
Ndjamena
Bokoro
Mongo
Goz Beïda
Abou-Deïa
Am Timan
Maiduguri
Bama
Biu
Potiskum
Bajoga
Kumo
Numan
Yola
Gashua
Geidam
Nguru
Nguigmi
Bosso
Mao
Lac Tchad
Moussoro
Massakory
Ati
Oum Hadjer
Abéché
Biltine
Zigey
Bahr el Ghazal
Erg du Djourab
Oum Chalouba
Zagaoua
Fada
Ennedi
1310
Dépression du Mourdi
Ounianga Sérir
Faya-Largeau
Borkou
Grand Erg du Bilma
Bilma
Fachi
Chirfa
Madama
Toummo
Aozou Strip
Aozou
Bardaï
Pic Toussidé 3265
Tarso Emissi 2160
Tibesti
Zouar
Emi Koussi 3415
Ma'tan as Sarra
J. Uweinat 1893
1082
1200
Al Junaynah
Zalingei
Jebel Marra 3088
Nyâlâ
Kutum
1954
Malha
Darfur
El Fâsher
Umm Keddada
1325
2259
2187
2578
1830
3202
3606
2160
3187
Sahara
8
9
10
11
12
13
14
15
20
25
30
35
40
A
B
C
D
E
F
G
H

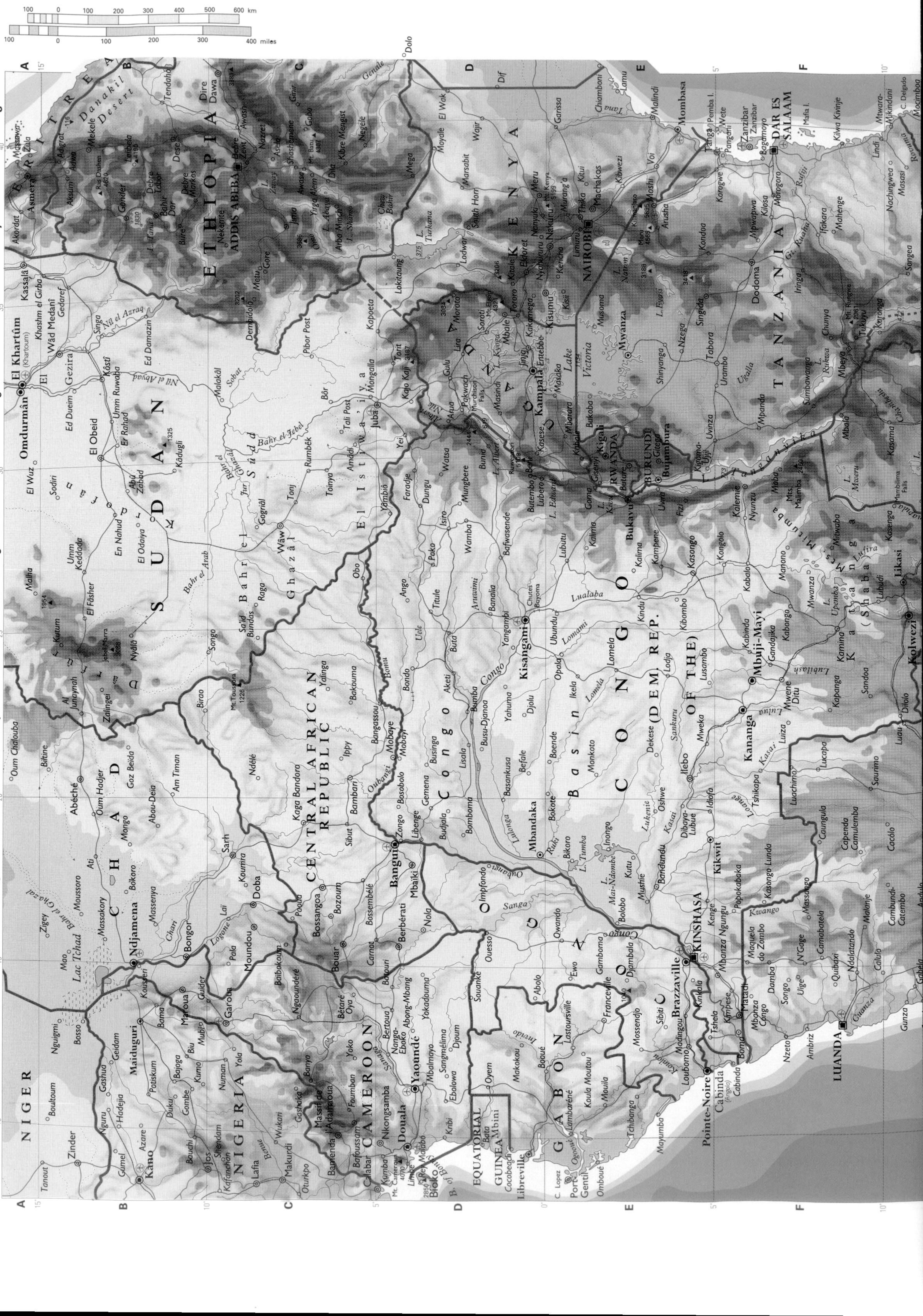
100 0 100 200 300 400 500 600 km
100 0 100 200 300 400 miles
SUDAN
ETHIOPIA
ERITREA
KENYA
UGANDA
TANZANIA
RWANDA
BURUNDI
CONGO (DEM. REP. OF THE)
CONGO
GABON
EQUATORIAL GUINEA
CAMEROON
CENTRAL AFRICAN REPUBLIC
CHAD
NIGERIA
NIGER
ADDIS ABEBA
NAIROBI
Kampala
Kigali
Bujumbura
DAR ES SALAAM
KINSHASA
Brazzaville
LUANDA
Libreville
Yaoundé
Bangui
Ndjamena
El Khartûm
Omdurmân
Asmera
Mombasa
Kisangani
Lake Victoria
Congo Basin
Dolo

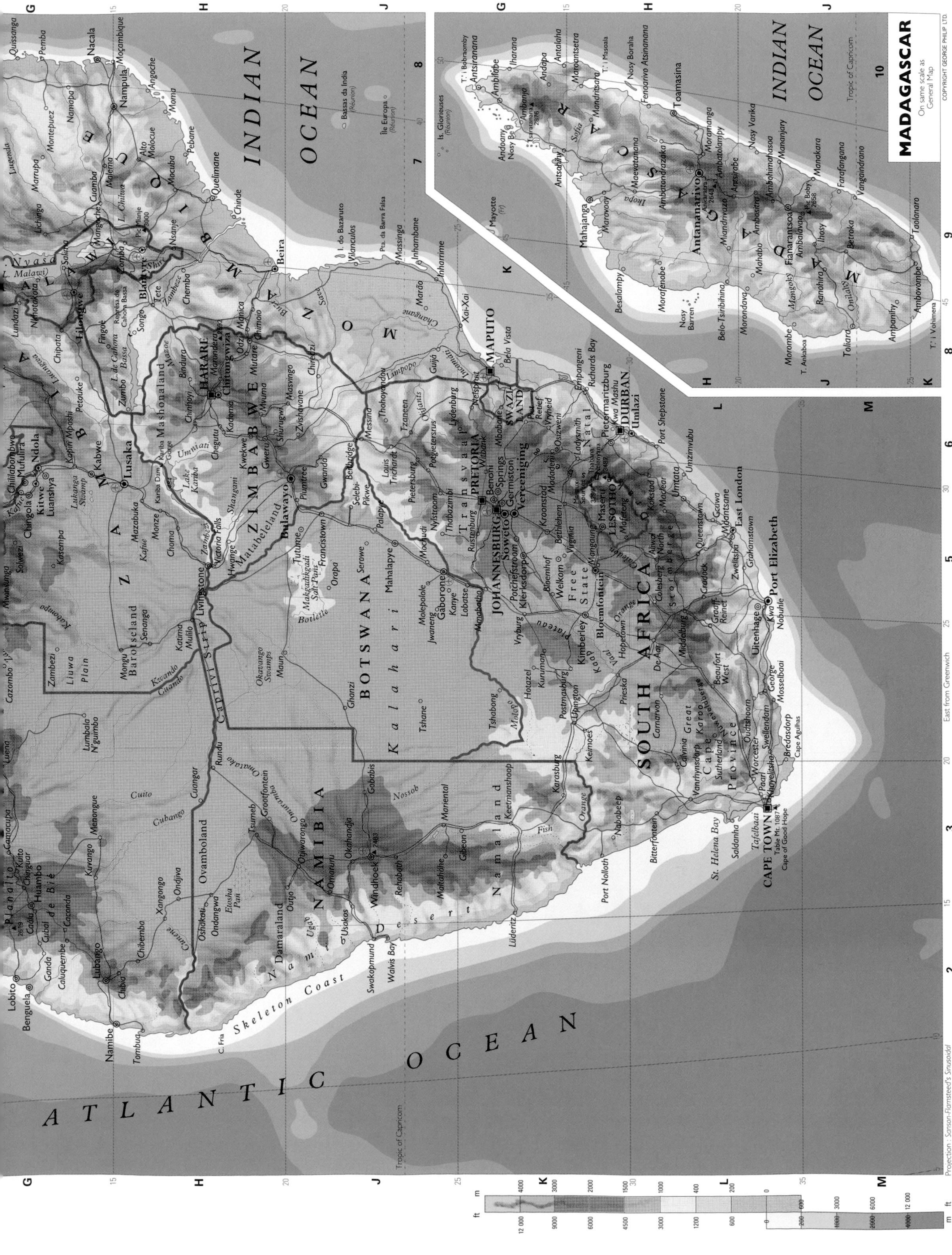
MADAGASCAR
On same scale as General Map
ATLANTIC OCEAN
INDIAN OCEAN
NAMIBIA
BOTSWANA
ZIMBABWE
ZAMBIA
MOZAMBIQUE
SOUTH AFRICA
LESOTHO
SWAZILAND
Kalahari
Namib Desert
Skeleton Coast
Tropic of Capricorn
East from Greenwich
Projection : Sanson-Flamsteed's Sinusoidal
COPYRIGHT GEORGE PHILIP LTD.
CAPE TOWN
Cape of Good Hope
JOHANNESBURG
PRETORIA
MAPUTO
HARARE
DURBAN
Windhoek
Gaborone
Lusaka
Bulawayo
Beira
Antananarivo
Port Elizabeth
Bloemfontein
Maseru
East London
Kimberley
Livingstone
Walvis Bay
Lüderitz
Toamasina
Fianarantsoa
Toliara
Mahajanga
Antsiranana
m
ft
4000
3000
2000
1500
1000
400
200
0
12 000
9000
6000
4500
3000
1200
600
0
200
600
1000
3000
2000
6000
4000
12 000

EAST AFRICA 1:8 000 000

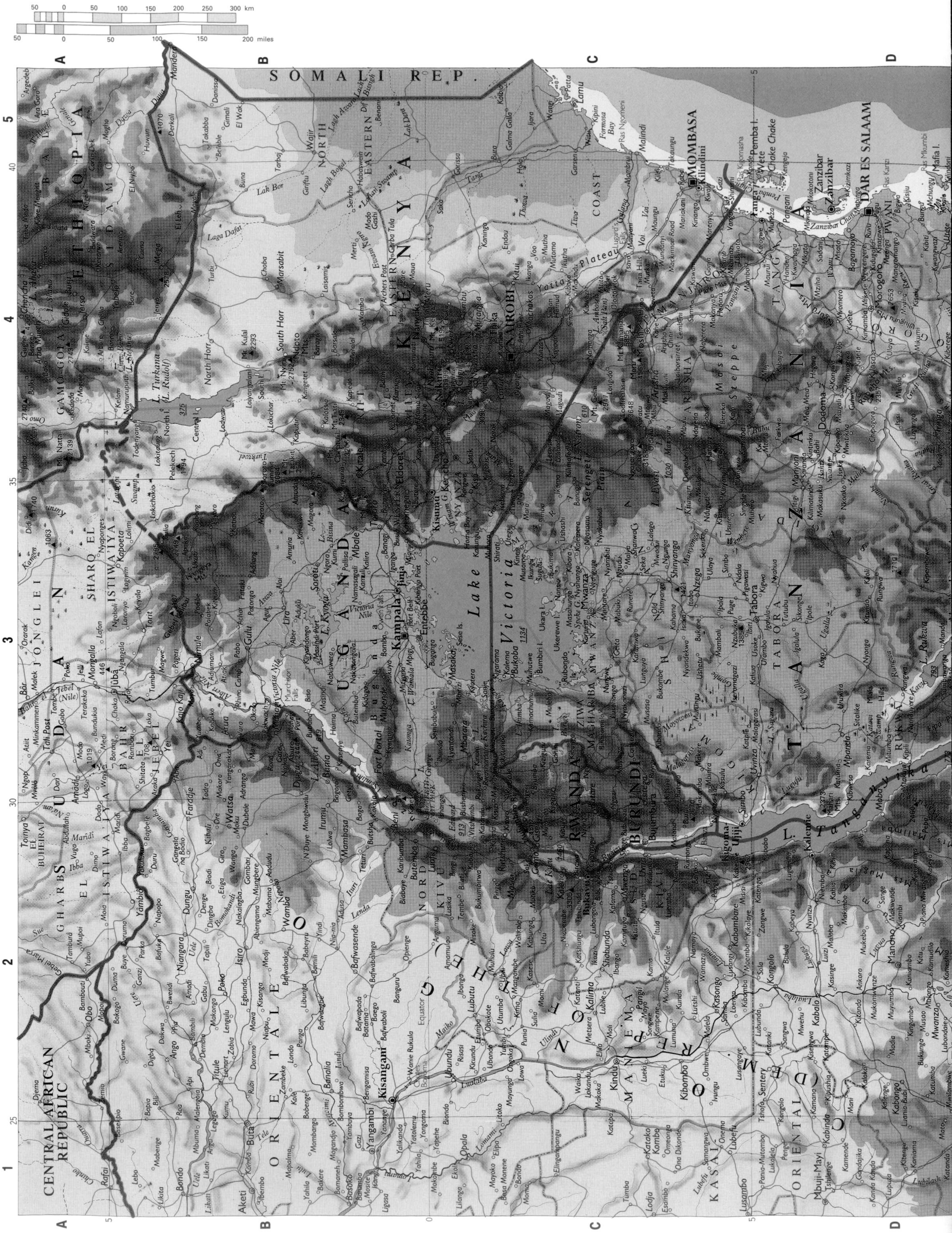

50 0 50 100 150 200 250 300 km
50 0 50 100 150 200 miles
SOMALI REP.
ETHIOPIA
KENYA
UGANDA
RWANDA
BURUNDI
CENTRAL AFRICAN REPUBLIC
NAIROBI
MOMBASA
DAR ES SALAAM
Zanzibar
Kampala
Kisangani
Lake Victoria
L. Turkana (L. Rudolf)

INDIAN OCEAN
Z A M B I A
Z I M B A B W E
M O Z A M B I Q U E
B O T S W A N A
SOUTH AFRICA
ANGOLA
NAMIBIA
L. Malawi
HARARE
Lusaka
BULAWAYO
Lubumbashi
Beira
Blantyre
Lilongwe
Projection: Lambert's Equivalent Azimuthal
East from Greenwich
COPYRIGHT GEORGE PHILIP LTD.

SOUTHERN AFRICA 1:8 000 000

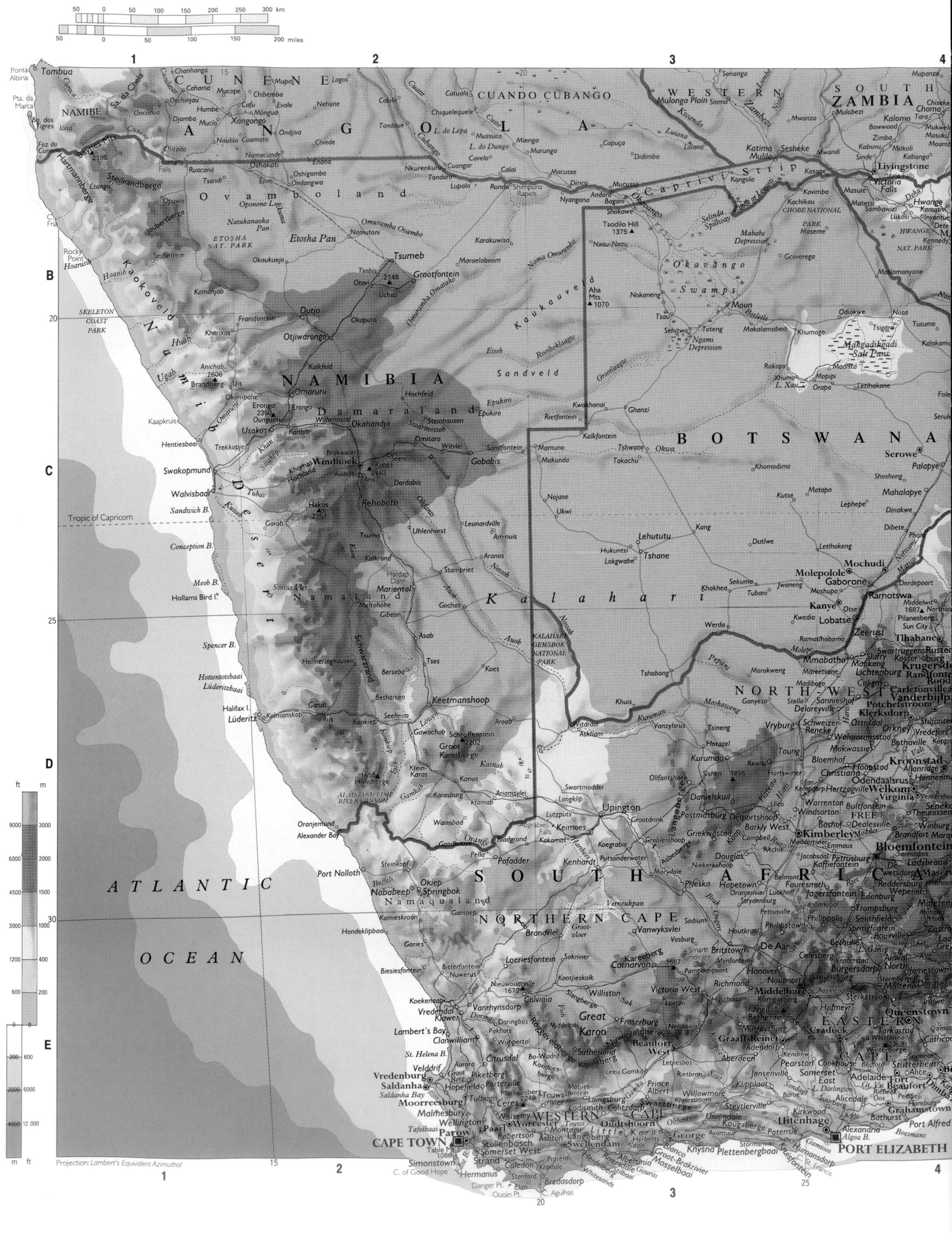

50 0 50 100 150 200 250 300 km
50 0 50 100 150 200 miles
1
2
3
4
B
C
D
E
ft m
9000 3000
6000 2000
4500 1500
3000 1000
1200 400
600 200
0 0
200 600
2000 6000
4000 12 000
m ft
Projection: Lambert's Equivalent Azimuthal
Ponta Albina
Tombua
Pta. da Marca
NAMIBE
Bg. dos Tigres
Foz do Cunene
C U N E N E
A N G O L A
CUANDO CUBANGO
Lubango
Sa. da Chela
Chibemba
Cahama
Humbe
Xangongo
Ondjiva
Mupa
Cafu
Mongua
Evale
Nehone
Chiede
Cuamato
Naulila
Chitado
Namacunde
Oshakati
Ondangwa
Oshigambo
Ruacana
Ruacana Falls
Tsandi
Elim
Baynes Mts.
2195
Hartmannberge
Steilrandberge
Etanga
Opuwo
Ovamboland
Oponono L.
Ekuma
Natukanaoka Pan
ETOSHA NAT. PARK
Etosha Pan
Namutoni
Omuramba Ovambo
Okaukuejo
Sesfontein
Joubertberge
Rocky Point
Hoarusib
Hoanib
Kaokoveld
Kamanjab
Tsumeb
Tsobis
Otavi
2148
Grootfontein
Uchab
Outjo
Okaputa
Otjiwarongo
Fransfontein
Khorixas
SKELETON COAST PARK
Huab
Ugab
Anichab
2606
Brandberg
Uis
Kalkfeld
Omaruru
Okombahe
Erongo
2350
Ounguati
Wilhelmstal
Okahandjo
Steinhausen
Karibib
Usakos
Kaapkruis
Hentiesbaai
Trekkopje
Khan
Swakop
Swakopmund
Walvisbaai
Sandwich B.
Tropic of Capricorn
Kuiseb
Tubas
Khomas Hochland
Windhoek
Brakwater
Seeis
Kobos
2463
Aris
Ausasberg
Dordabis
Hakos
2351
Rehoboth
Gobabis
Witvlei
Omitara
Garob
Tsumis
Uhlenhorst
Leonardville
Aminuis
Aranos
Conception B.
Meob B.
Hollams Bird I.
Sossus Vlei
Kalkrand
Hardap Dam
Mariental
Maltahöhe
Gibeon
Gochas
Auob
Nossob
Namaland
Spencer B.
Helmeringhausen
Schwarzrand
Bersebo
Asab
Tses
Koes
Hottentotsbaai
Lüderitzbaai
Halifax I.
Lüderitz
Kolmanskop
Garub
Aus
Bethanien
Keetmanshoop
Seeheim
Konkiep
Gawachab
Schroffenstein
2202
Groot Karasberge
Aroab
Klein-Karas
1655
Hunsberge
Kanus
Karasburg
Hamab
Ariamsvlei
AI-AIS AND FISH RIVER CANYON
Warmbad
Oranjemund
Alexander Bay
Goodhouse
Orange
Vioolsdrif
NAMIBIA
Damaraland
Namib
Desert
Kalahari
Sandveld
Kaukauveld
ATLANTIC
OCEAN
Cuatir
Catuala
Chiquelequele
Cuito
L. do Lipa
Mussuco
L. do Dungo
Mienga
Marunga
Cavelo
Cuangar
Cubango
Calai
Nkurenkuru
Tondoro
Lupala
Runda
Shimpuru Rapids
Macusse
Dirico
Mucusso
Andara
Bagani
Nyangana
Shakawe
Okavango
Tsodilo Hill
1375
Nxau-Nxau
Karakuwisa
Maroelaboom
Omuramba Omatako
Noma Omuramba
Aha Mts.
1070
Nokaneng
Okavango Swamps
Tsau
Sehitwa
Toteng
Ngami Depression
Maun
Eiseb
Rooibokvlei
Groote Laagte
Epukiro
Rietfontein
Kwakhanai
Ghanzi
Kalkfontein
Sandfontein
Mamuno
Makunda
Tshwane
Okwa
Takachu
Nojane
Ukwi
Lehututu
Hukuntsi
Lokgwabe
Tshane
Kang
Dutlwe
Sekuma
Tubani
Jwaneng
Khakhea
Werda
KALAHARI GEMSBOK NATIONAL PARK
Molopo
Tshabong
Khuis
Kuruman
Witdraai
Askham
Vanzylsrus
Tsineng
Hotazel
Kuruman
Sishen
1855
Reivilo
Olifantshoek
Daniëlskuil
Swartmodder
Langklip
Upington
Grootdrink
Lutzputs
Keimoes
Augrabies Falls
Kakamas
Bladgrond
Pofadder
Pella
Kenhardt
Koegrabie
Putsonderwater
Marydale
Prieska
Niekerkshoop
Groblershoop
Postmasburg
Steinkopf
Port Nolloth
Buffels
Okiep
Nababeep
Springbok
Namaqualand
Gamoep
Kamieskroon
Hondeklipbaai
Garies
Bitterfontein
Nuwerus
Biesiesfontein
Loeriesfontein
Brandvlei
Grootvloer
Verneukpan
NORTHERN CAPE
SOUTH AFRICA
Vanwyksvlei
Vosburg
Sakrivier
Kootjieskolk
Williston
Calvinia
Nieuwoudtville
1672
Koekenaap
Vredendal
Klawer
Vanrhynsdorp
Doring
Doringbos
Pakhuis
Lambert's Bay
Clanwilliam
Wuppertal
Citrusdal
St. Helena B.
Velddrif
Vredenburg
Saldanha
Saldanha Bay
Aurora
Piketberg
Porterville
Hopefield
Moorreesburg
Malmesbury
Tulbagh
Wellington
Paarl
Tafelbaai
Table Mt. 1086
CAPE TOWN
Parow
Stellenbosch
Somerset West
Strand
Simonstown
C. of Good Hope
False B.
Hermanus
Caledon
Kleinmond
Stanford
Danger Pt.
Elim
Quoin Pt.
Bredasdorp
C. Agulhas
Worcester
Wolseley
Robertson
Ashton
Swellendam
Montagu
Touws
Touwsrivier
Matjiesfontein
Laingsburg
Ladismith
Calitzdorp
Oudtshoorn
Langeberg
Riversdale
Heidelberg
Albertinia
Stilbaai
Mosselbaai
George
Knysna
Plettenbergbaai
Groot-Brakrivier
Little Karoo
Swartberge
Uniondale
Kougaberge
Willowmore
Steytlerville
Klipplaat
Jansenville
Kirkwood
Uitenhage
PORT ELIZABETH
Algoa B.
Humansdorp
Kareedouw
Jeffreys Bay
C. St. Francis
Gamtoos
Fraserburg
Great Karoo
Sutherland
Nuweveldberge
Komsberg
Beaufort West
Nelspoort
Koo Bokkeveld
Roggeveldberge
Middelpos
Carnarvon
Kareeberg
Loxton
Victoria West
Richmond
Hanover
Noupoort
Middelburg
Murraysburg
Graaff-Reinet
Aberdeen
Letjiesbos
Leeu Gamka
Prince Albert
Rietbron
Pearston
Somerset East
Cookhouse
Bedford
Adelaide
Fort Beaufort
Alicedale
Grahamstown
Port Alfred
Kenton
Bathurst
Cradock
EASTERN CAPE
Queenstown
Tarkastad
Steynsburg
Burgersdorp
Aliwal North
Jamestown
Molteno
Sterkstroom
Hofmeyr
Colesberg
De Aar
Britstown
Philipstown
Petrusville
Hopetown
Strydenburg
Douglas
Kimberley
Modder
Jacobsdal
Koffiefontein
Petrusburg
Fauresmith
Jagersfontein
Reddersburg
Edenburg
Trompsburg
Philippolis
Smithfield
Springfontein
Rouxville
Zastron
Wepener
Bloemfontein
Dewetsdorp
Ladybrand
Brandfort
Winburg
Theunissen
Welkom
Virginia
Odendaalsrus
Hennenman
Allanridge
Kroonstad
Hoopstad
Bultfontein
Warrenton
Windsorton
Boshof
Dealesville
Christiana
Bloemhof
Hertzogville
Jan Kempdorp
Barkly West
Delportshoop
Campbell
Griekwastad
Ulco
Hartswater
Taung
Vryburg
Schweizer-Reneke
Wolmaransstad
Makwassie
Bothaville
Orkney
Klerksdorp
Vredefort
Stilfontein
Potchefstroom
Ventersdorp
Carletonville
Vanderbijlpark
Ottosdal
Delareyville
Sannieshof
Lichtenburg
Coligny
Ganyesa
Stella
Madibogo
Mareetsane
Mmabatho
Mafikeng
NORTH-WEST
Zeerust
Swartruggens
Koster
Krugersdorp
Randfontein
Tlhabane
Rustenburg
Sun City
Pilanesberg
Ramatlhabama
Lobatse
Otse
Kanye
Moshupa
Gaborone
Molepolole
Mochudi
Ramotswa
Derdepoort
Middelwit
1687
Notwane
Marico
Letlhakeng
Kweneng
Dibete
Phala
Dinokwe
Lephepe
Mahalapye
Shoshong
Kutse
Matapa
Khomodimo
BOTSWANA
Serowe
Palapye
Falesa
Serule
Rakops
Xhumo
L. Xau
Mopipi
Orapa
Letlhakane
Makgadikgadi Salt Pans
Madista
Tsigaro
Khumaga
Makalamabedi
Boteti
Odiakwe
Nata
Tutume
Kalakamati
Maitlamanyane
Gcoverega
Mababe Depression
PARK
Maseme
Selinda Spillway
Kavimba
Kachikau
CHOBE NATIONAL
Kasane
Kazungula
Caprivi Strip
Katima Mulilo
Sesheke
Kongola
Linyanti
Chobe or Linyanti
Luiana
Kwando
Lialana
Didimbo
Capuça
Mwanza
WESTERN
Zambezi
Luanginga
Lumbe
Njoko
Mulonga Plain
Sioma
Senanga
Mwandi
SOUTH
ZAMBIA
Mulobezi
Kalomo
Choma
Chisekesi
Tara
Mapanza
Bowwood
Zimba
Kabuvu
Mokoli
Mukwela
Masuku
Maamba
Sinde
Kabango
Livingstone
Victoria Falls
Masuie
Matetsi
Sambawizi
Lukosi
Kamativi
Hwange
Inyantue
Dete
HWANGE
NAT. PARK
Kennedy
Deka

Port Elizabeth

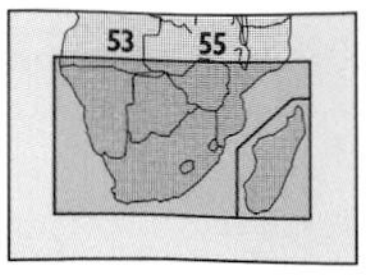
53
55

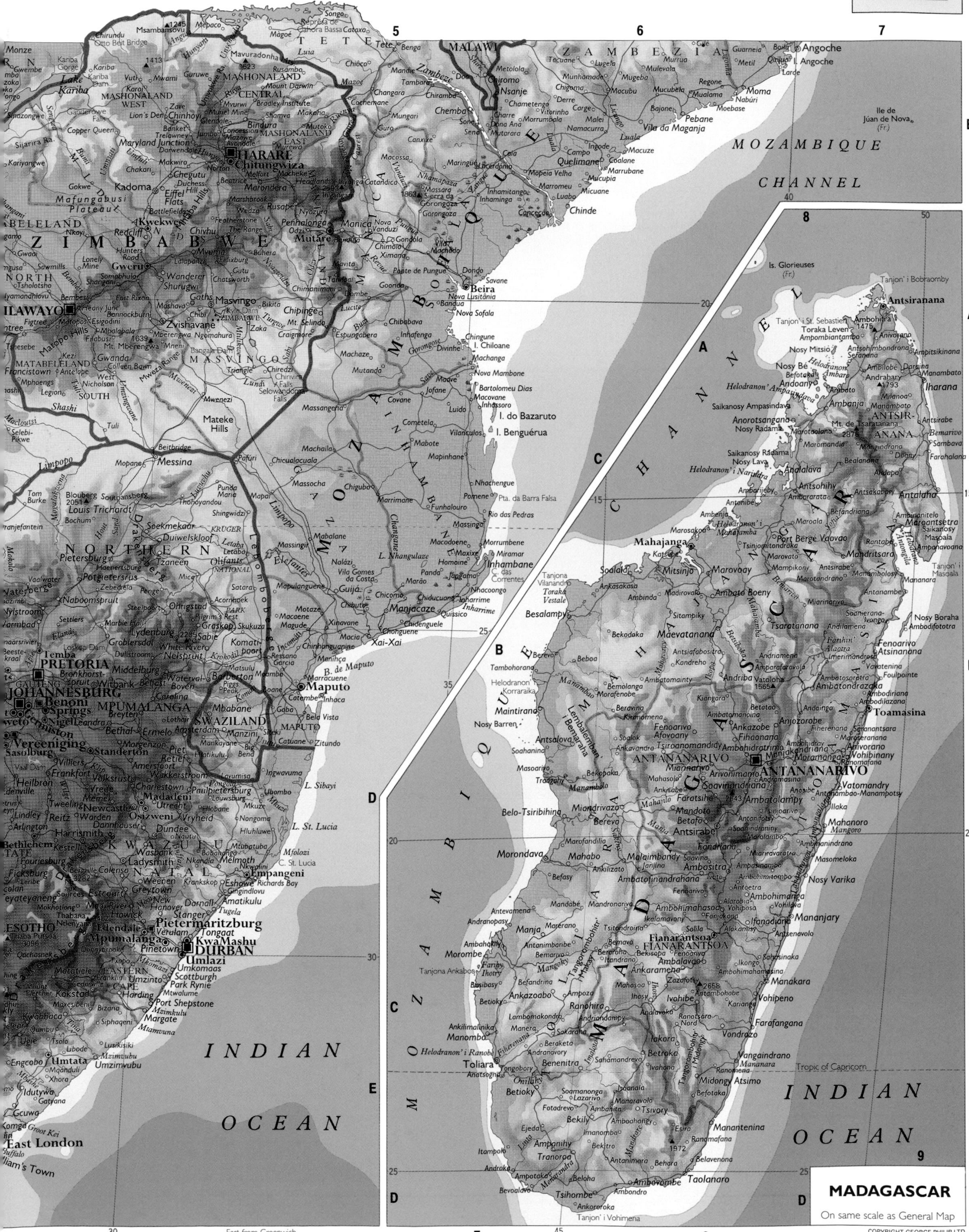
ZIMBABWE
MOZAMBIQUE
MALAWI
SWAZILAND
LESOTHO
MADAGASCAR
HARARE
Chitungwiza
Bulawayo
Gweru
Mutare
Masvingo
Kadoma
Chegutu
Zvishavane
Beira
Chimoio
Tete
Quelimane
Chinde
Angoche
Moma
Pebane
Inhambane
Maputo
Xai-Xai
Manjacaze
Messina
Louis Trichardt
Pietersburg
Tzaneen
Nelspruit
Middelburg
PRETORIA
JOHANNESBURG
Vereeniging
Benoni
Springs
Standerton
Ermelo
Mbabane
Manzini
Newcastle
Ladysmith
Pietermaritzburg
DURBAN
Umlazi
Empangeni
Richards Bay
Port Shepstone
Margate
Umtata
East London
NORTHERN
MPUMALANGA
KWAZULU NATAL
EASTERN CAPE
GAUTENG
Limpopo
Zambeze
I. do Bazaruto
I. Benguérua
MOZAMBIQUE CHANNEL
INDIAN OCEAN
Ile de Júan de Nova (Fr.)
Is. Glorieuses (Fr.)
Antsiranana
Mahajanga
Toamasina
ANTANANARIVO
Antsirabe
Fianarantsoa
Toliara
Morondava
Taolanaro
Manakara
Farafangana
Mananjary
Maintirano
Besalampy
Morombe
Ambovombe
Tropic of Capricorn
MADAGASCAR
On same scale as General Map
East from Greenwich

COPYRIGHT GEORGE PHILIP LTD.

AUSTRALIA AND OCEANIA : Physical and Political 1:50 000 000

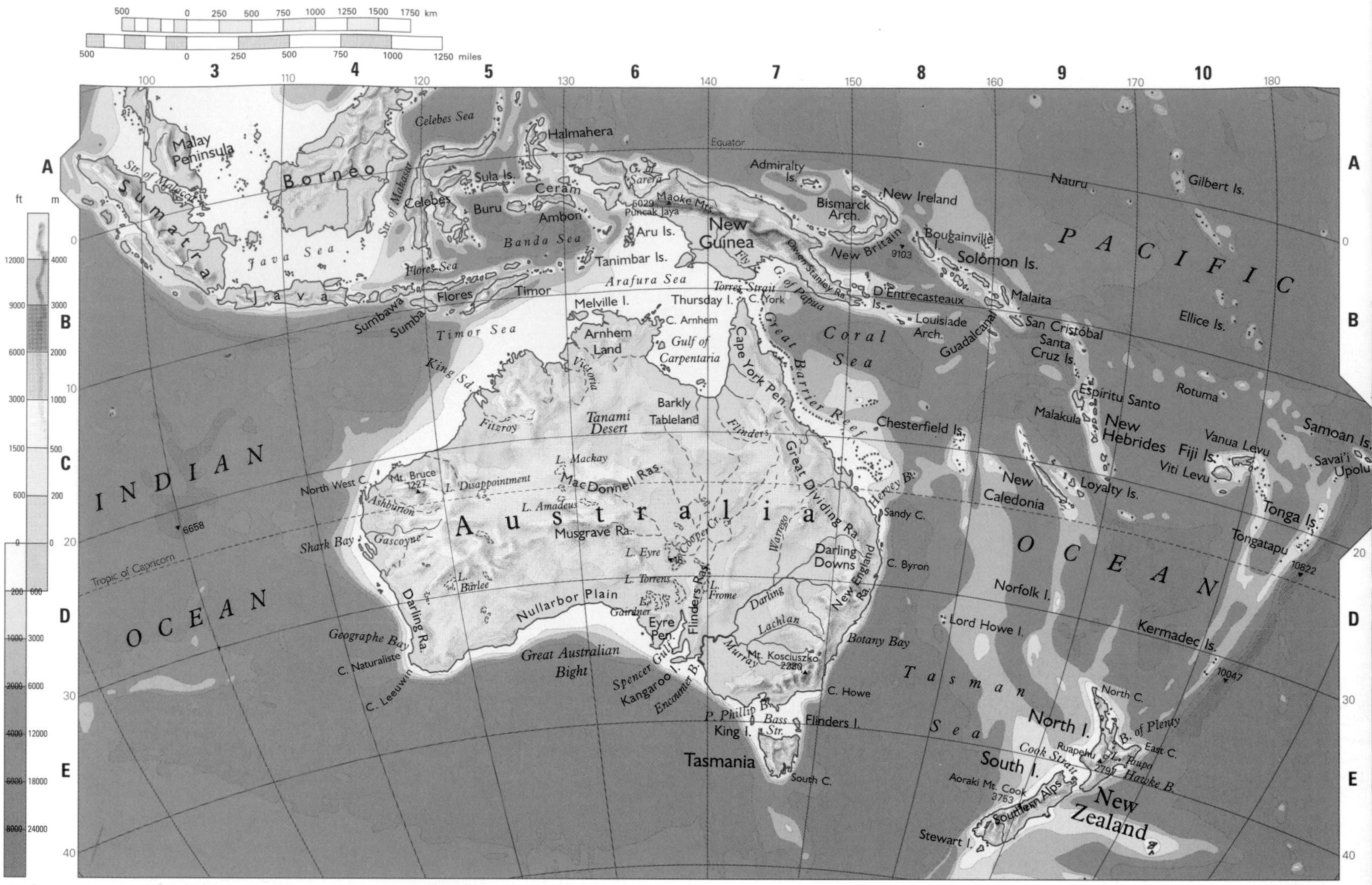

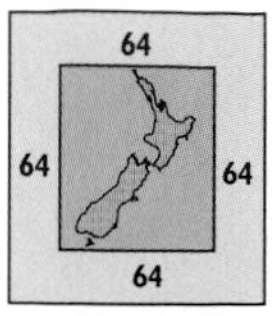

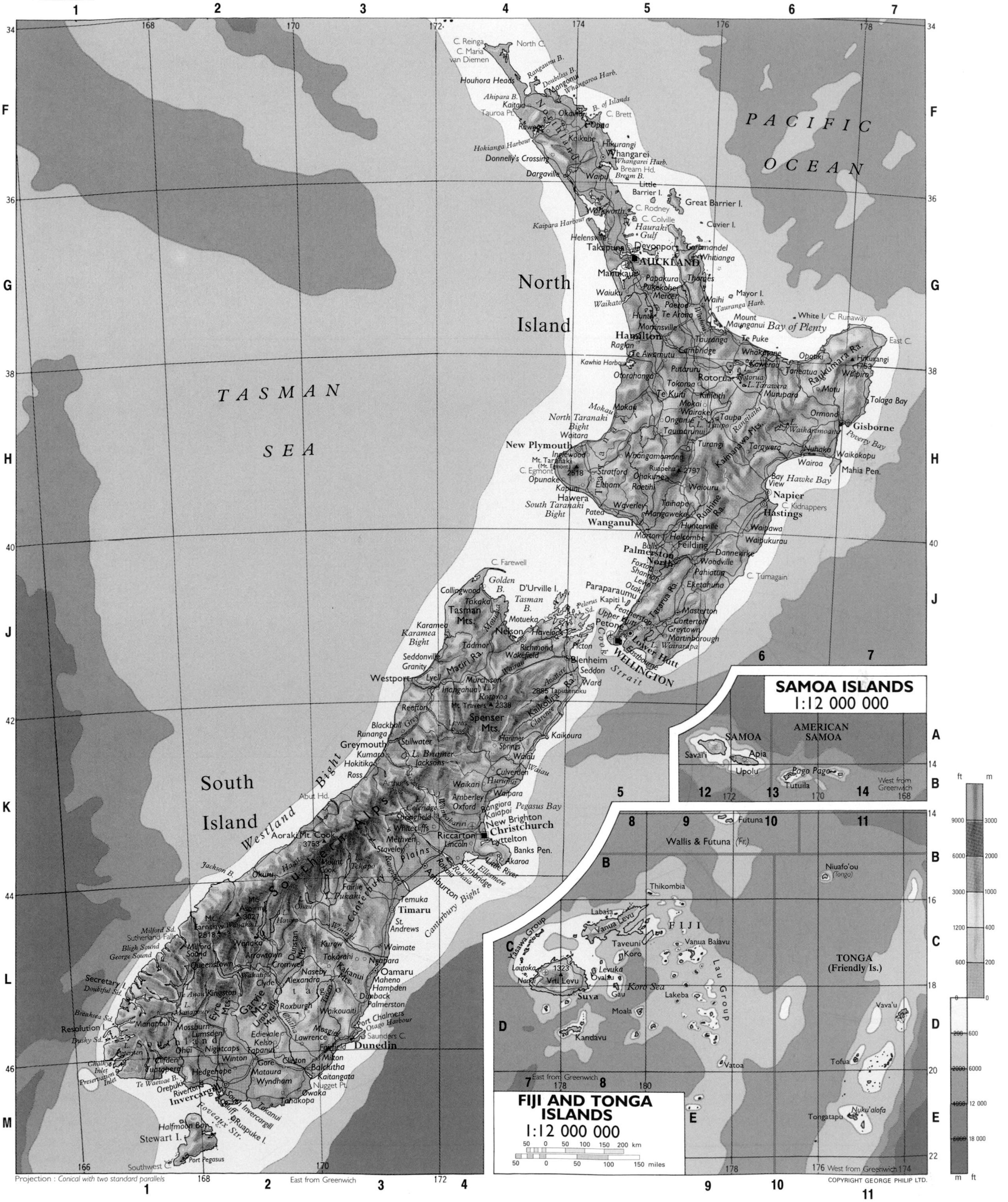

PACIFIC OCEAN
TASMAN SEA
North Island
South Island
C. Reinga
North C.
Houhora Heads
Kaitaia
Kaikohe
B. of Islands
Whangarei
Dargaville
Great Barrier I.
Hauraki Gulf
AUCKLAND
Manukau
Thames
Hamilton
Bay of Plenty
Tauranga
Rotorua
Taupo
Gisborne
New Plymouth
Mt. Taranaki
Hawke Bay
Napier
Hastings
Wanganui
Palmerston North
Masterton
WELLINGTON
Cook Strait
Lower Hutt
C. Farewell
Nelson
Blenheim
Westport
Greymouth
Hokitika
Kaikoura
Christchurch
Banks Pen.
Aoraki Mt. Cook
Southern Alps
Canterbury Plains
Ashburton
Timaru
Canterbury Bight
Westland Bight
Oamaru
Queenstown
Otago
Dunedin
Invercargill
Foveaux Str.
Stewart I.
SAMOA ISLANDS
1:12 000 000
SAMOA
AMERICAN SAMOA
Savai'i
Apia
Upolu
Pago Pago
Tutuila
Wallis & Futuna (Fr.)
FIJI
Vanua Levu
Viti Levu
Suva
Koro Sea
Lau Group
Kandavu
TONGA (Friendly Is.)
Vava'u
Tofua
Nuku'alofa
Tongatapu
FIJI AND TONGA ISLANDS
1:12 000 000
Projection : Conical with two standard parallels
East from Greenwich
COPYRIGHT GEORGE PHILIP LTD.

50 0 50 100 150 200 250 300 km
50 0 50 100 150 200 miles
TIMOR SEA
INDIAN OCEAN
INDONESIA
NORTHERN TERRITORY
Tanami Desert
Great Sandy Desert
Gibson Desert
Kimberley
King Leopold Ranges
Hamersley Range
Pilbara
Bonaparte Archipelago
Joseph Bonaparte Gulf
Eighty Mile Beach
Darwin
Katherine
Kununurra
Wyndham
Derby
Broome
Port Hedland
Karratha
Kupang
Timor
Sumba
Sumbawa
Lombok
Bali
Melville I.
Bathurst I.
Rowley Shoals
Lake Mackay
Lake Disappointment
Exmouth Gulf

WESTERN AUSTRALIA
SOUTH AUSTRALIA
INDIAN OCEAN
SOUTHERN OCEAN
Great Australian Bight
Great Victoria Desert
Nullarbor Plain
Hampton Tableland
PERTH
Fremantle
Kwinana
Rockingham
Mandurah
Bunbury
Busselton
Albany
Esperance
Geraldton
Carnarvon
Kalgoorlie-Boulder
Norseman
Northam
Merredin
Ayers Rock 868
Mt. Olga 1069
Uluru Nat. Park
Petermann Ranges
Musgrave Ranges
Everard Ranges
Shark Bay
Dirk Hartog I.
Archipelago of the Recherche
L. Carnegie
L. Austin
L. Moore
L. Barlee
L. Carey
L. Cowan
L. Dundas
Projection: Bonne
East from Greenwich
COPYRIGHT GEORGE PHILIP LTD.

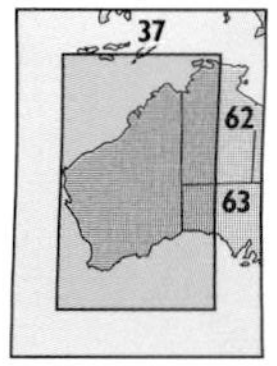
37
62
63

EASTERN AUSTRALIA 1:8 000 000

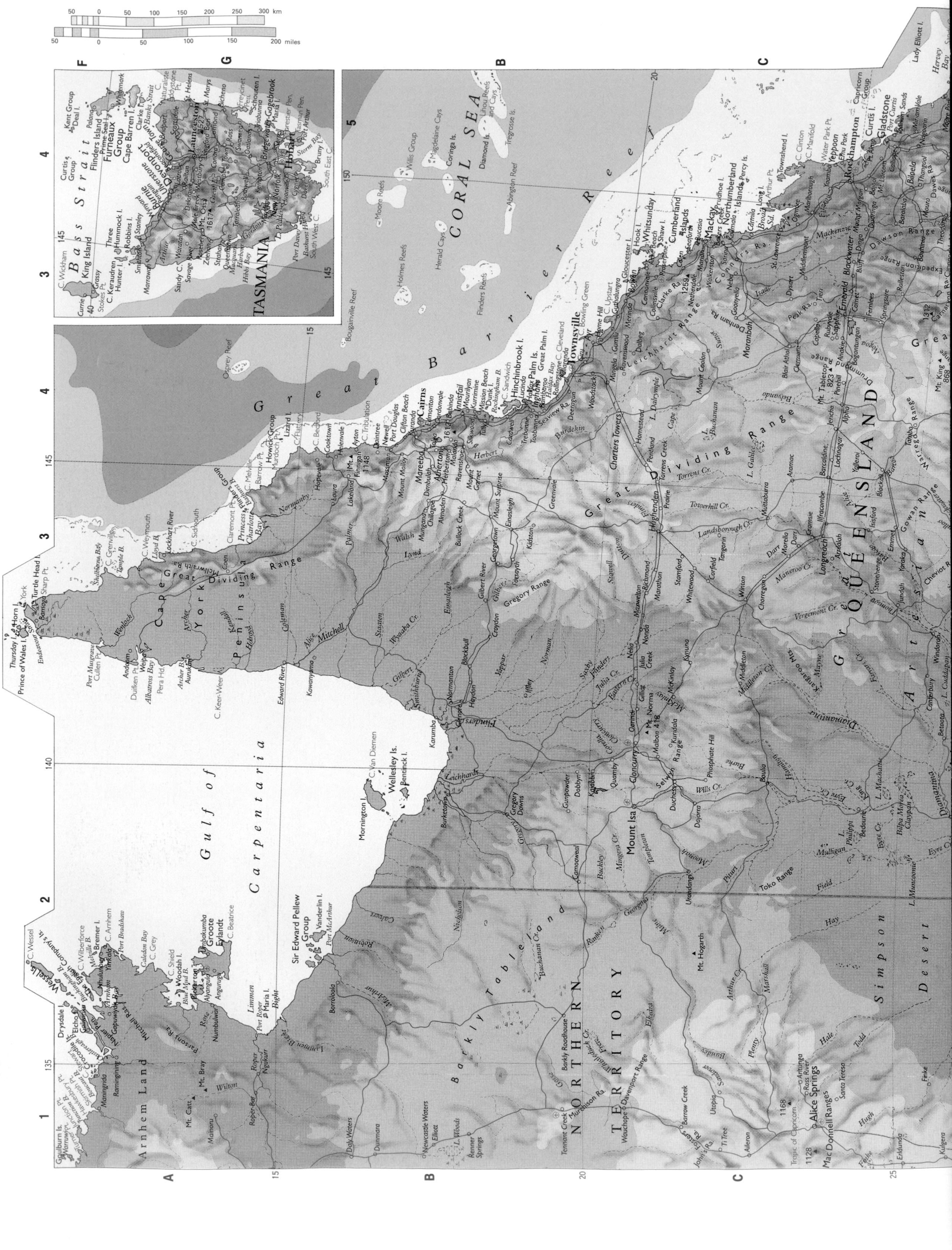

50 0 50 100 150 200 250 300 km
50 0 50 100 150 200 miles
TASMANIA
Bass Strait
King Island
Flinders Island
Furneaux Group
Launceston
Hobart
Devonport
Burnie
CORAL SEA
Great Barrier Reef
Gulf of Carpentaria
Cape York Peninsula
Great Dividing Range
QUEENSLAND
NORTHERN TERRITORY
Barkly Tableland
Simpson Desert
Arnhem Land
Great Artesian Basin
Townsville
Cairns
Mackay
Rockhampton
Gladstone
Mount Isa
Cloncurry
Alice Springs
Longreach
Charters Towers
Tennant Creek
Groote Eylandt
Mornington I.
Wellesley Is.
Whitsunday I.
Hinchinbrook I.
Tropic of Capricorn

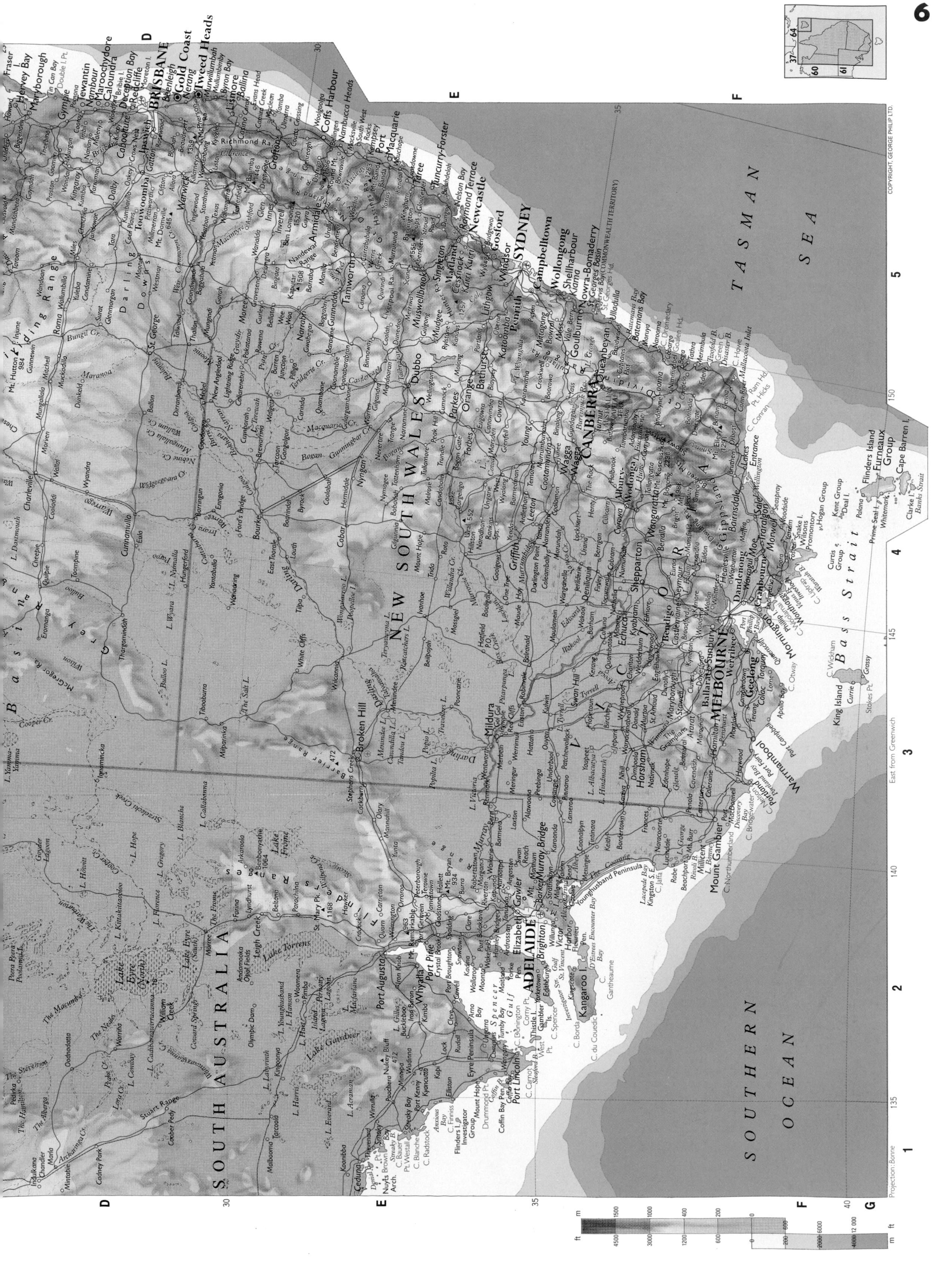
TASMAN SEA
SOUTHERN OCEAN
NEW SOUTH WALES
SOUTH AUSTRALIA
VICTORIA
SYDNEY
MELBOURNE
ADELAIDE
CANBERRA
BRISBANE
Bass Strait
Kangaroo I.
King Island
Flinders Island
Furneaux Group
Gold Coast
Newcastle
Wollongong
Broken Hill
Mildura
Port Augusta
Geelong
Warrnambool
Mount Gambier
Dubbo
Wagga Wagga
Bendigo
Ballarat
Great Dividing Range
Flinders Ranges
Lake Eyre (North)
Lake Eyre (South)
Lake Torrens
Lake Frome
Lake Gairdner
Projection: Bonne
East from Greenwich
COPYRIGHT, GEORGE PHILIP LTD.
m
ft
1500
4500
1000
3000
400
1200
200
600
0
0
200
600
2000
6000
4000
12 000

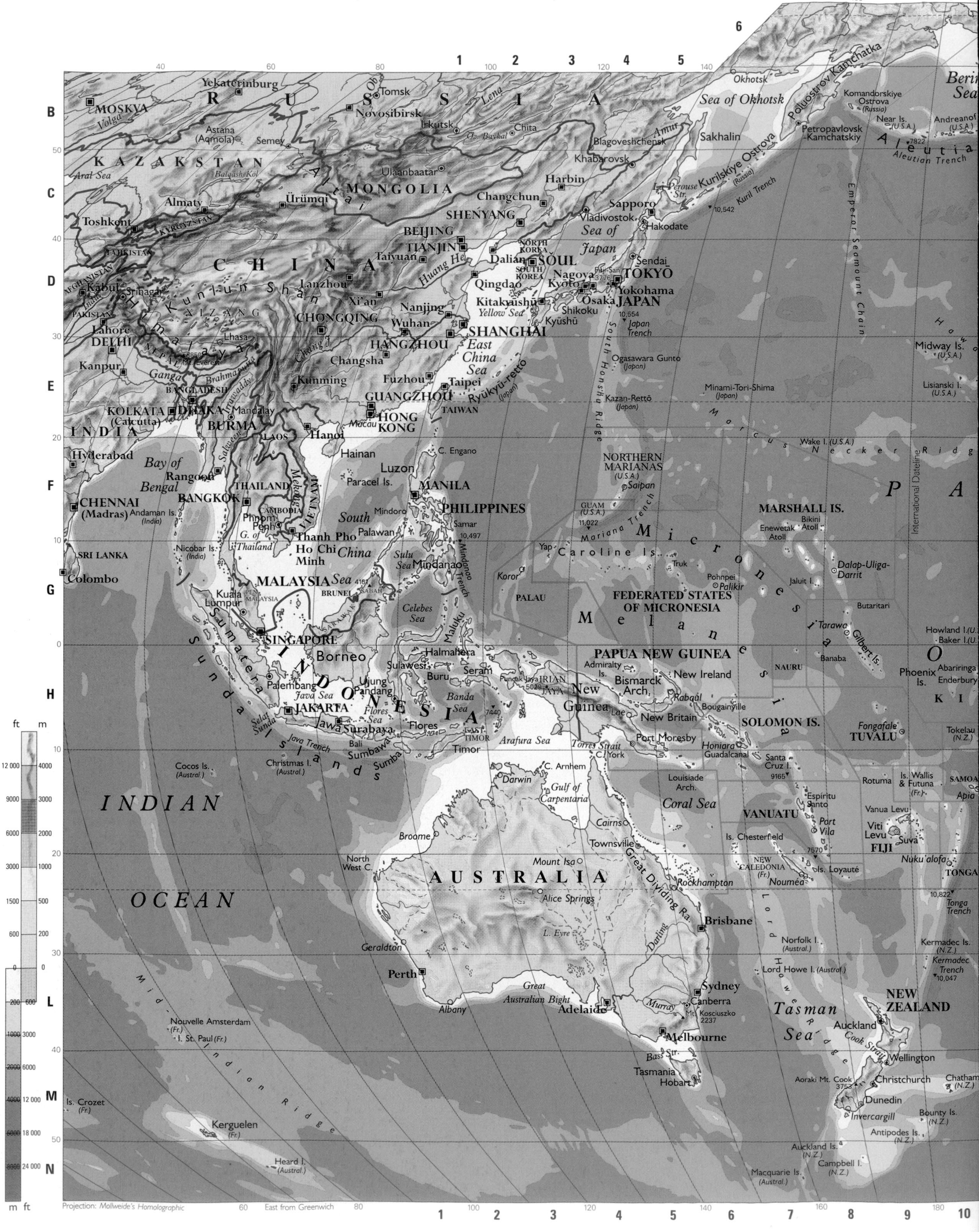
RUSSIA
MOSKVA
Volga
Yekaterinburg
Tomsk
Novosibirsk
Irkutsk
Oz. Baykal
Chita
Lena
Ob
Astana (Aqmola)
Semey
KAZAKSTAN
Aral Sea
Balqash Kol
Altai
Ulaanbaatar
MONGOLIA
Ürümqi
Almaty
Toshkent
KYRGYZSTAN
TAJIKISTAN
AFGHANISTAN
Kabul
Srinagar
PAKISTAN
Lahore
DELHI
Kanpur
Ganga
Himalaya
Kunlun Shan
XIZANG
Lhasa
Everest
NEPAL
Brahmaputra
BANGLADESH
DHAKA
KOLKATA (Calcutta)
INDIA
Hyderabad
CHENNAI (Madras)
SRI LANKA
Colombo
Bay of Bengal
Andaman Is. (India)
Nicobar Is. (India)
Mandalay
BURMA
Rangoon
Irrawaddy
Salween
THAILAND
BANGKOK
LAOS
Hanoi
Mekong
VIETNAM
CAMBODIA
Phnom Penh
G. of Thailand
Thanh Pho Ho Chi Minh
CHINA
Lanzhou
Xi'an
Huang He
Taiyuan
BEIJING
TIANJIN
Chang Jiang
CHONGQING
Wuhan
Nanjing
SHANGHAI
HANGZHOU
Changsha
Kunming
Fuzhou
Taipei
TAIWAN
GUANGZHOU
HONG KONG
Macau
Hainan
Paracel Is.
South China Sea
East China Sea
Yellow Sea
Qingdao
Dalian
SHENYANG
Changchun
Harbin
Amur
Khabarovsk
Blagoveshchensk
Vladivostok
NORTH KOREA
SOUTH KOREA
SŎUL
Sea of Japan
JAPAN
TŌKYŌ
Yokohama
Ōsaka
Kyōto
Nagoya
Fuji-San 3776
Kitakyūshū
Shikoku
Kyūshū
Sendai
Hakodate
Sapporo
La Pérouse Str.
Sakhalin
Sea of Okhotsk
Okhotsk
Kurilskiye Ostrova (Russia)
Kuril Trench
10,542
Poluostrov Kamchatka
Petropavlovsk-Kamchatskiy
Komandorskiye Ostrova (Russia)
Near Is. (U.S.A.)
Andreanof (U.S.A.)
7822
Aleutian Trench
Bering Sea
Emperor Seamount Chain
Ryūkyū-rettō (Japan)
10,554
Japan Trench
South Honshu Ridge
Ogasawara Gunto (Japan)
Kazan-Rettō (Japan)
Minami-Tori-Shima (Japan)
Marcus Necker Ridge
Wake I. (U.S.A.)
Midway Is. (U.S.A.)
Lisianski I. (U.S.A.)
Luzon
C. Engano
MANILA
PHILIPPINES
Mindoro
Samar
Palawan
Sulu Sea
Mindanao
Mindanao Trench
10,497
NORTHERN MARIANAS (U.S.A.)
Saipan
GUAM (U.S.A.)
11,022
Mariana Trench
Micronesia
Caroline Is.
Yap
Koror
PALAU
Truk
Pohnpei
Palikir
FEDERATED STATES OF MICRONESIA
MARSHALL IS.
Bikini Atoll
Enewetak Atoll
Dalap-Uliga-Darrit
Jaluit I.
Butaritari
Tarawa
Gilbert Is.
NAURU
Banaba
Howland I. (U.S.A.)
Baker I. (U.S.A.)
Phoenix Is.
Abariringa
Enderbury
KIRIBATI
International Dateline
PACIFIC OCEAN
MALAYSIA
Kuala Lumpur
BRUNEI
SABAH
SARAWAK
SINGAPORE
Borneo
Sumatera
Sunda Islands
Palembang
Java Sea
JAKARTA
Selat Sunda
Jawa
Surabaya
Bali
Sumbawa
Sumba
Flores
Flores Sea
Java Trench
INDONESIA
Sulawesi
Ujung Pandang
Celebes Sea
Maluku
Halmahera
Buru
Seram
Banda Sea
EAST TIMOR
Timor
7440
4161
Puncak Jaya 5029
IRIAN JAYA
New Guinea
PAPUA NEW GUINEA
Melanesia
Admiralty Is.
Bismarck Arch.
New Ireland
Rabaul
New Britain
Bougainville
Lae
Port Moresby
SOLOMON IS.
Honiara
Guadalcanal
Santa Cruz I.
9165
Torres Strait
C. York
Arafura Sea
Darwin
C. Arnhem
Gulf of Carpentaria
Louisiade Arch.
Coral Sea
VANUATU
Espíritu Santo
Port Vila
Is. Chesterfield
7570
NEW CALEDONIA (Fr.)
Nouméa
Is. Loyauté
Fongafale
TUVALU
Tokelau (N.Z.)
Rotuma
Is. Wallis & Futuna (Fr.)
SAMOA
Apia
Vanua Levu
Viti Levu
Suva
FIJI
Nuku'alofa
TONGA
10,822
Tonga Trench
Kermadec Is. (N.Z.)
Kermadec Trench
10,047
Cairns
Townsville
Great Dividing Ra.
Rockhampton
Broome
North West C.
Mount Isa
AUSTRALIA
Alice Springs
L. Eyre
Brisbane
Darling
Geraldton
Perth
Great Australian Bight
Albany
Adelaide
Murray
Sydney
Canberra
Mt. Kosciuszko 2237
Melbourne
Bass Str.
Tasmania
Hobart
Lord Howe Rise
Norfolk I. (Austral.)
Lord Howe I. (Austral.)
Tasman Sea
NEW ZEALAND
Auckland
Cook Strait
Wellington
Christchurch
Aoraki Mt. Cook 3753
Dunedin
Invercargill
Chatham Is. (N.Z.)
Bounty Is. (N.Z.)
Antipodes Is. (N.Z.)
Auckland Is. (N.Z.)
Campbell I. (N.Z.)
Macquarie Is. (Austral.)
Cocos Is. (Austral.)
Christmas I. (Austral.)
INDIAN OCEAN
Mid-Indian Ridge
Nouvelle Amsterdam (Fr.)
I. St. Paul (Fr.)
Is. Crozet (Fr.)
Kerguelen (Fr.)
Heard I. (Austral.)
ft m
12 000 4000
9000 3000
6000 2000
3000 1000
1500 500
600 200
0 0
200 600
1000 3000
2000 6000
4000 12 000
6000 18 000
8000 24 000
m ft
Projection: Mollweide's Homolographic
East from Greenwich

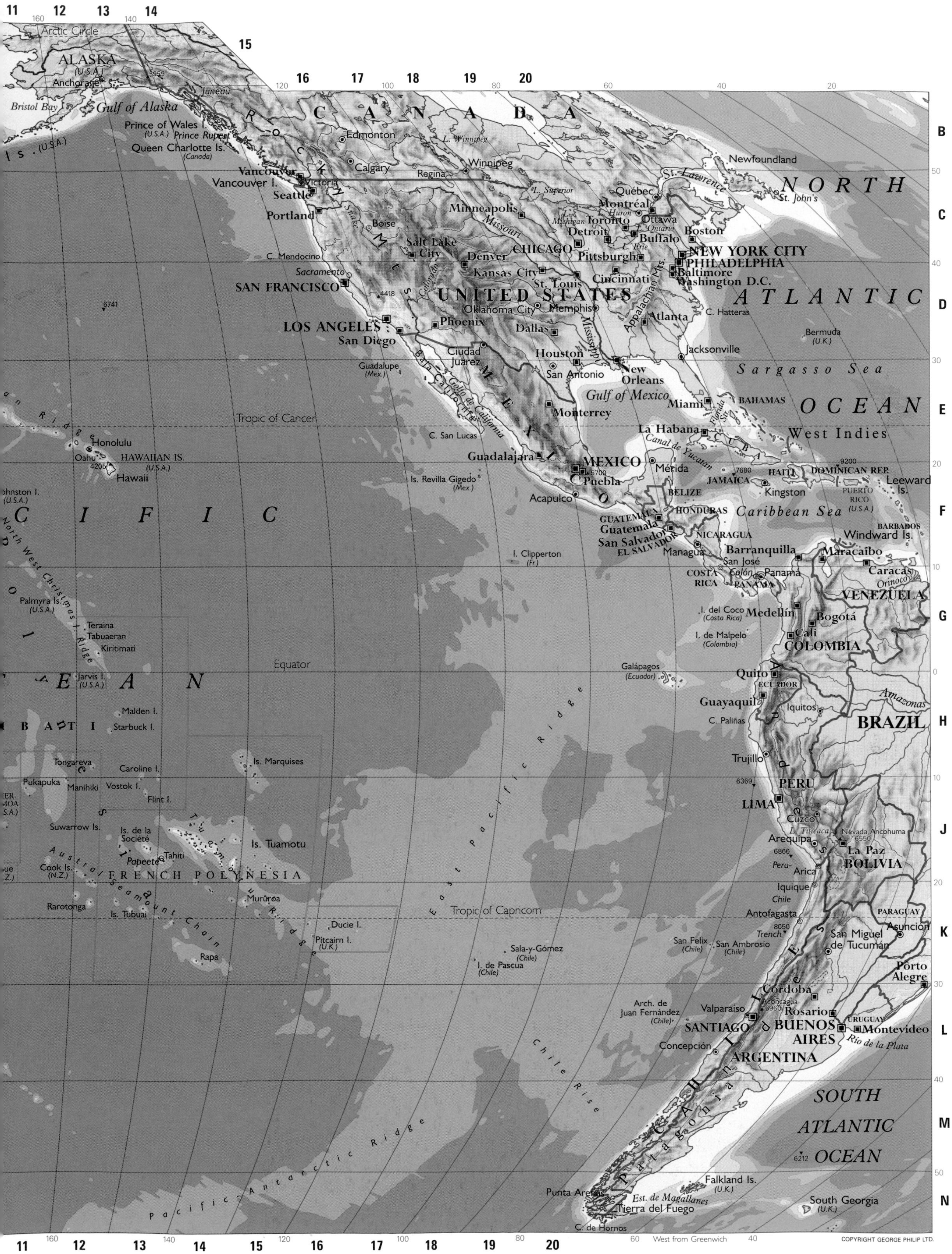
Arctic Circle
ALASKA
(U.S.A.)
Anchorage
5959
Bristol Bay
Gulf of Alaska
Juneau
Prince of Wales I.
(U.S.A.)
Prince Rupert
Queen Charlotte Is.
(Canada)
C A N A D A
Edmonton
Calgary
L. Winnipeg
Winnipeg
Regina
Vancouver
Vancouver I.
Victoria
Seattle
Portland
Boise
Salt Lake City
C. Mendocino
Sacramento
SAN FRANCISCO
4418
LOS ANGELES
San Diego
Phoenix
Denver
Kansas City
Minneapolis
Missouri
CHICAGO
L. Superior
L. Michigan
L. Huron
L. Ontario
L. Erie
Toronto
Detroit
Ottawa
Montréal
Québec
Buffalo
Boston
Pittsburgh
Cincinnati
St. Louis
NEW YORK CITY
PHILADELPHIA
Baltimore
Washington D.C.
UNITED STATES
Oklahoma City
Memphis
Dallas
Atlanta
Appalachian Mts.
Mississippi
C. Hatteras
Jacksonville
Houston
San Antonio
New Orleans
Ciudad Juárez
Guadalupe
(Mex.)
Baja California
Golfo de California
Gulf of Mexico
Miami
Florida Str.
Monterrey
M E X I C O
C. San Lucas
Guadalajara
MEXICO
5700
Puebla
Acapulco
Mérida
Canal de Yucatán
La Habana
C U B A
BAHAMAS
Newfoundland
St. Lawrence
St. John's
N O R T H
A T L A N T I C
O C E A N
Bermuda
(U.K.)
Sargasso Sea
West Indies
7680
JAMAICA
Kingston
HAITI
9200
DOMINICAN REP.
PUERTO RICO
(U.S.A.)
Leeward Is.
BARBADOS
Windward Is.
Caribbean Sea
BELIZE
GUATEMALA
Guatemala
HONDURAS
San Salvador
EL SALVADOR
NICARAGUA
Managua
COSTA RICA
San José
Colón
Panama
PANAMA
Barranquilla
Maracaibo
Caracas
Orinoco
VENEZUELA
Medellín
Bogotá
Cali
COLOMBIA
Is. Revilla Gigedo
(Mex.)
I. Clipperton
(Fr.)
I. del Coco
(Costa Rica)
I. de Malpelo
(Colombia)
Galápagos
(Ecuador)
Quito
ECUADOR
Guayaquil
Iquitos
C. Pariñas
Amazonas
BRAZIL
Trujillo
6369
PERU
LIMA
Cuzco
L. Titicaca
Arequipa
6866
Nevada Ancohuma
6550
La Paz
BOLIVIA
Peru-Chile Trench
Arica
Iquique
Antofagasta
8050
PARAGUAY
Asunción
San Felix
(Chile)
San Ambrosio
(Chile)
San Miguel de Tucumán
Porto Alegre
Córdoba
Aconcagua
6960
Rosario
Valparaíso
SANTIAGO
BUENOS AIRES
URUGUAY
Montevideo
Río de la Plata
Concepción
ARGENTINA
Arch. de Juan Fernández
(Chile)
Patagonia
SOUTH ATLANTIC OCEAN
6212
Falkland Is.
(U.K.)
Punta Arenas
Est. de Magallanes
Tierra del Fuego
C. de Hornos
South Georgia
(U.K.)
Chile Rise
East Pacific Ridge
Pacific-Antarctic Ridge
Sala-y-Gómez
(Chile)
I. de Pascua
(Chile)
Tropic of Capricorn
Tropic of Cancer
Equator
6741
Honolulu
Oahu
4205
HAWAIIAN IS.
(U.S.A.)
Hawaii
Johnston I.
(U.S.A.)
P A C I F I C
O C E A N
Palmyra Is.
(U.S.A.)
Teraina
Tabuaeran
Kiritimati
Christmas Ridge
Jarvis I.
(U.S.A.)
Malden I.
Starbuck I.
Tongareva
Pukapuka
Manihiki
Caroline I.
Vostok I.
Flint I.
Is. Marquises
Suwarrow Is.
Is. de la Société
Papeete
Tahiti
Is. Tuamotu
Tuamotu Ridge
Cook Is.
(N.Z.)
Austral Seamount Chain
FRENCH POLYNESIA
Rarotonga
Is. Tubuai
Mururoa
Ducie I.
Pitcairn I.
(U.K.)
Rapa
West from Greenwich
11
12
13
14
15
16
17
18
19
20
B
C
D
E
F
G
H
J
K
L
M
N
COPYRIGHT GEORGE PHILIP LTD.

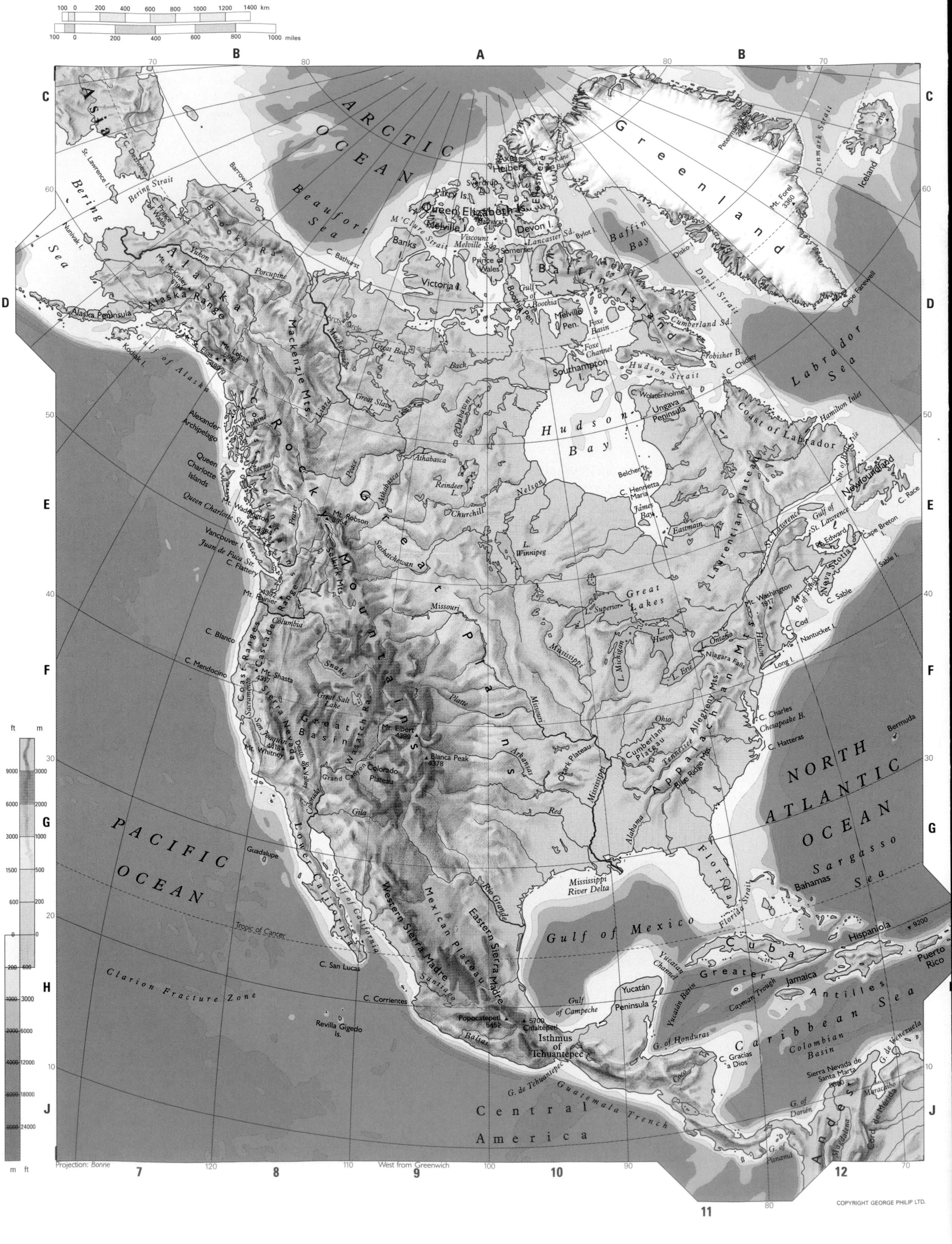
100 0 200 400 600 800 1000 1200 1400 km
100 0 200 400 600 800 1000 miles
ARCTIC OCEAN
Beaufort Sea
Greenland
Iceland
Denmark Strait
Petermann Peak
Mt. Forel 3360
Baffin Bay
Davis Strait
Cape Farewell
Asia
C. Dezhnev
St. Lawrence I.
Bering Strait
Bering Sea
Nunivak I.
C. Prince of Wales
Barrow Pt.
Brooks Ra.
Yukon
Porcupine
Alaska
Mt. McKinley
Alaska Range
Alaska Peninsula
Kodiak I.
Gulf of Alaska
Mt. St. Elias
Mt. Logan
Axel Heiberg I.
Sverdrup Is.
Ellesmere I.
Kane Basin
Parry Is.
Queen Elizabeth Is.
Melville I.
Bathurst I.
Devon I.
M'Clure Strait
Viscount Melville Sd.
Lancaster Sd.
Bylot I.
Banks I.
C. Bathurst
Somerset I.
Prince of Wales I.
Victoria I.
Baffin Island
Disko I.
Gulf of Boothia
Boothia Pen.
Melville Pen.
Foxe Basin
Foxe Channel
Cumberland Sd.
Frobisher B.
Southampton I.
Hudson Strait
C. Chidley
C. Wolstenholme
Ungava Peninsula
Labrador Sea
Hamilton Inlet
Coast of Labrador
Str. of Belle Isle
Newfoundland
C. Race
Mackenzie
Arctic Circle
Great Bear L.
Back
Mackenzie Mts.
Great Slave L.
Liard
Dubawnt
Hudson Bay
Belcher Is.
C. Henrietta Maria
James Bay
Eastmain
Laurentian Plateau
Alexander Archipelago
Queen Charlotte Islands
Queen Charlotte Str.
Stikine
Skeena
Coast Mountains
Rocky Mountains
Mt. Waddington 3994
Fraser
Mt. Robson 3954
Peace
Athabasca
L. Athabasca
Reindeer L.
Churchill
Nelson
Great Plains
Saskatchewan
L. Winnipeg
Vancouver I.
Juan de Fuca Str.
C. Flattery
Selkirk Mts.
St. Lawrence
Gulf of St. Lawrence
Pr. Edward I.
Cape Breton I.
Nova Scotia
Sable I.
B. of Fundy
Mt. Rainier 4392
Cascade Range
Columbia
C. Blanco
Missouri
L. Superior
Great Lakes
L. Huron
L. Michigan
L. Ontario
L. Erie
Niagara Falls
Mt. Washington 1917
C. Cod
Nantucket I.
Hudson
Long I.
Appalachian Mts.
Allegheny Mts.
C. Mendocino
Coast Ranges
Mt. Shasta 4317
Snake
Great Salt Lake
Sierra Nevada
Sacramento
San Joaquin
Mt. Whitney 4418
Great Basin
Wasatch Ra.
Platte
Mt. Elbert 4399
Blanca Peak 4378
Mississippi
Ohio
Cumberland Plateau
Tennessee
Blue Ridge Mts.
C. Charles
Chesapeake B.
C. Hatteras
Bermuda
Death Valley
Grand Canyon
Colorado Plateau
Colorado
Arkansas
Ozark Plateau
Red
Gila
Alabama
Florida
NORTH ATLANTIC OCEAN
Sargasso Sea
Bahamas
PACIFIC OCEAN
Guadalupe
Lower California
Gulf of California
Rio Grande
Mississippi River Delta
Florida Strait
Gulf of Mexico
Tropic of Cancer
Western Sierra Madre
Mexican Plateau
Eastern Sierra Madre
Santiago
C. San Lucas
Clarion Fracture Zone
C. Corrientes
Revilla Gigedo Is.
Cuba
Hispaniola
Puerto Rico
Yucatan Channel
Greater Antilles
Jamaica
Cayman Trough
Yucatán Basin
Yucatán Peninsula
Gulf of Campeche
Popocatepetl 5452
Citlaltepetl 5700
Balsas
Isthmus of Tehuantepec
G. of Honduras
Caribbean Sea
Colombian Basin
C. Gracias a Dios
Coco
G. de Tehuantepec
Guatemala Trench
Central America
G. de Venezuela
Sierra Nevada de Santa Marta 5800
Maracaibo
Cord. de Mérida
Andes
Magdalena
G. of Darién
G. of Panamá
Projection: Bonne
West from Greenwich
ft m
9000 3000
6000 2000
3000 1000
1500 500
600 200
0 0
200 600
1000 3000
2000 6000
4000 12000
6000 18000
8000 24000
m ft

100 0 200 400 600 800 1000 1200 1400 km
100 0 200 400 600 800 1000 miles
ARCTIC OCEAN
RUSSIA
Asia
International Date Line
St. Lawrence I.
Bering Strait
Bering Sea
Beaufort Sea
Queen Elizabeth Is.
Ellesmere I.
GREENLAND (Denmark)
Denmark Strait
ICELAND
Reykjavik
Baffin Bay
Baffin Island
Davis Strait
Nuuk
Cape Farewell
Victoria I.
NUNAVUT
ALASKA (U.S.A.)
Yukon
Porcupine
Fairbanks
Anchorage
Kodiak I.
Gulf of Alaska
YUKON TERRITORY
Whitehorse
Juneau
NORTHWEST TERRITORIES
Arctic Circle
Mackenzie
Great Bear L.
Back
Yellowknife
Great Slave L.
Liard
Dubawnt
Hudson Strait
Hudson Bay
CANADA
BRITISH COLUMBIA
Skeena
Peace
Athabasca
Fraser
ALBERTA
Edmonton
Calgary
Churchill
Nelson
MANITOBA
SASKATCHEWAN
Saskatchewan
Regina
L. Winnipeg
Winnipeg
ONTARIO
Eastmain
QUÉBEC
Labrador
NEWFOUNDLAND
St. John's
St. Pierre Et Miquelon (Fr.)
PRINCE EDWARD I.
Charlottetown
NEW BRUNSWICK
NOVA SCOTIA
Halifax
C. Sable
Fredericton
Québec
Montréal
Ottawa
Toronto
St. Lawrence
Vancouver
Victoria
WASHINGTON
Olympia
Seattle
Portland
Salem
Columbia
OREGON
IDAHO
Boise
Snake
MONTANA
Missouri
Helena
NORTH DAKOTA
Bismarck
MINNESOTA
Minneapolis
SOUTH DAKOTA
WYOMING
Cheyenne
NEBRASKA
IOWA
WISCONSIN
Madison
Milwaukee
L. Superior
L. Michigan
MICHIGAN
Lansing
Huron
Detroit
L. Erie
L. Ontario
Buffalo
NEW YORK
MAINE
Augusta
VER.
N.H.
Concord
MASS.
Boston
Providence
Hartford
NEW YORK CITY
PHILADELPHIA
PA.
Pittsburgh
Cleveland
Toledo
CHICAGO
OHIO
Columbus
INDIANA
Indianapolis
ILLINOIS
Springfield
Cincinnati
Baltimore
Washington D.C.
MD.
N.J.
W.V.
Richmond
VIRGINIA
KENTUCKY
Nashville
TENNESSEE
NORTH CAROLINA
Raleigh
Charlotte
SOUTH CAROLINA
Columbia
Charleston
Atlanta
GEORGIA
ALABAMA
Montgomery
Birmingham
MISSISSIPPI
Jackson
Mississippi
Memphis
ARKANSAS
Little Rock
MISSOURI
St. Louis
Kansas City
Topeka
KANSAS
UNITED STATES
Sacramento
SAN FRANCISCO
San Jose
Carson City
NEVADA
Salt Lake City
UTAH
Denver
COLORADO
Lincoln
CALIFORNIA
Las Vegas
LOS ANGELES
San Diego
Colorado
ARIZONA
Phoenix
Tucson
NEW MEXICO
Santa Fe
Albuquerque
OKLAHOMA
Oklahoma City
TEXAS
El Paso
Dallas
Austin
Houston
Baton Rouge
LOUISIANA
New Orleans
Tallahassee
Jacksonville
FLORIDA
Tampa
Miami
Florida Str.
Nassau
BAHAMAS
Turks & Caicos Is. (U.K.)
Bermuda (U.K.)
NORTH ATLANTIC OCEAN
PACIFIC OCEAN
Guadalupe (Mex.)
Hermosillo
Rio Grande
Tropic of Cancer
MEXICO
Culiacan
Monterrey
Gulf of Mexico
Guadalajara
MÉXICO
Puebla
Acapulco
Revilla Gigedo Is. (Mex.)
Mérida
Belmopan
BELIZE
GUATEMALA
Guatemala
HONDURAS
Tegucigalpa
San Salvador
EL SALVADOR
NICARAGUA
Managua
L. Nicaragua
COSTA RICA
San José
PANAMA
Panamá
Havana
CUBA
Cayman Is. (U.K.)
JAMAICA
Kingston
HAITI
Port-au-Prince
DOMINICAN REP.
Santo Domingo
PUERTO RICO (U.S.A.)
San Juan
Caribbean Sea
Barranquilla
Maracaibo
VENEZUELA
COLOMBIA
Medellín
South America
Projection: Bonne
West from Greenwich
COPYRIGHT GEORGE PHILIP LTD.

■ MÉXICO Capital Cities

CANADA 1:15 000 000

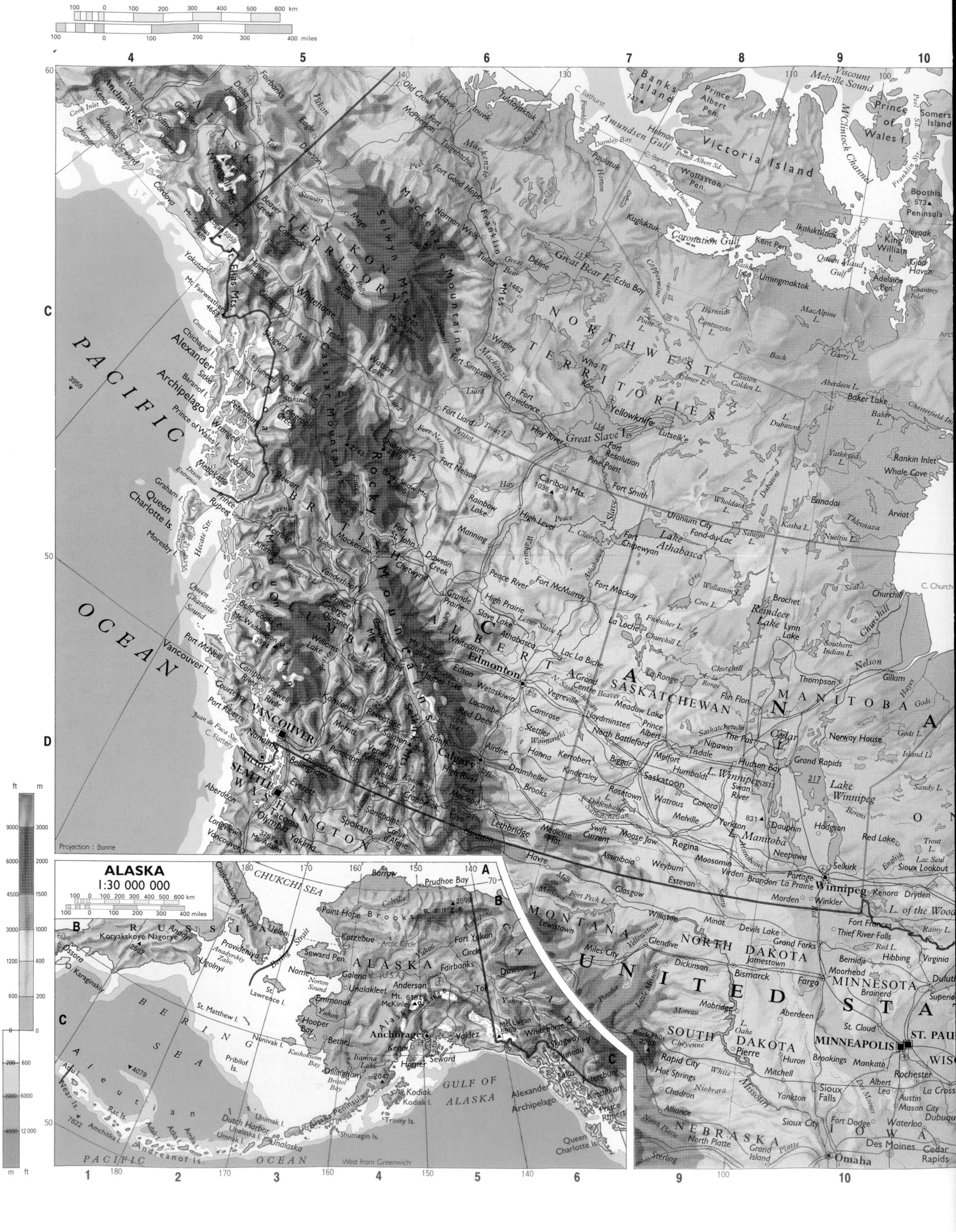

PACIFIC
OCEAN
ALASKA
YUKON TERRITORY
NORTHWEST TERRITORIES
BRITISH COLUMBIA
ALBERTA
SASKATCHEWAN
MANITOBA
WASHINGTON
MONTANA
NORTH DAKOTA
SOUTH DAKOTA
NEBRASKA
MINNESOTA
IOWA
UNITED STATES
Rocky Mountains
Mackenzie Mountains
Selwyn Mts.
Cassiar Mountains
Coast Mountains
Selkirk Mts.
Caribou Mts.
Alexander Archipelago
Queen Charlotte Is.
Vancouver I.
Victoria Island
Banks Island
Prince of Wales I.
Great Bear L.
Great Slave L.
Lake Athabasca
Reindeer Lake
Lake Winnipeg
Coronation Gulf
Amundsen Gulf
Viscount Melville Sound
M'Clintock Channel
Boothia Peninsula
King William I.
Anchorage
Fairbanks
Juneau
Whitehorse
Dawson
Inuvik
Yellowknife
Edmonton
Calgary
VANCOUVER
Victoria
SEATTLE
Spokane
Regina
Saskatoon
Winnipeg
Churchill
Prince George
Prince Rupert
Fort McMurray
Lethbridge
Medicine Hat
Moose Jaw
Bismarck
Fargo
Pierre
Rapid City
MINNEAPOLIS
ST. PAUL
Omaha
Des Moines
Projection: Bonne
ALASKA
1:30 000 000
CHUKCHI SEA
BERING SEA
GULF OF ALASKA
PACIFIC OCEAN
Brooks Range
Mt. McKinley 6194
Aleutian Is.
Kodiak I.
Nome
Barrow
Prudhoe Bay
West from Greenwich

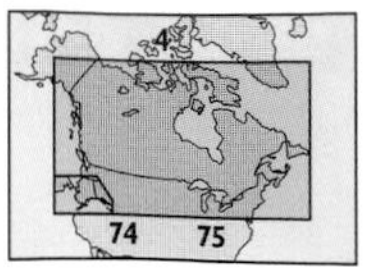
74
75

11
12
13
14
15
16
B
C
D
E
Baffin Bay
Lancaster Sound
Devon I.
Bylot I.
Arctic Bay
Nanisivik
Borden Pen.
Brodeur Peninsula
Pond Inlet
Clyde River
C. Adair
C. Raper
Home B.
Baffin Island
Fury and Hecla Str.
Igloolik
Sanirajak
Simpson Pen.
Pelly Bay
Committee B.
Melville Peninsula
Foxe Basin
Prince Charles I.
Air Force I.
Nettilling L.
Rae Isthmus
Repulse Bay
NUNAVUT
C. Dorchester
Amadjuak L.
Foxe Pen.
Cape Dorset
Foxe Channel
Roes Welcome Sd.
Wager B.
Southampton I.
Sallig
Bell Pen.
Salisbury I.
Nottingham I.
Hudson Strait
Iqaluit
Meta Incognita Peninsula
Kimmirut
Hall Peninsula
Frobisher Bay
Resolution I.
Cumberland Peninsula
Pangnirtung
Qikiqtarjuaq
Cumberland Sd.
Hoare B.
Mercy C.
C. Dyer
Davis Strait
Coats I.
Mansel I.
Ivujivik
Salluit
Kangiqsujuaq
Quaqtaq
Akpatok I.
C. Chidley
Péninsule d'Ungava
Ungava Bay
Kangirsuk
Puvirnituq
L. Payne
Kuujjuaq
Kangiqsualujjuaq
Hebron
Nain
Hopedale
C. Harrison
Labrador Sea
Hudson Bay
Ottawa Is.
Inukjuak
Sleeper Is.
King George Is.
Baker's Dozen Is.
Sanikiluaq
Belcher Is.
Kuujjuarapik
L. Minto
Caniapiscau
Baleine
George
Feuilles
Koksoak
Schefferville
Esker
Labrador City
Fermont
Churchill Falls
Smallwood Res.
North West River
Happy Valley-Goose Bay
Churchill
Rigolet
Cartwright
Port Hope Simpson
Belle Isle
C. Bauld
St. Anthony
Str. of Belle Isle
NEWFOUNDLAND
Labrador
L. Bienville
Rés. de Caniapiscau
L. à l'Eau Claire
Grande Baleine
C. Henrietta Maria
Pte. Louis XIV
Kanaaupscow
La Grande
Chisasibi
James Bay
Akimiski I.
Wemindji
Eastmain
Charlton I.
Waskaganish
Moosonee
Fort Albany
Attawapiskat
Big Trout L.
Peawanuck
Winisk
Severn
QUÉBEC
Gagnon
Rés. Manicouagan
Moisie
Romaine
Natashquan
St-Augustin
Havre-St-Pierre
I. d'Anticosti
Sept-Îles
Port-Cartier
Baie Comeau
Gulf of St. Lawrence
L. Mistassini
L. Albanel
Chibougamau
Rupert
Nottaway
Harricana
Matagami
L. Matagami
Chicoutimi
Dolbeau
Roberval
Jonquière
Québec
La Tuque
Rés. Gouin
Amos
Val-d'Or
Rouyn-Noranda
Kirkland Lake
Timmins
Cochrane
Hearst
Kapuskasing
Nakina
Geraldton
Nipigon
L. Nipigon
Marathon
Thunder Bay
Lake Superior
Wawa
Chapleau
New Liskeard
Sudbury
Sault Ste. Marie
Elliot Lake
North Bay
Parry Sound
Manitoulin I.
Georgian Bay
Lake Huron
Barrie
Owen Sound
Peterborough
Oshawa
TORONTO
Kitchener
Hamilton
London
Sarnia
Windsor
DETROIT
Toledo
CLEVELAND
CHICAGO
Gary
South Bend
MILWAUKEE
Racine
Kenosha
Grand Rapids
Lansing
Flint
Saginaw
Cadillac
Traverse City
Petoskey
MICHIGAN
L. Michigan
Green Bay
Appleton
Sheboygan
Escanaba
Menominee
Marquette
Houghton
Ironwood
Wausau
Lake Ontario
Kingston
Belleville
OTTAWA
Hull
Pembroke
Huntsville
MONTRÉAL
Trois-Rivières
Shawinigan
Mont-Laurier
Joliette
St-Hyacinthe
Sherbrooke
Granby
Cornwall
Burlington
Montpelier
L. Champlain
VERMONT
NEW HAMPSHIRE
Concord
Manchester
MAINE
Augusta
Bangor
Lewiston
Portland
BOSTON
Providence
C. Cod
MASS.
Springfield
Albany
HARTFORD
CONN.
New Haven
Bridgeport
NEW YORK
Newark
N.J.
Trenton
Allentown
Scranton
Binghamton
Elmira
Syracuse
Rochester
BUFFALO
Niagara Falls
Erie
Jamestown
L. Erie
PENNSYLVANIA
OHIO
INDIANA
Lévis
Thetford Mines
Rimouski
Matane
Gaspé
Pén. de Gaspé
Campbellton
Bathurst
Rivière-du-Loup
Edmundston
Grand Falls
Woodstock
Fredericton
NEW BRUNSWICK
Saint John
Moncton
Miramichi
Amherst
Truro
Kentville
Halifax
Dartmouth
Bridgewater
Liverpool
Yarmouth
Digby
B. of Fundy
C. Sable
NOVA SCOTIA
Summerside
Charlottetown
PR. EDWARD I.
New Glasgow
Antigonish
Port Hawkesbury
Sydney
Glace Bay
Cape Breton I.
Îs. de la Madeleine
Cabot Str.
C. Ray
Channel-Port aux Basques
Stephenville
Corner Brook
Deer Lake
Baie Verte
Grand Falls
Gander
Lewisporte
Notre Dame B.
Bonavista
Trinity B.
Carbonear
St. John's
Placentia
Marystown
C. Race
Newfoundland
ST-PIERRE et MIQUELON (Fr.)
Sable I. (Nova Scotia)
ATLANTIC OCEAN
GREENLAND (KALAALLIT NUNAAT) (Denmark)
Nunavik
Uummannaq
Qeqertarsuaq
Ilulissat
Qasigiannguit
Kangerlussuaq
Sisimiut
Maniitsoq
Nuuk
Paamiut
Arsuk
Qaqortoq
Nanortalik
Qeqertarsuatsiaat
Tasiilaq
Kong Frederik VI's Kyst
Uummannarsuaq
2136
1890
2591
2850
3809
1852
257
1135
1190
814
6309
183
174
90
80
70
60
50
40
30
West from Greenwich

COPYRIGHT GEORGE PHILIP LTD.

EASTERN CANADA 1:7 000 000

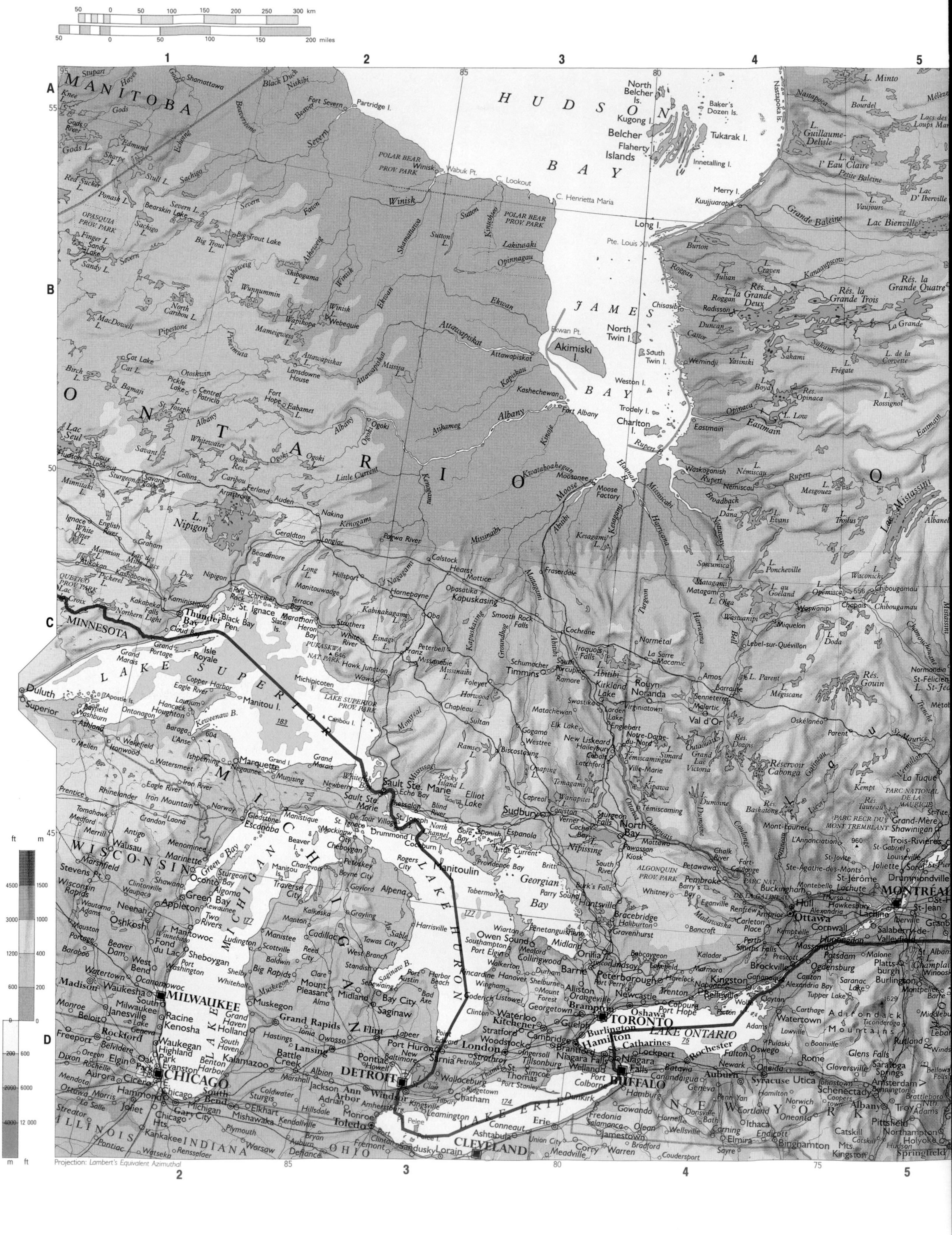

50 0 50 100 150 200 250 300 km
50 0 50 100 150 200 miles
1 2 3 4 5
A B C D
HUDSON BAY
JAMES BAY
MANITOBA
ONTARIO
MINNESOTA
WISCONSIN
MICHIGAN
ILLINOIS
INDIANA
OHIO
NEW YORK
LAKE SUPERIOR
LAKE MICHIGAN
LAKE HURON
LAKE ONTARIO
LAKE ERIE
Georgian Bay
Belcher Islands
Akimiski I.
L. Nipigon
Manitoulin
Thunder Bay
Sault Ste. Marie
Sudbury
Timmins
North Bay
Ottawa
MONTRÉAL
TORONTO
Hamilton
BUFFALO
DETROIT
CLEVELAND
MILWAUKEE
CHICAGO
Duluth
Moosonee
Kapuskasing
Rouyn-Noranda
Val d'Or
Kingston
London
Windsor
Toledo
Rochester
Syracuse
Grand Rapids
Lansing
Flint
Saginaw
Green Bay
Lac Mistassini
Rés. Gouin
Trois-Rivières
Projection: Lambert's Equivalent Azimuthal
ft m
4500 1500
3000 1000
1200 400
600 200
200 600
2000 6000
4000 12 000

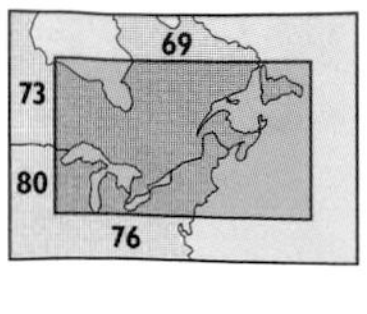
69
73
80
76

6
7
8
9
A
B
C
D
LABRADOR
SEA
ATLANTIC
OCEAN
GULF OF
ST. LAWRENCE
NEWFOUNDLAND
Labrador
Newfoundland
QUEBEC
NEW BRUNSWICK
NOVA SCOTIA
MAINE
PRINCE EDWARD ISLAND
UNITED STATES
Smallwood Reservoir
Rés. de Caniapiscau
Rés. Manicouagan
Nain
Hopedale
Makkovik
Postville
Rigolet
Cartwright
Happy Valley-Goose Bay
North West River
Churchill Falls
Labrador City
Wabush
Fermont
Schefferville
Sept-Îles
Port-Cartier
Baie Comeau
Havre-St-Pierre
Natashquan
Blanc-Sablon
St. Anthony
Corner Brook
Stephenville
Deer Lake
Gander
Grand Falls Windsor
Botwood
Lewisporte
Clarenville
St. John's
Mt. Pearl
Carbonear
Marystown
Burin
Channel-Port aux Basques
ST-PIERRE ET MIQUELON (France)
Î. d'Anticosti
Gaspé
Matane
Rimouski
Rivière-du-Loup
Chicoutimi
Jonquière
Québec
Lévis
Sherbrooke
Edmundston
Bathurst
Campbellton
Miramichi
Moncton
Fredericton
Saint John
Charlottetown
Summerside
Halifax
Dartmouth
Truro
New Glasgow
Sydney
Glace Bay
Cape Breton Island
Yarmouth
Sable I. (Nova Scotia)
Bangor
Augusta
Portland
BOSTON
Manchester
Bay of Fundy
Cabot Strait
Str. of Belle Isle
Long Range Mts.
Mealy Mts.
Îs. de la Madeleine
70
65
60
55
50
45
West from Greenwich

0 50 100 150 200 250 300 km
50 0 50 100 150 200 miles
YUKON TERRITORY
NORTHWEST TERRITORIES
BRITISH COLUMBIA
ALBERTA
ALASKA (USA)
WASHINGTON
IDAHO
UNITED STATES
PACIFIC OCEAN
GREAT SLAVE LAKE
Queen Charlotte Islands
Queen Charlotte Sound
Hecate Strait
Dixon Entrance
Alexander Arch.
Vancouver Island
Coast Mountains
Skeena Mountains
Cassiar Mountains
Rocky Mountains
Cariboo Mts.
Columbia Mountains
Monashee Mts.
Selkirk Mts.
Purcell Mts.
Caribou Mts.
Birch Mountains
Clear Hills
Swan Hills
Cameron Hills
Horn Mts.
WOOD BUFFALO NATIONAL PARK
Whitehorse
Juneau
Yellowknife
Fort Nelson
Fort St. John
Dawson Creek
Grande Prairie
Prince George
Prince Rupert
Kamloops
Kelowna
Vancouver
Victoria
Seattle
Edmonton
Calgary
Red Deer
Lethbridge
Peace River
Fort McMurray
Hay River
Fort Smith
Mt. Waddington 3994
Mt. Robson 3954
Mt. Fairweather 4663
Mt. Columbia 3747
Projection: Lambert's Equivalent Azimuthal
West from Greenwich

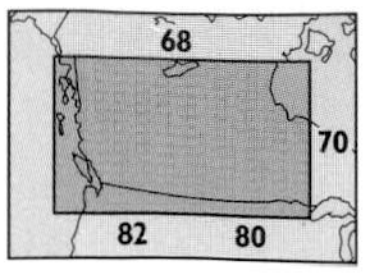

68
70
82
80

7
8
9
10
11
A
B
C
D
NUNAVUT
HUDSON BAY
MANITOBA
SASKATCHEWAN
ONTARIO
MINNESOTA
NORTH DAKOTA
MONTANA
LAKE WINNIPEG
Lake Athabasca
Reindeer Lake
Wollaston L.
Cedar Lake
Lake Winnipegosis
Lake Manitoba
Lake of the Woods
Lac Seul
Churchill
C. Churchill
C. Tatnam
Hubbart Pt.
Button B.
Whale Cove
Pistol B.
Bibby I.
Dawson Inlet
Austin I.
Maguse Pt.
Arviat
Nueltin L.
Kasba L.
Thompson
The Pas
Flin Flon
Lynn Lake
Norway House
Winnipeg
Brandon
Portage la Prairie
Selkirk
Steinbach
Dauphin
Swan River
Regina
Saskatoon
Moose Jaw
Prince Albert
North Battleford
Lloydminster
Swift Current
Yorkton
Estevan
Weyburn
Uranium City
Fort Chipewyan
La Ronge
Kenora
Dryden
Fort Frances
International Falls
Sioux Lookout
Red Lake
Grand Forks
Minot
Williston
Bemidji
Duluth
Superior
Hibbing
Cypress Hills
GRASSLANDS NAT. PARK
PRINCE ALBERT NAT. PARK
RIDING MOUNTAIN NATIONAL PARK
WOODLAND CARIBOU PROV. PARK
OPASQUIA PROV. PARK
QUETICO PROV. PARK
110
105
100
95
90
60
55
50
COPYRIGHT GEORGE PHILIP LTD.

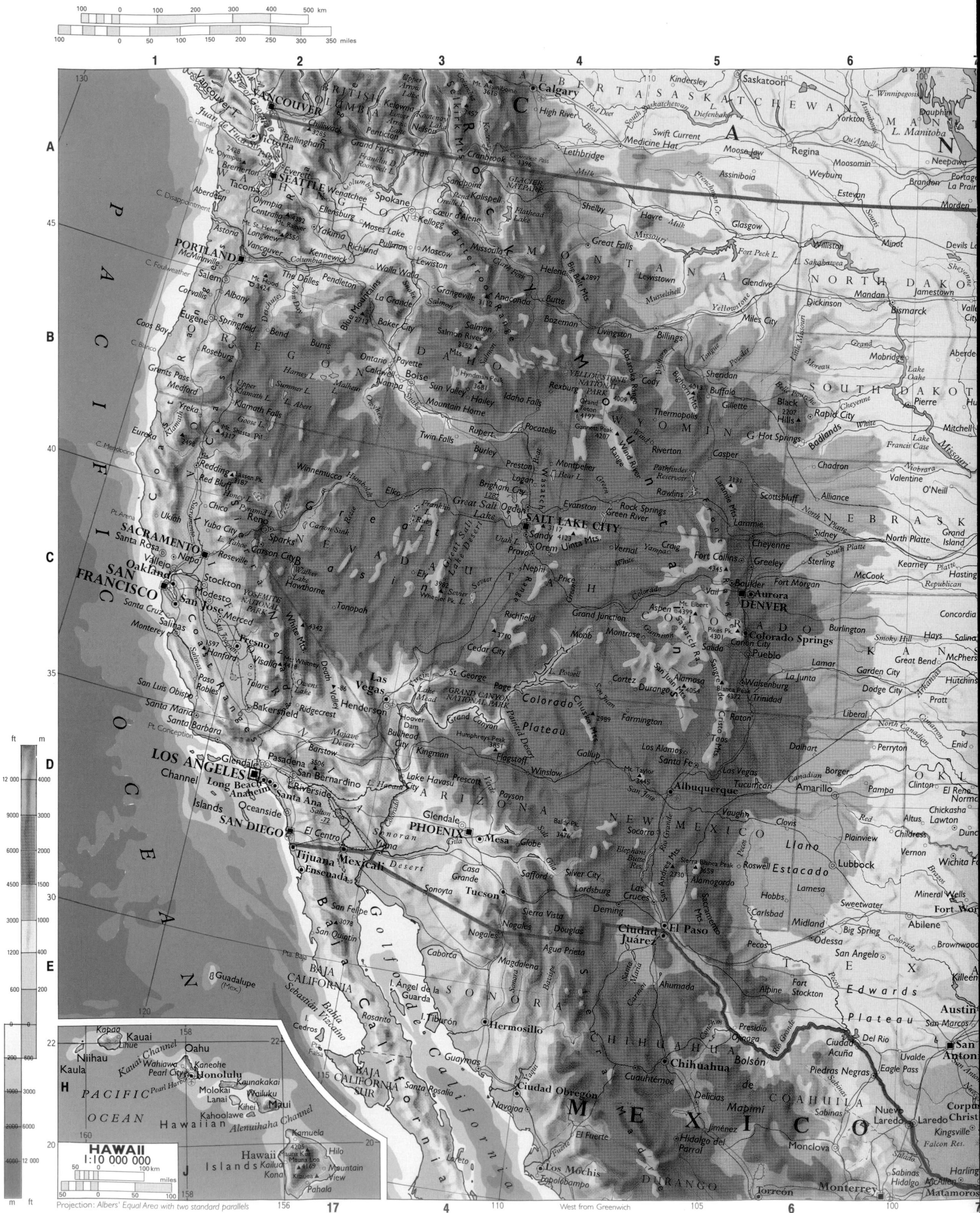

Projection: Albers' Equal Area with two standard parallels

15 16 17 4 5 6 7

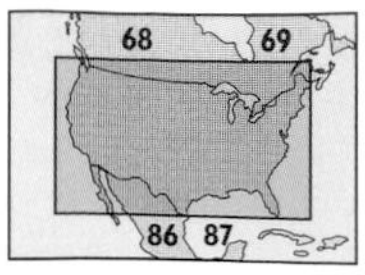

68
69
86
87

8
9
10
11
12
13
A
B
C
D
E
F
45
40
35
30
25
95
90
85
80
75
CANADA
ONTARIO
QUEBEC
Lake Winnipeg
Winnipeg
Kenora
Dryden
Lake of the Woods
Sioux Lookout
Lake Nipigon
Nipigon
Geraldton
Nakina
Marathon
Hearst
Moosonee
Thunder Bay
I. Royale
Fort Frances
International Falls
Thief River Falls
Grand Forks
Red Lake
Bemidji
Hibbing
Virginia
Lake Superior
Two Harbors
Houghton
Keweenaw Bay
Duluth
Superior
Apostle Is.
Marquette
Ishpeming
Ashland
Ironwood
Iron Mountain
Sault Ste. Marie
Whitefish B.
Wawa
Michipicoten I.
Timmins
Cochrane
Kirkland Lake
Rouyn-Noranda
Amos
Chibougamau
L. Chibougamau
L. Matagami
Sudbury
North Bay
L. Nipissing
North Channel
Manitoulin I.
Parry Sound
Georgian Bay
Huntsville
Pembroke
Ottawa
Hull
Montreal
Mont-Laurier
Trois-Rivières
Shawinigan
Joliette
Québec
La Tuque
Roberval
Jonquière
Alma
Chicoutimi
Baie-Comeau
St. Lawrence
Matane
Rimouski
Rivière-du-Loup
Edmundston
NEW BRUNSWICK
Fort Kent
Caribou
Presque Isle
Houlton
Millinocket
Saint John
Calais
Moorhead
Fargo
MINNESOTA
Fergus Falls
Brainerd
Mille Lacs L.
St. Cloud
Big Stone Lake
Willmar
MINNEAPOLIS
ST. PAUL
Coon Rapids
Red Wing
Owatonna
Rochester
Austin
Mankato
Winona
Brookings
Madison
Albert Lea
Mason City
Worthington
Spencer
Cherokee
Fort Dodge
Sioux City
IOWA
Waterloo
Cedar Rapids
Ames
Des Moines
Iowa City
Davenport
Council Bluffs
Ottumwa
Red Oak
Creston
Dubuque
Rockford
Clinton
Galesburg
Rock Island
Burlington
Rice Lake
Rhinelander
Merrill
Wausau
Stevens Point
Eau Claire
Green Bay
Appleton
Manitowoc
Oshkosh
Sheboygan
WISCONSIN
La Crosse
Portage
Madison
MILWAUKEE
Janesville
Racine
Kenosha
Elgin
CHICAGO
Aurora
Joliet
Gary
South Bend
Kankakee
Lake Michigan
Menominee
Escanaba
Manistique
Petoskey
Traverse City
Manistee
Cadillac
Ludington
Midland
Saginaw
Bay City
Flint
Port Huron
Muskegon
Grand Rapids
Lansing
Battle Creek
Kalamazoo
Jackson
Ann Arbor
DETROIT
Windsor
Alpena
Lake Huron
Owen Sound
Barrie
Orillia
Peterborough
Kingston
Oshawa
TORONTO
Kitchener
Hamilton
London
Niagara Falls
Lake Ontario
Lake Erie
Rochester
BUFFALO
Erie
Toledo
Sandusky
Elkhart
Fort Wayne
Findlay
Lima
Marion
Mansfield
Canton
Akron
Youngstown
CLEVELAND
Ashtabula
Warren
Oil City
Jamestown
Bradford
Elmira
Binghamton
Ithaca
Syracuse
Utica
Schenectady
Albany
Troy
Oswego
Watertown
Ogdensburg
Cornwall
Plattsburgh
Burlington
Montpelier
Adirondack Mts.
Glens Falls
Rutland
Catskill Mts.
Poughkeepsie
Kingston
Scranton
Wilkes-Barre
Williamsport
PENNSYLVANIA
Altoona
Johnstown
Harrisburg
Allentown
Reading
Lancaster
PHILADELPHIA
Trenton
Newark
Jersey City
NEW YORK
Paterson
Yonkers
Bridgeport
New Haven
HARTFORD
Springfield
Worcester
Providence
Fall River
New Bedford
Martha's Vineyard
Nantucket I.
C. Cod
BOSTON
Lowell
Lawrence
Manchester
Nashua
Concord
NEW HAMPSHIRE
White Mts.
VERMONT
Berlin
Lewiston
Portland
Brunswick
Augusta
Waterville
Belfast
Penobscot Bay
Bangor
MAINE
Farmington
Moosehead L.
Sherbrooke
Drummondville
Granby
L. Champlain
Long I.
Atlantic City
Wilmington
Dover
BALTIMORE
Annapolis
WASHINGTON D.C.
C. May
Delaware B.
Salisbury
Frederick
Cumberland
PITTSBURGH
Wheeling
Morgantown
Clarksburg
Elkins
Zanesville
COLUMBUS
Springfield
Dayton
Richmond
INDIANAPOLIS
Muncie
Kokomo
Lafayette
Bloomington
Danville
Champaign
Decatur
Springfield
Peoria
Terre Haute
Bloomington
Columbus
CINCINNATI
Midwest
ILLINOIS
INDIANA
OHIO
Maysville
Portsmouth
Parkersburg
Huntington
Charleston
WEST VIRGINIA
Harrisonburg
Charlottesville
Richmond
Lynchburg
Petersburg
Roanoke
Newport News
Virginia Beach
Norfolk
Elizabeth City
Albemarle Sd.
Pamlico Sd.
C. Hatteras
C. Charles
Danville
Durham
Rocky Mount
Greenville
Raleigh
Goldsboro
New Bern
Fayetteville
Jacksonville
Onslow Bay
Wilmington
C. Fear
Greensboro
Winston-Salem
CHARLOTTE
NORTH CAROLINA
Hickory
Asheville
Spartanburg
Greenville
Rock Hill
Anderson
Columbia
Sumter
Florence
Myrtle Beach
Long Bay
Georgetown
C. Romain
Charleston
Orangeburg
SOUTH CAROLINA
Augusta
Athens
Savannah
Statesboro
ATLANTA
Rome
Gainesville
Roswell
Macon
Columbus
Dublin
La Grange
GEORGIA
Albany
Cordele
Douglas
Waycross
Brunswick
Tifton
Valdosta
Thomasville
Tallahassee
Lake City
Jacksonville
St. Augustine
Daytona Beach
Gainesville
Ocala
Deltona
C. Canaveral
Orlando
Lakeland
Melbourne
Palm Bay
Fort Pierce
TAMPA
Clearwater
St. Petersburg
Tampa B.
Sarasota
Charlotte Harbor
Cape Coral
Fort Myers
L. Okeechobee
West Palm Beach
Fort Lauderdale
MIAMI
Naples
C. Sable
Florida Bay
Florida Keys
Key West
Straits of Florida
Grand Bahama I.
Freeport
Little Abaco I.
Great Abaco I.
N.E. Providence Channel
N.W. Providence Channel
BAHAMAS
Eleuthera I.
Nassau
New Providence I.
Andros I.
Exuma Sound
Cat I.
Great Exuma
Long I.
ATLANTIC OCEAN
GULF OF MEXICO
Panama City
Pensacola
Apalachicola
Apalachee B.
C. San Blas
Mobile
Biloxi
Gulfport
Pontchartrain
NEW ORLEANS
Breton Sd.
Mississippi River Delta
Baton Rouge
Lafayette
New Iberia
Morgan City
Houma
Atchafalaya B.
Marsh I.
Port Arthur
Beaumont
Lake Charles
LOUISIANA
Alexandria
Natchitoches
Shreveport
Monroe
Vicksburg
Natchez
Jackson
McComb
Hattiesburg
Laurel
Bogalusa
Meridian
MISSISSIPPI
Greenville
Greenwood
Cleveland
Clarksdale
Oxford
Tupelo
Columbus
Tuscaloosa
Birmingham
Anniston
Gadsden
Huntsville
Florence
Decatur
Corinth
ALABAMA
Demopolis
Selma
Montgomery
Auburn
Troy
Dothan
Andalusia
Greenville
Memphis
Jackson
Dyersburg
Columbia
Nashville
Murfreesboro
Clarksville
TENNESSEE
Chattanooga
Knoxville
Oak Ridge
Athens
Johnson City
Kingsport
Bristol
Appalachian Mts.
Cumberland Plateau
Blue Ridge
Allegheny Mts.
Louisville
Frankfort
Lexington
Richmond
Danville
Hazard
Somerset
KENTUCKY
Bowling Green
Middlesboro
Hopkinsville
Owensboro
Evansville
Henderson
Mount Vernon
Vincennes
Paducah
Mayfield
Marion
Bluefield
Beckley
Pulaski
Radford
Carbondale
Cape Girardeau
Poplar Bluff
East St. Louis
ST. LOUIS
Alton
Effingham
Mattoon
Quincy
Hannibal
Columbia
Jefferson City
Rolla
MISSOURI
Sedalia
Lake of the Ozarks
Ozark Plateau
West Plains
Springfield
Joplin
Lebanon
KANSAS CITY
Lawrence
Topeka
Leavenworth
St. Joseph
Chillicothe
Kirksville
Maryville
Beatrice
Manhattan
Emporia
Fort Scott
Nevada
Pittsburg
Parsons
Wichita
Arkansas City
Bartlesville
Ponca City
Tulsa
Muskogee
Fayetteville
Boston Mts.
Ozark Mts.
Paragould
Jonesboro
Blytheville
Newport
Russellville
Conway
Fort Smith
Little Rock
Pine Bluff
Stuttgart
Hot Springs
Ouachita Mts.
ARKANSAS
McAlester
Shawnee
Oklahoma City
Ardmore
Durant
Paris
Sherman
Texarkana
Hope
Camden
El Dorado
Marshall
Longview
Tyler
DALLAS
Arlington
Corsicana
Waco
Palestine
Nacogdoches
Lufkin
Toledo Bend Res.
De Ridder
Huntsville
Bryan
HOUSTON
Pasadena
Galveston
Freeport
Port Lavaca
Matagorda I.
Aransas Pass
Victoria
Laguna Madre
Brownsville
Rio Grande
Des Moines
Omaha
Lincoln
Sioux Falls

EASTERN UNITED STATES 1:6 000 000

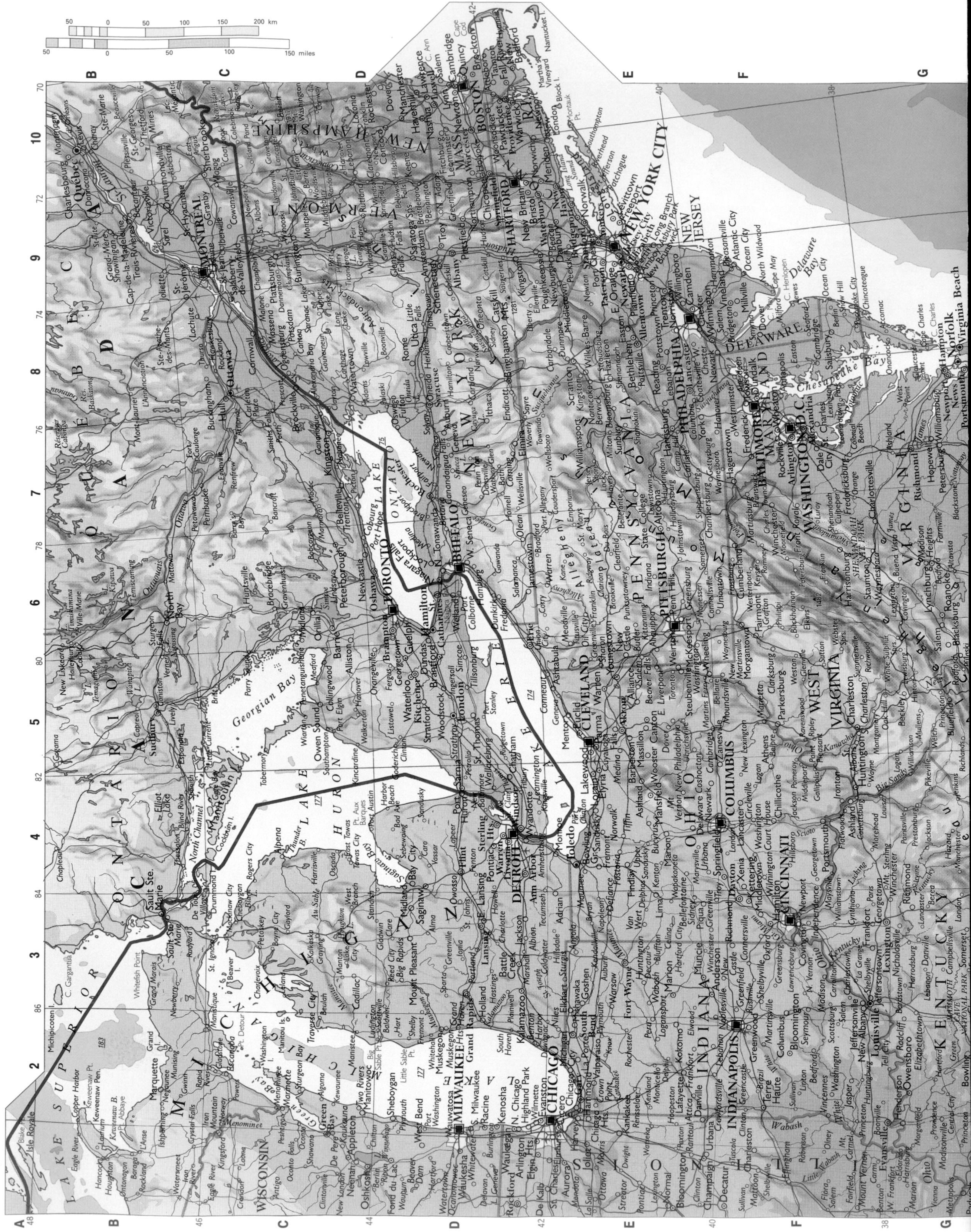
50 0 50 100 150 200 km
50 0 50 100 150 miles
LAKE SUPERIOR
LAKE HURON
LAKE MICHIGAN
LAKE ERIE
LAKE ONTARIO
Georgian Bay
ONTARIO
QUEBEC
MICHIGAN
WISCONSIN
ILLINOIS
INDIANA
OHIO
KENTUCKY
WEST VIRGINIA
VIRGINIA
PENNSYLVANIA
NEW YORK
NEW JERSEY
DELAWARE
MARYLAND
VERMONT
NEW HAMPSHIRE
MASS.
CONN.
R.I.
NEW YORK CITY
BOSTON
PHILADELPHIA
BALTIMORE
WASHINGTON D.C.
PITTSBURGH
CLEVELAND
DETROIT
TORONTO
MONTREAL
CHICAGO
MILWAUKEE
INDIANAPOLIS
COLUMBUS
CINCINNATI
BUFFALO
HARTFORD
Ottawa
Québec
Chesapeake Bay
Delaware Bay

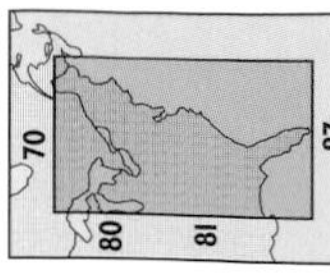

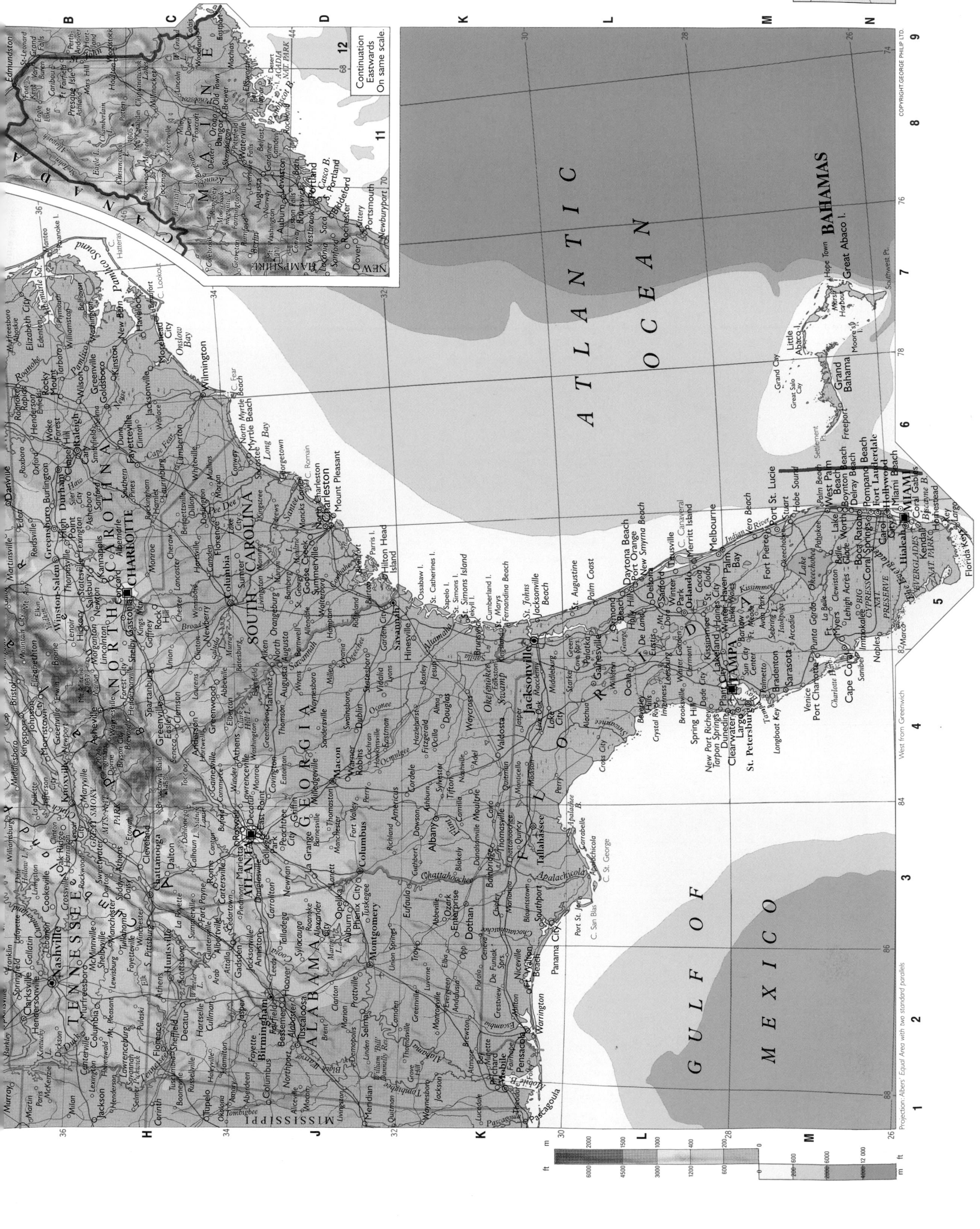
ATLANTIC OCEAN
GULF OF MEXICO
BAHAMAS
TENNESSEE
NORTH CAROLINA
SOUTH CAROLINA
GEORGIA
ALABAMA
FLORIDA
MISSISSIPPI
MAINE
CHARLOTTE
ATLANTA
JACKSONVILLE
TAMPA
MIAMI
Continuation Eastwards On same scale.
West from Greenwich
Projection: Albers' Equal Area with two standard parallels
COPYRIGHT GEORGE PHILIP LTD.

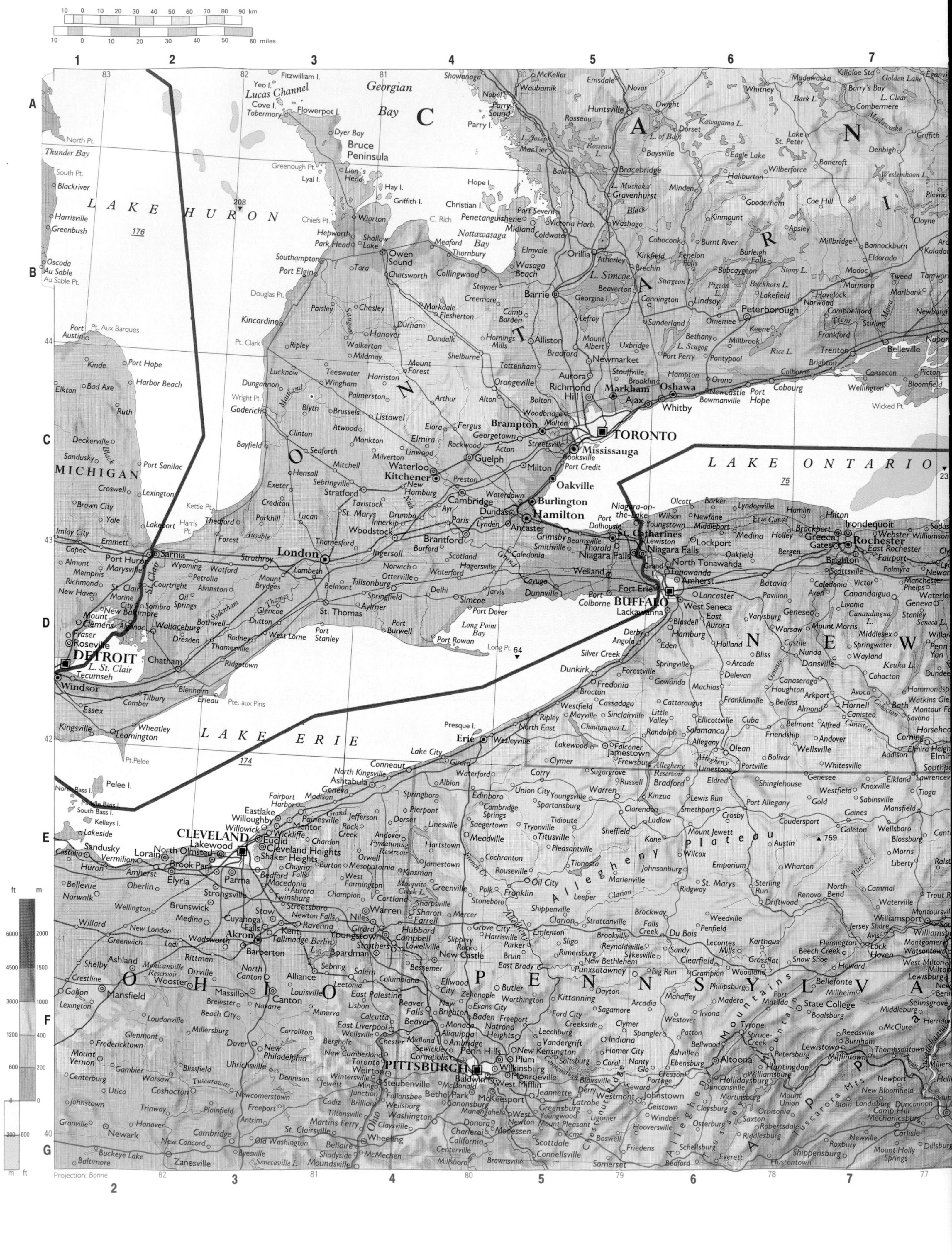

10 0 10 20 30 40 50 60 70 80 90 km
10 0 10 20 30 40 50 60 miles
LAKE HURON
LAKE ONTARIO
LAKE ERIE
Georgian Bay
Nottawasaga Bay
Bruce Peninsula
ONTARIO
CANADA
MICHIGAN
OHIO
PENNSYLVANIA
NEW YORK
TORONTO
Mississauga
Hamilton
Burlington
Oakville
Brampton
Kitchener
Waterloo
Guelph
Cambridge
London
Sarnia
Port Huron
DETROIT
Windsor
L. St. Clair
Chatham
St. Catharines
Niagara Falls
BUFFALO
Rochester
Erie
CLEVELAND
Lakewood
Akron
Canton
Youngstown
PITTSBURGH
Altoona
State College
Williamsport
Barrie
L. Simcoe
Peterborough
Oshawa
Belleville
Allegheny Plateau
Allegheny Mountains
Appalachian Mts.
Tuscarora Mts.
Projection: Bonne

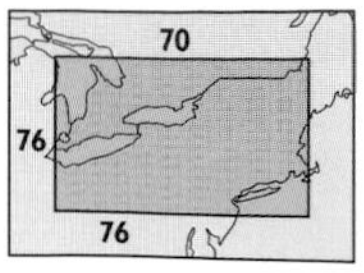
70
76
76

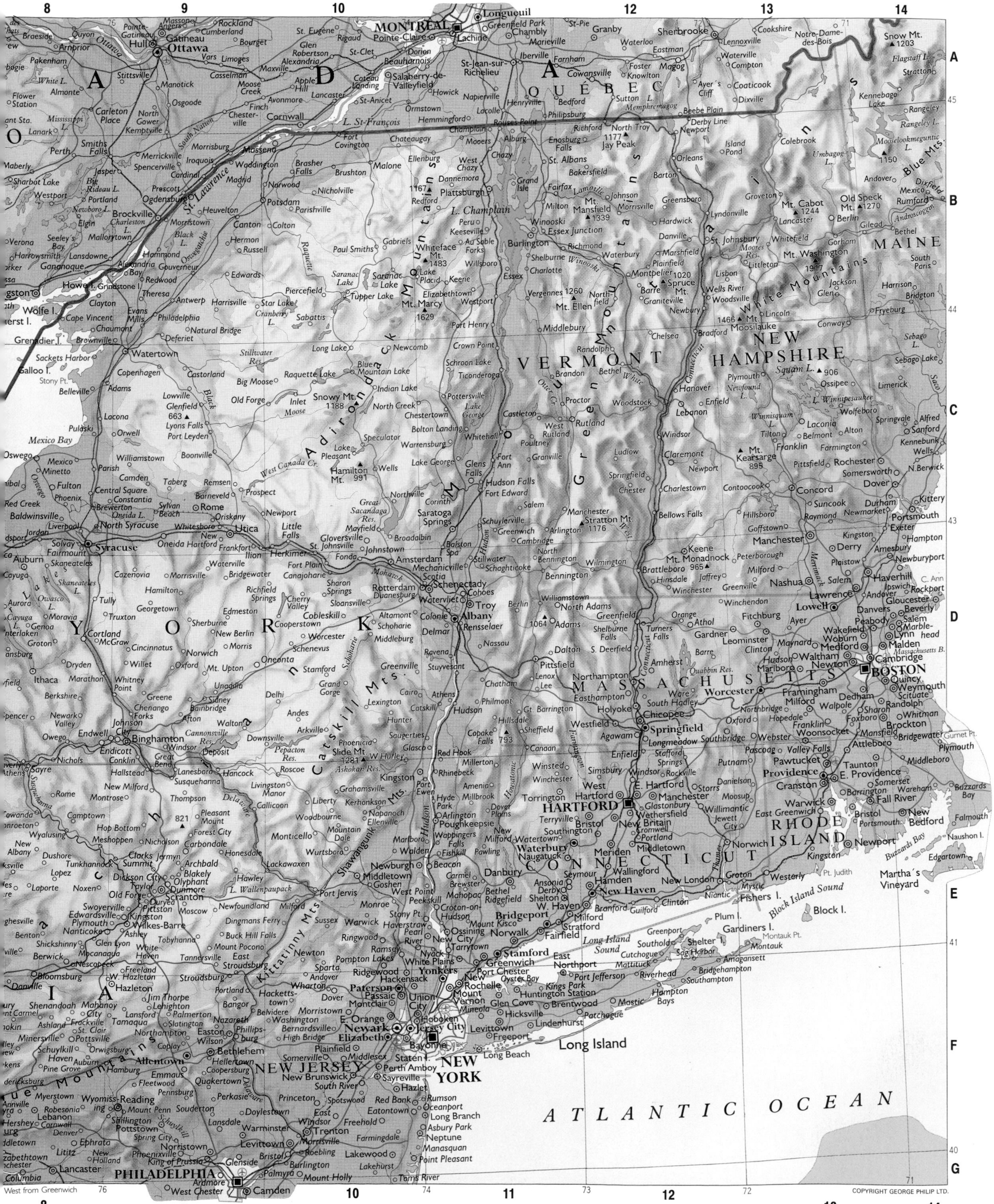
8
9
10
11
12
13
14
A
B
C
D
E
F
G
45
44
43
41
40
QUÉBEC
VERMONT
NEW HAMPSHIRE
MAINE
MASSACHUSETTS
CONNECTICUT
RHODE ISLAND
NEW JERSEY
NEW YORK
ATLANTIC OCEAN
Adirondack Mountains
Green Mountains
White Mountains
Catskill Mts.
Kittatinny Mts.
Shawangunk Mts.
Blue Mountains
Appalachian Mountains
Long Island
Long Island Sound
Block Island Sound
Block I.
Martha's Vineyard
Nantucket Sound
L. Champlain
Lake George
L. Winnipesaukee
Mt. Washington 1917
Mt. Marcy 1629
Mt. Mansfield 1339
Slide Mt. 1281
MONTREAL
Ottawa
Hull
Sherbrooke
Burlington
Plattsburgh
Montpelier
Rutland
Concord
Manchester
Portsmouth
Portland
BOSTON
Worcester
Springfield
Providence
HARTFORD
New Haven
Bridgeport
Stamford
Albany
Schenectady
Troy
Utica
Syracuse
Binghamton
Scranton
Wilkes-Barre
Allentown
Bethlehem
Reading
Lancaster
PHILADELPHIA
Camden
Trenton
Newark
Jersey City
Paterson
Yonkers
NEW YORK
Poughkeepsie
Kingston
Watertown
Newport
New Bedford
Fall River
Cambridge
Lowell
Lawrence
Nashua
West from Greenwich
76
74
73
72
71

COPYRIGHT GEORGE PHILIP LTD.

MIDDLE UNITED STATES 1:6 000 000

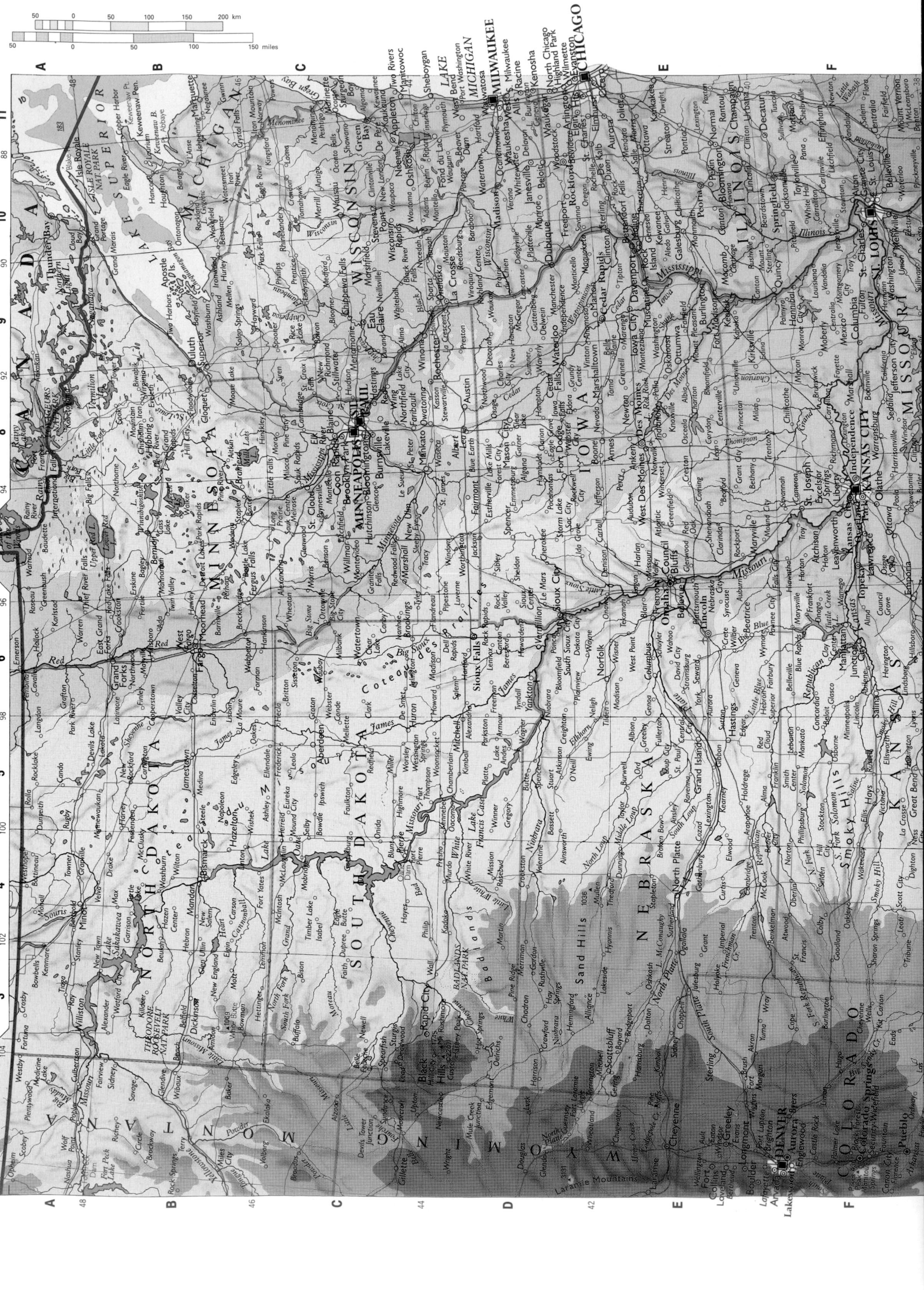

OKLAHOMA
ARKANSAS
TENNESSEE
MISSISSIPPI
LOUISIANA
TEXAS
NEW MEXICO
MEXICO
COAHUILA
CHIHUAHUA
GULF OF MEXICO
Oklahoma City
Tulsa
Wichita
Amarillo
Lubbock
DALLAS
Fort Worth
Austin
SAN ANTONIO
HOUSTON
Corpus Christi
Galveston
Shreveport
Little Rock
Memphis
Jackson
Baton Rouge
NEW ORLEANS
Springfield
Laredo
El Paso
Llano Estacado
Edwards Plateau
Stockton Plateau
Balcones Escarpment
Boston Mts.
Ozark Plateau
Ouachita Mts.
Sangre de Cristo Mts.
Bolsón de Mapimí
Rio Grande
Red
Arkansas
Mississippi
Continuation Southwards on same scale
Projection: Albers' Equal Area with two standard parallels
West from Greenwich
COPYRIGHT.GEORGE PHILIP LTD.

WESTERN UNITED STATES 1:6 000 000

50 0 50 100 150 200 km

50 0 50 100 150 miles

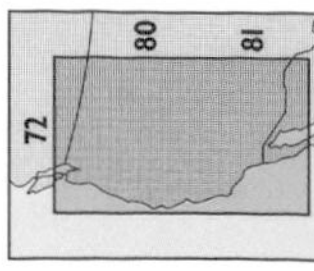

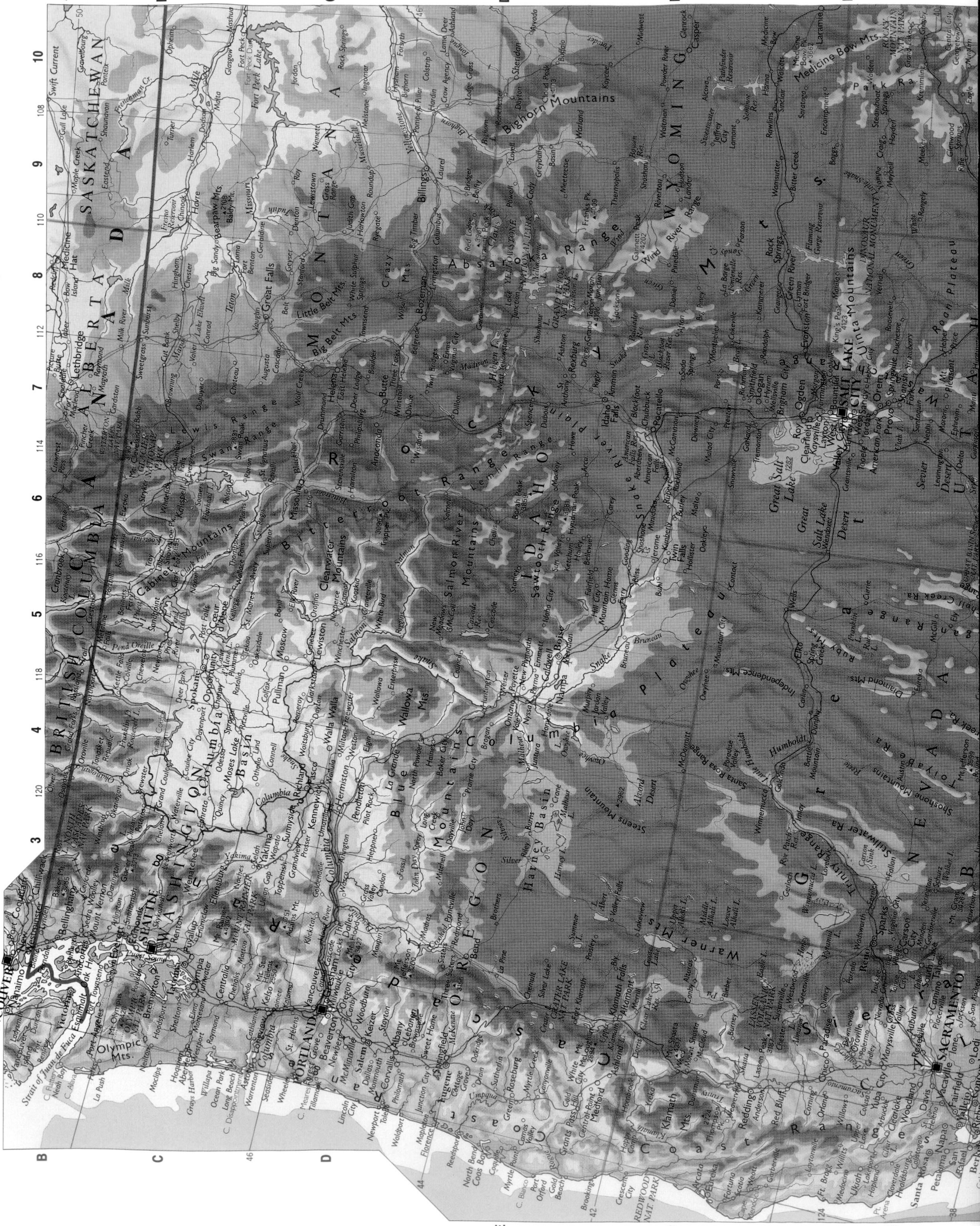

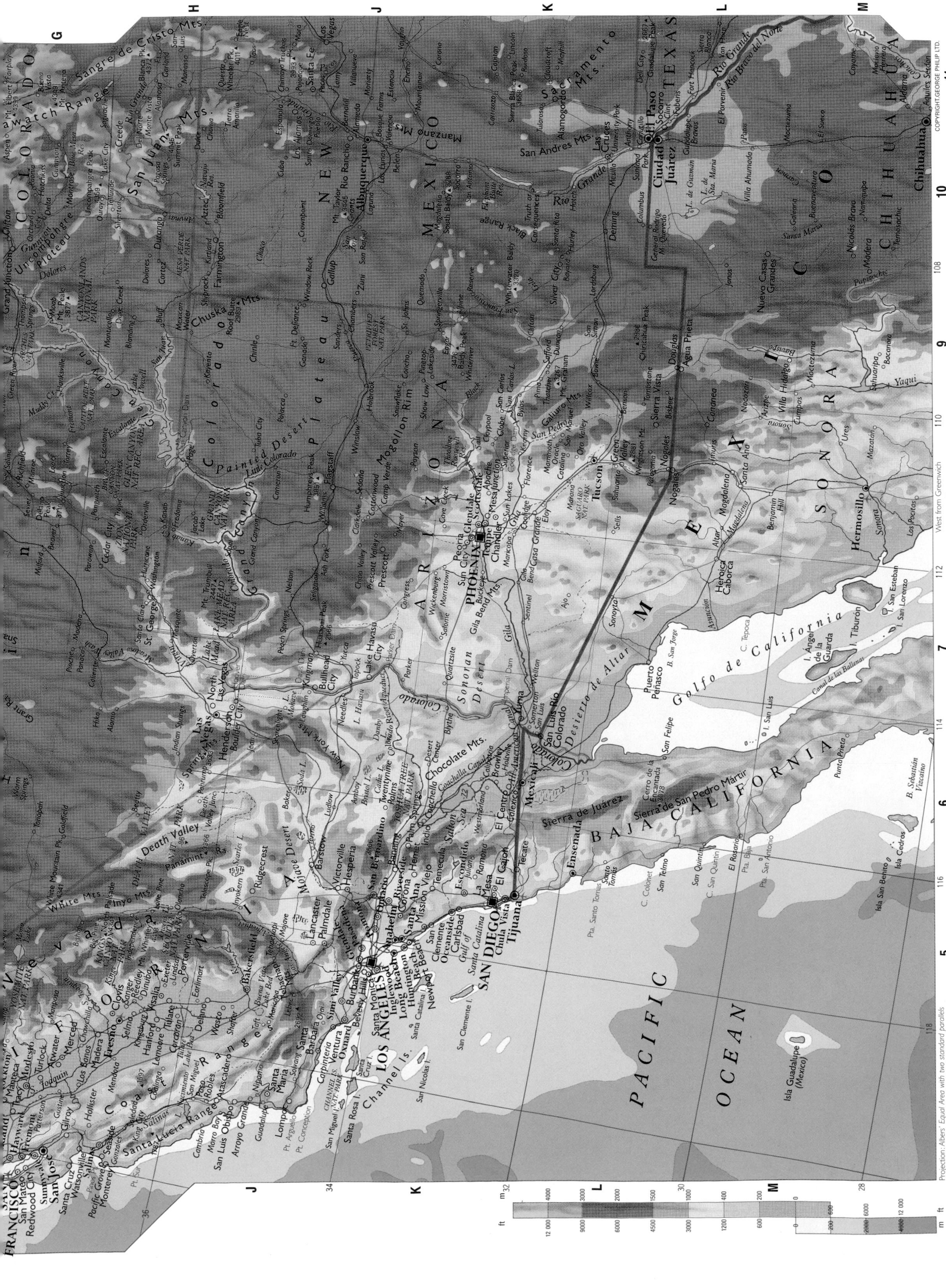
COLORADO
NEW MEXICO
ARIZONA
TEXAS
SONORA
CHIHUAHUA
BAJA CALIFORNIA
MEXICO
PACIFIC OCEAN
Golfo de California
Colorado Plateau
Painted Desert
Mojave Desert
Sonoran Desert
Death Valley
Grand Canyon
Sangre de Cristo Mts.
San Juan Mts.
Sacramento Mts.
Mogollon Rim
Sierra de San Pedro Mártir
Sierra de Juárez
Desierto de Altar
Chocolate Mts.
Chuska Mts.
Rio Grande
Colorado
Gila
Yaqui
Channel Is.
LOS ANGELES
SAN DIEGO
PHOENIX
Tijuana
Mexicali
Ensenada
Tucson
Nogales
Hermosillo
Chihuahua
Ciudad Juárez
El Paso
Las Cruces
Albuquerque
Santa Fe
Flagstaff
Yuma
Las Vegas
Henderson
Bakersfield
Fresno
San Jose
SAN FRANCISCO
Santa Barbara
Isla Guadalupe (Mexico)
Isla Tiburón
Projection: Albers' Equal Area with two standard parallels
West from Greenwich
COPYRIGHT GEORGE PHILIP LTD.
m
ft

CENTRAL AND SOUTHERN CALIFORNIA AND WESTERN WASHINGTON 1:2 500 000

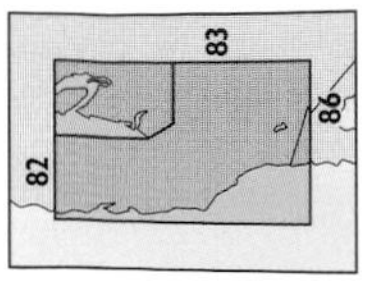
82
83
86

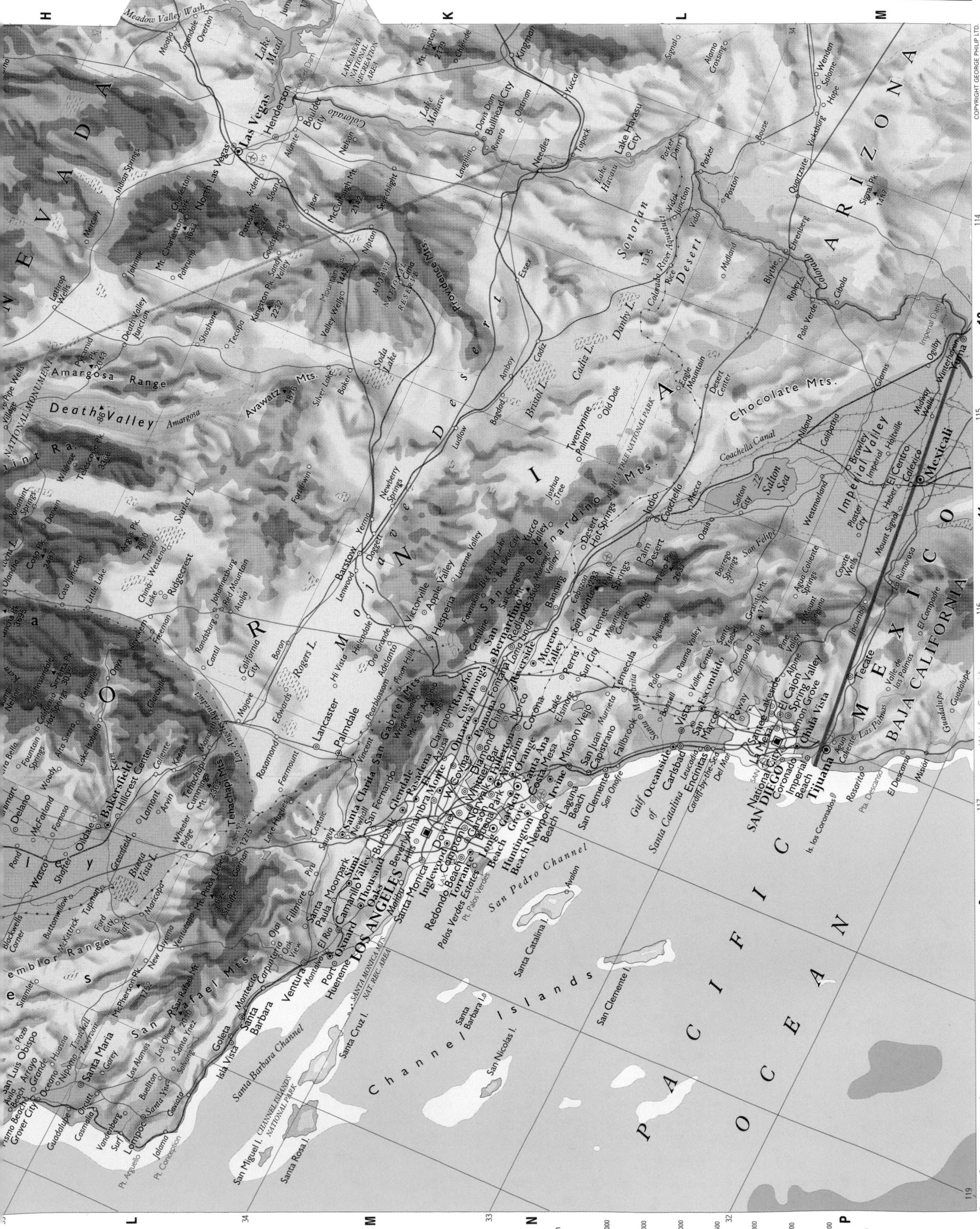
km 10 0 10 20 30 40 50 60 70 80 90
miles 10 0 10 20 30 40 50 60
H
J
K
L
M
N
P
NEVADA
ARIZONA
CALIFORNIA
MEXICO
BAJA CALIFORNIA
Mojave Desert
Sonoran Desert
PACIFIC OCEAN
Channel Islands
Las Vegas
Henderson
North Las Vegas
Boulder City
Lake Mead
Kingman
Bullhead City
Needles
Lake Havasu City
Parker
Blythe
Quartzsite
Death Valley
Amargosa Range
Avawatz Mts.
Soda Lake
Barstow
Victorville
Apple Valley
Hesperia
Ridgecrest
Bakersfield
Oildale
Delano
Wasco
Tehachapi Mts.
Lancaster
Palmdale
Mojave
San Gabriel Mts.
San Bernardino Mts.
San Bernardino
Riverside
Palm Springs
Palm Desert
Indio
Salton Sea
Imperial Valley
Chocolate Mts.
El Centro
Calexico
Mexicali
Yuma
Santa Barbara
Santa Maria
San Luis Obispo
Lompoc
Ventura
Oxnard
Santa Clarita
LOS ANGELES
Long Beach
Pasadena
Glendale
Burbank
Anaheim
Santa Ana
Irvine
Huntington Beach
Oceanside
Escondido
SAN DIEGO
Chula Vista
Tijuana
Tecate
Ensenada
Santa Catalina I.
San Clemente I.
San Nicolas I.
Santa Cruz I.
Santa Rosa I.
San Miguel I.
Santa Barbara Channel
San Pedro Channel
Gulf of Santa Catalina
Projection: Bonne
West from Greenwich
COPYRIGHT GEORGE PHILIP LTD.

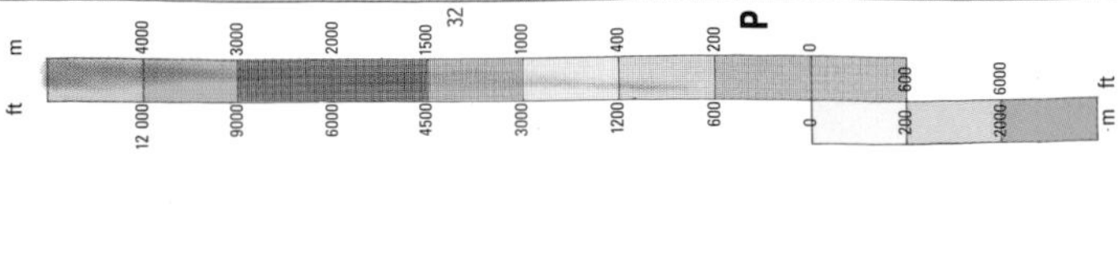
m
4000
3000
2000
1500
1000
400
200
0
ft
12 000
9000
6000
4500
3000
1200
600
0
200 600
2000 6000
m ft

MEXICO 1:8 000 000

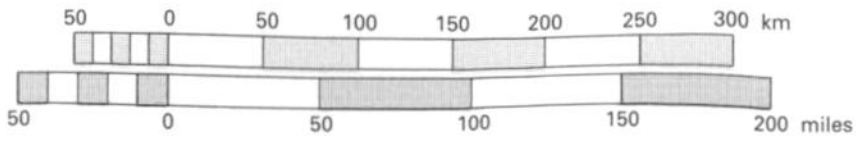

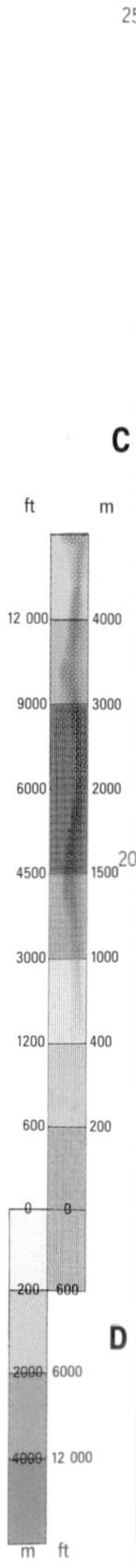

Projection: *Bi-polar oblique Conical Orthomorphic*

2 3 4

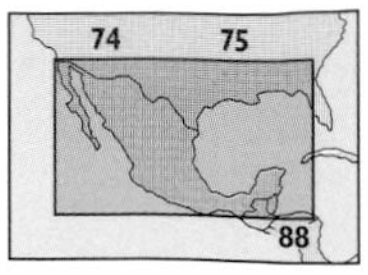
74
75
88

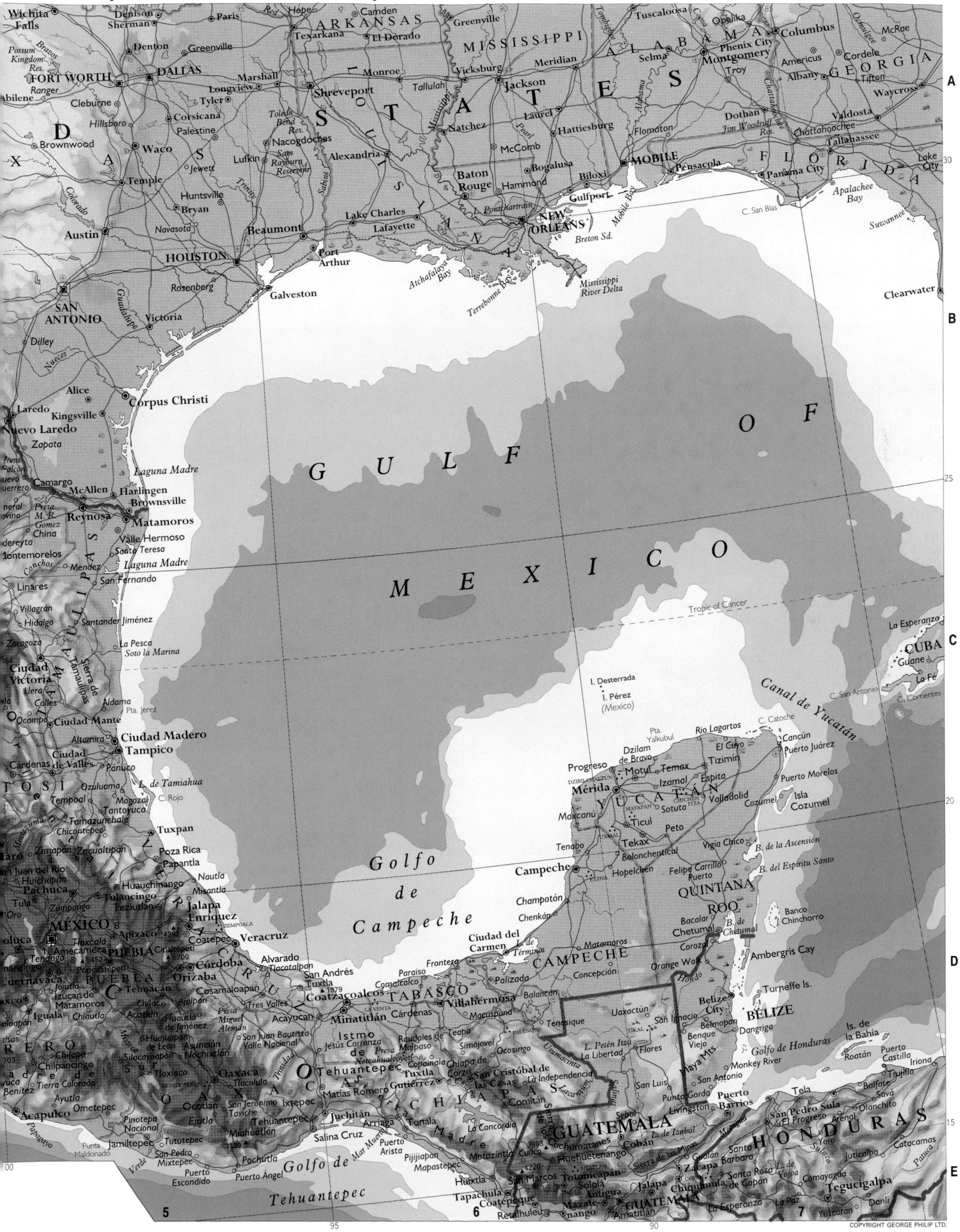
5
6
7
8
A
B
C
D
E
UNITED STATES
ARKANSAS
MISSISSIPPI
ALABAMA
GEORGIA
LOUISIANA
TEXAS
FLORIDA
Wichita Falls
Denison
Sherman
Paris
Hope
Camden
Texarkana
El Dorado
Greenville
Tuscaloosa
Opelika
Columbus
Denton
Greenville
Phenix City
Montgomery
Selma
Meridian
FORT WORTH
DALLAS
Marshall
Shreveport
Monroe
Vicksburg
Jackson
Longview
Tyler
Tallulah
Troy
Americus
Albany
Cordele
Tifton
Ranger
Cleburne
Hillsboro
Corsicana
Palestine
Natchez
Laurel
Hattiesburg
Dothan
Valdosta
Waycross
Brownwood
Waco
Nacogdoches
Alexandria
McComb
Flomaton
Tallahassee
Lufkin
Jewett
Bogalusa
Biloxi
MOBILE
Pensacola
Panama City
Lake City
Temple
Baton Rouge
Hammond
Gulfport
Huntsville
Bryan
Navasota
Lake Charles
Lafayette
NEW ORLEANS
Apalachee Bay
Austin
Beaumont
Port Arthur
Breton Sd.
C. San Blas
HOUSTON
Galveston
Atchafalaya Bay
Terrebonne Bay
Mississippi River Delta
Rosenberg
SAN ANTONIO
Victoria
Clearwater
Dilley
Alice
Corpus Christi
Laredo
Kingsville
Nuevo Laredo
Zapata
GULF OF MEXICO
Laguna Madre
Camargo
McAllen
Harlingen
Brownsville
Reynosa
Matamoros
Valle Hermoso
Santa Teresa
Laguna Madre
Mendez
San Fernando
Linares
Tropic of Cancer
Santander Jiménez
La Esperanza
CUBA
Guane
La Fé
La Pesca
Soto la Marina
Ciudad Victoria
I. Desterrada
I. Pérez (Mexico)
Canal de Yucatán
C. San Antonio
C. Corrientes
Aldama
Pta. Jerez
Ciudad Mante
Ciudad Madero
Tampico
Rio Lagartos
C. Catoche
Cancún
Puerto Juárez
Progreso
Dzilam de Bravo
Motul
Temax
Tizimín
El Cuyo
Mérida
Izamal
Espita
Valladolid
Puerto Morelos
YUCATÁN
Cozumel
Isla Cozumel
Maxcanú
Ticul
Sotuta
Peto
Tuxpan
Poza Rica
Papantla
Tekax
Tenabo
Vigia Chico
Bolonchenticul
Golfo de Campeche
Campeche
Hopelchén
Felipe Carrillo Puerto
B. de la Ascensión
B. del Espíritu Santo
QUINTANA ROO
Champotón
Chenkán
Bacalar
Chetumal
Banco Chinchorro
Pachuca
Tulancingo
Jalapa Enriquez
Veracruz
Ciudad del Carmen
L. de Términos
CAMPECHE
Corozal
Ambergris Cay
MÉXICO
PUEBLA
Córdoba
Orizaba
Alvarado
San Andrés Tuxtla
Coatzacoalcos
Frontera
TABASCO
Villahermosa
Concepción
Orange Walk
Turneffe Is.
Minatitlán
Cárdenas
Acayucan
Uaxactún
Belize City
BELIZE
Tenosique
Belmopan
San Ignacio
Is. de la Bahía
Oaxaca
Tehuantepec
Tuxtla Gutiérrez
San Cristóbal de las Casas
Flores
Dangriga
Golfo de Honduras
Roatán
Puerto Castilla
Iriona
Trujillo
CHIAPAS
Comitán
San Luis
Punta Gorda
Puerto Barrios
Tela
Balfate
Acapulco
Juchitán
Arriaga
Tonalá
Livingston
San Pedro Sula
Olanchito
GUATEMALA
Cobán
HONDURAS
Salina Cruz
Golfo de Tehuantepec
Puerto Ángel
Puerto Escondido
Huehuetenango
Zacapa
Santa Bárbara
Tapachula
Huixtla
Quetzaltenango
GUATEMALA
Chiquimula
Comayagua
Tegucigalpa
Retalhuleu
Mazatenango
Amatitlán
Catacamas
Juticalpa
95
90
25
20
15
30

COPYRIGHT GEORGE PHILIP LTD.

CENTRAL AMERICA AND THE WEST INDIES

1:8 000 000

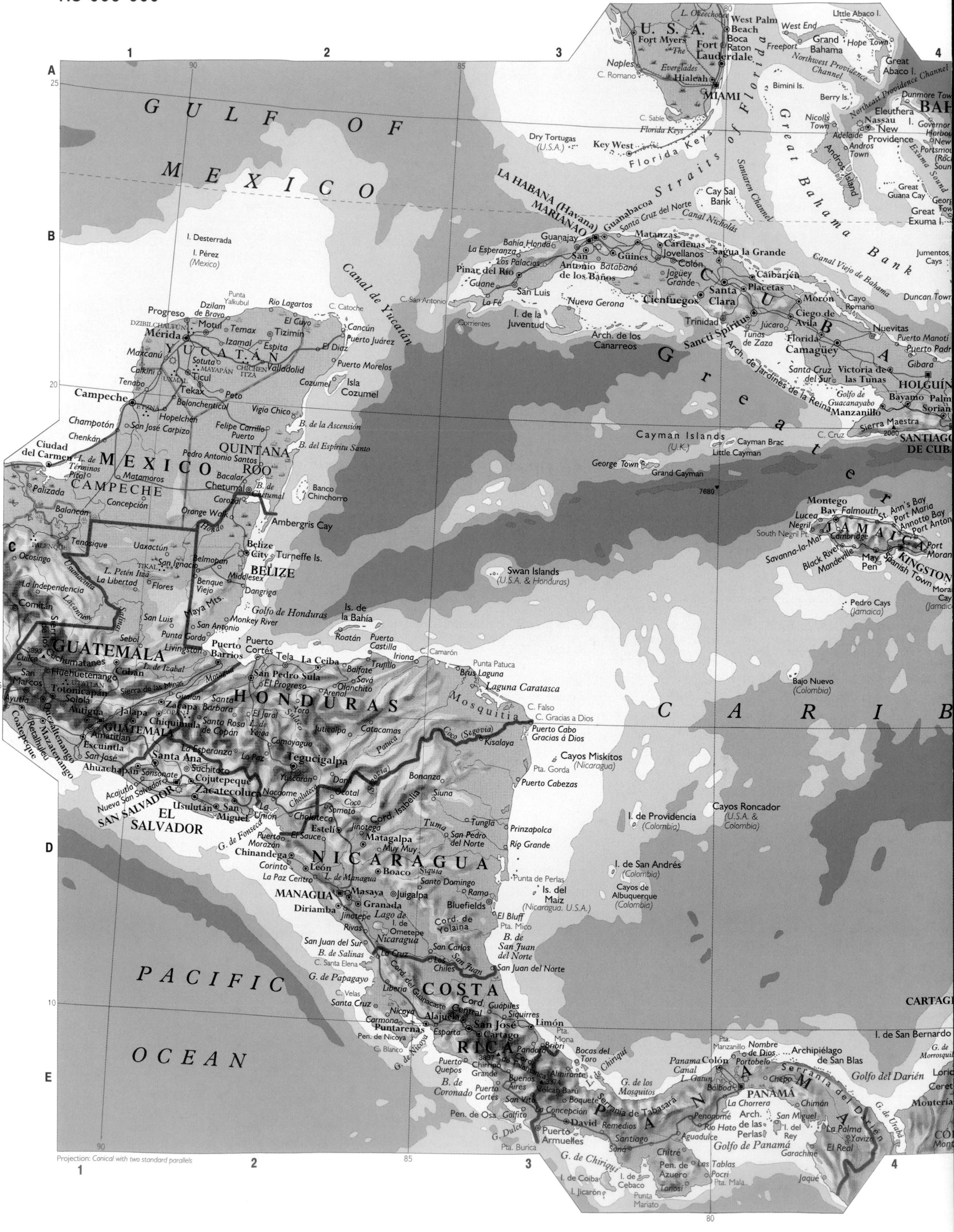

Projection: Conical with two standard parallels

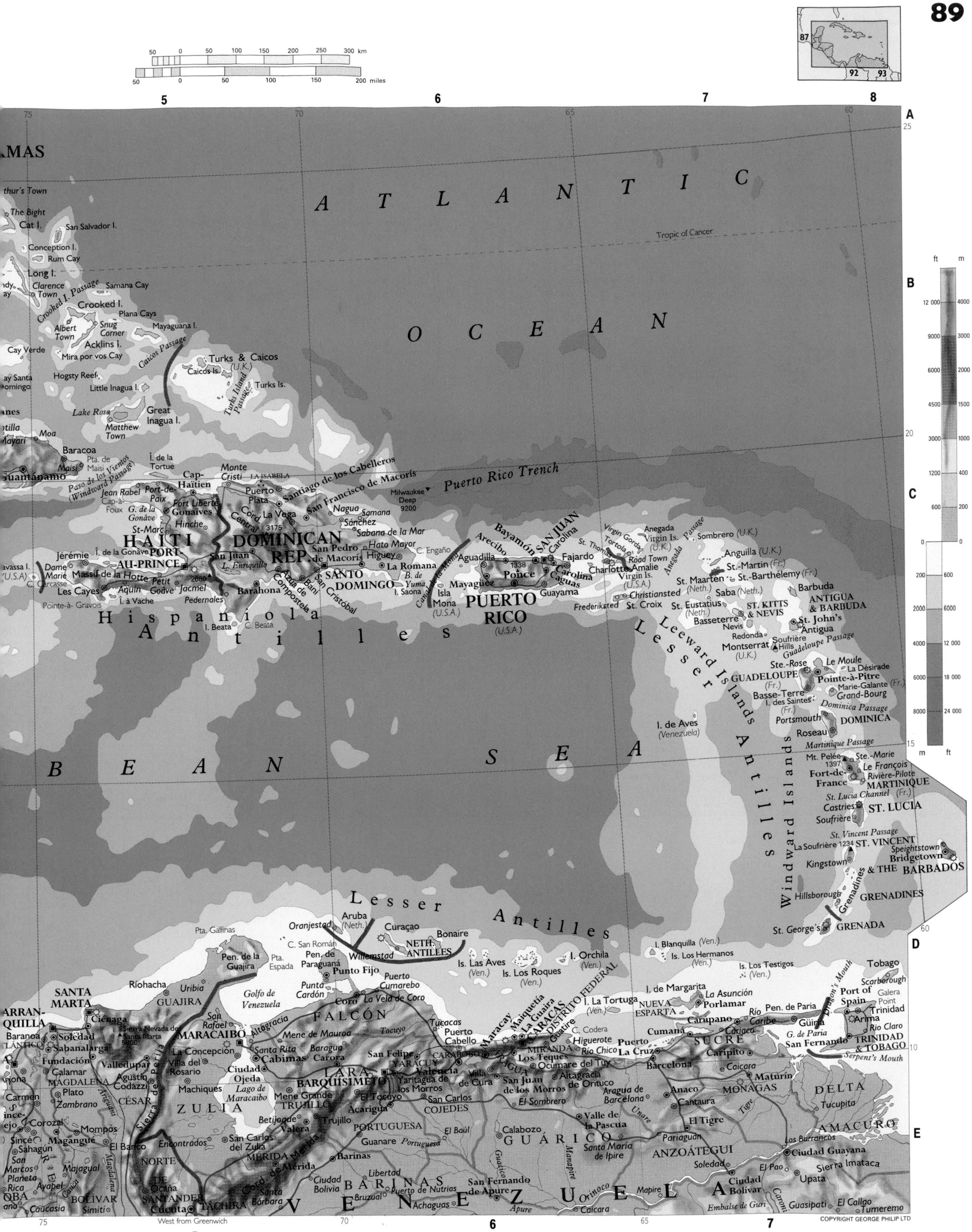

50 0 50 100 150 200 250 300 km
50 0 50 100 150 200 miles
5
6
7
8
87
92
93
A
B
C
D
E
75
70
65
60
25
20
15
10
A T L A N T I C
O C E A N
Tropic of Cancer
Puerto Rico Trench
Milwaukee Deep 9200
ft
m
12 000
9000
6000
4500
3000
1200
600
0
200
2000
4000
6000
8000
4000
3000
2000
1500
1000
400
200
600
6000
12 000
18 000
24 000
MAS
thur's Town
The Bight
Cat I.
San Salvador I.
Conception I.
Rum Cay
Long I.
Clarence Town
Samana Cay
Crooked I. Passage
Crooked I.
Plana Cays
Albert Town
Snug Corner
Acklins I.
Mayaguana I.
Cay Verde
Mira por vos Cay
Caicos Passage
Turks & Caicos (U.K.)
Caicos Is.
Turks Island Passage
Turks Is.
Hogsty Reef
Little Inagua I.
Lake Rosa
Great Inagua I.
Matthew Town
Moa
Baracoa
Pta. de Maisí
Maisí
Guantánamo
Paso de los Vientos (Windward Passage)
Î. de la Tortue
Cap-Haïtien
Port-de-Paix
Jean Rabel
Cap-à-Foux
Monte Cristi
LA ISABELA
Puerto Plata
Santiago de los Caballeros
San Francisco de Macorís
Fort Liberté
Gonaïves
G. de la Gonâve
Hinche
St-Marc
Cord. Central
La Vega
Nagua
Samana
Sánchez
Sabana de la Mar
Hato Mayor
HAITI
DOMINICAN REP.
Î. de la Gonâve
Jérémie
PORT-AU-PRINCE
San Juan
L. Enriquillo
San Pedro de Macorís
Higüey
C. Engaño
La Romana
Dame Marie
Massif de la Hotte
C. Carcasse
Les Cayes
Aquin
Petit Goâve
Jacmel
Barahona
Azua de Compostela
Baní
San Cristóbal
SANTO DOMINGO
B. de Yuma
I. Saona
Pointe-à-Gravois
Î. à Vache
Pedernales
Hispaniola
I. Beata
C. Beata
Antilles
Mona Passage
Isla Mona (U.S.A.)
Aguadilla
Arecibo
Bayamón
SAN JUAN
Carolina
Mayagüez
Ponce
Caguas
Guayama
Fajardo
PUERTO RICO (U.S.A.)
St. Thomas
Virgin Gorda
Tortola
Anegada
Virgin Is. (U.K.)
Anegada Passage
Road Town
Charlotte Amalie
Virgin Is. (U.S.A.)
Christiansted
Frederiksted
St. Croix
Sombrero (U.K.)
Anguilla (U.K.)
St.-Martin (Fr.)
St. Maarten (Neth.)
St.-Barthélemy (Fr.)
Saba (Neth.)
Barbuda
St. Eustatius (Neth.)
ST. KITTS & NEVIS
ANTIGUA & BARBUDA
Basseterre
Nevis
St. John's
Antigua
Redonda
Montserrat (U.K.)
Soufrière Hills
Guadeloupe Passage
Leeward Islands
Lesser Antilles
Ste.-Rose
Le Moule
La Désirade
GUADELOUPE (Fr.)
Pointe-à-Pitre
Marie-Galante (Fr.)
Basse-Terre
Grand-Bourg
I. des Saintes (Fr.)
Dominica Passage
Portsmouth
DOMINICA
Roseau
I. de Aves (Venezuela)
Martinique Passage
Mt. Pelée 1397
Ste.-Marie
Le François
Fort-de-France
Rivière-Pilote
MARTINIQUE (Fr.)
St. Lucia Channel
Castries
ST. LUCIA
Soufrière
St. Vincent Passage
La Soufrière 1234
ST. VINCENT & THE GRENADINES
Speightstown
Bridgetown
BARBADOS
Kingstown
Windward Islands
Grenadines
Hillsborough
GRENADINES
St. George's
GRENADA
B E A N S E A
Lesser Antilles
Pta. Gallinas
Aruba (Neth.)
Oranjestad
Curaçao
Bonaire
NETH. ANTILLES
Willemstad
C. San Román
Pen. de la Guajira
Pta. Espada
Pen. de Paraguaná
Punto Fijo
Is. Las Aves (Ven.)
Is. Los Roques (Ven.)
I. Orchila (Ven.)
I. Blanquilla (Ven.)
Is. Los Hermanos (Ven.)
Is. Los Testigos (Ven.)
Tobago
Scarborough
Riohacha
Uribia
GUAJIRA
Golfo de Venezuela
Punta Cardón
Puerto Cumarebo
Coro
La Vela de Coro
SANTA MARTA
BARRANQUILLA
Ciénaga
Sierra Nevada de Santa Marta 5800
San Rafael
MARACAIBO
Altagracia
FALCÓN
I. de Margarita
La Asunción
Porlamar
I. La Tortuga (Ven.)
NUEVA ESPARTA
DISTRITO FEDERAL
Soledad
Sabanalarga
Fundación
Valledupar
Villa del Rosario
La Concepción
Santa Rita
Cabimas
Mene de Mauroa
Baragua
Carora
Tocuyo
Tucacas
Puerto Cabello
Maracay
Maiquetía
La Guaira
CARACAS
Guatire
C. Codera
Higuerote
Río Chico
Puerto La Cruz
Cumaná
Carúpano
Río Caribe
Pen. de Paria
Güiria
Dragon's Mouth
Port of Spain
Galera Point
Trinidad
Arima
Rio Claro
G. de Paria
San Fernando
TRINIDAD & TOBAGO
Serpent's Mouth
SUCRE
Cariaco
Caripito
Caicara
Maturín
MONAGAS
Calamar
MAGDALENA
Plato
Zambrano
Agustín Codazzi
CÉSAR
Sierra de Perijá
Machiques
Ciudad Ojeda
Lago de Maracaibo
ZULIA
BARQUISIMETO
LARA
Yaritagua
San Felipe
YARACUY
CARABOBO
Valencia
ARAGUA
Villa de Cura
Los Teques
MIRANDA
Ocumare del Tuy
San Juan de los Morros
Altagracia de Orituco
Aragua de Barcelona
Barcelona
Anaco
Cantaura
DELTA AMACURO
Tucupita
Mene Grande
TRUJILLO
El Tocuyo
Acarigua
San Carlos
COJEDES
El Sombrero
Unare
Valle de la Pascua
El Tigre
Pariaguán
Corozal
Mompós
Sincé
Magangué
Sahagún
El Banco
Encontrados
Betijoque
Valera
Trujillo
PORTUGUESA
El Baúl
Calabozo
GUÁRICO
Santa María de Ipire
ANZOÁTEGUI
Los Barrancos
Ciudad Guayana
Sierra Imataca
San Marcos
Planeta Rica
Ayapel
Majagual
Cauca
BOLÍVAR
Simití
Caucasia
NORTE DE SANTANDER
Ocaña
San Carlos del Zulia
MÉRIDA
Mérida
Cord. de Mérida
Barinas
Guanare
Portuguesa
BARINAS
Libertad
Ciudad Bolivia
Bruzual
Puerto de Nutrias
San Fernando de Apure
Achaguas
Apure
Guárico
Manapire
Orinoco
Caicara
Mapire
Soledad
Ciudad Bolívar
El Pao
Upata
Caroní
Embalse de Guri
Guasipati
El Callao
Tumeremo
Cúcuta
TÁCHIRA
Santa Bárbara
V E N E Z U E L A
West from Greenwich

SOUTH AMERICA : Physical 1:35 000 000

NORTH ATLANTIC OCEAN
SOUTH ATLANTIC OCEAN
PACIFIC OCEAN
Caribbean Sea
Greater Antilles
Lesser Antilles
Cuba
Hispaniola
Puerto Rico
Jamaica
Turks & Caicos Is.
Guadeloupe
Dominica
Martinique
St. Lucia
Barbados
St. Vincent
Grenada
Tobago
Trinidad
I. Margarita
Yucatán Peninsula
Yucatan Channel
Gulf of Campeche
Isthmus of Tehuantepec
G. de Honduras
C. Gracias a Dios
L. Nicaragua
Guatemala Trench
Panama Canal
G. of Darién
Gulf of Panamá
C. de la Aguja
Sierra Nevada de Santa Marta
Maracaibo
Cordillera Occidental
Cordillera Central
Cordillera Oriental
Cord. de Mérida
Magdalena
Llanos
Orinoco
Meta
Guaviare
Guiana Highlands
Sierra Pacaraima
Mt. Roraima
2810
Serra Tumucumaque
C. Orange
Equator
Marajó I.
Amazon
Negro
Japurá
Caquetá
Putumayo
Napo
Marañón
Branco
Essequibo
Courantyne
C. de San Francisco
Cotopaxi
5897
Chimborazo
6267
G. of Guayaquil
Galapagos Is.
Pta. Pariñas
Pta. Negra
Selvas
Juruá
Purus
Madeira
Tapajós
Xingu
Tocantins
Araguaia
Parnaíba
Aripuanã
Roosevelt
Teles Pires
Arinos
Madre de Dios
Ucayali
Huascarán
6768
Guaporé
Mamoré
Plateau of Mato Grosso
C. de São Roque
Plat. of Borborema
São Francisco
Brazilian Highlands
Chile Peru Trench
Chincha Alta
L. Titicaca
Nevada Ancohuma
6550
L. de Poopó
Bolivian Plateau
Atacama Desert
Andes
Abrolhos Bank
Gran Chaco
Paraguay
Paraná
Pilcomayo
Serra da Mantiqueira
2890
Pico da Bandeira
C. Frio
Iguaçu Falls
Uruguay
Serra do Mar
Tropic of Cancer
Tropic of Capricorn
8050
San Félix
San Ambrosio
Cerro Ojos del Salado
6863
Salinas Grandes
Salado
Entre Rios
Sierra de Córdoba
L. Mar Chiquita
Mt. Aconcagua
6960
Pampas
L. dos Patos
Arch. de Juan Fernández
Río de la Plata
Colorado
Bahía Blanca
Negro
G. San Matías
Valdés Peninsula
Chubut
Patagonia
Chile Rise
Chiloé I.
Chonos Archipelago
Mte. San Valentín
4058
Taitao Peninsula
Gulf of Penas
Gulf of San Jorge
Argentine Basin
6212
Wellington I.
Madre de Dios I.
Magellan's St.
West Falkland
Falkland Is.
East Falkland
Santa Inés I.
Tierra del Fuego
Staten I.
Canal Cockburn
Canal Beagle
C. Horn
South Georgia
9200
Projection: Lambert's Azimuthal Equal Area
60 West from Greenwich
CARTOGRAPHY BY PHILIP'S.

1:35 000 000 Political : SOUTH AMERICA

NORTH ATLANTIC OCEAN
Caribbean Sea
PACIFIC OCEAN
SOUTH ATLANTIC OCEAN
BRAZIL
ARGENTINA
CHILE
PERU
BOLIVIA
COLOMBIA
VENEZUELA
ECUADOR
PARAGUAY
URUGUAY
GUYANA
SURINAM
FRENCH GUIANA
MEXICO
BELIZE
GUATEMALA
HONDURAS
EL SALVADOR
NICARAGUA
COSTA RICA
PANAMA
CUBA
JAMAICA
HAITI
DOMINICAN REP.
BAHAMAS
Havana
Kingston
Port-au-Prince
San Juan
Caracas
Bogotá
Quito
LIMA
La Paz
Santiago
BUENOS AIRES
Montevideo
Asunción
Brasília
RIO DE JANEIRO
SÃO PAULO
Manaus
Belém
Salvador
Recife
Fortaleza
Falkland Is. (U.K.)
Galapagos Is. (Ecuador)
South Georgia (U.K.)
Tropic of Cancer
Equator
Tropic of Capricorn
Projection: Lambert's Azimuthal Equal Area
West from Greenwich
CARTOGRAPHY BY PHILIP'S.
LIMA Capital Cities

SOUTH AMERICA-NORTH 1:16 000 000

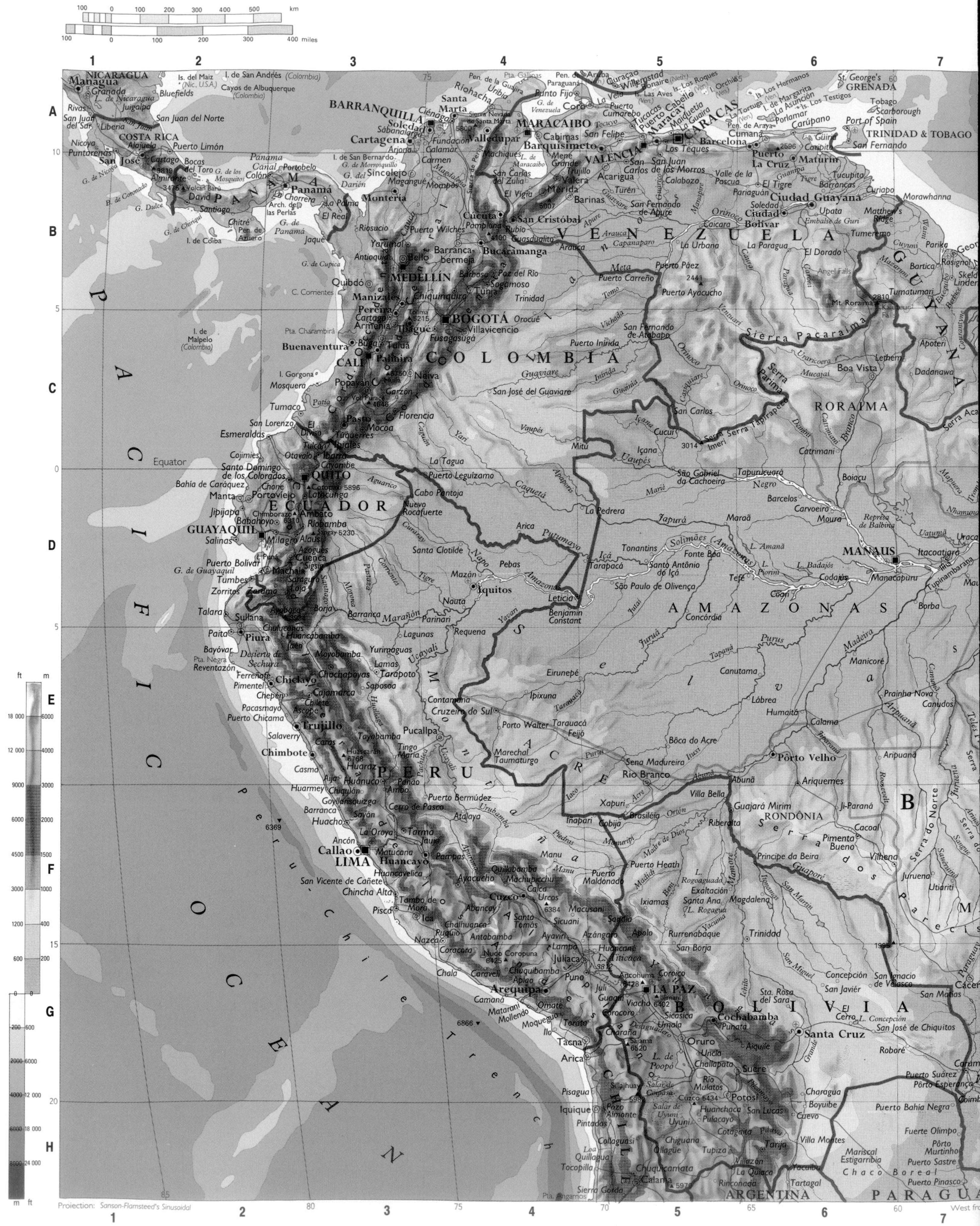

100 0 100 200 300 400 500 km
100 0 100 200 300 400 miles
NICARAGUA
Managua
Granada
L. de Nicaragua
Bluefields
Is. del Maiz (Nic. U.S.A.)
I. de San Andrés (Colombia)
Cayos de Albuquerque (Colombia)
San Juan del Norte
COSTA RICA
Puerto Limón
San José
Cartago
Bocas del Toro
Panama Canal
Portobelo
Colón
PANAMA
Panamá
David
Santiago
Chitré
Pen. de Azuero
I. de Coiba
G. de Panamá
Arch. de las Perlas
BARRANQUILLA
Cartagena
Santa Marta
Ciénaga
Soledad
Sincelejo
Montería
Magangué
Mompós
Riohacha
Pen. de la Guajira
Pta. Gallinas
Valledupar
MARACAIBO
L. de Maracaibo
Cabimas
Barquisimeto
Punto Fijo
Pen. de Paraguana
Coro
Aruba
Curaçao
Willemstad
Bonaire
Puerto Cabello
VALENCIA
Maracay
La Guaira
CARACAS
Los Teques
Barcelona
Cumaná
Carúpano
Is. Los Roques
I. de Margarita
La Asunción
Porlamar
St. George's
GRENADA
Tobago
Scarborough
Port of Spain
TRINIDAD & TOBAGO
San Fernando
San Felipe
Acarigua
Trujillo
Mérida
Barinas
San Cristóbal
Cúcuta
San Fernando de Apure
Calabozo
Valle de la Pascua
El Tigre
Puerto La Cruz
Maturín
Tucupita
Ciudad Guayana
Ciudad Bolívar
Upata
Embalse de Guri
Morawhanna
Matthew's Ridge
Tumeremo
VENEZUELA
Caicara
La Urbana
La Paragua
El Dorado
Angel Falls
Puerto Páez
Puerto Carreño
Puerto Ayacucho
Mt. Roraima 2810
Sierra Pacaraima
Serra Parima
GUYANA
Lethem
Bucaramanga
Barrancabermeja
MEDELLÍN
Bello
Quibdó
Manizales
Pereira
Armenia
Tunja
Sogamoso
BOGOTÁ
Villavicencio
Fusagasugá
Ibagué
Buenaventura
CALI
Palmira
Popayán
Neiva
Pasto
Tumaco
Mocoa
Florencia
COLOMBIA
Puerto Inírida
San José del Guaviare
Mitú
San Carlos
Cucuí
Boa Vista
RORAIMA
Caracaraí
I. de Malpelo (Colombia)
I. Gorgona
Esmeraldas
Ibarra
Equator
Santo Domingo de los Colorados
QUITO
Manta
Portoviejo
Latacunga
Ambato
Chimborazo 6310
Riobamba
ECUADOR
GUAYAQUIL
Salinas
Cuenca
Machala
G. de Guayaquil
Tumbes
Loja
Talara
Sullana
Paita
Piura
Desierto de Sechura
Chiclayo
Cajamarca
Chachapoyas
Moyobamba
Tarapoto
Trujillo
Chimbote
Huaraz
Huascarán 6768
Huánuco
Pucallpa
Cerro de Pasco
La Oroya
Tarma
Huancayo
Callao
LIMA
Huancavelica
Ayacucho
Cuzco
Machupicchu
Nazca
Arequipa
Tacna
Arica
Iquitos
Leticia
Benjamin Constant
Tabatinga
Nauta
Requena
PERU
Juliaca
Puno
L. Titicaca
LA PAZ
Oruro
Cochabamba
Sucre
Potosí
Tarija
Santa Cruz
BOLIVIA
Trinidad
Riberalta
Guajará Mirim
Porto Velho
RONDÔNIA
Rio Branco
ACRE
Cruzeiro do Sul
Tefé
MANAUS
AMAZONAS
Purus
Madeira
Japurá
Solimões
Amazonas
Negro
Iquique
Calama
Antofagasta
CHILE
ARGENTINA
PARAGUAY
Puerto Suárez
PACIFIC OCEAN
Peru-Chile Trench
Projection: Sanson-Flamsteed's Sinusoidal

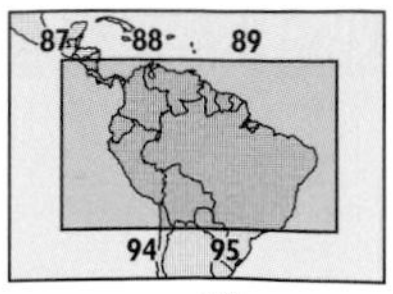
87
88
89
94
95

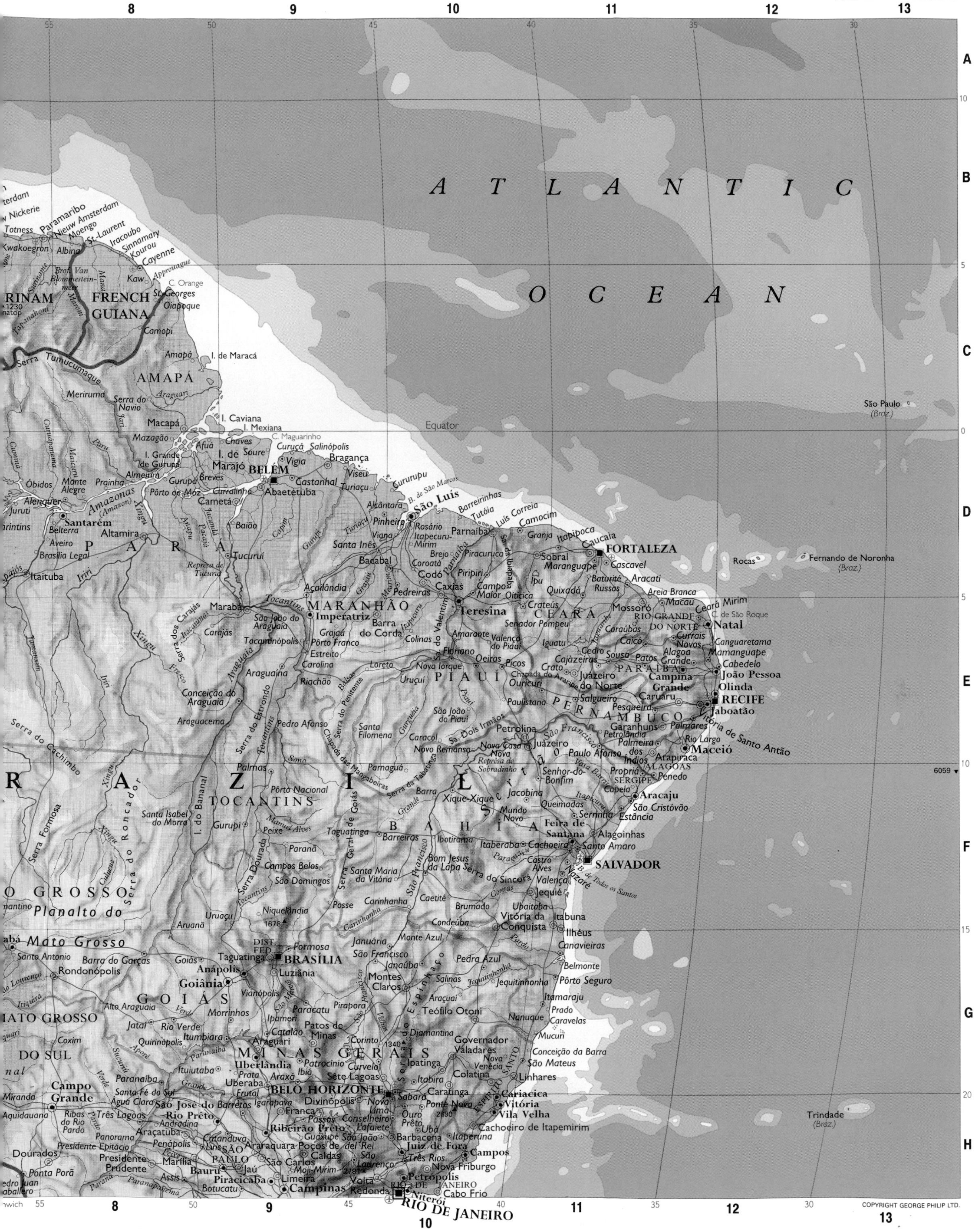
8
9
10
11
12
13
A
B
C
D
E
F
G
H
ATLANTIC
OCEAN
Equator
São Paulo
(Braz.)
Rocas
Fernando de Noronha
(Braz.)
Trindade
(Braz.)
6059
Paramaribo
Nieuw Amsterdam
Moengo
Totness
Nieuw Nickerie
St-Laurent
Iracoubo
Sinnamary
Kourou
Cayenne
Kwakoegron
Albina
Kaw
C. Orange
St-Georges
Oiapoque
SURINAM
FRENCH
GUIANA
Camopi
Amapá
I. de Maracá
AMAPÁ
Serra Tumucumaque
Merirumã
Serra do Navio
Macapá
I. Caviana
I. Mexiana
C. Maguarinho
Mazagão
Afuá
Chaves
Soure
Curuçá
Salinópolis
Bragança
I. de Marajó
Vigia
BELÉM
Castanhal
Viseu
Gurupi
Breves
Gurupá
Almeirim
Óbidos
Monte Alegre
Prainha
Pôrto de Moz
Curralinho
Abaetetuba
Cametá
Turiaçu
Alenquer
Juruti
Santarém
Belterra
Aveiro
Brasília Legal
Altamira
Itaituba
Amazonas
(Amazon)
Baião
Tucuruí
Represa de Tucuruí
PARÁ
Marabá
Carajás
Acailândia
MARANHÃO
Imperatriz
São João do Araguaia
Tocantinópolis
Pôrto Franco
Estreito
Carolina
Barra do Corda
Grajaú
Colinas
Araguaína
Riachão
Conceição do Araguaia
Araguacema
Pedro Afonso
Palmas
TOCANTINS
Pôrto Nacional
Gurupi
Peixe
Paranã
Campos Belos
São Domingos
Santa Isabel do Morro
Serra do Roncador
Serra Formosa
Serra do Cachimbo
MATO GROSSO
Planalto do Mato Grosso
Niquelândia
1678
Uruaçu
Aruanã
DIST. FED.
BRASÍLIA
Formosa
Taguatinga
Luziânia
Goiás
Anápolis
Goiânia
GOIÁS
Rondonópolis
Barra do Garças
Santo Antônio
Alto Araguaia
Jataí
Rio Verde
Itumbiara
Quirinópolis
Vianópolis
Morrinhos
Ipameri
Catalão
Paracatu
Patos de Minas
Araguari
MINAS GERAIS
Uberlândia
Uberaba
Prata
Araxá
Ituiutaba
Paranaíba
Santo Fé do Sul
Água Clara
São José do Barretos
Três Lagoas
Rio Prêto
Andradina
Araçatuba
Penápolis
Presidente Epitácio
Presidente Prudente
Marília
Bauru
Lins
SÃO PAULO
Catanduva
Araraquara
Ribeirão Prêto
Franca
São Carlos
Piracicaba
Jaú
Botucatu
Limeira
Campinas
Campo Grande
MATO GROSSO DO SUL
Coxim
Miranda
Aquidauana
Ribas do Rio Pardo
Dourados
Ponta Porã
Pedro Juan Caballero
Panorama
Assis
BELO HORIZONTE
Sete Lagoas
Divinópolis
Sabará
Itabira
Ipatinga
Caratinga
Curvelo
Diamantina
Corinto
Montes Claros
Janaúba
Januária
São Francisco
Pirapora
Teófilo Otoni
Governador Valadares
Colatina
Linhares
São Mateus
Conceição da Barra
Nova Venécia
ESPÍRITO SANTO
Cariacica
Vitória
Vila Velha
Cachoeiro de Itapemirim
Campos
Nova Friburgo
Petrópolis
Niterói
RIO DE JANEIRO
Cabo Frio
Volta Redonda
Juiz de Fora
Barbacena
Três Rios
Poços de Caldas
São Lourenço
Lafaiete
Conselheiro
Ouro Prêto
Ubá
Ponte Nova
2890
2787
Pedra Azul
Jequitinhonha
Araçuaí
Salinas
Nanuque
Mucuri
Caravelas
Prado
Itamaraju
Pôrto Seguro
Belmonte
Canavieiras
Ilhéus
Itabuna
Vitória da Conquista
Condeúba
Brumado
Caetité
Monte Azul
Jequié
Valença
Nazaré
SALVADOR
Santo Amaro
Cachoeira
Feira de Santana
Alagoinhas
Castro Alves
B. de Todos os Santos
Itaberaba
Ibotirama
Bom Jesus da Lapa
Santa Maria da Vitória
Carinhanha
Posse
Barreiras
BAHIA
Barra
Xique-Xique
Jacobina
Mundo Novo
Queimadas
Serrinha
Estância
Senhor-do-Bonfim
Juazeiro
Petrolina
Represa de Sobradinho
Remanso
Casa Nova
Paulo Afonso
Propriá
Penedo
SERGIPE
Aracaju
São Cristóvão
ALAGOAS
Arapiraca
Palmeira dos Índios
Maceió
Rio Largo
Garanhuns
Palmares
Caruaru
Vitória de Santo Antão
RECIFE
Jaboatão
Olinda
PERNAMBUCO
Salgueiro
Pesqueira
Petrolândia
João Pessoa
Cabedelo
Campina Grande
PARAÍBA
Patos
Sousa
Cajàzeiras
Juazeiro do Norte
Crato
Ouricuri
Paulistano
Picos
Oeiras
Floriano
PIAUÍ
Nova Iorque
Uruçuí
Loreto
Teresina
Caxias
Campo Maior
Piripiri
Piracuruca
Parnaíba
Tutóia
Barreirinhas
São Luís
B. de São Marcos
Gurupi
Alcântara
Pinheiro
Viana
Rosário
Itapecuru-Mirim
Brejo
Coroatá
Codó
Pedreiras
Bacabal
Santa Inês
Luís Correia
Camocim
Granja
Itapipoca
Caucaia
FORTALEZA
Cascavel
Sobral
Maranguape
Baturité
Russas
Quixadá
Aracati
Ipu
Crateús
CEARÁ
Senador Pompeu
Iguatu
Cedro
Mossoró
Areia Branca
Macau
Ceará Mirim
C. de São Roque
Natal
RIO GRANDE DO NORTE
Caraúbas
Caicó
Currais Novos
Canguaretama
Mamanguape
Alagoa Grande
Serra Geral de Goiás
Serra do Espinhaço
Chapada das Mangabeiras
Serra dos Carajás
Serra do Estrondo
Serra Dourada
Serra da Tabatinga
Sa. Dois Irmãos
Chapada do Araripe
Tocantins
Araguaia
Xingu
Iriri
São Francisco
Parnaíba
Paraná
Grande
Doce
Paranaíba
Jari
Greenwich
55
50
45
40
35
30
10
5
0
15
20

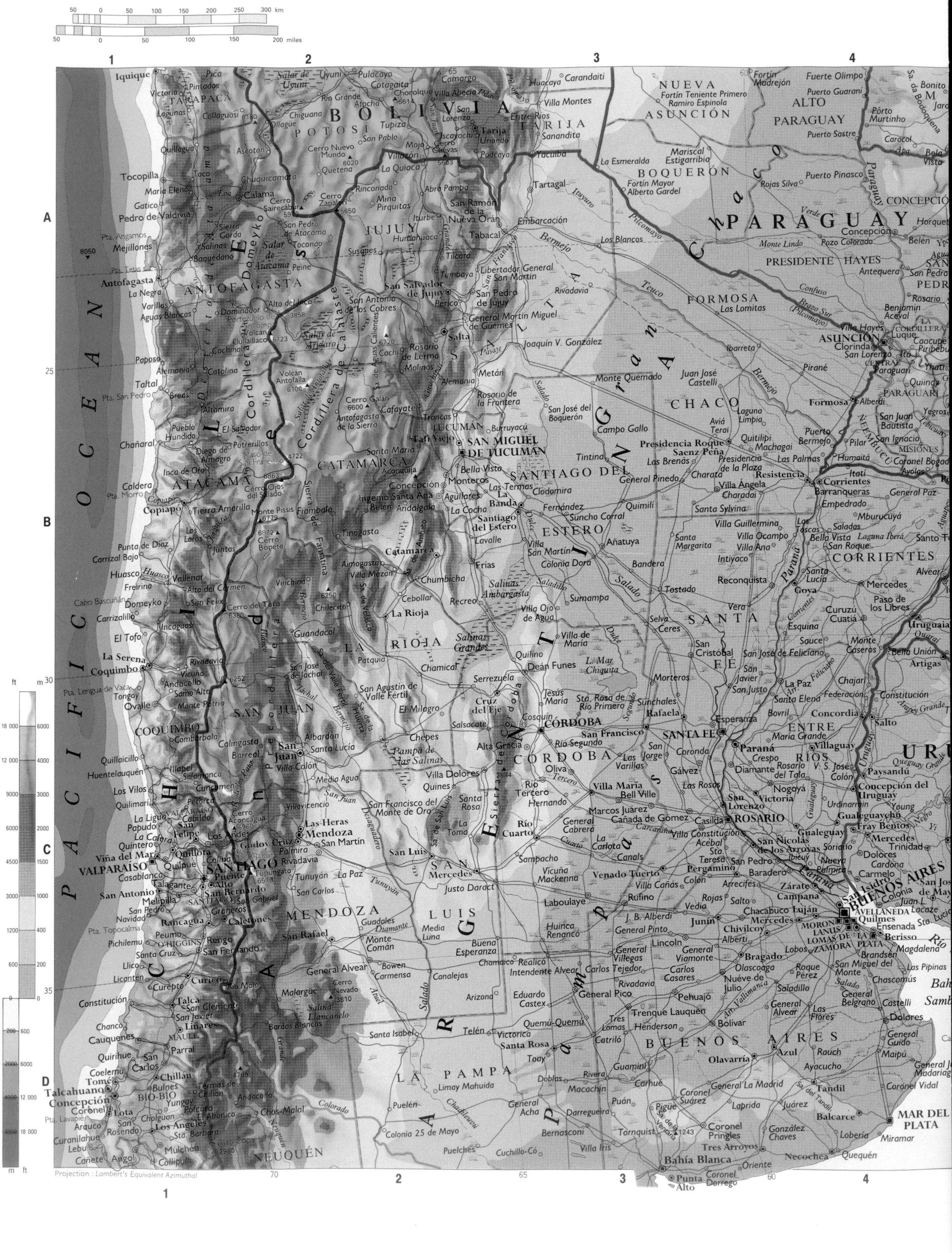

50 0 50 100 150 200 250 300 km
50 0 50 100 150 200 miles
1 2 3 4
A B C D
25 30 70 65 60
Projection : Lambert's Equivalent Azimuthal
ft m
18 000 6000
12 000 4000
9000 3000
6000 2000
4500 1500
3000 1000
1200 400
600 200
35
200 600
2000 6000
4000 12 000
6000 18 000
m ft
PACIFIC OCEAN
CHILE
ARGENTINA
BOLIVIA
PARAGUAY
URU
Gran Chaco
Andes
Cordillera Domeyko
Salar de Atacama
Cordillera de Calalaste
Pampa de las Salinas
Sierras de Córdoba
Salinas Grandes
Salar de Uyuni
TARAPACÁ
ANTOFAGASTA
ATACAMA
COQUIMBO
VALPARAÍSO
SANTIAGO
O'HIGGINS
MAULE
BÍO-BÍO
POTOSÍ
TARIJA
JUJUY
SALTA
TUCUMÁN
CATAMARCA
LA RIOJA
SAN JUAN
MENDOZA
SAN LUIS
CÓRDOBA
SANTIAGO DEL ESTERO
CHACO
FORMOSA
SANTA FE
CORRIENTES
ENTRE RÍOS
BUENOS AIRES
LA PAMPA
NEUQUÉN
NUEVA ASUNCIÓN
BOQUERÓN
ALTO PARAGUAY
PRESIDENTE HAYES
Iquique
Antofagasta
Copiapó
La Serena
Coquimbo
VALPARAÍSO
SANTIAGO
Talcahuano
Concepción
San Antonio
Rancagua
Talca
Chillán
Los Angeles
Calama
Tocopilla
Mejillones
Taltal
Chañaral
Caldera
Vallenar
Ovalle
Tarija
SAN MIGUEL DE TUCUMÁN
San Salvador de Jujuy
Salta
Catamarca
La Rioja
San Juan
Mendoza
San Luis
CÓRDOBA
Santiago del Estero
Resistencia
Corrientes
Formosa
ASUNCIÓN
Concepción
SANTA FE
Paraná
ROSARIO
BUENOS AIRES
La Plata
MAR DEL PLATA
Bahía Blanca
Santa Rosa
Río Cuarto
Villa María
San Rafael
Tandil
Olavarría
Azul
Pergamino
Junín
Punta Alto

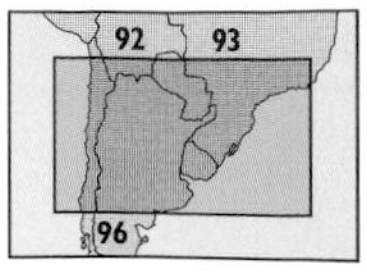
92
93
96

5
6
7
BELO HORIZONTE
Nova Lima
Itabirito
Três Lagoas
Andradina
Mirassol
Olímpia
Passos
Congonhas
Conselheiro Lafaiete
Ouro Prêto
Ponte Nova
Vitória
Vila Velha
Guarapari
Sidrolândia
Nioaque
MATO GROSSO DO SUL
Xavantina
Mirandópolis
Araçatuba
São José do Rio Prêto
Catanduva
Bebedouro
Batatais
São Sebastião do Paraíso
Oliveira
Campo Belo
São João del Rei
Lavras
Três Pontas
Barbacena
Cataguases
Ubá
Muriaé
Carangola
Alegre
Castelo
Cachoeiro de Itapemirim
Itaperuna
Campos
Cabo de São Tomé
Maracaju
Nova Alvorada do Sul
Panorama
Birigui
Taquaritinga
Novo Horizonte
Jaboticabal
Ribeirão Prêto
Guaxupé
Alfenas
Varginha
Três Corações
Juiz de Fora
Santos Dumont
Leopoldina
Cambuci
Guarus
Rio Brilhante
Dourados
Ponta Porã
Pedro Juan Caballero
Presidente Epitácio
Adamantina
Santo Anastácio
Presidente Prudente
Tupã
Penápolis
Lins
Araraquara
Mococa
Casa Branca
Poços de Caldas
Pouso Alegre
Itajubá
Volta Redonda
Barra do Piraí
Petrópolis
Nova Friburgo
Macaé
RIO DE JANEIRO
Nova Andradina
Euclides da Cunha Paulista
Martinópolis
Marília
Garça
São Carlos
São João da Boa Vista
Araras
Pinhal
Ouro Fino
Mogi-Mirim
Guaratinguetá
Barra Mansa
Três Rios
Além Paraíba
Ivinhema
Rosana
Rancharia
Paraguaçu Paulista
Bauru
Jaú
Rio Claro
Limeira
Americana
Piracicaba
Bragança Paulista
Taubaté
NOVA IGUAÇU
DUQUE DE CAXIAS
SÃO GONÇALO
NITERÓI
RIO DE JANEIRO
Cabo Frio
Amambaí
Naviraí
Pôrto São José
Centenário do Sul
Porecatu
Assis
Santa Cruz do Rio Pardo
CAMPINAS
Botucatu
Jundiaí
São José dos Campos
Jacareí
Angra dos Reis
Ilha Grande
Paranavaí
Sertanópolis
Cambará
Ourinhos
Avaré
Tatuí
Itu
Sorocaba
SÃO PAULO
Mogi das Cruzes
SANTO ANDRÉ
Nova Esperança
Londrina
Rolândia
Maringá
Arapongas
Cornélio Procópio
Jacarèzinho
Itapetininga
São Bernardo do Campo
São Vicente
SANTOS
Guarujá
Ilha de São Sebastião
Tropic of Capricorn
Umuarama
Cianorte
Cruzeiro do Oeste
Mandaguari
Apucarana
Joaquim Távora
Itaporanga
Itapeva
Itararé
Juquiá
Itanhaém
Guaíra
Salto del Guairá
Goio-Erê
Campo Mourão
PARANÁ
BRAZIL
Ibaiti
Tibagi
Jaguariaíva
Registro
Iguape
Ilha Comprida
Ilha do Cardoso
Toledo
Cascavel
Cândido de Abreu
Pitanga
Castro
Ponta Grossa
Prudentópolis
Guarapuava
Foz do Iguaçu
Ciudad del Este
Medianeira
Laranjeiras do Sul
Irati
Palmeira
CURITIBA
Antonina
Paranaguá
Matinhos
Guaratuba
Francisco Beltrão
Pato Branco
União da Vitória
São Mateus do Sul
Rio Negro
Mafra
Joinville
São Francisco do Sul
Clevelândia
Palmas
Pôrto União
Xanxerê
Caçador
Chapecó
Joaçaba
SANTA CATARINA
Blumenau
Itajaí
Brusque
Curitibanos
Rio do Sul
Campos Novos
São José
Ilha de Santa Catarina
Florianópolis
Erechim
Lajes
Santo Ângelo
Carazinho
Passo Fundo
Lagoa Vermelha
São Joaquim
Cruz Alta
Vacaria
Tubarão
Laguna
Cabo Santa Marta Grande
Criciúma
Araranguá
São Borja
Santiago
RIO GRANDE DO SUL
Bento Gonçalves
Caxias do Sul
Torres
Alegrete
Santa Maria
Santa Cruz do Sul
Montenegro
Nôvo Hamburgo
Taquara
São Leopoldo
Canoas
Osorio
Cachoeira do Sul
Rio Pardo
Viamão
PÔRTO ALEGRE
São Gabriel
Santana do Livramento
Rivera
Caçapava do Sul
Camaquã
Tapes
Dom Pedrito
Bagé
Mostardas
São Lourenço do Sul
Canguçu
Lagoa dos Patos
Pelotas
São José do Norte
Rio Grande
Tacuarembó
Melo
Jaguarão
Río Branco
Lagoa Mirim
Lagoa Mangueira
Treinta y Tres
Santa Vitória do Palmar
Chuy
Lascano
Castillos
Rocha
Minas
San Carlos
Maldonado
MONTEVIDEO
ATLANTIC OCEAN
5304
A
B
C
D
25
30
35
55
50
45
40
West from Greenwich
COPYRIGHT GEORGE PHILIP LTD
5
6
7

PACIFIC OCEAN
SOUTH ATLANTIC OCEAN
Peru-Chile Trench
PARAGUAY
URUGUAY
ARGENTINA
CHILE
BRAZIL
PATAGONIA
GRAN CHACO
PAMPAS
Chaco Boreal
Chaco Central
Chaco Austral
SÃO PAULO
PARANÁ
SANTA CATARINA
RIO GRANDE DO SUL
Asunción
BUENOS AIRES
MONTEVIDEO
SANTIAGO
SÃO PAULO
RIO DE JANEIRO
NOVA IGUAÇU
CURITIBA
PORTO ALEGRE
CÓRDOBA
ROSARIO
Mendoza
San Miguel de Tucumán
Salta
San Salvador de Jujuy
Santiago del Estero
Corrientes
Posadas
Resistencia
Formosa
Santa Fe
Paraná
San Juan
La Rioja
Catamarca
San Luis
Río Cuarto
La Plata
Avellaneda
Mar del Plata
Bahía Blanca
Neuquén
Viedma
Puerto Madryn
Trelew
Rawson
Comodoro Rivadavia
Puerto Deseado
Puerto San Julián
Puerto Santa Cruz
Río Gallegos
Punta Arenas
Ushuaia
Antofagasta
Calama
Chuquicamata
Copiapó
La Serena
Coquimbo
Valparaíso
Viña del Mar
Rancagua
Talca
Chillán
Concepción
Talcahuano
Los Angeles
Temuco
Valdivia
Osorno
Puerto Montt
I. de Chiloé
Arch. de los Chonos
Pen. de Taitao
Golfo San Jorge
Golfo San Matías
Pen. Valdés
Isla Grande de Tierra del Fuego
Estrecho de Magallanes
C. de Hornos (C. Horn)
I. de Los Estados (Staten I.)
FALKLAND ISLANDS (U.K.) (ISLAS MALVINAS)
West Falkland
East Falkland
Stanley
South Georgia (U.K.)
Río de la Plata
Cerro Aconcagua 6960
Ojos del Salado 6863
Tropic of Capricorn
Pelotas
Rio Grande
Florianópolis
Joinville
Campinas
Santos
Londrina
Foz do Iguaçu
Encarnación
Salto
Paysandú
Rivera
Melo

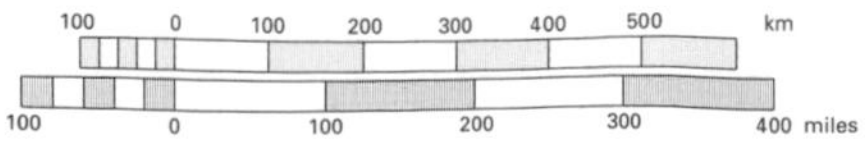

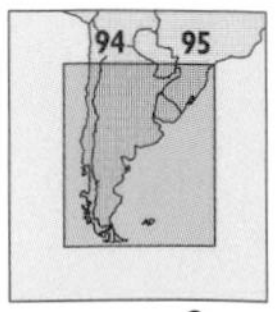

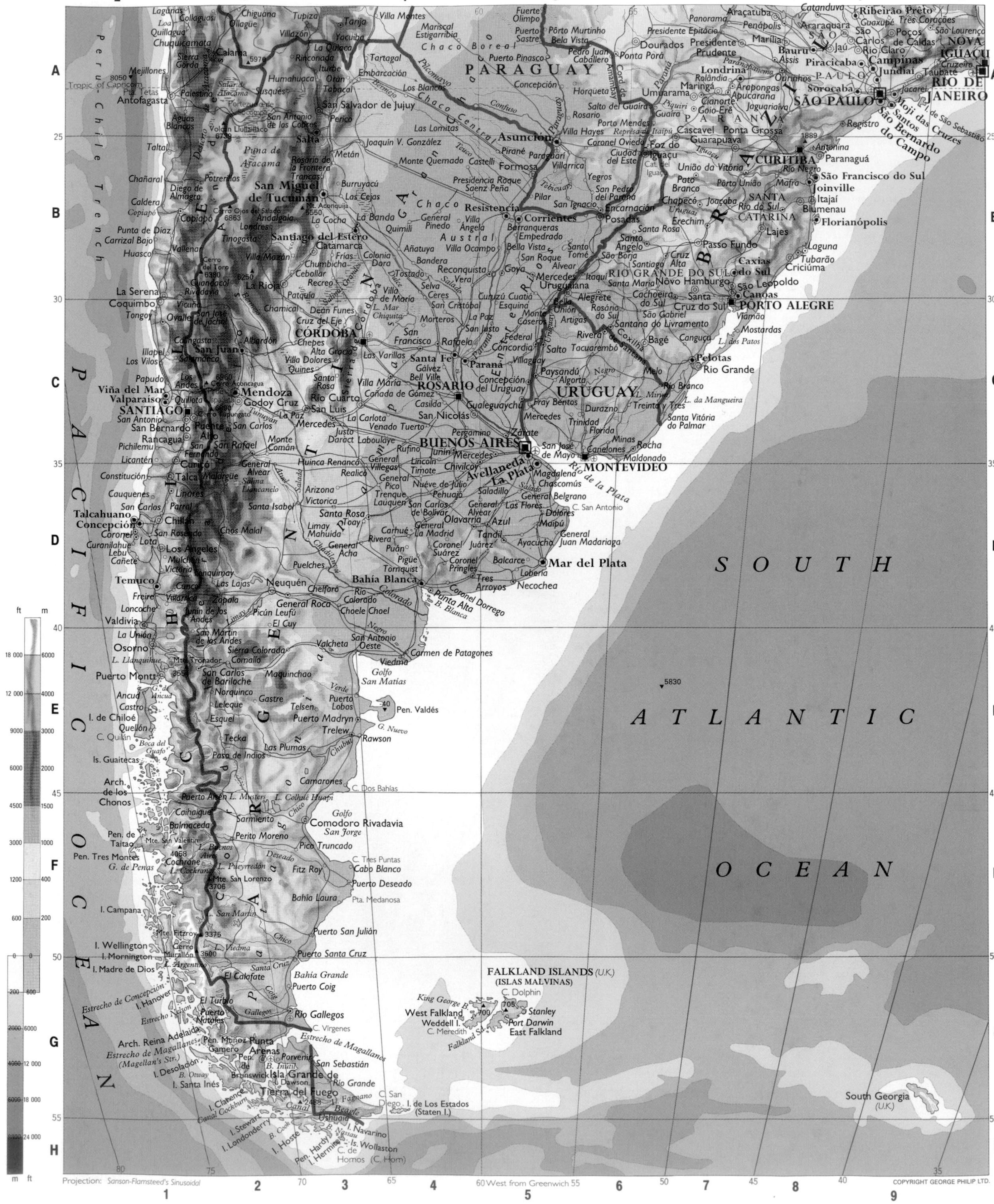

Projection: Sanson-Flamsteed's Sinusoidal

INDEX

The index contains the names of all the principal places and features shown on the World Maps. Each name is followed by an additional entry in italics giving the country or region within which it is located. The alphabetical order of names composed of two or more words is governed primarily by the first word and then by the second. This is an example of the rule:

Mīr Kūh, *Iran*	**45 E8**	26 22N	58 55 E
Mīr Shahdād, *Iran*	**45 E8**	26 15N	58 29 E
Mira, *Italy*	**20 B5**	45 26N	12 8 E
Mira por vos Cay, *Bahamas*	**89 B5**	22 9N	74 30W
Miraj, *India*	**40 L9**	16 50N	74 45 E

Physical features composed of a proper name (Erie) and a description (Lake) are positioned alphabetically by the proper name. The description is positioned after the proper name and is usually abbreviated:

Erie, L., *N. Amer.*	**78 D4**	42 15N	81 0W

Where a description forms part of a settlement or administrative name however, it is always written in full and put in its true alphabetic position:

Mount Morris, *U.S.A.*	**78 D7**	42 44N	77 52W

Names beginning with M' and Mc are indexed as if they were spelled Mac. Names beginning St. are alphabetised under Saint, but Sankt, Sint, Sant', Santa and San are all spelt in full and are alphabetised accordingly. If the same place name occurs two or more times in the index and all are in the same country, each is followed by the name of the administrative subdivision in which it is located. The names are placed in the alphabetical order of the subdivisions. For example:

Jackson, *Ky., U.S.A.*	**76 G4**	37 33N	83 23W
Jackson, *Mich., U.S.A.*	**76 D3**	42 15N	84 24W
Jackson, *Minn., U.S.A.*	**80 D7**	43 37N	95 1W

The number in bold type which follows each name in the index refers to the number of the map page where that feature or place will be found. This is usually the largest scale at which the place or feature appears.

The letter and figure which are in bold type immediately after the page number give the grid square on the map page, within which the feature is situated. The letter represents the latitude and the figure the longitude.

In some cases the feature itself may fall within the specified square, while the name is outside. This is usually the case only with features which are larger than a grid square.

For a more precise location the geographical coordinates which follow the letter/figure references give the latitude and the longitude of each place. The first set of figures represent the latitude which is the distance north or south of the Equator measured as an angle at the centre of the earth. The Equator is latitude 0°, the North Pole is 90°N, and the South Pole 90°S.

The second set of figures represent the longitude, which is the distance East or West of the prime meridian, which runs through Greenwich, England. Longitude is also measured as an angle at the centre of the earth and is given East or West of the prime meridian, from 0° to 180° in either direction.

The unit of measurement for latitude and longitude is the degree, which is subdivided into 60 minutes. Each index entry states the position of a place in degrees and minutes, a space being left between the degrees and the minutes.

The latitude is followed by N(orth) or S(outh) and the longitude by E(ast) or W(est).

Rivers are indexed to their mouths or confluences, and carry the symbol → after their names. A solid square ■ follows the name of a country, while an open square □ refers to a first order administrative area.

Abbreviations used in the index

A.C.T. – Australian Capital Territory
Afghan. – Afghanistan
Ala. – Alabama
Alta. – Alberta
Amer. – America(n)
Arch. – Archipelago
Ariz. – Arizona
Ark. – Arkansas
Atl. Oc. – Atlantic Ocean
B. – Baie, Bahía, Bay, Bucht, Bugt
B.C. – British Columbia
Bangla. – Bangladesh
Barr. – Barrage
Bos.-H. – Bosnia-Herzegovina
C. – Cabo, Cap, Cape, Coast
C.A.R. – Central African Republic
C. Prov. – Cape Province
Calif. – California
Cent. – Central
Chan. – Channel
Colo. – Colorado
Conn. – Connecticut
Cord. – Cordillera
Cr. – Creek
Czech. – Czech Republic
D.C. – District of Columbia
Del. – Delaware
Dep. – Dependency
Des. – Desert
Dist. – District
Dj. – Djebel
Domin. – Dominica
Dom. Rep. – Dominican Republic
E. – East
E. Salv. – El Salvador
Eq. Guin. – Equatorial Guinea
Fla. – Florida
Falk. Is. – Falkland Is.
G. – Golfe, Golfo, Gulf, Guba, Gebel
Ga. – Georgia
Gt. – Great, Greater
Guinea-Biss. – Guinea-Bissau
H.K. – Hong Kong
H.P. – Himachal Pradesh
Hants. – Hampshire
Harb. – Harbor, Harbour
Hd. – Head
Hts. – Heights
I.(s). – Île, Ilha, Insel, Isla, Island, Isle
Ill. – Illinois
Ind. – Indiana
Ind. Oc. – Indian Ocean
Ivory C. – Ivory Coast
J. – Jabal, Jebel, Jazira
Junc. – Junction
K. – Kap, Kapp
Kans. – Kansas
Kep. – Kepulauan
Ky. – Kentucky
L. – Lac, Lacul, Lago, Lagoa, Lake, Limni, Loch, Lough
La. – Louisiana
Liech. – Liechtenstein
Lux. – Luxembourg
Mad. P. – Madhya Pradesh
Madag. – Madagascar
Man. – Manitoba
Mass. – Massachusetts
Md. – Maryland
Me. – Maine
Medit. S. – Mediterranean Sea
Mich. – Michigan
Minn. – Minnesota
Miss. – Mississippi
Mo. – Missouri
Mont. – Montana
Mozam. – Mozambique
Mt.(e) – Mont, Monte, Monti, Montaña, Mountain
N. – Nord, Norte, North, Northern, Nouveau
N.B. – New Brunswick
N.C. – North Carolina
N. Cal. – New Caledonia
N. Dak. – North Dakota
N.H. – New Hampshire
N.I. – North Island
N.J. – New Jersey
N. Mex. – New Mexico
N.S. – Nova Scotia
N.S.W. – New South Wales
N.W.T. – North West Territory
N.Y. – New York
N.Z. – New Zealand
Nebr. – Nebraska
Neths. – Netherlands
Nev. – Nevada
Nfld. – Newfoundland
Nic. – Nicaragua
O. – Oued, Ouadi
Occ. – Occidentale
Okla. – Oklahoma
Ont. – Ontario
Or. – Orientale
Oreg. – Oregon
Os. – Ostrov
Oz. – Ozero
P. – Pass, Passo, Pasul, Pulau
P.E.I. – Prince Edward Island
Pa. – Pennsylvania
Pac. Oc. – Pacific Ocean
Papua N.G. – Papua New Guinea
Pass. – Passage
Pen. – Peninsula, Péninsule
Phil. – Philippines
Pk. – Park, Peak
Plat. – Plateau
Prov. – Province, Provincial
Pt. – Point
Pta. – Ponta, Punta
Pte. – Pointe
Qué. – Québec
Queens. – Queensland
R. – Rio, River
R.I. – Rhode Island
Ra.(s). – Range(s)
Raj. – Rajasthan
Reg. – Region
Rep. – Republic
Res. – Reserve, Reservoir
S. – San, South, Sea
Si. Arabia – Saudi Arabia
S.C. – South Carolina
S. Dak. – South Dakota
S.I. – South Island
S. Leone – Sierra Leone
Sa. – Serra, Sierra
Sask. – Saskatchewan
Scot. – Scotland
Sd. – Sound
Sev. – Severnaya
Sib. – Siberia
Sprs. – Springs
St. – Saint
Sta. – Santa, Station
Ste. – Sainte
Sto. – Santo
Str. – Strait, Stretto
Switz. – Switzerland
Tas. – Tasmania
Tenn. – Tennessee
Tex. – Texas
Tg. – Tanjung
Trin. & Tob. – Trinidad & Tobago
U.A.E. – United Arab Emirates
U.K. – United Kingdom
U.S.A. – United States of America
Ut. P. – Uttar Pradesh
Va. – Virginia
Vdkhr. – Vodokhranilishche
Vf. – Vírful
Vic. – Victoria
Vol. – Volcano
Vt. – Vermont
W. – Wadi, West
W. Va. – West Virginia
Wash. – Washington
Wis. – Wisconsin
Wlkp. – Wielkopolski
Wyo. – Wyoming
Yorks. – Yorkshire
Yug. – Yugoslavia

A

A Coruña, Spain 19 A1 43 20N 8 25W
A Estrada, Spain 19 A1 42 43N 8 27W
A Fonsagrada, Spain 19 A2 43 8N 7 4W
Aachen, Germany 16 C4 50 45N 6 6 E
Aalborg = Ålborg, Denmark 9 H13 57 2N 9 54 E
Aalen, Germany 16 D6 48 51N 10 6 E
Aalst, Belgium 15 D4 50 56N 4 2 E
Aalten, Neths. 15 C6 51 56N 6 35 E
Aalter, Belgium 15 C3 51 5N 3 28 E
Äänekoski, Finland 9 E21 62 36N 25 44 E
Aarau, Switz. 18 C8 47 23N 8 4 E
Aare →, Switz. 18 C8 47 33N 8 14 E
Aarhus = Århus, Denmark 9 H14 56 8N 10 11 E
Aarschot, Belgium 15 D4 50 59N 4 49 E
Aba, Dem. Rep. of the Congo 54 B3 3 58N 30 17 E
Aba, Nigeria 50 G7 5 10N 7 19 E
Ābādān, Iran 45 D6 30 22N 48 20 E
Ābādeh, Iran 45 D7 31 8N 52 40 E
Abadla, Algeria 50 B5 31 2N 2 45W
Abaetetuba, Brazil 93 D9 1 40S 48 50W
Abagnar Qi, China 34 C9 43 52N 116 2 E
Abai, Paraguay 95 B4 25 58S 55 54W
Abakan, Russia 27 D10 53 40N 91 10 E
Abancay, Peru 92 F4 13 35S 72 55W
Abariringa, Kiribati 64 H10 2 50S 171 40W
Abarqū, Iran 45 D7 31 10N 53 20 E
Abashiri, Japan 30 B12 44 0N 144 15 E
Abashiri-Wan, Japan 30 C12 44 0N 144 30 E
Ābay = Nîl el Azraq →, Sudan 51 E12 15 38N 32 31 E
Abay, Kazakstan 26 E8 49 38N 72 53 E
Abaya, L., Ethiopia 46 F2 6 30N 37 50 E
Abaza, Russia 26 D9 52 39N 90 6 E
'Abbāsābād, Iran 45 C8 33 34N 58 23 E
Abbay = Nîl el Azraq →,
Sudan 51 E12 15 38N 32 31 E
Abbaye, Pt., U.S.A. 76 B1 46 58N 88 8W
Abbé, L., Ethiopia 46 E3 11 8N 41 47 E
Abbeville, France 18 A4 50 6N 1 49 E
Abbeville, Ala., U.S.A. 77 K3 31 34N 85 15W
Abbeville, La., U.S.A. 81 L8 29 58N 92 8W
Abbeville, S.C., U.S.A. 77 H4 34 11N 82 23W
Abbot Ice Shelf, Antarctica 5 D16 73 0S 92 0W
Abbottabad, Pakistan 42 B5 34 10N 73 15 E
Abd al Kūrī, Yemen 46 E5 12 5N 52 20 E
Ābdar, Iran 45 D7 30 16N 55 19 E
'Abdolābād, Iran 45 C8 34 12N 56 30 E
Abdulpur, Bangla. 43 G13 24 15N 88 59 E
Abéché, Chad 51 F10 13 50N 20 35 E
Abengourou, Ivory C. 50 G5 6 42N 3 27W
Åbenrå, Denmark 9 J13 55 3N 9 25 E
Abeokuta, Nigeria 50 G6 7 3N 3 19 E
Aber, Uganda 54 B3 2 12N 32 25 E
Aberaeron, U.K. 11 E3 52 15N 4 15W
Aberayron = Aberaeron, U.K. 11 E3 52 15N 4 15W
Aberchirder, U.K. 12 D6 57 34N 2 37W
Abercorn = Mbala, Zambia 55 D3 8 46S 31 24 E
Abercorn, Australia 63 D5 25 12S 151 5 E
Aberdare, U.K. 11 F4 51 43N 3 27W
Aberdare Ra., Kenya 54 C4 0 15S 36 50 E
Aberdeen, Australia 63 E5 32 9S 150 56 E
Aberdeen, Canada 73 C7 52 20N 106 8W
Aberdeen, S. Africa 56 E3 32 28S 24 2 E
Aberdeen, U.K. 12 D6 57 9N 2 5W
Aberdeen, Ala., U.S.A. 77 J1 33 49N 88 33W
Aberdeen, Idaho, U.S.A. 82 E7 42 57N 112 50W
Aberdeen, Md., U.S.A. 76 F7 39 31N 76 10W
Aberdeen, S. Dak., U.S.A. 80 C5 45 28N 98 29W
Aberdeen, Wash., U.S.A. 84 D3 46 59N 123 50W
Aberdeen, City of □, U.K. 12 D6 57 10N 2 10W
Aberdeenshire □, U.K. 12 D6 57 17N 2 36W
Aberdovey = Aberdyfi, U.K. 11 E3 52 33N 4 3W
Aberdyfi, U.K. 11 E3 52 33N 4 3W
Aberfeldy, U.K. 12 E5 56 37N 3 51W
Abergavenny, U.K. 11 F4 51 49N 3 1W
Abergele, U.K. 10 D4 53 17N 3 35W
Abernathy, U.S.A. 81 J4 33 50N 101 51W
Abert, L., U.S.A. 82 E3 42 38N 120 14W
Aberystwyth, U.K. 11 E3 52 25N 4 5W
Abhā, Si. Arabia 46 D3 18 0N 42 34 E
Abhar, Iran 45 B6 36 9N 49 13 E
Abhayapuri, India 43 F14 26 24N 90 38 E
Abidjan, Ivory C. 50 G5 5 26N 3 58W
Abilene, Kans., U.S.A. 80 F6 38 55N 97 13W
Abilene, Tex., U.S.A. 81 J5 32 28N 99 43W
Abingdon, U.K. 11 F6 51 40N 1 17W
Abingdon, U.S.A. 77 G5 36 43N 81 59W
Abington Reef, Australia 62 B4 18 0S 149 35 E
Abitau →, Canada 73 B7 59 53N 109 3W
Abitibi →, Canada 70 B3 51 3N 80 55W
Abitibi, L., Canada 70 C4 48 40N 79 40W
Abkhaz Republic =
Abkhazia □, Georgia 25 F7 43 12N 41 5 E
Abkhazia □, Georgia 25 F7 43 12N 41 5 E
Abminga, Australia 63 D1 26 8S 134 51 E
Åbo = Turku, Finland 9 F20 60 30N 22 19 E
Abohar, India 42 D6 30 10N 74 10 E
Abomey, Benin 50 G6 7 10N 2 5 E
Abong-Mbang, Cameroon 52 D2 4 0N 13 8 E
Abou-Deïa, Chad 51 F9 11 20N 19 20 E
Aboyne, U.K. 12 D6 57 4N 2 47W
Abra Pampa, Argentina 94 A2 22 43S 65 42W
Abraham L., Canada 72 C5 52 15N 116 35W
Abreojos, Pta., Mexico 86 B2 26 50N 113 40W
Abrud, Romania 17 E12 46 19N 23 5 E
Absaroka Range, U.S.A. 82 D9 44 45N 109 50W
Abu, India 42 G5 24 41N 72 50 E
Abū al Abyad, U.A.E. 45 E7 24 11N 53 50 E
Abū al Khaṣīb, Iraq 45 D6 30 25N 48 0 E
Abū 'Alī, Si. Arabia 45 E6 27 20N 49 27 E
Abū 'Alī →, Lebanon 47 A4 34 25N 35 50 E
Abu Dhabi = Abū Ẓāby, U.A.E. 46 C5 24 28N 54 22 E
Abū Du'ān, Syria 44 B3 36 25N 38 15 E
Abu el Gairi, W. →, Egypt 47 F2 29 35N 33 30 E
Abu Ga'da, W. →, Egypt 47 F1 29 15N 32 53 E
Abū Ḥadrīyah, Si. Arabia 45 E6 27 20N 48 58 E
Abu Hamed, Sudan 51 E12 19 32N 33 13 E
Abū Kamāl, Syria 44 C4 34 30N 41 0 E
Abū Madd, Ra's, Si. Arabia 44 E3 24 50N 37 7 E
Abū Mūsā, U.A.E. 45 E7 25 52N 55 3 E
Abū Qaṣr, Si. Arabia 44 D3 30 21N 38 34 E
Abu Ṣafāt, W. →, Jordan 47 E5 30 24N 36 7 E
Abu Simbel, Egypt 51 D12 22 18N 31 40 E
Abū Şukhayr, Iraq 44 D5 31 54N 44 30 E
Abu Zabad, Sudan 51 F11 12 25N 29 10 E
Abū Ẓāby, U.A.E. 46 C5 24 28N 54 22 E
Abū Zeydābād, Iran 45 C6 33 54N 51 45 E
Abuja, Nigeria 50 G7 9 5N 7 32 E
Abukuma-Gawa →, Japan 30 E10 38 6N 140 52 E
Abukuma-Sammyaku, Japan 30 F10 37 30N 140 45 E
Abunã, Brazil 92 E5 9 40S 65 20W
Abunã →, Brazil 92 E5 9 41S 65 20W
Aburo, Dem. Rep. of
the Congo 54 B3 2 4N 30 53 E
Abut Hd., N.Z. 59 K3 43 7S 170 15 E
Acadia Nat. Park, U.S.A. 77 C11 44 20N 68 13W
Açailândia, Brazil 93 D9 4 57S 47 0W
Acajutla, El Salv. 88 D2 13 36N 89 50W
Acámbaro, Mexico 86 D4 20 0N 100 40W
Acaponeta, Mexico 86 C3 22 30N 105 20W
Acapulco, Mexico 87 D5 16 51N 99 56W
Acarai, Serra, Brazil 92 C7 1 50N 57 50W
Acarigua, Venezuela 92 B5 9 33N 69 12W
Acatlán, Mexico 87 D5 18 10N 98 3W
Acayucan, Mexico 87 D6 17 59N 94 58W
Accomac, U.S.A. 76 G8 37 43N 75 40W
Accra, Ghana 50 G5 5 35N 0 6W
Accrington, U.K. 10 D5 53 45N 2 22W
Acebal, Argentina 94 C3 33 20S 60 50W
Aceh □, Indonesia 36 D1 4 15N 97 30 E
Achalpur, India 40 J10 21 22N 77 32 E
Acheng, China 35 B14 45 30N 126 58 E
Acher, India 42 H5 23 10N 72 32 E
Achill Hd., Ireland 13 C1 53 58N 10 15W
Achill I., Ireland 13 C1 53 58N 10 1W
Achinsk, Russia 27 D10 56 20N 90 20 E
Acireale, Italy 20 F6 37 37N 15 10 E
Ackerman, U.S.A. 81 J10 33 19N 89 11W
Acklins I., Bahamas 89 B5 22 30N 74 0W
Acme, Canada 72 C6 51 33N 113 30W
Acme, U.S.A. 78 F5 40 8N 79 26W
Aconcagua, Cerro, Argentina 94 C2 32 39S 70 0W
Aconquija, Mt., Argentina 94 B2 27 0S 66 0W
Açores, Is. dos, Atl. Oc. 50 A1 38 0N 27 0W
Acornhoek, S. Africa 57 C5 24 37S 31 2 E
Acraman, L., Australia 63 E2 32 2S 135 23 E
Acre = 'Akko, Israel 47 C4 32 55N 35 4 E
Acre □, Brazil 92 E4 9 1S 71 0W
Acre →, Brazil 92 E5 8 45S 67 22W
Acton, Canada 78 C4 43 38N 80 3W
Acuña, Mexico 86 B4 29 18N 100 55W
Ad Dammām, Si. Arabia 45 E6 26 20N 50 5 E
Ad Dāmūr, Lebanon 47 B4 33 44N 35 27 E
Ad Dawādimī, Si. Arabia 44 E5 24 35N 44 15 E
Ad Dawḥah, Qatar 46 B5 25 15N 51 35 E
Ad Dawr, Iraq 44 C4 34 27N 43 47 E
Ad Dir'iyah, Si. Arabia 44 E5 24 44N 46 35 E
Ad Dīwānīyah, Iraq 44 D5 32 0N 45 0 E
Ad Dujayl, Iraq 44 C5 33 51N 44 14 E
Ad Duwayd, Si. Arabia 44 D4 30 15N 42 17 E
Ada, Minn., U.S.A. 80 B6 47 18N 96 31W
Ada, Okla., U.S.A. 81 H6 34 46N 96 41W
Adabiya, Egypt 47 F1 29 53N 32 28 E
Adair, C., Canada 69 A12 71 31N 71 24W
Adaja →, Spain 19 B3 41 32N 4 52W
Adak I., U.S.A. 68 C2 51 45N 176 45W
Adamaoua, Massif de l',
Cameroon 51 G7 7 20N 12 20 E
Adamawa Highlands =
Adamaoua, Massif de l',
Cameroon 51 G7 7 20N 12 20 E
Adamello, Mte., Italy 18 C9 46 9N 10 30 E
Adaminaby, Australia 63 F4 36 0S 148 45 E
Adams, Mass., U.S.A. 79 D11 42 38N 73 7W
Adams, N.Y., U.S.A. 79 C8 43 49N 76 1W
Adams, Wis., U.S.A. 80 D10 43 57N 89 49W
Adam's Bridge, Sri Lanka 40 Q11 9 15N 79 40 E
Adams L., Canada 72 C5 51 10N 119 40W
Adams Mt., U.S.A. 84 D5 46 12N 121 30W
Adam's Peak, Sri Lanka 40 R12 6 48N 80 30 E
Adana, Turkey 25 G6 37 0N 35 16 E
Adapazarı = Sakarya, Turkey 25 F5 40 48N 30 25 E
Adarama, Sudan 51 E12 17 10N 34 52 E
Adare, C., Antarctica 5 D11 71 0S 171 0 E
Adaut, Indonesia 37 F8 8 8S 131 7 E
Adavale, Australia 63 D3 25 52S 144 32 E
Adda →, Italy 18 D8 45 8N 9 53 E
Addis Ababa = Addis Abeba,
Ethiopia 46 F2 9 2N 38 42 E
Addis Abeba, Ethiopia 46 F2 9 2N 38 42 E
Addison, U.S.A. 78 D7 42 1N 77 14W
Addo, S. Africa 56 E4 33 32S 25 45 E
Ādeh, Iran 44 B5 37 42N 45 11 E
Adel, U.S.A. 77 K4 31 8N 83 25W
Adelaide, Australia 63 E2 34 52S 138 30 E
Adelaide, Bahamas 88 A4 25 4N 77 31W
Adelaide, S. Africa 56 E4 32 42S 26 20 E
Adelaide I., Antarctica 5 C17 67 15S 68 30W
Adelaide Pen., Canada 68 B10 68 15N 97 30W
Adelaide River, Australia 60 B5 13 15S 131 7 E
Adelanto, U.S.A. 85 L9 34 35N 117 22W
Adele I., Australia 60 C3 15 32S 123 9 E
Adélie, Terre, Antarctica 5 C10 68 0S 140 0 E
Adélie Land = Adélie, Terre,
Antarctica 5 C10 68 0S 140 0 E
Aden = Al 'Adan, Yemen 46 E4 12 45N 45 0 E
Aden, G. of, Asia 46 E4 12 30N 47 30 E
Adendorp, S. Africa 56 E3 32 15S 24 30 E
Adh Dhayd, U.A.E. 45 E7 25 17N 55 53 E
Adhoi, India 42 H4 23 26N 70 32 E
Adi, Indonesia 37 E8 4 15S 133 30 E
Adieu, C., Australia 61 F5 32 0S 132 10 E
Adieu Pt., Australia 60 C3 15 14S 124 35 E
Adige →, Italy 20 B5 45 9N 12 20 E
Adigrat, Ethiopia 46 E2 14 20N 39 26 E
Adilabad, India 40 K11 19 33N 78 20 E
Adirondack Mts., U.S.A. 79 C10 44 0N 74 0W
Adjumani, Uganda 54 B3 3 20N 31 50 E
Adlavik Is., Canada 71 B8 55 0N 58 40W
Admiralty G., Australia 60 B4 14 20S 125 55 E
Admiralty I., U.S.A. 72 B2 57 30N 134 30W
Admiralty Is., Papua N. G. 64 H6 2 0S 147 0 E
Adonara, Indonesia 37 F6 8 15S 123 5 E
Adoni, India 40 M10 15 33N 77 18 E
Adour →, France 18 E3 43 32N 1 32W
Adra, India 43 H12 23 30N 86 42 E
Adra, Spain 19 D4 36 43N 3 3W
Adrano, Italy 20 F6 37 40N 14 50 E
Adrar, Mauritania 50 D3 20 30N 7 30 E
Adrar des Iforas, Algeria 50 C5 27 51N 0 11 E
Adrian, Mich., U.S.A. 76 E3 41 54N 84 2W
Adrian, Tex., U.S.A. 81 H3 35 16N 102 40W
Adriatic Sea, Medit. S. 20 C6 43 0N 16 0 E
Adua, Indonesia 37 E7 1 45S 129 50 E
Adwa, Ethiopia 46 E2 14 15N 38 52 E
Adygea □, Russia 25 F7 45 0N 40 0 E
Adzhar Republic = Ajaria □,
Georgia 25 F7 41 30N 42 0 E
Adzopé, Ivory C. 50 G5 6 7N 3 49W
Ægean Sea, Medit. S. 21 E11 38 30N 25 0 E
Aerhtai Shan, Mongolia 32 B4 46 40N 92 45 E
'Afak, Iraq 44 C5 32 4N 45 15 E
Afándou, Greece 23 C10 36 18N 28 12 E
Afghanistan ■, Asia 40 C4 33 0N 65 0 E
Aflou, Algeria 50 B6 34 7N 2 3 E
Africa 48 E6 10 0N 20 0 E
'Afrīn, Syria 44 B3 36 32N 36 50 E
Afton, N.Y., U.S.A. 79 D9 42 14N 75 32W
Afton, Wyo., U.S.A. 82 E8 42 44N 110 56W
Afuá, Brazil 93 D8 0 15S 50 20W
'Afula, Israel 47 C4 32 37N 35 17 E
Afyon, Turkey 25 G5 38 45N 30 33 E
Afyonkarahisar = Afyon,
Turkey 25 G5 38 45N 30 33 E
Agadès = Agadez, Niger 50 E7 16 58N 7 59 E
Agadez, Niger 50 E7 16 58N 7 59 E
Agadir, Morocco 50 B4 30 28N 9 55W
Agaete, Canary Is. 22 F4 28 6N 15 43W
Agar, India 42 H7 23 40N 76 2 E
Agartala, India 41 H17 23 50N 91 23 E
Agassiz, Canada 72 D4 49 14N 121 46W
Agats, Indonesia 37 F9 5 33S 138 0 E
Agawam, U.S.A. 79 D12 42 5N 72 37W
Agboville, Ivory C. 50 G5 5 55N 4 15W
Ağdam, Azerbaijan 44 B5 40 0N 46 58 E
Agde, France 18 E5 43 19N 3 28 E
Agen, France 18 D4 44 12N 0 38 E
Āgh Kand, Iran 45 B6 37 15N 48 4 E
Aginskoye, Russia 27 D12 51 6N 114 32 E
Agnew, Australia 61 E3 28 1S 120 31 E
Agori, India 43 G10 24 33N 82 57 E
Agra, India 42 F7 27 17N 77 58 E
Ağri, Turkey 25 G7 39 44N 43 3 E
Agri →, Italy 20 D7 40 13N 16 44 E
Ağrı Dağı, Turkey 25 G7 39 50N 44 15 E
Ağrı Karakose = Ağri, Turkey 25 G7 39 44N 43 3 E
Agrigento, Italy 20 F5 37 19N 13 34 E
Agrínion, Greece 21 E9 38 37N 21 27 E
Agua Caliente, Baja Calif.,
Mexico 85 N10 32 29N 116 59W
Agua Caliente, Sinaloa,
Mexico 86 B3 26 30N 108 20W
Agua Caliente Springs, U.S.A. 85 N10 32 56N 116 19W
Água Clara, Brazil 93 H8 20 25S 52 45W
Agua Hechicero, Mexico 85 N10 32 26N 116 14W
Agua Prieta, Mexico 86 A3 31 20N 109 32W
Aguadilla, Puerto Rico 89 C6 18 26N 67 10W
Aguadulce, Panama 88 E3 8 15N 80 32W
Aguanga, U.S.A. 85 M10 33 27N 116 51W
Aguanish, Canada 71 B7 50 14N 62 2W
Aguanus →, Canada 71 B7 50 13N 62 5W
Aguapey →, Argentina 94 B4 29 7S 56 36W
Aguaray Guazú →, Paraguay 94 A4 24 47S 57 19W
Aguarico →, Ecuador 92 D3 0 59S 75 11W
Aguas Blancas, Chile 94 A2 24 15S 69 55W
Aguas Calientes, Sierra de,
Argentina 94 B2 25 26S 66 40W
Aguascalientes, Mexico 86 C4 21 53N 102 12W
Aguascalientes □, Mexico 86 C4 22 0N 102 20W
Aguilares, Argentina 94 B2 27 26S 65 35W
Águilas, Spain 19 D5 37 23N 1 35W
Agüimes, Canary Is. 22 G4 27 58N 15 27W
Aguja, C. de la, Colombia 90 B3 11 18N 74 12W
Agulhas, C., S. Africa 56 E3 34 52S 20 0 E
Agulo, Canary Is. 22 F2 28 11N 17 12W
Agung, Gunung, Indonesia 36 F5 8 20S 115 28 E
Agur, Uganda 54 B3 2 28N 32 55 E
Agusan →, Phil. 37 C7 9 0N 125 30 E
Aha Mts., Botswana 56 B3 19 45S 21 0 E
Ahaggar, Algeria 50 D7 23 0N 6 30 E
Ahar, Iran 44 B5 38 35N 47 0 E
Ahipara B., N.Z. 59 F4 35 5S 173 5 E
Ahiri, India 40 K12 19 30N 80 0 E
Ahmad Wal, Pakistan 42 E1 29 18N 65 58 E
Ahmadabad, India 42 H5 23 0N 72 40 E
Aḥmadābād, Khorāsān, Iran 45 C9 35 3N 60 50 E
Aḥmadābād, Khorāsān, Iran 45 C8 35 49N 59 42 E
Aḥmadī, Iran 45 E8 27 56N 56 42 E
Ahmadnagar, India 40 K9 19 7N 74 46 E
Ahmadpur, Pakistan 42 E4 29 12N 71 10 E
Ahmadpur Lamma, Pakistan 42 E4 28 19N 70 3 E
Ahmedabad = Ahmadabad,
India 42 H5 23 0N 72 40 E
Ahmednagar = Ahmadnagar,
India 40 K9 19 7N 74 46 E
Ahome, Mexico 86 B3 25 55N 109 11W
Ahoskie, U.S.A. 77 G7 36 17N 76 59W
Ahram, Iran 45 D6 28 52N 51 16 E
Ahrax Pt., Malta 23 D1 36 0N 14 22 E
Āhū, Iran 45 C6 34 33N 50 2 E
Ahuachapán, El Salv. 88 D2 13 54N 89 52W
Ahvāz, Iran 45 D6 31 20N 48 40 E
Ahvenanmaa = Åland, Finland 9 F19 60 15N 20 0 E
Aḥwar, Yemen 46 E4 13 30N 46 40 E
Ai →, India 43 F14 26 26N 90 44 E
Ai-Ais, Namibia 56 D2 27 54S 17 59 E
Aichi □, Japan 31 G8 35 0N 137 15 E
Aigua, Uruguay 95 C5 34 13S 54 46W
Aigues-Mortes, France 18 E6 43 35N 4 12 E
Aihui, China 33 A7 50 10N 127 30 E
Aija, Peru 92 E3 9 50S 77 45W
Aikawa, Japan 30 E9 38 2N 138 15 E
Aiken, U.S.A. 77 J5 33 34N 81 43W
Aileron, Australia 62 C1 22 39S 133 20 E
Aillik, Canada 71 A8 55 11N 59 18W
Ailsa Craig, U.K. 12 F3 55 15N 5 6W
'Ailūn, Jordan 47 C4 32 18N 35 47 E
Aim, Russia 27 D14 59 0N 133 55 E
Aimere, Indonesia 37 F6 8 45S 121 3 E
Aimogasta, Argentina 94 B2 28 33S 66 50W
Aïn Ben Tili, Mauritania 50 C4 25 59N 9 27W
Aïn Sefra, Algeria 50 B5 32 47N 0 37W
Ain Sudr, Egypt 47 F2 29 50N 33 6 E
Ainaži, Latvia 9 H21 57 50N 24 24 E
Ainsworth, U.S.A. 80 D5 42 33N 99 52W
Aiquile, Bolivia 92 G5 18 10S 65 10W
Aïr, Niger 50 E7 18 30N 8 0 E
Air Force I., Canada 69 B12 67 58N 74 5W
Air Hitam, Malaysia 39 M4 1 55N 103 11 E
Airdrie, Canada 72 C6 51 18N 114 2W
Airdrie, U.K. 12 F5 55 52N 3 57W
Aire →, U.K. 10 D7 53 43N 0 55W
Aire, I. de l', Spain 22 B11 39 48N 4 16 E
Airlie Beach, Australia 62 C4 20 16S 148 43 E
Aisne →, France 18 B5 49 26N 2 50 E
Ait, India 43 G8 25 54N 79 14 E
Aitkin, U.S.A. 80 B8 46 32N 93 42W
Aiud, Romania 17 E12 46 19N 23 44 E
Aix-en-Provence, France 18 E6 43 32N 5 27 E
Aix-la-Chapelle = Aachen,
Germany 16 C4 50 45N 6 6 E
Aix-les-Bains, France 18 D6 45 41N 5 53 E
Aíyion, Greece 21 E10 38 15N 22 5 E
Aizawl, India 41 H18 23 40N 92 44 E
Aizkraukle, Latvia 9 H21 56 36N 25 11 E
Aizpute, Latvia 9 H19 56 43N 21 40 E
Aizuwakamatsu, Japan 30 F9 37 30N 139 56 E
Ajaccio, France 18 F8 41 55N 8 40 E
Ajalgarh, India 43 G9 24 52N 80 16 E
Ajalpan, Mexico 87 D5 18 22N 97 15W
Ajanta Ra., India 40 J9 20 28N 75 50 E
Ajari Rep. = Ajaria □, Georgia 25 F7 41 30N 42 0 E
Ajaria □, Georgia 25 F7 41 30N 42 0 E
Ajax, Canada 78 C5 43 50N 79 1W
Ajdābiyā, Libya 51 B10 30 54N 20 4 E
Ajka, Hungary 17 E9 47 4N 17 31 E
'Ajmān, U.A.E. 45 E7 25 25N 55 30 E
Ajmer, India 42 F6 26 28N 74 37 E
Ajnala, India 42 D6 31 50N 74 48 E
Ajo, U.S.A. 83 K7 32 22N 112 52W
Ajo, C. de, Spain 19 A4 43 31N 3 35W
Akabira, Japan 30 C11 43 33N 142 5 E
Akamas, Cyprus 23 D11 35 3N 32 18 E
Akanthou, Cyprus 23 D12 35 22N 33 45 E
Akaroa, N.Z. 59 K4 43 49S 172 59 E
Akashi, Japan 31 G7 34 45N 134 58 E
Akbarpur, Bihar, India 43 G10 24 39N 83 58 E
Akbarpur, Ut. P., India 43 F10 26 25N 82 32 E
Akelamo, Indonesia 37 D7 1 35N 129 40 E
Aketi, Dem. Rep. of the Congo 52 D4 2 38N 23 47 E
Akharnai, Greece 21 E10 38 5N 23 44 E
Akhelóös →, Greece 21 E9 38 19N 21 7 E
Akhisar, Turkey 21 E12 38 56N 27 48 E
Akhnur, India 43 C6 32 52N 74 45 E
Akhtyrka = Okhtyrka, Ukraine 25 D5 50 25N 35 0 E
Aki, Japan 31 H6 33 30N 133 54 E
Akimiski I., Canada 70 B3 52 50N 81 30W
Akita, Japan 30 E10 39 45N 140 7 E
Akita □, Japan 30 E10 39 40N 140 30 E
Akjoujt, Mauritania 50 E3 19 45N 14 15W
Akkeshi, Japan 30 C12 43 2N 144 51 E
'Akko, Israel 47 C4 32 55N 35 4 E
Aklavik, Canada 68 B6 68 12N 135 0W
Aklera, India 42 G7 24 26N 76 32 E
Akmolinsk = Astana,
Kazakstan 26 D8 51 10N 71 30 E
Akō, Japan 31 G7 34 45N 134 24 E
Akola, India 40 J10 20 42N 77 2 E
Akordat, Eritrea 46 D2 15 30N 37 40 E
Akpatok I., Canada 69 B13 60 25N 68 8W
Åkrahamn, Norway 9 G11 59 15N 5 10 E
Akranes, Iceland 8 D2 64 19N 22 5W
Akron, Colo., U.S.A. 80 E3 40 10N 103 13W
Akron, Ohio, U.S.A. 78 E3 41 5N 81 31W
Akrotiri, Cyprus 23 E11 34 36N 32 57 E
Akrotiri Bay, Cyprus 23 E12 34 35N 33 10 E
Aksai Chin, China 43 B8 35 15N 79 55 E
Aksaray, Turkey 25 G5 38 25N 34 2 E
Aksay, Kazakstan 25 D9 51 11N 53 0 E
Akşehir, Turkey 44 B1 38 18N 31 30 E
Akşehir Gölü, Turkey 25 G5 38 30N 31 25 E
Aksu, China 32 B3 41 5N 80 10 E
Aksum, Ethiopia 46 E2 14 5N 38 40 E
Aktogay, Kazakstan 26 E8 46 57N 79 40 E
Aktsyabrski, Belarus 17 B15 52 38N 28 53 E
Aktyubinsk = Aqtöbe,
Kazakstan 25 D10 50 17N 57 10 E
Akure, Nigeria 50 G7 7 15N 5 5 E
Akureyri, Iceland 8 D4 65 40N 18 6W
Akuseki-Shima, Japan 31 K4 29 27N 129 37 E
Akyab = Sittwe, Burma 41 J18 20 18N 92 45 E
Al 'Adan, Yemen 46 E4 12 45N 45 0 E
Al Aḥsā = Hasa □, Si. Arabia 45 E6 25 50N 49 0 E
Al Ajfar, Si. Arabia 44 E4 27 26N 43 0 E
Al Amādīyah, Iraq 44 B4 37 5N 43 30 E
Al 'Amārah, Iraq 44 D5 31 55N 47 15 E
Al 'Aqabah, Jordan 47 F4 29 31N 35 0 E
Al Arak, Syria 44 C3 34 38N 38 35 E
Al 'Aramah, Si. Arabia 44 E5 25 30N 46 0 E
Al Arṭāwīyah, Si. Arabia 44 E5 26 31N 45 20 E
Al 'Āṣimah = 'Ammān □,
Jordan 47 D5 31 40N 36 30 E
Al 'Assāfīyah, Si. Arabia 44 D3 28 17N 38 59 E
Al 'Ayn, Oman 45 E7 24 15N 55 45 E
Al 'Ayn, Si. Arabia 44 E3 25 4N 38 6 E
Al 'Aẓamīyah, Iraq 44 C5 33 22N 44 22 E
Al 'Azīzīyah, Iraq 44 C5 32 54N 45 4 E
Al Bāb, Syria 44 B3 36 23N 37 29 E
Al Bad', Si. Arabia 44 D2 28 28N 35 1 E
Al Bādī, Iraq 44 C4 35 56N 41 32 E
Al Baḥrah, Kuwait 44 D5 29 40N 47 52 E
Al Baḥral Mayyit = Dead Sea,
Asia 47 D4 31 30N 35 30 E
Al Balqā' □, Jordan 47 C4 32 5N 35 45 E
Al Bārūk, J., Lebanon 47 B4 33 39N 35 40 E
Al Baṣrah, Iraq 44 D5 30 30N 47 50 E
Al Baṭḥā, Iraq 44 D5 31 6N 45 53 E
Al Batrūn, Lebanon 47 A4 34 15N 35 40 E
Al Bayḍā, Libya 51 B10 32 50N 21 44 E
Al Biqā, Lebanon 47 A5 34 10N 36 10 E
Al Bi'r, Si. Arabia 44 D3 28 51N 36 16 E
Al Burayj, Syria 47 A5 34 15N 36 46 E
Al Faḍilī, Si. Arabia 45 E6 26 58N 49 10 E
Al Fallūjah, Iraq 44 C4 33 20N 43 55 E
Al Fāw, Iraq 45 D6 30 0N 48 30 E
Al Fujayrah, U.A.E. 45 E8 25 7N 56 18 E
Al Ghadaf, W. →, Jordan 47 D5 31 26N 36 43 E
Al Ghammās, Iraq 44 D5 31 45N 44 37 E

Antsenavolo, Madag. 57 C8 21 24S 48 3 E
Antsiafabositra, Madag. 57 B8 17 18S 46 57 E
Antsirabe, Antananarivo, Madag. 57 B8 19 55S 47 2 E
Antsirabe, Antsiranana, Madag. 57 A8 14 0S 49 59 E
Antsirabe, Mahajanga, Madag. 57 B8 15 57S 48 58 E
Antsiranana, Madag. 57 A8 12 25S 49 20 E
Antsiranana □, Madag. 57 A8 12 16S 49 17 E
Antsohihy, Madag. 57 A8 14 50S 47 59 E
Antsohimbondrona Seranana, Madag. 57 A8 13 7S 48 48 E
Antu, China 35 C15 42 30N 128 20 E
Antwerp = Antwerpen, Belgium 15 C4 51 13N 4 25 E
Antwerp, U.S.A. 79 B9 44 12N 75 37W
Antwerpen, Belgium 15 C4 51 13N 4 25 E
Antwerpen □, Belgium 15 C4 51 15N 4 40 E
Anupgarh, India 42 E5 29 10N 73 10 E
Anuppur, India 43 H9 23 6N 81 41 E
Anuradhapura, Sri Lanka 40 Q12 8 22N 80 28 E
Anveh, Iran 45 E7 27 23N 54 11 E
Anvers = Antwerpen, Belgium 15 C4 51 13N 4 25 E
Anvers I., Antarctica 5 C17 64 30S 63 40W
Anxi, China 32 B4 40 30N 95 43 E
Anxious B., Australia 63 E1 33 24S 134 45 E
Anyang, China 34 F8 36 5N 114 21 E
Anyer-Kidul, Indonesia 37 G11 6 4S 105 53 E
Anyi, China 34 G6 35 2N 111 2 E
Anza, U.S.A. 85 M10 33 35N 116 39W
Anze, China 34 F7 36 10N 112 12 E
Anzhero-Sudzhensk, Russia 26 D9 56 10N 86 0 E
Ánzio, Italy 20 D5 41 27N 12 37 E
Aoga-Shima, Japan 31 H9 32 28N 139 46 E
Aomen = Macau, China 33 D6 22 12N 113 33 E
Aomori, Japan 30 D10 40 45N 140 45 E
Aomori □, Japan 30 D10 40 45N 140 40 E
Aonla, India 43 E8 28 16N 79 11 E
Aoraki Mount Cook, N.Z. 59 K3 43 36S 170 9 E
Aosta, Italy 18 D7 45 45N 7 20 E
Aoukâr, Mauritania 50 E4 17 40N 10 0W
Apa →, S. Amer. 94 A4 22 6S 58 2W
Apache, U.S.A. 81 H5 34 54N 98 22W
Apache Junction, U.S.A. 83 K8 33 25N 111 33W
Apalachee B., U.S.A. 77 L4 30 0N 84 0W
Apalachicola, U.S.A. 77 L3 29 43N 84 59W
Apalachicola →, U.S.A. 77 L3 29 43N 84 58W
Apaporis →, Colombia 92 D5 1 23S 69 25W
Aparri, Phil. 37 A6 18 22N 121 38 E
Apatity, Russia 24 A5 67 34N 33 22 E
Apatzingán, Mexico 86 D4 19 0N 102 20W
Apeldoorn, Neths. 15 B5 52 13N 5 57 E
Apennines = Appennini, Italy 20 B4 44 0N 10 0 E
Apia, Samoa 59 A13 13 50S 171 50W
Apiacás, Serra dos, Brazil 92 E7 9 50S 57 0W
Apies →, S. Africa 57 D4 25 15S 28 8 E
Apizaco, Mexico 87 D5 19 26N 98 9W
Aplao, Peru 92 G4 16 0S 72 40W
Apo, Mt., Phil. 37 C7 6 53N 125 14 E
Apolakkiá, Greece 23 C9 36 5N 27 48 E
Apolakkiá, Órmos, Greece 23 C9 36 5N 27 45 E
Apolo, Bolivia 92 F5 14 30S 68 30W
Aporé →, Brazil 93 G8 19 27S 50 57W
Apostle Is., U.S.A. 80 B9 47 0N 90 40W
Apóstoles, Argentina 95 B4 28 0S 56 0W
Apostolos Andreas, C., Cyprus 23 D13 35 42N 34 35 E
Apoteri, Guyana 92 C7 4 2N 58 32W
Appalachian Mts., U.S.A. 76 G6 38 0N 80 0W
Appennini, Italy 20 B4 44 0N 10 0 E
Apple Hill, Canada 79 A10 45 13N 74 46W
Apple Valley, U.S.A. 85 L9 34 32N 117 14W
Appleby-in-Westmorland, U.K. 10 C5 54 35N 2 29W
Appleton, U.S.A. 76 C1 44 16N 88 25W
Approuague →, Fr. Guiana 93 C8 4 30N 51 57W
Aprília, Italy 20 D5 41 36N 12 39 E
Apsley, Canada 78 B6 44 45N 78 6W
Apucarana, Brazil 95 A5 23 55S 51 33W
Apure →, Venezuela 92 B5 7 37N 66 25W
Apurimac →, Peru 92 F4 12 17S 73 56W
Āqā Jari, Iran 45 D6 30 42N 49 50 E
Aqaba = Al 'Aqabah, Jordan 47 F4 29 31N 35 0 E
Aqaba, G. of, Red Sea 44 D2 28 15N 33 20 E
'Aqabah, Khalīj al = Aqaba, G. of, Red Sea 44 D2 28 15N 33 20 E
'Aqdā, Iran 45 C7 32 26N 53 37 E
Aqmola = Astana, Kazakstan 26 D8 51 10N 71 30 E
'Aqrah, Iraq 44 B4 36 46N 43 45 E
Aqtaū, Kazakstan 26 E6 43 39N 51 12 E
Aqtöbe, Kazakstan 25 D10 50 17N 57 10 E
Aquidauana, Brazil 93 H7 20 30S 55 50W
Aquiles Serdán, Mexico 86 B3 28 37N 105 54W
Aquin, Haiti 89 C5 18 16N 73 24W
Aquitain, Bassin, France 18 D3 44 0N 0 30W
Aqviligjuaq = Pelly Bay, Canada 69 B11 68 38N 89 50W
Ar Rachidiya = Er Rachidia, Morocco 50 B5 31 58N 4 20W
Ar Rafid, Syria 47 C4 32 57N 35 52 E
Ar Raḩḩālīyah, Iraq 44 C4 32 44N 43 23 E
Ar Ramādī, Iraq 44 C4 33 25N 43 20 E
Ar Ramthā, Jordan 47 C5 32 34N 36 0 E
Ar Raqqah, Syria 44 C3 35 59N 39 8 E
Ar Rass, Si. Arabia 44 E4 25 50N 43 40 E
Ar Rifā'ī, Iraq 44 D5 31 50N 46 10 E
Ar Riyāḑ, Si. Arabia 46 C4 24 41N 46 42 E
Ar Ru'ays, Qatar 45 E6 26 8N 51 12 E
Ar Rukhaymīyah, Iraq 44 D5 29 22N 45 38 E
Ar Ruşāfah, Syria 44 C3 35 45N 38 49 E
Ar Ruţbah, Iraq 44 C4 33 0N 40 15 E
Ara, India 43 G11 25 35N 84 32 E
Arab, U.S.A. 77 H2 34 19N 86 30W
'Arab, Bahr el →, Sudan 51 G11 9 0N 29 30 E
Arab, Shatt al →, Asia 45 D6 30 0N 48 31 E
'Arabābād, Iran 45 C8 33 2N 57 41 E
Arabia, Asia 28 G8 25 0N 45 0 E
Arabian Desert = Es Sahrâ' Esh Sharqîya, Egypt 51 C12 27 30N 32 30 E
Arabian Gulf = Gulf, The, Asia 45 E6 27 0N 50 0 E
Arabian Sea, Ind. Oc. 29 H10 16 0N 65 0 E
Aracaju, Brazil 93 F11 10 55S 37 4W
Aracati, Brazil 93 D11 4 30S 37 44W
Araçatuba, Brazil 95 A5 21 10S 50 30W
Aracena, Spain 19 D2 37 53N 6 38W
Araçuai, Brazil 93 G10 16 52S 42 4W
'Arad, Israel 47 D4 31 15N 35 12 E
Arad, Romania 17 E11 46 10N 21 20 E
Arādān, Iran 45 C7 35 21N 52 30 E
Aradhippou, Cyprus 23 E12 34 57N 33 36 E
Arafura Sea, E. Indies 28 K17 9 0S 135 0 E
Aragón □, Spain 19 B5 41 25N 0 40W
Aragón →, Spain 19 A5 42 13N 1 44W
Araguacema, Brazil 93 E9 8 50S 49 20W
Araguaia →, Brazil 93 E9 5 21S 48 41W
Araguaína, Brazil 93 E9 7 12S 48 12W
Araguari, Brazil 93 G9 18 38S 48 11W
Araguari →, Brazil 93 C9 1 15N 49 55W
Arain, India 42 F6 26 27N 75 2 E
Arak, Algeria 50 C6 25 20N 3 45 E
Arāk, Iran 45 C6 34 0N 49 40 E
Arakan Coast, Burma 41 K19 19 0N 94 0 E
Arakan Yoma, Burma 41 K19 20 0N 94 40 E
Araks = Aras, Rūd-e →, Asia 44 B5 40 5N 48 29 E
Aral, Kazakstan 26 E7 46 41N 61 45 E
Aral Sea, Asia 26 E7 44 30N 60 0 E
Aral Tengizi = Aral Sea, Asia 26 E7 44 30N 60 0 E
Aralsk = Aral, Kazakstan 26 E7 46 41N 61 45 E
Aralskoye More = Aral Sea, Asia 26 E7 44 30N 60 0 E
Aramac, Australia 62 C4 22 58S 145 14 E
Aran I., Ireland 13 A3 55 0N 8 30W
Aran Is., Ireland 13 C2 53 6N 9 38W
Aranda de Duero, Spain 19 B4 41 39N 3 42W
Arandān, Iran 44 C5 35 23N 46 55 E
Aranjuez, Spain 19 B4 40 1N 3 40W
Aranos, Namibia 56 C2 24 9S 19 7 E
Aransas Pass, U.S.A. 81 M6 27 55N 97 9W
Aranyaprathet, Thailand 38 F4 13 41N 102 30 E
Arapahoe, U.S.A. 80 E5 40 18N 99 54W
Arapey Grande →, Uruguay 94 C4 30 55S 57 49W
Arapgir, Turkey 44 B3 39 5N 38 30 E
Arapiraca, Brazil 93 E11 9 45S 36 39W
Arapongas, Brazil 95 A5 23 29S 51 28W
Ar'ar, Si. Arabia 44 D4 30 59N 41 2 E
Araranguá, Brazil 95 B6 29 0S 49 30W
Araraquara, Brazil 93 H9 21 50S 48 0W
Ararás, Serra das, Brazil 95 B5 25 0S 53 10W
Ararat, Australia 63 F3 37 16S 143 0 E
Ararat, Mt. = Ağrı Dağı, Turkey 25 G7 39 50N 44 15 E
Araria, India 43 F12 26 9N 87 33 E
Araripe, Chapada do, Brazil 93 E11 7 20S 40 0W
Araruama, L. de, Brazil 95 A7 22 53S 42 12W
Aras, Rūd-e →, Asia 44 B5 40 5N 48 29 E
Arauca, Colombia 92 B4 7 0N 70 40W
Arauca →, Venezuela 92 B5 7 24N 66 35W
Arauco, Chile 94 D1 37 16S 73 25W
Araxá, Brazil 93 G9 19 35S 46 55W
Araya, Pen. de, Venezuela 92 A6 10 40N 64 0W
Arba Minch, Ethiopia 46 F2 6 0N 37 30 E
Arbat, Iraq 44 C5 35 25N 45 35 E
Árbatax, Italy 20 E3 39 56N 9 42 E
Arbīl, Iraq 44 B5 36 15N 44 5 E
Arborfield, Canada 73 C8 53 6N 103 39W
Arborg, Canada 73 C9 50 54N 97 13W
Arbroath, U.K. 12 E6 56 34N 2 35W
Arbuckle, U.S.A. 84 F4 39 1N 122 3W
Arcachon, France 18 D3 44 40N 1 10W
Arcade, Calif., U.S.A. 85 L8 34 2N 118 15W
Arcade, N.Y., U.S.A. 78 D6 42 32N 78 25W
Arcadia, Fla., U.S.A. 77 M5 27 13N 81 52W
Arcadia, La., U.S.A. 81 J8 32 33N 92 55W
Arcadia, Pa., U.S.A. 78 F6 40 47N 78 51W
Arcata, U.S.A. 82 F1 40 52N 124 5W
Archangel = Arkhangelsk, Russia 24 B7 64 38N 40 36 E
Archbald, U.S.A. 79 E9 41 30N 75 32W
Archer →, Australia 62 A3 13 28S 141 41 E
Archer B., Australia 62 A3 13 20S 141 30 E
Archers Post, Kenya 54 B4 0 35N 37 35 E
Arches Nat. Park, U.S.A. 83 G9 38 45N 109 25W
Arckaringa Cr. →, Australia 63 D2 28 10S 135 22 E
Arco, U.S.A. 82 E7 43 38N 113 18W
Arcos de la Frontera, Spain 19 D3 36 45N 5 49W
Arcot, India 40 N11 12 53N 79 20 E
Arctic Bay, Canada 69 A11 73 1N 85 7W
Arctic Ocean, Arctic 4 B18 78 0N 160 0W
Arctic Red River = Tsiigehtchic, Canada 68 B6 67 15N 134 0W
Arda →, Bulgaria 21 D12 41 40N 26 30 E
Ardabīl, Iran 45 B6 38 15N 48 18 E
Ardakān = Sepīdān, Iran 45 D7 30 20N 52 5 E
Ardakān, Iran 45 C7 32 19N 53 59 E
Ardee, Ireland 13 C5 53 52N 6 33W
Arden, Canada 78 B8 44 43N 76 56W
Arden, Calif., U.S.A. 84 G5 38 36N 121 33W
Arden, Nev., U.S.A. 85 J11 36 1N 115 14W
Ardenne, Belgium 16 D3 49 50N 5 5 E
Ardennes = Ardenne, Belgium 16 D3 49 50N 5 5 E
Arderin, Ireland 13 C4 53 2N 7 39W
Ardestān, Iran 45 C7 33 20N 52 25 E
Ardivachar Pt., U.K. 12 D1 57 23N 7 26W
Ardlethan, Australia 63 E4 34 22S 146 53 E
Ardmore, Okla., U.S.A. 81 H6 34 10N 97 8W
Ardmore, Pa., U.S.A. 79 G9 39 58N 75 18W
Ardnamurchan, Pt. of, U.K. 12 E2 56 43N 6 14W
Ardnave Pt., U.K. 12 F2 55 53N 6 20W
Ardrossan, Australia 63 E2 34 26S 137 53 E
Ardrossan, U.K. 12 F4 55 39N 4 49W
Ards Pen., U.K. 13 B6 54 33N 5 34W
Arecibo, Puerto Rico 89 C6 18 29N 66 43W
Areia Branca, Brazil 93 E11 5 0S 37 0W
Arena, Pt., U.S.A. 84 G3 38 57N 123 44W
Arenal, Honduras 88 C2 15 21N 86 50W
Arendal, Norway 9 G13 58 28N 8 46 E
Arequipa, Peru 92 G4 16 20S 71 30W
Arévalo, Spain 19 B3 41 3N 4 43W
Arezzo, Italy 20 C4 43 25N 11 53 E
Arga, Turkey 44 B3 38 21N 37 59 E
Arganda, Spain 19 B4 40 19N 3 26W
Argenta, Canada 72 C5 50 11N 116 56W
Argentan, France 18 B3 48 45N 0 1W
Argentário, Mte., Italy 20 C4 42 24N 11 9 E
Argentia, Canada 71 C9 47 18N 53 58W
Argentina ■, S. Amer. 96 D3 35 0S 66 0W
Argentino, L., Argentina 96 G2 50 10S 73 0W
Argeş →, Romania 17 F14 44 5N 26 38 E
Arghandab →, Afghan. 42 D1 31 30N 64 15 E
Argolikós Kólpos, Greece 21 F10 37 20N 22 52 E
Árgos, Greece 21 F10 37 40N 22 43 E
Argostólion, Greece 21 E9 38 11N 20 29 E
Arguello, Pt., U.S.A. 85 L6 34 35N 120 39W
Arguineguín, Canary Is. 22 G4 27 46N 15 41W
Argun →, Russia 27 D13 53 20N 121 28 E
Argus Pk., U.S.A. 85 K9 35 52N 117 26W
Argyle, L., Australia 60 C4 16 20S 128 40 E
Argyll & Bute □, U.K. 12 E3 56 13N 5 28W
Århus, Denmark 9 H14 56 8N 10 11 E
Ariadnoye, Russia 30 B7 45 8N 134 25 E
Ariamsvlei, Namibia 56 D2 28 9S 19 51 E
Ariana, Tunisia 51 A8 36 52N 10 12 E
Arica, Chile 92 G4 18 32S 70 20W
Arica, Colombia 92 D4 2 0S 71 50W
Arico, Canary Is. 22 F3 28 9N 16 29W
Arid, C., Australia 61 F3 34 1S 123 10 E
Arida, Japan 31 G7 34 5N 135 8 E
Arilla, Ákra, Greece 23 A3 39 43N 19 39 E
Arima, Trin. & Tob. 89 D7 10 38N 61 17W
Arinos →, Brazil 92 F7 10 25S 58 20W
Ario de Rosales, Mexico 86 D4 19 12N 102 0W
Aripuanã, Brazil 92 E6 9 25S 60 30W
Aripuanã →, Brazil 92 E6 5 7S 60 25W
Ariquemes, Brazil 92 E6 9 55S 63 6W
Arisaig, U.K. 12 E3 56 55N 5 51W
Aristazabal I., Canada 72 C3 52 40N 129 10W
Arivonimamo, Madag. 57 B8 19 1S 47 11 E
Arizaro, Salar de, Argentina 94 A2 24 40S 67 50W
Arizona, Argentina 94 D2 35 45S 65 25W
Arizona □, U.S.A. 83 J8 34 0N 112 0W
Arizpe, Mexico 86 A2 30 20N 110 11W
Arjeplog, Sweden 8 D18 66 3N 18 2 E
Arjona, Colombia 92 A3 10 14N 75 22W
Arjuna, Indonesia 37 G15 7 49S 112 34 E
Arka, Russia 27 C15 60 15N 142 0 E
Arkadelphia, U.S.A. 81 H8 34 7N 93 4W
Arkaig, L., U.K. 12 E3 56 59N 5 10W
Arkalyk = Arqalyk, Kazakstan 26 D7 50 13N 66 50 E
Arkansas □, U.S.A. 81 H8 35 0N 92 30W
Arkansas →, U.S.A. 81 J9 33 47N 91 4W
Arkansas City, U.S.A. 81 G6 37 4N 97 2W
Arkaroola, Australia 63 E2 30 20S 139 22 E
Arkhángelos, Greece 23 C10 36 13N 28 7 E
Arkhangelsk, Russia 24 B7 64 38N 40 36 E
Arki, India 42 D7 31 9N 76 58 E
Arklow, Ireland 13 D5 52 48N 6 10W
Arkport, U.S.A. 78 D7 42 24N 77 42W
Arkticheskiy, Mys, Russia 27 A10 81 10N 95 0 E
Arkville, U.S.A. 79 D10 42 9N 74 37W
Arlanzón →, Spain 19 A3 42 3N 4 17W
Arlbergpass, Austria 16 E6 47 9N 10 12 E
Arles, France 18 E6 43 41N 4 40 E
Arlington, S. Africa 57 D4 28 1S 27 53 E
Arlington, N.Y., U.S.A. 79 E11 41 42N 73 54W
Arlington, Oreg., U.S.A. 82 D3 45 43N 120 12W
Arlington, S. Dak., U.S.A. 80 C6 44 22N 97 8W
Arlington, Tex., U.S.A. 81 J6 32 44N 97 7W
Arlington, Va., U.S.A. 76 F7 38 53N 77 7W
Arlington, Vt., U.S.A. 79 C11 43 5N 73 9W
Arlington, Wash., U.S.A. 84 B4 48 12N 122 8W
Arlington Heights, U.S.A. 76 D2 42 5N 87 59W
Arlit, Niger 50 E7 19 0N 7 38 E
Arlon, Belgium 15 E5 49 42N 5 49 E
Arltunga, Australia 62 C1 23 26S 134 41 E
Armagh, U.K. 13 B5 54 21N 6 39W
Armagh □, U.K. 13 B5 54 18N 6 37W
Armavir, Russia 25 E7 45 2N 41 7 E
Armenia, Colombia 92 C3 4 35N 75 45W
Armenia ■, Asia 25 F7 40 20N 45 0 E
Armenistís, Ákra, Greece 23 C9 36 8N 27 42 E
Armidale, Australia 63 E5 30 30S 151 40 E
Armour, U.S.A. 80 D5 43 19N 98 21W
Armstrong, B.C., Canada 72 C5 50 25N 119 10W
Armstrong, Ont., Canada 70 B2 50 18N 89 4W
Arnarfjörður, Iceland 8 D2 65 48N 23 40W
Arnaud →, Canada 69 B12 60 0N 70 0W
Arnauti, C., Cyprus 23 D11 35 6N 32 17 E
Arnett, U.S.A. 81 G5 36 8N 99 46W
Arnhem, Neths. 15 C5 51 58N 5 55 E
Arnhem, C., Australia 62 A2 12 20S 137 30 E
Arnhem B., Australia 62 A2 12 20S 136 10 E
Arnhem Land, Australia 62 A1 13 10S 134 30 E
Arno →, Italy 20 C4 43 41N 10 17 E
Arno Bay, Australia 63 E2 33 54S 136 34 E
Arnold, U.K. 10 D6 53 1N 1 7W
Arnold, U.S.A. 84 G6 38 15N 120 20W
Arnot, Canada 73 B9 55 56N 96 41W
Arnøy, Norway 8 A19 70 9N 20 40 E
Arnprior, Canada 79 A8 45 26N 76 21W
Arnsberg, Germany 16 C5 51 24N 8 5 E
Aroab, Namibia 56 D2 26 41S 19 39 E
Aron, India 42 G6 25 57N 77 56 E
Arqalyk, Kazakstan 26 D7 50 13N 66 50 E
Arrah = Ara, India 43 G11 25 35N 84 32 E
Arran, U.K. 12 F3 55 34N 5 12W
Arras, France 18 A5 50 17N 2 46 E
Arrecife, Canary Is. 22 F6 28 57N 13 37W
Arrecifes, Argentina 94 C3 34 6S 60 9W
Arrée, Mts. d', France 18 B2 48 26N 3 55W
Arriaga, Chiapas, Mexico 87 D6 16 15N 93 52W
Arriaga, San Luis Potosí, Mexico 86 C4 21 55N 101 23W
Arrilalah, Australia 62 C3 23 43S 143 54 E
Arrino, Australia 61 E2 29 30S 115 40 E
Arrow, L., Ireland 13 B3 54 3N 8 19W
Arrowhead, L., U.S.A. 85 L9 34 16N 117 10W
Arrowtown, N.Z. 59 L2 44 57S 168 50 E
Arroyo Grande, U.S.A. 85 K6 35 7N 120 35W
Ars, Iran 44 B5 37 9N 47 46 E
Arsenault L., Canada 73 B7 55 6N 108 32W
Arsenev, Russia 30 B6 44 10N 133 15 E
Árta, Greece 21 E9 39 8N 21 2 E
Artà, Spain 22 B10 39 41N 3 21 E
Arteaga, Mexico 86 D4 18 50N 102 20W
Artem, Russia 30 C6 43 22N 132 13 E
Artemovsk, Russia 27 D10 54 45N 93 35 E
Artemovsk, Ukraine 25 E6 48 35N 38 0 E
Artesia = Mosomane, Botswana 56 C4 24 2S 26 19 E
Artesia, U.S.A. 81 J2 32 51N 104 24W
Arthur, Canada 78 C4 43 50N 80 32W
Arthur →, Australia 62 G3 41 2S 144 40 E
Arthur Cr. →, Australia 62 C2 22 30S 136 25 E
Arthur Pt., Australia 62 C5 22 7S 150 3 E
Arthur River, Australia 61 F2 33 20S 117 2 E
Arthur's Pass, N.Z. 59 K3 42 54S 171 35 E
Arthur's Town, Bahamas 89 B4 24 38N 75 42W
Artigas, Uruguay 94 C4 30 20S 56 30W
Artillery L., Canada 73 A7 63 9N 107 52W
Artois, France 18 A5 50 20N 2 30 E
Artrutx, C. de, Spain 22 B10 39 55N 3 49 E
Artsyz, Ukraine 17 E15 46 4N 29 26 E
Artvin, Turkey 25 F7 41 14N 41 44 E
Aru, Kepulauan, Indonesia 37 F8 6 0S 134 30 E
Aru Is. = Aru, Kepulauan, Indonesia 37 F8 6 0S 134 30 E
Arua, Uganda 54 B3 3 1N 30 58 E
Aruanã, Brazil 93 F8 14 54S 51 10W
Aruba ■, W. Indies 89 D6 12 30N 70 0W
Arucas, Canary Is. 22 F4 28 7N 15 32W
Arun →, Nepal 43 F12 26 55N 87 10 E
Arun →, U.K. 11 G7 50 49N 0 33W
Arunachal Pradesh □, India 41 F19 28 0N 95 0 E
Arusha, Tanzania 54 C4 3 20S 36 40 E
Arusha □, Tanzania 54 C4 4 0S 36 30 E
Arusha Chini, Tanzania 54 C4 3 32S 37 20 E
Aruwimi →, Dem. Rep. of the Congo 54 B1 1 13N 23 36 E
Arvada, Colo., U.S.A. 80 F2 39 48N 105 5W
Arvada, Wyo., U.S.A. 82 D10 44 39N 106 8W
Árvi, Greece 23 E7 34 59N 25 28 E
Arviat, Canada 73 A10 61 6N 93 59W
Arvidsjaur, Sweden 8 D18 65 35N 19 10 E
Arvika, Sweden 9 G15 59 40N 12 36 E
Arvin, U.S.A. 85 K8 35 12N 118 50W
Arwal, India 43 G11 25 15N 84 41 E
Arxan, China 33 B6 47 11N 119 57 E
Aryirádhes, Greece 23 B3 39 27N 19 58 E
Aryiroúpolis, Greece 23 D6 35 17N 24 20 E
Arys, Kazakstan 26 E7 42 26N 68 48 E
Arzamas, Russia 24 C7 55 27N 43 55 E
Aş Şafā, Syria 47 B6 33 10N 37 0 E
As Saffānīyah, Si. Arabia 45 E6 27 55N 48 50 E
As Safīrah, Syria 44 B3 36 5N 37 21 E
Aş Şahm, Oman 45 E8 24 10N 56 53 E
As Sājir, Si. Arabia 44 E5 25 11N 44 36 E
As Salamīyah, Syria 44 C3 35 1N 37 2 E
As Salmān, Iraq 44 D5 30 30N 44 32 E
As Salţ, Jordan 47 C4 32 2N 35 43 E
As Sal'w'a, Qatar 45 E6 24 23N 50 50 E
As Samāwah, Iraq 44 D5 31 15N 45 15 E
As Sanamayn, Syria 47 B5 33 3N 36 10 E
As Sohar = Şuḩār, Oman 46 C6 24 20N 56 40 E
As Sukhnah, Syria 44 C3 34 52N 38 52 E
As Sulaymānīyah, Iraq 44 C5 35 35N 45 29 E
As Sulaymī, Si. Arabia 44 E4 26 17N 41 21 E
As Sulayyil, Si. Arabia 46 C4 20 27N 45 34 E
As Summān, Si. Arabia 44 E5 25 0N 47 0 E
As Suwaydā', Syria 47 C5 32 40N 36 30 E
As Suwaydā' □, Syria 47 C5 32 45N 36 45 E
As Suwayq, Oman 45 F8 23 51N 57 26 E
As Şuwayrah, Iraq 44 C5 32 55N 45 0 E
Asab, Namibia 56 D2 25 30S 18 0 E
Asad, Buḩayrat al, Syria 44 C3 36 0N 38 15 E
Asahi-Gawa →, Japan 31 G6 34 36N 133 58 E
Asahigawa, Japan 30 C11 43 46N 142 22 E
Asamankese, Ghana 50 G5 5 50N 0 40W
Asan →, India 43 F8 26 37N 78 24 E
Asansol, India 43 H12 23 40N 87 1 E
Asbesberge, S. Africa 56 D3 29 0S 23 0 E
Asbestos, Canada 71 C5 45 47N 71 58W
Asbury Park, U.S.A. 79 F10 40 13N 74 1W
Ascensión, Mexico 86 A3 31 6N 107 59W
Ascensión, B. de la, Mexico 87 D7 19 50N 87 20W
Ascension I., Atl. Oc. 49 G2 7 57S 14 23W
Aschaffenburg, Germany 16 D5 49 58N 9 6 E
Aschersleben, Germany 16 C6 51 45N 11 29 E
Áscoli Piceno, Italy 20 C5 42 51N 13 34 E
Ascope, Peru 92 E3 7 46S 79 8W
Ascotán, Chile 94 A2 21 45S 68 17W
Aseb, Eritrea 46 E3 13 0N 42 40 E
Asela, Ethiopia 46 F2 8 0N 39 0 E
Asenovgrad, Bulgaria 21 C11 42 1N 24 51 E
Aserradero, Mexico 86 C3 23 40N 105 43W
Asgata, Cyprus 23 E12 34 46N 33 15 E
Ash Fork, U.S.A. 83 J7 35 13N 112 29W
Ash Grove, U.S.A. 81 G8 37 19N 93 35W
Ash Shabakah, Iraq 44 D4 30 49N 43 39 E
Ash Shamāl □, Lebanon 47 A5 34 25N 36 0 E
Ash Shāmīyah, Iraq 44 D5 31 55N 44 35 E
Ash Shāriqah, U.A.E. 46 B6 25 23N 55 26 E
Ash Sharmah, Si. Arabia 44 D2 28 1N 35 16 E
Ash Sharqāt, Iraq 44 C4 35 27N 43 16 E
Ash Sharqi, Al Jabal, Lebanon 47 B5 33 40N 36 10 E
Ash Shaţrah, Iraq 44 D5 31 30N 46 10 E
Ash Shawbak, Jordan 44 D2 30 32N 35 34 E
Ash Shawmari, J., Jordan 47 E5 30 35N 36 35 E
Ash Shināfīyah, Iraq 44 D5 31 35N 44 39 E
Ash Shu'bah, Si. Arabia 44 D5 28 54N 44 44 E
Ash Shumlūl, Si. Arabia 44 E5 26 31N 47 20 E
Ash Shūr'a, Iraq 44 C4 35 58N 43 13 E
Ash Shurayf, Si. Arabia 44 E3 25 43N 39 14 E
Ash Shuwayfāt, Lebanon 47 B4 33 45N 35 30 E
Asha, Russia 24 D10 55 0N 57 16 E
Ashau, Vietnam 38 D6 16 6N 107 22 E
Ashbourne, U.K. 10 D6 53 2N 1 43W
Ashburn, U.S.A. 77 K4 31 43N 83 39W
Ashburton, N.Z. 59 K3 43 53S 171 48 E
Ashburton →, Australia 60 D1 21 40S 114 56 E
Ashcroft, Canada 72 C4 50 40N 121 20W
Ashdod, Israel 47 D3 31 49N 34 35 E
Ashdown, U.S.A. 81 J7 33 40N 94 8W
Asheboro, U.S.A. 77 H6 35 43N 79 49W
Ashern, Canada 73 C9 51 11N 98 21W
Asherton, U.S.A. 81 L5 28 27N 99 46W
Asheville, U.S.A. 77 H4 35 36N 82 33W
Ashewat, Pakistan 42 D3 31 22N 68 32 E
Asheweig →, Canada 70 B2 54 17N 87 12W
Ashford, Australia 63 D5 29 15S 151 3 E
Ashford, U.K. 11 F8 51 8N 0 53 E
Ashgabat, Turkmenistan 26 F6 38 0N 57 50 E
Ashibetsu, Japan 30 C11 43 31N 142 11 E
Ashikaga, Japan 31 F9 36 28N 139 29 E
Ashington, U.K. 10 B6 55 11N 1 33W
Ashizuri-Zaki, Japan 31 H6 32 44N 133 0 E
Ashkarkot, Afghan. 42 C2 33 3N 67 58 E
Ashkhabad = Ashgabat, Turkmenistan 26 F6 38 0N 57 50 E

Āshkhāneh, Iran 45 B8 37 26N 56 55 E
Ashland, Kans., U.S.A. 81 G5 37 11N 99 46W
Ashland, Ky., U.S.A. 76 F4 38 28N 82 38W
Ashland, Mont., U.S.A. 82 D10 45 36N 106 16W
Ashland, Ohio, U.S.A. 78 F2 40 52N 82 19W
Ashland, Oreg., U.S.A. 82 E2 42 12N 122 43W
Ashland, Pa., U.S.A. 79 F8 40 45N 76 22W
Ashland, Va., U.S.A. 76 G7 37 46N 77 29W
Ashland, Wis., U.S.A. 80 B9 46 35N 90 53W
Ashley, N. Dak., U.S.A. 80 B5 46 2N 99 22W
Ashley, Pa., U.S.A. 79 E9 41 12N 75 55W
Ashmore Reef, Australia 60 B3 12 14S 123 5 E
Ashmyany, Belarus 9 J21 54 26N 25 52 E
Ashokan Reservoir, U.S.A. 79 E10 41 56N 74 13W
Ashqelon, Israel 47 D3 31 42N 34 35 E
Ashta, India 42 H7 23 1N 76 43 E
Ashtabula, U.S.A. 78 E4 41 52N 80 47W
Ashton, S. Africa 56 E3 33 50S 20 5 E
Ashton, U.S.A. 82 D8 44 4N 111 27W
Ashuanipi, L., Canada 71 B6 52 45N 66 15W
Ashville, U.S.A. 78 F6 40 34N 78 33W
Asia 28 E11 45 0N 75 0 E
Asia, Kepulauan, Indonesia 37 D8 1 0N 131 13 E
Āsīā Bak, Iran 45 C6 35 19N 50 30 E
Asifabad, India 40 K11 19 20N 79 24 E
Asinara, Italy 20 D3 41 4N 8 16 E
Asinara, G. dell', Italy 20 D3 41 0N 8 30 E
Asino, Russia 26 D9 57 0N 86 0 E
Asipovichy, Belarus 17 B15 53 19N 28 33 E
'Asīr □, Si. Arabia 46 D3 18 40N 42 30 E
Asir, Ras, Somali Rep. 46 E5 11 55N 51 10 E
Askersund, Sweden 9 G16 58 53N 14 55 E
Askham, S. Africa 56 D3 26 59S 20 47 E
Askim, Norway 9 G14 59 35N 11 10 E
Askja, Iceland 8 D5 65 3N 16 48W
Askøy, Norway 9 F11 60 29N 5 10 E
Asmara = Asmera, Eritrea 46 D2 15 19N 38 55 E
Asmera, Eritrea 46 D2 15 19N 38 55 E
Åsnen, Sweden 9 H16 56 37N 14 45 E
Aspen, U.S.A. 83 G10 39 11N 106 49W
Aspermont, U.S.A. 81 J4 33 8N 100 14W
Aspiring, Mt., N.Z. 59 L2 44 23S 168 46 E
Asprókavos, Ákra, Greece 23 B4 39 21N 20 6 E
Aspur, India 42 H6 23 58N 74 7 E
Asquith, Canada 73 C7 52 8N 107 13W
Assab = Aseb, Eritrea 46 E3 13 0N 42 40 E
Assam □, India 41 G18 26 0N 93 0 E
Asse, Belgium 15 D4 50 24N 4 10 E
Assen, Neths. 15 A6 53 0N 6 35 E
Assiniboia, Canada 73 D7 49 40N 105 59W
Assiniboine →, Canada 73 D9 49 53N 97 8W
Assiniboine, Mt., Canada 72 C5 50 52N 115 39W
Assis, Brazil 95 A5 22 40S 50 20W
Assisi, Italy 20 C5 43 4N 12 37 E
Assynt, L., U.K. 12 C3 58 10N 5 3W
Astana, Kazakstan 26 D8 51 10N 71 30 E
Āstāneh, Iran 45 B6 37 17N 49 59 E
Astara, Azerbaijan 25 G8 38 30N 48 50 E
Asteroúsia, Greece 23 E7 34 59N 25 3 E
Asti, Italy 18 D8 44 54N 8 12 E
Astipálaia, Greece 21 F12 36 32N 26 22 E
Astorga, Spain 19 A2 42 29N 6 8W
Astoria, U.S.A. 84 D3 46 11N 123 50W
Astrakhan, Russia 25 E8 46 25N 48 5 E
Asturias □, Spain 19 A3 43 15N 6 0W
Asunción, Paraguay 94 B4 25 10S 57 30W
Asunción Nochixtlán, Mexico 87 D5 17 28N 97 14W
Aswa →, Uganda 54 B3 3 43N 31 55 E
Aswân, Egypt 51 D12 24 4N 32 57 E
Aswân High Dam = Sadd el Aali, Egypt 51 D12 23 54N 32 54 E
Asyût, Egypt 51 C12 27 11N 31 4 E
At Ṭafīlah, Jordan 47 E4 30 45N 35 30 E
Aṭ Ṭā'if, Si. Arabia 46 C3 21 5N 40 27 E
Aṭ Ṭirāq, Si. Arabia 44 E5 27 19N 44 33 E
Aṭ Ṭubayq, Si. Arabia 44 D3 29 30N 37 0 E
Atacama □, Chile 94 B2 27 30S 70 0W
Atacama, Desierto de, Chile 94 A2 24 0S 69 20W
Atacama, Salar de, Chile 94 A2 23 30S 68 20W
Atalaya, Peru 92 F4 10 45S 73 50W
Atalaya de Femes, Canary Is. 22 F6 28 56N 13 47W
Atami, Japan 31 G9 35 5N 139 4 E
Atapupu, E. Timor 37 F6 9 0S 124 51 E
Atâr, Mauritania 50 D3 20 30N 13 5W
Atari, Pakistan 42 D6 30 56N 74 2 E
Atascadero, U.S.A. 84 K6 35 29N 120 40W
Atasu, Kazakstan 26 E8 48 30N 71 0 E
Atatürk Barajı, Turkey 25 G6 37 28N 38 30 E
Atauro, E. Timor 37 F7 8 10S 125 30 E
'Atbara, Sudan 51 E12 17 42N 33 59 E
'Atbara, Nahr →, Sudan 51 E12 17 40N 33 56 E
Atbasar, Kazakstan 26 D7 51 48N 68 20 E
Atchafalaya B., U.S.A. 81 L9 29 25N 91 25W
Atchison, U.S.A. 80 F7 39 34N 95 7W
Āteshān, Iran 45 C7 35 35N 52 37 E
Ath, Belgium 15 D3 50 38N 3 47 E
Athabasca, Canada 72 C6 54 45N 113 20W
Athabasca →, Canada 73 B6 58 40N 110 50W
Athabasca, L., Canada 73 B7 59 15N 109 15W
Athboy, Ireland 13 C5 53 37N 6 56W
Athenry, Ireland 13 C3 53 18N 8 44W
Athens = Athínai, Greece 21 F10 37 58N 23 46 E
Athens, Ala., U.S.A. 77 H2 34 48N 86 58W
Athens, Ga., U.S.A. 77 J4 33 57N 83 23W
Athens, N.Y., U.S.A. 79 D11 42 16N 73 49W
Athens, Ohio, U.S.A. 76 F4 39 20N 82 6W
Athens, Pa., U.S.A. 79 E8 41 57N 76 31W
Athens, Tenn., U.S.A. 77 H3 35 27N 84 36W
Athens, Tex., U.S.A. 81 J7 32 12N 95 51W
Atherley, Canada 78 B5 44 37N 79 20W
Atherton, Australia 62 B4 17 17S 145 30 E
Athienou, Cyprus 23 D12 35 3N 33 32 E
Athínai, Greece 21 F10 37 58N 23 46 E
Athlone, Ireland 13 C4 53 25N 7 56W
Athna, Cyprus 23 D12 35 3N 33 47 E
Athol, U.S.A. 79 D12 42 36N 72 14W
Atholl, Forest of, U.K. 12 E5 56 51N 3 50W
Atholville, Canada 71 C6 47 59N 66 43W
Áthos, Greece 21 D11 40 9N 24 22 E
Athy, Ireland 13 C5 53 0N 7 0W
Ati, Chad 51 F9 13 13N 18 20 E
Atiak, Uganda 54 B3 3 12N 32 2 E
Atik L., Canada 73 B9 55 15N 96 0W
Atikameg →, Canada 70 B3 52 30N 82 46W
Atikokan, Canada 70 C1 48 45N 91 37W
Atikonak L., Canada 71 B7 52 40N 64 32W
Atka, Russia 27 C16 60 50N 151 48 E
Atka I., U.S.A. 68 C2 52 7N 174 30W
Atkinson, U.S.A. 80 D5 42 32N 98 59W
Atlanta, Ga., U.S.A. 77 J3 33 45N 84 23W
Atlanta, Tex., U.S.A. 81 J7 33 7N 94 10W
Atlantic, U.S.A. 80 E7 41 24N 95 1W
Atlantic City, U.S.A. 76 F8 39 21N 74 27W
Atlantic Ocean 2 E9 0 0 20 0W
Atlas Mts. = Haut Atlas, Morocco 50 B4 32 30N 5 0W
Atlin, Canada 72 B2 59 31N 133 41W
Atlin, L., Canada 72 B2 59 26N 133 45W
Atlin Prov. Park, Canada 72 B2 59 10N 134 30W
Atmore, U.S.A. 77 K2 31 2N 87 29W
Atoka, U.S.A. 81 H6 34 23N 96 8W
Atolia, U.S.A. 85 K9 35 19N 117 37W
Atrai →, Bangla. 43 G13 24 7N 89 22 E
Atrak = Atrek →, Turkmenistan 45 B8 37 35N 53 58 E
Atrauli, India 42 E8 28 2N 78 20 E
Atrek →, Turkmenistan 45 B8 37 35N 53 58 E
Atsuta, Japan 30 C10 43 24N 141 26 E
Attalla, U.S.A. 77 H2 34 1N 86 6W
Attapu, Laos 38 E6 14 48N 106 50 E
Attáviros, Greece 23 C9 36 12N 27 50 E
Attawapiskat, Canada 70 B3 52 56N 82 24W
Attawapiskat →, Canada 70 B3 52 57N 82 18W
Attawapiskat L., Canada 70 B2 52 18N 87 54W
Attica, Ind., U.S.A. 76 E2 40 18N 87 15W
Attica, Ohio, U.S.A. 78 E2 41 4N 82 53W
Attikamagen L., Canada 71 B6 55 0N 66 30W
Attleboro, U.S.A. 79 E13 41 57N 71 17W
Attock, Pakistan 42 C5 33 52N 72 20 E
Attopeu = Attapu, Laos 38 E6 14 48N 106 50 E
Attu I., U.S.A. 68 C1 52 55N 172 55 E
Attur, India 40 P11 11 35N 78 30 E
Atuel →, Argentina 94 D2 36 17S 66 50W
Åtvidaberg, Sweden 9 G17 58 12N 16 0 E
Atwater, U.S.A. 84 H6 37 21N 120 37W
Atwood, Canada 78 C3 43 40N 81 1W
Atwood, U.S.A. 80 F4 39 48N 101 3W
Atyraū, Kazakstan 25 E9 47 5N 52 0 E
Au Sable, U.S.A. 78 B1 44 25N 83 20W
Au Sable →, U.S.A. 76 C4 44 25N 83 20W
Au Sable Forks, U.S.A. 79 B11 44 27N 73 41W
Au Sable Pt., U.S.A. 78 B1 44 20N 83 20W
Aubagne, France 18 E6 43 17N 5 37 E
Aubarca, C. d', Spain 22 B7 39 4N 1 22 E
Aube →, France 18 B5 48 34N 3 43 E
Auberry, U.S.A. 84 H7 37 7N 119 29W
Auburn, Ala., U.S.A. 77 J3 32 36N 85 29W
Auburn, Calif., U.S.A. 84 G5 38 54N 121 4W
Auburn, Ind., U.S.A. 76 E3 41 22N 85 4W
Auburn, Maine, U.S.A. 77 C10 44 6N 70 14W
Auburn, N.Y., U.S.A. 79 D8 42 56N 76 34W
Auburn, Nebr., U.S.A. 80 E7 40 23N 95 51W
Auburn, Pa., U.S.A. 79 F8 40 36N 76 6W
Auburn, Wash., U.S.A. 84 C4 47 18N 122 14W
Auburn Ra., Australia 63 D5 25 15S 150 30 E
Auburndale, U.S.A. 77 L5 28 4N 81 48W
Aubusson, France 18 D5 45 57N 2 11 E
Auch, France 18 E4 43 39N 0 36 E
Auckland, N.Z. 59 G5 36 52S 174 46 E
Auckland Is., Pac. Oc. 64 N8 50 40S 166 5 E
Aude →, France 18 E5 43 13N 3 14 E
Auden, Canada 70 B2 50 14N 87 53W
Audubon, U.S.A. 80 E7 41 43N 94 56W
Augathella, Australia 63 D4 25 48S 146 35 E
Aughnacloy, U.K. 13 B5 54 25N 6 59W
Augrabies Falls, S. Africa 56 D3 28 35S 20 20 E
Augsburg, Germany 16 D6 48 25N 10 52 E
Augusta, Australia 61 F2 34 19S 115 9 E
Augusta, Italy 20 F6 37 13N 15 13 E
Augusta, Ark., U.S.A. 81 H9 35 17N 91 22W
Augusta, Ga., U.S.A. 77 J5 33 28N 81 58W
Augusta, Kans., U.S.A. 81 G6 37 41N 96 59W
Augusta, Maine, U.S.A. 69 D13 44 19N 69 47W
Augusta, Mont., U.S.A. 82 C7 47 30N 112 24W
Augustów, Poland 17 B12 53 51N 23 0 E
Augustus, Mt., Australia 61 D2 24 20S 116 50 E
Augustus I., Australia 60 C3 15 20S 124 30 E
Aukum, U.S.A. 84 G6 38 34N 120 43W
Auld, L., Australia 60 D3 22 25S 123 50 E
Ault, U.S.A. 80 E2 40 35N 104 44W
Aunis, France 18 C3 46 5N 0 50W
Auponhia, Indonesia 37 E7 1 58S 125 27 E
Aur, Pulau, Malaysia 39 L5 2 35N 104 10 E
Auraiya, India 43 F8 26 28N 79 33 E
Aurangabad, Bihar, India 43 G11 24 45N 84 18 E
Aurangabad, Maharashtra, India 40 K9 19 50N 75 23 E
Aurich, Germany 16 B4 53 28N 7 28 E
Aurillac, France 18 D5 44 55N 2 26 E
Aurora, Canada 78 C5 44 0N 79 28W
Aurora, S. Africa 56 E2 32 40S 18 29 E
Aurora, Colo., U.S.A. 80 F2 39 44N 104 52W
Aurora, Ill., U.S.A. 76 E1 41 45N 88 19W
Aurora, Mo., U.S.A. 81 G8 36 58N 93 43W
Aurora, N.Y., U.S.A. 79 D8 42 45N 76 42W
Aurora, Nebr., U.S.A. 80 E6 40 52N 98 0W
Aurora, Ohio, U.S.A. 78 E3 41 21N 81 20W
Aurukun, Australia 62 A3 13 20S 141 45 E
Aus, Namibia 56 D2 26 35S 16 12 E
Ausable →, Canada 78 C3 43 19N 81 46W
Auschwitz = Oświęcim, Poland 17 C10 50 2N 19 11 E
Austin, Minn., U.S.A. 80 D8 43 40N 92 58W
Austin, Nev., U.S.A. 82 G5 39 30N 117 4W
Austin, Pa., U.S.A. 78 E6 41 38N 78 6W
Austin, Tex., U.S.A. 81 K6 30 17N 97 45W
Austin, L., Australia 61 E2 27 40S 118 0 E
Austin I., Canada 73 A10 61 10N 94 0W
Austra, Norway 8 D14 65 8N 11 55 E
Austral Is. = Tubuai Is., Pac. Oc. 65 K13 25 0S 150 0W
Austral Seamount Chain, Pac. Oc. 65 K13 24 0S 150 0W
Australia ■, Oceania 63 E3 23 0S 135 0 E
Australian Capital Territory □, Australia 63 F4 35 30S 149 0 E
Australind, Australia 61 F2 33 17S 115 42 E
Austria ■, Europe 16 E8 47 0N 14 0 E
Austvågøy, Norway 8 B16 68 20N 14 40 E
Autlán, Mexico 86 D4 19 40N 104 30W
Autun, France 18 C6 46 58N 4 17 E
Auvergne, France 18 D5 45 20N 3 15 E
Auvergne, Mts. d', France 18 D5 45 20N 2 55 E
Auxerre, France 18 C5 47 48N 3 32 E
Ava, U.S.A. 81 G8 36 57N 92 40W
Avallon, France 18 C5 47 30N 3 53 E
Avalon, U.S.A. 85 M8 33 21N 118 20W
Avalon Pen., Canada 71 C9 47 30N 53 20W
Avanos, Turkey 44 B2 38 43N 34 51 E
Avaré, Brazil 95 A6 23 4S 48 58W
Avawatz Mts., U.S.A. 85 K10 35 40N 116 30W
Aveiro, Brazil 93 D7 3 10S 55 5W
Aveiro, Portugal 19 B1 40 37N 8 38W
Āvej, Iran 45 C6 35 40N 49 15 E
Avellaneda, Argentina 94 C4 34 50S 58 10W
Avellino, Italy 20 D6 40 54N 14 47 E
Avenal, U.S.A. 84 K6 36 0N 120 8W
Aversa, Italy 20 D6 40 58N 14 12 E
Avery, U.S.A. 82 C6 47 15N 115 49W
Aves, Is. las, Venezuela 89 D6 12 0N 67 30W
Avesta, Sweden 9 F17 60 9N 16 10 E
Avezzano, Italy 20 C5 42 2N 13 25 E
Aviá Terai, Argentina 94 B3 26 45S 60 50W
Aviemore, U.K. 12 D5 57 12N 3 50W
Avignon, France 18 E6 43 57N 4 50 E
Ávila, Spain 19 B3 40 39N 4 43W
Avila Beach, U.S.A. 85 K6 35 11N 120 44W
Avilés, Spain 19 A3 43 35N 5 57W
Avis, U.S.A. 78 E7 41 11N 77 19W
Avoca, U.S.A. 78 D7 42 25N 77 25W
Avoca →, Australia 63 F3 35 40S 143 43 E
Avoca →, Ireland 13 D5 52 48N 6 10W
Avola, Canada 72 C5 51 45N 119 19W
Avola, Italy 20 F6 36 56N 15 7 E
Avon, U.S.A. 78 D7 42 55N 77 45W
Avon →, Australia 61 F2 31 40S 116 7 E
Avon →, Bristol, U.K. 11 F5 51 29N 2 41W
Avon →, Dorset, U.K. 11 G6 50 44N 1 46W
Avon →, Warks., U.K. 11 E5 52 0N 2 8W
Avon Park, U.S.A. 77 M5 27 36N 81 31W
Avondale, Zimbabwe 55 F3 17 43S 30 58 E
Avonlea, Canada 73 D8 50 0N 105 0W
Avonmore, Canada 79 A10 45 10N 74 58W
Avranches, France 18 B3 48 40N 1 20W
A'waj →, Syria 47 B5 33 23N 36 20 E
Awaji-Shima, Japan 31 G7 34 30N 134 50 E
'Awālī, Bahrain 45 E6 26 0N 50 30 E
Awantipur, India 43 C6 33 55N 75 3 E
Awasa, Ethiopia 46 F2 7 2N 38 28 E
Awash, Ethiopia 46 F3 9 1N 40 10 E
Awatere →, N.Z. 59 J5 41 37S 174 10 E
Awbārī, Libya 51 C8 26 46N 12 57 E
Awe, L., U.K. 12 E3 56 17N 5 16W
Awjilah, Libya 51 C10 29 8N 21 7 E
Axe →, U.K. 11 F5 50 42N 3 4W
Axel Heiberg I., Canada 4 B3 80 0N 90 0W
Axim, Ghana 50 H5 4 51N 2 15W
Axiós →, Greece 21 D10 40 57N 22 35 E
Axminster, U.K. 11 G4 50 46N 3 0W
Ayabaca, Peru 92 D3 4 40S 79 53W
Ayabe, Japan 31 G7 35 20N 135 20 E
Ayacucho, Argentina 94 D4 37 5S 58 20W
Ayacucho, Peru 92 F4 13 0S 74 0W
Ayaguz, Kazakstan 26 E9 48 10N 80 10 E
Ayamonte, Spain 19 D2 37 12N 7 24W
Ayan, Russia 27 D14 56 30N 138 16 E
Ayaviri, Peru 92 F4 14 50S 70 35W
Aydın, Turkey 21 F12 37 51N 27 51 E
Aydin □, Turkey 25 G4 37 50N 28 0 E
Ayer, U.S.A. 79 D13 42 34N 71 35W
Ayer's Cliff, Canada 79 A12 45 10N 72 3W
Ayers Rock, Australia 61 E5 25 23S 131 5 E
Ayia Aikateríni, Ákra, Greece 23 A3 39 50N 19 50 E
Ayia Dhéka, Greece 23 D6 35 3N 24 58 E
Ayia Gálini, Greece 23 D6 35 6N 24 41 E
Ayia Napa, Cyprus 23 E13 34 59N 34 0 E
Ayia Phyla, Cyprus 23 E12 34 43N 33 1 E
Ayia Varvára, Greece 23 D7 35 8N 25 1 E
Áyios Amvrósios, Cyprus 23 D12 35 20N 33 35 E
Áyios Evstrátios, Greece 21 E11 39 34N 24 58 E
Áyios Ioánnis, Ákra, Greece 23 D7 35 20N 25 40 E
Áyios Isidhoros, Greece 23 C9 36 9N 27 51 E
Áyios Matthaíos, Greece 23 B3 39 30N 19 47 E
Áyios Nikólaos, Greece 23 D7 35 11N 25 41 E
Áyios Seryios, Cyprus 23 D12 35 12N 33 53 E
Áyios Theodhoros, Cyprus 23 D13 35 22N 34 1 E
Aykino, Russia 24 B8 62 15N 49 56 E
Aylesbury, U.K. 11 F7 51 49N 0 49W
Aylmer, Canada 78 D4 42 46N 80 59W
Aylmer, L., Canada 68 B8 64 0N 110 8W
'Ayn, Wādī al, Oman 45 F7 22 15N 55 28 E
Ayn Dār, Si. Arabia 45 E7 25 55N 49 10 E
Ayn Zālah, Iraq 44 B4 36 45N 42 35 E
Ayolas, Paraguay 94 B4 27 10S 56 59W
Ayon, Ostrov, Russia 27 C17 69 50N 169 0 E
'Ayoûn el 'Atroûs, Mauritania 50 E4 16 38N 9 37W
Ayr, Australia 62 B4 19 35S 147 25 E
Ayr, Canada 78 C4 43 17N 80 27W
Ayr, U.K. 12 F4 55 28N 4 38W
Ayr →, U.K. 12 F4 55 28N 4 38W
Ayre, Pt. of, U.K. 10 C3 54 25N 4 21W
Ayton, Australia 62 B4 15 56S 145 22 E
Aytos, Bulgaria 21 C12 42 42N 27 16 E
Ayu, Kepulauan, Indonesia 37 D8 0 35N 131 5 E
Ayutla, Guatemala 88 D1 14 40N 92 10W
Ayutla, Mexico 87 D5 16 58N 99 17W
Ayvacık, Turkey 21 E12 39 36N 26 24 E
Ayvalık, Turkey 21 E12 39 20N 26 46 E
Az Zabadānī, Syria 47 B5 33 43N 36 5 E
Aẓ Ẓāhirīyah, West Bank 47 D3 31 25N 34 58 E
Aẓ Ẓahrān, Si. Arabia 45 E6 26 10N 50 7 E
Az Zarqā, Jordan 47 C5 32 5N 36 4 E
Az Zarqā', U.A.E. 45 E7 24 53N 53 4 E
Az Zībār, Iraq 44 B5 36 52N 44 4 E
Az Zilfī, Si. Arabia 44 E5 26 12N 44 52 E
Az Zubayr, Iraq 44 D5 30 26N 47 40 E
Azamgarh, India 43 F10 26 5N 83 13 E
Azangaro, Peru 92 F4 14 55S 70 13W
Āzār Shahr, Iran 44 B5 37 45N 45 59 E
Azarān, Iran 44 B5 37 25N 47 16 E
Azärbayjan = Azerbaijan ■, Asia 25 F8 40 20N 48 0 E
Āzarbāyjān-e Gharbī □, Iran 44 B5 37 0N 44 30 E
Āzarbāyjān-e Sharqī □, Iran 44 B5 37 20N 47 0 E
Azare, Nigeria 50 F8 11 55N 10 10 E
A'zāz, Syria 44 B3 36 36N 37 4 E
Azbine = Aïr, Niger 50 E7 18 30N 8 0 E
Azerbaijan ■, Asia 25 F8 40 20N 48 0 E
Azerbaijchan = Azerbaijan ■, Asia 25 F8 40 20N 48 0 E
Azimganj, India 43 G13 24 14N 88 16 E
Azogues, Ecuador 92 D3 2 35S 78 0W
Azores = Açores, Is. dos, Atl. Oc. 50 A1 38 0N 27 0W
Azov, Russia 25 E6 47 3N 39 25 E
Azov, Sea of, Europe 25 E6 46 0N 36 30 E
Azovskoye More = Azov, Sea of, Europe 25 E6 46 0N 36 30 E
Azraq ash Shīshān, Jordan 47 D5 31 50N 36 49 E
Aztec, U.S.A. 83 H10 36 49N 107 59W
Azúa de Compostela, Dom. Rep. 89 C5 18 25N 70 44W
Azuaga, Spain 19 C3 38 16N 5 39W
Azuero, Pen. de, Panama 88 E3 7 30N 80 30W
Azul, Argentina 94 D4 36 42S 59 43W
Azusa, U.S.A. 85 L9 34 8N 117 52W

B

Ba Don, Vietnam 38 D6 17 45N 106 26 E
Ba Dong, Vietnam 39 H6 9 40N 106 33 E
Ba Ngoi = Cam Lam, Vietnam 39 G7 11 54N 109 10 E
Ba Tri, Vietnam 39 G6 10 2N 106 36 E
Ba Xian = Bazhou, China 34 E9 39 8N 116 22 E
Baa, Indonesia 37 F6 10 50S 123 0 E
Baardeere = Bardera, Somali Rep. 46 G3 2 20N 42 27 E
Baarle-Nassau, Belgium 15 C4 51 27N 4 56 E
Bab el Mandeb, Red Sea 46 E3 12 35N 43 25 E
Bābā, Koh-i-, Afghan. 40 B5 34 30N 67 0 E
Baba Burnu, Turkey 21 E12 39 29N 26 2 E
Bābā Kalū, Iran 45 D6 30 7N 50 49 E
Babadag, Romania 17 F15 44 53N 28 44 E
Babadayhan, Turkmenistan 26 F7 37 42N 60 23 E
Babaeski, Turkey 21 D12 41 26N 27 6 E
Babahoyo, Ecuador 92 D3 1 40S 79 30W
Babai = Sarju →, India 43 F9 27 21N 81 23 E
Babar, Indonesia 37 F7 8 0S 129 30 E
Babar, Pakistan 42 D3 31 7N 69 32 E
Babarkach, Pakistan 42 E2 29 45N 68 0 E
Babb, U.S.A. 82 B7 48 51N 113 27W
Baberu, India 43 G9 25 33N 80 43 E
Babi Besar, Pulau, Malaysia 39 L4 2 25N 103 59 E
Babinda, Australia 62 B4 17 20S 145 56 E
Babine, Canada 72 B3 55 22N 126 37W
Babine →, Canada 72 B3 55 45N 127 44W
Babine L., Canada 72 C3 54 48N 126 0W
Babo, Indonesia 37 E8 2 30S 133 30 E
Bābol, Iran 45 B7 36 40N 52 50 E
Bābol Sar, Iran 45 B7 36 45N 52 45 E
Babruysk, Belarus 17 B15 53 10N 29 15 E
Babuhri, India 42 F3 26 49N 69 43 E
Babusar Pass, Pakistan 43 B5 35 12N 73 59 E
Babuyan Chan., Phil. 37 A6 18 40N 121 30 E
Babylon, Iraq 44 C5 32 34N 44 22 E
Bac Can, Vietnam 38 A5 22 8N 105 49 E
Bac Giang, Vietnam 38 B6 21 16N 106 11 E
Bac Lieu, Vietnam 39 H5 9 17N 105 43 E
Bac Ninh, Vietnam 38 B6 21 13N 106 4 E
Bac Phan, Vietnam 38 B5 22 0N 105 0 E
Bac Quang, Vietnam 38 A5 22 30N 104 48 E
Bacabal, Brazil 93 D10 4 15S 44 45W
Bacalar, Mexico 87 D7 18 50N 87 27W
Bacan, Kepulauan, Indonesia 37 E7 0 35S 127 30 E
Bacarra, Phil. 37 A6 18 15N 120 37 E
Bacău, Romania 17 E14 46 35N 26 55 E
Bacerac, Mexico 86 A3 30 18N 108 50W
Bach Long Vi, Dao, Vietnam 38 B6 20 10N 107 40 E
Bachelina, Russia 26 D7 57 45N 67 20 E
Bachhwara, India 43 G11 25 35N 85 54 E
Back →, Canada 68 B9 65 10N 104 0W
Bacolod, Phil. 37 B6 10 40N 122 57 E
Bacuk, Malaysia 39 J4 6 4N 102 25 E
Bād, Iran 45 C7 33 41N 52 1 E
Bad →, U.S.A. 80 C4 44 21N 100 22W
Bad Axe, U.S.A. 78 C2 43 48N 83 0W
Bad Ischl, Austria 16 E7 47 44N 13 38 E
Bad Kissingen, Germany 16 C6 50 11N 10 4 E
Bad Lands, U.S.A. 80 D3 43 40N 102 10W
Bada Barabil, India 43 H11 22 7N 85 24 E
Badagara, India 40 P9 11 35N 75 40 E
Badajós, L., Brazil 92 D6 3 15S 62 50W
Badajoz, Spain 19 C2 38 50N 6 59W
Badakhshān □, Afghan. 40 A7 36 30N 71 0 E
Badalona, Spain 19 B7 41 26N 2 15 E
Badalzai, Afghan. 42 E1 29 50N 65 35 E
Badampahar, India 41 H15 22 10N 86 10 E
Badanah, Si. Arabia 44 D4 30 58N 41 30 E
Badarinath, India 43 D8 30 45N 79 30 E
Badas, Kepulauan, Indonesia 36 D3 0 45N 107 5 E
Baddo →, Pakistan 40 F4 28 0N 64 20 E
Bade, Indonesia 37 F9 7 10S 139 35 E
Baden, Austria 16 D9 48 1N 16 13 E
Baden, U.S.A. 78 F4 40 38N 80 14W
Baden-Baden, Germany 16 D5 48 44N 8 13 E
Baden-Württemberg □, Germany 16 D5 48 20N 8 40 E
Badgastein, Austria 16 E7 47 7N 13 9 E
Badger, Canada 71 C8 49 0N 56 4W
Badger, U.S.A. 84 J7 36 38N 119 1W
Bādghīs □, Afghan. 40 B3 35 0N 63 0 E
Badgom, India 43 B6 34 1N 74 45 E
Badin, Pakistan 42 G3 24 38N 68 54 E
Badlands Nat. Park, U.S.A. 80 D3 43 38N 102 56W
Badrah, Iraq 44 C5 33 6N 45 58 E
Badrinath, India 43 D8 30 44N 79 29 E
Badulla, Sri Lanka 40 R12 7 1N 81 7 E
Baena, Spain 19 D3 37 37N 4 20W
Baeza, Spain 19 D4 37 57N 3 25W
Baffin B., Canada 69 A13 72 0N 64 0W
Baffin I., Canada 69 B12 68 0N 75 0W
Bafing →, Mali 50 F3 13 49N 10 50W
Bafliyūn, Syria 44 B3 36 37N 36 59 E
Bafoulabé, Mali 50 F3 13 50N 10 55W
Bāfq, Iran 45 D7 31 40N 55 25 E
Bafra, Turkey 25 F6 41 34N 35 56 E
Bāft, Iran 45 D8 29 15N 56 38 E
Bafwasende, Dem. Rep. of the Congo 54 B2 1 3N 27 5 E

Bagamoyo, *Tanzania* 54 D4 6 28S 38 55 E
Bagan Datoh, *Malaysia* 39 L3 3 59N 100 47 E
Bagan Serai, *Malaysia* 39 K3 5 1N 100 32 E
Baganga, *Phil.* 37 C7 7 34N 126 33 E
Bagani, *Namibia* 56 B3 18 7S 21 41 E
Bagansiapiapi, *Indonesia* 36 D2 2 12N 100 50 E
Bagasra, *India* 42 J4 21 30N 71 0 E
Bagaud, *India* 42 H6 22 19N 75 53 E
Bagdad, *U.S.A.* 85 L11 34 35N 115 53W
Bagdarin, *Russia* 27 D12 54 26N 113 36 E
Bagé, *Brazil* 95 C5 31 20S 54 15W
Bagenalstown = Muine Bheag, *Ireland* 13 D5 52 42N 6 58W
Baggs, *U.S.A.* 82 F10 41 2N 107 39W
Bagh, *Pakistan* 43 C5 33 59N 73 45 E
Baghain →, *India* 43 G9 25 32N 81 1 E
Baghdād, *Iraq* 44 C5 33 20N 44 30 E
Bagheria, *Italy* 20 E5 38 5N 13 30 E
Baghlān, *Afghan.* 40 A6 32 12N 68 46 E
Baghlān □, *Afghan.* 40 B6 36 0N 68 30 E
Bagley, *U.S.A.* 80 B7 47 32N 95 24W
Bago = Pegu, *Burma* 41 L20 17 20N 96 29 E
Bagodar, *India* 43 G11 24 5N 85 52 E
Bagrationovsk, *Russia* 9 J19 54 23N 20 39 E
Baguio, *Phil.* 37 A6 16 26N 120 34 E
Bah, *India* 43 F8 26 53N 78 36 E
Bahadurganj, *India* 43 F12 26 16N 87 49 E
Bahadurgarh, *India* 42 E7 28 40N 76 57 E
Bahama, Canal Viejo de, *W. Indies* 88 B4 22 10N 77 30W
Bahamas ■, *N. Amer.* 89 B5 24 0N 75 0W
Baharampur, *India* 43 G13 24 2N 88 27 E
Bahawalnagar, *Pakistan* 42 E5 30 0N 73 15 E
Bahawalpur, *Pakistan* 42 E4 29 24N 71 40 E
Baheri, *India* 43 E8 28 45N 79 34 E
Bahgul →, *India* 43 F8 27 45N 79 36 E
Bahi, *Tanzania* 54 D4 5 58S 35 21 E
Bahi Swamp, *Tanzania* 54 D4 6 10S 35 0 E
Bahia = Salvador, *Brazil* 93 F11 13 0S 38 30W
Bahia □, *Brazil* 93 F10 12 0S 42 0W
Bahía, Is. de la, *Honduras* 88 C2 16 45N 86 15W
Bahía Blanca, *Argentina* 94 D3 38 35S 62 13W
Bahía de Caráquez, *Ecuador* 92 D2 0 40S 80 27W
Bahía Honda, *Cuba* 88 B3 22 54N 83 10W
Bahía Laura, *Argentina* 96 F3 48 10S 66 30W
Bahía Negra, *Paraguay* 92 H7 20 5S 58 5W
Bahir Dar, *Ethiopia* 46 E2 11 37N 37 10 E
Bahmanzād, *Iran* 45 D6 31 15N 51 47 E
Bahr el Ghazâl □, *Sudan* 51 G11 7 0N 28 0 E
Bahraich, *India* 43 F9 27 38N 81 37 E
Bahrain ■, *Asia* 46 B5 26 0N 50 35 E
Bahror, *India* 42 F7 27 51N 76 20 E
Bāhū Kalāt, *Iran* 45 E9 25 43N 61 25 E
Bai Bung, Mui = Ca Mau, Mui, *Vietnam* 39 H5 8 38N 104 44 E
Bai Duc, *Vietnam* 38 C5 18 3N 105 49 E
Bai Thuong, *Vietnam* 38 C5 19 54N 105 23 E
Baia Mare, *Romania* 17 E12 47 40N 23 35 E
Baião, *Brazil* 93 D9 2 40S 49 40W
Baïbokoum, *Chad* 51 G9 7 46N 15 43 E
Baicheng, *China* 35 B12 45 38N 122 42 E
Baidoa, *Somali Rep.* 46 G3 3 8N 43 30 E
Baie Comeau, *Canada* 71 C6 49 12N 68 10W
Baie-St-Paul, *Canada* 71 C5 47 28N 70 32W
Baie Trinité, *Canada* 71 C6 49 25N 67 20W
Baie Verte, *Canada* 71 C8 49 55N 56 12W
Baihar, *India* 43 H9 22 6N 80 33 E
Baihe, *China* 34 H6 32 50N 110 5 E
Ba'ījī, *Iraq* 44 C4 35 0N 43 30 E
Baijnath, *India* 43 E8 29 55N 79 37 E
Baikal, L. = Baykal, Oz., *Russia* 27 D11 53 0N 108 0 E
Baikunthpur, *India* 43 H10 23 15N 82 33 E
Baile Atha Cliath = Dublin, *Ireland* 13 C5 53 21N 6 15W
Băileşti, *Romania* 17 F12 44 1N 23 20 E
Bainbridge, *Ga., U.S.A.* 77 K3 30 55N 84 35W
Bainbridge, *N.Y., U.S.A.* 79 D9 42 18N 75 29W
Baing, *Indonesia* 37 F6 10 14S 120 34 E
Bainiu, *China* 34 H7 32 50N 112 15 E
Bā'ir, *Jordan* 47 E5 30 45N 36 55 E
Bairin Youqi, *China* 35 C10 43 30N 118 35 E
Bairin Zuoqi, *China* 35 C10 43 58N 119 15 E
Bairnsdale, *Australia* 63 F4 37 48S 147 36 E
Baisha, *China* 34 G7 34 20N 112 32 E
Baitadi, *Nepal* 43 E9 29 35N 80 25 E
Baiyin, *China* 34 F3 36 45N 104 14 E
Baiyu Shan, *China* 34 F4 37 15N 107 30 E
Baj Baj, *India* 43 H13 22 30N 88 5 E
Baja, *Hungary* 17 E10 46 12N 18 59 E
Baja, Pta., *Mexico* 86 B1 29 50N 116 0W
Baja California, *Mexico* 86 A1 31 10N 115 12W
Baja California □, *Mexico* 86 B2 30 0N 115 0W
Baja California Sur □, *Mexico* 86 B2 25 50N 111 50W
Bajag, *India* 43 H9 22 40N 81 21 E
Bajamar, *Canary Is.* 22 F3 28 33N 16 20W
Bajana, *India* 42 H4 23 7N 71 49 E
Bājgīrān, *Iran* 45 B8 37 36N 58 24 E
Bajimba, Mt., *Australia* 63 D5 29 17S 152 6 E
Bajo Nuevo, *Caribbean* 88 C4 15 40N 78 50W
Bajoga, *Nigeria* 51 F8 10 57N 11 20 E
Bajool, *Australia* 62 C5 23 40S 150 35 E
Bakel, *Senegal* 50 F3 14 56N 12 20W
Baker, *Calif., U.S.A.* 85 K10 35 16N 116 4W
Baker, *Mont., U.S.A.* 80 B2 46 22N 104 17W
Baker, L., *Canada* 68 B10 64 0N 96 0W
Baker City, *U.S.A.* 82 D5 44 47N 117 50W
Baker I., *Pac. Oc.* 64 G10 0 10N 176 35W
Baker I., *U.S.A.* 72 B2 55 20N 133 40W
Baker L., *Australia* 61 E4 26 54S 126 5 E
Baker Lake, *Canada* 68 B10 64 20N 96 3W
Baker Mt., *U.S.A.* 82 B3 48 50N 121 49W
Bakers Creek, *Australia* 62 C4 21 13S 149 7 E
Baker's Dozen Is., *Canada* 70 A4 56 45N 78 45W
Bakersfield, *Calif., U.S.A.* 85 K8 35 23N 119 1W
Bakersfield, *Vt., U.S.A.* 79 B12 44 45N 72 48W
Bākhtarān, *Iran* 44 C5 34 23N 47 0 E
Bākhtarān □, *Iran* 44 C5 34 0N 46 30 E
Bakı, *Azerbaijan* 25 F8 40 29N 49 56 E
Bakkafjörður, *Iceland* 8 C6 66 2N 14 48W
Bakony, *Hungary* 17 E9 47 10N 17 30 E
Bakony Forest = Bakony, *Hungary* 17 E9 47 10N 17 30 E
Bakouma, *C.A.R.* 52 C4 5 40N 22 56 E
Bakswaho, *India* 43 G8 24 15N 79 18 E
Baku = Bakı, *Azerbaijan* 25 F8 40 29N 49 56 E
Bakutis Coast, *Antarctica* 5 D15 74 0S 120 0W
Baky = Bakı, *Azerbaijan* 25 F8 40 29N 49 56 E
Bala, *Canada* 78 A5 45 1N 79 37W
Bala, *U.K.* 10 E4 52 54N 3 36W
Bala, L., *U.K.* 10 E4 52 53N 3 37W
Balabac I., *Phil.* 36 C5 8 0N 117 0 E
Balabac Str., *E. Indies* 36 C5 7 53N 117 5 E
Balabagh, *Afghan.* 42 B4 34 25N 70 12 E
Ba'labakk, *Lebanon* 47 B5 34 0N 36 10 E
Balabalangan, Kepulauan, *Indonesia* 36 E5 2 20S 117 30 E
Balad, *Iraq* 44 C5 34 1N 44 9 E
Balad Rūz, *Iraq* 44 C5 33 42N 45 5 E
Bālādeh, *Fārs, Iran* 45 D6 29 17N 51 56 E
Bālādeh, *Māzandaran, Iran* 45 B6 36 12N 51 48 E
Balaghat, *India* 40 J12 21 49N 80 12 E
Balaghat Ra., *India* 40 K10 18 50N 76 30 E
Balaguer, *Spain* 19 B6 41 50N 0 50 E
Balaklava, *Ukraine* 25 F5 44 30N 33 30 E
Balakovo, *Russia* 24 D8 52 4N 47 55 E
Balamau, *India* 43 F9 27 10N 80 21 E
Balancán, *Mexico* 87 D6 17 48N 91 32W
Balashov, *Russia* 25 D7 51 30N 43 10 E
Balasinor, *India* 42 H5 22 57N 73 23 E
Balasore = Baleshwar, *India* 41 J15 21 35N 87 3 E
Balaton, *Hungary* 17 E9 46 50N 17 40 E
Balbina, Reprêsa de, *Brazil* 92 D7 2 0S 59 30W
Balboa, *Panama* 88 E4 8 57N 79 34W
Balbriggan, *Ireland* 13 C5 53 37N 6 11W
Balcarce, *Argentina* 94 D4 38 0S 58 10W
Balcarres, *Canada* 73 C8 50 50N 103 35W
Balchik, *Bulgaria* 21 C13 43 28N 28 11 E
Balclutha, *N.Z.* 59 M2 46 15S 169 45 E
Balcones Escarpment, *U.S.A.* 81 L5 29 30N 99 15W
Bald Hd., *Australia* 61 G2 35 6S 118 1 E
Bald I., *Australia* 61 F2 34 57S 118 27 E
Bald Knob, *U.S.A.* 81 H9 35 19N 91 34W
Baldock L., *Canada* 73 B9 56 33N 97 57W
Baldwin, *Mich., U.S.A.* 76 D3 43 54N 85 51W
Baldwin, *Pa., U.S.A.* 78 F5 40 23N 79 59W
Baldwinsville, *U.S.A.* 79 C8 43 10N 76 20W
Baldy Mt., *U.S.A.* 82 B9 48 9N 109 39W
Baldy Peak, *U.S.A.* 83 K9 33 54N 109 34W
Baleares, Is., *Spain* 22 B10 39 30N 3 0 E
Balearic Is. = Baleares, Is., *Spain* 22 B10 39 30N 3 0 E
Baleine = Whale →, *Canada* 71 A6 58 15N 67 40W
Baler, *Phil.* 37 A6 15 46N 121 34 E
Baleshare, *U.K.* 12 D1 57 31N 7 22W
Baleshwar, *India* 41 J15 21 35N 87 3 E
Balfate, *Honduras* 88 C2 15 48N 86 25W
Bali, *Greece* 23 D6 35 25N 24 47 E
Bali, *India* 42 G5 25 11N 73 17 E
Bali, *Indonesia* 36 F4 8 20S 115 0 E
Bali □, *Indonesia* 36 F5 8 20S 115 0 E
Bali, Selat, *Indonesia* 37 H16 8 18S 114 25 E
Baliapal, *India* 43 J12 21 40N 87 17 E
Balikeşir, *Turkey* 21 E12 39 39N 27 53 E
Balikpapan, *Indonesia* 36 E5 1 10S 116 55 E
Balimbing, *Phil.* 37 C5 5 5N 119 58 E
Baling, *Malaysia* 39 K3 5 41N 100 55 E
Balipara, *India* 41 F18 26 50N 92 45 E
Balkan Mts. = Stara Planina, *Bulgaria* 21 C10 43 15N 23 0 E
Balkhash = Balqash, *Kazakstan* 26 E8 46 50N 74 50 E
Balkhash, Ozero = Balqash Köl, *Kazakstan* 26 E8 46 0N 74 50 E
Balla, *Bangla.* 41 G17 24 10N 91 35 E
Ballachulish, *U.K.* 12 E3 56 41N 5 8W
Balladonia, *Australia* 61 F3 32 27S 123 51 E
Ballaghaderreen, *Ireland* 13 C3 53 55N 8 34W
Ballarat, *Australia* 63 F3 37 33S 143 50 E
Ballard, L., *Australia* 61 E3 29 20S 120 40 E
Ballater, *U.K.* 12 D5 57 3N 3 3W
Ballenas, Canal de, *Mexico* 86 B2 29 10N 113 45W
Balleny Is., *Antarctica* 5 C11 66 30S 163 0 E
Ballia, *India* 43 G11 25 46N 84 12 E
Ballina, *Australia* 63 D5 28 50S 153 31 E
Ballina, *Ireland* 13 B2 54 7N 9 9W
Ballinasloe, *Ireland* 13 C3 53 20N 8 13W
Ballinger, *U.S.A.* 81 K5 31 45N 99 57W
Ballinrobe, *Ireland* 13 C2 53 38N 9 13W
Ballinskelligs B., *Ireland* 13 E1 51 48N 10 13W
Ballston Spa, *U.S.A.* 79 D11 43 0N 73 51W
Ballycastle, *U.K.* 13 A5 55 12N 6 15W
Ballyclare, *U.K.* 13 B5 54 46N 6 0W
Ballyhaunis, *Ireland* 13 C3 53 46N 8 46W
Ballymena, *U.K.* 13 B5 54 52N 6 17W
Ballymoney, *U.K.* 13 A5 55 5N 6 31W
Ballymote, *Ireland* 13 B3 54 5N 8 31W
Ballynahinch, *U.K.* 13 B6 54 24N 5 54W
Ballyquintin Pt., *U.K.* 13 B6 54 20N 5 30W
Ballyshannon, *Ireland* 13 B3 54 30N 8 11W
Balmaceda, *Chile* 96 F2 46 0S 71 50W
Balmertown, *Canada* 73 C10 51 4N 93 41W
Balmoral, *Australia* 63 F3 37 15S 141 48 E
Balmorhea, *U.S.A.* 81 K3 30 59N 103 45W
Balochistan = Baluchistan □, *Pakistan* 40 F4 27 30N 65 0 E
Balonne →, *Australia* 63 D4 28 47S 147 56 E
Balotra, *India* 42 G5 25 50N 72 14 E
Balqash, *Kazakstan* 26 E8 46 50N 74 50 E
Balqash Köl, *Kazakstan* 26 E8 46 0N 74 50 E
Balrampur, *India* 43 F10 27 30N 82 20 E
Balranald, *Australia* 63 E3 34 38S 143 33 E
Balsas, *Mexico* 87 D5 18 0N 99 40W
Balsas →, *Brazil* 93 E9 7 15S 44 35W
Balsas →, *Mexico* 86 D4 17 55N 102 10W
Balston Spa, *U.S.A.* 79 D11 43 0N 73 52W
Balta, *Ukraine* 17 D15 48 2N 29 45 E
Bălţi, *Moldova* 17 E14 47 48N 27 58 E
Baltic Sea, *Europe* 9 H18 57 0N 19 0 E
Baltimore, *Ireland* 13 E2 51 29N 9 22W
Baltimore, *Md., U.S.A.* 76 F7 39 17N 76 37W
Baltimore, *Ohio, U.S.A.* 78 G2 39 51N 82 36W
Baltit, *Pakistan* 43 A6 36 15N 74 40 E
Baltiysk, *Russia* 9 J18 54 41N 19 58 E
Baluchistan □, *Pakistan* 40 F4 27 30N 65 0 E
Balurghat, *India* 43 G13 25 15N 88 44 E
Balvi, *Latvia* 9 H22 57 8N 27 15 E
Balya, *Turkey* 21 E12 39 44N 27 35 E
Bam, *Iran* 45 D8 29 7N 58 14 E
Bama, *Nigeria* 51 F8 11 33N 13 41 E
Bamaga, *Australia* 62 A3 10 50S 142 25 E
Bamaji L., *Canada* 70 B1 51 9N 91 25W
Bamako, *Mali* 50 F4 12 34N 7 55W
Bambari, *C.A.R.* 52 C4 5 40N 20 35 E
Bambaroo, *Australia* 62 B4 18 50S 146 10 E
Bamberg, *Germany* 16 D6 49 54N 10 53 E
Bamberg, *U.S.A.* 77 J5 33 18N 81 2W
Bambili, *Dem. Rep. of the Congo* 54 B2 3 40N 26 0 E
Bamfield, *Canada* 72 D3 48 45N 125 10W
Bāmīān □, *Afghan.* 40 B5 35 0N 67 0 E
Bamiancheng, *China* 35 C13 43 15N 124 2 E
Bampūr, *Iran* 45 E9 27 15N 60 21 E
Ban Ban, *Laos* 38 C4 19 31N 103 30 E
Ban Bang Hin, *Thailand* 39 H2 9 32N 98 35 E
Ban Chiang Klang, *Thailand* 38 C3 19 25N 100 55 E
Ban Chik, *Laos* 38 D4 17 15N 102 22 E
Ban Choho, *Thailand* 38 E4 15 2N 102 9 E
Ban Dan Lan Hoi, *Thailand* 38 D2 17 0N 99 35 E
Ban Don = Surat Thani, *Thailand* 39 H2 9 6N 99 20 E
Ban Don, *Vietnam* 38 F6 12 53N 107 48 E
Ban Don, Ao →, *Thailand* 39 H2 9 20N 99 25 E
Ban Dong, *Thailand* 38 C3 19 30N 100 59 E
Ban Hong, *Thailand* 38 C2 18 18N 98 50 E
Ban Kaeng, *Thailand* 38 D3 17 29N 100 7 E
Ban Kantang, *Thailand* 39 J2 7 25N 99 31 E
Ban Keun, *Laos* 38 C4 18 22N 102 35 E
Ban Khai, *Thailand* 38 F3 12 46N 101 18 E
Ban Kheun, *Laos* 38 B3 20 13N 101 7 E
Ban Khlong Kua, *Thailand* 39 J3 6 57N 100 8 E
Ban Khuan Mao, *Thailand* 39 J2 7 50N 99 37 E
Ban Ko Yai Chim, *Thailand* 39 G2 11 17N 99 26 E
Ban Kok, *Thailand* 38 D4 16 40N 103 40 E
Ban Laem, *Thailand* 38 F2 13 13N 99 59 E
Ban Lao Ngam, *Laos* 38 E6 15 28N 106 10 E
Ban Le Kathe, *Thailand* 38 E2 15 49N 98 53 E
Ban Mae Chedi, *Thailand* 38 C2 19 11N 99 31 E
Ban Mae Laeng, *Thailand* 38 B2 20 1N 99 17 E
Ban Mae Sariang, *Thailand* 38 C1 18 10N 97 56 E
Ban Mê Thuôt = Buon Ma Thuot, *Vietnam* 38 F7 12 40N 108 3 E
Ban Mi, *Thailand* 38 E3 15 3N 100 32 E
Ban Muong Mo, *Laos* 38 C4 19 4N 103 58 E
Ban Na Mo, *Laos* 38 D5 17 7N 105 40 E
Ban Na San, *Thailand* 39 H2 8 53N 99 52 E
Ban Na Tong, *Laos* 38 B3 20 56N 101 47 E
Ban Nam Bac, *Laos* 38 B4 20 38N 102 20 E
Ban Nam Ma, *Laos* 38 A3 22 2N 101 37 E
Ban Ngang, *Laos* 38 E6 15 59N 106 11 E
Ban Nong Bok, *Laos* 38 D5 17 5N 104 48 E
Ban Nong Boua, *Laos* 38 E6 15 40N 106 33 E
Ban Nong Pling, *Thailand* 38 E3 15 40N 100 10 E
Ban Pak Chan, *Thailand* 39 G2 10 32N 98 51 E
Ban Phai, *Thailand* 38 D4 16 4N 102 44 E
Ban Pong, *Thailand* 38 F2 13 50N 99 55 E
Ban Ron Phibun, *Thailand* 39 H2 8 9N 99 51 E
Ban Sanam Chai, *Thailand* 39 J3 7 33N 100 25 E
Ban Sangkha, *Thailand* 38 E4 14 37N 103 52 E
Ban Tak, *Thailand* 38 D2 17 2N 99 4 E
Ban Tako, *Thailand* 38 E4 14 5N 102 40 E
Ban Tha Dua, *Thailand* 38 D2 17 59N 98 39 E
Ban Tha Li, *Thailand* 38 D3 17 37N 101 25 E
Ban Tha Nun, *Thailand* 39 H2 8 12N 98 18 E
Ban Thahine, *Laos* 38 E5 14 12N 105 33 E
Ban Xien Kok, *Laos* 38 B3 20 54N 100 39 E
Ban Yen Nhan, *Vietnam* 38 B6 20 57N 106 2 E
Banaba, *Kiribati* 64 H8 0 45S 169 50 E
Banalia, *Dem. Rep. of the Congo* 54 B2 1 32N 25 5 E
Banam, *Cambodia* 39 G5 11 20N 105 17 E
Bananal, I. do, *Brazil* 93 F8 11 30S 50 30W
Banaras = Varanasi, *India* 43 G10 25 22N 83 0 E
Banas →, *Gujarat, India* 42 H4 23 45N 71 25 E
Banas →, *Mad. P., India* 43 G9 24 15N 81 30 E
Bânâs, Ras, *Egypt* 51 D13 23 57N 35 59 E
Banbridge, *U.K.* 13 B5 54 22N 6 16W
Banbury, *U.K.* 11 E6 52 4N 1 20W
Banchory, *U.K.* 12 D6 57 3N 2 29W
Bancroft, *Canada* 78 A7 45 3N 77 51W
Band Bonī, *Iran* 45 E8 25 30N 59 33 E
Band Qīr, *Iran* 45 D6 31 39N 48 53 E
Banda, *Mad. P., India* 43 G8 24 3N 78 57 E
Banda, *Ut. P., India* 43 G9 25 30N 80 26 E
Banda, Kepulauan, *Indonesia* 37 E7 4 37S 129 50 E
Banda Aceh, *Indonesia* 36 C1 5 35N 95 20 E
Banda Banda, Mt., *Australia* 63 E5 31 10S 152 28 E
Banda Elat, *Indonesia* 37 F8 5 40S 133 5 E
Banda Is. = Banda, Kepulauan, *Indonesia* 37 E7 4 37S 129 50 E
Banda Sea, *Indonesia* 37 F7 6 0S 130 0 E
Bandai-San, *Japan* 30 F10 37 36N 140 4 E
Bandān, *Iran* 45 D9 31 23N 60 44 E
Bandanaira, *Indonesia* 37 E7 4 32S 129 54 E
Bandanwara, *India* 42 F6 26 9N 74 38 E
Bandar = Machilipatnam, *India* 41 L12 16 12N 81 8 E
Bandār 'Abbās, *Iran* 45 E8 27 15N 56 15 E
Bandar-e Anzalī, *Iran* 45 B6 37 30N 49 30 E
Bandar-e Bushehr = Būshehr, *Iran* 45 D6 28 55N 50 55 E
Bandar-e Chārak, *Iran* 45 E7 26 45N 54 20 E
Bandar-e Deylam, *Iran* 45 D6 30 5N 50 10 E
Bandar-e Khomeynı, *Iran* 45 D6 30 30N 49 5 E
Bandar-e Lengeh, *Iran* 45 E7 26 35N 54 58 E
Bandar-e Maqām, *Iran* 45 E7 26 56N 53 29 E
Bandar-e Ma'shur, *Iran* 45 D6 30 35N 49 10 E
Bandar-e Rīg, *Iran* 45 D6 29 29N 50 38 E
Bandar-e Torkeman, *Iran* 45 B7 37 0N 54 10 E
Bandar Maharani = Muar, *Malaysia* 39 L4 2 3N 102 34 E
Bandar Penggaram = Batu Pahat, *Malaysia* 39 M4 1 50N 102 56 E
Bandar Seri Begawan, *Brunei* 36 C4 4 52N 115 0 E
Bandar Sri Aman, *Malaysia* 36 D4 1 15N 111 32 E
Bandawe, *Malawi* 55 E3 11 58S 34 5 E
Bandeira, Pico da, *Brazil* 95 A7 20 26S 41 47W
Bandera, *Argentina* 94 B3 28 55S 62 20W
Banderas, B. de, *Mexico* 86 C3 20 40N 105 30W
Bandhogarh, *India* 43 H9 23 40N 81 2 E
Bandi →, *India* 42 F6 26 12N 75 47 E
Bandikui, *India* 42 F7 27 3N 76 34 E
Bandırma, *Turkey* 21 D13 40 20N 28 0 E
Bandon, *Ireland* 13 E3 51 44N 8 44W
Bandon →, *Ireland* 13 E3 51 43N 8 37W
Bandula, *Mozam.* 55 F3 19 0S 33 7 E
Bandundu, *Dem. Rep. of the Congo* 52 E3 3 15S 17 22 E
Bandung, *Indonesia* 36 F3 6 54S 107 36 E
Bāneh, *Iran* 44 C5 35 59N 45 53 E
Banes, *Cuba* 89 B4 21 0N 75 42W
Banff, *Canada* 72 C5 51 10N 115 34W
Banff, *U.K.* 12 D6 57 40N 2 33W
Banff Nat. Park, *Canada* 72 C5 51 30N 116 15W
Bang Fai →, *Laos* 38 D5 16 57N 104 45 E
Bang Hieng →, *Laos* 38 D5 16 10N 105 10 E
Bang Krathum, *Thailand* 38 D3 16 34N 100 18 E
Bang Lamung, *Thailand* 38 F3 13 3N 100 56 E
Bang Mun Nak, *Thailand* 38 D3 16 2N 100 23 E
Bang Pa In, *Thailand* 38 E3 14 14N 100 35 E
Bang Rakam, *Thailand* 38 D3 16 45N 100 7 E
Bang Saphan, *Thailand* 39 G2 11 14N 99 28 E
Bangaduni I., *India* 43 J13 21 34N 88 52 E
Bangala Dam, *Zimbabwe* 55 G3 21 7S 31 25 E
Bangalore, *India* 40 N10 12 59N 77 40 E
Banganga →, *India* 42 F6 27 6N 77 25 E
Bangaon, *India* 43 H13 23 0N 88 47 E
Bangassou, *C.A.R.* 52 D4 4 55N 23 7 E
Banggai, *Indonesia* 37 E6 1 34S 123 30 E
Banggai, Kepulauan, *Indonesia* 37 E6 1 40S 123 30 E
Banggai Arch. = Banggai, Kepulauan, *Indonesia* 37 E6 1 40S 123 30 E
Banggi, *Malaysia* 36 C5 7 17N 117 5 E
Banghāzī, *Libya* 51 B10 32 11N 20 3 E
Bangka, *Sulawesi, Indonesia* 37 D7 1 50N 125 5 E
Bangka, *Sumatera, Indonesia* 36 E3 2 0S 105 50 E
Bangka, Selat, *Indonesia* 36 E3 2 30S 105 30 E
Bangkalan, *Indonesia* 37 G15 7 2S 112 46 E
Bangkinang, *Indonesia* 36 D2 0 18N 101 5 E
Bangko, *Indonesia* 36 E2 2 5S 102 9 E
Bangkok, *Thailand* 38 F3 13 45N 100 35 E
Bangladesh ■, *Asia* 41 H17 24 0N 90 0 E
Bangong Co, *India* 43 B8 35 50N 79 20 E
Bangor, *Down, U.K.* 13 B6 54 40N 5 40W
Bangor, *Gwynedd, U.K.* 10 D3 53 14N 4 8W
Bangor, *Maine, U.S.A.* 69 D13 44 48N 68 46W
Bangor, *Pa., U.S.A.* 79 F9 40 52N 75 13W
Bangued, *Phil.* 37 A6 17 40N 120 37 E
Bangui, *C.A.R.* 52 D3 4 23N 18 35 E
Banguru, *Dem. Rep. of the Congo* 54 B2 0 30N 27 10 E
Bangweulu, L., *Zambia* 55 E3 11 0S 30 0 E
Bangweulu Swamp, *Zambia* 55 E3 11 20S 30 15 E
Bani, *Dom. Rep.* 89 C5 18 16N 70 22W
Banī Sa'd, *Iraq* 44 C5 33 34N 44 32 E
Banihal Pass, *India* 43 C6 33 30N 75 12 E
Bāniyās, *Syria* 44 C3 35 10N 36 0 E
Banja Luka, *Bos.-H.* 20 B7 44 49N 17 11 E
Banjar, *India* 42 D7 31 38N 77 21 E
Banjar →, *India* 43 H9 22 36N 80 22 E
Banjarmasin, *Indonesia* 36 E4 3 20S 114 35 E
Banjul, *Gambia* 50 F2 13 28N 16 40W
Banka, *India* 43 G12 24 53N 86 55 E
Banket, *Zimbabwe* 55 F3 17 27S 30 19 E
Bankipore, *India* 41 G14 25 35N 85 10 E
Banks I., *B.C., Canada* 72 C3 53 20N 130 0W
Banks I., *N.W.T., Canada* 68 A7 73 15N 121 30W
Banks Pen., *N.Z.* 59 K4 43 45S 173 15 E
Banks Str., *Australia* 62 G4 40 40S 148 10 E
Bankura, *India* 43 H12 23 11N 87 18 E
Banmankhi, *India* 43 G12 25 53N 87 11 E
Bann →, *Arm., U.K.* 13 B5 54 30N 6 31W
Bann →, *L'derry., U.K.* 13 A5 55 8N 6 41W
Bannang Sata, *Thailand* 39 J3 6 16N 101 16 E
Banning, *U.S.A.* 85 M10 33 56N 116 53W
Banningville = Bandundu, *Dem. Rep. of the Congo* 52 E3 3 15S 17 22 E
Bannockburn, *Canada* 78 B7 44 39N 77 33W
Bannockburn, *U.K.* 12 E5 56 5N 3 55W
Bannockburn, *Zimbabwe* 55 G2 20 17S 29 48 E
Bannu, *Pakistan* 40 C7 33 0N 70 18 E
Bano, *India* 43 H11 22 40N 84 55 E
Bansgaon, *India* 43 F10 26 33N 83 21 E
Banská Bystrica, *Slovak Rep.* 17 D10 48 46N 19 14 E
Banswara, *India* 42 H6 23 32N 74 24 E
Bantaeng, *Indonesia* 37 F5 5 32S 119 56 E
Bantry, *Ireland* 13 E2 51 41N 9 27W
Bantry B., *Ireland* 13 E2 51 37N 9 44W
Bantul, *Indonesia* 37 G14 7 55S 110 19 E
Bantva, *India* 42 J4 21 29N 70 12 E
Banyak, Kepulauan, *Indonesia* 36 D1 2 10N 97 10 E
Banyalbufar, *Spain* 22 B9 39 42N 2 31 E
Banyo, *Cameroon* 52 C2 6 52N 11 45 E
Banyumas, *Indonesia* 37 G13 7 32S 109 18 E
Banyuwangi, *Indonesia* 37 H16 8 13S 114 21 E
Banzare Coast, *Antarctica* 5 C9 68 0S 125 0 E
Bao Ha, *Vietnam* 38 A5 22 11N 104 21 E
Bao Lac, *Vietnam* 38 A5 22 57N 105 40 E
Bao Loc, *Vietnam* 39 G6 11 32N 107 48 E
Baocheng, *China* 34 H4 33 12N 106 56 E
Baode, *China* 34 E6 39 1N 111 5 E
Baodi, *China* 35 E9 39 38N 117 20 E
Baoding, *China* 34 E8 38 50N 115 28 E
Baoji, *China* 34 G4 34 20N 107 5 E
Baoshan, *China* 32 D4 25 10N 99 5 E
Baotou, *China* 34 D6 40 32N 110 2 E
Baoying, *China* 35 H10 33 17N 119 20 E
Bap, *India* 42 F5 27 23N 72 18 E
Bapatla, *India* 41 M12 15 55N 80 30 E
Bāqerābād, *Iran* 45 C6 33 2N 51 58 E
Ba'qūbah, *Iraq* 44 C5 33 45N 44 50 E
Baquedano, *Chile* 94 A2 23 20S 69 52W
Bar, *Montenegro, Yug.* 21 C8 42 8N 19 6 E
Bar, *Ukraine* 17 D14 49 4N 27 40 E
Bar Bigha, *India* 43 G11 25 21N 85 47 E
Bar Harbor, *U.S.A.* 77 C11 44 23N 68 13W
Bar-le-Duc, *France* 18 B6 48 47N 5 10 E
Bara, *India* 43 G9 25 16N 81 43 E
Bara Banki, *India* 43 F9 26 55N 81 12 E
Barabai, *Indonesia* 36 E5 2 32S 115 34 E
Baraboo, *U.S.A.* 80 D10 43 28N 89 45W
Baracoa, *Cuba* 89 B5 20 20N 74 30W
Baradā →, *Syria* 47 B5 33 33N 36 34 E
Baradero, *Argentina* 94 C4 33 52S 59 29W
Baraga, *U.S.A.* 80 B10 46 47N 88 30W
Barah →, *India* 42 F6 27 42N 77 5 E
Barahona, *Dom. Rep.* 89 C5 18 13N 71 7W
Barail Range, *India* 41 G18 25 15N 93 20 E
Barakaldo, *Spain* 19 A4 43 18N 2 59W
Barakar →, *India* 43 G12 24 7N 86 14 E
Barakhola, *India* 41 G18 25 0N 92 45 E
Barakot, *India* 43 J11 21 33N 84 59 E

Barakpur, India 43 H13 22 44N 88 30 E
Baralaba, Australia 62 C4 24 13S 149 50 E
Baralzon L., Canada 73 B9 60 0N 98 3W
Baramula, India 43 B6 34 15N 74 20 E
Baran, India 42 G7 25 9N 76 40 E
Baran →, Pakistan 42 G3 25 13N 68 17 E
Baranavichy, Belarus 17 B14 53 10N 26 0 E
Baranof, U.S.A. 72 B2 57 5N 134 50W
Baranof I., U.S.A. 68 C6 57 0N 135 0W
Barapasi, Indonesia 37 E9 2 15S 137 5 E
Barasat, India 43 H13 22 46N 88 31 E
Barat Daya, Kepulauan, Indonesia 37 F7 7 30S 128 0 E
Barataria B., U.S.A. 81 L10 29 20N 89 55W
Barauda, India 42 H6 23 33N 75 15 E
Baraut, India 42 E7 29 13N 77 7 E
Barbacena, Brazil 95 A7 21 15S 43 56W
Barbados ■, W. Indies 89 D8 13 10N 59 30W
Barbària, C. de, Spain 22 C7 38 39N 1 24 E
Barbastro, Spain 19 A6 42 2N 0 5 E
Barberton, S. Africa 57 D5 25 42S 31 2 E
Barberton, U.S.A. 78 E3 41 0N 81 39W
Barbosa, Colombia 92 B4 5 57N 73 37W
Barbourville, U.S.A. 77 G4 36 52N 83 53W
Barbuda, W. Indies 89 C7 17 30N 61 40W
Barcaldine, Australia 62 C4 23 43S 145 6 E
Barcellona Pozzo di Gotto, Italy 20 E6 38 9N 15 13 E
Barcelona, Spain 19 B7 41 21N 2 10 E
Barcelona, Venezuela 92 A6 10 10N 64 40W
Barcelos, Brazil 92 D6 1 0S 63 0W
Barcoo →, Australia 62 D3 25 30S 142 50 E
Bardaï, Chad 51 D9 21 25N 17 0 E
Bardas Blancas, Argentina 94 D2 35 49S 69 45W
Bardawîl, Sabkhet el, Egypt 47 D2 31 10N 33 15 E
Barddhaman, India 43 H12 23 14N 87 39 E
Bardejov, Slovak Rep. 17 D11 49 18N 21 15 E
Bardera, Somali Rep. 46 G3 2 20N 42 27 E
Bardīyah, Libya 51 B10 31 45N 25 5 E
Bardsey I., U.K. 10 E3 52 45N 4 47W
Bardstown, U.S.A. 76 G3 37 49N 85 28W
Bareilly, India 43 E8 28 22N 79 27 E
Barela, India 43 H9 23 6N 80 3 E
Barents Sea, Arctic 4 B9 73 0N 39 0 E
Barfleur, Pte. de, France 18 B3 49 42N 1 16W
Bargara, Australia 62 C5 24 50S 152 25 E
Barguzin, Russia 27 D11 53 37N 109 37 E
Barh, India 43 G11 25 29N 85 46 E
Barhaj, India 43 F10 26 18N 83 44 E
Barharwa, India 43 G12 24 52N 87 47 E
Barhi, India 43 G11 24 15N 85 25 E
Bari, India 42 F7 26 39N 77 39 E
Bari, Italy 20 D7 41 8N 16 51 E
Bari Doab, Pakistan 42 D5 30 20N 73 0 E
Bari Sadri, India 42 G6 24 28N 74 30 E
Barīdī, Ra's, Si. Arabia 44 E3 24 17N 37 31 E
Barīm, Yemen 48 E8 12 39N 43 25 E
Barinas, Venezuela 92 B4 8 36N 70 15W
Baring, C., Canada 68 B8 70 0N 117 30W
Baringo, Kenya 54 B4 0 47N 36 16 E
Baringo, L., Kenya 54 B4 0 47N 36 16 E
Barisal, Bangla. 41 H17 22 45N 90 20 E
Barisan, Bukit, Indonesia 36 E2 3 30S 102 15 E
Barito →, Indonesia 36 E4 4 0S 114 50 E
Bark L., Canada 78 A7 45 27N 77 51W
Barkakana, India 43 H11 23 37N 85 29 E
Barker, U.S.A. 78 C6 43 20N 78 33W
Barkley, L., U.S.A. 77 G2 37 1N 88 14W
Barkley Sound, Canada 72 D3 48 50N 125 10W
Barkly East, S. Africa 56 E4 30 58S 27 33 E
Barkly Roadhouse, Australia 62 B2 19 52S 135 50 E
Barkly Tableland, Australia 62 B2 17 50S 136 40 E
Barkly West, S. Africa 56 D3 28 5S 24 31 E
Barkol Kazak Zizhixian, China 32 B4 43 37N 93 2 E
Bârlad, Romania 17 E14 46 15N 27 38 E
Bârlad →, Romania 17 F14 45 38N 27 32 E
Barlee, L., Australia 61 E2 29 15S 119 30 E
Barlee, Mt., Australia 61 D4 24 38S 128 13 E
Barletta, Italy 20 D7 41 19N 16 17 E
Barlovento, Canary Is. 22 F2 28 48N 17 48W
Barlow L., Canada 73 A8 62 0N 103 0W
Barmedman, Australia 63 E4 34 9S 147 21 E
Barmer, India 42 G4 25 45N 71 20 E
Barmera, Australia 63 E3 34 15S 140 28 E
Barmouth, U.K. 10 E3 52 44N 4 4W
Barna →, India 43 G10 25 21N 83 3 E
Barnagar, India 42 H6 23 7N 75 19 E
Barnala, India 42 D6 30 23N 75 33 E
Barnard Castle, U.K. 10 C6 54 33N 1 55W
Barnaul, Russia 26 D9 53 20N 83 40 E
Barnesville, U.S.A. 77 J3 33 3N 84 9W
Barnet □, U.K. 11 F7 51 38N 0 9W
Barneveld, Neths. 15 B5 52 7N 5 36 E
Barneveld, U.S.A. 79 C9 43 16N 75 14W
Barnhart, U.S.A. 81 K4 31 8N 101 10W
Barnsley, U.K. 10 D6 53 34N 1 27W
Barnstaple, U.K. 11 F3 51 5N 4 4W
Barnstaple Bay = Bideford Bay, U.K. 11 F3 51 5N 4 20W
Barnsville, U.S.A. 80 B6 46 43N 96 28W
Barnwell, U.S.A. 77 J5 33 15N 81 23W
Baro, Nigeria 50 G7 8 35N 6 18 E
Baroda = Vadodara, India 42 H5 22 20N 73 10 E
Baroda, India 42 G7 25 29N 76 35 E
Baroe, S. Africa 56 E3 33 13S 24 33 E
Baron Ra., Australia 60 D4 23 30S 127 45 E
Barotseland, Zambia 53 H4 15 0S 24 0 E
Barpeta, India 41 F17 26 20N 91 10 E
Barques, Pt. Aux, U.S.A. 78 B2 44 4N 82 58W
Barquísimeto, Venezuela 92 A5 10 4N 69 19W
Barr Smith Range, Australia 61 E3 27 4S 120 20 E
Barra, Brazil 93 F10 11 5S 43 10W
Barra, U.K. 12 E1 57 0N 7 29W
Barra, Sd. of, U.K. 12 D1 57 4N 7 25W
Barra de Navidad, Mexico 86 D4 19 12N 104 41W
Barra do Corda, Brazil 93 E9 5 30S 45 10W
Barra do Piraí, Brazil 95 A7 22 30S 43 50W
Barra Falsa, Pta. da, Mozam. 57 C6 22 58S 35 37 E
Barra Hd., U.K. 12 E1 56 47N 7 40W
Barra Mansa, Brazil 95 A7 22 35S 44 12W
Barraba, Australia 63 E5 30 21S 150 35 E
Barrackpur = Barakpur, India 43 H13 22 44N 88 30 E
Barradale Roadhouse, Australia 60 D1 22 42S 114 58 E
Barraigh = Barra, U.K. 12 E1 57 0N 7 29W
Barranca, Lima, Peru 92 F3 10 45S 77 50W
Barranca, Loreto, Peru 92 D3 4 50S 76 50W
Barrancabermeja, Colombia 92 B4 7 0N 73 50W
Barrancas, Venezuela 92 B6 8 55N 62 5W
Barrancos, Portugal 19 C2 38 10N 6 58W
Barranqueras, Argentina 94 B4 27 30S 59 0W
Barranquilla, Colombia 92 A4 11 0N 74 50W
Barraute, Canada 70 C4 48 26N 77 38W
Barre, Mass., U.S.A. 79 D12 42 25N 72 6W
Barre, Vt., U.S.A. 79 B12 44 12N 72 30W
Barreal, Argentina 94 C2 31 33S 69 28W
Barreiras, Brazil 93 F10 12 8S 45 0W
Barreirinhas, Brazil 93 D10 2 30S 42 50W
Barreiro, Portugal 19 C1 38 40N 9 6W
Barren, Nosy, Madag. 57 B7 18 25S 43 40 E
Barretos, Brazil 93 H9 20 30S 48 35W
Barrhead, Canada 72 C6 54 10N 114 24W
Barrie, Canada 78 B5 44 24N 79 40W
Barrier Ra., Australia 63 E3 31 0S 141 30 E
Barrière, Canada 72 C4 51 12N 120 7W
Barrington, U.S.A. 79 E13 41 44N 71 18W
Barrington L., Canada 73 B8 56 55N 100 15W
Barrington Tops, Australia 63 E5 32 6S 151 28 E
Barringun, Australia 63 D4 29 1S 145 41 E
Barro do Garças, Brazil 93 G8 15 54S 52 16W
Barron, U.S.A. 80 C9 45 24N 91 51W
Barrow, U.S.A. 68 A4 71 18N 156 47W
Barrow →, Ireland 13 D5 52 25N 6 58W
Barrow Creek, Australia 62 C1 21 30S 133 55 E
Barrow I., Australia 60 D2 20 45S 115 20 E
Barrow-in-Furness, U.K. 10 C4 54 7N 3 14W
Barrow Pt., Australia 62 A3 14 20S 144 40 E
Barrow Pt., U.S.A. 66 B4 71 10N 156 20W
Barrow Ra., Australia 61 E4 26 0S 127 40 E
Barrow Str., Canada 4 B3 74 20N 95 0W
Barry, U.K. 11 F4 51 24N 3 16W
Barry's Bay, Canada 78 A7 45 29N 77 41W
Barsat, Pakistan 43 A5 36 10N 72 45 E
Barsham, Syria 44 C4 35 21N 40 33 E
Barsi, India 40 K9 18 10N 75 50 E
Barsoi, India 41 G15 25 48N 87 57 E
Barstow, U.S.A. 85 L9 34 54N 117 1W
Barthélemy, Col, Vietnam 38 C5 19 26N 104 6 E
Bartica, Guyana 92 B7 6 25N 58 40W
Bartlesville, U.S.A. 81 G7 36 45N 95 59W
Bartlett, U.S.A. 84 J8 36 29N 118 2W
Bartlett, L., Canada 72 A5 63 5N 118 20W
Bartolomeu Dias, Mozam. 55 G4 21 10S 35 8 E
Barton, U.S.A. 79 B12 44 45N 72 11W
Barton upon Humber, U.K. 10 D7 53 41N 0 25W
Bartow, U.S.A. 77 M5 27 54N 81 50W
Barú, Volcan, Panama 88 E3 8 55N 82 35W
Barumba, Dem. Rep. of the Congo 54 B1 1 3N 23 37 E
Baruunsuu, Mongolia 34 C3 43 43N 105 35 E
Barwani, India 42 H6 22 2N 74 57 E
Barysaw, Belarus 17 A15 54 17N 28 28 E
Barzān, Iraq 44 B5 36 55N 44 3 E
Bāsa'idū, Iran 45 E7 26 35N 55 20 E
Basal, Pakistan 42 C5 33 33N 72 13 E
Basankusa, Dem. Rep. of the Congo 52 D3 1 5N 19 50 E
Basarabeasca, Moldova 17 E15 46 21N 28 58 E
Basarabia = Bessarabiya, Moldova 17 E15 47 0N 28 10 E
Basawa, Afghan. 42 B4 34 15N 70 50 E
Bascuñán, C., Chile 94 B1 28 52S 71 35W
Basel, Switz. 18 C7 47 35N 7 35 E
Bashākerd, Kūhhā-ye, Iran 45 E8 26 42N 58 35 E
Bashaw, Canada 72 C6 52 35N 112 58W
Bāshī, Iran 45 D6 28 41N 51 4 E
Bashkir Republic = Bashkortostan □, Russia 24 D10 54 0N 57 0 E
Bashkortostan □, Russia 24 D10 54 0N 57 0 E
Basibasy, Madag. 57 C7 22 10S 43 40 E
Basilan I., Phil. 37 C6 6 35N 122 0 E
Basilan Str., Phil. 37 C6 6 50N 122 0 E
Basildon, U.K. 11 F8 51 34N 0 28 E
Basim = Washim, India 40 J10 20 3N 77 0 E
Basin, U.S.A. 82 D9 44 23N 108 2W
Basingstoke, U.K. 11 F6 51 15N 1 5W
Baskatong, Rés., Canada 70 C4 46 46N 75 50W
Basle = Basel, Switz. 18 C7 47 35N 7 35 E
Basoda, India 42 H7 23 52N 77 54 E
Basoko, Dem. Rep. of the Congo 54 B1 1 16N 23 40 E
Basque Provinces = País Vasco □, Spain 19 A4 42 50N 2 45W
Basra = Al Başrah, Iraq 44 D5 30 30N 47 50 E
Bass Str., Australia 62 F4 39 15S 146 30 E
Bassano, Canada 72 C6 50 48N 112 20W
Bassano del Grappa, Italy 20 B4 45 46N 11 44 E
Bassas da India, Ind. Oc. 53 J7 22 0S 39 0 E
Basse-Terre, Guadeloupe 89 C7 16 0N 61 44W
Bassein, Burma 41 L19 16 45N 94 30 E
Basseterre, St. Kitts & Nevis 89 C7 17 17N 62 43W
Bassett, U.S.A. 80 D5 42 35N 99 32W
Bassi, India 42 D7 30 44N 76 21 E
Bastak, Iran 45 E7 27 15N 54 25 E
Baştām, Iran 45 B7 36 29N 55 4 E
Bastar, India 41 K12 19 15N 81 40 E
Basti, India 43 F10 26 52N 82 55 E
Bastia, France 18 E8 42 40N 9 30 E
Bastogne, Belgium 15 D5 50 1N 5 43 E
Bastrop, La., U.S.A. 81 J9 32 47N 91 55W
Bastrop, Tex., U.S.A. 81 K6 30 7N 97 19W
Bat Yam, Israel 47 C3 32 2N 34 44 E
Bata, Eq. Guin. 52 D1 1 57N 9 50 E
Bataan □, Phil. 37 B6 14 40N 120 25 E
Batabanó, Cuba 88 B3 22 40N 82 20W
Batabanó, G. de, Cuba 88 B3 22 30N 82 30W
Batac, Phil. 37 A6 18 3N 120 34 E
Batagai, Russia 27 C14 67 38N 134 38 E
Batala, India 42 D6 31 48N 75 12 E
Batama, Dem. Rep. of the Congo 54 B2 0 58N 26 33 E
Batamay, Russia 27 C13 63 30N 129 15 E
Batang, Indonesia 37 G13 6 55S 109 45 E
Batangas, Phil. 37 B6 13 35N 121 10 E
Batanta, Indonesia 37 E8 0 55S 130 40 E
Batatais, Brazil 95 A6 20 54S 47 37W
Batavia, U.S.A. 78 D6 43 0N 78 11W
Batchelor, Australia 60 B5 13 4S 131 1 E
Batdambang, Cambodia 38 F4 13 7N 103 12 E
Batemans B., Australia 63 F5 35 40S 150 12 E
Batemans Bay, Australia 63 F5 35 44S 150 11 E
Bates Ra., Australia 61 E3 27 27S 121 5 E
Batesburg-Leesville, U.S.A. 77 J5 33 54N 81 33W
Batesville, Ark., U.S.A. 81 H9 35 46N 91 39W
Batesville, Miss., U.S.A. 81 H10 34 19N 89 57W
Batesville, Tex., U.S.A. 81 L5 28 58N 99 37W
Bath, Canada 79 B8 44 11N 76 47W
Bath, U.K. 11 F5 51 23N 2 22W
Bath, Maine, U.S.A. 77 D11 43 55N 69 49W
Bath, N.Y., U.S.A. 78 D7 42 20N 77 19W
Bath & North East Somerset □, U.K. 11 F5 51 21N 2 27W
Batheay, Cambodia 39 G5 11 59N 104 57 E
Bathurst = Banjul, Gambia 50 F2 13 28N 16 40W
Bathurst, Australia 63 E4 33 25S 149 31 E
Bathurst, Canada 71 C6 47 37N 65 43W
Bathurst, S. Africa 56 E4 33 30S 26 50 E
Bathurst, C., Canada 68 A7 70 34N 128 0W
Bathurst B., Australia 62 A3 14 16S 144 25 E
Bathurst Harb., Australia 62 G4 43 15S 146 10 E
Bathurst I., Australia 60 B5 11 30S 130 10 E
Bathurst I., Canada 4 B2 76 0N 100 30W
Bathurst Inlet, Canada 68 B9 66 50N 108 1W
Batlow, Australia 63 F4 35 31S 148 9 E
Batman, Turkey 25 G7 37 55N 41 5 E
Baţn al Ghūl, Jordan 47 F4 29 36N 35 56 E
Batna, Algeria 50 A7 35 34N 6 15 E
Batoka, Zambia 55 F2 16 45S 27 15 E
Baton Rouge, U.S.A. 81 K9 30 27N 91 11W
Batong, Ko, Thailand 39 J2 6 32N 99 12 E
Batopilas, Mexico 86 B3 27 0N 107 45W
Batouri, Cameroon 52 D2 4 30N 14 25 E
Båtsfjord, Norway 8 A23 70 38N 29 39 E
Battambang = Batdambang, Cambodia 38 F4 13 7N 103 12 E
Batticaloa, Sri Lanka 40 R12 7 43N 81 45 E
Battipáglia, Italy 20 D6 40 37N 14 58 E
Battle, U.K. 11 G8 50 55N 0 30 E
Battle →, Canada 73 C7 52 43N 108 15W
Battle Creek, U.S.A. 76 D3 42 19N 85 11W
Battle Ground, U.S.A. 84 E4 45 47N 122 32W
Battle Harbour, Canada 71 B8 52 16N 55 35W
Battle Lake, U.S.A. 80 B7 46 17N 95 43W
Battle Mountain, U.S.A. 82 F5 40 38N 116 56W
Battlefields, Zimbabwe 55 F2 18 37S 29 47 E
Battleford, Canada 73 C7 52 45N 108 15W
Batu, Ethiopia 46 F2 6 55N 39 45 E
Batu, Kepulauan, Indonesia 36 E1 0 30S 98 25 E
Batu Caves, Malaysia 39 L3 3 15N 101 40 E
Batu Gajah, Malaysia 39 K3 4 28N 101 3 E
Batu Is. = Batu, Kepulauan, Indonesia 36 E1 0 30S 98 25 E
Batu Pahat, Malaysia 39 M4 1 50N 102 56 E
Batuata, Indonesia 37 F6 6 12S 122 42 E
Batumi, Georgia 25 F7 41 39N 41 44 E
Baturaja, Indonesia 36 E2 4 11S 104 15 E
Baturité, Brazil 93 D11 4 28S 38 45W
Bau, Malaysia 36 D4 1 26N 110 9 E
Baubau, Indonesia 37 F6 5 25S 122 38 E
Baucau, E. Timor 37 F7 8 27S 126 27 E
Bauchi, Nigeria 50 F7 10 22N 9 48 E
Baudette, U.S.A. 80 A7 48 43N 94 36W
Bauer, C., Australia 63 E1 32 44S 134 4 E
Bauhinia, Australia 62 C4 24 35S 149 18 E
Baukau = Baucau, E. Timor 37 F7 8 27S 126 27 E
Bauld, C., Canada 69 C14 51 38N 55 26W
Bauru, Brazil 95 A6 22 10S 49 0W
Bausi, India 43 G12 24 48N 87 1 E
Bauska, Latvia 9 H21 56 24N 24 15 E
Bautzen, Germany 16 C8 51 10N 14 26 E
Bavānāt, Iran 45 D7 30 28N 53 27 E
Bavaria = Bayern □, Germany 16 D6 48 50N 12 0 E
Bavispe →, Mexico 86 B3 29 30N 109 11W
Bawdwin, Burma 41 H20 23 5N 97 20 E
Bawean, Indonesia 36 F4 5 46S 112 35 E
Bawku, Ghana 50 F5 11 3N 0 19W
Bawlake, Burma 41 K20 19 11N 97 21 E
Baxley, U.S.A. 77 K4 31 47N 82 21W
Baxter, U.S.A. 80 B7 46 21N 94 17W
Baxter Springs, U.S.A. 81 G7 37 2N 94 44W
Bay City, Mich., U.S.A. 76 D4 43 36N 83 54W
Bay City, Tex., U.S.A. 81 L7 28 59N 95 58W
Bay Minette, U.S.A. 77 K2 30 53N 87 46W
Bay Roberts, Canada 71 C9 47 36N 53 16W
Bay St. Louis, U.S.A. 81 K10 30 19N 89 20W
Bay Springs, U.S.A. 81 K10 31 59N 89 17W
Bay View, N.Z. 59 H6 39 25S 176 50 E
Baya, Dem. Rep. of the Congo 55 E2 11 53S 27 25 E
Bayamo, Cuba 88 B4 20 20N 76 40W
Bayamón, Puerto Rico 89 C6 18 24N 66 10W
Bayan Har Shan, China 32 C4 34 0N 98 0 E
Bayan Hot = Alxa Zuoqi, China 34 E3 38 50N 105 40 E
Bayan Obo, China 34 D5 41 52N 109 59 E
Bayan-Ovoo = Erdenetsogt, Mongolia 34 C4 42 55N 106 5 E
Bayana, India 42 F7 26 55N 77 18 E
Bayanaūyl, Kazakstan 26 D8 50 45N 75 45 E
Bayandalay, Mongolia 34 C2 43 30N 103 29 E
Bayanhongor, Mongolia 32 B5 46 8N 102 43 E
Bayard, N. Mex., U.S.A. 83 K9 32 46N 108 8W
Bayard, Nebr., U.S.A. 80 E3 41 45N 103 20W
Baybay, Phil. 37 B6 10 40N 124 55 E
Baydhabo = Baidoa, Somali Rep. 46 G3 3 8N 43 30 E
Bayern □, Germany 16 D6 48 50N 12 0 E
Bayeux, France 18 B3 49 17N 0 42W
Bayfield, Canada 78 C3 43 34N 81 42W
Bayfield, U.S.A. 80 B9 46 49N 90 49W
Bayındır, Turkey 21 E12 38 13N 27 39 E
Baykal, Oz., Russia 27 D11 53 0N 108 0 E
Baykan, Turkey 44 B4 38 7N 41 44 E
Baykonur = Bayqongyr, Kazakstan 26 E7 47 48N 65 50 E
Baymak, Russia 24 D10 52 36N 58 19 E
Baynes Mts., Namibia 56 B1 17 15S 13 0 E
Bayombong, Phil. 37 A6 16 30N 121 10 E
Bayonne, France 18 E3 43 30N 1 28W
Bayonne, U.S.A. 79 F10 40 40N 74 7W
Bayovar, Peru 92 E2 5 50S 81 0W
Bayqongyr, Kazakstan 26 E7 47 48N 65 50 E
Bayram-Ali = Bayramaly, Turkmenistan 26 F7 37 37N 62 10 E
Bayramaly, Turkmenistan 26 F7 37 37N 62 10 E
Bayramiç, Turkey 21 E12 39 48N 26 36 E
Bayreuth, Germany 16 D6 49 56N 11 35 E
Bayrūt, Lebanon 47 B4 33 53N 35 31 E
Bays, L. of, Canada 78 A5 45 15N 79 4W
Baysville, Canada 78 A5 45 9N 79 7W
Bayt Lahm, West Bank 47 D4 31 43N 35 12 E
Baytown, U.S.A. 81 L7 29 43N 94 59W
Baza, Spain 19 D4 37 30N 2 47W
Bazaruto, I. do, Mozam. 57 C6 21 40S 35 28 E
Bazhou, China 34 E9 39 8N 116 22 E
Bazmān, Kūh-e, Iran 45 D9 28 4N 60 1 E
Beach, U.S.A. 80 B3 46 58N 104 0W
Beach City, U.S.A. 78 F3 40 39N 81 35W
Beachport, Australia 63 F3 37 29S 140 0 E
Beachy Hd., U.K. 11 G8 50 44N 0 15 E
Beacon, Australia 61 F2 30 26S 117 52 E
Beacon, U.S.A. 79 E11 41 30N 73 58W
Beaconsfield, Australia 62 G4 41 11S 146 48 E
Beagle, Canal, S. Amer. 96 H3 55 0S 68 30W
Beagle Bay, Australia 60 C3 16 58S 122 40 E
Bealanana, Madag. 57 A8 14 33S 48 44 E
Beals Cr. →, U.S.A. 81 J4 32 10N 100 51W
Beamsville, Canada 78 C5 43 12N 79 28W
Bear →, Calif., U.S.A. 84 G5 38 56N 121 36W
Bear →, Utah, U.S.A. 74 B4 41 30N 112 8W
Bear I., Ireland 13 E2 51 38N 9 50W
Bear L., Canada 73 B9 55 8N 96 0W
Bear L., U.S.A. 82 F8 41 59N 111 21W
Beardmore, Canada 70 C2 49 36N 87 57W
Beardmore Glacier, Antarctica 5 E11 84 30S 170 0 E
Beardstown, U.S.A. 80 F9 40 1N 90 26W
Bearma →, India 43 G8 24 20N 79 51 E
Béarn, France 18 E3 43 20N 0 30W
Bearpaw Mts., U.S.A. 82 B9 48 12N 109 30W
Bearskin Lake, Canada 70 B1 53 58N 91 2W
Beas →, India 42 D6 31 10N 74 59 E
Beata, C., Dom. Rep. 89 C5 17 40N 71 30W
Beata, I., Dom. Rep. 89 C5 17 34N 71 31W
Beatrice, U.S.A. 80 E6 40 16N 96 45W
Beatrice, Zimbabwe 55 F3 18 15S 30 55 E
Beatrice, C., Australia 62 A2 14 20S 136 55 E
Beatton →, Canada 72 B4 56 15N 120 45W
Beatton River, Canada 72 B4 57 26N 121 20W
Beatty, U.S.A. 84 J10 36 54N 116 46W
Beauce, Plaine de la, France 18 B4 48 10N 1 45 E
Beauceville, Canada 71 C5 46 13N 70 46W
Beaudesert, Australia 63 D5 27 59S 153 0 E
Beaufort, Malaysia 36 C5 5 30N 115 40 E
Beaufort, N.C., U.S.A. 77 H7 34 43N 76 40W
Beaufort, S.C., U.S.A. 77 J5 32 26N 80 40W
Beaufort Sea, Arctic 4 B1 72 0N 140 0W
Beaufort West, S. Africa 56 E3 32 18S 22 36 E
Beauharnois, Canada 79 A11 45 20N 73 52W
Beaulieu →, Canada 72 A6 62 3N 113 11W
Beauly, U.K. 12 D4 57 30N 4 28W
Beauly →, U.K. 12 D4 57 29N 4 27W
Beaumaris, U.K. 10 D3 53 16N 4 6W
Beaumont, Belgium 15 D4 50 15N 4 14 E
Beaumont, U.S.A. 81 K7 30 5N 94 6W
Beaune, France 18 C6 47 2N 4 50 E
Beaupré, Canada 71 C5 47 3N 70 54W
Beauraing, Belgium 15 D4 50 7N 4 57 E
Beauséjour, Canada 73 C9 50 5N 96 35W
Beauvais, France 18 B5 49 25N 2 8 E
Beauval, Canada 73 B7 55 9N 107 37W
Beaver, Okla., U.S.A. 81 G4 36 49N 100 31W
Beaver, Pa., U.S.A. 78 F4 40 42N 80 19W
Beaver, Utah, U.S.A. 83 G7 38 17N 112 38W
Beaver →, B.C., Canada 72 B4 59 52N 124 20W
Beaver →, Ont., Canada 70 A2 55 55N 87 48W
Beaver →, Sask., Canada 73 B7 55 26N 107 45W
Beaver →, U.S.A. 81 G5 36 35N 99 30W
Beaver City, U.S.A. 80 E5 40 8N 99 50W
Beaver Creek, Canada 68 B5 63 0N 141 0W
Beaver Dam, U.S.A. 80 D10 43 28N 88 50W
Beaver Falls, U.S.A. 78 F4 40 46N 80 20W
Beaver Hill L., Canada 73 C10 54 5N 94 50W
Beaver I., U.S.A. 76 C3 45 40N 85 33W
Beaverhill L., Canada 72 C6 53 27N 112 32W
Beaverlodge, Canada 72 B5 55 11N 119 29W
Beaverstone →, Canada 70 B2 54 59N 89 25W
Beaverton, Canada 78 B5 44 26N 79 9W
Beaverton, U.S.A. 84 E4 45 29N 122 48W
Beawar, India 42 F6 26 3N 74 18 E
Bebedouro, Brazil 95 A6 21 0S 48 25W
Beboa, Madag. 57 B7 17 22S 44 33 E
Beccles, U.K. 11 E9 52 27N 1 35 E
Bečej, Serbia, Yug. 21 B9 45 36N 20 3 E
Béchar, Algeria 50 B5 31 38N 2 18W
Beckley, U.S.A. 76 G5 37 47N 81 11W
Beddouza, Ras, Morocco 50 B4 32 33N 9 9W
Bedford, Canada 79 A12 45 7N 72 59W
Bedford, S. Africa 56 E4 32 40S 26 10 E
Bedford, U.K. 11 E7 52 8N 0 28W
Bedford, Ind., U.S.A. 76 F2 38 52N 86 29W
Bedford, Iowa, U.S.A. 80 E7 40 40N 94 44W
Bedford, Ohio, U.S.A. 78 E3 41 23N 81 32W
Bedford, Pa., U.S.A. 78 F6 40 1N 78 30W
Bedford, Va., U.S.A. 76 G6 37 20N 79 31W
Bedford, C., Australia 62 B4 15 14S 145 21 E
Bedfordshire □, U.K. 11 E7 52 4N 0 28W
Bedourie, Australia 62 C2 24 30S 139 30 E
Bedum, Neths. 15 A6 53 18N 6 36 E
Beebe Plain, Canada 79 A12 45 1N 72 9W
Beech Creek, U.S.A. 78 E7 41 5N 77 36W
Beenleigh, Australia 63 D5 27 43S 153 10 E
Be'er Menuha, Israel 44 D2 30 19N 35 8 E
Be'er Sheva, Israel 47 D3 31 15N 34 48 E
Beersheba = Be'er Sheva, Israel 47 D3 31 15N 34 48 E
Beestekraal, S. Africa 57 D4 25 23S 27 38 E
Beeston, U.K. 10 E6 52 56N 1 14W
Beeville, U.S.A. 81 L6 28 24N 97 45W
Befale, Dem. Rep. of the Congo 52 D4 0 25N 20 45 E
Befandriana, Mahajanga, Madag. 57 B8 15 16S 48 32 E
Befandriana, Toliara, Madag. 57 C7 21 55S 44 0 E
Befasy, Madag. 57 C7 20 33S 44 23 E
Befotaka, Antsiranana, Madag. 57 A8 13 15S 48 16 E
Befotaka, Fianarantsoa, Madag. 57 C8 23 49S 47 0 E
Bega, Australia 63 F4 36 41S 149 51 E
Begusarai, India 43 G12 25 24N 86 9 E
Behābād, Iran 45 C8 32 24N 59 47 E

Behala, *India* **43 H13** 22 30N 88 20 E
Behara, *Madag.* **57 C8** 24 55S 46 20 E
Behbehān, *Iran* **45 D6** 30 30N 50 15 E
Behm Canal, *U.S.A.* **72 B2** 55 10N 131 0W
Behshahr, *Iran* **45 B7** 36 45N 53 35 E
Bei Jiang →, *China* **33 D6** 23 2N 112 58 E
Bei'an, *China* **33 B7** 48 10N 126 20 E
Beihai, *China* **33 D5** 21 28N 109 6 E
Beijing, *China* **34 E9** 39 55N 116 20 E
Beijing □, *China* **34 E9** 39 55N 116 20 E
Beilen, *Neths.* **15 B6** 52 52N 6 27 E
Beilpajah, *Australia* **63 E3** 32 54S 143 52 E
Beinn na Faoghla = Benbecula, *U.K.* **12 D1** 57 26N 7 21W
Beipiao, *China* **35 D11** 41 52N 120 32 E
Beira, *Mozam.* **55 F3** 19 50S 34 52 E
Beirut = Bayrūt, *Lebanon* **47 B4** 33 53N 35 31 E
Beiseker, *Canada* **72 C6** 51 23N 113 32W
Beitaolaizhao, *China* **35 B13** 44 58N 125 58 E
Beitbridge, *Zimbabwe* **55 G3** 22 12S 30 0 E
Beizhen = Binzhou, *China* **35 F10** 37 20N 118 2 E
Beizhen, *China* **35 D11** 41 38N 121 54 E
Beizhengzhen, *China* **35 B12** 44 31N 123 30 E
Beja, *Portugal* **19 C2** 38 2N 7 53W
Béja, *Tunisia* **51 A7** 36 43N 9 12 E
Bejaïa, *Algeria* **50 A7** 36 42N 5 2 E
Béjar, *Spain* **19 B3** 40 23N 5 46W
Bejestān, *Iran* **45 C8** 34 30N 58 5 E
Békéscsaba, *Hungary* **17 E11** 46 40N 21 5 E
Bekily, *Madag.* **57 C8** 24 13S 45 19 E
Bekisopa, *Madag.* **57 C8** 21 40S 45 54 E
Bekitro, *Madag.* **57 C8** 24 33S 45 18 E
Bekodoka, *Madag.* **57 B8** 16 58S 45 7 E
Bekok, *Malaysia* **39 L4** 2 20N 103 7 E
Bekopaka, *Madag.* **57 B7** 19 9S 44 48 E
Bela, *India* **43 G10** 25 50N 82 0 E
Bela, *Pakistan* **42 F2** 26 12N 66 20 E
Bela Crkva, *Serbia, Yug.* **21 B9** 44 55N 21 27 E
Bela Vista, *Brazil* **94 A4** 22 12S 56 20W
Bela Vista, *Mozam.* **57 D5** 26 10S 32 44 E
Belan →, *India* **43 G9** 24 2N 81 45 E
Belarus ■, *Europe* **17 B14** 53 30N 27 0 E
Belau = Palau ■, *Pac. Oc.* **28 J17** 7 30N 134 30 E
Belavenona, *Madag.* **57 C8** 24 50S 47 4 E
Belawan, *Indonesia* **36 D1** 3 33N 98 32 E
Belaya →, *Russia* **24 C9** 54 40N 56 0 E
Belaya Tserkov = Bila Tserkva, *Ukraine* **17 D16** 49 45N 30 10 E
Belcher Is., *Canada* **70 A3** 56 15N 78 45W
Belden, *U.S.A.* **84 E5** 40 2N 121 17W
Belebey, *Russia* **24 D9** 54 7N 54 7 E
Beled Weyne = Belet Uen, *Somali Rep.* **46 G4** 4 30N 45 5 E
Belém, *Brazil* **93 D9** 1 20S 48 30W
Belén, *Argentina* **94 B2** 27 40S 67 5W
Belén, *Paraguay* **94 A4** 23 30S 57 6W
Belen, *U.S.A.* **83 J10** 34 40N 106 46W
Belet Uen, *Somali Rep.* **46 G4** 4 30N 45 5 E
Belev, *Russia* **24 D6** 53 50N 36 5 E
Belfair, *U.S.A.* **84 C4** 47 27N 122 50W
Belfast, *S. Africa* **57 D5** 25 42S 30 2 E
Belfast, *U.K.* **13 B6** 54 37N 5 56W
Belfast, *Maine, U.S.A.* **77 C11** 44 26N 69 1W
Belfast, *N.Y., U.S.A.* **78 D6** 42 21N 78 7W
Belfast L., *U.K.* **13 B6** 54 40N 5 50W
Belfield, *U.S.A.* **80 B3** 46 53N 103 12W
Belfort, *France* **18 C7** 47 38N 6 50 E
Belfry, *U.S.A.* **82 D9** 45 9N 109 1W
Belgaum, *India* **40 M9** 15 55N 74 35 E
Belgium ■, *Europe* **15 D4** 50 30N 5 0 E
Belgorod, *Russia* **25 D6** 50 35N 36 35 E
Belgorod-Dnestrovskiy = Bilhorod-Dnistrovskyy, *Ukraine* **25 E5** 46 11N 30 23 E
Belgrade = Beograd, *Serbia, Yug.* **21 B9** 44 50N 20 37 E
Belgrade, *U.S.A.* **82 D8** 45 47N 111 11W
Belhaven, *U.S.A.* **77 H7** 35 33N 76 37W
Beli Drim →, *Europe* **21 C9** 42 6N 20 25 E
Belinyu, *Indonesia* **36 E3** 1 35S 105 50 E
Beliton Is. = Belitung, *Indonesia* **36 E3** 3 10S 107 50 E
Belitung, *Indonesia* **36 E3** 3 10S 107 50 E
Belize ■, *Cent. Amer.* **87 D7** 17 0N 88 30W
Belize City, *Belize* **87 D7** 17 25N 88 0W
Belkovskiy, Ostrov, *Russia* **27 B14** 75 32N 135 44 E
Bell →, *Canada* **70 C4** 49 48N 77 38W
Bell I., *Canada* **71 B8** 50 46N 55 35W
Bell-Irving →, *Canada* **72 B3** 56 12N 129 5W
Bell Peninsula, *Canada* **69 B11** 63 50N 82 0W
Bell Ville, *Argentina* **94 C3** 32 40S 62 40W
Bella Bella, *Canada* **72 C3** 52 10N 128 10W
Bella Coola, *Canada* **72 C3** 52 25N 126 40W
Bella Unión, *Uruguay* **94 C4** 30 15S 57 40W
Bella Vista, *Corrientes, Argentina* **94 B4** 28 33S 59 0W
Bella Vista, *Tucuman, Argentina* **94 B2** 27 10S 65 25W
Bellaire, *U.S.A.* **78 F4** 40 1N 80 45W
Bellary, *India* **40 M10** 15 10N 76 56 E
Bellata, *Australia* **63 D4** 29 53S 149 46 E
Belle-Chasse, *U.S.A.* **81 L10** 29 51N 89 59W
Belle Fourche, *U.S.A.* **80 C3** 44 40N 103 51W
Belle Fourche →, *U.S.A.* **80 C3** 44 26N 102 18W
Belle Glade, *U.S.A.* **77 M5** 26 41N 80 40W
Belle-Île, *France* **18 C2** 47 20N 3 10W
Belle Isle, *Canada* **71 B8** 51 57N 55 25W
Belle Isle, Str. of, *Canada* **71 B8** 51 30N 56 30W
Belle Plaine, *U.S.A.* **80 E8** 41 54N 92 17W
Bellefontaine, *U.S.A.* **76 E4** 40 22N 83 46W
Bellefonte, *U.S.A.* **78 F7** 40 55N 77 47W
Belleoram, *Canada* **71 C8** 47 31N 55 25W
Belleville, *Canada* **78 B7** 44 10N 77 23W
Belleville, *Ill., U.S.A.* **80 F10** 38 31N 89 59W
Belleville, *Kans., U.S.A.* **80 F6** 39 50N 97 38W
Belleville, *N.Y., U.S.A.* **79 C8** 43 46N 76 10W
Bellevue, *Canada* **72 D6** 49 35N 114 22W
Bellevue, *Idaho, U.S.A.* **82 E6** 43 28N 114 16W
Bellevue, *Nebr., U.S.A.* **80 E7** 41 8N 95 53W
Bellevue, *Ohio, U.S.A.* **78 E2** 41 17N 82 51W
Bellevue, *Wash., U.S.A.* **84 C4** 47 37N 122 12W
Bellin = Kangirsuk, *Canada* **69 B13** 60 0N 70 0W
Bellingen, *Australia* **63 E5** 30 25S 152 50 E
Bellingham, *U.S.A.* **68 D7** 48 46N 122 29W
Bellingshausen Sea, *Antarctica* **5 C17** 66 0S 80 0W
Bellinzona, *Switz.* **18 C8** 46 11N 9 1 E
Bello, *Colombia* **92 B3** 6 20N 75 33W
Bellows Falls, *U.S.A.* **79 C12** 43 8N 72 27W
Bellpat, *Pakistan* **42 E3** 29 0N 68 5 E
Belluno, *Italy* **20 A5** 46 9N 12 13 E
Bellwood, *U.S.A.* **78 F6** 40 36N 78 20W
Belmont, *Canada* **78 D3** 42 53N 81 5W
Belmont, *S. Africa* **56 D3** 29 28S 24 22 E
Belmont, *U.S.A.* **78 D6** 42 14N 78 2W
Belmonte, *Brazil* **93 G11** 16 0S 39 0W
Belmopan, *Belize* **87 D7** 17 18N 88 30W
Belmullet, *Ireland* **13 B2** 54 14N 9 58W
Belo Horizonte, *Brazil* **93 G10** 19 55S 43 56W
Belo-sur-Mer, *Madag.* **57 C7** 20 42S 44 0 E
Belo-Tsiribihina, *Madag.* **57 B7** 19 40S 44 30 E
Belogorsk, *Russia* **27 D13** 51 0N 128 20 E
Beloha, *Madag.* **57 D8** 25 10S 45 3 E
Beloit, *Kans., U.S.A.* **80 F5** 39 28N 98 6W
Beloit, *Wis., U.S.A.* **80 D10** 42 31N 89 2W
Belokorovichi, *Ukraine* **17 C15** 51 7N 28 2 E
Belomorsk, *Russia* **24 B5** 64 35N 34 54 E
Belonia, *India* **41 H17** 23 15N 91 30 E
Beloretsk, *Russia* **24 D10** 53 58N 58 24 E
Belorussia = Belarus ■, *Europe* **17 B14** 53 30N 27 0 E
Belovo, *Russia* **26 D9** 54 30N 86 0 E
Beloye, Ozero, *Russia* **24 B6** 60 10N 37 35 E
Beloye More, *Russia* **24 A6** 66 30N 38 0 E
Belozersk, *Russia* **24 B6** 60 1N 37 45 E
Belpre, *U.S.A.* **76 F5** 39 17N 81 34W
Belrain, *India* **43 E9** 28 23N 80 55 E
Belt, *U.S.A.* **82 C8** 47 23N 110 55W
Beltana, *Australia* **63 E2** 30 48S 138 25 E
Belterra, *Brazil* **93 D8** 2 45S 55 0W
Belton, *U.S.A.* **81 K6** 31 3N 97 28W
Belton L., *U.S.A.* **81 K6** 31 8N 97 32W
Beltsy = Bălţi, *Moldova* **17 E14** 47 48N 27 58 E
Belturbet, *Ireland* **13 B4** 54 6N 7 26W
Belukha, *Russia* **26 E9** 49 50N 86 50 E
Beluran, *Malaysia* **36 C5** 5 48N 117 35 E
Belvidere, *Ill., U.S.A.* **80 D10** 42 15N 88 50W
Belvidere, *N.J., U.S.A.* **79 F9** 40 50N 75 5W
Belyando →, *Australia* **62 C4** 21 38S 146 50 E
Belyy, Ostrov, *Russia* **26 B8** 73 30N 71 0 E
Belyy Yar, *Russia* **26 D9** 58 26N 84 39 E
Belzoni, *U.S.A.* **81 J9** 33 11N 90 29W
Bemaraha, Lembalemban' i, *Madag.* **57 B7** 18 40S 44 45 E
Bemarivo, *Madag.* **57 C7** 21 45S 44 45 E
Bemarivo →, *Antsiranana, Madag.* **57 A9** 14 9S 50 9 E
Bemarivo →, *Mahajanga, Madag.* **57 B8** 15 27S 47 40 E
Bemavo, *Madag.* **57 C8** 21 33S 45 25 E
Bembéréke, *Benin* **50 F6** 10 11N 2 43 E
Bembesi, *Zimbabwe* **55 G2** 20 0S 28 58 E
Bembesi →, *Zimbabwe* **55 F2** 18 57S 27 47 E
Bemetara, *India* **43 J9** 21 42N 81 32 E
Bemidji, *U.S.A.* **80 B7** 47 28N 94 53W
Bemolanga, *Madag.* **57 B8** 17 44S 45 6 E
Ben, *Iran* **45 C6** 32 32N 50 45 E
Ben Cruachan, *U.K.* **12 E3** 56 26N 5 8W
Ben Dearg, *U.K.* **12 D4** 57 47N 4 56W
Ben Hope, *U.K.* **12 C4** 58 25N 4 36W
Ben Lawers, *U.K.* **12 E4** 56 32N 4 14W
Ben Lomond, *N.S.W., Australia* **63 E5** 30 1S 151 43 E
Ben Lomond, *Tas., Australia* **62 G4** 41 38S 147 42 E
Ben Lomond, *U.K.* **12 E4** 56 11N 4 38W
Ben Luc, *Vietnam* **39 G6** 10 39N 106 29 E
Ben Macdhui, *U.K.* **12 D5** 57 4N 3 40W
Ben Mhor, *U.K.* **12 D1** 57 15N 7 18W
Ben More, *Arg. & Bute, U.K.* **12 E2** 56 26N 6 1W
Ben More, *Stirl., U.K.* **12 E4** 56 23N 4 32W
Ben More Assynt, *U.K.* **12 C4** 58 8N 4 52W
Ben Nevis, *U.K.* **12 E3** 56 48N 5 1W
Ben Quang, *Vietnam* **38 D6** 17 3N 106 55 E
Ben Vorlich, *U.K.* **12 E4** 56 21N 4 14W
Ben Wyvis, *U.K.* **12 D4** 57 40N 4 35W
Bena, *Nigeria* **50 F7** 11 20N 5 50 E
Benalla, *Australia* **63 F4** 36 30S 146 0 E
Benares = Varanasi, *India* **43 G10** 25 22N 83 0 E
Benavente, *Spain* **19 A3** 42 2N 5 43W
Benavides, *U.S.A.* **81 M5** 27 36N 98 25W
Benbecula, *U.K.* **12 D1** 57 26N 7 21W
Benbonyathe, *Australia* **63 E2** 30 25S 139 11 E
Bend, *U.S.A.* **82 D3** 44 4N 121 19W
Bender Beila, *Somali Rep.* **46 F5** 9 30N 50 48 E
Bendery = Tighina, *Moldova* **17 E15** 46 50N 29 30 E
Bendigo, *Australia* **63 F3** 36 40S 144 15 E
Benē Beraq, *Israel* **47 C3** 32 6N 34 51 E
Benenitra, *Madag.* **57 C8** 23 27S 45 5 E
Benevento, *Italy* **20 D6** 41 8N 14 45 E
Benga, *Mozam.* **55 F3** 16 11S 33 40 E
Bengal, Bay of, *Ind. Oc.* **41 M17** 15 0N 90 0 E
Bengbu, *China* **35 H9** 32 58N 117 20 E
Benghazi = Banghāzī, *Libya* **51 B10** 32 11N 20 3 E
Bengkalis, *Indonesia* **36 D2** 1 30N 102 10 E
Bengkulu, *Indonesia* **36 E2** 3 50S 102 12 E
Bengkulu □, *Indonesia* **36 E2** 3 48S 102 16 E
Bengough, *Canada* **73 D7** 49 25N 105 10W
Benguela, *Angola* **53 G2** 12 37S 13 25 E
Benguérua, I., *Mozam.* **57 C6** 21 58S 35 28 E
Beni, *Dem. Rep. of the Congo* **54 B2** 0 30N 29 27 E
Beni →, *Bolivia* **92 F5** 10 23S 65 24W
Beni Mellal, *Morocco* **50 B4** 32 21N 6 21W
Beni Suef, *Egypt* **51 C12** 29 5N 31 6 E
Beniah L., *Canada* **72 A6** 63 23N 112 17W
Benicia, *U.S.A.* **84 G4** 38 3N 122 9W
Benidorm, *Spain* **19 C5** 38 33N 0 9W
Benin ■, *Africa* **50 G6** 10 0N 2 0 E
Benin, Bight of, *W. Afr.* **50 H6** 5 0N 3 0 E
Benin City, *Nigeria* **50 G7** 6 20N 5 31 E
Benitses, *Greece* **23 A3** 39 32N 19 55 E
Benjamin Aceval, *Paraguay* **94 A4** 24 58S 57 34W
Benjamin Constant, *Brazil* **92 D4** 4 40S 70 15W
Benjamin Hill, *Mexico* **86 A2** 30 10N 111 10W
Benkelman, *U.S.A.* **80 E4** 40 3N 101 32W
Bennett, *Canada* **72 B2** 59 56N 134 53W
Bennett, L., *Australia* **60 D5** 22 50S 131 2 E
Bennetta, Ostrov, *Russia* **27 B15** 76 21N 148 56 E
Bennettsville, *U.S.A.* **77 H6** 34 37N 79 41W
Bennington, *N.H., U.S.A.* **79 D11** 43 0N 71 55W
Bennington, *Vt., U.S.A.* **79 D11** 42 53N 73 12W
Benoni, *S. Africa* **57 D4** 26 11S 28 18 E
Benque Viejo, *Belize* **87 D7** 17 5N 89 8W
Benson, *Ariz., U.S.A.* **83 L8** 31 58N 110 18W
Benson, *Minn., U.S.A.* **80 C7** 45 19N 95 36W
Bent, *Iran* **45 E8** 26 20N 59 31 E
Benteng, *Indonesia* **37 F6** 6 10S 120 30 E
Bentinck I., *Australia* **62 B2** 17 3S 139 35 E
Bento Gonçalves, *Brazil* **95 B5** 29 10S 51 31W
Benton, *Ark., U.S.A.* **81 H8** 34 34N 92 35W
Benton, *Calif., U.S.A.* **84 H8** 37 48N 118 32W
Benton, *Ill., U.S.A.* **80 G10** 38 0N 88 55W
Benton, *Pa., U.S.A.* **79 E8** 41 12N 76 23W
Benton Harbor, *U.S.A.* **76 D2** 42 6N 86 27W
Bentonville, *U.S.A.* **81 G7** 36 22N 94 13W
Bentung, *Malaysia* **39 L3** 3 31N 101 55 E
Benue →, *Nigeria* **50 G7** 7 48N 6 46 E
Benxi, *China* **35 D12** 41 20N 123 48 E
Beo, *Indonesia* **37 D7** 4 25N 126 50 E
Beograd, *Serbia, Yug.* **21 B9** 44 50N 20 37 E
Beppu, *Japan* **31 H5** 33 15N 131 30 E
Beqaa Valley = Al Biqā, *Lebanon* **47 A5** 34 10N 36 10 E
Ber Mota, *India* **42 H3** 23 27N 68 34 E
Berach →, *India* **42 G6** 25 15N 75 2 E
Beraketa, *Madag.* **57 C7** 23 7S 44 25 E
Berat, *Albania* **21 D8** 40 43N 19 59 E
Berau, Teluk, *Indonesia* **37 E8** 2 30S 132 30 E
Beravina, *Madag.* **57 B8** 18 10S 45 14 E
Berber, *Sudan* **51 E12** 18 0N 34 0 E
Berbera, *Somali Rep.* **46 E4** 10 30N 45 2 E
Berbérati, *C.A.R.* **52 D3** 4 15N 15 40 E
Berbice →, *Guyana* **92 B7** 6 20N 57 32W
Berdichev = Berdychiv, *Ukraine* **17 D15** 49 57N 28 30 E
Berdsk, *Russia* **26 D9** 54 47N 83 2 E
Berdyansk, *Ukraine* **25 E6** 46 45N 36 50 E
Berdychiv, *Ukraine* **17 D15** 49 57N 28 30 E
Berea, *U.S.A.* **76 G3** 37 34N 84 17W
Berebere, *Indonesia* **37 D7** 2 25N 128 45 E
Bereda, *Somali Rep.* **46 E5** 11 45N 51 0 E
Berehove, *Ukraine* **17 D12** 48 15N 22 35 E
Berekum, *Ghana* **50 G5** 7 29N 2 34W
Berens →, *Canada* **73 C9** 52 25N 97 2W
Berens I., *Canada* **73 C9** 52 18N 97 18W
Berens River, *Canada* **73 C9** 52 25N 97 0W
Beresford, *U.S.A.* **80 D6** 43 5N 96 47W
Berestechko, *Ukraine* **17 C13** 50 22N 25 5 E
Berevo, *Mahajanga, Madag.* **57 B7** 17 14S 44 17 E
Berevo, *Toliara, Madag.* **57 B7** 19 44S 44 58 E
Bereza = Byaroza, *Belarus* **17 B13** 52 31N 24 51 E
Berezhany, *Ukraine* **17 D13** 49 26N 24 58 E
Berezina = Byarezina →, *Belarus* **17 B16** 52 33N 30 14 E
Bereznik, *Russia* **24 B7** 62 51N 42 40 E
Berezniki, *Russia* **24 C10** 59 24N 56 46 E
Berezovo, *Russia* **26 C7** 64 0N 65 0 E
Berga, *Spain* **19 A6** 42 6N 1 48 E
Bergama, *Turkey* **21 E12** 39 8N 27 11 E
Bérgamo, *Italy* **18 D8** 45 41N 9 43 E
Bergen, *Neths.* **15 B4** 52 40N 4 43 E
Bergen, *Norway* **9 F11** 60 20N 5 20 E
Bergen, *U.S.A.* **78 C7** 43 5N 77 57W
Bergen op Zoom, *Neths.* **15 C4** 51 28N 4 18 E
Bergerac, *France* **18 D4** 44 51N 0 30 E
Bergholz, *U.S.A.* **78 F4** 40 31N 80 53W
Bergisch Gladbach, *Germany* **15 D7** 50 59N 7 8 E
Bergville, *S. Africa* **57 D4** 28 52S 29 18 E
Berhala, Selat, *Indonesia* **36 E2** 1 0S 104 15 E
Berhampore = Baharampur, *India* **43 G13** 24 2N 88 27 E
Berhampur = Brahmapur, *India* **41 K14** 19 15N 84 54 E
Bering Sea, *Pac. Oc.* **68 C1** 58 0N 171 0 E
Bering Strait, *Pac. Oc.* **68 B3** 65 30N 169 0W
Beringovskiy, *Russia* **27 C18** 63 3N 179 19 E
Berisso, *Argentina* **94 C4** 34 56S 57 50W
Berja, *Spain* **19 D4** 36 50N 2 56W
Berkeley, *U.S.A.* **84 H4** 37 52N 122 16W
Berkner I., *Antarctica* **5 D18** 79 30S 50 0W
Berkshire, *U.S.A.* **79 D8** 42 19N 76 11W
Berkshire Downs, *U.K.* **11 F6** 51 33N 1 29W
Berlin, *Germany* **16 B7** 52 30N 13 25 E
Berlin, *Md., U.S.A.* **76 F8** 38 20N 75 13W
Berlin, *N.H., U.S.A.* **79 B13** 44 28N 71 11W
Berlin, *N.Y., U.S.A.* **79 D11** 42 42N 73 23W
Berlin, *Wis., U.S.A.* **76 D1** 43 58N 88 57W
Berlin L., *U.S.A.* **78 E4** 41 3N 81 0W
Bermejo →, *Formosa, Argentina* **94 B4** 26 51S 58 23W
Bermejo →, *San Juan, Argentina* **94 C2** 32 30S 67 30W
Bermen, L., *Canada* **71 B6** 53 35N 68 55W
Bermuda ■, *Atl. Oc.* **66 F13** 32 45N 65 0W
Bern, *Switz.* **18 C7** 46 57N 7 28 E
Bernalillo, *U.S.A.* **83 J10** 35 18N 106 33W
Bernardo de Irigoyen, *Argentina* **95 B5** 26 15S 53 40W
Bernardo O'Higgins □, *Chile* **94 C1** 34 15S 70 45W
Bernardsville, *U.S.A.* **79 F10** 40 43N 74 34W
Bernasconi, *Argentina* **94 D3** 37 55S 63 44W
Bernburg, *Germany* **16 C6** 51 47N 11 44 E
Berne = Bern, *Switz.* **18 C7** 46 57N 7 28 E
Berneray, *U.K.* **12 D1** 57 43N 7 11W
Bernier I., *Australia* **61 D1** 24 50S 113 12 E
Bernina, Piz, *Switz.* **18 C8** 46 20N 9 54 E
Beroroha, *Madag.* **57 C8** 21 40S 45 10 E
Beroun, *Czech Rep.* **16 D8** 49 57N 14 5 E
Berri, *Australia* **63 E3** 34 14S 140 35 E
Berriane, *Algeria* **50 B6** 32 50N 3 46 E
Berry, *Australia* **63 E5** 34 46S 150 43 E
Berry, *France* **18 C5** 46 50N 2 0 E
Berry Is., *Bahamas* **88 A4** 25 40N 77 50W
Berryessa L., *U.S.A.* **84 G4** 38 31N 122 6W
Berryville, *U.S.A.* **81 G8** 36 22N 93 34W
Berseba, *Namibia* **56 D2** 26 0S 17 46 E
Bershad, *Ukraine* **17 D15** 48 22N 29 31 E
Berthold, *U.S.A.* **80 A4** 48 19N 101 44W
Berthoud, *U.S.A.* **80 E2** 40 19N 105 5W
Bertoua, *Cameroon* **52 D2** 4 30N 13 45 E
Bertraghboy B., *Ireland* **13 C2** 53 22N 9 54W
Berwick, *U.S.A.* **79 E8** 41 3N 76 14W
Berwick-upon-Tweed, *U.K.* **10 B6** 55 46N 2 0W
Berwyn Mts., *U.K.* **10 E4** 52 54N 3 26W
Besal, *Pakistan* **43 B5** 35 4N 73 56 E
Besalampy, *Madag.* **57 B7** 16 43S 44 29 E
Besançon, *France* **18 C7** 47 15N 6 2 E
Besar, *Indonesia* **36 E5** 2 40S 116 0 E
Besnard L., *Canada* **73 B7** 55 25N 106 0W
Besni, *Turkey* **44 B3** 37 41N 37 52 E
Besor, N. →, *Egypt* **47 D3** 31 28N 34 22 E
Bessarabiya, *Moldova* **17 E15** 47 0N 28 10 E
Bessarabka = Basarabeasca, *Moldova* **17 E15** 46 21N 28 58 E
Bessemer, *Ala., U.S.A.* **77 J2** 33 24N 86 58W
Bessemer, *Mich., U.S.A.* **80 B9** 46 29N 90 3W
Bessemer, *Pa., U.S.A.* **78 F4** 40 59N 80 30W
Beswick, *Australia* **60 B5** 14 34S 132 53 E
Bet She'an, *Israel* **47 C4** 32 30N 35 30 E
Bet Shemesh, *Israel* **47 D4** 31 44N 35 0 E
Betafo, *Madag.* **57 B8** 19 50S 46 51 E
Betancuria, *Canary Is.* **22 F5** 28 25N 14 3W
Betanzos, *Spain* **19 A1** 43 15N 8 12W
Bétaré Oya, *Cameroon* **52 C2** 5 40N 14 5 E
Betatao, *Madag.* **57 B8** 18 11S 47 52 E
Bethal, *S. Africa* **57 D4** 26 27S 29 28 E
Bethanien, *Namibia* **56 D2** 26 31S 17 8 E
Bethany, *Canada* **78 B6** 44 11N 78 34W
Bethany, *U.S.A.* **80 E7** 40 16N 94 2W
Bethel, *Alaska, U.S.A.* **68 B3** 60 48N 161 45W
Bethel, *Conn., U.S.A.* **79 E11** 41 22N 73 25W
Bethel, *Maine, U.S.A.* **79 B14** 44 25N 70 47W
Bethel, *Vt., U.S.A.* **79 C12** 43 50N 72 38W
Bethel Park, *U.S.A.* **78 F4** 40 20N 80 1W
Bethlehem = Bayt Lahm, *West Bank* **47 D4** 31 43N 35 12 E
Bethlehem, *S. Africa* **57 D4** 28 14S 28 18 E
Bethlehem, *U.S.A.* **79 F9** 40 37N 75 23W
Bethulie, *S. Africa* **56 E4** 30 30S 25 59 E
Béthune, *France* **18 A5** 50 30N 2 38 E
Betioky, *Madag.* **57 C7** 23 48S 44 20 E
Betong, *Thailand* **39 K3** 5 45N 101 5 E
Betoota, *Australia* **62 D3** 25 45S 140 42 E
Betroka, *Madag.* **57 C8** 23 16S 46 0 E
Betsiamites, *Canada* **71 C6** 48 56N 68 40W
Betsiamites →, *Canada* **71 C6** 48 56N 68 38W
Betsiboka →, *Madag.* **57 B8** 16 3S 46 36 E
Bettendorf, *U.S.A.* **80 E9** 41 32N 90 30W
Bettiah, *India* **43 F11** 26 48N 84 33 E
Betul, *India* **40 J10** 21 58N 77 59 E
Betung, *Malaysia* **36 D4** 1 24N 111 31 E
Betws-y-Coed, *U.K.* **10 D4** 53 5N 3 48W
Beulah, *Mich., U.S.A.* **76 C2** 44 38N 86 6W
Beulah, *N. Dak., U.S.A.* **80 B4** 47 16N 101 47W
Beveren, *Belgium* **15 C4** 51 12N 4 16 E
Beverley, *Australia* **61 F2** 32 9S 116 56 E
Beverley, *U.K.* **10 D7** 53 51N 0 26W
Beverley Hills, *U.S.A.* **77 L4** 28 56N 82 28W
Beverly, *U.S.A.* **79 D14** 42 33N 70 53W
Beverly Hills, *U.S.A.* **85 L8** 34 4N 118 25W
Bevoalavo, *Madag.* **57 D7** 25 13S 45 26 E
Bewas →, *India* **43 H8** 23 59N 79 21 E
Bexhill, *U.K.* **11 G8** 50 51N 0 29 E
Beyānlū, *Iran* **44 C5** 36 0N 47 51 E
Beyneu, *Kazakstan* **25 E10** 45 18N 55 9 E
Beypazarı, *Turkey* **25 F5** 40 10N 31 56 E
Beyşehir Gölü, *Turkey* **25 G5** 37 41N 31 33 E
Béziers, *France* **18 E5** 43 20N 3 12 E
Bezwada = Vijayawada, *India* **41 L12** 16 31N 80 39 E
Bhabua, *India* **43 G10** 25 3N 83 37 E
Bhachau, *India* **40 H7** 23 20N 70 16 E
Bhadar →, *Gujarat, India* **42 H5** 22 17N 72 20 E
Bhadar →, *Gujarat, India* **42 J3** 21 27N 69 47 E
Bhadarwah, *India* **43 C6** 32 58N 75 46 E
Bhadohi, *India* **43 G10** 25 25N 82 34 E
Bhadra, *India* **42 E6** 29 8N 75 14 E
Bhadrakh, *India* **41 J15** 21 10N 86 30 E
Bhadran, *India* **42 H5** 22 19N 72 6 E
Bhadravati, *India* **40 N9** 13 49N 75 40 E
Bhag, *Pakistan* **42 E2** 29 2N 67 49 E
Bhagalpur, *India* **43 G12** 25 10N 87 0 E
Bhagirathi →, *Uttaranchal, India* **43 D8** 30 8N 78 35 E
Bhagirathi →, *W. Bengal, India* **43 H13** 23 25N 88 23 E
Bhakkar, *Pakistan* **42 D4** 31 40N 71 5 E
Bhakra Dam, *India* **42 D7** 31 30N 76 45 E
Bhaktapur, *Nepal* **43 F11** 27 38N 85 24 E
Bhamo, *Burma* **41 G20** 24 15N 97 15 E
Bhandara, *India* **40 J11** 21 5N 79 42 E
Bhanpura, *India* **42 G6** 24 31N 75 44 E
Bhanrer Ra., *India* **43 H8** 23 40N 79 45 E
Bhaptiahi, *India* **43 F12** 26 19N 86 44 E
Bharat = India ■, *Asia* **40 K11** 20 0N 78 0 E
Bharatpur, *Chhattisgarh, India* **43 H9** 23 44N 81 46 E
Bharatpur, *Raj., India* **42 F7** 27 15N 77 30 E
Bharno, *India* **43 H11** 23 14N 84 53 E
Bhatinda, *India* **42 D6** 30 15N 74 57 E
Bhatpara, *India* **43 H13** 22 50N 88 25 E
Bhattu, *India* **42 E6** 29 36N 75 19 E
Bhaun, *Pakistan* **42 C5** 32 55N 72 40 E
Bhaunagar = Bhavnagar, *India* **40 J8** 21 45N 72 10 E
Bhavnagar, *India* **40 J8** 21 45N 72 10 E
Bhawari, *India* **42 G5** 25 42N 73 4 E
Bhayavadar, *India* **42 J4** 21 51N 70 15 E
Bhera, *Pakistan* **42 C5** 32 29N 72 57 E
Bhikangaon, *India* **42 J6** 21 52N 75 57 E
Bhilsa = Vidisha, *India* **42 H7** 23 28N 77 53 E
Bhilwara, *India* **42 G6** 25 25N 74 38 E
Bhima →, *India* **40 L10** 16 25N 77 17 E
Bhimbar, *Pakistan* **43 C6** 32 59N 74 3 E
Bhind, *India* **43 F8** 26 30N 78 46 E
Bhinga, *India* **43 F9** 27 43N 81 56 E
Bhinmal, *India* **42 G5** 25 0N 72 15 E
Bhiwandi, *India* **40 K8** 19 20N 73 0 E
Bhiwani, *India* **42 E7** 28 50N 76 9 E
Bhogava →, *India* **42 H5** 22 26N 72 20 E
Bhola, *Bangla.* **41 H17** 22 45N 90 35 E
Bholari, *Pakistan* **42 G3** 25 19N 68 13 E
Bhopal, *India* **42 H7** 23 20N 77 30 E
Bhubaneshwar, *India* **41 J14** 20 15N 85 50 E
Bhuj, *India* **42 H3** 23 15N 69 49 E
Bhusaval, *India* **40 J9** 21 3N 75 46 E
Bhutan ■, *Asia* **41 F17** 27 25N 90 30 E
Biafra, B. of = Bonny, Bight of, *Africa* **52 D1** 3 30N 9 20 E
Biak, *Indonesia* **37 E9** 1 10S 136 6 E
Biała Podlaska, *Poland* **17 B12** 52 4N 23 6 E
Białogard, *Poland* **16 A8** 54 2N 15 58 E
Białystok, *Poland* **17 B12** 53 10N 23 10 E
Biaora, *India* **42 H7** 23 56N 76 56 E

Boggabri, *Australia* 63 E5 30 45S 150 5 E
Boggeragh Mts., *Ireland* 13 D3 52 2N 8 55W
Boglan = Solhan, *Turkey* 44 B4 38 57N 41 3 E
Bognor Regis, *U.K.* 11 G7 50 47N 0 40W
Bogo, *Phil.* 37 B6 11 3N 124 0 E
Bogong, Mt., *Australia* 63 F4 36 47S 147 17 E
Bogor, *Indonesia* 36 F3 6 36S 106 48 E
Bogotá, *Colombia* 92 C4 4 34N 74 0W
Bogotol, *Russia* 26 D9 56 15N 89 50 E
Bogra, *Bangla.* 41 G16 24 51N 89 22 E
Boguchany, *Russia* 27 D10 58 40N 97 30 E
Bohemian Forest = Böhmerwald, *Germany* 16 D7 49 8N 13 14 E
Böhmerwald, *Germany* 16 D7 49 8N 13 14 E
Bohol □, *Phil.* 37 C6 9 50N 124 10 E
Bohol Sea, *Phil.* 37 C6 9 0N 124 0 E
Bohuslän, *Sweden* 9 G14 58 25N 12 0 E
Boi, Pta. de, *Brazil* 95 A6 23 55S 45 15W
Boiaçu, *Brazil* 92 D6 0 27S 61 46W
Boileau, C., *Australia* 60 C3 17 40S 122 7 E
Boise, *U.S.A.* 82 E5 43 37N 116 13W
Boise City, *U.S.A.* 81 G3 36 44N 102 31W
Boissevain, *Canada* 73 D8 49 15N 100 5W
Bojador, C., *W. Sahara* 50 C3 26 0N 14 30W
Bojana →, *Albania* 21 D8 41 52N 19 22 E
Bojnūrd, *Iran* 45 B8 37 30N 57 20 E
Bojonegoro, *Indonesia* 37 G14 7 11S 111 54 E
Bokaro, *India* 43 H11 23 46N 85 55 E
Bokhara →, *Australia* 63 D4 29 55S 146 42 E
Boknafjorden, *Norway* 9 G11 59 14N 5 40 E
Bokoro, *Chad* 51 F9 12 25N 17 14 E
Bokpyin, *Burma* 39 G2 11 18N 98 42 E
Bolan →, *Pakistan* 42 E2 28 38N 67 42 E
Bolan Pass, *Pakistan* 40 E5 29 50N 67 20 E
Bolaños →, *Mexico* 86 C4 21 14N 104 8W
Bolbec, *France* 18 B4 49 30N 0 30 E
Boldājī, *Iran* 45 D6 31 56N 51 3 E
Bole, *China* 32 B3 45 11N 81 37 E
Bolekhiv, *Ukraine* 17 D12 49 0N 23 57 E
Bolesławiec, *Poland* 16 C8 51 17N 15 37 E
Bolgrad = Bolhrad, *Ukraine* 17 F15 45 40N 28 32 E
Bolhrad, *Ukraine* 17 F15 45 40N 28 32 E
Bolívar, *Argentina* 94 D3 36 15S 60 53W
Bolivar, *Mo., U.S.A.* 81 G8 37 37N 93 25W
Bolivar, *N.Y., U.S.A.* 78 D6 42 4N 78 10W
Bolivar, *Tenn., U.S.A.* 81 H10 35 12N 89 0W
Bolivia ■, *S. Amer.* 92 G6 17 6S 64 0W
Bolivian Plateau, *S. Amer.* 90 E4 20 0S 67 30W
Bollnäs, *Sweden* 9 F17 61 21N 16 24 E
Bollon, *Australia* 63 D4 28 2S 147 29 E
Bolmen, *Sweden* 9 H15 56 55N 13 40 E
Bolobo, *Dem. Rep. of the Congo* 52 E3 2 6S 16 20 E
Bologna, *Italy* 20 B4 44 29N 11 20 E
Bologoye, *Russia* 24 C5 57 55N 34 5 E
Bolonchenticul, *Mexico* 87 D7 20 0N 89 49W
Boloven, Cao Nguyen, *Laos* 38 E6 15 10N 106 30 E
Bolpur, *India* 43 H12 23 40N 87 45 E
Bolsena, L. di, *Italy* 20 C4 42 36N 11 56 E
Bolshevik, Ostrov, *Russia* 27 B11 78 30N 102 0 E
Bolshoi Kavkas = Caucasus Mountains, *Eurasia* 25 F7 42 50N 44 0 E
Bolshoy Anyuy →, *Russia* 27 C17 68 30N 160 49 E
Bolshoy Begichev, Ostrov, *Russia* 27 B12 74 20N 112 30 E
Bolshoy Lyakhovskiy, Ostrov, *Russia* 27 B15 73 35N 142 0 E
Bolshoy Tyuters, Ostrov, *Russia* 9 G22 59 51N 27 13 E
Bolsward, *Neths.* 15 A5 53 3N 5 32 E
Bolt Head, *U.K.* 11 G4 50 12N 3 48W
Bolton, *Canada* 78 C5 43 54N 79 45W
Bolton, *U.K.* 10 D5 53 35N 2 26W
Bolton Landing, *U.S.A.* 79 C11 43 32N 73 35W
Bolu, *Turkey* 25 F5 40 45N 31 35 E
Bolungavík, *Iceland* 8 C2 66 9N 23 15W
Bolvadin, *Turkey* 25 G5 38 45N 31 4 E
Bolzano, *Italy* 20 A4 46 31N 11 22 E
Bom Jesus da Lapa, *Brazil* 93 F10 13 15S 43 25W
Boma, *Dem. Rep. of the Congo* 52 F2 5 50S 13 4 E
Bombala, *Australia* 63 F4 36 56S 149 15 E
Bombay = Mumbai, *India* 40 K8 18 55N 72 50 E
Bomboma, *Dem. Rep. of the Congo* 52 D3 2 25N 18 55 E
Bombombwa, *Dem. Rep. of the Congo* 54 B2 1 40N 25 40 E
Bomili, *Dem. Rep. of the Congo* 54 B2 1 45N 27 5 E
Bømlo, *Norway* 9 G11 59 37N 5 13 E
Bomokandi →, *Dem. Rep. of the Congo* 54 B2 3 39N 26 8 E
Bomu →, *C.A.R.* 52 D4 4 40N 22 30 E
Bon, C., *Tunisia* 48 C5 37 1N 11 2 E
Bon Sar Pa, *Vietnam* 38 F6 12 24N 107 35 E
Bonaigarh, *India* 43 J11 21 50N 84 57 E
Bonaire, *Neth. Ant.* 89 D6 12 10N 68 15W
Bonang, *Australia* 63 F4 37 11S 148 41 E
Bonanza, *Nic.* 88 D3 13 54N 84 35W
Bonaparte Arch., *Australia* 60 B3 14 0S 124 30 E
Bonaventure, *Canada* 71 C6 48 5N 65 32W
Bonavista, *Canada* 71 C9 48 40N 53 5W
Bonavista, C., *Canada* 71 C9 48 42N 53 5W
Bonavista B., *Canada* 71 C9 48 45N 53 25W
Bondo, *Dem. Rep. of the Congo* 54 B1 3 55N 23 53 E
Bondoukou, *Ivory C.* 50 G5 8 2N 2 47W
Bondowoso, *Indonesia* 37 G15 7 55S 113 49 E
Bone, Teluk, *Indonesia* 37 E6 4 10S 120 50 E
Bonerate, *Indonesia* 37 F6 7 25S 121 5 E
Bonerate, Kepulauan, *Indonesia* 37 F6 6 30S 121 10 E
Bo'ness, *U.K.* 12 E5 56 1N 3 37W
Bonete, Cerro, *Argentina* 94 B2 27 55S 68 40W
Bong Son = Hoai Nhon, *Vietnam* 38 E7 14 28N 109 1 E
Bongor, *Chad* 51 F9 10 35N 15 20 E
Bonham, *U.S.A.* 81 J6 33 35N 96 11W
Bonifacio, *France* 18 F8 41 24N 9 10 E
Bonifacio, Bouches de, *Medit. S.* 20 D3 41 12N 9 15 E
Bonin Is. = Ogasawara Gunto, *Pac. Oc.* 28 G18 27 0N 142 0 E
Bonn, *Germany* 16 C4 50 46N 7 6 E
Bonne Terre, *U.S.A.* 81 G9 37 55N 90 33W
Bonners Ferry, *U.S.A.* 82 B5 48 42N 116 19W
Bonney, L., *Australia* 63 F3 37 50S 140 20 E
Bonnie Rock, *Australia* 61 F2 30 29S 118 22 E
Bonny, Bight of, *Africa* 52 D1 3 30N 9 20 E
Bonnyrigg, *U.K.* 12 F5 55 53N 3 6W
Bonnyville, *Canada* 73 C6 54 20N 110 45W
Bonoi, *Indonesia* 37 E9 1 45S 137 41 E
Bonsall, *U.S.A.* 85 M9 33 16N 117 14W
Bontang, *Indonesia* 36 D5 0 10N 117 30 E
Bonthe, *S. Leone* 50 G3 7 30N 12 33W
Bontoc, *Phil.* 37 A6 17 7N 120 58 E
Bonython Ra., *Australia* 60 D4 23 40S 128 45 E
Bookabie, *Australia* 61 F5 31 50S 132 41 E
Booker, *U.S.A.* 81 G4 36 27N 100 32W
Boolaboolka L., *Australia* 63 E3 32 38S 143 10 E
Booligal, *Australia* 63 E3 33 58S 144 53 E
Boonah, *Australia* 63 D5 27 58S 152 41 E
Boone, *Iowa, U.S.A.* 80 D8 42 4N 93 53W
Boone, *N.C., U.S.A.* 77 G5 36 13N 81 41W
Booneville, *Ark., U.S.A.* 81 H8 35 8N 93 55W
Booneville, *Miss., U.S.A.* 77 H1 34 39N 88 34W
Boonville, *Calif., U.S.A.* 84 F3 39 1N 123 22W
Boonville, *Ind., U.S.A.* 76 F2 38 3N 87 16W
Boonville, *Mo., U.S.A.* 80 F8 38 58N 92 44W
Boonville, *N.Y., U.S.A.* 79 C9 43 29N 75 20W
Boorindal, *Australia* 63 E4 30 22S 146 11 E
Boorowa, *Australia* 63 E4 34 28S 148 44 E
Boosaaso = Bosaso, *Somali Rep.* 46 E4 11 12N 49 18 E
Boothia, Gulf of, *Canada* 69 A11 71 0N 90 0W
Boothia Pen., *Canada* 68 A10 71 0N 94 0W
Bootle, *U.K.* 10 D4 53 28N 3 1W
Booué, *Gabon* 52 E2 0 5S 11 55 E
Boquete, *Panama* 88 E3 8 46N 82 27W
Boquilla, Presa de la, *Mexico* 86 B3 27 40N 105 30W
Boquillas del Carmen, *Mexico* 86 B4 29 17N 102 53W
Bor, *Serbia, Yug.* 21 B10 44 5N 22 7 E
Bôr, *Sudan* 51 G12 6 10N 31 40 E
Bor Mashash, *Israel* 47 D3 31 7N 34 50 E
Borah Peak, *U.S.A.* 82 D7 44 8N 113 47W
Borås, *Sweden* 9 H15 57 43N 12 56 E
Borāzjān, *Iran* 45 D6 29 22N 51 10 E
Borba, *Brazil* 92 D7 4 12S 59 34W
Borborema, Planalto da, *Brazil* 90 D7 7 0S 37 0W
Bord Khūn-e Now, *Iran* 45 D6 28 3N 51 28 E
Borda, C., *Australia* 63 F2 35 45S 136 34 E
Bordeaux, *France* 18 D3 44 50N 0 36W
Borden, *Australia* 61 F2 34 3S 118 12 E
Borden, *Canada* 71 C7 46 18N 63 47W
Borden I., *Canada* 4 B2 78 30N 111 30W
Borden Pen., *Canada* 69 A11 73 0N 83 0W
Borders = Scottish Borders □, *U.K.* 12 F6 55 35N 2 50W
Bordertown, *Australia* 63 F3 36 19S 140 45 E
Borðeyri, *Iceland* 8 D3 65 12N 21 6W
Bordj Fly Ste. Marie, *Algeria* 50 C5 27 19N 2 32W
Bordj-in-Eker, *Algeria* 50 D7 24 9N 5 3 E
Bordj Omar Driss, *Algeria* 50 C7 28 10N 6 40 E
Borehamwood, *U.K.* 11 F7 51 40N 0 15W
Borgå = Porvoo, *Finland* 9 F21 60 24N 25 40 E
Borgarfjörður, *Iceland* 8 D7 65 31N 13 49W
Borgarnes, *Iceland* 8 D3 64 32N 21 55W
Børgefjellet, *Norway* 8 D15 65 20N 13 45 E
Borger, *Neths.* 15 B6 52 54N 6 44 E
Borger, *U.S.A.* 81 H4 35 39N 101 24W
Borgholm, *Sweden* 9 H17 56 52N 16 39 E
Borhoyn Tal, *Mongolia* 34 C6 43 50N 111 58 E
Borikhane, *Laos* 38 C4 18 33N 103 43 E
Borisoglebsk, *Russia* 25 D7 51 27N 42 5 E
Borisov = Barysaw, *Belarus* 17 A15 54 17N 28 28 E
Borja, *Peru* 92 D3 4 20S 77 40W
Borkou, *Chad* 51 E9 18 15N 18 50 E
Borkum, *Germany* 16 B4 53 34N 6 40 E
Borlänge, *Sweden* 9 F16 60 29N 15 26 E
Borley, C., *Antarctica* 5 C5 66 15S 52 30 E
Borneo, *E. Indies* 36 D5 1 0N 115 0 E
Bornholm, *Denmark* 9 J16 55 10N 15 0 E
Borogontsy, *Russia* 27 C14 62 42N 131 8 E
Boron, *U.S.A.* 85 L9 35 0N 117 39W
Borongan, *Phil.* 37 B7 11 37N 125 26 E
Borovichi, *Russia* 24 C5 58 25N 33 55 E
Borrego Springs, *U.S.A.* 85 M10 33 15N 116 23W
Borroloola, *Australia* 62 B2 16 4S 136 17 E
Borşa, *Romania* 17 E13 47 41N 24 50 E
Borsad, *India* 42 H5 22 25N 72 54 E
Borth, *U.K.* 11 E3 52 29N 4 2W
Borūjerd, *Iran* 45 C6 33 55N 48 50 E
Boryslav, *Ukraine* 17 D12 49 18N 23 28 E
Borzya, *Russia* 27 D12 50 24N 116 31 E
Bosa, *Italy* 20 D3 40 18N 8 30 E
Bosanska Gradiška, *Bos.-H.* 20 B7 45 10N 17 15 E
Bosaso, *Somali Rep.* 46 E4 11 12N 49 18 E
Boscastle, *U.K.* 11 G3 50 41N 4 42W
Boshan, *China* 35 F9 36 28N 117 49 E
Boshof, *S. Africa* 56 D4 28 31S 25 13 E
Boshrūyeh, *Iran* 45 C8 33 50N 57 30 E
Bosna →, *Bos.-H.* 21 B8 45 4N 18 29 E
Bosna i Hercegovina = Bosnia-Herzegovina ■, *Europe* 20 B7 44 0N 18 0 E
Bosnia-Herzegovina ■, *Europe* 20 B7 44 0N 18 0 E
Bosnik, *Indonesia* 37 E9 1 5S 136 10 E
Bosobolo, *Dem. Rep. of the Congo* 52 D3 4 15N 19 50 E
Bosporus = İstanbul Boğazı, *Turkey* 21 D13 41 10N 29 10 E
Bosque Farms, *U.S.A.* 83 J10 34 53N 106 40W
Bossangoa, *C.A.R.* 52 C3 6 35N 17 30 E
Bossier City, *U.S.A.* 81 J8 32 31N 93 44W
Bosso, *Niger* 51 F8 13 43N 13 19 E
Bostan, *Pakistan* 42 D2 30 26N 67 2 E
Bostānābād, *Iran* 44 B5 37 50N 46 50 E
Bosten Hu, *China* 32 B3 41 55N 87 40 E
Boston, *U.K.* 10 E7 52 59N 0 2W
Boston, *U.S.A.* 79 D13 42 22N 71 4W
Boston Bar, *Canada* 72 D4 49 52N 121 30W
Boston Mts., *U.S.A.* 81 H8 35 42N 93 15W
Boswell, *Canada* 72 D5 49 28N 116 45W
Boswell, *U.S.A.* 78 F5 40 10N 79 2W
Botad, *India* 42 H4 22 15N 71 40 E
Botene, *Laos* 38 D3 17 35N 101 12 E
Bothaville, *S. Africa* 56 D4 27 23S 26 34 E
Bothnia, G. of, *Europe* 8 E19 63 0N 20 15 E
Bothwell, *Australia* 62 G4 42 20S 147 1 E
Bothwell, *Canada* 78 D3 42 38N 81 52W
Botletle →, *Botswana* 56 C3 20 10S 23 15 E
Botoşani, *Romania* 17 E14 47 42N 26 41 E
Botou, *Burkina Faso* 50 F6 12 42N 1 59 E
Botswana ■, *Africa* 56 C3 22 0S 24 0 E
Bottineau, *U.S.A.* 80 A4 48 50N 100 27W
Bottrop, *Germany* 15 C6 51 31N 6 58 E
Botucatu, *Brazil* 95 A6 22 55S 48 30W
Botwood, *Canada* 71 C8 49 6N 55 23W
Bouaflé, *Ivory C.* 50 G4 7 1N 5 47W
Bouaké, *Ivory C.* 50 G4 7 40N 5 2W
Bouar, *C.A.R.* 52 C3 6 0N 15 40 E
Bouârfa, *Morocco* 50 B5 32 32N 1 58W
Boucaut B., *Australia* 62 A1 12 0S 134 25 E
Bougainville, C., *Australia* 60 B4 13 57S 126 4 E
Bougainville I., *Papua N. G.* 64 H7 6 0S 155 0 E
Bougainville Reef, *Australia* 62 B4 15 30S 147 5 E
Bougie = Bejaïa, *Algeria* 50 A7 36 42N 5 2 E
Bougouni, *Mali* 50 F4 11 30N 7 20W
Bouillon, *Belgium* 15 E5 49 44N 5 3 E
Boulder, *Colo., U.S.A.* 80 E2 40 1N 105 17W
Boulder, *Mont., U.S.A.* 82 C7 46 14N 112 7W
Boulder City, *U.S.A.* 85 K12 35 59N 114 50W
Boulder Creek, *U.S.A.* 84 H4 37 7N 122 7W
Boulder Dam = Hoover Dam, *U.S.A.* 85 K12 36 1N 114 44W
Boulia, *Australia* 62 C2 22 52S 139 51 E
Boulogne-sur-Mer, *France* 18 A4 50 42N 1 36 E
Boultoum, *Niger* 51 F8 14 45N 10 25 E
Boun Neua, *Laos* 38 B3 21 38N 101 54 E
Boun Tai, *Laos* 38 B3 21 23N 101 58 E
Bouna, *Ivory C.* 50 G5 9 10N 3 0W
Boundary Peak, *U.S.A.* 84 H8 37 51N 118 21W
Boundiali, *Ivory C.* 50 G4 9 30N 6 20W
Bountiful, *U.S.A.* 82 F8 40 53N 111 53W
Bounty Is., *Pac. Oc.* 64 M9 48 0S 178 30 E
Bourbonnais, *France* 18 C5 46 28N 3 0 E
Bourdel L., *Canada* 70 A5 56 43N 74 10W
Bourem, *Mali* 50 E5 17 0N 0 24W
Bourg-en-Bresse, *France* 18 C6 46 13N 5 12 E
Bourg-St-Maurice, *France* 18 D7 45 35N 6 46 E
Bourges, *France* 18 C5 47 9N 2 25 E
Bourget, *Canada* 79 A9 45 26N 75 9W
Bourgogne, *France* 18 C6 47 0N 4 50 E
Bourke, *Australia* 63 E4 30 8S 145 55 E
Bourne, *U.K.* 10 E7 52 47N 0 22W
Bournemouth, *U.K.* 11 G6 50 43N 1 52W
Bournemouth □, *U.K.* 11 G6 50 43N 1 52W
Bouse, *U.S.A.* 85 M13 33 56N 114 0W
Bouvet I. = Bouvetøya, *Antarctica* 3 G10 54 26S 3 24 E
Bouvetøya, *Antarctica* 3 G10 54 26S 3 24 E
Bovill, *U.S.A.* 82 C5 46 51N 116 24W
Bovril, *Argentina* 94 C4 31 21S 59 26W
Bow →, *Canada* 72 C6 49 57N 111 41W
Bow Island, *Canada* 72 D6 49 50N 111 23W
Bowbells, *U.S.A.* 80 A3 48 48N 102 15W
Bowdle, *U.S.A.* 80 C5 45 27N 99 39W
Bowelling, *Australia* 61 F2 33 25S 116 30 E
Bowen, *Argentina* 94 D2 35 0S 67 31W
Bowen, *Australia* 62 C4 20 0S 148 16 E
Bowen Mts., *Australia* 63 F4 37 0S 147 50 E
Bowie, *Ariz., U.S.A.* 83 K9 32 19N 109 29W
Bowie, *Tex., U.S.A.* 81 J6 33 34N 97 51W
Bowkān, *Iran* 44 B5 36 31N 46 12 E
Bowland, Forest of, *U.K.* 10 D5 54 0N 2 30W
Bowling Green, *Ky., U.S.A.* 76 G2 36 59N 86 27W
Bowling Green, *Ohio, U.S.A.* 76 E4 41 23N 83 39W
Bowling Green, C., *Australia* 62 B4 19 19S 147 25 E
Bowman, *U.S.A.* 80 B3 46 11N 103 24W
Bowman I., *Antarctica* 5 C8 65 0S 104 0 E
Bowmanville, *Canada* 78 C6 43 55N 78 41W
Bowmore, *U.K.* 12 F2 55 45N 6 17W
Bowral, *Australia* 63 E5 34 26S 150 27 E
Bowraville, *Australia* 63 E5 30 37S 152 52 E
Bowron →, *Canada* 72 C4 54 3N 121 50W
Bowron Lake Prov. Park, *Canada* 72 C4 53 10N 121 5W
Bowser L., *Canada* 72 B3 56 30N 129 30W
Bowsman, *Canada* 73 C8 52 14N 101 12W
Bowwood, *Zambia* 55 F2 17 5S 26 20 E
Box Cr. →, *Australia* 63 E3 34 10S 143 50 E
Boxmeer, *Neths.* 15 C5 51 38N 5 56 E
Boxtel, *Neths.* 15 C5 51 36N 5 20 E
Boyce, *U.S.A.* 81 K8 31 23N 92 40W
Boyd L., *Canada* 70 B4 52 46N 76 42W
Boyle, *Canada* 72 C6 54 35N 112 49W
Boyle, *Ireland* 13 C3 53 59N 8 18W
Boyne →, *Ireland* 13 C5 53 43N 6 15W
Boyne City, *U.S.A.* 76 C3 45 13N 85 1W
Boynton Beach, *U.S.A.* 77 M5 26 32N 80 4W
Boyolali, *Indonesia* 37 G14 7 32S 110 35 E
Boyoma, Chutes, *Dem. Rep. of the Congo* 54 B2 0 35N 25 23 E
Boysen Reservoir, *U.S.A.* 82 E9 43 25N 108 11W
Boyuibe, *Bolivia* 92 G6 20 25S 63 17W
Boyup Brook, *Australia* 61 F2 33 50S 116 23 E
Boz Dağları, *Turkey* 21 E13 38 20N 28 0 E
Bozburun, *Turkey* 21 F13 36 43N 28 4 E
Bozcaada, *Turkey* 21 E12 39 49N 26 3 E
Bozdoğan, *Turkey* 21 F13 37 40N 28 17 E
Bozeman, *U.S.A.* 82 D8 45 41N 111 2W
Bozen = Bolzano, *Italy* 20 A4 46 31N 11 22 E
Bozhou, *China* 34 H8 33 55N 115 41 E
Bozoum, *C.A.R.* 52 C3 6 25N 16 35 E
Bra, *Italy* 18 D7 44 42N 7 51 E
Brabant □, *Belgium* 15 D4 50 46N 4 30 E
Brabant L., *Canada* 73 B8 55 58N 103 43W
Brač, *Croatia* 20 C7 43 20N 16 40 E
Bracadale, L., *U.K.* 12 D2 57 20N 6 30W
Bracciano, L. di, *Italy* 20 C5 42 7N 12 14 E
Bracebridge, *Canada* 78 A5 45 2N 79 19W
Brach, *Libya* 51 C8 27 31N 14 20 E
Bräcke, *Sweden* 9 E16 62 45N 15 26 E
Brackettville, *U.S.A.* 81 L4 29 19N 100 25W
Bracknell, *U.K.* 11 F7 51 25N 0 43W
Bracknell Forest □, *U.K.* 11 F7 51 25N 0 44W
Brad, *Romania* 17 E12 46 10N 22 50 E
Bradenton, *U.S.A.* 77 M4 27 30N 82 34W
Bradford, *Canada* 78 B5 44 7N 79 34W
Bradford, *U.K.* 10 D6 53 47N 1 45W
Bradford, *Pa., U.S.A.* 78 E6 41 58N 78 38W
Bradford, *Vt., U.S.A.* 79 C12 43 59N 72 9W
Bradley, *Ark., U.S.A.* 81 J8 33 6N 93 39W
Bradley, *Calif., U.S.A.* 84 K6 35 52N 120 48W
Bradley Institute, *Zimbabwe* 55 F3 17 7S 31 25 E
Brady, *U.S.A.* 81 K5 31 9N 99 20W
Braeside, *Canada* 79 A8 45 28N 76 24W
Braga, *Portugal* 19 B1 41 35N 8 25W
Bragado, *Argentina* 94 D3 35 2S 60 27W
Bragança, *Brazil* 93 D9 1 0S 47 2W
Bragança, *Portugal* 19 B2 41 48N 6 50W
Bragança Paulista, *Brazil* 95 A6 22 55S 46 32W
Brahmanbaria, *Bangla.* 41 H17 23 58N 91 15 E
Brahmani →, *India* 41 J15 20 39N 86 46 E
Brahmapur, *India* 41 K14 19 15N 84 54 E
Brahmaputra →, *India* 41 F19 27 48N 95 30 E
Braich-y-pwll, *U.K.* 10 E3 52 47N 4 46W
Braidwood, *Australia* 63 F4 35 27S 149 49 E
Brăila, *Romania* 17 F14 45 19N 27 59 E
Brainerd, *U.S.A.* 80 B7 46 22N 94 12W
Braintree, *U.K.* 11 F8 51 53N 0 34 E
Braintree, *U.S.A.* 79 D14 42 13N 71 0W
Brak →, *S. Africa* 56 D3 29 35S 22 55 E
Brakwater, *Namibia* 56 C2 22 28S 17 3 E
Brampton, *Canada* 78 C5 43 45N 79 45W
Brampton, *U.K.* 10 C5 54 57N 2 44W
Branco →, *Brazil* 92 D6 1 20S 61 50W
Brandberg, *Namibia* 56 B2 21 10S 14 33 E
Brandenburg = Neubrandenburg, *Germany* 16 B7 53 33N 13 15 E
Brandenburg, *Germany* 16 B7 52 25N 12 33 E
Brandenburg □, *Germany* 16 B6 52 50N 13 0 E
Brandfort, *S. Africa* 56 D4 28 40S 26 30 E
Brandon, *Canada* 73 D9 49 50N 99 57W
Brandon, *U.S.A.* 79 C11 43 48N 73 4W
Brandon B., *Ireland* 13 D1 52 17N 10 8W
Brandon Mt., *Ireland* 13 D1 52 15N 10 15W
Brandsen, *Argentina* 94 D4 35 10S 58 15W
Brandvlei, *S. Africa* 56 E3 30 25S 20 30 E
Branford, *U.S.A.* 79 E12 41 17N 72 49W
Braniewo, *Poland* 17 A10 54 25N 19 50 E
Bransfield Str., *Antarctica* 5 C18 63 0S 59 0W
Branson, *U.S.A.* 81 G8 36 39N 93 13W
Brantford, *Canada* 78 C4 43 10N 80 15W
Bras d'Or L., *Canada* 71 C7 45 50N 60 50W
Brasher Falls, *U.S.A.* 79 B10 44 49N 74 47W
Brasil, Planalto, *Brazil* 90 E6 18 0S 46 30W
Brasiléia, *Brazil* 92 F5 11 0S 68 45W
Brasília, *Brazil* 93 G9 15 47S 47 55W
Brasília Legal, *Brazil* 93 D7 3 49S 55 36W
Braslaw, *Belarus* 9 J22 55 38N 27 0 E
Braşov, *Romania* 17 F13 45 38N 25 35 E
Brasschaat, *Belgium* 15 C4 51 19N 4 27 E
Brassey, Banjaran, *Malaysia* 36 D5 5 0N 117 15 E
Brassey Ra., *Australia* 61 E3 25 8S 122 15 E
Brasstown Bald, *U.S.A.* 77 H4 34 53N 83 49W
Brastad, *Sweden* 9 G14 58 23N 11 30 E
Bratislava, *Slovak Rep.* 17 D9 48 10N 17 7 E
Bratsk, *Russia* 27 D11 56 10N 101 30 E
Brattleboro, *U.S.A.* 79 D12 42 51N 72 34W
Braunau, *Austria* 16 D7 48 15N 13 3 E
Braunschweig, *Germany* 16 B6 52 15N 10 31 E
Braunton, *U.K.* 11 F3 51 7N 4 10W
Bravo del Norte, Rio = Grande, Rio →, *U.S.A.* 81 N6 25 58N 97 9W
Brawley, *U.S.A.* 85 N11 32 59N 115 31W
Bray, *Ireland* 13 C5 53 13N 6 7W
Bray, Mt., *Australia* 62 A1 14 0S 134 30 E
Bray, Pays de, *France* 18 B4 49 46N 1 26 E
Brazeau →, *Canada* 72 C5 52 55N 115 14W
Brazil, *U.S.A.* 76 F2 39 32N 87 8W
Brazil ■, *S. Amer.* 93 F9 12 0S 50 0W
Brazilian Highlands = Brasil, Planalto, *Brazil* 90 E6 18 0S 46 30W
Brazo Sur →, *S. Amer.* 94 B4 25 21S 57 42W
Brazos →, *U.S.A.* 81 L7 28 53N 95 23W
Brazzaville, *Congo* 52 E3 4 9S 15 12 E
Brčko, *Bos.-H.* 21 B8 44 54N 18 46 E
Breaden, L., *Australia* 61 E4 25 51S 125 28 E
Breaksea Sd., *N.Z.* 59 L1 45 35S 166 35 E
Bream B., *N.Z.* 59 F5 35 56S 174 28 E
Bream Hd., *N.Z.* 59 F5 35 51S 174 36 E
Breas, *Chile* 94 B1 25 29S 70 24W
Brebes, *Indonesia* 37 G13 6 52S 109 3 E
Brechin, *Canada* 78 B5 44 32N 79 10W
Brechin, *U.K.* 12 E6 56 44N 2 39W
Brecht, *Belgium* 15 C4 51 21N 4 38 E
Breckenridge, *Colo., U.S.A.* 82 G10 39 29N 106 3W
Breckenridge, *Minn., U.S.A.* 80 B6 46 16N 96 35W
Breckenridge, *Tex., U.S.A.* 81 J5 32 45N 98 54W
Breckland, *U.K.* 11 E8 52 30N 0 40 E
Brecon, *U.K.* 11 F4 51 57N 3 23W
Brecon Beacons, *U.K.* 11 F4 51 53N 3 26W
Breda, *Neths.* 15 C4 51 35N 4 45 E
Bredasdorp, *S. Africa* 56 E3 34 33S 20 2 E
Bree, *Belgium* 15 C5 51 8N 5 35 E
Bregenz, *Austria* 16 E5 47 30N 9 45 E
Breiðafjörður, *Iceland* 8 D2 65 15N 23 15W
Brejo, *Brazil* 93 D10 3 41S 42 47W
Bremen, *Germany* 16 B5 53 4N 8 47 E
Bremer Bay, *Australia* 61 F2 34 21S 119 20 E
Bremer I., *Australia* 62 A2 12 5S 136 45 E
Bremerhaven, *Germany* 16 B5 53 33N 8 36 E
Bremerton, *U.S.A.* 84 C4 47 34N 122 38W
Brenham, *U.S.A.* 81 K6 30 10N 96 24W
Brennerpass, *Austria* 16 E6 47 2N 11 30 E
Brent, *U.S.A.* 77 J2 32 56N 87 10W
Brentwood, *U.K.* 11 F8 51 37N 0 19 E
Brentwood, *Calif., U.S.A.* 84 H5 37 56N 121 42W
Brentwood, *N.Y., U.S.A.* 79 F11 40 47N 73 15W
Bréscia, *Italy* 18 D9 45 33N 10 15 E
Breskens, *Neths.* 15 C3 51 23N 3 33 E
Breslau = Wrocław, *Poland* 17 C9 51 5N 17 5 E
Bressanone, *Italy* 20 A4 46 43N 11 39 E
Bressay, *U.K.* 12 A7 60 9N 1 6W
Brest, *Belarus* 17 B12 52 10N 23 40 E
Brest, *France* 18 B1 48 24N 4 31W
Brest-Litovsk = Brest, *Belarus* 17 B12 52 10N 23 40 E
Bretagne, *France* 18 B2 48 10N 3 0W
Breton, *Canada* 72 C6 53 7N 114 28W
Breton Sd., *U.S.A.* 81 L10 29 35N 89 15W
Brett, C., *N.Z.* 59 F5 35 10S 174 20 E
Brevard, *U.S.A.* 77 H4 35 14N 82 44W
Breves, *Brazil* 93 D8 1 40S 50 29W
Brewarrina, *Australia* 63 E4 30 0S 146 51 E
Brewer, *U.S.A.* 77 C11 44 48N 68 46W
Brewer, Mt., *U.S.A.* 84 J8 36 44N 118 28W
Brewster, *N.Y., U.S.A.* 79 E11 41 23N 73 37W

Butte Creek →, *U.S.A.* **84 F5** 39 12N 121 56W
Butterworth = Gcuwa,
S. Africa ..... **57 E4** 32 20S 28 11 E
Butterworth, *Malaysia* ..... **39 K3** 5 24N 100 23 E
Buttevant, *Ireland* **13 D3** 52 14N 8 40W
Buttfield, Mt., *Australia* ..... **61 D4** 24 45S 128 9 E
Button B., *Canada* **73 B10** 58 45N 94 23W
Buttonwillow, *U.S.A.* **85 K7** 35 24N 119 28W
Butty Hd., *Australia* ..... **61 F3** 33 54S 121 39 E
Butuan, *Phil.* ..... **37 C7** 8 57N 125 33 E
Butung = Buton, *Indonesia* .. **37 E6** 5 0S 122 45 E
Buturlinovka, *Russia* ..... **25 D7** 50 50N 40 35 E
Buur Hakaba = Bur Acaba,
Somali Rep. ..... **46 G3** 3 12N 44 20 E
Buxa Duar, *India* ..... **43 F13** 27 45N 89 35 E
Buxar, *India* ..... **43 G10** 25 34N 83 58 E
Buxtehude, *Germany* ..... **16 B5** 53 28N 9 39 E
Buxton, *U.K.* **10 D6** 53 16N 1 54W
Buy, *Russia* ..... **24 C7** 58 28N 41 28 E
Büyük Menderes →, *Turkey* **21 F12** 37 28N 27 11 E
Büyükçekmece, *Turkey* ..... **21 D13** 41 2N 28 35 E
Buzău, *Romania* ..... **17 F14** 45 10N 26 50 E
Buzău →, *Romania* ..... **17 F14** 45 26N 27 44 E
Buzen, *Japan* ..... **31 H5** 33 35N 131 5 E
Buzi →, *Mozam.* ..... **55 F3** 19 50S 34 43 E
Buzuluk, *Russia* ..... **24 D9** 52 48N 52 12 E
Buzzards B., *U.S.A.* **79 E14** 41 45N 70 37W
Buzzards Bay, *U.S.A.* **79 E14** 41 44N 70 37W
Bwana Mkubwe, *Dem. Rep. of the Congo* ..... **55 E2** 13 8S 28 38 E
Byarezina →, *Belarus* ..... **17 B16** 52 33N 30 14 E
Byaroza, *Belarus* ..... **17 B13** 52 31N 24 51 E
Bydgoszcz, *Poland* ..... **17 B9** 53 10N 18 0 E
Byelarus = Belarus ■, *Europe* **17 B14** 53 30N 27 0 E
Byelorussia = Belarus ■,
Europe ..... **17 B14** 53 30N 27 0 E
Byers, *U.S.A.* **80 F2** 39 43N 104 14W
Byesville, *U.S.A.* **78 G3** 39 58N 81 32W
Byford, *Australia* ..... **61 F2** 32 15S 116 0 E
Bykhaw, *Belarus* ..... **17 B16** 53 31N 30 14 E
Bykhov = Bykhaw, *Belarus* .. **17 B16** 53 31N 30 14 E
Bylas, *U.S.A.* **83 K8** 33 8N 110 7W
Bylot, *Canada* **73 B10** 58 25N 94 8W
Bylot I., *Canada* **69 A12** 73 13N 78 34W
Byrd, C., *Antarctica* **5 C17** 69 38S 76 7W
Byrock, *Australia* ..... **63 E4** 30 40S 146 27 E
Byron Bay, *Australia* ..... **63 D5** 28 43S 153 37 E
Byrranga, Gory, *Russia* ..... **27 B11** 75 0N 100 0 E
Byrranga Mts. = Byrranga,
Gory, *Russia* ..... **27 B11** 75 0N 100 0 E
Byske, *Sweden* ..... **8 D19** 64 57N 21 11 E
Byske älv →, *Sweden* ..... **8 D19** 64 57N 21 13 E
Bytom, *Poland* ..... **17 C10** 50 25N 18 54 E
Bytów, *Poland* ..... **17 A9** 54 10N 17 30 E
Byumba, *Rwanda* ..... **54 C3** 1 35S 30 4 E

C

Ca →, *Vietnam* ..... **38 C5** 18 45N 105 45 E
Ca Mau, *Vietnam* ..... **39 H5** 9 7N 105 8 E
Ca Mau, Mui, *Vietnam* ..... **39 H5** 8 38N 104 44 E
Ca Na, *Vietnam* ..... **39 G7** 11 20N 108 54 E
Caacupé, *Paraguay* **94 B4** 25 23S 57 5W
Caála, *Angola* ..... **53 G3** 12 46S 15 30 E
Caamano Sd., *Canada* **72 C3** 52 55N 129 25W
Caazapá, *Paraguay* **94 B4** 26 8S 56 19W
Caazapá □, *Paraguay* **95 B4** 26 10S 56 0W
Caballeria, C. de, *Spain* ..... **22 A11** 40 5N 4 5 E
Cabanatuan, *Phil.* ..... **37 A6** 15 30N 120 58 E
Cabano, *Canada* **71 C6** 47 40N 68 56W
Cabazon, *U.S.A.* **85 M10** 33 55N 116 47W
Cabedelo, *Brazil* **93 E12** 7 0S 34 50W
Cabildo, *Chile* **94 C1** 32 30S 71 5W
Cabimas, *Venezuela* **92 A4** 10 23N 71 25W
Cabinda, *Angola* ..... **52 F2** 5 33S 12 11 E
Cabinda □, *Angola* ..... **52 F2** 5 0S 12 30 E
Cabinet Mts., *U.S.A.* **82 C6** 48 0N 115 30W
Cabo Blanco, *Argentina* **96 F3** 47 15S 65 47W
Cabo Frio, *Brazil* **95 A7** 22 51S 42 3W
Cabo Pantoja, *Peru* **92 D3** 1 0S 75 10W
Cabonga, Réservoir, *Canada* **70 C4** 47 20N 76 40W
Cabool, *U.S.A.* **81 G8** 37 7N 92 6W
Caboolture, *Australia* ..... **63 D5** 27 5S 152 58 E
Cabora Bassa Dam = Cahora
Bassa, Représa de, *Mozam.* **55 F3** 15 20S 32 50 E
Caborca, *Mexico* **86 A2** 30 40N 112 10W
Cabot, Mt., *U.S.A.* **79 B13** 44 30N 71 25W
Cabot Hd., *Canada* **78 A3** 45 14N 81 17W
Cabot Str., *Canada* **71 C8** 47 15N 59 40W
Cabra, *Spain* **19 D3** 37 30N 4 28W
Cabrera, *Spain* ..... **22 B9** 39 8N 2 57 E
Cabri, *Canada* **73 C7** 50 35N 108 25W
Cabriel →, *Spain* **19 C5** 39 14N 1 3W
Caçador, *Brazil* **95 B5** 26 47S 51 0W
Čačak, *Serbia, Yug.* ..... **21 C9** 43 54N 20 20 E
Caçapava do Sul, *Brazil* **95 C5** 30 30S 53 30W
Cáceres, *Brazil* **92 G7** 16 5S 57 40W
Cáceres, *Spain* **19 C2** 39 26N 6 23W
Cache Bay, *Canada* **70 C4** 46 22N 80 0W
Cache Cr. →, *U.S.A.* **84 G5** 38 42N 121 42W
Cache Creek, *Canada* **72 C4** 50 48N 121 19W
Cachi, *Argentina* **94 B2** 25 5S 66 10W
Cachimbo, Serra do, *Brazil* .. **93 E7** 9 30S 55 30W
Cachinal de la Sierra, *Chile* . **94 A2** 24 58S 69 32W
Cachoeira, *Brazil* **93 F11** 12 30S 39 0W
Cachoeira do Sul, *Brazil* **95 C5** 30 3S 52 53W
Cachoeiro de Itapemirim,
Brazil **95 A7** 20 51S 41 7W
Cacoal, *Brazil* **92 F6** 11 32S 61 18W
Cacólo, *Angola* ..... **52 G3** 10 9S 19 21 E
Caconda, *Angola* ..... **53 G3** 13 48S 15 8 E
Caddo, *U.S.A.* **81 H6** 34 7N 96 16W
Cader Idris, *U.K.* **11 E4** 52 42N 3 53W
Cadereyta, *Mexico* **86 B5** 25 36N 100 0W
Cadibarrawirracanna, L.,
Australia ..... **63 D2** 28 52S 135 27 E
Cadillac, *U.S.A.* **76 C3** 44 15N 85 24W
Cadiz, *Phil.* ..... **37 B6** 10 57N 123 15 E
Cádiz, *Spain* **19 D2** 36 30N 6 20W
Cadiz, *Calif., U.S.A.* **85 L11** 34 30N 115 28W
Cadiz, *Ohio, U.S.A.* **78 F4** 40 22N 81 0W
Cádiz, G. de, *Spain* **19 D2** 36 40N 7 0W
Cadiz L., *U.S.A.* **83 J6** 34 18N 115 24W
Cadney Park, *Australia* ..... **63 D1** 27 55S 134 3 E
Cadomin, *Canada* **72 C5** 53 2N 117 20W
Cadotte Lake, *Canada* **72 B5** 56 26N 116 23W
Cadoux, *Australia* ..... **61 F2** 30 46S 117 7 E
Caen, *France* **18 B3** 49 10N 0 22W
Caernarfon, *U.K.* **10 D3** 53 8N 4 16W
Caernarfon B., *U.K.* **10 D3** 53 4N 4 40W
Caernarvon = Caernarfon,
U.K. **10 D3** 53 8N 4 16W
Caerphilly, *U.K.* **11 F4** 51 35N 3 13W
Caerphilly □, *U.K.* **11 F4** 51 37N 3 12W
Caesarea, *Israel* ..... **47 C3** 32 30N 34 53 E
Caetité, *Brazil* **93 F10** 13 50S 42 32W
Cafayate, *Argentina* **94 B2** 26 2S 66 0W
Cafu, *Angola* ..... **56 B2** 16 30S 15 8 E
Cagayan de Oro, *Phil.* ..... **37 C6** 8 30N 124 40 E
Cagayan Is., *Phil.* ..... **37 C5** 9 40N 121 16 E
Cágliari, *Italy* ..... **20 E3** 39 13N 9 7 E
Cágliari, G. di, *Italy* ..... **20 E3** 39 8N 9 11 E
Caguán →, *Colombia* **92 D4** 0 8S 74 18W
Caguas, *Puerto Rico* **89 C6** 18 14N 66 2W
Caha Mts., *Ireland* **13 E2** 51 45N 9 40W
Cahama, *Angola* ..... **56 B1** 16 17S 14 19 E
Caher, *Ireland* **13 D4** 52 22N 7 56W
Caherciveen, *Ireland* **13 E1** 51 56N 10 14W
Cahora Bassa, L. de, *Mozam.* **55 F3** 15 35S 32 0 E
Cahora Bassa, Représa de,
Mozam. ..... **55 F3** 15 20S 32 50 E
Cahore Pt., *Ireland* **13 D5** 52 33N 6 12W
Cahors, *France* ..... **18 D4** 44 27N 1 27 E
Cahul, *Moldova* ..... **17 F15** 45 50N 28 15 E
Cai Bau, Dao, *Vietnam* ..... **38 B6** 21 10N 107 27 E
Cai Nuoc, *Vietnam* ..... **39 H5** 8 56N 105 1 E
Caia, *Mozam.* ..... **55 F4** 17 51S 35 24 E
Caianda, *Angola* ..... **55 E1** 11 2S 23 31 E
Caibarién, *Cuba* **88 B4** 22 30N 79 30W
Caicara, *Venezuela* **92 B5** 7 38N 66 10W
Caicó, *Brazil* **93 E11** 6 20S 37 0W
Caicos Is., *Turks & Caicos* .. **89 B5** 21 40N 71 40W
Caicos Passage, *W. Indies* .. **89 B5** 22 45N 72 45W
Caird Coast, *Antarctica* **5 D1** 75 0S 25 0W
Cairn Gorm, *U.K.* **12 D5** 57 7N 3 39W
Cairngorm Mts., *U.K.* **12 D5** 57 6N 3 42W
Cairnryan, *U.K.* **12 G3** 54 59N 5 1W
Cairns, *Australia* ..... **62 B4** 16 57S 145 45 E
Cairns L., *Canada* **73 C10** 51 42N 94 30W
Cairo = El Qâhira, *Egypt* ..... **51 B12** 30 1N 31 14 E
Cairo, *Ga., U.S.A.* **77 K3** 30 52N 84 13W
Cairo, *Ill., U.S.A.* **81 G10** 37 0N 89 11W
Cairo, *N.Y., U.S.A.* **79 D11** 42 18N 74 0W
Caithness, Ord of, *U.K.* **12 C5** 58 8N 3 36W
Cajamarca, *Peru* **92 E3** 7 5S 78 28W
Cajàzeiras, *Brazil* **93 E11** 6 52S 38 30W
Cala d'Or, *Spain* ..... **22 B10** 39 23N 3 14 E
Cala en Porter, *Spain* ..... **22 B11** 39 52N 4 8 E
Cala Figuera, C. de, *Spain* .. **22 B9** 39 27N 2 31 E
Cala Forcat, *Spain* ..... **22 B10** 40 0N 3 47 E
Cala Major, *Spain* ..... **22 B9** 39 33N 2 37 E
Cala Mezquida = Sa
Mesquida, *Spain* ..... **22 B11** 39 55N 4 16 E
Cala Millor, *Spain* ..... **22 B10** 39 35N 3 22 E
Cala Ratjada, *Spain* ..... **22 B10** 39 43N 3 27 E
Cala Santa Galdana, *Spain* .. **22 B10** 39 56N 3 58 E
Calabar, *Nigeria* ..... **50 H7** 4 57N 8 20 E
Calabogie, *Canada* **79 A8** 45 18N 76 43W
Calabozo, *Venezuela* **92 B5** 9 0N 67 28W
Calábria □, *Italy* ..... **20 E7** 39 0N 16 30 E
Calafate, *Argentina* **96 G2** 50 19S 72 15W
Calahorra, *Spain* **19 A5** 42 18N 1 59W
Calais, *France* ..... **18 A4** 50 57N 1 56 E
Calais, *U.S.A.* **77 C12** 45 11N 67 17W
Calalaste, Cord. de, *Argentina* **94 B2** 25 0S 67 0W
Calama, *Brazil* **92 E6** 8 0S 62 50W
Calama, *Chile* **94 A2** 22 30S 68 55W
Calamar, *Colombia* **92 A4** 10 15N 74 55W
Calamian Group, *Phil.* ..... **37 B5** 11 50N 119 55 E
Calamocha, *Spain* **19 B5** 40 50N 1 17W
Calang, *Indonesia* ..... **36 D1** 4 37N 95 37 E
Calapan, *Phil.* ..... **37 B6** 13 25N 121 7 E
Călăraşi, *Romania* ..... **17 F14** 44 12N 27 20 E
Calatayud, *Spain* **19 B5** 41 20N 1 40W
Calauag, *Phil.* ..... **37 B6** 13 55N 122 15 E
Calavite, C., *Phil.* ..... **37 B6** 13 26N 120 20 E
Calbayog, *Phil.* ..... **37 B6** 12 4N 124 38 E
Calca, *Peru* **92 F4** 13 22S 72 0W
Calcasieu L., *U.S.A.* **81 L8** 29 55N 93 18W
Calcutta = Kolkata, *India* ..... **43 H13** 22 36N 88 24 E
Calcutta, *U.S.A.* **78 F4** 40 40N 80 34W
Caldas da Rainha, *Portugal* .. **19 C1** 39 24N 9 8W
Calder →, *U.K.* **10 D6** 53 44N 1 22W
Caldera, *Chile* **94 B1** 27 5S 70 55W
Caldwell, *Idaho, U.S.A.* **82 E5** 43 40N 116 41W
Caldwell, *Kans., U.S.A.* **81 G6** 37 2N 97 37W
Caldwell, *Tex., U.S.A.* **81 K6** 30 32N 96 42W
Caledon, *S. Africa* ..... **56 E2** 34 14S 19 26 E
Caledon →, *S. Africa* ..... **56 E4** 30 31S 26 5 E
Caledon B., *Australia* ..... **62 A2** 12 45S 137 0 E
Caledonia, *Canada* **78 C5** 43 7N 79 58W
Caledonia, *U.S.A.* **78 D7** 42 58N 77 51W
Calemba, *Angola* ..... **56 B2** 16 0S 15 44 E
Calen, *Australia* ..... **62 C4** 20 56S 148 48 E
Caletones, *Chile* **94 C1** 34 6S 70 27W
Calexico, *U.S.A.* **85 N11** 32 40N 115 30W
Calf of Man, *U.K.* **10 C3** 54 3N 4 48W
Calgary, *Canada* **72 C6** 51 0N 114 10W
Calheta, *Madeira* **22 D2** 32 44N 17 11W
Calhoun, *U.S.A.* **77 H3** 34 30N 84 57W
Cali, *Colombia* **92 C3** 3 25N 76 35W
Calicut, *India* ..... **40 P9** 11 15N 75 43 E
Caliente, *U.S.A.* **83 H6** 37 37N 114 31W
California, *Mo., U.S.A.* **80 F8** 38 38N 92 34W
California, *Pa., U.S.A.* **78 F5** 40 4N 79 54W
California □, *U.S.A.* **84 H7** 37 30N 119 30W
California, Baja, *Mexico* **86 A1** 32 10N 115 12W
California, Baja, T.N. = Baja
California □, *Mexico* **86 B2** 30 0N 115 0W
California, Baja, T.S. = Baja
California Sur □, *Mexico* **86 B2** 25 50N 111 50W
California, G. de, *Mexico* **86 B2** 27 0N 111 0W
California City, *U.S.A.* **85 K9** 35 10N 117 55W
California Hot Springs, *U.S.A.* **85 K8** 35 51N 118 41W
Calingasta, *Argentina* **94 C2** 31 15S 69 30W
Calipatria, *U.S.A.* **85 M11** 33 8N 115 31W
Calistoga, *U.S.A.* **84 G4** 38 35N 122 35W
Calitzdorp, *S. Africa* ..... **56 E3** 33 33S 21 42 E
Callabonna, L., *Australia* ..... **63 D3** 29 40S 140 5 E
Callan, *Ireland* **13 D4** 52 32N 7 24W
Callander, *U.K.* **12 E4** 56 15N 4 13W
Callao, *Peru* **92 F3** 12 0S 77 0W
Calles, *Mexico* **87 C5** 23 2N 98 42W
Callicoon, *U.S.A.* **79 E9** 41 46N 75 3W
Calling Lake, *Canada* **72 B6** 55 15N 113 12W
Calliope, *Australia* ..... **62 C5** 24 0S 151 16 E
Calne, *U.K.* **11 F6** 51 26N 2 0W
Calola, *Angola* ..... **56 B2** 16 25S 17 48 E
Caloundra, *Australia* ..... **63 D5** 26 45S 153 10 E
Calpella, *U.S.A.* **84 F3** 39 14N 123 12W
Calpine, *U.S.A.* **84 F6** 39 40N 120 27W
Calstock, *Canada* **70 C3** 49 47N 84 9W
Caltagirone, *Italy* ..... **20 F6** 37 14N 14 31 E
Caltanissetta, *Italy* ..... **20 F6** 37 29N 14 4 E
Calulo, *Angola* ..... **52 G2** 10 1S 14 56 E
Calvert →, *Australia* ..... **62 B2** 16 17S 137 44 E
Calvert I., *Canada* **72 C3** 51 30N 128 0W
Calvert Ra., *Australia* ..... **60 D3** 24 0S 122 30 E
Calvi, *France* ..... **18 E8** 42 34N 8 45 E
Calviá, *Spain* ..... **19 C7** 39 34N 2 31 E
Calvillo, *Mexico* **86 C4** 21 51N 102 43W
Calvinia, *S. Africa* ..... **56 E2** 31 28S 19 45 E
Calwa, *U.S.A.* **84 J7** 36 42N 119 46W
Cam →, *U.K.* ..... **11 E8** 52 21N 0 16 E
Cam Lam, *Vietnam* ..... **39 G7** 11 54N 109 10 E
Cam Pha, *Vietnam* ..... **38 B6** 21 7N 107 18 E
Cam Ranh, *Vietnam* ..... **39 G7** 11 54N 109 12 E
Cam Xuyen, *Vietnam* ..... **38 C6** 18 15N 106 0 E
Camabatela, *Angola* ..... **52 F3** 8 20S 15 26 E
Camacha, *Madeira* **22 D3** 32 41N 16 49W
Camacho, *Mexico* **86 C4** 24 25N 102 18W
Camacupa, *Angola* ..... **53 G3** 11 58S 17 22 E
Camagüey, *Cuba* **88 B4** 21 20N 78 0W
Camaná, *Peru* **92 G4** 16 30S 72 50W
Camanche Reservoir, *U.S.A.* **84 G6** 38 14N 121 1W
Camaquã, *Brazil* **95 C5** 30 51S 51 49W
Camaquã →, *Brazil* **95 C5** 31 17S 51 47W
Câmara de Lobos, *Madeira* . **22 D3** 32 39N 16 59W
Camargo, *Mexico* **87 B5** 26 19N 98 50W
Camargue, *France* ..... **18 E6** 43 34N 4 34 E
Camarillo, *U.S.A.* **85 L7** 34 13N 119 2W
Camarón, C., *Honduras* **88 C2** 16 0N 85 5W
Camarones, *Argentina* **96 E3** 44 50S 65 40W
Camas, *U.S.A.* **84 E4** 45 35N 122 24W
Camas Valley, *U.S.A.* **82 E2** 43 2N 123 40W
Camballin, *Australia* ..... **60 C3** 17 59S 124 12 E
Cambará, *Brazil* **95 A5** 23 2S 50 5W
Cambay = Khambhat, *India* . **42 H5** 22 23N 72 33 E
Cambay, G. of = Khambhat,
G. of, *India* ..... **40 J8** 20 45N 72 30 E
Cambodia ■, *Asia* ..... **38 F5** 12 15N 105 0 E
Camborne, *U.K.* **11 G2** 50 12N 5 19W
Cambrai, *France* ..... **18 A5** 50 11N 3 14 E
Cambria, *U.S.A.* **84 K5** 35 34N 121 5W
Cambrian Mts., *U.K.* **11 E4** 52 3N 3 57W
Cambridge, *Canada* **78 C4** 43 23N 80 15W
Cambridge, *Jamaica* **88 C4** 18 18N 77 54W
Cambridge, *N.Z.* ..... **59 G5** 37 54S 175 29 E
Cambridge, *U.K.* ..... **11 E8** 52 12N 0 8 E
Cambridge, *Mass., U.S.A.* .. **79 D13** 42 22N 71 6W
Cambridge, *Minn., U.S.A.* .. **80 C8** 45 34N 93 13W
Cambridge, *N.Y., U.S.A.* ... **79 C11** 43 2N 73 22W
Cambridge, *Nebr., U.S.A.* ... **80 E4** 40 17N 100 10W
Cambridge, *Ohio, U.S.A.* **78 F3** 40 2N 81 35W
Cambridge Bay = Ikaluktutiak,
Canada **68 B9** 69 10N 105 0W
Cambridge G., *Australia* ..... **60 B4** 14 55S 128 15 E
Cambridge Springs, *U.S.A.* . **78 E4** 41 48N 80 4W
Cambridgeshire □, *U.K.* **11 E7** 52 25N 0 7W
Cambuci, *Brazil* **95 A7** 21 35S 41 55W
Cambundi-Catembo, *Angola* **52 G3** 10 10S 17 35 E
Camden, *Ala., U.S.A.* **77 K2** 31 59N 87 17W
Camden, *Ark., U.S.A.* **81 J8** 33 35N 92 50W
Camden, *Maine, U.S.A.* **77 C11** 44 13N 69 4W
Camden, *N.J., U.S.A.* **79 G9** 39 56N 75 7W
Camden, *N.Y., U.S.A.* **79 C9** 43 20N 75 45W
Camden, *S.C., U.S.A.* **77 H5** 34 16N 80 36W
Camden Sd., *Australia* ..... **60 C3** 15 27S 124 25 E
Camdenton, *U.S.A.* **81 F8** 38 1N 92 45W
Cameron, *Ariz., U.S.A.* **83 J8** 35 53N 111 25W
Cameron, *La., U.S.A.* **81 L8** 29 48N 93 20W
Cameron, *Mo., U.S.A.* **80 F7** 39 44N 94 14W
Cameron, *Tex., U.S.A.* **81 K6** 30 51N 96 59W
Cameron Highlands, *Malaysia* **39 K3** 4 27N 101 22 E
Cameron Hills, *Canada* **72 B5** 59 48N 118 0W
Cameroon ■, *Africa* ..... **52 C2** 6 0N 12 30 E
Cameroun, Mt., *Cameroon* .. **52 D1** 4 13N 9 10 E
Cametá, *Brazil* **93 D9** 2 12S 49 30W
Camiguin I., *Phil.* ..... **37 C6** 18 56N 121 55 E
Camilla, *U.S.A.* **77 K3** 31 14N 84 12W
Caminha, *Portugal* **19 B1** 41 50N 8 50W
Camino, *U.S.A.* **84 G6** 38 44N 120 41W
Camira Creek, *Australia* ..... **63 D5** 29 15S 152 58 E
Cammal, *U.S.A.* **78 E7** 41 24N 77 28W
Camocim, *Brazil* **93 D10** 2 55S 40 50W
Camooweal, *Australia* ..... **62 B2** 19 56S 138 7 E
Camopi, *Fr. Guiana* **93 C8** 3 12N 52 17W
Camp Borden, *Canada* **78 B5** 44 18N 79 56W
Camp Hill, *U.S.A.* **78 F8** 40 14N 76 55W
Camp Nelson, *U.S.A.* **85 J8** 36 8N 118 39W
Camp Pendleton, *U.S.A.* **85 M9** 33 16N 117 23W
Camp Verde, *U.S.A.* **83 J8** 34 34N 111 51W
Camp Wood, *U.S.A.* **81 L5** 29 40N 100 1W
Campana, *Argentina* **94 C4** 34 10S 58 55W
Campana, I., *Chile* **96 F1** 48 20S 75 20W
Campanário, *Madeira* **22 D2** 32 39N 17 2W
Campánia □, *Italy* ..... **20 D6** 41 0N 14 30 E
Campbell, *S. Africa* ..... **56 D3** 28 48S 23 44 E
Campbell, *Calif., U.S.A.* **84 H5** 37 17N 121 57W
Campbell, *Ohio, U.S.A.* **78 E4** 41 5N 80 37W
Campbell I., *Pac. Oc.* ..... **64 N8** 52 30S 169 0 E
Campbell L., *Canada* **73 A7** 63 14N 106 55W
Campbell River, *Canada* **72 C3** 50 5N 125 20W
Campbell Town, *Australia* ... **62 G4** 41 52S 147 30 E
Campbellford, *Canada* **78 B7** 44 18N 77 48W
Campbellpur, *Pakistan* ..... **42 C5** 33 46N 72 26 E
Campbellsville, *U.S.A.* **76 G3** 37 21N 85 20W
Campbellton, *Canada* **71 C6** 47 57N 66 43W
Campbelltown, *Australia* ..... **63 E5** 34 4S 150 49 E
Campbeltown, *U.K.* **12 F3** 55 26N 5 36W
Campeche, *Mexico* **87 D6** 19 50N 90 32W
Campeche □, *Mexico* **87 D6** 19 50N 90 32W
Campeche, Golfo de, *Mexico* **87 D6** 19 30N 93 0W
Camperdown, *Australia* ..... **63 F3** 38 14S 143 9 E
Camperville, *Canada* **73 C8** 51 59N 100 9W
Câmpina, *Romania* ..... **17 F13** 45 10N 25 45 E
Campina Grande, *Brazil* **93 E11** 7 20S 35 47W
Campinas, *Brazil* **95 A6** 22 50S 47 0W
Campo Grande, *Brazil* **93 H8** 20 25S 54 40W
Campo Maíor, *Brazil* **93 D10** 4 50S 42 12W
Campo Mourão, *Brazil* **95 A5** 24 3S 52 22W
Campobasso, *Italy* ..... **20 D6** 41 34N 14 39 E
Campos, *Brazil* **95 A7** 21 50S 41 20W
Campos Belos, *Brazil* **93 F9** 13 10S 47 3W
Campos del Port, *Spain* ..... **22 B10** 39 26N 3 1 E
Campos Novos, *Brazil* **95 B5** 27 21S 51 50W
Camptonville, *U.S.A.* **84 F5** 39 27N 121 3W
Camptown, *U.S.A.* **79 E8** 41 44N 76 14W
Câmpulung, *Romania* ..... **17 F13** 45 17N 25 3 E
Camrose, *Canada* **72 C6** 53 0N 112 50W
Camsell Portage, *Canada* ... **73 B7** 59 37N 109 15W
Çan, *Turkey* ..... **21 D12** 40 2N 27 3 E
Can Clavo, *Spain* ..... **22 C7** 38 57N 1 27 E
Can Creu, *Spain* ..... **22 C7** 38 58N 1 28 E
Can Gio, *Vietnam* ..... **39 G6** 10 25N 106 58 E
Can Tho, *Vietnam* ..... **39 G5** 10 2N 105 46 E
Canaan, *U.S.A.* **79 D11** 42 2N 73 20W
Canada ■, *N. Amer.* **68 C10** 60 0N 100 0W
Cañada de Gómez, *Argentina* **94 C3** 32 40S 61 30W
Canadian, *U.S.A.* **81 H4** 35 55N 100 23W
Canadian →, *U.S.A.* **81 H7** 35 28N 95 3W
Canajoharie, *U.S.A.* **79 D10** 42 54N 74 35W
Çanakkale, *Turkey* ..... **21 D12** 40 8N 26 24 E
Çanakkale Boğazı, *Turkey* ... **21 D12** 40 17N 26 32 E
Canal Flats, *Canada* **72 C5** 50 10N 115 48W
Canalejas, *Argentina* **94 D2** 35 15S 66 34W
Canals, *Argentina* **94 C3** 33 35S 62 53W
Canandaigua, *U.S.A.* **78 D7** 42 54N 77 17W
Canandaigua L., *U.S.A.* **78 D7** 42 47N 77 19W
Cananea, *Mexico* **86 A2** 31 0N 110 20W
Canarias, Is., *Atl. Oc.* **22 F4** 28 30N 16 0W
Canarreos, Arch. de los, *Cuba* **88 B3** 21 35N 81 40W
Canary Is. = Canarias, Is.,
Atl. Oc. **22 F4** 28 30N 16 0W
Canaseraga, *U.S.A.* **78 D7** 42 27N 77 45W
Canatlán, *Mexico* **86 C4** 24 31N 104 47W
Canaveral, C., *U.S.A.* **77 L5** 28 27N 80 32W
Canavieiras, *Brazil* **93 G11** 15 39S 39 0W
Canberra, *Australia* ..... **63 F4** 35 15S 149 8 E
Canby, *Calif., U.S.A.* **82 F3** 41 27N 120 52W
Canby, *Minn., U.S.A.* **80 C6** 44 43N 96 16W
Canby, *Oreg., U.S.A.* **84 E4** 45 16N 122 42W
Cancún, *Mexico* **87 C7** 21 8N 86 44W
Candelaria, *Argentina* **95 B4** 27 29S 55 44W
Candelaria, *Canary Is.* **22 F3** 28 22N 16 22W
Candelo, *Australia* ..... **63 F4** 36 47S 149 43 E
Candia = Iráklion, *Greece* ... **23 D7** 35 20N 25 12 E
Candle L., *Canada* **73 C7** 53 50N 105 18W
Candlemas I., *Antarctica* **5 B1** 57 3S 26 40W
Cando, *U.S.A.* **80 A5** 48 32N 99 12W
Canea = Khaniá, *Greece* ..... **23 D6** 35 30N 24 4 E
Canelones, *Uruguay* **95 C4** 34 32S 56 17W
Cañete, *Chile* **94 D1** 37 50S 73 30W
Cañete, *Peru* **92 F3** 13 8S 76 30W
Cangas de Narcea, *Spain* **19 A2** 43 10N 6 32W
Canguaretama, *Brazil* **93 E11** 6 20S 35 5W
Canguçu, *Brazil* **95 C5** 31 22S 52 43W
Canguçu, Serra do, *Brazil* ... **95 C5** 31 20S 52 40W
Cangzhou, *China* ..... **34 E9** 38 19N 116 52 E
Caniapiscau →, *Canada* **71 A6** 56 40N 69 30W
Caniapiscau, Rés. de, *Canada* **71 B6** 54 10N 69 55W
Canicattì, *Italy* ..... **20 F5** 37 21N 13 51 E
Canim Lake, *Canada* **72 C4** 51 47N 120 54W
Canindeyu □, *Paraguay* **95 A5** 24 10S 55 0W
Canisteo, *U.S.A.* **78 D7** 42 16N 77 36W
Canisteo →, *U.S.A.* **78 D7** 42 7N 77 8W
Cañitas, *Mexico* **86 C4** 23 36N 102 43W
Çankırı, *Turkey* ..... **25 F5** 40 40N 33 37 E
Cankuzo, *Burundi* ..... **54 C3** 3 10S 30 31 E
Canmore, *Canada* **72 C5** 51 7N 115 18W
Cann River, *Australia* ..... **63 F4** 37 35S 149 7 E
Canna, *U.K.* **12 D2** 57 3N 6 33W
Cannanore, *India* ..... **40 P9** 11 53N 75 27 E
Cannes, *France* ..... **18 E7** 43 32N 7 1 E
Canning Town = Port
Canning, *India* ..... **43 H13** 22 23N 88 40 E
Cannington, *Canada* **78 B5** 44 20N 79 2W
Cannock, *U.K.* **11 E5** 52 41N 2 1W
Cannon Ball →, *U.S.A.* **80 B4** 46 20N 100 38W
Cannondale Mt., *Australia* ... **62 D4** 25 13S 148 57 E
Cannonsville Reservoir,
U.S.A. **79 D9** 42 4N 75 22W
Cannonvale, *Australia* ..... **62 C4** 20 17S 148 43 E
Canoas, *Brazil* **95 B5** 29 56S 51 11W
Canoe L., *Canada* **73 B7** 55 10N 108 15W
Canon City, *U.S.A.* **80 F2** 38 27N 105 14W
Canora, *Canada* **73 C8** 51 40N 102 30W
Canowindra, *Australia* ..... **63 E4** 33 35S 148 38 E
Canso, *Canada* **71 C7** 45 20N 61 0W
Cantabria □, *Spain* **19 A4** 43 10N 4 0W
Cantabrian Mts. = Cantábrica,
Cordillera, *Spain* **19 A3** 43 0N 5 10W
Cantábrica, Cordillera, *Spain* **19 A3** 43 0N 5 10W
Cantal, Plomb du, *France* ... **18 D5** 45 3N 2 45 E
Canterbury, *Australia* ..... **62 D3** 25 23S 141 53 E
Canterbury, *U.K.* ..... **11 F9** 51 16N 1 6 E
Canterbury Bight, *N.Z.* ..... **59 L3** 44 16S 171 55 E
Canterbury Plains, *N.Z.* ..... **59 K3** 43 55S 171 22 E
Cantil, *U.S.A.* **85 K9** 35 18N 117 58W
Canton = Guangzhou, *China* **33 D6** 23 5N 113 10 E
Canton, *Ga., U.S.A.* **77 H3** 34 14N 84 29W
Canton, *Ill., U.S.A.* **80 E9** 40 33N 90 2W
Canton, *Miss., U.S.A.* **81 J9** 32 37N 90 2W
Canton, *Mo., U.S.A.* **80 E9** 40 8N 91 32W
Canton, *N.Y., U.S.A.* **79 B9** 44 36N 75 10W
Canton, *Ohio, U.S.A.* **78 F3** 40 48N 81 23W
Canton, *Pa., U.S.A.* **78 E8** 41 39N 76 51W
Canton, *S. Dak., U.S.A.* **80 D6** 43 18N 96 35W
Canton L., *U.S.A.* **81 G5** 36 6N 98 35W
Canudos, *Brazil* **92 E7** 7 13S 58 5W
Canumã →, *Brazil* **92 D7** 3 55S 59 10W
Canutama, *Brazil* **92 E6** 6 30S 64 20W
Canutillo, *U.S.A.* **83 L10** 31 55N 106 36W
Canvey, *U.K.* ..... **11 F8** 51 32N 0 37 E
Canyon, *U.S.A.* **81 H4** 34 59N 101 55W
Canyonlands Nat. Park,
U.S.A. **83 G9** 38 15N 110 0W
Canyonville, *U.S.A.* **82 E2** 42 56N 123 17W

Cao Bang, *Vietnam* 38 A6 22 40N 106 15 E
Cao He →, *China* 35 D13 40 10N 124 32 E
Cao Lanh, *Vietnam* 39 G5 10 27N 105 38 E
Cao Xian, *China* 34 G8 34 50N 115 35 E
Cap-aux-Meules, *Canada* 71 C7 47 23N 61 52W
Cap-Chat, *Canada* 71 C6 49 6N 66 40W
Cap-de-la-Madeleine, *Canada* 70 C5 46 22N 72 31W
Cap-Haïtien, *Haiti* 89 C5 19 40N 72 20W
Capac, *U.S.A.* 78 C2 43 1N 82 56W
Capanaparo →, *Venezuela* 92 B5 7 1N 67 7W
Cape →, *Australia* 62 C4 20 59S 146 51 E
Cape Barren I., *Australia* 62 G4 40 25S 148 15 E
Cape Breton Highlands Nat. Park, *Canada* 71 C7 46 50N 60 40W
Cape Breton I., *Canada* 71 C7 46 0N 60 30W
Cape Charles, *U.S.A.* 76 G8 37 16N 76 1W
Cape Coast, *Ghana* 50 G5 5 5N 1 15W
Cape Coral, *U.S.A.* 77 M5 26 33N 81 57W
Cape Dorset, *Canada* 69 B12 64 14N 76 32W
Cape Fear →, *U.S.A.* 77 H6 33 53N 78 1W
Cape Girardeau, *U.S.A.* 81 G10 37 19N 89 32W
Cape May, *U.S.A.* 76 F8 38 56N 74 56W
Cape May Point, *U.S.A.* 76 F8 38 56N 74 58W
Cape Province, *S. Africa* 53 L3 32 0S 23 0 E
Cape Tormentine, *Canada* 71 C7 46 8N 63 47W
Cape Town, *S. Africa* 56 E2 33 55S 18 22 E
Cape Verde Is. ■, *Atl. Oc.* 49 E1 16 0N 24 0W
Cape Vincent, *U.S.A.* 79 B8 44 8N 76 20W
Cape York Peninsula, *Australia* 62 A3 12 0S 142 30 E
Capela, *Brazil* 93 F11 10 30S 37 0W
Capella, *Australia* 62 C4 23 2S 148 1 E
Capim →, *Brazil* 93 D9 1 40S 47 47W
Capitan, *U.S.A.* 83 K11 33 35N 105 35W
Capitol Reef Nat. Park, *U.S.A.* 83 G8 38 15N 111 10W
Capitola, *U.S.A.* 84 J5 36 59N 121 57W
Capoche →, *Mozam.* 55 F3 15 35S 33 0 E
Capraia, *Italy* 18 E8 43 2N 9 50 E
Capreol, *Canada* 70 C3 46 43N 80 56W
Capri, *Italy* 20 D6 40 33N 14 14 E
Capricorn Group, *Australia* 62 C5 23 30S 151 55 E
Capricorn Ra., *Australia* 60 D2 23 20S 116 50 E
Caprivi Strip, *Namibia* 56 B3 18 0S 23 0 E
Captain's Flat, *Australia* 63 F4 35 35S 149 27 E
Caquetá →, *Colombia* 92 D5 1 15S 69 15W
Caracal, *Romania* 17 F13 44 8N 24 22 E
Caracas, *Venezuela* 92 A5 10 30N 66 55W
Caracol, *Mato Grosso do Sul, Brazil* 94 A4 22 18S 57 1W
Caracol, *Piauí, Brazil* 93 E10 9 15S 43 22W
Carajas, *Brazil* 93 E8 6 5S 50 23W
Carajás, Serra dos, *Brazil* 93 E8 6 0S 51 30W
Carangola, *Brazil* 95 A7 20 44S 42 5W
Caransebeş, *Romania* 17 F12 45 28N 22 18 E
Caraquet, *Canada* 71 C6 47 48N 64 57W
Caras, *Peru* 92 E3 9 3S 77 47W
Caratasca, L., *Honduras* 88 C3 15 20N 83 40W
Caratinga, *Brazil* 93 G10 19 50S 42 10W
Caraúbas, *Brazil* 93 E11 5 43S 37 33W
Caravaca = Caravaca de la Cruz, *Spain* 19 C5 38 8N 1 52W
Caravaca de la Cruz, *Spain* 19 C5 38 8N 1 52W
Caravelas, *Brazil* 93 G11 17 45S 39 15W
Caraveli, *Peru* 92 G4 15 45S 73 25W
Caràzinho, *Brazil* 95 B5 28 16S 52 46W
Carballo, *Spain* 19 A1 43 13N 8 41W
Carberry, *Canada* 73 D9 49 50N 99 25W
Carbó, *Mexico* 86 B2 29 42N 110 58W
Carbonara, C., *Italy* 20 E3 39 6N 9 31 E
Carbondale, *Colo., U.S.A.* 82 G10 39 24N 107 13W
Carbondale, *Ill., U.S.A.* 81 G10 37 44N 89 13W
Carbondale, *Pa., U.S.A.* 79 E9 41 35N 75 30W
Carbonear, *Canada* 71 C9 47 42N 53 13W
Carbónia, *Italy* 20 E3 39 10N 8 30 E
Carcajou, *Canada* 72 B5 57 47N 117 6W
Carcarana →, *Argentina* 94 C3 32 27S 60 48W
Carcasse, C., *Haiti* 89 C5 18 30N 74 28W
Carcassonne, *France* 18 E5 43 13N 2 20 E
Carcross, *Canada* 72 A2 60 13N 134 45W
Cardamon Hills, *India* 40 Q10 9 30N 77 15 E
Cárdenas, *Cuba* 88 B3 23 0N 81 30W
Cárdenas, *San Luis Potosí, Mexico* 87 C5 22 0N 99 41W
Cárdenas, *Tabasco, Mexico* 87 D6 17 59N 93 21W
Cardiff, *U.K.* 11 F4 51 29N 3 10W
Cardiff □, *U.K.* 11 F4 51 31N 3 12W
Cardiff-by-the-Sea, *U.S.A.* 85 M9 33 1N 117 17W
Cardigan, *U.K.* 11 E3 52 5N 4 40W
Cardigan B., *U.K.* 11 E3 52 30N 4 30W
Cardinal, *Canada* 79 B9 44 47N 75 23W
Cardona, *Uruguay* 94 C4 33 53S 57 18W
Cardoso, Ilha do, *Brazil* 95 B5 25 8S 47 58W
Cardston, *Canada* 72 D6 49 15N 113 20W
Cardwell, *Australia* 62 B4 18 14S 146 2 E
Careen L., *Canada* 73 B7 57 0N 108 11W
Carei, *Romania* 17 E12 47 40N 22 29 E
Careme = Ciremai, *Indonesia* 37 G13 6 55S 108 27 E
Carey, *U.S.A.* 82 E7 43 19N 113 57W
Carey, L., *Australia* 61 E3 29 0S 122 15 E
Carey L., *Canada* 73 A8 62 12N 102 55W
Carhué, *Argentina* 94 D3 37 10S 62 50W
Caria, *Turkey* 21 F13 37 20N 28 10 E
Cariacica, *Brazil* 93 H10 20 16S 40 25W
Caribbean Sea, *W. Indies* 89 D5 15 0N 75 0W
Cariboo Mts., *Canada* 72 C4 53 0N 121 0W
Caribou, *U.S.A.* 77 B12 46 52N 68 1W
Caribou →, *Man., Canada* 73 B10 59 20N 94 44W
Caribou →, *N.W.T., Canada* 72 A3 61 27N 125 45W
Caribou I., *Canada* 70 C2 47 22N 85 49W
Caribou Is., *Canada* 72 A6 61 55N 113 15W
Caribou L., *Man., Canada* 73 B9 59 21N 96 10W
Caribou L., *Ont., Canada* 70 B2 50 25N 89 5W
Caribou Mts., *Canada* 72 B5 59 12N 115 40W
Carichic, *Mexico* 86 B3 27 56N 107 3W
Carillo, *Mexico* 86 B4 26 50N 103 55W
Carinda, *Australia* 63 E4 30 28S 147 41 E
Carinhanha, *Brazil* 93 F10 14 15S 44 46W
Carinhanha →, *Brazil* 93 F10 14 20S 43 47W
Carinthia = Kärnten □, *Austria* 16 E8 46 52N 13 30 E
Caripito, *Venezuela* 92 A6 10 8N 63 6W
Carleton, Mt., *Canada* 71 C6 47 23N 66 53W
Carleton Place, *Canada* 79 A8 45 8N 76 9W
Carletonville, *S. Africa* 56 D4 26 23S 27 22 E
Carlin, *U.S.A.* 82 F5 40 43N 116 7W
Carlingford L., *U.K.* 13 B5 54 3N 6 9W
Carlinville, *U.S.A.* 80 F10 39 17N 89 53W
Carlisle, *U.K.* 10 C5 54 54N 2 56W
Carlisle, *U.S.A.* 78 F7 40 12N 77 12W
Carlos Casares, *Argentina* 94 D3 35 32S 61 20W
Carlos Tejedor, *Argentina* 94 D3 35 25S 62 25W
Carlow, *Ireland* 13 D5 52 50N 6 56W
Carlow □, *Ireland* 13 D5 52 43N 6 50W
Carlsbad, *Calif., U.S.A.* 85 M9 33 10N 117 21W
Carlsbad, *N. Mex., U.S.A.* 81 J2 32 25N 104 14W
Carlsbad Caverns Nat. Park, *U.S.A.* 81 J2 32 10N 104 35W
Carluke, *U.K.* 12 F5 55 45N 3 50W
Carlyle, *Canada* 73 D8 49 40N 102 20W
Carmacks, *Canada* 68 B6 62 5N 136 16W
Carman, *Canada* 73 D9 49 30N 98 0W
Carmarthen, *U.K.* 11 F3 51 52N 4 19W
Carmarthen B., *U.K.* 11 F3 51 40N 4 30W
Carmarthenshire □, *U.K.* 11 F3 51 55N 4 13W
Carmaux, *France* 18 D5 44 3N 2 10 E
Carmel, *U.S.A.* 79 E11 41 26N 73 41W
Carmel-by-the-Sea, *U.S.A.* 84 J5 36 33N 121 55W
Carmel Valley, *U.S.A.* 84 J5 36 29N 121 43W
Carmelo, *Uruguay* 94 C4 34 0S 58 20W
Carmen, *Colombia* 92 B3 9 43N 75 8W
Carmen, *Paraguay* 95 B4 27 13S 56 12W
Carmen →, *Mexico* 86 A3 30 42N 106 29W
Carmen, I., *Mexico* 86 B2 26 0N 111 20W
Carmen de Patagones, *Argentina* 96 E4 40 50S 63 0W
Carmensa, *Argentina* 94 D2 35 15S 67 40W
Carmi, *Canada* 72 D5 49 36N 119 8W
Carmi, *U.S.A.* 76 F1 38 5N 88 10W
Carmichael, *U.S.A.* 84 G5 38 38N 121 19W
Carmila, *Australia* 62 C4 21 55S 149 24 E
Carmona, *Costa Rica* 88 E2 10 0N 85 15W
Carmona, *Spain* 19 D3 37 28N 5 42W
Carn Ban, *U.K.* 12 D4 57 7N 4 15W
Carn Eige, *U.K.* 12 D3 57 17N 5 8W
Carnac, *France* 18 C2 47 35N 3 6W
Carnamah, *Australia* 61 E2 29 41S 115 53 E
Carnarvon, *Australia* 61 D1 24 51S 113 42 E
Carnarvon, *S. Africa* 56 E3 30 56S 22 8 E
Carnarvon Ra., *Queens., Australia* 62 D4 25 15S 148 30 E
Carnarvon Ra., *W. Austral., Australia* 61 E3 25 20S 120 45 E
Carnation, *U.S.A.* 84 C5 47 39N 121 55W
Carndonagh, *Ireland* 13 A4 55 16N 7 15W
Carnduff, *Canada* 73 D8 49 10N 101 50W
Carnegie, *U.S.A.* 78 F4 40 24N 80 5W
Carnegie, L., *Australia* 61 E3 26 5S 122 30 E
Carnic Alps = Karnische Alpen, *Europe* 16 E7 46 36N 13 0 E
Carniche Alpi = Karnische Alpen, *Europe* 16 E7 46 36N 13 0 E
Carnot, *C.A.R.* 52 D3 4 59N 15 56 E
Carnot, C., *Australia* 63 E2 34 57S 135 38 E
Carnot B., *Australia* 60 C3 17 20S 122 15 E
Carnoustie, *U.K.* 12 E6 56 30N 2 42W
Carnsore Pt., *Ireland* 13 D5 52 10N 6 22W
Caro, *U.S.A.* 76 D4 43 29N 83 24W
Carol City, *U.S.A.* 77 N5 25 56N 80 16W
Carolina, *Brazil* 93 E9 7 10S 47 30W
Carolina, *Puerto Rico* 89 C6 18 23N 65 58W
Carolina, *S. Africa* 57 D5 26 5S 30 6 E
Caroline I., *Kiribati* 65 H12 9 58S 150 13W
Caroline Is., *Micronesia* 28 J17 8 0N 150 0 E
Caroni →, *Venezuela* 92 B6 8 21N 62 43W
Caronie = Nébrodi, Monti, *Italy* 20 F6 37 54N 14 35 E
Caroona, *Australia* 63 E5 31 24S 150 26 E
Carpathians, *Europe* 17 D11 49 30N 21 0 E
Carpaţii Meridionali, *Romania* 17 F13 45 30N 25 0 E
Carpentaria, G. of, *Australia* 62 A2 14 0S 139 0 E
Carpentras, *France* 18 D6 44 3N 5 2 E
Carpi, *Italy* 20 B4 44 47N 10 53 E
Carpinteria, *U.S.A.* 85 L7 34 24N 119 31W
Carr Boyd Ra., *Australia* 60 C4 16 15S 128 35 E
Carrabelle, *U.S.A.* 77 L3 29 51N 84 40W
Carranza, Presa V., *Mexico* 86 B4 27 20N 100 50W
Carrara, *Italy* 18 D9 44 5N 10 6 E
Carrauntoohill, *Ireland* 13 D2 52 0N 9 45W
Carrick-on-Shannon, *Ireland* 13 C3 53 57N 8 5W
Carrick-on-Suir, *Ireland* 13 D4 52 21N 7 24W
Carrickfergus, *U.K.* 13 B6 54 43N 5 49W
Carrickmacross, *Ireland* 13 C5 53 59N 6 43W
Carrieton, *Australia* 63 E2 32 25S 138 31 E
Carrington, *U.S.A.* 80 B5 47 27N 99 8W
Carrizal Bajo, *Chile* 94 B1 28 5S 71 20W
Carrizalillo, *Chile* 94 B1 29 5S 71 30W
Carrizo Cr. →, *U.S.A.* 81 G3 36 55N 103 55W
Carrizo Springs, *U.S.A.* 81 L5 28 31N 99 52W
Carrizozo, *U.S.A.* 83 K11 33 38N 105 53W
Carroll, *U.S.A.* 80 D7 42 4N 94 52W
Carrollton, *Ga., U.S.A.* 77 J3 33 35N 85 5W
Carrollton, *Ill., U.S.A.* 80 F9 39 18N 90 24W
Carrollton, *Ky., U.S.A.* 76 F3 38 41N 85 11W
Carrollton, *Mo., U.S.A.* 80 F8 39 22N 93 30W
Carrollton, *Ohio, U.S.A.* 78 F3 40 34N 81 5W
Carron →, *U.K.* 12 D4 57 53N 4 22W
Carron, L., *U.K.* 12 D3 57 22N 5 35W
Carrot →, *Canada* 73 C8 53 50N 101 17W
Carrot River, *Canada* 73 C8 53 17N 103 35W
Carruthers, *Canada* 73 C7 52 52N 109 16W
Carson, *Calif., U.S.A.* 85 M8 33 48N 118 17W
Carson, *N. Dak., U.S.A.* 80 B4 46 25N 101 34W
Carson →, *U.S.A.* 84 F8 39 45N 118 40W
Carson City, *U.S.A.* 84 F7 39 10N 119 46W
Carson Sink, *U.S.A.* 82 G4 39 50N 118 25W
Cartagena, *Colombia* 92 A3 10 25N 75 33W
Cartagena, *Spain* 19 D5 37 38N 0 59W
Cartago, *Colombia* 92 C3 4 45N 75 55W
Cartago, *Costa Rica* 88 E3 9 50N 83 55W
Cartersville, *U.S.A.* 77 H3 34 10N 84 48W
Carterton, *N.Z.* 59 J5 41 2S 175 31 E
Carthage, *Tunisia* 51 A8 36 50N 10 21 E
Carthage, *Ill., U.S.A.* 80 E9 40 25N 91 8W
Carthage, *Mo., U.S.A.* 81 G7 37 11N 94 19W
Carthage, *N.Y., U.S.A.* 76 D8 43 59N 75 37W
Carthage, *Tex., U.S.A.* 81 J7 32 9N 94 20W
Cartier I., *Australia* 60 B3 12 31S 123 29 E
Cartwright, *Canada* 71 B8 53 41N 56 58W
Caruaru, *Brazil* 93 E11 8 15S 35 55W
Carúpano, *Venezuela* 92 A6 10 39N 63 15W
Caruthersville, *U.S.A.* 81 G10 36 11N 89 39W
Carvoeiro, *Brazil* 92 D6 1 30S 61 59W
Carvoeiro, C., *Portugal* 19 C1 39 21N 9 24W
Cary, *U.S.A.* 77 H6 35 47N 78 46W
Casa Grande, *U.S.A.* 83 K8 32 53N 111 45W
Casablanca, *Chile* 94 C1 33 20S 71 25W
Casablanca, *Morocco* 50 B4 33 36N 7 36W
Cascade, *Idaho, U.S.A.* 82 D5 44 31N 116 2W
Cascade, *Mont., U.S.A.* 82 C8 47 16N 111 42W
Cascade Locks, *U.S.A.* 84 E5 45 40N 121 54W
Cascade Ra., *U.S.A.* 84 D5 47 0N 121 30W
Cascade Reservoir, *U.S.A.* 82 D5 44 32N 116 3W
Cascais, *Portugal* 19 C1 38 41N 9 25W
Cascavel, *Brazil* 95 A5 24 57S 53 28W
Cáscina, *Italy* 20 C4 43 41N 10 33 E
Casco B., *U.S.A.* 77 D10 43 45N 70 0W
Caserta, *Italy* 20 D6 41 4N 14 20 E
Caseyr, Raas = Asir, Ras, *Somali Rep.* 46 E5 11 55N 51 10 E
Cashel, *Ireland* 13 D4 52 30N 7 53W
Casiguran, *Phil.* 37 A6 16 22N 122 7 E
Casilda, *Argentina* 94 C3 33 10S 61 10W
Casino, *Australia* 63 D5 28 52S 153 3 E
Casiquiare →, *Venezuela* 92 C5 2 1N 67 7W
Casma, *Peru* 92 E3 9 30S 78 20W
Casmalia, *U.S.A.* 85 L6 34 50N 120 32W
Caspe, *Spain* 19 B5 41 14N 0 1W
Casper, *U.S.A.* 82 E10 42 51N 106 19W
Caspian Depression, *Eurasia* 25 E8 47 0N 48 0 E
Caspian Sea, *Eurasia* 25 F9 43 0N 50 0 E
Cass Lake, *U.S.A.* 80 B7 47 23N 94 37W
Cassadaga, *U.S.A.* 78 D5 42 20N 79 19W
Casselman, *Canada* 79 A9 45 19N 75 5W
Casselton, *U.S.A.* 80 B6 46 54N 97 13W
Cassiar, *Canada* 72 B3 59 16N 129 40W
Cassiar Mts., *Canada* 72 B2 59 30N 130 30W
Cassino, *Italy* 20 D5 41 30N 13 49 E
Cassville, *U.S.A.* 81 G8 36 41N 93 52W
Castaic, *U.S.A.* 85 L8 34 30N 118 38W
Castalia, *U.S.A.* 78 E2 41 24N 82 49W
Castanhal, *Brazil* 93 D9 1 18S 47 55W
Castellammare di Stábia, *Italy* 20 D6 40 42N 14 29 E
Castelli, *Argentina* 94 D4 36 7S 57 47W
Castelló de la Plana, *Spain* 19 C5 39 58N 0 3W
Castelo, *Brazil* 95 A7 20 33S 41 14W
Castelo Branco, *Portugal* 19 C2 39 50N 7 31W
Castelsarrasin, *France* 18 E4 44 2N 1 7 E
Castelvetrano, *Italy* 20 F5 37 41N 12 47 E
Casterton, *Australia* 63 F3 37 30S 141 30 E
Castile, *U.S.A.* 78 D6 42 38N 78 3W
Castilla-La Mancha □, *Spain* 19 C4 39 30N 3 30W
Castilla y Leon □, *Spain* 19 B3 42 0N 5 0W
Castillos, *Uruguay* 95 C5 34 12S 53 52W
Castle Dale, *U.S.A.* 82 G8 39 13N 111 1W
Castle Douglas, *U.K.* 12 G5 54 56N 3 56W
Castle Rock, *Colo., U.S.A.* 80 F2 39 22N 104 51W
Castle Rock, *Wash., U.S.A.* 84 D4 46 17N 122 54W
Castlebar, *Ireland* 13 C2 53 52N 9 18W
Castleblaney, *Ireland* 13 B5 54 7N 6 44W
Castlederg, *U.K.* 13 B4 54 42N 7 35W
Castleford, *U.K.* 10 D6 53 43N 1 21W
Castlegar, *Canada* 72 D5 49 20N 117 40W
Castlemaine, *Australia* 63 F3 37 2S 144 12 E
Castlepollard, *Ireland* 13 C4 53 41N 7 19W
Castlerea, *Ireland* 13 C3 53 46N 8 29W
Castlereagh →, *Australia* 63 E4 30 12S 147 32 E
Castlereagh B., *Australia* 62 A2 12 10S 135 10 E
Castleton, *U.S.A.* 79 C11 43 37N 73 11W
Castletown, *U.K.* 10 C3 54 5N 4 38W
Castletown Bearhaven, *Ireland* 13 E2 51 39N 9 55W
Castor, *Canada* 72 C6 52 15N 111 50W
Castor →, *Canada* 70 B4 53 24N 78 58W
Castorland, *U.S.A.* 79 C9 43 53N 75 31W
Castres, *France* 18 E5 43 37N 2 13 E
Castricum, *Neths.* 15 B4 52 33N 4 40 E
Castries, *St. Lucia* 89 D7 14 2N 60 58W
Castro, *Brazil* 95 A6 24 45S 50 0W
Castro, *Chile* 96 E2 42 30S 73 50W
Castro Alves, *Brazil* 93 F11 12 46S 39 33W
Castroville, *U.S.A.* 84 J5 36 46N 121 45W
Castuera, *Spain* 19 C3 38 43N 5 37W
Cat Ba, Dao, *Vietnam* 38 B6 20 50N 107 0 E
Cat I., *Bahamas* 89 B4 24 30N 75 30W
Cat L., *Canada* 70 B1 51 40N 91 50W
Cat Lake, *Canada* 70 B1 51 40N 91 50W
Catacamas, *Honduras* 88 D2 14 54N 85 56W
Cataguases, *Brazil* 95 A7 21 23S 42 39W
Catalão, *Brazil* 93 G9 18 10S 47 57W
Çatalca, *Turkey* 21 D13 41 8N 28 27 E
Catalina, *Canada* 71 C9 48 31N 53 4W
Catalina, *Chile* 94 B2 25 13S 69 43W
Catalina, *U.S.A.* 83 K8 32 30N 110 50W
Catalonia = Cataluña □, *Spain* 19 B6 41 40N 1 15 E
Cataluña □, *Spain* 19 B6 41 40N 1 15 E
Catamarca, *Argentina* 94 B2 28 30S 65 50W
Catamarca □, *Argentina* 94 B2 27 0S 65 50W
Catanduanes □, *Phil.* 37 B6 13 50N 124 20 E
Catanduva, *Brazil* 95 A6 21 5S 48 58W
Catánia, *Italy* 20 F6 37 30N 15 6 E
Catanzaro, *Italy* 20 E7 38 54N 16 35 E
Catarman, *Phil.* 37 B6 12 28N 124 35 E
Cateel, *Phil.* 37 C7 7 47N 126 24 E
Catembe, *Mozam.* 57 D5 26 0S 32 33 E
Caterham, *U.K.* 11 F7 51 15N 0 4W
Cathcart, *S. Africa* 56 E4 32 18S 27 10 E
Cathlamet, *U.S.A.* 84 D3 46 12N 123 23W
Catlettsburg, *U.S.A.* 76 F4 38 25N 82 36W
Catoche, C., *Mexico* 87 C7 21 40N 87 8W
Catriló, *Argentina* 94 D3 36 26S 63 24W
Catrimani, *Brazil* 92 C6 0 27N 61 41W
Catrimani →, *Brazil* 92 C6 0 28N 61 44W
Catskill, *U.S.A.* 79 D11 42 14N 73 52W
Catskill Mts., *U.S.A.* 79 D10 42 10N 74 25W
Catt, Mt., *Australia* 62 A1 13 49S 134 23 E
Cattaraugus, *U.S.A.* 78 D6 42 22N 78 52W
Catuala, *Angola* 56 B2 16 25S 19 2 E
Catuane, *Mozam.* 57 D5 26 48S 32 18 E
Catur, *Mozam.* 55 E4 13 45S 35 30 E
Catwick Is., *Vietnam* 39 G7 10 0N 109 0 E
Cauca →, *Colombia* 92 B4 8 54N 74 28W
Caucaia, *Brazil* 93 D11 3 40S 38 35W
Caucasus Mountains, *Eurasia* 25 F7 42 50N 44 0 E
Caungula, *Angola* 52 F3 8 26S 18 38 E
Cauquenes, *Chile* 94 D1 36 0S 72 22W
Caura →, *Venezuela* 92 B6 7 38N 64 53W
Cauresi →, *Mozam.* 55 F3 17 8S 33 0 E
Causapscal, *Canada* 71 C6 48 19N 67 12W
Cauvery →, *India* 40 P11 11 9N 78 52 E
Caux, Pays de, *France* 18 B4 49 38N 0 35 E
Cavalier, *U.S.A.* 80 A6 48 48N 97 37W
Cavan, *Ireland* 13 B4 54 0N 7 22W
Cavan □, *Ireland* 13 C4 54 1N 7 16W
Cave Creek, *U.S.A.* 83 K7 33 50N 111 57W
Cavenagh Ra., *Australia* 61 E4 26 12S 127 55 E
Cavendish, *Australia* 63 F3 37 31S 142 2 E
Caviana, I., *Brazil* 93 C8 0 10N 50 10W
Cavite, *Phil.* 37 B6 14 29N 120 55 E
Cawndilla L., *Australia* 63 E3 32 30S 142 15 E
Cawnpore = Kanpur, *India* 43 F9 26 28N 80 20 E
Caxias, *Brazil* 93 D10 4 55S 43 20W
Caxias do Sul, *Brazil* 95 B5 29 10S 51 10W
Cay Sal Bank, *Bahamas* 88 B4 23 45N 80 0W
Cayambe, *Ecuador* 92 C3 0 3N 78 8W
Cayenne, *Fr. Guiana* 93 B8 5 5N 52 18W
Cayman Brac, *Cayman Is.* 88 C4 19 43N 79 49W
Cayman Is. ■, *W. Indies* 88 C3 19 40N 80 30W
Cayo Romano, *Cuba* 88 B4 22 0N 78 0W
Cayuga, *Canada* 78 D5 42 59N 79 50W
Cayuga, *U.S.A.* 79 D8 42 54N 76 44W
Cayuga L., *U.S.A.* 79 D8 42 41N 76 41W
Cazenovia, *U.S.A.* 79 D9 42 56N 75 51W
Cazombo, *Angola* 53 G4 11 54S 22 56 E
Ceananus Mor, *Ireland* 13 C5 53 44N 6 53W
Ceará = Fortaleza, *Brazil* 93 D11 3 45S 38 35W
Ceará □, *Brazil* 93 E11 5 0S 40 0W
Ceará Mirim, *Brazil* 93 E11 5 38S 35 25W
Cebaco, I. de, *Panama* 88 E3 7 33N 81 9W
Cebollar, *Argentina* 94 B2 29 10S 66 35W
Cebu, *Phil.* 37 B6 10 18N 123 54 E
Cecil Plains, *Australia* 63 D5 27 30S 151 11 E
Cedar →, *U.S.A.* 80 E9 41 17N 91 21W
Cedar City, *U.S.A.* 83 H7 37 41N 113 4W
Cedar Creek Reservoir, *U.S.A.* 81 J6 32 11N 96 4W
Cedar Falls, *Iowa, U.S.A.* 80 D8 42 32N 92 27W
Cedar Falls, *Wash., U.S.A.* 84 C5 47 25N 121 45W
Cedar Key, *U.S.A.* 77 L4 29 8N 83 2W
Cedar L., *Canada* 73 C9 53 10N 100 0W
Cedar Rapids, *U.S.A.* 80 E9 41 59N 91 40W
Cedartown, *U.S.A.* 77 H3 34 1N 85 15W
Cedarvale, *Canada* 72 B3 55 1N 128 22W
Cedarville, *S. Africa* 57 E4 30 23S 29 3 E
Cedral, *Mexico* 86 C4 23 50N 100 42W
Cedro, *Brazil* 93 E11 6 34S 39 3W
Cedros, I. de, *Mexico* 86 B1 28 10N 115 20W
Ceduna, *Australia* 63 E1 32 7S 133 46 E
Ceerigaabo = Erigavo, *Somali Rep.* 46 E4 10 35N 47 20 E
Cefalù, *Italy* 20 E6 38 2N 14 1 E
Cegléd, *Hungary* 17 E10 47 11N 19 47 E
Celaya, *Mexico* 86 C4 20 31N 100 37W
Celebes Sea, *Indonesia* 37 D6 3 0N 123 0 E
Celina, *U.S.A.* 76 E3 40 33N 84 35W
Celje, *Slovenia* 16 E8 46 16N 15 18 E
Celle, *Germany* 16 B6 52 37N 10 4 E
Cenderwasih, Teluk, *Indonesia* 37 E9 3 0S 135 20 E
Center, *N. Dak., U.S.A.* 80 B4 47 7N 101 18W
Center, *Tex., U.S.A.* 81 K7 31 48N 94 11W
Centerburg, *U.S.A.* 78 F2 40 18N 82 42W
Centerville, *Calif., U.S.A.* 84 J7 36 44N 119 30W
Centerville, *Iowa, U.S.A.* 80 E8 40 44N 92 52W
Centerville, *Pa., U.S.A.* 78 F5 40 3N 79 59W
Centerville, *Tenn., U.S.A.* 77 H2 35 47N 87 28W
Centerville, *Tex., U.S.A.* 81 K7 31 16N 95 59W
Central □, *Kenya* 54 C4 0 30S 37 30 E
Central □, *Malawi* 55 E3 13 30S 33 30 E
Central □, *Zambia* 55 E2 14 25S 28 50 E
Central, Cordillera, *Colombia* 92 C4 5 0N 75 0W
Central, Cordillera, *Costa Rica* 88 D3 10 10N 84 5W
Central, Cordillera, *Dom. Rep.* 89 C5 19 15N 71 0W
Central African Rep. ■, *Africa* 52 C4 7 0N 20 0 E
Central America, *America* 66 H11 12 0N 85 0W
Central Butte, *Canada* 73 C7 50 48N 106 31W
Central City, *Colo., U.S.A.* 82 G11 39 48N 105 31W
Central City, *Ky., U.S.A.* 76 G2 37 18N 87 7W
Central City, *Nebr., U.S.A.* 80 E6 41 7N 98 0W
Central I., *Kenya* 54 B4 3 30N 36 0 E
Central Makran Range, *Pakistan* 40 F4 26 30N 64 15 E
Central Patricia, *Canada* 70 B1 51 30N 90 9W
Central Point, *U.S.A.* 82 E2 42 23N 122 55W
Central Russian Uplands, *Europe* 6 E13 54 0N 36 0 E
Central Siberian Plateau, *Russia* 28 C14 65 0N 105 0 E
Central Square, *U.S.A.* 79 C8 43 17N 76 9W
Centralia, *Ill., U.S.A.* 80 F10 38 32N 89 8W
Centralia, *Mo., U.S.A.* 80 F8 39 13N 92 8W
Centralia, *Wash., U.S.A.* 84 D4 46 43N 122 58W
Cephalonia = Kefallinia, *Greece* 21 E9 38 15N 20 30 E
Cepu, *Indonesia* 37 G14 7 9S 111 35 E
Ceram = Seram, *Indonesia* 37 E7 3 10S 129 0 E
Ceram Sea = Seram Sea, *Indonesia* 37 E7 2 30S 128 30 E
Ceredigion □, *U.K.* 11 E3 52 16N 4 15W
Ceres, *Argentina* 94 B3 29 55S 61 55W
Ceres, *S. Africa* 56 E2 33 21S 19 18 E
Ceres, *U.S.A.* 84 H6 37 35N 120 57W
Cerignola, *Italy* 20 D6 41 17N 15 53 E
Cerigo = Kíthira, *Greece* 21 F10 36 8N 23 0 E
Çerkezköy, *Turkey* 21 D12 41 17N 28 0 E
Cerralvo, I., *Mexico* 86 C3 24 20N 109 45W
Cerritos, *Mexico* 86 C4 22 27N 100 20W
Cerro Chato, *Uruguay* 95 C4 33 6S 55 8W
Cerventes, *Australia* 61 F2 30 31S 115 3 E
Cervera, *Spain* 19 B6 41 40N 1 16 E
Cesena, *Italy* 20 B5 44 8N 12 15 E
Cēsis, *Latvia* 9 H21 57 18N 25 15 E
České Budějovice, *Czech Rep.* 16 D8 48 55N 14 25 E
Českomoravská Vrchovina, *Czech Rep.* 16 D8 49 30N 15 40 E
Çeşme, *Turkey* 21 E12 38 20N 26 23 E
Cessnock, *Australia* 63 E5 32 50S 151 21 E
Cetinje, *Montenegro, Yug.* 21 C8 42 23N 18 59 E
Cetraro, *Italy* 20 E6 39 31N 15 55 E
Ceuta, *N. Afr.* 19 E3 35 52N 5 18W
Cévennes, *France* 18 D5 44 10N 3 50 E
Ceyhan, *Turkey* 44 B2 37 4N 35 47 E
Ceylon = Sri Lanka ■, *Asia* 40 R12 7 30N 80 50 E

Cha-am, Thailand 38 F2 12 48N 99 58 E
Cha Pa, Vietnam 38 A4 22 20N 103 47 E
Chacabuco, Argentina 94 C3 34 40S 60 27W
Chachapoyas, Peru 92 E3 6 15S 77 50W
Chachoengsao, Thailand 38 F3 13 42N 101 5 E
Chachran, Pakistan 40 E7 28 55N 70 30 E
Chachro, Pakistan 42 G4 25 5N 70 15 E
Chaco □, Argentina 94 B3 26 30S 61 0W
Chaco □, Paraguay 94 B4 26 0S 60 0W
Chaco →, U.S.A. 83 H9 36 46N 108 39W
Chaco Austral, S. Amer. 96 B4 27 0S 61 30W
Chaco Boreal, S. Amer. 92 H6 22 0S 60 0W
Chaco Central, S. Amer. 96 A4 24 0S 61 0W
Chacon, C., U.S.A. 72 C2 54 42N 132 0W
Chad ■, Africa 51 F8 15 0N 17 15 E
Chad, L. = Tchad, L., Chad 51 F8 13 30N 14 30 E
Chadan, Russia 27 D10 51 17N 91 35 E
Chadileuvú →, Argentina 94 D2 37 46S 66 0W
Chadiza, Zambia 55 E3 14 45S 32 27 E
Chadron, U.S.A. 80 D3 42 50N 103 0W
Chadyr-Lunga = Ciadâr-Lunga, Moldova 17 E15 46 3N 28 51 E
Chae Hom, Thailand 38 C2 18 43N 99 35 E
Chaem →, Thailand 38 C2 18 11N 98 38 E
Chaeryŏng, N. Korea 35 E13 38 24N 125 36 E
Chagai Hills = Chāh Gay Hills, Afghan. 40 E3 29 30N 64 0 E
Chagda, Russia 27 D14 58 45N 130 38 E
Chaghcharān, Afghan. 40 B4 34 31N 65 15 E
Chagos Arch., Ind. Oc. 29 K11 6 0S 72 0 E
Chagrin Falls, U.S.A. 78 E3 41 26N 81 24W
Chāh Ākhvor, Iran 45 C8 32 41N 59 40 E
Chāh Bahar, Iran 45 E9 25 20N 60 40 E
Chāh-e Kavīr, Iran 45 C8 34 29N 56 52 E
Chāh Gay Hills, Afghan. 40 E3 29 30N 64 0 E
Chahar Burjak, Afghan. 40 D3 30 15N 62 0 E
Chahār Mahāll va Bakhtīarī □, Iran 45 C6 32 0N 49 0 E
Chaibasa, India 41 H14 22 42N 85 49 E
Chainat, Thailand 38 E3 15 11N 100 8 E
Chaiya, Thailand 39 H2 9 23N 99 14 E
Chaj Doab, Pakistan 42 C5 32 15N 73 0 E
Chajari, Argentina 94 C4 30 42S 58 0W
Chak Amru, Pakistan 42 C6 32 22N 75 11 E
Chakar →, Pakistan 42 E3 29 29N 68 2 E
Chakari, Zimbabwe 57 B4 18 5S 29 51 E
Chake Chake, Tanzania 54 D4 5 15S 39 45 E
Chakhānsūr, Afghan. 40 D3 31 10N 62 0 E
Chakonipau, L., Canada 71 A6 56 18N 68 30W
Chakradharpur, India 43 H11 22 45N 85 40 E
Chakrata, India 42 D7 30 42N 77 51 E
Chakwal, Pakistan 42 C5 32 56N 72 53 E
Chala, Peru 92 G4 15 48S 74 20W
Chalchihuites, Mexico 86 C4 23 29N 103 53W
Chalcis = Khalkis, Greece 21 E10 38 27N 23 42 E
Chaleur B., Canada 71 C6 47 55N 65 30W
Chalfant, U.S.A. 84 H8 37 32N 118 21W
Chalhuanca, Peru 92 F4 14 15S 73 15W
Chalisgaon, India 40 J9 20 30N 75 10 E
Chalk River, Canada 70 C4 46 1N 77 27W
Chalky Inlet, N.Z. 59 M1 46 3S 166 31 E
Challapata, Bolivia 92 G5 18 53S 66 50W
Challis, U.S.A. 82 D6 44 30N 114 14W
Chalmette, U.S.A. 81 L10 29 56N 89 58W
Chalon-sur-Saône, France 18 C6 46 48N 4 50 E
Châlons-en-Champagne, France 18 B6 48 58N 4 20 E
Chalyaphum, Thailand 38 E4 15 48N 102 2 E
Cham, Cu Lao, Vietnam 38 E7 15 57N 108 30 E
Chama, U.S.A. 83 H10 36 54N 106 35W
Chamaicó, Argentina 94 D3 35 3S 64 58W
Chaman, Pakistan 40 D5 30 58N 66 25 E
Chamba, India 42 C7 32 35N 76 10 E
Chamba, Tanzania 55 E4 11 37S 37 0 E
Chambal →, India 43 F8 26 29N 79 15 E
Chamberlain, U.S.A. 80 D5 43 49N 99 20W
Chamberlain →, Australia 60 C4 15 30S 127 54 E
Chamberlain L., U.S.A. 77 B11 46 14N 69 19W
Chambers, U.S.A. 83 J9 35 11N 109 26W
Chambersburg, U.S.A. 76 F7 39 56N 77 40W
Chambéry, France 18 D6 45 34N 5 55 E
Chambeshi →, Zambia 52 G6 11 53S 29 48 E
Chambly, Canada 79 A11 45 27N 73 17W
Chambord, Canada 71 C5 48 25N 72 6W
Chamchamal, Iraq 44 C5 35 32N 44 50 E
Chamela, Mexico 86 D3 19 32N 105 5W
Chamical, Argentina 94 C2 30 22S 66 27W
Chamkar Luong, Cambodia 39 G4 11 0N 103 45 E
Chamoli, India 43 D8 30 24N 79 21 E
Chamonix-Mont Blanc, France 18 D7 45 55N 6 51 E
Chamouchouane →, Canada 70 C5 48 37N 72 20W
Champa, India 43 H10 22 2N 82 43 E
Champagne, Canada 72 A1 60 49N 136 30W
Champagne, France 18 B6 48 40N 4 20 E
Champaign, U.S.A. 76 E1 40 7N 88 15W
Champassak, Laos 38 E5 14 53N 105 52 E
Champawat, India 43 E9 29 20N 80 6 E
Champdoré, L., Canada 71 A6 55 55N 65 49W
Champion, U.S.A. 78 E4 41 19N 80 51W
Champlain, U.S.A. 79 B11 44 59N 73 27W
Champlain, L., U.S.A. 79 B11 44 40N 73 20W
Champotón, Mexico 87 D6 19 20N 90 50W
Champua, India 43 H11 22 5N 85 40 E
Chana, Thailand 39 J3 6 55N 100 44 E
Chañaral, Chile 94 B1 26 23S 70 40W
Chanārān, Iran 45 B8 36 39N 59 6 E
Chanasma, India 42 H5 23 44N 72 5 E
Chanco, Chile 94 D1 35 44S 72 32W
Chand, India 43 J8 21 57N 79 7 E
Chandan, India 43 G12 24 38N 86 40 E
Chandan Chauki, India 43 E9 28 33N 80 47 E
Chandannagar, India 43 H13 22 52N 88 24 E
Chandausi, India 43 E8 28 27N 78 49 E
Chandeleur Is., U.S.A. 81 L10 29 55N 88 57W
Chandeleur Sd., U.S.A. 81 L10 29 55N 89 0W
Chandigarh, India 42 D7 30 43N 76 47 E
Chandil, India 43 H12 22 58N 86 3 E
Chandler, Australia 63 D1 27 0S 133 19 E
Chandler, Canada 71 C7 48 18N 64 46W
Chandler, Ariz., U.S.A. 83 K8 33 18N 111 50W
Chandler, Okla., U.S.A. 81 H6 35 42N 96 53W
Chandod, India 42 J5 21 59N 73 28 E
Chandpur, Bangla. 41 H17 23 8N 90 45 E
Chandrapur, India 40 K11 19 57N 79 25 E
Chānf, Iran 45 E9 26 38N 60 29 E
Chang, Pakistan 42 F3 26 59N 68 30 E
Chang, Ko, Thailand 39 F4 12 0N 102 23 E
Ch'ang Chiang = Chang Jiang →, China 33 C7 31 48N 121 10 E
Chang Jiang →, China 33 C7 31 48N 121 10 E
Changa, India 43 C7 33 53N 77 35 E
Changanacheri, India 40 Q10 9 25N 76 31 E
Changane →, Mozam. 57 C5 24 30S 33 30 E
Changbai, China 35 D15 41 25N 128 5 E
Changbai Shan, China 35 C15 42 20N 129 0 E
Changchiak'ou = Zhangjiakou, China 34 D8 40 48N 114 55 E
Ch'angchou = Changzhou, China 33 C6 31 47N 119 58 E
Changchun, China 35 C13 43 57N 125 17 E
Changchunling, China 35 B13 45 18N 125 27 E
Changde, China 33 D6 29 4N 111 35 E
Changdo-ri, N. Korea 35 E14 38 30N 127 40 E
Changhai = Shanghai, China 33 C7 31 15N 121 26 E
Changhua, Taiwan 33 D7 24 2N 120 30 E
Changhŭng, S. Korea 35 G14 34 41N 126 52 E
Changhŭngni, N. Korea 35 D15 40 24N 128 19 E
Changjiang, China 38 C7 19 20N 108 55 E
Changjin, N. Korea 35 D14 40 23N 127 15 E
Changjin-chŏsuji, N. Korea 35 D14 40 30N 127 15 E
Changli, China 35 E10 39 40N 119 13 E
Changling, China 35 B12 44 20N 123 58 E
Changlun, Malaysia 39 J3 6 25N 100 26 E
Changping, China 34 D9 40 14N 116 12 E
Changsha, China 33 D6 28 12N 113 0 E
Changwu, China 34 G4 35 10N 107 45 E
Changyi, China 35 F10 36 40N 119 30 E
Changyŏn, N. Korea 35 E13 38 15N 125 6 E
Changyuan, China 34 G8 35 15N 114 42 E
Changzhi, China 34 F7 36 10N 113 6 E
Changzhou, China 33 C6 31 47N 119 58 E
Chanhanga, Angola 56 B1 16 0S 14 8 E
Channapatna, India 40 N10 12 40N 77 15 E
Channel Is., U.K. 11 H5 49 19N 2 24W
Channel Is., U.S.A. 85 M7 33 40N 119 15W
Channel Islands Nat. Park, U.S.A. 85 M8 33 30N 119 0W
Channel-Port aux Basques, Canada 71 C8 47 30N 59 9W
Channel Tunnel, Europe 11 F9 51 0N 1 30 E
Channing, U.S.A. 81 H3 35 41N 102 20W
Chantada, Spain 19 A2 42 36N 7 46W
Chanthaburi, Thailand 38 F4 12 38N 102 12 E
Chantrey Inlet, Canada 68 B10 67 48N 96 20W
Chanute, U.S.A. 81 G7 37 41N 95 27W
Chao Phraya →, Thailand 38 F3 13 32N 100 36 E
Chao Phraya Lowlands, Thailand 38 E3 15 30N 100 0 E
Chaocheng, China 34 F8 36 4N 115 37 E
Chaoyang, China 35 D11 41 35N 120 22 E
Chaozhou, China 33 D6 23 42N 116 32 E
Chapais, Canada 70 C5 49 47N 74 51W
Chapala, Mozam. 55 F4 15 50S 37 35 E
Chapala, L. de, Mexico 86 C4 20 10N 103 20W
Chapayev, Kazakstan 25 D9 50 25N 51 10 E
Chapayevsk, Russia 24 D8 53 0N 49 40 E
Chapecó, Brazil 95 B5 27 14S 52 41W
Chapel Hill, U.S.A. 77 H6 35 55N 79 4W
Chapleau, Canada 70 C3 47 50N 83 24W
Chaplin, Canada 73 C7 50 28N 106 40W
Chaplin L., Canada 73 C7 50 22N 106 36W
Chappell, U.S.A. 80 E3 41 6N 102 28W
Chapra = Chhapra, India 43 G11 25 48N 84 44 E
Chara, Russia 27 D12 56 54N 118 20 E
Charadai, Argentina 94 B4 27 35S 59 55W
Charagua, Bolivia 92 G6 19 45S 63 10W
Charambirá, Punta, Colombia 92 C3 4 16N 77 32W
Charaña, Bolivia 92 G5 17 30S 69 25W
Charanwala, India 42 F5 27 51N 72 10 E
Charata, Argentina 94 B3 27 13S 61 14W
Charcas, Mexico 86 C4 23 10N 101 20W
Chard, U.K. 11 G5 50 52N 2 58W
Chardon, U.S.A. 78 E3 41 35N 81 12W
Chardzhou = Chärjew, Turkmenistan 26 F7 39 6N 63 34 E
Charente →, France 18 D3 45 57N 1 5W
Chari →, Chad 51 F8 12 58N 14 31 E
Chārīkār, Afghan. 40 B6 35 0N 69 10 E
Chariton →, U.S.A. 80 F8 39 19N 92 58W
Chärjew, Turkmenistan 26 F7 39 6N 63 34 E
Charkhari, India 43 G8 25 24N 79 45 E
Charkhi Dadri, India 42 E7 28 37N 76 17 E
Charleroi, Belgium 15 D4 50 24N 4 27 E
Charleroi, U.S.A. 78 F5 40 9N 79 57W
Charles, C., U.S.A. 76 G8 37 7N 75 58W
Charles City, U.S.A. 80 D8 43 4N 92 41W
Charles L., Canada 73 B6 59 50N 110 33W
Charles Town, U.S.A. 76 F7 39 17N 77 52W
Charleston, Ill., U.S.A. 76 F1 39 30N 88 10W
Charleston, Miss., U.S.A. 81 H9 34 1N 90 4W
Charleston, Mo., U.S.A. 81 G10 36 55N 89 21W
Charleston, S.C., U.S.A. 77 J6 32 46N 79 56W
Charleston, W. Va., U.S.A. 76 F5 38 21N 81 38W
Charleston L., Canada 79 B9 44 32N 76 0W
Charleston Peak, U.S.A. 85 J11 36 16N 115 42W
Charlestown, Ireland 13 C3 53 58N 8 48W
Charlestown, S. Africa 57 D4 27 26S 29 53 E
Charlestown, Ind., U.S.A. 76 F3 38 27N 85 40W
Charlestown, N.H., U.S.A. 79 C12 43 14N 72 25W
Charleville = Rath Luirc, Ireland 13 D3 52 21N 8 40W
Charleville, Australia 63 D4 26 24S 146 15 E
Charleville-Mézières, France 18 B6 49 44N 4 40 E
Charlevoix, U.S.A. 76 C3 45 19N 85 16W
Charlotte, Mich., U.S.A. 76 D3 42 34N 84 50W
Charlotte, N.C., U.S.A. 77 H5 35 13N 80 51W
Charlotte, Vt., U.S.A. 79 B11 44 19N 73 14W
Charlotte Amalie, U.S. Virgin Is. 89 C7 18 21N 64 56W
Charlotte Harbor, U.S.A. 77 M4 26 50N 82 10W
Charlotte L., Canada 72 C3 52 12N 125 19W
Charlottesville, U.S.A. 76 F6 38 2N 78 30W
Charlottetown, Nfld., Canada 71 B8 52 46N 56 7W
Charlottetown, P.E.I., Canada 71 C7 46 14N 63 8W
Charlton, Australia 63 F3 36 16S 143 24 E
Charlton, U.S.A. 80 E8 40 59N 93 20W
Charlton I., Canada 70 B4 52 0N 79 20W
Charny, Canada 71 C5 46 43N 71 15W
Charolles, France 18 C6 46 27N 4 16 E
Charre, Mozam. 55 F4 17 13S 35 10 E
Charsadda, Pakistan 42 B4 34 7N 71 45 E
Charters Towers, Australia 62 C4 20 5S 146 13 E
Chartres, France 18 B4 48 29N 1 30 E
Chascomús, Argentina 94 D4 35 30S 58 0W
Chasefu, Zambia 55 E3 11 55S 33 8 E
Chashma Barrage, Pakistan 42 C4 32 27N 71 20 E
Chāt, Iran 45 B7 37 59N 55 16 E
Châteaubriant, France 18 C3 47 43N 1 23W
Chateaugay, U.S.A. 79 B10 44 56N 74 5W
Châteauguay, L., Canada 71 A5 56 26N 70 3W
Châteaulin, France 18 B1 48 11N 4 8W
Châteauroux, France 18 C4 46 50N 1 40 E
Châtellerault, France 18 C4 46 50N 0 30 E
Chatham = Miramichi, Canada 71 C6 47 2N 65 28W
Chatham, Canada 78 D2 42 24N 82 11W
Chatham, U.K. 11 F8 51 22N 0 32 E
Chatham, U.S.A. 79 D11 42 21N 73 36W
Chatham Is., Pac. Oc. 64 M10 44 0S 176 40W
Chatmohar, Bangla. 43 G13 24 15N 89 15 E
Chatra, India 43 G11 24 12N 84 56 E
Chatrapur, India 41 K14 19 22N 85 2 E
Chats, L. des, Canada 79 A8 45 30N 76 20W
Chatsu, India 42 F6 26 36N 75 57 E
Chatsworth, Canada 78 B4 44 27N 80 54W
Chatsworth, Zimbabwe 55 F3 19 38S 31 13 E
Chattahoochee, U.S.A. 77 K3 30 42N 84 51W
Chattahoochee →, U.S.A. 77 K3 30 54N 84 57W
Chattanooga, U.S.A. 77 H3 35 3N 85 19W
Chatteris, U.K. 11 E8 52 28N 0 2 E
Chaturat, Thailand 38 E3 15 40N 101 51 E
Chau Doc, Vietnam 39 G5 10 42N 105 7 E
Chaukan Pass, Burma 41 F20 27 0N 97 15 E
Chaumont, France 18 B6 48 7N 5 8 E
Chaumont, U.S.A. 79 B8 44 4N 76 8W
Chautauqua L., U.S.A. 78 D5 42 10N 79 24W
Chauvin, Canada 73 C6 52 45N 110 10W
Chaves, Brazil 93 D9 0 15S 49 55W
Chaves, Portugal 19 B2 41 45N 7 32W
Chawang, Thailand 39 H2 8 25N 99 30 E
Chaykovskiy, Russia 24 C9 56 47N 54 9 E
Chazy, U.S.A. 79 B11 44 53N 73 26W
Cheb, Czech Rep. 16 C7 50 9N 12 28 E
Cheboksary, Russia 24 C8 56 8N 47 12 E
Cheboygan, U.S.A. 76 C3 45 39N 84 29W
Chech, Erg, Africa 50 D5 25 0N 2 15W
Chechenia □, Russia 25 F8 43 30N 45 29 E
Checheno-Ingush Republic = Chechenia □, Russia 25 F8 43 30N 45 29 E
Chechnya = Chechenia □, Russia 25 F8 43 30N 45 29 E
Chech'ŏn, S. Korea 35 F15 37 8N 128 12 E
Checotah, U.S.A. 81 H7 35 28N 95 31W
Chedabucto B., Canada 71 C7 45 25N 61 8W
Cheduba I., Burma 41 K18 18 45N 93 40 E
Cheepie, Australia 63 D4 26 33S 145 1 E
Chegdomyn, Russia 27 D14 51 7N 133 1 E
Chegga, Mauritania 50 C4 25 27N 5 40W
Chegutu, Zimbabwe 55 F3 18 10S 30 14 E
Chehalis, U.S.A. 84 D4 46 40N 122 58W
Chehalis →, U.S.A. 84 D3 46 57N 123 50W
Cheju do, S. Korea 35 H14 33 29N 126 34 E
Chekiang = Zhejiang □, China 33 D7 29 0N 120 0 E
Chela, Sa. da, Angola 56 B1 16 20S 13 20 E
Chelan, U.S.A. 82 C4 47 51N 120 1W
Chelan, L., U.S.A. 82 B3 48 11N 120 30W
Cheleken, Turkmenistan 25 G9 39 34N 53 16 E
Cheleken Yarymadasy, Turkmenistan 45 B7 39 30N 53 15 E
Chelforó, Argentina 96 D3 39 0S 66 33W
Chelkar = Shalqar, Kazakstan 26 E6 47 48N 59 39 E
Chelkar Tengiz, Solonchak, Kazakstan 26 E7 48 5N 63 7 E
Chełm, Poland 17 C12 51 8N 23 30 E
Chełmno, Poland 17 B10 53 20N 18 30 E
Chelmsford, U.K. 11 F8 51 44N 0 29 E
Chelsea, U.S.A. 79 C12 43 59N 72 27W
Cheltenham, U.K. 11 F5 51 54N 2 4W
Chelyabinsk, Russia 26 D7 55 10N 61 24 E
Chelyuskin, C., Russia 28 B14 77 30N 103 0 E
Chemainus, Canada 84 B3 48 55N 123 42W
Chemba, Mozam. 53 H6 17 9S 34 53 E
Chemnitz, Germany 16 C7 50 51N 12 54 E
Chemult, U.S.A. 82 E3 43 14N 121 47W
Chen, Gora, Russia 27 C15 65 16N 141 50 E
Chenab →, Pakistan 42 D4 30 23N 71 2 E
Chenango Forks, U.S.A. 79 D9 42 15N 75 51W
Cheney, U.S.A. 82 C5 47 30N 117 35W
Cheng Xian, China 34 H3 33 43N 105 42 E
Chengcheng, China 34 G5 35 8N 109 56 E
Chengchou = Zhengzhou, China 34 G7 34 45N 113 34 E
Chengde, China 35 D9 40 59N 117 58 E
Chengdu, China 32 C5 30 38N 104 2 E
Chenggu, China 34 H4 33 10N 107 21 E
Chengjiang, China 32 D5 24 39N 103 0 E
Ch'engmai, China 38 C7 19 50N 109 58 E
Ch'engtu = Chengdu, China 32 C5 30 38N 104 2 E
Chengwu, China 34 G8 34 58N 115 50 E
Chengyang, China 35 F11 36 18N 120 21 E
Chenjiagang, China 35 G10 34 23N 119 47 E
Chenkán, Mexico 87 D6 19 8N 90 58W
Chennai, India 40 N12 13 8N 80 19 E
Cheo Reo, Vietnam 36 B3 13 25N 108 28 E
Cheom Ksan, Cambodia 38 E5 14 13N 104 56 E
Chepén, Peru 92 E3 7 15S 79 23W
Chepes, Argentina 94 C2 31 20S 66 35W
Chepo, Panama 88 E4 9 10N 79 6W
Chepstow, U.K. 11 F5 51 38N 2 41W
Cheptulil, Mt., Kenya 54 B4 1 25N 35 35 E
Chequamegon B., U.S.A. 80 B9 46 40N 90 30W
Cher →, France 18 C4 47 21N 0 29 E
Cheraw, U.S.A. 77 H6 34 42N 79 53W
Cherbourg, France 18 B3 49 39N 1 40W
Cherdyn, Russia 24 B10 60 24N 56 29 E
Cheremkhovo, Russia 27 D11 53 8N 103 1 E
Cherepanovo, Russia 26 D9 54 15N 83 30 E
Cherepovets, Russia 24 C6 59 5N 37 55 E
Chergui, Chott ech, Algeria 50 B6 34 21N 0 25 E
Cherikov = Cherykaw, Belarus 17 B16 53 32N 31 20 E
Cherkasy, Ukraine 25 E5 49 27N 32 4 E
Cherkessk, Russia 25 F7 44 15N 42 5 E
Cherlak, Russia 26 D8 54 15N 74 55 E
Chernaya, Russia 27 B9 70 30N 89 10 E
Chernigov = Chernihiv, Ukraine 24 D5 51 28N 31 20 E
Chernihiv, Ukraine 24 D5 51 28N 31 20 E
Chernivtsi, Ukraine 17 D13 48 15N 25 52 E
Chernobyl = Chornobyl, Ukraine 17 C16 51 20N 30 15 E
Chernogorsk, Russia 27 D10 53 49N 91 18 E
Chernovtsy = Chernivtsi, Ukraine 17 D13 48 15N 25 52 E
Chernyakhovsk, Russia 9 J19 54 36N 21 48 E
Chernysheyskiy, Russia 27 C12 63 0N 112 30 E
Cherokee, Iowa, U.S.A. 80 D7 42 45N 95 33W
Cherokee, Okla., U.S.A. 81 G5 36 45N 98 21W
Cherokee Village, U.S.A. 81 G9 36 17N 91 30W
Cherokees, Grand Lake O' The, U.S.A. 81 G7 36 28N 95 2W
Cherrapunji, India 41 G17 25 17N 91 47 E
Cherry Valley, Calif., U.S.A. 85 M10 33 59N 116 57W
Cherry Valley, N.Y., U.S.A. 79 D10 42 48N 74 45W
Cherskiy, Russia 27 C17 68 45N 161 18 E
Cherskogo Khrebet, Russia 27 C15 65 0N 143 0 E
Cherven, Belarus 17 B15 53 45N 28 28 E
Chervonohrad, Ukraine 17 C13 50 25N 24 10 E
Cherwell →, U.K. 11 F6 51 44N 1 14W
Cherykaw, Belarus 17 B16 53 32N 31 20 E
Chesapeake, U.S.A. 76 G7 36 50N 76 17W
Chesapeake B., U.S.A. 76 G7 38 0N 76 10W
Cheshire □, U.K. 10 D5 53 14N 2 30W
Cheshskaya Guba, Russia 24 A8 67 20N 47 0 E
Cheshunt, U.K. 11 F7 51 43N 0 1W
Chesil Beach, U.K. 11 G5 50 37N 2 33W
Chesley, Canada 78 B3 44 17N 81 5W
Chester, U.K. 10 D5 53 12N 2 53W
Chester, Calif., U.S.A. 82 F3 40 19N 121 14W
Chester, Ill., U.S.A. 81 G10 37 55N 89 49W
Chester, Mont., U.S.A. 82 B8 48 31N 110 58W
Chester, Pa., U.S.A. 76 F8 39 51N 75 22W
Chester, S.C., U.S.A. 77 H5 34 43N 81 12W
Chester, Vt., U.S.A. 79 C12 43 16N 72 36W
Chester, W. Va., U.S.A. 78 F4 40 37N 80 34W
Chester-le-Street, U.K. 10 C6 54 51N 1 34W
Chesterfield, U.K. 10 D6 53 15N 1 25W
Chesterfield, Is., N. Cal. 64 J7 19 52S 158 15 E
Chesterfield Inlet, Canada 68 B10 63 30N 90 45W
Chesterton Ra., Australia 63 D4 25 30S 147 27 E
Chestertown, U.S.A. 79 C11 43 40N 73 48W
Chesterville, Canada 79 A9 45 6N 75 14W
Chestnut Ridge, U.S.A. 78 F5 40 20N 79 10W
Chesuncook L., U.S.A. 77 C11 46 0N 69 21W
Chéticamp, Canada 71 C7 46 37N 60 59W
Chetumal, Mexico 87 D7 18 30N 88 20W
Chetumal, B. de, Mexico 87 D7 18 40N 88 10W
Chetwynd, Canada 72 B4 55 45N 121 36W
Cheviot, The, U.K. 10 B5 55 29N 2 9W
Cheviot Hills, U.K. 10 B5 55 20N 2 30W
Cheviot Ra., Australia 62 D3 25 20S 143 45 E
Chew Bahir, Ethiopia 46 G2 4 40N 36 50 E
Chewelah, U.S.A. 82 B5 48 17N 117 43W
Cheyenne, Okla., U.S.A. 81 H5 35 37N 99 40W
Cheyenne, Wyo., U.S.A. 80 E2 41 8N 104 49W
Cheyenne →, U.S.A. 80 C4 44 41N 101 18W
Cheyenne Wells, U.S.A. 80 F3 38 49N 102 21W
Cheyne B., Australia 61 F2 34 35S 118 50 E
Chhabra, India 42 G7 24 40N 76 54 E
Chhaktala, India 42 H6 22 6N 74 11 E
Chhapra, India 43 G11 25 48N 84 44 E
Chhata, India 42 F7 27 42N 77 30 E
Chhatarpur, Jharkhand, India 43 G11 24 23N 84 11 E
Chhatarpur, Mad. P., India 43 G8 24 55N 79 35 E
Chhattisgarh □, India 43 J10 22 0N 82 0 E
Chhep, Cambodia 38 F5 13 45N 105 24 E
Chhindwara, Mad. P., India 43 H8 23 3N 79 29 E
Chhindwara, Mad. P., India 43 H8 22 2N 78 59 E
Chhlong, Cambodia 39 F5 12 15N 105 58 E
Chhota Tawa →, India 42 H7 22 14N 76 36 E
Chhoti Kali Sindh →, India 42 G6 24 2N 75 31 E
Chhuikhadan, India 43 J9 21 32N 80 59 E
Chhuk, Cambodia 39 G5 10 46N 104 28 E
Chi →, Thailand 38 E5 15 11N 104 43 E
Chiai, Taiwan 33 D7 23 29N 120 25 E
Chiamboni, Somali Rep. 52 E8 1 39S 41 35 E
Chiamussu = Jiamusi, China 33 B8 46 40N 130 26 E
Chiang Dao, Thailand 38 C2 19 22N 98 58 E
Chiang Kham, Thailand 38 C3 19 32N 100 18 E
Chiang Khan, Thailand 38 D3 17 52N 101 36 E
Chiang Khong, Thailand 38 B3 20 17N 100 24 E
Chiang Mai, Thailand 38 C2 18 47N 98 59 E
Chiang Rai, Thailand 38 C2 19 52N 99 50 E
Chiang Saen, Thailand 38 B3 20 16N 100 5 E
Chiapa →, Mexico 87 D6 16 42N 93 0W
Chiapa de Corzo, Mexico 87 D6 16 42N 93 0W
Chiapas □, Mexico 87 D6 17 0N 92 45W
Chiautla, Mexico 87 D5 18 18N 98 34W
Chiávari, Italy 18 D8 44 19N 9 19 E
Chiavenna, Italy 18 C8 46 19N 9 24 E
Chiba, Japan 31 G10 35 30N 140 7 E
Chiba □, Japan 31 G10 35 30N 140 20 E
Chibabava, Mozam. 57 C5 20 17S 33 35 E
Chibemba, Cunene, Angola 53 H2 15 48S 14 8 E
Chibemba, Huila, Angola 56 B2 16 20S 15 20 E
Chibi, Zimbabwe 57 C5 20 18S 30 25 E
Chibia, Angola 53 H2 15 10S 13 42 E
Chibougamau, Canada 70 C5 49 56N 74 24W
Chibougamau, L., Canada 70 C5 49 50N 74 20W
Chibuto, Mozam. 57 C5 24 40S 33 33 E
Chic-Chocs, Mts., Canada 71 C6 48 55N 66 0W
Chicacole = Srikakulam, India 41 K13 18 14N 83 58 E
Chicago, U.S.A. 76 E2 41 53N 87 38W
Chicago Heights, U.S.A. 76 E2 41 30N 87 38W
Chichagof I., U.S.A. 68 C6 57 30N 135 30W
Chichén-Itzá, Mexico 87 C7 20 40N 88 36W
Chicheng, China 34 D8 40 55N 115 55 E
Chichester, U.K. 11 G7 50 50N 0 47W
Chichester Ra., Australia 60 D2 22 12S 119 15 E
Chichibu, Japan 31 F9 35 59N 139 10 E
Ch'ich'ihaerh = Qiqihar, China 27 E13 47 26N 124 0 E
Chicholi, India 42 H8 22 1N 77 40 E
Chickasha, U.S.A. 81 H6 35 3N 97 58W
Chiclana de la Frontera, Spain 19 D2 36 26N 6 9W
Chiclayo, Peru 92 E3 6 42S 79 50W
Chico, U.S.A. 84 F5 39 44N 121 50W
Chico →, Chubut, Argentina 96 E3 44 0S 67 0W
Chico →, Santa Cruz, Argentina 96 G3 50 0S 68 30W
Chicomo, Mozam. 57 C5 24 31S 34 6 E
Chicontepec, Mexico 87 C5 20 58N 98 10W
Chicopee, U.S.A. 79 D12 42 9N 72 37W

Chicoutimi, Canada 71 C5 48 28N 71 5W
Chicualacuala, Mozam. 57 C5 22 6S 31 42 E
Chidambaram, India 40 P11 11 20N 79 45 E
Chidenguele, Mozam. 57 C5 24 55S 34 11 E
Chidley, C., Canada 69 B13 60 23N 64 26W
Chiducuane, Mozam. 57 C5 24 35S 34 25 E
Chiede, Angola 56 B2 17 15S 16 22 E
Chiefs Pt., Canada 78 B3 44 41N 81 18W
Chiem Hoa, Vietnam 38 A5 22 12N 105 17 E
Chiemsee, Germany 16 E7 47 53N 12 28 E
Chiengi, Zambia 55 D2 8 45S 29 10 E
Chiengmai = Chiang Mai, Thailand 38 C2 18 47N 98 59 E
Chiese →, Italy 18 D9 45 8N 10 25 E
Chieti, Italy 20 C6 42 21N 14 10 E
Chifeng, China 35 C10 42 18N 118 58 E
Chignecto B., Canada 71 C7 45 30N 64 40W
Chiguana, Bolivia 94 A2 21 0S 67 58W
Chigwell, U.K. 11 F8 51 37N 0 5 E
Chiha-ri, N. Korea 35 E14 38 40N 126 30 E
Chihli, G. of = Bo Hai, China 35 E10 39 0N 119 0 E
Chihuahua, Mexico 86 B3 28 40N 106 3W
Chihuahua □, Mexico 86 B3 28 40N 106 3W
Chiili = Shīeli, Kazakstan 26 E7 44 20N 66 15 E
Chik Bollapur, India 40 N10 13 25N 77 45 E
Chikmagalur, India 40 N9 13 15N 75 45 E
Chikwawa, Malawi 55 F3 16 2S 34 50 E
Chilac, Mexico 87 D5 18 20N 97 24W
Chilam Chavki, Pakistan 43 B6 35 5N 75 5 E
Chilanga, Zambia 55 F2 15 33S 28 16 E
Chilapa, Mexico 87 D5 17 40N 99 11W
Chilas, Pakistan 43 B6 35 25N 74 5 E
Chilaw, Sri Lanka 40 R11 7 30N 79 50 E
Chilcotin →, Canada 72 C4 51 44N 122 23W
Childers, Australia 63 D5 25 15S 152 17 E
Childress, U.S.A. 81 H4 34 25N 100 13W
Chile ■, S. Amer. 96 D2 35 0S 72 0W
Chile Rise, Pac. Oc. 65 L18 38 0S 92 0W
Chilecito, Argentina 94 B2 29 10S 67 30W
Chilete, Peru 92 E3 7 10S 78 50W
Chililabombwe, Zambia 55 E2 12 18S 27 43 E
Chilin = Jilin, China 35 C14 43 44N 126 30 E
Chilka L., India 41 K14 19 40N 85 25 E
Chilko →, Canada 72 C4 52 0N 123 40W
Chilko L., Canada 72 C4 51 20N 124 10W
Chillagoe, Australia 62 B3 17 7S 144 33 E
Chillán, Chile 94 D1 36 40S 72 10W
Chillicothe, Ill., U.S.A. 80 E10 40 55N 89 29W
Chillicothe, Mo., U.S.A. 80 F8 39 48N 93 33W
Chillicothe, Ohio, U.S.A. 76 F4 39 20N 82 59W
Chilliwack, Canada 72 D4 49 10N 121 54W
Chilo, India 42 F5 27 25N 73 32 E
Chiloane, I., Mozam. 57 C5 20 40S 34 55 E
Chiloé, I. de, Chile 96 E2 42 30S 73 50W
Chilpancingo, Mexico 87 D5 17 30N 99 30W
Chiltern Hills, U.K. 11 F7 51 40N 0 53W
Chilton, U.S.A. 76 C1 44 2N 88 10W
Chilubi, Zambia 55 E2 11 5S 29 58 E
Chilubula, Zambia 55 E3 10 14S 30 51 E
Chilumba, Malawi 55 E3 10 28S 34 12 E
Chilung, Taiwan 33 D7 25 3N 121 45 E
Chilwa, L., Malawi 55 F4 15 15S 35 40 E
Chimaltitán, Mexico 86 C4 21 46N 103 50W
Chimán, Panama 88 E4 8 45N 78 40W
Chimanimani, Zimbabwe 57 B5 19 48S 32 52 E
Chimay, Belgium 15 D4 50 3N 4 20 E
Chimayo, U.S.A. 83 H11 36 0N 105 56W
Chimbay, Uzbekistan 26 E6 42 57N 59 47 E
Chimborazo, Ecuador 92 D3 1 29S 78 55W
Chimbote, Peru 92 E3 9 0S 78 35W
Chimkent = Shymkent, Kazakstan 26 E7 42 18N 69 36 E
Chimoio, Mozam. 55 F3 19 4S 33 30 E
Chimpembe, Zambia 55 D2 9 31S 29 33 E
Chin □, Burma 41 J18 22 0N 93 0 E
Chin Ling Shan = Qinling Shandi, China 34 H5 33 50N 108 10 E
China, Mexico 87 B5 25 40N 99 20W
China ■, Asia 33 C6 30 0N 110 0 E
China Lake, U.S.A. 85 K9 35 44N 117 37W
Chinan = Jinan, China 34 F9 36 38N 117 1 E
Chinandega, Nic. 88 D2 12 35N 87 12W
Chinati Peak, U.S.A. 81 L2 29 57N 104 29W
Chincha Alta, Peru 92 F3 13 25S 76 7W
Chinchaga →, Canada 72 B5 58 53N 118 20W
Chinchilla, Australia 63 D5 26 45S 150 38 E
Chinchorro, Banco, Mexico 87 D7 18 35N 87 20W
Chinchou = Jinzhou, China 35 D11 41 5N 121 3 E
Chincoteague, U.S.A. 76 G8 37 56N 75 23W
Chinde, Mozam. 55 F4 18 35S 36 30 E
Chindo, S. Korea 35 G14 34 28N 126 15 E
Chindwin →, Burma 41 J19 21 26N 95 15 E
Chineni, India 43 C6 33 2N 75 15 E
Chinga, Mozam. 55 F4 15 13S 38 35 E
Chingola, Zambia 55 E2 12 31S 27 53 E
Chingole, Malawi 55 E3 13 4S 34 17 E
Ch'ingtao = Qingdao, China 35 F11 36 5N 120 20 E
Chinguetti, Mauritania 50 D3 20 25N 12 24W
Chingune, Mozam. 57 C5 20 33S 34 58 E
Chinhae, S. Korea 35 G15 35 9N 128 47 E
Chinhanguanine, Mozam. 57 D5 25 21S 32 30 E
Chinhoyi, Zimbabwe 55 F3 17 20S 30 8 E
Chini, India 42 D8 31 32N 78 15 E
Chiniot, Pakistan 42 D5 31 45N 73 0 E
Chínipas, Mexico 86 B3 27 22N 108 32W
Chinji, Pakistan 42 C5 32 42N 72 22 E
Chinju, S. Korea 35 G15 35 12N 128 2 E
Chinle, U.S.A. 83 H9 36 9N 109 33W
Chinnampo = Namp'o, N. Korea 35 E13 38 52N 125 10 E
Chino, Japan 31 G9 35 59N 138 9 E
Chino, U.S.A. 85 L9 34 1N 117 41W
Chino Valley, U.S.A. 83 J7 34 45N 112 27W
Chinon, France 18 C4 47 10N 0 15 E
Chinook, U.S.A. 82 B9 48 35N 109 14W
Chinsali, Zambia 55 E3 10 30S 32 2 E
Chióggia, Italy 20 B5 45 13N 12 17 E
Chíos = Khíos, Greece 21 E12 38 27N 26 9 E
Chipata, Zambia 55 E3 13 38S 32 28 E
Chipinge, Zimbabwe 55 G3 20 13S 32 28 E
Chipley, U.S.A. 77 K3 30 47N 85 32W
Chipman, Canada 71 C6 46 6N 65 53W
Chipoka, Malawi 55 E3 13 57S 34 28 E
Chippenham, U.K. 11 F5 51 27N 2 6W
Chippewa →, U.S.A. 80 C8 44 25N 92 5W
Chippewa Falls, U.S.A. 80 C9 44 56N 91 24W
Chipping Norton, U.K. 11 F6 51 56N 1 32W
Chiputneticook Lakes, U.S.A. 77 C11 45 35N 67 35W
Chiquián, Peru 92 F3 10 10S 77 0W
Chiquimula, Guatemala 88 D2 14 51N 89 37W
Chiquinquira, Colombia 92 B4 5 37N 73 50W
Chirala, India 40 M12 15 50N 80 26 E
Chiramba, Mozam. 55 F3 16 55S 34 39 E
Chirawa, India 42 E6 28 14N 75 42 E
Chirchiq, Uzbekistan 26 E7 41 29N 69 35 E
Chiredzi, Zimbabwe 57 C5 21 0S 31 38 E
Chiricahua Peak, U.S.A. 83 L9 31 51N 109 18W
Chiriquí, G. de, Panama 88 E3 8 0N 82 10W
Chiriquí, L. de, Panama 88 E3 9 10N 82 0W
Chirivira Falls, Zimbabwe 55 G3 21 10S 32 12 E
Chirmiri, India 41 H13 23 15N 82 20 E
Chirripó Grande, Cerro, Costa Rica 88 E3 9 29N 83 29W
Chirundu, Zimbabwe 57 B4 16 3S 28 50 E
Chisamba, Zambia 55 E2 14 55S 28 20 E
Chisapani Garhi, Nepal 41 F14 27 30N 84 2 E
Chisasibi, Canada 70 B4 53 50N 79 0W
Chisholm, Canada 72 C6 54 55N 114 10W
Chisholm, U.S.A. 80 B8 47 29N 92 53W
Chishtian Mandi, Pakistan 42 E5 29 50N 72 55 E
Chisimaio, Somali Rep. 49 G8 0 22S 42 32 E
Chisimba Falls, Zambia 55 E3 10 12S 30 56 E
Chişinău, Moldova 17 E15 47 2N 28 50 E
Chisos Mts., U.S.A. 81 L3 29 5N 103 15W
Chistopol, Russia 24 C9 55 25N 50 38 E
Chita, Russia 27 D12 52 0N 113 35 E
Chitipa, Malawi 55 D3 9 41S 33 19 E
Chitose, Japan 30 C10 42 49N 141 39 E
Chitral, Pakistan 40 B7 35 50N 71 56 E
Chitré, Panama 88 E3 7 59N 80 27W
Chittagong, Bangla. 41 H17 22 19N 91 48 E
Chittagong □, Bangla. 41 G17 24 5N 91 0 E
Chittaurgarh, India 42 G6 24 52N 74 38 E
Chittoor, India 40 N11 13 15N 79 5 E
Chitungwiza, Zimbabwe 55 F3 18 0S 31 6 E
Chiusi, Italy 20 C4 43 1N 11 57 E
Chivasso, Italy 18 D7 45 11N 7 53 E
Chivhu, Zimbabwe 55 F3 19 2S 30 52 E
Chivilcoy, Argentina 94 C4 34 55S 60 0W
Chiwanda, Tanzania 55 E3 11 23S 34 55 E
Chizarira, Zimbabwe 55 F2 17 36S 27 45 E
Chizera, Zambia 55 E2 13 10S 25 0 E
Chkalov = Orenburg, Russia 24 D10 51 45N 55 6 E
Chloride, U.S.A. 85 K12 35 25N 114 12W
Cho Bo, Vietnam 38 B5 20 46N 105 10 E
Cho-do, N. Korea 35 E13 38 30N 124 40 E
Cho Phuoc Hai, Vietnam 39 G6 10 26N 107 18 E
Choba, Kenya 54 B4 2 30N 38 5 E
Choch'iwŏn, S. Korea 35 F14 36 37N 127 18 E
Chocolate Mts., U.S.A. 85 M11 33 15N 115 15W
Choctawhatchee →, U.S.A. 77 K3 30 25N 86 8W
Choele Choel, Argentina 96 D3 39 11S 65 40W
Choix, Mexico 86 B3 26 40N 108 23W
Chojnice, Poland 17 B9 53 42N 17 32 E
Chōkai-San, Japan 30 E10 39 6N 140 3 E
Choke Canyon L., U.S.A. 81 L5 28 30N 98 20W
Chokurdakh, Russia 27 B15 70 38N 147 55 E
Cholame, U.S.A. 84 K6 35 44N 120 18W
Cholet, France 18 C3 47 4N 0 52W
Cholguan, Chile 94 D1 37 10S 72 3W
Choluteca, Honduras 88 D2 13 20N 87 14W
Choluteca →, Honduras 88 D2 13 0N 87 20W
Chom Bung, Thailand 38 F2 13 37N 99 36 E
Chom Thong, Thailand 38 C2 18 25N 98 41 E
Choma, Zambia 55 F2 16 48S 26 59 E
Chomun, India 42 F6 27 15N 75 40 E
Chomutov, Czech Rep. 16 C7 50 28N 13 23 E
Chon Buri, Thailand 38 F3 13 21N 101 1 E
Chon Thanh, Vietnam 39 G6 11 24N 106 36 E
Ch'onan, S. Korea 35 F14 36 48N 127 9 E
Chone, Ecuador 92 D3 0 40S 80 0W
Chong Kai, Cambodia 38 F4 13 57N 103 35 E
Chong Mek, Thailand 38 E5 15 10N 105 27 E
Chŏngdo, S. Korea 35 G15 35 38N 128 42 E
Chŏngha, S. Korea 35 F15 36 12N 129 21 E
Chŏngjin, N. Korea 35 D15 41 47N 129 50 E
Chŏngjiu, S. Korea 35 F14 36 39N 127 27 E
Chŏngju, N. Korea 35 E13 39 40N 125 5 E
Chongli, China 34 D8 40 58N 115 15 E
Chongqing, China 32 D5 29 35N 106 25 E
Chongqing Shi □, China 32 C5 30 0N 108 0 E
Chonguene, Mozam. 57 C5 25 3S 33 49 E
Chŏngŭp, S. Korea 35 G14 35 35N 126 50 E
Chŏnju, S. Korea 35 G14 35 50N 127 4 E
Chonos, Arch. de los, Chile 96 F2 45 0S 75 0W
Chop, Ukraine 17 D12 48 26N 22 12 E
Chopim →, Brazil 95 B5 25 35S 53 5W
Chor, Pakistan 42 G3 25 31N 69 46 E
Chorbat La, India 43 B7 34 42N 76 37 E
Chorley, U.K. 10 D5 53 39N 2 38W
Chornobyl, Ukraine 17 C16 51 20N 30 15 E
Chorolque, Cerro, Bolivia 94 A2 20 59S 66 5W
Chorregon, Australia 62 C3 22 40S 143 32 E
Chortkiv, Ukraine 17 D13 49 2N 25 46 E
Ch'ŏrwon, S. Korea 35 E14 38 15N 127 10 E
Chorzów, Poland 17 C10 50 18N 18 57 E
Chos-Malal, Argentina 94 D1 37 20S 70 15W
Ch'osan, N. Korea 35 D13 40 50N 125 47 E
Choszczno, Poland 16 B8 53 7N 15 25 E
Choteau, U.S.A. 82 C7 47 49N 112 11W
Chotila, India 42 H4 22 23N 71 15 E
Chotta Udepur, India 42 H6 22 19N 74 1 E
Chowchilla, U.S.A. 84 H6 37 7N 120 16W
Choybalsan, Mongolia 33 B6 48 4N 114 30 E
Christchurch, N.Z. 59 K4 43 33S 172 47 E
Christchurch, U.K. 11 G6 50 44N 1 47W
Christian I., Canada 78 B4 44 50N 80 12W
Christiana, S. Africa 56 D4 27 52S 25 8 E
Christiansted, U.S. Virgin Is. 89 C7 17 45N 64 42W
Christie B., Canada 73 A6 62 32N 111 10W
Christina →, Canada 73 B6 56 40N 111 3W
Christmas Cr. →, Australia 60 C4 18 29S 125 23 E
Christmas I. = Kiritimati, Kiribati 65 G12 1 58N 157 27W
Christmas I., Ind. Oc. 64 J2 10 30S 105 40 E
Christopher L., Australia 61 D4 24 49S 127 42 E
Chtimba, Malawi 55 E3 10 35S 34 13 E
Chu = Shū, Kazakstan 26 E8 43 36N 73 42 E
Chu →, Vietnam 38 C5 19 53N 105 45 E
Chu Lai, Vietnam 38 E7 15 28N 108 45 E
Ch'uanchou = Quanzhou, China 33 D6 24 55N 118 34 E
Chuankou, China 34 G6 34 20N 110 59 E
Chubbuck, U.S.A. 82 E7 42 55N 112 28W
Chūbu □, Japan 31 F8 36 45N 137 30 E
Chubut →, Argentina 96 E3 43 20S 65 5W
Chuchi L., Canada 72 B4 55 12N 124 30W
Chuda, India 42 H4 22 29N 71 41 E
Chudskoye, Ozero, Russia 9 G22 58 13N 27 30 E
Chūgoku □, Japan 31 G6 35 0N 133 0 E
Chūgoku-Sanchi, Japan 31 G6 35 0N 133 0 E
Chugwater, U.S.A. 80 E2 41 46N 104 50W
Chukchi Sea, Russia 27 C19 68 0N 175 0W
Chukotskoye Nagorye, Russia 27 C18 68 0N 175 0 E
Chula Vista, U.S.A. 85 N9 32 39N 117 5W
Chulucanas, Peru 92 E2 5 8S 80 10W
Chulym →, Russia 26 D9 57 43N 83 51 E
Chum Phae, Thailand 38 D4 16 40N 102 6 E
Chum Saeng, Thailand 38 E3 15 55N 100 15 E
Chumar, India 43 C8 32 40N 78 35 E
Chumbicha, Argentina 94 B2 29 0S 66 10W
Chumikan, Russia 27 D14 54 40N 135 10 E
Chumphon, Thailand 39 G2 10 35N 99 14 E
Chumuare, Mozam. 55 E3 14 31S 31 50 E
Chumunjin, S. Korea 35 F15 37 55N 128 54 E
Chuna →, Russia 27 D10 57 47N 94 37 E
Ch'unch'ŏn, S. Korea 35 F14 37 58N 127 44 E
Chunchura, India 43 H13 22 53N 88 27 E
Chunga, Zambia 55 F2 15 0S 26 2 E
Chunggang-ŭp, N. Korea 35 D14 41 48N 126 48 E
Chunghwa, N. Korea 35 E13 38 52N 125 47 E
Ch'ungju, S. Korea 35 F14 36 58N 127 58 E
Chungking = Chongqing, China 32 D5 29 35N 106 25 E
Ch'ungmu, S. Korea 35 G15 34 50N 128 20 E
Chungt'iaoshan = Zhongtiao Shan, China 34 G6 35 0N 111 10 E
Chunian, Pakistan 42 D6 30 57N 74 0 E
Chunya, Tanzania 55 D3 8 30S 33 27 E
Chunyang, China 35 C15 43 38N 129 23 E
Chuquibamba, Peru 92 G4 15 47S 72 44W
Chuquicamata, Chile 94 A2 22 15S 69 0W
Chur, Switz. 18 C8 46 52N 9 32 E
Churachandpur, India 41 G18 24 20N 93 40 E
Churchill, Canada 73 B10 58 47N 94 11W
Churchill →, Man., Canada 73 B10 58 47N 94 12W
Churchill →, Nfld., Canada 71 B7 53 19N 60 10W
Churchill, C., Canada 73 B10 58 46N 93 12W
Churchill Falls, Canada 71 B7 53 36N 64 19W
Churchill L., Canada 73 B7 55 55N 108 20W
Churchill Pk., Canada 72 B3 58 10N 125 10W
Churki, India 43 H10 23 50N 83 12 E
Churu, India 42 E6 28 20N 74 50 E
Churún Merú = Angel Falls, Venezuela 92 B6 5 57N 62 30W
Chushal, India 43 C8 33 40N 78 40 E
Chuska Mts., U.S.A. 83 H9 36 15N 108 50W
Chusovoy, Russia 24 C10 58 22N 57 50 E
Chute-aux-Outardes, Canada 71 C6 49 7N 68 24W
Chuuronjang, N. Korea 35 D15 41 35N 129 40 E
Chuvash Republic = Chuvashia □, Russia 24 C8 55 30N 47 0 E
Chuvashia □, Russia 24 C8 55 30N 47 0 E
Chuwārtah, Iraq 44 C5 35 43N 45 34 E
Chüy = Shū →, Kazakstan 28 E10 45 0N 67 44 E
Chuy, Uruguay 95 C5 33 41S 53 27W
Ci Xian, China 34 F8 36 20N 114 25 E
Ciadâr-Lunga, Moldova 17 E15 46 3N 28 51 E
Ciamis, Indonesia 37 G13 7 20S 108 21 E
Cianjur, Indonesia 37 G12 6 49S 107 8 E
Cianorte, Brazil 95 A5 23 37S 52 37W
Cibola, U.S.A. 85 M12 33 17N 114 42W
Cicero, U.S.A. 76 E2 41 51N 87 45W
Ciechanów, Poland 17 B11 52 52N 20 38 E
Ciego de Avila, Cuba 88 B4 21 50N 78 50W
Ciénaga, Colombia 92 A4 11 1N 74 15W
Cienfuegos, Cuba 88 B3 22 10N 80 30W
Cieszyn, Poland 17 D10 49 45N 18 35 E
Cieza, Spain 19 C5 38 17N 1 23W
Cihuatlán, Mexico 86 D4 19 14N 104 35W
Cijara, Embalse de, Spain 19 C3 39 18N 4 52W
Cijulang, Indonesia 37 G13 7 42S 108 27 E
Cilacap, Indonesia 37 G13 7 43S 109 0 E
Cill Chainnigh = Kilkenny, Ireland 13 D4 52 39N 7 15W
Cilo Dağı, Turkey 25 G7 37 28N 43 55 E
Cima, U.S.A. 85 K11 35 14N 115 30W
Cimarron, Kans., U.S.A. 81 G4 37 48N 100 21W
Cimarron, N. Mex., U.S.A. 81 G2 36 31N 104 55W
Cimarron →, U.S.A. 81 G6 36 10N 96 17W
Cimişlia, Moldova 17 E15 46 34N 28 44 E
Cimone, Mte., Italy 20 B4 44 12N 10 42 E
Cinca →, Spain 19 B6 41 26N 0 21 E
Cincar, Bos.-H. 20 C7 43 55N 17 5 E
Cincinnati, U.S.A. 76 F3 39 6N 84 31W
Cincinnatus, U.S.A. 79 D9 42 33N 75 54W
Çine, Turkey 21 F13 37 37N 28 2 E
Ciney, Belgium 15 D5 50 18N 5 5 E
Cinto, Mte., France 18 E8 42 24N 8 54 E
Circle, Alaska, U.S.A. 68 B5 65 50N 144 4W
Circle, Mont., U.S.A. 80 B2 47 25N 105 35W
Circleville, U.S.A. 76 F4 39 36N 82 57W
Cirebon, Indonesia 36 F3 6 45S 108 32 E
Ciremai, Indonesia 37 G13 6 55S 108 27 E
Cirencester, U.K. 11 F6 51 43N 1 57W
Cirium, Cyprus 23 E11 34 40N 32 53 E
Cisco, U.S.A. 81 J5 32 23N 98 59W
Citlaltépetl, Mexico 87 D5 19 0N 97 20W
Citrus Heights, U.S.A. 84 G5 38 42N 121 17W
Citrusdal, S. Africa 56 E2 32 35S 19 0 E
Città di Castello, Italy 20 C5 43 27N 12 14 E
Ciudad Altamirano, Mexico 86 D4 18 20N 100 40W
Ciudad Bolívar, Venezuela 92 B6 8 5N 63 36W
Ciudad Camargo, Mexico 86 B3 27 41N 105 10W
Ciudad de Valles, Mexico 87 C5 22 0N 99 0W
Ciudad del Carmen, Mexico 87 D6 18 38N 91 50W
Ciudad del Este, Paraguay 95 B5 25 30S 54 50W
Ciudad Delicias = Delicias, Mexico 86 B3 28 10N 105 30W
Ciudad Guayana, Venezuela 92 B6 8 0N 62 30W
Ciudad Guerrero, Mexico 86 B3 28 33N 107 28W
Ciudad Guzmán, Mexico 86 D4 19 40N 103 30W
Ciudad Juárez, Mexico 86 A3 31 40N 106 28W
Ciudad Madero, Mexico 87 C5 22 19N 97 50W
Ciudad Mante, Mexico 87 C5 22 50N 99 0W
Ciudad Obregón, Mexico 86 B3 27 28N 109 59W
Ciudad Real, Spain 19 C4 38 59N 3 55W
Ciudad Rodrigo, Spain 19 B2 40 35N 6 32W
Ciudad Trujillo = Santo Domingo, Dom. Rep. 89 C6 18 30N 69 59W
Ciudad Victoria, Mexico 87 C5 23 41N 99 9W
Ciudadela, Spain 22 B10 40 0N 3 50 E
Civitanova Marche, Italy 20 C5 43 18N 13 44 E
Civitavécchia, Italy 20 C4 42 6N 11 48 E
Cizre, Turkey 25 G7 37 19N 42 10 E
Clackmannanshire □, U.K. 12 E5 56 10N 3 43W
Clacton-on-Sea, U.K. 11 F9 51 47N 1 11 E
Claire, L., Canada 72 B6 58 35N 112 5W
Clairton, U.S.A. 78 F5 40 18N 79 53W
Clallam Bay, U.S.A. 84 B2 48 15N 124 16W
Clanton, U.S.A. 77 J2 32 51N 86 38W
Clanwilliam, S. Africa 56 E2 32 11S 18 52 E
Clara, Ireland 13 C4 53 21N 7 37W
Claraville, U.S.A. 85 K8 35 24N 118 20W
Clare, Australia 63 E2 33 50S 138 37 E
Clare, U.S.A. 76 D3 43 49N 84 46W
Clare □, Ireland 13 D3 52 45N 9 0W
Clare →, Ireland 13 C2 53 20N 9 2W
Clare I., Ireland 13 C1 53 49N 10 0W
Claremont, Calif., U.S.A. 85 L9 34 6N 117 43W
Claremont, N.H., U.S.A. 79 C12 43 23N 72 20W
Claremont Pt., Australia 62 A3 14 1S 143 41 E
Claremore, U.S.A. 81 G7 36 19N 95 36W
Claremorris, Ireland 13 C3 53 45N 9 0W
Clarence →, Australia 63 D5 29 25S 153 22 E
Clarence →, N.Z. 59 K4 42 10S 173 56 E
Clarence, I., Chile 96 G2 54 0S 72 0W
Clarence I., Antarctica 5 C18 61 10S 54 0W
Clarence Str., Australia 60 B5 12 0S 131 0 E
Clarence Town, Bahamas 89 B5 23 6N 74 59W
Clarendon, Pa., U.S.A. 78 E5 41 47N 79 6W
Clarendon, Tex., U.S.A. 81 H4 34 56N 100 53W
Clarenville, Canada 71 C9 48 10N 54 1W
Claresholm, Canada 72 D6 50 0N 113 33W
Clarie Coast, Antarctica 5 C9 68 0S 135 0 E
Clarinda, U.S.A. 80 E7 40 44N 95 2W
Clarion, Iowa, U.S.A. 80 D8 42 44N 93 44W
Clarion, Pa., U.S.A. 78 E5 41 13N 79 23W
Clarion →, U.S.A. 78 E5 41 7N 79 41W
Clark, U.S.A. 80 C6 44 53N 97 44W
Clark, Pt., Canada 78 B3 44 4N 81 45W
Clark Fork, U.S.A. 82 B5 48 9N 116 11W
Clark Fork →, U.S.A. 82 B5 48 9N 116 15W
Clarkdale, U.S.A. 83 J7 34 46N 112 3W
Clarke City, Canada 71 B6 50 12N 66 38W
Clarke I., Australia 62 G4 40 32S 148 10 E
Clarke Ra., Australia 62 C4 20 40S 148 30 E
Clark's Fork →, U.S.A. 82 D9 45 39N 108 43W
Clark's Harbour, Canada 71 D6 43 25N 65 38W
Clarks Hill L., U.S.A. 77 J4 33 40N 82 12W
Clarks Summit, U.S.A. 79 E9 41 30N 75 42W
Clarksburg, U.S.A. 76 F5 39 17N 80 30W
Clarksdale, U.S.A. 81 H9 34 12N 90 35W
Clarksville, Ark., U.S.A. 81 H8 35 28N 93 28W
Clarksville, Tenn., U.S.A. 77 G2 36 32N 87 21W
Clarksville, Tex., U.S.A. 81 J7 33 37N 95 3W
Clatskanie, U.S.A. 84 D3 46 6N 123 12W
Claude, U.S.A. 81 H4 35 7N 101 22W
Claveria, Phil. 37 A6 18 37N 121 4 E
Clay, U.S.A. 84 G5 38 17N 121 10W
Clay Center, U.S.A. 80 F6 39 23N 97 8W
Claypool, U.S.A. 83 K8 33 25N 110 51W
Claysburg, U.S.A. 78 F6 40 17N 78 27W
Claysville, U.S.A. 78 F4 40 7N 80 25W
Clayton, N. Mex., U.S.A. 81 G3 36 27N 103 11W
Clayton, N.Y., U.S.A. 79 B8 44 14N 76 5W
Clear, C., Ireland 13 E2 51 25N 9 32W
Clear, L., Canada 78 A7 45 26N 77 12W
Clear Hills, Canada 72 B5 56 40N 119 30W
Clear I., Ireland 13 E2 51 26N 9 30W
Clear L., U.S.A. 84 F4 39 2N 122 47W
Clear Lake, Iowa, U.S.A. 80 D8 43 8N 93 23W
Clear Lake, S. Dak., U.S.A. 80 C6 44 45N 96 41W
Clear Lake Reservoir, U.S.A. 82 F3 41 56N 121 5W
Clearfield, Pa., U.S.A. 78 E6 41 2N 78 27W
Clearfield, Utah, U.S.A. 82 F8 41 7N 112 2W
Clearlake, U.S.A. 82 G2 38 57N 122 38W
Clearlake Highlands, U.S.A. 84 G4 38 57N 122 38W
Clearwater, Canada 72 C4 51 38N 120 2W
Clearwater, U.S.A. 77 M4 27 58N 82 48W
Clearwater →, Alta., Canada 72 C6 52 22N 114 57W
Clearwater →, Alta., Canada 73 B6 56 44N 111 23W
Clearwater L., Canada 73 C9 53 34N 99 49W
Clearwater Mts., U.S.A. 82 C6 46 5N 115 20W
Clearwater Prov. Park, Canada 73 C8 54 0N 101 0W
Clearwater River Prov. Park, Canada 73 B7 56 55N 109 10W
Cleburne, U.S.A. 81 J6 32 21N 97 23W
Clee Hills, U.K. 11 E5 52 26N 2 35W
Cleethorpes, U.K. 10 D7 53 33N 0 3W
Cleeve Cloud, U.K. 11 F6 51 56N 2 0W
Clemson, U.S.A. 77 H4 34 41N 82 50W
Clerke Reef, Australia 60 C2 17 22S 119 20 E
Clermont, Australia 62 C4 22 49S 147 39 E
Clermont, U.S.A. 77 L5 28 33N 81 46W
Clermont-Ferrand, France 18 D5 45 46N 3 4 E
Clervaux, Lux. 15 D6 50 4N 6 2 E
Clevedon, U.K. 11 F5 51 26N 2 52W
Cleveland, Miss., U.S.A. 81 J9 33 45N 90 43W
Cleveland, Ohio, U.S.A. 78 E3 41 30N 81 42W
Cleveland, Okla., U.S.A. 81 G6 36 19N 96 28W
Cleveland, Tenn., U.S.A. 77 H3 35 10N 84 53W
Cleveland, Tex., U.S.A. 81 K7 30 21N 95 5W
Cleveland, C., Australia 62 B4 19 11S 147 1 E
Cleveland, Mt., U.S.A. 82 B7 48 56N 113 51W
Cleveland Heights, U.S.A. 78 E3 41 30N 81 34W
Clevelândia, Brazil 95 B5 26 24S 52 23W
Clew B., Ireland 13 C2 53 50N 9 49W
Clewiston, U.S.A. 77 M5 26 45N 80 56W
Clifden, Ireland 13 C1 53 29N 10 1W
Clifden, N.Z. 59 M1 46 1S 167 42 E
Cliffdell, U.S.A. 84 D5 46 56N 121 5W
Cliffy Hd., Australia 61 G2 35 1S 116 29 E
Clifton, Australia 63 D5 27 59S 151 53 E
Clifton, Ariz., U.S.A. 83 K9 33 3N 109 18W
Clifton, Colo., U.S.A. 83 G9 39 7N 108 25W
Clifton, Tex., U.S.A. 81 K6 31 47N 97 35W
Clifton Beach, Australia 62 B4 16 46S 145 39 E
Climax, Canada 73 D7 49 10N 108 20W

Coral Springs, U.S.A. **77 M5** 26 16N 80 13W
Coraopolis, U.S.A. **78 F4** 40 31N 80 10W
Corato, Italy **20 D7** 41 9N 16 25 E
Corbin, U.S.A. **76 G3** 36 57N 84 6W
Corby, U.K. **11 E7** 52 30N 0 41W
Corcaigh = Cork, Ireland **13 E3** 51 54N 8 29W
Corcoran, U.S.A. **84 J7** 36 6N 119 33W
Corcubión, Spain **19 A1** 42 56N 9 12W
Cordele, U.S.A. **77 K4** 31 58N 83 47W
Cordell, U.S.A. **81 H5** 35 17N 98 59W
Córdoba, Argentina **94 C3** 31 20S 64 10W
Córdoba, Mexico **87 D5** 18 50N 97 0W
Córdoba, Spain **19 D3** 37 50N 4 50W
Córdoba □, Argentina **94 C3** 31 22S 64 15W
Córdoba, Sierra de, Argentina **94 C3** 31 10S 64 25W
Cordova, U.S.A. **68 B5** 60 33N 145 45W
Corella →, Australia **62 B3** 19 34S 140 47 E
Corfield, Australia **62 C3** 21 40S 143 21 E
Corfu = Kérkira, Greece **23 A3** 39 38N 19 50 E
Corfu, Str. of, Greece **23 A4** 39 34N 20 0 E
Coria, Spain **19 C2** 39 58N 6 33W
Corigliano Cálabro, Italy **20 E7** 39 36N 16 31 E
Coringa Is., Australia **62 B4** 16 58S 149 58 E
Corinth = Kórinthos, Greece **21 F10** 37 56N 22 55 E
Corinth, Miss., U.S.A. **77 H1** 34 56N 88 31W
Corinth, N.Y., U.S.A. **79 C11** 43 15N 73 49W
Corinth, G. of = Korinthiakós Kólpos, Greece **21 E10** 38 16N 22 30 E
Corinto, Brazil **93 G10** 18 20S 44 30W
Corinto, Nic. **88 D2** 12 30N 87 10W
Cork, Ireland **13 E3** 51 54N 8 29W
Cork □, Ireland **13 E3** 51 57N 8 40W
Cork Harbour, Ireland **13 E3** 51 47N 8 16W
Çorlu, Turkey **21 D12** 41 11N 27 49 E
Cormack L., Canada **72 A4** 60 56N 121 37W
Cormorant, Canada **73 C8** 54 14N 100 35W
Cormorant L., Canada **73 C8** 54 15N 100 50W
Corn Is. = Maíz, Is. del, Nic. **88 D3** 12 15N 83 4W
Cornélio Procópio, Brazil **95 A5** 23 7S 50 40W
Corner Brook, Canada **71 C8** 48 57N 57 58W
Corneşti, Moldova **17 E15** 47 21N 28 1 E
Corning, Ark., U.S.A. **81 G9** 36 25N 90 35W
Corning, Calif., U.S.A. **82 G2** 39 56N 122 11W
Corning, Iowa, U.S.A. **80 E7** 40 59N 94 44W
Corning, N.Y., U.S.A. **78 D7** 42 9N 77 3W
Cornwall, Canada **79 A10** 45 2N 74 44W
Cornwall, U.S.A. **79 F8** 40 17N 76 25W
Cornwall □, U.K. **11 G3** 50 26N 4 40W
Corny Pt., Australia **63 E2** 34 55S 137 0 E
Coro, Venezuela **92 A5** 11 25N 69 41W
Coroatá, Brazil **93 D10** 4 8S 44 0W
Corocoro, Bolivia **92 G5** 17 15S 68 28W
Coroico, Bolivia **92 G5** 16 0S 67 50W
Coromandel, N.Z. **59 G5** 36 45S 175 31 E
Coromandel Coast, India **40 N12** 12 30N 81 0 E
Corona, Calif., U.S.A. **85 M9** 33 53N 117 34W
Corona, N. Mex., U.S.A. **83 J11** 34 15N 105 36W
Coronach, Canada **73 D7** 49 7N 105 31W
Coronado, U.S.A. **85 N9** 32 41N 117 11W
Coronado, B. de, Costa Rica **88 E3** 9 0N 83 40W
Coronados, Is. los, U.S.A. **85 N9** 32 25N 117 15W
Coronation, Canada **72 C6** 52 5N 111 27W
Coronation Gulf, Canada **68 B8** 68 25N 110 0W
Coronation I., Antarctica **5 C18** 60 45S 46 0W
Coronation Is., Australia **60 B3** 14 57S 124 55 E
Coronda, Argentina **94 C3** 31 58S 60 56W
Coronel, Chile **94 D1** 37 0S 73 10W
Coronel Bogado, Paraguay **94 B4** 27 11S 56 18W
Coronel Dorrego, Argentina **94 D3** 38 40S 61 10W
Coronel Oviedo, Paraguay **94 B4** 25 24S 56 30W
Coronel Pringles, Argentina **94 D3** 38 0S 61 30W
Coronel Suárez, Argentina **94 D3** 37 30S 61 52W
Coronel Vidal, Argentina **94 D4** 37 28S 57 45W
Coropuna, Nevado, Peru **92 G4** 15 30S 72 41W
Corowa, Australia **63 F4** 35 58S 146 21 E
Corozal, Belize **87 D7** 18 23N 88 23W
Corpus, Argentina **95 B4** 27 10S 55 30W
Corpus Christi, U.S.A. **81 M6** 27 47N 97 24W
Corpus Christi, L., U.S.A. **81 L6** 28 2N 97 52W
Corralejo, Canary Is. **22 F6** 28 43N 13 53W
Corraun Pen., Ireland **13 C2** 53 54N 9 54W
Correntes, C. das, Mozam. **57 C6** 24 6S 35 34 E
Corrib, L., Ireland **13 C2** 53 27N 9 16W
Corrientes, Argentina **94 B4** 27 30S 58 45W
Corrientes □, Argentina **94 B4** 28 0S 57 0W
Corrientes →, Argentina **94 C4** 30 42S 59 38W
Corrientes →, Peru **92 D4** 3 43S 74 35W
Corrientes, C., Colombia **92 B3** 5 30N 77 34W
Corrientes, C., Cuba **88 B3** 21 43N 84 30W
Corrientes, C., Mexico **86 C3** 20 25N 105 42W
Corrigan, U.S.A. **81 K7** 31 0N 94 52W
Corrigin, Australia **61 F2** 32 20S 117 53 E
Corry, U.S.A. **78 E5** 41 55N 79 39W
Corse, France **18 F8** 42 0N 9 0 E
Corse, C., France **18 E8** 43 1N 9 25 E
Corsica = Corse, France **18 F8** 42 0N 9 0 E
Corsicana, U.S.A. **81 J6** 32 6N 96 28W
Corte, France **18 E8** 42 19N 9 11 E
Cortez, U.S.A. **83 H9** 37 21N 108 35W
Cortland, N.Y., U.S.A. **79 D8** 42 36N 76 11W
Cortland, Ohio, U.S.A. **78 E4** 41 20N 80 44W
Çorum, Turkey **25 F5** 40 30N 34 57 E
Corumbá, Brazil **92 G7** 19 0S 57 30W
Corunna = A Coruña, Spain **19 A1** 43 20N 8 25W
Corvallis, U.S.A. **82 D2** 44 34N 123 16W
Corvette, L. de la, Canada **70 B5** 53 25N 74 3W
Corydon, U.S.A. **80 E8** 40 46N 93 19W
Cosalá, Mexico **86 C3** 24 28N 106 40W
Cosamaloapan, Mexico **87 D5** 18 23N 95 50W
Cosenza, Italy **20 E7** 39 18N 16 15 E
Coshocton, U.S.A. **78 F3** 40 16N 81 51W
Cosmo Newberry, Australia **61 E3** 28 0S 122 54 E
Coso Junction, U.S.A. **85 J9** 36 3N 117 57W
Coso Pk., U.S.A. **85 J9** 36 13N 117 44W
Cosquín, Argentina **94 C3** 31 15S 64 30W
Costa Blanca, Spain **19 C5** 38 25N 0 10W
Costa Brava, Spain **19 B7** 41 30N 3 0 E
Costa del Sol, Spain **19 D3** 36 30N 4 30W
Costa Dorada, Spain **19 B6** 41 12N 1 15 E
Costa Mesa, U.S.A. **85 M9** 33 38N 117 55W
Costa Rica ■, Cent. Amer. **88 E3** 10 0N 84 0W
Cosumnes →, U.S.A. **84 G5** 38 16N 121 26W
Cotabato, Phil. **37 C6** 7 14N 124 15 E
Cotagaita, Bolivia **94 A2** 20 45S 65 40W
Côte d'Azur, France **18 E7** 43 25N 7 10 E
Côte-d'Ivoire = Ivory Coast ■, Africa **50 G4** 7 30N 5 0W
Coteau des Prairies, U.S.A. **80 C6** 45 20N 97 50W
Coteau du Missouri, U.S.A. **80 B4** 47 0N 100 0W
Coteau Landing, Canada **79 A10** 45 15N 74 13W
Cotentin, France **18 B3** 49 15N 1 30W
Cotillo, Canary Is. **22 F5** 28 41N 14 1W
Cotonou, Benin **50 G6** 6 20N 2 25 E
Cotopaxi, Ecuador **92 D3** 0 40S 78 30W
Cotswold Hills, U.K. **11 F5** 51 42N 2 10W
Cottage Grove, U.S.A. **82 E2** 43 48N 123 3W
Cottbus, Germany **16 C8** 51 45N 14 20 E
Cottonwood, U.S.A. **83 J7** 34 45N 112 1W
Cotulla, U.S.A. **81 L5** 28 26N 99 14W
Coudersport, U.S.A. **78 E6** 41 46N 78 1W
Couedic, C. du, Australia **63 F2** 36 5S 136 40 E
Coulee City, U.S.A. **82 C4** 47 37N 119 17W
Coulman I., Antarctica **5 D11** 73 35S 170 0 E
Coulonge →, Canada **70 C4** 45 52N 76 46W
Coulterville, U.S.A. **84 H6** 37 43N 120 12W
Council, U.S.A. **82 D5** 44 44N 116 26W
Council Bluffs, U.S.A. **80 E7** 41 16N 95 52W
Council Grove, U.S.A. **80 F6** 38 40N 96 29W
Coupeville, U.S.A. **84 B4** 48 13N 122 41W
Courantyne →, S. Amer. **92 B7** 5 55N 57 5W
Courcelles, Belgium **15 D4** 50 28N 4 22 E
Courtenay, Canada **72 D4** 49 45N 125 0W
Courtland, U.S.A. **84 G5** 38 20N 121 34W
Courtrai = Kortrijk, Belgium **15 D3** 50 50N 3 17 E
Courtright, Canada **78 D2** 42 49N 82 28W
Coushatta, U.S.A. **81 J8** 32 1N 93 21W
Coutts Crossing, Australia **63 D5** 29 49S 152 55 E
Couvin, Belgium **15 D4** 50 3N 4 29 E
Cove I., Canada **78 A3** 45 17N 81 44W
Coventry, U.K. **11 E6** 52 25N 1 28W
Covilhã, Portugal **19 B2** 40 17N 7 31W
Covington, Ga., U.S.A. **77 J4** 33 36N 83 51W
Covington, Ky., U.S.A. **76 F3** 39 5N 84 31W
Covington, Okla., U.S.A. **81 G6** 36 18N 97 35W
Covington, Tenn., U.S.A. **81 H10** 35 34N 89 39W
Covington, Va., U.S.A. **76 G5** 37 47N 79 59W
Cowal, L., Australia **63 E4** 33 40S 147 25 E
Cowan, L., Australia **61 F3** 31 45S 121 45 E
Cowan L., Canada **73 C7** 54 0N 107 15W
Cowangie, Australia **63 F3** 35 12S 141 26 E
Cowansville, Canada **79 A12** 45 14N 72 46W
Coward Springs, Australia **63 D2** 29 24S 136 49 E
Cowcowing Lakes, Australia **61 F2** 30 55S 117 20 E
Cowdenbeath, U.K. **12 E5** 56 7N 3 21W
Cowell, Australia **63 E2** 33 39S 136 56 E
Cowes, U.K. **11 G6** 50 45N 1 18W
Cowichan L., Canada **84 B2** 48 53N 124 17W
Cowlitz →, U.S.A. **84 D4** 46 6N 122 55W
Cowra, Australia **63 E4** 33 49S 148 42 E
Coxilha Grande, Brazil **95 B5** 28 18S 51 30W
Coxim, Brazil **93 G8** 18 30S 54 55W
Cox's Bazar, Bangla. **41 J17** 21 26N 91 59 E
Coyote Wells, U.S.A. **85 N11** 32 44N 115 58W
Coyuca de Benítez, Mexico **87 D4** 17 1N 100 8W
Coyuca de Catalan, Mexico **86 D4** 18 18N 100 41W
Cozad, U.S.A. **80 E5** 40 52N 99 59W
Cozumel, Mexico **87 C7** 20 31N 86 55W
Cozumel, Isla, Mexico **87 C7** 20 30N 86 40W
Cracow = Kraków, Poland **17 C10** 50 4N 19 57 E
Cracow, Australia **63 D5** 25 17S 150 17 E
Cradock, Australia **63 E2** 32 6S 138 31 E
Cradock, S. Africa **56 E4** 32 8S 25 36 E
Craig, U.S.A. **82 F10** 40 31N 107 33W
Craigavon, U.K. **13 B5** 54 27N 6 23W
Craigmore, Zimbabwe **55 G3** 20 28S 32 50 E
Craik, Canada **73 C7** 51 3N 105 49W
Crailsheim, Germany **16 D6** 49 8N 10 5 E
Craiova, Romania **17 F12** 44 21N 23 48 E
Cramsie, Australia **62 C3** 23 20S 144 15 E
Cranberry L., U.S.A. **79 B10** 44 11N 74 50W
Cranberry Portage, Canada **73 C8** 54 35N 101 23W
Cranbrook, Australia **61 F2** 34 18S 117 33 E
Cranbrook, Canada **72 D5** 49 30N 115 46W
Crandon, U.S.A. **80 C10** 45 34N 88 54W
Crane, Oreg., U.S.A. **82 E4** 43 25N 118 35W
Crane, Tex., U.S.A. **81 K3** 31 24N 102 21W
Cranston, U.S.A. **79 E13** 41 47N 71 26W
Crater L., U.S.A. **82 E2** 42 56N 122 6W
Crater Lake Nat. Park, U.S.A. **82 E2** 42 55N 122 10W
Crateús, Brazil **93 E10** 5 10S 40 39W
Crato, Brazil **93 E11** 7 10S 39 25W
Craven, L., Canada **70 B4** 54 20N 76 56W
Crawford, U.S.A. **80 D3** 42 41N 103 25W
Crawfordsville, U.S.A. **76 E2** 40 2N 86 54W
Crawley, U.K. **11 F7** 51 7N 0 11W
Crazy Mts., U.S.A. **82 C8** 46 12N 110 20W
Crean L., Canada **73 C7** 54 5N 106 9W
Crediton, Canada **78 C3** 43 17N 81 33W
Cree →, Canada **73 B7** 58 57N 105 47W
Cree →, U.K. **12 G4** 54 55N 4 25W
Cree L., Canada **73 B7** 57 30N 106 30W
Creede, U.S.A. **83 H10** 37 51N 106 56W
Creekside, U.S.A. **78 F5** 40 40N 79 11W
Creel, Mexico **86 B3** 27 45N 107 38W
Creemore, Canada **78 B4** 44 19N 80 6W
Creighton, Canada **73 C8** 54 45N 101 54W
Creighton, U.S.A. **80 D6** 42 28N 97 54W
Crema, Italy **18 D8** 45 22N 9 41 E
Cremona, Italy **18 D9** 45 7N 10 2 E
Cres, Croatia **16 F8** 44 58N 14 25 E
Crescent City, U.S.A. **82 F1** 41 45N 124 12W
Crespo, Argentina **94 C3** 32 2S 60 19W
Cresson, U.S.A. **78 F6** 40 28N 78 36W
Crestline, Calif., U.S.A. **85 L9** 34 14N 117 18W
Crestline, Ohio, U.S.A. **78 F2** 40 47N 82 44W
Creston, Canada **72 D5** 49 10N 116 31W
Creston, Calif., U.S.A. **84 K6** 35 32N 120 33W
Creston, Iowa, U.S.A. **80 E7** 41 4N 94 22W
Crestview, Calif., U.S.A. **84 H8** 37 46N 118 58W
Crestview, Fla., U.S.A. **77 K2** 30 46N 86 34W
Crete = Kríti, Greece **23 D7** 35 15N 25 0 E
Crete, U.S.A. **80 E6** 40 38N 96 58W
Créteil, France **18 B5** 48 47N 2 28 E
Creus, C. de, Spain **19 A7** 42 20N 3 19 E
Creuse →, France **18 C4** 47 0N 0 34 E
Crewe, U.K. **10 D5** 53 6N 2 26W
Crewkerne, U.K. **11 G5** 50 53N 2 48W
Criciúma, Brazil **95 B6** 28 40S 49 23W
Crieff, U.K. **12 E5** 56 22N 3 50W
Crimea □, Ukraine **25 E5** 45 30N 33 10 E
Crimean Pen. = Krymskyy Pivostriv, Ukraine **25 F5** 45 0N 34 0 E
Crişul Alb →, Romania **17 E11** 46 42N 21 17 E
Crişul Negru →, Romania **17 E11** 46 42N 21 16 E
Crna →, Macedonia **21 D9** 41 33N 21 59 E
Crna Gora = Montenegro □, Yugoslavia **21 C8** 42 40N 19 20 E
Crna Gora, Macedonia **21 C9** 42 10N 21 30 E
Crna Reka = Crna →, Macedonia **21 D9** 41 33N 21 59 E
Croagh Patrick, Ireland **13 C2** 53 46N 9 40W
Croatia ■, Europe **16 F9** 45 20N 16 0 E
Crocker, Banjaran, Malaysia **36 C5** 5 40N 116 30 E
Crockett, U.S.A. **81 K7** 31 19N 95 27W
Crocodile = Krokodil →, Mozam. **57 D5** 25 14S 32 18 E
Crocodile Is., Australia **62 A1** 12 3S 134 58 E
Crohy Hd., Ireland **13 B3** 54 55N 8 26W
Croix, L. La, Canada **70 C1** 48 20N 92 15W
Croker, C., Australia **60 B5** 10 58S 132 35 E
Croker, C., Canada **78 B4** 44 58N 80 59W
Croker I., Australia **60 B5** 11 12S 132 32 E
Cromarty, U.K. **12 D4** 57 40N 4 2W
Cromer, U.K. **10 E9** 52 56N 1 17 E
Cromwell, N.Z. **59 L2** 45 3S 169 14 E
Cromwell, U.S.A. **79 E12** 41 36N 72 39W
Crook, U.K. **10 C6** 54 43N 1 45W
Crooked →, Canada **72 C4** 54 50N 122 54W
Crooked →, U.S.A. **82 D3** 44 32N 121 16W
Crooked I., Bahamas **89 B5** 22 50N 74 10W
Crooked Island Passage, Bahamas **89 B5** 23 0N 74 30W
Crookston, Minn., U.S.A. **80 B6** 47 47N 96 37W
Crookston, Nebr., U.S.A. **80 D4** 42 56N 100 45W
Crookwell, Australia **63 E4** 34 28S 149 24 E
Crosby, U.K. **10 D4** 53 30N 3 3W
Crosby, N. Dak., U.S.A. **80 A3** 48 55N 103 18W
Crosby, Pa., U.S.A. **78 E6** 41 45N 78 23W
Crosbyton, U.S.A. **81 J4** 33 40N 101 14W
Cross City, U.S.A. **77 L4** 29 38N 83 7W
Cross Fell, U.K. **10 C5** 54 43N 2 28W
Cross L., Canada **73 C9** 54 45N 97 30W
Cross Lake, Canada **73 C9** 54 37N 97 47W
Cross Sound, U.S.A. **68 C6** 58 0N 135 0W
Crossett, U.S.A. **81 J9** 33 8N 91 58W
Crosshaven, Ireland **13 E3** 51 47N 8 17W
Crossville, U.S.A. **77 G3** 35 57N 85 2W
Croswell, U.S.A. **78 C2** 43 16N 82 37W
Croton-on-Hudson, U.S.A. **79 E11** 41 12N 73 55W
Crotone, Italy **20 E7** 39 5N 17 8 E
Crow →, Canada **72 B4** 59 41N 124 20W
Crow Agency, U.S.A. **82 D10** 45 36N 107 28W
Crow Hd., Ireland **13 E1** 51 35N 10 9W
Crowell, U.S.A. **81 J5** 33 59N 99 43W
Crowley, U.S.A. **81 K8** 30 13N 92 22W
Crowley, L., U.S.A. **84 H8** 37 35N 118 42W
Crown Point, Ind., U.S.A. **76 E2** 41 25N 87 22W
Crown Point, N.Y., U.S.A. **79 C11** 43 57N 73 26W
Crownpoint, U.S.A. **83 J9** 35 41N 108 9W
Crows Landing, U.S.A. **84 H5** 37 23N 121 6W
Crows Nest, Australia **63 D5** 27 16S 152 4 E
Crowsnest Pass, Canada **72 D6** 49 40N 114 40W
Croydon, Australia **62 B3** 18 13S 142 14 E
Croydon □, U.K. **11 F7** 51 22N 0 5W
Crozet, Is., Ind. Oc. **3 G12** 46 27S 52 0 E
Cruz, C., Cuba **88 C4** 19 50N 77 50W
Cruz Alta, Brazil **95 B5** 28 45S 53 40W
Cruz del Eje, Argentina **94 C3** 30 45S 64 50W
Cruzeiro, Brazil **95 A7** 22 33S 45 0W
Cruzeiro do Oeste, Brazil **95 A5** 23 46S 53 4W
Cruzeiro do Sul, Brazil **92 E4** 7 35S 72 35W
Cry L., Canada **72 B3** 58 45N 129 0W
Crystal Bay, U.S.A. **84 F7** 39 15N 120 0W
Crystal Brook, Australia **63 E2** 33 21S 138 12 E
Crystal City, U.S.A. **81 L5** 28 41N 99 50W
Crystal Falls, U.S.A. **76 B1** 46 5N 88 20W
Crystal River, U.S.A. **77 L4** 28 54N 82 35W
Crystal Springs, U.S.A. **81 K9** 31 59N 90 21W
Csongrád, Hungary **17 E11** 46 43N 20 12 E
Cu Lao Hon, Vietnam **39 G7** 10 54N 108 18 E
Cua Rao, Vietnam **38 C5** 19 16N 104 27 E
Cuácua →, Mozam. **55 F4** 17 54S 37 0 E
Cuamato, Angola **56 B2** 17 2S 15 7 E
Cuamba, Mozam. **55 E4** 14 45S 36 22 E
Cuando →, Angola **53 H4** 17 30S 23 15 E
Cuando Cubango □, Angola **56 B3** 16 25S 20 0 E
Cuangar, Angola **56 B2** 17 36S 18 39 E
Cuango = Kwango →, Dem. Rep. of the Congo **52 E3** 3 14S 17 22 E
Cuanza →, Angola **52 F2** 9 21S 13 9 E
Cuarto →, Argentina **94 C3** 33 25S 63 2W
Cuatrociénegas, Mexico **86 B4** 26 59N 102 5W
Cuauhtémoc, Mexico **86 B3** 28 25N 106 52W
Cuba, N. Mex., U.S.A. **83 J10** 36 1N 107 4W
Cuba, N.Y., U.S.A. **78 D6** 42 13N 78 17W
Cuba ■, W. Indies **88 B4** 22 0N 79 0W
Cubango →, Africa **56 B3** 18 50S 22 25 E
Cuchumatanes, Sierra de los, Guatemala **88 C1** 15 35N 91 25W
Cuckfield, U.K. **11 F7** 51 1N 0 8W
Cucuí, Brazil **92 C5** 1 12N 66 50W
Cucurpe, Mexico **86 A2** 30 20N 110 43W
Cúcuta, Colombia **92 B4** 7 54N 72 31W
Cuddalore, India **40 P11** 11 46N 79 45 E
Cuddapah, India **40 M11** 14 30N 78 47 E
Cuddapan, L., Australia **62 D3** 25 45S 141 26 E
Cue, Australia **61 E2** 27 25S 117 54 E
Cuenca, Ecuador **92 D3** 2 50S 79 9W
Cuenca, Spain **19 B4** 40 5N 2 10W
Cuenca, Serranía de, Spain **19 C5** 39 55N 1 50W
Cuernavaca, Mexico **87 D5** 18 55N 99 15W
Cuero, U.S.A. **81 L6** 29 6N 97 17W
Cuevas del Almanzora, Spain **19 D5** 37 18N 1 58W
Cuevo, Bolivia **92 H6** 20 15S 63 30W
Cuiabá, Brazil **93 G7** 15 30S 56 0W
Cuiabá →, Brazil **93 G7** 17 5S 56 36W
Cuijk, Neths. **15 C5** 51 44N 5 50 E
Cuilco, Guatemala **88 C1** 15 24N 91 58W
Cuillin Hills, U.K. **12 D2** 57 13N 6 15W
Cuillin Sd., U.K. **12 D2** 57 4N 6 20W
Cuito →, Angola **56 B3** 18 1S 20 48 E
Cuitzeo, L. de, Mexico **86 D4** 19 55N 101 5W
Cukai, Malaysia **39 K4** 4 13N 103 25 E
Culbertson, U.S.A. **80 A2** 48 9N 104 31W
Culcairn, Australia **63 F4** 35 41S 147 3 E
Culgoa →, Australia **63 D4** 29 56S 146 20 E
Culiacán, Mexico **86 C3** 24 50N 107 23W
Culiacán →, Mexico **86 C3** 24 30N 107 42W
Culion, Phil. **37 B6** 11 54N 119 58 E
Cullarin Ra., Australia **63 E4** 34 30S 149 30 E
Cullen, U.K. **12 D6** 57 42N 2 49W
Cullen Pt., Australia **62 A3** 11 57S 141 54 E
Cullera, Spain **19 C5** 39 9N 0 17W
Cullman, U.S.A. **77 H2** 34 11N 86 51W
Culpeper, U.S.A. **76 F7** 38 30N 78 0W
Culuene →, Brazil **93 F8** 12 56S 52 51W
Culver, Pt., Australia **61 F3** 32 54S 124 43 E
Culverden, N.Z. **59 K4** 42 47S 172 49 E
Cumaná, Venezuela **92 A6** 10 30N 64 5W
Cumberland, B.C., Canada **72 D4** 49 40N 125 0W
Cumberland, Ont., Canada **79 A9** 45 29N 75 24W
Cumberland, U.S.A. **76 F6** 39 39N 78 46W
Cumberland →, U.S.A. **77 G2** 36 15N 87 0W
Cumberland, L., U.S.A. **77 G3** 36 57N 84 55W
Cumberland I., U.S.A. **77 K5** 30 50N 81 25W
Cumberland Is., Australia **62 C4** 20 35S 149 10 E
Cumberland L., Canada **73 C8** 54 3N 102 18W
Cumberland Pen., Canada **69 B13** 67 0N 64 0W
Cumberland Plateau, U.S.A. **77 H3** 36 0N 85 0W
Cumberland Sd., Canada **69 B13** 65 30N 66 0W
Cumbernauld, U.K. **12 F5** 55 57N 3 58W
Cumborah, Australia **63 D4** 29 40S 147 45 E
Cumbria □, U.K. **10 C5** 54 42N 2 52W
Cumbrian Mts., U.K. **10 C5** 54 30N 3 0W
Cumbum, India **40 M11** 15 40N 79 10 E
Cuminá →, Brazil **93 D7** 1 30S 56 0W
Cummings Mt., U.S.A. **85 K8** 35 2N 118 34W
Cummins, Australia **63 E2** 34 16S 135 43 E
Cumnock, Australia **63 E4** 32 59S 148 46 E
Cumnock, U.K. **12 F4** 55 28N 4 17W
Cumpas, Mexico **86 B3** 30 0N 109 48W
Cumplida, Pta., Canary Is. **22 F2** 28 50N 17 48W
Cunco, Chile **96 D2** 38 55S 72 2W
Cuncumén, Chile **94 C1** 31 53S 70 38W
Cunderdin, Australia **61 F2** 31 37S 117 12 E
Cunene →, Angola **56 B1** 17 20S 11 50 E
Cúneo, Italy **18 D7** 44 23N 7 32 E
Çüngüş, Turkey **44 B3** 38 13N 39 17 E
Cunillera, I. = Sa Conillera, Spain **22 C7** 38 59N 1 13 E
Cunnamulla, Australia **63 D4** 28 2S 145 38 E
Cupar, Canada **73 C8** 50 57N 104 10W
Cupar, U.K. **12 E5** 56 19N 3 1W
Cupica, G. de, Colombia **92 B3** 6 25N 77 30W
Curaçao, Neth. Ant. **89 D6** 12 10N 69 0W
Curanilahue, Chile **94 D1** 37 29S 73 28W
Curaray →, Peru **92 D4** 2 20S 74 5W
Curepto, Chile **94 D1** 35 8S 72 1W
Curiapo, Venezuela **92 B6** 8 33N 61 5W
Curicó, Chile **94 C1** 34 55S 71 20W
Curitiba, Brazil **95 B6** 25 20S 49 10W
Curitibanos, Brazil **95 B5** 27 18S 50 36W
Currabubula, Australia **63 E5** 31 16S 150 44 E
Currais Novos, Brazil **93 E11** 6 13S 36 30W
Curralinho, Brazil **93 D9** 1 45S 49 46W
Currant, U.S.A. **82 G6** 38 51N 115 32W
Current →, U.S.A. **81 G9** 36 15N 90 55W
Currie, Australia **62 F3** 39 56S 143 53 E
Currie, U.S.A. **82 F6** 40 16N 114 45W
Curtea de Argeş, Romania **17 F13** 45 12N 24 42 E
Curtis, U.S.A. **80 E4** 40 38N 100 31W
Curtis Group, Australia **62 F4** 39 30S 146 37 E
Curtis I., Australia **62 C5** 23 35S 151 10 E
Curuápanema →, Brazil **93 D7** 2 25S 55 2W
Curuçá, Brazil **93 D9** 0 43S 47 50W
Curuguaty, Paraguay **95 A4** 24 31S 55 42W
Curup, Indonesia **36 E2** 4 26S 102 13 E
Cururupu, Brazil **93 D10** 1 50S 44 50W
Curuzú Cuatiá, Argentina **94 B4** 29 50S 58 5W
Curvelo, Brazil **93 G10** 18 45S 44 27W
Cushing, U.S.A. **81 H6** 35 59N 96 46W
Cushing, Mt., Canada **72 B3** 57 35N 126 57W
Cusihuiriáchic, Mexico **86 B3** 28 10N 106 50W
Custer, U.S.A. **80 D3** 43 46N 103 36W
Cut Bank, U.S.A. **82 B7** 48 38N 112 20W
Cutchogue, U.S.A. **79 E12** 41 1N 72 30W
Cuthbert, U.S.A. **77 K3** 31 46N 84 48W
Cutler, U.S.A. **84 J7** 36 31N 119 17W
Cuttaburra →, Australia **63 D3** 29 43S 144 22 E
Cuttack, India **41 J14** 20 25N 85 57 E
Cuvier, C., Australia **61 D1** 23 14S 113 22 E
Cuvier I., N.Z. **59 G5** 36 27S 175 50 E
Cuxhaven, Germany **16 B5** 53 51N 8 41 E
Cuyahoga Falls, U.S.A. **78 E3** 41 8N 81 29W
Cuyo, Phil. **37 B6** 10 50N 121 5 E
Cuyuni →, Guyana **92 B7** 6 23N 58 41W
Cuzco, Bolivia **92 H5** 20 0S 66 50W
Cuzco, Peru **92 F4** 13 32S 72 0W
Cwmbran, U.K. **11 F4** 51 39N 3 2W
Cyangugu, Rwanda **54 C2** 2 29S 28 54 E
Cyclades = Kikládhes, Greece **21 F11** 37 0N 24 30 E
Cygnet, Australia **62 G4** 43 8S 147 1 E
Cynthiana, U.S.A. **76 F3** 38 23N 84 18W
Cypress Hills, Canada **73 D7** 49 40N 109 30W
Cypress Hills Prov. Park, Canada **73 D7** 49 40N 109 30W
Cyprus ■, Asia **23 E12** 35 0N 33 0 E
Cyrenaica, Libya **51 C10** 27 0N 23 0 E
Czar, Canada **73 C6** 52 27N 110 50W
Czech Rep. ■, Europe **16 D8** 50 0N 15 0 E
Częstochowa, Poland **17 C10** 50 49N 19 7 E

D

Da →, Vietnam **38 B5** 21 15N 105 20 E
Da Hinggan Ling, China **33 B7** 48 0N 121 0 E
Da Lat, Vietnam **39 G7** 11 56N 108 25 E
Da Nang, Vietnam **38 D7** 16 4N 108 13 E
Da Qaidam, China **32 C4** 37 50N 95 15 E
Da Yunhe →, China **35 G11** 34 25N 120 5 E
Da'an, China **35 B13** 45 30N 124 7 E
Daba Shan, China **33 C5** 32 0N 109 0 E
Dabbagh, Jabal, Si. Arabia **44 E2** 27 52N 35 45 E
Dabhoi, India **42 H5** 22 10N 73 20 E
Dabo = Pasirkuning, Indonesia **36 E2** 0 30S 104 33 E
Dabola, Guinea **50 F3** 10 50N 11 5W
Dabung, Malaysia **39 K4** 5 23N 102 1 E

Dacca = Dhaka, *Bangla.* **43 H14** 23 43N 90 26 E
Dacca = Dhaka □, *Bangla.* **43 G14** 24 25N 90 25 E
Dachau, *Germany* **16 D6** 48 15N 11 26 E
Dadanawa, *Guyana* **92 C7** 2 50N 59 30W
Dade City, *U.S.A.* **77 L4** 28 22N 82 11W
Dadhar, *Pakistan* **42 E2** 29 28N 67 39 E
Dadra & Nagar Haveli □, *India* **40 J8** 20 5N 73 0 E
Dadri = Charkhi Dadri, *India* **42 E7** 28 37N 76 17 E
Dadu, *Pakistan* **42 F2** 26 45N 67 45 E
Daet, *Phil.* **37 B6** 14 2N 122 55 E
Dagana, *Senegal* **50 E2** 16 30N 15 35W
Dagestan □, *Russia* **25 F8** 42 30N 47 0 E
Daggett, *U.S.A.* **85 L10** 34 52N 116 52W
Daghestan Republic = Dagestan □, *Russia* **25 F8** 42 30N 47 0 E
Dağlıq Qarabağ = Nagorno-Karabakh, *Azerbaijan* **25 F8** 39 55N 46 45 E
Dagö = Hiiumaa, *Estonia* **9 G20** 58 50N 22 45 E
Dagu, *China* **35 E9** 38 59N 117 40 E
Dagupan, *Phil.* **37 A6** 16 3N 120 20 E
Daguragu, *Australia* **60 C5** 17 33S 130 30 E
Dahlak Kebir, *Eritrea* **46 D3** 15 50N 40 10 E
Dahlonega, *U.S.A.* **77 H4** 34 32N 83 59W
Dahod, *India* **42 H6** 22 50N 74 15 E
Dahomey = Benin ■, *Africa* **50 G6** 10 0N 2 0 E
Dahūk, *Iraq* **44 B3** 36 50N 43 1 E
Dai Hao, *Vietnam* **38 C6** 18 1N 106 25 E
Dai-Sen, *Japan* **31 G6** 35 22N 133 32 E
Dai Xian, *China* **34 E7** 39 4N 112 58 E
Daicheng, *China* **34 E9** 38 42N 116 38 E
Daingean, *Ireland* **13 C4** 53 18N 7 17W
Daintree, *Australia* **62 B4** 16 20S 145 20 E
Daiō-Misaki, *Japan* **31 G8** 34 15N 136 45 E
Daisetsu-Zan, *Japan* **30 C11** 43 30N 142 57 E
Dajarra, *Australia* **62 C2** 21 42S 139 30 E
Dak Dam, *Cambodia* **38 F6** 12 20N 107 21 E
Dak Nhe, *Vietnam* **38 E6** 15 28N 107 48 E
Dak Pek, *Vietnam* **38 E6** 15 4N 107 44 E
Dak Song, *Vietnam* **39 F6** 12 19N 107 35 E
Dak Sui, *Vietnam* **38 E6** 14 55N 107 43 E
Dakar, *Senegal* **50 F2** 14 34N 17 29W
Dakhla, *W. Sahara* **50 D2** 23 50N 15 53W
Dakhla, El Wâhât el-, *Egypt* **51 C11** 25 30N 28 50 E
Dakor, *India* **42 H5** 22 45N 73 11 E
Dakota City, *U.S.A.* **80 D6** 42 25N 96 25W
Đakovica, *Kosovo, Yug.* **21 C9** 42 22N 20 26 E
Dalachi, *China* **34 F3** 36 48N 105 0 E
Dalai Nur, *China* **34 C9** 43 20N 116 45 E
Dālakī, *Iran* **45 D6** 29 26N 51 17 E
Dalälven →, *Sweden* **9 F17** 60 12N 16 43 E
Dalaman →, *Turkey* **21 F13** 36 41N 28 43 E
Dalandzadgad, *Mongolia* **34 C3** 43 27N 104 30 E
Dalap-Uliga-Darrit, *Marshall Is.* **64 G9** 7 7N 171 24 E
Dalarna, *Sweden* **9 F16** 61 0N 14 0 E
Dālbandīn, *Pakistan* **40 E4** 29 0N 64 23 E
Dalbeattie, *U.K.* **12 G5** 54 56N 3 50W
Dalbeg, *Australia* **62 C4** 20 16S 147 18 E
Dalby, *Australia* **63 D5** 27 10S 151 17 E
Dale City, *U.S.A.* **76 F7** 38 38N 77 18W
Dale Hollow L., *U.S.A.* **77 G3** 36 32N 85 27W
Dalgān, *Iran* **45 E8** 27 31N 59 19 E
Dalhart, *U.S.A.* **81 G3** 36 4N 102 31W
Dalhousie, *Canada* **71 C6** 48 5N 66 26W
Dalhousie, *India* **42 C6** 32 38N 75 58 E
Dali, *Shaanxi, China* **34 G5** 34 48N 109 58 E
Dali, *Yunnan, China* **32 D5** 25 40N 100 10 E
Dalian, *China* **35 E11** 38 50N 121 40 E
Daliang Shan, *China* **32 D5** 28 0N 102 45 E
Daling He →, *China* **35 D11** 40 55N 121 40 E
Dāliyat el Karmel, *Israel* **47 C4** 32 43N 35 2 E
Dalkeith, *U.K.* **12 F5** 55 54N 3 4W
Dallas, *Oreg., U.S.A.* **82 D2** 44 55N 123 19W
Dallas, *Tex., U.S.A.* **81 J6** 32 47N 96 49W
Dalmā, *U.A.E.* **45 E7** 24 30N 52 20 E
Dalmacija, *Croatia* **20 C7** 43 20N 17 0 E
Dalmas, L., *Canada* **71 B5** 53 30N 71 50W
Dalmatia = Dalmacija, *Croatia* **20 C7** 43 20N 17 0 E
Dalmau, *India* **43 F9** 26 4N 81 2 E
Dalmellington, *U.K.* **12 F4** 55 19N 4 23W
Dalnegorsk, *Russia* **27 E14** 44 32N 135 33 E
Dalnerechensk, *Russia* **27 E14** 45 50N 133 40 E
Daloa, *Ivory C.* **50 G4** 7 0N 6 30W
Dalry, *U.K.* **12 F4** 55 42N 4 43W
Dalrymple, L., *Australia* **62 C4** 20 40S 147 0 E
Dalsland, *Sweden* **9 G14** 58 50N 12 15 E
Daltenganj, *India* **43 H11** 24 0N 84 4 E
Dalton, *Ga., U.S.A.* **77 H3** 34 46N 84 58W
Dalton, *Mass., U.S.A.* **79 D11** 42 28N 73 11W
Dalton, *Nebr., U.S.A.* **80 E3** 41 25N 102 58W
Dalton-in-Furness, *U.K.* **10 C4** 54 10N 3 11W
Dalvík, *Iceland* **8 D4** 65 58N 18 32W
Dalwallinu, *Australia* **61 F2** 30 17S 116 40 E
Daly →, *Australia* **60 B5** 13 35S 130 19 E
Daly City, *U.S.A.* **84 H4** 37 42N 122 28W
Daly L., *Canada* **73 B7** 56 32N 105 39W
Daly River, *Australia* **60 B5** 13 46S 130 42 E
Daly Waters, *Australia* **62 B1** 16 15S 133 24 E
Dam Doi, *Vietnam* **39 H5** 8 50N 105 12 E
Dam Ha, *Vietnam* **38 B6** 21 21N 107 36 E
Daman, *India* **40 J8** 20 25N 72 57 E
Dāmaneh, *Iran* **45 C6** 33 1N 50 29 E
Damanhûr, *Egypt* **51 B12** 31 0N 30 30 E
Damant L., *Canada* **73 A7** 61 45N 105 5W
Damanzhuang, *China* **34 E9** 38 5N 116 35 E
Damar, *Indonesia* **37 F7** 7 7S 128 40 E
Damaraland, *Namibia* **56 C2** 20 0S 15 0 E
Damascus = Dimashq, *Syria* **47 B5** 33 30N 36 18 E
Damāvand, *Iran* **45 C7** 35 47N 52 0 E
Damāvand, Qolleh-ye, *Iran* **45 C7** 35 56N 52 10 E
Damba, *Angola* **52 F3** 6 44S 15 20 E
Dâmboviţa →, *Romania* **17 F14** 44 12N 26 26 E
Dame Marie, *Haiti* **89 C5** 18 36N 74 26W
Dāmghān, *Iran* **45 B7** 36 10N 54 17 E
Damiel, *Spain* **19 C4** 39 4N 3 37W
Damietta = Dumyât, *Egypt* **51 B12** 31 24N 31 48 E
Daming, *China* **34 F8** 36 15N 115 6 E
Damīr Qābū, *Syria* **44 B4** 36 58N 41 51 E
Dammam = Ad Dammām, *Si. Arabia* **45 E6** 26 20N 50 5 E
Damodar →, *India* **43 H12** 23 17N 87 35 E
Damoh, *India* **43 H8** 23 50N 79 28 E
Dampier, *Australia* **60 D2** 20 41S 116 42 E
Dampier, Selat, *Indonesia* **37 E8** 0 40S 131 0 E
Dampier Arch., *Australia* **60 D2** 20 38S 116 32 E
Damrei, Chuor Phnum, *Cambodia* **39 G4** 11 30N 103 0 E
Dan Xian, *China* **38 C7** 19 31N 109 33 E
Dana, *Indonesia* **37 F6** 11 0S 122 52 E
Dana, L., *Canada* **70 B4** 50 53N 77 20W
Dana, Mt., *U.S.A.* **84 H7** 37 54N 119 12W
Danakil Desert, *Ethiopia* **46 E3** 12 45N 41 0 E
Danané, *Ivory C.* **50 G4** 7 16N 8 9W
Danau Poso, *Indonesia* **37 E6** 1 52S 120 35 E
Danbury, *U.S.A.* **79 E11** 41 24N 73 28W
Danby L., *U.S.A.* **83 J6** 34 13N 115 5W
Dand, *Afghan.* **42 D1** 31 28N 65 32 E
Dandeldhura, *Nepal* **43 E9** 29 20N 80 35 E
Dandeli, *India* **40 M9** 15 5N 74 30 E
Dandenong, *Australia* **63 F4** 38 0S 145 15 E
Dandong, *China* **35 D13** 40 10N 124 20 E
Danfeng, *China* **34 H6** 33 45N 110 25 E
Danger Is. = Pukapuka, *Cook Is.* **65 J11** 10 53S 165 49W
Danger Pt., *S. Africa* **56 E2** 34 40S 19 17 E
Dangla Shan = Tanggula Shan, *China* **32 C4** 32 40N 92 10 E
Dangrek, Phnom, *Thailand* **38 E5** 14 15N 105 0 E
Dangriga, *Belize* **87 D7** 17 0N 88 13W
Dangshan, *China* **34 G9** 34 27N 116 22 E
Daniel, *U.S.A.* **82 E8** 42 52N 110 4W
Daniel's Harbour, *Canada* **71 B8** 50 13N 57 35W
Danielskuil, *S. Africa* **56 D3** 28 11S 23 33 E
Danielson, *U.S.A.* **79 E13** 41 48N 71 53W
Danilov, *Russia* **24 C7** 58 16N 40 13 E
Daning, *China* **34 F6** 36 28N 110 45 E
Danissa, *Kenya* **54 B5** 3 15N 40 58 E
Ḑank, *Oman* **45 F8** 23 33N 56 16 E
Dankhar Gompa, *India* **40 C11** 32 10N 78 10 E
Danlí, *Honduras* **88 D2** 14 4N 86 35W
Dannemora, *U.S.A.* **79 B11** 44 43N 73 44W
Dannevirke, *N.Z.* **59 J6** 40 12S 176 8 E
Dannhauser, *S. Africa* **57 D5** 28 0S 30 3 E
Dansville, *U.S.A.* **78 D7** 42 34N 77 42W
Danta, *India* **42 G5** 24 11N 72 46 E
Dantan, *India* **43 J12** 21 57N 87 20 E
Danube = Dunărea →, *Europe* **17 F15** 45 20N 29 40 E
Danvers, *U.S.A.* **79 D14** 42 34N 70 56W
Danville, *Ill., U.S.A.* **76 E2** 40 8N 87 37W
Danville, *Ky., U.S.A.* **76 G3** 37 39N 84 46W
Danville, *Pa., U.S.A.* **79 F8** 40 58N 76 37W
Danville, *Va., U.S.A.* **77 G6** 36 36N 79 23W
Danville, *Vt., U.S.A.* **79 B12** 44 25N 72 9W
Danzig = Gdańsk, *Poland* **17 A10** 54 22N 18 40 E
Dapaong, *Togo* **50 F6** 10 55N 0 16 E
Daqing Shan, *China* **34 D6** 40 40N 111 0 E
Dar Banda, *Africa* **48 F6** 8 0N 23 0 E
Dar el Beida = Casablanca, *Morocco* **50 B4** 33 36N 7 36W
Dar es Salaam, *Tanzania* **54 D4** 6 50S 39 12 E
Dar Mazār, *Iran* **45 D8** 29 14N 57 20 E
Dar'ā, *Syria* **47 C5** 32 36N 36 7 E
Dar'ā □, *Syria* **47 C5** 32 55N 36 10 E
Dārāb, *Iran* **45 D7** 28 50N 54 30 E
Daraban, *Pakistan* **42 D4** 31 44N 70 20 E
Daraina, *Madag.* **57 A8** 13 12S 49 40 E
Daraj, *Libya* **51 B8** 30 10N 10 28 E
Dārān, *Iran* **45 C6** 32 59N 50 24 E
Dārayyā, *Syria* **47 B5** 33 28N 36 15 E
Darband, *Pakistan* **42 B5** 34 20N 72 50 E
Darband, Kūh-e, *Iran* **45 D8** 31 34N 57 8 E
Darbhanga, *India* **43 F11** 26 15N 85 55 E
D'Arcy, *Canada* **72 C4** 50 27N 122 35W
Dardanelle, *Ark., U.S.A.* **81 H8** 35 13N 93 9W
Dardanelle, *Calif., U.S.A.* **84 G7** 38 20N 119 50W
Dardanelles = Çanakkale Boğazı, *Turkey* **21 D12** 40 17N 26 32 E
Dārestān, *Iran* **45 D8** 29 9N 58 42 E
Dârfûr, *Sudan* **51 F10** 13 40N 24 0 E
Dargai, *Pakistan* **42 B4** 34 25N 71 55 E
Dargan Ata, *Turkmenistan* **26 E7** 40 29N 62 10 E
Dargaville, *N.Z.* **59 F4** 35 57S 173 52 E
Darhan, *Mongolia* **32 B5** 49 37N 106 21 E
Darhan Muminggan Lianheqi, *China* **34 D6** 41 40N 110 28 E
Darıca, *Turkey* **21 D13** 40 45N 29 23 E
Darién, G. del, *Colombia* **92 B3** 9 0N 77 0W
Dariganga = Ovoot, *Mongolia* **34 B7** 45 21N 113 45 E
Darjeeling = Darjiling, *India* **43 F13** 27 3N 88 18 E
Darjiling, *India* **43 F13** 27 3N 88 18 E
Darkan, *Australia* **61 F2** 33 20S 116 43 E
Darkhana, *Pakistan* **42 D5** 30 39N 72 11 E
Darkhazīneh, *Iran* **45 D6** 31 54N 48 39 E
Darkot Pass, *Pakistan* **43 A5** 36 45N 73 26 E
Darling →, *Australia* **63 E3** 34 4S 141 54 E
Darling Downs, *Australia* **63 D5** 27 30S 150 30 E
Darling Ra., *Australia* **61 F2** 32 30S 116 0 E
Darlington, *U.K.* **10 C6** 54 32N 1 33W
Darlington, *U.S.A.* **77 H6** 34 18N 79 52W
Darlington □, *U.K.* **10 C6** 54 32N 1 33W
Darlington, L., *S. Africa* **56 E4** 33 10S 25 9 E
Darlot, L., *Australia* **61 E3** 27 48S 121 35 E
Darłowo, *Poland* **16 A9** 54 25N 16 25 E
Darmstadt, *Germany* **16 D5** 49 51N 8 39 E
Darnah, *Libya* **51 B10** 32 45N 22 45 E
Darnall, *S. Africa* **57 D5** 29 23S 31 18 E
Darnley, C., *Antarctica* **5 C6** 68 0S 69 0 E
Darnley B., *Canada* **68 B7** 69 30N 123 30W
Darr →, *Australia* **62 C3** 23 39S 143 50 E
Darra Pezu, *Pakistan* **42 C4** 32 19N 70 44 E
Darrequeira, *Argentina* **94 D3** 37 42S 63 10W
Darrington, *U.S.A.* **82 B3** 48 15N 121 36W
Dart →, *U.K.* **11 G4** 50 24N 3 39W
Dart, C., *Antarctica* **5 D14** 73 6S 126 20W
Dartford, *U.K.* **11 F8** 51 26N 0 13 E
Dartmoor, *U.K.* **11 G4** 50 38N 3 57W
Dartmouth, *Canada* **71 D7** 44 40N 63 30W
Dartmouth, *U.K.* **11 G4** 50 21N 3 36W
Dartmouth, L., *Australia* **63 D4** 26 4S 145 18 E
Dartuch, C. = Artrutx, C. de, *Spain* **22 B10** 39 55N 3 49 E
Darvaza, *Turkmenistan* **26 E6** 40 11N 58 24 E
Darvel, Teluk = Lahad Datu, Teluk, *Malaysia* **37 D5** 4 50N 118 20 E
Darwen, *U.K.* **10 D5** 53 42N 2 29W
Darwendale, *Zimbabwe* **57 B5** 17 41S 30 33 E
Darwha, *India* **40 J10** 20 15N 77 45 E
Darwin, *Australia* **60 B5** 12 25S 130 51 E
Darwin, *U.S.A.* **85 J9** 36 15N 117 35W
Darya Khan, *Pakistan* **42 D4** 31 48N 71 6 E
Daryoi Amu = Amudarya →, *Uzbekistan* **26 E6** 43 58N 59 34 E
Dās, *U.A.E.* **45 E7** 25 20N 53 30 E
Dashen, Ras, *Ethiopia* **46 E2** 13 8N 38 26 E
Dashetai, *China* **34 D5** 41 0N 109 5 E
Dashhowuz, *Turkmenistan* **26 E6** 41 49N 59 58 E
Dashköpri, *Turkmenistan* **45 B9** 36 16N 62 8 E
Dasht, *Iran* **45 B8** 37 17N 56 7 E
Dasht →, *Pakistan* **40 G2** 25 10N 61 40 E
Daska, *Pakistan* **42 C6** 32 20N 74 20 E
Dasuya, *India* **42 D6** 31 49N 75 38 E
Datça, *Turkey* **21 F12** 36 46N 27 40 E
Datia, *India* **43 G8** 25 39N 78 27 E
Datong, *China* **34 D7** 40 6N 113 18 E
Dattakhel, *Pakistan* **42 C3** 32 54N 69 46 E
Datu, Tanjung, *Indonesia* **36 D3** 2 5N 109 39 E
Datu Piang, *Phil.* **37 C6** 7 2N 124 30 E
Datuk, Tanjong = Datu, Tanjung, *Indonesia* **36 D3** 2 5N 109 39 E
Daud Khel, *Pakistan* **42 C4** 32 53N 71 34 E
Daudnagar, *India* **43 G11** 25 2N 84 24 E
Daugava →, *Latvia* **9 H21** 57 4N 24 3 E
Daugavpils, *Latvia* **9 J22** 55 53N 26 32 E
Daulpur, *India* **42 F7** 26 45N 77 59 E
Dauphin, *Canada* **73 C8** 51 9N 100 5W
Dauphin, *U.S.A.* **78 F8** 40 22N 76 56W
Dauphin L., *Canada* **73 C9** 51 20N 99 45W
Dauphiné, *France* **18 D6** 45 15N 5 25 E
Dausa, *India* **42 F7** 26 52N 76 20 E
Davangere, *India* **40 M9** 14 25N 75 55 E
Davao, *Phil.* **37 C7** 7 0N 125 40 E
Davao G., *Phil.* **37 C7** 6 30N 125 48 E
Dāvar Panāh, *Iran* **45 E9** 27 25N 62 15 E
Davenport, *Calif., U.S.A.* **84 H4** 37 1N 122 12W
Davenport, *Iowa, U.S.A.* **80 E9** 41 32N 90 35W
Davenport, *Wash., U.S.A.* **82 C4** 47 39N 118 9W
Davenport Ra., *Australia* **62 C1** 20 28S 134 0 E
Daventry, *U.K.* **11 E6** 52 16N 1 10W
David, *Panama* **88 E3** 8 30N 82 30W
David City, *U.S.A.* **80 E6** 41 15N 97 8W
David Gorodok = Davyd Haradok, *Belarus* **17 B14** 52 4N 27 8 E
Davidson, *Canada* **73 C7** 51 16N 105 59W
Davis, *U.S.A.* **84 G5** 38 33N 121 44W
Davis Dam, *U.S.A.* **85 K12** 35 11N 114 34W
Davis Inlet, *Canada* **71 A7** 55 50N 60 59W
Davis Mts., *U.S.A.* **81 K2** 30 50N 103 55W
Davis Sea, *Antarctica* **5 C7** 66 0S 92 0 E
Davis Str., *N. Amer.* **69 B14** 65 0N 58 0W
Davos, *Switz.* **18 C8** 46 48N 9 49 E
Davy L., *Canada* **73 B7** 58 53N 108 18W
Davyd Haradok, *Belarus* **17 B14** 52 4N 27 8 E
Dawei, *Burma* **38 E2** 14 2N 98 12 E
Dawes Ra., *Australia* **62 C5** 24 40S 150 40 E
Dawlish, *U.K.* **11 G4** 50 35N 3 28W
Dawna Ra., *Burma* **38 D2** 16 30N 98 30 E
Dawros Hd., *Ireland* **13 B3** 54 50N 8 33W
Dawson, *Canada* **68 B6** 64 10N 139 30W
Dawson, *U.S.A.* **77 K3** 31 46N 84 27W
Dawson, I., *Chile* **96 G2** 53 50S 70 50W
Dawson B., *Canada* **73 C8** 52 53N 100 49W
Dawson Creek, *Canada* **72 B4** 55 45N 120 15W
Dawson Inlet, *Canada* **73 A10** 61 50N 93 25W
Dawson Ra., *Australia* **62 C4** 24 30S 149 48 E
Dax, *France* **18 E3** 43 44N 1 3W
Daxian, *China* **32 C5** 31 15N 107 23 E
Daxindian, *China* **35 F11** 37 30N 120 50 E
Daxinggou, *China* **35 C15** 43 25N 129 40 E
Daxue Shan, *China* **32 C5** 30 30N 101 30 E
Daylesford, *Australia* **63 F3** 37 21S 144 9 E
Dayr az Zawr, *Syria* **44 C4** 35 20N 40 5 E
Daysland, *Canada* **72 C6** 52 50N 112 20W
Dayton, *Nev., U.S.A.* **84 F7** 39 14N 119 36W
Dayton, *Ohio, U.S.A.* **76 F3** 39 45N 84 12W
Dayton, *Pa., U.S.A.* **78 F5** 40 53N 79 15W
Dayton, *Tenn., U.S.A.* **77 H3** 35 30N 85 1W
Dayton, *Wash., U.S.A.* **82 C4** 46 19N 117 59W
Dayton, *Wyo., U.S.A.* **82 D10** 44 53N 107 16W
Daytona Beach, *U.S.A.* **77 L5** 29 13N 81 1W
Dayville, *U.S.A.* **82 D4** 44 28N 119 32W
De Aar, *S. Africa* **56 E3** 30 39S 24 0 E
De Funiak Springs, *U.S.A.* **77 K2** 30 43N 86 7W
De Grey →, *Australia* **60 D2** 20 12S 119 13 E
De Haan, *Belgium* **15 C3** 51 16N 3 2 E
De Kalb, *U.S.A.* **80 E10** 41 56N 88 46W
De Land, *U.S.A.* **77 L5** 29 2N 81 18W
De Leon, *U.S.A.* **81 J5** 32 7N 98 32W
De Panne, *Belgium* **15 C2** 51 6N 2 34 E
De Pere, *U.S.A.* **76 C1** 44 27N 88 4W
De Queen, *U.S.A.* **81 H7** 34 2N 94 21W
De Quincy, *U.S.A.* **81 K8** 30 27N 93 26W
De Ridder, *U.S.A.* **81 K8** 30 51N 93 17W
De Smet, *U.S.A.* **80 C6** 44 23N 97 33W
De Soto, *U.S.A.* **80 F9** 38 8N 90 34W
De Tour Village, *U.S.A.* **76 C4** 46 0N 83 56W
De Witt, *U.S.A.* **81 H9** 34 18N 91 20W
Dead Sea, *Asia* **47 D4** 31 30N 35 30 E
Deadwood, *U.S.A.* **80 C3** 44 23N 103 44W
Deadwood L., *Canada* **72 B3** 59 10N 128 30W
Deal, *U.K.* **11 F9** 51 13N 1 25 E
Deal I., *Australia* **62 F4** 39 30S 147 20 E
Dealesville, *S. Africa* **56 D4** 28 41S 25 44 E
Dean →, *Canada* **72 C3** 52 49N 126 58W
Dean, Forest of, *U.K.* **11 F5** 51 45N 2 33W
Dean Chan., *Canada* **72 C3** 52 30N 127 15W
Deán Funes, *Argentina* **94 C3** 30 20S 64 20W
Dease →, *Canada* **72 B3** 59 56N 128 32W
Dease L., *Canada* **72 B2** 58 40N 130 5W
Dease Lake, *Canada* **72 B2** 58 25N 130 6W
Death Valley, *U.S.A.* **85 J10** 36 15N 116 50W
Death Valley Junction, *U.S.A.* **85 J10** 36 20N 116 25W
Death Valley Nat. Park, *U.S.A.* **85 J10** 36 45N 117 15W
Debar, *Macedonia* **21 D9** 41 31N 20 30 E
Debden, *Canada* **73 C7** 53 30N 106 50W
Dębica, *Poland* **17 C11** 50 2N 21 25 E
Debolt, *Canada* **72 B5** 55 12N 118 1W
Deborah East, L., *Australia* **61 F2** 30 45S 119 0 E
Deborah West, L., *Australia* **61 F2** 30 45S 118 50 E
Debre Markos, *Ethiopia* **46 E2** 10 20N 37 40 E
Debre Tabor, *Ethiopia* **46 E2** 11 50N 38 26 E
Debre Zeyit, *Ethiopia* **46 F2** 11 48N 38 30 E
Debrecen, *Hungary* **17 E11** 47 33N 21 42 E
Decatur, *Ala., U.S.A.* **77 H2** 34 36N 86 59W
Decatur, *Ga., U.S.A.* **77 J3** 33 47N 84 18W
Decatur, *Ill., U.S.A.* **80 F10** 39 51N 88 57W
Decatur, *Ind., U.S.A.* **76 E3** 40 50N 84 56W
Decatur, *Tex., U.S.A.* **81 J6** 33 14N 97 35W
Deccan, *India* **40 L11** 18 0N 79 0 E
Deception Bay, *Australia* **63 D5** 27 10S 153 5 E
Deception L., *Canada* **73 B8** 56 33N 104 13W
Dechhu, *India* **42 F5** 26 46N 72 20 E
Děčín, *Czech Rep.* **16 C8** 50 47N 14 12 E
Deckerville, *U.S.A.* **78 C2** 43 32N 82 44W
Decorah, *U.S.A.* **80 D9** 43 18N 91 48W
Dedéagach = Alexandroúpolis, *Greece* **21 D11** 40 50N 25 54 E
Dedham, *U.S.A.* **79 D13** 42 15N 71 10W
Dedza, *Malawi* **55 E3** 14 20S 34 20 E
Dee →, *Aberds., U.K.* **12 D6** 57 9N 2 5W
Dee →, *Dumf. & Gall., U.K.* **12 G4** 54 51N 4 3W
Dee →, *Wales, U.K.* **10 D4** 53 22N 3 17W
Deep B., *Canada* **72 A5** 61 15N 116 35W
Deepwater, *Australia* **63 D5** 29 25S 151 51 E
Deer →, *Canada* **73 B10** 58 23N 94 13W
Deer L., *Canada* **73 C10** 52 40N 94 20W
Deer Lake, *Nfld., Canada* **71 C8** 49 11N 57 27W
Deer Lake, *Ont., Canada* **73 C10** 52 36N 94 20W
Deer Lodge, *U.S.A.* **82 C7** 46 24N 112 44W
Deer Park, *U.S.A.* **82 C5** 47 57N 117 28W
Deer River, *U.S.A.* **80 B8** 47 20N 93 48W
Deeragun, *Australia* **62 B4** 19 16S 146 33 E
Deerdepoort, *S. Africa* **56 C4** 24 37S 26 27 E
Deferiet, *U.S.A.* **79 B9** 44 2N 75 41W
Defiance, *U.S.A.* **76 E3** 41 17N 84 22W
Degana, *India* **42 F6** 26 50N 74 20 E
Dégelis, *Canada* **71 C6** 47 30N 68 35W
Deggendorf, *Germany* **16 D7** 48 50N 12 57 E
Degh →, *Pakistan* **42 D5** 31 3N 73 21 E
Deh Bīd, *Iran* **45 D7** 30 39N 53 11 E
Deh-e Shīr, *Iran* **45 D7** 31 29N 53 45 E
Dehaj, *Iran* **45 D7** 30 42N 54 53 E
Dehak, *Iran* **45 E9** 27 11N 62 37 E
Dehdez, *Iran* **45 D6** 31 43N 50 17 E
Dehej, *India* **42 J5** 21 44N 72 40 E
Dehestān, *Iran* **45 D7** 28 30N 55 35 E
Dehgolān, *Iran* **44 C5** 35 17N 47 25 E
Dehibat, *Tunisia* **51 B8** 32 0N 10 47 E
Dehlorān, *Iran* **44 C5** 32 41N 47 16 E
Dehnow-e Kūhestān, *Iran* **45 E8** 27 58N 58 32 E
Dehra Dun, *India* **42 D8** 30 20N 78 4 E
Dehri, *India* **43 G11** 24 50N 84 15 E
Dehui, *China* **35 B13** 44 30N 125 40 E
Deinze, *Belgium* **15 D3** 50 59N 3 32 E
Dej, *Romania* **17 E12** 47 10N 23 52 E
Deka →, *Zimbabwe* **56 B4** 18 4S 26 42 E
Dekese, *Dem. Rep. of the Congo* **52 E4** 3 24S 21 24 E
Del Mar, *U.S.A.* **85 N9** 32 58N 117 16W
Del Norte, *U.S.A.* **83 H10** 37 41N 106 21W
Del Rio, *U.S.A.* **81 L4** 29 22N 100 54W
Delambre I., *Australia* **60 D2** 20 26S 117 5 E
Delano, *U.S.A.* **85 K7** 35 46N 119 15W
Delano Peak, *U.S.A.* **83 G7** 38 22N 112 22W
Delareyville, *S. Africa* **56 D4** 26 41S 25 26 E
Delaronde L., *Canada* **73 C7** 54 3N 107 3W
Delavan, *U.S.A.* **80 D10** 42 38N 88 39W
Delaware, *U.S.A.* **76 E4** 40 18N 83 4W
Delaware □, *U.S.A.* **76 F8** 39 0N 75 20W
Delaware →, *U.S.A.* **79 G9** 39 15N 75 20W
Delaware B., *U.S.A.* **76 F8** 39 0N 75 10W
Delay →, *Canada* **71 A5** 56 56N 71 28W
Delegate, *Australia* **63 F4** 37 4S 148 56 E
Delevan, *U.S.A.* **78 D6** 42 29N 78 29W
Delft, *Neths.* **15 B4** 52 1N 4 22 E
Delfzijl, *Neths.* **15 A6** 53 20N 6 55 E
Delgado, C., *Mozam.* **55 E5** 10 45S 40 40 E
Delgerhet, *Mongolia* **34 B6** 45 50N 110 30 E
Delgo, *Sudan* **51 D12** 20 6N 30 40 E
Delhi, *Canada* **78 D4** 42 51N 80 30W
Delhi, *India* **42 E7** 28 38N 77 17 E
Delhi, *La., U.S.A.* **81 J9** 32 28N 91 30W
Delhi, *N.Y., U.S.A.* **79 D10** 42 17N 74 55W
Delia, *Canada* **72 C6** 51 38N 112 23W
Delice, *Turkey* **25 G5** 39 54N 34 2 E
Delicias, *Mexico* **86 B3** 28 10N 105 30W
Delījān, *Iran* **45 C6** 33 59N 50 40 E
Déline, *Canada* **68 B7** 65 10N 123 30W
Delisle, *Canada* **73 C7** 51 55N 107 8W
Dell City, *U.S.A.* **83 L11** 31 56N 105 12W
Dell Rapids, *U.S.A.* **80 D6** 43 50N 96 43W
Delmar, *U.S.A.* **79 D11** 42 37N 73 47W
Delmenhorst, *Germany* **16 B5** 53 3N 8 37 E
Delonga, Ostrova, *Russia* **27 B15** 76 40N 149 20 E
Deloraine, *Australia* **62 G4** 41 30S 146 40 E
Deloraine, *Canada* **73 D8** 49 15N 100 29W
Delphi, *U.S.A.* **76 E2** 40 36N 86 41W
Delphos, *U.S.A.* **76 E3** 40 51N 84 21W
Delportshoop, *S. Africa* **56 D3** 28 22S 24 20 E
Delray Beach, *U.S.A.* **77 M5** 26 28N 80 4W
Delta, *Colo., U.S.A.* **83 G9** 38 44N 108 4W
Delta, *Utah, U.S.A.* **82 G7** 39 21N 112 35W
Delta Junction, *U.S.A.* **68 B5** 64 2N 145 44W
Deltona, *U.S.A.* **77 L5** 28 54N 81 16W
Delungra, *Australia* **63 D5** 29 39S 150 51 E
Delvada, *India* **42 J4** 20 46N 71 2 E
Delvinë, *Albania* **21 E9** 39 59N 20 6 E
Demak, *Indonesia* **37 G14** 6 53S 110 38 E
Demanda, Sierra de la, *Spain* **19 A4** 42 15N 3 0W
Demavand = Damāvand, *Iran* **45 C7** 35 47N 52 0 E
Dembia, *Dem. Rep. of the Congo* **54 B2** 3 33N 25 48 E
Dembidolo, *Ethiopia* **46 F1** 8 34N 34 50 E
Demchok, *India* **43 C8** 32 42N 79 29 E
Demer →, *Belgium* **15 D4** 50 57N 4 42 E
Deming, *N. Mex., U.S.A.* **83 K10** 32 16N 107 46W
Deming, *Wash., U.S.A.* **84 B4** 48 50N 122 13W
Demini →, *Brazil* **92 D6** 0 46S 62 56W
Demirci, *Turkey* **21 E13** 39 2N 28 38 E
Demirköy, *Turkey* **21 D12** 41 49N 27 45 E
Demopolis, *U.S.A.* **77 J2** 32 31N 87 50W
Dempo, *Indonesia* **36 E2** 4 2S 103 15 E
Den Burg, *Neths.* **15 A4** 53 3N 4 47 E
Den Chai, *Thailand* **38 D3** 17 59N 100 4 E
Den Haag = 's-Gravenhage, *Neths.* **15 B4** 52 7N 4 17 E
Den Helder, *Neths.* **15 B4** 52 57N 4 45 E
Den Oever, *Neths.* **15 B5** 52 56N 5 2 E
Denair, *U.S.A.* **84 H6** 37 32N 120 48W
Denau, *Uzbekistan* **26 F7** 38 16N 67 54 E

Donnybrook, *Australia* 61 F2 33 34S 115 48 E
Donnybrook, *S. Africa* 57 D4 29 59S 29 48 E
Donora, *U.S.A.* 78 F5 40 11N 79 52W
Donostia = Donostia-San Sebastián, *Spain* 19 A5 43 17N 1 58W
Donostia-San Sebastián, *Spain* 19 A5 43 17N 1 58W
Doon →, *U.K.* 12 F4 55 27N 4 39W
Dora, L., *Australia* 60 D3 22 0S 123 0 E
Dora Báltea →, *Italy* 18 D8 45 11N 8 3 E
Doran L., *Canada* 73 A7 61 13N 108 6W
Dorchester, *U.K.* 11 G5 50 42N 2 27W
Dorchester, C., *Canada* 69 B12 65 27N 77 27W
Dordabis, *Namibia* 56 C2 22 52S 17 38 E
Dordogne →, *France* 18 D3 45 2N 0 36W
Dordrecht, *Neths.* 15 C4 51 48N 4 39 E
Dordrecht, *S. Africa* 56 E4 31 20S 27 3 E
Doré L., *Canada* 73 C7 54 46N 107 17W
Doré Lake, *Canada* 73 C7 54 38N 107 36W
Dori, *Burkina Faso* 50 F5 14 3N 0 2W
Doring →, *S. Africa* 56 E2 31 54S 18 39 E
Doringbos, *S. Africa* 56 E2 31 59S 19 16 E
Dorion, *Canada* 79 A10 45 23N 74 3W
Dornbirn, *Austria* 16 E5 47 25N 9 45 E
Dornie, *U.K.* 12 D3 57 17N 5 31W
Dornoch, *U.K.* 12 D4 57 53N 4 2W
Dornoch Firth, *U.K.* 12 D4 57 51N 4 4W
Dornogovĭ □, *Mongolia* 34 C6 44 0N 110 0 E
Dorohoi, *Romania* 17 E14 47 56N 26 23 E
Döröö Nuur, *Mongolia* 32 B4 48 0N 93 0 E
Dorr, *Iran* 45 C6 33 17N 50 38 E
Dorre I., *Australia* 61 E1 25 13S 113 12 E
Dorrigo, *Australia* 63 E5 30 20S 152 44 E
Dorris, *U.S.A.* 82 F3 41 58N 121 55W
Dorset, *Canada* 78 A6 45 14N 78 54W
Dorset, *U.S.A.* 78 E4 41 40N 80 40W
Dorset □, *U.K.* 11 G5 50 45N 2 26W
Dortmund, *Germany* 16 C4 51 30N 7 28 E
Doruma, *Dem. Rep. of the Congo* 54 B2 4 42N 27 33 E
Dorūneh, *Iran* 45 C8 35 10N 57 18 E
Dos Bahías, C., *Argentina* 96 E3 44 58S 65 32W
Dos Hermanas, *Spain* 19 D3 37 16N 5 55W
Dos Palos, *U.S.A.* 84 J6 36 59N 120 37W
Dosso, *Niger* 50 F6 13 0N 3 13 E
Dothan, *U.S.A.* 77 K3 31 13N 85 24W
Doty, *U.S.A.* 84 D3 46 38N 123 17W
Douai, *France* 18 A5 50 21N 3 4 E
Douala, *Cameroon* 52 D1 4 0N 9 45 E
Douarnenez, *France* 18 B1 48 6N 4 21W
Double Island Pt., *Australia* 63 D5 25 56S 153 11 E
Double Mountain Fork →, *U.S.A.* 81 J4 33 16N 100 0W
Doubs →, *France* 18 C6 46 53N 5 1 E
Doubtful Sd., *N.Z.* 59 L1 45 20S 166 49 E
Doubtless B., *N.Z.* 59 F4 34 55S 173 26 E
Douglas, *S. Africa* 56 D3 29 4S 23 46 E
Douglas, *U.K.* 10 C3 54 10N 4 28W
Douglas, *Ariz., U.S.A.* 83 L9 31 21N 109 33W
Douglas, *Ga., U.S.A.* 77 K4 31 31N 82 51W
Douglas, *Wyo., U.S.A.* 80 D2 42 45N 105 24W
Douglas Chan., *Canada* 72 C3 53 40N 129 20W
Douglas Pt., *Canada* 78 B3 44 19N 81 37W
Douglasville, *U.S.A.* 77 J3 33 45N 84 45W
Dounreay, *U.K.* 12 C5 58 35N 3 44W
Dourada, Serra, *Brazil* 93 F9 13 10S 48 45W
Dourados, *Brazil* 95 A5 22 9S 54 50W
Dourados →, *Brazil* 95 A5 21 58S 54 18W
Dourados, Serra dos, *Brazil* 95 A5 23 30S 53 30W
Douro →, *Europe* 19 B1 41 8N 8 40W
Dove →, *U.K.* 10 E6 52 51N 1 36W
Dove Creek, *U.S.A.* 83 H9 37 46N 108 54W
Dover, *Australia* 62 G4 43 18S 147 2 E
Dover, *U.K.* 11 F9 51 7N 1 19 E
Dover, *Del., U.S.A.* 76 F8 39 10N 75 32W
Dover, *N.H., U.S.A.* 79 C14 43 12N 70 56W
Dover, *N.J., U.S.A.* 79 F10 40 53N 74 34W
Dover, *Ohio, U.S.A.* 78 F3 40 32N 81 29W
Dover, Pt., *Australia* 61 F4 32 32S 125 32 E
Dover, Str. of, *Europe* 11 G9 51 0N 1 30 E
Dover-Foxcroft, *U.S.A.* 77 C11 45 11N 69 13W
Dover Plains, *U.S.A.* 79 E11 41 43N 73 35W
Dovey = Dyfi →, *U.K.* 11 E3 52 32N 4 3W
Dovrefjell, *Norway* 9 E13 62 15N 9 33 E
Dow Rūd, *Iran* 45 C6 33 28N 49 4 E
Dowa, *Malawi* 55 E3 13 38S 33 58 E
Dowagiac, *U.S.A.* 76 E2 41 59N 86 6W
Dowerin, *Australia* 61 F2 31 12S 117 2 E
Dowgha'i, *Iran* 45 B8 36 54N 58 32 E
Dowlatābād, *Iran* 45 D8 28 20N 56 40 E
Down □, *U.K.* 13 B5 54 23N 6 2W
Downey, *Calif., U.S.A.* 85 M8 33 56N 118 7W
Downey, *Idaho, U.S.A.* 82 E7 42 26N 112 7W
Downham Market, *U.K.* 11 E8 52 37N 0 23 E
Downieville, *U.S.A.* 84 F6 39 34N 120 50W
Downpatrick, *U.K.* 13 B6 54 20N 5 43W
Downpatrick Hd., *Ireland* 13 B2 54 20N 9 21W
Downsville, *U.S.A.* 79 D10 42 5N 74 50W
Downton, Mt., *Canada* 72 C4 52 42N 124 52W
Dowsārī, *Iran* 45 D8 28 25N 57 59 E
Doyle, *U.S.A.* 84 E6 40 2N 120 6W
Doylestown, *U.S.A.* 79 F9 40 21N 75 10W
Dozois, Rés., *Canada* 70 C4 47 30N 77 5W
Dra Khel, *Pakistan* 42 F2 27 58N 66 45 E
Drachten, *Neths.* 15 A6 53 7N 6 5 E
Drăgăşani, *Romania* 17 F13 44 39N 24 17 E
Dragichyn, *Belarus* 17 B13 52 15N 25 8 E
Dragoman, Prokhod, *Bulgaria* 21 C10 42 58N 22 53 E
Draguignan, *France* 18 E7 43 32N 6 27 E
Drain, *U.S.A.* 82 E2 43 40N 123 19W
Drake, *U.S.A.* 80 B4 47 55N 100 23W
Drake Passage, *S. Ocean* 5 B17 58 0S 68 0W
Drakensberg, *S. Africa* 57 D4 31 0S 28 0 E
Dráma, *Greece* 21 D11 41 9N 24 10 E
Drammen, *Norway* 9 G14 59 42N 10 12 E
Drangajökull, *Iceland* 8 C2 66 9N 22 15W
Dras, *India* 43 B6 34 25N 75 48 E
Drau = Drava →, *Croatia* 21 B8 45 33N 18 55 E
Drava →, *Croatia* 21 B8 45 33N 18 55 E
Drayton Valley, *Canada* 72 C6 53 12N 114 58W
Drenthe □, *Neths.* 15 B6 52 52N 6 40 E
Drepanum, C., *Cyprus* 23 E11 34 54N 32 19 E
Dresden, *Canada* 78 D2 42 35N 82 11W
Dresden, *Germany* 16 C7 51 3N 13 44 E
Dreux, *France* 18 B4 48 44N 1 23 E
Driffield, *U.K.* 10 C7 54 0N 0 26W
Driftwood, *U.S.A.* 78 E6 41 20N 78 8W
Driggs, *U.S.A.* 82 E8 43 44N 111 6W
Drin →, *Albania* 21 C8 42 1N 19 38 E
Drina →, *Bos.-H.* 21 B8 44 53N 19 21 E
Drøbak, *Norway* 9 G14 59 39N 10 39 E
Drobeta-Turnu Severin, *Romania* 17 F12 44 39N 22 41 E
Drochia, *Moldova* 17 D14 48 2N 27 48 E
Drogheda, *Ireland* 13 C5 53 43N 6 22W
Drogichin = Dragichyn, *Belarus* 17 B13 52 15N 25 8 E
Drogobych = Drohobych, *Ukraine* 17 D12 49 20N 23 30 E
Drohobych, *Ukraine* 17 D12 49 20N 23 30 E
Droichead Atha = Drogheda, *Ireland* 13 C5 53 43N 6 22W
Droichead Nua, *Ireland* 13 C5 53 11N 6 48W
Droitwich, *U.K.* 11 E5 52 16N 2 8W
Dromedary, C., *Australia* 63 F5 36 17S 150 10 E
Dromore, *U.K.* 13 B4 54 31N 7 28W
Dromore West, *Ireland* 13 B3 54 15N 8 52W
Dronfield, *U.K.* 10 D6 53 19N 1 27W
Dronten, *Neths.* 15 B5 52 32N 5 43 E
Drumbo, *Canada* 78 C4 43 16N 80 35W
Drumheller, *Canada* 72 C6 51 25N 112 40W
Drummond, *U.S.A.* 82 C7 46 40N 113 9W
Drummond I., *U.S.A.* 76 C4 46 1N 83 39W
Drummond Pt., *Australia* 63 E2 34 9S 135 16 E
Drummond Ra., *Australia* 62 C4 23 45S 147 10 E
Drummondville, *Canada* 70 C5 45 55N 72 25W
Drumright, *U.S.A.* 81 H6 35 59N 96 36W
Druskininkai, *Lithuania* 9 J20 54 3N 23 58 E
Drut →, *Belarus* 17 B16 53 8N 30 5 E
Druzhina, *Russia* 27 C15 68 14N 145 18 E
Dry Tortugas, *U.S.A.* 88 B3 24 38N 82 55W
Dryden, *Canada* 73 D10 49 47N 92 50W
Dryden, *U.S.A.* 79 D8 42 30N 76 18W
Drygalski I., *Antarctica* 5 C7 66 0S 92 0 E
Drysdale →, *Australia* 60 B4 13 59S 126 51 E
Drysdale I., *Australia* 62 A2 11 41S 136 0 E
Du Bois, *U.S.A.* 78 E6 41 8N 78 46W
Du Gué →, *Canada* 70 A5 57 21N 70 45W
Du Quoin, *U.S.A.* 80 G10 38 1N 89 14W
Duanesburg, *U.S.A.* 79 D10 42 45N 74 11W
Duaringa, *Australia* 62 C4 23 42S 149 42 E
Ḍubā, *Si. Arabia* 44 E2 27 10N 35 40 E
Dubai = Dubayy, *U.A.E.* 46 B6 25 18N 55 20 E
Dubăsari, *Moldova* 17 E15 47 15N 29 10 E
Dubăsari Vdkhr., *Moldova* 17 E15 47 30N 29 0 E
Dubawnt →, *Canada* 73 A8 64 33N 100 6W
Dubawnt, L., *Canada* 73 A8 63 4N 101 42W
Dubayy, *U.A.E.* 46 B6 25 18N 55 20 E
Dubbo, *Australia* 63 E4 32 11S 148 35 E
Dubele, *Dem. Rep. of the Congo* 54 B2 2 56N 29 35 E
Dublin, *Ireland* 13 C5 53 21N 6 15W
Dublin, *Ga., U.S.A.* 77 J4 32 32N 82 54W
Dublin, *Tex., U.S.A.* 81 J5 32 5N 98 21W
Dublin □, *Ireland* 13 C5 53 24N 6 20W
Dubno, *Ukraine* 17 C13 50 25N 25 45 E
Dubois, *U.S.A.* 82 D7 44 10N 112 14W
Dubossary = Dubăsari, *Moldova* 17 E15 47 15N 29 10 E
Dubossary Vdkhr. = Dubăsari Vdkhr., *Moldova* 17 E15 47 30N 29 0 E
Dubovka, *Russia* 25 E7 49 5N 44 50 E
Dubrajpur, *India* 43 H12 23 48N 87 25 E
Dubréka, *Guinea* 50 G3 9 46N 13 31W
Dubrovitsa = Dubrovytsya, *Ukraine* 17 C14 51 31N 26 35 E
Dubrovnik, *Croatia* 21 C8 42 39N 18 6 E
Dubrovytsya, *Ukraine* 17 C14 51 31N 26 35 E
Dubuque, *U.S.A.* 80 D9 42 30N 90 41W
Duchesne, *U.S.A.* 82 F8 40 10N 110 24W
Duchess, *Australia* 62 C2 21 20S 139 50 E
Ducie I., *Pac. Oc.* 65 K15 24 40S 124 48W
Duck →, *U.S.A.* 77 G2 36 2N 87 52W
Duck Cr. →, *Australia* 60 D2 22 37S 116 53 E
Duck Lake, *Canada* 73 C7 52 50N 106 16W
Duck Mountain Prov. Park, *Canada* 73 C8 51 45N 101 0W
Duckwall, Mt., *U.S.A.* 84 H6 37 58N 120 7W
Dudhi, *India* 41 G13 24 15N 83 10 E
Dudinka, *Russia* 27 C9 69 30N 86 13 E
Dudley, *U.K.* 11 E5 52 31N 2 5W
Dudwa, *India* 43 E9 28 30N 80 41 E
Duero = Douro →, *Europe* 19 B1 41 8N 8 40W
Dufftown, *U.K.* 12 D5 57 27N 3 8W
Dūghī Kalā, *Afghan.* 40 C3 32 20N 62 50 E
Dugi Otok, *Croatia* 16 G8 44 0N 15 3 E
Duifken Pt., *Australia* 62 A3 12 33S 141 38 E
Duisburg, *Germany* 16 C4 51 26N 6 45 E
Duiwelskloof, *S. Africa* 57 C5 23 42S 30 10 E
Dūkdamīn, *Iran* 45 C8 35 59N 57 43 E
Dukelský Průsmyk, *Slovak Rep.* 17 D11 49 25N 21 42 E
Dukhān, *Qatar* 45 E6 25 25N 50 50 E
Duki, *Pakistan* 40 D6 30 14N 68 25 E
Duku, *Nigeria* 51 F8 10 43N 10 43 E
Dulce, *U.S.A.* 83 H10 36 56N 107 0W
Dulce →, *Argentina* 94 C3 30 32S 62 33W
Dulce, G., *Costa Rica* 88 E3 8 40N 83 20W
Dulf, *Iraq* 44 C5 35 7N 45 51 E
Dulit, Banjaran, *Malaysia* 36 D4 3 15N 114 30 E
Duliu, *China* 34 E9 39 2N 116 55 E
Dullewala, *Pakistan* 42 D4 31 50N 71 25 E
Dullstroom, *S. Africa* 57 D5 25 27S 30 7 E
Dulq Maghār, *Syria* 44 B3 36 22N 38 39 E
Duluth, *U.S.A.* 80 B8 46 47N 92 6W
Dum Dum, *India* 43 H13 22 39N 88 33 E
Dum Duma, *India* 41 F19 27 40N 95 40 E
Dūmā, *Syria* 47 B5 33 34N 36 24 E
Dumaguete, *Phil.* 37 C6 9 17N 123 15 E
Dumai, *Indonesia* 36 D2 1 35N 101 28 E
Dumaran, *Phil.* 37 B5 10 33N 119 50 E
Dumas, *Ark., U.S.A.* 81 J9 33 53N 91 29W
Dumas, *Tex., U.S.A.* 81 H4 35 52N 101 58W
Ḍumayr, *Syria* 47 B5 33 39N 36 42 E
Dumbarton, *U.K.* 12 F4 55 57N 4 33W
Dumbleyung, *Australia* 61 F2 33 17S 117 42 E
Dumfries, *U.K.* 12 F5 55 4N 3 37W
Dumfries & Galloway □, *U.K.* 12 F5 55 9N 3 58W
Dumka, *India* 43 G12 24 12N 87 15 E
Dumoine →, *Canada* 70 C4 46 13N 77 51W
Dumoine, L., *Canada* 70 C4 46 55N 77 55W
Dumraon, *India* 43 G11 25 33N 84 8 E
Dumyât, *Egypt* 51 B12 31 24N 31 48 E
Dún Dealgan = Dundalk, *Ireland* 13 B5 54 1N 6 24W
Dun Laoghaire, *Ireland* 13 C5 53 17N 6 8W
Duna = Dunărea →, *Europe* 17 F15 45 20N 29 40 E
Dunagiri, *India* 43 D8 30 31N 79 52 E
Dunaj = Dunărea →, *Europe* 17 F15 45 20N 29 40 E
Dunakeszi, *Hungary* 17 E10 47 37N 19 8 E
Dunărea →, *Europe* 17 F15 45 20N 29 40 E
Dunaújváros, *Hungary* 17 E10 46 58N 18 57 E
Dunav = Dunărea →, *Europe* 17 F15 45 20N 29 40 E
Dunay, *Russia* 30 C6 42 52N 132 22 E
Dunback, *N.Z.* 59 L3 45 23S 170 36 E
Dunbar, *U.K.* 12 E6 56 0N 2 31W
Dunblane, *U.K.* 12 E5 56 11N 3 58W
Duncan, *Canada* 72 D4 48 45N 123 40W
Duncan, *Ariz., U.S.A.* 83 K9 32 43N 109 6W
Duncan, *Okla., U.S.A.* 81 H6 34 30N 97 57W
Duncan, L., *Canada* 70 B4 53 29N 77 58W
Duncan L., *Canada* 72 A6 62 51N 113 58W
Duncan Town, *Bahamas* 88 B4 22 15N 75 45W
Duncannon, *U.S.A.* 78 F7 40 23N 77 2W
Duncansby Head, *U.K.* 12 C5 58 38N 3 1W
Duncansville, *U.S.A.* 78 F6 40 25N 78 26W
Dundalk, *Canada* 78 B4 44 10N 80 24W
Dundalk, *Ireland* 13 B5 54 1N 6 24W
Dundalk, *U.S.A.* 76 F7 39 16N 76 32W
Dundalk Bay, *Ireland* 13 C5 53 55N 6 15W
Dundas, *Canada* 78 C5 43 17N 79 59W
Dundas, L., *Australia* 61 F3 32 35S 121 50 E
Dundas I., *Canada* 72 C2 54 30N 130 50W
Dundas Str., *Australia* 60 B5 11 15S 131 35 E
Dundee, *S. Africa* 57 D5 28 11S 30 15 E
Dundee, *U.K.* 12 E6 56 28N 2 59W
Dundee, *U.S.A.* 78 D8 42 32N 76 59W
Dundee City □, *U.K.* 12 E6 56 30N 2 58W
Dundgovĭ □, *Mongolia* 34 B4 45 10N 106 0 E
Dundrum, *U.K.* 13 B6 54 16N 5 52W
Dundrum B., *U.K.* 13 B6 54 13N 5 47W
Dunedin, *N.Z.* 59 L3 45 50S 170 33 E
Dunedin, *U.S.A.* 77 L4 28 1N 82 47W
Dunfermline, *U.K.* 12 E5 56 5N 3 27W
Dungannon, *Canada* 78 C3 43 51N 81 36W
Dungannon, *U.K.* 13 B5 54 31N 6 46W
Dungarpur, *India* 42 H5 23 52N 73 45 E
Dungarvan, *Ireland* 13 D4 52 5N 7 37W
Dungarvan Harbour, *Ireland* 13 D4 52 4N 7 35W
Dungeness, *U.K.* 11 G8 50 54N 0 59 E
Dungo, L. do, *Angola* 56 B2 17 15S 19 0 E
Dungog, *Australia* 63 E5 32 22S 151 46 E
Dungu, *Dem. Rep. of the Congo* 54 B2 3 40N 28 32 E
Dungun, *Malaysia* 39 K4 4 45N 103 25 E
Dunhua, *China* 35 C15 43 20N 128 14 E
Dunhuang, *China* 32 B4 40 8N 94 36 E
Dunk I., *Australia* 62 B4 17 59S 146 29 E
Dunkeld, *Australia* 63 E4 33 25S 149 29 E
Dunkeld, *U.K.* 12 E5 56 34N 3 35W
Dunkerque, *France* 18 A5 51 2N 2 20 E
Dunkery Beacon, *U.K.* 11 F4 51 9N 3 36W
Dunkirk = Dunkerque, *France* 18 A5 51 2N 2 20 E
Dunkirk, *U.S.A.* 78 D5 42 29N 79 20W
Dúnleary = Dun Laoghaire, *Ireland* 13 C5 53 17N 6 8W
Dunleer, *Ireland* 13 C5 53 50N 6 24W
Dunmanus B., *Ireland* 13 E2 51 31N 9 50W
Dunmanway, *Ireland* 13 E2 51 43N 9 6W
Dunmara, *Australia* 62 B1 16 42S 133 25 E
Dunmore, *U.S.A.* 79 E9 41 25N 75 38W
Dunmore Hd., *Ireland* 13 D1 52 10N 10 35W
Dunmore Town, *Bahamas* 88 A4 25 30N 76 39W
Dunn, *U.S.A.* 77 H6 35 19N 78 37W
Dunnellon, *U.S.A.* 77 L4 29 3N 82 28W
Dunnet Hd., *U.K.* 12 C5 58 40N 3 21W
Dunning, *U.S.A.* 80 E4 41 50N 100 6W
Dunnville, *Canada* 78 D5 42 54N 79 36W
Dunolly, *Australia* 63 F3 36 51S 143 44 E
Dunoon, *U.K.* 12 F4 55 57N 4 56W
Dunphy, *U.S.A.* 82 F5 40 42N 116 31W
Duns, *U.K.* 12 F6 55 47N 2 20W
Dunseith, *U.S.A.* 80 A4 48 50N 100 3W
Dunsmuir, *U.S.A.* 82 F2 41 13N 122 16W
Dunstable, *U.K.* 11 F7 51 53N 0 32W
Dunstan Mts., *N.Z.* 59 L2 44 53S 169 35 E
Dunster, *Canada* 72 C5 53 8N 119 50W
Dunvegan L., *Canada* 73 A7 60 8N 107 10W
Duolun, *China* 34 C9 42 12N 116 28 E
Duong Dong, *Vietnam* 39 G4 10 13N 103 58 E
Dupree, *U.S.A.* 80 C4 45 4N 101 35W
Dupuyer, *U.S.A.* 82 B7 48 13N 112 30W
Duque de Caxias, *Brazil* 95 A7 22 45S 43 19W
Durack →, *Australia* 60 C4 15 33S 127 52 E
Durack Ra., *Australia* 60 C4 16 50S 127 40 E
Durance →, *France* 18 E6 43 55N 4 45 E
Durand, *U.S.A.* 80 C9 44 38N 91 58W
Durango, *Mexico* 86 C4 24 3N 104 39W
Durango, *U.S.A.* 83 H10 37 16N 107 53W
Durango □, *Mexico* 86 C4 25 0N 105 0W
Durant, *Miss., U.S.A.* 81 J10 33 4N 89 51W
Durant, *Okla., U.S.A.* 81 J6 33 59N 96 25W
Durazno, *Uruguay* 94 C4 33 25S 56 31W
Durazzo = Durrës, *Albania* 21 D8 41 19N 19 28 E
Durban, *S. Africa* 57 D5 29 49S 31 1 E
Durbuy, *Belgium* 15 D5 50 21N 5 28 E
Düren, *Germany* 16 C4 50 48N 6 29 E
Durg, *India* 41 J12 21 15N 81 22 E
Durgapur, *India* 43 H12 23 30N 87 20 E
Durham, *Canada* 78 B4 44 10N 80 49W
Durham, *U.K.* 10 C6 54 47N 1 34W
Durham, *Calif., U.S.A.* 84 F5 39 39N 121 48W
Durham, *N.C., U.S.A.* 77 H6 35 59N 78 54W
Durham, *N.H., U.S.A.* 79 C14 43 8N 70 56W
Durham □, *U.K.* 10 C6 54 42N 1 45W
Ḍurmā, *Si. Arabia* 44 E5 24 37N 46 8 E
Durmitor, *Montenegro, Yug.* 21 C8 43 10N 19 0 E
Durness, *U.K.* 12 C4 58 34N 4 45W
Durrës, *Albania* 21 D8 41 19N 19 28 E
Durrow, *Ireland* 13 D4 52 51N 7 24W
Dursey I., *Ireland* 13 E1 51 36N 10 12W
Dursunbey, *Turkey* 21 E13 39 35N 28 37 E
Duru, *Dem. Rep. of the Congo* 54 B2 4 14N 28 50 E
Durūz, Jabal ad, *Jordan* 47 C5 32 35N 36 40 E
D'Urville, Tanjung, *Indonesia* 37 E9 1 28S 137 54 E
D'Urville I., *N.Z.* 59 J4 40 50S 173 55 E
Duryea, *U.S.A.* 79 E9 41 20N 75 45W
Dushak, *Turkmenistan* 26 F7 37 13N 60 1 E
Dushanbe, *Tajikistan* 26 F7 38 33N 68 48 E
Dushore, *U.S.A.* 79 E8 41 31N 76 24W
Dusky Sd., *N.Z.* 59 L1 45 47S 166 30 E
Dussejour, C., *Australia* 60 B4 14 45S 128 13 E
Düsseldorf, *Germany* 16 C4 51 14N 6 47 E
Dutch Harbor, *U.S.A.* 68 C3 53 53N 166 32W
Dutlwe, *Botswana* 56 C3 23 58S 23 46 E
Dutton, *Canada* 78 D3 42 39N 81 30W
Dutton →, *Australia* 62 C3 20 44S 143 10 E
Duwayhin, Khawr, *U.A.E.* 45 E6 24 20N 51 25 E
Duyun, *China* 32 D5 26 18N 107 29 E
Duzdab = Zāhedān, *Iran* 45 D9 29 30N 60 50 E
Dvina, Severnaya →, *Russia* 24 B7 64 32N 40 30 E
Dvinsk = Daugavpils, *Latvia* 9 J22 55 53N 26 32 E
Dvinskaya Guba, *Russia* 24 B6 65 0N 39 0 E
Dwarka, *India* 42 H3 22 18N 69 8 E
Dwellingup, *Australia* 61 F2 32 43S 116 4 E
Dwight, *Canada* 78 A5 45 20N 79 1W
Dwight, *U.S.A.* 76 E1 41 5N 88 26W
Dyatlovo = Dzyatlava, *Belarus* 17 B13 53 28N 25 28 E
Dyce, *U.K.* 12 D6 57 13N 2 12W
Dyer, C., *Canada* 69 B13 66 40N 61 0W
Dyer Bay, *Canada* 78 A3 45 10N 81 20W
Dyer Plateau, *Antarctica* 5 D17 70 45S 65 30W
Dyersburg, *U.S.A.* 81 G10 36 3N 89 23W
Dyfi →, *U.K.* 11 E3 52 32N 4 3W
Dymer, *Ukraine* 17 C16 50 47N 30 18 E
Dysart, *Australia* 62 C4 22 32S 148 23 E
Dzamin Üüd = Borhoyn Tal, *Mongolia* 34 C6 43 50N 111 58 E
Dzerzhinsk, *Russia* 24 C7 56 14N 43 30 E
Dzhalinda, *Russia* 27 D13 53 26N 124 0 E
Dzhambul = Taraz, *Kazakstan* 26 E8 42 54N 71 22 E
Dzhankoy, *Ukraine* 25 E5 45 40N 34 20 E
Dzhezkazgan = Zhezqazghan, *Kazakstan* 26 E7 47 44N 67 40 E
Dzhizak = Jizzakh, *Uzbekistan* 26 E7 40 6N 67 50 E
Dzhugdzur, Khrebet, *Russia* 27 D14 57 30N 138 0 E
Dzhungarskiye Vorota = Dzungarian Gates, *Asia* 32 B3 45 0N 82 0 E
Działdowo, *Poland* 17 B11 53 15N 20 15 E
Dzibilchaltun, *Mexico* 87 C7 21 5N 89 36W
Dzierżoniów, *Poland* 17 C9 50 45N 16 39 E
Dzilam de Bravo, *Mexico* 87 C7 21 24N 88 53W
Dzungaria = Junggar Pendi, *China* 32 B3 44 30N 86 0 E
Dzungarian Gates, *Asia* 32 B3 45 0N 82 0 E
Dzuumod, *Mongolia* 32 B5 47 45N 106 58 E
Dzyarzhynsk, *Belarus* 17 B14 53 40N 27 1 E
Dzyatlava, *Belarus* 17 B13 53 28N 25 28 E

E

Eabamet L., *Canada* 70 B2 51 30N 87 46W
Eads, *U.S.A.* 80 F3 38 29N 102 47W
Eagar, *U.S.A.* 83 J9 34 6N 109 17W
Eagle, *Alaska, U.S.A.* 68 B5 64 47N 141 12W
Eagle, *Colo., U.S.A.* 82 G10 39 39N 106 50W
Eagle →, *Canada* 71 B8 53 36N 57 26W
Eagle Butte, *U.S.A.* 80 C4 45 0N 101 10W
Eagle Grove, *U.S.A.* 80 D8 42 40N 93 54W
Eagle L., *Canada* 73 D10 49 42N 93 13W
Eagle L., *Calif., U.S.A.* 82 F3 40 39N 120 45W
Eagle L., *Maine, U.S.A.* 77 B11 46 20N 69 22W
Eagle Lake, *Canada* 78 A6 45 8N 78 29W
Eagle Lake, *Maine, U.S.A.* 77 B11 47 3N 68 36W
Eagle Lake, *Tex., U.S.A.* 81 L6 29 35N 96 20W
Eagle Mountain, *U.S.A.* 85 M11 33 49N 115 27W
Eagle Nest, *U.S.A.* 83 H11 36 33N 105 16W
Eagle Pass, *U.S.A.* 81 L4 28 43N 100 30W
Eagle Pk., *U.S.A.* 84 G7 38 10N 119 25W
Eagle Pt., *Australia* 60 C3 16 11S 124 23 E
Eagle River, *Mich., U.S.A.* 76 B1 47 24N 88 18W
Eagle River, *Wis., U.S.A.* 80 C10 45 55N 89 15W
Eaglehawk, *Australia* 63 F3 36 44S 144 15 E
Eagles Mere, *U.S.A.* 79 E8 41 25N 76 33W
Ealing □, *U.K.* 11 F7 51 31N 0 20W
Ear Falls, *Canada* 73 C10 50 38N 93 13W
Earle, *U.S.A.* 81 H9 35 16N 90 28W
Earlimart, *U.S.A.* 85 K7 35 53N 119 16W
Earn →, *U.K.* 12 E5 56 21N 3 18W
Earn, L., *U.K.* 12 E4 56 23N 4 13W
Earnslaw, Mt., *N.Z.* 59 L2 44 32S 168 27 E
Earth, *U.S.A.* 81 H3 34 14N 102 24W
Easley, *U.S.A.* 77 H4 34 50N 82 36W
East Anglia, *U.K.* 10 E9 52 30N 1 0 E
East Angus, *Canada* 71 C5 45 30N 71 40W
East Aurora, *U.S.A.* 78 D6 42 46N 78 37W
East Ayrshire □, *U.K.* 12 F4 55 26N 4 11W
East Bengal, *Bangla.* 41 H17 24 0N 90 0 E
East Beskids = Vychodné Beskydy, *Europe* 17 D11 49 20N 22 0 E
East Brady, *U.S.A.* 78 F5 40 59N 79 36W
East C., *N.Z.* 59 G7 37 42S 178 35 E
East Chicago, *U.S.A.* 76 E2 41 38N 87 27W
East China Sea, *Asia* 33 D7 30 0N 126 0 E
East Coulee, *Canada* 72 C6 51 23N 112 27W
East Dereham, *U.K.* 11 E8 52 41N 0 57 E
East Dunbartonshire □, *U.K.* 12 F4 55 57N 4 13W
East Falkland, *Falk. Is.* 96 G5 51 30S 58 30W
East Grand Forks, *U.S.A.* 80 B6 47 56N 97 1W
East Greenwich, *U.S.A.* 79 E13 41 40N 71 27W
East Grinstead, *U.K.* 11 F8 51 7N 0 0W
East Hartford, *U.S.A.* 79 E12 41 46N 72 39W
East Helena, *U.S.A.* 82 C8 46 35N 111 56W
East Indies, *Asia* 28 K15 0 0 120 0 E
East Kilbride, *U.K.* 12 F4 55 47N 4 11W
East Lansing, *U.S.A.* 76 D3 42 44N 84 29W
East Liverpool, *U.S.A.* 78 F4 40 37N 80 35W
East London, *S. Africa* 57 E4 33 0S 27 55 E
East Lothian □, *U.K.* 12 F6 55 58N 2 44W
East Main = Eastmain, *Canada* 70 B4 52 10N 78 30W
East Northport, *U.S.A.* 79 F11 40 53N 73 20W
East Orange, *U.S.A.* 79 F10 40 46N 74 13W
East Pacific Ridge, *Pac. Oc.* 65 J17 15 0S 110 0W
East Palestine, *U.S.A.* 78 F4 40 50N 80 33W
East Pine, *Canada* 72 B4 55 48N 120 12W
East Point, *U.S.A.* 77 J3 33 41N 84 27W
East Providence, *U.S.A.* 79 E13 41 49N 71 23W

East Pt., Canada 71 C7 46 27N 61 58W
East Renfrewshire □, U.K. 12 F4 55 46N 4 21W
East Retford = Retford, U.K. 10 D7 53 19N 0 56W
East Riding of Yorkshire □, U.K. 10 D7 53 55N 0 30W
East Rochester, U.S.A. 78 C7 43 7N 77 29W
East St. Louis, U.S.A. 80 F9 38 37N 90 9W
East Schelde = Oosterschelde →, Neths. 15 C4 51 33N 4 0 E
East Sea = Japan, Sea of, Asia 30 E7 40 0N 135 0 E
East Siberian Sea, Russia 27 B17 73 0N 160 0 E
East Stroudsburg, U.S.A. 79 E9 41 1N 75 11W
East Sussex □, U.K. 11 G8 50 56N 0 19 E
East Tawas, U.S.A. 76 C4 44 17N 83 29W
East Timor ■, Asia 37 F7 8 50S 126 0 E
East Toorale, Australia 63 E4 30 27S 145 28 E
East Walker →, U.S.A. 84 G7 38 52N 119 10W
East Windsor, U.S.A. 79 F10 40 17N 74 34W
Eastbourne, N.Z. 59 J5 41 19S 174 55 E
Eastbourne, U.K. 11 G8 50 46N 0 18 E
Eastend, Canada 73 D7 49 32N 108 50W
Easter I. = Pascua, I. de, Chile 65 K17 27 7S 109 23W
Eastern □, Kenya 54 C4 0 0 38 30 E
Eastern Cape □, S. Africa 56 E4 32 0S 26 0 E
Eastern Cr. →, Australia 62 C3 20 40S 141 35 E
Eastern Ghats, India 40 N11 14 0N 78 50 E
Eastern Group = Lau Group, Fiji 59 C9 17 0S 178 30W
Eastern Group, Australia 61 F3 33 30S 124 30 E
Eastern Transvaal = Mpumalanga □, S. Africa 57 B5 26 0S 30 0 E
Easterville, Canada 73 C9 53 8N 99 49W
Easthampton, U.S.A. 79 D12 42 16N 72 40W
Eastlake, U.S.A. 78 E3 41 40N 81 26W
Eastland, U.S.A. 81 J5 32 24N 98 49W
Eastleigh, U.K. 11 G6 50 58N 1 21W
Eastmain, Canada 70 B4 52 10N 78 30W
Eastmain →, Canada 70 B4 52 27N 78 26W
Eastman, Canada 79 A12 45 18N 72 19W
Eastman, U.S.A. 77 J4 32 12N 83 11W
Easton, Md., U.S.A. 76 F7 38 47N 76 5W
Easton, Pa., U.S.A. 79 F9 40 41N 75 13W
Easton, Wash., U.S.A. 84 C5 47 14N 121 11W
Eastpointe, U.S.A. 78 D2 42 27N 82 56W
Eastport, U.S.A. 77 C12 44 56N 67 0W
Eastsound, U.S.A. 84 B4 48 42N 122 55W
Eaton, U.S.A. 80 E2 40 32N 104 42W
Eatonia, Canada 73 C7 51 13N 109 25W
Eatonton, U.S.A. 77 J4 33 20N 83 23W
Eatontown, U.S.A. 79 F10 40 19N 74 4W
Eatonville, U.S.A. 84 D4 46 52N 122 16W
Eau Claire, U.S.A. 80 C9 44 49N 91 30W
Eau Claire, L. à l', Canada 70 A5 56 10N 74 25W
Ebbw Vale, U.K. 11 F4 51 46N 3 12W
Ebeltoft, Denmark 9 H14 56 12N 10 41 E
Ebensburg, U.S.A. 78 F6 40 29N 78 44W
Eberswalde-Finow, Germany 16 B7 52 50N 13 49 E
Ebetsu, Japan 30 C10 43 7N 141 34 E
Ebolowa, Cameroon 52 D2 2 55N 11 10 E
Ebro →, Spain 19 B6 40 43N 0 54 E
Eceabat, Turkey 21 D12 40 11N 26 21 E
Ech Chéliff, Algeria 50 A6 36 10N 1 20 E
Echigo-Sammyaku, Japan 31 F9 36 50N 139 50 E
Echizen-Misaki, Japan 31 G7 35 59N 135 57 E
Echo Bay, N.W.T., Canada 68 B8 66 5N 117 55W
Echo Bay, Ont., Canada 70 C3 46 29N 84 4W
Echoing →, Canada 70 B1 55 51N 92 5W
Echternach, Lux. 15 E6 49 49N 6 25 E
Echuca, Australia 63 F3 36 10S 144 45 E
Ecija, Spain 19 D3 37 30N 5 10W
Eclipse Is., Australia 60 B4 13 54S 126 19 E
Eclipse Sd., Canada 69 A11 72 38N 79 0W
Ecuador ■, S. Amer. 92 D3 2 0S 78 0W
Ed Damazin, Sudan 51 F12 11 46N 34 21 E
Ed Debba, Sudan 51 E12 18 0N 30 51 E
Ed Dueim, Sudan 51 F12 14 0N 32 10 E
Edam, Canada 73 C7 53 11N 108 46W
Edam, Neths. 15 B5 52 31N 5 3 E
Eday, U.K. 12 B6 59 11N 2 47W
Eddrachillis B., U.K. 12 C3 58 17N 5 14W
Eddystone Pt., Australia 62 G4 40 59S 148 20 E
Ede, Neths. 15 B5 52 4N 5 40 E
Edehon L., Canada 73 A9 60 25N 97 15W
Eden, Australia 63 F4 37 3S 149 55 E
Eden, N.C., U.S.A. 77 G6 36 29N 79 53W
Eden, N.Y., U.S.A. 78 D6 42 39N 78 55W
Eden, Tex., U.S.A. 81 K5 31 13N 99 51W
Eden →, U.K. 10 C4 54 57N 3 1W
Edenburg, S. Africa 56 D4 29 43S 25 58 E
Edendale, S. Africa 57 D5 29 39S 30 18 E
Edenderry, Ireland 13 C4 53 21N 7 4W
Edenton, U.S.A. 77 G7 36 4N 76 39W
Edenville, S. Africa 57 D4 27 37S 27 34 E
Eder →, Germany 16 C5 51 12N 9 28 E
Edgar, U.S.A. 80 E6 40 22N 97 58W
Edgartown, U.S.A. 79 E14 41 23N 70 31W
Edge Hill, U.K. 11 E6 52 8N 1 26W
Edgefield, U.S.A. 77 J5 33 47N 81 56W
Edgeley, U.S.A. 80 B5 46 22N 98 43W
Edgemont, U.S.A. 80 D3 43 18N 103 50W
Edgeøya, Svalbard 4 B9 77 45N 22 30 E
Édhessa, Greece 21 D10 40 48N 22 5 E
Edievale, N.Z. 59 L2 45 49S 169 22 E
Edina, U.S.A. 80 E8 40 10N 92 11W
Edinboro, U.S.A. 78 E4 41 52N 80 8W
Edinburg, U.S.A. 81 M5 26 18N 98 10W
Edinburgh, U.K. 12 F5 55 57N 3 13W
Edinburgh, City of □, U.K. 12 F5 55 57N 3 17W
Edineţ, Moldova 17 D14 48 9N 27 18 E
Edirne, Turkey 21 D12 41 40N 26 34 E
Edison, U.S.A. 84 B4 48 33N 122 27W
Edithburgh, Australia 63 F2 35 5S 137 43 E
Edmeston, U.S.A. 79 D9 42 42N 75 15W
Edmond, U.S.A. 81 H6 35 39N 97 29W
Edmonds, U.S.A. 84 C4 47 49N 122 23W
Edmonton, Australia 62 B4 17 2S 145 46 E
Edmonton, Canada 72 C6 53 30N 113 30W
Edmund L., Canada 70 B1 54 45N 93 17W
Edmundston, Canada 71 C6 47 23N 68 20W
Edna, U.S.A. 81 L6 28 59N 96 39W
Edremit, Turkey 21 E12 39 34N 27 0 E
Edremit Körfezi, Turkey 21 E12 39 30N 26 45 E
Edson, Canada 72 C5 53 35N 116 28W
Eduardo Castex, Argentina 94 D3 35 50S 64 18W
Edward →, Australia 63 F3 35 5S 143 30 E
Edward, L., Africa 54 C2 0 25S 29 40 E
Edward River, Australia 62 A3 14 59S 141 26 E
Edward VII Land, Antarctica 5 E13 80 0S 150 0W
Edwards, Calif., U.S.A. 85 L9 34 55N 117 51W
Edwards, N.Y., U.S.A. 79 B9 44 20N 75 15W
Edwards Air Force Base, U.S.A. 85 L9 34 50N 117 40W
Edwards Plateau, U.S.A. 81 K4 30 45N 101 20W
Edwardsville, U.S.A. 79 E9 41 15N 75 56W
Edzo, Canada 72 A5 62 49N 116 4W
Eeklo, Belgium 15 C3 51 11N 3 33 E
Effingham, U.S.A. 76 F1 39 7N 88 33W
Égadi, Ísole, Italy 20 F5 37 55N 12 16 E
Egan Range, U.S.A. 82 G6 39 35N 114 55W
Eganville, Canada 78 A7 45 32N 77 5W
Eger = Cheb, Czech Rep. 16 C7 50 9N 12 28 E
Eger, Hungary 17 E11 47 53N 20 27 E
Egersund, Norway 9 G12 58 26N 6 1 E
Egg L., Canada 73 B7 55 5N 105 30W
Éghezée, Belgium 15 D4 50 35N 4 55 E
Egmont, Canada 72 D4 49 45N 123 56W
Egmont, C., N.Z. 59 H4 39 16S 173 45 E
Egmont, Mt. = Taranaki, Mt., N.Z. 59 H5 39 17S 174 5 E
Egra, India 43 J12 21 54N 87 32 E
Eğridir, Turkey 25 G5 37 52N 30 51 E
Eğridir Gölü, Turkey 25 G5 37 53N 30 50 E
Egvekinot, Russia 27 C19 66 19N 179 50W
Egypt ■, Africa 51 C12 28 0N 31 0 E
Ehime □, Japan 31 H6 33 30N 132 40 E
Ehrenberg, U.S.A. 85 M12 33 36N 114 31W
Eibar, Spain 19 A4 43 11N 2 28W
Eidsvold, Australia 63 D5 25 25S 151 12 E
Eidsvoll, Norway 9 F14 60 19N 11 14 E
Eifel, Germany 16 C4 50 15N 6 50 E
Eiffel Flats, Zimbabwe 55 F3 18 20S 30 0 E
Eigg, U.K. 12 E2 56 54N 6 10W
Eighty Mile Beach, Australia 60 C3 19 30S 120 40 E
Eil, Somali Rep. 46 F4 8 0N 49 50 E
Eil, L., U.K. 12 E3 56 51N 5 16W
Eildon, L., Australia 63 F4 37 10S 146 0 E
Einasleigh, Australia 62 B3 18 32S 144 5 E
Einasleigh →, Australia 62 B3 17 30S 142 17 E
Eindhoven, Neths. 15 C5 51 26N 5 28 E
Eire = Ireland ■, Europe 13 C4 53 50N 7 52W
Eiríksjökull, Iceland 8 D3 64 46N 20 24W
Eirunepé, Brazil 92 E5 6 35S 69 53W
Eiseb →, Namibia 56 C2 20 33S 20 59 E
Eisenach, Germany 16 C6 50 58N 10 19 E
Eisenerz, Austria 16 E8 47 32N 14 54 E
Eivissa, Spain 22 C7 38 54N 1 26 E
Ejeda, Madag. 57 C7 24 20S 44 31 E
Ejutla, Mexico 87 D5 16 34N 96 44W
Ekalaka, U.S.A. 80 C2 45 53N 104 33W
Eketahuna, N.Z. 59 J5 40 38S 175 43 E
Ekibastuz, Kazakstan 26 D8 51 50N 75 10 E
Ekoli, Dem. Rep. of the Congo 54 C1 0 23S 24 13 E
Eksjö, Sweden 9 H16 57 40N 14 58 E
Ekuma →, Namibia 56 B2 18 40S 16 2 E
Ekwan →, Canada 70 B3 53 12N 82 15W
Ekwan Pt., Canada 70 B3 53 16N 82 7W
El Aaiún, W. Sahara 50 C3 27 9N 13 12W
El Abanico, Chile 94 D1 37 20S 71 31W
El 'Agrûd, Egypt 47 E3 30 14N 34 24 E
El Alamein, Egypt 51 B11 30 48N 28 58 E
El 'Aqaba, W. →, Egypt 47 E2 30 7N 33 54 E
El Arīḥā, West Bank 47 D4 31 52N 35 27 E
El 'Arîsh, Egypt 47 D2 31 8N 33 50 E
El 'Arîsh, W. →, Egypt 47 D2 31 8N 33 47 E
El Asnam = Ech Chéliff, Algeria 50 A6 36 10N 1 20 E
El Bayadh, Algeria 50 B6 33 40N 1 1 E
El Bluff, Nic. 88 D3 11 59N 83 40W
El Brûk, W. →, Egypt 47 E2 30 15N 33 50 E
El Cajon, U.S.A. 85 N10 32 48N 116 58W
El Campo, U.S.A. 81 L6 29 12N 96 16W
El Centro, U.S.A. 85 N11 32 48N 115 34W
El Cerro, Bolivia 92 G6 17 30S 61 40W
El Compadre, Mexico 85 N10 32 20N 116 14W
El Cuy, Argentina 96 D3 39 55S 68 25W
El Cuyo, Mexico 87 C7 21 30N 87 40W
El Daheir, Egypt 47 D3 31 13N 34 10 E
El Dátil, Mexico 86 B2 30 7N 112 15W
El Dere, Somali Rep. 46 G4 3 50N 47 8 E
El Descanso, Mexico 85 N10 32 12N 116 58W
El Desemboque, Mexico 86 A2 30 30N 112 57W
El Diviso, Colombia 92 C3 1 22N 78 14W
El Djouf, Mauritania 50 D4 20 0N 9 0W
El Dorado, Ark., U.S.A. 81 J8 33 12N 92 40W
El Dorado, Kans., U.S.A. 81 G6 37 49N 96 52W
El Dorado, Venezuela 92 B6 6 55N 61 37W
El Escorial, Spain 19 B3 40 35N 4 7W
El Faiyûm, Egypt 51 C12 29 19N 30 50 E
El Fâsher, Sudan 51 F11 13 33N 25 26 E
El Ferrol = Ferrol, Spain 19 A1 43 29N 8 15W
El Fuerte, Mexico 86 B3 26 30N 108 40W
El Gal, Somali Rep. 46 E5 10 58N 50 20 E
El Geneina = Al Junaynah, Sudan 51 F10 13 27N 22 45 E
El Gîza, Egypt 51 C12 30 0N 31 10 E
El Goléa, Algeria 50 B6 30 30N 2 50 E
El Iskandarîya, Egypt 51 B11 31 13N 29 58 E
El Istiwa'iya, Sudan 51 G11 5 0N 28 0 E
El Jadida, Morocco 50 B4 33 11N 8 17W
El Jardal, Honduras 88 D2 14 54N 88 50W
El Kabrît, G., Egypt 47 F2 29 42N 33 16 E
El Khârga, Egypt 51 C12 25 30N 30 33 E
El Khartûm, Sudan 51 E12 15 31N 32 35 E
El Kuntilla, Egypt 47 E3 30 1N 34 45 E
El Maestrazgo, Spain 19 B5 40 30N 0 25W
El Mahalla el Kubra, Egypt 51 B12 31 0N 31 0 E
El Mansûra, Egypt 51 B12 31 0N 31 19 E
El Medano, Canary Is. 22 F3 28 3N 16 32W
El Milagro, Argentina 94 C2 30 59S 65 59W
El Minyâ, Egypt 51 C12 28 7N 30 33 E
El Monte, U.S.A. 85 L8 34 4N 118 1W
El Obeid, Sudan 51 F12 13 8N 30 10 E
El Odaiya, Sudan 51 F11 12 8N 28 12 E
El Oro, Mexico 87 D4 19 48N 100 8W
El Oued, Algeria 50 B7 33 20N 6 58 E
El Palmito, Presa, Mexico 86 B3 25 40N 105 30W
El Paso, U.S.A. 83 L10 31 45N 106 29W
El Paso Robles, U.S.A. 84 K6 35 38N 120 41W
El Portal, U.S.A. 84 H7 37 41N 119 47W
El Porvenir, Mexico 86 A3 31 15N 105 51W
El Prat de Llobregat, Spain 19 B7 41 18N 2 3 E
El Progreso, Honduras 88 C2 15 26N 87 51W
El Pueblito, Mexico 86 B3 29 3N 105 4W
El Pueblo, Canary Is. 22 F2 28 36N 17 47W
El Puerto de Santa María, Spain 19 D2 36 36N 6 13W
El Qâhira, Egypt 51 B12 30 1N 31 14 E
El Qantara, Egypt 47 E1 30 51N 32 20 E
El Quseima, Egypt 47 E3 30 40N 34 15 E
El Real, Panama 92 B3 8 0N 77 40W
El Reno, U.S.A. 81 H6 35 32N 97 57W
El Rio, U.S.A. 85 L7 34 14N 119 10W
El Roque, Pta., Canary Is. 22 F4 28 10N 15 25W
El Rosarito, Mexico 86 B2 28 38N 114 4W
El Saheira, W. →, Egypt 47 E2 30 5N 33 25 E
El Salto, Mexico 86 C3 23 47N 105 22W
El Salvador ■, Cent. Amer. 88 D2 13 50N 89 0W
El Sauce, Nic. 88 D2 13 0N 86 40W
El Sueco, Mexico 86 B3 29 54N 106 24W
El Suweis, Egypt 51 C12 29 58N 32 31 E
El Tamarâni, W. →, Egypt 47 E3 30 7N 34 43 E
El Thamad, Egypt 47 F3 29 40N 34 28 E
El Tigre, Venezuela 92 B6 8 44N 64 15W
El Tîh, Gebal, Egypt 47 F2 29 40N 33 50 E
El Tîna, Khalîg, Egypt 47 D1 31 10N 32 40 E
El Tofo, Chile 94 B1 29 22S 71 18W
El Tránsito, Chile 94 B1 28 52S 70 17W
El Tûr, Egypt 44 D2 28 14N 33 36 E
El Turbio, Argentina 96 G2 51 45S 72 5W
El Uqsur, Egypt 51 C12 25 41N 32 38 E
El Venado, Mexico 86 C4 22 56N 101 10W
El Vergel, Mexico 86 B3 26 28N 106 22W
El Vigía, Venezuela 92 B4 8 38N 71 39W
El Wabeira, Egypt 47 F2 29 34N 33 6 E
El Wak, Kenya 54 B5 2 49N 40 56 E
El Wuz, Sudan 51 E12 15 5N 30 7 E
Elat, Israel 47 F3 29 30N 34 56 E
Elâzığ, Turkey 25 G6 38 37N 39 14 E
Elba, Italy 20 C4 42 46N 10 17 E
Elba, U.S.A. 77 K2 31 25N 86 4W
Elbasan, Albania 21 D9 41 9N 20 9 E
Elbe, U.S.A. 84 D4 46 45N 122 10W
Elbe →, Europe 16 B5 53 50N 9 0 E
Elbert, Mt., U.S.A. 83 G10 39 7N 106 27W
Elberton, U.S.A. 77 H4 34 7N 82 52W
Elbeuf, France 18 B4 49 17N 1 2 E
Elbidtan, Turkey 44 B3 38 13N 37 12 E
Elbing = Elbląg, Poland 17 A10 54 10N 19 25 E
Elbląg, Poland 17 A10 54 10N 19 25 E
Elbow, Canada 73 C7 51 7N 106 35W
Elbrus, Asia 25 F7 43 21N 42 30 E
Elburz Mts. = Alborz, Reshteh-ye Kūhhā-ye, Iran 45 C7 36 0N 52 0 E
Elche, Spain 19 C5 38 15N 0 42W
Elcho I., Australia 62 A2 11 55S 135 45 E
Elda, Spain 19 C5 38 29N 0 47W
Elde →, Germany 16 B6 53 7N 11 15 E
Eldon, Mo., U.S.A. 80 F8 38 21N 92 35W
Eldon, Wash., U.S.A. 84 C3 47 33N 123 3W
Eldora, U.S.A. 80 D8 42 22N 93 5W
Eldorado, Argentina 95 B5 26 28S 54 43W
Eldorado, Canada 78 B7 44 35N 77 31W
Eldorado, Mexico 86 C3 24 20N 107 22W
Eldorado, Ill., U.S.A. 76 G1 37 49N 88 26W
Eldorado, Tex., U.S.A. 81 K4 30 52N 100 36W
Eldorado Springs, U.S.A. 81 G8 37 52N 94 1W
Eldoret, Kenya 54 B4 0 30N 35 17 E
Eldred, U.S.A. 78 E6 41 58N 78 23W
Elea, C., Cyprus 23 D13 35 19N 34 4 E
Eleanora, Pk., Australia 61 F3 32 57S 121 9 E
Elefantes →, Mozam. 57 C5 24 10S 32 40 E
Elektrostal, Russia 24 C6 55 41N 38 32 E
Elephant Butte Reservoir, U.S.A. 83 K10 33 9N 107 11W
Elephant I., Antarctica 5 C18 61 0S 55 0W
Eleuthera, Bahamas 88 B4 25 0N 76 20W
Elgin, Canada 79 B8 44 36N 76 13W
Elgin, U.K. 12 D5 57 39N 3 19W
Elgin, Ill., U.S.A. 76 D1 42 2N 88 17W
Elgin, N. Dak., U.S.A. 80 B4 46 24N 101 51W
Elgin, Oreg., U.S.A. 82 D5 45 34N 117 55W
Elgin, Tex., U.S.A. 81 K6 30 21N 97 22W
Elgon, Mt., Africa 54 B3 1 10N 34 30 E
Eliase, Indonesia 37 F8 8 21S 130 48 E
Elim, Namibia 56 B2 17 48S 15 31 E
Elim, S. Africa 56 E2 34 35S 19 45 E
Elista, Russia 25 E7 46 16N 44 14 E
Elizabeth, Australia 63 E2 34 42S 138 41 E
Elizabeth, N.J., U.S.A. 79 F10 40 39N 74 13W
Elizabeth, N.J., U.S.A. 79 F10 40 40N 74 13W
Elizabeth City, U.S.A. 77 G7 36 18N 76 14W
Elizabethton, U.S.A. 77 G4 36 21N 82 13W
Elizabethtown, Ky., U.S.A. 76 G3 37 42N 85 52W
Elizabethtown, N.Y., U.S.A. 79 B11 44 13N 73 36W
Elizabethtown, Pa., U.S.A. 79 F8 40 9N 76 36W
Ełk, Poland 17 B12 53 50N 22 21 E
Elk →, Canada 72 C5 49 11N 115 14W
Elk →, U.S.A. 77 H2 34 46N 87 16W
Elk City, U.S.A. 81 H5 35 25N 99 25W
Elk Creek, U.S.A. 84 F4 39 36N 122 32W
Elk Grove, U.S.A. 84 G5 38 25N 121 22W
Elk Island Nat. Park, Canada 72 C6 53 35N 112 59W
Elk Lake, Canada 70 C3 47 40N 80 25W
Elk Point, Canada 73 C6 53 54N 110 55W
Elk River, Idaho, U.S.A. 82 C5 46 47N 116 11W
Elk River, Minn., U.S.A. 80 C8 45 18N 93 35W
Elkedra →, Australia 62 C2 21 8S 136 22 E
Elkhart, Ind., U.S.A. 76 E3 41 41N 85 58W
Elkhart, Kans., U.S.A. 81 G4 37 0N 101 54W
Elkhorn, Canada 73 D8 49 59N 101 14W
Elkhorn →, U.S.A. 80 E6 41 8N 96 19W
Elkhovo, Bulgaria 21 C12 42 10N 26 35 E
Elkin, U.S.A. 77 G5 36 15N 80 51W
Elkins, U.S.A. 76 F6 38 55N 79 51W
Elkland, U.S.A. 78 E7 41 59N 77 19W
Elko, Canada 72 D5 49 20N 115 10W
Elko, U.S.A. 82 F6 40 50N 115 46W
Elkton, U.S.A. 78 C1 43 49N 83 11W
Ell, L., Australia 61 E4 29 13S 127 46 E
Ellef Ringnes I., Canada 4 B2 78 30N 102 2W
Ellen, Mt., U.S.A. 79 B12 44 9N 72 56W
Ellenburg, U.S.A. 79 B11 44 54N 73 48W
Ellendale, U.S.A. 80 B5 46 0N 98 32W
Ellensburg, U.S.A. 82 C3 46 59N 120 34W
Ellenville, U.S.A. 79 E10 41 43N 74 24W
Ellery, Mt., Australia 63 F4 37 28S 148 47 E
Ellesmere, L., N.Z. 59 M4 43 47S 172 28 E
Ellesmere I., Canada 4 B4 79 30N 80 0W
Ellesmere Port, U.K. 10 D5 53 17N 2 54W
Ellice Is. = Tuvalu ■, Pac. Oc. 64 H9 8 0S 178 0 E
Ellicottville, U.S.A. 78 D6 42 17N 78 40W
Elliot, Australia 62 B1 17 33S 133 32 E
Elliot, S. Africa 57 E4 31 22S 27 48 E
Elliot Lake, Canada 70 C3 46 25N 82 35W
Elliotdale = Xhora, S. Africa 57 E4 31 55S 28 38 E
Ellis, U.S.A. 80 F5 38 56N 99 34W
Elliston, Australia 63 E1 33 39S 134 53 E
Ellisville, U.S.A. 81 K10 31 36N 89 12W
Ellon, U.K. 12 D6 57 22N 2 4W
Ellore = Eluru, India 41 L12 16 48N 81 8 E
Ellsworth, Kans., U.S.A. 80 F5 38 44N 98 14W
Ellsworth, Maine, U.S.A. 77 C11 44 33N 68 25W
Ellsworth Land, Antarctica 5 D16 76 0S 89 0W
Ellsworth Mts., Antarctica 5 D16 78 30S 85 0W
Ellwood City, U.S.A. 78 F4 40 52N 80 17W
Elma, Canada 73 D9 49 52N 95 55W
Elma, U.S.A. 84 D3 47 0N 123 25W
Elmalı, Turkey 25 G4 36 44N 29 56 E
Elmhurst, U.S.A. 76 E2 41 53N 87 56W
Elmira, Canada 78 C4 43 36N 80 33W
Elmira, U.S.A. 78 D8 42 6N 76 48W
Elmira Heights, U.S.A. 78 D8 42 8N 76 50W
Elmore, Australia 63 F3 36 30S 144 37 E
Elmore, U.S.A. 85 M11 33 7N 115 49W
Elmshorn, Germany 16 B5 53 43N 9 40 E
Elmvale, Canada 78 B5 44 35N 79 52W
Elora, Canada 78 C4 43 41N 80 26W
Eloúnda, Greece 23 D7 35 16N 25 42 E
Eloy, U.S.A. 83 K8 32 45N 111 33W
Elrose, Canada 73 C7 51 12N 108 0W
Elsie, U.S.A. 84 E3 45 52N 123 36W
Elsinore = Helsingør, Denmark 9 H15 56 2N 12 35 E
Eltham, N.Z. 59 H5 39 26S 174 19 E
Eluru, India 41 L12 16 48N 81 8 E
Elvas, Portugal 19 C2 38 50N 7 10W
Elverum, Norway 9 F14 60 53N 11 34 E
Elvire →, Australia 60 C4 17 51S 128 11 E
Elvire, Mt., Australia 61 E2 29 22S 119 36 E
Elwell, L., U.S.A. 82 B8 48 22N 111 17W
Elwood, Ind., U.S.A. 76 E3 40 17N 85 50W
Elwood, Nebr., U.S.A. 80 E5 40 36N 99 52W
Elx = Elche, Spain 19 C5 38 15N 0 42W
Ely, U.K. 11 E8 52 24N 0 16 E
Ely, Minn., U.S.A. 80 B9 47 55N 91 51W
Ely, Nev., U.S.A. 82 G6 39 15N 114 54W
Elyria, U.S.A. 78 E2 41 22N 82 7W
Emāmrūd, Iran 45 B7 36 30N 55 0 E
Emba, Kazakstan 26 E6 48 50N 58 8 E
Emba →, Kazakstan 25 E9 46 55N 53 28 E
Embarcación, Argentina 94 A3 23 10S 64 0W
Embarras Portage, Canada 73 B6 58 27N 111 28W
Embetsu, Japan 30 B10 44 44N 141 47 E
Embi = Emba, Kazakstan 26 E6 48 50N 58 8 E
Embi = Emba →, Kazakstan 25 E9 46 55N 53 28 E
Embóna, Greece 23 C9 36 13N 27 51 E
Embrun, France 18 D7 44 34N 6 30 E
Embu, Kenya 54 C4 0 32S 37 38 E
Emden, Germany 16 B4 53 21N 7 12 E
Emerald, Australia 62 C4 23 32S 148 10 E
Emerson, Canada 73 D9 49 0N 97 10W
Emet, Turkey 21 E13 39 20N 29 15 E
Emi Koussi, Chad 51 E9 19 45N 18 55 E
Eminabad, Pakistan 42 C6 32 2N 74 8 E
Emine, Nos, Bulgaria 21 C12 42 40N 27 56 E
Emissi, Tarso, Chad 51 D9 21 27N 18 36 E
Emlenton, U.S.A. 78 E5 41 11N 79 43W
Emmaus, S. Africa 56 D4 29 2S 25 15 E
Emmaus, U.S.A. 79 F9 40 32N 75 30W
Emmeloord, Neths. 15 B5 52 44N 5 46 E
Emmen, Neths. 15 B6 52 48N 6 57 E
Emmet, Australia 62 C3 24 45S 144 30 E
Emmetsburg, U.S.A. 80 D7 43 7N 94 41W
Emmett, Idaho, U.S.A. 82 E5 43 52N 116 30W
Emmett, Mich., U.S.A. 78 D2 42 59N 82 46W
Emmonak, U.S.A. 68 B3 62 46N 164 30W
Emo, Canada 73 D10 48 38N 93 50W
Empalme, Mexico 86 B2 28 1N 110 49W
Empangeni, S. Africa 57 D5 28 50S 31 52 E
Empedrado, Argentina 94 B4 28 0S 58 46W
Emperor Seamount Chain, Pac. Oc. 64 D9 40 0N 170 0 E
Emporia, Kans., U.S.A. 80 F6 38 25N 96 11W
Emporia, Va., U.S.A. 77 G7 36 42N 77 32W
Emporium, U.S.A. 78 E6 41 31N 78 14W
Empress, Canada 73 C7 50 57N 110 0W
Empty Quarter = Rub' al Khālī, Si. Arabia 46 D4 19 0N 48 0 E
Ems →, Germany 16 B4 53 20N 7 12 E
Emsdale, Canada 78 A5 45 32N 79 19W
Emu, China 35 C15 43 40N 128 6 E
Emu Park, Australia 62 C5 23 13S 150 50 E
'En 'Avrona, Israel 47 F4 29 43N 35 0 E
En Nahud, Sudan 51 F11 12 45N 28 25 E
Ena, Japan 31 G8 35 25N 137 25 E
Enana, Namibia 56 B2 17 30S 16 23 E
Enard B., U.K. 12 C3 58 5N 5 20W
Enare = Inarijärvi, Finland 8 B22 69 0N 28 0 E
Enarotali, Indonesia 37 E9 3 55S 136 21 E
Encampment, U.S.A. 82 F10 41 12N 106 47W
Encantadas, Serra, Brazil 95 C5 30 40S 53 0W
Encarnación, Paraguay 95 B4 27 15S 55 50W
Encarnación de Diaz, Mexico 86 C4 21 30N 102 13W
Encinitas, U.S.A. 85 M9 33 3N 117 17W
Encino, U.S.A. 83 J11 34 39N 105 28W
Encounter B., Australia 63 F2 35 45S 138 45 E
Endako, Canada 72 C3 54 6N 125 2W
Ende, Indonesia 37 F6 8 45S 121 40 E
Endeavour Str., Australia 62 A3 10 45S 142 0 E
Enderbury I., Kiribati 64 H10 3 8S 171 5W
Enderby, Canada 72 C5 50 35N 119 10W
Enderby I., Australia 60 D2 20 35S 116 30 E
Enderby Land, Antarctica 5 C5 66 0S 53 0 E
Enderlin, U.S.A. 80 B6 46 38N 97 36W
Endicott, U.S.A. 79 D8 42 6N 76 4W
Endwell, U.S.A. 79 D8 42 6N 76 2W
Endyalgout I., Australia 60 B5 11 40S 132 35 E
Eneabba, Australia 61 E2 29 49S 115 16 E
Enewetak Atoll, Marshall Is. 64 F8 11 30N 162 15 E
Enez, Turkey 21 D12 40 45N 26 5 E

F

Fort Yukon, U.S.A. **68 B5** 66 34N 145 16W
Fortaleza, Brazil **93 D11** 3 45S 38 35W
Forteau, Canada **71 B8** 51 28N 56 58W
Fortescue →, Australia **60 D2** 21 0S 116 4 E
Forth →, U.K. **12 E5** 56 9N 3 50W
Forth, Firth of, U.K. **12 E6** 56 5N 2 55W
Fortrose, U.K. **12 D4** 57 35N 4 9W
Fortuna, Calif., U.S.A. **82 F1** 40 36N 124 9W
Fortuna, N. Dak., U.S.A. **80 A3** 48 55N 103 47W
Fortune, Canada **71 C8** 47 4N 55 50W
Fortune B., Canada **71 C8** 47 30N 55 22W
Forūr, Iran **45 E7** 26 17N 54 32 E
Foshan, China **33 D6** 23 4N 113 5 E
Fosna, Norway **8 E14** 63 50N 10 20 E
Fosnavåg, Norway **9 E11** 62 22N 5 38 E
Fossano, Italy **18 D7** 44 33N 7 43 E
Fossil, U.S.A. **82 D3** 45 0N 120 9W
Foster, Canada **79 A12** 45 17N 72 30W
Foster →, Canada **73 B7** 55 47N 105 49W
Fosters Ra., Australia **62 C1** 21 35S 133 48 E
Fostoria, U.S.A. **76 E4** 41 10N 83 25W
Fotadrevo, Madag. **57 C8** 24 3S 45 1 E
Fougères, France **18 B3** 48 21N 1 14W
Foul Pt., Sri Lanka **40 Q12** 8 35N 81 18 E
Foula, U.K. **12 A6** 60 10N 2 5W
Foulness I., U.K. **11 F8** 51 36N 0 55 E
Foulpointe, Madag. **57 B8** 17 41S 49 31 E
Foulweather, C., U.S.A. **74 B2** 44 50N 124 5W
Foumban, Cameroon **52 C2** 5 45N 10 50 E
Fountain, U.S.A. **80 F2** 38 41N 104 42W
Fountain Springs, U.S.A. **85 K8** 35 54N 118 51W
Fouriesburg, S. Africa **56 D4** 28 38S 28 14 E
Foúrnoi, Greece **21 F12** 37 36N 26 32 E
Fourth Cataract, Sudan **51 E12** 18 47N 32 3 E
Fouta Djalon, Guinea **50 F3** 11 20N 12 10W
Foux, Cap-à-, Haiti **89 C5** 19 43N 73 27W
Foveaux Str., N.Z. **59 M2** 46 42S 168 10 E
Fowey, U.K. **11 G3** 50 20N 4 39W
Fowler, Calif., U.S.A. **84 J7** 36 38N 119 41W
Fowler, Colo., U.S.A. **80 F3** 38 8N 104 2W
Fowlers B., Australia **61 F5** 31 59S 132 34 E
Fowman, Iran **45 B6** 37 13N 49 19 E
Fox →, Canada **73 B10** 56 3N 93 18W
Fox Creek, Canada **72 C5** 54 24N 116 48W
Fox Lake, Canada **72 B6** 58 28N 114 31W
Fox Valley, Canada **73 C7** 50 30N 109 25W
Foxboro, U.S.A. **79 D13** 42 4N 71 16W
Foxe Basin, Canada **69 B12** 66 0N 77 0W
Foxe Chan., Canada **69 B11** 65 0N 80 0W
Foxe Pen., Canada **69 B12** 65 0N 76 0W
Foxton, N.Z. **59 J5** 40 29S 175 18 E
Foyle, Lough, U.K. **13 A4** 55 7N 7 4W
Foynes, Ireland **13 D2** 52 37N 9 7W
Foz do Cunene, Angola **56 B1** 17 15S 11 48 E
Foz do Iguaçu, Brazil **95 B5** 25 30S 54 30W
Frackville, U.S.A. **79 F8** 40 47N 76 14W
Fraile Muerto, Uruguay **95 C5** 32 31S 54 32W
Framingham, U.S.A. **79 D13** 42 17N 71 25W
Franca, Brazil **93 H9** 20 33S 47 30W
Francavilla Fontana, Italy **21 D7** 40 32N 17 35 E
France ■, Europe **18 C5** 47 0N 3 0 E
Frances, Australia **63 F3** 36 41S 140 55 E
Frances →, Canada **72 A3** 60 16N 129 10W
Frances L., Canada **72 A3** 61 23N 129 30W
Franceville, Gabon **52 E2** 1 40S 13 32 E
Franche-Comté, France **18 C6** 46 50N 5 55 E
Francis Case, L., U.S.A. **80 D5** 43 4N 98 34W
Francisco Beltrão, Brazil **95 B5** 26 5S 53 4W
Francisco I. Madero, Coahuila, Mexico **86 B4** 25 48N 103 18W
Francisco I. Madero, Durango, Mexico **86 C4** 24 32N 104 22W
Francistown, Botswana **57 C4** 21 7S 27 33 E
François, Canada **71 C8** 47 35N 56 45W
François L., Canada **72 C3** 54 0N 125 30W
Franeker, Neths. **15 A5** 53 12N 5 33 E
Frankford, Canada **78 B7** 44 12N 77 36W
Frankfort, S. Africa **57 D4** 27 17S 28 30 E
Frankfort, Ind., U.S.A. **76 E2** 40 17N 86 31W
Frankfort, Kans., U.S.A. **80 F6** 39 42N 96 25W
Frankfort, Ky., U.S.A. **76 F3** 38 12N 84 52W
Frankfort, N.Y., U.S.A. **79 C9** 43 2N 75 4W
Frankfurt, Brandenburg, Germany **16 B8** 52 20N 14 32 E
Frankfurt, Hessen, Germany **16 C5** 50 7N 8 41 E
Fränkische Alb, Germany **16 D6** 49 10N 11 23 E
Frankland →, Australia **61 G2** 35 0S 116 48 E
Franklin, Ky., U.S.A. **77 G2** 36 43N 86 35W
Franklin, La., U.S.A. **81 L9** 29 48N 91 30W
Franklin, Mass., U.S.A. **79 D13** 42 5N 71 24W
Franklin, N.H., U.S.A. **79 C13** 43 27N 71 39W
Franklin, Nebr., U.S.A. **80 E5** 40 6N 98 57W
Franklin, Pa., U.S.A. **78 E5** 41 24N 79 50W
Franklin, Va., U.S.A. **77 G7** 36 41N 76 56W
Franklin, W. Va., U.S.A. **76 F6** 38 39N 79 20W
Franklin B., Canada **68 B7** 69 45N 126 0W
Franklin D. Roosevelt L., U.S.A. **82 B4** 48 18N 118 9W
Franklin I., Antarctica **5 D11** 76 10S 168 30 E
Franklin L., U.S.A. **82 F6** 40 25N 115 22W
Franklin Mts., Canada **68 B7** 65 0N 125 0W
Franklin Str., Canada **68 A10** 72 0N 96 0W
Franklinton, U.S.A. **81 K9** 30 51N 90 9W
Franklinville, U.S.A. **78 D6** 42 20N 78 27W
Franks Pk., U.S.A. **82 E9** 43 58N 109 18W
Frankston, Australia **63 F4** 38 8S 145 8 E
Fransfontein, Namibia **56 C2** 20 12S 15 1 E
Frantsa Iosifa, Zemlya, Russia **26 A6** 82 0N 55 0 E
Franz, Canada **70 C3** 48 25N 84 30W
Franz Josef Land = Frantsa Iosifa, Zemlya, Russia **26 A6** 82 0N 55 0 E
Fraser, U.S.A. **78 D2** 42 32N 82 57W
Fraser →, B.C., Canada **72 D4** 49 7N 123 11W
Fraser →, Nfld., Canada **71 A7** 56 39N 62 10W
Fraser, Mt., Australia **61 E2** 25 35S 118 20 E
Fraser I., Australia **63 D5** 25 15S 153 10 E
Fraser Lake, Canada **72 C4** 54 0N 124 50W
Fraserburg, S. Africa **56 E3** 31 55S 21 30 E
Fraserburgh, U.K. **12 D6** 57 42N 2 1W
Fraserdale, Canada **70 C3** 49 55N 81 37W
Fray Bentos, Uruguay **94 C4** 33 10S 58 15W
Fredericia, Denmark **9 J13** 55 34N 9 45 E
Frederick, Md., U.S.A. **76 F7** 39 25N 77 25W
Frederick, Okla., U.S.A. **81 H5** 34 23N 99 1W
Frederick, S. Dak., U.S.A. **80 C5** 45 50N 98 31W
Fredericksburg, Pa., U.S.A. **79 F8** 40 27N 76 26W
Fredericksburg, Tex., U.S.A. **81 K5** 30 16N 98 52W
Fredericksburg, Va., U.S.A. **76 F7** 38 18N 77 28W
Fredericktown, Mo., U.S.A. **81 G9** 37 34N 90 18W
Fredericktown, Ohio, U.S.A. **78 F2** 40 29N 82 33W
Frederico I. Madero, Presa, Mexico **86 B3** 28 7N 105 40W
Frederico Westphalen, Brazil **95 B5** 27 22S 53 24W
Fredericton, Canada **71 C6** 45 57N 66 40W
Fredericton Junction, Canada **71 C6** 45 41N 66 40W
Frederikshåb = Paamiut, Greenland **4 C5** 62 0N 49 43W
Frederikshavn, Denmark **9 H14** 57 28N 10 31 E
Frederiksted, U.S. Virgin Is. **89 C7** 17 43N 64 53W
Fredonia, Ariz., U.S.A. **83 H7** 36 57N 112 32W
Fredonia, Kans., U.S.A. **81 G7** 37 32N 95 49W
Fredonia, N.Y., U.S.A. **78 D5** 42 26N 79 20W
Fredrikstad, Norway **9 G14** 59 13N 10 57 E
Free State □, S. Africa **56 D4** 28 30S 27 0 E
Freehold, U.S.A. **79 F10** 40 16N 74 17W
Freel Peak, U.S.A. **84 G7** 38 52N 119 54W
Freeland, U.S.A. **79 E9** 41 1N 75 54W
Freels, C., Canada **71 C9** 49 15N 53 30W
Freeman, Calif., U.S.A. **85 K9** 35 35N 117 53W
Freeman, S. Dak., U.S.A. **80 D6** 43 21N 97 26W
Freeport, Bahamas **88 A4** 26 30N 78 47W
Freeport, Ill., U.S.A. **80 D10** 42 17N 89 36W
Freeport, N.Y., U.S.A. **79 F11** 40 39N 73 35W
Freeport, Ohio, U.S.A. **78 F3** 40 12N 81 15W
Freeport, Pa., U.S.A. **78 F5** 40 41N 79 41W
Freeport, Tex., U.S.A. **81 L7** 28 57N 95 21W
Freetown, S. Leone **50 G3** 8 30N 13 17W
Frégate, L., Canada **70 B5** 53 15N 74 45W
Fregenal de la Sierra, Spain **19 C2** 38 10N 6 39W
Freibourg = Fribourg, Switz. **18 C7** 46 49N 7 9 E
Freiburg, Germany **16 E4** 47 59N 7 51 E
Freire, Chile **96 D2** 38 54S 72 38W
Freirina, Chile **94 B1** 28 30S 71 10W
Freising, Germany **16 D6** 48 24N 11 45 E
Freistadt, Austria **16 D8** 48 30N 14 30 E
Fréjus, France **18 E7** 43 25N 6 44 E
Fremantle, Australia **61 F2** 32 7S 115 47 E
Fremont, Calif., U.S.A. **84 H4** 37 32N 121 57W
Fremont, Mich., U.S.A. **76 D3** 43 28N 85 57W
Fremont, Nebr., U.S.A. **80 E6** 41 26N 96 30W
Fremont, Ohio, U.S.A. **76 E4** 41 21N 83 7W
Fremont →, U.S.A. **83 G8** 38 24N 110 42W
French Camp, U.S.A. **84 H5** 37 53N 121 16W
French Creek →, U.S.A. **78 E5** 41 24N 79 50W
French Guiana ■, S. Amer. **93 C8** 4 0N 53 0W
French Polynesia ■, Pac. Oc. **65 K13** 20 0S 145 0W
Frenchman Cr. →, N. Amer. **82 B10** 48 31N 107 10W
Frenchman Cr. →, U.S.A. **80 E4** 40 14N 100 50W
Fresco →, Brazil **93 E8** 7 15S 51 30W
Freshfield, C., Antarctica **5 C10** 68 25S 151 10 E
Fresnillo, Mexico **86 C4** 23 10N 103 0W
Fresno, U.S.A. **84 J7** 36 44N 119 47W
Fresno Reservoir, U.S.A. **82 B9** 48 36N 109 57W
Frew →, Australia **62 C2** 20 0S 135 38 E
Frewsburg, U.S.A. **78 D5** 42 3N 79 10W
Freycinet Pen., Australia **62 G4** 42 10S 148 25 E
Fria, C., Namibia **56 B1** 18 0S 12 0 E
Friant, U.S.A. **84 J7** 36 59N 119 43W
Frías, Argentina **94 B2** 28 40S 65 5W
Fribourg, Switz. **18 C7** 46 49N 7 9 E
Friday Harbor, U.S.A. **84 B3** 48 32N 123 1W
Friedens, U.S.A. **78 F6** 40 3N 78 59W
Friedrichshafen, Germany **16 E5** 47 39N 9 30 E
Friendly Is. = Tonga ■, Pac. Oc. **59 D11** 19 50S 174 30W
Friendship, U.S.A. **78 D6** 42 12N 78 8W
Friesland □, Neths. **15 A5** 53 5N 5 50 E
Frio →, U.S.A. **81 L5** 28 26N 98 11W
Frio, C., Brazil **90 F6** 22 50S 41 50W
Friona, U.S.A. **81 H3** 34 38N 102 43W
Fritch, U.S.A. **81 H4** 35 38N 101 36W
Frobisher B., Canada **69 B13** 62 30N 66 0W
Frobisher Bay = Iqaluit, Canada **69 B13** 63 44N 68 31W
Frobisher L., Canada **73 B7** 56 20N 108 15W
Frohavet, Norway **8 E13** 64 0N 9 30 E
Frome, U.K. **11 F5** 51 14N 2 19W
Frome →, U.K. **11 G5** 50 41N 2 6W
Frome, L., Australia **63 E2** 30 45S 139 45 E
Front Range, U.S.A. **74 C5** 40 25N 105 45W
Front Royal, U.S.A. **76 F6** 38 55N 78 12W
Frontera, Canary Is. **22 G2** 27 47N 17 59W
Frontera, Mexico **87 D6** 18 30N 92 40W
Fronteras, Mexico **86 A3** 30 56N 109 31W
Frosinone, Italy **20 D5** 41 38N 13 19 E
Frostburg, U.S.A. **76 F6** 39 39N 78 56W
Frostisen, Norway **8 B17** 68 14N 17 10 E
Frøya, Norway **8 E13** 63 43N 8 40 E
Frunze = Bishkek, Kyrgyzstan **26 E8** 42 54N 74 46 E
Frutal, Brazil **93 H9** 20 0S 49 0W
Frýdek-Místek, Czech Rep. **17 D10** 49 40N 18 20 E
Fryeburg, U.S.A. **79 B14** 44 1N 70 59W
Fu Xian = Wafangdian, China **35 E11** 39 38N 121 58 E
Fu Xian, China **34 G5** 36 0N 109 20 E
Fucheng, China **34 F9** 37 50N 116 10 E
Fuchou = Fuzhou, China **33 D6** 26 5N 119 16 E
Fuchū, Japan **31 G6** 34 34N 133 14 E
Fuencaliente, Canary Is. **22 F2** 28 28N 17 50W
Fuencaliente, Pta., Canary Is. **22 F2** 28 27N 17 51W
Fuengirola, Spain **19 D3** 36 32N 4 41W
Fuentes de Oñoro, Spain **19 B2** 40 33N 6 52W
Fuerte →, Mexico **86 B3** 25 50N 109 25W
Fuerte Olimpo, Paraguay **94 A4** 21 0S 57 51W
Fuerteventura, Canary Is. **22 F6** 28 30N 14 0W
Fufeng, China **34 G5** 34 22N 108 0 E
Fugou, China **34 G8** 34 3N 114 25 E
Fugu, China **34 E6** 39 2N 111 3 E
Fuhai, China **32 B3** 47 2N 87 25 E
Fuḩaymī, Iraq **44 C4** 34 16N 42 10 E
Fuji, Japan **31 G9** 35 9N 138 39 E
Fuji-San, Japan **31 G9** 35 22N 138 44 E
Fuji-Yoshida, Japan **31 G9** 35 30N 138 46 E
Fujian □, China **33 D6** 26 0N 118 0 E
Fujinomiya, Japan **31 G9** 35 10N 138 40 E
Fujisawa, Japan **31 G9** 35 22N 139 29 E
Fujiyama, Mt. = Fuji-San, Japan **31 G9** 35 22N 138 44 E
Fukien = Fujian □, China **33 D6** 26 0N 118 0 E
Fukuchiyama, Japan **31 G7** 35 19N 135 9 E
Fukue-Shima, Japan **31 H4** 32 40N 128 45 E
Fukui, Japan **31 F8** 36 5N 136 10 E
Fukui □, Japan **31 F8** 36 0N 136 12 E
Fukuoka, Japan **31 H5** 33 39N 130 21 E
Fukuoka □, Japan **31 H5** 33 30N 131 0 E
Fukushima, Japan **30 F10** 37 44N 140 28 E
Fukushima □, Japan **30 F10** 37 30N 140 15 E
Fukuyama, Japan **31 G6** 34 35N 133 20 E
Fulda, Germany **16 C5** 50 32N 9 40 E
Fulda →, Germany **16 C5** 51 25N 9 39 E
Fulford Harbour, Canada **84 B3** 48 47N 123 27W
Fullerton, Calif., U.S.A. **85 M9** 33 53N 117 56W
Fullerton, Nebr., U.S.A. **80 E6** 41 22N 97 58W
Fulongquan, China **35 B13** 44 20N 124 42 E
Fulton, Mo., U.S.A. **80 F9** 38 52N 91 57W
Fulton, N.Y., U.S.A. **79 C8** 43 19N 76 25W
Funabashi, Japan **31 G10** 35 45N 140 0 E
Funafuti = Fongafale, Tuvalu **64 H9** 8 31S 179 13 E
Funchal, Madeira **22 D3** 32 38N 16 54W
Fundación, Colombia **92 A4** 10 31N 74 11W
Fundão, Portugal **19 B2** 40 8N 7 30W
Fundy, B. of, Canada **71 D6** 45 0N 66 0W
Funhalouro, Mozam. **57 C5** 23 3S 34 25 E
Funing, Hebei, China **35 E10** 39 53N 119 12 E
Funing, Jiangsu, China **35 H10** 33 45N 119 50 E
Funiu Shan, China **34 H7** 33 30N 112 20 E
Funtua, Nigeria **50 F7** 11 30N 7 18 E
Fuping, Hebei, China **34 E8** 38 48N 114 12 E
Fuping, Shaanxi, China **34 G5** 34 42N 109 10 E
Furano, Japan **30 C11** 43 21N 142 23 E
Furāt, Nahr al →, Asia **44 D5** 31 0N 47 25 E
Fūrg, Iran **45 D7** 28 18N 55 13 E
Furnás, Spain **22 B8** 39 3N 1 32 E
Furnas, Reprêsa de, Brazil **95 A6** 20 50S 45 30W
Furneaux Group, Australia **62 G4** 40 10S 147 50 E
Furqlus, Syria **47 A6** 34 36N 37 8 E
Fürstenwalde, Germany **16 B8** 52 22N 14 3 E
Fürth, Germany **16 D6** 49 28N 10 59 E
Furukawa, Japan **30 E10** 38 34N 140 58 E
Fury and Hecla Str., Canada **69 B11** 69 56N 84 0W
Fusagasuga, Colombia **92 C4** 4 21N 74 22W
Fushan, Shandong, China **35 F11** 37 30N 121 15 E
Fushan, Shanxi, China **34 G6** 35 58N 111 51 E
Fushun, China **35 D12** 41 50N 123 56 E
Fusong, China **35 C14** 42 20N 127 15 E
Futuna, Wall. & F. Is. **59 B8** 14 25S 178 20W
Fuxin, China **35 C11** 42 5N 121 48 E
Fuyang, China **34 H8** 33 0N 115 48 E
Fuyang He →, China **34 E9** 38 12N 117 0 E
Fuyu, China **35 B13** 45 12N 124 43 E
Fuzhou, China **33 D6** 26 5N 119 16 E
Fylde, U.K. **10 D5** 53 50N 2 58W
Fyn, Denmark **9 J14** 55 20N 10 30 E
Fyne, L., U.K. **12 F3** 55 59N 5 23W

G

Gabela, Angola **52 G2** 11 0S 14 24 E
Gabès, Tunisia **51 B8** 33 53N 10 2 E
Gabès, G. de, Tunisia **51 B8** 34 0N 10 30 E
Gabon ■, Africa **52 E2** 0 10S 10 0 E
Gaborone, Botswana **56 C4** 24 45S 25 57 E
Gabriels, U.S.A. **79 B10** 44 26N 74 12W
Gābrīk, Iran **45 E8** 25 44N 58 28 E
Gabrovo, Bulgaria **21 C11** 42 52N 25 19 E
Gāch Sār, Iran **45 B6** 36 7N 51 19 E
Gachsārān, Iran **45 D6** 30 15N 50 45 E
Gadag, India **40 M9** 15 30N 75 45 E
Gadap, Pakistan **42 G2** 25 5N 67 28 E
Gadarwara, India **43 H8** 22 50N 78 50 E
Gadhada, India **42 J4** 22 0N 71 35 E
Gadra, Pakistan **42 G4** 25 40N 70 38 E
Gadsden, U.S.A. **77 H3** 34 1N 86 1W
Gadwal, India **40 L10** 16 10N 77 50 E
Gaffney, U.S.A. **77 H5** 35 5N 81 39W
Gafsa, Tunisia **50 B7** 34 24N 8 43 E
Gagaria, India **42 G4** 25 43N 70 46 E
Gagnoa, Ivory C. **50 G4** 6 56N 5 16W
Gagnon, Canada **71 B6** 51 50N 68 5W
Gagnon, L., Canada **73 A6** 62 3N 110 27W
Gahini, Rwanda **54 C3** 1 50S 30 30 E
Gahmar, India **43 G10** 25 27N 83 49 E
Gai Xian = Gaizhou, China **35 D12** 40 22N 122 20 E
Gaïdhouronisi, Greece **23 E7** 34 53N 25 41 E
Gail, U.S.A. **81 J4** 32 46N 101 27W
Gaillimh = Galway, Ireland **13 C2** 53 17N 9 3W
Gaines, U.S.A. **78 E7** 41 46N 77 35W
Gainesville, Fla., U.S.A. **77 L4** 29 40N 82 20W
Gainesville, Ga., U.S.A. **77 H4** 34 18N 83 50W
Gainesville, Mo., U.S.A. **81 G8** 36 36N 92 26W
Gainesville, Tex., U.S.A. **81 J6** 33 38N 97 8W
Gainsborough, U.K. **10 D7** 53 24N 0 46W
Gairdner, L., Australia **63 E2** 31 30S 136 0 E
Gairloch, L., U.K. **12 D3** 57 43N 5 45W
Gaizhou, China **35 D12** 40 22N 122 20 E
Gaj →, Pakistan **42 F2** 26 26N 67 21 E
Gakuch, Pakistan **43 A5** 36 7N 73 45 E
Galán, Cerro, Argentina **94 B2** 25 55S 66 52W
Galana →, Kenya **54 C5** 3 9S 40 8 E
Galápagos, Pac. Oc. **90 D1** 0 0 91 0W
Galashiels, U.K. **12 F6** 55 37N 2 49W
Galaţi, Romania **17 F15** 45 27N 28 2 E
Galatina, Italy **21 D8** 40 10N 18 10 E
Galax, U.S.A. **77 G5** 36 40N 80 56W
Galcaio, Somali Rep. **46 F4** 6 30N 47 30 E
Galdhøpiggen, Norway **9 F12** 61 38N 8 18 E
Galeana, Chihuahua, Mexico **86 A3** 30 7N 107 38W
Galeana, Nuevo León, Mexico **86 A3** 24 50N 100 4W
Galela, Indonesia **37 D7** 1 50N 127 49 E
Galena, U.S.A. **68 B4** 64 44N 156 56W
Galera Pt., Trin. & Tob. **89 D7** 10 49N 60 54W
Galesburg, U.S.A. **80 E9** 40 57N 90 22W
Galeton, U.S.A. **78 E7** 41 44N 77 39W
Galich, Russia **24 C7** 58 22N 42 24 E
Galicia □, Spain **19 A2** 42 43N 7 45W
Galilee = Hagalil, Israel **47 C4** 32 53N 35 18 E
Galilee, L., Australia **62 C4** 22 20S 145 50 E
Galilee, Sea of = Yam Kinneret, Israel **47 C4** 32 45N 35 35 E
Galinoporni, Cyprus **23 D13** 35 31N 34 18 E
Galion, U.S.A. **78 F2** 40 44N 82 47W
Galiuro Mts., U.S.A. **83 K8** 32 30N 110 20W
Galiwinku, Australia **62 A2** 12 2S 135 34 E
Gallan Hd., U.K. **12 C1** 58 15N 7 2W
Gallatin, U.S.A. **77 G2** 36 24N 86 27W
Galle, Sri Lanka **40 R12** 6 5N 80 10 E
Gállego →, Spain **19 B5** 41 39N 0 51W
Gallegos →, Argentina **96 G3** 51 35S 69 0W
Galley Hd., Ireland **13 E3** 51 32N 8 55W
Gallinas, Pta., Colombia **92 A4** 12 28N 71 40W
Gallipoli = Gelibolu, Turkey **21 D12** 40 28N 26 43 E
Gallipoli, Italy **21 D8** 40 3N 17 58 E
Gallipolis, U.S.A. **76 F4** 38 49N 82 12W
Gällivare, Sweden **8 C19** 67 9N 20 40 E
Galloo I., U.S.A. **79 C8** 43 55N 76 25W
Galloway, U.K. **12 F4** 55 1N 4 29W
Galloway, Mull of, U.K. **12 G4** 54 39N 4 52W
Gallup, U.S.A. **83 J9** 35 32N 108 45W
Galoya, Sri Lanka **40 Q12** 8 10N 80 55 E
Galt, U.S.A. **84 G5** 38 15N 121 18W
Galty Mts., Ireland **13 D3** 52 22N 8 10W
Galtymore, Ireland **13 D3** 52 21N 8 11W
Galva, U.S.A. **80 E9** 41 10N 90 3W
Galveston, U.S.A. **81 L7** 29 18N 94 48W
Galveston B., U.S.A. **81 L7** 29 36N 94 50W
Gálvez, Argentina **94 C3** 32 0S 61 14W
Galway, Ireland **13 C2** 53 17N 9 3W
Galway □, Ireland **13 C2** 53 22N 9 1W
Galway B., Ireland **13 C2** 53 13N 9 10W
Gam →, Vietnam **38 B5** 21 55N 105 12 E
Gamagōri, Japan **31 G8** 34 50N 137 14 E
Gambat, Pakistan **42 F3** 27 17N 68 26 E
Gambhir →, India **42 F6** 26 58N 77 27 E
Gambia ■, W. Afr. **50 F2** 13 25N 16 0W
Gambia →, W. Afr. **50 F2** 13 28N 16 34W
Gambier, U.S.A. **78 F2** 40 22N 82 23W
Gambier, C., Australia **60 B5** 11 56S 130 57 E
Gambier Is., Australia **63 F2** 35 3S 136 30 E
Gambo, Canada **71 C9** 48 47N 54 13W
Gamboli, Pakistan **42 E3** 29 53N 68 24 E
Gamboma, Congo **52 E3** 1 55S 15 52 E
Gamka →, S. Africa **56 E3** 33 18S 21 39 E
Gamkab →, Namibia **56 D2** 28 4S 17 54 E
Gamlakarleby = Kokkola, Finland **8 E20** 63 50N 23 8 E
Gammon →, Canada **73 C9** 51 24N 95 44W
Gamtoos →, S. Africa **56 E4** 33 58S 25 1 E
Gan Jiang →, China **33 D6** 29 15N 116 0 E
Ganado, U.S.A. **83 J9** 35 43N 109 33W
Gananoque, Canada **79 B8** 44 20N 76 10W
Ganāveh, Iran **45 D6** 29 35N 50 35 E
Gäncä, Azerbaijan **25 F8** 40 45N 46 20 E
Gancheng, China **38 C7** 18 51N 108 37 E
Gand = Gent, Belgium **15 C3** 51 2N 3 42 E
Ganda, Angola **53 G2** 13 3S 14 35 E
Gandajika, Dem. Rep. of the Congo **52 F4** 6 45S 23 57 E
Gandak →, India **43 G11** 25 39N 85 13 E
Gandava, Pakistan **42 E2** 28 32N 67 32 E
Gander, Canada **71 C9** 48 58N 54 35W
Gander L., Canada **71 C9** 48 58N 54 35W
Ganderowe Falls, Zimbabwe **55 F2** 17 20S 29 10 E
Gandhi Sagar, India **42 G6** 24 40N 75 40 E
Gandhinagar, India **42 H5** 23 15N 72 45 E
Gandía, Spain **19 C5** 38 58N 0 9W
Gando, Pta., Canary Is. **22 G4** 27 55N 15 22W
Ganedidalem = Gani, Indonesia **37 E7** 0 48S 128 14 E
Ganga →, India **43 H14** 23 20N 90 30 E
Ganga Sagar, India **43 J13** 21 38N 88 5 E
Gangan →, India **43 E8** 28 38N 78 58 E
Ganganagar, India **42 E5** 29 56N 73 56 E
Gangapur, India **42 F7** 26 32N 76 49 E
Gangaw, Burma **41 H19** 22 5N 94 5 E
Gangdisê Shan, China **41 D12** 31 20N 81 0 E
Ganges = Ganga →, India **43 H14** 23 20N 90 30 E
Ganges, Canada **72 D4** 48 51N 123 31W
Ganges, Mouths of the, India **43 J14** 21 30N 90 0 E
Gangoh, India **42 E7** 29 46N 77 18 E
Gangroti, India **43 D8** 30 50N 79 10 E
Gangtok, India **41 F16** 27 20N 88 37 E
Gangu, China **34 G3** 34 40N 105 15 E
Gangyao, China **35 B14** 44 12N 126 37 E
Gani, Indonesia **37 E7** 0 48S 128 14 E
Ganj, India **43 F8** 27 45N 78 57 E
Gannett Peak, U.S.A. **82 E9** 43 11N 109 39W
Ganquan, China **34 F5** 36 20N 109 20 E
Gansu □, China **34 G3** 36 0N 104 0 E
Ganta, Liberia **50 G4** 7 15N 8 59W
Gantheaume, C., Australia **63 F2** 36 4S 137 32 E
Gantheaume B., Australia **61 E1** 27 40S 114 10 E
Gantsevichi = Hantsavichy, Belarus **17 B14** 52 49N 26 30 E
Ganyem = Genyem, Indonesia **37 E10** 2 46S 140 12 E
Ganyu, China **35 G10** 34 50N 119 8 E
Ganzhou, China **33 D6** 25 51N 114 56 E
Gao, Mali **50 E5** 16 15N 0 5W
Gaomi, China **35 F10** 36 20N 119 42 E
Gaoping, China **34 G7** 35 45N 112 55 E
Gaotang, China **34 F9** 36 50N 116 15 E
Gaoua, Burkina Faso **50 F5** 10 20N 3 8W
Gaoual, Guinea **50 F3** 11 45N 13 25W
Gaoxiong = Kaohsiung, Taiwan **33 D7** 22 35N 120 16 E
Gaoyang, China **34 E8** 38 40N 115 45 E
Gaoyou Hu, China **35 H10** 32 45N 119 20 E
Gaoyuan, China **35 F9** 37 8N 117 58 E
Gap, France **18 D7** 44 33N 6 5 E
Gapat →, India **43 G10** 24 30N 82 28 E
Gapuwiyak, Australia **62 A2** 12 25S 135 43 E
Gar, China **32 C2** 32 10N 79 58 E
Garabogazköl Aylagy, Turkmenistan **25 F9** 41 0N 53 30 E
Garachico, Canary Is. **22 F3** 28 22N 16 46W
Garachiné, Panama **88 E4** 8 0N 78 12W
Garafia, Canary Is. **22 F2** 28 48N 17 57W
Garah, Australia **63 D4** 29 5S 149 38 E
Garajonay, Canary Is. **22 F2** 28 7N 17 14W
Garanhuns, Brazil **93 E11** 8 50S 36 30W
Garautha, India **43 G8** 25 34N 79 18 E
Garba Tula, Kenya **54 B4** 0 30N 38 32 E
Garberville, U.S.A. **82 F2** 40 6N 123 48W
Garbiyang, India **43 D9** 30 8N 80 54 E
Garda, L. di, Italy **20 B4** 45 40N 10 41 E
Garde L., Canada **73 A7** 62 50N 106 13W
Garden City, Ga., U.S.A. **77 J5** 32 6N 81 9W
Garden City, Kans., U.S.A. **81 G4** 37 58N 100 53W
Garden City, Tex., U.S.A. **81 K4** 31 52N 101 29W

Name	Map	Lat	Long
Garden Grove, *U.S.A.*	**85 M9**	33 47N	117 55W
Gardêz, *Afghan.*	**42 C3**	33 37N	69 9 E
Gardiner, *Maine, U.S.A.*	**77 C11**	44 14N	69 47W
Gardiner, *Mont., U.S.A.*	**82 D8**	45 2N	110 22W
Gardiners I., *U.S.A.*	**79 E12**	41 6N	72 6W
Gardner, *U.S.A.*	**79 D13**	42 34N	71 59W
Gardner Canal, *Canada*	**72 C3**	53 27N	128 8W
Gardnerville, *U.S.A.*	**84 G7**	38 56N	119 45W
Gardo, *Somali Rep.*	**46 F4**	9 30N	49 6 E
Garey, *U.S.A.*	**85 L6**	34 53N	120 19W
Garfield, *U.S.A.*	**82 C5**	47 1N	117 9W
Garforth, *U.K.*	**10 D6**	53 47N	1 24W
Gargano, Mte., *Italy*	**20 D6**	41 43N	15 43 E
Garibaldi Prov. Park, *Canada*	**72 D4**	49 50N	122 40W
Gariep, L., *S. Africa*	**56 E4**	30 40S	25 40 E
Garies, *S. Africa*	**56 E2**	30 32S	17 59 E
Garigliano →, *Italy*	**20 D5**	41 13N	13 45 E
Garissa, *Kenya*	**54 C4**	0 25S	39 40 E
Garland, *Tex., U.S.A.*	**81 J6**	32 55N	96 38W
Garland, *Utah, U.S.A.*	**82 F7**	41 47N	112 10W
Garm, *Tajikistan*	**26 F8**	39 0N	70 20 E
Garmāb, *Iran*	**45 C8**	35 25N	56 45 E
Garmisch-Partenkirchen, *Germany*	**16 E6**	47 30N	11 6 E
Garmo, Qullai = Kommunizma, Pik, *Tajikistan*	**26 F8**	39 0N	72 2 E
Garmsār, *Iran*	**45 C7**	35 20N	52 25 E
Garner, *U.S.A.*	**80 D8**	43 6N	93 36W
Garnett, *U.S.A.*	**80 F7**	38 17N	95 14W
Garo Hills, *India*	**43 G14**	25 30N	90 30 E
Garoe, *Somali Rep.*	**46 F4**	8 25N	48 33 E
Garonne →, *France*	**18 D3**	45 2N	0 36W
Garoowe = Garoe, *Somali Rep.*	**46 F4**	8 25N	48 33 E
Garot, *India*	**42 G6**	24 19N	75 41 E
Garoua, *Cameroon*	**51 G8**	9 19N	13 21 E
Garrauli, *India*	**43 G8**	25 5N	79 22 E
Garrison, *Mont., U.S.A.*	**82 C7**	46 31N	112 49W
Garrison, *N. Dak., U.S.A.*	**80 B4**	47 40N	101 25W
Garrison Res. = Sakakawea, L., *U.S.A.*	**80 B4**	47 30N	101 25W
Garron Pt., *U.K.*	**13 A6**	55 3N	5 59W
Garry →, *U.K.*	**12 E5**	56 44N	3 47W
Garry, L., *Canada*	**68 B9**	65 58N	100 18W
Garsen, *Kenya*	**54 C5**	2 20S	40 5 E
Garson L., *Canada*	**73 B6**	56 19N	110 2W
Garu, *India*	**43 H11**	23 40N	84 14 E
Garub, *Namibia*	**56 D2**	26 37S	16 0 E
Garut, *Indonesia*	**37 G12**	7 14S	107 53 E
Garvie Mts., *N.Z.*	**59 L2**	45 30S	168 50 E
Garwa = Garoua, *Cameroon*	**51 G8**	9 19N	13 21 E
Garwa, *India*	**43 G10**	24 11N	83 47 E
Gary, *U.S.A.*	**76 E2**	41 36N	87 20W
Garzê, *China*	**32 C5**	31 38N	100 1 E
Garzón, *Colombia*	**92 C3**	2 10N	75 40W
Gas-San, *Japan*	**30 E10**	38 32N	140 1 E
Gasan Kuli = Esenguly, *Turkmenistan*	**26 F6**	37 37N	53 59 E
Gascogne, *France*	**18 E4**	43 45N	0 20 E
Gascogne, G. de, *Europe*	**18 D2**	44 0N	2 0W
Gascony = Gascogne, *France*	**18 E4**	43 45N	0 20 E
Gascoyne →, *Australia*	**61 D1**	24 52S	113 37 E
Gascoyne Junction, *Australia*	**61 E2**	25 2S	115 17 E
Gashaka, *Nigeria*	**51 G8**	7 20N	11 29 E
Gasherbrum, *Pakistan*	**43 B7**	35 40N	76 40 E
Gashua, *Nigeria*	**51 F8**	12 54N	11 0 E
Gaspé, *Canada*	**71 C7**	48 52N	64 30W
Gaspé, C. de, *Canada*	**71 C7**	48 48N	64 7W
Gaspé, Pén. de, *Canada*	**71 C6**	48 45N	65 40W
Gaspésie, Parc de Conservation de la, *Canada*	**71 C6**	48 55N	65 50W
Gasteiz = Vitoria-Gasteiz, *Spain*	**19 A4**	42 50N	2 41W
Gastonia, *U.S.A.*	**77 H5**	35 16N	81 11W
Gastre, *Argentina*	**96 E3**	42 20S	69 15W
Gata, C., *Cyprus*	**23 E12**	34 34N	33 2 E
Gata, C. de, *Spain*	**19 D4**	36 41N	2 13W
Gata, Sierra de, *Spain*	**19 B2**	40 20N	6 45W
Gataga →, *Canada*	**72 B3**	58 35N	126 59W
Gatehouse of Fleet, *U.K.*	**12 G4**	54 53N	4 12W
Gates, *U.S.A.*	**78 C7**	43 9N	77 42W
Gateshead, *U.K.*	**10 C6**	54 57N	1 35W
Gatesville, *U.S.A.*	**81 K6**	31 26N	97 45W
Gaths, *Zimbabwe*	**55 G3**	20 2S	30 32 E
Gatico, *Chile*	**94 A1**	22 29S	70 20W
Gatineau, *Canada*	**79 A9**	45 29N	75 38W
Gatineau →, *Canada*	**70 C4**	45 27N	75 42W
Gatineau, Parc Nat. de la, *Canada*	**70 C4**	45 40N	76 0W
Gatton, *Australia*	**63 D5**	27 32S	152 17 E
Gatun, L., *Panama*	**88 E4**	9 7N	79 56W
Gatyana, *S. Africa*	**57 E4**	32 16S	28 31 E
Gau, *Fiji*	**59 D8**	18 2S	179 18 E
Gauer L., *Canada*	**73 B9**	57 0N	97 50W
Gauhati = Guwahati, *India*	**41 F17**	26 10N	91 45 E
Gauja →, *Latvia*	**9 H21**	57 10N	24 16 E
Gaula →, *Norway*	**8 E14**	63 21N	10 14 E
Gauri Phanta, *India*	**43 E9**	28 41N	80 36 E
Gausta, *Norway*	**9 G13**	59 48N	8 40 E
Gauteng □, *S. Africa*	**57 D4**	26 0S	28 0 E
Gāv Koshī, *Iran*	**45 D8**	28 38N	57 12 E
Gāvakān, *Iran*	**45 D7**	29 37N	53 10 E
Gavāter, *Iran*	**45 E9**	25 10N	61 31 E
Gāvbandī, *Iran*	**45 E7**	27 12N	53 4 E
Gavdhopoúla, *Greece*	**23 E6**	34 56N	24 0 E
Gávdhos, *Greece*	**23 E6**	34 50N	24 5 E
Gaviota, *U.S.A.*	**85 L6**	34 29N	120 13W
Gāvkhūnī, Bāţlāq-e, *Iran*	**45 C7**	32 6N	52 52 E
Gävle, *Sweden*	**9 F17**	60 40N	17 9 E
Gawachab, *Namibia*	**56 D2**	27 4S	17 55 E
Gawilgarh Hills, *India*	**40 J10**	21 15N	76 45 E
Gawler, *Australia*	**63 E2**	34 30S	138 42 E
Gaxun Nur, *China*	**32 B5**	42 22N	100 30 E
Gay, *Russia*	**24 D10**	51 27N	58 27 E
Gaya, *India*	**43 G11**	24 47N	85 4 E
Gaya, *Niger*	**50 F6**	11 52N	3 28 E
Gaylord, *U.S.A.*	**76 C3**	45 2N	84 41W
Gayndah, *Australia*	**63 D5**	25 35S	151 32 E
Gaysin = Haysyn, *Ukraine*	**17 D15**	48 57N	29 25 E
Gayvoron = Hayvoron, *Ukraine*	**17 D15**	48 22N	29 52 E
Gaza, *Gaza Strip*	**47 D3**	31 30N	34 28 E
Gaza □, *Mozam.*	**57 C5**	23 10S	32 45 E
Gaza Strip □, *Asia*	**47 D3**	31 29N	34 25 E
Gazanjyk, *Turkmenistan*	**45 B7**	39 16N	55 32 E
Gāzbor, *Iran*	**45 D8**	28 5N	58 51 E
Gazi, *Dem. Rep. of the Congo*	**54 B1**	1 3N	24 30 E
Gaziantep, *Turkey*	**25 G6**	37 6N	37 23 E
Gcoverega, *Botswana*	**56 B3**	19 8S	24 18 E
Gcuwa, *S. Africa*	**57 E4**	32 20S	28 11 E
Gdańsk, *Poland*	**17 A10**	54 22N	18 40 E
Gdańska, Zatoka, *Poland*	**17 A10**	54 30N	19 20 E
Gdov, *Russia*	**9 G22**	58 48N	27 55 E
Gdynia, *Poland*	**17 A10**	54 35N	18 33 E
Gebe, *Indonesia*	**37 D7**	0 5N	129 25 E
Gebze, *Turkey*	**21 D13**	40 47N	29 25 E
Gedaref, *Sudan*	**51 F13**	14 2N	35 28 E
Gediz →, *Turkey*	**21 E12**	38 35N	26 48 E
Gedser, *Denmark*	**9 J14**	54 35N	11 55 E
Geegully Cr. →, *Australia*	**60 C3**	18 32S	123 41 E
Geel, *Belgium*	**15 C4**	51 10N	4 59 E
Geelong, *Australia*	**63 F3**	38 10S	144 22 E
Geelvink B. = Cenderwasih, Teluk, *Indonesia*	**37 E9**	3 0S	135 20 E
Geelvink Chan., *Australia*	**61 E1**	28 30S	114 0 E
Geesthacht, *Germany*	**16 B6**	53 26N	10 22 E
Geidam, *Nigeria*	**51 F8**	12 57N	11 57 E
Geikie →, *Canada*	**73 B8**	57 45N	103 52W
Geistown, *U.S.A.*	**78 F6**	40 18N	78 52W
Geita, *Tanzania*	**54 C3**	2 48S	32 12 E
Gejiu, *China*	**32 D5**	23 20N	103 10 E
Gel, Meydān-e, *Iran*	**45 D7**	29 4N	54 50 E
Gela, *Italy*	**20 F6**	37 4N	14 15 E
Gelderland □, *Neths.*	**15 B6**	52 5N	6 10 E
Geldrop, *Neths.*	**15 C5**	51 25N	5 32 E
Geleen, *Neths.*	**15 D5**	50 57N	5 49 E
Gelibolu, *Turkey*	**21 D12**	40 28N	26 43 E
Gelsenkirchen, *Germany*	**16 C4**	51 32N	7 6 E
Gemas, *Malaysia*	**39 L4**	2 37N	102 36 E
Gembloux, *Belgium*	**15 D4**	50 34N	4 43 E
Gemena, *Dem. Rep. of the Congo*	**52 D3**	3 13N	19 48 E
Gemerek, *Turkey*	**44 B3**	39 15N	36 10 E
Gemlik, *Turkey*	**21 D13**	40 26N	29 9 E
Genale →, *Ethiopia*	**46 F2**	6 2N	39 1 E
General Acha, *Argentina*	**94 D3**	37 20S	64 38W
General Alvear, *Buenos Aires, Argentina*	**94 D4**	36 0S	60 0W
General Alvear, *Mendoza, Argentina*	**94 D2**	35 0S	67 40W
General Artigas, *Paraguay*	**94 B4**	26 52S	56 16W
General Belgrano, *Argentina*	**94 D4**	36 35S	58 47W
General Cabrera, *Argentina*	**94 C3**	32 53S	63 52W
General Cepeda, *Mexico*	**86 B4**	25 23N	101 27W
General Guido, *Argentina*	**94 D4**	36 40S	57 50W
General Juan Madariaga, *Argentina*	**94 D4**	37 0S	57 0W
General La Madrid, *Argentina*	**94 D3**	37 17S	61 20W
General MacArthur, *Phil.*	**37 B7**	11 18N	125 28 E
General Martin Miguel de Güemes, *Argentina*	**94 A3**	24 50S	65 0W
General Paz, *Argentina*	**94 B4**	27 45S	57 36W
General Pico, *Argentina*	**94 D3**	35 45S	63 50W
General Pinedo, *Argentina*	**94 B3**	27 15S	61 20W
General Pinto, *Argentina*	**94 C3**	34 45S	61 50W
General Roca, *Argentina*	**96 D3**	39 2S	67 35W
General Santos, *Phil.*	**37 C7**	6 5N	125 14 E
General Trevino, *Mexico*	**87 B5**	26 14N	99 29W
General Trías, *Mexico*	**86 B3**	28 21N	106 22W
General Viamonte, *Argentina*	**94 D3**	35 1S	61 3W
General Villegas, *Argentina*	**94 D3**	35 5S	63 0W
Genesee, *Idaho, U.S.A.*	**82 C5**	46 33N	116 56W
Genesee, *Pa., U.S.A.*	**78 E7**	41 59N	77 54W
Genesee →, *U.S.A.*	**78 C7**	43 16N	77 36W
Geneseo, *Ill., U.S.A.*	**80 E9**	41 27N	90 9W
Geneseo, *N.Y., U.S.A.*	**78 D7**	42 48N	77 49W
Geneva = Genève, *Switz.*	**18 C7**	46 12N	6 9 E
Geneva, *Ala., U.S.A.*	**77 K3**	31 2N	85 52W
Geneva, *N.Y., U.S.A.*	**78 D8**	42 52N	76 59W
Geneva, *Nebr., U.S.A.*	**80 E6**	40 32N	97 36W
Geneva, *Ohio, U.S.A.*	**78 E4**	41 48N	80 57W
Geneva, L. = Léman, L., *Europe*	**18 C7**	46 26N	6 30 E
Geneva, L., *U.S.A.*	**76 D1**	42 38N	88 30W
Genève, *Switz.*	**18 C7**	46 12N	6 9 E
Genil →, *Spain*	**19 D3**	37 42N	5 19W
Genk, *Belgium*	**15 D5**	50 58N	5 32 E
Gennargentu, Mti. del, *Italy*	**20 D3**	40 1N	9 19 E
Genoa = Génova, *Italy*	**18 D8**	44 25N	8 57 E
Genoa, *Australia*	**63 F4**	37 29S	149 35 E
Genoa, *N.Y., U.S.A.*	**79 D8**	42 40N	76 32W
Genoa, *Nebr., U.S.A.*	**80 E6**	41 27N	97 44W
Genoa, *Nev., U.S.A.*	**84 F7**	39 2N	119 50W
Génova, *Italy*	**18 D8**	44 25N	8 57 E
Génova, G. di, *Italy*	**20 C3**	44 0N	9 0 E
Genriyetty, Ostrov, *Russia*	**27 B16**	77 6N	156 30 E
Gent, *Belgium*	**15 C3**	51 2N	3 42 E
Genteng, *Indonesia*	**37 G12**	7 22S	106 24 E
Genyem, *Indonesia*	**37 E10**	2 46S	140 12 E
Geographe B., *Australia*	**61 F2**	33 30S	115 15 E
Geographe Chan., *Australia*	**61 D1**	24 30S	113 0 E
George, Zemlya, *Russia*	**26 A5**	80 30N	49 0 E
George, *S. Africa*	**56 E3**	33 58S	22 29 E
George →, *Canada*	**71 A6**	58 49N	66 10W
George, L., *N.S.W., Australia*	**63 F4**	35 10S	149 25 E
George, L., *S. Austral., Australia*	**63 F3**	37 25S	140 0 E
George, L., *W. Austral., Australia*	**60 D3**	22 45S	123 40 E
George, L., *Uganda*	**54 B3**	0 5N	30 10 E
George, L., *Fla., U.S.A.*	**77 L5**	29 17N	81 36W
George, L., *N.Y., U.S.A.*	**79 C11**	43 37N	73 33W
George Gill Ra., *Australia*	**60 D5**	24 22S	131 45 E
George River = Kangiqsualujjuaq, *Canada*	**69 C13**	58 30N	65 59W
George Sound, *N.Z.*	**59 L1**	44 52S	167 25 E
George Town, *Australia*	**62 G4**	41 6S	146 49 E
George Town, *Bahamas*	**88 B4**	23 33N	75 47W
George Town, *Cayman Is.*	**88 C3**	19 20N	81 24W
George Town, *Malaysia*	**39 K3**	5 25N	100 20 E
George V Land, *Antarctica*	**5 C10**	69 0S	148 0 E
George VI Sound, *Antarctica*	**5 D17**	71 0S	68 0W
George West, *U.S.A.*	**81 L5**	28 20N	98 7W
Georgetown, *Australia*	**62 B3**	18 17S	143 33 E
Georgetown, *Ont., Canada*	**78 C5**	43 40N	79 56W
Georgetown, *P.E.I., Canada*	**71 C7**	46 13N	62 24W
Georgetown, *Gambia*	**50 F3**	13 30N	14 47W
Georgetown, *Guyana*	**92 B7**	6 50N	58 12W
Georgetown, *Calif., U.S.A.*	**84 G6**	38 54N	120 50W
Georgetown, *Colo., U.S.A.*	**82 G11**	39 42N	105 42W
Georgetown, *Ky., U.S.A.*	**76 F3**	38 13N	84 33W
Georgetown, *N.Y., U.S.A.*	**79 D9**	42 46N	75 44W
Georgetown, *Ohio, U.S.A.*	**76 F4**	38 52N	83 54W
Georgetown, *S.C., U.S.A.*	**77 J6**	33 23N	79 17W
Georgetown, *Tex., U.S.A.*	**81 K6**	30 38N	97 41W
Georgia □, *U.S.A.*	**77 K5**	32 50N	83 15W
Georgia ■, *Asia*	**25 F7**	42 0N	43 0 E
Georgia, Str. of, *Canada*	**72 D4**	49 25N	124 0W
Georgian B., *Canada*	**78 A4**	45 15N	81 0W
Georgina →, *Australia*	**62 C2**	23 30S	139 47 E
Georgina I., *Canada*	**78 B5**	44 22N	79 17W
Georgiu-Dezh = Liski, *Russia*	**25 D6**	51 3N	39 30 E
Georgiyevsk, *Russia*	**25 F7**	44 12N	43 28 E
Gera, *Germany*	**16 C7**	50 53N	12 4 E
Geraardsbergen, *Belgium*	**15 D3**	50 45N	3 53 E
Geral, Serra, *Brazil*	**95 B6**	26 25S	50 0W
Geral de Goiás, Serra, *Brazil*	**93 F9**	12 0S	46 0W
Geraldine, *U.S.A.*	**82 C8**	47 36N	110 16W
Geraldton, *Australia*	**61 E1**	28 48S	114 32 E
Geraldton, *Canada*	**70 C2**	49 44N	86 59W
Gereshk, *Afghan.*	**40 D4**	31 47N	64 35 E
Gerik, *Malaysia*	**39 K3**	5 50N	101 15 E
Gering, *U.S.A.*	**80 E3**	41 50N	103 40W
Gerlach, *U.S.A.*	**82 F4**	40 39N	119 21W
Germansen Landing, *Canada*	**72 B4**	55 43N	124 40W
Germantown, *U.S.A.*	**81 M10**	35 5N	89 49W
Germany ■, *Europe*	**16 C6**	51 0N	10 0 E
Germī, *Iran*	**45 B6**	39 1N	48 3 E
Germiston, *S. Africa*	**57 D4**	26 15S	28 10 E
Gernika-Lumo, *Spain*	**19 A4**	43 19N	2 40W
Gero, *Japan*	**31 G8**	35 48N	137 14 E
Gerona = Girona, *Spain*	**19 B7**	41 58N	2 46 E
Gerrard, *Canada*	**72 C5**	50 30N	117 17W
Geser, *Indonesia*	**37 E8**	3 50S	130 54 E
Getafe, *Spain*	**19 B4**	40 18N	3 44W
Gettysburg, *Pa., U.S.A.*	**76 F7**	39 50N	77 14W
Gettysburg, *S. Dak., U.S.A.*	**80 C5**	45 1N	99 57W
Getxo, *Spain*	**19 A4**	43 21N	2 59W
Getz Ice Shelf, *Antarctica*	**5 D14**	75 0S	130 0W
Geyser, *U.S.A.*	**82 C8**	47 16N	110 30W
Geyserville, *U.S.A.*	**84 G4**	38 42N	122 54W
Ghaggar →, *India*	**42 E6**	29 30N	74 53 E
Ghaghara →, *India*	**43 G11**	25 45N	84 40 E
Ghaghat →, *Bangla.*	**43 G13**	25 19N	89 38 E
Ghagra, *India*	**43 H11**	23 17N	84 33 E
Ghagra →, *India*	**43 F9**	27 29N	81 9 E
Ghana ■, *W. Afr.*	**50 G5**	8 0N	1 0W
Ghansor, *India*	**43 H9**	22 39N	80 1 E
Ghanzi, *Botswana*	**56 C3**	21 50S	21 34 E
Ghardaïa, *Algeria*	**50 B6**	32 20N	3 37 E
Gharyān, *Libya*	**51 B8**	32 10N	13 0 E
Ghat, *Libya*	**51 D8**	24 59N	10 11 E
Ghatal, *India*	**43 H12**	22 40N	87 46 E
Ghatampur, *India*	**43 F9**	26 8N	80 13 E
Ghatsila, *India*	**43 H12**	22 36N	86 29 E
Ghaţţī, *Si. Arabia*	**44 D3**	31 16N	37 31 E
Ghawdex = Gozo, *Malta*	**23 C1**	36 3N	14 15 E
Ghazal, Bahr el →, *Chad*	**51 F9**	13 0N	15 47 E
Ghazâl, Bahr el →, *Sudan*	**51 G12**	9 31N	30 25 E
Ghaziabad, *India*	**42 E7**	28 42N	77 26 E
Ghazipur, *India*	**43 G10**	25 38N	83 35 E
Ghaznī, *Afghan.*	**42 C3**	33 30N	68 28 E
Ghaznī □, *Afghan.*	**40 C6**	32 10N	68 20 E
Ghent = Gent, *Belgium*	**15 C3**	51 2N	3 42 E
Gheorghe Gheorghiu-Dej = Oneşti, *Romania*	**17 E14**	46 17N	26 47 E
Ghīnah, Wādī al →, *Si. Arabia*	**44 D3**	30 27N	38 14 E
Ghizao, *Afghan.*	**42 C1**	33 20N	65 44 E
Ghizar →, *Pakistan*	**43 A5**	36 15N	73 43 E
Ghotaru, *India*	**42 F4**	27 20N	70 1 E
Ghotki, *Pakistan*	**42 E3**	28 5N	69 21 E
Ghowr □, *Afghan.*	**40 C4**	34 0N	64 20 E
Ghudaf, W. al →, *Iraq*	**44 C4**	32 56N	43 30 E
Ghudāmis, *Libya*	**49 C4**	30 11N	9 29 E
Ghughri, *India*	**43 H9**	22 39N	80 41 E
Ghugus, *India*	**40 K11**	19 58N	79 12 E
Ghulam Mohammad Barrage, *Pakistan*	**42 G3**	25 30N	68 20 E
Ghūrīān, *Afghan.*	**40 B2**	34 17N	61 25 E
Gia Dinh, *Vietnam*	**39 G6**	10 49N	106 42 E
Gia Lai = Plei Ku, *Vietnam*	**38 F7**	13 57N	108 0 E
Gia Nghia, *Vietnam*	**39 G6**	11 58N	107 42 E
Gia Ngoc, *Vietnam*	**38 E7**	14 50N	108 58 E
Gia Vuc, *Vietnam*	**38 E7**	14 42N	108 34 E
Giant Forest, *U.S.A.*	**84 J8**	36 36N	118 43W
Giants Causeway, *U.K.*	**13 A5**	55 16N	6 29W
Giarabub = Al Jaghbūb, *Libya*	**51 C10**	29 42N	24 38 E
Giarre, *Italy*	**20 F6**	37 43N	15 11 E
Gibara, *Cuba*	**88 B4**	21 9N	76 11W
Gibb River, *Australia*	**60 C4**	16 26S	126 26 E
Gibbon, *U.S.A.*	**80 E5**	40 45N	98 51W
Gibeon, *Namibia*	**56 D2**	25 9S	17 43 E
Gibraltar ■, *Europe*	**19 D3**	36 7N	5 22W
Gibraltar, Str. of, *Medit. S.*	**19 E3**	35 55N	5 40W
Gibson Desert, *Australia*	**60 D4**	24 0S	126 0 E
Gibsons, *Canada*	**72 D4**	49 24N	123 32W
Gibsonville, *U.S.A.*	**84 F6**	39 46N	120 54W
Giddings, *U.S.A.*	**81 K6**	30 11N	96 56W
Giebnegáisi = Kebnekaise, *Sweden*	**8 C18**	67 53N	18 33 E
Giessen, *Germany*	**16 C5**	50 34N	8 41 E
Gīfān, *Iran*	**45 B8**	37 54N	57 28 E
Gift Lake, *Canada*	**72 B5**	55 53N	115 49W
Gifu, *Japan*	**31 G8**	35 30N	136 45 E
Gifu □, *Japan*	**31 G8**	35 40N	137 0 E
Giganta, Sa. de la, *Mexico*	**86 B2**	25 30N	111 30W
Gigha, *U.K.*	**12 F3**	55 42N	5 44W
Giglio, *Italy*	**20 C4**	42 20N	10 52 E
Gijón, *Spain*	**19 A3**	43 32N	5 42W
Gil I., *Canada*	**72 C3**	53 12N	129 15W
Gila →, *U.S.A.*	**83 K6**	32 43N	114 33W
Gila Bend, *U.S.A.*	**83 K7**	32 57N	112 43W
Gila Bend Mts., *U.S.A.*	**83 K7**	33 10N	113 0W
Gīlān □, *Iran*	**45 B6**	37 0N	50 0 E
Gilbert →, *Australia*	**62 B3**	16 35S	141 15 E
Gilbert Is., *Kiribati*	**64 G9**	1 0N	172 0 E
Gilbert River, *Australia*	**62 B3**	18 9S	142 52 E
Gilead, *U.S.A.*	**79 B14**	44 24N	70 59W
Gilford I., *Canada*	**72 C3**	50 40N	126 30W
Gilgandra, *Australia*	**63 E4**	31 43S	148 39 E
Gilgil, *Kenya*	**54 C4**	0 30S	36 20 E
Gilgit, *India*	**43 B6**	35 50N	74 15 E
Gilgit →, *Pakistan*	**43 B6**	35 44N	74 37 E
Gillam, *Canada*	**73 B10**	56 20N	94 40W
Gillen, L., *Australia*	**61 E3**	26 11S	124 38 E
Gilles, L., *Australia*	**63 E2**	32 50S	136 45 E
Gillette, *U.S.A.*	**80 C2**	44 18N	105 30W
Gilliat, *Australia*	**62 C3**	20 40S	141 28 E
Gillingham, *U.K.*	**11 F8**	51 23N	0 33 E
Gilmer, *U.S.A.*	**81 J7**	32 44N	94 57W
Gilmore, L., *Australia*	**61 F3**	32 29S	121 37 E
Gilroy, *U.S.A.*	**84 H5**	37 1N	121 34W
Gimli, *Canada*	**73 C9**	50 40N	97 0W
Gin Gin, *Australia*	**63 D5**	25 0S	151 58 E
Gingin, *Australia*	**61 F2**	31 22S	115 54 E
Gingindlovu, *S. Africa*	**57 D5**	29 2S	31 30 E
Ginir, *Ethiopia*	**46 F3**	7 6N	40 40 E
Gióna, Óros, *Greece*	**21 E10**	38 38N	22 14 E
Gir Hills, *India*	**42 J4**	21 0N	71 0 E
Girab, *India*	**42 F4**	26 2N	70 38 E
Girâfi, W. →, *Egypt*	**47 F3**	29 58N	34 39 E
Girard, *Kans., U.S.A.*	**81 G7**	37 31N	94 51W
Girard, *Ohio, U.S.A.*	**78 E4**	41 9N	80 42W
Girard, *Pa., U.S.A.*	**78 E4**	42 0N	80 19W
Girdle Ness, *U.K.*	**12 D6**	57 9N	2 3W
Giresun, *Turkey*	**25 F6**	40 55N	38 30 E
Girga, *Egypt*	**51 C12**	26 17N	31 55 E
Giri →, *India*	**42 D7**	30 28N	77 41 E
Giridih, *India*	**43 G12**	24 10N	86 21 E
Girne = Kyrenia, *Cyprus*	**23 D12**	35 20N	33 20 E
Girona, *Spain*	**19 B7**	41 58N	2 46 E
Gironde →, *France*	**18 D3**	45 32N	1 7W
Giru, *Australia*	**62 B4**	19 30S	147 5 E
Girvan, *U.K.*	**12 F4**	55 14N	4 51W
Gisborne, *N.Z.*	**59 H7**	38 39S	178 5 E
Gisenyi, *Rwanda*	**54 C2**	1 41S	29 15 E
Gislaved, *Sweden*	**9 H15**	57 19N	13 32 E
Gitega, *Burundi*	**54 C2**	3 26S	29 56 E
Giuba →, *Somali Rep.*	**46 G3**	1 30N	42 35 E
Giurgiu, *Romania*	**17 G13**	43 52N	25 57 E
Giza = El Gîza, *Egypt*	**51 C12**	30 0N	31 10 E
Gizhiga, *Russia*	**27 C17**	62 3N	160 30 E
Gizhiginskaya Guba, *Russia*	**27 C16**	61 0N	158 0 E
Giżycko, *Poland*	**17 A11**	54 2N	21 48 E
Gjirokastër, *Albania*	**21 D9**	40 7N	20 10 E
Gjoa Haven, *Canada*	**68 B10**	68 20N	96 8W
Gjøvik, *Norway*	**9 F14**	60 47N	10 43 E
Glace Bay, *Canada*	**71 C8**	46 11N	59 58W
Glacier Bay Nat. Park and Preserve, *U.S.A.*	**72 B1**	58 45N	136 30W
Glacier Nat. Park, *Canada*	**72 C5**	51 15N	117 30W
Glacier Nat. Park, *U.S.A.*	**82 B7**	48 30N	113 18W
Glacier Peak, *U.S.A.*	**82 B3**	48 7N	121 7W
Gladewater, *U.S.A.*	**81 J7**	32 33N	94 56W
Gladstone, *Queens., Australia*	**62 C5**	23 52S	151 16 E
Gladstone, *S. Austral., Australia*	**63 E2**	33 15S	138 22 E
Gladstone, *Canada*	**73 C9**	50 13N	98 57W
Gladstone, *U.S.A.*	**76 C2**	45 51N	87 1W
Gladwin, *U.S.A.*	**76 D3**	43 59N	84 29W
Glåma = Glomma →, *Norway*	**9 G14**	59 12N	10 57 E
Gláma, *Iceland*	**8 D2**	65 48N	23 0W
Glamis, *U.S.A.*	**85 N11**	32 55N	115 5W
Glasco, *Kans., U.S.A.*	**80 F6**	39 22N	97 50W
Glasco, *N.Y., U.S.A.*	**79 D11**	42 3N	73 57W
Glasgow, *U.K.*	**12 F4**	55 51N	4 15W
Glasgow, *Ky., U.S.A.*	**76 G3**	37 0N	85 55W
Glasgow, *Mont., U.S.A.*	**82 B10**	48 12N	106 38W
Glasgow, City of □, *U.K.*	**12 F4**	55 51N	4 12W
Glaslyn, *Canada*	**73 C7**	53 22N	108 21W
Glastonbury, *U.K.*	**11 F5**	51 9N	2 43W
Glastonbury, *U.S.A.*	**79 E12**	41 43N	72 37W
Glazov, *Russia*	**24 C9**	58 9N	52 40 E
Gleichen, *Canada*	**72 C6**	50 52N	113 3W
Gleiwitz = Gliwice, *Poland*	**17 C10**	50 22N	18 41 E
Glen, *U.S.A.*	**79 B13**	44 7N	71 11W
Glen Affric, *U.K.*	**12 D3**	57 17N	5 1W
Glen Canyon, *U.S.A.*	**83 H8**	37 30N	110 40W
Glen Canyon Dam, *U.S.A.*	**83 H8**	36 57N	111 29W
Glen Canyon Nat. Recr. Area, *U.S.A.*	**83 H8**	37 15N	111 0W
Glen Coe, *U.K.*	**12 E3**	56 40N	5 0W
Glen Cove, *U.S.A.*	**79 F11**	40 52N	73 38W
Glen Garry, *U.K.*	**12 D3**	57 3N	5 7W
Glen Innes, *Australia*	**63 D5**	29 44S	151 44 E
Glen Lyon, *U.S.A.*	**79 E8**	41 10N	76 5W
Glen Mor, *U.K.*	**12 D4**	57 9N	4 37W
Glen Moriston, *U.K.*	**12 D4**	57 11N	4 52W
Glen Robertson, *Canada*	**79 A10**	45 22N	74 30W
Glen Spean, *U.K.*	**12 E4**	56 53N	4 40W
Glen Ullin, *U.S.A.*	**80 B4**	46 49N	101 50W
Glencoe, *Canada*	**78 D3**	42 45N	81 43W
Glencoe, *S. Africa*	**57 D5**	28 11S	30 11 E
Glencoe, *U.S.A.*	**80 C7**	44 46N	94 9W
Glendale, *Ariz., U.S.A.*	**83 K7**	33 32N	112 11W
Glendale, *Calif., U.S.A.*	**85 L8**	34 9N	118 15W
Glendale, *Zimbabwe*	**55 F3**	17 22S	31 5 E
Glendive, *U.S.A.*	**80 B2**	47 7N	104 43W
Glendo, *U.S.A.*	**80 D2**	42 30N	105 2W
Glenelg →, *Australia*	**63 F3**	38 4S	140 59 E
Glenfield, *U.S.A.*	**79 C9**	43 43N	75 24W
Glengarriff, *Ireland*	**13 E2**	51 45N	9 34W
Glenmont, *U.S.A.*	**78 F2**	40 31N	82 6W
Glenmorgan, *Australia*	**63 D4**	27 14S	149 42 E
Glenn, *U.S.A.*	**84 F4**	39 31N	122 1W
Glennallen, *U.S.A.*	**68 B5**	62 7N	145 33W
Glennamaddy, *Ireland*	**13 C3**	53 37N	8 33W
Glenns Ferry, *U.S.A.*	**82 E6**	42 57N	115 18W
Glenore, *Australia*	**62 B3**	17 50S	141 12 E
Glenreagh, *Australia*	**63 E5**	30 2S	153 1 E
Glenrock, *U.S.A.*	**82 E11**	42 52N	105 52W
Glenrothes, *U.K.*	**12 E5**	56 12N	3 10W
Glens Falls, *U.S.A.*	**79 C11**	43 19N	73 39W
Glenside, *U.S.A.*	**79 F9**	40 6N	75 9W
Glenties, *Ireland*	**13 B3**	54 49N	8 16W
Glenville, *U.S.A.*	**76 F5**	38 56N	80 50W
Glenwood, *Canada*	**71 C9**	49 0N	54 58W
Glenwood, *Ark., U.S.A.*	**81 H8**	34 20N	93 33W
Glenwood, *Iowa, U.S.A.*	**80 E7**	41 3N	95 45W
Glenwood, *Minn., U.S.A.*	**80 C7**	45 39N	95 23W
Glenwood, *Wash., U.S.A.*	**84 D5**	46 1N	121 17W
Glenwood Springs, *U.S.A.*	**82 G10**	39 33N	107 19W
Glettinganes, *Iceland*	**8 D7**	65 30N	13 37W
Gliwice, *Poland*	**17 C10**	50 22N	18 41 E
Globe, *U.S.A.*	**83 K8**	33 24N	110 47W
Głogów, *Poland*	**16 C9**	51 37N	16 5 E
Glomma →, *Norway*	**9 G14**	59 12N	10 57 E
Glorieuses, Is., *Ind. Oc.*	**57 A8**	11 30S	47 20 E
Glossop, *U.K.*	**10 D6**	53 27N	1 56W

Gloucester, Australia 63 E5 32 0S 151 59 E
Gloucester, U.K. 11 F5 51 53N 2 15W
Gloucester, U.S.A. 79 D14 42 37N 70 40W
Gloucester I., Australia 62 C4 20 0S 148 30 E
Gloucester Point, U.S.A. 76 G7 37 15N 76 29W
Gloucestershire □, U.K. 11 F5 51 46N 2 15W
Gloversville, U.S.A. 79 C10 43 3N 74 21W
Glovertown, Canada 71 C9 48 40N 54 3W
Glusk, Belarus 17 B15 52 53N 28 41 E
Gmünd, Austria 16 D8 48 45N 15 0 E
Gmunden, Austria 16 E7 47 55N 13 48 E
Gniezno, Poland 17 B9 52 30N 17 35 E
Gnowangerup, Australia 61 F2 33 58S 117 59 E
Go Cong, Vietnam 39 G6 10 22N 106 40 E
Gō-no-ura, Japan 31 H4 33 44N 129 40 E
Goa, India 40 M8 15 33N 73 59 E
Goa □, India 40 M8 15 33N 73 59 E
Goalen Hd., Australia 63 F5 36 33S 150 4 E
Goalpara, India 41 F17 26 10N 90 40 E
Goaltor, India 43 H12 22 43N 87 10 E
Goalundo Ghat, Bangla. 43 H13 23 50N 89 47 E
Goat Fell, U.K. 12 F3 55 38N 5 11W
Goba, Ethiopia 46 F2 7 1N 39 59 E
Goba, Mozam. 57 D5 26 15S 32 13 E
Gobabis, Namibia 56 C2 22 30S 19 0 E
Gobi, Asia 34 C6 44 0N 110 0 E
Gobō, Japan 31 H7 33 53N 135 10 E
Gochas, Namibia 56 C2 24 59S 18 55 E
Godavari →, India 41 L13 16 25N 82 18 E
Godavari Pt., India 41 L13 17 0N 82 20 E
Godbout, Canada 71 C6 49 20N 67 38W
Godda, India 43 G12 24 50N 87 13 E
Goderich, Canada 78 C3 43 45N 81 41W
Godfrey Ra., Australia 61 D2 24 0S 117 0 E
Godhavn = Qeqertarsuaq, Greenland 4 C5 69 15N 53 38W
Godhra, India 42 H5 22 49N 73 40 E
Godoy Cruz, Argentina 94 C2 32 56S 68 52W
Gods →, Canada 70 A1 56 22N 92 51W
Gods L., Canada 70 B1 54 40N 94 15W
Gods River, Canada 73 C10 54 50N 94 5W
Godthåb = Nuuk, Greenland 69 B14 64 10N 51 35W
Godwin Austen = K2, Pakistan 43 B7 35 58N 76 32 E
Goeie Hoop, Kaap die = Good Hope, C. of, S. Africa 56 E2 34 24S 18 30 E
Goéland, L. au, Canada 70 C4 49 50N 76 48W
Goeree, Neths. 15 C3 51 50N 4 0 E
Goes, Neths. 15 C3 51 30N 3 55 E
Goffstown, U.S.A. 79 C13 43 1N 71 36W
Gogama, Canada 70 C3 47 35N 81 43W
Gogebic, L., U.S.A. 80 B10 46 30N 89 35W
Gogra = Ghaghara →, India 43 G11 25 45N 84 40 E
Gogriāl, Sudan 51 G11 8 30N 28 8 E
Gohana, India 42 E7 29 8N 76 42 E
Goharganj, India 42 H7 23 1N 77 41 E
Goi →, India 42 H6 22 4N 74 46 E
Goiânia, Brazil 93 G9 16 43S 49 20W
Goiás, Brazil 93 G8 15 55S 50 10W
Goiás □, Brazil 93 F9 12 10S 48 0W
Goio-Erê, Brazil 95 A5 24 12S 53 1W
Gojō, Japan 31 G7 34 21N 135 42 E
Gojra, Pakistan 42 D5 31 10N 72 40 E
Gökçeada, Turkey 21 D11 40 10N 25 50 E
Gökova Körfezi, Turkey 21 F12 36 55N 27 50 E
Gokteik, Burma 41 H20 22 26N 97 0 E
Gokurt, Pakistan 42 E2 29 40N 67 26 E
Gokwe, Zimbabwe 57 B4 18 7S 28 58 E
Gola, India 43 E9 28 3N 80 32 E
Golakganj, India 43 F13 26 8N 89 52 E
Golan Heights = Hagolan, Syria 47 C4 33 0N 35 45 E
Golāshkerd, Iran 45 E8 27 59N 57 16 E
Golchikha, Russia 4 B12 71 45N 83 30 E
Golconda, U.S.A. 82 F5 40 58N 117 30W
Gold, U.S.A. 78 E7 41 52N 77 50W
Gold Beach, U.S.A. 82 E1 42 25N 124 25W
Gold Coast, W. Afr. 50 H5 4 0N 1 40W
Gold Hill, U.S.A. 82 E2 42 26N 123 3W
Gold River, Canada 72 D3 49 46N 126 3W
Golden, Canada 72 C5 51 20N 116 59W
Golden B., N.Z. 59 J4 40 40S 172 50 E
Golden Gate, U.S.A. 82 H2 37 54N 122 30W
Golden Hinde, Canada 72 D3 49 40N 125 44W
Golden Lake, Canada 78 A7 45 34N 77 21W
Golden Vale, Ireland 13 D3 52 33N 8 17W
Goldendale, U.S.A. 82 D3 45 49N 120 50W
Goldfield, U.S.A. 83 H5 37 42N 117 14W
Goldsand L., Canada 73 B8 57 2N 101 8W
Goldsboro, U.S.A. 77 H7 35 23N 77 59W
Goldsmith, U.S.A. 81 K3 31 59N 102 37W
Goldsworthy, Australia 60 D2 20 21S 119 30 E
Goldthwaite, U.S.A. 81 K5 31 27N 98 34W
Goleniów, Poland 16 B8 53 35N 14 50 E
Golestānak, Iran 45 D7 30 36N 54 14 E
Goleta, U.S.A. 85 L7 34 27N 119 50W
Golfito, Costa Rica 88 E3 8 41N 83 5W
Golfo Aranci, Italy 20 D3 40 59N 9 38 E
Goliad, U.S.A. 81 L6 28 40N 97 23W
Golpāyegān, Iran 45 C6 33 27N 50 18 E
Golra, Pakistan 42 C5 33 37N 72 56 E
Golspie, U.K. 12 D5 57 58N 3 59W
Goma, Dem. Rep. of the Congo 54 C2 1 37S 29 10 E
Gomal Pass, Pakistan 42 D3 31 56N 69 20 E
Gomati →, India 43 G10 25 32N 83 11 E
Gombari, Dem. Rep. of the Congo 54 B2 2 45N 29 3 E
Gombe, Nigeria 51 F8 10 19N 11 2 E
Gombe →, Tanzania 54 C3 4 38S 31 40 E
Gomel = Homyel, Belarus 17 B16 52 28N 31 0 E
Gomera, Canary Is. 22 F2 28 7N 17 14W
Gómez Palacio, Mexico 86 B4 25 40N 104 0W
Gomīshān, Iran 45 B7 37 4N 54 6 E
Gomogomo, Indonesia 37 F8 6 39S 134 43 E
Gomoh, India 41 H15 23 52N 86 10 E
Gompa = Ganta, Liberia 50 G4 7 15N 8 59W
Gonābād, Iran 45 C8 34 15N 58 45 E
Gonaïves, Haiti 89 C5 19 20N 72 42W
Gonâve, G. de la, Haiti 89 C5 19 29N 72 42W
Gonâve, I. de la, Haiti 89 C5 18 45N 73 0W
Gonbad-e Kāvūs, Iran 45 B7 37 20N 55 25 E
Gonda, India 43 F9 27 9N 81 58 E
Gondal, India 42 J4 21 58N 70 52 E
Gonder, Ethiopia 46 E2 12 39N 37 30 E
Gondia, India 40 J12 21 23N 80 10 E
Gondola, Mozam. 55 F3 19 10S 33 37 E
Gönen, Turkey 21 D12 40 6N 27 39 E
Gonghe, China 32 C5 36 18N 100 32 E
Gongolgon, Australia 63 E4 30 21S 146 54 E
Gongzhuling, China 35 C13 43 30N 124 40 E
Gonzales, Calif., U.S.A. 84 J5 36 30N 121 26W
Gonzales, Tex., U.S.A. 81 L6 29 30N 97 27W
González Chaves, Argentina 94 D3 38 2S 60 5W
Good Hope, C. of, S. Africa 56 E2 34 24S 18 30 E
Gooderham, Canada 78 B6 44 54N 78 21W
Goodhouse, S. Africa 56 D2 28 57S 18 13 E
Gooding, U.S.A. 82 E6 42 56N 114 43W
Goodland, U.S.A. 80 F4 39 21N 101 43W
Goodlow, Canada 72 B4 56 20N 120 8W
Goodooga, Australia 63 D4 29 3S 147 28 E
Goodsprings, U.S.A. 85 K11 35 49N 115 27W
Goole, U.K. 10 D7 53 42N 0 53W
Goolgowi, Australia 63 E4 33 58S 145 41 E
Goomalling, Australia 61 F2 31 15S 116 49 E
Goomeri, Australia 63 D5 26 12S 152 6 E
Goonda, Mozam. 55 F3 19 48S 33 57 E
Goondiwindi, Australia 63 D5 28 30S 150 21 E
Goongarrie, L., Australia 61 F3 30 3S 121 9 E
Goonyella, Australia 62 C4 21 47S 147 58 E
Goose →, Canada 71 B7 53 20N 60 35W
Goose Creek, U.S.A. 77 J5 32 59N 80 2W
Goose L., U.S.A. 82 F3 41 56N 120 26W
Gop, India 40 H6 22 5N 69 50 E
Gopalganj, India 43 F11 26 28N 84 30 E
Göppingen, Germany 16 D5 48 42N 9 39 E
Gorakhpur, India 43 F10 26 47N 83 23 E
Goražde, Bos.-H. 21 C8 43 38N 18 58 E
Gorda, U.S.A. 84 K5 35 53N 121 26W
Gorda, Pta., Canary Is. 22 F2 28 45N 18 0W
Gorda, Pta., Nic. 88 D3 14 20N 83 10W
Gordan B., Australia 60 B5 11 35S 130 10 E
Gordon, U.S.A. 80 D3 42 48N 102 12W
Gordon →, Australia 62 G4 42 27S 145 30 E
Gordon L., Alta., Canada 73 B6 56 30N 110 25W
Gordon L., N.W.T., Canada 72 A6 63 5N 113 11W
Gordonvale, Australia 62 B4 17 5S 145 50 E
Gore, Ethiopia 46 F2 8 12N 35 32 E
Gore, N.Z. 59 M2 46 5S 168 58 E
Gore Bay, Canada 70 C3 45 57N 82 28W
Gorey, Ireland 13 D5 52 41N 6 18W
Gorg, Iran 45 D8 29 29N 59 43 E
Gorgān, Iran 45 B7 36 50N 54 29 E
Gorgona, I., Colombia 92 C3 3 0N 78 10W
Gorham, U.S.A. 79 B13 44 23N 71 10W
Goriganga →, India 43 E9 29 45N 80 23 E
Gorinchem, Neths. 15 C4 51 50N 4 59 E
Goris, Armenia 25 G8 39 31N 46 22 E
Gorízia, Italy 20 B5 45 56N 13 37 E
Gorki = Nizhniy Novgorod, Russia 24 C7 56 20N 44 0 E
Gorkiy = Nizhniy Novgorod, Russia 24 C7 56 20N 44 0 E
Gorkovskoye Vdkhr., Russia 24 C7 57 2N 43 4 E
Görlitz, Germany 16 C8 51 9N 14 58 E
Gorlovka = Horlivka, Ukraine 25 E6 48 19N 38 5 E
Gorman, U.S.A. 85 L8 34 47N 118 51W
Gorna Dzhumayo = Blagoevgrad, Bulgaria 21 C10 42 2N 23 5 E
Gorna Oryakhovitsa, Bulgaria 21 C11 43 7N 25 40 E
Gorno-Altay □, Russia 26 D9 51 0N 86 0 E
Gorno-Altaysk, Russia 26 D9 51 50N 86 5 E
Gornyatski, Russia 24 A11 67 32N 64 3 E
Gornyy, Russia 30 B6 44 57N 133 59 E
Gorodenka = Horodenka, Ukraine 17 D13 48 41N 25 29 E
Gorodok = Horodok, Ukraine 17 D12 49 46N 23 32 E
Gorokhov = Horokhiv, Ukraine 17 C13 50 30N 24 45 E
Goromonzi, Zimbabwe 55 F3 17 52S 31 22 E
Gorong, Kepulauan, Indonesia 37 E8 3 59S 131 25 E
Gorongose →, Mozam. 57 C5 20 30S 34 40 E
Gorongoza, Mozam. 55 F3 18 44S 34 2 E
Gorongoza, Sa. da, Mozam. 55 F3 18 27S 34 2 E
Gorontalo, Indonesia 37 D6 0 35N 123 5 E
Gort, Ireland 13 C3 53 3N 8 49W
Gortis, Greece 23 D6 35 4N 24 58 E
Gorzów Wielkopolski, Poland 16 B8 52 43N 15 15 E
Gosford, Australia 63 E5 33 23S 151 18 E
Goshen, Calif., U.S.A. 84 J7 36 21N 119 25W
Goshen, Ind., U.S.A. 76 E3 41 35N 85 50W
Goshen, N.Y., U.S.A. 79 E10 41 24N 74 20W
Goshogawara, Japan 30 D10 40 48N 140 27 E
Goslar, Germany 16 C6 51 54N 10 25 E
Gospič, Croatia 16 F8 44 35N 15 23 E
Gosport, U.K. 11 G6 50 48N 1 9W
Gosse →, Australia 62 B1 19 32S 134 37 E
Göta älv →, Sweden 9 H14 57 42N 11 54 E
Göta kanal, Sweden 9 G16 58 30N 15 58 E
Götaland, Sweden 9 G15 57 30N 14 30 E
Göteborg, Sweden 9 H14 57 43N 11 59 E
Gotha, Germany 16 C6 50 56N 10 42 E
Gothenburg = Göteborg, Sweden 9 H14 57 43N 11 59 E
Gothenburg, U.S.A. 80 E4 40 56N 100 10W
Gotland, Sweden 9 H18 57 30N 18 33 E
Gotō-Rettō, Japan 31 H4 32 55N 129 5 E
Gotska Sandön, Sweden 9 G18 58 24N 19 15 E
Gōtsu, Japan 31 G6 35 0N 132 14 E
Gott Pk., Canada 72 C4 50 18N 122 16W
Göttingen, Germany 16 C5 51 31N 9 55 E
Gottwaldov = Zlín, Czech Rep. 17 D9 49 14N 17 40 E
Goubangzi, China 35 D11 41 20N 121 52 E
Gouda, Neths. 15 B4 52 1N 4 42 E
Goúdhoura, Ákra, Greece 23 E8 34 59N 26 6 E
Gough I., Atl. Oc. 2 G9 40 10S 9 45W
Gouin, Rés., Canada 70 C5 48 35N 74 40W
Goulburn, Australia 63 E4 34 44S 149 44 E
Goulburn Is., Australia 62 A1 11 40S 133 20 E
Goulimine, Morocco 50 C3 28 56N 10 0W
Gourits →, S. Africa 56 E3 34 21S 21 52 E
Goúrnais, Greece 23 D7 35 19N 25 16 E
Gouverneur, U.S.A. 79 B9 44 20N 75 28W
Gouviá, Greece 23 A3 39 39N 19 50 E
Governador Valadares, Brazil 93 G10 18 15S 41 57W
Governor's Harbour, Bahamas 88 A4 25 10N 76 14W
Govindgarh, India 43 G9 24 23N 81 18 E
Gowan Ra., Australia 62 D4 25 0S 145 0 E
Gowanda, U.S.A. 78 D6 42 28N 78 56W
Gower, U.K. 11 F3 51 35N 4 10W
Gowna, L., Ireland 13 C4 53 51N 7 34W
Goya, Argentina 94 B4 29 10S 59 10W
Goyder Lagoon, Australia 63 D2 27 3S 138 58 E
Goyllarisquisga, Peru 92 F3 10 31S 76 24W
Goz Beïda, Chad 51 F10 12 10N 21 20 E
Gozo, Malta 23 C1 36 3N 14 15 E
Graaff-Reinet, S. Africa 56 E3 32 13S 24 32 E
Gračac, Croatia 16 F8 44 18N 15 57 E
Gracias a Dios, C., Honduras 88 D3 15 0N 83 10W
Graciosa, I., Canary Is. 22 E6 29 15N 13 32W
Grado, Spain 19 A2 43 23N 6 4W
Grady, U.S.A. 81 H3 34 49N 103 19W
Grafham Water, U.K. 11 E7 52 19N 0 18W
Grafton, Australia 63 D5 29 38S 152 58 E
Grafton, N. Dak., U.S.A. 80 A6 48 25N 97 25W
Grafton, W. Va., U.S.A. 76 F5 39 21N 80 2W
Graham, Canada 70 C1 49 20N 90 30W
Graham, U.S.A. 81 J5 33 6N 98 35W
Graham, Mt., U.S.A. 83 K9 32 42N 109 52W
Graham Bell, Ostrov = Greem-Bell, Ostrov, Russia 26 A7 81 0N 62 0 E
Graham I., Canada 72 C2 53 40N 132 30W
Graham Land, Antarctica 5 C17 65 0S 64 0W
Grahamstown, S. Africa 56 E4 33 19S 26 31 E
Grahamsville, U.S.A. 79 E10 41 51N 74 33W
Grain Coast, W. Afr. 50 H3 4 20N 10 0W
Grajaú, Brazil 93 E9 5 50S 46 4W
Grajaú →, Brazil 93 D10 3 41S 44 48W
Grampian, U.S.A. 78 F6 40 58N 78 37W
Grampian Highlands = Grampian Mts., U.K. 12 E5 56 50N 4 0W
Grampian Mts., U.K. 12 E5 56 50N 4 0W
Grampians, The, Australia 63 F3 37 0S 142 20 E
Gran Canaria, Canary Is. 22 G4 27 55N 15 35W
Gran Chaco, S. Amer. 94 B3 25 0S 61 0W
Gran Paradiso, Italy 18 D7 45 33N 7 17 E
Gran Sasso d'Itália, Italy 20 C5 42 27N 13 42 E
Granada, Nic. 88 D2 11 58N 86 0W
Granada, Spain 19 D4 37 10N 3 35W
Granada, U.S.A. 81 F3 38 4N 102 19W
Granadilla de Abona, Canary Is. 22 F3 28 7N 16 33W
Granard, Ireland 13 C4 53 47N 7 30W
Granbury, U.S.A. 81 J6 32 27N 97 47W
Granby, Canada 79 A12 45 25N 72 45W
Granby, U.S.A. 82 F11 40 5N 105 56W
Grand →, Canada 78 D5 42 51N 79 34W
Grand →, Mo., U.S.A. 80 F8 39 23N 93 7W
Grand →, S. Dak., U.S.A. 80 C4 45 40N 100 45W
Grand Bahama, Bahamas 88 A4 26 40N 78 30W
Grand Bank, Canada 71 C8 47 6N 55 48W
Grand Bassam, Ivory C. 50 G5 5 10N 3 49W
Grand-Bourg, Guadeloupe 89 C7 15 53N 61 19W
Grand Canal = Yun Ho →, China 35 E9 39 10N 117 10 E
Grand Canyon, U.S.A. 83 H7 36 3N 112 9W
Grand Canyon Nat. Park, U.S.A. 83 H7 36 15N 112 30W
Grand Cayman, Cayman Is. 88 C3 19 20N 81 20W
Grand Centre, Canada 73 C6 54 25N 110 13W
Grand Coulee, U.S.A. 82 C4 47 57N 119 0W
Grand Coulee Dam, U.S.A. 82 C4 47 57N 118 59W
Grand Falls, Canada 71 C6 47 3N 67 44W
Grand Falls-Windsor, Canada 71 C8 48 56N 55 40W
Grand Forks, Canada 72 D5 49 0N 118 30W
Grand Forks, U.S.A. 80 B6 47 55N 97 3W
Grand Gorge, U.S.A. 79 D10 42 21N 74 29W
Grand Haven, U.S.A. 76 D2 43 4N 86 13W
Grand I., Mich., U.S.A. 76 B2 46 31N 86 40W
Grand I., N.Y., U.S.A. 78 D6 43 0N 78 58W
Grand Island, U.S.A. 80 E5 40 55N 98 21W
Grand Isle, La., U.S.A. 81 L9 29 14N 90 0W
Grand Isle, Vt., U.S.A. 79 B11 44 43N 73 18W
Grand Junction, U.S.A. 83 G9 39 4N 108 33W
Grand L., N.B., Canada 71 C6 45 57N 66 7W
Grand L., Nfld., Canada 71 C8 49 0N 57 30W
Grand L., Nfld., Canada 71 B7 53 40N 60 30W
Grand L., U.S.A. 81 L8 29 55N 92 47W
Grand Lake, U.S.A. 82 F11 40 15N 105 49W
Grand Manan I., Canada 71 D6 44 45N 66 52W
Grand Marais, Canada 80 B9 47 45N 90 25W
Grand Marais, U.S.A. 76 B3 46 40N 85 59W
Grand-Mère, Canada 70 C5 46 36N 72 40W
Grand Portage, U.S.A. 80 B10 47 58N 89 41W
Grand Prairie, U.S.A. 81 J6 32 47N 97 0W
Grand Rapids, Canada 73 C9 53 12N 99 19W
Grand Rapids, Mich., U.S.A. 76 D2 42 58N 85 40W
Grand Rapids, Minn., U.S.A. 80 B8 47 14N 93 31W
Grand St-Bernard, Col du, Europe 18 D7 45 50N 7 10 E
Grand Teton, U.S.A. 82 E8 43 54N 111 50W
Grand Teton Nat. Park, U.S.A. 82 D8 43 50N 110 50W
Grand Union Canal, U.K. 11 E7 52 7N 0 53W
Grand View, Canada 73 C8 51 10N 100 42W
Grande →, Jujuy, Argentina 94 A2 24 20S 65 2W
Grande →, Mendoza, Argentina 94 D2 36 52S 69 45W
Grande →, Bolivia 92 G6 15 51S 64 39W
Grande →, Bahia, Brazil 93 F10 11 30S 44 30W
Grande →, Minas Gerais, Brazil 93 H8 20 6S 51 4W
Grande, B., Argentina 96 G3 50 30S 68 20W
Grande, Rio →, U.S.A. 81 N6 25 58N 97 9W
Grande Baleine, R. de la →, Canada 70 A4 55 16N 77 47W
Grande Cache, Canada 72 C5 53 53N 119 8W
Grande-Entrée, Canada 71 C7 47 30N 61 40W
Grande Prairie, Canada 72 B5 55 10N 118 50W
Grande-Rivière, Canada 71 C7 48 26N 64 30W
Grande-Vallée, Canada 71 C6 49 14N 65 8W
Grandfalls, U.S.A. 81 K3 31 20N 102 51W
Grandview, U.S.A. 82 C4 46 15N 119 54W
Graneros, Chile 94 C1 34 5S 70 45W
Grangemouth, U.K. 12 E5 56 1N 3 42W
Granger, U.S.A. 82 F9 41 35N 109 58W
Grangeville, U.S.A. 82 D5 45 56N 116 7W
Granisle, Canada 72 C3 54 53N 126 13W
Granite City, U.S.A. 80 F9 38 42N 90 9W
Granite Falls, U.S.A. 80 C7 44 49N 95 33W
Granite L., Canada 71 C8 48 8N 57 5W
Granite Mt., U.S.A. 85 M10 33 5N 116 28W
Granite Pk., U.S.A. 82 D9 45 10N 109 48W
Graniteville, U.S.A. 79 B12 44 8N 72 29W
Granity, N.Z. 59 J3 41 39S 171 51 E
Granja, Brazil 93 D10 3 7S 40 50W
Granollers, Spain 19 B7 41 39N 2 18 E
Grant, U.S.A. 80 E4 40 53N 101 42W
Grant, Mt., U.S.A. 82 G4 38 34N 118 48W
Grant City, U.S.A. 80 E7 40 29N 94 25W
Grant I., Australia 60 B5 11 10S 132 52 E
Grant Range, U.S.A. 83 G6 38 30N 115 25W
Grantham, U.K. 10 E7 52 55N 0 38W
Grantown-on-Spey, U.K. 12 D5 57 20N 3 36W
Grants, U.S.A. 83 J10 35 9N 107 52W
Grants Pass, U.S.A. 82 E2 42 26N 123 19W
Grantsville, U.S.A. 82 F7 40 36N 112 28W
Granville, France 18 B3 48 50N 1 35W
Granville, N. Dak., U.S.A. 80 A4 48 16N 100 47W
Granville, N.Y., U.S.A. 79 C11 43 24N 73 16W
Granville, Ohio, U.S.A. 78 F2 40 4N 82 31W
Granville L., Canada 73 B8 56 18N 100 30W
Graskop, S. Africa 57 C5 24 56S 30 49 E
Grass →, Canada 73 B9 56 3N 96 33W
Grass Range, U.S.A. 82 C9 47 0N 109 0W
Grass River Prov. Park, Canada 73 C8 54 40N 100 50W
Grass Valley, Calif., U.S.A. 84 F6 39 13N 121 4W
Grass Valley, Oreg., U.S.A. 82 D3 45 22N 120 47W
Grasse, France 18 E7 43 38N 6 56 E
Grassflat, U.S.A. 78 F6 41 0N 78 6W
Grasslands Nat. Park, Canada 73 D7 49 11N 107 38W
Grassy, Australia 62 G3 40 3S 144 5 E
Graulhet, France 18 E4 43 45N 1 59 E
Gravelbourg, Canada 73 D7 49 50N 106 35W
's-Gravenhage, Neths. 15 B4 52 7N 4 17 E
Gravenhurst, Canada 78 B5 44 52N 79 20W
Gravesend, Australia 63 D5 29 35S 150 20 E
Gravesend, U.K. 11 F8 51 26N 0 22 E
Gravois, Pointe-à-, Haiti 89 C5 18 15N 73 56W
Grayling, U.S.A. 76 C3 44 40N 84 43W
Grays Harbor, U.S.A. 82 C1 46 59N 124 1W
Grays L., U.S.A. 82 E8 43 4N 111 26W
Grays River, U.S.A. 84 D3 46 21N 123 37W
Graz, Austria 16 E8 47 4N 15 27 E
Greasy L., Canada 72 A4 62 55N 122 12W
Great Abaco I., Bahamas 88 A4 26 25N 77 10W
Great Artesian Basin, Australia 62 C3 23 0S 144 0 E
Great Australian Bight, Australia 61 F5 33 30S 130 0 E
Great Bahama Bank, Bahamas 88 B4 23 15N 78 0W
Great Barrier I., N.Z. 59 G5 36 11S 175 25 E
Great Barrier Reef, Australia 62 B4 18 0S 146 50 E
Great Barrington, U.S.A. 79 D11 42 12N 73 22W
Great Basin, U.S.A. 82 G5 40 0N 117 0W
Great Basin Nat. Park, U.S.A. 82 G6 38 55N 114 14W
Great Bear →, Canada 68 B7 65 0N 124 0W
Great Bear L., Canada 68 B7 65 30N 120 0W
Great Belt = Store Bælt, Denmark 9 J14 55 20N 11 0 E
Great Bend, Kans., U.S.A. 80 F5 38 22N 98 46W
Great Bend, Pa., U.S.A. 79 E9 41 58N 75 45W
Great Blasket I., Ireland 13 D1 52 6N 10 32W
Great Britain, Europe 6 E5 54 0N 2 15W
Great Codroy, Canada 71 C8 47 51N 59 16W
Great Dividing Ra., Australia 62 C4 23 0S 146 0 E
Great Driffield = Driffield, U.K. 10 C7 54 0N 0 26W
Great Exuma I., Bahamas 88 B4 23 30N 75 50W
Great Falls, U.S.A. 82 C8 47 30N 111 17W
Great Fish = Groot Vis →, S. Africa 56 E4 33 28S 27 5 E
Great Guana Cay, Bahamas 88 B4 24 0N 76 20W
Great Inagua I., Bahamas 89 B5 21 0N 73 20W
Great Indian Desert = Thar Desert, India 42 F5 28 0N 72 0 E
Great Karoo, S. Africa 56 E3 31 55S 21 0 E
Great Lake, Australia 62 G4 41 50S 146 40 E
Great Lakes, N. Amer. 66 E11 46 0N 84 0W
Great Malvern, U.K. 11 E5 52 7N 2 18W
Great Miami →, U.S.A. 76 F3 39 20N 84 40W
Great Ormes Head, U.K. 10 D4 53 20N 3 52W
Great Ouse →, U.K. 10 E8 52 48N 0 21 E
Great Palm I., Australia 62 B4 18 45S 146 40 E
Great Plains, N. Amer. 74 A6 47 0N 105 0W
Great Ruaha →, Tanzania 54 D4 7 56S 37 52 E
Great Sacandaga Res., U.S.A. 79 C10 43 6N 74 16W
Great Saint Bernard Pass = Grand St-Bernard, Col du, Europe 18 D7 45 50N 7 10 E
Great Salt L., U.S.A. 82 F7 41 15N 112 40W
Great Salt Lake Desert, U.S.A. 82 F7 40 50N 113 30W
Great Salt Plains L., U.S.A. 81 G5 36 45N 98 8W
Great Sandy Desert, Australia 60 D3 21 0S 124 0 E
Great Sangi = Sangihe, Pulau, Indonesia 37 D7 3 35N 125 30 E
Great Skellig, Ireland 13 E1 51 47N 10 33W
Great Slave L., Canada 72 A5 61 23N 115 38W
Great Smoky Mts. Nat. Park, U.S.A. 77 H4 35 40N 83 40W
Great Snow Mt., Canada 72 B4 57 26N 124 0W
Great Stour = Stour →, U.K. 11 F9 51 18N 1 22 E
Great Victoria Desert, Australia 61 E4 29 30S 126 30 E
Great Wall, China 34 E5 38 30N 109 30 E
Great Whernside, U.K. 10 C6 54 10N 1 58W
Great Yarmouth, U.K. 11 E9 52 37N 1 44 E
Greater Antilles, W. Indies 89 C5 17 40N 74 0W
Greater London □, U.K. 11 F7 51 31N 0 6W
Greater Manchester □, U.K. 10 D5 53 30N 2 15W
Greater Sunda Is., Indonesia 36 F4 7 0S 112 0 E
Greco, C., Cyprus 23 E13 34 57N 34 5 E
Gredos, Sierra de, Spain 19 B3 40 20N 5 0W
Greece, U.S.A. 78 C7 43 13N 77 41W
Greece ■, Europe 21 E9 40 0N 23 0 E
Greeley, Colo., U.S.A. 80 E2 40 25N 104 42W
Greeley, Nebr., U.S.A. 80 E5 41 33N 98 32W
Greem-Bell, Ostrov, Russia 26 A7 81 0N 62 0 E
Green, U.S.A. 82 E2 43 9N 123 22W
Green →, Ky., U.S.A. 76 G2 37 54N 87 30W
Green →, Utah, U.S.A. 83 G9 38 11N 109 53W
Green B., U.S.A. 76 C2 45 0N 87 30W
Green Bay, U.S.A. 76 C2 44 31N 88 0W
Green C., Australia 63 F5 37 13S 150 1 E
Green Cove Springs, U.S.A. 77 L5 29 59N 81 42W
Green Lake, Canada 73 C7 54 17N 107 47W
Green Mts., U.S.A. 79 C12 43 45N 72 45W
Green River, Utah, U.S.A. 83 G8 38 59N 110 10W
Green River, Wyo., U.S.A. 82 F9 41 32N 109 28W

Green Valley, *U.S.A.* **83 L8** 31 52N 110 56W
Greenbank, *U.S.A.* **84 B4** 48 6N 122 34W
Greenbush, *Mich., U.S.A.* . . . **78 B1** 44 35N 83 19W
Greenbush, *Minn., U.S.A.* . . **80 A6** 48 42N 96 11W
Greencastle, *U.S.A.* **76 F2** 39 38N 86 52W
Greene, *U.S.A.* **79 D9** 42 20N 75 46W
Greenfield, *Calif., U.S.A.* **84 J5** 36 19N 121 15W
Greenfield, *Calif., U.S.A.* **85 K8** 35 15N 119 0W
Greenfield, *Ind., U.S.A.* **76 F3** 39 47N 85 46W
Greenfield, *Iowa, U.S.A.* **80 E7** 41 18N 94 28W
Greenfield, *Mass., U.S.A.* . . . **79 D12** 42 35N 72 36W
Greenfield, *Mo., U.S.A.* **81 G8** 37 25N 93 51W
Greenfield Park, *Canada* **79 A11** 45 29N 73 29W
Greenland ■, *N. Amer.* **4 C5** 66 0N 45 0W
Greenland Sea, *Arctic* **4 B7** 73 0N 10 0W
Greenock, *U.K.* **12 F4** 55 57N 4 46W
Greenore, *Ireland* **13 B5** 54 2N 6 8W
Greenore Pt., *Ireland* **13 D5** 52 14N 6 19W
Greenough, *Australia* . . . . . . **61 E1** 28 58S 114 43 E
Greenough →, *Australia* . . . . **61 E1** 28 51S 114 38 E
Greenough Pt., *Canada* **78 B3** 44 58N 81 26W
Greenport, *U.S.A.* **79 E12** 41 6N 72 22W
Greensboro, *Ga., U.S.A.* **77 J4** 33 35N 83 11W
Greensboro, *N.C., U.S.A.* **77 G6** 36 4N 79 48W
Greensboro, *Vt., U.S.A.* **79 B12** 44 36N 72 18W
Greensburg, *Ind., U.S.A.* . . . **76 F3** 39 20N 85 29W
Greensburg, *Kans., U.S.A.* . . **81 G5** 37 36N 99 18W
Greensburg, *Pa., U.S.A.* **78 F5** 40 18N 79 33W
Greenstone Pt., *U.K.* **12 D3** 57 55N 5 37W
Greenvale, *Australia* . . . . **62 B4** 18 59S 145 7 E
Greenville, *Ala., U.S.A.* **77 K2** 31 50N 86 38W
Greenville, *Calif., U.S.A.* **84 E6** 40 8N 120 57W
Greenville, *Maine, U.S.A.* . . . **77 C11** 45 28N 69 35W
Greenville, *Mich., U.S.A.* **76 D3** 43 11N 85 15W
Greenville, *Miss., U.S.A.* **81 J9** 33 24N 91 4W
Greenville, *Mo., U.S.A.* **81 G9** 37 8N 90 27W
Greenville, *N.C., U.S.A.* **77 H7** 35 37N 77 23W
Greenville, *N.H., U.S.A.* **79 D13** 42 46N 71 49W
Greenville, *N.Y., U.S.A.* **79 D10** 42 25N 74 1W
Greenville, *Ohio, U.S.A.* **76 E3** 40 6N 84 38W
Greenville, *Pa., U.S.A.* **78 E4** 41 24N 80 23W
Greenville, *S.C., U.S.A.* **77 H4** 34 51N 82 24W
Greenville, *Tenn., U.S.A.* . . . **77 G4** 36 13N 82 51W
Greenville, *Tex., U.S.A.* **81 J6** 33 8N 96 7W
Greenwater Lake Prov. Park,
Canada **73 C8** 52 32N 103 30W
Greenwich, *Conn., U.S.A.* . . . **79 E11** 41 2N 73 38W
Greenwich, *N.Y., U.S.A.* **79 C11** 43 5N 73 30W
Greenwich, *Ohio, U.S.A.* **78 E2** 41 2N 82 31W
Greenwich □, *U.K.* . . . . **11 F8** 51 29N 0 1 E
Greenwood, *Canada* **72 D5** 49 10N 118 40W
Greenwood, *Ark., U.S.A.* **81 H7** 35 13N 94 16W
Greenwood, *Ind., U.S.A.* **76 F2** 39 37N 86 7W
Greenwood, *Miss., U.S.A.* . . . **81 J9** 33 31N 90 11W
Greenwood, *S.C., U.S.A.* **77 H4** 34 12N 82 10W
Greenwood, Mt., *Australia* . . **60 B5** 13 48S 130 4 E
Gregory, *U.S.A.* **80 D5** 43 14N 99 20W
Gregory →, *Australia* . . . . . . **62 B2** 17 53S 139 17 E
Gregory, L., *S. Austral.,*
Australia . . . . **63 D2** 28 55S 139 0 E
Gregory, L., *W. Austral.,*
Australia . . . . **61 E2** 25 38S 119 58 E
Gregory Downs, *Australia* . . **62 B2** 18 35S 138 45 E
Gregory L., *Australia* . . . . . . **60 D4** 20 0S 127 40 E
Gregory Ra., *Queens.,*
Australia . . . . **62 B3** 19 30S 143 40 E
Gregory Ra., *W. Austral.,*
Australia . . . . **60 D3** 21 20S 121 12 E
Greifswald, *Germany* . . . . . . **16 A7** 54 5N 13 23 E
Greiz, *Germany* . . . . **16 C7** 50 39N 12 10 E
Gremikha, *Russia* . . . . **24 A6** 67 59N 39 47 E
Grenå, *Denmark* . . . . **9 H14** 56 25N 10 53 E
Grenada, *U.S.A.* **81 J10** 33 47N 89 49W
Grenada ■, *W. Indies* **89 D7** 12 10N 61 40W
Grenadier I., *U.S.A.* **79 B8** 44 3N 76 22W
Grenadines, *St. Vincent* **89 D7** 12 40N 61 20W
Grenen, *Denmark* . . . . **9 H14** 57 44N 10 40 E
Grenfell, *Australia* . . . . **63 E4** 33 52S 148 8 E
Grenfell, *Canada* **73 C8** 50 30N 102 56W
Grenoble, *France* . . . . **18 D6** 45 12N 5 42 E
Grenville, C., *Australia* . . . . . **62 A3** 12 0S 143 13 E
Grenville Chan., *Canada* **72 C3** 53 40N 129 46W
Gresham, *U.S.A.* **84 E4** 45 30N 122 26W
Gresik, *Indonesia* . . . . **37 G15** 7 13S 112 38 E
Gretna, *U.K.* **12 F5** 55 0N 3 3W
Grevenmacher, *Lux.* . . . . **15 E6** 49 41N 6 26 E
Grey →, *Canada* **71 C8** 47 34N 57 6W
Grey →, *N.Z.* . . . . **59 K3** 42 27S 171 12 E
Grey, C., *Australia* . . . . **62 A2** 13 0S 136 35 E
Grey Ra., *Australia* . . . . **63 D3** 27 0S 143 30 E
Greybull, *U.S.A.* **82 D9** 44 30N 108 3W
Greymouth, *N.Z.* . . . . **59 K3** 42 29S 171 13 E
Greystones, *Ireland* **13 C5** 53 9N 6 5W
Greytown, *N.Z.* . . . . **59 J5** 41 5S 175 29 E
Greytown, *S. Africa* . . . . **57 D5** 29 1S 30 36 E
Gribbell I., *Canada* **72 C3** 53 23N 129 0W
Gridley, *U.S.A.* **84 F5** 39 22N 121 42W
Griekwastad, *S. Africa* . . . . . **56 D3** 28 49S 23 15 E
Griffin, *U.S.A.* **77 J3** 33 15N 84 16W
Griffith, *Australia* . . . . **63 E4** 34 18S 146 2 E
Griffith, *Canada* **78 A7** 45 15N 77 10W
Griffith I., *Canada* **78 B4** 44 50N 80 55W
Grimaylov = Hrymayliv,
Ukraine . . . . **17 D14** 49 20N 26 5 E
Grimes, *U.S.A.* **84 F5** 39 4N 121 54W
Grimsay, *U.K.* **12 D1** 57 29N 7 14W
Grimsby, *Canada* **78 C5** 43 12N 79 34W
Grimsby, *U.K.* **10 D7** 53 34N 0 5W
Grimsey, *Iceland* **8 C5** 66 33N 17 58W
Grimshaw, *Canada* **72 B5** 56 10N 117 40W
Grimstad, *Norway* . . . . **9 G13** 58 20N 8 35 E
Grindstone I., *Canada* **79 B8** 44 43N 76 14W
Grinnell, *U.S.A.* **80 E8** 41 45N 92 43W
Gris-Nez, C., *France* . . . . **18 A4** 50 52N 1 35 E
Groais I., *Canada* **71 B8** 50 55N 55 35W
Groblersdal, *S. Africa* . . . . . . **57 D4** 25 15S 29 25 E
Grodno = Hrodna, *Belarus* . . **17 B12** 53 42N 23 52 E
Grodzyanka = Hrodzyanka,
Belarus . . . . **17 B15** 53 31N 28 42 E
Groesbeck, *U.S.A.* **81 K6** 30 48N 96 31W
Grójec, *Poland* . . . . **17 C11** 51 50N 20 58 E
Grong, *Norway* . . . . **8 D15** 64 25N 12 8 E
Groningen, *Neths.* . . . . **15 A6** 53 15N 6 35 E
Groningen □, *Neths.* . . . . **15 A6** 53 16N 6 40 E
Groom, *U.S.A.* **81 H4** 35 12N 101 6W
Groot →, *S. Africa* . . . . **56 E3** 33 45S 24 36 E
Groot Berg →, *S. Africa* . . . . **56 E2** 32 47S 18 8 E
Groot-Brakrivier, *S. Africa* . . . **56 E3** 34 2S 22 18 E
Groot Karasberge, *Namibia* . . **56 D2** 27 20S 18 40 E
Groot-Kei →, *S. Africa* . . . . . **57 E4** 32 41S 28 22 E
Groot Vis →, *S. Africa* . . . . . . **56 E4** 33 28S 27 5 E
Grootdrink, *S. Africa* . . . . . . **56 D3** 28 33S 21 42 E
Groote Eylandt, *Australia* . . . **62 A2** 14 0S 136 40 E
Grootfontein, *Namibia* . . . . . **56 B2** 19 31S 18 6 E
Grootlaagte →, *Africa* . . . . . **56 C3** 20 55S 21 27 E
Grootvloer →, *S. Africa* . . . . **56 E3** 30 0S 20 40 E
Gros C., *Canada* **72 A6** 61 59N 113 32W
Gros Morne Nat. Park,
Canada **71 C8** 49 40N 57 50W
Grossa, Pta., *Spain* . . . . **22 B8** 39 6N 1 36 E
Grosser Arber, *Germany* . . . . **16 D7** 49 6N 13 8 E
Grosseto, *Italy* . . . . **20 C4** 42 46N 11 8 E
Grossglockner, *Austria* . . . . . **16 E7** 47 5N 12 40 E
Groswater B., *Canada* **71 B8** 54 20N 57 40W
Groton, *Conn., U.S.A.* **79 E12** 41 21N 72 5W
Groton, *N.Y., U.S.A.* **79 D8** 42 36N 76 22W
Groton, *S. Dak., U.S.A.* **80 C5** 45 27N 98 6W
Grouard Mission, *Canada* . . . **72 B5** 55 33N 116 9W
Groundhog →, *Canada* **70 C3** 48 45N 82 58W
Grouw, *Neths.* . . . . **15 A5** 53 5N 5 51 E
Grove City, *U.S.A.* **78 E4** 41 10N 80 5W
Grove Hill, *U.S.A.* **77 K2** 31 42N 87 47W
Groveland, *U.S.A.* **84 H6** 37 50N 120 14W
Grover City, *U.S.A.* **85 K6** 35 7N 120 37W
Groves, *U.S.A.* **81 L8** 29 57N 93 54W
Groveton, *U.S.A.* **79 B13** 44 36N 71 31W
Groznyy, *Russia* . . . . **25 F8** 43 20N 45 45 E
Grudziądz, *Poland* . . . . **17 B10** 53 30N 18 47 E
Gruinard B., *U.K.* **12 D3** 57 56N 5 35W
Grundy Center, *U.S.A.* **80 D8** 42 22N 92 47W
Gruver, *U.S.A.* **81 G4** 36 16N 101 24W
Gryazi, *Russia* . . . . **24 D6** 52 30N 39 58 E
Gryazovets, *Russia* . . . . **24 C7** 58 50N 40 10 E
Gua, *India* . . . . **41 H14** 22 18N 85 20 E
Gua Musang, *Malaysia* . . . . . **39 K3** 4 53N 101 58 E
Guacanayabo, G. de, *Cuba* . . **88 B4** 20 40N 77 20W
Guachípas →, *Argentina* **94 B2** 25 40S 65 30W
Guadalajara, *Mexico* **86 C4** 20 40N 103 20W
Guadalajara, *Spain* **19 B4** 40 37N 3 12W
Guadalcanal, *Solomon Is.* . . . **64 H8** 9 32S 160 12 E
Guadales, *Argentina* **94 C2** 34 30S 67 55W
Guadalete →, *Spain* **19 D2** 36 35N 6 13W
Guadalquivir →, *Spain* **19 D2** 36 47N 6 22W
Guadalupe = Guadeloupe ■,
W. Indies **89 C7** 16 20N 61 40W
Guadalupe, *Mexico* **85 N10** 32 4N 116 32W
Guadalupe, *U.S.A.* **85 L6** 34 59N 120 33W
Guadalupe →, *Mexico* **85 N10** 32 6N 116 51W
Guadalupe →, *U.S.A.* **81 L6** 28 27N 96 47W
Guadalupe, Sierra de, *Spain* . **19 C3** 39 28N 5 30W
Guadalupe Bravos, *Mexico* . . **86 A3** 31 20N 106 10W
Guadalupe I., *Pac. Oc.* **66 G8** 29 0N 118 50W
Guadalupe Mts. Nat. Park,
U.S.A. **81 K2** 32 0N 104 30W
Guadalupe Peak, *U.S.A.* **81 K2** 31 50N 104 52W
Guadalupe y Calvo, *Mexico* . . **86 B3** 26 6N 106 58W
Guadarrama, Sierra de, *Spain* **19 B4** 41 0N 4 0W
Guadeloupe ■, *W. Indies* . . . **89 C7** 16 20N 61 40W
Guadeloupe Passage,
W. Indies **89 C7** 16 50N 62 15W
Guadiana →, *Portugal* **19 D2** 37 14N 7 22W
Guadix, *Spain* **19 D4** 37 18N 3 11W
Guafo, Boca del, *Chile* **96 E2** 43 35S 74 0W
Guainía →, *Colombia* **92 C5** 2 1N 67 7W
Guaíra, *Brazil* **95 A5** 24 5S 54 10W
Guaíra □, *Paraguay* **94 B4** 25 45S 56 30W
Guaitecas, Is., *Chile* **96 E2** 44 0S 74 30W
Guajará-Mirim, *Brazil* **92 F5** 10 50S 65 20W
Guajira, Pen. de la, *Colombia* **92 A4** 12 0N 72 0W
Gualán, *Guatemala* **88 C2** 15 8N 89 22W
Gualeguay, *Argentina* **94 C4** 33 10S 59 14W
Gualeguaychú, *Argentina* . . . **94 C4** 33 3S 59 31W
Gualequay →, *Argentina* . . . **94 C4** 33 19S 59 39W
Guam ■, *Pac. Oc.* . . . . **64 F6** 13 27N 144 45 E
Guaminí, *Argentina* **94 D3** 37 1S 62 28W
Guamúchil, *Mexico* **86 B3** 25 25N 108 3W
Guanabacoa, *Cuba* **88 B3** 23 8N 82 18W
Guanacaste, Cordillera del,
Costa Rica **88 D2** 10 40N 85 4W
Guanaceví, *Mexico* **86 B3** 25 40N 106 0W
Guanahani = San Salvador I.,
Bahamas **89 B5** 24 0N 74 40W
Guanajay, *Cuba* **88 B3** 22 56N 82 42W
Guanajuato, *Mexico* **86 C4** 21 0N 101 20W
Guanajuato □, *Mexico* **86 C4** 20 40N 101 20W
Guandacol, *Argentina* **94 B2** 29 30S 68 40W
Guane, *Cuba* **88 B3** 22 10N 84 7W
Guangdong □, *China* . . . . . . **33 D6** 23 0N 113 0 E
Guangling, *China* . . . . **34 E8** 39 47N 114 22 E
Guangrao, *China* . . . . **35 F10** 37 5N 118 25 E
Guangwu, *China* . . . . **34 F3** 37 48N 105 57 E
Guangxi Zhuangzu Zizhiqu □,
China . . . . **33 D5** 24 0N 109 0 E
Guangzhou, *China* . . . . **33 D6** 23 5N 113 10 E
Guanipa →, *Venezuela* **92 B6** 9 56N 62 26W
Guannan, *China* . . . . **35 G10** 34 8N 119 21 E
Guantánamo, *Cuba* **89 B4** 20 10N 75 14W
Guantao, *China* . . . . **34 F8** 36 42N 115 25 E
Guanyun, *China* . . . . **35 G10** 34 20N 119 18 E
Guápiles, *Costa Rica* **88 D3** 10 10N 83 46W
Guaporé, *Brazil* **95 B5** 28 51S 51 54W
Guaporé →, *Brazil* **92 F5** 11 55S 65 4W
Guaqui, *Bolivia* **92 G5** 16 41S 68 54W
Guarapari, *Brazil* **95 A7** 20 40S 40 30W
Guarapuava, *Brazil* **95 B5** 25 20S 51 30W
Guaratinguetá, *Brazil* **95 A6** 22 49S 45 9W
Guaratuba, *Brazil* **95 B6** 25 53S 48 38W
Guarda, *Portugal* **19 B2** 40 32N 7 20W
Guardafui, C. = Asir, Ras,
Somali Rep. . . . . **46 E5** 11 55N 51 10 E
Guárico □, *Venezuela* **92 B5** 8 40N 66 35W
Guarujá, *Brazil* **95 A6** 24 2S 46 25W
Guarus, *Brazil* **95 A7** 21 44S 41 20W
Guasave, *Mexico* **86 B3** 25 34N 108 27W
Guasdualito, *Venezuela* **92 B4** 7 15N 70 44W
Guatemala, *Guatemala* **88 D1** 14 40N 90 22W
Guatemala ■, *Cent. Amer.* . . . **88 C1** 15 40N 90 30W
Guaviare →, *Colombia* **92 C5** 4 3N 67 44W
Guaxupé, *Brazil* **95 A6** 21 10S 47 5W
Guayama, *Puerto Rico* **89 C6** 17 59N 66 7W
Guayaquil, *Ecuador* **92 D3** 2 15S 79 52W
Guayaquil, G. de, *Ecuador* . . **92 D2** 3 10S 81 0W
Guaymas, *Mexico* **86 B2** 27 59N 110 54W
Guba, *Dem. Rep. of*
the Congo . . . . **55 E2** 10 38S 26 27 E
Gubkin, *Russia* . . . . **25 D6** 51 17N 37 32 E
Gudbrandsdalen, *Norway* . . . **9 F14** 61 33N 10 10 E
Guddu Barrage, *Pakistan* . . . **40 E6** 28 30N 69 50 E
Gudur, *India* . . . . **40 M11** 14 12N 79 55 E
Guecho = Getxo, *Spain* **19 A4** 43 21N 2 59W
Guelmine = Goulimine,
Morocco **50 C3** 28 56N 10 0W
Guelph, *Canada* **78 C4** 43 35N 80 20W
Guéret, *France* . . . . **18 C4** 46 11N 1 51 E
Guerneville, *U.S.A.* **84 G4** 38 30N 123 0W
Guernica = Gernika-Lumo,
Spain **19 A4** 43 19N 2 40W
Guernsey, *U.K.* **11 H5** 49 26N 2 35W
Guernsey, *U.S.A.* **80 D2** 42 19N 104 45W
Guerrero □, *Mexico* **87 D5** 17 30N 100 0W
Gügher, *Iran* . . . . **45 D8** 29 28N 56 27 E
Guhakolak, Tanjung,
Indonesia . . . . **37 G11** 6 50S 105 14 E
Guia, *Canary Is.* **22 F4** 28 8N 15 38W
Guia de Isora, *Canary Is.* . . . **22 F3** 28 12N 16 46W
Guia Lopes da Laguna, *Brazil* **95 A4** 21 26S 56 7W
Guiana, *S. Amer.* **90 C4** 5 10N 60 40W
Guidónia-Montecélio, *Italy* . . **20 C5** 42 1N 12 45 E
Guijá, *Mozam.* . . . . **57 C5** 24 27S 33 0 E
Guildford, *U.K.* **11 F7** 51 14N 0 34W
Guilford, *U.S.A.* **79 E12** 41 17N 72 41W
Guilin, *China* . . . . **33 D6** 25 18N 110 15 E
Guillaume-Delisle L., *Canada* **70 A4** 56 15N 76 17W
Güimar, *Canary Is.* **22 F3** 28 18N 16 24W
Guimarães, *Portugal* **19 B1** 41 28N 8 24W
Guimaras □, *Phil.* . . . . **37 B6** 10 35N 122 37 E
Guinda, *U.S.A.* **84 G4** 38 50N 122 12W
Guinea, *Africa* . . . . **48 F4** 8 0N 8 0 E
Guinea ■, *W. Afr.* **50 F3** 10 20N 11 30W
Guinea, Gulf of, *Atl. Oc.* . . . . **49 F4** 3 0N 2 30 E
Guinea-Bissau ■, *Africa* **50 F3** 12 0N 15 0W
Güines, *Cuba* **88 B3** 22 50N 82 0W
Guingamp, *France* **18 B2** 48 34N 3 10W
Güiria, *Venezuela* **92 A6** 10 32N 62 18W
Guiuan, *Phil.* . . . . **37 B7** 11 5N 125 55 E
Guiyang, *China* . . . . **32 D5** 26 32N 106 40 E
Guizhou □, *China* . . . . **32 D5** 27 0N 107 0 E
Gujar Khan, *Pakistan* . . . . . . **42 C5** 33 16N 73 19 E
Gujarat □, *India* . . . . **42 H4** 23 20N 71 0 E
Gujranwala, *Pakistan* . . . . . . **42 C6** 32 10N 74 12 E
Gujrat, *Pakistan* . . . . **42 C6** 32 40N 74 2 E
Gulbarga, *India* . . . . **40 L10** 17 20N 76 50 E
Gulbene, *Latvia* . . . . **9 H22** 57 8N 26 52 E
Gulf, The, *Asia* . . . . **45 E6** 27 0N 50 0 E
Gulfport, *U.S.A.* **81 K10** 30 22N 89 6W
Gulgong, *Australia* . . . . **63 E4** 32 20S 149 49 E
Gulistan, *Pakistan* . . . . **42 D2** 30 30N 66 35 E
Gull Lake, *Canada* **73 C7** 50 10N 108 29W
Güllük, *Turkey* . . . . **21 F12** 37 14N 27 35 E
Gulmarg, *India* . . . . **43 B6** 34 3N 74 25 E
Gulshad, *Kazakstan* . . . . **26 E8** 46 45N 74 25 E
Gulu, *Uganda* . . . . **54 B3** 2 48N 32 17 E
Gulwe, *Tanzania* . . . . **54 D4** 6 30S 36 25 E
Gumal →, *Pakistan* . . . . **42 D4** 31 40N 71 50 E
Gumbaz, *Pakistan* . . . . **42 D3** 30 2N 69 0 E
Gumel, *Nigeria* . . . . **50 F7** 12 39N 9 22 E
Gumla, *India* . . . . **43 H11** 23 3N 84 33 E
Gumlu, *Australia* . . . . **62 B4** 19 53S 147 41 E
Gumma □, *Japan* . . . . **31 F9** 36 30N 138 20 E
Gumzai, *Indonesia* . . . . **37 F8** 5 28S 134 42 E
Guna, *India* . . . . **42 G7** 24 40N 77 19 E
Gunisao →, *Canada* **73 C9** 53 56N 97 53W
Gunisao L., *Canada* **73 C9** 53 33N 96 15W
Gunjyal, *Pakistan* . . . . **42 C4** 32 20N 71 55 E
Gunnbjørn Fjeld, *Greenland* . **4 C6** 68 55N 29 47W
Gunnedah, *Australia* . . . . **63 E5** 30 59S 150 15 E
Gunnewin, *Australia* . . . . **63 D4** 25 59S 148 33 E
Gunningbar Cr. →, *Australia* . **63 E4** 31 14S 147 6 E
Gunnison, *Colo., U.S.A.* **83 G10** 38 33N 106 56W
Gunnison, *Utah, U.S.A.* **82 G8** 39 9N 111 49W
Gunnison →, *U.S.A.* **83 G9** 39 4N 108 35W
Gunpowder, *Australia* . . . . . . **62 B2** 19 42S 139 22 E
Guntakal, *India* . . . . **40 M10** 15 11N 77 27 E
Guntersville, *U.S.A.* **77 H2** 34 21N 86 18W
Guntong, *Malaysia* . . . . **39 K3** 4 36N 101 3 E
Guntur, *India* . . . . **41 L12** 16 23N 80 30 E
Gunungapi, *Indonesia* . . . . . . **37 F7** 6 45S 126 30 E
Gunungsitoli, *Indonesia* . . . . **36 D1** 1 15N 97 30 E
Gunza, *Angola* . . . . **52 G2** 10 50S 13 50 E
Guo He →, *China* . . . . **35 H9** 32 59N 117 10 E
Guoyang, *China* . . . . **34 H9** 33 32N 116 12 E
Gupis, *Pakistan* . . . . **43 A5** 36 15N 73 20 E
Gurdaspur, *India* . . . . **42 C6** 32 5N 75 31 E
Gurdon, *U.S.A.* **81 J8** 33 55N 93 9W
Gurgaon, *India* . . . . **42 E7** 28 27N 77 1 E
Gurgueia →, *Brazil* **93 E10** 6 50S 43 24W
Gurha, *India* . . . . **42 G4** 25 12N 71 39 E
Guri, Embalse de, *Venezuela* **92 B6** 7 50N 62 52W
Gurkha, *Nepal* . . . . **43 E11** 28 5N 84 40 E
Gurley, *Australia* . . . . **63 D4** 29 45S 149 48 E
Gurnet Point, *U.S.A.* **79 D14** 42 1N 70 34W
Guro, *Mozam.* . . . . **55 F3** 17 26S 32 30 E
Gurué, *Mozam.* . . . . **55 F4** 15 25S 36 58 E
Gurun, *Malaysia* . . . . **39 K3** 5 49N 100 27 E
Gürün, *Turkey* . . . . **25 G6** 38 43N 37 15 E
Gurupá, *Brazil* **93 D8** 1 25S 51 35W
Gurupá, I. Grande de, *Brazil* . **93 D8** 1 25S 51 45W
Gurupi, *Brazil* **93 F9** 11 43S 49 4W
Gurupi →, *Brazil* **93 D9** 1 13S 46 6W
Guruwe, *Zimbabwe* . . . . **57 B5** 16 40S 30 42 E
Guryev = Atyraū, *Kazakstan* . **25 E9** 47 5N 52 0 E
Gusau, *Nigeria* . . . . **50 F7** 12 12N 6 40 E
Gusev, *Russia* . . . . **9 J20** 54 35N 22 10 E
Gushan, *China* . . . . **35 E12** 39 50N 123 35 E
Gushgy, *Turkmenistan* . . . . . **26 F7** 35 20N 62 18 E
Gusinoozersk, *Russia* . . . . . . **27 D11** 51 16N 106 27 E
Gustavus, *U.S.A.* **72 B1** 58 25N 135 44W
Gustine, *U.S.A.* **84 H6** 37 16N 121 0W
Güstrow, *Germany* . . . . **16 B7** 53 47N 12 10 E
Gütersloh, *Germany* . . . . **16 C5** 51 54N 8 24 E
Gutha, *Australia* . . . . **61 E2** 28 58S 115 55 E
Guthalungra, *Australia* . . . . . **62 B4** 19 52S 147 50 E
Guthrie, *Okla., U.S.A.* **81 H6** 35 53N 97 25W
Guthrie, *Tex., U.S.A.* **81 J4** 33 37N 100 19W
Guttenberg, *U.S.A.* **80 D9** 42 47N 91 6W
Gutu, *Zimbabwe* . . . . **57 B5** 19 41S 31 9 E
Guwahati, *India* . . . . **41 F17** 26 10N 91 45 E
Guyana ■, *S. Amer.* **92 C7** 5 0N 59 0W
Guyane française = French
Guiana ■, *S. Amer.* **93 C8** 4 0N 53 0W
Guyang, *China* . . . . **34 D6** 41 0N 110 5 E
Guyenne, *France* . . . . **18 D4** 44 30N 0 40 E
Guymon, *U.S.A.* **81 G4** 36 41N 101 29W
Guyra, *Australia* . . . . **63 E5** 30 15S 151 40 E
Guyuan, *Hebei, China* . . . . . . **34 D8** 41 37N 115 40 E
Guyuan, *Ningxia Huizu, China* **34 G4** 36 0N 106 20 E
Guzhen, *China* . . . . **35 H9** 33 22N 117 18 E
Guzmán, L. de, *Mexico* **86 A3** 31 25N 107 25W
Gvardeysk, *Russia* . . . . **9 J19** 54 39N 21 5 E
Gwa, *Burma* . . . . **41 L19** 17 36N 94 34 E
Gwaai, *Zimbabwe* . . . . **55 F2** 19 15S 27 45 E
Gwaai →, *Zimbabwe* . . . . **55 F2** 17 59S 26 52 E
Gwabegar, *Australia* . . . . **63 E4** 30 31S 149 0 E
Gwādar, *Pakistan* . . . . **40 G3** 25 10N 62 18 E
Gwalior, *India* . . . . **42 F8** 26 12N 78 10 E
Gwanda, *Zimbabwe* . . . . **55 G2** 20 55S 29 0 E
Gwane, *Dem. Rep. of*
the Congo . . . . **54 B2** 4 45N 25 48 E
Gweebarra B., *Ireland* **13 B3** 54 51N 8 23W
Gweedore, *Ireland* **13 A3** 55 3N 8 13W
Gweru, *Zimbabwe* . . . . **55 F2** 19 28S 29 45 E
Gwinn, *U.S.A.* **76 B2** 46 19N 87 27W
Gwydir →, *Australia* . . . . **63 D4** 29 27S 149 48 E
Gwynedd □, *U.K.* **10 E3** 52 52N 4 10W
Gyandzha = Gäncä,
Azerbaijan . . . . **25 F8** 40 45N 46 20 E
Gyaring Hu, *China* . . . . **32 C4** 34 50N 97 40 E
Gydanskiy Poluostrov, *Russia* **26 C8** 70 0N 78 0 E
Gympie, *Australia* . . . . **63 D5** 26 11S 152 38 E
Gyöngyös, *Hungary* . . . . **17 E10** 47 48N 19 56 E
Győr, *Hungary* . . . . **17 E9** 47 41N 17 40 E
Gypsum Pt., *Canada* **72 A6** 61 53N 114 35W
Gypsumville, *Canada* **73 C9** 51 45N 98 40W
Gyula, *Hungary* . . . . **17 E11** 46 38N 21 17 E
Gyumri, *Armenia* . . . . **25 F7** 40 47N 43 50 E
Gyzylarbat, *Turkmenistan* . . . **26 F6** 39 4N 56 23 E
Gyzyletrek, *Turkmenistan* . . . **45 B7** 37 36N 54 46 E

H

Ha 'Arava →, *Israel* . . . . **47 E4** 30 50N 35 20 E
Ha Coi, *Vietnam* . . . . **38 B6** 21 26N 107 46 E
Ha Dong, *Vietnam* . . . . **38 B5** 20 58N 105 46 E
Ha Giang, *Vietnam* . . . . **38 A5** 22 50N 104 59 E
Ha Tien, *Vietnam* . . . . **39 G5** 10 23N 104 29 E
Ha Tinh, *Vietnam* . . . . **38 C5** 18 20N 105 54 E
Ha Trung, *Vietnam* . . . . **38 C5** 19 58N 105 50 E
Haaksbergen, *Neths.* . . . . **15 B6** 52 9N 6 45 E
Haapsalu, *Estonia* . . . . **9 G20** 58 56N 23 30 E
Haarlem, *Neths.* . . . . **15 B4** 52 23N 4 39 E
Haast →, *N.Z.* . . . . **59 K2** 43 50S 169 2 E
Haast Bluff, *Australia* . . . . . . **60 D5** 23 22S 132 0 E
Hab →, *Pakistan* . . . . **42 G3** 24 53N 66 41 E
Hab Nadi Chauki, *Pakistan* . . **42 G2** 25 0N 66 50 E
Habaswein, *Kenya* . . . . **54 B4** 1 2N 39 30 E
Habay, *Canada* **72 B5** 58 50N 118 44W
Ḥabbānīyah, *Iraq* . . . . **44 C4** 33 17N 43 29 E
Haboro, *Japan* . . . . **30 B10** 44 22N 141 42 E
Ḥabshān, *U.A.E.* . . . . **45 F7** 23 50N 53 37 E
Hachijō-Jima, *Japan* . . . . **31 H9** 33 5N 139 45 E
Hachinohe, *Japan* . . . . **30 D10** 40 30N 141 29 E
Hachiōji, *Japan* . . . . **31 G9** 35 40N 139 20 E
Hachŏn, *N. Korea* . . . . **35 D15** 41 29N 129 2 E
Hackensack, *U.S.A.* **79 F10** 40 53N 74 3W
Hackettstown, *U.S.A.* **79 F10** 40 51N 74 50W
Hadali, *Pakistan* . . . . **42 C5** 32 16N 72 11 E
Hadarba, Ras, *Sudan* . . . . . . **51 D13** 22 4N 36 51 E
Hadarom □, *Israel* . . . . **47 E4** 31 0N 35 0 E
Ḥadd, Ra's al, *Oman* . . . . **46 C6** 22 35N 59 50 E
Hadejia, *Nigeria* . . . . **50 F7** 12 30N 10 5 E
Hadera, *Israel* . . . . **47 C3** 32 27N 34 55 E
Hadera, N. →, *Israel* . . . . **47 C3** 32 28N 34 52 E
Haderslev, *Denmark* . . . . **9 J13** 55 15N 9 30 E
Hadhramaut = Ḥaḍramawt,
Yemen . . . . **46 D4** 15 30N 49 30 E
Hadiboh, *Yemen* . . . . **46 E5** 12 39N 54 2 E
Hadong, *S. Korea* . . . . **35 G14** 35 5N 127 44 E
Ḥaḍramawt, *Yemen* . . . . **46 D4** 15 30N 49 30 E
Ḥadrānīyah, *Iraq* . . . . **44 C4** 35 38N 43 14 E
Hadrian's Wall, *U.K.* **10 B5** 55 0N 2 30W
Haeju, *N. Korea* . . . . **35 E13** 38 3N 125 45 E
Haenam, *S. Korea* . . . . **35 G14** 34 34N 126 35 E
Haenertsburg, *S. Africa* . . . . . **57 C4** 24 0S 29 50 E
Haerhpin = Harbin, *China* . . . **35 B14** 45 48N 126 40 E
Hafar al Bāṭin, *Si. Arabia* . . . **44 D5** 28 32N 45 52 E
Ḥafirat al 'Aydā, *Si. Arabia* . . **44 E3** 26 26N 39 12 E
Ḥafit, *Oman* . . . . **45 F7** 23 59N 55 49 E
Hafizabad, *Pakistan* . . . . **42 C5** 32 5N 73 40 E
Haflong, *India* . . . . **41 G18** 25 10N 93 5 E
Hafnarfjörður, *Iceland* **8 D3** 64 4N 21 57W
Haft Gel, *Iran* . . . . **45 D6** 31 30N 49 32 E
Hafun, Ras, *Somali Rep.* . . . . **46 E5** 10 29N 51 30 E
Hagalil, *Israel* . . . . **47 C4** 32 53N 35 18 E
Hagen, *Germany* . . . . **16 C4** 51 21N 7 27 E
Hagerman, *U.S.A.* **81 J2** 33 7N 104 20W
Hagerstown, *U.S.A.* **76 F7** 39 39N 77 43W
Hagersville, *Canada* **78 D4** 42 58N 80 3W
Hagfors, *Sweden* . . . . **9 F15** 60 3N 13 45 E
Hagi, *Japan* . . . . **31 G5** 34 30N 131 22 E
Hagolan, *Syria* . . . . **47 C4** 33 0N 35 45 E
Hagondange, *France* . . . . **18 B7** 49 16N 6 11 E
Hags Hd., *Ireland* **13 D2** 52 57N 9 28W
Hague, C. de la, *France* **18 B3** 49 44N 1 56W
Hague, The = 's-Gravenhage,
Neths. . . . . **15 B4** 52 7N 4 17 E
Haguenau, *France* . . . . **18 B7** 48 49N 7 47 E
Hai Duong, *Vietnam* . . . . **38 B6** 20 56N 106 19 E
Haicheng, *China* . . . . **35 D12** 40 50N 122 45 E
Haidar Khel, *Afghan.* . . . . **42 C3** 33 58N 68 38 E
Haidargarh, *India* . . . . **43 F9** 26 37N 81 22 E
Haifa = Ḥefa, *Israel* . . . . **47 C4** 32 46N 35 0 E
Haikou, *China* . . . . **33 D6** 20 1N 110 16 E
Ḥā'il, *Si. Arabia* . . . . **44 E4** 27 28N 41 45 E
Hailar, *China* . . . . **33 B6** 49 10N 119 38 E
Hailey, *U.S.A.* **82 E6** 43 31N 114 19W
Haileybury, *Canada* **70 C4** 47 30N 79 38W
Hailin, *China* . . . . **35 B15** 44 37N 129 30 E
Hailong, *China* . . . . **35 C13** 42 32N 125 40 E

Hailuoto, Finland 8 D21 65 3N 24 45 E
Hainan □, China 33 E5 19 0N 109 30 E
Hainaut □, Belgium 15 D4 50 30N 4 0 E
Haines, Alaska, U.S.A. 72 B1 59 14N 135 26W
Haines, Oreg., U.S.A. 82 D5 44 55N 117 56W
Haines City, U.S.A. 77 L5 28 7N 81 38W
Haines Junction, Canada 72 A1 60 45N 137 30W
Haiphong, Vietnam 32 D5 20 47N 106 41 E
Haiti ■, W. Indies 89 C5 19 0N 72 30W
Haiya, Sudan 51 E13 18 20N 36 21 E
Haiyang, China 35 F11 36 47N 121 9 E
Haiyuan, China 34 F3 36 35N 105 52 E
Haizhou, China 35 G10 34 37N 119 7 E
Haizhou Wan, China 35 G10 34 50N 119 20 E
Hajdúböszörmény, Hungary 17 E11 47 40N 21 30 E
Hajipur, India 43 G11 25 45N 85 13 E
Ḩājjī Muḩsin, Iraq 44 C5 32 35N 45 29 E
Ḩājjīābād, Iran 45 D7 28 19N 55 55 E
Ḩājjīābād-e Zarrīn, Iran 45 C7 33 9N 54 51 E
Hajnówka, Poland 17 B12 52 47N 23 35 E
Hakansson, Mts., Dem. Rep. of the Congo 55 D2 8 40S 25 45 E
Hakkâri, Turkey 44 B4 37 34N 43 44 E
Hakken-Zan, Japan 31 G7 34 10N 135 54 E
Hakodate, Japan 30 D10 41 45N 140 44 E
Hakos, Namibia 56 C2 23 13S 16 21 E
Haku-San, Japan 31 F8 36 9N 136 46 E
Hakui, Japan 31 F8 36 53N 136 47 E
Hala, Pakistan 40 G6 25 43N 68 20 E
Ḩalab, Syria 44 B3 36 10N 37 15 E
Ḩalabjah, Iraq 44 C5 35 10N 45 58 E
Halaib, Sudan 51 D13 22 12N 36 30 E
Hālat 'Ammār, Si. Arabia 44 D3 29 10N 36 4 E
Halbā, Lebanon 47 A5 34 34N 36 6 E
Halberstadt, Germany 16 C6 51 54N 11 3 E
Halcombe, N.Z. 59 J5 40 8S 175 30 E
Halcon, Phil. 37 B6 13 0N 121 30 E
Halden, Norway 9 G14 59 9N 11 23 E
Haldia, India 41 H16 22 5N 88 3 E
Haldwani, India 43 E8 29 31N 79 30 E
Hale ~▸, Australia 62 C2 24 56S 135 53 E
Halesowen, U.K. 11 E5 52 27N 2 3W
Haleyville, U.S.A. 77 H2 34 14N 87 37W
Halfmoon Bay, N.Z. 59 M2 46 50S 168 5 E
Halfway ~▸, Canada 72 B4 56 12N 121 32W
Halia, India 43 G10 24 50N 82 19 E
Haliburton, Canada 78 A6 45 3N 78 30W
Halifax, Australia 62 B4 18 32S 146 22 E
Halifax, Canada 71 D7 44 38N 63 35W
Halifax, U.K. 10 D6 53 43N 1 52W
Halifax, U.S.A. 78 F8 40 25N 76 55W
Halifax B., Australia 62 B4 18 50S 147 0 E
Halifax I., Namibia 56 D2 26 38S 15 4 E
Halīl ~▸, Iran 45 E8 27 40N 58 30 E
Halkirk, U.K. 12 C5 58 30N 3 29W
Hall Beach = Sanirajak, Canada 69 B11 68 46N 81 12W
Hall Pen., Canada 69 B13 63 30N 66 0W
Hall Pt., Australia 60 C3 15 40S 124 23 E
Halland, Sweden 9 H15 57 8N 12 47 E
Halle, Belgium 15 D4 50 44N 4 13 E
Halle, Germany 16 C6 51 30N 11 56 E
Hällefors, Sweden 9 G16 59 47N 14 31 E
Hallett, Australia 63 E2 33 25S 138 55 E
Hallettsville, U.S.A. 81 L6 29 27N 96 57W
Hallim, S. Korea 35 H14 33 24N 126 15 E
Hallingdalselvi ~▸, Norway 9 F13 60 23N 9 35 E
Hallock, U.S.A. 80 A6 48 47N 96 57W
Halls Creek, Australia 60 C4 18 16S 127 38 E
Hallsberg, Sweden 9 G16 59 5N 15 7 E
Hallstead, U.S.A. 79 E9 41 58N 75 45W
Halmahera, Indonesia 37 D7 0 40N 128 0 E
Halmstad, Sweden 9 H15 56 41N 12 52 E
Hälsingborg = Helsingborg, Sweden 9 H15 56 3N 12 42 E
Hälsingland, Sweden 9 F16 61 40N 16 5 E
Halstead, U.K. 11 F8 51 57N 0 40 E
Halti, Finland 8 B19 69 17N 21 18 E
Halton □, U.K. 10 D5 53 22N 2 45W
Haltwhistle, U.K. 10 C5 54 58N 2 26W
Ḩālūl, Qatar 45 E7 25 40N 52 40 E
Halvad, India 42 H4 23 1N 71 11 E
Ḩalvān, Iran 45 C8 33 57N 56 15 E
Ham Tan, Vietnam 39 G6 10 40N 107 45 E
Ham Yen, Vietnam 38 A5 22 4N 105 3 E
Hamab, Namibia 56 D2 28 7S 19 16 E
Hamada, Japan 31 G6 34 56N 132 4 E
Hamadān, Iran 45 C6 34 52N 48 32 E
Hamadān □, Iran 45 C6 35 0N 49 0 E
Ḩamāh, Syria 44 C3 35 5N 36 40 E
Hamamatsu, Japan 31 G8 34 45N 137 45 E
Hamar, Norway 9 F14 60 48N 11 7 E
Hamâta, Gebel, Egypt 44 E2 24 17N 35 0 E
Hambantota, Sri Lanka 40 R12 6 10N 81 10 E
Hamber Prov. Park, Canada 72 C5 52 20N 118 0W
Hamburg, Germany 16 B5 53 33N 9 59 E
Hamburg, Ark., U.S.A. 81 J9 33 14N 91 48W
Hamburg, N.Y., U.S.A. 78 D6 42 43N 78 50W
Hamburg, Pa., U.S.A. 79 F9 40 33N 75 59W
Ḩamḑ, W. al ~▸, Si. Arabia 44 E3 24 55N 36 20 E
Hamden, U.S.A. 79 E12 41 23N 72 54W
Häme, Finland 9 F20 61 38N 25 10 E
Hämeenlinna, Finland 9 F21 61 0N 24 28 E
Hamelin Pool, Australia 61 E1 26 22S 114 20 E
Hameln, Germany 16 B5 52 6N 9 21 E
Hamerkaz □, Israel 47 C3 32 15N 34 55 E
Hamersley Ra., Australia 60 D2 22 0S 117 45 E
Hamhung, N. Korea 35 E14 39 54N 127 30 E
Hami, China 32 B4 42 55N 93 25 E
Hamilton, Australia 63 F3 37 45S 142 2 E
Hamilton, Canada 78 C5 43 15N 79 50W
Hamilton, N.Z. 59 G5 37 47S 175 19 E
Hamilton, U.K. 12 F4 55 46N 4 2W
Hamilton, Ala., U.S.A. 77 H1 34 9N 87 59W
Hamilton, Mont., U.S.A. 82 C6 46 15N 114 10W
Hamilton, N.Y., U.S.A. 79 D9 42 50N 75 33W
Hamilton, Ohio, U.S.A. 76 F3 39 24N 84 34W
Hamilton, Tex., U.S.A. 81 K5 31 42N 98 7W
Hamilton ~▸, Australia 62 C2 23 30S 139 47 E
Hamilton City, U.S.A. 84 F4 39 45N 122 1W
Hamilton Inlet, Canada 71 B8 54 0N 57 30W
Hamilton Mt., U.S.A. 79 C10 43 25N 74 22W
Hamina, Finland 9 F22 60 34N 27 12 E
Hamirpur, H.P., India 42 D7 31 41N 76 31 E
Hamirpur, Ut. P., India 43 G9 25 57N 80 9 E
Hamlet, U.S.A. 77 H6 34 53N 79 42W
Hamley Bridge, Australia 63 E2 34 17S 138 35 E
Hamlin = Hameln, Germany 16 B5 52 6N 9 21 E
Hamlin, N.Y., U.S.A. 78 C7 43 17N 77 55W
Hamlin, Tex., U.S.A. 81 J4 32 53N 100 8W
Hamm, Germany 16 C4 51 40N 7 50 E
Ḩammār, Hawr al, Iraq 44 D5 30 50N 47 10 E
Hammerfest, Norway 8 A20 70 39N 23 41 E
Hammond, Ind., U.S.A. 76 E2 41 38N 87 30W
Hammond, La., U.S.A. 81 K9 30 30N 90 28W
Hammond, N.Y., U.S.A. 79 B9 44 27N 75 42W
Hammondsport, U.S.A. 78 D7 42 25N 77 13W
Hammonton, U.S.A. 76 F8 39 39N 74 48W
Hampden, N.Z. 59 L3 45 18S 170 50 E
Hampshire □, U.K. 11 F6 51 7N 1 23W
Hampshire Downs, U.K. 11 F6 51 15N 1 10W
Hampton, N.B., Canada 71 C6 45 32N 65 51W
Hampton, Ont., Canada 78 C6 43 58N 78 45W
Hampton, Ark., U.S.A. 81 J8 33 32N 92 28W
Hampton, Iowa, U.S.A. 80 D8 42 45N 93 13W
Hampton, N.H., U.S.A. 79 D14 42 57N 70 50W
Hampton, S.C., U.S.A. 77 J5 32 52N 81 7W
Hampton, Va., U.S.A. 76 G7 37 2N 76 21W
Hampton Bays, U.S.A. 79 F12 40 53N 72 30W
Hampton Tableland, Australia 61 F4 32 0S 127 0 E
Hamyang, S. Korea 35 G14 35 32N 127 42 E
Han Pijesak, Bos.-H. 21 B8 44 5N 18 57 E
Hanak, Si. Arabia 44 E3 25 32N 37 0 E
Hanamaki, Japan 30 E10 39 23N 141 7 E
Hanang, Tanzania 54 C4 4 30S 35 25 E
Hanau, Germany 16 C5 50 7N 8 56 E
Hanbogd = Ihbulag, Mongolia 34 C4 43 11N 107 10 E
Hancheng, China 34 G6 35 31N 110 25 E
Hancock, Mich., U.S.A. 80 B10 47 8N 88 35W
Hancock, N.Y., U.S.A. 79 E9 41 57N 75 17W
Handa, Japan 31 G8 34 53N 136 55 E
Handan, China 34 F8 36 35N 114 28 E
Handeni, Tanzania 54 D4 5 25S 38 2 E
Handwara, India 43 B6 34 21N 74 20 E
Hanegev, Israel 47 E4 30 50N 35 0 E
Hanford, U.S.A. 84 J7 36 20N 119 39W
Hang Chat, Thailand 38 C2 18 20N 99 21 E
Hang Dong, Thailand 38 C2 18 41N 98 55 E
Hangang ~▸, S. Korea 35 F14 37 50N 126 30 E
Hangayn Nuruu, Mongolia 32 B4 47 30N 99 0 E
Hangchou = Hangzhou, China 33 C7 30 18N 120 11 E
Hanggin Houqi, China 34 D4 40 58N 107 4 E
Hanggin Qi, China 34 E5 39 52N 108 50 E
Hangu, China 35 E9 39 18N 117 53 E
Hangzhou, China 33 C7 30 18N 120 11 E
Hangzhou Wan, China 33 C7 30 15N 120 45 E
Hanhongor, Mongolia 34 C3 43 55N 104 28 E
Ḩanīdh, Si. Arabia 45 E6 26 35N 48 38 E
Ḩanīsh, Yemen 46 E3 13 45N 42 46 E
Hankinson, U.S.A. 80 B6 46 4N 96 54W
Hanko, Finland 9 G20 59 50N 22 57 E
Hanksville, U.S.A. 83 G8 38 22N 110 43W
Hanle, India 43 C8 32 42N 79 4 E
Hanmer Springs, N.Z. 59 K4 42 32S 172 50 E
Hann ~▸, Australia 60 C4 17 26S 126 17 E
Hann, Mt., Australia 60 C4 15 45S 126 0 E
Hanna, Canada 72 C6 51 40N 111 54W
Hanna, U.S.A. 82 F10 41 52N 106 34W
Hannah B., Canada 70 B4 51 40N 80 0W
Hannibal, Mo., U.S.A. 80 F9 39 42N 91 22W
Hannibal, N.Y., U.S.A. 79 C8 43 19N 76 35W
Hannover, Germany 16 B5 52 22N 9 46 E
Hanoi, Vietnam 32 D5 21 5N 105 55 E
Hanover = Hannover, Germany 16 B5 52 22N 9 46 E
Hanover, Canada 78 B3 44 9N 81 2W
Hanover, S. Africa 56 E3 31 4S 24 29 E
Hanover, N.H., U.S.A. 79 C12 43 42N 72 17W
Hanover, Ohio, U.S.A. 78 F2 40 4N 82 16W
Hanover, Pa., U.S.A. 76 F7 39 48N 76 59W
Hanover, I., Chile 96 G2 51 0S 74 50W
Hansdiha, India 43 G12 24 36N 87 5 E
Hansi, India 42 E6 29 10N 75 57 E
Hanson, L., Australia 63 E2 31 0S 136 15 E
Hantsavichy, Belarus 17 B14 52 49N 26 30 E
Hanumangarh, India 42 E6 29 35N 74 19 E
Hanzhong, China 34 H4 33 10N 107 1 E
Hanzhuang, China 35 G9 34 33N 117 23 E
Haora, India 43 H13 22 37N 88 20 E
Haparanda, Sweden 8 D21 65 52N 24 8 E
Happy, U.S.A. 81 H4 34 45N 101 52W
Happy Camp, U.S.A. 82 F2 41 48N 123 23W
Happy Valley-Goose Bay, Canada 71 B7 53 15N 60 20W
Hapsu, N. Korea 35 D15 41 13N 128 51 E
Hapur, India 42 E7 28 45N 77 45 E
Ḩaql, Si. Arabia 47 F3 29 10N 34 58 E
Har, Indonesia 37 F8 5 16S 133 14 E
Har-Ayrag, Mongolia 34 B5 45 47N 109 16 E
Har Hu, China 32 C4 38 20N 97 38 E
Har Us Nuur, Mongolia 32 B4 48 0N 92 0 E
Har Yehuda, Israel 47 D3 31 35N 34 57 E
Ḩaraḑ, Si. Arabia 46 C4 24 22N 49 0 E
Haranomachi, Japan 30 F10 37 38N 140 58 E
Harare, Zimbabwe 55 F3 17 43S 31 2 E
Harbin, China 35 B14 45 48N 126 40 E
Harbor Beach, U.S.A. 78 C2 43 51N 82 39W
Harbour Breton, Canada 71 C8 47 29N 55 50W
Harbour Deep, Canada 71 B8 50 25N 56 32W
Harda, India 42 H7 22 27N 77 5 E
Hardangerfjorden, Norway 9 F12 60 5N 6 0 E
Hardangervidda, Norway 9 F12 60 7N 7 20 E
Hardap Dam, Namibia 56 C2 24 32S 17 50 E
Hardenberg, Neths. 15 B6 52 34N 6 37 E
Harderwijk, Neths. 15 B5 52 21N 5 38 E
Hardey ~▸, Australia 60 D2 22 45S 116 8 E
Hardin, U.S.A. 82 D10 45 44N 107 37W
Harding, S. Africa 57 E4 30 35S 29 55 E
Harding Ra., Australia 60 C3 16 17S 124 55 E
Hardisty, Canada 72 C6 52 40N 111 18W
Hardoi, India 43 F9 27 26N 80 6 E
Hardwar = Haridwar, India 42 E8 29 58N 78 9 E
Hardwick, U.S.A. 79 B12 44 30N 72 22W
Hardy, Pen., Chile 96 H3 55 30S 68 20W
Hare B., Canada 71 B8 51 15N 55 45W
Hareid, Norway 9 E12 62 22N 6 1 E
Harer, Ethiopia 46 F3 9 20N 42 8 E
Hargeisa, Somali Rep. 46 F3 9 30N 44 2 E
Hari ~▸, Indonesia 36 E2 1 16S 104 5 E
Haria, Canary Is. 22 E6 29 8N 13 32W
Haridwar, India 42 E8 29 58N 78 9 E
Harim, Jabal al, Oman 45 E8 25 58N 56 14 E
Haringhata ~▸, Bangla. 41 J16 22 0N 89 58 E
Harīrūd ~▸, Asia 40 A2 37 24N 60 38 E
Härjedalen, Sweden 9 E15 62 22N 13 5 E
Harlan, Iowa, U.S.A. 80 E7 41 39N 95 19W
Harlan, Ky., U.S.A. 77 G4 36 51N 83 19W
Harlech, U.K. 10 E3 52 52N 4 6W
Harlem, U.S.A. 82 B9 48 32N 108 47W
Harlingen, Neths. 15 A5 53 11N 5 25 E
Harlingen, U.S.A. 81 M6 26 12N 97 42W
Harlow, U.K. 11 F8 51 46N 0 8 E
Harlowton, U.S.A. 82 C9 46 26N 109 50W
Harnai, Pakistan 42 D2 30 6N 67 56 E
Harney Basin, U.S.A. 82 E4 43 30N 119 0W
Harney L., U.S.A. 82 E4 43 14N 119 8W
Harney Peak, U.S.A. 80 D3 43 52N 103 32W
Härnösand, Sweden 9 E17 62 38N 17 55 E
Haroldswick, U.K. 12 A8 60 48N 0 50W
Harp L., Canada 71 A7 55 5N 61 50W
Harper, Liberia 50 H4 4 25N 7 43W
Harrai, India 43 H8 22 37N 79 13 E
Harrand, Pakistan 42 E4 29 28N 70 3 E
Harricana ~▸, Canada 70 B4 50 56N 79 32W
Harriman, U.S.A. 77 H3 35 56N 84 33W
Harrington Harbour, Canada 71 B8 50 31N 59 30W
Harris, U.K. 12 D2 57 50N 6 55W
Harris, Sd. of, U.K. 12 D1 57 44N 7 6W
Harris L., Australia 63 E2 31 10S 135 10 E
Harris Pt., Canada 78 C2 43 6N 82 9W
Harrisburg, Ill., U.S.A. 81 G10 37 44N 88 32W
Harrisburg, Nebr., U.S.A. 80 E3 41 33N 103 44W
Harrisburg, Pa., U.S.A. 78 F8 40 16N 76 53W
Harrismith, S. Africa 57 D4 28 15S 29 8 E
Harrison, Ark., U.S.A. 81 G8 36 14N 93 7W
Harrison, Maine, U.S.A. 79 B14 44 7N 70 39W
Harrison, Nebr., U.S.A. 80 D3 42 41N 103 53W
Harrison, C., Canada 71 B8 54 55N 57 55W
Harrison L., Canada 72 D4 49 33N 121 50W
Harrisonburg, U.S.A. 76 F6 38 27N 78 52W
Harrisonville, U.S.A. 80 F7 38 39N 94 21W
Harriston, Canada 78 C4 43 57N 80 53W
Harrisville, Mich., U.S.A. 78 B1 44 39N 83 17W
Harrisville, N.Y., U.S.A. 79 B9 44 9N 75 19W
Harrisville, Pa., U.S.A. 78 E5 41 8N 80 0W
Harrodsburg, U.S.A. 76 G3 37 46N 84 51W
Harrogate, U.K. 10 C6 54 0N 1 33W
Harrow □, U.K. 11 F7 51 35N 0 21W
Harrowsmith, Canada 79 B8 44 24N 76 40W
Harry S. Truman Reservoir, U.S.A. 80 F7 38 16N 93 24W
Harsin, Iran 44 C5 34 18N 47 33 E
Harstad, Norway 8 B17 68 48N 16 30 E
Harsud, India 42 H7 22 6N 76 44 E
Hart, U.S.A. 76 D2 43 42N 86 22W
Hart, L., Australia 63 E2 31 10S 136 25 E
Hartbees ~▸, S. Africa 56 D3 28 45S 20 32 E
Hartford, Conn., U.S.A. 79 E12 41 46N 72 41W
Hartford, Ky., U.S.A. 76 G2 37 27N 86 55W
Hartford, S. Dak., U.S.A. 80 D6 43 38N 96 57W
Hartford, Wis., U.S.A. 80 D10 43 19N 88 22W
Hartford City, U.S.A. 76 E3 40 27N 85 22W
Hartland, Canada 71 C6 46 20N 67 32W
Hartland Pt., U.K. 11 F3 51 1N 4 32W
Hartlepool, U.K. 10 C6 54 42N 1 13W
Hartlepool □, U.K. 10 C6 54 42N 1 17W
Hartley Bay, Canada 72 C3 53 25N 129 15W
Hartmannberge, Namibia 56 B1 17 0S 13 0 E
Hartney, Canada 73 D8 49 30N 100 35W
Harts ~▸, S. Africa 56 D3 28 24S 24 17 E
Hartselle, U.S.A. 77 H2 34 27N 86 56W
Hartshorne, U.S.A. 81 H7 34 51N 95 34W
Hartstown, U.S.A. 78 E4 41 33N 80 23W
Hartsville, U.S.A. 77 H5 34 23N 80 4W
Hartswater, S. Africa 56 D3 27 34S 24 43 E
Hartwell, U.S.A. 77 H4 34 21N 82 56W
Harunabad, Pakistan 42 E5 29 35N 73 8 E
Harvand, Iran 45 D7 28 25N 55 43 E
Harvey, Australia 61 F2 33 5S 115 54 E
Harvey, Ill., U.S.A. 76 E2 41 36N 87 50W
Harvey, N. Dak., U.S.A. 80 B5 47 47N 99 56W
Harwich, U.K. 11 F9 51 56N 1 17 E
Haryana □, India 42 E7 29 0N 76 10 E
Haryn ~▸, Belarus 17 B14 52 7N 27 17 E
Harz, Germany 16 C6 51 38N 10 44 E
Hasa □, Si. Arabia 45 E6 25 50N 49 0 E
Ḩasanābād, Iran 45 C7 32 8N 52 44 E
Hasdo ~▸, India 43 J10 21 44N 82 44 E
Hashimoto, Japan 31 G7 34 19N 135 37 E
Hashtjerd, Iran 45 C6 35 52N 50 40 E
Haskell, U.S.A. 81 J5 33 10N 99 44W
Haslemere, U.K. 11 F7 51 5N 0 43W
Hasselt, Belgium 15 D5 50 56N 5 21 E
Hassi Messaoud, Algeria 50 B7 31 51N 6 1 E
Hässleholm, Sweden 9 H15 56 10N 13 46 E
Hastings, N.Z. 59 H6 39 39S 176 52 E
Hastings, U.K. 11 G8 50 51N 0 35 E
Hastings, Mich., U.S.A. 76 D3 42 39N 85 17W
Hastings, Minn., U.S.A. 80 C8 44 44N 92 51W
Hastings, Nebr., U.S.A. 80 E5 40 35N 98 23W
Hastings Ra., Australia 63 E5 31 15S 152 14 E
Hat Yai, Thailand 39 J3 7 1N 100 27 E
Hatanbulag = Ergel, Mongolia 34 C5 43 8N 109 5 E
Hatay = Antalya, Turkey 25 G5 36 52N 30 45 E
Hatch, U.S.A. 83 K10 32 40N 107 9W
Hatchet L., Canada 73 B8 58 36N 103 40W
Hateruma-Shima, Japan 31 M1 24 3N 123 47 E
Hatfield P.O., Australia 63 E3 33 54S 143 49 E
Hatgal, Mongolia 32 A5 50 26N 100 9 E
Hathras, India 42 F8 27 36N 78 6 E
Hatia, Bangla. 41 H17 22 30N 91 5 E
Hato Mayor, Dom. Rep. 89 C6 18 46N 69 15W
Hatta, India 43 G8 24 7N 79 36 E
Hattah, Australia 63 E3 34 48S 142 17 E
Hatteras, C., U.S.A. 77 H8 35 14N 75 32W
Hattiesburg, U.S.A. 81 K10 31 20N 89 17W
Hatvan, Hungary 17 E10 47 40N 19 45 E
Hau Bon = Cheo Reo, Vietnam 36 B3 13 25N 108 28 E
Hau Duc, Vietnam 38 E7 15 20N 108 13 E
Haugesund, Norway 9 G11 59 23N 5 13 E
Haukipudas, Finland 8 D21 65 12N 25 20 E
Haultain ~▸, Canada 73 B7 55 51N 106 46W
Hauraki G., N.Z. 59 G5 36 35S 175 5 E
Haut Atlas, Morocco 50 B4 32 30N 5 0W
Haut-Zaïre = Orientale □, Dem. Rep. of the Congo 54 B2 2 20N 26 0 E
Hautes Fagnes = Hohe Venn, Belgium 15 D6 50 30N 6 5 E
Hauts Plateaux, Algeria 48 C4 35 0N 1 0 E
Havana = La Habana, Cuba 88 B3 23 8N 82 22W
Havana, U.S.A. 80 E9 40 18N 90 4W
Havant, U.K. 11 G7 50 51N 0 58W
Havasu, L., U.S.A. 85 L12 34 18N 114 28W
Havel ~▸, Germany 16 B7 52 50N 12 3 E
Havelian, Pakistan 42 B5 34 2N 73 10 E
Havelock, Canada 78 B7 44 26N 77 53W
Havelock, N.Z. 59 J4 41 17S 173 48 E
Havelock, U.S.A. 77 H7 34 53N 76 54W
Haverfordwest, U.K. 11 F3 51 48N 4 58W
Haverhill, U.S.A. 79 D13 42 47N 71 5W
Haverstraw, U.S.A. 79 E11 41 12N 73 58W
Havirga, Mongolia 34 B7 45 41N 113 5 E
Havířov, Czech Rep. 17 D10 49 46N 18 20 E
Havlíčkův Brod, Czech Rep. 16 D8 49 36N 15 33 E
Havre, U.S.A. 82 B9 48 33N 109 41W
Havre-Aubert, Canada 71 C7 47 12N 61 56W
Havre-St.-Pierre, Canada 71 B7 50 18N 63 33W
Haw ~▸, U.S.A. 77 H6 35 36N 79 3W
Hawaii □, U.S.A. 74 H16 19 30N 156 30W
Hawaii I., Pac. Oc. 74 J17 20 0N 155 0W
Hawaiian Is., Pac. Oc. 74 H17 20 30N 156 0W
Hawaiian Ridge, Pac. Oc. 65 E11 24 0N 165 0W
Hawarden, U.S.A. 80 D6 43 0N 96 29W
Hawea, L., N.Z. 59 L2 44 28S 169 19 E
Hawera, N.Z. 59 H5 39 35S 174 19 E
Hawick, U.K. 12 F6 55 26N 2 47W
Hawk Junction, Canada 70 C3 48 5N 84 38W
Hawke B., N.Z. 59 H6 39 25S 177 20 E
Hawker, Australia 63 E2 31 59S 138 22 E
Hawkesbury, Canada 70 C5 45 37N 74 37W
Hawkesbury I., Canada 72 C3 53 37N 129 3W
Hawkesbury Pt., Australia 62 A1 11 55S 134 5 E
Hawkinsville, U.S.A. 77 J4 32 17N 83 28W
Hawley, Minn., U.S.A. 80 B6 46 53N 96 19W
Hawley, Pa., U.S.A. 79 E9 41 28N 75 11W
Ḩawrān, W. ~▸, Iraq 44 C4 33 58N 42 34 E
Ḩawsh Mūssá, Lebanon 47 B4 33 45N 35 55 E
Hawthorne, U.S.A. 82 G4 38 32N 118 38W
Hay, Australia 63 E3 34 30S 144 51 E
Hay ~▸, Australia 62 C2 24 50S 138 0 E
Hay ~▸, Canada 72 A5 60 50N 116 26W
Hay, C., Australia 60 B4 14 5S 129 29 E
Hay I., Canada 78 B4 44 53N 80 58W
Hay L., Canada 72 B5 58 50N 118 50W
Hay-on-Wye, U.K. 11 E4 52 5N 3 8W
Hay River, Canada 72 A5 60 51N 115 44W
Hay Springs, U.S.A. 80 D3 42 41N 102 41W
Haya = Tehoru, Indonesia 37 E7 3 23S 129 30 E
Hayachine-San, Japan 30 E10 39 34N 141 29 E
Hayden, U.S.A. 82 F10 40 30N 107 16W
Haydon, Australia 62 B3 18 0S 141 30 E
Hayes, U.S.A. 80 C4 44 23N 101 1W
Hayes ~▸, Canada 70 A1 57 3N 92 12W
Hayes Creek, Australia 60 B5 13 43S 131 22 E
Hayle, U.K. 11 G2 50 11N 5 26W
Hayling I., U.K. 11 G7 50 48N 0 59W
Hayrabolu, Turkey 21 D12 41 12N 27 5 E
Hays, Canada 72 C6 50 6N 111 48W
Hays, U.S.A. 80 F5 38 53N 99 20W
Haysyn, Ukraine 17 D15 48 57N 29 25 E
Hayvoron, Ukraine 17 D15 48 22N 29 52 E
Hayward, Calif., U.S.A. 84 H4 37 40N 122 5W
Hayward, Wis., U.S.A. 80 B9 46 1N 91 29W
Haywards Heath, U.K. 11 G7 51 0N 0 5W
Haẕafon □, Israel 47 C4 32 40N 35 20 E
Hazārān, Kūh-e, Iran 45 D8 29 35N 57 20 E
Hazard, U.S.A. 76 G4 37 15N 83 12W
Hazaribag, India 43 H11 23 58N 85 26 E
Hazaribag Road, India 43 G11 24 12N 85 57 E
Hazelton, Canada 72 B3 55 20N 127 42W
Hazelton, U.S.A. 80 B4 46 29N 100 17W
Hazen, U.S.A. 80 B4 47 18N 101 38W
Hazlehurst, Ga., U.S.A. 77 K4 31 52N 82 36W
Hazlehurst, Miss., U.S.A. 81 K9 31 52N 90 24W
Hazlet, U.S.A. 79 F10 40 25N 74 12W
Hazleton, U.S.A. 79 F9 40 57N 75 59W
Hazlett, L., Australia 60 D4 21 30S 128 48 E
Hazro, Turkey 44 B4 38 15N 40 47 E
Head of Bight, Australia 61 F5 31 30S 131 25 E
Headlands, Zimbabwe 55 F3 18 15S 32 2 E
Healdsburg, U.S.A. 84 G4 38 37N 122 52W
Healdton, U.S.A. 81 H6 34 14N 97 29W
Healesville, Australia 63 F4 37 35S 145 30 E
Heany Junction, Zimbabwe 57 C4 20 6S 28 54 E
Heard I., Ind. Oc. 3 G13 53 0S 74 0 E
Hearne, U.S.A. 81 K6 30 53N 96 36W
Hearst, Canada 70 C3 49 40N 83 41W
Heart ~▸, U.S.A. 80 B4 46 46N 100 50W
Heart's Content, Canada 71 C9 47 54N 53 27W
Heath Pt., Canada 71 C7 49 8N 61 40W
Heavener, U.S.A. 81 H7 34 53N 94 36W
Hebbronville, U.S.A. 81 M5 27 18N 98 41W
Hebei □, China 34 E9 39 0N 116 0 E
Hebel, Australia 63 D4 28 58S 147 47 E
Heber, U.S.A. 85 N11 32 44N 115 32W
Heber City, U.S.A. 82 F8 40 31N 111 25W
Heber Springs, U.S.A. 81 H9 35 30N 92 2W
Hebert, Canada 73 C7 50 30N 107 10W
Hebgen L., U.S.A. 82 D8 44 52N 111 20W
Hebi, China 34 G8 35 57N 114 7 E
Hebrides, U.K. 6 D4 57 30N 7 0W
Hebrides, Sea of the, U.K. 12 D2 57 5N 7 0W
Hebron = Al Khalīl, West Bank 47 D4 31 32N 35 6 E
Hebron, Canada 69 C13 58 5N 62 30W
Hebron, N. Dak., U.S.A. 80 B3 46 54N 102 3W
Hebron, Nebr., U.S.A. 80 E6 40 10N 97 35W
Hecate Str., Canada 72 C2 53 10N 130 30W
Heceta I., U.S.A. 72 B2 55 46N 133 40W
Hechi, China 32 D5 24 40N 108 2 E
Hechuan, China 32 C5 30 2N 106 12 E
Hecla, U.S.A. 80 C5 45 53N 98 9W
Hecla I., Canada 73 C9 51 10N 96 43W
Hede, Sweden 9 E15 62 23N 13 30 E
Hedemora, Sweden 9 F16 60 18N 15 58 E
Heerde, Neths. 15 B6 52 24N 6 2 E
Heerenveen, Neths. 15 B5 52 57N 5 55 E
Heerhugowaard, Neths. 15 B4 52 40N 4 51 E
Heerlen, Neths. 18 A6 50 55N 5 58 E
Ḩefa, Israel 47 C4 32 46N 35 0 E
Ḩefa □, Israel 47 C4 32 40N 35 0 E
Hefei, China 33 C6 31 52N 117 18 E

Hegang, China 33 B8 47 20N 130 19 E
Heichengzhen, China 34 F4 36 24N 106 3 E
Heidelberg, Germany 16 D5 49 24N 8 42 E
Heidelberg, S. Africa 56 E3 34 6S 20 59 E
Heilbron, S. Africa 57 D4 27 16S 27 59 E
Heilbronn, Germany 16 D5 49 9N 9 13 E
Heilongjiang □, China 33 B7 48 0N 126 0 E
Heilunkiang = Heilongjiang □, China 33 B7 48 0N 126 0 E
Heimaey, Iceland 8 E3 63 26N 20 17W
Heinola, Finland 9 F22 61 13N 26 2 E
Heinze Kyun, Burma 38 E1 14 25N 97 45 E
Heishan, China 35 D12 41 40N 122 5 E
Heishui, China 35 C10 42 8N 119 30 E
Hejaz = Ḥijāz □, Si. Arabia 46 C2 24 0N 40 0 E
Hejian, China 34 E9 38 25N 116 5 E
Hejin, China 34 G6 35 35N 110 42 E
Hekımhan, Turkey 44 B3 38 50N 37 55 E
Hekla, Iceland 8 E4 63 56N 19 35W
Hekou, China 32 D5 22 30N 103 59 E
Helan Shan, China 34 E3 38 30N 105 55 E
Helen Atoll, Pac. Oc. 37 D8 2 40N 132 0 E
Helena, Ark., U.S.A. 81 H9 34 32N 90 36W
Helena, Mont., U.S.A. 82 C7 46 36N 112 2W
Helendale, U.S.A. 85 L9 34 44N 117 19W
Helensburgh, U.K. 12 E4 56 1N 4 43W
Helensville, N.Z. 59 G5 36 41S 174 29 E
Helenvale, Australia 62 B4 15 43S 145 14 E
Helgeland, Norway 8 C15 66 7N 13 29 E
Helgoland, Germany 16 A4 54 10N 7 53 E
Heligoland = Helgoland, Germany 16 A4 54 10N 7 53 E
Heligoland B. = Deutsche Bucht, Germany 16 A5 54 15N 8 0 E
Hella, Iceland 8 E3 63 50N 20 24W
Hellertown, U.S.A. 79 F9 40 35N 75 21W
Hellespont = Çanakkale Boğazı, Turkey 21 D12 40 17N 26 32 E
Hellevoetsluis, Neths. 15 C4 51 50N 4 8 E
Hellín, Spain 19 C5 38 31N 1 40W
Helmand □, Afghan. 40 D4 31 20N 64 0 E
Helmand →, Afghan. 40 D2 31 12N 61 34 E
Helmeringhausen, Namibia 56 D2 25 54S 16 57 E
Helmond, Neths. 15 C5 51 29N 5 41 E
Helmsdale, U.K. 12 C5 58 7N 3 39W
Helmsdale →, U.K. 12 C5 58 7N 3 40W
Helong, China 35 C15 42 40N 129 0 E
Helper, U.S.A. 82 G8 39 41N 110 51W
Helsingborg, Sweden 9 H15 56 3N 12 42 E
Helsingfors = Helsinki, Finland 9 F21 60 15N 25 3 E
Helsingør, Denmark 9 H15 56 2N 12 35 E
Helsinki, Finland 9 F21 60 15N 25 3 E
Helston, U.K. 11 G2 50 6N 5 17W
Helvellyn, U.K. 10 C4 54 32N 3 1W
Helwân, Egypt 51 C12 29 50N 31 20 E
Hemel Hempstead, U.K. 11 F7 51 44N 0 28W
Hemet, U.S.A. 85 M10 33 45N 116 58W
Hemingford, U.S.A. 80 D3 42 19N 103 4W
Hemmingford, Canada 79 A11 45 3N 73 35W
Hempstead, U.S.A. 81 K6 30 6N 96 5W
Hemse, Sweden 9 H18 57 15N 18 22 E
Henan □, China 34 H8 34 0N 114 0 E
Henares →, Spain 19 B4 40 24N 3 30W
Henashi-Misaki, Japan 30 D9 40 37N 139 51 E
Henderson, Argentina 94 D3 36 18S 61 43W
Henderson, Ky., U.S.A. 76 G2 37 50N 87 35W
Henderson, N.C., U.S.A. 77 G6 36 20N 78 25W
Henderson, Nev., U.S.A. 85 J12 36 2N 114 59W
Henderson, Tenn., U.S.A. 77 H1 35 26N 88 38W
Henderson, Tex., U.S.A. 81 J7 32 9N 94 48W
Hendersonville, N.C., U.S.A. 77 H4 35 19N 82 28W
Hendersonville, Tenn., U.S.A. 77 G2 36 18N 86 37W
Hendījān, Iran 45 D6 30 14N 49 43 E
Hendorābī, Iran 45 E7 26 40N 53 37 E
Hengcheng, China 34 E4 38 18N 106 28 E
Hengdaohezi, China 35 B15 44 52N 129 0 E
Hengelo, Neths. 15 B6 52 16N 6 48 E
Hengshan, China 34 F5 37 58N 109 5 E
Hengshui, China 34 F8 37 41N 115 40 E
Hengyang, China 33 D6 26 59N 112 22 E
Henlopen, C., U.S.A. 76 F8 38 48N 75 6W
Hennenman, S. Africa 56 D4 27 59S 27 1 E
Hennessey, U.S.A. 81 G6 36 6N 97 54W
Henrietta, U.S.A. 81 J5 33 49N 98 12W
Henrietta, Ostrov = Genriyetty, Ostrov, Russia 27 B16 77 6N 156 30 E
Henrietta Maria, C., Canada 70 A3 55 9N 82 20W
Henry, U.S.A. 80 E10 41 7N 89 22W
Henryetta, U.S.A. 81 H7 35 27N 95 59W
Henryville, Canada 79 A11 45 8N 73 11W
Hensall, Canada 78 C3 43 26N 81 30W
Hentiesbaai, Namibia 56 C1 22 8S 14 18 E
Hentiyn Nuruu, Mongolia 33 B5 48 30N 108 30 E
Henty, Australia 63 F4 35 30S 147 0 E
Henzada, Burma 41 L19 17 38N 95 26 E
Heppner, U.S.A. 82 D4 45 21N 119 33W
Hepworth, Canada 78 B3 44 37N 81 9W
Hequ, China 34 E6 39 20N 111 15 E
Héraðsflói, Iceland 8 D6 65 42N 14 12W
Héraðsvötn →, Iceland 8 D4 65 45N 19 25W
Herald Cays, Australia 62 B4 16 58S 149 9 E
Herāt, Afghan. 40 B3 34 20N 62 7 E
Herāt □, Afghan. 40 B3 35 0N 62 0 E
Herbert →, Australia 62 B4 18 31S 146 17 E
Herberton, Australia 62 B4 17 20S 145 25 E
Herbertsdale, S. Africa 56 E3 34 1S 21 46 E
Herceg-Novi, Montenegro, Yug. 21 C8 42 30N 18 33 E
Herchmer, Canada 73 B10 57 22N 94 10W
Herðubreið, Iceland 8 D5 65 11N 16 21W
Hereford, U.K. 11 E5 52 4N 2 43W
Hereford, U.S.A. 81 H3 34 49N 102 24W
Herefordshire □, U.K. 11 E5 52 8N 2 40W
Herentals, Belgium 15 C4 51 12N 4 51 E
Herford, Germany 16 B5 52 7N 8 39 E
Herington, U.S.A. 80 F6 38 40N 96 57W
Herkimer, U.S.A. 79 D10 43 0N 74 59W
Herlong, U.S.A. 84 E6 40 8N 120 8W
Herm, U.K. 11 H5 49 30N 2 28W
Hermann, U.S.A. 80 F9 38 42N 91 27W
Hermannsburg, Australia 60 D5 23 57S 132 45 E
Hermanus, S. Africa 56 E2 34 27S 19 12 E
Hermidale, Australia 63 E4 31 30S 146 42 E
Hermiston, U.S.A. 82 D4 45 51N 119 17W
Hermite, I., Chile 96 H3 55 50S 68 0W
Hermon, U.S.A. 79 B9 44 28N 75 14W
Hermon, Mt. = Shaykh, J. ash, Lebanon 47 B4 33 25N 35 50 E
Hermosillo, Mexico 86 B2 29 10N 111 0W
Hernád →, Hungary 17 D11 47 56N 21 8 E
Hernandarias, Paraguay 95 B5 25 20S 54 40W
Hernandez, U.S.A. 84 J6 36 24N 120 46W
Hernando, Argentina 94 C3 32 28S 63 40W
Hernando, U.S.A. 81 H10 34 50N 90 0W
Herndon, U.S.A. 78 F8 40 43N 76 51W
Herne, Germany 15 C7 51 32N 7 14 E
Herne Bay, U.K. 11 F9 51 21N 1 8 E
Herning, Denmark 9 H13 56 8N 8 58 E
Heroica = Caborca, Mexico 86 A2 30 40N 112 10W
Heroica Nogales = Nogales, Mexico 86 A2 31 20N 110 56W
Heron Bay, Canada 70 C2 48 40N 86 25W
Herradura, Pta. de la, Canary Is. 22 F5 28 26N 14 8W
Herreid, U.S.A. 80 C4 45 50N 100 4W
Herrin, U.S.A. 81 G10 37 48N 89 2W
Herriot, Canada 73 B8 56 22N 101 16W
Hershey, U.S.A. 79 F8 40 17N 76 39W
Hersonissos, Greece 23 D7 35 18N 25 22 E
Herstal, Belgium 15 D5 50 40N 5 38 E
Hertford, U.K. 11 F7 51 48N 0 4W
Hertfordshire □, U.K. 11 F7 51 51N 0 5W
's-Hertogenbosch, Neths. 15 C5 51 42N 5 17 E
Hertzogville, S. Africa 56 D4 28 9S 25 30 E
Hervey B., Australia 62 C5 25 0S 152 52 E
Herzliyya, Israel 47 C3 32 10N 34 50 E
Ḥeşār, Fārs, Iran 45 D6 29 52N 50 16 E
Ḥeşār, Markazī, Iran 45 C6 35 50N 49 12 E
Heshui, China 34 G5 35 48N 108 0 E
Heshun, China 34 F7 37 22N 113 32 E
Hesperia, U.S.A. 85 L9 34 25N 117 18W
Hesse = Hessen □, Germany 16 C5 50 30N 9 0 E
Hessen □, Germany 16 C5 50 30N 9 0 E
Hetch Hetchy Aqueduct, U.S.A. 84 H5 37 29N 122 19W
Hettinger, U.S.A. 80 C3 46 0N 102 42W
Heuvelton, U.S.A. 79 B9 44 37N 75 25W
Hewitt, U.S.A. 81 K6 31 27N 97 11W
Hexham, U.K. 10 C5 54 58N 2 4W
Hexigten Qi, China 35 C9 43 18N 117 30 E
Ḥeydarābād, Iran 45 D7 30 33N 55 38 E
Heysham, U.K. 10 C5 54 3N 2 53W
Heywood, Australia 63 F3 38 8S 141 37 E
Heze, China 34 G8 35 14N 115 20 E
Hi Vista, U.S.A. 85 L9 34 45N 117 46W
Hialeah, U.S.A. 77 N5 25 50N 80 17W
Hiawatha, U.S.A. 80 F7 39 51N 95 32W
Hibbing, U.S.A. 80 B8 47 25N 92 56W
Hibbs B., Australia 62 G4 42 35S 145 15 E
Hibernia Reef, Australia 60 B3 12 0S 123 23 E
Hickman, U.S.A. 81 G10 36 34N 89 11W
Hickory, U.S.A. 77 H5 35 44N 81 21W
Hicks, Pt., Australia 63 F4 37 49S 149 17 E
Hicks L., Canada 73 A9 61 25N 100 0W
Hicksville, U.S.A. 79 F11 40 46N 73 32W
Hida-Gawa →, Japan 31 G8 35 26N 137 3 E
Hida-Sammyaku, Japan 31 F8 36 30N 137 40 E
Hidaka-Sammyaku, Japan 30 C11 42 35N 142 45 E
Hidalgo, Mexico 87 C5 24 15N 99 26W
Hidalgo □, Mexico 87 C5 20 30N 99 10W
Hidalgo, Presa M., Mexico 86 B3 26 30N 108 35W
Hidalgo del Parral, Mexico 86 B3 26 58N 105 40W
Hierro, Canary Is. 22 G1 27 44N 18 0W
Higashiajima-San, Japan 30 F10 37 40N 140 10 E
Higashiōsaka, Japan 31 G7 34 40N 135 37 E
Higgins, U.S.A. 81 G4 36 7N 100 2W
Higgins Corner, U.S.A. 84 F5 39 2N 121 5W
High Atlas = Haut Atlas, Morocco 50 B4 32 30N 5 0W
High Bridge, U.S.A. 79 F10 40 40N 74 54W
High Level, Canada 72 B5 58 31N 117 8W
High Point, U.S.A. 77 H6 35 57N 80 0W
High Prairie, Canada 72 B5 55 30N 116 30W
High River, Canada 72 C6 50 30N 113 50W
High Tatra = Tatry, Slovak Rep. 17 D11 49 20N 20 0 E
High Veld, Africa 48 J6 27 0S 27 0 E
High Wycombe, U.K. 11 F7 51 37N 0 45W
Highland □, U.K. 12 D4 57 17N 4 21W
Highland Park, U.S.A. 76 D2 42 11N 87 48W
Highmore, U.S.A. 80 C5 44 31N 99 27W
Highrock L., Man., Canada 73 B8 55 45N 100 30W
Highrock L., Sask., Canada 73 B7 57 5N 105 32W
Higüey, Dom. Rep. 89 C6 18 37N 68 42W
Hiiumaa, Estonia 9 G20 58 50N 22 45 E
Ḥijāz □, Si. Arabia 46 C2 24 0N 40 0 E
Hijo = Tagum, Phil. 37 C7 7 33N 125 53 E
Hikari, Japan 31 H5 33 58N 131 58 E
Hiko, U.S.A. 84 H11 37 32N 115 14W
Hikone, Japan 31 G8 35 15N 136 10 E
Hikurangi, Gisborne, N.Z. 59 H6 37 55S 178 4 E
Hikurangi, Northland, N.Z. 59 F5 35 36S 174 17 E
Hildesheim, Germany 16 B5 52 9N 9 56 E
Hill →, Australia 61 F2 30 23S 115 3 E
Hill City, Idaho, U.S.A. 82 E6 43 18N 115 3W
Hill City, Kans., U.S.A. 80 F5 39 22N 99 51W
Hill City, S. Dak., U.S.A. 80 D3 43 56N 103 35W
Hill Island L., Canada 73 A7 60 30N 109 50W
Hillcrest Center, U.S.A. 85 K8 35 23N 118 57W
Hillegom, Neths. 15 B4 52 18N 4 35 E
Hillerød, Denmark 9 J15 55 56N 12 19 E
Hillsboro, Kans., U.S.A. 80 F6 38 21N 97 12W
Hillsboro, N. Dak., U.S.A. 80 B6 47 26N 97 3W
Hillsboro, N.H., U.S.A. 79 C13 43 7N 71 54W
Hillsboro, Ohio, U.S.A. 76 F4 39 12N 83 37W
Hillsboro, Oreg., U.S.A. 84 E4 45 31N 122 59W
Hillsboro, Tex., U.S.A. 81 J6 32 1N 97 8W
Hillsborough, Grenada 89 D7 12 28N 61 28W
Hillsdale, Mich., U.S.A. 76 E3 41 56N 84 38W
Hillsdale, N.Y., U.S.A. 79 D11 42 11N 73 30W
Hillsport, Canada 70 C2 49 27N 85 34W
Hillston, Australia 63 E4 33 30S 145 31 E
Hilo, U.S.A. 74 J17 19 44N 155 5W
Hilton, U.S.A. 78 C7 43 17N 77 48W
Hilton Head Island, U.S.A. 77 J5 32 13N 80 45W
Hilversum, Neths. 15 B5 52 14N 5 10 E
Himachal Pradesh □, India 42 D7 31 30N 77 0 E
Himalaya, Asia 43 E11 29 0N 84 0 E
Himatnagar, India 40 H8 23 37N 72 57 E
Himeji, Japan 31 G7 34 50N 134 40 E
Himi, Japan 31 F8 36 50N 136 55 E
Ḥimş, Syria 47 A5 34 40N 36 45 E
Ḥimş □, Syria 47 A6 34 30N 37 0 E
Hinche, Haiti 89 C5 19 9N 72 1W
Hinchinbrook I., Australia 62 B4 18 20S 146 15 E
Hinckley, U.K. 11 E6 52 33N 1 22W
Hinckley, U.S.A. 80 B8 46 1N 92 56W
Hindaun, India 42 F7 26 44N 77 5 E
Hindmarsh, L., Australia 63 F3 36 5S 141 55 E
Hindu Bagh, Pakistan 42 D2 30 56N 67 50 E
Hindu Kush, Asia 40 B7 36 0N 71 0 E
Hindubagh, Pakistan 40 D5 30 56N 67 57 E
Hindupur, India 40 N10 13 49N 77 32 E
Hines Creek, Canada 72 B5 56 20N 118 40W
Hinesville, U.S.A. 77 K5 31 51N 81 36W
Hinganghat, India 40 J11 20 30N 78 52 E
Hingham, U.S.A. 82 B8 48 33N 110 25W
Hingir, India 43 J10 21 57N 83 41 E
Hingoli, India 40 K10 19 41N 77 15 E
Hinna = Imi, Ethiopia 46 F3 6 28N 42 10 E
Hinnøya, Norway 8 B16 68 35N 15 50 E
Hinojosa del Duque, Spain 19 C3 38 30N 5 9W
Hinsdale, U.S.A. 79 D12 42 47N 72 29W
Hinton, Canada 72 C5 53 26N 117 34W
Hinton, U.S.A. 76 G5 37 40N 80 54W
Hirado, Japan 31 H4 33 22N 129 33 E
Hirakud Dam, India 41 J13 21 32N 83 45 E
Hiran →, India 43 H8 23 6N 79 21 E
Hirapur, India 43 G8 24 22N 79 13 E
Hiratsuka, Japan 31 G9 35 19N 139 21 E
Hiroo, Japan 30 C11 42 17N 143 19 E
Hirosaki, Japan 30 D10 40 34N 140 28 E
Hiroshima, Japan 31 G6 34 24N 132 30 E
Hiroshima □, Japan 31 G6 34 50N 133 0 E
Hisar, India 42 E6 29 12N 75 45 E
Hisb →, Iraq 44 D5 31 45N 44 17 E
Ḥismá, Si. Arabia 44 D3 28 30N 36 0 E
Hispaniola, W. Indies 89 C5 19 0N 71 0W
Hīt, Iraq 44 C4 33 38N 42 49 E
Hita, Japan 31 H5 33 20N 130 58 E
Hitachi, Japan 31 F10 36 36N 140 39 E
Hitchin, U.K. 11 F7 51 58N 0 16W
Hitoyoshi, Japan 31 H5 32 13N 130 45 E
Hitra, Norway 8 E13 63 30N 8 45 E
Hixon, Canada 72 C4 53 25N 122 35W
Ḥiyyon, N. →, Israel 47 E4 30 25N 35 10 E
Hjalmar L., Canada 73 A7 61 33N 109 25W
Hjälmaren, Sweden 9 G16 59 18N 15 40 E
Hjørring, Denmark 9 H13 57 29N 9 59 E
Hkakabo Razi, Burma 41 E20 28 25N 97 23 E
Hlobane, S. Africa 57 D5 27 42S 31 0 E
Hluhluwe, S. Africa 57 D5 28 1S 32 15 E
Hlyboka, Ukraine 17 D13 48 5N 25 56 E
Ho Chi Minh City = Thanh Pho Ho Chi Minh, Vietnam 39 G6 10 58N 106 40 E
Ho Thuong, Vietnam 38 C5 19 32N 105 48 E
Hoa Binh, Vietnam 38 B5 20 50N 105 20 E
Hoa Da, Vietnam 39 G7 11 16N 108 40 E
Hoa Hiep, Vietnam 39 G5 11 34N 105 51 E
Hoai Nhon, Vietnam 38 E7 14 28N 109 1 E
Hoang Lien Son, Vietnam 38 A4 22 0N 104 0 E
Hoanib →, Namibia 56 B2 19 27S 12 46 E
Hoare B., Canada 69 B13 65 17N 62 30W
Hoarusib →, Namibia 56 B2 19 3S 12 36 E
Hobart, Australia 62 G4 42 50S 147 21 E
Hobart, U.S.A. 81 H5 35 1N 99 6W
Hobbs, U.S.A. 81 J3 32 42N 103 8W
Hobbs Coast, Antarctica 5 D14 74 50S 131 0W
Hobe Sound, U.S.A. 77 M5 27 4N 80 8W
Hoboken, U.S.A. 79 F10 40 45N 74 4W
Hobro, Denmark 9 H13 56 39N 9 46 E
Hoburgen, Sweden 9 H18 56 55N 18 7 E
Hochfeld, Namibia 56 C2 21 28S 17 58 E
Hodaka-Dake, Japan 31 F8 36 17N 137 39 E
Hodeida = Al Ḥudaydah, Yemen 46 E3 14 50N 43 0 E
Hodgeville, Canada 73 C7 50 7N 106 58W
Hodgson, Canada 73 C9 51 13N 97 36W
Hódmezővásárhely, Hungary 17 E11 46 28N 20 22 E
Hodna, Chott el, Algeria 50 A6 35 26N 4 43 E
Hodonín, Czech Rep. 17 D9 48 50N 17 10 E
Hoeamdong, N. Korea 35 C16 42 30N 130 16 E
Hoek van Holland, Neths. 15 C4 52 0N 4 7 E
Hoengsŏng, S. Korea 35 F14 37 29N 127 59 E
Hoeryong, N. Korea 35 C15 42 30N 129 45 E
Hoeyang, N. Korea 35 E14 38 43N 127 36 E
Hof, Germany 16 C6 50 19N 11 55 E
Hofmeyr, S. Africa 56 E4 31 39S 25 50 E
Höfn, Iceland 8 D6 64 15N 15 13W
Hofors, Sweden 9 F17 60 31N 16 15 E
Hofsjökull, Iceland 8 D4 64 49N 18 48W
Hōfu, Japan 31 G5 34 3N 131 34 E
Hogan Group, Australia 63 F4 39 13S 147 1 E
Hogarth, Mt., Australia 62 C2 21 48S 136 58 E
Hoggar = Ahaggar, Algeria 50 D7 23 0N 6 30 E
Hogsty Reef, Bahamas 89 B5 21 41N 73 48W
Hoh →, U.S.A. 84 C2 47 45N 124 29W
Hohe Venn, Belgium 15 D6 50 30N 6 5 E
Hohenwald, U.S.A. 77 H2 35 33N 87 33W
Hoher Rhön = Rhön, Germany 16 C5 50 24N 9 58 E
Hohhot, China 34 D6 40 52N 111 40 E
Hóhlakas, Greece 23 D9 35 57N 27 53 E
Hoi An, Vietnam 38 E7 15 30N 108 19 E
Hoi Xuan, Vietnam 38 B5 20 25N 105 9 E
Hoisington, U.S.A. 80 F5 38 31N 98 47W
Hōjō, Japan 31 H6 33 58N 132 46 E
Hokianga Harbour, N.Z. 59 F4 35 31S 173 22 E
Hokitika, N.Z. 59 K3 42 42S 171 0 E
Hokkaidō □, Japan 30 C11 43 30N 143 0 E
Holbrook, Australia 63 F4 35 42S 147 18 E
Holbrook, U.S.A. 83 J8 34 54N 110 10W
Holden, U.S.A. 82 G7 39 6N 112 16W
Holdenville, U.S.A. 81 H6 35 5N 96 24W
Holdrege, U.S.A. 80 E5 40 26N 99 23W
Holguín, Cuba 88 B4 20 50N 76 20W
Hollams Bird I., Namibia 56 C1 24 40S 14 30 E
Holland, Mich., U.S.A. 76 D2 42 47N 86 7W
Holland, N.Y., U.S.A. 78 D6 42 38N 78 32W
Hollandale, U.S.A. 81 J9 33 10N 90 51W
Hollandia = Jayapura, Indonesia 37 E10 2 28S 140 38 E
Holley, U.S.A. 78 C6 43 14N 78 2W
Hollidaysburg, U.S.A. 78 F6 40 26N 78 24W
Hollis, U.S.A. 81 H5 34 41N 99 55W
Hollister, Calif., U.S.A. 84 J5 36 51N 121 24W
Hollister, Idaho, U.S.A. 82 E6 42 21N 114 35W
Holly Hill, U.S.A. 77 L5 29 16N 81 3W
Holly Springs, U.S.A. 81 H10 34 46N 89 27W
Hollywood, U.S.A. 77 N5 26 1N 80 9W
Holman, Canada 68 A8 70 44N 117 44W
Hólmavík, Iceland 8 D3 65 42N 21 40W
Holmen, U.S.A. 80 D9 43 58N 91 15W
Holmes Reefs, Australia 62 B4 16 27S 148 0 E
Holmsund, Sweden 8 E19 63 41N 20 20 E
Holroyd →, Australia 62 A3 14 10S 141 36 E
Holstebro, Denmark 9 H13 56 22N 8 37 E
Holsworthy, U.K. 11 G3 50 48N 4 22W
Holton, Canada 71 B8 54 31N 57 12W
Holton, U.S.A. 80 F7 39 28N 95 44W
Holtville, U.S.A. 85 N11 32 49N 115 23W
Holwerd, Neths. 15 A5 53 22N 5 54 E
Holy I., Angl., U.K. 10 D3 53 17N 4 37W
Holy I., Northumb., U.K. 10 B6 55 40N 1 47W
Holyhead, U.K. 10 D3 53 18N 4 38W
Holyoke, Colo., U.S.A. 80 E3 40 35N 102 18W
Holyoke, Mass., U.S.A. 79 D12 42 12N 72 37W
Holyrood, Canada 71 C9 47 27N 53 8W
Homa Bay, Kenya 54 C3 0 36S 34 30 E
Homalin, Burma 41 G19 24 55N 95 0 E
Homand, Iran 45 C8 32 28N 59 37 E
Homathko →, Canada 72 C4 51 0N 124 56W
Hombori, Mali 50 E5 15 20N 1 38W
Home B., Canada 69 B13 68 40N 67 10W
Home Hill, Australia 62 B4 19 43S 147 25 E
Homedale, U.S.A. 82 E5 43 37N 116 56W
Homer, Alaska, U.S.A. 68 C4 59 39N 151 33W
Homer, La., U.S.A. 81 J8 32 48N 93 4W
Homer City, U.S.A. 78 F5 40 32N 79 10W
Homestead, Australia 62 C4 20 20S 145 40 E
Homestead, U.S.A. 77 N5 25 28N 80 29W
Homewood, U.S.A. 84 F6 39 4N 120 8W
Homoine, Mozam. 57 C6 23 55S 35 8 E
Homs = Ḥimş, Syria 47 A5 34 40N 36 45 E
Homyel, Belarus 17 B16 52 28N 31 0 E
Hon Chong, Vietnam 39 G5 10 25N 104 30 E
Hon Me, Vietnam 38 C5 19 23N 105 56 E
Honan = Henan □, China 34 H8 34 0N 114 0 E
Honbetsu, Japan 30 C11 43 7N 143 37 E
Honcut, U.S.A. 84 F5 39 20N 121 32W
Hondeklipbaai, S. Africa 56 E2 30 19S 17 17 E
Hondo, Japan 31 H5 32 27N 130 12 E
Hondo, U.S.A. 81 L5 29 21N 99 9W
Hondo →, Belize 87 D7 18 25N 88 21W
Honduras ■, Cent. Amer. 88 D2 14 40N 86 30W
Honduras, G. de, Caribbean 88 C2 16 50N 87 0W
Hønefoss, Norway 9 F14 60 10N 10 18 E
Honesdale, U.S.A. 79 E9 41 34N 75 16W
Honey L., U.S.A. 84 E6 40 15N 120 19W
Honfleur, France 18 B4 49 25N 0 13 E
Hong →, Vietnam 32 D5 22 0N 104 0 E
Hong Gai, Vietnam 38 B6 20 57N 107 5 E
Hong He →, China 34 H8 32 25N 115 35 E
Hong Kong □, China 33 D6 22 11N 114 14 E
Hongch'ŏn, S. Korea 35 F14 37 44N 127 53 E
Hongjiang, China 33 D5 27 7N 109 59 E
Hongliu He →, China 34 F5 38 0N 109 50 E
Hongor, Mongolia 34 B7 45 45N 112 50 E
Hongsa, Laos 38 C3 19 43N 101 20 E
Hongshui He →, China 33 D5 23 48N 109 30 E
Hongsŏng, S. Korea 35 F14 36 37N 126 38 E
Hongtong, China 34 F6 36 16N 111 40 E
Honguedo, Détroit d', Canada 71 C7 49 15N 64 0W
Hongwon, N. Korea 35 E14 40 0N 127 56 E
Hongze Hu, China 35 H10 33 15N 118 35 E
Honiara, Solomon Is. 64 H7 9 27S 159 57 E
Honiton, U.K. 11 G4 50 47N 3 11W
Honjō, Japan 30 E10 39 23N 140 3 E
Honningsvåg, Norway 8 A21 70 59N 25 59 E
Honolulu, U.S.A. 74 H16 21 19N 157 52W
Honshū, Japan 33 C8 36 0N 138 0 E
Hood, Mt., U.S.A. 82 D3 45 23N 121 42W
Hood, Pt., Australia 61 F2 34 23S 119 34 E
Hood River, U.S.A. 82 D3 45 43N 121 31W
Hoodsport, U.S.A. 84 C3 47 24N 123 9W
Hoogeveen, Neths. 15 B6 52 44N 6 28 E
Hoogezand-Sappemeer, Neths. 15 A6 53 9N 6 45 E
Hooghly = Hugli →, India 43 J13 21 56N 88 4 E
Hooghly-Chinsura = Chunchura, India 43 H13 22 53N 88 27 E
Hook Hd., Ireland 13 D5 52 7N 6 56W
Hook I., Australia 62 C4 20 4S 149 0 E
Hook of Holland = Hoek van Holland, Neths. 15 C4 52 0N 4 7 E
Hooker, U.S.A. 81 G4 36 52N 101 13W
Hooker Creek, Australia 60 C5 18 23S 130 38 E
Hoonah, U.S.A. 72 B1 58 7N 135 27W
Hooper Bay, U.S.A. 68 B3 61 32N 166 6W
Hoopeston, U.S.A. 76 E2 40 28N 87 40W
Hoopstad, S. Africa 56 D4 27 50S 25 55 E
Hoorn, Neths. 15 B5 52 38N 5 4 E
Hoover, U.S.A. 77 J2 33 20N 86 11W
Hoover Dam, U.S.A. 85 K12 36 1N 114 44W
Hooversville, U.S.A. 78 F6 40 9N 78 55W
Hop Bottom, U.S.A. 79 E9 41 42N 75 46W
Hope, Canada 72 D4 49 25N 121 25W
Hope, Ariz., U.S.A. 85 M13 33 43N 113 42W
Hope, Ark., U.S.A. 81 J8 33 40N 93 36W
Hope, L., S. Austral., Australia 63 D2 28 24S 139 18 E
Hope, L., W. Austral., Australia 61 F3 32 35S 120 15 E
Hope I., Canada 78 B4 44 55N 80 11W
Hope Town, Bahamas 88 A4 26 35N 76 57W
Hopedale, Canada 71 A7 55 28N 60 13W
Hopedale, U.S.A. 79 D13 42 8N 71 33W
Hopefield, S. Africa 56 E2 33 3S 18 22 E
Hopei = Hebei □, China 34 E9 39 0N 116 0 E
Hopelchén, Mexico 87 D7 19 46N 89 50W
Hopetoun, Vic., Australia 63 F3 35 42S 142 22 E
Hopetoun, W. Austral., Australia 61 F3 33 57S 120 7 E
Hopetown, S. Africa 56 D3 29 34S 24 3 E
Hopevale, Australia 62 B4 15 16S 145 20 E
Hopewell, U.S.A. 76 G7 37 18N 77 17W
Hopkins, L., Australia 60 D4 24 15S 128 35 E
Hopkinsville, U.S.A. 77 G2 36 52N 87 29W
Hopland, U.S.A. 84 G3 38 58N 123 7W
Hoquiam, U.S.A. 84 D3 46 59N 123 53W
Horden Hills, Australia 60 D5 20 15S 130 0 E

Horinger, China 34 D6 40 28N 111 48 E
Horlick Mts., Antarctica 5 E15 84 0S 102 0W
Horlivka, Ukraine 25 E6 48 19N 38 5 E
Hormak, Iran 45 D9 29 58N 60 51 E
Hormoz, Iran 45 E7 27 35N 55 0 E
Hormoz, Jaz.-ye, Iran 45 E8 27 8N 56 28 E
Hormozgān □, Iran 45 E8 27 30N 56 0 E
Hormuz, Kūh-e, Iran 45 E7 27 27N 55 10 E
Hormuz, Str. of, The Gulf 45 E8 26 30N 56 30 E
Horn, Austria 16 D8 48 39N 15 40 E
Horn, Iceland 8 C2 66 28N 22 28W
Horn →, Canada 72 A5 61 30N 118 1W
Horn, Cape = Hornos, C. de, Chile 96 H3 55 50S 67 30W
Horn Head, Ireland 13 A3 55 14N 8 0W
Horn I., Australia 62 A3 10 37S 142 17 E
Horn Mts., Canada 72 A5 62 15N 119 15W
Hornavan, Sweden 8 C17 66 15N 17 30 E
Hornbeck, U.S.A. 81 K8 31 20N 93 24W
Hornbrook, U.S.A. 82 F2 41 55N 122 33W
Horncastle, U.K. 10 D7 53 13N 0 7W
Hornell, U.S.A. 78 D7 42 20N 77 40W
Hornell L., Canada 72 A5 62 20N 119 25W
Hornepayne, Canada 70 C3 49 14N 84 48W
Hornings Mills, Canada 78 B4 44 9N 80 12W
Hornitos, U.S.A. 84 H6 37 30N 120 14W
Hornos, C. de, Chile 96 H3 55 50S 67 30W
Hornsea, U.K. 10 D7 53 55N 0 11W
Horobetsu, Japan 30 C10 42 24N 141 6 E
Horodenka, Ukraine 17 D13 48 41N 25 29 E
Horodok, Khmelnytskyy, Ukraine 17 D14 49 10N 26 34 E
Horodok, Lviv, Ukraine 17 D12 49 46N 23 32 E
Horokhiv, Ukraine 17 C13 50 30N 24 45 E
Horqin Youyi Qianqi, China 35 A12 46 5N 122 3 E
Horqueta, Paraguay 94 A4 23 15S 56 55W
Horse Creek, U.S.A. 80 E3 41 57N 105 10W
Horse Is., Canada 71 B8 50 15N 55 50W
Horsefly L., Canada 72 C4 52 25N 121 0W
Horseheads, U.S.A. 78 D8 42 10N 76 49W
Horsens, Denmark 9 J13 55 52N 9 51 E
Horsham, Australia 63 F3 36 44S 142 13 E
Horsham, U.K. 11 F7 51 4N 0 20W
Horten, Norway 9 G14 59 25N 10 32 E
Horton, U.S.A. 80 F7 39 40N 95 32W
Horton →, Canada 68 B7 69 56N 126 52W
Horwood L., Canada 70 C3 48 5N 82 20W
Hose, Gunung-Gunung, Malaysia 36 D4 2 5N 114 6 E
Ḩoseynābād, Khuzestān, Iran 45 C6 32 45N 48 20 E
Ḩoseynābād, Kordestān, Iran 44 C5 35 33N 47 8 E
Hoshangabad, India 42 H7 22 45N 77 45 E
Hoshiarpur, India 42 D6 31 30N 75 58 E
Hospet, India 40 M10 15 15N 76 20 E
Hoste, I., Chile 96 H3 55 0S 69 0W
Hot, Thailand 38 C2 18 8N 98 29 E
Hot Creek Range, U.S.A. 82 G6 38 40N 116 20W
Hot Springs, Ark., U.S.A. 81 H8 34 31N 93 3W
Hot Springs, S. Dak., U.S.A. 80 D3 43 26N 103 29W
Hotagen, Sweden 8 E16 63 50N 14 30 E
Hotan, China 32 C2 37 25N 79 55 E
Hotazel, S. Africa 56 D3 27 17S 22 58 E
Hotchkiss, U.S.A. 83 G10 38 48N 107 43W
Hotham, C., Australia 60 B5 12 2S 131 18 E
Hoting, Sweden 8 D17 64 8N 16 15 E
Hotte, Massif de la, Haiti 89 C5 18 30N 73 45W
Hottentotsbaai, Namibia 56 D1 26 8S 14 59 E
Houei Sai, Laos 38 B3 20 18N 100 26 E
Houffalize, Belgium 15 D5 50 8N 5 48 E
Houghton, Mich., U.S.A. 80 B10 47 7N 88 34W
Houghton, N.Y., U.S.A. 78 D6 42 25N 78 10W
Houghton L., U.S.A. 76 C3 44 21N 84 44W
Houhora Heads, N.Z. 59 F4 34 49S 173 9 E
Houlton, U.S.A. 77 B12 46 8N 67 51W
Houma, U.S.A. 81 L9 29 36N 90 43W
Housatonic →, U.S.A. 79 E11 41 10N 73 7W
Houston, Canada 72 C3 54 25N 126 39W
Houston, Mo., U.S.A. 81 G9 37 22N 91 58W
Houston, Tex., U.S.A. 81 L7 29 46N 95 22W
Hout →, S. Africa 57 C4 23 4S 29 36 E
Houtkraal, S. Africa 56 E3 30 23S 24 5 E
Houtman Abrolhos, Australia 61 E1 28 43S 113 48 E
Hovd, Mongolia 32 B4 48 2N 91 37 E
Hove, U.K. 11 G7 50 50N 0 10W
Hoveyzeh, Iran 45 D6 31 27N 48 4 E
Hövsgöl, Mongolia 34 C5 43 37N 109 39 E
Hövsgöl Nuur, Mongolia 32 A5 51 0N 100 30 E
Howard, Australia 63 D5 25 16S 152 32 E
Howard, Pa., U.S.A. 78 F7 41 1N 77 40W
Howard, S. Dak., U.S.A. 80 C6 44 1N 97 32W
Howe, U.S.A. 82 E7 43 48N 113 0W
Howe, C., Australia 63 F5 37 30S 150 0 E
Howe I., Canada 79 B8 44 16N 76 17W
Howell, U.S.A. 76 D4 42 36N 83 56W
Howick, Canada 79 A11 45 11N 73 51W
Howick, S. Africa 57 D5 29 28S 30 14 E
Howick Group, Australia 62 A4 14 20S 145 30 E
Howitt, L., Australia 63 D2 27 40S 138 40 E
Howland I., Pac. Oc. 64 G10 0 48N 176 38W
Howrah = Haora, India 43 H13 22 37N 88 20 E
Howth Hd., Ireland 13 C5 53 22N 6 3W
Höxter, Germany 16 C5 51 46N 9 22 E
Hoy, U.K. 12 C5 58 50N 3 15W
Høyanger, Norway 9 F12 61 13N 6 4 E
Hoyerswerda, Germany 16 C8 51 26N 14 14 E
Hoylake, U.K. 10 D4 53 24N 3 10W
Hpa-an = Pa-an, Burma 41 L20 16 51N 97 40 E
Hpungan Pass, Burma 41 F20 27 30N 96 55 E
Hradec Králové, Czech Rep. 16 C8 50 15N 15 50 E
Hrodna, Belarus 17 B12 53 42N 23 52 E
Hrodzyanka, Belarus 17 B15 53 31N 28 42 E
Hron →, Slovak Rep. 17 E10 47 49N 18 45 E
Hrvatska = Croatia ■, Europe 16 F9 45 20N 16 0 E
Hrymayliv, Ukraine 17 D14 49 20N 26 5 E
Hsenwi, Burma 41 H20 23 22N 97 55 E
Hsiamen = Xiamen, China 33 D6 24 25N 118 4 E
Hsian = Xi'an, China 34 G5 34 15N 109 0 E
Hsinchu, Taiwan 33 D7 24 48N 120 58 E
Hsinhailien = Lianyungang, China 35 G10 34 40N 119 11 E
Hsüchou = Xuzhou, China 35 G9 34 18N 117 10 E
Hu Xian, China 34 G5 34 8N 108 42 E
Hua Hin, Thailand 38 F2 12 34N 99 58 E
Hua Xian, Henan, China 34 G8 35 30N 114 30 E
Hua Xian, Shaanxi, China 34 G5 34 30N 109 48 E
Huab →, Namibia 56 B2 20 52S 13 25 E
Huachinera, Mexico 86 A3 30 9N 108 55W
Huacho, Peru 92 F3 11 10S 77 35W
Huade, China 34 D7 41 55N 113 59 E
Huadian, China 35 C14 43 0N 126 40 E
Huai He →, China 33 C6 33 0N 118 30 E
Huai Yot, Thailand 39 J2 7 45N 99 37 E
Huai'an, Hebei, China 34 D8 40 30N 114 20 E
Huai'an, Jiangsu, China 35 H10 33 30N 119 10 E
Huaibei, China 34 G9 34 0N 116 48 E
Huaide = Gongzhuling, China 35 C13 43 30N 124 40 E
Huaidezhen, China 35 C13 43 48N 124 50 E
Huainan, China 33 C6 32 38N 116 58 E
Huairen, China 34 E7 39 48N 113 20 E
Huairou, China 34 D9 40 20N 116 35 E
Huaiyang, China 34 H8 33 40N 114 52 E
Huaiyin, China 35 H10 33 30N 119 2 E
Huaiyuan, China 35 H9 32 55N 117 10 E
Huajianzi, China 35 D13 41 23N 125 20 E
Huajuapan de Leon, Mexico 87 D5 17 50N 97 48W
Hualapai Peak, U.S.A. 83 J7 35 5N 113 54W
Huallaga →, Peru 92 E3 5 15S 75 30W
Huambo, Angola 53 G3 12 42S 15 54 E
Huan Jiang →, China 34 G5 34 28N 109 0 E
Huan Xian, China 34 F4 36 33N 107 7 E
Huancabamba, Peru 92 E3 5 10S 79 15W
Huancane, Peru 92 G5 15 10S 69 44W
Huancavelica, Peru 92 F3 12 50S 75 5W
Huancayo, Peru 92 F3 12 5S 75 12W
Huanchaca, Bolivia 92 H5 20 15S 66 40W
Huang Hai = Yellow Sea, China 35 G12 35 0N 123 0 E
Huang He →, China 35 F10 37 55N 118 50 E
Huang Xian, China 35 F11 37 38N 120 30 E
Huangling, China 34 G5 35 34N 109 15 E
Huanglong, China 34 G5 35 30N 109 59 E
Huangshan, China 33 D6 29 42N 118 25 E
Huangshi, China 33 C6 30 10N 115 3 E
Huangsongdian, China 35 C14 43 45N 127 25 E
Huantai, China 35 F9 36 58N 117 56 E
Huánuco, Peru 92 E3 9 55S 76 15W
Huaraz, Peru 92 E3 9 30S 77 32W
Huarmey, Peru 92 F3 10 5S 78 5W
Huascarán, Peru 92 E3 9 8S 77 36W
Huasco, Chile 94 B1 28 30S 71 15W
Huasco →, Chile 94 B1 28 27S 71 13W
Huasna, U.S.A. 85 K6 35 6N 120 24W
Huatabampo, Mexico 86 B3 26 50N 109 50W
Huauchinango, Mexico 87 C5 20 11N 98 3W
Huautla de Jiménez, Mexico 87 D5 18 8N 96 51W
Huay Namota, Mexico 86 C4 21 56N 104 30W
Huayin, China 34 G6 34 35N 110 5 E
Hubbard, Ohio, U.S.A. 78 E4 41 9N 80 34W
Hubbard, Tex., U.S.A. 81 K6 31 51N 96 48W
Hubbart Pt., Canada 73 B10 59 21N 94 41W
Hubei □, China 33 C6 31 0N 112 0 E
Huch'ang, N. Korea 35 D14 41 25N 127 2 E
Hucknall, U.K. 10 D6 53 3N 1 13W
Huddersfield, U.K. 10 D6 53 39N 1 47W
Hudiksvall, Sweden 9 F17 61 43N 17 10 E
Hudson, Canada 70 B1 50 6N 92 9W
Hudson, Mass., U.S.A. 79 D13 42 23N 71 34W
Hudson, N.Y., U.S.A. 79 D11 42 15N 73 46W
Hudson, Wis., U.S.A. 80 C8 44 58N 92 45W
Hudson, Wyo., U.S.A. 82 E9 42 54N 108 35W
Hudson →, U.S.A. 79 F10 40 42N 74 2W
Hudson Bay, Nunavut, Canada 69 C11 60 0N 86 0W
Hudson Bay, Sask., Canada 73 C8 52 51N 102 23W
Hudson Falls, U.S.A. 79 C11 43 18N 73 35W
Hudson Mts., Antarctica 5 D16 74 32S 99 20W
Hudson Str., Canada 69 B13 62 0N 70 0W
Hudson's Hope, Canada 72 B4 56 0N 121 54W
Hue, Vietnam 38 D6 16 30N 107 35 E
Huehuetenango, Guatemala 88 C1 15 20N 91 28W
Huejúcar, Mexico 86 C4 22 21N 103 13W
Huelva, Spain 19 D2 37 18N 6 57W
Huentelauquén, Chile 94 C1 31 38S 71 33W
Huerta, Sa. de la, Argentina 94 C2 31 10S 67 30W
Huesca, Spain 19 A5 42 8N 0 25W
Huetamo, Mexico 86 D4 18 36N 100 54W
Hugh →, Australia 62 D1 25 1S 134 1 E
Hughenden, Australia 62 C3 20 52S 144 10 E
Hughes, Australia 61 F4 30 42S 129 31 E
Hughesville, U.S.A. 79 E8 41 14N 76 44W
Hugli →, India 43 J13 21 56N 88 4 E
Hugo, Colo., U.S.A. 80 F3 39 8N 103 28W
Hugo, Okla., U.S.A. 81 H7 34 1N 95 31W
Hugoton, U.S.A. 81 G4 37 11N 101 21W
Hui Xian = Huixian, China 34 G7 35 27N 113 12 E
Hui Xian, China 34 H4 33 50N 106 4 E
Hui'anbu, China 34 F4 37 28N 106 38 E
Huichapán, Mexico 87 C5 20 24N 99 40W
Huifa He →, China 35 C14 43 0N 127 50 E
Huila, Nevado del, Colombia 92 C3 3 0N 76 0W
Huimin, China 35 F9 37 27N 117 28 E
Huinan, China 35 C14 42 40N 126 2 E
Huinca Renancó, Argentina 94 C3 34 51S 64 22W
Huining, China 34 G3 35 38N 105 0 E
Huinong, China 34 E4 39 5N 106 35 E
Huisache, Mexico 86 C4 22 55N 100 25W
Huiting, China 34 G9 34 5N 116 5 E
Huixian, China 34 G7 35 27N 113 12 E
Huixtla, Mexico 87 D6 15 9N 92 28W
Huize, China 32 D5 26 24N 103 15 E
Hukawng Valley, Burma 41 F20 26 30N 96 30 E
Hŭksan-chedo, S. Korea 35 G13 34 40N 125 30 E
Hukuntsi, Botswana 56 C3 23 58S 21 45 E
Ḩulayfā', Si. Arabia 44 E4 25 58N 40 45 E
Huld = Ulaanjirem, Mongolia 34 B3 45 5N 105 30 E
Hulin He →, China 35 B12 45 0N 122 10 E
Hull = Kingston upon Hull, U.K. 10 D7 53 45N 0 21W
Hull, Canada 79 A9 45 25N 75 44W
Hull →, U.K. 10 D7 53 44N 0 20W
Hulst, Neths. 15 C4 51 17N 4 2 E
Hulun Nur, China 33 B6 49 0N 117 30 E
Humahuaca, Argentina 94 A2 23 10S 65 25W
Humaitá, Brazil 92 E6 7 35S 63 1W
Humaitá, Paraguay 94 B4 27 2S 58 31W
Humansdorp, S. Africa 56 E3 34 2S 24 46 E
Humbe, Angola 56 B1 16 40S 14 55 E
Humber →, U.K. 10 D7 53 42N 0 27W
Humboldt, Canada 73 C7 52 15N 105 9W
Humboldt, Iowa, U.S.A. 80 D7 42 44N 94 13W
Humboldt, Tenn., U.S.A. 81 H10 35 50N 88 55W
Humboldt →, U.S.A. 82 F4 39 59N 118 36W
Humboldt Gletscher, Greenland 4 B4 79 30N 62 0W
Hume, U.S.A. 84 J8 36 48N 118 54W
Hume, L., Australia 63 F4 36 0S 147 5 E
Humenné, Slovak Rep. 17 D11 48 55N 21 50 E
Humphreys, Mt., U.S.A. 84 H8 37 17N 118 40W
Humphreys Peak, U.S.A. 83 J8 35 21N 111 41W
Humptulips, U.S.A. 84 C3 47 14N 123 57W
Hūn, Libya 51 C9 29 2N 16 0 E
Hun Jiang →, China 35 D13 40 50N 125 38 E
Húnaflói, Iceland 8 D3 65 50N 20 50W
Hunan □, China 33 D6 27 30N 112 0 E
Hunchun, China 35 C16 42 52N 130 28 E
Hundewali, Pakistan 42 D5 31 55N 72 38 E
Hundred Mile House, Canada 72 C4 51 38N 121 18W
Hunedoara, Romania 17 F12 45 40N 22 50 E
Hung Yen, Vietnam 38 B6 20 39N 106 4 E
Hungary ■, Europe 17 E10 47 20N 19 20 E
Hungary, Plain of, Europe 6 F10 47 0N 20 0 E
Hungerford, Australia 63 D3 28 58S 144 24 E
Hŭngnam, N. Korea 35 E14 39 49N 127 45 E
Hunsberge, Namibia 56 D2 27 45S 17 12 E
Hunsrück, Germany 16 D4 49 56N 7 27 E
Hunstanton, U.K. 10 E8 52 56N 0 29 E
Hunter, U.S.A. 79 D10 42 13N 74 13W
Hunter I., Australia 62 G3 40 30S 144 45 E
Hunter I., Canada 72 C3 51 55N 128 0W
Hunter Ra., Australia 63 E5 32 45S 150 15 E
Hunters Road, Zimbabwe 55 F2 19 9S 29 49 E
Hunterville, N.Z. 59 H5 39 56S 175 35 E
Huntingburg, U.S.A. 76 F2 38 18N 86 57W
Huntingdon, Canada 70 C5 45 6N 74 10W
Huntingdon, U.K. 11 E7 52 20N 0 11W
Huntingdon, U.S.A. 78 F6 40 30N 78 1W
Huntington, Ind., U.S.A. 76 E3 40 53N 85 30W
Huntington, Oreg., U.S.A. 82 D5 44 21N 117 16W
Huntington, Utah, U.S.A. 82 G8 39 20N 110 58W
Huntington, W. Va., U.S.A. 76 F4 38 25N 82 27W
Huntington Beach, U.S.A. 85 M9 33 40N 118 5W
Huntington Station, U.S.A. 79 F11 40 52N 73 26W
Huntly, N.Z. 59 G5 37 34S 175 11 E
Huntly, U.K. 12 D6 57 27N 2 47W
Huntsville, Canada 78 A5 45 20N 79 14W
Huntsville, Ala., U.S.A. 77 H2 34 44N 86 35W
Huntsville, Tex., U.S.A. 81 K7 30 43N 95 33W
Hunyani →, Zimbabwe 55 F3 15 57S 30 39 E
Hunyuan, China 34 E7 39 42N 113 42 E
Hunza →, India 43 B6 35 54N 74 20 E
Huo Xian = Huozhou, China 34 F6 36 36N 111 42 E
Huong Hoa, Vietnam 38 D6 16 37N 106 45 E
Huong Khe, Vietnam 38 C5 18 13N 105 41 E
Huonville, Australia 62 G4 43 0S 147 5 E
Huozhou, China 34 F6 36 36N 111 42 E
Hupeh = Hubei □, China 33 C6 31 0N 112 0 E
Ḩūr, Iran 45 D8 30 50N 57 7 E
Hurd, C., Canada 78 A3 45 13N 81 44W
Hure Qi, China 35 C11 42 45N 121 45 E
Hurghada, Egypt 51 C12 27 15N 33 50 E
Hurley, N. Mex., U.S.A. 83 K9 32 42N 108 8W
Hurley, Wis., U.S.A. 80 B9 46 27N 90 11W
Huron, Calif., U.S.A. 84 J6 36 12N 120 6W
Huron, Ohio, U.S.A. 78 E2 41 24N 82 33W
Huron, S. Dak., U.S.A. 80 C5 44 22N 98 13W
Huron, L., U.S.A. 78 B2 44 30N 82 40W
Hurricane, U.S.A. 83 H7 37 11N 113 17W
Hurunui →, N.Z. 59 K4 42 54S 173 18 E
Húsavík, Iceland 8 C5 66 3N 17 21W
Huşi, Romania 17 E15 46 41N 28 7 E
Huskvarna, Sweden 9 H16 57 47N 14 15 E
Hustadvika, Norway 8 E12 63 0N 7 0 E
Hustontown, U.S.A. 78 F6 40 3N 78 2W
Hutchinson, Kans., U.S.A. 81 F6 38 5N 97 56W
Hutchinson, Minn., U.S.A. 80 C7 44 54N 94 22W
Hutte Sauvage, L. de la, Canada 71 A7 56 15N 64 45W
Hutton, Mt., Australia 63 D4 25 51S 148 20 E
Huy, Belgium 15 D5 50 31N 5 15 E
Huzhou, China 33 C7 30 51N 120 8 E
Hvammstangi, Iceland 8 D3 65 24N 20 57W
Hvar, Croatia 20 C7 43 11N 16 28 E
Hvítá →, Iceland 8 D3 64 30N 21 58W
Hwachŏn-chŏsuji, S. Korea 35 E14 38 5N 127 50 E
Hwang Ho = Huang He →, China 35 F10 37 55N 118 50 E
Hwange, Zimbabwe 55 F2 18 18S 26 30 E
Hwange Nat. Park, Zimbabwe 56 B4 19 0S 26 30 E
Hyannis, Mass., U.S.A. 76 E10 41 39N 70 17W
Hyannis, Nebr., U.S.A. 80 E4 42 0N 101 46W
Hyargas Nuur, Mongolia 32 B4 49 0N 93 0 E
Hydaburg, U.S.A. 72 B2 55 15N 132 50W
Hyde Park, U.S.A. 79 E11 41 47N 73 56W
Hyden, Australia 61 F2 32 24S 118 53 E
Hyder, U.S.A. 72 B2 55 55N 130 5W
Hyderabad, India 40 L11 17 22N 78 29 E
Hyderabad, Pakistan 42 G3 25 23N 68 24 E
Hyères, France 18 E7 43 8N 6 9 E
Hyères, Îs. d', France 18 E7 43 0N 6 20 E
Hyesan, N. Korea 35 D15 41 20N 128 10 E
Hyland →, Canada 72 B3 59 52N 128 12W
Hymia, India 43 C8 33 40N 78 2 E
Hyndman Peak, U.S.A. 82 E6 43 45N 114 8W
Hyōgo □, Japan 31 G7 35 15N 134 50 E
Hyrum, U.S.A. 82 F8 41 38N 111 51W
Hysham, U.S.A. 82 C10 46 18N 107 14W
Hythe, U.K. 11 F9 51 4N 1 5 E
Hyūga, Japan 31 H5 32 25N 131 35 E
Hyvinge = Hyvinkää, Finland 9 F21 60 38N 24 50 E
Hyvinkää, Finland 9 F21 60 38N 24 50 E

I

I-n-Gall, Niger 50 E7 16 51N 7 1 E
Iaco →, Brazil 92 E5 9 3S 68 34W
Iakora, Madag. 57 C8 23 6S 46 40 E
Ialomiţa →, Romania 17 F14 44 42N 27 51 E
Iaşi, Romania 17 E14 47 10N 27 40 E
Ib →, India 43 J10 21 34N 83 48 E
Iba, Phil. 37 A6 15 22N 120 0 E
Ibadan, Nigeria 50 G6 7 22N 3 58 E
Ibagué, Colombia 92 C3 4 20N 75 20W
Ibar →, Serbia, Yug. 21 C9 43 43N 20 45 E
Ibaraki □, Japan 31 F10 36 10N 140 10 E
Ibarra, Ecuador 92 C3 0 21N 78 7W
Ibembo, Dem. Rep. of the Congo 54 B1 2 35N 23 35 E
Ibera, L., Argentina 94 B4 28 30S 57 9W
Iberian Peninsula, Europe 6 H5 40 0N 5 0W
Iberville, Canada 79 A11 45 19N 73 17W
Iberville, Lac d', Canada 70 A5 55 55N 73 15W
Ibiá, Brazil 93 G9 19 30S 46 30W
Ibiapaba, Sa. da, Brazil 93 D10 4 0S 41 30W
Ibicuí →, Brazil 95 B4 29 25S 56 47W
Ibicuy, Argentina 94 C4 33 55S 59 10W
Ibiza = Eivissa, Spain 22 C7 38 54N 1 26 E
Ibo, Mozam. 55 E5 12 22S 40 40 E
Ibonma, Indonesia 37 E8 3 29S 133 31 E
Ibotirama, Brazil 93 F10 12 13S 43 12W
Ibrāhīm →, Lebanon 47 A4 34 4N 35 38 E
'Ibrī, Oman 45 F8 23 14N 56 30 E
Ibu, Indonesia 37 D7 1 35N 127 33 E
Ibusuki, Japan 31 J5 31 12N 130 40 E
Ica, Peru 92 F3 14 0S 75 48W
Iça →, Brazil 92 D5 2 55S 67 58W
Içana, Brazil 92 C5 0 21N 67 19W
Içana →, Brazil 92 C5 0 26N 67 19W
Içel = Mersin, Turkey 25 G5 36 51N 34 36 E
Iceland ■, Europe 8 D4 64 45N 19 0W
Ich'ang = Yichang, China 33 C6 30 40N 111 20 E
Ichchapuram, India 41 K14 19 10N 84 40 E
Ichhawar, India 42 H7 23 1N 77 1 E
Ichihara, Japan 31 G10 35 28N 140 5 E
Ichikawa, Japan 31 G9 35 44N 139 55 E
Ichilo →, Bolivia 92 G6 15 57S 64 50W
Ichinohe, Japan 30 D10 40 13N 141 17 E
Ichinomiya, Japan 31 G8 35 18N 136 48 E
Ichinoseki, Japan 30 E10 38 55N 141 8 E
Icod, Canary Is. 22 F3 28 22N 16 43W
Ida Grove, U.S.A. 80 D7 42 21N 95 28W
Idabel, U.S.A. 81 J7 33 54N 94 50W
Idaho □, U.S.A. 82 D7 45 0N 115 0W
Idaho City, U.S.A. 82 E6 43 50N 115 50W
Idaho Falls, U.S.A. 82 E7 43 30N 112 2W
Idar-Oberstein, Germany 16 D4 49 43N 7 16 E
Idfû, Egypt 51 D12 24 55N 32 49 E
Ídhi Óros, Greece 23 D6 35 15N 24 45 E
Ídhra, Greece 21 F10 37 20N 23 28 E
Idi, Indonesia 36 C1 5 2N 97 37 E
Idiofa, Dem. Rep. of the Congo 52 E3 4 55S 19 42 E
Idlib, Syria 44 C3 35 55N 36 36 E
Idria, U.S.A. 84 J6 36 25N 120 41W
Idutywa, S. Africa 57 E4 32 8S 28 18 E
Ieper, Belgium 15 D2 50 51N 2 53 E
Ierápetra, Greece 23 E7 35 1N 25 44 E
Iesi, Italy 20 C5 43 31N 13 14 E
Ifakara, Tanzania 52 F7 8 8S 36 41 E
'Ifāl, W. al →, Si. Arabia 44 D2 28 7N 35 3 E
Ifanadiana, Madag. 57 C8 21 19S 47 39 E
Ife, Nigeria 50 G6 7 30N 4 31 E
Iffley, Australia 62 B3 18 53S 141 12 E
Iforas, Adrar des, Africa 50 E6 19 40N 1 40 E
Ifould, L., Australia 61 F5 30 52S 132 6 E
Iganga, Uganda 54 B3 0 37N 33 28 E
Igarapava, Brazil 93 H9 20 3S 47 47W
Igarka, Russia 26 C9 67 30N 86 33 E
Igatimi, Paraguay 95 A4 24 5S 55 40W
Iggesund, Sweden 9 F17 61 39N 17 10 E
Iglésias, Italy 20 E3 39 19N 8 32 E
Igloolik, Canada 69 B11 69 20N 81 49W
Igluligaarjuk, Canada 69 B10 63 21N 90 42W
Iglulik = Igloolik, Canada 69 B11 69 20N 81 49W
Ignace, Canada 70 C1 49 30N 91 40W
İğneada Burnu, Turkey 21 D13 41 53N 28 2 E
Igoumenítsa, Greece 21 E9 39 32N 20 18 E
Iguaçu →, Brazil 95 B5 25 36S 54 36W
Iguaçu, Cat. del, Brazil 95 B5 25 41S 54 26W
Iguaçu Falls = Iguaçu, Cat. del, Brazil 95 B5 25 41S 54 26W
Iguala, Mexico 87 D5 18 20N 99 40W
Igualada, Spain 19 B6 41 37N 1 37 E
Iguassu = Iguaçu →, Brazil 95 B5 25 36S 54 36W
Iguatu, Brazil 93 E11 6 20S 39 18W
Iharana, Madag. 57 A9 13 25S 50 0 E
Ihbulag, Mongolia 34 C4 43 11N 107 10 E
Iheya-Shima, Japan 31 L3 27 4N 127 58 E
Ihosy, Madag. 57 C8 22 24S 46 8 E
Ihotry, Farihy, Madag. 57 C7 21 56S 43 41 E
Ii, Finland 8 D21 65 19N 25 22 E
Ii-Shima, Japan 31 L3 26 43N 127 47 E
Iida, Japan 31 G8 35 35N 137 50 E
Iijoki →, Finland 8 D21 65 20N 25 20 E
Iisalmi, Finland 8 E22 63 32N 27 10 E
Iiyama, Japan 31 F9 36 51N 138 22 E
Iizuka, Japan 31 H5 33 38N 130 42 E
Ijebu-Ode, Nigeria 50 G6 6 47N 3 58 E
IJmuiden, Neths. 15 B4 52 28N 4 35 E
IJssel →, Neths. 15 B5 52 35N 5 50 E
IJsselmeer, Neths. 15 B5 52 45N 5 20 E
Ijuí, Brazil 95 B5 28 23S 53 55W
Ijuí →, Brazil 95 B4 27 58S 55 20W
Ikalamavony, Madag. 57 C8 21 9S 46 35 E
Ikaluktutiak, Canada 68 B9 69 10N 105 0W
Ikare, Nigeria 50 G7 7 32N 5 40 E
Ikaría, Greece 21 F12 37 35N 26 10 E
Ikeda, Japan 31 G6 34 1N 133 48 E
Ikela, Dem. Rep. of the Congo 52 E4 1 6S 23 6 E
Iki, Japan 31 H4 33 45N 129 42 E
Ikimba L., Tanzania 54 C3 1 30S 31 20 E
Ikongo, Madag. 57 C8 21 52S 47 27 E
Ikopa →, Madag. 57 B8 16 45S 46 40 E
Ikungu, Tanzania 54 C3 1 33S 33 42 E
Ilagan, Phil. 37 A6 17 7N 121 53 E
Ilaka, Madag. 57 B8 19 33S 48 52 E
Īlām, Iran 44 C5 33 36N 46 36 E
Ilam, Nepal 43 F12 26 58N 87 58 E
Īlām □, Iran 44 C5 33 0N 47 0 E
Ilanskiy, Russia 27 D10 56 14N 96 3 E
Iława, Poland 17 B10 53 36N 19 34 E
Ile →, Kazakstan 26 E8 45 53N 77 10 E
Île-à-la-Crosse, Canada 73 B7 55 27N 107 53W
Île-à-la-Crosse, Lac, Canada 73 B7 55 40N 107 45W
Île-de-France □, France 18 B5 49 0N 2 20 E
Ilebo, Dem. Rep. of the Congo 52 E4 4 17S 20 55 E
Ilek, Russia 26 D6 51 32N 53 21 E
Ilek →, Russia 24 D9 51 30N 53 22 E
Ilesha, Nigeria 50 G6 7 37N 4 40 E
Ilford, Canada 73 B9 56 4N 95 35W
Ilfracombe, Australia 62 C3 23 30S 144 30 E

J

Jaboatão, Brazil 93 E11 8 7S 35 1W
Jaboticabal, Brazil 95 A6 21 15S 48 17W
Jaca, Spain 19 A5 42 35N 0 33W
Jacareí, Brazil 95 A6 23 20S 46 0W
Jacarèzinho, Brazil 95 A6 23 5S 49 58W
Jackman, U.S.A. 77 C10 45 35N 70 17W
Jacksboro, U.S.A. 81 J5 33 14N 98 15W
Jackson, Ala., U.S.A. 77 K2 31 31N 87 53W
Jackson, Calif., U.S.A. 84 G6 38 21N 120 46W
Jackson, Ky., U.S.A. 76 G4 37 33N 83 23W
Jackson, Mich., U.S.A. 76 D3 42 15N 84 24W
Jackson, Minn., U.S.A. 80 D7 43 37N 95 1W
Jackson, Miss., U.S.A. 81 J9 32 18N 90 12W
Jackson, Mo., U.S.A. 81 G10 37 23N 89 40W
Jackson, N.H., U.S.A. 79 B13 44 10N 71 11W
Jackson, Ohio, U.S.A. 76 F4 39 3N 82 39W
Jackson, Tenn., U.S.A. 77 H1 35 37N 88 49W
Jackson, Wyo., U.S.A. 82 E8 43 29N 110 46W
Jackson B., N.Z. 59 K2 43 58S 168 42 E
Jackson L., U.S.A. 82 E8 43 52N 110 36W
Jacksons, N.Z. 59 K3 42 46S 171 32 E
Jackson's Arm, Canada 71 C8 49 52N 56 47W
Jacksonville, Ala., U.S.A. 77 J3 33 49N 85 46W
Jacksonville, Ark., U.S.A. 81 H8 34 52N 92 7W
Jacksonville, Calif., U.S.A. 84 H6 37 52N 120 24W
Jacksonville, Fla., U.S.A. 77 K5 30 20N 81 39W
Jacksonville, Ill., U.S.A. 80 F9 39 44N 90 14W
Jacksonville, N.C., U.S.A. 77 H7 34 45N 77 26W
Jacksonville, Tex., U.S.A. 81 K7 31 58N 95 17W
Jacksonville Beach, U.S.A. 77 K5 30 17N 81 24W
Jacmel, Haiti 89 C5 18 14N 72 32W
Jacob Lake, U.S.A. 83 H7 36 43N 112 13W
Jacobabad, Pakistan 42 E3 28 20N 68 29 E
Jacobina, Brazil 93 F10 11 11S 40 30W
Jacques Cartier, Dét. de, Canada 71 C7 50 0N 63 30W
Jacques Cartier, Mt., Canada 71 C6 48 57N 66 0W
Jacques Cartier, Parc Prov., Canada 71 C5 47 15N 71 33W
Jacuí →, Brazil 95 C5 30 2S 51 15W
Jacumba, U.S.A. 85 N10 32 37N 116 11W
Jacundá →, Brazil 93 D8 1 57S 50 26W
Jadotville = Likasi, Dem. Rep. of the Congo 55 E2 10 55S 26 48 E
Jaén, Peru 92 E3 5 25S 78 40W
Jaén, Spain 19 D4 37 44N 3 43W
Jafarabad, India 42 J4 20 52N 71 22 E
Jaffa = Tel Aviv-Yafo, Israel 47 C3 32 4N 34 48 E
Jaffa, C., Australia 63 F2 36 58S 139 40 E
Jaffna, Sri Lanka 40 Q12 9 45N 80 2 E
Jaffrey, U.S.A. 79 D12 42 49N 72 2W
Jagadhri, India 42 D7 30 10N 77 20 E
Jagadishpur, India 43 G11 25 30N 84 21 E
Jagdalpur, India 41 K13 19 3N 82 0 E
Jagersfontein, S. Africa 56 D4 29 44S 25 27 E
Jaghīn →, Iran 45 E8 27 17N 57 13 E
Jagodina, Serbia, Yug. 21 C9 44 5N 21 15 E
Jagraon, India 40 D9 30 50N 75 25 E
Jagtial, India 40 K11 18 50N 79 0 E
Jaguariaíva, Brazil 95 A6 24 10S 49 50W
Jaguaribe →, Brazil 93 D11 4 25S 37 45W
Jagüey Grande, Cuba 88 B3 22 35N 81 7W
Jahanabad, India 43 G11 25 13N 84 59 E
Jahazpur, India 42 G6 25 37N 75 17 E
Jahrom, Iran 45 D7 28 30N 53 31 E
Jaijon, India 42 D7 31 21N 76 9 E
Jailolo, Indonesia 37 D7 1 5N 127 30 E
Jailolo, Selat, Indonesia 37 D7 0 5N 129 5 E
Jaipur, India 42 F6 27 0N 75 50 E
Jais, India 43 F9 26 15N 81 32 E
Jaisalmer, India 42 F4 26 55N 70 54 E
Jaisinghnagar, India 43 H8 23 38N 78 34 E
Jaitaran, India 42 F5 26 12N 73 56 E
Jaithari, India 43 H8 23 14N 78 37 E
Jājarm, Iran 45 B8 36 58N 56 27 E
Jakam →, India 42 H6 23 54N 74 13 E
Jakarta, Indonesia 36 F3 6 9S 106 49 E
Jakhal, India 42 E6 29 48N 75 50 E
Jakhau, India 42 H3 23 13N 68 43 E
Jakobstad = Pietarsaari, Finland 8 E20 63 40N 22 43 E
Jal, U.S.A. 81 J3 32 7N 103 12W
Jalālābād, Afghan. 42 B4 34 30N 70 29 E
Jalalabad, India 43 F8 27 41N 79 42 E
Jalalpur Jattan, Pakistan 42 C6 32 38N 74 11 E
Jalama, U.S.A. 85 L6 34 29N 120 29W
Jalapa, Guatemala 88 D2 14 39N 89 59W
Jalapa Enríquez, Mexico 87 D5 19 32N 96 55W
Jalasjärvi, Finland 9 E20 62 29N 22 47 E
Jalaun, India 43 F8 26 8N 79 25 E
Jaldhaka →, Bangla. 43 F13 26 16N 89 16 E
Jalesar, India 42 F8 27 29N 78 19 E
Jaleswar, Nepal 43 F11 26 38N 85 48 E
Jalgaon, India 40 J9 21 0N 75 42 E
Jalibah, Iraq 44 D5 30 35N 46 32 E
Jalisco □, Mexico 86 D4 20 0N 104 0W
Jalkot, Pakistan 43 B5 35 14N 73 24 E
Jalna, India 40 K9 19 48N 75 38 E
Jalón →, Spain 19 B5 41 47N 1 4W
Jalor, India 42 G5 25 21N 72 37 E
Jalpa, Mexico 86 C4 21 38N 102 58W
Jalpaiguri, India 41 F16 26 32N 88 46 E
Jaluit I., Marshall Is. 64 G8 6 0N 169 30 E
Jalūlā, Iraq 44 C5 34 16N 45 10 E
Jamaica ■, W. Indies 88 C4 18 10N 77 30W
Jamalpur, Bangla. 41 G16 24 52N 89 56 E
Jamalpur, India 43 G12 25 18N 86 28 E
Jamalpurganj, India 43 H13 23 2N 87 59 E
Jamanxim →, Brazil 93 D7 4 43S 56 18W
Jambi, Indonesia 36 E2 1 38S 103 30 E
Jambi □, Indonesia 36 E2 1 30S 102 30 E
Jambusar, India 42 H5 22 3N 72 51 E
James →, S. Dak., U.S.A. 80 D6 42 52N 97 18W
James →, Va., U.S.A. 76 G7 36 56N 76 27W
James B., Canada 70 B3 54 0N 80 0W
James Ranges, Australia 60 D5 24 10S 132 30 E
James Ross I., Antarctica 5 C18 63 58S 57 50W
Jamesabad, Pakistan 42 G3 25 17N 69 15 E
Jamestown, Australia 63 E2 33 10S 138 32 E
Jamestown, S. Africa 56 E4 31 6S 26 45 E
Jamestown, N. Dak., U.S.A. 80 B5 46 54N 98 42W
Jamestown, N.Y., U.S.A. 78 D5 42 6N 79 14W
Jamestown, Pa., U.S.A. 78 E4 41 29N 80 27W
Jamīlābād, Iran 45 C6 34 24N 48 28 E
Jamiltepec, Mexico 87 D5 16 17N 97 49W
Jamira →, India 43 J13 21 35N 88 28 E
Jamkhandi, India 40 L9 16 30N 75 15 E
Jammu, India 42 C6 32 43N 74 54 E
Jammu & Kashmir □, India 43 B7 34 25N 77 0 E
Jamnagar, India 42 H4 22 30N 70 6 E
Jamni →, India 43 G8 25 13N 78 35 E
Jampur, Pakistan 42 E4 29 39N 70 40 E
Jamrud, Pakistan 42 C4 33 59N 71 24 E
Jämsä, Finland 9 F21 61 53N 25 10 E
Jamshedpur, India 43 H12 22 44N 86 12 E
Jamtara, India 43 H12 23 59N 86 49 E
Jämtland, Sweden 8 E15 63 31N 14 0 E
Jan L., Canada 73 C8 54 56N 102 55W
Jan Mayen, Arctic 4 B7 71 0N 9 0W
Janakkala, Finland 9 F21 60 54N 24 36 E
Janaúba, Brazil 93 G10 15 48S 43 19W
Jand, Pakistan 42 C5 33 30N 72 6 E
Jandaq, Iran 45 C7 34 3N 54 22 E
Jandia, Canary Is. 22 F5 28 6N 14 21W
Jandia, Pta. de, Canary Is. 22 F5 28 3N 14 31W
Jandola, Pakistan 42 C4 32 20N 70 9 E
Jandowae, Australia 63 D5 26 45S 151 7 E
Janesville, U.S.A. 80 D10 42 41N 89 1W
Jangamo, Mozam. 57 C6 24 6S 35 21 E
Janghai, India 43 G10 25 33N 82 19 E
Janīn, West Bank 47 C4 32 28N 35 18 E
Janjgir, India 43 J10 22 1N 82 34 E
Janjina, Madag. 57 C8 20 30S 45 50 E
Janos, Mexico 86 A3 30 45N 108 10W
Januária, Brazil 93 G10 15 25S 44 25W
Janubio, Canary Is. 22 F6 28 56N 13 50W
Jaora, India 42 H6 23 40N 75 10 E
Japan ■, Asia 31 G8 36 0N 136 0 E
Japan, Sea of, Asia 30 E7 40 0N 135 0 E
Japan Trench, Pac. Oc. 28 F18 32 0N 142 0 E
Japen = Yapen, Indonesia 37 E9 1 50S 136 0 E
Japla, India 43 G11 24 33N 84 1 E
Japurá →, Brazil 92 D5 3 8S 65 46W
Jaquarão, Brazil 95 C5 32 34S 53 23W
Jaqué, Panama 88 E4 7 27N 78 8W
Jarābulus, Syria 44 B3 36 49N 38 1 E
Jarama →, Spain 19 B4 40 24N 3 32W
Jaranwala, Pakistan 42 D5 31 15N 73 26 E
Jarash, Jordan 47 C4 32 17N 35 54 E
Jardim, Brazil 94 A4 21 28S 56 2W
Jardines de la Reina, Arch. de los, Cuba 88 B4 20 50N 78 50W
Jargalang, China 35 C12 43 5N 122 55 E
Jargalant = Hovd, Mongolia 32 B4 48 2N 91 37 E
Jari →, Brazil 93 D8 1 9S 51 54W
Jarīr, W. al →, Si. Arabia 44 E4 25 38N 42 30 E
Jarosław, Poland 17 C12 50 2N 22 42 E
Jarrahdale, Australia 61 F2 32 24S 116 5 E
Jarrahi →, Iran 45 D6 30 49N 48 48 E
Jarres, Plaine des, Laos 38 C4 19 27N 103 10 E
Jartai, China 34 E3 39 45N 105 48 E
Jarud Qi, China 35 B11 44 28N 120 50 E
Järvenpää, Finland 9 F21 60 29N 25 5 E
Jarvis, Canada 78 D4 42 53N 80 6W
Jarvis I., Pac. Oc. 65 H12 0 15S 160 5W
Jarwa, India 43 F10 27 38N 82 30 E
Jasdan, India 42 H4 22 2N 71 12 E
Jashpurnagar, India 43 H11 22 54N 84 9 E
Jasidih, India 43 G12 24 31N 86 39 E
Jāsimīyah, Iraq 44 C5 33 45N 44 41 E
Jasin, Malaysia 39 L4 2 20N 102 26 E
Jāsk, Iran 45 E8 25 38N 57 45 E
Jasło, Poland 17 D11 49 45N 21 30 E
Jaso, India 43 G9 24 30N 80 29 E
Jasper, Alta., Canada 72 C5 52 55N 118 5W
Jasper, Ont., Canada 79 B9 44 52N 75 57W
Jasper, Ala., U.S.A. 77 J2 33 50N 87 17W
Jasper, Fla., U.S.A. 77 K4 30 31N 82 57W
Jasper, Ind., U.S.A. 76 F2 38 24N 86 56W
Jasper, Tex., U.S.A. 81 K8 30 56N 94 1W
Jasper Nat. Park, Canada 72 C5 52 50N 118 8W
Jasrasar, India 42 F5 27 43N 73 49 E
Jászberény, Hungary 17 E10 47 30N 19 55 E
Jataí, Brazil 93 G8 17 58S 51 48W
Jati, Pakistan 42 G3 24 20N 68 19 E
Jatibarang, Indonesia 37 G13 6 28S 108 18 E
Jatinegara, Indonesia 37 G12 6 13S 106 52 E
Játiva = Xátiva, Spain 19 C5 38 59N 0 32W
Jaú, Brazil 95 A6 22 10S 48 30W
Jauja, Peru 92 F3 11 45S 75 15W
Jaunpur, India 43 G10 25 46N 82 44 E
Java = Jawa, Indonesia 36 F3 7 0S 110 0 E
Java Barat □, Indonesia 37 G12 7 0S 107 0 E
Java Sea, Indonesia 36 E3 4 35S 107 15 E
Java Tengah □, Indonesia 37 G14 7 0S 110 0 E
Java Timur □, Indonesia 37 G15 8 0S 113 0 E
Java Trench, Ind. Oc. 36 F3 9 0S 105 0 E
Javhlant = Ulyasutay, Mongolia 32 B4 47 56N 97 28 E
Jawa, Indonesia 36 F3 7 0S 110 0 E
Jawad, India 42 G6 24 36N 74 51 E
Jay Peak, U.S.A. 79 B12 44 55N 72 32W
Jaya, Puncak, Indonesia 37 E9 3 57S 137 17 E
Jayanti, India 41 F16 26 45N 89 40 E
Jayapura, Indonesia 37 E10 2 28S 140 38 E
Jayawijaya, Pegunungan, Indonesia 37 E9 5 0S 139 0 E
Jaynagar, India 41 F15 26 43N 86 9 E
Jayrūd, Syria 44 C3 33 49N 36 44 E
Jayton, U.S.A. 81 J4 33 15N 100 34W
Jāz Mūrīān, Hāmūn-e, Iran 45 E8 27 20N 58 55 E
Jazīreh-ye Shīf, Iran 45 D6 29 4N 50 54 E
Jazminal, Mexico 86 C4 24 56N 101 25W
Jazzin, Lebanon 47 B4 33 31N 35 35 E
Jean, U.S.A. 85 K11 35 47N 115 20W
Jean Marie River, Canada 72 A4 61 32N 120 38W
Jean Rabel, Haiti 89 C5 19 50N 73 5W
Jeanerette, U.S.A. 81 L9 29 55N 91 40W
Jeanette, Ostrov = Zhannetty, Ostrov, Russia 27 B16 76 43N 158 0 E
Jeannette, U.S.A. 78 F5 40 20N 79 36W
Jebāl Bārez, Kūh-e, Iran 45 D8 28 30N 58 20 E
Jebel, Bahr el →, Sudan 51 G12 9 30N 30 25 E
Jedburgh, U.K. 12 F6 55 29N 2 33W
Jedda = Jiddah, Si. Arabia 46 C2 21 29N 39 10 E
Jeddore L., Canada 71 C8 48 3N 55 55W
Jędrzejów, Poland 17 C11 50 35N 20 15 E
Jefferson, Iowa, U.S.A. 80 D7 42 1N 94 23W
Jefferson, Ohio, U.S.A. 78 E4 41 44N 80 46W
Jefferson, Tex., U.S.A. 81 J7 32 46N 94 21W
Jefferson, Mt., Nev., U.S.A. 82 G5 38 51N 117 0W
Jefferson, Mt., Oreg., U.S.A. 82 D3 44 41N 121 48W
Jefferson City, Mo., U.S.A. 80 F8 38 34N 92 10W
Jefferson City, Tenn., U.S.A. 77 G4 36 7N 83 30W
Jeffersontown, U.S.A. 76 F3 38 12N 85 35W
Jeffersonville, U.S.A. 76 F3 38 17N 85 44W
Jeffrey City, U.S.A. 82 E10 42 30N 107 49W
Jega, Nigeria 50 F6 12 15N 4 23 E
Jēkabpils, Latvia 9 H21 56 29N 25 57 E
Jekyll I., U.S.A. 77 K5 31 4N 81 25W
Jelenia Góra, Poland 16 C8 50 50N 15 45 E
Jelgava, Latvia 9 H20 56 41N 23 49 E
Jemaja, Indonesia 39 L5 3 5N 105 45 E
Jemaluang, Malaysia 39 L4 2 16N 103 52 E
Jember, Indonesia 37 H15 8 11S 113 41 E
Jembongan, Malaysia 36 C5 6 45N 117 20 E
Jena, Germany 16 C6 50 54N 11 35 E
Jena, U.S.A. 81 K8 31 41N 92 8W
Jenkins, U.S.A. 76 G4 37 10N 82 38W
Jenner, U.S.A. 84 G3 38 27N 123 7W
Jennings, U.S.A. 81 K8 30 13N 92 40W
Jepara, Indonesia 37 G14 7 40S 109 14 E
Jeparit, Australia 63 F3 36 8S 142 1 E
Jequié, Brazil 93 F10 13 51S 40 5W
Jequitinhonha, Brazil 93 G10 16 30S 41 0W
Jequitinhonha →, Brazil 93 G11 15 51S 38 53W
Jerantut, Malaysia 39 L4 3 56N 102 22 E
Jérémie, Haiti 89 C5 18 40N 74 10W
Jerez, Punta, Mexico 87 C5 22 58N 97 40W
Jerez de García Salinas, Mexico 86 C4 22 39N 103 0W
Jerez de la Frontera, Spain 19 D2 36 41N 6 7W
Jerez de los Caballeros, Spain 19 C2 38 20N 6 45W
Jericho = El Arīḥā, West Bank 47 D4 31 52N 35 27 E
Jericho, Australia 62 C4 23 38S 146 6 E
Jerid, Chott el = Djerid, Chott, Tunisia 50 B7 33 42N 8 30 E
Jerilderie, Australia 63 F4 35 20S 145 41 E
Jermyn, U.S.A. 79 E9 41 31N 75 31W
Jerome, U.S.A. 82 E6 42 44N 114 31W
Jerramungup, Australia 61 F2 33 55S 118 55 E
Jersey, U.K. 11 H5 49 11N 2 7W
Jersey City, U.S.A. 79 F10 40 44N 74 4W
Jersey Shore, U.S.A. 78 E7 41 12N 77 15W
Jerseyville, U.S.A. 80 F9 39 7N 90 20W
Jerusalem, Israel 47 D4 31 47N 35 10 E
Jervis B., Australia 63 F5 35 8S 150 46 E
Jervis Inlet, Canada 72 C4 50 0N 123 57W
Jesi = Iesi, Italy 20 C5 43 31N 13 14 E
Jesselton = Kota Kinabalu, Malaysia 36 C5 6 0N 116 4 E
Jessore, Bangla. 41 H16 23 10N 89 10 E
Jesup, U.S.A. 77 K5 31 36N 81 53W
Jesús Carranza, Mexico 87 D5 17 28N 95 1W
Jesús María, Argentina 94 C3 30 59S 64 5W
Jetmore, U.S.A. 81 F5 38 4N 99 54W
Jetpur, India 42 J4 21 45N 70 10 E
Jevnaker, Norway 9 F14 60 15N 10 26 E
Jewett, U.S.A. 78 F3 40 22N 81 2W
Jewett City, U.S.A. 79 E13 41 36N 72 0W
Jeyḥūnābād, Iran 45 C6 34 58N 48 59 E
Jeypore, India 41 K13 18 50N 82 38 E
Jha Jha, India 43 G12 24 46N 86 22 E
Jhaarkand = Jharkhand □, India 43 H11 24 0N 85 50 E
Jhabua, India 42 H6 22 46N 74 36 E
Jhajjar, India 42 E7 28 37N 76 42 E
Jhal, Pakistan 42 E2 28 17N 67 27 E
Jhal Jhao, Pakistan 40 F4 26 20N 65 35 E
Jhalawar, India 42 G7 24 40N 76 10 E
Jhalida, India 43 H11 23 22N 85 58 E
Jhalrapatan, India 42 G7 24 33N 76 10 E
Jhang Maghiana, Pakistan 42 D5 31 15N 72 22 E
Jhansi, India 43 G8 25 30N 78 36 E
Jhargram, India 43 H12 22 27N 86 59 E
Jharia, India 43 H12 23 45N 86 26 E
Jharkhand □, India 43 H11 24 0N 85 50 E
Jharsuguda, India 41 J14 21 56N 84 5 E
Jhelum, Pakistan 42 C5 33 0N 73 45 E
Jhelum →, Pakistan 42 D6 31 20N 72 10 E
Jhilmilli, India 43 H10 23 24N 82 51 E
Jhudo, Pakistan 42 G3 24 58N 69 18 E
Jhunjhunu, India 42 E6 28 10N 75 30 E
Ji-Paraná, Brazil 92 F6 10 52S 62 57W
Ji Xian, Hebei, China 34 F8 37 35N 115 30 E
Ji Xian, Henan, China 34 G8 35 22N 114 5 E
Ji Xian, Shanxi, China 34 F6 36 7N 110 40 E
Jia Xian, Henan, China 34 H7 33 59N 113 12 E
Jia Xian, Shaanxi, China 34 E6 38 12N 110 28 E
Jiamusi, China 33 B8 46 40N 130 26 E
Ji'an, Jiangxi, China 33 D6 27 6N 114 59 E
Ji'an, Jilin, China 35 D14 41 5N 126 10 E
Jianchang, China 35 D11 40 55N 120 35 E
Jianchangying, China 35 D10 40 10N 118 50 E
Jiangcheng, China 32 D5 22 36N 101 52 E
Jiangmen, China 33 D6 22 32N 113 0 E
Jiangsu □, China 35 H11 33 0N 120 0 E
Jiangxi □, China 33 D6 27 30N 116 0 E
Jiao Xian = Jiaozhou, China 35 F11 36 18N 120 1 E
Jiaohe, Hebei, China 34 E9 38 2N 116 20 E
Jiaohe, Jilin, China 35 C14 43 40N 127 22 E
Jiaozhou, China 35 F11 36 18N 120 1 E
Jiaozhou Wan, China 35 F11 36 5N 120 10 E
Jiaozuo, China 34 G7 35 16N 113 12 E
Jiawang, China 35 G9 34 28N 117 26 E
Jiaxiang, China 34 G9 35 25N 116 20 E
Jiaxing, China 33 C7 30 49N 120 45 E
Jiayi = Chiai, Taiwan 33 D7 23 29N 120 25 E
Jibuti = Djibouti ■, Africa 46 E3 12 0N 43 0 E
Jicarón, I., Panama 88 E3 7 10N 81 50W
Jiddah, Si. Arabia 46 C2 21 29N 39 10 E
Jido, India 41 E19 29 2N 94 58 E
Jieshou, China 34 H8 33 18N 115 22 E
Jiexiu, China 34 F6 37 2N 111 55 E
Jiggalong, Australia 60 D3 23 21S 120 47 E
Jigni, India 43 G8 25 45N 79 25 E
Jihlava, Czech Rep. 16 D8 49 28N 15 35 E
Jihlava →, Czech Rep. 17 D9 48 55N 16 36 E
Jijiga, Ethiopia 46 F3 9 20N 42 50 E
Jilin, China 35 C14 43 44N 126 30 E
Jilin □, China 35 C14 44 0N 127 0 E
Jilong = Chilung, Taiwan 33 D7 25 3N 121 45 E
Jim Thorpe, U.S.A. 79 F9 40 52N 75 44W
Jima, Ethiopia 46 F2 7 40N 36 47 E
Jiménez, Mexico 86 B4 27 10N 104 54W
Jimo, China 35 F11 36 23N 120 30 E
Jin Xian = Jinzhou, China 34 E8 38 2N 115 2 E
Jin Xian, China 35 E11 38 55N 121 42 E
Jinan, China 34 F9 36 38N 117 1 E
Jinchang, China 32 C5 38 30N 102 10 E
Jincheng, China 34 G7 35 29N 112 50 E
Jind, India 42 E7 29 19N 76 22 E
Jindabyne, Australia 63 F4 36 25S 148 35 E
Jindřichův Hradec, Czech Rep. 16 D8 49 10N 15 2 E
Jing He →, China 34 G5 34 27N 109 4 E
Jingbian, China 34 F5 37 20N 108 30 E
Jingchuan, China 34 G4 35 20N 107 20 E
Jingdezhen, China 33 D6 29 20N 117 11 E
Jinggu, China 32 D5 23 35N 100 41 E
Jinghai, China 34 E9 38 55N 116 55 E
Jingle, China 34 E6 38 20N 111 55 E
Jingning, China 34 G3 35 30N 105 43 E
Jingpo Hu, China 35 C15 43 55N 128 55 E
Jingtai, China 34 F3 37 10N 104 6 E
Jingxing, China 34 E8 38 2N 114 8 E
Jingyang, China 34 G5 34 30N 108 50 E
Jingyu, China 35 C14 42 25N 126 45 E
Jingyuan, China 34 F3 36 30N 104 40 E
Jingziguan, China 34 H6 33 15N 111 0 E
Jinhua, China 33 D6 29 8N 119 38 E
Jining, Nei Monggol Zizhiqu, China 34 D7 41 5N 113 0 E
Jining, Shandong, China 34 G9 35 22N 116 34 E
Jinja, Uganda 54 B3 0 25N 33 12 E
Jinjang, Malaysia 39 L3 3 13N 101 39 E
Jinji, China 34 F4 37 58N 106 8 E
Jinnah Barrage, Pakistan 40 C7 32 58N 71 33 E
Jinotega, Nic. 88 D2 13 6N 85 59W
Jinotepe, Nic. 88 D2 11 50N 86 10W
Jinsha Jiang →, China 32 D5 28 50N 104 36 E
Jinxi, China 35 D11 40 52N 120 50 E
Jinxiang, China 34 G9 35 5N 116 22 E
Jinzhou, Hebei, China 34 E8 38 2N 115 2 E
Jinzhou, Liaoning, China 35 D11 41 5N 121 3 E
Jiparaná →, Brazil 92 E6 8 3S 62 52W
Jipijapa, Ecuador 92 D2 1 0S 80 40W
Jiquilpan, Mexico 86 D4 19 57N 102 42W
Jishan, China 34 G6 35 34N 110 58 E
Jisr ash Shughūr, Syria 44 C3 35 49N 36 18 E
Jitarning, Australia 61 F2 32 48S 117 57 E
Jitra, Malaysia 39 J3 6 16N 100 25 E
Jiu →, Romania 17 F12 43 47N 23 48 E
Jiudengkou, China 34 E4 39 56N 106 40 E
Jiujiang, China 33 D6 29 42N 115 58 E
Jiutai, China 35 B13 44 10N 125 50 E
Jiuxincheng, China 34 E8 39 17N 115 59 E
Jixi, China 35 B16 45 20N 130 50 E
Jiyang, China 35 F9 37 0N 117 12 E
Jiyuan, China 34 G7 35 7N 112 57 E
Jīzān, Si. Arabia 46 D3 17 0N 42 20 E
Jize, China 34 F8 36 54N 114 56 E
Jizl, Wādī al, Si. Arabia 44 E3 25 39N 38 25 E
Jizō-Zaki, Japan 31 G6 35 34N 133 20 E
Jizzakh, Uzbekistan 26 E7 40 6N 67 50 E
Joaçaba, Brazil 95 B5 27 5S 51 31W
João Pessoa, Brazil 93 E12 7 10S 34 52W
Joaquín V. González, Argentina 94 B3 25 10S 64 0W
Jobat, India 42 H6 22 25N 74 34 E
Jodhpur, India 42 F5 26 23N 73 8 E
Jodiya, India 42 H4 22 42N 70 18 E
Joensuu, Finland 24 B4 62 37N 29 49 E
Jōetsu, Japan 31 F9 37 12N 138 10 E
Jofane, Mozam. 57 C5 21 15S 34 18 E
Jogbani, India 43 F12 26 25N 87 15 E
Jõgeva, Estonia 9 G22 58 45N 26 24 E
Jogjakarta = Yogyakarta, Indonesia 36 F4 7 49S 110 22 E
Johannesburg, S. Africa 57 D4 26 10S 28 2 E
Johannesburg, U.S.A. 85 K9 35 22N 117 38W
Johilla →, India 43 H9 23 37N 81 14 E
John Day, U.S.A. 82 D4 44 25N 118 57W
John Day →, U.S.A. 82 D3 45 44N 120 39W
John D'Or Prairie, Canada 72 B5 58 30N 115 8W
John H. Kerr Reservoir, U.S.A. 77 G6 36 36N 78 18W
John o' Groats, U.K. 12 C5 58 38N 3 4W
Johnnie, U.S.A. 85 J10 36 25N 116 5W
John's Ra., Australia 62 C1 21 55S 133 23 E
Johnson, Kans., U.S.A. 81 G4 37 34N 101 45W
Johnson, Vt., U.S.A. 79 B12 44 38N 72 41W
Johnson City, N.Y., U.S.A. 79 D9 42 7N 75 58W
Johnson City, Tenn., U.S.A. 77 G4 36 19N 82 21W
Johnson City, Tex., U.S.A. 81 K5 30 17N 98 25W
Johnsonburg, U.S.A. 78 E6 41 29N 78 41W
Johnsondale, U.S.A. 85 K8 35 58N 118 32W
Johnson's Crossing, Canada 72 A2 60 29N 133 18W
Johnston, L., Australia 61 F3 32 25S 120 30 E
Johnston Falls = Mambilima Falls, Zambia 55 E2 10 31S 28 45 E
Johnston I., Pac. Oc. 65 F11 17 10N 169 8W
Johnstone Str., Canada 72 C3 50 28N 126 0W
Johnstown, N.Y., U.S.A. 79 C10 43 0N 74 22W
Johnstown, Ohio, U.S.A. 78 F2 40 9N 82 41W
Johnstown, Pa., U.S.A. 78 F6 40 20N 78 55W
Johor Baharu, Malaysia 39 M4 1 28N 103 46 E
Jõhvi, Estonia 9 G22 59 22N 27 27 E
Joinville, Brazil 95 B6 26 15S 48 55W
Joinville I., Antarctica 5 C18 65 0S 55 30W
Jojutla, Mexico 87 D5 18 37N 99 11W
Jokkmokk, Sweden 8 C18 66 35N 19 50 E
Jökulsá á Bru →, Iceland 8 D6 65 40N 14 16W
Jökulsá á Fjöllum →, Iceland 8 C5 66 10N 16 30W
Jolfā, Āzarbājān-e Sharqī, Iran 44 B5 38 57N 45 38 E
Jolfā, Eşfahan, Iran 45 C6 32 58N 51 37 E
Joliet, U.S.A. 76 E1 41 32N 88 5W
Joliette, Canada 70 C5 46 3N 73 24W
Jolo, Phil. 37 C6 6 0N 121 0 E
Jolon, U.S.A. 84 K5 35 58N 121 9W
Jombang, Indonesia 37 G15 7 33S 112 14 E
Jonava, Lithuania 9 J21 55 8N 24 12 E
Jones Sound, Canada 4 B3 76 0N 85 0W
Jonesboro, Ark., U.S.A. 81 H9 35 50N 90 42W
Jonesboro, La., U.S.A. 81 J8 32 15N 92 43W
Joniškis, Lithuania 9 H20 56 13N 23 35 E
Jönköping, Sweden 9 H16 57 45N 14 8 E
Jonquière, Canada 71 C5 48 27N 71 14W
Joplin, U.S.A. 81 G7 37 6N 94 31W

Jora, India 42 F6 26 20N 77 49 E
Jordan, Mont., U.S.A. 82 C10 47 19N 106 55W
Jordan, N.Y., U.S.A. 79 C8 43 4N 76 29W
Jordan ■, Asia 47 E5 31 0N 36 0 E
Jordan →, Asia 47 D4 31 48N 35 32 E
Jordan Valley, U.S.A. 82 E5 42 59N 117 3W
Jorhat, India 41 F19 26 45N 94 12 E
Jörn, Sweden 8 D19 65 4N 20 1 E
Jorong, Indonesia 36 E4 3 58S 114 56 E
Jørpeland, Norway 9 G11 59 3N 6 1 E
Jorquera →, Chile 94 B2 28 3S 69 58W
Jos, Nigeria 50 G7 9 53N 8 51 E
José Batlle y Ordóñez, Uruguay 95 C4 33 20S 55 10W
Joseph, L., Nfld., Canada 71 B6 52 45N 65 18W
Joseph, L., Ont., Canada 78 A5 45 10N 79 44W
Joseph Bonaparte G., Australia 60 B4 14 35S 128 50 E
Joshinath, India 43 D8 30 34N 79 34 E
Joshua Tree, U.S.A. 85 L10 34 8N 116 19W
Joshua Tree Nat. Park, U.S.A. 85 M10 33 55N 116 0W
Jostedalsbreen, Norway 9 F12 61 40N 6 59 E
Jotunheimen, Norway 9 F13 61 35N 8 25 E
Joubertberge, Namibia 56 B1 18 30S 14 0 E
Jourdanton, U.S.A. 81 L5 28 55N 98 33W
Jovellanos, Cuba 88 B3 22 40N 81 10W
Ju Xian, China 35 F10 36 35N 118 20 E
Juan Aldama, Mexico 86 C4 24 20N 103 23W
Juan Bautista Alberdi, Argentina 94 C3 34 26S 61 48W
Juan de Fuca Str., Canada 84 B3 48 15N 124 0W
Juan de Nova, Ind. Oc. 57 B7 17 3S 43 45 E
Juan Fernández, Arch. de, Pac. Oc. 90 G2 33 50S 80 0W
Juan José Castelli, Argentina 94 B3 25 27S 60 57W
Juan L. Lacaze, Uruguay 94 C4 34 26S 57 25W
Juankoski, Finland 8 E23 63 3N 28 19 E
Juárez, Argentina 94 D4 37 40S 59 43W
Juárez, Mexico 85 N11 32 20N 115 57W
Juárez, Sierra de, Mexico 86 A1 32 0N 116 0W
Juàzeiro, Brazil 93 E10 9 30S 40 30W
Juàzeiro do Norte, Brazil 93 E11 7 10S 39 18W
Juba = Giuba →, Somali Rep. 46 G3 1 30N 42 35 E
Juba, Sudan 51 H12 4 50N 31 35 E
Jubayl, Lebanon 47 A4 34 5N 35 39 E
Jubbah, Si. Arabia 44 D4 28 2N 40 56 E
Jubbal, India 42 D7 31 5N 77 40 E
Jubbulpore = Jabalpur, India 43 H8 23 9N 79 58 E
Jubilee L., Australia 61 E4 29 0S 126 50 E
Juby, C., Morocco 50 C3 28 0N 12 59W
Júcar = Xúquer →, Spain 19 C5 39 5N 0 10W
Júcaro, Cuba 88 B4 21 37N 78 51W
Juchitán, Mexico 87 D5 16 27N 95 5W
Judaea = Har Yehuda, Israel 47 D3 31 35N 34 57 E
Judith →, U.S.A. 82 C9 47 44N 109 39W
Judith, Pt., U.S.A. 79 E13 41 22N 71 29W
Judith Gap, U.S.A. 82 C9 46 41N 109 45W
Jugoslavia = Yugoslavia ■, Europe 21 B9 43 20N 20 0 E
Juigalpa, Nic. 88 D2 12 6N 85 26W
Juiz de Fora, Brazil 95 A7 21 43S 43 19W
Jujuy □, Argentina 94 A2 23 20S 65 40W
Julesburg, U.S.A. 80 E3 40 59N 102 16W
Juli, Peru 92 G5 16 10S 69 25W
Julia Cr. →, Australia 62 C3 20 0S 141 11 E
Julia Creek, Australia 62 C3 20 39S 141 44 E
Juliaca, Peru 92 G4 15 25S 70 10W
Julian, U.S.A. 85 M10 33 4N 116 38W
Julian L., Canada 70 B4 54 25N 77 57W
Julianatop, Surinam 93 C7 3 40N 56 30W
Julianehåb = Qaqortoq, Greenland 69 B6 60 43N 46 0W
Julimes, Mexico 86 B3 28 25N 105 27W
Jullundur, India 42 D6 31 20N 75 40 E
Julu, China 34 F8 37 15N 115 2 E
Jumbo, Zimbabwe 55 F3 17 30S 30 58 E
Jumbo Pk., U.S.A. 85 J12 36 12N 114 11W
Jumentos Cays, Bahamas 88 B4 23 0N 75 40W
Jumilla, Spain 19 C5 38 28N 1 19W
Jumla, Nepal 43 E10 29 15N 82 13 E
Jumna = Yamuna →, India 43 G9 25 30N 81 53 E
Junagadh, India 42 J4 21 30N 70 30 E
Junction, Tex., U.S.A. 81 K5 30 29N 99 46W
Junction, Utah, U.S.A. 83 G7 38 14N 112 13W
Junction B., Australia 62 A1 11 52S 133 55 E
Junction City, Kans., U.S.A. 80 F6 39 2N 96 50W
Junction City, Oreg., U.S.A. 82 D2 44 13N 123 12W
Junction Pt., Australia 62 A1 11 45S 133 50 E
Jundah, Australia 62 C3 24 46S 143 2 E
Jundiaí, Brazil 95 A6 24 30S 47 0W
Juneau, U.S.A. 72 B2 58 18N 134 25W
Junee, Australia 63 E4 34 53S 147 35 E
Jungfrau, Switz. 18 C7 46 32N 7 58 E
Junggar Pendi, China 32 B3 44 30N 86 0 E
Jungshahi, Pakistan 42 G2 24 52N 67 44 E
Juniata →, U.S.A. 78 F7 40 30N 77 40W
Junín, Argentina 94 C3 34 33S 60 57W
Junín de los Andes, Argentina 96 D2 39 45S 71 0W
Jūniyah, Lebanon 47 B4 33 59N 35 38 E
Juntas, Chile 94 B2 28 24S 69 58W
Juntura, U.S.A. 82 E4 43 45N 118 5W
Jur, Nahr el →, Sudan 51 G11 8 45N 29 15 E
Jura = Jura, Mts. du, Europe 18 C7 46 40N 6 5 E
Jura = Schwäbische Alb, Germany 16 D5 48 20N 9 30 E
Jura, U.K. 12 F3 56 0N 5 50W
Jura, Mts. du, Europe 18 C7 46 40N 6 5 E
Jura, Sd. of, U.K. 12 F3 55 57N 5 45W
Jurbarkas, Lithuania 9 J20 55 4N 22 46 E
Jurien, Australia 61 F2 30 18S 115 2 E
Jūrmala, Latvia 9 H20 56 58N 23 34 E
Juruá →, Brazil 92 D5 2 37S 65 44W
Juruena, Brazil 92 F7 13 0S 58 10W
Juruena →, Brazil 92 E7 7 20S 58 3W
Juruti, Brazil 93 D7 2 9S 56 4W
Justo Daract, Argentina 94 C2 33 52S 65 12W
Jutaí →, Brazil 92 D5 2 43S 66 57W
Juticalpa, Honduras 88 D2 14 40N 86 12W
Jutland = Jylland, Denmark 9 H13 56 25N 9 30 E
Juventud, I. de la, Cuba 88 B3 21 40N 82 40W
Jūy Zar, Iran 44 C5 33 50N 46 18 E
Juye, China 34 G9 35 22N 116 5 E
Jwaneng, Botswana 53 J4 24 45S 24 50 E
Jylland, Denmark 9 H13 56 25N 9 30 E
Jyväskylä, Finland 9 E21 62 14N 25 50 E

K

K2, Pakistan 43 B7 35 58N 76 32 E
Kaap Plateau, S. Africa 56 D3 28 30S 24 0 E
Kaapkruis, Namibia 56 C1 21 55S 13 57 E
Kaapstad = Cape Town, S. Africa 56 E2 33 55S 18 22 E
Kabaena, Indonesia 37 F6 5 15S 122 0 E
Kabala, S. Leone 50 G3 9 38N 11 37W
Kabale, Uganda 54 C3 1 15S 30 0 E
Kabalo, Dem. Rep. of the Congo 54 D2 6 0S 27 0 E
Kabambare, Dem. Rep. of the Congo 54 C2 4 41S 27 39 E
Kabango, Dem. Rep. of the Congo 55 D2 8 35S 28 30 E
Kabanjahe, Indonesia 36 D1 3 6N 98 30 E
Kabardino-Balkar Republic = Kabardino-Balkaria □, Russia 25 F7 43 30N 43 30 E
Kabardino-Balkaria □, Russia 25 F7 43 30N 43 30 E
Kabarega Falls = Murchison Falls, Uganda 54 B3 2 15N 31 30 E
Kabasalan, Phil. 37 C6 7 47N 122 44 E
Kabetogama, U.S.A. 80 A8 48 28N 92 59W
Kabin Buri, Thailand 38 F3 13 57N 101 43 E
Kabinakagami L., Canada 70 C3 48 54N 84 25W
Kabinda, Dem. Rep. of the Congo 52 F4 6 19S 24 20 E
Kabompo, Zambia 55 E1 13 36S 24 14 E
Kabompo →, Zambia 53 G4 14 10S 23 11 E
Kabondo, Dem. Rep. of the Congo 55 D2 8 58S 25 40 E
Kabongo, Dem. Rep. of the Congo 54 D2 7 22S 25 33 E
Kabūd Gonbad, Iran 45 B8 37 5N 59 45 E
Kābul, Afghan. 42 B3 34 28N 69 11 E
Kābul □, Afghan. 40 B6 34 30N 69 0 E
Kābul →, Pakistan 42 C5 33 55N 72 14 E
Kabunga, Dem. Rep. of the Congo 54 C2 1 38S 28 3 E
Kaburuang, Indonesia 37 D7 3 50N 126 30 E
Kabwe, Zambia 55 E2 14 30S 28 29 E
Kachchh, Gulf of, India 42 H3 22 50N 69 15 E
Kachchh, Rann of, India 42 H4 24 0N 70 0 E
Kachchhidhana, India 43 J8 21 44N 78 46 E
Kachebera, Zambia 55 E3 13 50S 32 50 E
Kachikau, Botswana 56 B3 18 8S 24 26 E
Kachin □, Burma 41 G20 26 0N 97 30 E
Kachira, L., Uganda 54 C3 0 40S 31 7 E
Kachiry, Kazakstan 26 D8 53 10N 75 50 E
Kachnara, India 42 H6 23 50N 75 6 E
Kachot, Cambodia 39 G4 11 30N 103 3 E
Kaçkar, Turkey 25 F7 40 45N 41 10 E
Kadan Kyun, Burma 38 F2 12 30N 98 20 E
Kadanai →, Afghan. 42 D1 31 22N 65 45 E
Kadavu, Fiji 59 D8 19 0S 178 15 E
Kadi, India 42 H5 23 18N 72 23 E
Kadina, Australia 63 E2 33 55S 137 43 E
Kadipur, India 43 F10 26 10N 82 23 E
Kadirli, Turkey 44 B3 37 23N 36 5 E
Kadiyevka = Stakhanov, Ukraine 25 E6 48 35N 38 40 E
Kadoka, U.S.A. 80 D4 43 50N 101 31W
Kadoma, Zimbabwe 55 F2 18 20S 29 52 E
Kâdugli, Sudan 51 F11 11 0N 29 45 E
Kaduna, Nigeria 50 F7 10 30N 7 21 E
Kaédi, Mauritania 50 E3 16 9N 13 28W
Kaeng Khoï, Thailand 38 E3 14 35N 101 0 E
Kaesŏng, N. Korea 35 F14 37 58N 126 35 E
Kāf, Si. Arabia 44 D3 31 25N 37 29 E
Kafan = Kapan, Armenia 25 G8 39 18N 46 27 E
Kafanchan, Nigeria 50 G7 9 40N 8 20 E
Kafinda, Zambia 55 E3 12 32S 30 20 E
Kafirévs, Ákra, Greece 21 E11 38 9N 24 38 E
Kafue, Zambia 55 F2 15 46S 28 9 E
Kafue →, Zambia 53 H5 15 30S 29 0 E
Kafue Flats, Zambia 55 F2 15 40S 27 25 E
Kafulwe, Zambia 55 D2 9 0S 29 1 E
Kaga, Afghan. 42 B4 34 14N 70 10 E
Kaga Bandoro, C.A.R. 52 C3 7 0N 19 10 E
Kagan, Uzbekistan 26 F7 39 43N 64 33 E
Kagawa □, Japan 31 G7 34 15N 134 0 E
Kagera = Ziwa Maghariba □, Tanzania 54 C3 2 0S 31 30 E
Kagera →, Uganda 54 C3 0 57S 31 47 E
Kağızman, Turkey 44 B4 40 5N 43 10 E
Kagoshima, Japan 31 J5 31 35N 130 33 E
Kagoshima □, Japan 31 J5 31 30N 130 30 E
Kagul = Cahul, Moldova 17 F15 45 50N 28 15 E
Kahak, Iran 45 B6 36 6N 49 46 E
Kahama, Tanzania 54 C3 4 8S 32 30 E
Kahan, Pakistan 42 E3 29 18N 68 54 E
Kahang, Malaysia 39 L4 2 12N 103 32 E
Kahayan →, Indonesia 36 E4 3 40S 114 0 E
Kahe, Tanzania 54 C4 3 30S 37 25 E
Kahnūj, Iran 45 E8 27 55N 57 40 E
Kahoka, U.S.A. 80 E9 40 25N 91 44W
Kahoolawe, U.S.A. 74 H16 20 33N 156 37W
Kahramanmaraş, Turkey 25 G6 37 37N 36 53 E
Kahuta, Pakistan 42 C5 33 35N 73 24 E
Kai, Kepulauan, Indonesia 37 F8 5 55S 132 45 E
Kai Besar, Indonesia 37 F8 5 35S 133 0 E
Kai Is. = Kai, Kepulauan, Indonesia 37 F8 5 55S 132 45 E
Kai Kecil, Indonesia 37 F8 5 45S 132 40 E
Kaiapoi, N.Z. 59 K4 43 24S 172 40 E
Kaieteur Falls, Guyana 92 B7 5 1N 59 10W
Kaifeng, China 34 G8 34 48N 114 21 E
Kaikohe, N.Z. 59 F4 35 25S 173 49 E
Kaikoura, N.Z. 59 K4 42 25S 173 43 E
Kaikoura Ra., N.Z. 59 J4 41 59S 173 41 E
Kailu, China 35 C11 43 38N 121 18 E
Kailua Kona, U.S.A. 74 J17 19 39N 155 59W
Kaimana, Indonesia 37 E8 3 39S 133 45 E
Kaimanawa Mts., N.Z. 59 H5 39 15S 175 56 E
Kaimganj, India 43 F8 27 33N 79 24 E
Kaimur Hills, India 43 G10 24 30N 82 0 E
Kainab →, Namibia 56 D2 28 32S 19 34 E
Kainji Res., Nigeria 50 F6 10 1N 4 40 E
Kainuu, Finland 8 D23 64 30N 29 7 E
Kaipara Harbour, N.Z. 59 G5 36 25S 174 14 E
Kaipokok B., Canada 71 B8 54 54N 59 47W
Kaira, India 42 H5 22 45N 72 50 E
Kairana, India 42 E7 29 24N 77 15 E
Kaironi, Indonesia 37 E8 0 47S 133 40 E
Kairouan, Tunisia 51 A8 35 45N 10 5 E
Kaiserslautern, Germany 16 D4 49 26N 7 45 E
Kaitaia, N.Z. 59 F4 35 8S 173 17 E
Kaitangata, N.Z. 59 M2 46 17S 169 51 E
Kaithal, India 42 E7 29 48N 76 26 E
Kaitu →, Pakistan 42 C4 33 10N 70 30 E
Kaiyuan, China 35 C13 42 28N 124 1 E
Kajaani, Finland 8 D22 64 17N 27 46 E
Kajabbi, Australia 62 C3 20 0S 140 1 E
Kajana = Kajaani, Finland 8 D22 64 17N 27 46 E
Kajang, Malaysia 39 L3 2 59N 101 48 E
Kajiado, Kenya 54 C4 1 53S 36 48 E
Kajo Kaji, Sudan 51 H12 3 58N 31 40 E
Kakabeka Falls, Canada 70 C2 48 24N 89 37W
Kakamas, S. Africa 56 D3 28 45S 20 33 E
Kakamega, Kenya 54 B3 0 20N 34 46 E
Kakanui Mts., N.Z. 59 L3 45 10S 170 30 E
Kakdwip, India 43 J13 21 53N 88 11 E
Kake, Japan 31 G6 34 36N 132 19 E
Kake, U.S.A. 72 B2 56 59N 133 57W
Kakegawa, Japan 31 G9 34 45N 138 1 E
Kakeroma-Jima, Japan 31 K4 28 8N 129 14 E
Kakhovka, Ukraine 25 E5 46 45N 33 30 E
Kakhovske Vdskh., Ukraine 25 E5 47 5N 34 0 E
Kakinada, India 41 L13 16 57N 82 11 E
Kakisa →, Canada 72 A5 61 3N 118 10W
Kakisa L., Canada 72 A5 60 56N 117 43W
Kakogawa, Japan 31 G7 34 46N 134 51 E
Kakwa →, Canada 72 C5 54 37N 118 28W
Kāl Gūsheh, Iran 45 D8 30 59N 58 12 E
Kal Safīd, Iran 44 C5 34 52N 47 23 E
Kalaallit Nunaat = Greenland ■, N. Amer. 4 C5 66 0N 45 0W
Kalabagh, Pakistan 42 C4 33 0N 71 28 E
Kalabahi, Indonesia 37 F6 8 13S 124 31 E
Kalach, Russia 25 D7 50 22N 41 0 E
Kaladan →, Burma 41 J18 20 20N 93 5 E
Kaladar, Canada 78 B7 44 37N 77 5W
Kalahari, Africa 56 C3 24 0S 21 30 E
Kalajoki, Finland 8 D20 64 12N 24 10 E
Kālak, Iran 45 E8 25 29N 59 22 E
Kalakamati, Botswana 57 C4 20 40S 27 25 E
Kalakan, Russia 27 D12 55 15N 116 45 E
K'alak'unlun Shank'ou = Karakoram Pass, Asia 43 B7 35 33N 77 50 E
Kalam, Pakistan 43 B5 35 34N 72 30 E
Kalama, Dem. Rep. of the Congo 54 C2 2 52S 28 35 E
Kalama, U.S.A. 84 E4 46 1N 122 51W
Kalámai, Greece 21 F10 37 3N 22 10 E
Kalamata = Kalámai, Greece 21 F10 37 3N 22 10 E
Kalamazoo, U.S.A. 76 D3 42 17N 85 35W
Kalamazoo →, U.S.A. 76 D2 42 40N 86 10W
Kalambo Falls, Tanzania 55 D3 8 37S 31 35 E
Kalan, Turkey 44 B3 39 7N 39 32 E
Kalannie, Australia 61 F2 30 22S 117 5 E
Kalāntarī, Iran 45 C7 32 10N 54 8 E
Kalao, Indonesia 37 F6 7 21S 121 0 E
Kalaotoa, Indonesia 37 F6 7 20S 121 50 E
Kalasin, Thailand 38 D4 16 26N 103 30 E
Kalat, Pakistan 40 E5 29 8N 66 31 E
Kalāteh, Iran 45 B7 36 33N 55 41 E
Kalāteh-ye Ganj, Iran 45 E8 27 31N 57 55 E
Kalbarri, Australia 61 E1 27 40S 114 10 E
Kalce, Slovenia 16 F8 45 54N 14 13 E
Kale, Turkey 21 F13 37 27N 28 49 E
Kalegauk Kyun, Burma 41 M20 15 33N 97 35 E
Kalehe, Dem. Rep. of the Congo 54 C2 2 6S 28 50 E
Kalema, Tanzania 54 C3 1 12S 31 55 E
Kalemie, Dem. Rep. of the Congo 54 D2 5 55S 29 9 E
Kalewa, Burma 41 H19 23 10N 94 15 E
Kaleybar, Iran 44 B5 38 47N 47 2 E
Kalgan = Zhangjiakou, China 34 D8 40 48N 114 55 E
Kalgoorlie-Boulder, Australia 61 F3 30 40S 121 22 E
Kali →, India 43 F8 27 6N 79 55 E
Kali Sindh →, India 42 G6 25 32N 76 17 E
Kaliakra, Nos, Bulgaria 21 C13 43 21N 28 30 E
Kalianda, Indonesia 36 F3 5 50S 105 45 E
Kalibo, Phil. 37 B6 11 43N 122 22 E
Kalima, Dem. Rep. of the Congo 54 C2 2 33S 26 32 E
Kalimantan □, Indonesia 36 E4 0 0 114 0 E
Kalimantan Barat □, Indonesia 36 E4 0 0 110 30 E
Kalimantan Selatan □, Indonesia 36 E5 2 30S 115 30 E
Kalimantan Tengah □, Indonesia 36 E4 2 0S 113 30 E
Kalimantan Timur □, Indonesia 36 D5 1 30N 116 30 E
Kálimnos, Greece 21 F12 37 0N 27 0 E
Kalimpong, India 43 F13 27 4N 88 35 E
Kalinin = Tver, Russia 24 C6 56 55N 35 55 E
Kaliningrad, Russia 9 J19 54 42N 20 32 E
Kalinkavichy, Belarus 17 B15 52 12N 29 20 E
Kalinkovichi = Kalinkavichy, Belarus 17 B15 52 12N 29 20 E
Kaliro, Uganda 54 B3 0 56N 33 30 E
Kalispell, U.S.A. 82 B6 48 12N 114 19W
Kalisz, Poland 17 C10 51 45N 18 8 E
Kaliua, Tanzania 54 D3 5 5S 31 48 E
Kalix, Sweden 8 D20 65 53N 23 12 E
Kalix →, Sweden 8 D20 65 50N 23 11 E
Kalka, India 42 D7 30 46N 76 57 E
Kalkarindji, Australia 60 C5 17 30S 130 47 E
Kalkaska, U.S.A. 76 C3 44 44N 85 11W
Kalkfeld, Namibia 56 C2 20 57S 16 14 E
Kalkfontein, Botswana 56 C3 22 4S 20 57 E
Kalkrand, Namibia 56 C2 24 1S 17 35 E
Kallavesi, Finland 8 E22 62 58N 27 30 E
Kallsjön, Sweden 8 E15 63 38N 13 0 E
Kalmar, Sweden 9 H17 56 40N 16 20 E
Kalmyk Republic = Kalmykia □, Russia 25 E8 46 5N 46 1 E
Kalmykia □, Russia 25 E8 46 5N 46 1 E
Kalmykovo, Kazakstan 25 E9 49 0N 51 47 E
Kalna, India 43 H13 23 13N 88 25 E
Kalnai, India 43 H10 22 46N 83 30 E
Kalocsa, Hungary 17 E10 46 32N 19 0 E
Kalokhorio, Cyprus 23 E12 34 51N 33 2 E
Kaloko, Dem. Rep. of the Congo 54 D2 6 47S 25 48 E
Kalol, Gujarat, India 42 H5 22 37N 73 31 E
Kalol, Gujarat, India 42 H5 23 15N 72 33 E
Kalomo, Zambia 55 F2 17 0S 26 30 E
Kalpi, India 43 F8 26 8N 79 47 E
Kalu, Pakistan 42 G2 25 5N 67 39 E
Kaluga, Russia 24 D6 54 35N 36 10 E
Kalulushi, Zambia 55 E2 12 50S 28 3 E
Kalundborg, Denmark 9 J14 55 41N 11 5 E
Kalush, Ukraine 17 D13 49 3N 24 23 E
Kalutara, Sri Lanka 40 R12 6 35N 80 0 E
Kalya, Russia 24 B10 60 15N 59 59 E
Kama, Dem. Rep. of the Congo 54 C2 3 30S 27 5 E
Kama →, Russia 24 C9 55 45N 52 0 E
Kamachumu, Tanzania 54 C3 1 37S 31 37 E
Kamaishi, Japan 30 E10 39 16N 141 53 E
Kamalia, Pakistan 42 D5 30 44N 72 42 E
Kaman, India 42 F6 27 39N 77 16 E
Kamanjab, Namibia 56 B2 19 35S 14 51 E
Kamapanda, Zambia 55 E1 12 5S 24 0 E
Kamarān, Yemen 46 D3 15 21N 42 35 E
Kamativi, Zimbabwe 56 B4 18 20S 27 6 E
Kambalda, Australia 61 F3 31 10S 121 37 E
Kambar, Pakistan 42 F3 27 37N 68 1 E
Kambarka, Russia 24 C9 56 15N 54 11 E
Kambolé, Zambia 55 D3 8 47S 30 48 E
Kambos, Cyprus 23 D11 35 2N 32 44 E
Kambove, Dem. Rep. of the Congo 55 E2 10 51S 26 33 E
Kamchatka, Poluostrov, Russia 27 D16 57 0N 160 0 E
Kamchatka Pen. = Kamchatka, Poluostrov, Russia 27 D16 57 0N 160 0 E
Kamchiya →, Bulgaria 21 C12 43 4N 27 44 E
Kamen, Russia 26 D9 53 50N 81 30 E
Kamen-Rybolov, Russia 30 B6 44 46N 132 2 E
Kamenjak, Rt, Croatia 16 F7 44 47N 13 55 E
Kamenka, Russia 24 A7 65 58N 44 0 E
Kamenka Bugskaya = Kamyanka-Buzka, Ukraine 17 C13 50 8N 24 16 E
Kamensk Uralskiy, Russia 26 D7 56 25N 62 2 E
Kamenskoye, Russia 27 C17 62 45N 165 30 E
Kameoka, Japan 31 G7 35 0N 135 35 E
Kamiah, U.S.A. 82 C5 46 14N 116 2W
Kamieskroon, S. Africa 56 E2 30 9S 17 56 E
Kamilukuak, L., Canada 73 A8 62 22N 101 40W
Kamin-Kashyrskyy, Ukraine 17 C13 51 39N 24 56 E
Kamina, Dem. Rep. of the Congo 55 D2 8 45S 25 0 E
Kaminak L., Canada 73 A10 62 10N 95 0W
Kaministiquia, Canada 70 C1 48 32N 89 35W
Kaminoyama, Japan 30 E10 38 9N 140 17 E
Kamiros, Greece 23 C9 36 20N 27 56 E
Kamituga, Dem. Rep. of the Congo 54 C2 3 2S 28 10 E
Kamla →, India 43 G12 25 35N 86 36 E
Kamloops, Canada 72 C4 50 40N 120 20W
Kamo, Japan 30 F9 37 39N 139 3 E
Kamoke, Pakistan 42 C6 32 4N 74 4 E
Kampala, Uganda 54 B3 0 20N 32 30 E
Kampang Chhnang, Cambodia 39 F5 12 20N 104 35 E
Kampar, Malaysia 39 K3 4 18N 101 9 E
Kampar →, Indonesia 36 D2 0 30N 103 8 E
Kampen, Neths. 15 B5 52 33N 5 53 E
Kampene, Dem. Rep. of the Congo 52 E5 3 36S 26 40 E
Kamphaeng Phet, Thailand 38 D2 16 28N 99 30 E
Kampolombo, L., Zambia 55 E2 11 37S 29 42 E
Kampong Saom, Cambodia 39 G4 10 38N 103 30 E
Kampong Saom, Chaak, Cambodia 39 G4 10 50N 103 32 E
Kampong To, Thailand 39 J3 6 3N 101 13 E
Kampot, Cambodia 39 G5 10 36N 104 10 E
Kampuchea = Cambodia ■, Asia 38 F5 12 15N 105 0 E
Kampung Air Putih, Malaysia 39 K4 4 15N 103 10 E
Kampung Jerangau, Malaysia 39 K4 4 50N 103 10 E
Kampung Raja, Malaysia 39 K4 5 45N 102 35 E
Kampungbaru = Tolitoli, Indonesia 37 D6 1 5N 120 50 E
Kamrau, Teluk, Indonesia 37 E8 3 30S 133 36 E
Kamsack, Canada 73 C8 51 34N 101 54W
Kamskoye Vdkhr., Russia 24 C10 58 41N 56 7 E
Kamuchawie L., Canada 73 B8 56 18N 101 59W
Kamui-Misaki, Japan 30 C10 43 20N 140 21 E
Kamyanets-Podilskyy, Ukraine 17 D14 48 45N 26 40 E
Kamyanka-Buzka, Ukraine 17 C13 50 8N 24 16 E
Kāmyārān, Iran 44 C5 34 47N 46 56 E
Kamyshin, Russia 25 D8 50 10N 45 24 E
Kanaaupscow, Canada 70 B4 54 2N 76 30W
Kanaaupscow →, Canada 69 C12 53 39N 77 9W
Kanab, U.S.A. 83 H7 37 3N 112 32W
Kanab →, U.S.A. 83 H7 36 24N 112 38W
Kanagi, Japan 30 D10 40 54N 140 27 E
Kanairiktok →, Canada 71 A7 55 2N 60 18W
Kananga, Dem. Rep. of the Congo 52 F4 5 55S 22 18 E
Kanash, Russia 24 C8 55 30N 47 32 E
Kanaskat, U.S.A. 84 C5 47 19N 121 54W
Kanastraíon, Ákra = Palioúrion, Ákra, Greece 21 E10 39 57N 23 45 E
Kanawha →, U.S.A. 76 F4 38 50N 82 9W
Kanazawa, Japan 31 F8 36 30N 136 38 E
Kanchanaburi, Thailand 38 E2 14 2N 99 31 E
Kanchenjunga, Nepal 43 F13 27 50N 88 10 E
Kanchipuram, India 40 N11 12 52N 79 45 E
Kandaghat, India 42 D7 30 59N 77 7 E
Kandahar = Qandahār, Afghan. 40 D4 31 32N 65 43 E
Kandalaksha, Russia 24 A5 67 9N 32 30 E
Kandalakshskiy Zaliv, Russia 24 A6 66 0N 35 0 E
Kandangan, Indonesia 36 E5 2 50S 115 20 E
Kandanghaur, Indonesia 37 G13 6 21S 108 6 E
Kandanos, Greece 23 D5 35 19N 23 44 E
Kandavu = Kadavu, Fiji 59 D8 19 0S 178 15 E
Kandhkot, Pakistan 42 E3 28 16N 69 8 E
Kandhla, India 42 E7 29 18N 77 19 E
Kandi, Benin 50 F6 11 7N 2 55 E
Kandi, India 43 H13 23 58N 88 5 E
Kandiaro, Pakistan 42 F3 27 4N 68 13 E
Kandla, India 42 H4 23 0N 70 10 E
Kandos, Australia 63 E4 32 45S 149 58 E
Kandreho, Madag. 57 B8 17 29S 46 6 E

Kandy, *Sri Lanka* 40 R12 7 18N 80 43 E
Kane, *U.S.A.* 78 E6 41 40N 78 49W
Kane Basin, *Greenland* 4 B4 79 1N 70 0W
Kaneohe, *U.S.A.* 74 H16 21 25N 157 48W
Kang, *Botswana* 56 C3 23 41S 22 50 E
Kangān, *Fārs, Iran* 45 E7 27 50N 52 3 E
Kangān, *Hormozgān, Iran* 45 E8 25 48N 57 28 E
Kangar, *Malaysia* 39 J3 6 27N 100 12 E
Kangaroo I., *Australia* 63 F2 35 45S 137 0 E
Kangaroo Mts., *Australia* 62 C3 23 29S 141 51 E
Kangasala, *Finland* 9 F21 61 28N 24 4 E
Kangāvar, *Iran* 45 C6 34 40N 48 0 E
Kangdong, *N. Korea* 35 E14 39 9N 126 5 E
Kangean, Kepulauan, *Indonesia* 36 F5 6 55S 115 23 E
Kangean Is. = Kangean, Kepulauan, *Indonesia* 36 F5 6 55S 115 23 E
Kanggye, *N. Korea* 35 D14 41 0N 126 35 E
Kanggyŏng, *S. Korea* 35 F14 36 10N 127 0 E
Kanghwa, *S. Korea* 35 F14 37 45N 126 30 E
Kangikajik, *Greenland* 4 B6 70 7N 22 0W
Kangiqsliniq = Rankin Inlet, *Canada* 68 B10 62 30N 93 0W
Kangiqsualujjuaq, *Canada* 69 C13 58 30N 65 59W
Kangiqsujuaq, *Canada* 69 B12 61 30N 72 0W
Kangiqtugaapik = Clyde River, *Canada* 69 A13 70 30N 68 30W
Kangirsuk, *Canada* 69 B13 60 0N 70 0W
Kangnŭng, *S. Korea* 35 F15 37 45N 128 54 E
Kangping, *China* 35 C12 42 43N 123 18 E
Kangra, *India* 42 C7 32 6N 76 16 E
Kangto, *India* 41 F18 27 50N 92 35 E
Kanhar →, *India* 43 G10 24 28N 83 8 E
Kaniama, *Dem. Rep. of the Congo* 54 D1 7 30S 24 12 E
Kaniapiskau = Caniapiscau →, *Canada* 71 A6 56 40N 69 30W
Kaniapiskau, Res. = Caniapiscau, Rés. de, *Canada* 71 B6 54 10N 69 55W
Kanin, Poluostrov, *Russia* 24 A8 68 0N 45 0 E
Kanin Nos, Mys, *Russia* 24 A7 68 39N 43 32 E
Kanin Pen. = Kanin, Poluostrov, *Russia* 24 A8 68 0N 45 0 E
Kaniva, *Australia* 63 F3 36 22S 141 18 E
Kanjut Sar, *Pakistan* 43 A6 36 7N 75 25 E
Kankaanpää, *Finland* 9 F20 61 44N 22 50 E
Kankakee, *U.S.A.* 76 E2 41 7N 87 52W
Kankakee →, *U.S.A.* 76 E1 41 23N 88 15W
Kankan, *Guinea* 50 F4 10 23N 9 15W
Kankendy = Xankändi, *Azerbaijan* 25 G8 39 52N 46 49 E
Kanker, *India* 41 J12 20 10N 81 40 E
Kankroli, *India* 42 G5 25 4N 73 53 E
Kannapolis, *U.S.A.* 77 H5 35 30N 80 37W
Kannauj, *India* 43 F8 27 3N 79 56 E
Kannod, *India* 40 H10 22 45N 76 40 E
Kano, *Nigeria* 50 F7 12 2N 8 30 E
Kan'onji, *Japan* 31 G6 34 7N 133 39 E
Kanowit, *Malaysia* 36 D4 2 14N 112 20 E
Kanoya, *Japan* 31 J5 31 25N 130 50 E
Kanpetlet, *Burma* 41 J18 21 10N 93 59 E
Kanpur, *India* 43 F9 26 28N 80 20 E
Kansas □, *U.S.A.* 80 F6 38 30N 99 0W
Kansas →, *U.S.A.* 80 F7 39 7N 94 37W
Kansas City, *Kans., U.S.A.* 80 F7 39 7N 94 38W
Kansas City, *Mo., U.S.A.* 80 F7 39 6N 94 35W
Kansenia, *Dem. Rep. of the Congo* 55 E2 10 20S 26 0 E
Kansk, *Russia* 27 D10 56 20N 95 37 E
Kansŏng, *S. Korea* 35 E15 38 24N 128 30 E
Kansu = Gansu □, *China* 34 G3 36 0N 104 0 E
Kantaphor, *India* 42 H7 22 35N 76 34 E
Kantharalak, *Thailand* 38 E5 14 39N 104 39 E
Kantli →, *India* 42 E6 28 20N 75 30 E
Kantō □, *Japan* 31 F9 36 15N 139 30 E
Kantō-Sanchi, *Japan* 31 G9 35 59N 138 50 E
Kanturk, *Ireland* 13 D3 52 11N 8 54W
Kanuma, *Japan* 31 F9 36 34N 139 42 E
Kanus, *Namibia* 56 D2 27 50S 18 39 E
Kanye, *Botswana* 56 C4 24 55S 25 28 E
Kanzenze, *Dem. Rep. of the Congo* 55 E2 10 30S 25 12 E
Kanzi, Ras, *Tanzania* 54 D4 7 1S 39 33 E
Kaohsiung, *Taiwan* 33 D7 22 35N 120 16 E
Kaokoveld, *Namibia* 56 B1 19 15S 14 30 E
Kaolack, *Senegal* 50 F2 14 5N 16 8W
Kaoshan, *China* 35 B13 44 38N 124 50 E
Kapaa, *U.S.A.* 74 G15 22 5N 159 19W
Kapadvanj, *India* 42 H5 23 5N 73 0 E
Kapan, *Armenia* 25 G8 39 18N 46 27 E
Kapanga, *Dem. Rep. of the Congo* 52 F4 8 30S 22 40 E
Kapchagai = Qapshaghay, *Kazakstan* 26 E8 43 51N 77 14 E
Kapela = Velika Kapela, *Croatia* 16 F8 45 10N 15 5 E
Kapema, *Dem. Rep. of the Congo* 55 E2 10 45S 28 22 E
Kapfenberg, *Austria* 16 E8 47 26N 15 18 E
Kapiri Mposhi, *Zambia* 55 E2 13 59S 28 43 E
Kāpīsā □, *Afghan.* 40 B6 35 0N 69 20 E
Kapiskau →, *Canada* 70 B3 52 47N 81 55W
Kapit, *Malaysia* 36 D4 2 0N 112 55 E
Kapiti I., *N.Z.* 59 J5 40 50S 174 56 E
Kaplan, *U.S.A.* 81 K8 30 0N 92 17W
Kapoe, *Thailand* 39 H2 9 34N 98 32 E
Kapoeta, *Sudan* 51 H12 4 50N 33 35 E
Kaposvár, *Hungary* 17 E9 46 25N 17 47 E
Kapowsin, *U.S.A.* 84 D4 46 59N 122 13W
Kapps, *Namibia* 56 C2 22 32S 17 18 E
Kapsan, *N. Korea* 35 D15 41 4N 128 19 E
Kapsukas = Marijampolė, *Lithuania* 9 J20 54 33N 23 19 E
Kapuas →, *Indonesia* 36 E3 0 25S 109 20 E
Kapuas Hulu, Pegunungan, *Malaysia* 36 D4 1 30N 113 30 E
Kapuas Hulu Ra. = Kapuas Hulu, Pegunungan, *Malaysia* 36 D4 1 30N 113 30 E
Kapulo, *Dem. Rep. of the Congo* 55 D2 8 18S 29 15 E
Kapunda, *Australia* 63 E2 34 20S 138 56 E
Kapuni, *N.Z.* 59 H5 39 29S 174 8 E
Kapurthala, *India* 42 D6 31 23N 75 25 E
Kapuskasing, *Canada* 70 C3 49 25N 82 30W
Kapuskasing →, *Canada* 70 C3 49 49N 82 0W
Kaputar, *Australia* 63 E5 30 15S 150 10 E
Kaputir, *Kenya* 54 B4 2 5N 35 28 E
Kara, *Russia* 26 C7 69 10N 65 0 E
Kara Bogaz Gol, Zaliv = Garabogazköl Aylagy, *Turkmenistan* 25 F9 41 0N 53 30 E
Kara Kalpak Republic = Qoraqalpoghistan □, *Uzbekistan* 26 E6 43 0N 58 0 E
Kara Kum, *Turkmenistan* 26 F6 39 30N 60 0 E
Kara Sea, *Russia* 26 B7 75 0N 70 0 E
Karabiğa, *Turkey* 21 D12 40 23N 27 17 E
Karabük, *Turkey* 25 F5 41 12N 32 37 E
Karaburun, *Turkey* 21 E12 38 41N 26 28 E
Karabutak = Qarabutaq, *Kazakstan* 26 E7 49 59N 60 14 E
Karacabey, *Turkey* 21 D13 40 12N 28 21 E
Karacasu, *Turkey* 21 F13 37 43N 28 35 E
Karachey-Cherkessia □, *Russia* 25 F7 43 40N 41 30 E
Karachi, *Pakistan* 42 G2 24 53N 67 0 E
Karad, *India* 40 L9 17 15N 74 10 E
Karaganda = Qaraghandy, *Kazakstan* 26 E8 49 50N 73 10 E
Karagayly, *Kazakstan* 26 E8 49 26N 76 0 E
Karaginskiy, Ostrov, *Russia* 27 D17 58 45N 164 0 E
Karagiye, Vpadina, *Kazakstan* 25 F9 43 27N 51 45 E
Karagiye Depression = Karagiye, Vpadina, *Kazakstan* 25 F9 43 27N 51 45 E
Karagola Road, *India* 43 G12 25 29N 87 23 E
Karaikal, *India* 40 P11 10 59N 79 50 E
Karaikkudi, *India* 40 P11 10 5N 78 45 E
Karaj, *Iran* 45 C6 35 48N 51 0 E
Karak, *Malaysia* 39 L4 3 25N 102 2 E
Karakalpakstan = Qoraqalpoghistan □, *Uzbekistan* 26 E6 43 0N 58 0 E
Karakelong, *Indonesia* 37 D7 4 35N 126 50 E
Karakitang, *Indonesia* 37 D7 3 14N 125 28 E
Karaklis = Vanadzor, *Armenia* 25 F7 40 48N 44 30 E
Karakol, *Kyrgyzstan* 26 E8 42 30N 78 20 E
Karakoram Pass, *Asia* 43 B7 35 33N 77 50 E
Karakoram Ra., *Pakistan* 43 B7 35 30N 77 0 E
Karakuwisa, *Namibia* 56 B2 18 56S 19 40 E
Karalon, *Russia* 27 D12 57 5N 115 50 E
Karama, *Jordan* 47 D4 31 57N 35 35 E
Karaman, *Turkey* 25 G5 37 14N 33 13 E
Karamay, *China* 32 B3 45 30N 84 58 E
Karambu, *Indonesia* 36 E5 3 53S 116 6 E
Karamea Bight, *N.Z.* 59 J3 41 22S 171 40 E
Karamnasa →, *India* 43 G10 25 31N 83 52 E
Karand, *Iran* 44 C5 34 16N 46 15 E
Karanganyar, *Indonesia* 37 G13 7 38S 109 37 E
Karanjia, *India* 43 J11 21 47N 85 58 E
Karasburg, *Namibia* 56 D2 28 0S 18 44 E
Karasino, *Russia* 26 C9 66 50N 86 50 E
Karasjok, *Norway* 8 B21 69 27N 25 30 E
Karasuk, *Russia* 26 D8 53 44N 78 2 E
Karasuyama, *Japan* 31 F10 36 39N 140 9 E
Karatau, Khrebet = Qarataū, *Kazakstan* 26 E7 43 30N 69 30 E
Karatsu, *Japan* 31 H4 33 26N 129 58 E
Karaul, *Russia* 26 B9 70 6N 82 15 E
Karauli, *India* 42 F7 26 30N 77 4 E
Karavostasi, *Cyprus* 23 D11 35 8N 32 50 E
Karawang, *Indonesia* 37 G12 6 30S 107 15 E
Karawanken, *Europe* 16 E8 46 30N 14 40 E
Karayazı, *Turkey* 25 G7 39 41N 42 9 E
Karazhal, *Kazakstan* 26 E8 48 2N 70 49 E
Karbalā', *Iraq* 44 C5 32 36N 44 3 E
Karcag, *Hungary* 17 E11 47 19N 20 57 E
Karcha →, *Pakistan* 43 B7 34 45N 76 10 E
Karchana, *India* 43 G9 25 17N 81 56 E
Kardhítsa, *Greece* 21 E9 39 23N 21 54 E
Kärdla, *Estonia* 9 G20 58 50N 22 40 E
Kareeberge, *S. Africa* 56 E3 30 59S 21 50 E
Kareha →, *India* 43 G12 25 44N 86 21 E
Kareima, *Sudan* 51 E12 18 30N 31 49 E
Karelia □, *Russia* 24 A5 65 30N 32 30 E
Karelian Republic = Karelia □, *Russia* 24 A5 65 30N 32 30 E
Karera, *India* 42 G8 25 32N 78 9 E
Kārevāndar, *Iran* 45 E9 27 53N 60 44 E
Kargasok, *Russia* 26 D9 59 3N 80 53 E
Kargat, *Russia* 26 D9 55 10N 80 15 E
Kargil, *India* 43 B7 34 32N 76 12 E
Kargopol, *Russia* 24 B6 61 30N 38 58 E
Karhal, *India* 43 F8 27 1N 78 57 E
Kariān, *Iran* 45 E8 26 57N 57 14 E
Karianga, *Madag.* 57 C8 22 25S 47 22 E
Kariba, *Zimbabwe* 55 F2 16 28S 28 50 E
Kariba, L., *Zimbabwe* 55 F2 16 40S 28 25 E
Kariba Dam, *Zimbabwe* 55 F2 16 30S 28 35 E
Kariba Gorge, *Zambia* 55 F2 16 30S 28 50 E
Karibib, *Namibia* 56 C2 22 0S 15 56 E
Karimata, Kepulauan, *Indonesia* 36 E3 1 25S 109 0 E
Karimata, Selat, *Indonesia* 36 E3 2 0S 108 40 E
Karimata Is. = Karimata, Kepulauan, *Indonesia* 36 E3 1 25S 109 0 E
Karimnagar, *India* 40 K11 18 26N 79 10 E
Karimunjawa, Kepulauan, *Indonesia* 36 F4 5 50S 110 30 E
Karin, *Somali Rep.* 46 E4 10 50N 45 52 E
Karīt, *Iran* 45 C8 33 29N 56 55 E
Kariya, *Japan* 31 G8 34 58N 137 1 E
Kariyangwe, *Zimbabwe* 57 B4 18 0S 27 38 E
Karkaralinsk = Qarqaraly, *Kazakstan* 26 E8 49 26N 75 30 E
Karkheh →, *Iran* 44 D5 31 2N 47 29 E
Karkinitska Zatoka, *Ukraine* 25 E5 45 56N 33 0 E
Karkinitskiy Zaliv = Karkinitska Zatoka, *Ukraine* 25 E5 45 56N 33 0 E
Karl-Marx-Stadt = Chemnitz, *Germany* 16 C7 50 51N 12 54 E
Karlovac, *Croatia* 16 F8 45 31N 15 36 E
Karlovo, *Bulgaria* 21 C11 42 38N 24 47 E
Karlovy Vary, *Czech Rep.* 16 C7 50 13N 12 51 E
Karlsbad = Karlovy Vary, *Czech Rep.* 16 C7 50 13N 12 51 E
Karlsborg, *Sweden* 9 G16 58 33N 14 33 E
Karlshamn, *Sweden* 9 H16 56 10N 14 51 E
Karlskoga, *Sweden* 9 G16 59 28N 14 33 E
Karlskrona, *Sweden* 9 H16 56 10N 15 35 E
Karlsruhe, *Germany* 16 D5 49 0N 8 23 E
Karlstad, *Sweden* 9 G15 59 23N 13 30 E
Karlstad, *U.S.A.* 80 A6 48 35N 96 31W
Karmi'el, *Israel* 47 C4 32 55N 35 18 E
Karnak, *Egypt* 51 C12 25 43N 32 39 E
Karnal, *India* 42 E7 29 42N 77 2 E
Karnali →, *Nepal* 43 E9 28 45N 81 16 E
Karnaphuli Res., *Bangla.* 41 H18 22 40N 92 20 E
Karnaprayag, *India* 43 D8 30 16N 79 15 E
Karnataka □, *India* 40 N10 13 15N 77 0 E
Karnes City, *U.S.A.* 81 L6 28 53N 97 54W
Karnische Alpen, *Europe* 16 E7 46 36N 13 0 E
Kärnten □, *Austria* 16 E8 46 52N 13 30 E
Karoi, *Zimbabwe* 55 F2 16 48S 29 45 E
Karonga, *Malawi* 55 D3 9 57S 33 55 E
Karoonda, *Australia* 63 F2 35 1S 139 59 E
Karor, *Pakistan* 42 D4 31 15N 70 59 E
Karora, *Sudan* 51 E13 17 44N 38 15 E
Karpasia, *Cyprus* 23 D13 35 32N 34 15 E
Kárpathos, *Greece* 21 G12 35 37N 27 10 E
Karpinsk, *Russia* 24 C11 59 45N 60 1 E
Karpogory, *Russia* 24 B7 64 0N 44 27 E
Karpuz Burnu = Apostolos Andreas, C., *Cyprus* 23 D13 35 42N 34 35 E
Karratha, *Australia* 60 D2 20 53S 116 40 E
Kars, *Turkey* 25 F7 40 40N 43 5 E
Karsakpay, *Kazakstan* 26 E7 47 55N 66 40 E
Karshi = Qarshi, *Uzbekistan* 26 F7 38 53N 65 48 E
Karsiyang, *India* 43 F13 26 56N 88 18 E
Karsog, *India* 42 D7 31 23N 77 12 E
Kartaly, *Russia* 26 D7 53 3N 60 40 E
Kartapur, *India* 42 D6 31 27N 75 32 E
Karthaus, *U.S.A.* 78 E6 41 8N 78 9W
Karufa, *Indonesia* 37 E8 3 50S 133 20 E
Karumba, *Australia* 62 B3 17 31S 140 50 E
Karumo, *Tanzania* 54 C3 2 25S 32 50 E
Karumwa, *Tanzania* 54 C3 3 12S 32 38 E
Kārūn →, *Iran* 45 D6 30 26N 48 10 E
Karungu, *Kenya* 54 C3 0 50S 34 10 E
Karviná, *Czech Rep.* 17 D10 49 53N 18 31 E
Karwan →, *India* 42 F8 27 26N 78 4 E
Karwar, *India* 40 M9 14 55N 74 13 E
Karwi, *India* 43 G9 25 12N 80 57 E
Kasache, *Malawi* 55 E3 13 25S 34 20 E
Kasai →, *Dem. Rep. of the Congo* 52 E3 3 30S 16 10 E
Kasai-Oriental □, *Dem. Rep. of the Congo* 54 D1 5 0S 24 30 E
Kasaji, *Dem. Rep. of the Congo* 55 E1 10 25S 23 27 E
Kasama, *Zambia* 55 E3 10 16S 31 9 E
Kasan-dong, *N. Korea* 35 D14 41 18N 126 55 E
Kasane, *Namibia* 56 B3 17 34S 24 50 E
Kasanga, *Tanzania* 55 D3 8 30S 31 10 E
Kasaragod, *India* 40 N9 12 30N 74 58 E
Kasba L., *Canada* 73 A8 60 20N 102 10W
Kāseh Garān, *Iran* 44 C5 34 5N 46 2 E
Kasempa, *Zambia* 55 E2 13 30S 25 44 E
Kasenga, *Dem. Rep. of the Congo* 55 E2 10 20S 28 45 E
Kasese, *Uganda* 54 B3 0 13N 30 3 E
Kasewa, *Zambia* 55 E2 14 28S 28 53 E
Kasganj, *India* 43 F8 27 48N 78 42 E
Kashabowie, *Canada* 70 C1 48 40N 90 26W
Kashaf, *Iran* 45 C9 35 58N 61 7 E
Kāshān, *Iran* 45 C6 34 5N 51 30 E
Kashechewan, *Canada* 70 B3 52 18N 81 37W
Kashgar = Kashi, *China* 32 C2 39 30N 76 2 E
Kashi, *China* 32 C2 39 30N 76 2 E
Kashimbo, *Dem. Rep. of the Congo* 55 E2 11 12S 26 19 E
Kashipur, *India* 43 E8 29 15N 79 0 E
Kashiwazaki, *Japan* 31 F9 37 22N 138 33 E
Kashk-e Kohneh, *Afghan.* 40 B3 34 55N 62 30 E
Kashkū'īyeh, *Iran* 45 D7 30 31N 55 40 E
Kāshmar, *Iran* 45 C8 35 16N 58 26 E
Kashmir, *Asia* 43 C7 34 0N 76 0 E
Kashmor, *Pakistan* 42 E3 28 28N 69 32 E
Kashun Noerh = Gaxun Nur, *China* 32 B5 42 22N 100 30 E
Kasiari, *India* 43 H12 22 8N 87 14 E
Kasimov, *Russia* 24 D7 54 55N 41 20 E
Kasinge, *Dem. Rep. of the Congo* 54 D2 6 15S 26 58 E
Kasiruta, *Indonesia* 37 E7 0 25S 127 12 E
Kaskaskia →, *U.S.A.* 80 G10 37 58N 89 57W
Kaskattama →, *Canada* 73 B10 57 3N 90 4W
Kaskinen, *Finland* 9 E19 62 22N 21 15 E
Kaslo, *Canada* 72 D5 49 55N 116 55W
Kasmere L., *Canada* 73 B8 59 34N 101 10W
Kasongo, *Dem. Rep. of the Congo* 54 C2 4 30S 26 33 E
Kasongo Lunda, *Dem. Rep. of the Congo* 52 F3 6 35S 16 49 E
Kásos, *Greece* 21 G12 35 20N 26 55 E
Kassalâ, *Sudan* 51 E13 15 30N 36 0 E
Kassel, *Germany* 16 C5 51 18N 9 26 E
Kassiópi, *Greece* 23 A3 39 48N 19 53 E
Kasson, *U.S.A.* 80 C8 44 2N 92 45W
Kastamonu, *Turkey* 25 F5 41 25N 33 43 E
Kastéli, *Greece* 23 D5 35 29N 23 38 E
Kastéllion, *Greece* 23 D7 35 12N 25 20 E
Kasterlee, *Belgium* 15 C4 51 15N 4 59 E
Kastoría, *Greece* 21 D9 40 30N 21 19 E
Kasulu, *Tanzania* 54 C3 4 37S 30 5 E
Kasumi, *Japan* 31 G7 35 38N 134 38 E
Kasungu, *Malawi* 55 E3 13 0S 33 29 E
Kasur, *Pakistan* 42 D6 31 5N 74 25 E
Kataba, *Zambia* 55 F2 16 5S 25 10 E
Katahdin, Mt., *U.S.A.* 77 C11 45 54N 68 56W
Katako Kombe, *Dem. Rep. of the Congo* 54 C1 3 25S 24 20 E
Katale, *Tanzania* 54 C3 4 52S 31 7 E
Katanda, *Katanga, Dem. Rep. of the Congo* 54 D1 7 52S 24 13 E
Katanda, *Nord-Kivu, Dem. Rep. of the Congo* 54 C2 0 55S 29 21 E
Katanga □, *Dem. Rep. of the Congo* 54 D2 8 0S 25 0 E
Katangi, *India* 40 J11 21 56N 79 50 E
Katanning, *Australia* 61 F2 33 40S 117 33 E
Katavi Swamp, *Tanzania* 54 D3 6 50S 31 10 E
Katerini, *Greece* 21 D10 40 18N 22 37 E
Katghora, *India* 43 H10 22 30N 82 33 E
Katha, *Burma* 41 G20 24 10N 96 30 E
Katherîna, Gebel, *Egypt* 44 D2 28 30N 33 57 E
Katherine, *Australia* 60 B5 14 27S 132 20 E
Katherine Gorge, *Australia* 60 B5 14 18S 132 28 E
Kathi, *India* 42 J6 21 47N 74 3 E
Kathiawar, *India* 42 H4 22 20N 71 0 E
Kathikas, *Cyprus* 23 E11 34 55N 32 25 E
Kathmandu = Katmandu, *Nepal* 43 F11 27 45N 85 20 E
Kathua, *India* 42 C6 32 23N 75 34 E
Katihar, *India* 43 G12 25 34N 87 36 E
Katima Mulilo, *Zambia* 56 B3 17 28S 24 13 E
Katimbira, *Malawi* 55 E3 12 40S 34 0 E
Katingan = Mendawai →, *Indonesia* 36 E4 3 30S 113 0 E
Katiola, *Ivory C.* 50 G4 8 10N 5 10W
Katmandu, *Nepal* 43 F11 27 45N 85 20 E
Katni, *India* 43 H9 23 51N 80 24 E
Káto Arkhánai, *Greece* 23 D7 35 15N 25 10 E
Káto Khorió, *Greece* 23 D7 35 3N 25 47 E
Káto Pyrgos, *Cyprus* 23 D11 35 11N 32 41 E
Katompe, *Dem. Rep. of the Congo* 54 D2 6 2S 26 23 E
Katonga →, *Uganda* 54 B3 0 34N 31 50 E
Katoomba, *Australia* 63 E5 33 41S 150 19 E
Katowice, *Poland* 17 C10 50 17N 19 5 E
Katrine, L., *U.K.* 12 E4 56 15N 4 30W
Katrineholm, *Sweden* 9 G17 59 9N 16 12 E
Katsepe, *Madag.* 57 B8 15 45S 46 15 E
Katsina, *Nigeria* 50 F7 13 0N 7 32 E
Katsumoto, *Japan* 31 H4 33 51N 129 42 E
Katsuura, *Japan* 31 G10 35 10N 140 20 E
Katsuyama, *Japan* 31 F8 36 3N 136 30 E
Kattaviá, *Greece* 23 D9 35 57N 27 46 E
Kattegat, *Denmark* 9 H14 56 40N 11 20 E
Katumba, *Dem. Rep. of the Congo* 54 D2 7 40S 25 17 E
Katungu, *Kenya* 54 C5 2 55S 40 3 E
Katwa, *India* 43 H13 23 30N 88 5 E
Katwijk, *Neths.* 15 B4 52 12N 4 24 E
Kauai, *U.S.A.* 74 H15 22 3N 159 30W
Kauai Channel, *U.S.A.* 74 H15 21 45N 158 50W
Kaufman, *U.S.A.* 81 J6 32 35N 96 19W
Kauhajoki, *Finland* 9 E20 62 25N 22 10 E
Kaukauna, *U.S.A.* 76 C1 44 17N 88 17W
Kaukauveld, *Namibia* 56 C3 20 0S 20 15 E
Kaunakakai, *U.S.A.* 74 H16 21 6N 157 1W
Kaunas, *Lithuania* 9 J20 54 54N 23 54 E
Kaunia, *Bangla.* 43 G13 25 46N 89 26 E
Kautokeino, *Norway* 8 B20 69 0N 23 4 E
Kauwapur, *India* 43 F10 27 31N 82 18 E
Kavacha, *Russia* 27 C17 60 16N 169 51 E
Kavalerovo, *Russia* 30 B7 44 15N 135 4 E
Kavali, *India* 40 M12 14 55N 80 1 E
Kavála, *Greece* 21 D11 40 57N 24 28 E
Kavār, *Iran* 45 D7 29 11N 52 44 E
Kavi, *India* 42 H5 22 12N 72 38 E
Kavimba, *Botswana* 56 B3 18 2S 24 38 E
Kavīr, Dasht-e, *Iran* 45 C7 34 30N 55 0 E
Kavos, *Greece* 23 B4 39 23N 20 3 E
Kaw, *Fr. Guiana* 93 C8 4 30N 52 15W
Kawagama L., *Canada* 78 A6 45 18N 78 45W
Kawagoe, *Japan* 31 G9 35 55N 139 29 E
Kawaguchi, *Japan* 31 G9 35 52N 139 45 E
Kawambwa, *Zambia* 55 D2 9 48S 29 3 E
Kawanoe, *Japan* 31 G6 34 1N 133 34 E
Kawardha, *India* 43 J9 22 0N 81 17 E
Kawasaki, *Japan* 31 G9 35 35N 139 42 E
Kawasi, *Indonesia* 37 E7 1 38S 127 28 E
Kawerau, *N.Z.* 59 H6 38 7S 176 42 E
Kawhia Harbour, *N.Z.* 59 H5 38 5S 174 51 E
Kawio, Kepulauan, *Indonesia* 37 D7 4 30N 125 30 E
Kawnro, *Burma* 41 H21 22 48N 99 8 E
Kawthaung, *Burma* 39 H2 10 5N 98 36 E
Kawthoolei = Kayin □, *Burma* 41 L20 18 0N 97 30 E
Kawthule = Kayin □, *Burma* 41 L20 18 0N 97 30 E
Kaya, *Burkina Faso* 50 F5 13 4N 1 10W
Kayah □, *Burma* 41 K20 19 15N 97 15 E
Kayan →, *Indonesia* 36 D5 2 55N 117 35 E
Kaycee, *U.S.A.* 82 E10 43 43N 106 38W
Kayeli, *Indonesia* 37 E7 3 20S 127 10 E
Kayenta, *U.S.A.* 83 H8 36 44N 110 15W
Kayes, *Mali* 50 F3 14 25N 11 30W
Kayin □, *Burma* 41 L20 18 0N 97 30 E
Kayoa, *Indonesia* 37 D7 0 1N 127 28 E
Kayomba, *Zambia* 55 E1 13 11S 24 2 E
Kayseri, *Turkey* 25 G6 38 45N 35 30 E
Kaysville, *U.S.A.* 82 F8 41 2N 111 56W
Kazachye, *Russia* 27 B14 70 52N 135 58 E
Kazakstan ■, *Asia* 26 E7 50 0N 70 0 E
Kazan, *Russia* 24 C8 55 50N 49 10 E
Kazan →, *Canada* 73 A9 64 3N 95 35W
Kazan-Rettō, *Pac. Oc.* 64 E6 25 0N 141 0 E
Kazanlŭk, *Bulgaria* 21 C11 42 38N 25 20 E
Kazatin = Kozyatyn, *Ukraine* 17 D15 49 45N 28 50 E
Kāzerūn, *Iran* 45 D6 29 38N 51 40 E
Kazi Magomed = Qazimämmäd, *Azerbaijan* 45 A6 40 3N 49 0 E
Kazuno, *Japan* 30 D10 40 10N 140 45 E
Kazym →, *Russia* 26 C7 63 54N 65 50 E
Kéa, *Greece* 21 F11 37 35N 24 22 E
Keady, *U.K.* 13 B5 54 15N 6 42W
Kearney, *U.S.A.* 80 E5 40 42N 99 5W
Kearny, *U.S.A.* 83 K8 33 3N 110 55W
Kearsarge, Mt., *U.S.A.* 79 C13 43 22N 71 50W
Keban, *Turkey* 25 G6 38 50N 38 50 E
Keban Barajı, *Turkey* 25 G6 38 41N 38 33 E
Kebnekaise, *Sweden* 8 C18 67 53N 18 33 E
Kebri Dehar, *Ethiopia* 46 F3 6 45N 44 17 E
Kebumen, *Indonesia* 37 G13 7 42S 109 40 E
Kechika →, *Canada* 72 B3 59 41N 127 12W
Kecskemét, *Hungary* 17 E10 46 57N 19 42 E
Kėdainiai, *Lithuania* 9 J21 55 15N 24 2 E
Kedarnath, *India* 43 D8 30 44N 79 4 E
Kedgwick, *Canada* 71 C6 47 40N 67 20W
Kédhros Óros, *Greece* 23 D6 35 11N 24 37 E
Kediri, *Indonesia* 36 F4 7 51S 112 1 E
Keeler, *U.S.A.* 84 J9 36 29N 117 52W
Keeley L., *Canada* 73 C7 54 54N 108 8W
Keeling Is. = Cocos Is., *Ind. Oc.* 64 J1 12 10S 96 55 E
Keelung = Chilung, *Taiwan* 33 D7 25 3N 121 45 E
Keene, *Canada* 78 B6 44 15N 78 10W
Keene, *Calif., U.S.A.* 85 K8 35 13N 118 33W
Keene, *N.H., U.S.A.* 79 D12 42 56N 72 17W

Keene, N.Y., U.S.A. 79 B11 44 16N 73 46W
Keeper Hill, Ireland 13 D3 52 45N 8 16W
Keer-Weer, C., Australia 62 A3 14 0S 141 32 E
Keeseville, U.S.A. 79 B11 44 29N 73 30W
Keetmanshoop, Namibia 56 D2 26 35S 18 8 E
Keewatin, Canada 73 D10 49 46N 94 34W
Keewatin →, Canada 73 B8 56 29N 100 46W
Kefallinía, Greece 21 E9 38 15N 20 30 E
Kefamenanu, Indonesia 37 F6 9 28S 124 29 E
Kefar Sava, Israel 47 C3 32 11N 34 54 E
Keffi, Nigeria 50 G7 8 55N 7 43 E
Keflavík, Iceland 8 D2 64 2N 22 35W
Keg River, Canada 72 B5 57 54N 117 55W
Kegaska, Canada 71 B7 50 9N 61 18W
Keighley, U.K. 10 D6 53 52N 1 54W
Keila, Estonia 9 G21 59 18N 24 25 E
Keimoes, S. Africa 56 D3 28 41S 20 59 E
Keitele, Finland 8 E22 63 10N 26 20 E
Keith, Australia 63 F3 36 6S 140 20 E
Keith, U.K. 12 D6 57 32N 2 57W
Keizer, U.S.A. 82 D2 44 57N 123 1W
Kejimkujik Nat. Park, Canada 71 D6 44 25N 65 25W
Kejserr Franz Joseph Fd., Greenland 4 B6 73 30N 24 30W
Kekri, India 42 G6 26 0N 75 10 E
Kelan, China 34 E6 38 43N 111 31 E
Kelang, Malaysia 39 L3 3 2N 101 26 E
Kelantan →, Malaysia 39 J4 6 13N 102 14 E
Kelkit →, Turkey 25 F6 40 45N 36 32 E
Kellerberrin, Australia 61 F2 31 36S 117 38 E
Kellett, C., Canada 4 B1 72 0N 126 0W
Kelleys I., U.S.A. 78 E2 41 36N 82 42W
Kellogg, U.S.A. 82 C5 47 32N 116 7W
Kells = Ceanannus Mor, Ireland 13 C5 53 44N 6 53W
Kelokedhara, Cyprus 23 E11 34 48N 32 39 E
Kelowna, Canada 72 D5 49 50N 119 25W
Kelseyville, U.S.A. 84 G4 38 59N 122 50W
Kelso, N.Z. 59 L2 45 54S 169 15 E
Kelso, U.K. 12 F6 55 36N 2 26W
Kelso, U.S.A. 84 D4 46 9N 122 54W
Keluang, Malaysia 39 L4 2 3N 103 18 E
Kelvington, Canada 73 C8 52 10N 103 30W
Kem, Russia 24 B5 65 0N 34 38 E
Kem →, Russia 24 B5 64 57N 34 41 E
Kema, Indonesia 37 D7 1 22N 125 8 E
Kemah, Turkey 44 B3 39 32N 39 5 E
Kemaman, Malaysia 36 D2 4 12N 103 18 E
Kemano, Canada 72 C3 53 35N 128 0W
Kemasik, Malaysia 39 K4 4 25N 103 27 E
Kemerovo, Russia 26 D9 55 20N 86 5 E
Kemi, Finland 8 D21 65 44N 24 34 E
Kemi älv = Kemijoki →, Finland 8 D21 65 47N 24 32 E
Kemijärvi, Finland 8 C22 66 43N 27 22 E
Kemijoki →, Finland 8 D21 65 47N 24 32 E
Kemmerer, U.S.A. 82 F8 41 48N 110 32W
Kemmuna = Comino, Malta 23 C1 36 1N 14 20 E
Kemp, L., U.S.A. 81 J5 33 46N 99 9W
Kemp Land, Antarctica 5 C5 69 0S 55 0 E
Kempsey, Australia 63 E5 31 1S 152 50 E
Kempt, L., Canada 70 C5 47 25N 74 22W
Kempten, Germany 16 E6 47 45N 10 17 E
Kempton, Australia 62 G4 42 31S 147 12 E
Kemptville, Canada 79 B9 45 0N 75 38W
Ken →, India 43 G9 25 13N 80 27 E
Kenai, U.S.A. 68 B4 60 33N 151 16W
Kendai, India 43 H10 22 45N 82 37 E
Kendal, Indonesia 37 G14 6 56S 110 14 E
Kendal, U.K. 10 C5 54 20N 2 44W
Kendall, Australia 63 E5 31 35S 152 44 E
Kendall, U.S.A. 77 N5 25 41N 80 19W
Kendall →, Australia 62 A3 14 4S 141 35 E
Kendallville, U.S.A. 76 E3 41 27N 85 16W
Kendari, Indonesia 37 E6 3 50S 122 30 E
Kendawangan, Indonesia 36 E4 2 32S 110 17 E
Kendrapara, India 41 J15 20 35N 86 30 E
Kendrew, S. Africa 56 E3 32 32S 24 30 E
Kene Thao, Laos 38 D3 17 44N 101 10 E
Kenedy, U.S.A. 81 L6 28 49N 97 51W
Kenema, S. Leone 50 G3 7 50N 11 14W
Keng Kok, Laos 38 D5 16 26N 105 12 E
Keng Tawng, Burma 41 J21 20 45N 98 18 E
Keng Tung, Burma 41 J21 21 0N 99 30 E
Kengeja, Tanzania 54 D4 5 26S 39 45 E
Kenhardt, S. Africa 56 D3 29 19S 21 12 E
Kenitra, Morocco 50 B4 34 15N 6 40W
Kenli, China 35 F10 37 30N 118 20 E
Kenmare, Ireland 13 E2 51 53N 9 36W
Kenmare, U.S.A. 80 A3 48 41N 102 5W
Kenmare River, Ireland 13 E2 51 48N 9 51W
Kennebago Lake, U.S.A. 79 A14 45 4N 70 40W
Kennebec, U.S.A. 80 D5 43 54N 99 52W
Kennebec →, U.S.A. 77 D11 43 45N 69 46W
Kennebunk, U.S.A. 79 C14 43 23N 70 33W
Kennedy, Zimbabwe 56 B4 18 52S 27 10 E
Kennedy Ra., Australia 61 D2 24 45S 115 10 E
Kennedy Taungdeik, Burma 41 H18 23 15N 93 45 E
Kenner, U.S.A. 81 L9 29 59N 90 15W
Kennet →, U.K. 11 F7 51 27N 0 57W
Kenneth Ra., Australia 61 D2 23 50S 117 8 E
Kennett, U.S.A. 81 G9 36 14N 90 3W
Kennewick, U.S.A. 82 C4 46 12N 119 7W
Kenogami →, Canada 70 B3 51 6N 84 28W
Kenora, Canada 73 D10 49 47N 94 29W
Kenosha, U.S.A. 76 D2 42 35N 87 49W
Kensington, Canada 71 C7 46 28N 63 34W
Kent, Ohio, U.S.A. 78 E3 41 9N 81 22W
Kent, Tex., U.S.A. 81 K2 31 4N 104 13W
Kent, Wash., U.S.A. 84 C4 47 23N 122 14W
Kent □, U.K. 11 F8 51 12N 0 40 E
Kent Group, Australia 62 F4 39 30S 147 20 E
Kent Pen., Canada 68 B9 68 30N 107 0W
Kentaū, Kazakstan 26 E7 43 32N 68 36 E
Kentland, U.S.A. 76 E2 40 46N 87 27W
Kenton, U.S.A. 76 E4 40 39N 83 37W
Kentucky □, U.S.A. 76 G3 37 0N 84 0W
Kentucky →, U.S.A. 76 F3 38 41N 85 11W
Kentucky L., U.S.A. 77 G2 37 1N 88 16W
Kentville, Canada 71 C7 45 6N 64 29W
Kentwood, U.S.A. 81 K9 30 56N 90 31W
Kenya ■, Africa 54 B4 1 0N 38 0 E
Kenya, Mt., Kenya 54 C4 0 10S 37 18 E
Keo Neua, Deo, Vietnam 38 C5 18 23N 105 10 E
Keokuk, U.S.A. 80 E9 40 24N 91 24W
Keonjhargarh, India 43 J11 21 28N 85 35 E
Kep, Cambodia 39 G5 10 29N 104 19 E
Kep, Vietnam 38 B6 21 24N 106 16 E
Kepi, Indonesia 37 F9 6 32S 139 19 E
Kerala □, India 40 P10 11 0N 76 15 E
Kerama-Rettō, Japan 31 L3 26 5N 127 15 E
Keran, Pakistan 43 B5 34 35N 73 59 E
Kerang, Australia 63 F3 35 40S 143 55 E
Keraudren, C., Australia 60 C2 19 58S 119 45 E
Kerava, Finland 9 F21 60 25N 25 5 E
Kerch, Ukraine 25 E6 45 20N 36 20 E
Kerguelen, Ind. Oc. 3 G13 49 15S 69 10 E
Kericho, Kenya 54 C4 0 22S 35 15 E
Kerinci, Indonesia 36 E2 1 40S 101 15 E
Kerki, Turkmenistan 26 F7 37 50N 65 12 E
Kérkira, Greece 23 A3 39 38N 19 50 E
Kerkrade, Neths. 15 D6 50 53N 6 4 E
Kermadec Is., Pac. Oc. 64 L10 30 0S 178 15W
Kermadec Trench, Pac. Oc. 64 L10 30 30S 176 0W
Kermān, Iran 45 D8 30 15N 57 1 E
Kerman, U.S.A. 84 J6 36 43N 120 4W
Kermān □, Iran 45 D8 30 0N 57 0 E
Kermān, Bīābān-e, Iran 45 D8 28 45N 59 45 E
Kermānshāh = Bākhtarān, Iran 44 C5 34 23N 47 0 E
Kermit, U.S.A. 81 K3 31 52N 103 6W
Kern →, U.S.A. 85 K7 35 16N 119 18W
Kernow = Cornwall □, U.K. 11 G3 50 26N 4 40W
Kernville, U.S.A. 85 K8 35 45N 118 26W
Keroh, Malaysia 39 K3 5 43N 101 1 E
Kerrera, U.K. 12 E3 56 24N 5 33W
Kerrobert, Canada 73 C7 51 56N 109 8W
Kerrville, U.S.A. 81 K5 30 3N 99 8W
Kerry □, Ireland 13 D2 52 7N 9 35W
Kerry Hd., Ireland 13 D2 52 25N 9 56W
Kerulen →, Asia 33 B6 48 48N 117 0 E
Kerzaz, Algeria 50 C5 29 29N 1 37W
Kesagami →, Canada 70 B4 51 40N 79 45W
Kesagami L., Canada 70 B3 50 23N 80 15W
Keşan, Turkey 21 D12 40 49N 26 38 E
Kesennuma, Japan 30 E10 38 54N 141 35 E
Keshit, Iran 45 D8 29 43N 58 17 E
Kestell, S. Africa 57 D4 28 17S 28 42 E
Kestenga, Russia 24 A5 65 50N 31 45 E
Keswick, U.K. 10 C4 54 36N 3 8W
Ket →, Russia 26 D9 58 55N 81 32 E
Ketapang, Indonesia 36 E4 1 55S 110 0 E
Ketchikan, U.S.A. 72 B2 55 21N 131 39W
Ketchum, U.S.A. 82 E6 43 41N 114 22W
Ketef, Khalîg Umm el, Egypt 44 F2 23 40N 35 35 E
Keti Bandar, Pakistan 42 G2 24 8N 67 27 E
Ketri, India 42 E6 28 1N 75 50 E
Kętrzyn, Poland 17 A11 54 7N 21 22 E
Kettering, U.K. 11 E7 52 24N 0 43W
Kettering, U.S.A. 76 F3 39 41N 84 10W
Kettle →, Canada 73 B11 56 40N 89 34W
Kettle Falls, U.S.A. 82 B4 48 37N 118 3W
Kettle Pt., Canada 78 C2 43 13N 82 1W
Kettleman City, U.S.A. 84 J7 36 1N 119 58W
Keuka L., U.S.A. 78 D7 42 30N 77 9W
Keuruu, Finland 9 E21 62 16N 24 41 E
Kewanee, U.S.A. 80 E10 41 14N 89 56W
Kewaunee, U.S.A. 76 C2 44 27N 87 31W
Keweenaw B., U.S.A. 76 B1 47 0N 88 15W
Keweenaw Pen., U.S.A. 76 B2 47 30N 88 0W
Keweenaw Pt., U.S.A. 76 B2 47 25N 87 43W
Key Largo, U.S.A. 77 N5 25 5N 80 27W
Key West, U.S.A. 75 F10 24 33N 81 48W
Keynsham, U.K. 11 F5 51 24N 2 29W
Keyser, U.S.A. 76 F6 39 26N 78 59W
Kezhma, Russia 27 D11 58 59N 101 9 E
Kezi, Zimbabwe 57 C4 20 58S 28 32 E
Khabarovsk, Russia 27 E14 48 30N 135 5 E
Khabr, Iran 45 D8 28 51N 56 22 E
Khābūr →, Syria 44 C4 35 17N 40 35 E
Khachmas = Xaçmaz, Azerbaijan 25 F8 41 31N 48 42 E
Khachrod, India 42 H6 23 25N 75 20 E
Khadro, Pakistan 42 F3 26 11N 68 50 E
Khadzhilyangar, China 43 B8 35 45N 79 20 E
Khaga, India 43 G9 25 47N 81 7 E
Khagaria, India 43 G12 25 30N 86 32 E
Khaipur, Pakistan 42 E5 29 34N 72 17 E
Khair, India 42 F7 27 57N 77 46 E
Khairabad, India 43 F9 27 33N 80 47 E
Khairagarh, India 43 J9 21 27N 81 2 E
Khairpur, Pakistan 42 F3 27 32N 68 49 E
Khairpur Nathan Shah, Pakistan 42 F2 27 6N 67 44 E
Khairwara, India 42 H5 23 58N 73 38 E
Khaisor →, Pakistan 42 D3 31 17N 68 59 E
Khajuri Kach, Pakistan 42 C3 32 4N 69 51 E
Khakassia □, Russia 26 D9 53 0N 90 0 E
Khakhea, Botswana 56 C3 24 48S 23 22 E
Khalafābād, Iran 45 D6 30 54N 49 24 E
Khalilabad, India 43 F10 26 48N 83 5 E
Khalīlī, Iran 45 E7 27 38N 53 17 E
Khalkhāl, Iran 45 B6 37 37N 48 32 E
Khalkís, Greece 21 E10 38 27N 23 42 E
Khalmer-Sede = Tazovskiy, Russia 26 C8 67 30N 78 44 E
Khalmer Yu, Russia 26 C7 67 58N 65 1 E
Khalturin, Russia 24 C8 58 40N 48 50 E
Khalūf, Oman 46 C6 20 30N 58 13 E
Kham Keut, Laos 38 C5 18 15N 104 43 E
Khamaria, India 43 H9 23 5N 80 48 E
Khambhaliya, India 42 H3 22 14N 69 41 E
Khambhat, India 42 H5 22 23N 72 33 E
Khambhat, G. of, India 40 J8 20 45N 72 30 E
Khamir, Iran 45 E7 26 57N 55 36 E
Khamir, Yemen 46 D3 16 2N 44 0 E
Khamsa, Egypt 47 E1 30 27N 32 23 E
Khan →, Namibia 56 C2 22 37S 14 56 E
Khān Abū Shāmat, Syria 47 B5 33 39N 36 53 E
Khān Azād, Iraq 44 C5 33 7N 44 22 E
Khān Mujīddah, Iraq 44 C4 32 21N 43 48 E
Khān Shaykhūn, Syria 44 C3 35 26N 36 38 E
Khān Yūnis, Gaza Strip 47 D3 31 21N 34 18 E
Khanai, Pakistan 42 D2 30 30N 67 8 E
Khānaqīn, Iraq 44 C5 34 23N 45 25 E
Khānbāghī, Iran 45 B7 36 10N 55 25 E
Khandwa, India 40 J10 21 49N 76 22 E
Khandyga, Russia 27 C14 62 42N 135 35 E
Khāneh, Iran 44 B5 36 41N 45 8 E
Khanewal, Pakistan 42 D4 30 20N 71 55 E
Khangah Dogran, Pakistan 42 D5 31 50N 73 37 E
Khanh Duong, Vietnam 38 F7 12 44N 108 44 E
Khaniá, Greece 23 D6 35 30N 24 4 E
Khaniá □, Greece 23 D6 35 30N 24 0 E
Khaniadhana, India 42 G8 25 1N 78 8 E
Khanion, Kólpos, Greece 23 D5 35 33N 23 55 E
Khanka, L., Asia 27 E14 45 0N 132 24 E
Khankendy = Xankändi, Azerbaijan 25 G8 39 52N 46 49 E
Khanna, India 42 D7 30 42N 76 16 E
Khanozai, Pakistan 42 D2 30 37N 67 19 E
Khanpur, Pakistan 42 E4 28 42N 70 35 E
Khanty-Mansiysk, Russia 26 C7 61 0N 69 0 E
Khapalu, Pakistan 43 B7 35 10N 76 20 E
Khapcheranga, Russia 27 E12 49 42N 112 24 E
Kharaghoda, India 42 H4 23 11N 71 46 E
Kharagpur, India 43 H12 22 20N 87 25 E
Khárakas, Greece 23 D7 35 1N 25 7 E
Kharan Kalat, Pakistan 40 E4 28 34N 65 21 E
Kharānaq, Iran 45 C7 32 20N 54 45 E
Kharda, India 40 K9 18 40N 75 34 E
Khardung La, India 43 B7 34 20N 77 43 E
Khârga, El Wâhât-el, Egypt 51 C12 25 10N 30 35 E
Khargon, India 40 J9 21 45N 75 40 E
Khari →, India 42 G6 25 54N 74 31 E
Kharian, Pakistan 42 C5 32 49N 73 52 E
Khārk, Jazīreh-ye, Iran 45 D6 29 15N 50 28 E
Kharkiv, Ukraine 25 E6 49 58N 36 20 E
Kharkov = Kharkiv, Ukraine 25 E6 49 58N 36 20 E
Kharovsk, Russia 24 C7 59 56N 40 13 E
Kharsawangarh, India 43 H11 22 48N 85 50 E
Kharta, Turkey 21 D13 40 55N 29 7 E
Khartoum = El Khartûm, Sudan 51 E12 15 31N 32 35 E
Khasan, Russia 30 C5 42 25N 130 40 E
Khāsh, Iran 40 E2 28 15N 61 15 E
Khashm el Girba, Sudan 51 F13 14 59N 35 58 E
Khaskovo, Bulgaria 21 D11 41 56N 25 30 E
Khatanga, Russia 27 B11 72 0N 102 20 E
Khatanga →, Russia 27 B11 72 55N 106 0 E
Khatauli, India 42 E7 29 17N 77 43 E
Khatra, India 43 H12 22 59N 86 51 E
Khātūnābād, Iran 45 D7 30 1N 55 25 E
Khatyrka, Russia 27 C18 62 3N 175 15 E
Khavda, India 42 H3 23 51N 69 43 E
Khaybar, Ḥarrat, Si. Arabia 44 E4 25 45N 40 0 E
Khayelitsha, S. Africa 53 L3 34 5S 18 42 E
Khāzimiyah, Iraq 44 C4 34 46N 43 37 E
Khe Bo, Vietnam 38 C5 19 8N 104 41 E
Khe Long, Vietnam 38 B5 21 29N 104 46 E
Khed Brahma, India 40 G8 24 7N 73 5 E
Khekra, India 42 E7 28 52N 77 20 E
Khemarak Phouminville, Cambodia 39 G4 11 37N 102 59 E
Khemisset, Morocco 50 B4 33 50N 6 1W
Khemmarat, Thailand 38 D5 16 10N 105 15 E
Khenāmān, Iran 45 D8 30 27N 56 29 E
Khenchela, Algeria 50 A7 35 28N 7 11 E
Khersān →, Iran 45 D6 31 33N 50 22 E
Kherson, Ukraine 25 E5 46 35N 32 35 E
Khersónisos Akrotiri, Greece 23 D6 35 30N 24 10 E
Kheta →, Russia 27 B11 71 54N 102 6 E
Khewari, Pakistan 42 F3 26 36N 68 52 E
Khilchipur, India 42 G7 24 2N 76 34 E
Khilok, Russia 27 D12 51 30N 110 45 E
Khíos, Greece 21 E12 38 27N 26 9 E
Khirsadoh, India 43 H8 22 11N 78 47 E
Khiuma = Hiiumaa, Estonia 9 G20 58 50N 22 45 E
Khiva, Uzbekistan 26 E7 41 30N 60 18 E
Khiyāv, Iran 44 B5 38 30N 47 45 E
Khlong Khlung, Thailand 38 D2 16 12N 99 43 E
Khmelnik, Ukraine 17 D14 49 33N 27 58 E
Khmelnitskiy = Khmelnytskyy, Ukraine 17 D14 49 23N 27 0 E
Khmelnytskyy, Ukraine 17 D14 49 23N 27 0 E
Khmer Rep. = Cambodia ■, Asia 38 F5 12 15N 105 0 E
Khoai, Hon, Vietnam 39 H5 8 26N 104 50 E
Khodoriv, Ukraine 17 D13 49 24N 24 19 E
Khodzent = Khŭjand, Tajikistan 26 E7 40 17N 69 37 E
Khojak Pass, Afghan. 42 D2 30 51N 66 34 E
Khok Kloi, Thailand 39 H2 8 17N 98 19 E
Khok Pho, Thailand 39 J3 6 43N 101 6 E
Kholm, Russia 24 C5 57 10N 31 15 E
Kholmsk, Russia 27 E15 47 40N 142 5 E
Khomas Hochland, Namibia 56 C2 22 40S 16 0 E
Khomeyn, Iran 45 C6 33 40N 50 7 E
Khomeyni Shahr, Iran 45 C6 32 41N 51 31 E
Khomodino, Botswana 56 C3 22 46S 23 52 E
Khon Kaen, Thailand 38 D4 16 30N 102 47 E
Khong →, Cambodia 38 F5 13 32N 105 58 E
Khong Sedone, Laos 38 E5 15 34N 105 49 E
Khonuu, Russia 27 C15 66 30N 143 12 E
Khoper →, Russia 25 D6 49 30N 42 20 E
Khóra Sfakion, Greece 23 D6 35 15N 24 9 E
Khorāsān □, Iran 45 C8 34 0N 58 0 E
Khorat = Nakhon Ratchasima, Thailand 38 E4 14 59N 102 12 E
Khorat, Cao Nguyen, Thailand 38 E4 15 30N 102 50 E
Khorixas, Namibia 56 C1 20 16S 14 59 E
Khorramābād, Khorāsān, Iran 45 C8 35 6N 57 57 E
Khorramābād, Lorestān, Iran 45 C6 33 30N 48 25 E
Khorrāmshahr, Iran 45 D6 30 29N 48 15 E
Khorugh, Tajikistan 26 F8 37 30N 71 36 E
Khosravī, Iran 45 D6 30 48N 51 28 E
Khosrowābād, Khuzestān, Iran 45 D6 30 10N 48 25 E
Khosrowābād, Kordestān, Iran 44 C5 35 31N 47 38 E
Khost, Pakistan 42 D2 30 13N 67 35 E
Khosūyeh, Iran 45 D7 28 32N 54 26 E
Khotyn, Ukraine 17 D14 48 31N 26 27 E
Khouribga, Morocco 50 B4 32 58N 6 57W
Khowst, Afghan. 42 C3 33 22N 69 58 E
Khowst □, Afghan. 40 C6 33 20N 70 0 E
Khoyniki, Belarus 17 C15 51 54N 29 55 E
Khrysokhou B., Cyprus 23 D11 35 6N 32 25 E
Khu Khan, Thailand 38 E5 14 42N 104 12 E
Khudzhand = Khŭjand, Tajikistan 26 E7 40 17N 69 37 E
Khuff, Si. Arabia 44 E5 24 55N 44 53 E
Khūgīānī, Afghan. 42 D2 31 37N 65 41 E
Khuis, Botswana 56 D3 26 40S 21 49 E
Khuiyala, India 42 F4 27 9N 70 25 E
Khŭjand, Tajikistan 26 E7 40 17N 69 37 E
Khujner, India 42 H7 23 47N 76 36 E
Khulna, Bangla. 41 H16 22 45N 89 34 E
Khulna □, Bangla. 41 H16 22 25N 89 35 E
Khumago, Botswana 56 C3 20 26S 24 32 E
Khūnsorkh, Iran 45 E8 27 9N 56 7 E
Khunti, India 43 H11 23 5N 85 17 E
Khūr, Iran 45 C8 32 55N 58 18 E
Khurai, India 42 G8 24 3N 78 23 E
Khurayş, Si. Arabia 45 E6 25 6N 48 2 E
Khurīyā Murīyā, Jazā'ir, Oman 46 D6 17 30N 55 58 E
Khurja, India 42 E7 28 15N 77 58 E
Khūrmāl, Iraq 44 C5 35 18N 46 2 E
Khurr, Wādī al, Iraq 44 C4 32 3N 43 52 E
Khūsf, Iran 45 C8 32 46N 58 53 E
Khush, Afghan. 40 C3 32 55N 62 10 E
Khushab, Pakistan 42 C5 32 20N 72 20 E
Khust, Ukraine 17 D12 48 10N 23 18 E
Khuzdar, Pakistan 42 F2 27 52N 66 30 E
Khūzestān □, Iran 45 D6 31 0N 49 0 E
Khvāf, Iran 45 C9 34 33N 60 8 E
Khvājeh, Iran 44 B5 38 9N 46 35 E
Khvānsār, Iran 45 D7 29 56N 54 8 E
Khvor, Iran 45 C7 33 45N 55 0 E
Khvorgū, Iran 45 E8 27 34N 56 27 E
Khvormūj, Iran 45 D6 28 40N 51 30 E
Khvoy, Iran 44 B5 38 35N 45 0 E
Khyber Pass, Afghan. 42 B4 34 10N 71 8 E
Kiabukwa, Dem. Rep. of the Congo 55 D1 8 40S 24 48 E
Kiama, Australia 63 E5 34 40S 150 50 E
Kiamba, Phil. 37 C6 6 2N 124 46 E
Kiambi, Dem. Rep. of the Congo 54 D2 7 15S 28 0 E
Kiambu, Kenya 54 C4 1 8S 36 50 E
Kiangara, Madag. 57 B8 17 58S 47 2 E
Kiangsi = Jiangxi □, China 33 D6 27 30N 116 0 E
Kiangsu = Jiangsu □, China 35 H11 33 0N 120 0 E
Kibanga Port, Uganda 54 B3 0 10N 32 58 E
Kibara, Tanzania 54 C3 2 8S 33 30 E
Kibare, Mts., Dem. Rep. of the Congo 54 D2 8 25S 27 10 E
Kibombo, Dem. Rep. of the Congo 54 C2 3 57S 25 53 E
Kibondo, Tanzania 54 C3 3 35S 30 45 E
Kibre Mengist, Ethiopia 46 F2 5 54N 38 59 E
Kibumbu, Burundi 54 C2 3 32S 29 45 E
Kibungo, Rwanda 54 C3 2 10S 30 32 E
Kibuye, Burundi 54 C2 3 39S 29 59 E
Kibuye, Rwanda 54 C2 2 3S 29 21 E
Kibwesa, Tanzania 54 D2 6 30S 29 58 E
Kibwezi, Kenya 54 C4 2 27S 37 57 E
Kichha, India 43 E8 28 53N 79 30 E
Kichha →, India 43 E8 28 41N 79 18 E
Kichmengskiy Gorodok, Russia 24 B8 59 59N 45 48 E
Kicking Horse Pass, Canada 72 C5 51 28N 116 16W
Kidal, Mali 50 E6 18 26N 1 22 E
Kidderminster, U.K. 11 E5 52 24N 2 15W
Kidete, Tanzania 54 D4 6 25S 37 17 E
Kidnappers, C., N.Z. 59 H6 39 38S 177 5 E
Kidsgrove, U.K. 10 D5 53 5N 2 14W
Kidston, Australia 62 B3 18 52S 144 8 E
Kidugallo, Tanzania 54 D4 6 49S 38 15 E
Kiel, Germany 16 A6 54 19N 10 8 E
Kiel Canal = Nord-Ostsee-Kanal, Germany 16 A5 54 12N 9 32 E
Kielce, Poland 17 C11 50 52N 20 42 E
Kielder Water, U.K. 10 B5 55 11N 2 31W
Kieler Bucht, Germany 16 A6 54 35N 10 25 E
Kien Binh, Vietnam 39 H5 9 55N 105 19 E
Kien Tan, Vietnam 39 G5 10 7N 105 17 E
Kienge, Dem. Rep. of the Congo 55 E2 10 30S 27 30 E
Kiev = Kyyiv, Ukraine 17 C16 50 30N 30 28 E
Kiffa, Mauritania 50 E3 16 37N 11 24W
Kifrī, Iraq 44 C5 34 45N 45 0 E
Kigali, Rwanda 54 C3 1 59S 30 4 E
Kigarama, Tanzania 54 C3 1 1S 31 50 E
Kigoma □, Tanzania 54 D3 5 0S 30 0 E
Kigoma-Ujiji, Tanzania 54 C2 4 55S 29 36 E
Kigomasha, Ras, Tanzania 54 C4 4 58S 38 58 E
Kığızı, Turkey 44 B4 38 18N 43 25 E
Kihei, U.S.A. 74 H16 20 47N 156 28W
Kihnu, Estonia 9 G21 58 9N 24 1 E
Kii-Sanchi, Japan 31 G8 34 20N 136 0 E
Kii-Suidō, Japan 31 H7 33 40N 134 45 E
Kikaiga-Shima, Japan 31 K4 28 19N 129 59 E
Kikinda, Serbia, Yug. 21 B9 45 50N 20 30 E
Kikládhes, Greece 21 F11 37 0N 24 30 E
Kikwit, Dem. Rep. of the Congo 52 E3 5 0S 18 45 E
Kilar, India 42 C7 33 6N 76 25 E
Kilauea Crater, U.S.A. 74 J17 19 25N 155 17W
Kilbrannan Sd., U.K. 12 F3 55 37N 5 26W
Kilchu, N. Korea 35 D15 40 57N 129 25 E
Kilcoy, Australia 63 D5 26 59S 152 30 E
Kildare, Ireland 13 C5 53 9N 6 55W
Kildare □, Ireland 13 C5 53 10N 6 50W
Kilfinnane, Ireland 13 D3 52 21N 8 28W
Kilgore, U.S.A. 81 J7 32 23N 94 53W
Kilifi, Kenya 54 C4 3 40S 39 48 E
Kilimanjaro, Tanzania 54 C4 3 7S 37 20 E
Kilimanjaro □, Tanzania 54 C4 4 0S 38 0 E
Kilindini, Kenya 54 C4 4 4S 39 40 E
Kilis, Turkey 44 B3 36 42N 37 6 E
Kiliya, Ukraine 17 F15 45 28N 29 16 E
Kilkee, Ireland 13 D2 52 41N 9 39W
Kilkeel, U.K. 13 B5 54 4N 6 0W
Kilkenny, Ireland 13 D4 52 39N 7 15W
Kilkenny □, Ireland 13 D4 52 35N 7 15W
Kilkieran B., Ireland 13 C2 53 20N 9 41W
Kilkís, Greece 21 D10 40 58N 22 57 E
Killala, Ireland 13 B2 54 13N 9 12W
Killala B., Ireland 13 B2 54 16N 9 8W
Killaloe, Ireland 13 D3 52 48N 8 28W
Killaloe Station, Canada 78 A7 45 33N 77 25W
Killarney, Australia 63 D5 28 20S 152 18 E
Killarney, Canada 73 D9 49 10N 99 40W
Killarney, Ireland 13 D2 52 4N 9 30W
Killary Harbour, Ireland 13 C2 53 38N 9 52W
Killdeer, U.S.A. 80 B3 47 26N 102 48W
Killeen, U.S.A. 81 K6 31 7N 97 44W
Killin, U.K. 12 E4 56 28N 4 19W
Killíni, Greece 21 F10 37 54N 22 25 E
Killorglin, Ireland 13 D2 52 6N 9 47W
Killybegs, Ireland 13 B3 54 38N 8 26W
Kilmarnock, U.K. 12 F4 55 37N 4 29W
Kilmore, Australia 63 F3 37 25S 144 53 E

Köneürgench, Turkmenistan 26 E6 42 19N 59 10 E
Konevo, Russia 24 B6 62 8N 39 20 E
Kong = Khong →, Cambodia 38 F5 13 32N 105 58 E
Kong, Ivory C. 50 G5 8 54N 4 36W
Kong, Koh, Cambodia 39 G4 11 20N 103 0 E
Kong Christian IX Land, Greenland 4 C6 68 0N 36 0W
Kong Christian X Land, Greenland 4 B6 74 0N 29 0W
Kong Frederik IX Land, Greenland 4 C5 67 0N 52 0W
Kong Frederik VI Kyst, Greenland 4 C5 63 0N 43 0W
Kong Frederik VIII Land, Greenland 4 B6 78 30N 26 0W
Kong Oscar Fjord, Greenland 4 B6 72 20N 24 0W
Kongju, S. Korea 35 F14 36 30N 127 0 E
Konglu, Burma 41 F20 27 13N 97 57 E
Kongola, Namibia 56 B3 17 45S 23 20 E
Kongolo, Kasai-Or., Dem. Rep. of the Congo 54 D1 5 26S 24 49 E
Kongolo, Katanga, Dem. Rep. of the Congo 54 D2 5 22S 27 0 E
Kongsberg, Norway 9 G13 59 39N 9 39 E
Kongsvinger, Norway 9 F15 60 12N 12 2 E
Kongwa, Tanzania 54 D4 6 11S 36 26 E
Koni, Dem. Rep. of the Congo 55 E2 10 40S 27 11 E
Koni, Mts., Dem. Rep. of the Congo 55 E2 10 36S 27 10 E
Königsberg = Kaliningrad, Russia 9 J19 54 42N 20 32 E
Konin, Poland 17 B10 52 12N 18 15 E
Konjic, Bos.-H. 21 C7 43 42N 17 58 E
Konkiep, Namibia 56 D2 26 49S 17 15 E
Konosha, Russia 24 B7 61 0N 40 5 E
Kōnosu, Japan 31 F9 36 3N 139 31 E
Konotop, Ukraine 25 D5 51 12N 33 7 E
Końskie, Poland 17 C11 51 15N 20 23 E
Konstanz, Germany 16 E5 47 40N 9 10 E
Kont, Iran 45 E9 26 55N 61 50 E
Kontagora, Nigeria 50 F7 10 23N 5 27 E
Konya, Turkey 25 G5 37 52N 32 35 E
Konza, Kenya 54 C4 1 45S 37 7 E
Koocanusa, L., Canada 82 B6 49 20N 115 15W
Kookynie, Australia 61 E3 29 17S 121 22 E
Koolyanobbing, Australia 61 F2 30 48S 119 36 E
Koonibba, Australia 63 E1 31 54S 133 25 E
Koorawatha, Australia 63 E4 34 2S 148 33 E
Koorda, Australia 61 F2 30 48S 117 35 E
Kooskia, U.S.A. 82 C6 46 9N 115 59W
Kootenay →, U.S.A. 72 D5 49 19N 117 39W
Kootenay L., Canada 72 D5 49 45N 116 50W
Kootenay Nat. Park, Canada 72 C5 51 0N 116 0W
Kootjieskolk, S. Africa 56 E3 31 15S 20 21 E
Kopaonik, Yugoslavia 21 C9 43 10N 20 50 E
Kópavogur, Iceland 8 D3 64 6N 21 55W
Koper, Slovenia 16 F7 45 31N 13 44 E
Kopervik, Norway 9 G11 59 17N 5 17 E
Kopet Dagh, Asia 45 B8 38 0N 58 0 E
Kopi, Australia 63 E2 33 24S 135 40 E
Köping, Sweden 9 G17 59 31N 16 3 E
Koppeh Dāgh = Kopet Dagh, Asia 45 B8 38 0N 58 0 E
Koppies, S. Africa 57 D4 27 20S 27 30 E
Koprivnica, Croatia 20 A7 46 12N 16 45 E
Kopychyntsi, Ukraine 17 D13 49 7N 25 58 E
Korab, Macedonia 21 D9 41 44N 20 40 E
Korakiána, Greece 23 A3 39 42N 19 45 E
Koral, India 42 J5 21 50N 73 12 E
Korba, India 43 H10 22 20N 82 45 E
Korbu, G., Malaysia 39 K3 4 41N 101 18 E
Korce = Korçë, Albania 21 D9 40 37N 20 50 E
Korçë, Albania 21 D9 40 37N 20 50 E
Korčula, Croatia 20 C7 42 56N 16 57 E
Kord Kūy, Iran 45 B7 36 48N 54 7 E
Kord Sheykh, Iran 45 D7 28 31N 52 53 E
Kordestān □, Iran 44 C5 36 0N 47 0 E
Kordofân, Sudan 51 F11 13 0N 29 0 E
Korea, North ■, Asia 35 E14 40 0N 127 0 E
Korea, South ■, Asia 35 G15 36 0N 128 0 E
Korea Bay, Korea 35 E13 39 0N 124 0 E
Korea Strait, Asia 35 H15 34 0N 129 30 E
Korets, Ukraine 17 C14 50 40N 27 5 E
Korhogo, Ivory C. 50 G4 9 29N 5 28W
Korinthiakós Kólpos, Greece 21 E10 38 16N 22 30 E
Kórinthos, Greece 21 F10 37 56N 22 55 E
Korissa, Límni, Greece 23 B3 39 27N 19 53 E
Kōriyama, Japan 30 F10 37 24N 140 23 E
Korla, China 32 B3 41 45N 86 4 E
Kormakiti, C., Cyprus 23 D11 35 23N 32 56 E
Korneshty = Corneşti, Moldova 17 E15 47 21N 28 1 E
Koro, Fiji 59 C8 17 19S 179 23 E
Koro, Ivory C. 50 G4 8 32N 7 30W
Koro Sea, Fiji 59 C9 17 30S 179 45W
Korogwe, Tanzania 54 D4 5 5S 38 25 E
Koronadal, Phil. 37 C6 6 12N 125 1 E
Koror, Palau 64 G5 7 20N 134 28 E
Körös →, Hungary 17 E11 46 43N 20 12 E
Korosten, Ukraine 17 C15 50 54N 28 36 E
Korostyshev, Ukraine 17 C15 50 19N 29 4 E
Korraraika, Helodranon' i, Madag. 57 B7 17 45S 43 57 E
Korsakov, Russia 27 E15 46 36N 142 42 E
Korshunovo, Russia 27 D12 58 37N 110 10 E
Korsør, Denmark 9 J14 55 20N 11 9 E
Kortrijk, Belgium 15 D3 50 50N 3 17 E
Korwai, India 42 G8 24 7N 78 5 E
Koryakskoye Nagorye, Russia 27 C18 61 0N 171 0 E
Koryŏng, S. Korea 35 G15 35 44N 128 15 E
Kos, Greece 21 F12 36 50N 27 15 E
Koschagyl, Kazakstan 25 E9 46 40N 54 0 E
Kościan, Poland 17 B9 52 5N 16 40 E
Kosciusko, U.S.A. 81 J10 33 4N 89 35W
Kosciuszko, Mt., Australia 63 F4 36 27S 148 16 E
Kosha, Sudan 51 D12 20 50N 30 30 E
K'oshih = Kashi, China 32 C2 39 30N 76 2 E
Koshiki-Rettō, Japan 31 J4 31 45N 129 49 E
Kosi, India 42 F7 27 48N 77 29 E
Kosi →, India 43 E8 28 41N 78 57 E
Košice, Slovak Rep. 17 D11 48 42N 21 15 E
Koskhinoú, Greece 23 C10 36 23N 28 13 E
Koslan, Russia 24 B8 63 34N 49 14 E
Kosŏng, N. Korea 35 E15 38 40N 128 22 E
Kosovo □, Yugoslavia 21 C9 42 30N 21 0 E
Kosovska Mitrovica, Kosovo, Yug. 21 C9 42 54N 20 52 E
Kossou, L. de, Ivory C. 50 G4 6 59N 5 31W
Koster, S. Africa 56 D4 25 52S 26 54 E
Kôstî, Sudan 51 F12 13 8N 32 43 E
Kostopil, Ukraine 17 C14 50 51N 26 22 E
Kostroma, Russia 24 C7 57 50N 40 58 E
Kostrzyn, Poland 16 B8 52 35N 14 39 E
Koszalin, Poland 16 A9 54 11N 16 8 E
Kot Addu, Pakistan 42 D4 30 30N 71 0 E
Kot Kapura, India 42 D6 30 35N 74 50 E
Kot Moman, Pakistan 42 C5 32 13N 73 0 E
Kot Sultan, Pakistan 42 D4 30 46N 70 56 E
Kota, India 42 G6 25 14N 75 49 E
Kota Baharu, Malaysia 39 J4 6 7N 102 14 E
Kota Barrage, India 42 G6 25 6N 75 51 E
Kota Belud, Malaysia 36 C5 6 21N 116 26 E
Kota Kinabalu, Malaysia 36 C5 6 0N 116 4 E
Kota Kubu Baharu, Malaysia 39 L3 3 34N 101 39 E
Kota Tinggi, Malaysia 39 M4 1 44N 103 53 E
Kotaagung, Indonesia 36 F2 5 38S 104 29 E
Kotabaru, Indonesia 36 E5 3 20S 116 20 E
Kotabumi, Indonesia 36 E2 4 49S 104 54 E
Kotamobagu, Indonesia 37 D6 0 57N 124 31 E
Kotcho L., Canada 72 B4 59 7N 121 12W
Kotdwara, India 43 E8 29 45N 78 32 E
Kotelnich, Russia 24 C8 58 22N 48 24 E
Kotelnikovo, Russia 25 E7 47 38N 43 8 E
Kotelnyy, Ostrov, Russia 27 B14 75 10N 139 0 E
Kothari →, India 42 G6 25 20N 75 4 E
Kothi, Chhattisgarh, India 43 H10 23 21N 82 3 E
Kothi, Mad. P., India 43 G9 24 45N 80 40 E
Kotiro, Pakistan 42 F2 26 17N 67 13 E
Kotka, Finland 9 F22 60 28N 26 58 E
Kotlas, Russia 24 B8 61 17N 46 43 E
Kotli, Pakistan 42 C5 33 30N 73 55 E
Kotma, India 43 H9 23 12N 81 58 E
Kotmul, Pakistan 43 B6 35 32N 75 10 E
Kotor, Montenegro, Yug. 21 C8 42 25N 18 47 E
Kotovsk, Ukraine 17 E15 47 45N 29 35 E
Kotputli, India 42 F7 27 43N 76 12 E
Kotri, Pakistan 42 G3 25 22N 68 22 E
Kotturu, India 40 M10 14 45N 76 10 E
Kotuy →, Russia 27 B11 71 54N 102 6 E
Kotzebue, U.S.A. 68 B3 66 53N 162 39W
Koudougou, Burkina Faso 50 F5 12 10N 2 20W
Koufonísi, Greece 23 E8 34 56N 26 8 E
Kougaberge, S. Africa 56 E3 33 48S 23 50 E
Kouilou →, Congo 52 E2 4 10S 12 5 E
Koula Moutou, Gabon 52 E2 1 15S 12 25 E
Koulen = Kulen, Cambodia 38 F5 13 50N 104 40 E
Kouloúra, Greece 23 A3 39 42N 19 54 E
Koúm-bournoú, Ákra, Greece 23 C10 36 15N 28 11 E
Koumala, Australia 62 C4 21 38S 149 15 E
Koumra, Chad 51 G9 8 50N 17 35 E
Kounradskiy, Kazakstan 26 E8 46 59N 75 0 E
Kountze, U.S.A. 81 K7 30 22N 94 19W
Kouris →, Cyprus 23 E11 34 38N 32 54 E
Kourou, Fr. Guiana 93 B8 5 9N 52 39W
Kousseri, Cameroon 51 F8 12 0N 14 55 E
Kouvola, Finland 9 F22 60 52N 26 43 E
Kovdor, Russia 24 A5 67 34N 30 24 E
Kovel, Ukraine 17 C13 51 11N 24 38 E
Kovrov, Russia 24 C7 56 25N 41 25 E
Kowanyama, Australia 62 B3 15 29S 141 44 E
Kowŏn, N. Korea 35 E14 39 26N 127 14 E
Köyceğiz, Turkey 21 F13 36 57N 28 40 E
Koza, Japan 31 L3 26 19N 127 46 E
Kozan, Turkey 44 B2 37 26N 35 50 E
Kozáni, Greece 21 D9 40 19N 21 47 E
Kozhikode = Calicut, India 40 P9 11 15N 75 43 E
Kozhva, Russia 24 A10 65 10N 57 0 E
Kozyatyn, Ukraine 17 D15 49 45N 28 50 E
Kra, Isthmus of = Kra, Kho Khot, Thailand 39 G2 10 15N 99 30 E
Kra, Kho Khot, Thailand 39 G2 10 15N 99 30 E
Kra Buri, Thailand 39 G2 10 22N 98 46 E
Kraai →, S. Africa 56 E4 30 40S 26 45 E
Krabi, Thailand 39 H2 8 4N 98 55 E
Kracheh, Cambodia 38 F6 12 32N 106 10 E
Kragan, Indonesia 37 G14 6 43S 111 38 E
Kragerø, Norway 9 G13 58 52N 9 25 E
Kragujevac, Serbia, Yug. 21 B9 44 2N 20 56 E
Krajina, Bos.-H. 20 B7 44 45N 16 35 E
Krakatau = Rakata, Pulau, Indonesia 36 F3 6 10S 105 20 E
Krakatoa = Rakata, Pulau, Indonesia 36 F3 6 10S 105 20 E
Krakor, Cambodia 38 F5 12 32N 104 12 E
Kraków, Poland 17 C10 50 4N 19 57 E
Kralanh, Cambodia 38 F4 13 35N 103 25 E
Kraljevo, Serbia, Yug. 21 C9 43 44N 20 41 E
Kramatorsk, Ukraine 25 E6 48 50N 37 30 E
Kramfors, Sweden 9 E17 62 55N 17 48 E
Kranj, Slovenia 16 E8 46 16N 14 22 E
Krankskop, S. Africa 57 D5 28 0S 30 47 E
Krasavino, Russia 24 B8 60 58N 46 29 E
Kraskino, Russia 27 E14 42 44N 130 48 E
Kraśnik, Poland 17 C12 50 55N 22 15 E
Krasnoarmeysk, Russia 26 D5 51 0N 45 42 E
Krasnodar, Russia 25 E6 45 5N 39 0 E
Krasnokamsk, Russia 24 C10 58 4N 55 48 E
Krasnoperekopsk, Ukraine 25 E5 46 0N 33 54 E
Krasnorechenskiy, Russia 30 B7 44 41N 135 14 E
Krasnoselkup, Russia 26 C9 65 20N 82 10 E
Krasnoturinsk, Russia 24 C11 59 46N 60 12 E
Krasnoufimsk, Russia 24 C10 56 36N 57 38 E
Krasnouralsk, Russia 24 C11 58 21N 60 3 E
Krasnovishersk, Russia 24 B10 60 23N 57 3 E
Krasnovodsk = Türkmenbashi, Turkmenistan 25 G9 40 5N 53 5 E
Krasnoyarsk, Russia 27 D10 56 8N 93 0 E
Krasnyy Kut, Russia 25 D8 50 50N 47 0 E
Krasnyy Luch, Ukraine 25 E6 48 13N 39 0 E
Krasnyy Yar, Russia 25 E8 46 43N 48 23 E
Kratie = Kracheh, Cambodia 38 F6 12 32N 106 10 E
Krau, Indonesia 37 E10 3 19S 140 5 E
Kravanh, Chuor Phnum, Cambodia 39 G4 12 0N 103 32 E
Krefeld, Germany 16 C4 51 20N 6 33 E
Kremen, Croatia 16 F8 44 28N 15 53 E
Kremenchuk, Ukraine 25 E5 49 5N 33 25 E
Kremenchuksk Vdskh., Ukraine 25 E5 49 20N 32 30 E
Kremenets, Ukraine 17 C13 50 8N 25 43 E
Kremmling, U.S.A. 82 F10 40 4N 106 24W
Krems, Austria 16 D8 48 25N 15 36 E
Kretinga, Lithuania 9 J19 55 53N 21 15 E
Kribi, Cameroon 52 D1 2 57N 9 56 E
Krichev = Krychaw, Belarus 17 B16 53 40N 31 41 E
Kriós, Ákra, Greece 23 D5 35 13N 23 34 E
Krishna →, India 41 M12 15 57N 80 59 E
Krishnanagar, India 43 H13 23 24N 88 33 E
Kristiansand, Norway 9 G13 58 8N 8 1 E
Kristianstad, Sweden 9 H16 56 2N 14 9 E
Kristiansund, Norway 8 E12 63 7N 7 45 E
Kristiinankaupunki, Finland 9 E19 62 16N 21 21 E
Kristinehamn, Sweden 9 G16 59 18N 14 7 E
Kristinestad = Kristiinankaupunki, Finland 9 E19 62 16N 21 21 E
Kríti, Greece 23 D7 35 15N 25 0 E
Kritsá, Greece 23 D7 35 10N 25 41 E
Krivoy Rog = Kryvyy Rih, Ukraine 25 E5 47 51N 33 20 E
Krk, Croatia 16 F8 45 8N 14 40 E
Krokodil →, Mozam. 57 D5 25 14S 32 18 E
Krong Kaoh Kong, Cambodia 36 B2 11 35N 103 0 E
Kronprins Olav Kyst, Antarctica 5 C5 69 0S 42 0 E
Kronshtadt, Russia 24 B4 59 57N 29 51 E
Kroonstad, S. Africa 56 D4 27 43S 27 19 E
Kropotkin, Russia 25 E7 45 28N 40 28 E
Krosno, Poland 17 D11 49 42N 21 46 E
Krotoszyn, Poland 17 C9 51 42N 17 23 E
Kroussón, Greece 23 D6 35 13N 24 59 E
Krugersdorp, S. Africa 57 D4 26 5S 27 46 E
Kruisfontein, S. Africa 56 E3 33 59S 24 43 E
Krung Thep = Bangkok, Thailand 38 F3 13 45N 100 35 E
Krupki, Belarus 17 A15 54 19N 29 8 E
Kruševac, Serbia, Yug. 21 C9 43 35N 21 28 E
Krychaw, Belarus 17 B16 53 40N 31 41 E
Krymskiy Poluostrov = Krymskyy Pivostriv, Ukraine 25 F5 45 0N 34 0 E
Krymskyy Pivostriv, Ukraine 25 F5 45 0N 34 0 E
Kryvyy Rih, Ukraine 25 E5 47 51N 33 20 E
Ksar el Kebir, Morocco 50 B4 35 0N 6 0W
Ksar es Souk = Er Rachidia, Morocco 50 B5 31 58N 4 20W
Kuala Belait, Malaysia 36 D4 4 35N 114 11 E
Kuala Berang, Malaysia 39 K4 5 5N 103 1 E
Kuala Dungun = Dungun, Malaysia 39 K4 4 45N 103 25 E
Kuala Kangsar, Malaysia 39 K3 4 46N 100 56 E
Kuala Kelawang, Malaysia 39 L4 2 56N 102 5 E
Kuala Kerai, Malaysia 39 K4 5 30N 102 12 E
Kuala Lipis, Malaysia 39 K4 4 10N 102 3 E
Kuala Lumpur, Malaysia 39 L3 3 9N 101 41 E
Kuala Nerang, Malaysia 39 J3 6 16N 100 37 E
Kuala Pilah, Malaysia 39 L4 2 45N 102 15 E
Kuala Rompin, Malaysia 39 L4 2 49N 103 29 E
Kuala Selangor, Malaysia 39 L3 3 20N 101 15 E
Kuala Sepetang, Malaysia 39 K3 4 49N 100 28 E
Kuala Terengganu, Malaysia 39 K4 5 20N 103 8 E
Kualajelai, Indonesia 36 E4 2 58S 110 46 E
Kualakapuas, Indonesia 36 E4 2 55S 114 20 E
Kualakurun, Indonesia 36 E4 1 10S 113 50 E
Kualapembuang, Indonesia 36 E4 3 14S 112 38 E
Kualasimpang, Indonesia 36 D1 4 17N 98 3 E
Kuancheng, China 35 D10 40 37N 118 30 E
Kuandang, Indonesia 37 D6 0 56N 123 1 E
Kuandian, China 35 D13 40 45N 124 45 E
Kuangchou = Guangzhou, China 33 D6 23 5N 113 10 E
Kuantan, Malaysia 39 L4 3 49N 103 20 E
Kuba = Quba, Azerbaijan 25 F8 41 21N 48 32 E
Kuban →, Russia 25 E6 45 20N 37 30 E
Kubokawa, Japan 31 H6 33 12N 133 8 E
Kucha Gompa, India 43 B7 34 25N 76 56 E
Kuchaman, India 42 F6 27 13N 74 47 E
Kuchinda, India 43 J11 21 44N 84 21 E
Kuching, Malaysia 36 D4 1 33N 110 25 E
Kuchino-eruba-Jima, Japan 31 J5 30 28N 130 12 E
Kuchino-Shima, Japan 31 K4 29 57N 129 55 E
Kuchinotsu, Japan 31 H5 32 36N 130 11 E
Kucing = Kuching, Malaysia 36 D4 1 33N 110 25 E
Kud →, Pakistan 42 F2 26 5N 66 20 E
Kuda, India 40 H7 23 10N 71 15 E
Kudat, Malaysia 36 C5 6 55N 116 55 E
Kudus, Indonesia 37 G14 6 48S 110 51 E
Kudymkar, Russia 24 C9 59 1N 54 39 E
Kueiyang = Guiyang, China 32 D5 26 32N 106 40 E
Kufra Oasis = Al Kufrah, Libya 51 D10 24 17N 23 15 E
Kufstein, Austria 16 E7 47 35N 12 11 E
Kugluktuk, Canada 68 B8 67 50N 115 5W
Kugong I., Canada 70 A4 56 18N 79 50W
Kūhak, Iran 40 F3 27 12N 63 10 E
Kuhan, Pakistan 42 E2 28 19N 67 14 E
Kūhbonān, Iran 45 D8 31 23N 56 19 E
Kūhestak, Iran 45 E8 26 47N 57 2 E
Kuhin, Iran 45 B6 36 22N 49 40 E
Kūhīrī, Iran 45 E9 26 55N 61 2 E
Kūhpāyeh, Eşfahan, Iran 45 C7 32 44N 52 20 E
Kūhpāyeh, Kermān, Iran 45 D8 30 35N 57 15 E
Kūhrān, Kūh-e, Iran 45 E8 26 46N 58 12 E
Kui Buri, Thailand 39 F2 12 3N 99 52 E
Kuiseb →, Namibia 56 C1 22 59S 14 31 E
Kuito, Angola 53 G3 12 22S 16 55 E
Kuiu I., U.S.A. 72 B2 57 45N 134 10W
Kujang, N. Korea 35 E14 39 57N 126 1 E
Kuji, Japan 30 D10 40 11N 141 46 E
Kujū-San, Japan 31 H5 33 5N 131 15 E
Kukës, Albania 21 C9 42 5N 20 27 E
Kukup, Malaysia 39 M4 1 20N 103 27 E
Kula, Turkey 21 E13 38 32N 28 40 E
Kulachi, Pakistan 42 D4 31 56N 70 27 E
Kulai, Malaysia 39 M4 1 44N 103 35 E
Kulal, Mt., Kenya 54 B4 2 42N 36 57 E
Kulasekarappattinam, India 40 Q11 8 20N 78 5 E
Kuldīga, Latvia 9 H19 56 58N 21 59 E
Kuldja = Yining, China 26 E9 43 58N 81 10 E
Kulen, Cambodia 38 F5 13 50N 104 40 E
Kulgam, India 43 C6 33 36N 75 2 E
Kulgera, Australia 62 D1 25 50S 133 18 E
Kulim, Malaysia 39 K3 5 22N 100 34 E
Kulin, Australia 61 F2 32 40S 118 2 E
Kŭlob, Tajikistan 26 F7 37 55N 69 50 E
Kulsary, Kazakstan 25 E9 46 59N 54 1 E
Kulti, India 43 H12 23 43N 86 50 E
Kulu, India 42 D7 31 58N 77 6 E
Kulumbura, Australia 60 B4 13 55S 126 35 E
Kulunda, Russia 26 D8 52 35N 78 57 E
Kulungar, Afghan. 42 C3 34 0N 69 2 E
Kūlvand, Iran 45 D7 31 21N 54 35 E
Kulwin, Australia 63 F3 35 0S 142 42 E
Kulyab = Kŭlob, Tajikistan 26 F7 37 55N 69 50 E
Kuma →, Russia 25 F8 44 55N 47 0 E
Kumagaya, Japan 31 F9 36 9N 139 22 E
Kumai, Indonesia 36 E4 2 44S 111 43 E
Kumamba, Kepulauan, Indonesia 37 E9 1 36S 138 45 E
Kumamoto, Japan 31 H5 32 45N 130 45 E
Kumamoto □, Japan 31 H5 32 55N 130 55 E
Kumanovo, Macedonia 21 C9 42 9N 21 42 E
Kumara, N.Z. 59 K3 42 37S 171 12 E
Kumarina, Australia 61 D2 24 41S 119 32 E
Kumasi, Ghana 50 G5 6 41N 1 38W
Kumayri = Gyumri, Armenia 25 F7 40 47N 43 50 E
Kumba, Cameroon 52 D1 4 36N 9 24 E
Kumbakonam, India 40 P11 10 58N 79 25 E
Kumbarilla, Australia 63 D5 27 15S 150 55 E
Kumbhraj, India 42 G7 24 22N 77 3 E
Kumbia, Australia 63 D5 26 41S 151 39 E
Kŭmch'ŏn, N. Korea 35 E14 38 10N 126 29 E
Kumdok, India 43 C8 33 32N 78 10 E
Kume-Shima, Japan 31 L3 26 20N 126 47 E
Kumertau, Russia 24 D10 52 45N 55 57 E
Kumharsain, India 42 D7 31 19N 77 27 E
Kŭmhwa, S. Korea 35 E14 38 17N 127 28 E
Kumi, Uganda 54 B3 1 30N 33 58 E
Kumla, Sweden 9 G16 59 8N 15 10 E
Kumo, Nigeria 51 F8 10 1N 11 12 E
Kumon Bum, Burma 41 F20 26 30N 97 15 E
Kunashir, Ostrov, Russia 27 E15 44 0N 146 0 E
Kunda, Estonia 9 G22 59 30N 26 34 E
Kunda, India 43 G9 25 43N 81 31 E
Kundar →, Pakistan 42 D3 31 56N 69 19 E
Kundian, Pakistan 42 C4 32 27N 71 28 E
Kundla, India 42 J4 21 21N 71 25 E
Kunga →, Bangla. 43 J13 21 46N 89 30 E
Kunghit I., Canada 72 C2 52 6N 131 3W
Kungrad = Qŭnghirot, Uzbekistan 26 E6 43 6N 58 54 E
Kungsbacka, Sweden 9 H15 57 30N 12 5 E
Kungur, Russia 24 C10 57 25N 56 57 E
Kunhar →, Pakistan 43 B5 34 20N 73 30 E
Kuningan, Indonesia 37 G13 6 59S 108 29 E
Kunlong, Burma 41 H21 23 20N 98 50 E
Kunlun Shan, Asia 32 C3 36 0N 86 30 E
Kunming, China 32 D5 25 1N 102 41 E
Kunsan, S. Korea 35 G14 35 59N 126 45 E
Kununurra, Australia 60 C4 15 40S 128 50 E
Kunwari →, India 43 F8 26 26N 79 11 E
Kunya-Urgench = Köneürgench, Turkmenistan 26 E6 42 19N 59 10 E
Kuopio, Finland 8 E22 62 53N 27 35 E
Kupa →, Croatia 16 F9 45 28N 16 24 E
Kupang, Indonesia 37 F6 10 19S 123 39 E
Kupreanof I., U.S.A. 72 B2 56 50N 133 30W
Kupyansk-Uzlovoi, Ukraine 25 E6 49 40N 37 43 E
Kuqa, China 32 B3 41 35N 82 30 E
Kür →, Azerbaijan 25 G8 39 29N 49 15 E
Kür Dili, Azerbaijan 45 B6 39 3N 49 13 E
Kura = Kür →, Azerbaijan 25 G8 39 29N 49 15 E
Kuranda, Australia 62 B4 16 48S 145 35 E
Kuranga, India 42 H3 22 4N 69 10 E
Kurashiki, Japan 31 G6 34 40N 133 50 E
Kurayoshi, Japan 31 G6 35 26N 133 50 E
Kŭrdzhali, Bulgaria 21 D11 41 38N 25 21 E
Kure, Japan 31 G6 34 14N 132 32 E
Kuressaare, Estonia 9 G20 58 15N 22 30 E
Kurgan, Russia 26 D7 55 26N 65 18 E
Kuri, India 42 F4 26 37N 70 43 E
Kuria Maria Is. = Khurīyā Murīyā, Jazā'ir, Oman 46 D6 17 30N 55 58 E
Kuridala, Australia 62 C3 21 16S 140 29 E
Kurigram, Bangla. 41 G16 25 49N 89 39 E
Kurikka, Finland 9 E20 62 36N 22 24 E
Kuril Is. = Kurilskiye Ostrova, Russia 27 E15 45 0N 150 0 E
Kuril Trench, Pac. Oc. 28 E19 44 0N 153 0 E
Kurilsk, Russia 27 E15 45 14N 147 53 E
Kurilskiye Ostrova, Russia 27 E15 45 0N 150 0 E
Kurino, Japan 31 J5 31 57N 130 43 E
Kurinskaya Kosa = Kür Dili, Azerbaijan 45 B6 39 3N 49 13 E
Kurnool, India 40 M11 15 45N 78 0 E
Kuro-Shima, Kagoshima, Japan 31 J4 30 50N 129 57 E
Kuro-Shima, Okinawa, Japan 31 M2 24 14N 124 1 E
Kurow, N.Z. 59 L3 44 44S 170 29 E
Kurram →, Pakistan 42 C4 32 36N 71 20 E
Kurri Kurri, Australia 63 E5 32 50S 151 28 E
Kurrimine, Australia 62 B4 17 47S 146 6 E
Kurshskiy Zaliv, Russia 9 J19 55 9N 21 6 E
Kursk, Russia 24 D6 51 42N 36 11 E
Kuruçay, Turkey 44 B3 39 39N 38 29 E
Kuruktag, China 32 B3 41 0N 89 0 E
Kuruman, S. Africa 56 D3 27 28S 23 28 E
Kuruman →, S. Africa 56 D3 26 56S 20 39 E
Kurume, Japan 31 H5 33 15N 130 30 E
Kurunegala, Sri Lanka 40 R12 7 30N 80 23 E
Kurya, Russia 24 B10 61 42N 57 9 E
Kus Gölü, Turkey 21 D12 40 10N 27 55 E
Kuşadası, Turkey 21 F12 37 52N 27 15 E
Kusatsu, Japan 31 F9 36 37N 138 36 E
Kusawa L., Canada 72 A1 60 20N 136 13W
Kushalgarh, India 42 H6 23 10N 74 27 E
Kushikino, Japan 31 J5 31 44N 130 16 E
Kushima, Japan 31 J5 31 29N 131 14 E
Kushimoto, Japan 31 H7 33 28N 135 47 E
Kushiro, Japan 30 C12 43 0N 144 25 E
Kushiro-Gawa →, Japan 30 C12 42 59N 144 23 E
Kūshk, Iran 45 D8 28 46N 56 51 E
Kushka = Gushgy, Turkmenistan 26 F7 35 20N 62 18 E
Kūshkī, Iran 44 C5 33 31N 47 13 E
Kushol, India 43 C7 33 40N 76 36 E
Kushtia, Bangla. 41 H16 23 55N 89 5 E
Kushva, Russia 24 C10 58 18N 59 45 E
Kuskokwim B., U.S.A. 68 C3 59 45N 162 25W
Kusmi, India 43 H10 23 17N 83 55 E
Kussharo-Ko, Japan 30 C12 43 38N 144 21 E
Kustanay = Qostanay, Kazakstan 26 D7 53 10N 63 35 E

Kut, Ko, *Thailand* **39 G4** 11 40N 102 35 E
Kütahya, *Turkey* **25 G5** 39 30N 30 2 E
Kutaisi, *Georgia* **25 F7** 42 19N 42 40 E
Kutaraja = Banda Aceh, *Indonesia* **36 C1** 5 35N 95 20 E
Kutch, Gulf of = Kachchh, Gulf of, *India* **42 H3** 22 50N 69 15 E
Kutch, Rann of = Kachchh, Rann of, *India* **42 H4** 24 0N 70 0 E
Kutiyana, *India* **42 J4** 21 36N 70 2 E
Kutno, *Poland* **17 B10** 52 15N 19 23 E
Kutse, *Botswana* **56 C3** 21 7S 22 16 E
Kutu, *Dem. Rep. of the Congo* **52 E3** 2 40S 18 11 E
Kutum, *Sudan* **51 F10** 14 10N 24 40 E
Kuujjuaq, *Canada* **69 C13** 58 6N 68 15W
Kuujjuarapik, *Canada* **70 A4** 55 20N 77 35W
Kuŭp-tong, *N. Korea* **35 D14** 40 45N 126 1 E
Kuusamo, *Finland* **8 D23** 65 57N 29 8 E
Kuusankoski, *Finland* **9 F22** 60 55N 26 38 E
Kuwait = Al Kuwayt, *Kuwait* **46 B4** 29 30N 48 0 E
Kuwait ■, *Asia* **46 B4** 29 30N 47 30 E
Kuwana, *Japan* **31 G8** 35 5N 136 43 E
Kuwana →, *India* **43 F10** 26 25N 83 15 E
Kuybyshev = Samara, *Russia* **24 D9** 53 8N 50 6 E
Kuybyshev, *Russia* **26 D8** 55 27N 78 19 E
Kuybyshevskoye Vdkhr., *Russia* **24 C8** 55 2N 49 30 E
Kuye He →, *China* **34 E6** 38 23N 110 46 E
Kūyeh, *Iran* **44 B5** 38 45N 47 57 E
Küysanjaq, *Iraq* **44 B5** 36 5N 44 38 E
Kuyto, Ozero, *Russia* **24 B5** 65 6N 31 20 E
Kuyumba, *Russia* **27 C10** 60 58N 96 59 E
Kuzey Anadolu Dağları, *Turkey* **25 F6** 41 30N 35 0 E
Kuznetsk, *Russia* **24 D8** 53 12N 46 40 E
Kuzomen, *Russia* **24 A6** 66 22N 36 50 E
Kvænangen, *Norway* **8 A19** 70 5N 21 15 E
Kvaløy, *Norway* **8 B18** 69 40N 18 30 E
Kvarner, *Croatia* **16 F8** 44 50N 14 10 E
Kvarnerič, *Croatia* **16 F8** 44 43N 14 37 E
Kwa-Nobuhle, *S. Africa* **53 L5** 33 50S 25 22 E
Kwabhaca, *S. Africa* **57 E4** 30 51S 29 0 E
Kwakhanai, *Botswana* **56 C3** 21 39S 21 16 E
Kwakoegron, *Surinam* **93 B7** 5 12N 55 25W
Kwale, *Kenya* **54 C4** 4 15S 39 31 E
KwaMashu, *S. Africa* **57 D5** 29 45S 30 58 E
Kwando →, *Africa* **56 B3** 18 27S 23 32 E
Kwangdaeri, *N. Korea* **35 D14** 40 31N 127 32 E
Kwangju, *S. Korea* **35 G14** 35 9N 126 54 E
Kwango →, *Dem. Rep. of the Congo* **52 E3** 3 14S 17 22 E
Kwangsi-Chuang = Guangxi Zhuangzu Zizhiqu □, *China* **33 D5** 24 0N 109 0 E
Kwangtung = Guangdong □, *China* **33 D6** 23 0N 113 0 E
Kwataboahegan →, *Canada* **70 B3** 51 9N 80 50W
Kwatisore, *Indonesia* **37 E8** 3 18S 134 50 E
KwaZulu Natal □, *S. Africa* **57 D5** 29 0S 30 0 E
Kweichow = Guizhou □, *China* **32 D5** 27 0N 107 0 E
Kwekwe, *Zimbabwe* **55 F2** 18 58S 29 48 E
Kwidzyn, *Poland* **17 B10** 53 44N 18 55 E
Kwinana New Town, *Australia* **61 F2** 32 15S 115 47 E
Kwoka, *Indonesia* **37 E8** 0 31S 132 27 E
Kyabra Cr. →, *Australia* **63 D3** 25 36S 142 55 E
Kyabram, *Australia* **63 F4** 36 19S 145 4 E
Kyaikto, *Burma* **38 D1** 17 20N 97 3 E
Kyakhta, *Russia* **27 D11** 50 30N 106 25 E
Kyancutta, *Australia* **63 E2** 33 8S 135 33 E
Kyaukpadaung, *Burma* **41 J19** 20 52N 95 8 E
Kyaukpyu, *Burma* **41 K18** 19 28N 93 30 E
Kyaukse, *Burma* **41 J20** 21 36N 96 10 E
Kyburz, *U.S.A.* **84 G6** 38 47N 120 18W
Kyelang, *India* **42 C7** 32 35N 77 2 E
Kyenjojo, *Uganda* **54 B3** 0 40N 30 37 E
Kyle, *Canada* **73 C7** 50 50N 108 2W
Kyle Dam, *Zimbabwe* **55 G3** 20 15S 31 0 E
Kyle of Lochalsh, *U.K.* **12 D3** 57 17N 5 44W
Kymijoki →, *Finland* **9 F22** 60 30N 26 55 E
Kyneton, *Australia* **63 F3** 37 10S 144 29 E
Kynuna, *Australia* **62 C3** 21 37S 141 55 E
Kyō-ga-Saki, *Japan* **31 G7** 35 45N 135 15 E
Kyoga, L., *Uganda* **54 B3** 1 35N 33 0 E
Kyogle, *Australia* **63 D5** 28 40S 153 0 E
Kyongju, *S. Korea* **35 G15** 35 51N 129 14 E
Kyongpyaw, *Burma* **41 L19** 17 12N 95 10 E
Kyŏngsŏng, *N. Korea* **35 D15** 41 35N 129 36 E
Kyōto, *Japan* **31 G7** 35 0N 135 45 E
Kyōto □, *Japan* **31 G7** 35 15N 135 45 E
Kyparissovouno, *Cyprus* **23 D12** 35 19N 33 10 E
Kyperounda, *Cyprus* **23 E11** 34 56N 32 58 E
Kyrenia, *Cyprus* **23 D12** 35 20N 33 20 E
Kyrgyzstan ■, *Asia* **26 E8** 42 0N 75 0 E
Kyrönjoki →, *Finland* **8 E19** 63 14N 21 45 E
Kystatyam, *Russia* **27 C13** 67 20N 123 10 E
Kythréa, *Cyprus* **23 D12** 35 15N 33 29 E
Kyunhla, *Burma* **41 H19** 23 25N 95 15 E
Kyuquot Sound, *Canada* **72 D3** 50 2N 127 22W
Kyūshū, *Japan* **31 H5** 33 0N 131 0 E
Kyūshū □, *Japan* **31 H5** 33 0N 131 0 E
Kyūshū-Sanchi, *Japan* **31 H5** 32 35N 131 17 E
Kyustendil, *Bulgaria* **21 C10** 42 16N 22 41 E
Kyusyur, *Russia* **27 B13** 70 19N 127 30 E
Kyyiv, *Ukraine* **17 C16** 50 30N 30 28 E
Kyyivske Vdskh., *Ukraine* **17 C16** 51 0N 30 25 E
Kyzyl, *Russia* **27 D10** 51 50N 94 30 E
Kyzyl Kum, *Uzbekistan* **26 E7** 42 30N 65 0 E
Kyzyl-Kyya, *Kyrgyzstan* **26 E8** 40 16N 72 8 E
Kzyl-Orda = Qyzylorda, *Kazakstan* **26 E7** 44 48N 65 28 E

L

La Alcarria, *Spain* **19 B4** 40 31N 2 45W
La Asunción, *Venezuela* **92 A6** 11 2N 63 53W
La Baie, *Canada* **71 C5** 48 19N 70 53W
La Banda, *Argentina* **94 B3** 27 45S 64 10W
La Barca, *Mexico* **86 C4** 20 20N 102 40W
La Barge, *U.S.A.* **82 E8** 42 16N 110 12W
La Belle, *U.S.A.* **77 M5** 26 46N 81 26W
La Biche →, *Canada* **72 B4** 59 57N 123 50W
La Biche, L., *Canada* **72 C6** 54 50N 112 5W
La Bomba, *Mexico* **86 A1** 31 53N 115 2W
La Calera, *Chile* **94 C1** 32 50S 71 10W
La Canal = Sa Canal, *Spain* **22 C7** 38 51N 1 23 E
La Carlota, *Argentina* **94 C3** 33 30S 63 20W
La Ceiba, *Honduras* **88 C2** 15 40N 86 50W
La Chaux-de-Fonds, *Switz.* **18 C7** 47 7N 6 50 E
La Chorrera, *Panama* **88 E4** 8 53N 79 47W
La Cocha, *Argentina* **94 B2** 27 50S 65 40W
La Concepción, *Panama* **88 E3** 8 31N 82 37W
La Concordia, *Mexico* **87 D6** 16 8N 92 38W
La Coruña = A Coruña, *Spain* **19 A1** 43 20N 8 25W
La Crescent, *U.S.A.* **80 D9** 43 50N 91 18W
La Crete, *Canada* **72 B5** 58 11N 116 24W
La Crosse, *Kans., U.S.A.* **80 F5** 38 32N 99 18W
La Crosse, *Wis., U.S.A.* **80 D9** 43 48N 91 15W
La Cruz, *Costa Rica* **88 D2** 11 4N 85 39W
La Cruz, *Mexico* **86 C3** 23 55N 106 54W
La Désirade, *Guadeloupe* **89 C7** 16 18N 61 3W
La Escondida, *Mexico* **86 C5** 24 6N 99 55W
La Esmeralda, *Paraguay* **94 A3** 22 16S 62 33W
La Esperanza, *Cuba* **88 B3** 22 46N 83 44W
La Esperanza, *Honduras* **88 D2** 14 15N 88 10W
La Estrada = A Estrada, *Spain* **19 A1** 42 43N 8 27W
La Fayette, *U.S.A.* **77 H3** 34 42N 85 17W
La Fé, *Cuba* **88 B3** 22 2N 84 15W
La Follette, *U.S.A.* **77 G3** 36 23N 84 7W
La Grande, *U.S.A.* **82 D4** 45 20N 118 5W
La Grande →, *Canada* **70 B5** 53 50N 79 0W
La Grande Deux, Rés., *Canada* **70 B4** 53 40N 76 55W
La Grande Quatre, Rés., *Canada* **70 B5** 54 0N 73 15W
La Grande Trois, Rés., *Canada* **70 B4** 53 40N 75 10W
La Grange, *Calif., U.S.A.* **84 H6** 37 42N 120 27W
La Grange, *Ga., U.S.A.* **77 J3** 33 2N 85 2W
La Grange, *Ky., U.S.A.* **76 F3** 38 25N 85 23W
La Grange, *Tex., U.S.A.* **81 L6** 29 54N 96 52W
La Guaira, *Venezuela* **92 A5** 10 36N 66 56W
La Habana, *Cuba* **88 B3** 23 8N 82 22W
La Independencia, *Mexico* **87 D6** 16 31N 91 47W
La Isabela, *Dom. Rep.* **89 C5** 19 58N 71 2W
La Junta, *U.S.A.* **81 F3** 37 59N 103 33W
La Laguna, *Canary Is.* **22 F3** 28 28N 16 18W
La Libertad, *Guatemala* **88 C1** 16 47N 90 7W
La Libertad, *Mexico* **86 B2** 29 55N 112 41W
La Ligua, *Chile* **94 C1** 32 30S 71 16W
La Línea de la Concepción, *Spain* **19 D3** 36 15N 5 23W
La Loche, *Canada* **73 B7** 56 29N 109 26W
La Louvière, *Belgium* **15 D4** 50 27N 4 10 E
La Malbaie, *Canada* **71 C5** 47 40N 70 10W
La Mancha, *Spain* **19 C4** 39 10N 2 54W
La Martre, L., *Canada* **72 A5** 63 15N 117 55W
La Mesa, *U.S.A.* **85 N9** 32 46N 117 3W
La Misión, *Mexico* **86 A1** 32 5N 116 50W
La Moure, *U.S.A.* **80 B5** 46 21N 98 18W
La Negra, *Chile* **94 A1** 23 46S 70 18W
La Oliva, *Canary Is.* **22 F6** 28 36N 13 57W
La Orotava, *Canary Is.* **22 F3** 28 22N 16 31W
La Oroya, *Peru* **92 F3** 11 32S 75 54W
La Palma, *Canary Is.* **22 F2** 28 40N 17 50W
La Palma, *Panama* **88 E4** 8 15N 78 0W
La Palma del Condado, *Spain* **19 D2** 37 21N 6 38W
La Paloma, *Chile* **94 C1** 30 35S 71 0W
La Pampa □, *Argentina* **94 D2** 36 50S 66 0W
La Paragua, *Venezuela* **92 B6** 6 50N 63 20W
La Paz, *Entre Ríos, Argentina* **94 C4** 30 50S 59 45W
La Paz, *San Luis, Argentina* **94 C2** 33 30S 67 20W
La Paz, *Bolivia* **92 G5** 16 20S 68 10W
La Paz, *Honduras* **88 D2** 14 20N 87 47W
La Paz, *Mexico* **86 C2** 24 10N 110 20W
La Paz Centro, *Nic.* **88 D2** 12 20N 86 41W
La Pedrera, *Colombia* **92 D5** 1 18S 69 43W
La Pérade, *Canada* **71 C5** 46 35N 72 12W
La Perouse Str., *Asia* **30 B11** 45 40N 142 0 E
La Pesca, *Mexico* **87 C5** 23 46N 97 47W
La Piedad, *Mexico* **86 C4** 20 20N 102 1W
La Pine, *U.S.A.* **82 E3** 43 40N 121 30W
La Plata, *Argentina* **94 D4** 35 0S 57 55W
La Pocatière, *Canada* **71 C5** 47 22N 70 2W
La Porte, *Ind., U.S.A.* **76 E2** 41 36N 86 43W
La Porte, *Tex., U.S.A.* **81 L7** 29 39N 95 1W
La Purísima, *Mexico* **86 B2** 26 10N 112 4W
La Push, *U.S.A.* **84 C2** 47 55N 124 38W
La Quiaca, *Argentina* **94 A2** 22 5S 65 35W
La Restinga, *Canary Is.* **22 G2** 27 38N 17 59W
La Rioja, *Argentina* **94 B2** 29 20S 67 0W
La Rioja □, *Argentina* **94 B2** 29 30S 67 0W
La Rioja □, *Spain* **19 A4** 42 20N 2 20W
La Robla, *Spain* **19 A3** 42 50N 5 41W
La Roche-en-Ardenne, *Belgium* **15 D5** 50 11N 5 35 E
La Roche-sur-Yon, *France* **18 C3** 46 40N 1 25W
La Rochelle, *France* **18 C3** 46 10N 1 9W
La Roda, *Spain* **19 C4** 39 13N 2 15W
La Romana, *Dom. Rep.* **89 C6** 18 27N 68 57W
La Ronge, *Canada* **73 B7** 55 5N 105 20W
La Rumorosa, *Mexico* **85 N10** 32 33N 116 4W
La Sabina = Sa Savina, *Spain* **22 C7** 38 44N 1 25 E
La Salle, *U.S.A.* **80 E10** 41 20N 89 6W
La Santa, *Canary Is.* **22 E6** 29 5N 13 40W
La Sarre, *Canada* **70 C4** 48 45N 79 15W
La Scie, *Canada* **71 C8** 49 57N 55 36W
La Selva Beach, *U.S.A.* **84 J5** 36 56N 121 51W
La Serena, *Chile* **94 B1** 29 55S 71 10W
La Seu d'Urgell, *Spain* **19 A6** 42 22N 1 23 E
La Seyne-sur-Mer, *France* **18 E6** 43 7N 5 52 E
La Soufrière, *St. Vincent* **89 D7** 13 20N 61 11W
La Spézia, *Italy* **18 D8** 44 7N 9 50 E
La Tagua, *Colombia* **92 C4** 0 3N 74 40W
La Tortuga, *Venezuela* **89 D6** 11 0N 65 22W
La Tuque, *Canada* **70 C5** 47 30N 72 50W
La Unión, *Chile* **96 E2** 40 10S 73 0W
La Unión, *El Salv.* **88 D2** 13 20N 87 50W
La Unión, *Mexico* **86 D4** 17 58N 101 49W
La Urbana, *Venezuela* **92 B5** 7 8N 66 56W
La Vall d'Uixó, *Spain* **19 C5** 39 49N 0 15W
La Vega, *Dom. Rep.* **89 C5** 19 20N 70 30W
La Vela de Coro, *Venezuela* **92 A5** 11 27N 69 34W
La Venta, *Mexico* **87 D6** 18 8N 94 3W
La Ventura, *Mexico* **86 C4** 24 38N 100 54W
Laas Caanood = Las Anod, *Somali Rep.* **46 F4** 8 26N 47 19 E
Labasa, *Fiji* **59 C8** 16 30S 179 27 E
Labe = Elbe →, *Europe* **16 B5** 53 50N 9 0 E
Labé, *Guinea* **50 F3** 11 24N 12 16W
Laberge, L., *Canada* **72 A1** 61 11N 135 12W
Labinsk, *Russia* **25 F7** 44 40N 40 48 E
Labis, *Malaysia* **39 L4** 2 22N 103 2 E
Laboulaye, *Argentina* **94 C3** 34 10S 63 30W
Labrador, *Canada* **71 B7** 53 20N 61 0W
Labrador City, *Canada* **71 B6** 52 57N 66 55W
Labrador Sea, *Atl. Oc.* **69 C14** 57 0N 54 0W
Lábrea, *Brazil* **92 E6** 7 15S 64 51W
Labuan, *Malaysia* **36 C5** 5 20N 115 14 E
Labuan, Pulau, *Malaysia* **36 C5** 5 21N 115 13 E
Labuha, *Indonesia* **37 E7** 0 30S 127 30 E
Labuhan, *Indonesia* **37 G11** 6 22S 105 50 E
Labuhanbajo, *Indonesia* **37 F6** 8 28S 119 54 E
Labuk, Telok, *Malaysia* **36 C5** 6 10N 117 50 E
Labyrinth, L., *Australia* **63 E2** 30 40S 135 11 E
Labytnangi, *Russia* **26 C7** 66 39N 66 21 E
Lac Bouchette, *Canada* **71 C5** 48 16N 72 11W
Lac Édouard, *Canada* **70 C5** 47 40N 72 16W
Lac La Biche, *Canada* **72 C6** 54 45N 111 58W
Lac la Martre = Wha Ti, *Canada* **68 B8** 63 8N 117 16W
Lac La Ronge Prov. Park, *Canada* **73 B7** 55 9N 104 41W
Lac-Mégantic, *Canada* **71 C5** 45 35N 70 53W
Lac Thien, *Vietnam* **38 F7** 12 25N 108 11 E
Lacanau, *France* **18 D3** 44 58N 1 5W
Lacantúm →, *Mexico* **87 D6** 16 36N 90 40W
Laccadive Is. = Lakshadweep Is., *India* **29 H11** 10 0N 72 30 E
Lacepede B., *Australia* **63 F2** 36 40S 139 40 E
Lacepede Is., *Australia* **60 C3** 16 55S 122 0 E
Lacerdónia, *Mozam.* **55 F4** 18 3S 35 35 E
Lacey, *U.S.A.* **84 C4** 47 7N 122 49W
Lachhmangarh, *India* **42 F6** 27 50N 75 4 E
Lachi, *Pakistan* **42 C4** 33 25N 71 20 E
Lachine, *Canada* **79 A11** 45 30N 73 40W
Lachlan →, *Australia* **63 E3** 34 22S 143 55 E
Lachute, *Canada* **70 C5** 45 39N 74 21W
Lackawanna, *U.S.A.* **78 D6** 42 50N 78 50W
Lackawaxen, *U.S.A.* **79 E10** 41 29N 74 59W
Lacolle, *Canada* **79 A11** 45 5N 73 22W
Lacombe, *Canada* **72 C6** 52 30N 113 44W
Lacona, *U.S.A.* **79 C8** 43 39N 76 10W
Laconia, *U.S.A.* **79 C13** 43 32N 71 28W
Ladakh Ra., *India* **43 C8** 34 0N 78 0 E
Ladismith, *S. Africa* **56 E3** 33 28S 21 15 E
Lādīz, *Iran* **45 D9** 28 55N 61 15 E
Ladnun, *India* **42 F6** 27 38N 74 25 E
Ladoga, L. = Ladozhskoye Ozero, *Russia* **24 B5** 61 15N 30 30 E
Ladozhskoye Ozero, *Russia* **24 B5** 61 15N 30 30 E
Lady Elliott I., *Australia* **62 C5** 24 7S 152 42 E
Lady Grey, *S. Africa* **56 E4** 30 43S 27 13 E
Ladybrand, *S. Africa* **56 D4** 29 9S 27 29 E
Ladysmith, *Canada* **72 D4** 49 0N 123 49W
Ladysmith, *S. Africa* **57 D4** 28 32S 29 46 E
Ladysmith, *U.S.A.* **80 C9** 45 28N 91 12W
Lae, *Papua N. G.* **64 H6** 6 40S 147 2 E
Laem Ngop, *Thailand* **39 F4** 12 10N 102 26 E
Laem Pho, *Thailand* **39 J3** 6 55N 101 19 E
Læsø, *Denmark* **9 H14** 57 15N 11 5 E
Lafayette, *Colo., U.S.A.* **80 F2** 39 58N 105 12W
Lafayette, *Ind., U.S.A.* **76 E2** 40 25N 86 54W
Lafayette, *La., U.S.A.* **81 K9** 30 14N 92 1W
Lafayette, *Tenn., U.S.A.* **77 G2** 36 31N 86 2W
Laferte →, *Canada* **72 A5** 61 53N 117 44W
Lafia, *Nigeria* **50 G7** 8 30N 8 34 E
Lafleche, *Canada* **73 D7** 49 45N 106 40W
Lagan →, *U.K.* **13 B6** 54 36N 5 55W
Lagarfljót →, *Iceland* **8 D6** 65 40N 14 18W
Lågen →, *Oppland, Norway* **9 F14** 61 8N 10 25 E
Lågen →, *Vestfold, Norway* **9 G14** 59 3N 10 3 E
Laghouat, *Algeria* **50 B6** 33 50N 2 59 E
Lagoa Vermelha, *Brazil* **95 B5** 28 13S 51 32W
Lagonoy G., *Phil.* **37 B6** 13 35N 123 50 E
Lagos, *Nigeria* **50 G6** 6 25N 3 27 E
Lagos, *Portugal* **19 D1** 37 5N 8 41W
Lagos de Moreno, *Mexico* **86 C4** 21 21N 101 55W
Lagrange, *Australia* **60 C3** 18 45S 121 43 E
Lagrange B., *Australia* **60 C3** 18 38S 121 42 E
Laguna, *Brazil* **95 B6** 28 30S 48 50W
Laguna, *U.S.A.* **83 J10** 35 2N 107 25W
Laguna Beach, *U.S.A.* **85 M9** 33 33N 117 47W
Laguna Limpia, *Argentina* **94 B4** 26 32S 59 45W
Lagunas, *Chile* **94 A2** 21 0S 69 45W
Lagunas, *Peru* **92 E3** 5 10S 75 35W
Lahad Datu, *Malaysia* **37 C5** 5 0N 118 20 E
Lahad Datu, Teluk, *Malaysia* **37 D5** 4 50N 118 20 E
Lahan Sai, *Thailand* **38 E4** 14 25N 102 52 E
Lahanam, *Laos* **38 D5** 16 16N 105 16 E
Lahar, *India* **43 F8** 26 12N 78 57 E
Laharpur, *India* **43 F9** 27 43N 80 56 E
Lahat, *Indonesia* **36 E2** 3 45S 103 30 E
Lahewa, *Indonesia* **36 D1** 1 22N 97 12 E
Lāhījān, *Iran* **45 B6** 37 10N 50 6 E
Lahn →, *Germany* **16 C4** 50 19N 7 37 E
Laholm, *Sweden* **9 H15** 56 30N 13 2 E
Lahore, *Pakistan* **42 D6** 31 32N 74 22 E
Lahri, *Pakistan* **42 E3** 29 11N 68 13 E
Lahti, *Finland* **9 F21** 60 58N 25 40 E
Lahtis = Lahti, *Finland* **9 F21** 60 58N 25 40 E
Laï, *Chad* **51 G9** 9 25N 16 18 E
Lai Chau, *Vietnam* **38 A4** 22 5N 103 3 E
Laila = Layla, *Si. Arabia* **46 C4** 22 10N 46 40 E
Laingsburg, *S. Africa* **56 E3** 33 9S 20 52 E
Lainio älv →, *Sweden* **8 C20** 67 35N 22 40 E
Lairg, *U.K.* **12 C4** 58 2N 4 24W
Laishui, *China* **34 E8** 39 23N 115 45 E
Laiwu, *China* **35 F9** 36 15N 117 40 E
Laixi, *China* **35 F11** 36 50N 120 31 E
Laiyang, *China* **35 F11** 36 59N 120 45 E
Laiyuan, *China* **34 E8** 39 20N 114 40 E
Laizhou, *China* **35 F10** 37 8N 119 57 E
Laizhou Wan, *China* **35 F10** 37 30N 119 30 E
Laja →, *Mexico* **86 C4** 20 55N 100 46W
Lajes, *Brazil* **95 B5** 27 48S 50 20W
Lak Sao, *Laos* **38 C5** 18 11N 104 59 E
Lakaband, *Pakistan* **42 D3** 31 2N 69 15 E
Lake Alpine, *U.S.A.* **84 G7** 38 29N 120 0W
Lake Andes, *U.S.A.* **80 D5** 43 9N 98 32W
Lake Arthur, *U.S.A.* **81 K8** 30 5N 92 41W
Lake Cargelligo, *Australia* **63 E4** 33 15S 146 22 E
Lake Charles, *U.S.A.* **81 K8** 30 14N 93 13W
Lake City, *Colo., U.S.A.* **83 G10** 38 2N 107 19W
Lake City, *Fla., U.S.A.* **77 K4** 30 11N 82 38W
Lake City, *Mich., U.S.A.* **76 C3** 44 20N 85 13W
Lake City, *Minn., U.S.A.* **80 C8** 44 27N 92 16W
Lake City, *Pa., U.S.A.* **78 D4** 42 1N 80 21W
Lake City, *S.C., U.S.A.* **77 J6** 33 52N 79 45W
Lake Cowichan, *Canada* **72 D4** 48 49N 124 3W
Lake District, *U.K.* **10 C4** 54 35N 3 20 E
Lake Elsinore, *U.S.A.* **85 M9** 33 38N 117 20W
Lake George, *U.S.A.* **79 C11** 43 26N 73 43W
Lake Grace, *Australia* **61 F2** 33 7S 118 28 E
Lake Harbour = Kimmirut, *Canada* **69 B13** 62 50N 69 50W
Lake Havasu City, *U.S.A.* **85 L12** 34 27N 114 22W
Lake Hughes, *U.S.A.* **85 L8** 34 41N 118 26W
Lake Isabella, *U.S.A.* **85 K8** 35 38N 118 28W
Lake Jackson, *U.S.A.* **81 L7** 29 3N 95 27W
Lake Junction, *U.S.A.* **82 D8** 44 35N 110 28W
Lake King, *Australia* **61 F2** 33 5S 119 45 E
Lake Lenore, *Canada* **73 C8** 52 24N 104 59W
Lake Louise, *Canada* **72 C5** 51 30N 116 10W
Lake Mead Nat. Recr. Area, *U.S.A.* **85 K12** 36 15N 114 30W
Lake Mills, *U.S.A.* **80 D8** 43 25N 93 32W
Lake Placid, *U.S.A.* **79 B11** 44 17N 73 59W
Lake Pleasant, *U.S.A.* **79 C10** 43 28N 74 25W
Lake Providence, *U.S.A.* **81 J9** 32 48N 91 10W
Lake St. Peter, *Canada* **78 A6** 45 18N 78 2W
Lake Superior Prov. Park, *Canada* **70 C3** 47 45N 84 45W
Lake Village, *U.S.A.* **81 J9** 33 20N 91 17W
Lake Wales, *U.S.A.* **77 M5** 27 54N 81 35W
Lake Worth, *U.S.A.* **77 M5** 26 37N 80 3W
Lakeba, *Fiji* **59 D9** 18 13S 178 47W
Lakefield, *Canada* **78 B6** 44 25N 78 16W
Lakehurst, *U.S.A.* **79 F10** 40 1N 74 19W
Lakeland, *Australia* **62 B3** 15 49S 144 57 E
Lakeland, *U.S.A.* **77 M5** 28 3N 81 57W
Lakemba = Lakeba, *Fiji* **59 D9** 18 13S 178 47W
Lakeport, *Calif., U.S.A.* **84 F4** 39 3N 122 55W
Lakeport, *Mich., U.S.A.* **78 C2** 43 7N 82 30W
Lakes Entrance, *Australia* **63 F4** 37 50S 148 0 E
Lakeside, *Ariz., U.S.A.* **83 J9** 34 9N 109 58W
Lakeside, *Calif., U.S.A.* **85 N10** 32 52N 116 55W
Lakeside, *Nebr., U.S.A.* **80 D3** 42 3N 102 26W
Lakeside, *Ohio, U.S.A.* **78 E2** 41 32N 82 46W
Lakeview, *U.S.A.* **82 E3** 42 11N 120 21W
Lakeville, *U.S.A.* **80 C8** 44 39N 93 14W
Lakewood, *Colo., U.S.A.* **80 F2** 39 44N 105 5W
Lakewood, *N.J., U.S.A.* **79 F10** 40 6N 74 13W
Lakewood, *N.Y., U.S.A.* **78 D5** 42 6N 79 19W
Lakewood, *Ohio, U.S.A.* **78 E3** 41 29N 81 48W
Lakewood, *Wash., U.S.A.* **84 C4** 47 11N 122 32W
Lakha, *India* **42 F4** 26 9N 70 54 E
Lakhaniá, *Greece* **23 D9** 35 58N 27 54 E
Lakhimpur, *India* **43 F9** 27 57N 80 46 E
Lakhnadon, *India* **43 H8** 22 36N 79 36 E
Lakhonpheng, *Laos* **38 E5** 15 54N 105 34 E
Lakhpat, *India* **42 H3** 23 48N 68 47 E
Lakin, *U.S.A.* **81 G4** 37 57N 101 15W
Lakitusaki →, *Canada* **70 B3** 54 21N 82 25W
Lakki, *Pakistan* **42 C4** 32 36N 70 55 E
Lákkoi, *Greece* **23 D5** 35 24N 23 57 E
Lakonikós Kólpos, *Greece* **21 F10** 36 40N 22 40 E
Lakor, *Indonesia* **37 F7** 8 15S 128 17 E
Lakota, *Ivory C.* **50 G4** 5 50N 5 30W
Lakota, *U.S.A.* **80 A5** 48 2N 98 21W
Laksar, *India* **42 E8** 29 46N 78 3 E
Laksefjorden, *Norway* **8 A22** 70 45N 26 50 E
Lakselv, *Norway* **8 A21** 70 2N 25 0 E
Lakshadweep Is., *India* **29 H11** 10 0N 72 30 E
Lakshmanpur, *India* **43 H10** 22 58N 83 3 E
Lakshmikantapur, *India* **43 H13** 22 5N 88 20 E
Lala Ghat, *India* **41 G18** 24 30N 92 40 E
Lala Musa, *Pakistan* **42 C5** 32 40N 73 57 E
Lalago, *Tanzania* **54 C3** 3 28S 33 58 E
Lalapanzi, *Zimbabwe* **55 F3** 19 20S 30 15 E
L'Albufera, *Spain* **19 C5** 39 20N 0 27W
Lalganj, *India* **43 G11** 25 52N 85 13 E
Lalgola, *India* **43 G13** 24 25N 88 15 E
Lālī, *Iran* **45 C6** 32 21N 49 6 E
Lalibela, *Ethiopia* **46 E2** 12 3N 39 0 E
Lalin, *China* **35 B14** 45 12N 127 0 E
Lalín, *Spain* **19 A1** 42 40N 8 5W
Lalin He →, *China* **35 B13** 45 32N 125 40 E
Lalitapur, *Nepal* **43 F11** 27 40N 85 20 E
Lalitpur, *India* **43 G8** 24 42N 78 28 E
Lalkua, *India* **43 E8** 29 5N 79 31 E
Lalsot, *India* **42 F7** 26 34N 76 20 E
Lam, *Vietnam* **38 B6** 21 21N 106 31 E
Lam Pao Res., *Thailand* **38 D4** 16 50N 103 15 E
Lamaing, *Burma* **41 M20** 15 25N 97 53 E
Lamar, *Colo., U.S.A.* **80 F3** 38 5N 102 37W
Lamar, *Mo., U.S.A.* **81 G7** 37 30N 94 16W
Lamas, *Peru* **92 E3** 6 28S 76 31W
Lambaréné, *Gabon* **52 E2** 0 41S 10 12 E
Lambasa = Labasa, *Fiji* **59 C8** 16 30S 179 27 E
Lambay I., *Ireland* **13 C5** 53 29N 6 1W
Lambert Glacier, *Antarctica* **5 D6** 71 0S 70 0 E
Lambert's Bay, *S. Africa* **56 E2** 32 5S 18 17 E
Lambeth, *Canada* **78 D3** 42 54N 81 18W
Lambomakondro, *Madag.* **57 C7** 22 41S 44 44 E
Lame Deer, *U.S.A.* **82 D10** 45 37N 106 40W
Lamego, *Portugal* **19 B2** 41 5N 7 52W
Lamèque, *Canada* **71 C7** 47 45N 64 38W
Lameroo, *Australia* **63 F3** 35 19S 140 33 E
Lamesa, *U.S.A.* **81 J4** 32 44N 101 58W
Lamía, *Greece* **21 E10** 38 55N 22 26 E
Lammermuir Hills, *U.K.* **12 F6** 55 50N 2 40W
Lamoille →, *U.S.A.* **79 B11** 44 38N 73 13W
Lamon B., *Phil.* **37 B6** 14 30N 122 20 E
Lamont, *Canada* **72 C6** 53 46N 112 50W
Lamont, *Calif., U.S.A.* **85 K8** 35 15N 118 55W
Lamont, *Wyo., U.S.A.* **82 E10** 42 13N 107 29W
Lampa, *Peru* **92 G4** 15 22S 70 22W
Lampang, *Thailand* **38 C2** 18 16N 99 32 E
Lampasas, *U.S.A.* **81 K5** 31 4N 98 11W
Lampazos de Naranjo, *Mexico* **86 B4** 27 2N 100 32W
Lampedusa, *Medit. S.* **20 G5** 35 36N 12 40 E
Lampeter, *U.K.* **11 E3** 52 7N 4 4W
Lampione, *Medit. S.* **20 G5** 35 33N 12 20 E
Lampman, *Canada* **73 D8** 49 25N 102 50W
Lampung □, *Indonesia* **36 F2** 5 30S 104 30 E
Lamta, *India* **43 H9** 22 8N 80 7 E
Lamu, *Kenya* **54 C5** 2 16S 40 55 E
Lamy, *U.S.A.* **83 J11** 35 29N 105 53W
Lan Xian, *China* **34 E6** 38 15N 111 35 E
Lanak La, *China* **43 B8** 34 27N 79 32 E

Lanak'o Shank'ou = Lanak La, *China* 43 B8 34 27N 79 32 E
Lanark, *Canada* 79 A8 45 1N 76 22W
Lanark, *U.K.* 12 F5 55 40N 3 47W
Lanbi Kyun, *Burma* 39 G2 10 50N 98 20 E
Lancang Jiang →, *China* 32 D5 21 40N 101 10 E
Lancashire □, *U.K.* 10 D5 53 50N 2 48W
Lancaster, *Canada* 79 A10 45 10N 74 30W
Lancaster, *U.K.* 10 C5 54 3N 2 48W
Lancaster, *Calif., U.S.A.* 85 L8 34 42N 118 8W
Lancaster, *Ky., U.S.A.* 76 G3 37 37N 84 35W
Lancaster, *N.H., U.S.A.* 79 B13 44 29N 71 34W
Lancaster, *N.Y., U.S.A.* 78 D6 42 54N 78 40W
Lancaster, *Ohio, U.S.A.* 76 F4 39 43N 82 36W
Lancaster, *Pa., U.S.A.* 79 F8 40 2N 76 19W
Lancaster, *S.C., U.S.A.* 77 H5 34 43N 80 46W
Lancaster, *Wis., U.S.A.* 80 D9 42 51N 90 43W
Lancaster Sd., *Canada* 69 A11 74 13N 84 0W
Lancelin, *Australia* 61 F2 31 0S 115 18 E
Lanchow = Lanzhou, *China* 34 F2 36 1N 103 52 E
Lanciano, *Italy* 20 C6 42 14N 14 23 E
Lancun, *China* 35 F11 36 25N 120 10 E
Landeck, *Austria* 16 E6 47 9N 10 34 E
Lander, *U.S.A.* 82 E9 42 50N 108 44W
Lander →, *Australia* 60 D5 22 0S 132 0 E
Landes, *France* 18 D3 44 0N 1 0W
Landi Kotal, *Pakistan* 42 B4 34 7N 71 6 E
Landisburg, *U.S.A.* 78 F7 40 21N 77 19W
Land's End, *U.K.* 11 G2 50 4N 5 44W
Landsborough Cr. →, *Australia* 62 C3 22 28S 144 35 E
Landshut, *Germany* 16 D7 48 34N 12 8 E
Landskrona, *Sweden* 9 J15 55 53N 12 50 E
Lanesboro, *U.S.A.* 79 E9 41 57N 75 34W
Lanett, *U.S.A.* 77 J3 32 52N 85 12W
Lang Qua, *Vietnam* 38 A5 22 16N 104 27 E
Lang Shan, *China* 34 D4 41 0N 106 30 E
Lang Son, *Vietnam* 38 B6 21 52N 106 42 E
Lang Suan, *Thailand* 39 H2 9 57N 99 4 E
La'nga Co, *China* 41 D12 30 45N 81 15 E
Langar, *Iran* 45 C9 35 23N 60 25 E
Langara I., *Canada* 72 C2 54 14N 133 1W
Langdon, *U.S.A.* 80 A5 48 45N 98 22W
Langeberg, *S. Africa* 56 E3 33 55S 21 0 E
Langeberge, *S. Africa* 56 D3 28 15S 22 33 E
Langeland, *Denmark* 9 J14 54 56N 10 48 E
Langenburg, *Canada* 73 C8 50 51N 101 43W
Langholm, *U.K.* 12 F5 55 9N 3 0W
Langjökull, *Iceland* 8 D3 64 39N 20 12W
Langkawi, Pulau, *Malaysia* 39 J2 6 25N 99 45 E
Langklip, *S. Africa* 56 D3 28 12S 20 20 E
Langkon, *Malaysia* 36 C5 6 30N 116 40 E
Langlade, *St- P. & M.* 71 C8 46 50N 56 20W
Langley, *Canada* 84 A4 49 7N 122 39W
Langøya, *Norway* 8 B16 68 45N 14 50 E
Langreo, *Spain* 19 A3 43 18N 5 40W
Langres, *France* 18 C6 47 52N 5 20 E
Langres, Plateau de, *France* 18 C6 47 45N 5 3 E
Langsa, *Indonesia* 36 D1 4 30N 97 57 E
Langtry, *U.S.A.* 81 L4 29 49N 101 34W
Langu, *Thailand* 39 J2 6 53N 99 47 E
Languedoc, *France* 18 E5 43 58N 3 55 E
Langxiangzhen, *China* 34 E9 39 43N 116 8 E
Lanigan, *Canada* 73 C7 51 51N 105 2W
Lankao, *China* 34 G8 34 48N 114 50 E
Länkäran, *Azerbaijan* 25 G8 38 48N 48 52 E
Lannion, *France* 18 B2 48 46N 3 29W
L'Annonciation, *Canada* 70 C5 46 25N 74 55W
Lansdale, *U.S.A.* 79 F9 40 14N 75 17W
Lansdowne, *Australia* 63 E5 31 48S 152 30 E
Lansdowne, *Canada* 79 B8 44 24N 76 1W
Lansdowne, *India* 43 E8 29 50N 78 41 E
Lansdowne House, *Canada* 70 B2 52 14N 87 53W
L'Anse, *U.S.A.* 76 B1 46 45N 88 27W
L'Anse au Loup, *Canada* 71 B8 51 32N 56 50W
L'Anse aux Meadows, *Canada* 71 B8 51 36N 55 32W
Lansford, *U.S.A.* 79 F9 40 50N 75 53W
Lansing, *U.S.A.* 76 D3 42 44N 84 33W
Lanta Yai, Ko, *Thailand* 39 J2 7 35N 99 3 E
Lantian, *China* 34 G5 34 11N 109 20 E
Lanus, *Argentina* 94 C4 34 44S 58 27W
Lanusei, *Italy* 20 E3 39 52N 9 34 E
Lanzarote, *Canary Is.* 22 F6 29 0N 13 40W
Lanzhou, *China* 34 F2 36 1N 103 52 E
Lao Bao, *Laos* 38 D6 16 35N 106 30 E
Lao Cai, *Vietnam* 38 A4 22 30N 103 57 E
Laoag, *Phil.* 37 A6 18 7N 120 34 E
Laoang, *Phil.* 37 B7 12 32N 125 8 E
Laoha He →, *China* 35 C11 43 25N 120 35 E
Laois □, *Ireland* 13 D4 52 57N 7 36W
Laon, *France* 18 B5 49 33N 3 35 E
Laona, *U.S.A.* 76 C1 45 34N 88 40W
Laos ■, *Asia* 38 D5 17 45N 105 0 E
Lapa, *Brazil* 95 B6 25 46S 49 44W
Lapeer, *U.S.A.* 76 D4 43 3N 83 19W
Lapithos, *Cyprus* 23 D12 35 21N 33 11 E
Lapland = Lappland, *Europe* 8 B21 68 7N 24 0 E
Laporte, *U.S.A.* 79 E8 41 25N 76 30W
Lappeenranta, *Finland* 9 F23 61 3N 28 12 E
Lappland, *Europe* 8 B21 68 7N 24 0 E
Laprida, *Argentina* 94 D3 37 34S 60 45W
Lapseki, *Turkey* 21 D12 40 20N 26 41 E
Laptev Sea, *Russia* 27 B13 76 0N 125 0 E
Lapua, *Finland* 8 E20 62 58N 23 0 E
L'Áquila, *Italy* 20 C5 42 22N 13 22 E
Lār, *Āzarbājān-e Sharqī, Iran* 44 B5 38 30N 47 52 E
Lār, *Fārs, Iran* 45 E7 27 40N 54 14 E
Laramie, *U.S.A.* 80 E2 41 19N 105 35W
Laramie →, *U.S.A.* 82 F11 42 13N 104 33W
Laramie Mts., *U.S.A.* 80 E2 42 0N 105 30W
Laranjeiras do Sul, *Brazil* 95 B5 25 23S 52 23W
Larantuka, *Indonesia* 37 F6 8 21S 122 55 E
Larat, *Indonesia* 37 F8 7 0S 132 0 E
Larde, *Mozam.* 55 F4 16 28S 39 43 E
Larder Lake, *Canada* 70 C4 48 5N 79 40W
Lardhos, Ákra = Líndhos, Ákra, *Greece* 23 C10 36 4N 28 10 E
Lardhos, Órmos, *Greece* 23 C10 36 4N 28 2 E
Laredo, *U.S.A.* 81 M5 27 30N 99 30W
Laredo Sd., *Canada* 72 C3 52 30N 128 53W
Largo, *U.S.A.* 77 M4 27 55N 82 47W
Largs, *U.K.* 12 F4 55 47N 4 52W
Lariang, *Indonesia* 37 E5 1 26S 119 17 E
Larimore, *U.S.A.* 80 B6 47 54N 97 38W
Lārīn, *Iran* 45 C7 35 55N 52 19 E
Lárisa, *Greece* 21 E10 39 36N 22 27 E
Larkana, *Pakistan* 42 F3 27 32N 68 18 E
Larnaca, *Cyprus* 23 E12 34 55N 33 38 E
Larnaca Bay, *Cyprus* 23 E12 34 53N 33 45 E
Larne, *U.K.* 13 B6 54 51N 5 51W
Larned, *U.S.A.* 80 F5 38 11N 99 6W
Larose, *U.S.A.* 81 L9 29 34N 90 23W
Larrimah, *Australia* 60 C5 15 35S 133 12 E
Larsen Ice Shelf, *Antarctica* 5 C17 67 0S 62 0W
Larvik, *Norway* 9 G14 59 4N 10 2 E
Las Animas, *U.S.A.* 80 F3 38 4N 103 13W
Las Anod, *Somali Rep.* 46 F4 8 26N 47 19 E
Las Aves, Is., *W. Indies* 89 C7 15 45N 63 55W
Las Brenãs, *Argentina* 94 B3 27 5S 61 7W
Las Cejas, *Argentina* 96 B4 26 53S 64 44W
Las Chimeneas, *Mexico* 85 N10 32 8N 116 5W
Las Cruces, *U.S.A.* 83 K10 32 19N 106 47W
Las Flores, *Argentina* 94 D4 36 10S 59 7W
Las Heras, *Argentina* 94 C2 32 51S 68 49W
Las Lajas, *Argentina* 96 D2 38 30S 70 25W
Las Lomitas, *Argentina* 94 A3 24 43S 60 35W
Las Palmas, *Argentina* 94 B4 27 8S 58 45W
Las Palmas, *Canary Is.* 22 F4 28 7N 15 26W
Las Palmas →, *Mexico* 85 N10 32 26N 116 54W
Las Piedras, *Uruguay* 95 C4 34 44S 56 14W
Las Pipinas, *Argentina* 94 D4 35 30S 57 19W
Las Plumas, *Argentina* 96 E3 43 40S 67 15W
Las Rosas, *Argentina* 94 C3 32 30S 61 35W
Las Tablas, *Panama* 88 E3 7 49N 80 14W
Las Termas, *Argentina* 94 B3 27 29S 64 52W
Las Toscas, *Argentina* 94 B4 28 21S 59 18W
Las Truchas, *Mexico* 86 D4 17 57N 102 13W
Las Varillas, *Argentina* 94 C3 31 50S 62 50W
Las Vegas, *N. Mex., U.S.A.* 83 J11 35 36N 105 13W
Las Vegas, *Nev., U.S.A.* 85 J11 36 10N 115 9W
Lascano, *Uruguay* 95 C5 33 35S 54 12W
Lash-e Joveyn, *Afghan.* 40 D2 31 45N 61 30 E
Lashburn, *Canada* 73 C7 53 10N 109 40W
Lashio, *Burma* 41 H20 22 56N 97 45 E
Lashkar, *India* 42 F8 26 10N 78 10 E
Lasíthi, *Greece* 23 D7 35 11N 25 31 E
Lasíthi □, *Greece* 23 D7 35 5N 25 50 E
Lāsjerd, *Iran* 45 C7 35 24N 53 4 E
Lassen Pk., *U.S.A.* 82 F3 40 29N 121 31W
Lassen Volcanic Nat. Park, *U.S.A.* 82 F3 40 30N 121 20W
Last Mountain L., *Canada* 73 C7 51 5N 105 14W
Lastchance Cr. →, *U.S.A.* 84 E5 40 2N 121 15W
Lastoursville, *Gabon* 52 E2 0 55S 12 38 E
Lastovo, *Croatia* 20 C7 42 46N 16 55 E
Lat Yao, *Thailand* 38 E2 15 45N 99 48 E
Latacunga, *Ecuador* 92 D3 0 50S 78 35W
Latakia = Al Lādhiqīyah, *Syria* 44 C2 35 30N 35 45 E
Latchford, *Canada* 70 C4 47 20N 79 50W
Latehar, *India* 43 H11 23 45N 84 30 E
Latham, *Australia* 61 E2 29 44S 116 20 E
Lathi, *India* 42 F4 27 43N 71 23 E
Lathrop Wells, *U.S.A.* 85 J10 36 39N 116 24W
Latina, *Italy* 20 D5 41 28N 12 52 E
Latium = Lazio □, *Italy* 20 C5 42 10N 12 30 E
Laton, *U.S.A.* 84 J7 36 26N 119 41W
Latouche Treville, C., *Australia* 60 C3 18 27S 121 49 E
Latrobe, *Australia* 62 G4 41 14S 146 30 E
Latrobe, *U.S.A.* 78 F5 40 19N 79 23W
Latvia ■, *Europe* 9 H20 56 50N 24 0 E
Lau Group, *Fiji* 59 C9 17 0S 178 30W
Lauchhammer, *Germany* 16 C7 51 29N 13 47 E
Laughlin, *U.S.A.* 83 J6 35 8N 114 35W
Laukaa, *Finland* 9 E21 62 24N 25 56 E
Launceston, *Australia* 62 G4 41 24S 147 8 E
Launceston, *U.K.* 11 G3 50 38N 4 22W
Laune →, *Ireland* 13 D2 52 7N 9 47W
Launglon Bok, *Burma* 38 F1 13 50N 97 54 E
Laura, *Australia* 62 B3 15 32S 144 32 E
Laurel, *Miss., U.S.A.* 81 K10 31 41N 89 8W
Laurel, *Mont., U.S.A.* 82 D9 45 40N 108 46W
Laurencekirk, *U.K.* 12 E6 56 50N 2 28W
Laurens, *U.S.A.* 77 H4 34 30N 82 1W
Laurentian Plateau, *Canada* 71 B6 52 0N 70 0W
Lauria, *Italy* 20 E6 40 2N 15 50 E
Laurie L., *Canada* 73 B8 56 35N 101 57W
Laurinburg, *U.S.A.* 77 H6 34 47N 79 28W
Laurium, *U.S.A.* 76 B1 47 14N 88 27W
Lausanne, *Switz.* 18 C7 46 32N 6 38 E
Laut, *Indonesia* 39 K6 4 45N 108 0 E
Laut, Pulau, *Indonesia* 36 E5 3 40S 116 10 E
Laut Kecil, Kepulauan, *Indonesia* 36 E5 4 45S 115 40 E
Lautoka, *Fiji* 59 C7 17 37S 177 27 E
Lavagh More, *Ireland* 13 B3 54 46N 8 6W
Laval, *France* 18 B3 48 4N 0 48W
Lavalle, *Argentina* 94 B2 28 15S 65 15W
Lavant Station, *Canada* 79 A8 45 3N 76 42W
Lāvar Meydān, *Iran* 45 D7 30 20N 54 30 E
Laverton, *Australia* 61 E3 28 44S 122 29 E
Lavras, *Brazil* 95 A7 21 20S 45 0W
Lávrion, *Greece* 21 F11 37 40N 24 4 E
Lávris, *Greece* 23 D6 35 25N 24 40 E
Lavumisa, *Swaziland* 57 D5 27 20S 31 55 E
Lawas, *Malaysia* 36 D5 4 55N 115 25 E
Lawele, *Indonesia* 37 F6 5 13S 122 57 E
Lawng Pit, *Burma* 41 G20 25 30N 97 25 E
Lawqah, *Si. Arabia* 44 D4 29 49N 42 45 E
Lawrence, *N.Z.* 59 L2 45 55S 169 41 E
Lawrence, *Kans., U.S.A.* 80 F7 38 58N 95 14W
Lawrence, *Mass., U.S.A.* 79 D13 42 43N 71 10W
Lawrenceburg, *Ind., U.S.A.* 76 F3 39 6N 84 52W
Lawrenceburg, *Tenn., U.S.A.* 77 H2 35 14N 87 20W
Lawrenceville, *Ga., U.S.A.* 77 J4 33 57N 83 59W
Lawrenceville, *Pa., U.S.A.* 78 E7 41 59N 77 8W
Laws, *U.S.A.* 84 H8 37 24N 118 20W
Lawton, *U.S.A.* 81 H5 34 37N 98 25W
Lawu, *Indonesia* 37 G14 7 40S 111 13 E
Laxford, L., *U.K.* 12 C3 58 24N 5 6W
Layla, *Si. Arabia* 46 C4 22 10N 46 40 E
Laylān, *Iraq* 44 C5 35 18N 44 31 E
Layton, *U.S.A.* 82 F7 41 4N 111 58W
Laytonville, *U.S.A.* 82 G2 39 41N 123 29W
Lazarivo, *Madag.* 57 C8 23 54S 44 59 E
Lazio □, *Italy* 20 C5 42 10N 12 30 E
Lazo, *Russia* 30 C6 43 25N 133 55 E
Le Creusot, *France* 18 C6 46 48N 4 24 E
Le François, *Martinique* 89 D7 14 38N 60 57W
Le Havre, *France* 18 B4 49 30N 0 5 E
Le Mans, *France* 18 C4 48 0N 0 10 E
Le Mars, *U.S.A.* 80 D6 42 47N 96 10W
Le Mont-St-Michel, *France* 18 B3 48 40N 1 30W
Le Moule, *Guadeloupe* 89 C7 16 20N 61 22W
Le Puy-en-Velay, *France* 18 D5 45 3N 3 52 E
Le Sueur, *U.S.A.* 80 C8 44 28N 93 55W
Le Thuy, *Vietnam* 38 D6 17 14N 106 49 E
Le Touquet-Paris-Plage, *France* 18 A4 50 30N 1 36 E
Le Tréport, *France* 18 A4 50 3N 1 20 E
Le Verdon-sur-Mer, *France* 18 D3 45 33N 1 4W
Lea →, *U.K.* 11 F8 51 31N 0 1 E
Leach, *Cambodia* 39 F4 12 21N 103 46 E
Lead, *U.S.A.* 80 C3 44 21N 103 46W
Leader, *Canada* 73 C7 50 50N 109 30W
Leadville, *U.S.A.* 83 G10 39 15N 106 18W
Leaf →, *U.S.A.* 81 K10 30 59N 88 44W
Leaf Rapids, *Canada* 73 B9 56 30N 99 59W
Leamington, *Canada* 78 D2 42 3N 82 36W
Leamington, *U.S.A.* 82 G7 39 32N 112 17W
Leamington Spa = Royal Leamington Spa, *U.K.* 11 E6 52 18N 1 31W
Leandro Norte Alem, *Argentina* 95 B4 27 34S 55 15W
Leane, L., *Ireland* 13 D2 52 2N 9 32W
Learmonth, *Australia* 60 D1 22 13S 114 10 E
Leask, *Canada* 73 C7 53 5N 106 45W
Leatherhead, *U.K.* 11 F7 51 18N 0 20W
Leavenworth, *Kans., U.S.A.* 80 F7 39 19N 94 55W
Leavenworth, *Wash., U.S.A.* 82 C3 47 36N 120 40W
Lebak, *Phil.* 37 C6 6 32N 124 5 E
Lebam, *U.S.A.* 84 D3 46 34N 123 33W
Lebanon, *Ind., U.S.A.* 76 E2 40 3N 86 28W
Lebanon, *Kans., U.S.A.* 80 F5 39 49N 98 33W
Lebanon, *Ky., U.S.A.* 76 G3 37 34N 85 15W
Lebanon, *Mo., U.S.A.* 81 G8 37 41N 92 40W
Lebanon, *N.H., U.S.A.* 79 C12 43 39N 72 15W
Lebanon, *Oreg., U.S.A.* 82 D2 44 32N 122 55W
Lebanon, *Pa., U.S.A.* 79 F8 40 20N 76 26W
Lebanon, *Tenn., U.S.A.* 77 G2 36 12N 86 18W
Lebanon ■, *Asia* 47 B5 34 0N 36 0 E
Lebec, *U.S.A.* 85 L8 34 50N 118 52W
Lebel-sur-Quévillon, *Canada* 70 C4 49 3N 76 59W
Lebomboberge, *S. Africa* 57 C5 24 30S 32 0 E
Lębork, *Poland* 17 A9 54 33N 17 46 E
Lebrija, *Spain* 19 D2 36 53N 6 5W
Lebu, *Chile* 94 D1 37 40S 73 47W
Lecce, *Italy* 21 D8 40 23N 18 11 E
Lecco, *Italy* 18 D8 45 51N 9 23 E
Lech →, *Germany* 16 D6 48 43N 10 56 E
Lecontes Mills, *U.S.A.* 78 E6 41 5N 78 17W
Łęczyca, *Poland* 17 B10 52 5N 19 15 E
Ledong, *China* 38 C7 18 41N 109 5 E
Leduc, *Canada* 72 C6 53 15N 113 30W
Lee, *U.S.A.* 79 D11 42 19N 73 15W
Lee →, *Ireland* 13 E3 51 53N 8 56W
Lee Vining, *U.S.A.* 84 H7 37 58N 119 7W
Leech L., *U.S.A.* 80 B7 47 10N 94 24W
Leechburg, *U.S.A.* 78 F5 40 37N 79 36W
Leeds, *U.K.* 10 D6 53 48N 1 33W
Leeds, *U.S.A.* 77 J2 33 33N 86 33W
Leek, *Neths.* 15 A6 53 10N 6 24 E
Leek, *U.K.* 10 D5 53 7N 2 1W
Leeman, *Australia* 61 E1 29 57S 114 58 E
Leeper, *U.S.A.* 78 E5 41 22N 79 18W
Leer, *Germany* 16 B4 53 13N 7 26 E
Leesburg, *U.S.A.* 77 L5 28 49N 81 53W
Leesville, *U.S.A.* 81 K8 31 9N 93 16W
Leeton, *Australia* 63 E4 34 33S 146 23 E
Leetonia, *U.S.A.* 78 F4 40 53N 80 45W
Leeu Gamka, *S. Africa* 56 E3 32 47S 21 59 E
Leeuwarden, *Neths.* 15 A5 53 15N 5 48 E
Leeuwin, C., *Australia* 61 F2 34 20S 115 9 E
Leeward Is., *Atl. Oc.* 89 C7 16 30N 63 30W
Lefka, *Cyprus* 23 D11 35 6N 32 51 E
Lefkoniko, *Cyprus* 23 D12 35 18N 33 44 E
Lefroy, *Canada* 78 B5 44 16N 79 34W
Lefroy, L., *Australia* 61 F3 31 21S 121 40 E
Leganés, *Spain* 19 B4 40 19N 3 45W
Legazpi, *Phil.* 37 B6 13 10N 123 45 E
Legendre I., *Australia* 60 D2 20 22S 116 55 E
Leghorn = Livorno, *Italy* 20 C4 43 33N 10 19 E
Legionowo, *Poland* 17 B11 52 25N 20 50 E
Legnago, *Italy* 20 B4 45 11N 11 18 E
Legnica, *Poland* 16 C9 51 12N 16 10 E
Leh, *India* 43 B7 34 9N 77 35 E
Lehigh Acres, *U.S.A.* 77 M5 26 36N 81 39W
Lehighton, *U.S.A.* 79 F9 40 50N 75 43W
Lehututu, *Botswana* 56 C3 23 54S 21 55 E
Leiah, *Pakistan* 42 D4 30 58N 70 58 E
Leicester, *U.K.* 11 E6 52 38N 1 8W
Leicester City □, *U.K.* 11 E6 52 38N 1 8W
Leicestershire □, *U.K.* 11 E6 52 41N 1 17W
Leichhardt →, *Australia* 62 B2 17 35S 139 48 E
Leichhardt Ra., *Australia* 62 C4 20 46S 147 40 E
Leiden, *Neths.* 15 B4 52 9N 4 30 E
Leie →, *Belgium* 15 C3 51 2N 3 45 E
Leine →, *Germany* 16 B5 52 43N 9 36 E
Leinster, *Australia* 61 E3 27 51S 120 36 E
Leinster □, *Ireland* 13 C4 53 3N 7 8W
Leinster, Mt., *Ireland* 13 D5 52 37N 6 46W
Leipzig, *Germany* 16 C7 51 18N 12 22 E
Leiria, *Portugal* 19 C1 39 46N 8 53W
Leirvik, *Norway* 9 G11 59 47N 5 28 E
Leisler, Mt., *Australia* 60 D4 23 23S 129 20 E
Leith, *U.K.* 12 F5 55 59N 3 11W
Leith Hill, *U.K.* 11 F7 51 11N 0 22W
Leitrim, *Ireland* 13 B3 54 0N 8 5W
Leitrim □, *Ireland* 13 B4 54 8N 8 0W
Leizhou Bandao, *China* 33 D6 21 0N 110 0 E
Lek →, *Neths.* 15 C4 51 54N 4 35 E
Leka, *Norway* 8 D14 65 5N 11 35 E
Lékva Óros, *Greece* 23 D6 35 18N 24 3 E
Leland, *Mich., U.S.A.* 76 C3 45 1N 85 45W
Leland, *Miss., U.S.A.* 81 J9 33 24N 90 54W
Leleque, *Argentina* 96 E2 42 28S 71 0W
Lelystad, *Neths.* 15 B5 52 30N 5 25 E
Léman, L., *Europe* 18 C7 46 26N 6 30 E
Lemera, *Dem. Rep. of the Congo* 54 C2 3 0S 28 55 E
Lemhi Ra., *U.S.A.* 82 D7 44 30N 113 30W
Lemmer, *Neths.* 15 B5 52 51N 5 43 E
Lemmon, *U.S.A.* 80 C3 45 57N 102 10W
Lemon Grove, *U.S.A.* 85 N9 32 45N 117 2W
Lemoore, *U.S.A.* 84 J7 36 18N 119 46W
Lemvig, *Denmark* 9 H13 56 33N 8 20 E
Lena →, *Russia* 27 B13 72 52N 126 40 E
Léndas, *Greece* 23 E6 34 56N 24 56 E
Lendeh, *Iran* 45 D6 30 58N 50 25 E
Lenggong, *Malaysia* 39 K3 5 6N 100 58 E
Lengua de Vaca, Pta., *Chile* 94 C1 30 14S 71 38W
Leninabad = Khŭjand, *Tajikistan* 26 E7 40 17N 69 37 E
Leninakan = Gyumri, *Armenia* 25 F7 40 47N 43 50 E
Leningrad = Sankt-Peterburg, *Russia* 24 C5 59 55N 30 20 E
Leninogorsk, *Kazakstan* 26 D9 50 20N 83 30 E
Leninsk, *Russia* 25 E8 48 40N 45 15 E
Leninsk-Kuznetskiy, *Russia* 26 D9 54 44N 86 10 E
Lenkoran = Länkäran, *Azerbaijan* 25 G8 38 48N 48 52 E
Lenmalu, *Indonesia* 37 E8 1 45S 130 15 E
Lennox, *U.S.A.* 80 D6 43 21N 96 53W
Lennoxville, *Canada* 79 A13 45 22N 71 51W
Lenoir, *U.S.A.* 77 H5 35 55N 81 32W
Lenoir City, *U.S.A.* 77 H3 35 48N 84 16W
Lenore L., *Canada* 73 C8 52 30N 104 59W
Lenox, *U.S.A.* 79 D11 42 22N 73 17W
Lens, *France* 18 A5 50 26N 2 50 E
Lensk, *Russia* 27 C12 60 48N 114 55 E
Lentini, *Italy* 20 F6 37 17N 15 0 E
Lenwood, *U.S.A.* 85 L9 34 53N 117 7W
Lenya, *Burma* 36 B1 11 33N 98 57 E
Leoben, *Austria* 16 E8 47 22N 15 5 E
Leodhas = Lewis, *U.K.* 12 C2 58 9N 6 40W
Leola, *U.S.A.* 80 C5 45 43N 98 56W
Leominster, *U.K.* 11 E5 52 14N 2 43W
Leominster, *U.S.A.* 79 D13 42 32N 71 46W
León, *Mexico* 86 C4 21 7N 101 40W
León, *Nic.* 88 D2 12 20N 86 51W
León, *Spain* 19 A3 42 38N 5 34W
Leon, *U.S.A.* 80 E8 40 44N 93 45W
Leon →, *U.S.A.* 81 K6 31 14N 97 28W
León, Montes de, *Spain* 19 A2 42 30N 6 18W
Leonardtown, *U.S.A.* 76 F7 38 17N 76 38W
Leonardville, *Namibia* 56 C2 23 29S 18 49 E
Leongatha, *Australia* 63 F4 38 30S 145 58 E
Leonora, *Australia* 61 E3 28 49S 121 19 E
Leopoldina, *Brazil* 95 A7 21 28S 42 40W
Leopoldsburg, *Belgium* 15 C5 51 7N 5 13 E
Leoti, *U.S.A.* 80 F4 38 29N 101 21W
Leova, *Moldova* 17 E15 46 28N 28 15 E
Leoville, *Canada* 73 C7 53 39N 107 33W
Lepel = Lyepyel, *Belarus* 24 D4 54 50N 28 40 E
Lépo, L. do, *Angola* 56 B2 17 0S 19 0 E
Leppävirta, *Finland* 9 E22 62 29N 27 46 E
Lerdo, *Mexico* 86 B4 25 32N 103 32W
Leribe, *Lesotho* 57 D4 28 51S 28 3 E
Lérida = Lleida, *Spain* 19 B6 41 37N 0 39 E
Lerwick, *U.K.* 12 A7 60 9N 1 9W
Les Cayes, *Haiti* 89 C5 18 15N 73 46W
Les Sables-d'Olonne, *France* 18 C3 46 30N 1 45W
Lesbos = Lésvos, *Greece* 21 E12 39 10N 26 20 E
Leshan, *China* 32 D5 29 33N 103 41 E
Leshukonskoye, *Russia* 24 B8 64 54N 45 46 E
Leskov I., *Antarctica* 5 B1 56 0S 28 0W
Leskovac, *Serbia, Yug.* 21 C9 43 0N 21 58 E
Lesopilnoye, *Russia* 30 A7 46 44N 134 20 E
Lesotho ■, *Africa* 57 D4 29 40S 28 0 E
Lesozavodsk, *Russia* 27 E14 45 30N 133 29 E
Lesse →, *Belgium* 15 D4 50 15N 4 54 E
Lesser Antilles, *W. Indies* 89 D7 15 0N 61 0W
Lesser Slave L., *Canada* 72 B5 55 30N 115 25W
Lesser Sunda Is., *Indonesia* 37 F6 8 0S 120 0 E
Lessines, *Belgium* 15 D3 50 42N 3 50 E
Lester, *U.S.A.* 84 C5 47 12N 121 29W
Lestock, *Canada* 73 C8 51 19N 103 59W
Lesuer I., *Australia* 60 B4 13 50S 127 17 E
Lésvos, *Greece* 21 E12 39 10N 26 20 E
Leszno, *Poland* 17 C9 51 50N 16 30 E
Letaba, *S. Africa* 57 C5 23 59S 31 50 E
Letchworth, *U.K.* 11 F7 51 59N 0 13W
Lethbridge, *Canada* 72 D6 49 45N 112 45W
Lethem, *Guyana* 92 C7 3 20N 59 50W
Leti, Kepulauan, *Indonesia* 37 F7 8 10S 128 0 E
Leti Is. = Leti, Kepulauan, *Indonesia* 37 F7 8 10S 128 0 E
Letiahau →, *Botswana* 56 C3 21 16S 24 0 E
Leticia, *Colombia* 92 D5 4 9S 70 0W
Leting, *China* 35 E10 39 23N 118 55 E
Letjiesbos, *S. Africa* 56 E3 32 34S 22 16 E
Letlhakane, *Botswana* 56 C4 21 27S 25 30 E
Letlhakeng, *Botswana* 56 C3 24 0S 24 59 E
Letong, *Indonesia* 36 D3 2 58N 105 42 E
Letpadan, *Burma* 41 L19 17 45N 95 45 E
Letpan, *Burma* 41 K19 19 28N 94 10 E
Letsôk-aw Kyun, *Burma* 39 G2 11 30N 98 25 E
Letterkenny, *Ireland* 13 B4 54 57N 7 45W
Leucadia, *U.S.A.* 85 M9 33 4N 117 18W
Leuser, G., *Indonesia* 36 D1 3 46N 97 12 E
Leuven, *Belgium* 15 D4 50 52N 4 42 E
Leuze-en-Hainaut, *Belgium* 15 D3 50 36N 3 37 E
Levádhia, *Greece* 21 E10 38 27N 22 54 E
Levanger, *Norway* 8 E14 63 45N 11 19 E
Levelland, *U.S.A.* 81 J3 33 35N 102 23W
Leven, *U.K.* 12 E6 56 12N 3 0W
Leven, L., *U.K.* 12 E5 56 12N 3 22W
Leven, Toraka, *Madag.* 57 A8 12 30S 47 45 E
Leveque C., *Australia* 60 C3 16 20S 123 0 E
Levice, *Slovak Rep.* 17 D10 48 13N 18 35 E
Levin, *N.Z.* 59 J5 40 37S 175 18 E
Lévis, *Canada* 71 C5 46 48N 71 9W
Levis, L., *Canada* 72 A5 62 37N 117 58W
Levittown, *N.Y., U.S.A.* 79 F11 40 44N 73 31W
Levittown, *Pa., U.S.A.* 79 F10 40 9N 74 51W
Levkás, *Greece* 21 E9 38 40N 20 43 E
Levkímmi, *Greece* 23 B4 39 25N 20 3 E
Levkímmi, Ákra, *Greece* 23 B4 39 29N 20 4 E
Levkôsia = Nicosia, *Cyprus* 23 D12 35 10N 33 25 E
Levskigrad = Karlovo, *Bulgaria* 21 C11 42 38N 24 47 E
Lewes, *U.K.* 11 G8 50 52N 0 1 E
Lewes, *U.S.A.* 76 F8 38 46N 75 9W
Lewis, *U.K.* 12 C2 58 9N 6 40W
Lewis →, *U.S.A.* 84 E4 45 51N 122 48W
Lewis, Butt of, *U.K.* 12 C2 58 31N 6 16W
Lewis Ra., *Australia* 60 D4 20 3S 128 50 E
Lewis Range, *U.S.A.* 82 C7 48 5N 113 5W
Lewis Run, *U.S.A.* 78 E6 41 52N 78 40W
Lewisburg, *Pa., U.S.A.* 78 F8 40 58N 76 54W
Lewisburg, *Tenn., U.S.A.* 77 H2 35 27N 86 48W
Lewisburg, *W. Va., U.S.A.* 76 G5 37 48N 80 27W
Lewisporte, *Canada* 71 C8 49 15N 55 3W
Lewiston, *Idaho, U.S.A.* 82 C5 46 25N 117 1W

Lynden, U.S.A. 84 B4 48 57N 122 27W
Lyndhurst, Australia 63 E2 30 15S 138 18 E
Lyndon →, Australia 61 D1 23 29S 114 6 E
Lyndonville, N.Y., U.S.A. 78 C6 43 20N 78 23W
Lyndonville, Vt., U.S.A. 79 B12 44 31N 72 1W
Lyngen, Norway 8 B19 69 45N 20 30 E
Lynher Reef, Australia 60 C3 15 27S 121 55 E
Lynn, U.S.A. 79 D14 42 28N 70 57W
Lynn Lake, Canada 73 B8 56 51N 101 3W
Lynnwood, U.S.A. 84 C4 47 49N 122 19W
Lynton, U.K. 11 F4 51 13N 3 50W
Lyntupy, Belarus 9 J22 55 4N 26 23 E
Lynx L., Canada 73 A7 62 25N 106 15W
Lyon, France 18 D6 45 46N 4 50 E
Lyonnais, France 18 D6 45 45N 4 15 E
Lyons = Lyon, France 18 D6 45 46N 4 50 E
Lyons, Ga., U.S.A. 77 J4 32 12N 82 19W
Lyons, Kans., U.S.A. 80 F5 38 21N 98 12W
Lyons, N.Y., U.S.A. 78 C8 43 5N 77 0W
Lyons →, Australia 61 E2 25 2S 115 9 E
Lyons Falls, U.S.A. 79 C9 43 37N 75 22W
Lys = Leie →, Belgium 15 C3 51 2N 3 45 E
Lysva, Russia 24 C10 58 7N 57 49 E
Lysychansk, Ukraine 25 E6 48 55N 38 30 E
Lytham St. Anne's, U.K. 10 D4 53 45N 3 0W
Lyttelton, N.Z. 59 K4 43 35S 172 44 E
Lytton, Canada 72 C4 50 13N 121 31W
Lyubertsy, Russia 24 C6 55 39N 37 50 E
Lyuboml, Ukraine 17 C13 51 11N 24 4 E

M

M.R. Gomez, Presa, Mexico 87 B5 26 10N 99 0W
Ma →, Vietnam 38 C5 19 47N 105 56 E
Ma'adaba, Jordan 47 E4 30 43N 35 47 E
Maamba, Zambia 56 B4 17 17S 26 28 E
Ma'ān, Jordan 47 E4 30 12N 35 44 E
Ma'ān □, Jordan 47 F5 30 0N 36 0 E
Maanselkä, Finland 8 C23 63 52N 28 32 E
Ma'anshan, China 33 C6 31 44N 118 29 E
Maarianhamina, Finland 9 F18 60 5N 19 55 E
Ma'arrat an Nu'mān, Syria 44 C3 35 43N 36 43 E
Maas →, Neths. 15 C4 51 45N 4 32 E
Maaseik, Belgium 15 C5 51 6N 5 45 E
Maasin, Phil. 37 B6 10 8N 124 50 E
Maastricht, Neths. 18 A6 50 50N 5 40 E
Maave, Mozam. 57 C5 21 4S 34 47 E
Mababe Depression, Botswana 56 B3 18 50S 24 15 E
Mabalane, Mozam. 57 C5 23 37S 32 31 E
Mabel L., Canada 72 C5 50 35N 118 43W
Mabenge, Dem. Rep. of the Congo 54 B1 4 15N 24 12 E
Maberly, Canada 79 B8 44 50N 76 32W
Mablethorpe, U.K. 10 D8 53 20N 0 15 E
Maboma, Dem. Rep. of the Congo 54 B2 2 30N 28 10 E
Mac Bac, Vietnam 39 H6 9 46N 106 7 E
Macachín, Argentina 94 D3 37 10S 63 43W
Macaé, Brazil 95 A7 22 20S 41 43W
McAlester, U.S.A. 81 H7 34 56N 95 46W
McAllen, U.S.A. 81 M5 26 12N 98 14W
MacAlpine L., Canada 68 B9 66 40N 102 50W
Macamic, Canada 70 C4 48 45N 79 0W
Macao = Macau, China 33 D6 22 12N 113 33 E
Macapá, Brazil 93 C8 0 5N 51 4W
McArthur →, Australia 62 B2 15 54S 136 40 E
McArthur, Port, Australia 62 B2 16 4S 136 23 E
Macau, Brazil 93 E11 5 15S 36 40W
Macau, China 33 D6 22 12N 113 33 E
McBride, Canada 72 C4 53 20N 120 19W
McCall, U.S.A. 82 D5 44 55N 116 6W
McCamey, U.S.A. 81 K3 31 8N 102 14W
McCammon, U.S.A. 82 E7 42 39N 112 12W
McCauley I., Canada 72 C2 53 40N 130 15W
McCleary, U.S.A. 84 C3 47 3N 123 16W
Macclenny, U.S.A. 77 K4 30 17N 82 7W
Macclesfield, U.K. 10 D5 53 15N 2 8W
M'Clintock Chan., Canada 68 A9 72 0N 102 0W
McClintock Ra., Australia 60 C4 18 44S 127 38 E
McCloud, U.S.A. 82 F2 41 15N 122 8W
McCluer I., Australia 60 B5 11 5S 133 0 E
McClure, U.S.A. 78 F7 40 42N 77 19W
McClure, L., U.S.A. 84 H6 37 35N 120 16W
M'Clure Str., Canada 4 B2 75 0N 119 0W
McClusky, U.S.A. 80 B4 47 29N 100 27W
McComb, U.S.A. 81 K9 31 15N 90 27W
McConaughy, L., U.S.A. 80 E4 41 14N 101 40W
McCook, U.S.A. 80 E4 40 12N 100 38W
McCreary, Canada 73 C9 50 47N 99 29W
McCullough Mt., U.S.A. 85 K11 35 35N 115 13W
McCusker →, Canada 73 B7 55 32N 108 39W
McDame, Canada 72 B3 59 44N 128 59W
McDermitt, U.S.A. 82 F5 41 59N 117 43W
McDonald, U.S.A. 78 F4 40 22N 80 14W
Macdonald, L., Australia 60 D4 23 30S 129 0 E
McDonald Is., Ind. Oc. 3 G13 53 0S 73 0 E
MacDonnell Ranges, Australia 60 D5 23 40S 133 0 E
MacDowell L., Canada 70 B1 52 15N 92 45W
Macduff, U.K. 12 D6 57 40N 2 31W
Macedonia = Makedhonia □, Greece 21 D10 40 39N 22 0 E
Macedonia, U.S.A. 78 E3 41 19N 81 31W
Macedonia ■, Europe 21 D9 41 53N 21 40 E
Maceió, Brazil 93 E11 9 40S 35 41W
Macerata, Italy 20 C5 43 18N 13 27 E
McFarland, U.S.A. 85 K7 35 41N 119 14W
McFarlane →, Canada 73 B7 59 12N 107 58W
Macfarlane, L., Australia 63 E2 32 0S 136 40 E
McGehee, U.S.A. 81 J9 33 38N 91 24W
McGill, U.S.A. 82 G6 39 23N 114 47W
Macgillycuddy's Reeks, Ireland 13 E2 51 58N 9 45W
McGraw, U.S.A. 79 D8 42 36N 76 8W
McGregor, U.S.A. 80 D9 43 1N 91 11W
McGregor Ra., Australia 63 D3 27 0S 142 45 E
Mach, Pakistan 40 E5 29 50N 67 20 E
Māch Kowr, Iran 45 E9 25 48N 61 28 E
Machado = Jiparaná →, Brazil 92 E6 8 3S 62 52W
Machagai, Argentina 94 B3 26 56S 60 2W
Machakos, Kenya 54 C4 1 30S 37 15 E
Machala, Ecuador 92 D3 3 20S 79 57W
Machanga, Mozam. 57 C6 20 59S 35 0 E
Machattie, L., Australia 62 C2 24 50S 139 48 E
Machava, Mozam. 57 D5 25 54S 32 28 E
Machece, Mozam. 55 F4 19 15S 35 32 E
Macheke, Zimbabwe 57 B5 18 5S 31 51 E
Machhu →, India 42 H4 23 6N 70 46 E
Machias, Maine, U.S.A. 77 C12 44 43N 67 28W
Machias, N.Y., U.S.A. 78 D6 42 25N 78 30W
Machichi →, Canada 73 B10 57 3N 92 6W
Machico, Madeira 22 D3 32 43N 16 44W
Machilipatnam, India 41 L12 16 12N 81 8 E
Machiques, Venezuela 92 A4 10 4N 72 34W
Machupicchu, Peru 92 F4 13 8S 72 30W
Machynlleth, U.K. 11 E4 52 35N 3 50W
Macia, Mozam. 57 D5 25 2S 33 8 E
McIlwraith Ra., Australia 62 A3 13 50S 143 20 E
McInnes L., Canada 73 C10 52 13N 93 45W
McIntosh, U.S.A. 80 C4 45 55N 101 21W
McIntosh L., Canada 73 B8 55 45N 105 0W
Macintosh Ra., Australia 61 E4 27 39S 125 32 E
Macintyre →, Australia 63 D5 28 37S 150 47 E
Mackay, Australia 62 C4 21 8S 149 11 E
Mackay, U.S.A. 82 E7 43 55N 113 37W
MacKay →, Canada 72 B6 57 10N 111 38W
Mackay, L., Australia 60 D4 22 30S 129 0 E
McKay Ra., Australia 60 D3 23 0S 122 30 E
McKeesport, U.S.A. 78 F5 40 21N 79 52W
McKellar, Canada 78 A5 45 30N 79 55W
McKenna, U.S.A. 84 D4 46 56N 122 33W
Mackenzie, Canada 72 B4 55 20N 123 5W
McKenzie, U.S.A. 77 G1 36 8N 88 31W
Mackenzie →, Australia 62 C4 23 38S 149 46 E
Mackenzie →, Canada 68 B6 69 10N 134 20W
McKenzie →, U.S.A. 82 D2 44 7N 123 6W
Mackenzie Bay, Canada 4 B1 69 0N 137 30W
Mackenzie City = Linden, Guyana 92 B7 6 0N 58 10W
Mackenzie Mts., Canada 68 B6 64 0N 130 0W
Mackinaw City, U.S.A. 76 C3 45 47N 84 44W
McKinlay, Australia 62 C3 21 16S 141 18 E
McKinlay →, Australia 62 C3 20 50S 141 28 E
McKinley, Mt., U.S.A. 68 B4 63 4N 151 0W
McKinley Sea, Arctic 4 A7 82 0N 0 0W
McKinney, U.S.A. 81 J6 33 12N 96 37W
Mackinnon Road, Kenya 54 C4 3 40S 39 1 E
McKittrick, U.S.A. 85 K7 35 18N 119 37W
Macklin, Canada 73 C7 52 20N 109 56W
Macksville, Australia 63 E5 30 40S 152 56 E
McLaughlin, U.S.A. 80 C4 45 49N 100 49W
Maclean, Australia 63 D5 29 26S 153 16 E
McLean, U.S.A. 81 H4 35 14N 100 36W
McLeansboro, U.S.A. 80 F10 38 6N 88 32W
Maclear, S. Africa 57 E4 31 2S 28 23 E
Macleay →, Australia 63 E5 30 56S 153 0 E
McLennan, Canada 72 B5 55 42N 116 50W
McLeod →, Canada 72 C5 54 9N 115 44W
MacLeod, B., Canada 73 A7 62 53N 110 0W
McLeod, L., Australia 61 D1 24 9S 113 47 E
MacLeod Lake, Canada 72 C4 54 58N 123 0W
McLoughlin, Mt., U.S.A. 82 E2 42 27N 122 19W
McMechen, U.S.A. 78 G4 39 57N 80 44W
McMinnville, Oreg., U.S.A. 82 D2 45 13N 123 12W
McMinnville, Tenn., U.S.A. 77 H3 35 41N 85 46W
McMurdo Sd., Antarctica 5 D11 77 0S 170 0 E
McMurray = Fort McMurray, Canada 72 B6 56 44N 111 7W
McMurray, U.S.A. 84 B4 48 19N 122 14W
Macodoene, Mozam. 57 C6 23 32S 35 5 E
Macomb, U.S.A. 80 E9 40 27N 90 40W
Mâcon, France 18 C6 46 19N 4 50 E
Macon, Ga., U.S.A. 77 J4 32 51N 83 38W
Macon, Miss., U.S.A. 77 J1 33 7N 88 34W
Macon, Mo., U.S.A. 80 F8 39 44N 92 28W
Macossa, Mozam. 55 F3 17 55S 33 56 E
Macoun L., Canada 73 B8 56 32N 103 40W
Macovane, Mozam. 57 C6 21 30S 35 2 E
McPherson, U.S.A. 80 F6 38 22N 97 40W
McPherson Pk., U.S.A. 85 L7 34 53N 119 53W
McPherson Ra., Australia 63 D5 28 15S 153 15 E
Macquarie →, Australia 63 E4 30 5S 147 30 E
Macquarie Harbour, Australia 62 G4 42 15S 145 23 E
Macquarie Is., Pac. Oc. 64 N7 54 36S 158 55 E
MacRobertson Land, Antarctica 5 D6 71 0S 64 0 E
Macroom, Ireland 13 E3 51 54N 8 57W
MacTier, Canada 78 A5 45 9N 79 46W
Macubela, Mozam. 55 F4 16 53S 37 49 E
Macuiza, Mozam. 55 F3 18 7S 34 29 E
Macusani, Peru 92 F4 14 4S 70 29W
Macuse, Mozam. 55 F4 17 45S 37 10 E
Macuspana, Mexico 87 D6 17 46N 92 36W
Macusse, Angola 56 B3 17 48S 20 23 E
Madadeni, S. Africa 57 D5 27 43S 30 3 E
Madagascar ■, Africa 57 C8 20 0S 47 0 E
Madā'in Sālih, Si. Arabia 44 E3 26 46N 37 57 E
Madama, Niger 51 D8 22 0N 13 40 E
Madame I., Canada 71 C7 45 30N 60 58W
Madaripur, Bangla. 41 H17 23 19N 90 15 E
Madauk, Burma 41 L20 17 56N 96 52 E
Madawaska, Canada 78 A7 45 30N 78 0W
Madawaska →, Canada 78 A8 45 27N 76 21W
Madaya, Burma 41 H20 22 12N 96 10 E
Maddalena, Italy 20 D3 41 16N 9 23 E
Madeira, Atl. Oc. 22 D3 32 50N 17 0W
Madeira →, Brazil 92 D7 3 22S 58 45W
Madeleine, Îs. de la, Canada 71 C7 47 30N 61 40W
Madera, Mexico 86 B3 29 12N 108 7W
Madera, Calif., U.S.A. 84 J6 36 57N 120 3W
Madera, Pa., U.S.A. 78 F6 40 49N 78 26W
Madha, India 40 L9 18 0N 75 30 E
Madhavpur, India 42 J3 21 15N 69 58 E
Madhepura, India 43 F12 26 11N 86 23 E
Madhubani, India 43 F12 26 21N 86 7 E
Madhupur, India 43 G12 24 16N 86 39 E
Madhya Pradesh □, India 42 J8 22 50N 78 0 E
Madidi →, Bolivia 92 F5 12 32S 66 52W
Madikeri, India 40 N9 12 30N 75 45 E
Madill, U.S.A. 81 H6 34 6N 96 46W
Madimba, Dem. Rep. of the Congo 52 E3 4 58S 15 5 E
Ma'din, Syria 44 C3 35 45N 39 36 E
Madingou, Congo 52 E2 4 10S 13 33 E
Madirovalo, Madag. 57 B8 16 26S 46 32 E
Madison, Calif., U.S.A. 84 G5 38 41N 121 59W
Madison, Fla., U.S.A. 77 K4 30 28N 83 25W
Madison, Ind., U.S.A. 76 F3 38 44N 85 23W
Madison, Nebr., U.S.A. 80 E6 41 50N 97 27W
Madison, Ohio, U.S.A. 78 E3 41 46N 81 3W
Madison, S. Dak., U.S.A. 80 D6 44 0N 97 7W
Madison, Wis., U.S.A. 80 D10 43 4N 89 24W
Madison →, U.S.A. 82 D8 45 56N 111 31W
Madison Heights, U.S.A. 76 G6 37 25N 79 8W
Madisonville, Ky., U.S.A. 76 G2 37 20N 87 30W
Madisonville, Tex., U.S.A. 81 K7 30 57N 95 55W
Madista, Botswana 56 C4 21 15S 25 6 E
Madiun, Indonesia 36 F4 7 38S 111 32 E
Madoc, Canada 78 B7 44 30N 77 28W
Madona, Latvia 9 H22 56 53N 26 5 E
Madrakah, Ra's al, Oman 46 D6 19 0N 57 50 E
Madras = Chennai, India 40 N12 13 8N 80 19 E
Madras = Tamil Nadu □, India 40 P10 11 0N 77 0 E
Madras, U.S.A. 82 D3 44 38N 121 8W
Madre, Laguna, U.S.A. 81 M6 27 0N 97 30W
Madre, Sierra, Phil. 37 A6 17 0N 122 0 E
Madre de Dios →, Bolivia 92 F5 10 59S 66 8W
Madre de Dios, I., Chile 96 G1 50 20S 75 10W
Madre del Sur, Sierra, Mexico 87 D5 17 30N 100 0W
Madre Occidental, Sierra, Mexico 86 B3 27 0N 107 0W
Madre Oriental, Sierra, Mexico 86 C5 25 0N 100 0W
Madri, India 42 G5 24 16N 73 32 E
Madrid, Spain 19 B4 40 25N 3 45W
Madrid, U.S.A. 79 B9 44 45N 75 8W
Madura, Australia 61 F4 31 55S 127 0 E
Madura, Indonesia 37 G15 7 30S 114 0 E
Madura, Selat, Indonesia 37 G15 7 30S 113 20 E
Madurai, India 40 Q11 9 55N 78 10 E
Madurantakam, India 40 N11 12 30N 79 50 E
Mae Chan, Thailand 38 B2 20 9N 99 52 E
Mae Hong Son, Thailand 38 C2 19 16N 97 56 E
Mae Khlong →, Thailand 38 F3 13 24N 100 0 E
Mae Phrik, Thailand 38 D2 17 27N 99 7 E
Mae Ramat, Thailand 38 D2 16 58N 98 31 E
Mae Rim, Thailand 38 C2 18 54N 98 57 E
Mae Sot, Thailand 38 D2 16 43N 98 34 E
Mae Suai, Thailand 38 C2 19 39N 99 33 E
Mae Tha, Thailand 38 C2 18 28N 99 8 E
Maebashi, Japan 31 F9 36 24N 139 4 E
Maesteg, U.K. 11 F4 51 36N 3 40W
Maestra, Sierra, Cuba 88 B4 20 15N 77 0W
Maevatanana, Madag. 57 B8 16 56S 46 49 E
Mafeking = Mafikeng, S. Africa 56 D4 25 50S 25 38 E
Mafeking, Canada 73 C8 52 40N 101 10W
Mafeteng, Lesotho 56 D4 29 51S 27 15 E
Maffra, Australia 63 F4 37 53S 146 58 E
Mafia I., Tanzania 54 D4 7 45S 39 50 E
Mafikeng, S. Africa 56 D4 25 50S 25 38 E
Mafra, Brazil 95 B6 26 10S 49 55W
Mafra, Portugal 19 C1 38 55N 9 20W
Mafungabusi Plateau, Zimbabwe 55 F2 18 30S 29 8 E
Magadan, Russia 27 D16 59 38N 150 50 E
Magadi, Kenya 54 C4 1 54S 36 19 E
Magadi, L., Kenya 54 C4 1 54S 36 19 E
Magaliesburg, S. Africa 57 D4 26 0S 27 32 E
Magallanes, Estrecho de, Chile 96 G2 52 30S 75 0W
Magangué, Colombia 92 B4 9 14N 74 45W
Magdalen Is. = Madeleine, Îs. de la, Canada 71 C7 47 30N 61 40W
Magdalena, Argentina 94 D4 35 5S 57 30W
Magdalena, Bolivia 92 F6 13 13S 63 57W
Magdalena, Mexico 86 A2 30 50N 112 0W
Magdalena, U.S.A. 83 J10 34 7N 107 15W
Magdalena →, Colombia 92 A4 11 6N 74 51W
Magdalena →, Mexico 86 A2 30 40N 112 25W
Magdalena, B., Mexico 86 C2 24 30N 112 10W
Magdalena, Llano de la, Mexico 86 C2 25 0N 111 30W
Magdeburg, Germany 16 B6 52 7N 11 38 E
Magdelaine Cays, Australia 62 B5 16 33S 150 18 E
Magee, U.S.A. 81 K10 31 52N 89 44W
Magelang, Indonesia 36 F4 7 29S 110 13 E
Magellan's Str. = Magallanes, Estrecho de, Chile 96 G2 52 30S 75 0W
Magenta, L., Australia 61 F2 33 30S 119 2 E
Magerøya, Norway 8 A21 71 3N 25 40 E
Maggiore, Lago, Italy 18 D8 45 57N 8 39 E
Maghâgha, Egypt 51 C12 28 38N 30 50 E
Magherafelt, U.K. 13 B5 54 45N 6 37W
Maghreb, N. Afr. 50 B5 32 0N 4 0W
Magistralnyy, Russia 27 D11 56 16N 107 36 E
Magnetic Pole (North) = North Magnetic Pole, Canada 4 B2 77 58N 102 8W
Magnetic Pole (South) = South Magnetic Pole, Antarctica 5 C9 64 8S 138 8 E
Magnitogorsk, Russia 24 D10 53 27N 59 4 E
Magnolia, Ark., U.S.A. 81 J8 33 16N 93 14W
Magnolia, Miss., U.S.A. 81 K9 31 9N 90 28W
Magog, Canada 79 A12 45 18N 72 9W
Magoro, Uganda 54 B3 1 45N 34 12 E
Magosa = Famagusta, Cyprus 23 D12 35 8N 33 55 E
Magoulādhes, Greece 23 A3 39 45N 19 42 E
Magoye, Zambia 55 F2 16 1S 27 30 E
Magozal, Mexico 87 C5 21 34N 97 59W
Magpie, L., Canada 71 B7 51 0N 64 41W
Magrath, Canada 72 D6 49 25N 112 50W
Maguarinho, C., Brazil 93 D9 0 15S 48 30W
Magude, Mozam. 57 D5 25 2S 32 40 E
Mağusa = Famagusta, Cyprus 23 D12 35 8N 33 55 E
Maguse L., Canada 73 A9 61 40N 95 10W
Maguse Pt., Canada 73 A10 61 20N 93 50W
Magvana, India 42 H3 23 13N 69 22 E
Magwe, Burma 41 J19 20 10N 95 0 E
Maha Sarakham, Thailand 38 D4 16 12N 103 16 E
Mahābād, Iran 44 B5 36 50N 45 45 E
Mahabharat Lekh, Nepal 43 E10 28 30N 82 0 E
Mahabo, Madag. 57 C7 20 23S 44 40 E
Mahadeo Hills, India 43 H8 22 20N 78 30 E
Mahaffey, U.S.A. 78 F6 40 53N 78 44W
Mahagi, Dem. Rep. of the Congo 54 B3 2 20N 31 0 E
Mahajamba →, Madag. 57 B8 15 33S 47 8 E
Mahajamba, Helodranon' i, Madag. 57 B8 15 24S 47 5 E
Mahajan, India 42 E5 28 48N 73 56 E
Mahajanga, Madag. 57 B8 15 40S 46 25 E
Mahajanga □, Madag. 57 B8 17 0S 47 0 E
Mahajilo →, Madag. 57 B8 19 42S 45 22 E
Mahakam →, Indonesia 36 E5 0 35S 117 17 E
Mahalapye, Botswana 56 C4 23 1S 26 51 E
Mahallāt, Iran 45 C6 33 55N 50 30 E
Māhān, Iran 45 D8 30 5N 57 18 E
Mahan →, India 43 H10 23 30N 82 50 E
Mahanadi →, India 41 J15 20 20N 86 25 E
Mahananda →, India 43 G12 25 12N 87 52 E
Mahanoro, Madag. 57 B8 19 54S 48 48 E
Mahanoy City, U.S.A. 79 F8 40 49N 76 9W
Maharashtra □, India 40 J9 20 30N 75 30 E
Mahari Mts., Tanzania 54 D3 6 20S 30 0 E
Mahasham, W. →, Egypt 47 E3 30 15N 34 10 E
Mahasoa, Madag. 57 C8 22 12S 46 6 E
Mahasolo, Madag. 57 B8 19 7S 46 22 E
Mahattat ash Shīdiyah, Jordan 47 F4 29 55N 35 55 E
Mahattat 'Unayzah, Jordan 47 E4 30 30N 35 47 E
Mahavavy →, Madag. 57 B8 15 57S 45 54 E
Mahaxay, Laos 38 D5 17 22N 105 12 E
Mahbubnagar, India 40 L10 16 45N 77 59 E
Maḩḑah, Oman 45 E7 24 24N 55 59 E
Mahdia, Tunisia 51 A8 35 28N 11 0 E
Mahe, India 43 C8 33 10N 78 32 E
Mahendragarh, India 42 E7 28 17N 76 14 E
Mahenge, Tanzania 55 D4 8 45S 36 41 E
Maheno, N.Z. 59 L3 45 10S 170 50 E
Mahesana, India 42 H5 23 39N 72 26 E
Maheshwar, India 42 H6 22 11N 75 35 E
Mahgawan, India 43 F8 26 29N 78 37 E
Mahi →, India 42 H5 22 30N 72 55 E
Mahia Pen., N.Z. 59 H6 39 9S 177 55 E
Mahilyow, Belarus 17 B16 53 55N 30 18 E
Mahmud Kot, Pakistan 42 D4 30 16N 71 0 E
Mahnomen, U.S.A. 80 B7 47 19N 95 58W
Mahoba, India 43 G8 25 15N 79 55 E
Mahón = Maó, Spain 22 B11 39 53N 4 16 E
Mahone Bay, Canada 71 D7 44 30N 64 20W
Mahopac, U.S.A. 79 E11 41 22N 73 45W
Mahuva, India 42 J4 21 5N 71 48 E
Mai-Ndombe, L., Dem. Rep. of the Congo 52 E3 2 0S 18 20 E
Mai-Sai, Thailand 38 B2 20 20N 99 55 E
Maicurú →, Brazil 93 D8 2 14S 54 17W
Maidan Khula, Afghan. 42 C3 33 36N 69 50 E
Maidenhead, U.K. 11 F7 51 31N 0 42W
Maidstone, Canada 73 C7 53 5N 109 20W
Maidstone, U.K. 11 F8 51 16N 0 32 E
Maiduguri, Nigeria 51 F8 12 0N 13 20 E
Maihar, India 43 G9 24 16N 80 45 E
Maijdi, Bangla. 41 H17 22 48N 91 10 E
Maikala Ra., India 41 J12 22 0N 81 0 E
Mailani, India 43 E9 28 17N 80 21 E
Mailsi, Pakistan 42 E5 29 48N 72 15 E
Main →, Germany 16 C5 50 0N 8 18 E
Main →, U.K. 13 B5 54 48N 6 18W
Maine, France 18 C3 48 20N 0 15W
Maine □, U.S.A. 77 C11 45 20N 69 0W
Maine →, Ireland 13 D2 52 9N 9 45W
Maingkwan, Burma 41 F20 26 15N 96 37 E
Mainit, L., Phil. 37 C7 9 31N 125 30 E
Mainland, Orkney, U.K. 12 C5 58 59N 3 8W
Mainland, Shet., U.K. 12 A7 60 15N 1 22W
Mainoru, Australia 62 A1 14 0S 134 6 E
Mainpuri, India 43 F8 27 18N 79 4 E
Maintirano, Madag. 57 B7 18 3S 44 1 E
Mainz, Germany 16 C5 50 1N 8 14 E
Maipú, Argentina 94 D4 36 52S 57 50W
Maiquetía, Venezuela 92 A5 10 36N 66 57W
Mairabari, India 41 F18 26 30N 92 22 E
Maisí, Cuba 89 B5 20 17N 74 9W
Maisí, Pta. de, Cuba 89 B5 20 10N 74 10W
Maitland, N.S.W., Australia 63 E5 32 33S 151 36 E
Maitland, S. Austral., Australia 63 E2 34 23S 137 40 E
Maitland →, Canada 78 C3 43 45N 81 43W
Maiz, Is. del, Nic. 88 D3 12 15N 83 4W
Maizuru, Japan 31 G7 35 25N 135 22 E
Majalengka, Indonesia 37 G13 6 50S 108 13 E
Majene, Indonesia 37 E5 3 38S 118 57 E
Majorca = Mallorca, Spain 22 B10 39 30N 3 0 E
Makaha, Zimbabwe 57 B5 17 20S 32 39 E
Makalamabedi, Botswana 56 C3 20 19S 23 51 E
Makale, Indonesia 37 E5 3 6S 119 51 E
Makamba, Burundi 54 C2 4 8S 29 49 E
Makarikari = Makgadikgadi Salt Pans, Botswana 56 C4 20 40S 25 45 E
Makarovo, Russia 27 D11 57 40N 107 45 E
Makasar = Ujung Pandang, Indonesia 37 F5 5 10S 119 20 E
Makasar, Selat, Indonesia 37 E5 1 0S 118 20 E
Makasar, Str. of = Makasar, Selat, Indonesia 37 E5 1 0S 118 20 E
Makat, Kazakstan 25 E9 47 39N 53 19 E
Makedhonia □, Greece 21 D10 40 39N 22 0 E
Makedonija = Macedonia ■, Europe 21 D9 41 53N 21 40 E
Makeyevka = Makiyivka, Ukraine 25 E6 48 0N 38 0 E
Makgadikgadi Salt Pans, Botswana 56 C4 20 40S 25 45 E
Makhachkala, Russia 25 F8 43 0N 47 30 E
Makhmūr, Iraq 44 C4 35 46N 43 35 E
Makian, Indonesia 37 D7 0 20N 127 20 E
Makindu, Kenya 54 C4 2 18S 37 50 E
Makinsk, Kazakstan 26 D8 52 37N 70 26 E
Makiyivka, Ukraine 25 E6 48 0N 38 0 E
Makkah, Si. Arabia 46 C2 21 30N 39 54 E
Makkovik, Canada 71 A8 55 10N 59 10W
Makó, Hungary 17 E11 46 14N 20 33 E
Makokou, Gabon 52 D2 0 40N 12 50 E
Makongo, Dem. Rep. of the Congo 54 B2 3 25N 26 17 E
Makoro, Dem. Rep. of the Congo 54 B2 3 10N 29 59 E
Makrai, India 40 H10 22 2N 77 0 E
Makran Coast Range, Pakistan 40 G4 25 40N 64 0 E
Makrana, India 42 F6 27 2N 74 46 E
Makriyialos, Greece 23 D7 35 2N 25 59 E
Mākū, Iran 44 B5 39 15N 44 31 E
Makunda, Botswana 56 C3 22 30S 20 7 E
Makurazaki, Japan 31 J5 31 15N 130 20 E
Makurdi, Nigeria 50 G7 7 43N 8 35 E
Makūyeh, Iran 45 D7 28 7N 53 9 E
Makwassie, S. Africa 56 D4 27 17S 26 0 E
Makwiro, Zimbabwe 57 B5 17 58S 30 25 E

Mal B., Ireland 13 D2 52 50N 9 30W
Mala, Pta., Panama 88 E3 7 28N 80 2W
Malabar Coast, India 40 P9 11 0N 75 0 E
Malabo = Rey Malabo, Eq. Guin. 52 D1 3 45N 8 50 E
Malacca, Str. of, Indonesia 39 L3 3 0N 101 0 E
Malad City, U.S.A. 82 E7 42 12N 112 15W
Maladzyechna, Belarus 17 A14 54 20N 26 50 E
Málaga, Spain 19 D3 36 43N 4 23W
Malagarasi, Tanzania 54 D3 5 5S 30 50 E
Malagarasi →, Tanzania 54 D2 5 12S 29 47 E
Malagasy Rep. = Madagascar ■, Africa 57 C8 20 0S 47 0 E
Malahide, Ireland 13 C5 53 26N 6 9W
Malaimbandy, Madag. 57 C8 20 20S 45 36 E
Malakâl, Sudan 51 G12 9 33N 31 40 E
Malakand, Pakistan 42 B4 34 40N 71 55 E
Malakwal, Pakistan 42 C5 32 34N 73 13 E
Malamala, Indonesia 37 E6 3 21S 120 55 E
Malanda, Australia 62 B4 17 22S 145 35 E
Malang, Indonesia 36 F4 7 59S 112 45 E
Malangen, Norway 8 B18 69 24N 18 37 E
Malanje, Angola 52 F3 9 36S 16 17 E
Mälaren, Sweden 9 G17 59 30N 17 10 E
Malargüe, Argentina 94 D2 35 32S 69 30W
Malartic, Canada 70 C4 48 9N 78 9W
Malaryta, Belarus 17 C13 51 50N 24 3 E
Malatya, Turkey 25 G6 38 25N 38 20 E
Malawi ■, Africa 55 E3 11 55S 34 0 E
Malawi, L. = Nyasa, L., Africa 55 E3 12 30S 34 30 E
Malay Pen., Asia 39 J3 7 25N 100 0 E
Malaya Vishera, Russia 24 C5 58 55N 32 25 E
Malaybalay, Phil. 37 C7 8 5N 125 7 E
Malāyer, Iran 45 C6 34 19N 48 51 E
Malaysia ■, Asia 39 K4 5 0N 110 0 E
Malazgirt, Turkey 25 G7 39 10N 42 33 E
Malbon, Australia 62 C3 21 5S 140 17 E
Malbooma, Australia 63 E1 30 41S 134 11 E
Malbork, Poland 17 B10 54 3N 19 1 E
Malcolm, Australia 61 E3 28 51S 121 25 E
Malcolm, Pt., Australia 61 F3 33 48S 123 45 E
Maldah, India 43 G13 25 2N 88 9 E
Maldegem, Belgium 15 C3 51 14N 3 26 E
Malden, Mass., U.S.A. 79 D13 42 26N 71 4W
Malden, Mo., U.S.A. 81 G10 36 34N 89 57W
Malden I., Kiribati 65 H12 4 3S 155 1W
Maldives ■, Ind. Oc. 29 J11 5 0N 73 0 E
Maldonado, Uruguay 95 C5 34 59S 55 0W
Maldonado, Punta, Mexico 87 D5 16 19N 98 35W
Malé, Maldives 29 J11 4 0N 73 28 E
Malé Karpaty, Slovak Rep. 17 D9 48 30N 17 20 E
Maléa, Ákra, Greece 21 F10 36 28N 23 7 E
Malegaon, India 40 J9 20 30N 74 38 E
Malei, Mozam. 55 F4 17 12S 36 58 E
Malek Kandī, Iran 44 B5 37 9N 46 6 E
Malela, Dem. Rep. of the Congo 54 C2 4 22S 26 8 E
Malema, Mozam. 55 E4 14 57S 37 20 E
Máleme, Greece 23 D5 35 31N 23 49 E
Maleny, Australia 63 D5 26 45S 152 52 E
Malerkotla, India 42 D6 30 32N 75 58 E
Máles, Greece 23 D7 35 6N 25 35 E
Malgomaj, Sweden 8 D17 64 40N 16 30 E
Malha, Sudan 51 E11 15 8N 25 10 E
Malhargarh, India 42 G6 24 17N 74 59 E
Malheur →, U.S.A. 82 D5 44 4N 116 59W
Malheur L., U.S.A. 82 E4 43 20N 118 48W
Mali ■, Africa 50 E5 17 0N 3 0W
Mali →, Burma 41 G20 25 40N 97 40 E
Mali Kyun, Burma 38 F2 13 0N 98 20 E
Malibu, U.S.A. 85 L8 34 2N 118 41W
Maliku, Indonesia 37 E6 0 39S 123 16 E
Malili, Indonesia 37 E6 2 42S 121 6 E
Malimba, Mts., Dem. Rep. of the Congo 54 D2 7 30S 29 30 E
Malin Hd., Ireland 13 A4 55 23N 7 23W
Malin Pen., Ireland 13 A4 55 20N 7 17W
Malindi, Kenya 54 C5 3 12S 40 5 E
Malines = Mechelen, Belgium 15 C4 51 2N 4 29 E
Malino, Indonesia 37 D6 1 0N 121 0 E
Malinyi, Tanzania 55 D4 8 56S 36 0 E
Malita, Phil. 37 C7 6 19N 125 39 E
Maliwun, Burma 36 B1 10 17N 98 40 E
Maliya, India 42 H4 23 5N 70 46 E
Malkara, Turkey 21 D12 40 53N 26 53 E
Mallacoota Inlet, Australia 63 F4 37 34S 149 40 E
Mallaig, U.K. 12 D3 57 0N 5 50W
Mallawan, India 43 F9 27 4N 80 12 E
Mallawi, Egypt 51 C12 27 44N 30 44 E
Mállia, Greece 23 D7 35 17N 25 32 E
Mallión, Kólpos, Greece 23 D7 35 19N 25 27 E
Mallorca, Spain 22 B10 39 30N 3 0 E
Mallorytown, Canada 79 B9 44 29N 75 53W
Mallow, Ireland 13 D3 52 8N 8 39W
Malmberget, Sweden 8 C19 67 11N 20 40 E
Malmédy, Belgium 15 D6 50 25N 6 2 E
Malmesbury, S. Africa 56 E2 33 28S 18 41 E
Malmö, Sweden 9 J15 55 36N 12 59 E
Malolos, Phil. 37 B6 14 50N 120 49 E
Malombe L., Malawi 55 E4 14 40S 35 15 E
Malone, U.S.A. 79 B10 44 51N 74 18W
Måløy, Norway 9 F11 61 57N 5 6 E
Malpaso, Canary Is. 22 G1 27 43N 18 3W
Malpelo, I. de, Colombia 92 C2 4 3N 81 35W
Malpur, India 42 H5 23 21N 73 27 E
Malpura, India 42 F6 26 17N 75 23 E
Malta, Idaho, U.S.A. 82 E7 42 18N 113 22W
Malta, Mont., U.S.A. 82 B10 48 21N 107 52W
Malta ■, Europe 23 D2 35 55N 14 26 E
Maltahöhe, Namibia 56 C2 24 55S 17 0 E
Malton, Canada 78 C5 43 42N 79 38W
Malton, U.K. 10 C7 54 8N 0 49W
Maluku, Indonesia 37 E7 1 0S 127 0 E
Maluku □, Indonesia 37 E7 3 0S 128 0 E
Maluku Sea = Molucca Sea, Indonesia 37 E6 0 0 125 0 E
Malvan, India 40 L8 16 2N 73 30 E
Malvern, U.S.A. 81 H8 34 22N 92 49W
Malvern Hills, U.K. 11 E5 52 0N 2 19W
Malvinas, Is. = Falkland Is. □, Atl. Oc. 96 G5 51 30S 59 0W
Malya, Tanzania 54 C3 3 5S 33 38 E
Malyn, Ukraine 17 C15 50 46N 29 3 E
Malyy Lyakhovskiy, Ostrov, Russia 27 B15 74 7N 140 36 E
Mama, Russia 27 D12 58 18N 112 54 E
Mamanguape, Brazil 93 E11 6 50S 35 4W
Mamarr Mitlā, Egypt 47 E1 30 2N 32 54 E
Mamasa, Indonesia 37 E5 2 55S 119 20 E
Mambasa, Dem. Rep. of the Congo 54 B2 1 22N 29 3 E
Mamberamo →, Indonesia 37 E9 2 0S 137 50 E
Mambilima Falls, Zambia 55 E2 10 31S 28 45 E
Mambirima, Dem. Rep. of the Congo 55 E2 11 25S 27 33 E
Mambo, Tanzania 54 C4 4 52S 38 22 E
Mambrui, Kenya 54 C5 3 5S 40 5 E
Mamburao, Phil. 37 B6 13 13N 120 39 E
Mameigwess L., Canada 70 B2 52 35N 87 50W
Mammoth, U.S.A. 83 K8 32 43N 110 39W
Mammoth Cave Nat. Park, U.S.A. 76 G3 37 8N 86 13W
Mamoré →, Bolivia 92 F5 10 23S 65 53W
Mamou, Guinea 50 F3 10 15N 12 0W
Mamoudzou, Mayotte 49 H8 12 48S 45 14 E
Mampikony, Madag. 57 B8 16 6S 47 38 E
Mamuju, Indonesia 37 E5 2 41S 118 50 E
Mamuno, Botswana 56 C3 22 16S 20 1 E
Man, Ivory C. 50 G4 7 30N 7 40W
Man, I. of, U.K. 10 C3 54 15N 4 30W
Man-Bazar, India 43 H12 23 4N 86 39 E
Man Na, Burma 41 H20 23 27N 97 19 E
Mana →, Fr. Guiana 93 B8 5 45N 53 55W
Manaar, G. of = Mannar, G. of, Asia 40 Q11 8 30N 79 0 E
Manacapuru, Brazil 92 D6 3 16S 60 37W
Manacor, Spain 22 B10 39 34N 3 13 E
Manado, Indonesia 37 D6 1 29N 124 51 E
Managua, Nic. 88 D2 12 6N 86 20W
Managua, L. de, Nic. 88 D2 12 20N 86 30W
Manakara, Madag. 57 C8 22 8S 48 1 E
Manali, India 42 C7 32 16N 77 10 E
Manama = Al Manāmah, Bahrain 46 B5 26 10N 50 30 E
Manambao →, Madag. 57 B7 17 35S 44 0 E
Manambato, Madag. 57 A8 13 43S 49 7 E
Manambolo →, Madag. 57 B7 19 18S 44 22 E
Manambolosy, Madag. 57 B8 16 2S 49 40 E
Mananara, Madag. 57 B8 16 10S 49 46 E
Mananara →, Madag. 57 C8 23 21S 47 42 E
Mananjary, Madag. 57 C8 21 13S 48 20 E
Manantenina, Madag. 57 C8 24 17S 47 19 E
Manaos = Manaus, Brazil 92 D7 3 0S 60 0W
Manapire →, Venezuela 92 B5 7 42N 66 7W
Manapouri, N.Z. 59 L1 45 34S 167 39 E
Manapouri, L., N.Z. 59 L1 45 32S 167 32 E
Manār, Jabal, Yemen 46 E3 14 2N 44 17 E
Manaravolo, Madag. 57 C8 23 59S 45 39 E
Manas, China 32 B3 44 17N 85 56 E
Manas →, India 41 F17 26 12N 90 40 E
Manaslu, Nepal 43 E11 28 33N 84 33 E
Manasquan, U.S.A. 79 F10 40 8N 74 3W
Manassa, U.S.A. 83 H11 37 11N 105 56W
Manaung, Burma 41 K18 18 45N 93 40 E
Manaus, Brazil 92 D7 3 0S 60 0W
Manawan L., Canada 73 B8 55 24N 103 14W
Manbij, Syria 44 B3 36 31N 37 57 E
Manchegorsk, Russia 26 C4 67 54N 32 58 E
Manchester, U.K. 10 D5 53 29N 2 12W
Manchester, Calif., U.S.A. 84 G3 38 58N 123 41W
Manchester, Conn., U.S.A. 79 E12 41 47N 72 31W
Manchester, Ga., U.S.A. 77 J3 32 51N 84 37W
Manchester, Iowa, U.S.A. 80 D9 42 29N 91 27W
Manchester, Ky., U.S.A. 76 G4 37 9N 83 46W
Manchester, N.H., U.S.A. 79 D13 42 59N 71 28W
Manchester, N.Y., U.S.A. 78 D7 42 56N 77 16W
Manchester, Pa., U.S.A. 79 F8 40 4N 76 43W
Manchester, Tenn., U.S.A. 77 H2 35 29N 86 5W
Manchester, Vt., U.S.A. 79 C11 43 10N 73 5W
Manchester L., Canada 73 A7 61 28N 107 29W
Manchhar L., Pakistan 42 F2 26 25N 67 39 E
Manchuria = Dongbei, China 35 D13 45 0N 125 0 E
Manchurian Plain, China 28 E16 47 0N 124 0 E
Mand →, India 43 J10 21 42N 83 15 E
Mand →, Iran 45 D7 28 20N 52 30 E
Manda, Ludewe, Tanzania 55 E3 10 30S 34 40 E
Manda, Mbeya, Tanzania 54 D3 7 58S 32 29 E
Manda, Mbeya, Tanzania 55 D3 8 30S 32 49 E
Mandabé, Madag. 57 C7 21 0S 44 55 E
Mandaguari, Brazil 95 A5 23 32S 51 42W
Mandah = Töhöm, Mongolia 34 B5 44 27N 108 2 E
Mandal, Norway 9 G12 58 2N 7 25 E
Mandala, Puncak, Indonesia 37 E10 4 44S 140 20 E
Mandalay, Burma 41 J20 22 0N 96 4 E
Mandale = Mandalay, Burma 41 J20 22 0N 96 4 E
Mandalgarh, India 42 G6 25 12N 75 6 E
Mandalgovi, Mongolia 34 B4 45 45N 106 10 E
Mandalī, Iraq 44 C5 33 43N 45 28 E
Mandan, U.S.A. 80 B4 46 50N 100 54W
Mandar, Teluk, Indonesia 37 E5 3 35S 119 15 E
Mandaue, Phil. 37 B6 10 20N 123 56 E
Mandera, Kenya 54 B5 3 55N 41 53 E
Mandi, India 42 D7 31 39N 76 58 E
Mandi Dabwali, India 42 E6 29 58N 74 42 E
Mandimba, Mozam. 55 E4 14 20S 35 40 E
Mandioli, Indonesia 37 E7 0 40S 127 20 E
Mandla, India 43 H9 22 39N 80 30 E
Mandorah, Australia 60 B5 12 32S 130 42 E
Mandoto, Madag. 57 B8 19 34S 46 17 E
Mandra, Pakistan 42 C5 33 23N 73 12 E
Mandrare →, Madag. 57 D8 25 10S 46 30 E
Mandritsara, Madag. 57 B8 15 50S 48 49 E
Mandronarivo, Madag. 57 C8 21 7S 45 38 E
Mandsaur, India 42 G6 24 3N 75 8 E
Mandurah, Australia 61 F2 32 36S 115 48 E
Mandvi, India 42 H3 22 51N 69 22 E
Mandya, India 40 N10 12 30N 77 0 E
Mandzai, Pakistan 42 D2 30 55N 67 6 E
Maneh, Iran 45 B8 37 39N 57 7 E
Manera, Madag. 57 C7 22 55S 44 20 E
Maneroo Cr. →, Australia 62 C3 23 21S 143 53 E
Manfalût, Egypt 51 C12 27 20N 30 52 E
Manfredónia, Italy 20 D6 41 38N 15 55 E
Mangabeiras, Chapada das, Brazil 93 F9 10 0S 46 30W
Mangalia, Romania 17 G15 43 50N 28 35 E
Mangalore, India 40 N9 12 55N 74 47 E
Mangan, India 43 F13 27 31N 88 32 E
Mangaung, S. Africa 53 K5 29 10S 26 25 E
Mangawan, India 43 G9 24 41N 81 33 E
Mangaweka, N.Z. 59 H5 39 48S 175 47 E
Manggar, Indonesia 36 E3 2 50S 108 10 E
Manggawitu, Indonesia 37 E8 4 8S 133 32 E
Mangindrano, Madag. 57 A8 14 17S 48 58 E
Mangkalihat, Tanjung, Indonesia 37 D5 1 2N 118 59 E
Mangla, Pakistan 42 C5 33 7N 73 39 E
Mangla Dam, Pakistan 43 C5 33 9N 73 44 E
Manglaur, India 42 E7 29 44N 77 49 E
Mangnai, China 32 C4 37 52N 91 43 E
Mango, Togo 50 F6 10 20N 0 30 E
Mangoche, Malawi 55 E4 14 25S 35 16 E
Mangoky →, Madag. 57 C7 21 29S 43 41 E
Mangole, Indonesia 37 E6 1 50S 125 55 E
Mangombe, Dem. Rep. of the Congo 54 C2 1 20S 26 48 E
Mangonui, N.Z. 59 F4 35 1S 173 32 E
Mangoro →, Madag. 57 B8 20 0S 48 45 E
Mangrol, Mad. P., India 42 J4 21 7N 70 7 E
Mangrol, Raj., India 42 G6 25 20N 76 31 E
Mangueira, L. da, Brazil 95 C5 33 0S 52 50W
Mangum, U.S.A. 81 H5 34 53N 99 30W
Mangyshlak Poluostrov, Kazakstan 26 E6 44 30N 52 30 E
Manhattan, U.S.A. 80 F6 39 11N 96 35W
Manhiça, Mozam. 57 D5 25 23S 32 49 E
Mania →, Madag. 57 B8 19 42S 45 22 E
Manica, Mozam. 57 B5 18 58S 32 59 E
Manica □, Mozam. 57 B5 19 10S 33 45 E
Manicaland □, Zimbabwe 55 F3 19 0S 32 30 E
Manicoré, Brazil 92 E6 5 48S 61 16W
Manicouagan →, Canada 71 C6 49 30N 68 30W
Manicouagan, Rés., Canada 71 B6 51 5N 68 40W
Maniema □, Dem. Rep. of the Congo 54 C2 3 0S 26 0 E
Manīfah, Si. Arabia 45 E6 27 44N 49 0 E
Manifold, C., Australia 62 C5 22 41S 150 50 E
Manigotagan, Canada 73 C9 51 6N 96 18W
Manigotagan →, Canada 73 C9 51 7N 96 20W
Manihari, India 43 G12 25 21N 87 38 E
Manihiki, Cook Is. 65 J11 10 24S 161 1W
Manika, Plateau de la, Dem. Rep. of the Congo 55 E2 10 0S 25 5 E
Manikpur, India 43 G9 25 4N 81 7 E
Manila, Phil. 37 B6 14 40N 121 3 E
Manila, U.S.A. 82 F9 40 59N 109 43W
Manila B., Phil. 37 B6 14 40N 120 35 E
Manilla, Australia 63 E5 30 45S 150 43 E
Maningrida, Australia 62 A1 12 3S 134 13 E
Manipur □, India 41 G19 25 0N 94 0 E
Manipur →, Burma 41 H19 23 45N 94 20 E
Manisa, Turkey 21 E12 38 38N 27 30 E
Manistee, U.S.A. 76 C2 44 15N 86 19W
Manistee →, U.S.A. 76 C2 44 15N 86 21W
Manistique, U.S.A. 76 C2 45 57N 86 15W
Manito L., Canada 73 C7 52 43N 109 43W
Manitoba □, Canada 73 B9 55 30N 97 0W
Manitoba, L., Canada 73 C9 51 0N 98 45W
Manitou, Canada 73 D9 49 15N 98 32W
Manitou, L., Canada 71 B6 50 55N 65 17W
Manitou Is., U.S.A. 76 C3 45 8N 86 0W
Manitou Springs, U.S.A. 80 F2 38 52N 104 55W
Manitoulin I., Canada 70 C3 45 40N 82 30W
Manitouwadge, Canada 70 C2 49 8N 85 48W
Manitowoc, U.S.A. 76 C2 44 5N 87 40W
Manizales, Colombia 92 B3 5 5N 75 32W
Manja, Madag. 57 C7 21 26S 44 20 E
Manjacaze, Mozam. 57 C5 24 45S 34 0 E
Manjakandriana, Madag. 57 B8 18 55S 47 47 E
Manjhand, Pakistan 42 G3 25 50N 68 10 E
Manjil, Iran 45 B6 36 46N 49 30 E
Manjimup, Australia 61 F2 34 15S 116 6 E
Manjra →, India 40 K10 18 49N 77 52 E
Mankato, Kans., U.S.A. 80 F5 39 47N 98 13W
Mankato, Minn., U.S.A. 80 C8 44 10N 94 0W
Mankayane, Swaziland 57 D5 26 40S 31 4 E
Mankera, Pakistan 42 D4 31 23N 71 26 E
Mankota, Canada 73 D7 49 25N 107 5W
Manlay = Üydzin, Mongolia 34 B4 44 9N 107 0 E
Manmad, India 40 J9 20 18N 74 28 E
Mann Ranges, Australia 61 E5 26 6S 130 5 E
Manna, Indonesia 36 E2 4 25S 102 55 E
Mannahill, Australia 63 E3 32 25S 140 0 E
Mannar, Sri Lanka 40 Q11 9 1N 79 54 E
Mannar, G. of, Asia 40 Q11 8 30N 79 0 E
Mannar I., Sri Lanka 40 Q11 9 5N 79 45 E
Mannheim, Germany 16 D5 49 29N 8 29 E
Manning, Canada 72 B5 56 53N 117 39W
Manning, Oreg., U.S.A. 84 E3 45 45N 123 13W
Manning, S.C., U.S.A. 77 J5 33 42N 80 13W
Manning Prov. Park, Canada 72 D4 49 5N 120 45W
Mannum, Australia 63 E2 34 50S 139 20 E
Manoharpur, India 43 H11 22 23N 85 12 E
Manokwari, Indonesia 37 E8 0 54S 134 0 E
Manombo, Madag. 57 C7 22 57S 43 28 E
Manono, Dem. Rep. of the Congo 54 D2 7 15S 27 25 E
Manosque, France 18 E6 43 49N 5 47 E
Manotick, Canada 79 A9 45 13N 75 41W
Manouane →, Canada 71 C5 49 30N 71 10W
Manouane, L., Canada 71 B5 50 45N 70 45W
Manp'o, N. Korea 35 D14 41 6N 126 24 E
Manpojin = Manp'o, N. Korea 35 D14 41 6N 126 24 E
Manpur, Chhattisgarh, India 43 H10 23 17N 83 35 E
Manpur, Mad. P., India 42 H6 22 26N 75 37 E
Manresa, Spain 19 B6 41 48N 1 50 E
Mansa, Gujarat, India 42 H5 23 27N 72 45 E
Mansa, Punjab, India 42 E6 30 0N 75 27 E
Mansa, Zambia 55 E2 11 13S 28 55 E
Mansehra, Pakistan 42 B5 34 20N 73 15 E
Mansel I., Canada 69 B11 62 0N 80 0W
Mansfield, Australia 63 F4 37 4S 146 6 E
Mansfield, U.K. 10 D6 53 9N 1 11W
Mansfield, La., U.S.A. 81 J8 32 2N 93 43W
Mansfield, Mass., U.S.A. 79 D13 42 2N 71 13W
Mansfield, Ohio, U.S.A. 78 F2 40 45N 82 31W
Mansfield, Pa., U.S.A. 78 E7 41 48N 77 5W
Mansfield, Mt., U.S.A. 79 B12 44 33N 72 49W
Manson Creek, Canada 72 B4 55 37N 124 32W
Manta, Ecuador 92 D2 1 0S 80 40W
Mantalingajan, Mt., Phil. 36 C5 8 55N 117 45 E
Mantare, Tanzania 54 C3 2 42S 33 13 E
Manteca, U.S.A. 84 H5 37 48N 121 13W
Manteo, U.S.A. 77 H8 35 55N 75 40W
Mantes-la-Jolie, France 18 B4 48 58N 1 41 E
Manthani, India 40 K11 18 40N 79 35 E
Manti, U.S.A. 82 G8 39 16N 111 38W
Mantiqueira, Serra da, Brazil 95 A7 22 0S 44 0W
Manton, U.S.A. 76 C3 44 25N 85 24W
Mántova, Italy 20 B4 45 9N 10 48 E
Mänttä, Finland 9 E21 62 0N 24 40 E
Mantua = Mántova, Italy 20 B4 45 9N 10 48 E
Manu, Peru 92 F4 12 10S 70 51W
Manu →, Peru 92 F4 12 16S 70 55W
Manu'a Is., Amer. Samoa 59 B14 14 13S 169 35W
Manuel Alves →, Brazil 93 F9 11 19S 48 28W
Manui, Indonesia 37 E6 3 35S 123 5 E
Manukau, N.Z. 59 G5 40 43S 175 13 E
Manuripi →, Bolivia 92 F5 11 6S 67 36W
Many, U.S.A. 81 K8 31 34N 93 29W
Manyara, L., Tanzania 54 C4 3 40S 35 50 E
Manych-Gudilo, Ozero, Russia 25 E7 46 24N 42 38 E
Manyonga →, Tanzania 54 C3 4 10S 34 15 E
Manyoni, Tanzania 54 D3 5 45S 34 55 E
Manzai, Pakistan 42 C4 32 12N 70 15 E
Manzanares, Spain 19 C4 39 2N 3 22W
Manzanillo, Cuba 88 B4 20 20N 77 31W
Manzanillo, Mexico 86 D4 19 0N 104 20W
Manzanillo, Pta., Panama 88 E4 9 30N 79 40W
Manzano Mts., U.S.A. 83 J10 34 40N 106 20W
Manzarīyeh, Iran 45 C6 34 53N 50 50 E
Manzhouli, China 33 B6 49 35N 117 25 E
Manzini, Swaziland 57 D5 26 30S 31 25 E
Mao, Chad 51 F9 14 4N 15 19 E
Maó, Spain 22 B11 39 53N 4 16 E
Maoke, Pegunungan, Indonesia 37 E9 3 40S 137 30 E
Maolin, China 35 C12 43 58N 123 30 E
Maoming, China 33 D6 21 50N 110 54 E
Maoxing, China 35 B13 45 28N 124 40 E
Mapam Yumco, China 32 C3 30 45N 81 28 E
Mapastepec, Mexico 87 D6 15 26N 92 54W
Mapia, Kepulauan, Indonesia 37 D8 0 50N 134 20 E
Mapimí, Mexico 86 B4 25 50N 103 50W
Mapimí, Bolsón de, Mexico 86 B4 27 30N 104 15W
Mapinga, Tanzania 54 D4 6 40S 39 12 E
Mapinhane, Mozam. 57 C6 22 20S 35 0 E
Maple Creek, Canada 73 D7 49 55N 109 29W
Maple Valley, U.S.A. 84 C4 47 25N 122 3W
Mapleton, U.S.A. 82 D2 44 2N 123 52W
Mapuera →, Brazil 92 D7 1 5S 57 2W
Mapulanguene, Mozam. 57 C5 24 29S 32 6 E
Maputo, Mozam. 57 D5 25 58S 32 32 E
Maputo □, Mozam. 57 D5 26 0S 32 25 E
Maputo, B. de, Mozam. 57 D5 25 50S 32 45 E
Maqiaohe, China 35 B16 44 40N 130 30 E
Maqnā, Si. Arabia 44 D2 28 25N 34 50 E
Maquela do Zombo, Angola 52 F3 6 0S 15 15 E
Maquinchao, Argentina 96 E3 41 15S 68 50W
Maquoketa, U.S.A. 80 D9 42 4N 90 40W
Mar, Serra do, Brazil 95 B6 25 30S 49 0W
Mar Chiquita, L., Argentina 94 C3 30 40S 62 50W
Mar del Plata, Argentina 94 D4 38 0S 57 30W
Mar Menor, Spain 19 D5 37 40N 0 45W
Mara, Tanzania 54 C3 1 30S 34 32 E
Mara □, Tanzania 54 C3 1 45S 34 20 E
Maraã, Brazil 92 D5 1 52S 65 25W
Marabá, Brazil 93 E9 5 20S 49 5W
Maracá, I. de, Brazil 93 C8 2 10N 50 30W
Maracaibo, Venezuela 92 A4 10 40N 71 37W
Maracaibo, L. de, Venezuela 92 B4 9 40N 71 30W
Maracaju, Brazil 95 A4 21 38S 55 9W
Maracay, Venezuela 92 A5 10 15N 67 28W
Maradi, Niger 50 F7 13 29N 7 20 E
Marāgheh, Iran 44 B5 37 30N 46 12 E
Marāh, Si. Arabia 44 E5 25 0N 45 35 E
Marajó, I. de, Brazil 93 D9 1 0S 49 30W
Marākand, Iran 44 B5 38 51N 45 16 E
Maralal, Kenya 54 B4 1 0N 36 38 E
Maralinga, Australia 61 F5 30 13S 131 32 E
Maran, Malaysia 39 L4 3 35N 102 45 E
Marana, U.S.A. 83 K8 32 27N 111 13W
Maranboy, Australia 60 B5 14 40S 132 39 E
Marand, Iran 44 B5 38 30N 45 45 E
Marang, Malaysia 39 K4 5 12N 103 13 E
Maranguape, Brazil 93 D11 3 55S 38 50W
Maranhão = São Luís, Brazil 93 D10 2 39S 44 15W
Maranhão □, Brazil 93 E9 5 0S 46 0W
Maranoa →, Australia 63 D4 27 50S 148 37 E
Marañón →, Peru 92 D4 4 30S 73 35W
Marão, Mozam. 57 C5 24 18S 34 2 E
Maraş = Kahramanmaraş, Turkey 25 G6 37 37N 36 53 E
Marathasa, Cyprus 23 E11 34 59N 32 51 E
Marathon, Australia 62 C3 20 51S 143 32 E
Marathon, Canada 70 C2 48 44N 86 23W
Marathon, N.Y., U.S.A. 79 D8 42 27N 76 2W
Marathon, Tex., U.S.A. 81 K3 30 12N 103 15W
Marathóvouno, Cyprus 23 D12 35 13N 33 37 E
Maratua, Indonesia 37 D5 2 10N 118 35 E
Maravatío, Mexico 86 D4 19 51N 100 25W
Marāwih, U.A.E. 45 E7 24 18N 53 18 E
Marbella, Spain 19 D3 36 30N 4 57W
Marble Bar, Australia 60 D2 21 9S 119 44 E
Marble Falls, U.S.A. 81 K5 30 35N 98 16W
Marblehead, U.S.A. 79 D14 42 30N 70 51W
Marburg, Germany 16 C5 50 47N 8 46 E
March, U.K. 11 E8 52 33N 0 5 E
Marche, France 18 C4 46 5N 1 20 E
Marche-en-Famenne, Belgium 15 D5 50 14N 5 19 E
Marchena, Spain 19 D3 37 18N 5 23W
Marco, U.S.A. 77 N5 25 58N 81 44W
Marcos Juárez, Argentina 94 C3 32 42S 62 5W
Marcus I. = Minami-Tori-Shima, Pac. Oc. 64 E7 24 20N 153 58 E
Marcus Necker Ridge, Pac. Oc. 64 F9 20 0N 175 0 E
Marcy, Mt., U.S.A. 79 B11 44 7N 73 56W
Mardan, Pakistan 42 B5 34 20N 72 0 E
Mardin, Turkey 25 G7 37 20N 40 43 E
Maree, L., U.K. 12 D3 57 40N 5 26W
Mareeba, Australia 62 B4 16 59S 145 28 E
Mareetsane, S. Africa 56 D4 26 9S 25 25 E
Marek = Stanke Dimitrov, Bulgaria 21 C10 42 17N 23 9 E
Marengo, U.S.A. 80 E8 41 48N 92 4W
Marenyi, Kenya 54 C4 4 22S 39 8 E
Marerano, Madag. 57 C7 21 23S 44 52 E
Marfa, U.S.A. 81 K2 30 19N 104 1W
Marfa Pt., Malta 23 D1 35 59N 14 19 E
Margaret →, Australia 60 C4 18 9S 125 41 E
Margaret Bay, Canada 72 C3 51 20N 127 35W

Margaret L., *Canada* **72 B5** 58 56N 115 25W
Margaret River, *Australia* . . . **61 F2** 33 57S 115 4 E
Margarita, I. de, *Venezuela* . . **92 A6** 11 0N 64 0W
Margaritovo, *Russia* . . . . . . **30 C7** 43 25N 134 45 E
Margate, *S. Africa* . . . . **57 E5** 30 50S 30 20 E
Margate, *U.K.* . . . . **11 F9** 51 23N 1 23 E
Mārgow, Dasht-e, *Afghan.* . . **40 D3** 30 40N 62 30 E
Marguerite, *Canada* **72 C4** 52 30N 122 25W
Mari El □, *Russia* . . . . **24 C8** 56 30N 48 0 E
Mari Indus, *Pakistan* . . . . . . **42 C4** 32 57N 71 34 E
Mari Republic = Mari El □,
Russia . . . . **24 C8** 56 30N 48 0 E
María Elena, *Chile* **94 A2** 22 18S 69 40W
María Grande, *Argentina* . . . **94 C4** 31 45S 59 55W
Maria I., *N. Terr., Australia* . . **62 A2** 14 52S 135 45 E
Maria I., *Tas., Australia* . . . . . **62 G4** 42 35S 148 0 E
Maria van Diemen, C., *N.Z.* . **59 F4** 34 29S 172 40 E
Mariakani, *Kenya* . . . . **54 C4** 3 50S 39 27 E
Marian, *Australia* . . . . **62 C4** 21 9S 148 57 E
Marian L., *Canada* **72 A5** 63 0N 116 15W
Mariana Trench, *Pac. Oc.* . . . **28 H18** 13 0N 145 0 E
Marianao, *Cuba* **88 B3** 23 8N 82 24W
Marianna, *Ark., U.S.A.* **81 H9** 34 46N 90 46W
Marianna, *Fla., U.S.A.* **77 K3** 30 46N 85 14W
Marias →, *U.S.A.* **82 C8** 47 56N 110 30W
Mariato, Punta, *Panama* **88 E3** 7 12N 80 52W
Maribor, *Slovenia* . . . . **16 E8** 46 36N 15 40 E
Marico →, *Africa* . . . . **56 C4** 23 35S 26 57 E
Maricopa, *Ariz., U.S.A.* **83 K7** 33 4N 112 3W
Maricopa, *Calif., U.S.A.* **85 K7** 35 4N 119 24W
Marié →, *Brazil* **92 D5** 0 27S 66 26W
Marie Byrd Land, *Antarctica* . **5 D14** 79 30S 125 0W
Marie-Galante, *Guadeloupe* . **89 C7** 15 56N 61 16W
Mariecourt = Kangiqsujuaq,
Canada **69 B12** 61 30N 72 0W
Mariembourg, *Belgium* . . . . **15 D4** 50 6N 4 31 E
Mariental, *Namibia* . . . . **56 C2** 24 36S 18 0 E
Marienville, *U.S.A.* **78 E5** 41 28N 79 8W
Mariestad, *Sweden* . . . . **9 G15** 58 43N 13 50 E
Marietta, *Ga., U.S.A.* **77 J3** 33 57N 84 33W
Marietta, *Ohio, U.S.A.* **76 F5** 39 25N 81 27W
Marieville, *Canada* **79 A11** 45 26N 73 10W
Mariinsk, *Russia* . . . . **26 D9** 56 10N 87 20 E
Marijampolė, *Lithuania* . . . . **9 J20** 54 33N 23 19 E
Marília, *Brazil* **95 A6** 22 13S 50 0W
Marín, *Spain* **19 A1** 42 23N 8 42W
Marina, *U.S.A.* **84 J5** 36 41N 121 48W
Marinduque, *Phil.* . . . . **37 B6** 13 25N 122 0 E
Marine City, *U.S.A.* **78 D2** 42 43N 82 30W
Marinette, *U.S.A.* **76 C2** 45 6N 87 38W
Maringá, *Brazil* **95 A5** 23 26S 52 2W
Marion, *Ala., U.S.A.* **77 J2** 32 38N 87 19W
Marion, *Ill., U.S.A.* **81 G10** 37 44N 88 56W
Marion, *Ind., U.S.A.* **76 E3** 40 32N 85 40W
Marion, *Iowa, U.S.A.* **80 D9** 42 2N 91 36W
Marion, *Kans., U.S.A.* **80 F6** 38 21N 97 1W
Marion, *N.C., U.S.A.* **77 H5** 35 41N 82 1W
Marion, *Ohio, U.S.A.* **76 E4** 40 35N 83 8W
Marion, *S.C., U.S.A.* **77 H6** 34 11N 79 24W
Marion, *Va., U.S.A.* **77 G5** 36 50N 81 31W
Marion, L., *U.S.A.* **77 J5** 33 28N 80 10W
Mariposa, *U.S.A.* **84 H7** 37 29N 119 58W
Mariscal Estigarribia,
Paraguay **94 A3** 22 3S 60 40W
Maritime Alps = Maritimes,
Alpes, *Europe* . . . . **18 D7** 44 10N 7 10 E
Maritimes, Alpes, *Europe* . . . **18 D7** 44 10N 7 10 E
Maritsa = Évros →, *Greece* . . **21 D12** 41 40N 26 34 E
Maritsá, *Greece* . . . . **23 C10** 36 22N 28 8 E
Mariupol, *Ukraine* . . . . **25 E6** 47 5N 37 31 E
Marīvān, *Iran* . . . . **44 C5** 35 30N 46 25 E
Marj 'Uyūn, *Lebanon* . . . . . . **47 B4** 33 20N 35 35 E
Marka = Merca, *Somali Rep.* . **46 G3** 1 48N 44 50 E
Markazī □, *Iran* . . . . **45 C6** 35 0N 49 30 E
Markdale, *Canada* **78 B4** 44 19N 80 39W
Marked Tree, *U.S.A.* **81 H9** 35 32N 90 25W
Market Drayton, *U.K.* **10 E5** 52 54N 2 29W
Market Harborough, *U.K.* . . . **11 E7** 52 29N 0 55W
Market Rasen, *U.K.* **10 D7** 53 24N 0 20W
Markham, *Canada* **78 C5** 43 52N 79 16W
Markham, Mt., *Antarctica* . . . **5 E11** 83 0S 164 0 E
Markleeville, *U.S.A.* **84 G7** 38 42N 119 47W
Markovo, *Russia* . . . . **27 C17** 64 40N 170 24 E
Marks, *Russia* . . . . **24 D8** 51 45N 46 50 E
Marksville, *U.S.A.* **81 K8** 31 8N 92 4W
Marla, *Australia* . . . . **63 D1** 27 19S 133 33 E
Marlbank, *Canada* **78 B7** 44 26N 77 6W
Marlboro, *Mass., U.S.A.* **79 D13** 42 19N 71 33W
Marlboro, *N.Y., U.S.A.* **79 E11** 41 36N 73 59W
Marlborough, *Australia* . . . . . **62 C4** 22 46S 149 52 E
Marlborough, *U.K.* **11 F6** 51 25N 1 43W
Marlborough Downs, *U.K.* . . . **11 F6** 51 27N 1 53W
Marlin, *U.S.A.* **81 K6** 31 18N 96 54W
Marlow, *U.S.A.* **81 H6** 34 39N 97 58W
Marmagao, *India* . . . . **40 M8** 15 25N 73 56 E
Marmara, *Turkey* . . . . **21 D12** 40 35N 27 34 E
Marmara, Sea of = Marmara
Denizi, *Turkey* . . . . **21 D13** 40 45N 28 15 E
Marmara Denizi, *Turkey* . . . . **21 D13** 40 45N 28 15 E
Marmaris, *Turkey* . . . . **21 F13** 36 50N 28 14 E
Marmion, Mt., *Australia* . . . . **61 E2** 29 16S 119 50 E
Marmion L., *Canada* **70 C1** 48 55N 91 20W
Marmolada, Mte., *Italy* . . . . . **20 A4** 46 26N 11 51 E
Marmora, *Canada* **78 B7** 44 28N 77 41W
Marne →, *France* . . . . **18 B5** 48 48N 2 24 E
Maroala, *Madag.* . . . . **57 B8** 15 23S 47 59 E
Maroantsetra, *Madag.* . . . . . . **57 B8** 15 26S 49 44 E
Maroelaboom, *Namibia* . . . . . **56 B2** 19 15S 18 53 E
Marofandilia, *Madag.* . . . . . . **57 C7** 20 7S 44 34 E
Marolambo, *Madag.* . . . . **57 C8** 20 2S 48 7 E
Maromandia, *Madag.* . . . . . . **57 A8** 14 13S 48 5 E
Marondera, *Zimbabwe* . . . . . **55 F3** 18 5S 31 42 E
Maroni →, *Fr. Guiana* **93 B8** 5 30N 54 0W
Maroochydore, *Australia* . . . **63 D5** 26 29S 153 5 E
Maroona, *Australia* . . . . **63 F3** 37 27S 142 54 E
Marosakoa, *Madag.* . . . . **57 B8** 15 26S 46 38 E
Maroseranana, *Madag.* . . . . . **57 B8** 18 32S 48 51 E
Marotandrano, *Madag.* . . . . . **57 B8** 16 10S 48 50 E
Marotaolano, *Madag.* . . . . . . **57 A8** 12 47S 49 15 E
Maroua, *Cameroon* . . . . **51 F8** 10 40N 14 20 E
Marovato, *Madag.* . . . . **57 B8** 15 48S 48 5 E
Marovoay, *Madag.* . . . . **57 B8** 16 6S 46 39 E
Marquard, *S. Africa* . . . . **56 D4** 28 40S 27 28 E
Marquesas Is. = Marquises,
Is., *Pac. Oc.* **65 H14** 9 30S 140 0W
Marquette, *U.S.A.* **76 B2** 46 33N 87 24W
Marquises, Is., *Pac. Oc.* **65 H14** 9 30S 140 0W
Marra, Djebel, *Sudan* . . . . . . **51 F10** 13 10N 24 22 E
Marracuene, *Mozam.* . . . . **57 D5** 25 45S 32 35 E
Marrakech, *Morocco* **50 B4** 31 9N 8 0W
Marrawah, *Australia* . . . . **62 G3** 40 55S 144 42 E
Marree, *Australia* . . . . **63 D2** 29 39S 138 1 E
Marrero, *U.S.A.* **81 L9** 29 54N 90 6W
Marrimane, *Mozam.* . . . . **57 C5** 22 58S 33 34 E
Marromeu, *Mozam.* . . . . **57 B6** 18 15S 36 25 E
Marrowie Cr. →, *Australia* . . **63 E4** 33 23S 145 40 E
Marrubane, *Mozam.* . . . . **55 F4** 18 0S 37 0 E
Marrupa, *Mozam.* . . . . **55 E4** 13 8S 37 30 E
Mars Hill, *U.S.A.* **77 B12** 46 31N 67 52W
Marsá Matrûh, *Egypt* . . . . . . **51 B11** 31 19N 27 9 E
Marsabit, *Kenya* . . . . **54 B4** 2 18N 38 0 E
Marsala, *Italy* . . . . **20 F5** 37 48N 12 26 E
Marsalforn, *Malta* . . . . **23 C1** 36 4N 14 16 E
Marsden, *Australia* . . . . **63 E4** 33 47S 147 32 E
Marseille, *France* . . . . **18 E6** 43 18N 5 23 E
Marseilles = Marseille, *France* **18 E6** 43 18N 5 23 E
Marsh I., *U.S.A.* **81 L9** 29 34N 91 53W
Marshall, *Ark., U.S.A.* **81 H8** 35 55N 92 38W
Marshall, *Mich., U.S.A.* **76 D3** 42 16N 84 58W
Marshall, *Minn., U.S.A.* **80 C7** 44 25N 95 45W
Marshall, *Mo., U.S.A.* **80 F8** 39 7N 93 12W
Marshall, *Tex., U.S.A.* **81 J7** 32 33N 94 23W
Marshall →, *Australia* . . . . . **62 C2** 22 59S 136 59 E
Marshall Is. ■, *Pac. Oc.* . . . . . **64 G9** 9 0N 171 0 E
Marshalltown, *U.S.A.* **80 D8** 42 3N 92 55W
Marshbrook, *Zimbabwe* . . . . . **57 B5** 18 33S 31 9 E
Marshfield, *Mo., U.S.A.* **81 G8** 37 15N 92 54W
Marshfield, *Vt., U.S.A.* **79 B12** 44 20N 72 20W
Marshfield, *Wis., U.S.A.* **80 C9** 44 40N 90 10W
Marshūn, *Iran* . . . . **45 B6** 36 19N 49 23 E
Märsta, *Sweden* . . . . **9 G17** 59 37N 17 52 E
Mart, *U.S.A.* **81 K6** 31 33N 96 50W
Martaban, *Burma* . . . . **41 L20** 16 30N 97 35 E
Martaban, G. of, *Burma* . . . . **41 L20** 16 5N 96 30 E
Martapura, *Kalimantan,*
Indonesia . . . . **36 E4** 3 22S 114 47 E
Martapura, *Sumatera,*
Indonesia . . . . **36 E2** 4 19S 104 22 E
Martelange, *Belgium* . . . . **15 E5** 49 49N 5 43 E
Martha's Vineyard, *U.S.A.* . . . **79 E14** 41 25N 70 38W
Martigny, *Switz.* . . . . **18 C7** 46 6N 7 3 E
Martigues, *France* . . . . **18 E6** 43 24N 5 4 E
Martin, *Slovak Rep.* . . . . **17 D10** 49 6N 18 58 E
Martin, *S. Dak., U.S.A.* **80 D4** 43 11N 101 44W
Martin, *Tenn., U.S.A.* **81 G10** 36 21N 88 51W
Martin, L., *U.S.A.* **77 J3** 32 41N 85 55W
Martina Franca, *Italy* . . . . . . **20 D7** 40 42N 17 20 E
Martinborough, *N.Z.* . . . . **59 J5** 41 14S 175 29 E
Martinez, *Calif., U.S.A.* **84 G4** 38 1N 122 8W
Martinez, *Ga., U.S.A.* **77 J4** 33 31N 82 4W
Martinique ■, *W. Indies* **89 D7** 14 40N 61 0W
Martinique Passage,
W. Indies **89 C7** 15 15N 61 0W
Martinópolis, *Brazil* **95 A5** 22 11S 51 12W
Martins Ferry, *U.S.A.* **78 F4** 40 6N 80 44W
Martinsburg, *Pa., U.S.A.* **78 F6** 40 19N 78 20W
Martinsburg, *W. Va., U.S.A.* . . **76 F7** 39 27N 77 58W
Martinsville, *Ind., U.S.A.* **76 F2** 39 26N 86 25W
Martinsville, *Va., U.S.A.* **77 G6** 36 41N 79 52W
Marton, *N.Z.* . . . . **59 J5** 40 4S 175 23 E
Martos, *Spain* **19 D4** 37 44N 3 58W
Marudi, *Malaysia* . . . . **36 D4** 4 11N 114 19 E
Maruf, *Afghan.* . . . . **40 D5** 31 30N 67 6 E
Marugame, *Japan* . . . . **31 G6** 34 15N 133 40 E
Marunga, *Angola* . . . . **56 B3** 17 28S 20 2 E
Marungu, Mts., *Dem. Rep. of*
the Congo . . . . **54 D3** 7 30S 30 0 E
Marv Dasht, *Iran* . . . . **45 D7** 29 50N 52 40 E
Marvast, *Iran* . . . . **45 D7** 30 30N 54 15 E
Marvel Loch, *Australia* . . . . . **61 F2** 31 28S 119 29 E
Marwar, *India* . . . . **42 G5** 25 43N 73 45 E
Mary, *Turkmenistan* . . . . **26 F7** 37 40N 61 50 E
Maryborough = Port Laoise,
Ireland **13 C4** 53 2N 7 18W
Maryborough, *Queens.,*
Australia . . . . **63 D5** 25 31S 152 37 E
Maryborough, *Vic., Australia* **63 F3** 37 0S 143 44 E
Maryfield, *Canada* **73 D8** 49 50N 101 35W
Maryland □, *U.S.A.* **76 F7** 39 0N 76 30W
Maryland Junction,
Zimbabwe . . . . **55 F3** 17 45S 30 31 E
Maryport, *U.K.* **10 C4** 54 44N 3 28W
Mary's Harbour, *Canada* **71 B8** 52 18N 55 51W
Marystown, *Canada* **71 C8** 47 10N 55 10W
Marysville, *Canada* **72 D5** 49 35N 116 0W
Marysville, *Calif., U.S.A.* **84 F5** 39 9N 121 35W
Marysville, *Kans., U.S.A.* **80 F6** 39 51N 96 39W
Marysville, *Mich., U.S.A.* **78 D2** 42 54N 82 29W
Marysville, *Ohio, U.S.A.* **76 E4** 40 14N 83 22W
Marysville, *Wash., U.S.A.* **84 B4** 48 3N 122 11W
Maryville, *Mo., U.S.A.* **80 E7** 40 21N 94 52W
Maryville, *Tenn., U.S.A.* **77 H4** 35 46N 83 58W
Marzūq, *Libya* . . . . **51 C8** 25 53N 13 57 E
Masahunga, *Tanzania* . . . . . . **54 C3** 2 6S 33 18 E
Masai Steppe, *Tanzania* . . . . **54 C4** 4 30S 36 30 E
Masaka, *Uganda* . . . . **54 C3** 0 21S 31 45 E
Masalembo, Kepulauan,
Indonesia . . . . **36 F4** 5 35S 114 30 E
Masalima, Kepulauan,
Indonesia . . . . **36 F5** 5 4S 117 5 E
Masamba, *Indonesia* . . . . **37 E6** 2 30S 120 15 E
Masan, *S. Korea* . . . . **35 G15** 35 11N 128 32 E
Masandam, Ra's, *Oman* . . . . **46 B6** 26 30N 56 30 E
Masasi, *Tanzania* . . . . **55 E4** 10 45S 38 52 E
Masaya, *Nic.* **88 D2** 12 0N 86 7W
Masbate, *Phil.* . . . . **37 B6** 12 21N 123 36 E
Mascara, *Algeria* . . . . **50 A6** 35 26N 0 6 E
Mascota, *Mexico* **86 C4** 20 30N 104 50W
Masela, *Indonesia* . . . . **37 F7** 8 9S 129 51 E
Maseru, *Lesotho* . . . . **56 D4** 29 18S 27 30 E
Mashaba, *Zimbabwe* . . . . **55 G3** 20 2S 30 29 E
Mashābih, *Si. Arabia* . . . . . . **44 E3** 25 35N 36 30 E
Masherbrum, *Pakistan* . . . . . **43 B7** 35 38N 76 18 E
Mashhad, *Iran* . . . . **45 B8** 36 20N 59 35 E
Mashīz, *Iran* . . . . **45 D8** 29 56N 56 37 E
Mashkel, Hāmūn-i-, *Pakistan* **40 E3** 28 20N 62 56 E
Mashki Chāh, *Pakistan* . . . . . **40 E3** 29 5N 62 30 E
Mashonaland, *Zimbabwe* . . . . **53 H6** 16 30S 31 0 E
Mashonaland Central □,
Zimbabwe . . . . **57 B5** 17 30S 31 0 E
Mashonaland East □,
Zimbabwe . . . . **57 B5** 18 0S 32 0 E
Mashonaland West □,
Zimbabwe . . . . **57 B4** 17 30S 29 30 E
Mashrakh, *India* . . . . **43 F11** 26 7N 84 48 E
Masindi, *Uganda* . . . . **54 B3** 1 40N 31 43 E
Masindi Port, *Uganda* . . . . . . **54 B3** 1 43N 32 2 E
Maşīrah, *Oman* . . . . **46 C6** 21 0N 58 50 E
Maşīrah, Khalīj, *Oman* . . . . . **46 C6** 20 10N 58 10 E
Masisi, *Dem. Rep. of*
the Congo . . . . **54 C2** 1 23S 28 49 E
Masjed Soleyman, *Iran* . . . . . **45 D6** 31 55N 49 18 E
Mask, L., *Ireland* **13 C2** 53 36N 9 22W
Maskin, *Oman* . . . . **45 F8** 23 30N 56 50 E
Masoala, Tanjon' i, *Madag.* . **57 B9** 15 59S 50 13 E
Masoarivo, *Madag.* . . . . **57 B7** 19 3S 44 19 E
Masohi = Amahai, *Indonesia* **37 E7** 3 20S 128 55 E
Masomeloka, *Madag.* . . . . **57 C8** 20 17S 48 37 E
Mason, *Nev., U.S.A.* **84 G7** 38 56N 119 8W
Mason, *Tex., U.S.A.* **81 K5** 30 45N 99 14W
Mason City, *U.S.A.* **80 D8** 43 9N 93 12W
Maspalomas, *Canary Is.* **22 G4** 27 46N 15 35W
Maspalomas, Pta., *Canary Is.* **22 G4** 27 43N 15 36W
Masqat, *Oman* . . . . **46 C6** 23 37N 58 36 E
Massa, *Italy* . . . . **18 D9** 44 1N 10 9 E
Massachusetts □, *U.S.A.* . . . **79 D13** 42 30N 72 0W
Massachusetts B., *U.S.A.* . . . **79 D14** 42 20N 70 50W
Massakory, *Chad* . . . . **51 F9** 13 0N 15 49 E
Massanella, *Spain* . . . . **22 B9** 39 48N 2 51 E
Massangena, *Mozam.* . . . . . . **57 C5** 21 34S 33 0 E
Massango, *Angola* . . . . **52 F3** 8 2S 16 21 E
Massawa = Mitsiwa, *Eritrea* . **46 D2** 15 35N 39 25 E
Massena, *U.S.A.* **79 B10** 44 56N 74 54W
Massénya, *Chad* . . . . **51 F9** 11 21N 16 9 E
Masset, *Canada* **72 C2** 54 2N 132 10W
Massif Central, *France* . . . . . **18 D5** 44 55N 3 0 E
Massillon, *U.S.A.* **78 F3** 40 48N 81 32W
Massinga, *Mozam.* . . . . **57 C6** 23 15S 35 22 E
Massingir, *Mozam.* . . . . **57 C5** 23 51S 32 4 E
Masson, *Canada* **79 A9** 45 32N 75 25W
Masson I., *Antarctica* . . . . . . **5 C7** 66 10S 93 20 E
Mastanli = Momchilgrad,
Bulgaria . . . . **21 D11** 41 33N 25 23 E
Masterton, *N.Z.* . . . . **59 J5** 40 56S 175 39 E
Mastic, *U.S.A.* **79 F12** 40 47N 72 54W
Mastuj, *Pakistan* . . . . **43 A5** 36 20N 72 36 E
Mastung, *Pakistan* . . . . **40 E5** 29 50N 66 56 E
Masty, *Belarus* . . . . **17 B13** 53 27N 24 38 E
Masuda, *Japan* . . . . **31 G5** 34 40N 131 51 E
Masvingo, *Zimbabwe* . . . . **55 G3** 20 8S 30 49 E
Masvingo □, *Zimbabwe* . . . . **55 G3** 21 0S 31 30 E
Maşyāf, *Syria* . . . . **44 C3** 35 4N 36 20 E
Matabeleland, *Zimbabwe* . . . . **53 H5** 18 0S 27 0 E
Matabeleland North □,
Zimbabwe . . . . **55 F2** 19 0S 28 0 E
Matabeleland South □,
Zimbabwe . . . . **55 G2** 21 0S 29 0 E
Matachewan, *Canada* **70 C3** 47 56N 80 39W
Matadi, *Dem. Rep. of*
the Congo . . . . **52 F2** 5 52S 13 31 E
Matagalpa, *Nic.* **88 D2** 13 0N 85 58W
Matagami, *Canada* **70 C4** 49 45N 77 34W
Matagami, L., *Canada* **70 C4** 49 50N 77 40W
Matagorda B., *U.S.A.* **81 L6** 28 40N 96 0W
Matagorda I., *U.S.A.* **81 L6** 28 15N 96 30W
Matak, *Indonesia* . . . . **39 L6** 3 18N 106 16 E
Mátala, *Greece* . . . . **23 E6** 34 59N 24 45 E
Matam, *Senegal* **50 E3** 15 34N 13 17W
Matamoros, *Campeche,*
Mexico **87 D6** 18 50N 90 50W
Matamoros, *Coahuila, Mexico* **86 B4** 25 33N 103 15W
Matamoros, *Tamaulipas,*
Mexico **87 B5** 25 50N 97 30W
Ma'ṭan as Sarra, *Libya* . . . . . **51 D10** 21 45N 22 0 E
Matandu →, *Tanzania* . . . . . **55 D3** 8 45S 34 19 E
Matane, *Canada* **71 C6** 48 50N 67 33W
Matanomadh, *India* . . . . **42 H3** 23 33N 68 57 E
Matanzas, *Cuba* **88 B3** 23 0N 81 40W
Matapa, *Botswana* . . . . **56 C3** 23 11S 24 39 E
Matapan, C. = Tainaron, Ákra,
Greece . . . . **21 F10** 36 22N 22 27 E
Matapédia, *Canada* **71 C6** 48 0N 66 59W
Matara, *Sri Lanka* . . . . **40 S12** 5 58N 80 30 E
Mataram, *Indonesia* . . . . **36 F5** 8 35S 116 7 E
Matarani, *Peru* **92 G4** 17 0S 72 10W
Mataranka, *Australia* . . . . **60 B5** 14 55S 133 4 E
Matarma, Râs, *Egypt* . . . . **47 E1** 30 27N 32 44 E
Mataró, *Spain* . . . . **19 B7** 41 32N 2 29 E
Matatiele, *S. Africa* . . . . **57 E4** 30 20S 28 49 E
Mataura, *N.Z.* . . . . **59 M2** 46 11S 168 51 E
Matehuala, *Mexico* **86 C4** 23 40N 100 40W
Mateke Hills, *Zimbabwe* . . . . **55 G3** 21 48S 31 0 E
Matera, *Italy* . . . . **20 D7** 40 40N 16 36 E
Matetsi, *Zimbabwe* . . . . **55 F2** 18 12S 26 0 E
Mathis, *U.S.A.* **81 L6** 28 6N 97 50W
Mathráki, *Greece* . . . . **23 A3** 39 48N 19 31 E
Mathura, *India* . . . . **42 F7** 27 30N 77 40 E
Mati, *Phil.* . . . . **37 C7** 6 55N 126 15 E
Matiali, *India* . . . . **43 F13** 26 56N 88 49 E
Matías Romero, *Mexico* **87 D5** 16 53N 95 2W
Matibane, *Mozam.* . . . . **55 E5** 14 49S 40 45 E
Matima, *Botswana* . . . . **56 C3** 20 15S 24 26 E
Matiri Ra., *N.Z.* . . . . **59 J4** 41 38S 172 20 E
Matjiesfontein, *S. Africa* . . . . **56 E3** 33 14S 20 35 E
Matla →, *India* . . . . **43 J13** 21 40N 88 40 E
Matlamanyane, *Botswana* . . . **56 B4** 19 33S 25 57 E
Matli, *Pakistan* . . . . **42 G3** 25 2N 68 39 E
Matlock, *U.K.* **10 D6** 53 9N 1 33W
Mato Grosso □, *Brazil* **93 F8** 14 0S 55 0W
Mato Grosso, Planalto do,
Brazil **93 G8** 15 0S 55 0W
Mato Grosso do Sul □, *Brazil* **93 G8** 18 0S 55 0W
Matochkin Shar, *Russia* . . . . . **26 B6** 73 10N 56 40 E
Matopo Hills, *Zimbabwe* . . . . **55 G2** 20 36S 28 20 E
Matopos, *Zimbabwe* . . . . **55 G2** 20 20S 28 29 E
Matosinhos, *Portugal* **19 B1** 41 11N 8 42W
Matroosberg, *S. Africa* . . . . . **56 E2** 33 23S 19 40 E
Maṭruḥ, *Oman* . . . . **46 C6** 23 37N 58 30 E
Matsue, *Japan* . . . . **31 G6** 35 25N 133 10 E
Matsumae, *Japan* . . . . **30 D10** 41 26N 140 7 E
Matsumoto, *Japan* . . . . **31 F9** 36 15N 138 0 E
Matsusaka, *Japan* . . . . **31 G8** 34 34N 136 32 E
Matsuura, *Japan* . . . . **31 H4** 33 20N 129 49 E
Matsuyama, *Japan* . . . . **31 H6** 33 45N 132 45 E
Mattagami →, *Canada* **70 B3** 50 43N 81 29W
Mattancheri, *India* . . . . **40 Q10** 9 50N 76 15 E
Mattawa, *Canada* **70 C4** 46 20N 78 45W
Matterhorn, *Switz.* . . . . **18 D7** 45 58N 7 39 E
Matthew Town, *Bahamas* . . . **89 B5** 20 57N 73 40W
Matthew's Ridge, *Guyana* . . . **92 B6** 7 37N 60 10W
Mattice, *Canada* **70 C3** 49 40N 83 20W
Mattituck, *U.S.A.* **79 F12** 40 59N 72 32W
Mattō, *Japan* . . . . **31 F8** 36 31N 136 34 E
Mattoon, *U.S.A.* **76 F1** 39 29N 88 23W
Matuba, *Mozam.* . . . . **57 C5** 24 28S 32 49 E
Matucana, *Peru* **92 F3** 11 55S 76 25W
Matūn = Khowst, *Afghan.* . . . **42 C3** 33 22N 69 58 E
Maturín, *Venezuela* **92 B6** 9 45N 63 11W
Mau, *Mad. P., India* . . . . **43 F8** 26 17N 78 41 E
Mau, *Ut. P., India* . . . . **43 G10** 25 56N 83 33 E
Mau, *Ut. P., India* . . . . **43 G9** 25 17N 81 23 E
Mau Escarpment, *Kenya* . . . . **54 C4** 0 40S 36 0 E
Mau Ranipur, *India* . . . . **43 G8** 25 16N 79 8 E
Maubeuge, *France* . . . . **18 A6** 50 17N 3 57 E
Maud, Pt., *Australia* . . . . **60 D1** 23 6S 113 45 E
Maude, *Australia* . . . . **63 E3** 34 29S 144 18 E
Maudin Sun, *Burma* . . . . **41 M19** 16 0N 94 30 E
Maués, *Brazil* **92 D7** 3 20S 57 45W
Mauganj, *India* . . . . **41 G12** 24 50N 81 55 E
Maughold Hd., *U.K.* **10 C3** 54 18N 4 18W
Maui, *U.S.A.* **74 H16** 20 48N 156 20W
Maulamyaing = Moulmein,
Burma . . . . **41 L20** 16 30N 97 40 E
Maule □, *Chile* **94 D1** 36 5S 72 30W
Maumee, *U.S.A.* **76 E4** 41 34N 83 39W
Maumee →, *U.S.A.* **76 E4** 41 42N 83 28W
Maumere, *Indonesia* . . . . **37 F6** 8 38S 122 13 E
Maun, *Botswana* . . . . **56 C3** 20 0S 23 26 E
Mauna Kea, *U.S.A.* **74 J17** 19 50N 155 28W
Mauna Loa, *U.S.A.* **74 J17** 19 30N 155 35W
Maungmagan Kyunzu, *Burma* **38 E1** 14 0N 97 48 E
Maupin, *U.S.A.* **82 D3** 45 11N 121 5W
Maurepas, L., *U.S.A.* **81 K9** 30 15N 90 30W
Maurice, L., *Australia* . . . . . . **61 E5** 29 30S 131 0 E
Mauricie, Parc Nat. de la,
Canada **70 C5** 46 45N 73 0W
Mauritania ■, *Africa* **50 E3** 20 50N 10 0W
Mauritius ■, *Ind. Oc.* . . . . **49 J9** 20 0S 57 0 E
Mauston, *U.S.A.* **80 D9** 43 48N 90 5W
Mavli, *India* . . . . **42 G5** 24 45N 73 55 E
Mavuradonha Mts.,
Zimbabwe . . . . **55 F3** 16 30S 31 30 E
Mawa, *Dem. Rep. of*
the Congo . . . . **54 B2** 2 45N 26 40 E
Mawai, *India* . . . . **43 H9** 22 30N 81 4 E
Mawana, *India* . . . . **42 E7** 29 6N 77 58 E
Mawand, *Pakistan* . . . . **42 E3** 29 33N 68 38 E
Mawk Mai, *Burma* . . . . **41 J20** 20 14N 97 37 E
Mawlaik, *Burma* . . . . **41 H19** 23 40N 94 26 E
Mawlamyine = Moulmein,
Burma . . . . **41 L20** 16 30N 97 40 E
Mawqaq, *Si. Arabia* . . . . **44 E4** 27 25N 41 8 E
Mawson Coast, *Antarctica* . . **5 C6** 68 30S 63 0 E
Max, *U.S.A.* **80 B4** 47 49N 101 18W
Maxcanú, *Mexico* **87 C6** 20 40N 92 0W
Maxesibeni, *S. Africa* . . . . **57 E4** 30 49S 29 23 E
Maxhamish L., *Canada* **72 B4** 59 50N 123 17W
Maxixe, *Mozam.* . . . . **57 C6** 23 54S 35 17 E
Maxville, *Canada* **79 A10** 45 17N 74 51W
Maxwell, *U.S.A.* **84 F4** 39 17N 122 11W
Maxwelton, *Australia* . . . . **62 C3** 20 43S 142 41 E
May, C., *U.S.A.* **76 F8** 38 56N 74 58W
May Pen, *Jamaica* **88 C4** 17 58N 77 15W
Maya →, *Russia* . . . . **27 D14** 60 28N 134 28 E
Maya Mts., *Belize* **87 D7** 16 30N 89 0W
Mayaguana, *Bahamas* **89 B5** 22 30N 72 44W
Mayagüez, *Puerto Rico* **89 C6** 18 12N 67 9W
Mayāmey, *Iran* . . . . **45 B7** 36 24N 55 42 E
Mayanup, *Australia* . . . . **61 F2** 33 57S 116 27 E
Mayapan, *Mexico* **87 C7** 20 30N 89 25W
Mayarí, *Cuba* **89 B4** 20 40N 75 41W
Maybell, *U.S.A.* **82 F9** 40 31N 108 5W
Maybole, *U.K.* **12 F4** 55 21N 4 42W
Maydān, *Iraq* . . . . **44 C5** 34 55N 45 37 E
Maydena, *Australia* . . . . **62 G4** 42 45S 146 30 E
Mayenne →, *France* **18 C3** 47 30N 0 32W
Mayer, *U.S.A.* **83 J7** 34 24N 112 14W
Mayerthorpe, *Canada* **72 C5** 53 57N 115 8W
Mayfield, *Ky., U.S.A.* **77 G1** 36 44N 88 38W
Mayfield, *N.Y., U.S.A.* **79 C10** 43 6N 74 16W
Mayhill, *U.S.A.* **83 K11** 32 53N 105 29W
Maykop, *Russia* . . . . **25 F7** 44 35N 40 10 E
Maymyo, *Burma* . . . . **38 A1** 22 2N 96 28 E
Maynard, *Mass., U.S.A.* **79 D13** 42 26N 71 27W
Maynard, *Wash., U.S.A.* **84 C4** 47 59N 122 55W
Maynard Hills, *Australia* . . . . **61 E2** 28 28S 119 49 E
Mayne →, *Australia* . . . . **62 C3** 23 40S 141 55 E
Maynooth, *Ireland* **13 C5** 53 23N 6 34W
Mayo, *Canada* **68 B6** 63 38N 135 57W
Mayo □, *Ireland* **13 C2** 53 53N 9 3W
Mayon Volcano, *Phil.* . . . . **37 B6** 13 15N 123 41 E
Mayor I., *N.Z.* . . . . **59 G6** 37 16S 176 17 E
Mayotte, *Ind. Oc.* . . . . **53 G9** 12 50S 45 10 E
Maysville, *U.S.A.* **76 F4** 38 39N 83 46W
Mayu, *Indonesia* . . . . **37 D7** 1 30N 126 30 E
Mayville, *N. Dak., U.S.A.* **80 B6** 47 30N 97 20W
Mayville, *N.Y., U.S.A.* **78 D5** 42 15N 79 30W
Mayya, *Russia* . . . . **27 C14** 61 44N 130 18 E
Mazabuka, *Zambia* . . . . **55 F2** 15 52S 27 44 E
Mazagán = El Jadida,
Morocco **50 B4** 33 11N 8 17W
Mazagão, *Brazil* **93 D8** 0 7S 51 16W
Mazán, *Peru* **92 D4** 3 30S 73 0W
Māzandarān □, *Iran* . . . . **45 B7** 36 30N 52 0 E
Mazapil, *Mexico* **86 C4** 24 38N 101 34W
Mazara del Vallo, *Italy* . . . . . **20 F5** 37 39N 12 35 E
Mazarrón, *Spain* **19 D5** 37 38N 1 19W
Mazaruni →, *Guyana* **92 B7** 6 25N 58 35W
Mazatán, *Mexico* **86 B2** 29 0N 110 8W
Mazatenango, *Guatemala* . . . **88 D1** 14 35N 91 30W
Mazatlán, *Mexico* **86 C3** 23 13N 106 25W
Mažeikiai, *Lithuania* . . . . **9 H20** 56 20N 22 20 E
Māzhān, *Iran* . . . . **45 C8** 32 30N 59 0 E
Mazīnān, *Iran* . . . . **45 B8** 36 19N 56 56 E
Mazoe, *Mozam.* . . . . **55 F3** 16 42S 33 7 E
Mazoe →, *Mozam.* . . . . **55 F3** 16 20S 33 30 E
Mazowe, *Zimbabwe* . . . . **55 F3** 17 28S 30 58 E
Mazurian Lakes = Mazurski,
Pojezierze, *Poland* . . . . **17 B11** 53 50N 21 0 E
Mazurski, Pojezierze, *Poland* **17 B11** 53 50N 21 0 E
Mazyr, *Belarus* . . . . **17 B15** 51 59N 29 15 E
Mbabane, *Swaziland* . . . . **57 D5** 26 18S 31 6 E
Mbaïki, *C.A.R.* . . . . **52 D3** 3 53N 18 1 E
Mbala, *Zambia* . . . . **55 D3** 8 46S 31 24 E

Monolith, U.S.A. 85 K8 35 7N 118 22W
Monólithos, Greece 23 C9 36 7N 27 45 E
Monongahela, U.S.A. 78 F5 40 12N 79 56W
Monópoli, Italy 20 D7 40 57N 17 18 E
Monroe, Ga., U.S.A. 77 J4 33 47N 83 43W
Monroe, La., U.S.A. 81 J8 32 30N 92 7W
Monroe, Mich., U.S.A. 76 E4 41 55N 83 24W
Monroe, N.C., U.S.A. 77 H5 34 59N 80 33W
Monroe, N.Y., U.S.A. 79 E10 41 20N 74 11W
Monroe, Utah, U.S.A. 83 G7 38 38N 112 7W
Monroe, Wash., U.S.A. 84 C5 47 51N 121 58W
Monroe, Wis., U.S.A. 80 D10 42 36N 89 38W
Monroe City, U.S.A. 80 F9 39 39N 91 44W
Monroeton, U.S.A. 79 E8 41 43N 76 29W
Monroeville, Ala., U.S.A. 77 K2 31 31N 87 20W
Monroeville, Pa., U.S.A. 78 F5 40 26N 79 45W
Monrovia, Liberia 50 G3 6 18N 10 47W
Mons, Belgium 15 D3 50 27N 3 58 E
Monse, Indonesia 37 E6 4 7S 123 15 E
Mont-de-Marsan, France 18 E3 43 54N 0 31W
Mont-Joli, Canada 71 C6 48 37N 68 10W
Mont-Laurier, Canada 70 C4 46 35N 75 30W
Mont-Louis, Canada 71 C6 49 15N 65 44W
Mont-St-Michel, Le = Le Mont-St-Michel, France 18 B3 48 40N 1 30W
Mont Tremblant, Parc Recr. du, Canada 70 C5 46 30N 74 30W
Montagu, S. Africa 56 E3 33 45S 20 8 E
Montagu I., Antarctica 5 B1 58 25S 26 20W
Montague, Canada 71 C7 46 10N 62 39W
Montague, I., Mexico 86 A2 31 40N 114 56W
Montague Ra., Australia 61 E2 27 15S 119 30 E
Montague Sd., Australia 60 B4 14 28S 125 20 E
Montalbán, Spain 19 B5 40 50N 0 45W
Montalvo, U.S.A. 85 L7 34 15N 119 12W
Montana, Bulgaria 21 C10 43 27N 23 16 E
Montaña, Peru 92 E4 6 0S 73 0W
Montana □, U.S.A. 82 C9 47 0N 110 0W
Montaña Clara, I., Canary Is. 22 E6 29 17N 13 33W
Montargis, France 18 C5 47 59N 2 43 E
Montauban, France 18 D4 44 2N 1 21 E
Montauk, U.S.A. 79 E13 41 3N 71 57W
Montauk Pt., U.S.A. 79 E13 41 4N 71 52W
Montbéliard, France 18 C7 47 31N 6 48 E
Montceau-les-Mines, France 18 C6 46 40N 4 23 E
Montclair, U.S.A. 79 F10 40 49N 74 13W
Monte Albán, Mexico 87 D5 17 2N 96 45W
Monte Alegre, Brazil 93 D8 2 0S 54 0W
Monte Azul, Brazil 93 G10 15 9S 42 53W
Monte Bello Is., Australia 60 D2 20 30S 115 45 E
Monte-Carlo, Monaco 18 E7 43 46N 7 23 E
Monte Caseros, Argentina 94 C4 30 10S 57 50W
Monte Comán, Argentina 94 C2 34 40S 67 53W
Monte Cristi, Dom. Rep. 89 C5 19 52N 71 39W
Monte Lindo →, Paraguay 94 A4 23 56S 57 12W
Monte Patria, Chile 94 C1 30 42S 70 58W
Monte Quemado, Argentina 94 B3 25 53S 62 41W
Monte Rio, U.S.A. 84 G4 38 28N 123 0W
Monte Santu, C. di, Italy 20 D3 40 5N 9 44 E
Monte Vista, U.S.A. 83 H10 37 35N 106 9W
Monteagudo, Argentina 95 B5 27 14S 54 8W
Montebello, Canada 70 C5 45 40N 74 55W
Montecito, U.S.A. 85 L7 34 26N 119 40W
Montecristo, Italy 20 C4 42 20N 10 19 E
Montego Bay, Jamaica 88 C4 18 30N 78 0W
Montélimar, France 18 D6 44 33N 4 45 E
Montello, U.S.A. 80 D10 43 48N 89 20W
Montemorelos, Mexico 87 B5 25 11N 99 42W
Montenegro, Brazil 95 B5 29 39S 51 29W
Montenegro □, Yugoslavia 21 C8 42 40N 19 20 E
Montepuez, Mozam. 55 E4 13 8S 38 59 E
Montepuez →, Mozam. 55 E5 12 32S 40 27 E
Monterey, U.S.A. 84 J5 36 37N 121 55W
Monterey B., U.S.A. 84 J5 36 45N 122 0W
Montería, Colombia 92 B3 8 46N 75 53W
Monteros, Argentina 94 B2 27 11S 65 30W
Monterrey, Mexico 86 B4 25 40N 100 30W
Montes Claros, Brazil 93 G10 16 30S 43 50W
Montesano, U.S.A. 84 D3 46 59N 123 36W
Montesilvano, Italy 20 C6 42 29N 14 8 E
Montevideo, Uruguay 95 C4 34 50S 56 11W
Montevideo, U.S.A. 80 C7 44 57N 95 43W
Montezuma, U.S.A. 80 E8 41 35N 92 32W
Montgomery = Sahiwal, Pakistan 42 D5 30 45N 73 8 E
Montgomery, U.K. 11 E4 52 34N 3 8W
Montgomery, Ala., U.S.A. 77 J2 32 23N 86 19W
Montgomery, Pa., U.S.A. 78 E8 41 10N 76 53W
Montgomery, W. Va., U.S.A. 76 F5 38 11N 81 19W
Montgomery City, U.S.A. 80 F9 38 59N 91 30W
Monticello, Ark., U.S.A. 81 J9 33 38N 91 47W
Monticello, Fla., U.S.A. 77 K4 30 33N 83 52W
Monticello, Ind., U.S.A. 76 E2 40 45N 86 46W
Monticello, Iowa, U.S.A. 80 D9 42 15N 91 12W
Monticello, Ky., U.S.A. 77 G3 36 50N 84 51W
Monticello, Minn., U.S.A. 80 C8 45 18N 93 48W
Monticello, Miss., U.S.A. 81 K9 31 33N 90 7W
Monticello, N.Y., U.S.A. 79 E10 41 39N 74 42W
Monticello, Utah, U.S.A. 83 H9 37 52N 109 21W
Montijo, Portugal 19 C1 38 41N 8 54W
Montilla, Spain 19 D3 37 36N 4 40W
Montluçon, France 18 C5 46 22N 2 36 E
Montmagny, Canada 71 C5 46 58N 70 34W
Montmartre, Canada 73 C8 50 14N 103 27W
Montmorillon, France 18 C4 46 26N 0 50 E
Monto, Australia 62 C5 24 52S 151 6 E
Montoro, Spain 19 C3 38 1N 4 27W
Montour Falls, U.S.A. 78 D8 42 21N 76 51W
Montoursville, U.S.A. 78 E8 41 15N 76 55W
Montpelier, Idaho, U.S.A. 82 E8 42 19N 111 18W
Montpelier, Vt., U.S.A. 79 B12 44 16N 72 35W
Montpellier, France 18 E5 43 37N 3 52 E
Montréal, Canada 79 A11 45 31N 73 34W
Montreal →, Canada 70 C3 47 14N 84 39W
Montreal L., Canada 73 C7 54 20N 105 45W
Montreal Lake, Canada 73 C7 54 3N 105 46W
Montreux, Switz. 18 C7 46 26N 6 55 E
Montrose, U.K. 12 E6 56 44N 2 27W
Montrose, Colo., U.S.A. 83 G10 38 29N 107 53W
Montrose, Pa., U.S.A. 79 E9 41 50N 75 53W
Monts, Pte. des, Canada 71 C6 49 20N 67 12W
Montserrat ■, W. Indies 89 C7 16 40N 62 10W
Montuiri, Spain 22 B9 39 34N 2 59 E
Monywa, Burma 41 H19 22 7N 95 11 E
Monza, Italy 18 D8 45 35N 9 16 E
Monze, Zambia 55 F2 16 17S 27 29 E
Monze, C., Pakistan 42 G2 24 47N 66 37 E
Monzón, Spain 19 B6 41 52N 0 10 E
Mooers, U.S.A. 79 B11 44 58N 73 35W
Mooi →, S. Africa 57 D5 28 45S 30 34 E
Mooi River, S. Africa 57 D4 29 13S 29 50 E
Moonah →, Australia 62 C2 22 3S 138 33 E
Moonda, L., Australia 62 D3 25 52S 140 25 E
Moonie, Australia 63 D5 27 46S 150 20 E
Moonie →, Australia 63 D4 29 19S 148 43 E
Moonta, Australia 63 E2 34 6S 137 32 E
Moora, Australia 61 F2 30 37S 115 58 E
Moorcroft, U.S.A. 80 C2 44 16N 104 57W
Moore →, Australia 61 F2 31 22S 115 30 E
Moore, L., Australia 61 E2 29 50S 117 35 E
Moore Park, Australia 62 C5 24 43S 152 17 E
Moore Reefs, Australia 62 B4 16 0S 149 5 E
Moorefield, U.S.A. 76 F6 39 5N 78 59W
Moores Res., U.S.A. 79 B13 44 45N 71 50W
Moorfoot Hills, U.K. 12 F5 55 44N 3 8W
Moorhead, U.S.A. 80 B6 46 53N 96 45W
Moorpark, U.S.A. 85 L8 34 17N 118 53W
Moorreesburg, S. Africa 56 E2 33 6S 18 38 E
Moose →, Canada 70 B3 51 20N 80 25W
Moose →, U.S.A. 79 C9 43 38N 75 24W
Moose Creek, Canada 79 A10 45 15N 74 58W
Moose Factory, Canada 70 B3 51 16N 80 32W
Moose Jaw, Canada 73 C7 50 24N 105 30W
Moose Jaw →, Canada 73 C7 50 34N 105 18W
Moose Lake, Canada 73 C8 53 43N 100 20W
Moose Lake, U.S.A. 80 B8 46 27N 92 46W
Moose Mountain Prov. Park, Canada 73 D8 49 48N 102 25W
Moosehead L., U.S.A. 77 C11 45 38N 69 40W
Mooselookmeguntic L., U.S.A. 77 C10 44 55N 70 49W
Moosilauke, Mt., U.S.A. 79 B13 44 3N 71 40W
Moosomin, Canada 73 C8 50 9N 101 40W
Moosonee, Canada 70 B3 51 17N 80 39W
Moosup, U.S.A. 79 E13 41 43N 71 53W
Mopane, S. Africa 57 C4 22 37S 29 52 E
Mopeia Velha, Mozam. 55 F4 17 30S 35 40 E
Mopipi, Botswana 56 C3 21 6S 24 55 E
Mopoi, C.A.R. 54 A2 5 6N 26 54 E
Mopti, Mali 50 F5 14 30N 4 0W
Moqor, Afghan. 42 C2 32 50N 67 42 E
Moquegua, Peru 92 G4 17 15S 70 46W
Mora, Sweden 9 F16 61 2N 14 38 E
Mora, Minn., U.S.A. 80 C8 45 53N 93 18W
Mora, N. Mex., U.S.A. 83 J11 35 58N 105 20W
Mora →, U.S.A. 81 H2 35 35N 104 25W
Moradabad, India 43 E8 28 50N 78 50 E
Morafenobe, Madag. 57 B7 17 50S 44 53 E
Moramanga, Madag. 57 B8 18 56S 48 12 E
Moran, Kans., U.S.A. 81 G7 37 55N 95 10W
Moran, Wyo., U.S.A. 82 E8 43 53N 110 37W
Moranbah, Australia 62 C4 22 1S 148 6 E
Morant Cays, Jamaica 88 C4 17 22N 76 0W
Morant Pt., Jamaica 88 C4 17 55N 76 12W
Morar, India 42 F8 26 14N 78 14 E
Morar, L., U.K. 12 E3 56 57N 5 40W
Moratuwa, Sri Lanka 40 R11 6 45N 79 55 E
Morava →, Serbia, Yug. 21 B9 44 36N 21 4 E
Morava →, Slovak Rep. 17 D9 48 10N 16 59 E
Moravia, U.S.A. 79 D8 42 43N 76 25W
Moravian Hts. = Českomoravská Vrchovina, Czech Rep. 16 D8 49 30N 15 40 E
Morawa, Australia 61 E2 29 13S 116 0 E
Morawhanna, Guyana 92 B7 8 30N 59 40W
Moray □, U.K. 12 D5 57 31N 3 18W
Moray Firth, U.K. 12 D5 57 40N 3 52W
Morbi, India 42 H4 22 50N 70 42 E
Morden, Canada 73 D9 49 15N 98 10W
Mordovian Republic = Mordvinia □, Russia 24 D7 54 20N 44 30 E
Mordvinia □, Russia 24 D7 54 20N 44 30 E
Morea, Greece 6 H10 37 45N 22 10 E
Moreau →, U.S.A. 80 C4 45 18N 100 43W
Morecambe, U.K. 10 C5 54 5N 2 52W
Morecambe B., U.K. 10 C5 54 7N 3 0W
Moree, Australia 63 D4 29 28S 149 54 E
Morehead, U.S.A. 76 F4 38 11N 83 26W
Morehead City, U.S.A. 77 H7 34 43N 76 43W
Morel →, India 42 F7 26 13N 76 36 E
Morelia, Mexico 86 D4 19 42N 101 7W
Morella, Australia 62 C3 23 0S 143 52 E
Morella, Spain 19 B5 40 35N 0 5W
Morelos, Mexico 86 B3 26 42N 107 40W
Morelos □, Mexico 87 D5 18 40N 99 10W
Morena, India 42 F8 26 30N 78 4 E
Morena, Sierra, Spain 19 C3 38 20N 4 0W
Moreno Valley, U.S.A. 85 M10 33 56N 117 15W
Moresby I., Canada 72 C2 52 30N 131 40W
Moreton I., Australia 63 D5 27 10S 153 25 E
Morey, Spain 22 B10 39 44N 3 20 E
Morgan, U.S.A. 82 F8 41 2N 111 41W
Morgan City, U.S.A. 81 L9 29 42N 91 12W
Morgan Hill, U.S.A. 84 H5 37 8N 121 39W
Morganfield, U.S.A. 76 G2 37 41N 87 55W
Morganton, U.S.A. 77 H5 35 45N 81 41W
Morgantown, U.S.A. 76 F6 39 38N 79 57W
Morgenzon, S. Africa 57 D4 26 45S 29 36 E
Morghak, Iran 45 D8 29 7N 57 54 E
Morhar →, India 43 G11 25 29N 85 11 E
Moriarty, U.S.A. 83 J10 34 59N 106 3W
Morice L., Canada 72 C3 53 50N 127 40W
Morinville, Canada 72 C6 53 49N 113 41W
Morioka, Japan 30 E10 39 45N 141 8 E
Moris, Mexico 86 B3 28 8N 108 32W
Morlaix, France 18 B2 48 36N 3 52W
Mornington, Australia 63 F4 38 15S 145 5 E
Mornington, I., Chile 96 F1 49 50S 75 30W
Mornington I., Australia 62 B2 16 30S 139 30 E
Moro, Pakistan 42 F2 26 40N 68 0 E
Moro →, Pakistan 42 E2 29 42N 67 22 E
Moro G., Phil. 37 C6 6 30N 123 0 E
Morocco ■, N. Afr. 50 B4 32 0N 5 50W
Morogoro, Tanzania 54 D4 6 50S 37 40 E
Morogoro □, Tanzania 54 D4 8 0S 37 0 E
Moroleón, Mexico 86 C4 20 8N 101 32W
Morombe, Madag. 57 C7 21 45S 43 22 E
Moron, Argentina 94 C4 34 39S 58 37W
Morón, Cuba 88 B4 22 8N 78 39W
Morón de la Frontera, Spain 19 D3 37 6N 5 28W
Morona →, Peru 92 D3 4 40S 77 10W
Morondava, Madag. 57 C7 20 17S 44 17 E
Morongo Valley, U.S.A. 85 L10 34 3N 116 37W
Moroni, Comoros Is. 49 H8 11 40S 43 16 E
Moroni, U.S.A. 82 G8 39 32N 111 35W
Morotai, Indonesia 37 D7 2 10N 128 30 E
Moroto, Uganda 54 B3 2 28N 34 42 E
Moroto Summit, Kenya 54 B3 2 30N 34 43 E
Morpeth, U.K. 10 B6 55 10N 1 41W
Morphou, Cyprus 23 D11 35 12N 32 59 E
Morphou Bay, Cyprus 23 D11 35 15N 32 50 E
Morrilton, U.S.A. 81 H8 35 9N 92 44W
Morrinhos, Brazil 93 G9 17 45S 49 10W
Morrinsville, N.Z. 59 G5 37 40S 175 32 E
Morris, Canada 73 D9 49 25N 97 22W
Morris, Ill., U.S.A. 80 E10 41 22N 88 26W
Morris, Minn., U.S.A. 80 C7 45 35N 95 55W
Morris, N.Y., U.S.A. 79 D9 42 33N 75 15W
Morris, Pa., U.S.A. 78 E7 41 35N 77 17W
Morris, Mt., Australia 61 E5 26 9S 131 4 E
Morrisburg, Canada 79 B9 44 55N 75 7W
Morristown, Ariz., U.S.A. 83 K7 33 51N 112 37W
Morristown, N.J., U.S.A. 79 F10 40 48N 74 29W
Morristown, N.Y., U.S.A. 79 B9 44 35N 75 39W
Morristown, Tenn., U.S.A. 77 G4 36 13N 83 18W
Morrisville, N.Y., U.S.A. 79 D9 42 53N 75 35W
Morrisville, Pa., U.S.A. 79 F10 40 13N 74 47W
Morrisville, Vt., U.S.A. 79 B12 44 34N 72 36W
Morro, Pta., Chile 94 B1 27 6S 71 0W
Morro Bay, U.S.A. 84 K6 35 22N 120 51W
Morro del Jable, Canary Is. 22 F5 28 3N 14 23W
Morro Jable, Pta. de, Canary Is. 22 F5 28 2N 14 20W
Morrosquillo, G. de, Colombia 88 E4 9 35N 75 40W
Morrumbene, Mozam. 57 C6 23 31S 35 16 E
Morshansk, Russia 24 D7 53 28N 41 50 E
Morteros, Argentina 94 C3 30 50S 62 0W
Mortlach, Canada 73 C7 50 27N 106 4W
Mortlake, Australia 63 F3 38 5S 142 50 E
Morton, Tex., U.S.A. 81 J3 33 44N 102 46W
Morton, Wash., U.S.A. 84 D4 46 34N 122 17W
Morundah, Australia 63 E4 34 57S 146 19 E
Moruya, Australia 63 F5 35 58S 150 3 E
Morvan, France 18 C6 47 5N 4 3 E
Morven, Australia 63 D4 26 22S 147 5 E
Morvern, U.K. 12 E3 56 38N 5 44W
Morwell, Australia 63 F4 38 10S 146 22 E
Morzhovets, Ostrov, Russia 24 A7 66 44N 42 35 E
Moscos Is., Burma 38 E1 14 0N 97 30 E
Moscow = Moskva, Russia 24 C6 55 45N 37 35 E
Moscow, Idaho, U.S.A. 82 C5 46 44N 117 0W
Moscow, Pa., U.S.A. 79 E9 41 20N 75 31W
Mosel →, Europe 18 A7 50 22N 7 36 E
Moselle = Mosel →, Europe 18 A7 50 22N 7 36 E
Moses Lake, U.S.A. 82 C4 47 8N 119 17W
Mosgiel, N.Z. 59 L3 45 53S 170 21 E
Moshaweng →, S. Africa 56 D3 26 35S 22 50 E
Moshi, Tanzania 54 C4 3 22S 37 18 E
Moshupa, Botswana 56 C4 24 46S 25 29 E
Mosjøen, Norway 8 D15 65 51N 13 12 E
Moskenesøya, Norway 8 C15 67 58N 13 0 E
Moskenstraumen, Norway 8 C15 67 47N 12 45 E
Moskva, Russia 24 C6 55 45N 37 35 E
Mosomane, Botswana 56 C4 24 2S 26 19 E
Mosonmagyaróvár, Hungary 17 E9 47 52N 17 18 E
Mosquera, Colombia 92 C3 2 35N 78 24W
Mosquero, U.S.A. 81 H3 35 47N 103 58W
Mosquitia, Honduras 88 C3 15 20N 84 10W
Mosquito Coast = Mosquitia, Honduras 88 C3 15 20N 84 10W
Mosquito Creek L., U.S.A. 78 E4 41 18N 80 46W
Mosquito L., Canada 73 A8 62 35N 103 20W
Mosquitos, G. de los, Panama 88 E3 9 15N 81 10W
Moss, Norway 9 G14 59 27N 10 40 E
Moss Vale, Australia 63 E5 34 32S 150 25 E
Mossbank, Canada 73 D7 49 56N 105 56W
Mossburn, N.Z. 59 L2 45 41S 168 15 E
Mosselbaai, S. Africa 56 E3 34 11S 22 8 E
Mossendjo, Congo 52 E2 2 55S 12 42 E
Mossgiel, Australia 63 E3 33 15S 144 5 E
Mossman, Australia 62 B4 16 21S 145 15 E
Mossoró, Brazil 93 E11 5 10S 37 15W
Mossuril, Mozam. 55 E5 14 58S 40 42 E
Most, Czech Rep. 16 C7 50 31N 13 38 E
Mosta, Malta 23 D1 35 55N 14 26 E
Mostaganem, Algeria 50 A6 35 54N 0 5 E
Mostar, Bos.-H. 21 C7 43 22N 17 50 E
Mostardas, Brazil 95 C5 31 2S 50 51W
Mostiska = Mostyska, Ukraine 17 D12 49 48N 23 4 E
Mosty = Masty, Belarus 17 B13 53 27N 24 38 E
Mostyska, Ukraine 17 D12 49 48N 23 4 E
Mosul = Al Mawşil, Iraq 44 B4 36 15N 43 5 E
Mosŭlpo, S. Korea 35 H14 33 20N 126 17 E
Motagua →, Guatemala 88 C2 15 44N 88 14W
Motala, Sweden 9 G16 58 32N 15 1 E
Motaze, Mozam. 57 C5 24 48S 32 52 E
Moth, India 43 G8 25 43N 78 57 E
Motherwell, U.K. 12 F5 55 47N 3 58W
Motihari, India 43 F11 26 30N 84 55 E
Motozintla de Mendoza, Mexico 87 D6 15 21N 92 14W
Motril, Spain 19 D4 36 31N 3 37W
Mott, U.S.A. 80 B3 46 23N 102 20W
Motueka, N.Z. 59 J4 41 7S 173 1 E
Motueka →, N.Z. 59 J4 41 5S 173 1 E
Motul, Mexico 87 C7 21 0N 89 20W
Mouchalagane →, Canada 71 B6 50 56N 68 41W
Moúdhros, Greece 21 E11 39 50N 25 18 E
Mouila, Gabon 52 E2 1 50S 11 0 E
Moulamein, Australia 63 F3 35 3S 144 1 E
Moulianá, Greece 23 D7 35 10N 25 59 E
Moulins, France 18 C5 46 35N 3 19 E
Moulmein, Burma 41 L20 16 30N 97 40 E
Moulouya, O. →, Morocco 50 B5 35 5N 2 25W
Moultrie, U.S.A. 77 K4 31 11N 83 47W
Moultrie, L., U.S.A. 77 J5 33 20N 80 5W
Mound City, Mo., U.S.A. 80 E7 40 7N 95 14W
Mound City, S. Dak., U.S.A. 80 C4 45 44N 100 4W
Moundou, Chad 51 G9 8 40N 16 10 E
Moundsville, U.S.A. 78 G4 39 55N 80 44W
Moung, Cambodia 38 F4 12 46N 103 27 E
Mount Airy, U.S.A. 77 G5 36 31N 80 37W
Mount Albert, Canada 78 B5 44 8N 79 19W
Mount Barker, S. Austral., Australia 63 F2 35 5S 138 52 E
Mount Barker, W. Austral., Australia 61 F2 34 38S 117 40 E
Mount Brydges, Canada 78 D3 42 54N 81 29W
Mount Burr, Australia 63 F3 37 34S 140 26 E
Mount Carmel, Ill., U.S.A. 76 F2 38 25N 87 46W
Mount Carmel, Pa., U.S.A. 79 F8 40 47N 76 24W
Mount Charleston, U.S.A. 85 J11 36 16N 115 37W
Mount Clemens, U.S.A. 78 D2 42 35N 82 53W
Mount Coolon, Australia 62 C4 21 25S 147 25 E
Mount Darwin, Zimbabwe 55 F3 16 47S 31 38 E
Mount Desert I., U.S.A. 77 C11 44 21N 68 20W
Mount Dora, U.S.A. 77 L5 28 48N 81 38W
Mount Edziza Prov. Park, Canada 72 B2 57 30N 130 45W
Mount Fletcher, S. Africa 57 E4 30 40S 28 30 E
Mount Forest, Canada 78 C4 43 59N 80 43W
Mount Gambier, Australia 63 F3 37 50S 140 46 E
Mount Garnet, Australia 62 B4 17 37S 145 6 E
Mount Holly, U.S.A. 79 G10 39 59N 74 47W
Mount Holly Springs, U.S.A. 78 F7 40 7N 77 12W
Mount Hope, N.S.W., Australia 63 E4 32 51S 145 51 E
Mount Hope, S. Austral., Australia 63 E2 34 7S 135 23 E
Mount Isa, Australia 62 C2 20 42S 139 26 E
Mount Jewett, U.S.A. 78 E6 41 44N 78 39W
Mount Kisco, U.S.A. 79 E11 41 12N 73 44W
Mount Laguna, U.S.A. 85 N10 32 52N 116 25W
Mount Larcom, Australia 62 C5 23 48S 150 59 E
Mount Lofty Ra., Australia 63 E2 34 35S 139 5 E
Mount Magnet, Australia 61 E2 28 2S 117 47 E
Mount Maunganui, N.Z. 59 G6 37 40S 176 14 E
Mount Molloy, Australia 62 B4 16 42S 145 20 E
Mount Morgan, Australia 62 C5 23 40S 150 25 E
Mount Morris, U.S.A. 78 D7 42 44N 77 52W
Mount Pearl, Canada 71 C9 47 31N 52 47W
Mount Penn, U.S.A. 79 F9 40 20N 75 54W
Mount Perry, Australia 63 D5 25 13S 151 42 E
Mount Pleasant, Iowa, U.S.A. 80 E9 40 58N 91 33W
Mount Pleasant, Mich., U.S.A. 76 D3 43 36N 84 46W
Mount Pleasant, Pa., U.S.A. 78 F5 40 9N 79 33W
Mount Pleasant, S.C., U.S.A. 77 J6 32 47N 79 52W
Mount Pleasant, Tenn., U.S.A. 77 H2 35 32N 87 12W
Mount Pleasant, Tex., U.S.A. 81 J7 33 9N 94 58W
Mount Pleasant, Utah, U.S.A. 82 G8 39 33N 111 27W
Mount Pocono, U.S.A. 79 E9 41 7N 75 22W
Mount Rainier Nat. Park, U.S.A. 84 D5 46 55N 121 50W
Mount Revelstoke Nat. Park, Canada 72 C5 51 5N 118 30W
Mount Robson Prov. Park, Canada 72 C5 53 0N 119 0W
Mount Selinda, Zimbabwe 57 C5 20 24S 32 43 E
Mount Shasta, U.S.A. 82 F2 41 19N 122 19W
Mount Signal, U.S.A. 85 N11 32 39N 115 37W
Mount Sterling, Ill., U.S.A. 80 F9 39 59N 90 45W
Mount Sterling, Ky., U.S.A. 76 F4 38 4N 83 56W
Mount Surprise, Australia 62 B3 18 10S 144 17 E
Mount Union, U.S.A. 78 F7 40 23N 77 53W
Mount Upton, U.S.A. 79 D9 42 26N 75 23W
Mount Vernon, Ill., U.S.A. 76 F1 38 19N 88 55W
Mount Vernon, Ind., U.S.A. 80 F10 38 17N 88 57W
Mount Vernon, N.Y., U.S.A. 79 F11 40 55N 73 50W
Mount Vernon, Ohio, U.S.A. 78 F2 40 23N 82 29W
Mount Vernon, Wash., U.S.A. 84 B4 48 25N 122 20W
Mountain Ash, U.K. 11 F4 51 40N 3 23W
Mountain Center, U.S.A. 85 M10 33 42N 116 44W
Mountain City, Nev., U.S.A. 82 F6 41 50N 115 58W
Mountain City, Tenn., U.S.A. 77 G5 36 29N 81 48W
Mountain Dale, U.S.A. 79 E10 41 41N 74 32W
Mountain Grove, U.S.A. 81 G8 37 8N 92 16W
Mountain Home, Ark., U.S.A. 81 G8 36 20N 92 23W
Mountain Home, Idaho, U.S.A. 82 E6 43 8N 115 41W
Mountain Iron, U.S.A. 80 B8 47 32N 92 37W
Mountain Pass, U.S.A. 85 K11 35 29N 115 35W
Mountain View, Ark., U.S.A. 81 H8 35 52N 92 7W
Mountain View, Calif., U.S.A. 84 H4 37 23N 122 5W
Mountain View, Hawaii, U.S.A. 74 J17 19 33N 155 7W
Mountainair, U.S.A. 83 J10 34 31N 106 15W
Mountlake Terrace, U.S.A. 84 C4 47 47N 122 19W
Mountmellick, Ireland 13 C4 53 7N 7 20W
Mountrath, Ireland 13 D4 53 0N 7 28W
Moura, Australia 62 C4 24 35S 149 58 E
Moura, Brazil 92 D6 1 32S 61 38W
Moura, Portugal 19 C2 38 7N 7 30W
Mourdi, Dépression du, Chad 51 E10 18 10N 23 0 E
Mourilyan, Australia 62 B4 17 35S 146 3 E
Mourne →, U.K. 13 B4 54 52N 7 26W
Mourne Mts., U.K. 13 B5 54 10N 6 0W
Mourniaí, Greece 23 D6 35 29N 24 1 E
Mournies = Mourniaí, Greece 23 D6 35 29N 24 1 E
Mouscron, Belgium 15 D3 50 45N 3 12 E
Moussoro, Chad 51 F9 13 41N 16 35 E
Moutong, Indonesia 37 D6 0 28N 121 13 E
Movas, Mexico 86 B3 28 10N 109 25W
Moville, Ireland 13 A4 55 11N 7 3W
Mowandjum, Australia 60 C3 17 22S 123 40 E
Moy →, Ireland 13 B2 54 8N 9 8W
Moyale, Kenya 54 B4 3 30N 39 0 E
Moyen Atlas, Morocco 50 B4 33 0N 5 0W
Moyne, L. le, Canada 71 A6 56 45N 68 47W
Moyo, Indonesia 36 F5 8 10S 117 40 E
Moyobamba, Peru 92 E3 6 0S 77 0W
Moyyero →, Russia 27 C11 68 44N 103 42 E
Moyynty, Kazakstan 26 E8 47 10N 73 18 E
Mozambique = Moçambique, Mozam. 55 F5 15 3S 40 42 E
Mozambique ■, Africa 55 F4 19 0S 35 0 E
Mozambique Chan., Africa 57 B7 17 30S 42 30 E
Mozdok, Russia 25 F7 43 45N 44 48 E
Mozdūrān, Iran 45 B9 36 9N 60 35 E
Mozhnābād, Iran 45 C9 34 7N 60 6 E
Mozyr = Mazyr, Belarus 17 B15 51 59N 29 15 E
Mpanda, Tanzania 54 D3 6 23S 31 1 E
Mphoengs, Zimbabwe 57 C4 21 10S 27 51 E
Mpika, Zambia 55 E3 11 51S 31 25 E
Mpulungu, Zambia 55 D3 8 51S 31 5 E
Mpumalanga, S. Africa 57 D5 29 50S 30 33 E
Mpumalanga □, S. Africa 57 B5 26 0S 30 0 E
Mpwapwa, Tanzania 54 D4 6 23S 36 30 E
Mqanduli, S. Africa 57 E4 31 49S 28 45 E
Msambansovu, Zimbabwe 55 F3 15 50S 30 3 E
M'sila →, Algeria 50 A6 35 30N 4 29 E
Msoro, Zambia 55 E3 13 35S 31 50 E
Mstislavl = Mstsislaw, Belarus 17 A16 54 0N 31 50 E
Mstsislaw, Belarus 17 A16 54 0N 31 50 E

Mtama, *Tanzania* **55 E4** 10 17S 39 21 E
Mtamvuna →, *S. Africa* **57 E5** 31 6S 30 12 E
Mtilikwe →, *Zimbabwe* **55 G3** 21 9S 31 30 E
Mtubatuba, *S. Africa* **57 D5** 28 30S 32 8 E
Mtwalume, *S. Africa* **57 E5** 30 30S 30 38 E
Mtwara-Mikindani, *Tanzania* **55 E5** 10 20S 40 20 E
Mu Gia, Deo, *Vietnam* **38 D5** 17 40N 105 47 E
Mu Us Shamo, *China* **34 E5** 39 0N 109 0 E
Muang Chiang Rai = Chiang Rai, *Thailand* **38 C2** 19 52N 99 50 E
Muang Khong, *Laos* **38 E5** 14 7N 105 51 E
Muang Lamphun, *Thailand* **38 C2** 18 40N 99 2 E
Muang Pak Beng, *Laos* **38 C3** 19 54N 101 8 E
Muar, *Malaysia* **39 L4** 2 3N 102 34 E
Muarabungo, *Indonesia* **36 E2** 1 28S 102 52 E
Muaraenim, *Indonesia* **36 E2** 3 40S 103 50 E
Muarajuloi, *Indonesia* **36 E4** 0 12S 114 3 E
Muarakaman, *Indonesia* **36 E5** 0 2S 116 45 E
Muaratebo, *Indonesia* **36 E2** 1 30S 102 26 E
Muaratembesi, *Indonesia* **36 E2** 1 42S 103 8 E
Muaratewe, *Indonesia* **36 E4** 0 58S 114 52 E
Mubarakpur, *India* **43 F10** 26 6N 83 18 E
Mubarraz = Al Mubarraz, *Si. Arabia* **45 E6** 25 30N 49 40 E
Mubende, *Uganda* **54 B3** 0 33N 31 22 E
Mubi, *Nigeria* **51 F8** 10 18N 13 16 E
Mubur, Pulau, *Indonesia* **39 L6** 3 20N 106 12 E
Mucajaí →, *Brazil* **92 C6** 2 25N 60 52W
Muchachos, Roque de los, *Canary Is.* **22 F2** 28 44N 17 52W
Muchinga Mts., *Zambia* **55 E3** 11 30S 31 30 E
Muck, *U.K.* **12 E2** 56 50N 6 15W
Muckadilla, *Australia* **63 D4** 26 35S 148 23 E
Mucuri, *Brazil* **93 G11** 18 0S 39 36W
Mucusso, *Angola* **56 B3** 18 1S 21 25 E
Muda, *Canary Is.* **22 F6** 28 34N 13 57W
Mudanjiang, *China* **35 B15** 44 38N 129 30 E
Mudanya, *Turkey* **21 D13** 40 25N 28 50 E
Muddy Cr. →, *U.S.A.* **83 H8** 38 24N 110 42W
Mudgee, *Australia* **63 E4** 32 32S 149 31 E
Mudjatik →, *Canada* **73 B7** 56 1N 107 36W
Muecate, *Mozam.* **55 E4** 14 55S 39 40 E
Mueda, *Mozam.* **55 E4** 11 36S 39 28 E
Mueller Ra., *Australia* **60 C4** 18 18S 126 46 E
Muende, *Mozam.* **55 E3** 14 28S 33 0 E
Muerto, Mar, *Mexico* **87 D6** 16 10N 94 10W
Mufulira, *Zambia* **55 E2** 12 32S 28 15 E
Mufumbiro Range, *Africa* **54 C2** 1 25S 29 30 E
Mughal Sarai, *India* **43 G10** 25 18N 83 7 E
Mughayrā', *Si. Arabia* **44 D3** 29 17N 37 41 E
Mugi, *Japan* **31 H7** 33 40N 134 25 E
Mugila, Mts., *Dem. Rep. of the Congo* **54 D2** 7 0S 28 50 E
Muğla, *Turkey* **21 F13** 37 15N 28 22 E
Mugu, *Nepal* **43 E10** 29 45N 82 30 E
Muhammad, Râs, *Egypt* **44 E2** 27 44N 34 16 E
Muhammad Qol, *Sudan* **51 D13** 20 53N 37 9 E
Muhammadabad, *India* **43 F10** 26 4N 83 25 E
Muhesi →, *Tanzania* **54 D4** 7 0S 35 20 E
Mühlhausen, *Germany* **16 C6** 51 12N 10 27 E
Mühlig Hofmann fjell, *Antarctica* **5 D3** 72 30S 5 0 E
Muhos, *Finland* **8 D22** 64 47N 25 59 E
Muhu, *Estonia* **9 G20** 58 36N 23 11 E
Muhutwe, *Tanzania* **54 C3** 1 35S 31 45 E
Muine Bheag, *Ireland* **13 D5** 52 42N 6 58W
Muir, L., *Australia* **61 F2** 34 30S 116 40 E
Mujnak = Muynak, *Uzbekistan* **26 E6** 43 44N 59 10 E
Mukacheve, *Ukraine* **17 D12** 48 27N 22 45 E
Mukachevo = Mukacheve, *Ukraine* **17 D12** 48 27N 22 45 E
Mukah, *Malaysia* **36 D4** 2 55N 112 5 E
Mukandwara, *India* **42 G6** 24 49N 75 59 E
Mukdahan, *Thailand* **38 D5** 16 32N 104 43 E
Mukden = Shenyang, *China* **35 D12** 41 48N 123 27 E
Mukerian, *India* **42 D6** 31 57N 75 37 E
Mukhtuya = Lensk, *Russia* **27 C12** 60 48N 114 55 E
Mukinbudin, *Australia* **61 F2** 30 55S 118 5 E
Mukishi, *Dem. Rep. of the Congo* **55 D1** 8 30S 24 44 E
Mukomuko, *Indonesia* **36 E2** 2 30S 101 10 E
Mukomwenze, *Dem. Rep. of the Congo* **54 D2** 6 49S 27 15 E
Muktsar, *India* **42 D6** 30 30N 74 30 E
Mukur = Moqor, *Afghan.* **42 C2** 32 50N 67 42 E
Mukutawa →, *Canada* **73 C9** 53 10N 97 24W
Mukwela, *Zambia* **55 F2** 17 0S 26 40 E
Mula, *Spain* **19 C5** 38 3N 1 33W
Mula →, *Pakistan* **42 F2** 27 57N 67 36 E
Mulange, *Dem. Rep. of the Congo* **54 C2** 3 40S 27 10 E
Mulanje, *Malawi* **55 F4** 16 2S 35 33 E
Mulchén, *Chile* **94 D1** 37 45S 72 20W
Mulde →, *Germany* **16 C7** 51 53N 12 15 E
Mule Creek Junction, *U.S.A.* **80 D2** 43 19N 104 8W
Muleba, *Tanzania* **54 C3** 1 50S 31 37 E
Mulejé, *Mexico* **86 B2** 26 53N 112 1W
Muleshoe, *U.S.A.* **81 H3** 34 13N 102 43W
Mulgrave, *Canada* **71 C7** 45 38N 61 31W
Mulhacén, *Spain* **19 D4** 37 4N 3 20W
Mülheim, *Germany* **33 C6** 51 25N 6 54 E
Mulhouse, *France* **18 C7** 47 40N 7 20 E
Muling, *China* **35 B16** 44 35N 130 10 E
Mull, *U.K.* **12 E3** 56 25N 5 56W
Mull, Sound of, *U.K.* **12 E3** 56 30N 5 50W
Mullaittivu, *Sri Lanka* **40 Q12** 9 15N 80 49 E
Mullen, *U.S.A.* **80 D4** 42 3N 101 1W
Mullens, *U.S.A.* **76 G5** 37 35N 81 23W
Muller, Pegunungan, *Indonesia* **36 D4** 0 30N 113 30 E
Mullet Pen., *Ireland* **13 B1** 54 13N 10 2W
Mullewa, *Australia* **61 E2** 28 29S 115 30 E
Mulligan →, *Australia* **62 D2** 25 0S 139 0 E
Mullingar, *Ireland* **13 C4** 53 31N 7 21W
Mullins, *U.S.A.* **77 H6** 34 12N 79 15W
Mullumbimby, *Australia* **63 D5** 28 30S 153 30 E
Mulobezi, *Zambia* **55 F2** 16 45S 25 7 E
Mulroy B., *Ireland* **13 A4** 55 15N 7 46W
Multan, *Pakistan* **42 D4** 30 15N 71 36 E
Mulumbe, Mts., *Dem. Rep. of the Congo* **55 D2** 8 40S 27 30 E
Mulungushi Dam, *Zambia* **55 E2** 14 48S 28 48 E
Mulvane, *U.S.A.* **81 G6** 37 29N 97 15W
Mumbai, *India* **40 K8** 18 55N 72 50 E
Mumbwa, *Zambia* **55 F2** 15 0S 27 0 E
Mun →, *Thailand* **38 E5** 15 19N 105 30 E
Muna, *Indonesia* **37 F6** 5 0S 122 30 E
Munabao, *India* **42 G4** 25 45N 70 17 E
Munamagi, *Estonia* **9 H22** 57 43N 27 4 E
München, *Germany* **16 D6** 48 8N 11 34 E
Munchen-Gladbach = Mönchengladbach, *Germany* **16 C4** 51 11N 6 27 E
Muncho Lake, *Canada* **72 B3** 59 0N 125 50W
Munch'ŏn, *N. Korea* **35 E14** 39 14N 127 19 E
Muncie, *U.S.A.* **76 E3** 40 12N 85 23W
Muncoonie, L., *Australia* **62 D2** 25 12S 138 40 E
Mundabbera, *Australia* **63 D5** 25 36S 151 18 E
Munday, *U.S.A.* **81 J5** 33 27N 99 38W
Münden, *Germany* **16 C5** 51 25N 9 38 E
Mundiwindi, *Australia* **60 D3** 23 47S 120 9 E
Mundo Novo, *Brazil* **93 F10** 11 50S 40 29W
Mundra, *India* **42 H3** 22 54N 69 48 E
Mundrabilla, *Australia* **61 F4** 31 52S 127 51 E
Mungallala, *Australia* **63 D4** 26 28S 147 34 E
Mungallala Cr. →, *Australia* **63 D4** 28 53S 147 5 E
Mungana, *Australia* **62 B3** 17 8S 144 27 E
Mungaoli, *India* **42 G8** 24 24N 78 7 E
Mungari, *Mozam.* **55 F3** 17 12S 33 30 E
Mungbere, *Dem. Rep. of the Congo* **54 B2** 2 36N 28 28 E
Mungeli, *India* **43 H9** 22 4N 81 41 E
Munger, *India* **43 G12** 25 23N 86 30 E
Munich = München, *Germany* **16 D6** 48 8N 11 34 E
Munising, *U.S.A.* **76 B2** 46 25N 86 40W
Munku-Sardyk, *Russia* **27 D11** 51 45N 100 20 E
Muñoz Gamero, Pen., *Chile* **96 G2** 52 30S 73 5W
Munroe L., *Canada* **73 B9** 59 13N 98 35W
Munsan, *S. Korea* **35 F14** 37 51N 126 48 E
Münster, *Germany* **16 C4** 51 58N 7 37 E
Munster □, *Ireland* **13 D3** 52 18N 8 44W
Muntadgin, *Australia* **61 F2** 31 45S 118 33 E
Muntok, *Indonesia* **36 E3** 2 5S 105 10 E
Munyama, *Zambia* **55 F2** 16 5S 28 31 E
Muong Beng, *Laos* **38 B3** 20 23N 101 46 E
Muong Boum, *Vietnam* **38 A4** 22 24N 102 49 E
Muong Et, *Laos* **38 B5** 20 49N 104 1 E
Muong Hai, *Laos* **38 B3** 21 3N 101 49 E
Muong Hiem, *Laos* **38 B4** 20 5N 103 22 E
Muong Houn, *Laos* **38 B3** 20 8N 101 23 E
Muong Hung, *Vietnam* **38 B4** 20 56N 103 53 E
Muong Kau, *Laos* **38 E5** 15 6N 105 47 E
Muong Khao, *Laos* **38 C4** 19 38N 103 32 E
Muong Khoua, *Laos* **38 B4** 21 5N 102 31 E
Muong Liep, *Laos* **38 C3** 18 29N 101 40 E
Muong May, *Laos* **38 E6** 14 49N 106 56 E
Muong Ngeun, *Laos* **38 B3** 20 36N 101 3 E
Muong Ngoi, *Laos* **38 B4** 20 43N 102 41 E
Muong Nhie, *Vietnam* **38 A4** 22 12N 102 28 E
Muong Nong, *Laos* **38 D6** 16 22N 106 30 E
Muong Ou Tay, *Laos* **38 A3** 22 7N 101 48 E
Muong Oua, *Laos* **38 C3** 18 18N 101 20 E
Muong Peun, *Laos* **38 B4** 20 13N 103 52 E
Muong Phalane, *Laos* **38 D5** 16 39N 105 34 E
Muong Phieng, *Laos* **38 C3** 19 6N 101 32 E
Muong Phine, *Laos* **38 D6** 16 32N 106 2 E
Muong Sai, *Laos* **38 B3** 20 42N 101 59 E
Muong Saiapoun, *Laos* **38 C3** 18 24N 101 31 E
Muong Sen, *Vietnam* **38 C5** 19 24N 104 8 E
Muong Sing, *Laos* **38 B3** 21 11N 101 9 E
Muong Son, *Laos* **38 B4** 20 27N 103 19 E
Muong Soui, *Laos* **38 C4** 19 33N 102 52 E
Muong Va, *Laos* **38 B4** 21 53N 102 19 E
Muong Xia, *Vietnam* **38 B5** 20 19N 104 50 E
Muonio, *Finland* **8 C20** 67 57N 23 40 E
Muonionjoki →, *Finland* **8 C20** 67 11N 23 34 E
Muping, *China* **35 F11** 37 22N 121 36 E
Muqdisho, *Somali Rep.* **46 G4** 2 2N 45 25 E
Mur →, *Austria* **17 E9** 46 18N 16 52 E
Murakami, *Japan* **30 E9** 38 14N 139 29 E
Murallón, Cerro, *Chile* **96 F2** 49 48S 73 30W
Muranda, *Rwanda* **54 C2** 1 52S 29 20 E
Murang'a, *Kenya* **54 C4** 0 45S 37 9 E
Murashi, *Russia* **24 C8** 59 30N 49 0 E
Murat →, *Turkey* **25 G7** 38 46N 40 0 E
Muratlı, *Turkey* **21 D12** 41 10N 27 29 E
Murayama, *Japan* **30 E10** 38 30N 140 25 E
Murchison →, *Australia* **61 E1** 27 45S 114 0 E
Murchison, Mt., *Antarctica* **5 D11** 73 0S 168 0 E
Murchison Falls, *Uganda* **54 B3** 2 15N 31 30 E
Murchison Ra., *Australia* **62 C1** 20 0S 134 10 E
Murchison Rapids, *Malawi* **55 F3** 15 55S 34 35 E
Murcia, *Spain* **19 D5** 38 5N 1 10W
Murcia □, *Spain* **19 D5** 37 50N 1 30W
Murdo, *U.S.A.* **80 D4** 43 53N 100 43W
Murdoch Pt., *Australia* **62 A3** 14 37S 144 55 E
Mureş →, *Romania* **17 E11** 46 15N 20 13 E
Mureşul = Mureş →, *Romania* **17 E11** 46 15N 20 13 E
Murewa, *Zimbabwe* **57 B5** 17 39S 31 47 E
Murfreesboro, *N.C., U.S.A.* **77 G7** 36 27N 77 6W
Murfreesboro, *Tenn., U.S.A.* **77 H2** 35 51N 86 24W
Murgab = Murghob, *Tajikistan* **26 F8** 38 10N 74 2 E
Murgab →, *Turkmenistan* **45 B9** 38 18N 61 12 E
Murgenella, *Australia* **60 B5** 11 34S 132 56 E
Murgha Kibzai, *Pakistan* **42 D3** 30 44N 69 25 E
Murghob, *Tajikistan* **26 F8** 38 10N 74 2 E
Murgon, *Australia* **63 D5** 26 15S 151 54 E
Muri, *India* **43 H11** 23 22N 85 52 E
Muria, *Indonesia* **37 G14** 6 36S 110 53 E
Muriaé, *Brazil* **95 A7** 21 8S 42 23W
Muriel Mine, *Zimbabwe* **55 F3** 17 14S 30 40 E
Müritz, *Germany* **16 B7** 53 25N 12 42 E
Murka, *Kenya* **54 C4** 3 27S 38 0 E
Murliganj, *India* **43 G12** 25 54N 86 59 E
Murmansk, *Russia* **24 A5** 68 57N 33 10 E
Muro, *Spain* **22 B10** 39 44N 3 3 E
Murom, *Russia* **24 C7** 55 35N 42 3 E
Muroran, *Japan* **30 C10** 42 25N 141 0 E
Muroto, *Japan* **31 H7** 33 18N 134 9 E
Muroto-Misaki, *Japan* **31 H7** 33 15N 134 10 E
Murphy, *U.S.A.* **82 E5** 43 13N 116 33W
Murphys, *U.S.A.* **84 G6** 38 8N 120 28W
Murray, *Ky., U.S.A.* **77 G1** 36 37N 88 19W
Murray, *Utah, U.S.A.* **82 F8** 40 40N 111 53W
Murray →, *Australia* **63 F2** 35 20S 139 22 E
Murray, L., *U.S.A.* **77 H5** 34 3N 81 13W
Murray Bridge, *Australia* **63 F2** 35 6S 139 14 E
Murray Harbour, *Canada* **71 C7** 46 0N 62 28W
Murraysburg, *S. Africa* **56 E3** 31 58S 23 47 E
Murree, *Pakistan* **42 C5** 33 56N 73 28 E
Murrieta, *U.S.A.* **85 M9** 33 33N 117 13W
Murrumbidgee →, *Australia* **63 E3** 34 43S 143 12 E
Murrumburrah, *Australia* **63 E4** 34 32S 148 22 E
Murrurundi, *Australia* **63 E5** 31 42S 150 51 E
Murshidabad, *India* **43 G13** 24 11N 88 19 E
Murtle L., *Canada* **72 C5** 52 8N 119 38W
Murtoa, *Australia* **63 F3** 36 35S 142 28 E
Murungu, *Tanzania* **54 C3** 4 12S 31 10 E
Mururoa, *Pac. Oc.* **65 K14** 21 52S 138 55W
Murwara, *India* **43 H9** 23 46N 80 28 E
Murwillumbah, *Australia* **63 D5** 28 18S 153 27 E
Mürzzuschlag, *Austria* **16 E8** 47 36N 15 41 E
Muş, *Turkey* **25 G7** 38 45N 41 30 E
Mûsa, Gebel, *Egypt* **44 D2** 28 33N 33 59 E
Musa Khel, *Pakistan* **42 D3** 30 59N 69 52 E
Mūsa Qal'eh, *Afghan.* **40 C4** 32 20N 64 50 E
Musafirkhana, *India* **43 F9** 26 22N 81 48 E
Musala, *Bulgaria* **21 C10** 42 13N 23 37 E
Musala, *Indonesia* **36 D1** 1 41N 98 28 E
Musan, *N. Korea* **35 C15** 42 12N 129 12 E
Musangu, *Dem. Rep. of the Congo* **55 E1** 10 28S 23 55 E
Musasa, *Tanzania* **54 C3** 3 25S 31 30 E
Musay'īd, *Qatar* **45 E6** 25 0N 51 33 E
Muscat = Masqat, *Oman* **46 C6** 23 37N 58 36 E
Muscat & Oman = Oman ■, *Asia* **46 C6** 23 0N 58 0 E
Muscatine, *U.S.A.* **80 E9** 41 25N 91 3W
Musgrave Harbour, *Canada* **71 C9** 49 27N 53 58W
Musgrave Ranges, *Australia* **61 E5** 26 0S 132 0 E
Mushie, *Dem. Rep. of the Congo* **52 E3** 2 56S 16 55 E
Musi →, *Indonesia* **36 E2** 2 20S 104 56 E
Muskeg →, *Canada* **72 A4** 60 20N 123 20W
Muskegon, *U.S.A.* **76 D2** 43 14N 86 16W
Muskegon →, *U.S.A.* **76 D2** 43 14N 86 21W
Muskegon Heights, *U.S.A.* **76 D2** 43 12N 86 16W
Muskogee, *U.S.A.* **81 H7** 35 45N 95 22W
Muskoka, L., *Canada* **78 B5** 45 0N 79 25W
Muskwa →, *Canada* **72 B4** 58 47N 122 48W
Muslimiyah, *Syria* **44 B3** 36 19N 37 12 E
Musofu, *Zambia* **55 E2** 13 30S 29 0 E
Musoma, *Tanzania* **54 C3** 1 30S 33 48 E
Musquaro, L., *Canada* **71 B7** 50 38N 61 5W
Musquodoboit Harbour, *Canada* **71 D7** 44 50N 63 9W
Musselburgh, *U.K.* **12 F5** 55 57N 3 2W
Musselshell →, *U.S.A.* **82 C10** 47 21N 107 57W
Mussoorie, *India* **42 D8** 30 27N 78 6 E
Mussuco, *Angola* **56 B2** 17 2S 19 3 E
Mustafakemalpaşa, *Turkey* **21 D13** 40 2N 28 24 E
Mustang, *Nepal* **43 E10** 29 10N 83 55 E
Musters, L., *Argentina* **96 F3** 45 20S 69 25W
Musudan, *N. Korea* **35 D15** 40 50N 129 43 E
Muswellbrook, *Australia* **63 E5** 32 16S 150 56 E
Mût, *Egypt* **51 C11** 25 28N 28 58 E
Mut, *Turkey* **44 B2** 36 40N 33 28 E
Mutanda, *Mozam.* **57 C5** 21 0S 33 34 E
Mutanda, *Zambia* **55 E2** 12 24S 26 13 E
Mutare, *Zimbabwe* **55 F3** 18 58S 32 38 E
Muting, *Indonesia* **37 F10** 7 23S 140 20 E
Mutoko, *Zimbabwe* **57 B5** 17 24S 32 13 E
Mutoray, *Russia* **27 C11** 60 56N 101 0 E
Mutshatsha, *Dem. Rep. of the Congo* **55 E1** 10 35S 24 20 E
Mutsu, *Japan* **30 D10** 41 5N 140 55 E
Mutsu-Wan, *Japan* **30 D10** 41 5N 140 55 E
Muttaburra, *Australia* **62 C3** 22 38S 144 29 E
Mutton I., *Ireland* **13 D2** 52 49N 9 32W
Mutuáli, *Mozam.* **55 E4** 14 55S 37 0 E
Muweilih, *Egypt* **47 E3** 30 42N 34 19 E
Muy Muy, *Nic.* **88 D2** 12 39N 85 36W
Muyinga, *Burundi* **54 C3** 3 14S 30 33 E
Muynak, *Uzbekistan* **26 E6** 43 44N 59 10 E
Muzaffarabad, *Pakistan* **43 B5** 34 25N 73 30 E
Muzaffargarh, *Pakistan* **42 D4** 30 5N 71 14 E
Muzaffarnagar, *India* **42 E7** 29 26N 77 40 E
Muzaffarpur, *India* **43 F11** 26 7N 85 23 E
Muzafirpur, *Pakistan* **42 D3** 30 58N 69 9 E
Muzhi, *Russia* **24 A11** 65 25N 64 40 E
Mvuma, *Zimbabwe* **55 F3** 19 16S 30 30 E
Mvurwi, *Zimbabwe* **55 F3** 17 0S 30 57 E
Mwadui, *Tanzania* **54 C3** 3 26S 33 32 E
Mwambo, *Tanzania* **55 E5** 10 30S 40 22 E
Mwandi, *Zambia* **55 F1** 17 30S 24 51 E
Mwanza, *Dem. Rep. of the Congo* **54 D2** 7 55S 26 43 E
Mwanza, *Tanzania* **54 C3** 2 30S 32 58 E
Mwanza, *Zambia* **55 F1** 16 58S 24 28 E
Mwanza □, *Tanzania* **54 C3** 2 0S 33 0 E
Mwaya, *Tanzania* **55 D3** 9 32S 33 55 E
Mweelrea, *Ireland* **13 C2** 53 39N 9 49W
Mweka, *Dem. Rep. of the Congo* **52 E4** 4 50S 21 34 E
Mwenezi, *Zimbabwe* **55 G3** 21 15S 30 48 E
Mwenezi →, *Mozam.* **55 G3** 22 40S 31 50 E
Mwenga, *Dem. Rep. of the Congo* **54 C2** 3 1S 28 28 E
Mweru, L., *Zambia* **55 D2** 9 0S 28 40 E
Mweza Range, *Zimbabwe* **55 G3** 21 0S 30 0 E
Mwilambwe, *Dem. Rep. of the Congo* **54 D2** 8 7S 25 5 E
Mwimbi, *Tanzania* **55 D3** 8 38S 31 39 E
Mwinilunga, *Zambia* **55 E1** 11 43S 24 25 E
My Tho, *Vietnam* **39 G6** 10 29N 106 23 E
Myajlar, *India* **42 F4** 26 15N 70 20 E
Myanaung, *Burma* **41 K19** 18 18N 95 22 E
Myanmar = Burma ■, *Asia* **41 J20** 21 0N 96 30 E
Myaungmya, *Burma* **41 L19** 16 30N 94 40 E
Mycenæ, *Greece* **21 F10** 37 39N 22 52 E
Myeik Kyunzu, *Burma* **39 G1** 11 30N 97 30 E
Myers Chuck, *U.S.A.* **72 B2** 55 44N 132 11W
Myerstown, *U.S.A.* **79 F8** 40 22N 76 19W
Myingyan, *Burma* **41 J19** 21 30N 95 20 E
Myitkyina, *Burma* **41 G20** 25 24N 97 26 E
Mykines, *Færoe Is.* **8 E9** 62 7N 7 35W
Mykolayiv, *Ukraine* **25 E5** 46 58N 32 0 E
Mymensingh, *Bangla.* **41 G17** 24 45N 90 24 E
Mynydd Du, *U.K.* **11 F4** 51 52N 3 50W
Mýrdalsjökull, *Iceland* **8 E4** 63 40N 19 6W
Myrtle Beach, *U.S.A.* **77 J6** 33 42N 78 53W
Myrtle Creek, *U.S.A.* **82 E2** 43 1N 123 17W
Myrtle Point, *U.S.A.* **82 E1** 43 4N 124 8W
Myrtou, *Cyprus* **23 D12** 35 18N 33 4 E
Mysia, *Turkey* **21 E12** 39 50N 27 0 E
Mysore = Karnataka □, *India* **40 N10** 13 15N 77 0 E
Mysore, *India* **40 N10** 12 17N 76 41 E
Mystic, *U.S.A.* **79 E13** 41 21N 71 58W
Myszków, *Poland* **17 C10** 50 45N 19 22 E
Mytishchi, *Russia* **24 C6** 55 50N 37 50 E
Mývatn, *Iceland* **8 D5** 65 36N 17 0W
Mzimba, *Malawi* **55 E3** 11 55S 33 39 E
Mzimkulu →, *S. Africa* **57 E5** 30 44S 30 28 E
Mzimvubu →, *S. Africa* **57 E4** 31 38S 29 33 E
Mzuzu, *Malawi* **55 E3** 11 30S 33 55 E

N

Na Hearadh = Harris, *U.K.* **12 D2** 57 50N 6 55W
Na Noi, *Thailand* **38 C3** 18 19N 100 43 E
Na Phao, *Laos* **38 D5** 17 35N 105 44 E
Na Sam, *Vietnam* **38 A6** 22 3N 106 37 E
Na San, *Vietnam* **38 B5** 21 12N 104 2 E
Naab →, *Germany* **16 D6** 49 1N 12 2 E
Naantali, *Finland* **9 F19** 60 29N 22 2 E
Naas, *Ireland* **13 C5** 53 12N 6 40W
Nababeep, *S. Africa* **56 D2** 29 36S 17 46 E
Nabadwip = Navadwip, *India* **43 H13** 23 34N 88 20 E
Nabari, *Japan* **31 G8** 34 37N 136 5 E
Nabawa, *Australia* **61 E1** 28 30S 114 48 E
Nabberu, L., *Australia* **61 E3** 25 50S 120 30 E
Naberezhnyye Chelny, *Russia* **24 C9** 55 42N 52 19 E
Nabeul, *Tunisia* **51 A8** 36 30N 10 44 E
Nabha, *India* **42 D7** 30 26N 76 14 E
Nabīd, *Iran* **45 D8** 29 40N 57 38 E
Nabire, *Indonesia* **37 E9** 3 15S 135 26 E
Nabisar, *Pakistan* **42 G3** 25 8N 69 40 E
Nabisipi →, *Canada* **71 B7** 50 14N 62 13W
Nabiswera, *Uganda* **54 B3** 1 27N 32 15 E
Nablus = Nābulus, *West Bank* **47 C4** 32 14N 35 15 E
Naboomspruit, *S. Africa* **57 C4** 24 32S 28 40 E
Nābulus, *West Bank* **47 C4** 32 14N 35 15 E
Nacala, *Mozam.* **55 E5** 14 31S 40 34 E
Nacala-Velha, *Mozam.* **55 E5** 14 32S 40 34 E
Nacaome, *Honduras* **88 D2** 13 31N 87 30W
Nacaroa, *Mozam.* **55 E4** 14 22S 39 56 E
Naches, *U.S.A.* **82 C3** 46 44N 120 42W
Naches →, *U.S.A.* **84 D6** 46 38N 120 31W
Nachicapau, L., *Canada* **71 A6** 56 40N 68 5W
Nachingwea, *Tanzania* **55 E4** 10 23S 38 49 E
Nachna, *India* **42 F4** 27 34N 71 41 E
Nacimiento L., *U.S.A.* **84 K6** 35 46N 120 53W
Naco, *Mexico* **86 A3** 31 20N 109 56W
Nacogdoches, *U.S.A.* **81 K7** 31 36N 94 39W
Nácori Chico, *Mexico* **86 B3** 29 39N 109 1W
Nacozari, *Mexico* **86 A3** 30 24N 109 39W
Nadi, *Fiji* **59 C7** 17 42S 177 20 E
Nadiad, *India* **42 H5** 22 41N 72 56 E
Nador, *Morocco* **50 B5** 35 14N 2 58W
Nadur, *Malta* **23 C1** 36 2N 14 18 E
Nadūshan, *Iran* **45 C7** 32 2N 53 35 E
Nadvirna, *Ukraine* **17 D13** 48 37N 24 30 E
Nadvoitsy, *Russia* **24 B5** 63 52N 34 14 E
Nadvornaya = Nadvirna, *Ukraine* **17 D13** 48 37N 24 30 E
Nadym, *Russia* **26 C8** 65 35N 72 42 E
Nadym →, *Russia* **26 C8** 66 12N 72 0 E
Nærbø, *Norway* **9 G11** 58 40N 5 39 E
Næstved, *Denmark* **9 J14** 55 13N 11 44 E
Naft-e Safīd, *Iran* **45 D6** 31 40N 49 17 E
Naftshahr, *Iran* **44 C5** 34 0N 45 30 E
Nafud Desert = An Nafūd, *Si. Arabia* **44 D4** 28 15N 41 0 E
Naga, *Phil.* **37 B6** 13 38N 123 15 E
Nagahama, *Japan* **31 G8** 35 23N 136 16 E
Nagai, *Japan* **30 E10** 38 6N 140 2 E
Nagaland □, *India* **41 G19** 26 0N 94 30 E
Nagano, *Japan* **31 F9** 36 40N 138 10 E
Nagano □, *Japan* **31 F9** 36 15N 138 0 E
Nagaoka, *Japan* **31 F9** 37 27N 138 51 E
Nagappattinam, *India* **40 P11** 10 46N 79 51 E
Nagar →, *Bangla.* **43 G13** 24 27N 89 12 E
Nagar Parkar, *Pakistan* **42 G4** 24 28N 70 46 E
Nagasaki, *Japan* **31 H4** 32 47N 129 50 E
Nagasaki □, *Japan* **31 H4** 32 50N 129 40 E
Nagato, *Japan* **31 G5** 34 19N 131 5 E
Nagaur, *India* **42 F5** 27 15N 73 45 E
Nagda, *India* **42 H6** 23 27N 75 25 E
Nagercoil, *India* **40 Q10** 8 12N 77 26 E
Nagina, *India* **43 E8** 29 30N 78 30 E
Nagineh, *Iran* **45 C8** 34 20N 57 15 E
Nagir, *Pakistan* **43 A6** 36 12N 74 42 E
Nagod, *India* **43 G9** 24 34N 80 36 E
Nagoorin, *Australia* **62 C5** 24 17S 151 15 E
Nagorno-Karabakh, *Azerbaijan* **25 F8** 39 55N 46 45 E
Nagornyy, *Russia* **27 D13** 55 58N 124 57 E
Nagoya, *Japan* **31 G8** 35 10N 136 50 E
Nagpur, *India* **40 J11** 21 8N 79 10 E
Nagua, *Dom. Rep.* **89 C6** 19 23N 69 50W
Nagykanizsa, *Hungary* **17 E9** 46 28N 17 0 E
Nagykőrös, *Hungary* **17 E10** 47 5N 19 48 E
Naha, *Japan* **31 L3** 26 13N 127 42 E
Nahan, *India* **42 D7** 30 33N 77 18 E
Nahanni Butte, *Canada* **72 A4** 61 2N 123 31W
Nahanni Nat. Park, *Canada* **72 A4** 61 15N 125 0W
Nahargarh, *Mad. P., India* **42 G6** 24 10N 75 14 E
Nahargarh, *Raj., India* **42 G7** 24 55N 76 50 E
Nahariyya, *Israel* **44 C2** 33 1N 35 5 E
Nahāvand, *Iran* **45 C6** 34 10N 48 22 E
Naicá, *Mexico* **86 B3** 27 53N 105 31W
Naicam, *Canada* **73 C8** 52 30N 104 30W
Naikoon Prov. Park, *Canada* **72 C2** 53 55N 131 55W
Naimisharanya, *India* **43 F9** 27 21N 80 30 E
Nain, *Canada* **71 A7** 56 34N 61 40W
Nā'īn, *Iran* **45 C7** 32 54N 53 0 E
Naini Tal, *India* **43 E8** 29 30N 79 30 E
Nainpur, *India* **40 H12** 22 30N 80 10 E
Nainwa, *India* **42 G6** 25 46N 75 51 E
Nairn, *U.K.* **12 D5** 57 35N 3 53W
Nairobi, *Kenya* **54 C4** 1 17S 36 48 E
Naissaar, *Estonia* **9 G21** 59 34N 24 29 E
Naivasha, *Kenya* **54 C4** 0 40S 36 30 E
Naivasha, L., *Kenya* **54 C4** 0 48S 36 20 E
Najafābād, *Iran* **45 C6** 32 40N 51 15 E
Najd, *Si. Arabia* **46 B3** 26 30N 42 0 E
Najibabad, *India* **42 E8** 29 40N 78 20 E
Najin, *N. Korea* **35 C16** 42 12N 130 15 E
Najmah, *Si. Arabia* **45 E6** 26 42N 50 6 E

Neuquén □, *Argentina* **94 D2** 38 0S 69 50W
Neuruppin, *Germany* **16 B7** 52 55N 12 48 E
Neuse →, *U.S.A.* **77 H7** 35 6N 76 29W
Neusiedler See, *Austria* **17 E9** 47 50N 16 47 E
Neustrelitz, *Germany* **16 B7** 53 21N 13 4 E
Neva →, *Russia* **24 C5** 59 50N 30 30 E
Nevada, *Iowa, U.S.A.* **80 D8** 42 1N 93 27W
Nevada, *Mo., U.S.A.* **81 G7** 37 51N 94 22W
Nevada □, *U.S.A.* **82 G5** 39 0N 117 0W
Nevada City, *U.S.A.* **84 F6** 39 16N 121 1W
Nevado, Cerro, *Argentina* **94 D2** 35 30S 68 32W
Nevel, *Russia* **24 C4** 56 0N 29 55 E
Nevers, *France* **18 C5** 47 0N 3 9 E
Nevertire, *Australia* **63 E4** 31 50S 147 44 E
Neville, *Canada* **73 D7** 49 58N 107 39W
Nevinnomyssk, *Russia* **25 F7** 44 40N 42 0 E
Nevis, *St. Kitts & Nevis* **89 C7** 17 0N 62 30W
Nevşehir, *Turkey* **44 B2** 38 33N 34 40 E
Nevyansk, *Russia* **24 C11** 57 30N 60 13 E
New →, *U.S.A.* **76 F5** 38 10N 81 12W
New Aiyansh, *Canada* **72 B3** 55 12N 129 4W
New Albany, *Ind., U.S.A.* **76 F3** 38 18N 85 49W
New Albany, *Miss., U.S.A.* **81 H10** 34 29N 89 0W
New Albany, *Pa., U.S.A.* **79 E8** 41 36N 76 27W
New Amsterdam, *Guyana* **92 B7** 6 15N 57 36W
New Angledool, *Australia* **63 D4** 29 5S 147 55 E
New Baltimore, *U.S.A.* **78 D2** 42 41N 82 44W
New Bedford, *U.S.A.* **79 E14** 41 38N 70 56W
New Berlin, *N.Y., U.S.A.* **79 D9** 42 37N 75 20W
New Berlin, *Pa., U.S.A.* **78 F8** 40 50N 76 57W
New Bern, *U.S.A.* **77 H7** 35 7N 77 3W
New Bethlehem, *U.S.A.* **78 F5** 41 0N 79 20W
New Bloomfield, *U.S.A.* **78 F7** 40 25N 77 11W
New Boston, *U.S.A.* **81 J7** 33 28N 94 25W
New Braunfels, *U.S.A.* **81 L5** 29 42N 98 8W
New Brighton, *N.Z.* **59 K4** 43 29S 172 43 E
New Brighton, *U.S.A.* **78 F4** 40 42N 80 19W
New Britain, *Papua N. G.* **64 H7** 5 50S 150 20 E
New Britain, *U.S.A.* **79 E12** 41 40N 72 47W
New Brunswick, *U.S.A.* **79 F10** 40 30N 74 27W
New Brunswick □, *Canada* **71 C6** 46 50N 66 30W
New Caledonia ■, *Pac. Oc.* **64 K8** 21 0S 165 0 E
New Castile = Castilla-La Mancha □, *Spain* **19 C4** 39 30N 3 30W
New Castle, *Ind., U.S.A.* **76 F3** 39 55N 85 22W
New Castle, *Pa., U.S.A.* **78 F4** 41 0N 80 21W
New City, *U.S.A.* **79 E11** 41 9N 73 59W
New Concord, *U.S.A.* **78 G3** 39 59N 81 54W
New Cumberland, *U.S.A.* **78 F4** 40 30N 80 36W
New Cuyama, *U.S.A.* **85 L7** 34 57N 119 38W
New Delhi, *India* **42 E7** 28 37N 77 13 E
New Denver, *Canada* **72 D5** 50 0N 117 25W
New Don Pedro Reservoir, *U.S.A.* **84 H6** 37 43N 120 24W
New England, *U.S.A.* **80 B3** 46 32N 102 52W
New England Ra., *Australia* **63 E5** 30 20S 151 45 E
New Forest, *U.K.* **11 G6** 50 53N 1 34W
New Galloway, *U.K.* **12 F4** 55 5N 4 9W
New Glasgow, *Canada* **71 C7** 45 35N 62 36W
New Guinea, *Oceania* **28 K17** 4 0S 136 0 E
New Hamburg, *Canada* **78 C4** 43 23N 80 42W
New Hampshire □, *U.S.A.* **79 C13** 44 0N 71 30W
New Hampton, *U.S.A.* **80 D8** 43 3N 92 19W
New Hanover, *S. Africa* **57 D5** 29 22S 30 31 E
New Hartford, *U.S.A.* **79 C9** 43 4N 75 18W
New Haven, *Conn., U.S.A.* **79 E12** 41 18N 72 55W
New Haven, *Mich., U.S.A.* **78 D2** 42 44N 82 48W
New Hazelton, *Canada* **72 B3** 55 20N 127 30W
New Hebrides = Vanuatu ■, *Pac. Oc.* **64 J8** 15 0S 168 0 E
New Holland, *U.S.A.* **79 F8** 40 6N 76 5W
New Iberia, *U.S.A.* **81 K9** 30 1N 91 49W
New Ireland, *Papua N. G.* **64 H7** 3 20S 151 50 E
New Jersey □, *U.S.A.* **76 E8** 40 0N 74 30W
New Kensington, *U.S.A.* **78 F5** 40 34N 79 46W
New Lexington, *U.S.A.* **76 F4** 39 43N 82 13W
New Liskeard, *Canada* **70 C4** 47 31N 79 41W
New London, *Conn., U.S.A.* **79 E12** 41 22N 72 6W
New London, *Ohio, U.S.A.* **78 E2** 41 5N 82 24W
New London, *Wis., U.S.A.* **80 C10** 44 23N 88 45W
New Madrid, *U.S.A.* **81 G10** 36 36N 89 32W
New Martinsville, *U.S.A.* **76 F5** 39 39N 80 52W
New Meadows, *U.S.A.* **82 D5** 44 58N 116 18W
New Melones L., *U.S.A.* **84 H6** 37 57N 120 31W
New Mexico □, *U.S.A.* **83 J10** 34 30N 106 0W
New Milford, *Conn., U.S.A.* **79 E11** 41 35N 73 25W
New Milford, *Pa., U.S.A.* **79 E9** 41 52N 75 44W
New Norcia, *Australia* **61 F2** 30 57S 116 13 E
New Norfolk, *Australia* **62 G4** 42 46S 147 2 E
New Orleans, *U.S.A.* **81 L9** 29 58N 90 4W
New Philadelphia, *U.S.A.* **78 F3** 40 30N 81 27W
New Plymouth, *N.Z.* **59 H5** 39 4S 174 5 E
New Plymouth, *U.S.A.* **82 E5** 43 58N 116 49W
New Port Richey, *U.S.A.* **77 L4** 28 16N 82 43W
New Providence, *Bahamas* **88 A4** 25 25N 78 35W
New Quay, *U.K.* **11 E3** 52 13N 4 21W
New Radnor, *U.K.* **11 E4** 52 15N 3 9W
New Richmond, *Canada* **71 C6** 48 15N 65 45W
New Richmond, *U.S.A.* **80 C8** 45 7N 92 32W
New Roads, *U.S.A.* **81 K9** 30 42N 91 26W
New Rochelle, *U.S.A.* **79 F11** 40 55N 73 47W
New Rockford, *U.S.A.* **80 B5** 47 41N 99 8W
New Romney, *U.K.* **11 G8** 50 59N 0 57 E
New Ross, *Ireland* **13 D5** 52 23N 6 57W
New Salem, *U.S.A.* **80 B4** 46 51N 101 25W
New Scone, *U.K.* **12 E5** 56 25N 3 24W
New Siberian I. = Novaya Sibir, Ostrov, *Russia* **27 B16** 75 10N 150 0 E
New Siberian Is. = Novosibirskiye Ostrova, *Russia* **27 B15** 75 0N 142 0 E
New Smyrna Beach, *U.S.A.* **77 L5** 29 1N 80 56W
New South Wales □, *Australia* **63 E4** 33 0S 146 0 E
New Town, *U.S.A.* **80 B3** 47 59N 102 30W
New Tredegar, *U.K.* **11 F4** 51 44N 3 16W
New Ulm, *U.S.A.* **80 C7** 44 19N 94 28W
New Waterford, *Canada* **71 C7** 46 13N 60 4W
New Westminster, *Canada* **84 A4** 49 13N 122 55W
New York, *U.S.A.* **79 F11** 40 45N 74 0W
New York □, *U.S.A.* **79 D9** 43 0N 75 0W
New York Mts., *U.S.A.* **83 J6** 35 0N 115 20W
New Zealand ■, *Oceania* **59 J6** 40 0S 176 0 E
Newaj →, *India* **42 G7** 24 24N 76 49 E
Newala, *Tanzania* **55 E4** 10 58S 39 18 E
Newark, *Del., U.S.A.* **76 F8** 39 41N 75 46W
Newark, *N.J., U.S.A.* **79 F10** 40 44N 74 10W
Newark, *N.Y., U.S.A.* **78 C7** 43 3N 77 6W
Newark, *Ohio, U.S.A.* **78 F2** 40 3N 82 24W
Newark-on-Trent, *U.K.* **10 D7** 53 5N 0 48W
Newark Valley, *U.S.A.* **79 D8** 42 14N 76 11W
Newberg, *U.S.A.* **82 D2** 45 18N 122 58W
Newberry, *Mich., U.S.A.* **76 B3** 46 21N 85 30W
Newberry, *S.C., U.S.A.* **77 H5** 34 17N 81 37W
Newberry Springs, *U.S.A.* **85 L10** 34 50N 116 41W
Newboro L., *Canada* **79 B8** 44 38N 76 20W
Newbridge = Droichead Nua, *Ireland* **13 C5** 53 11N 6 48W
Newburgh, *Canada* **78 B8** 44 19N 76 52W
Newburgh, *U.S.A.* **79 E10** 41 30N 74 1W
Newbury, *U.K.* **11 F6** 51 24N 1 20W
Newbury, *N.H., U.S.A.* **79 B12** 43 19N 72 3W
Newbury, *Vt., U.S.A.* **79 B12** 44 5N 72 4W
Newburyport, *U.S.A.* **77 D10** 42 49N 70 53W
Newcastle, *Australia* **63 E5** 33 0S 151 46 E
Newcastle, *N.B., Canada* **71 C6** 47 1N 65 38W
Newcastle, *Ont., Canada* **70 D4** 43 55N 78 35W
Newcastle, *S. Africa* **57 D4** 27 45S 29 58 E
Newcastle, *U.K.* **13 B6** 54 13N 5 54W
Newcastle, *Calif., U.S.A.* **84 G5** 38 53N 121 8W
Newcastle, *Wyo., U.S.A.* **80 D2** 43 50N 104 11W
Newcastle Emlyn, *U.K.* **11 E3** 52 2N 4 28W
Newcastle Ra., *Australia* **60 C5** 15 45S 130 15 E
Newcastle-under-Lyme, *U.K.* **10 D5** 53 1N 2 14W
Newcastle-upon-Tyne, *U.K.* **10 C6** 54 58N 1 36W
Newcastle Waters, *Australia* **62 B1** 17 30S 133 28 E
Newcastle West, *Ireland* **13 D2** 52 27N 9 3W
Newcomb, *U.S.A.* **79 C10** 43 58N 74 10W
Newcomerstown, *U.S.A.* **78 F3** 40 16N 81 36W
Newdegate, *Australia* **61 F2** 33 6S 119 0 E
Newell, *Australia* **62 B4** 16 20S 145 16 E
Newell, *U.S.A.* **80 C3** 44 43N 103 25W
Newfane, *U.S.A.* **78 C6** 43 17N 78 43W
Newfield, *U.S.A.* **79 D8** 42 18N 76 33W
Newfound L., *U.S.A.* **79 C13** 43 40N 71 47W
Newfoundland, *Canada* **66 E14** 49 0N 55 0W
Newfoundland, *U.S.A.* **79 E9** 41 18N 75 19W
Newfoundland □, *Canada* **71 B8** 53 0N 58 0W
Newhall, *U.S.A.* **85 L8** 34 23N 118 32W
Newhaven, *U.K.* **11 G8** 50 47N 0 3 E
Newkirk, *U.S.A.* **81 G6** 36 53N 97 3W
Newlyn, *U.K.* **11 G2** 50 6N 5 34W
Newman, *Australia* **60 D2** 23 18S 119 45 E
Newman, *U.S.A.* **84 H5** 37 19N 121 1W
Newmarket, *Canada* **78 B5** 44 3N 79 28W
Newmarket, *Ireland* **13 D2** 52 13N 9 0W
Newmarket, *U.K.* **11 E8** 52 15N 0 25 E
Newmarket, *U.S.A.* **79 C14** 43 4N 70 56W
Newnan, *U.S.A.* **77 J3** 33 23N 84 48W
Newport, *Ireland* **13 C2** 53 53N 9 33W
Newport, *I. of W., U.K.* **11 G6** 50 42N 1 17W
Newport, *Newp., U.K.* **11 F5** 51 35N 3 0W
Newport, *Ark., U.S.A.* **81 H9** 35 37N 91 16W
Newport, *Ky., U.S.A.* **76 F3** 39 5N 84 30W
Newport, *N.H., U.S.A.* **79 C12** 43 22N 72 10W
Newport, *N.Y., U.S.A.* **79 C9** 43 11N 75 1W
Newport, *Oreg., U.S.A.* **82 D1** 44 39N 124 3W
Newport, *Pa., U.S.A.* **78 F7** 40 29N 77 8W
Newport, *R.I., U.S.A.* **79 E13** 41 29N 71 19W
Newport, *Tenn., U.S.A.* **77 H4** 35 58N 83 11W
Newport, *Vt., U.S.A.* **79 B12** 44 56N 72 13W
Newport, *Wash., U.S.A.* **82 B5** 48 11N 117 3W
Newport □, *U.K.* **11 F4** 51 33N 3 1W
Newport Beach, *U.S.A.* **85 M9** 33 37N 117 56W
Newport News, *U.S.A.* **76 G7** 36 59N 76 25W
Newport Pagnell, *U.K.* **11 E7** 52 5N 0 43W
Newquay, *U.K.* **11 G2** 50 25N 5 6W
Newry, *U.K.* **13 B5** 54 11N 6 21W
Newton, *Ill., U.S.A.* **80 F10** 38 59N 88 10W
Newton, *Iowa, U.S.A.* **80 E8** 41 42N 93 3W
Newton, *Kans., U.S.A.* **81 F6** 38 3N 97 21W
Newton, *Mass., U.S.A.* **79 D13** 42 21N 71 12W
Newton, *Miss., U.S.A.* **81 J10** 32 19N 89 10W
Newton, *N.C., U.S.A.* **77 H5** 35 40N 81 13W
Newton, *N.J., U.S.A.* **79 E10** 41 3N 74 45W
Newton, *Tex., U.S.A.* **81 K8** 30 51N 93 46W
Newton Abbot, *U.K.* **11 G4** 50 32N 3 37W
Newton Aycliffe, *U.K.* **10 C6** 54 37N 1 34W
Newton Falls, *U.S.A.* **78 E4** 41 11N 80 59W
Newton Stewart, *U.K.* **12 G4** 54 57N 4 30W
Newtonmore, *U.K.* **12 D4** 57 4N 4 8W
Newtown, *U.K.* **11 E4** 52 31N 3 19W
Newtownabbey, *U.K.* **13 B6** 54 40N 5 56W
Newtownards, *U.K.* **13 B6** 54 36N 5 42W
Newtownbarry = Bunclody, *Ireland* **13 D5** 52 39N 6 40W
Newtownstewart, *U.K.* **13 B4** 54 43N 7 23W
Newville, *U.S.A.* **78 F7** 40 10N 77 24W
Neya, *Russia* **24 C7** 58 21N 43 49 E
Neyrīz, *Iran* **45 D7** 29 15N 54 19 E
Neyshābūr, *Iran* **45 B8** 36 10N 58 50 E
Nezhin = Nizhyn, *Ukraine* **25 D5** 51 5N 31 55 E
Nezperce, *U.S.A.* **82 C5** 46 14N 116 14W
Ngabang, *Indonesia* **36 D3** 0 23N 109 55 E
Ngabordamlu, Tanjung, *Indonesia* **37 F8** 6 56S 134 11 E
N'Gage, *Angola* **52 F3** 7 46S 15 16 E
Ngami Depression, *Botswana* **56 C3** 20 30S 22 46 E
Ngamo, *Zimbabwe* **55 F2** 19 3S 27 32 E
Nganglong Kangri, *China* **41 C12** 33 0N 81 0 E
Ngao, *Thailand* **38 C2** 18 46N 99 59 E
Ngaoundéré, *Cameroon* **52 C2** 7 15N 13 35 E
Ngapara, *N.Z.* **59 L3** 44 57S 170 46 E
Ngara, *Tanzania* **54 C3** 2 29S 30 40 E
Ngawi, *Indonesia* **37 G14** 7 24S 111 26 E
Nghia Lo, *Vietnam* **38 B5** 21 33N 104 28 E
Ngoma, *Malawi* **55 E3** 13 8S 33 45 E
Ngomahura, *Zimbabwe* **55 G3** 20 26S 30 43 E
Ngomba, *Tanzania* **55 D3** 8 20S 32 53 E
Ngoring Hu, *China* **32 C4** 34 55N 97 5 E
Ngorongoro, *Tanzania* **54 C4** 3 11S 35 32 E
Ngozi, *Burundi* **54 C2** 2 54S 29 50 E
Ngudu, *Tanzania* **54 C3** 2 58S 33 25 E
Nguigmi, *Niger* **51 F8** 14 20N 13 20 E
Nguiu, *Australia* **60 B5** 11 46S 130 38 E
Ngukurr, *Australia* **62 A1** 14 44S 134 44 E
Ngunga, *Tanzania* **54 C3** 3 37S 33 37 E
Nguru, *Nigeria* **51 F8** 12 56N 10 29 E
Nguru Mts., *Tanzania* **54 D4** 6 0S 37 30 E
Ngusi, *Malawi* **55 E3** 14 0S 34 50 E
Nguyen Binh, *Vietnam* **38 A5** 22 39N 105 56 E
Nha Trang, *Vietnam* **39 F7** 12 16N 109 10 E
Nhacoongo, *Mozam.* **57 C6** 24 18S 35 14 E
Nhamaabué, *Mozam.* **55 F4** 17 25S 35 5 E
Nhamundá →, *Brazil* **93 D7** 2 12S 56 41W
Nhangulaze, L., *Mozam.* **57 C5** 24 0S 34 30 E
Nhill, *Australia* **63 F3** 36 18S 141 40 E
Nho Quan, *Vietnam* **38 B5** 20 18N 105 45 E
Nhulunbuy, *Australia* **62 A2** 12 10S 137 20 E
Nia-nia, *Dem. Rep. of the Congo* **54 B2** 1 30N 27 40 E
Niagara Falls, *Canada* **78 C5** 43 7N 79 5W
Niagara Falls, *U.S.A.* **78 C6** 43 5N 79 4W
Niagara-on-the-Lake, *Canada* **78 C5** 43 15N 79 4W
Niah, *Malaysia* **36 D4** 3 58N 113 46 E
Niamey, *Niger* **50 F6** 13 27N 2 6 E
Niangara, *Dem. Rep. of the Congo* **54 B2** 3 42N 27 50 E
Niantic, *U.S.A.* **79 E12** 41 20N 72 11W
Nias, *Indonesia* **36 D1** 1 0N 97 30 E
Niassa □, *Mozam.* **55 E4** 13 30S 36 0 E
Nibāk, *Si. Arabia* **45 E7** 24 25N 50 50 E
Nicaragua ■, *Cent. Amer.* **88 D2** 11 40N 85 30W
Nicaragua, L. de, *Nic.* **88 D2** 12 0N 85 30W
Nicastro, *Italy* **20 E7** 38 59N 16 19 E
Nice, *France* **18 E7** 43 42N 7 14 E
Niceville, *U.S.A.* **77 K2** 30 31N 86 30W
Nichicun, L., *Canada* **71 B5** 53 5N 71 0W
Nichinan, *Japan* **31 J5** 31 38N 131 23 E
Nicholás, Canal, *W. Indies* **88 B3** 23 30N 80 5W
Nicholasville, *U.S.A.* **76 G3** 37 53N 84 34W
Nichols, *U.S.A.* **79 D8** 42 1N 76 22W
Nicholson, *Australia* **60 C4** 18 2S 128 54 E
Nicholson, *U.S.A.* **79 E9** 41 37N 75 47W
Nicholson →, *Australia* **62 B2** 17 31S 139 36 E
Nicholson L., *Canada* **73 A8** 62 40N 102 40W
Nicholson Ra., *Australia* **61 E2** 27 15S 116 45 E
Nicholville, *U.S.A.* **79 B10** 44 41N 74 39W
Nicobar Is., *Ind. Oc.* **29 J13** 8 0N 93 30 E
Nicola, *Canada* **72 C4** 50 12N 120 40W
Nicolls Town, *Bahamas* **88 A4** 25 8N 78 0W
Nicosia, *Cyprus* **23 D12** 35 10N 33 25 E
Nicoya, *Costa Rica* **88 D2** 10 9N 85 27W
Nicoya, G. de, *Costa Rica* **88 E3** 10 0N 85 0W
Nicoya, Pen. de, *Costa Rica* **88 E2** 9 45N 85 40W
Nidd →, *U.K.* **10 D6** 53 59N 1 23W
Niedersachsen □, *Germany* **16 B5** 52 50N 9 0 E
Niekerkshoop, *S. Africa* **56 D3** 29 19S 22 51 E
Niemba, *Dem. Rep. of the Congo* **54 D2** 5 58S 28 24 E
Niemen = Neman →, *Lithuania* **9 J19** 55 25N 21 10 E
Nienburg, *Germany* **16 B5** 52 39N 9 13 E
Nieu Bethesda, *S. Africa* **56 E3** 31 51S 24 34 E
Nieuw Amsterdam, *Surinam* **93 B7** 5 53N 55 5W
Nieuw Nickerie, *Surinam* **93 B7** 6 0N 56 59W
Nieuwoudtville, *S. Africa* **56 E2** 31 23S 19 7 E
Nieuwpoort, *Belgium* **15 C2** 51 8N 2 45 E
Nieves, Pico de las, *Canary Is.* **22 G4** 27 57N 15 35W
Niğde, *Turkey* **25 G5** 37 58N 34 40 E
Nigel, *S. Africa* **57 D4** 26 27S 28 25 E
Niger ■, *W. Afr.* **50 E7** 17 30N 10 0 E
Niger →, *W. Afr.* **50 G7** 5 33N 6 33 E
Nigeria ■, *W. Afr.* **50 G7** 8 30N 8 0 E
Nighasin, *India* **43 E9** 28 14N 80 52 E
Nightcaps, *N.Z.* **59 L2** 45 57S 168 2 E
Nii-Jima, *Japan* **31 G9** 34 20N 139 15 E
Niigata, *Japan* **30 F9** 37 58N 139 0 E
Niigata □, *Japan* **31 F9** 37 15N 138 45 E
Niihama, *Japan* **31 H6** 33 55N 133 16 E
Niihau, *U.S.A.* **74 H14** 21 54N 160 9W
Niimi, *Japan* **31 G6** 34 59N 133 28 E
Niitsu, *Japan* **30 F9** 37 48N 139 7 E
Nijil, *Jordan* **47 E4** 30 32N 35 33 E
Nijkerk, *Neths.* **15 B5** 52 13N 5 30 E
Nijmegen, *Neths.* **15 C5** 51 50N 5 52 E
Nijverdal, *Neths.* **15 B6** 52 22N 6 28 E
Nīk Pey, *Iran* **45 B6** 36 50N 48 10 E
Nikiniki, *Indonesia* **37 F6** 9 49S 124 30 E
Nikkō, *Japan* **31 F9** 36 45N 139 35 E
Nikolayev = Mykolayiv, *Ukraine* **25 E5** 46 58N 32 0 E
Nikolayevsk, *Russia* **25 E8** 50 0N 45 35 E
Nikolayevsk-na-Amur, *Russia* **27 D15** 53 8N 140 44 E
Nikolskoye, *Russia* **27 D17** 55 12N 166 0 E
Nikopol, *Ukraine* **25 E5** 47 35N 34 25 E
Nīkshahr, *Iran* **45 E9** 26 15N 60 10 E
Nikšić, *Montenegro, Yug.* **21 C8** 42 50N 18 57 E
Nîl, Nahr en →, *Africa* **51 B12** 30 10N 31 6 E
Nîl el Abyad →, *Sudan* **51 E12** 15 38N 32 31 E
Nîl el Azraq →, *Sudan* **51 E12** 15 38N 32 31 E
Nila, *Indonesia* **37 F7** 6 44S 129 31 E
Niland, *U.S.A.* **85 M11** 33 14N 115 31W
Nile = Nîl, Nahr en →, *Africa* **51 B12** 30 10N 31 6 E
Niles, *Mich., U.S.A.* **76 E2** 41 50N 86 15W
Niles, *Ohio, U.S.A.* **78 E4** 41 11N 80 46W
Nim Ka Thana, *India* **42 F6** 27 44N 75 48 E
Nimach, *India* **42 G6** 24 30N 74 56 E
Nimbahera, *India* **42 G6** 24 37N 74 45 E
Nîmes, *France* **18 E6** 43 50N 4 23 E
Nimfaíon, Ákra = Pínnes, Ákra, *Greece* **21 D11** 40 5N 24 20 E
Nimmitabel, *Australia* **63 F4** 36 29S 149 15 E
Ninawá, *Iraq* **44 B4** 36 25N 43 10 E
Nindigully, *Australia* **63 D4** 28 21S 148 50 E
Nineveh = Nīnawá, *Iraq* **44 B4** 36 25N 43 10 E
Ning Xian, *China* **34 G4** 35 30N 107 58 E
Ning'an, *China* **35 B15** 44 22N 129 20 E
Ningbo, *China* **33 D7** 29 51N 121 28 E
Ningcheng, *China* **35 D10** 41 32N 119 53 E
Ningjin, *China* **34 F8** 37 35N 114 57 E
Ningjing Shan, *China* **32 D4** 30 0N 98 20 E
Ningling, *China* **34 G8** 34 25N 115 22 E
Ningpo = Ningbo, *China* **33 D7** 29 51N 121 28 E
Ningqiang, *China* **34 H4** 32 47N 106 15 E
Ningshan, *China* **34 H5** 33 21N 108 21 E
Ningsia Hui A.R. = Ningxia Huizu Zizhiqu □, *China* **34 F4** 38 0N 106 0 E
Ningwu, *China* **34 E7** 39 0N 112 18 E
Ningxia Huizu Zizhiqu □, *China* **34 F4** 38 0N 106 0 E
Ningyang, *China* **34 G9** 35 47N 116 45 E
Ninh Binh, *Vietnam* **38 B5** 20 15N 105 55 E
Ninh Giang, *Vietnam* **38 B6** 20 44N 106 24 E
Ninh Hoa, *Vietnam* **38 F7** 12 30N 109 7 E
Ninh Ma, *Vietnam* **38 F7** 12 48N 109 21 E
Ninove, *Belgium* **15 D4** 50 51N 4 2 E
Nioaque, *Brazil* **95 A4** 21 5S 55 50W
Niobrara, *U.S.A.* **80 D6** 42 45N 98 2W
Niobrara →, *U.S.A.* **80 D6** 42 46N 98 3W
Nioro du Sahel, *Mali* **50 E4** 15 15N 9 30W
Niort, *France* **18 C3** 46 19N 0 29W
Nipawin, *Canada* **73 C8** 53 20N 104 0W
Nipigon, *Canada* **70 C2** 49 0N 88 17W
Nipigon, L., *Canada* **70 C2** 49 50N 88 30W
Nipishish L., *Canada* **71 B7** 54 12N 60 45W
Nipissing, L., *Canada* **70 C4** 46 20N 80 0W
Nipomo, *U.S.A.* **85 K6** 35 3N 120 29W
Nipton, *U.S.A.* **85 K11** 35 28N 115 16W
Niquelândia, *Brazil* **93 F9** 14 33S 48 23W
Nīr, *Iran* **44 B5** 38 2N 47 59 E
Nirasaki, *Japan* **31 G9** 35 42N 138 27 E
Nirmal, *India* **40 K11** 19 3N 78 20 E
Nirmali, *India* **43 F12** 26 20N 86 35 E
Niš, *Serbia, Yug.* **21 C9** 43 19N 21 58 E
Nişāb, *Si. Arabia* **44 D5** 29 11N 44 43 E
Nişāb, *Yemen* **46 E4** 14 25N 46 29 E
Nishinomiya, *Japan* **31 G7** 34 45N 135 20 E
Nishino'omote, *Japan* **31 J5** 30 43N 130 59 E
Nishiwaki, *Japan* **31 G7** 34 59N 134 58 E
Niskibi →, *Canada* **70 A2** 56 29N 88 9W
Nisqually →, *U.S.A.* **84 C4** 47 6N 122 42W
Nissáki, *Greece* **23 A3** 39 43N 19 52 E
Nissum Bredning, *Denmark* **9 H13** 56 40N 8 20 E
Nistru = Dnister →, *Europe* **17 E16** 46 18N 30 17 E
Nisutlin →, *Canada* **72 A2** 60 14N 132 34W
Nitchequon, *Canada* **71 B5** 53 10N 70 58W
Niterói, *Brazil* **95 A7** 22 52S 43 0W
Nith →, *Canada* **78 C4** 43 12N 80 23W
Nith →, *U.K.* **12 F5** 55 14N 3 33W
Nitra, *Slovak Rep.* **17 D10** 48 19N 18 4 E
Nitra →, *Slovak Rep.* **17 E10** 47 46N 18 10 E
Niuafo'ou, *Tonga* **59 B11** 15 30S 175 58W
Niue, *Cook Is.* **65 J11** 19 2S 169 54W
Niut, *Indonesia* **36 D4** 0 55N 110 6 E
Niuzhuang, *China* **35 D12** 40 58N 122 28 E
Nivala, *Finland* **8 E21** 63 56N 24 57 E
Nivelles, *Belgium* **15 D4** 50 35N 4 20 E
Nivernais, *France* **18 C5** 47 15N 3 30 E
Niwas, *India* **43 H9** 23 3N 80 26 E
Nixon, *U.S.A.* **81 L6** 29 16N 97 46W
Nizamabad, *India* **40 K11** 18 45N 78 7 E
Nizamghat, *India* **41 E19** 28 20N 95 45 E
Nizhne Kolymsk, *Russia* **27 C17** 68 34N 160 55 E
Nizhnekamsk, *Russia* **24 C9** 55 38N 51 49 E
Nizhneudinsk, *Russia* **27 D10** 54 54N 99 3 E
Nizhnevartovsk, *Russia* **26 C8** 60 56N 76 38 E
Nizhniy Novgorod, *Russia* **24 C7** 56 20N 44 0 E
Nizhniy Tagil, *Russia* **24 C10** 57 55N 59 57 E
Nizhyn, *Ukraine* **25 D5** 51 5N 31 55 E
Nizip, *Turkey* **44 B3** 37 5N 37 50 E
Nízké Tatry, *Slovak Rep.* **17 D10** 48 55N 19 30 E
Njakwa, *Malawi* **55 E3** 11 1S 33 56 E
Njanji, *Zambia* **55 E3** 14 25S 31 46 E
Njinjo, *Tanzania* **55 D4** 8 48S 38 54 E
Njombe, *Tanzania* **55 D3** 9 20S 34 50 E
Njombe →, *Tanzania* **54 D4** 6 56S 35 6 E
Nkana, *Zambia* **55 E2** 12 50S 28 8 E
Nkandla, *S. Africa* **57 D5** 28 37S 31 5 E
Nkayi, *Zimbabwe* **55 F2** 19 41S 29 20 E
Nkhotakota, *Malawi* **55 E3** 12 56S 34 15 E
Nkongsamba, *Cameroon* **52 D1** 4 55N 9 55 E
Nkurenkuru, *Namibia* **56 B2** 17 42S 18 32 E
Nmai →, *Burma* **41 G20** 25 30N 97 25 E
Noakhali = Maijdi, *Bangla.* **41 H17** 22 48N 91 10 E
Nobel, *Canada* **78 A4** 45 25N 80 6W
Nobeoka, *Japan* **31 H5** 32 36N 131 41 E
Noblesville, *U.S.A.* **76 E3** 40 3N 86 1W
Nocera Inferiore, *Italy* **20 D6** 40 44N 14 38 E
Nocona, *U.S.A.* **81 J6** 33 47N 97 44W
Noda, *Japan* **31 G9** 35 56N 139 52 E
Nogales, *Mexico* **86 A2** 31 20N 110 56W
Nogales, *U.S.A.* **83 L8** 31 20N 110 56W
Nōgata, *Japan* **31 H5** 33 48N 130 44 E
Noggerup, *Australia* **61 F2** 33 32S 116 5 E
Noginsk, *Russia* **27 C10** 64 30N 90 50 E
Nogoa →, *Australia* **62 C4** 23 40S 147 55 E
Nogoyá, *Argentina* **94 C4** 32 24S 59 48W
Nohar, *India* **42 E6** 29 11N 74 49 E
Nohta, *India* **43 H8** 23 40N 79 34 E
Noires, Mts., *France* **18 B2** 48 11N 3 40W
Noirmoutier, Î. de, *France* **18 C2** 46 58N 2 10W
Nojane, *Botswana* **56 C3** 23 15S 20 14 E
Nojima-Zaki, *Japan* **31 G9** 34 54N 139 53 E
Nok Kundi, *Pakistan* **40 E3** 28 50N 62 45 E
Nokaneng, *Botswana* **56 B3** 19 40S 22 17 E
Nokia, *Finland* **9 F20** 61 30N 23 30 E
Nokomis, *Canada* **73 C8** 51 35N 105 0W
Nokomis L., *Canada* **73 B8** 57 0N 103 0W
Nola, *C.A.R.* **52 D3** 3 35N 16 4 E
Noma Omuramba →, *Namibia* **56 B3** 18 52S 20 53 E
Nombre de Dios, *Panama* **88 E4** 9 34N 79 28W
Nome, *U.S.A.* **68 B3** 64 30N 165 25W
Nomo-Zaki, *Japan* **31 H4** 32 35N 129 44 E
Nonacho L., *Canada* **73 A7** 61 42N 109 40W
Nonda, *Australia* **62 C3** 20 40S 142 28 E
Nong Chang, *Thailand* **38 E2** 15 23N 99 51 E
Nong Het, *Laos* **38 C4** 19 29N 103 59 E
Nong Khai, *Thailand* **38 D4** 17 50N 102 46 E
Nong'an, *China* **35 B13** 44 25N 125 5 E
Nongoma, *S. Africa* **57 D5** 27 58S 31 35 E
Nonoava, *Mexico* **86 B3** 27 28N 106 44W
Nonoava →, *Mexico* **86 B3** 27 29N 106 45W
Nonthaburi, *Thailand* **38 F3** 13 51N 100 34 E
Noonamah, *Australia* **60 B5** 12 40S 131 4 E
Noord Brabant □, *Neths.* **15 C5** 51 40N 5 0 E
Noord Holland □, *Neths.* **15 B4** 52 30N 4 45 E
Noordbeveland, *Neths.* **15 C3** 51 35N 3 50 E
Noordoostpolder, *Neths.* **15 B5** 52 45N 5 45 E
Noordwijk, *Neths.* **15 B4** 52 14N 4 26 E
Nootka I., *Canada* **72 D3** 49 32N 126 42W
Nopiming Prov. Park, *Canada* **73 C9** 50 30N 95 37W
Noralee, *Canada* **72 C3** 53 59N 126 26W
Noranda = Rouyn-Noranda, *Canada* **70 C4** 48 20N 79 0W
Norco, *U.S.A.* **85 M9** 33 56N 117 33W
Nord-Kivu □, *Dem. Rep. of the Congo* **54 C2** 1 0S 29 0 E
Nord-Ostsee-Kanal, *Germany* **16 A5** 54 12N 9 32 E
Nordaustlandet, *Svalbard* **4 B9** 79 14N 23 0 E
Nordegg, *Canada* **72 C5** 52 29N 116 5W
Norderney, *Germany* **16 B4** 53 42N 7 9 E
Norderstedt, *Germany* **16 B5** 53 42N 10 1 E

Nordfjord, *Norway* 9 F11 61 55N 5 30 E
Nordfriesische Inseln, *Germany* 16 A5 54 40N 8 20 E
Nordhausen, *Germany* 16 C6 51 30N 10 47 E
Norðoyar, *Færoe Is.* 8 E9 62 17N 6 35W
Nordkapp, *Norway* 8 A21 71 10N 25 50 E
Nordkapp, *Svalbard* 4 A9 80 31N 20 0 E
Nordkinn = Kinnarodden, *Norway* 6 A11 71 8N 27 40 E
Nordkinn-halvøya, *Norway* 8 A22 70 55N 27 40 E
Nordrhein-Westfalen □, *Germany* 16 C4 51 45N 7 30 E
Nordvik, *Russia* 27 B12 74 2N 111 32 E
Nore →, *Ireland* 13 D4 52 25N 6 58W
Norfolk, *Nebr., U.S.A.* 80 D6 42 2N 97 25W
Norfolk, *Va., U.S.A.* 76 G7 36 51N 76 17W
Norfolk □, *U.K.* 11 E8 52 39N 0 54 E
Norfolk I., *Pac. Oc.* 64 K8 28 58S 168 3 E
Norfork L., *U.S.A.* 81 G8 36 15N 92 14W
Norilsk, *Russia* 27 C9 69 20N 88 6 E
Norma, Mt., *Australia* 62 C3 20 55S 140 42 E
Normal, *U.S.A.* 80 E10 40 31N 88 59W
Norman, *U.S.A.* 81 H6 35 13N 97 26W
Norman →, *Australia* 62 B3 19 18S 141 51 E
Norman Wells, *Canada* 68 B7 65 17N 126 51W
Normanby →, *Australia* 62 A3 14 23S 144 10 E
Normandie, *France* 18 B4 48 45N 0 10 E
Normandin, *Canada* 70 C5 48 49N 72 31W
Normandy = Normandie, *France* 18 B4 48 45N 0 10 E
Normanhurst, Mt., *Australia* 61 E3 25 4S 122 30 E
Normanton, *Australia* 62 B3 17 40S 141 10 E
Normétal, *Canada* 70 C4 49 0N 79 22W
Norquay, *Canada* 73 C8 51 53N 102 5W
Norquinco, *Argentina* 96 E2 41 51S 70 55W
Norrbotten □, *Sweden* 8 C19 66 30N 22 30 E
Norris Point, *Canada* 71 C8 49 31N 57 53W
Norristown, *U.S.A.* 79 F9 40 7N 75 21W
Norrköping, *Sweden* 9 G17 58 37N 16 11 E
Norrland, *Sweden* 9 E16 62 15N 15 45 E
Norrtälje, *Sweden* 9 G18 59 46N 18 42 E
Norseman, *Australia* 61 F3 32 8S 121 43 E
Norsk, *Russia* 27 D14 52 30N 130 5 E
Norte, Pta. del, *Canary Is.* 22 G2 27 51N 17 57W
Norte, Serra do, *Brazil* 92 F7 11 20S 59 0W
North, C., *Canada* 71 C7 47 2N 60 20W
North Adams, *U.S.A.* 79 D11 42 42N 73 7W
North Arm, *Canada* 72 A5 62 0N 114 30W
North Augusta, *U.S.A.* 77 J5 33 30N 81 59W
North Ayrshire □, *U.K.* 12 F4 55 45N 4 44W
North Bass I., *U.S.A.* 78 E2 41 44N 82 53W
North Battleford, *Canada* 73 C7 52 50N 108 17W
North Bay, *Canada* 70 C4 46 20N 79 30W
North Belcher Is., *Canada* 70 A4 56 50N 79 50W
North Bend, *Oreg., U.S.A.* 82 E1 43 24N 124 14W
North Bend, *Pa., U.S.A.* 78 E7 41 20N 77 42W
North Bend, *Wash., U.S.A.* 84 C5 47 30N 121 47W
North Bennington, *U.S.A.* 79 D11 42 56N 73 15W
North Berwick, *U.K.* 12 E6 56 4N 2 42W
North Berwick, *U.S.A.* 79 C14 43 18N 70 44W
North C., *Canada* 71 C7 47 5N 64 0W
North C., *N.Z.* 59 F4 34 23S 173 4 E
North Canadian →, *U.S.A.* 81 H7 35 16N 95 31W
North Canton, *U.S.A.* 78 F3 40 53N 81 24W
North Cape = Nordkapp, *Norway* 8 A21 71 10N 25 50 E
North Cape = Nordkapp, *Svalbard* 4 A9 80 31N 20 0 E
North Caribou L., *Canada* 70 B1 52 50N 90 40W
North Carolina □, *U.S.A.* 77 H6 35 30N 80 0W
North Cascades Nat. Park, *U.S.A.* 82 B3 48 45N 121 10W
North Channel, *Canada* 70 C3 46 0N 83 0W
North Channel, *U.K.* 12 F3 55 13N 5 52W
North Charleston, *U.S.A.* 77 J6 32 53N 79 58W
North Chicago, *U.S.A.* 76 D2 42 19N 87 51W
North Creek, *U.S.A.* 79 C11 43 41N 73 59W
North Dakota □, *U.S.A.* 80 B5 47 30N 100 15W
North Downs, *U.K.* 11 F8 51 19N 0 21 E
North East, *U.S.A.* 78 D5 42 13N 79 50W
North East Frontier Agency = Arunachal Pradesh □, *India* 41 F19 28 0N 95 0 E
North East Lincolnshire □, *U.K.* 10 D7 53 34N 0 2W
North Eastern □, *Kenya* 54 B5 1 30N 40 0 E
North Esk →, *U.K.* 12 E6 56 46N 2 24W
North European Plain, *Europe* 6 E10 55 0N 25 0 E
North Foreland, *U.K.* 11 F9 51 22N 1 28 E
North Fork, *U.S.A.* 84 H7 37 14N 119 21W
North Fork American →, *U.S.A.* 84 G5 38 57N 120 59W
North Fork Feather →, *U.S.A.* 84 F5 38 33N 121 30W
North Fork Grand →, *U.S.A.* 80 C3 45 47N 102 16W
North Fork Red →, *U.S.A.* 81 H5 34 24N 99 14W
North Frisian Is. = Nordfriesische Inseln, *Germany* 16 A5 54 40N 8 20 E
North Gower, *Canada* 79 A9 45 8N 75 43W
North Hd., *Australia* 61 F1 30 14S 114 59 E
North Henik L., *Canada* 73 A9 61 45N 97 40W
North Highlands, *U.S.A.* 84 G5 38 40N 121 23W
North Horr, *Kenya* 54 B4 3 20N 37 8 E
North I., *Kenya* 54 B4 4 5N 36 5 E
North I., *N.Z.* 59 H5 38 0S 175 0 E
North Kingsville, *U.S.A.* 78 E4 41 54N 80 42W
North Knife →, *Canada* 73 B10 58 53N 94 45W
North Koel →, *India* 43 G10 24 45N 83 50 E
North Korea ■, *Asia* 35 E14 40 0N 127 0 E
North Lakhimpur, *India* 41 F19 27 14N 94 7 E
North Lanarkshire □, *U.K.* 12 F5 55 52N 3 56W
North Las Vegas, *U.S.A.* 85 J11 36 12N 115 7W
North Lincolnshire □, *U.K.* 10 D7 53 36N 0 30W
North Little Rock, *U.S.A.* 81 H8 34 45N 92 16W
North Loup →, *U.S.A.* 80 E5 41 17N 98 24W
North Magnetic Pole, *Canada* 4 B2 77 58N 102 8W
North Minch, *U.K.* 12 C3 58 5N 5 55W
North Moose L., *Canada* 73 C8 54 11N 100 6W
North Myrtle Beach, *U.S.A.* 77 J6 33 48N 78 42W
North Nahanni →, *Canada* 72 A4 62 15N 123 20W
North Olmsted, *U.S.A.* 78 E3 41 25N 81 56W
North Ossetia □, *Russia* 25 F7 43 30N 44 30 E
North Pagai, I. = Pagai Utara, Pulau, *Indonesia* 36 E2 2 35S 100 0 E
North Palisade, *U.S.A.* 84 H8 37 6N 118 31W
North Platte, *U.S.A.* 80 E4 41 8N 100 46W
North Platte →, *U.S.A.* 80 E4 41 7N 100 42W
North Pole, *Arctic* 4 A 90 0N 0 0W
North Portal, *Canada* 73 D8 49 0N 102 33W
North Powder, *U.S.A.* 82 D5 45 2N 117 55W
North Pt., *U.S.A.* 78 A1 45 2N 83 16W
North Rhine Westphalia = Nordrhein-Westfalen □, *Germany* 16 C4 51 45N 7 30 E
North River, *Canada* 71 B8 53 49N 57 6W
North Ronaldsay, *U.K.* 12 B6 59 22N 2 26W
North Saskatchewan →, *Canada* 73 C7 53 15N 105 5W
North Sea, *Europe* 6 D6 56 0N 4 0 E
North Seal →, *Canada* 73 B9 58 50N 98 7W
North Somerset □, *U.K.* 11 F5 51 24N 2 45W
North Sporades = Vóriai Sporádhes, *Greece* 21 E10 39 15N 23 30 E
North Sydney, *Canada* 71 C7 46 12N 60 15W
North Syracuse, *U.S.A.* 79 C8 43 8N 76 7W
North Taranaki Bight, *N.Z.* 59 H5 38 50S 174 15 E
North Thompson →, *Canada* 72 C4 50 40N 120 20W
North Tonawanda, *U.S.A.* 78 C6 43 2N 78 53W
North Troy, *U.S.A.* 79 B12 45 0N 72 24W
North Truchas Pk., *U.S.A.* 83 J11 36 0N 105 30W
North Twin I., *Canada* 70 B4 53 20N 80 0W
North Tyne →, *U.K.* 10 B5 55 0N 2 8W
North Uist, *U.K.* 12 D1 57 40N 7 15W
North Vancouver, *Canada* 72 D4 49 19N 123 4W
North Vernon, *U.S.A.* 76 F3 39 0N 85 38W
North Wabasca L., *Canada* 72 B6 56 0N 113 55W
North Walsham, *U.K.* 10 E9 52 50N 1 22 E
North-West □, *S. Africa* 56 D4 27 0S 25 0 E
North West C., *Australia* 60 D1 21 45S 114 9 E
North West Christmas I. Ridge, *Pac. Oc.* 65 G11 6 30N 165 0W
North West Frontier □, *Pakistan* 42 C4 34 0N 72 0 E
North West Highlands, *U.K.* 12 D4 57 33N 4 58W
North West River, *Canada* 71 B7 53 30N 60 10W
North Western □, *Zambia* 55 E2 13 30S 25 30 E
North Wildwood, *U.S.A.* 76 F8 39 0N 74 48W
North York Moors, *U.K.* 10 C7 54 23N 0 53W
North Yorkshire □, *U.K.* 10 C6 54 15N 1 25W
Northallerton, *U.K.* 10 C6 54 20N 1 26W
Northam, *Australia* 61 F2 31 35S 116 42 E
Northam, *S. Africa* 56 C4 24 56S 27 18 E
Northampton, *Australia* 61 E1 28 27S 114 33 E
Northampton, *U.K.* 11 E7 52 15N 0 53W
Northampton, *Mass., U.S.A.* 79 D12 42 19N 72 38W
Northampton, *Pa., U.S.A.* 79 F9 40 41N 75 30W
Northamptonshire □, *U.K.* 11 E7 52 16N 0 55W
Northbridge, *U.S.A.* 79 D13 42 9N 71 39W
Northcliffe, *Australia* 61 F2 34 39S 116 7 E
Northeast Providence Chan., *W. Indies* 88 A4 26 0N 76 0W
Northern □, *Malawi* 55 E3 11 0S 34 0 E
Northern □, *Zambia* 55 E3 10 30S 31 0 E
Northern Areas □, *Pakistan* 43 A5 36 30N 73 0 E
Northern Cape □, *S. Africa* 56 D3 30 0S 20 0 E
Northern Circars, *India* 41 L13 17 30N 82 30 E
Northern Indian L., *Canada* 73 B9 57 20N 97 20W
Northern Ireland □, *U.K.* 13 B5 54 45N 7 0W
Northern Light L., *Canada* 70 C1 48 15N 90 39W
Northern Marianas ■, *Pac. Oc.* 64 F6 17 0N 145 0 E
Northern Province □, *S. Africa* 57 C4 24 0S 29 0 E
Northern Territory □, *Australia* 60 D5 20 0S 133 0 E
Northfield, *Minn., U.S.A.* 80 C8 44 27N 93 9W
Northfield, *Vt., U.S.A.* 79 B12 44 9N 72 40W
Northland □, *N.Z.* 59 F4 35 30S 173 30 E
Northome, *U.S.A.* 80 B7 47 52N 94 17W
Northport, *Ala., U.S.A.* 77 J2 33 14N 87 35W
Northport, *Wash., U.S.A.* 82 B5 48 55N 117 48W
Northumberland □, *U.K.* 10 B6 55 12N 2 0W
Northumberland, C., *Australia* 63 F3 38 5S 140 40 E
Northumberland Is., *Australia* 62 C4 21 30S 149 50 E
Northumberland Str., *Canada* 71 C7 46 20N 64 0W
Northville, *U.S.A.* 79 C10 43 13N 74 11W
Northwest Providence Channel, *W. Indies* 88 A4 26 0N 78 0W
Northwest Territories □, *Canada* 68 B9 63 0N 118 0W
Northwood, *Iowa, U.S.A.* 80 D8 43 27N 93 13W
Northwood, *N. Dak., U.S.A.* 80 B6 47 44N 97 34W
Norton, *U.S.A.* 80 F5 39 50N 99 53W
Norton, *Zimbabwe* 55 F3 17 52S 30 40 E
Norton Sd., *U.S.A.* 68 B3 63 50N 164 0W
Norwalk, *Calif., U.S.A.* 85 M8 33 54N 118 5W
Norwalk, *Conn., U.S.A.* 79 E11 41 7N 73 22W
Norwalk, *Iowa, U.S.A.* 80 E8 41 29N 93 41W
Norwalk, *Ohio, U.S.A.* 78 E2 41 15N 82 37W
Norway, *Maine, U.S.A.* 77 C10 44 13N 70 32W
Norway, *Mich., U.S.A.* 76 C2 45 47N 87 55W
Norway ■, *Europe* 8 E14 63 0N 11 0 E
Norway House, *Canada* 73 C9 53 59N 97 50W
Norwegian Sea, *Atl. Oc.* 4 C8 66 0N 1 0 E
Norwich, *Canada* 78 D4 42 59N 80 36W
Norwich, *U.K.* 11 E9 52 38N 1 18 E
Norwich, *Conn., U.S.A.* 79 E12 41 31N 72 5W
Norwich, *N.Y., U.S.A.* 79 D9 42 32N 75 32W
Norwood, *Canada* 78 B7 44 23N 77 59W
Norwood, *U.S.A.* 79 B10 44 45N 75 0W
Noshiro, *Japan* 30 D10 40 12N 140 0 E
Noşratābād, *Iran* 45 D8 29 55N 60 0 E
Noss Hd., *U.K.* 12 C5 58 28N 3 3W
Nossob →, *S. Africa* 56 D3 26 55S 20 45 E
Nosy Barren, *Madag.* 53 H8 18 25S 43 40 E
Nosy Be, *Madag.* 53 G9 13 25S 48 15 E
Nosy Boraha, *Madag.* 57 B8 16 50S 49 55 E
Nosy Lava, *Madag.* 57 A8 14 33S 47 36 E
Nosy Varika, *Madag.* 57 C8 20 35S 48 32 E
Noteć →, *Poland* 16 B8 52 44N 15 26 E
Notikewin →, *Canada* 72 B5 57 2N 117 38W
Notodden, *Norway* 9 G13 59 35N 9 17 E
Notre Dame B., *Canada* 71 C8 49 45N 55 30W
Notre Dame de Koartac = Quaqtaq, *Canada* 69 B13 60 55N 69 40W
Notre-Dame-des-Bois, *Canada* 79 A13 45 24N 71 4W
Notre Dame d'Ivugivic = Ivujivik, *Canada* 69 B12 62 24N 77 55W
Notre-Dame-du-Nord, *Canada* 70 C4 47 36N 79 30W
Nottawasaga B., *Canada* 78 B4 44 35N 80 15W
Nottaway →, *Canada* 70 B4 51 22N 78 55W
Nottingham, *U.K.* 10 E6 52 58N 1 10W
Nottingham, City of □, *U.K.* 10 E6 52 58N 1 10W
Nottingham I., *Canada* 69 B12 63 20N 77 55W
Nottinghamshire □, *U.K.* 10 D6 53 10N 1 3W
Nottoway →, *U.S.A.* 76 G7 36 33N 76 55W
Notwane →, *Botswana* 56 C4 23 35S 26 58 E
Nouâdhibou, *Mauritania* 50 D2 20 54N 17 0W
Nouâdhibou, Ras, *Mauritania* 50 D2 20 50N 17 0W
Nouakchott, *Mauritania* 50 E2 18 9N 15 58W
Nouméa, *N. Cal.* 64 K8 22 17S 166 30 E
Noupoort, *S. Africa* 56 E3 31 10S 24 57 E
Nouveau Comptoir = Wemindji, *Canada* 70 B4 53 0N 78 49W
Nouvelle-Amsterdam, I., *Ind. Oc.* 3 F13 38 30S 77 30 E
Nouvelle-Calédonie = New Caledonia ■, *Pac. Oc.* 64 K8 21 0S 165 0 E
Nova Casa Nova, *Brazil* 93 E10 9 25S 41 5W
Nova Esperança, *Brazil* 95 A5 23 8S 52 24W
Nova Friburgo, *Brazil* 95 A7 22 16S 42 30W
Nova Gaia = Cambundi-Catembo, *Angola* 52 G3 10 10S 17 35 E
Nova Iguaçu, *Brazil* 95 A7 22 45S 43 28W
Nova Iorque, *Brazil* 93 E10 7 0S 44 5W
Nova Lima, *Brazil* 95 A7 19 59S 43 51W
Nova Lisboa = Huambo, *Angola* 53 G3 12 42S 15 54 E
Nova Lusitânia, *Mozam.* 55 F3 19 50S 34 34 E
Nova Mambone, *Mozam.* 57 C6 21 0S 35 3 E
Nova Scotia □, *Canada* 71 C7 45 10N 63 0W
Nova Sofala, *Mozam.* 57 C5 20 7S 34 42 E
Nova Venécia, *Brazil* 93 G10 18 45S 40 24W
Nova Zagora, *Bulgaria* 21 C11 42 32N 26 1 E
Novar, *Canada* 78 A5 45 27N 79 15W
Novara, *Italy* 18 D8 45 28N 8 38 E
Novato, *U.S.A.* 84 G4 38 6N 122 35W
Novaya Ladoga, *Russia* 24 B5 60 7N 32 16 E
Novaya Lyalya, *Russia* 24 C11 59 4N 60 45 E
Novaya Sibir, Ostrov, *Russia* 27 B16 75 10N 150 0 E
Novaya Zemlya, *Russia* 26 B6 75 0N 56 0 E
Nové Zámky, *Slovak Rep.* 17 D10 48 2N 18 8 E
Novgorod, *Russia* 24 C5 58 30N 31 25 E
Novgorod-Severskiy = Novhorod-Siverskyy, *Ukraine* 24 D5 52 2N 33 10 E
Novhorod-Siverskyy, *Ukraine* 24 D5 52 2N 33 10 E
Novi Lígure, *Italy* 18 D8 44 46N 8 47 E
Novi Pazar, *Serbia, Yug.* 21 C9 43 12N 20 28 E
Novi Sad, *Serbia, Yug.* 21 B8 45 18N 19 52 E
Novo Hamburgo, *Brazil* 95 B5 29 37S 51 7W
Novo Mesto, *Slovenia* 20 B6 45 47N 15 12 E
Novo Remanso, *Brazil* 93 E10 9 41S 42 4W
Novoataysk, *Russia* 26 D9 53 30N 84 0 E
Novocherkassk, *Russia* 25 E7 47 27N 40 15 E
Novogrudok = Navahrudak, *Belarus* 17 B13 53 40N 25 50 E
Novohrad-Volynskyy, *Ukraine* 17 C14 50 34N 27 35 E
Novokachalinsk, *Russia* 30 B6 45 5N 132 0 E
Novokazalinsk = Zhangaqazaly, *Kazakstan* 26 E7 45 48N 62 6 E
Novokuybyshevsk, *Russia* 24 D8 53 7N 49 58 E
Novokuznetsk, *Russia* 26 D9 53 45N 87 10 E
Novomoskovsk, *Russia* 24 D6 54 5N 38 15 E
Novorossiysk, *Russia* 25 F6 44 43N 37 46 E
Novorybnoye, *Russia* 27 B11 72 50N 105 50 E
Novoselytsya, *Ukraine* 17 D14 48 14N 26 15 E
Novoshakhtinsk, *Russia* 25 E6 47 46N 39 58 E
Novosibirsk, *Russia* 26 D9 55 0N 83 5 E
Novosibirskiye Ostrova, *Russia* 27 B15 75 0N 142 0 E
Novotroitsk, *Russia* 24 D10 51 10N 58 15 E
Novouzensk, *Russia* 25 D8 50 32N 48 17 E
Novovolynsk, *Ukraine* 17 C13 50 45N 24 4 E
Novska, *Croatia* 20 B7 45 19N 17 0 E
Novvy Urengoy, *Russia* 26 C8 65 48N 76 52 E
Novyy Bor, *Russia* 24 A9 66 43N 52 19 E
Novyy Port, *Russia* 26 C8 67 40N 72 30 E
Now Shahr, *Iran* 45 B6 36 40N 51 30 E
Nowa Sól, *Poland* 16 C8 51 48N 15 44 E
Nowata, *U.S.A.* 81 G7 36 42N 95 38W
Nowbarān, *Iran* 45 C6 35 8N 49 42 E
Nowghāb, *Iran* 45 C8 33 53N 59 4 E
Nowgong, *Assam, India* 41 F18 26 20N 92 50 E
Nowgong, *Mad. P., India* 43 G8 25 4N 79 27 E
Nowra, *Australia* 63 E5 34 53S 150 35 E
Nowshera, *Pakistan* 40 C8 34 0N 72 0 E
Nowy Sącz, *Poland* 17 D11 49 40N 20 41 E
Nowy Targ, *Poland* 17 D11 49 29N 20 2 E
Nowy Tomyśl, *Poland* 16 B9 52 19N 16 10 E
Noxen, *U.S.A.* 79 E8 41 25N 76 4W
Noxon, *U.S.A.* 82 C6 48 0N 115 43W
Noyabr'sk, *Russia* 26 C8 64 34N 76 21 E
Noyon, *France* 18 B5 49 34N 2 59 E
Noyon, *Mongolia* 34 C2 43 2N 102 4 E
Nqutu, *S. Africa* 57 D5 28 13S 30 32 E
Nsanje, *Malawi* 55 F4 16 55S 35 12 E
Nsomba, *Zambia* 55 E2 10 45S 29 51 E
Nu Jiang →, *China* 32 D4 29 58N 97 25 E
Nu Shan, *China* 32 D4 26 0N 99 20 E
Nubia, *Africa* 48 D7 21 0N 32 0 E
Nubian Desert = Nûbîya, Es Sahrâ en, *Sudan* 51 D12 21 30N 33 30 E
Nûbîya, Es Sahrâ en, *Sudan* 51 D12 21 30N 33 30 E
Nuboai, *Indonesia* 37 E9 2 10S 136 30 E
Nubra →, *India* 43 B7 34 35N 77 35 E
Nueces →, *U.S.A.* 81 M6 27 51N 97 30W
Nueltin L., *Canada* 73 A9 60 30N 99 30W
Nueva Asunción □, *Paraguay* 94 A3 21 0S 61 0W
Nueva Gerona, *Cuba* 88 B3 21 53N 82 49W
Nueva Palmira, *Uruguay* 94 C4 33 52S 58 20W
Nueva Rosita, *Mexico* 86 B4 28 0N 101 11W
Nueva San Salvador, *El Salv.* 88 D2 13 40N 89 18W
Nuéve de Julio, *Argentina* 94 D3 35 30S 61 0W
Nuevitas, *Cuba* 88 B4 21 30N 77 20W
Nuevo, G., *Argentina* 96 E4 43 0S 64 30W
Nuevo Casas Grandes, *Mexico* 86 A3 30 22N 108 0W
Nuevo Guerrero, *Mexico* 87 B5 26 34N 99 15W
Nuevo Laredo, *Mexico* 87 B5 27 30N 99 30W
Nuevo León □, *Mexico* 86 C5 25 0N 100 0W
Nuevo Rocafuerte, *Ecuador* 92 D3 0 55S 75 27W
Nugget Pt., *N.Z.* 59 M2 46 27S 169 50 E
Nuhaka, *N.Z.* 59 H6 39 3S 177 45 E
Nukey Bluff, *Australia* 63 E2 32 26S 135 29 E
Nukhuyb, *Iraq* 44 C4 32 4N 42 3 E
Nuku'alofa, *Tonga* 59 E12 21 10S 174 0W
Nukus, *Uzbekistan* 26 E6 42 27N 59 41 E
Nullagine, *Australia* 60 D3 21 53S 120 7 E
Nullagine →, *Australia* 60 D3 21 20S 120 20 E
Nullarbor, *Australia* 61 F5 31 28S 130 55 E
Nullarbor Plain, *Australia* 61 F4 31 10S 129 0 E
Numalla, L., *Australia* 63 D3 28 43S 144 20 E
Numan, *Nigeria* 51 G8 9 29N 12 3 E
Numata, *Japan* 31 F9 36 45N 139 4 E
Numazu, *Japan* 31 G9 35 7N 138 51 E
Numbulwar, *Australia* 62 A2 14 15S 135 45 E
Numfoor, *Indonesia* 37 E8 1 0S 134 50 E
Numurkah, *Australia* 63 F4 36 5S 145 26 E
Nunaksaluk I., *Canada* 71 A7 55 49N 60 20W
Nunap Isua, *Greenland* 69 C15 59 48N 43 55W
Nunavut □, *Canada* 69 B11 66 0N 85 0W
Nunda, *U.S.A.* 78 D7 42 35N 77 56W
Nungarin, *Australia* 61 F2 31 12S 118 6 E
Nungo, *Mozam.* 55 E4 13 23S 37 43 E
Nungwe, *Tanzania* 54 C3 2 48S 32 2 E
Nunivak I., *U.S.A.* 68 B3 60 10N 166 30W
Nunkun, *India* 43 C7 33 57N 76 2 E
Núoro, *Italy* 20 D3 40 20N 9 20 E
Nūrābād, *Iran* 45 E8 27 47N 57 12 E
Nuremberg = Nürnberg, *Germany* 16 D6 49 27N 11 3 E
Nuri, *Mexico* 86 B3 28 2N 109 22W
Nuriootpa, *Australia* 63 E2 34 27S 139 0 E
Nuristān □, *Afghan.* 40 B7 35 20N 71 0 E
Nurmes, *Finland* 8 E23 63 33N 29 10 E
Nürnberg, *Germany* 16 D6 49 27N 11 3 E
Nurpur, *Pakistan* 42 D4 31 53N 71 54 E
Nurran, L. = Terewah, L., *Australia* 63 D4 29 52S 147 35 E
Nurrari Lakes, *Australia* 61 E5 29 1S 130 5 E
Nusa Barung, *Indonesia* 37 H15 8 30S 113 30 E
Nusa Kambangan, *Indonesia* 37 G13 7 40S 108 10 E
Nusa Tenggara Barat □, *Indonesia* 36 F5 8 50S 117 30 E
Nusa Tenggara Timur □, *Indonesia* 37 F6 9 30S 122 0 E
Nusaybin, *Turkey* 25 G7 37 3N 41 10 E
Nushki, *Pakistan* 42 E2 29 35N 66 0 E
Nuuk, *Greenland* 69 B14 64 10N 51 35W
Nuwakot, *Nepal* 43 E10 28 10N 83 55 E
Nuweiba', *Egypt* 44 D2 28 59N 34 39 E
Nuwerus, *S. Africa* 56 E2 31 8S 18 24 E
Nuweveldberge, *S. Africa* 56 E3 32 10S 21 45 E
Nuyts, C., *Australia* 61 F5 32 2S 132 21 E
Nuyts, Pt., *Australia* 61 G2 35 4S 116 38 E
Nuyts Arch., *Australia* 63 E1 32 35S 133 20 E
Nxau-Nxau, *Botswana* 56 B3 18 57S 21 4 E
Nyabing, *Australia* 61 F2 33 33S 118 9 E
Nyack, *U.S.A.* 79 E11 41 5N 73 55W
Nyagan, *Russia* 26 C7 62 30N 65 38 E
Nyahanga, *Tanzania* 54 C3 2 20S 33 37 E
Nyahua, *Tanzania* 54 D3 5 25S 33 23 E
Nyahururu, *Kenya* 54 B4 0 2N 36 27 E
Nyainqentanglha Shan, *China* 32 D4 30 0N 90 0 E
Nyakanazi, *Tanzania* 54 C3 3 2S 31 10 E
Nyâlâ, *Sudan* 51 F10 12 2N 24 58 E
Nyamandhlovu, *Zimbabwe* 55 F2 19 55S 28 16 E
Nyambiti, *Tanzania* 54 C3 2 48S 33 27 E
Nyamwaga, *Tanzania* 54 C3 1 27S 34 33 E
Nyandekwa, *Tanzania* 54 C3 3 57S 32 32 E
Nyandoma, *Russia* 24 B7 61 40N 40 12 E
Nyangana, *Namibia* 56 B3 18 0S 20 40 E
Nyanguge, *Tanzania* 54 C3 2 30S 33 12 E
Nyanza, *Rwanda* 54 C2 2 20S 29 42 E
Nyanza □, *Kenya* 54 C3 0 10S 34 15 E
Nyanza-Lac, *Burundi* 54 C2 4 21S 29 36 E
Nyasa, L., *Africa* 55 E3 12 30S 34 30 E
Nyasvizh, *Belarus* 17 B14 53 14N 26 38 E
Nyazepetrovsk, *Russia* 24 C10 56 3N 59 36 E
Nyazura, *Zimbabwe* 55 F3 18 40S 32 16 E
Nyazwidzi →, *Zimbabwe* 55 G3 20 0S 31 17 E
Nybro, *Sweden* 9 H16 56 44N 15 55 E
Nyda, *Russia* 26 C8 66 40N 72 58 E
Nyeri, *Kenya* 54 C4 0 23S 36 56 E
Nyíregyháza, *Hungary* 17 E11 47 58N 21 47 E
Nykøbing, *Storstrøm, Denmark* 9 J14 54 56N 11 52 E
Nykøbing, *Vestsjælland, Denmark* 9 J14 55 55N 11 40 E
Nykøbing, *Viborg, Denmark* 9 H13 56 48N 8 51 E
Nyköping, *Sweden* 9 G17 58 45N 17 1 E
Nylstroom, *S. Africa* 57 C4 24 42S 28 22 E
Nymagee, *Australia* 63 E4 32 7S 146 20 E
Nynäshamn, *Sweden* 9 G17 58 54N 17 57 E
Nyngan, *Australia* 63 E4 31 30S 147 8 E
Nyoma Rap, *India* 43 C8 33 10N 78 40 E
Nyoman = Neman →, *Lithuania* 9 J19 55 25N 21 10 E
Nysa, *Poland* 17 C9 50 30N 17 22 E
Nysa →, *Europe* 16 B8 52 4N 14 46 E
Nyssa, *U.S.A.* 82 E5 43 53N 117 0W
Nyunzu, *Dem. Rep. of the Congo* 54 D2 5 57S 27 58 E
Nyurba, *Russia* 27 C12 63 17N 118 28 E
Nzega, *Tanzania* 54 C3 4 10S 33 12 E
Nzérékoré, *Guinea* 50 G4 7 49N 8 48W
Nzeto, *Angola* 52 F2 7 10S 12 52 E
Nzilo, Chutes de, *Dem. Rep. of the Congo* 55 E2 10 18S 25 27 E
Nzubuka, *Tanzania* 54 C3 4 45S 32 50 E

O

Ō-Shima, *Japan* 31 G9 34 44N 139 24 E
Oa, Mull of, *U.K.* 12 F2 55 35N 6 20W
Oacoma, *U.S.A.* 80 D5 43 48N 99 24W
Oahe, L., *U.S.A.* 80 C4 44 27N 100 24W
Oahe Dam, *U.S.A.* 80 C4 44 27N 100 24W
Oahu, *U.S.A.* 74 H16 21 28N 157 58W
Oak Harbor, *U.S.A.* 84 B4 48 18N 122 39W
Oak Hill, *U.S.A.* 76 G5 37 59N 81 9W
Oak Ridge, *U.S.A.* 77 G3 36 1N 84 16W
Oak View, *U.S.A.* 85 L7 34 24N 119 18W
Oakan-Dake, *Japan* 30 C12 43 27N 144 10 E
Oakdale, *Calif., U.S.A.* 84 H6 37 46N 120 51W
Oakdale, *La., U.S.A.* 81 K8 30 49N 92 40W
Oakes, *U.S.A.* 80 B5 46 8N 98 6W
Oakesdale, *U.S.A.* 82 C5 47 8N 117 15W
Oakey, *Australia* 63 D5 27 25S 151 43 E
Oakfield, *U.S.A.* 78 C6 43 4N 78 16W
Oakham, *U.K.* 11 E7 52 40N 0 43W

P

Palma de Mallorca, *Spain* **22 B9** 39 35N 2 39 E
Palma Soriano, *Cuba* **88 B4** 20 15N 76 0W
Palmares, *Brazil* **93 E11** 8 41S 35 28W
Palmas, *Brazil* **95 B5** 26 29S 52 0W
Palmas, C., *Liberia* **50 H4** 4 27N 7 46W
Pálmas, G. di, *Italy* **20 E3** 39 0N 8 30 E
Palmdale, *U.S.A.* **85 L8** 34 35N 118 7W
Palmeira das Missões, *Brazil* **95 B5** 27 55S 53 17W
Palmeira dos Índios, *Brazil* **93 E11** 9 25S 36 37W
Palmer, *U.S.A.* **68 B5** 61 36N 149 7W
Palmer →, *Australia* **62 B3** 16 0S 142 26 E
Palmer Arch., *Antarctica* **5 C17** 64 15S 65 0W
Palmer Lake, *U.S.A.* **80 F2** 39 7N 104 55W
Palmer Land, *Antarctica* **5 D18** 73 0S 63 0W
Palmerston, *Canada* **78 C4** 43 50N 80 51W
Palmerston, *N.Z.* **59 L3** 45 29S 170 43 E
Palmerston North, *N.Z.* **59 J5** 40 21S 175 39 E
Palmerton, *U.S.A.* **79 F9** 40 48N 75 37W
Palmetto, *U.S.A.* **77 M4** 27 31N 82 34W
Palmi, *Italy* **20 E6** 38 21N 15 51 E
Palmira, *Argentina* **94 C2** 32 59S 68 34W
Palmira, *Colombia* **92 C3** 3 32N 76 16W
Palmyra = Tudmur, *Syria* **44 C3** 34 36N 38 15 E
Palmyra, *Mo., U.S.A.* **80 F9** 39 48N 91 32W
Palmyra, *N.J., U.S.A.* **79 F9** 40 1N 75 1W
Palmyra, *N.Y., U.S.A.* **78 C7** 43 5N 77 18W
Palmyra, *Pa., U.S.A.* **79 F8** 40 18N 76 36W
Palmyra Is., *Pac. Oc.* **65 G11** 5 52N 162 5W
Palo Alto, *U.S.A.* **84 H4** 37 27N 122 10W
Palo Verde, *U.S.A.* **85 M12** 33 26N 114 44W
Palopo, *Indonesia* **37 E6** 3 0S 120 16 E
Palos, C. de, *Spain* **19 D5** 37 38N 0 40W
Palos Verdes, *U.S.A.* **85 M8** 33 48N 118 23W
Palos Verdes, Pt., *U.S.A.* **85 M8** 33 43N 118 26W
Palu, *Indonesia* **37 E5** 1 0S 119 52 E
Palu, *Turkey* **25 G7** 38 45N 40 0 E
Palwal, *India* **42 E7** 28 8N 77 19 E
Pamanukan, *Indonesia* **37 G12** 6 16S 107 49 E
Pamiers, *France* **18 E4** 43 7N 1 39 E
Pamir, *Tajikistan* **26 F8** 37 40N 73 0 E
Pamlico →, *U.S.A.* **77 H7** 35 20N 76 28W
Pamlico Sd., *U.S.A.* **77 H8** 35 20N 76 0W
Pampa, *U.S.A.* **81 H4** 35 32N 100 58W
Pampa de las Salinas,
Argentina **94 C2** 32 1S 66 58W
Pampanua, *Indonesia* **37 E6** 4 16S 120 8 E
Pampas, *Argentina* **94 D3** 35 0S 63 0W
Pampas, *Peru* **92 F4** 12 20S 74 50W
Pamplona, *Colombia* **92 B4** 7 23N 72 39W
Pamplona, *Spain* **19 A5** 42 48N 1 38W
Pampoenpoort, *S. Africa* **56 E3** 31 3S 22 40 E
Pana, *U.S.A.* **80 F10** 39 23N 89 5W
Panaca, *U.S.A.* **83 H6** 37 47N 114 23W
Panaitan, *Indonesia* **37 G11** 6 36S 105 12 E
Panaji, *India* **40 M8** 15 25N 73 50 E
Panamá, *Panama* **88 E4** 9 0N 79 25W
Panama ■, *Cent. Amer.* **88 E4** 8 48N 79 55W
Panamá, G. de, *Panama* **88 E4** 8 4N 79 20W
Panama Canal, *Panama* **88 E4** 9 10N 79 37W
Panama City, *U.S.A.* **77 K3** 30 10N 85 40W
Panamint Range, *U.S.A.* **85 J9** 36 20N 117 20W
Panamint Springs, *U.S.A.* **85 J9** 36 20N 117 28W
Panão, *Peru* **92 E3** 9 55S 75 55W
Panare, *Thailand* **39 J3** 6 51N 101 30 E
Panay, *Phil.* **37 B6** 11 10N 122 30 E
Panay, G., *Phil.* **37 B6** 11 0N 122 30 E
Pančevo, *Serbia, Yug.* **21 B9** 44 52N 20 41 E
Panda, *Mozam.* **57 C5** 24 2S 34 45 E
Pandan, *Phil.* **37 B6** 11 45N 122 10 E
Pandegelang, *Indonesia* **37 G12** 6 25S 106 5 E
Pandhana, *India* **42 J7** 21 42N 76 13 E
Pandharpur, *India* **40 L9** 17 41N 75 20 E
Pando, *Uruguay* **95 C4** 34 44S 56 0W
Pando, L. = Hope, L., *Australia* **63 D2** 28 24S 139 18 E
Pandokrátor, *Greece* **23 A3** 39 45N 19 50 E
Pandora, *Costa Rica* **88 E3** 9 43N 83 3W
Panevėžys, *Lithuania* **9 J21** 55 42N 24 25 E
Panfilov, *Kazakstan* **26 E8** 44 10N 80 0 E
Pang-Long, *Burma* **41 H21** 23 11N 98 45 E
Pang-Yang, *Burma* **41 H21** 22 7N 98 48 E
Panga, *Dem. Rep. of*
the Congo **54 B2** 1 52N 26 18 E
Pangalanes, Canal des =
Ampangalana,
Lakandranon', *Madag.* **57 C8** 22 48S 47 50 E
Pangani, *Tanzania* **54 D4** 5 25S 38 58 E
Pangani →, *Tanzania* **54 D4** 5 26S 38 58 E
Pangfou = Bengbu, *China* **35 H9** 32 58N 117 20 E
Pangil, *Dem. Rep. of*
the Congo **54 C2** 3 10S 26 35 E
Pangkah, Tanjung, *Indonesia* **37 G15** 6 51S 112 33 E
Pangkajene, *Indonesia* **37 E5** 4 46S 119 34 E
Pangkalanbrandan, *Indonesia* **36 D1** 4 1N 98 20 E
Pangkalanbuun, *Indonesia* **36 E4** 2 41S 111 37 E
Pangkalpinang, *Indonesia* **36 E3** 2 0S 106 0 E
Pangnirtung, *Canada* **69 B13** 66 8N 65 54W
Pangong Tso, *India* **42 B8** 34 40N 78 40 E
Panguitch, *U.S.A.* **83 H7** 37 50N 112 26W
Pangutaran Group, *Phil.* **37 C6** 6 18N 120 34 E
Panhandle, *U.S.A.* **81 H4** 35 21N 101 23W
Pani Mines, *India* **42 H5** 22 29N 73 50 E
Pania-Mutombo, *Dem. Rep.*
of the Congo **54 D1** 5 11S 23 51 E
Panikota I., *India* **42 J4** 20 46N 71 21 E
Panipat, *India* **42 E7** 29 25N 77 2 E
Panjal Range = Pir Panjal
Range, *India* **42 C7** 32 30N 76 50 E
Panjang, Hon, *Vietnam* **39 H4** 9 20N 103 28 E
Panjgur, *Pakistan* **40 F4** 27 0N 64 5 E
Panjim = Panaji, *India* **40 M8** 15 25N 73 50 E
Panjin, *China* **35 D12** 41 3N 122 2 E
Panjinad Barrage, *Pakistan* **42 E7** 29 22N 71 15 E
Panjnad →, *Pakistan* **42 E4** 28 57N 70 30 E
Panjwai, *Afghan.* **42 D1** 31 26N 65 27 E
Panmunjŏm, *N. Korea* **35 F14** 37 59N 126 38 E
Panna, *India* **43 G9** 24 40N 80 15 E
Panna Hills, *India* **43 G9** 24 40N 81 15 E
Pannawonica, *Australia* **60 D2** 21 39S 116 19 E
Pannirtuuq = Pangnirtung,
Canada **69 B13** 66 8N 65 54W
Pano Akil, *Pakistan* **42 F3** 27 51N 69 7 E
Pano Lefkara, *Cyprus* **23 E12** 34 53N 33 20 E
Pano Panayia, *Cyprus* **23 E11** 34 55N 32 38 E
Panorama, *Brazil* **95 A5** 21 21S 51 51W
Pánormon, *Greece* **23 D6** 35 25N 24 41 E
Pansemal, *India* **42 J6** 21 39N 74 42 E
Panshan = Panjin, *China* **35 D12** 41 3N 122 2 E
Panshi, *China* **35 C14** 42 58N 126 5 E
Pantanal, *Brazil* **92 H7** 17 30S 57 40W
Pantar, *Indonesia* **37 F6** 8 28S 124 10 E
Pante Macassar, *E. Timor* **37 F6** 9 30S 123 58 E
Pante Makasar = Pante
Macassar, *E. Timor* **37 F6** 9 30S 123 58 E
Pantelleria, *Italy* **20 F4** 36 50N 11 57 E
Pánuco, *Mexico* **87 C5** 22 0N 98 15W
Paola, *Malta* **23 D2** 35 52N 14 30 E
Paola, *U.S.A.* **80 F7** 38 35N 94 53W
Paonia, *U.S.A.* **83 G10** 38 52N 107 36W
Paoting = Baoding, *China* **34 E8** 38 50N 115 28 E
Paot'ou = Baotou, *China* **34 D6** 40 32N 110 2 E
Paoua, *C.A.R.* **52 C3** 7 9N 16 20 E
Pápa, *Hungary* **17 E9** 47 22N 17 30 E
Papa Stour, *U.K.* **12 A7** 60 20N 1 42W
Papa Westray, *U.K.* **12 B6** 59 20N 2 55W
Papagayo →, *Mexico* **87 D5** 16 36N 99 43W
Papagayo, G. de, *Costa Rica* **88 D2** 10 30N 85 50W
Papakura, *N.Z.* **59 G5** 37 4S 174 59 E
Papantla, *Mexico* **87 C5** 20 30N 97 30W
Papar, *Malaysia* **36 C5** 5 45N 116 0 E
Papeete, *Tahiti* **65 J13** 17 32S 149 34W
Paphos, *Cyprus* **23 E11** 34 46N 32 25 E
Papien Chiang = Da →,
Vietnam **38 B5** 21 15N 105 20 E
Papigochic →, *Mexico* **86 B3** 29 9N 109 40W
Paposo, *Chile* **94 B1** 25 0S 70 30W
Papoutsa, *Cyprus* **23 E12** 34 54N 33 4 E
Papua New Guinea ■,
Oceania **64 H6** 8 0S 145 0 E
Papudo, *Chile* **94 C1** 32 29S 71 27W
Papun, *Burma* **41 K20** 18 2N 97 30 E
Papunya, *Australia* **60 D5** 23 15S 131 54 E
Pará = Belém, *Brazil* **93 D9** 1 20S 48 30W
Pará □, *Brazil* **93 D8** 3 20S 52 0W
Paraburdoo, *Australia* **60 D2** 23 14S 117 32 E
Paracatu, *Brazil* **93 G9** 17 10S 46 50W
Paracel Is., *S. China Sea* **36 A4** 15 50N 112 0 E
Parachilna, *Australia* **63 E2** 31 10S 138 21 E
Parachinar, *Pakistan* **42 C4** 33 55N 70 5 E
Paradhísi, *Greece* **23 C10** 36 18N 28 7 E
Paradip, *India* **41 J15** 20 15N 86 35 E
Paradise, *Calif., U.S.A.* **84 F5** 39 46N 121 37W
Paradise, *Nev., U.S.A.* **85 J11** 36 9N 115 10W
Paradise →, *Canada* **71 B8** 53 27N 57 19W
Paradise Hill, *Canada* **73 C7** 53 32N 109 28W
Paradise River, *Canada* **71 B8** 53 27N 57 17W
Paradise Valley, *U.S.A.* **82 F5** 41 30N 117 32W
Parado, *Indonesia* **37 F5** 8 42S 118 30 E
Paragould, *U.S.A.* **81 G9** 36 3N 90 29W
Paragua →, *Venezuela* **92 B6** 6 55N 62 55W
Paraguaçu →, *Brazil* **93 F11** 12 45S 38 54W
Paraguaçu Paulista, *Brazil* **95 A5** 22 22S 50 35W
Paraguaná, Pen. de,
Venezuela **92 A5** 12 0N 70 0W
Paraguarí, *Paraguay* **94 B4** 25 36S 57 0W
Paraguarí □, *Paraguay* **94 B4** 26 0S 57 10W
Paraguay ■, *S. Amer.* **94 A4** 23 0S 57 0W
Paraguay →, *Paraguay* **94 B4** 27 18S 58 38W
Paraíba = João Pessoa, *Brazil* **93 E12** 7 10S 34 52W
Paraíba □, *Brazil* **93 E11** 7 0S 36 0W
Paraíba do Sul →, *Brazil* **95 A7** 21 37S 41 3W
Parainen, *Finland* **9 F20** 60 18N 22 18 E
Paraiso, *Mexico* **87 D6** 18 24N 93 14W
Parak, *Iran* **45 E7** 27 38N 52 25 E
Parakou, *Benin* **50 G6** 9 25N 2 40 E
Paralimni, *Cyprus* **23 D12** 35 2N 33 58 E
Paramaribo, *Surinam* **93 B7** 5 50N 55 10W
Paramushir, Ostrov, *Russia* **27 D16** 50 24N 156 0 E
Paran →, *Israel* **47 E4** 30 20N 35 10 E
Paraná, *Argentina* **94 C3** 31 45S 60 30W
Paraná, *Brazil* **93 F9** 12 30S 47 48W
Paraná □, *Brazil* **95 A5** 24 30S 51 0W
Paraná →, *Argentina* **94 C4** 33 43S 59 15W
Paranaguá, *Brazil* **95 B6** 25 30S 48 30W
Paranaíba, *Brazil* **93 G8** 19 40S 51 11W
Paranaíba →, *Brazil* **93 H8** 20 6S 51 4W
Paranapanema →, *Brazil* **95 A5** 22 40S 53 9W
Paranapiacaba, Serra do,
Brazil **95 A6** 24 31S 48 35W
Paranavaí, *Brazil* **95 A5** 23 4S 52 56W
Parang, *Maguindanao, Phil.* **37 C6** 7 23N 124 16 E
Parang, *Sulu, Phil.* **37 C6** 5 55N 120 54 E
Parângul Mare, Vf., *Romania* **17 F12** 45 20N 23 37 E
Paraparaumu, *N.Z.* **59 J5** 40 57S 175 3 E
Parbati →, *Mad. P., India* **42 G7** 25 50N 76 30 E
Parbati →, *Raj., India* **42 F7** 26 54N 77 53 E
Parbhani, *India* **40 K10** 19 8N 76 52 E
Parchim, *Germany* **16 B6** 53 26N 11 52 E
Pardes Hanna-Karkur, *Israel* **47 C3** 32 28N 34 57 E
Pardo →, *Bahia, Brazil* **93 G11** 15 40S 39 0W
Pardo →, *Mato Grosso, Brazil* **95 A5** 21 46S 52 9W
Pardubice, *Czech Rep.* **16 C8** 50 3N 15 45 E
Pare, *Indonesia* **37 G15** 7 43S 112 12 E
Pare Mts., *Tanzania* **54 C4** 4 0S 37 45 E
Parecis, Serra dos, *Brazil* **92 F7** 13 0S 60 0W
Paren, *Russia* **27 C17** 62 30N 163 15 E
Parent, *Canada* **70 C5** 47 55N 74 35W
Parent, L., *Canada* **70 C4** 48 31N 77 1W
Parepare, *Indonesia* **37 E5** 4 0S 119 40 E
Párga, *Greece* **21 E9** 39 15N 20 29 E
Pargo, Pta. do, *Madeira* **22 D2** 32 49N 17 17W
Pariaguán, *Venezuela* **92 B6** 8 51N 64 34W
Paricutín, Cerro, *Mexico* **86 D4** 19 28N 102 15W
Parigi, *Indonesia* **37 E6** 0 50S 120 5 E
Parika, *Guyana* **92 B7** 6 50N 58 20W
Parima, Serra, *Brazil* **92 C6** 2 30N 64 0W
Parinari, *Peru* **92 D4** 4 35S 74 25W
Pariñas, Pta., *S. Amer.* **90 D2** 4 30S 82 0W
Parintins, *Brazil* **93 D7** 2 40S 56 50W
Pariparit Kyun, *Burma* **41 M18** 14 55N 93 45 E
Paris, *Canada* **78 C4** 43 12N 80 25W
Paris, *France* **18 B5** 48 50N 2 20 E
Paris, *Idaho, U.S.A.* **82 E8** 42 14N 111 24W
Paris, *Ky., U.S.A.* **76 F3** 38 13N 84 15W
Paris, *Tenn., U.S.A.* **77 G1** 36 18N 88 19W
Paris, *Tex., U.S.A.* **81 J7** 33 40N 95 33W
Parish, *U.S.A.* **79 C8** 43 25N 76 8W
Parishville, *U.S.A.* **79 B10** 44 38N 74 49W
Park, *U.S.A.* **84 B4** 48 45N 122 18W
Park City, *U.S.A.* **81 G6** 37 48N 97 20W
Park Falls, *U.S.A.* **80 C9** 45 56N 90 27W
Park Head, *Canada* **78 B3** 44 36N 81 9W
Park Hills, *U.S.A.* **81 G9** 37 53N 90 28W
Park Range, *U.S.A.* **82 G10** 40 0N 106 30W
Park Rapids, *U.S.A.* **80 B7** 46 55N 95 4W
Park River, *U.S.A.* **80 A6** 48 24N 97 45W
Park Rynie, *S. Africa* **57 E5** 30 25S 30 45 E
Parkā Bandar, *Iran* **45 E8** 25 55N 59 35 E
Parkano, *Finland* **9 E20** 62 1N 23 0 E
Parker, *Ariz., U.S.A.* **85 L12** 34 9N 114 17W
Parker, *Pa., U.S.A.* **78 E5** 41 5N 79 41W
Parker Dam, *U.S.A.* **85 L12** 34 18N 114 8W
Parkersburg, *U.S.A.* **76 F5** 39 16N 81 34W
Parkes, *Australia* **63 E4** 33 9S 148 11 E
Parkfield, *U.S.A.* **84 K6** 35 54N 120 26W
Parkhill, *Canada* **78 C3** 43 15N 81 38W
Parkland, *U.S.A.* **84 C4** 47 9N 122 26W
Parkston, *U.S.A.* **80 D6** 43 24N 97 59W
Parksville, *Canada* **72 D4** 49 20N 124 21W
Parla, *Spain* **19 B4** 40 14N 3 46W
Parma, *Italy* **18 D9** 44 48N 10 20 E
Parma, *Idaho, U.S.A.* **82 E5** 43 47N 116 57W
Parma, *Ohio, U.S.A.* **78 E3** 41 23N 81 43W
Parnaguá, *Brazil* **93 F10** 10 10S 44 38W
Parnaíba, *Brazil* **93 D10** 2 54S 41 47W
Parnaíba →, *Brazil* **93 D10** 3 0S 41 50W
Parnassós, *Greece* **21 E10** 38 35N 22 30 E
Pärnu, *Estonia* **9 G21** 58 28N 24 33 E
Paroo →, *Australia* **63 E3** 31 28S 143 32 E
Páros, *Greece* **21 F11** 37 5N 25 12 E
Parowan, *U.S.A.* **83 H7** 37 51N 112 50W
Parral, *Chile* **94 D1** 36 10S 71 52W
Parras, *Mexico* **86 B4** 25 30N 102 20W
Parrett →, *U.K.* **11 F4** 51 12N 3 1W
Parris I., *U.S.A.* **77 J5** 32 20N 80 41W
Parrsboro, *Canada* **71 C7** 45 30N 64 25W
Parry I., *Canada* **78 A4** 45 18N 80 10W
Parry Is., *Canada* **4 B2** 77 0N 110 0W
Parry Sound, *Canada* **78 A5** 45 20N 80 0W
Parsnip →, *Canada* **72 B4** 55 10N 123 2W
Parsons, *U.S.A.* **81 G7** 37 20N 95 16W
Parsons Ra., *Australia* **62 A2** 13 30S 135 15 E
Partinico, *Italy* **20 E5** 38 3N 13 7 E
Partridge I., *Canada* **70 A2** 55 59N 87 37W
Paru →, *Brazil* **93 D8** 1 33S 52 38W
Parvān □, *Afghan.* **40 B6** 35 0N 69 0 E
Parvatipuram, *India* **41 K13** 18 50N 83 25 E
Parvatsar, *India* **42 F6** 26 52N 74 49 E
Parys, *S. Africa* **56 D4** 26 52S 27 29 E
Pas, Pta. des, *Spain* **22 C7** 38 46N 1 26 E
Pasadena, *Canada* **71 C8** 49 1N 57 36W
Pasadena, *Calif., U.S.A.* **85 L8** 34 9N 118 9W
Pasadena, *Tex., U.S.A.* **81 L7** 29 43N 95 13W
Pasaje →, *Argentina* **94 B3** 25 39S 63 56W
Pascagoula, *U.S.A.* **81 K10** 30 21N 88 33W
Pascagoula →, *U.S.A.* **81 K10** 30 23N 88 37W
Paşcani, *Romania* **17 E14** 47 14N 26 45 E
Pasco, *U.S.A.* **82 C4** 46 14N 119 6W
Pasco, Cerro de, *Peru* **92 F3** 10 45S 76 10W
Pasco I., *Australia* **60 D2** 20 57S 115 20 E
Pascoag, *U.S.A.* **79 E13** 41 57N 71 42W
Pascua, I. de, *Chile* **65 K17** 27 7S 109 23W
Pasfield L., *Canada* **73 B7** 58 24N 105 20W
Pashmakli = Smolyan,
Bulgaria **21 D11** 41 36N 24 38 E
Pasir Mas, *Malaysia* **39 J4** 6 2N 102 8 E
Pasir Putih, *Malaysia* **39 K4** 5 50N 102 24 E
Pasirian, *Indonesia* **37 H15** 8 13S 113 8 E
Pasirkuning, *Indonesia* **36 E2** 0 30S 104 33 E
Paskūh, *Iran* **45 E9** 27 34N 61 39 E
Pasley, C., *Australia* **61 F3** 33 52S 123 35 E
Pašman, *Croatia* **16 G8** 43 58N 15 20 E
Pasni, *Pakistan* **40 G3** 25 15N 63 27 E
Paso Cantinela, *Mexico* **85 N11** 32 33N 115 47W
Paso de Indios, *Argentina* **96 E3** 43 55S 69 0W
Paso de los Libres, *Argentina* **94 B4** 29 44S 57 10W
Paso de los Toros, *Uruguay* **94 C4** 32 45S 56 30W
Paso Robles, *U.S.A.* **83 J3** 35 38N 120 41W
Paspébiac, *Canada* **71 C6** 48 3N 65 17W
Pasrur, *Pakistan* **42 C6** 32 16N 74 43 E
Passage West, *Ireland* **13 E3** 51 52N 8 21W
Passaic, *U.S.A.* **79 F10** 40 51N 74 7W
Passau, *Germany* **16 D7** 48 34N 13 28 E
Passero, C., *Italy* **20 F6** 36 41N 15 10 E
Passo Fundo, *Brazil* **95 B5** 28 10S 52 20W
Passos, *Brazil* **93 H9** 20 45S 46 37W
Pastavy, *Belarus* **9 J22** 55 4N 26 50 E
Pastaza →, *Peru* **92 D3** 4 50S 76 52W
Pasto, *Colombia* **92 C3** 1 13N 77 17W
Pasuruan, *Indonesia* **37 G15** 7 40S 112 44 E
Patagonia, *Argentina* **96 F3** 45 0S 69 0W
Patagonia, *U.S.A.* **83 L8** 31 33N 110 45W
Patambar, *Iran* **45 D9** 29 45N 60 17 E
Patan = Lalitapur, *Nepal* **43 F11** 27 40N 85 20 E
Patan, *Gujarat, India* **40 H8** 23 54N 72 14 E
Patan, *Maharashtra, India* **42 H5** 23 54N 72 14 E
Patani, *Indonesia* **37 D7** 0 20N 128 50 E
Pataudi, *India* **42 E7** 28 18N 76 48 E
Patchewollock, *Australia* **63 F3** 35 22S 142 12 E
Patchogue, *U.S.A.* **79 F11** 40 46N 73 1W
Patea, *N.Z.* **59 H5** 39 45S 174 30 E
Patensie, *S. Africa* **56 E3** 33 46S 24 49 E
Paternò, *Italy* **20 F6** 37 34N 14 54 E
Pateros, *U.S.A.* **82 B4** 48 3N 119 54W
Paterson, *U.S.A.* **79 F10** 40 55N 74 11W
Paterson Ra., *Australia* **60 D3** 21 45S 122 10 E
Pathankot, *India* **42 C6** 32 18N 75 45 E
Pathein = Bassein, *Burma* **41 L19** 16 45N 94 30 E
Pathfinder Reservoir, *U.S.A.* **82 E10** 42 28N 106 51W
Pathiu, *Thailand* **39 G2** 10 42N 99 19 E
Pathum Thani, *Thailand* **38 E3** 14 1N 100 32 E
Pati, *Indonesia* **37 G14** 6 45S 111 1 E
Patía →, *Colombia* **92 C3** 2 13N 78 40W
Patiala, *Punjab, India* **42 D7** 30 23N 76 26 E
Patiala, *Ut. P., India* **43 F8** 27 43N 79 1 E
Patkai Bum, *India* **41 F19** 27 0N 95 30 E
Pátmos, *Greece* **21 F12** 37 21N 26 36 E
Patna, *India* **43 G11** 25 35N 85 12 E
Pato Branco, *Brazil* **95 B5** 26 13S 52 40W
Patonga, *Uganda* **54 B3** 2 45N 33 15 E
Patos, *Brazil* **93 E11** 6 55S 37 16W
Patos, L. dos, *Brazil* **95 C5** 31 20S 51 0W
Patos, Río de los →,
Argentina **94 C2** 31 18S 69 25W
Patos de Minas, *Brazil* **93 G9** 18 35S 46 32W
Patquía, *Argentina* **94 C2** 30 2S 66 55W
Pátrai, *Greece* **21 E9** 38 14N 21 47 E
Pátraikós Kólpos, *Greece* **21 E9** 38 17N 21 30 E
Patras = Pátrai, *Greece* **21 E9** 38 14N 21 47 E
Patrocínio, *Brazil* **93 G9** 18 57S 47 0W
Patta, *Kenya* **54 C5** 2 10S 41 0 E
Pattani, *Thailand* **39 J3** 6 48N 101 15 E
Pattaya, *Thailand* **36 B2** 12 52N 100 55 E
Patten, *U.S.A.* **77 C11** 46 0N 68 38W
Patterson, *Calif., U.S.A.* **84 H5** 37 28N 121 8W
Patterson, *La., U.S.A.* **81 L9** 29 42N 91 18W
Patterson, Mt., *U.S.A.* **84 G7** 38 29N 119 20W
Patti, *Punjab, India* **42 D6** 31 17N 74 54 E
Patti, *Ut. P., India* **43 G10** 25 55N 82 12 E
Pattoki, *Pakistan* **42 D5** 31 5N 73 52 E
Patton, *U.S.A.* **78 F6** 40 38N 78 39W
Patuakhali, *Bangla.* **41 H17** 22 20N 90 25 E
Patuanak, *Canada* **73 B7** 55 55N 107 43W
Patuca →, *Honduras* **88 C3** 15 50N 84 18W
Patuca, Punta, *Honduras* **88 C3** 15 49N 84 14W
Pátzcuaro, *Mexico* **86 D4** 19 30N 101 40W
Pau, *France* **18 E3** 43 19N 0 25W
Pauk, *Burma* **41 J19** 21 27N 94 30 E
Paul I., *Canada* **71 A7** 56 30N 61 20W
Paul Smiths, *U.S.A.* **79 B10** 44 26N 74 15W
Paulatuk, *Canada* **68 B7** 69 25N 124 0W
Paulis = Isiro, *Dem. Rep. of*
the Congo **54 B2** 2 53N 27 40 E
Paulistana, *Brazil* **93 E10** 8 9S 41 9W
Paulo Afonso, *Brazil* **93 E11** 9 21S 38 15W
Paulpietersburg, *S. Africa* **57 D5** 27 23S 30 50 E
Pauls Valley, *U.S.A.* **81 H6** 34 44N 97 13W
Pauma Valley, *U.S.A.* **85 M10** 33 16N 116 58W
Pauri, *India* **43 D8** 30 9N 78 47 E
Pāveh, *Iran* **44 C5** 35 3N 46 22 E
Pavia, *Italy* **18 D8** 45 7N 9 8 E
Pavilion, *U.S.A.* **78 D6** 42 52N 78 1W
Pāvilosta, *Latvia* **9 H19** 56 53N 21 14 E
Pavlodar, *Kazakstan* **26 D8** 52 33N 77 0 E
Pavlograd = Pavlohrad,
Ukraine **25 E6** 48 30N 35 52 E
Pavlohrad, *Ukraine* **25 E6** 48 30N 35 52 E
Pavlovo, *Russia* **24 C7** 55 58N 43 5 E
Pavlovsk, *Russia* **25 D7** 50 26N 40 5 E
Pavlovskaya, *Russia* **25 E6** 46 17N 39 47 E
Pawayan, *India* **43 E9** 28 4N 80 6 E
Pawhuska, *U.S.A.* **81 G6** 36 40N 96 20W
Pawling, *U.S.A.* **79 E11** 41 34N 73 36W
Pawnee, *U.S.A.* **81 G6** 36 20N 96 48W
Pawnee City, *U.S.A.* **80 E6** 40 7N 96 9W
Pawtucket, *U.S.A.* **79 E13** 41 53N 71 23W
Paximádhia, *Greece* **23 E6** 35 0N 24 35 E
Paxoí, *Greece* **21 E9** 39 14N 20 12 E
Paxton, *Ill., U.S.A.* **76 E1** 40 27N 88 6W
Paxton, *Nebr., U.S.A.* **80 E4** 41 7N 101 21W
Payakumbuh, *Indonesia* **36 E2** 0 20S 100 35 E
Payette, *U.S.A.* **82 D5** 44 5N 116 56W
Payne Bay = Kangirsuk,
Canada **69 B13** 60 0N 70 0W
Payne L., *Canada* **69 C12** 59 30N 74 30W
Paynes Find, *Australia* **61 E2** 29 15S 117 42 E
Paynesville, *U.S.A.* **80 C7** 45 23N 94 43W
Paysandú, *Uruguay* **94 C4** 32 19S 58 8W
Payson, *U.S.A.* **83 J8** 34 14N 111 20W
Paz →, *Guatemala* **88 D1** 13 44N 90 10W
Paz, B. de la, *Mexico* **86 C2** 24 15N 110 25W
Pāzanān, *Iran* **45 D6** 30 35N 49 59 E
Pazardzhik, *Bulgaria* **21 C11** 42 12N 24 20 E
Pe Ell, *U.S.A.* **84 D3** 46 34N 123 18W
Peabody, *U.S.A.* **79 D14** 42 31N 70 56W
Peace →, *Canada* **72 B6** 59 0N 111 25W
Peace Point, *Canada* **72 B6** 59 7N 112 27W
Peace River, *Canada* **72 B5** 56 15N 117 18W
Peach Springs, *U.S.A.* **83 J7** 35 32N 113 25W
Peachland, *Canada* **72 D5** 49 47N 119 45W
Peachtree City, *U.S.A.* **77 J3** 33 25N 84 35W
Peak, The = Kinder Scout,
U.K. **10 D6** 53 24N 1 52W
Peak District, *U.K.* **10 D6** 53 10N 1 50W
Peak Hill, *N.S.W., Australia* **63 E4** 32 47S 148 11 E
Peak Hill, *W. Austral.,*
Australia **61 E2** 25 35S 118 43 E
Peak Ra., *Australia* **62 C4** 22 50S 148 20 E
Peake Cr. →, *Australia* **63 D2** 28 2S 136 7 E
Peale, Mt., *U.S.A.* **83 G9** 38 26N 109 14W
Pearblossom, *U.S.A.* **85 L9** 34 30N 117 55W
Pearl →, *U.S.A.* **81 K10** 30 11N 89 32W
Pearl City, *U.S.A.* **74 H16** 21 24N 157 59W
Pearl Harbor, *U.S.A.* **74 H16** 21 21N 157 57W
Pearl River, *U.S.A.* **79 E10** 41 4N 74 2W
Pearsall, *U.S.A.* **81 L5** 28 54N 99 6W
Peary Land, *Greenland* **4 A6** 82 40N 33 0W
Pease →, *U.S.A.* **81 H5** 34 12N 99 2W
Peawanuck, *Canada* **69 C11** 55 15N 85 12W
Pebane, *Mozam.* **55 F4** 17 10S 38 8 E
Pebas, *Peru* **92 D4** 3 10S 71 46W
Pebble Beach, *U.S.A.* **84 J5** 36 34N 121 57W
Peć, *Kosovo, Yug.* **21 C9** 42 40N 20 17 E
Pechenga, *Russia* **24 A5** 69 29N 31 4 E
Pechenizhyn, *Ukraine* **17 D13** 48 30N 24 48 E
Pechiguera, Pta., *Canary Is.* **22 F6** 28 51N 13 53W
Pechora, *Russia* **24 A10** 65 10N 57 11 E
Pechora →, *Russia* **24 A9** 68 13N 54 15 E
Pechorskaya Guba, *Russia* **24 A9** 68 40N 54 0 E
Pečory, *Russia* **9 H22** 57 48N 27 40 E
Pecos, *U.S.A.* **81 K3** 31 26N 103 30W
Pecos →, *U.S.A.* **81 L3** 29 42N 101 22W
Pécs, *Hungary* **17 E10** 46 5N 18 15 E
Pedder, L., *Australia* **62 G4** 42 55S 146 10 E
Peddie, *S. Africa* **57 E4** 33 14S 27 7 E
Pedernales, *Dom. Rep.* **89 C5** 18 2N 71 44W
Pedieos →, *Cyprus* **23 D12** 35 10N 33 54 E
Pedirka, *Australia* **63 D2** 26 40S 135 14 E
Pedra Azul, *Brazil* **93 G10** 16 2S 41 17W
Pedreiras, *Brazil* **93 D10** 4 32S 44 40W
Pedro Afonso, *Brazil* **93 E9** 9 0S 48 10W
Pedro Cays, *Jamaica* **88 C4** 17 5N 77 48W
Pedro de Valdivia, *Chile* **94 A2** 22 55S 69 38W
Pedro Juan Caballero,
Paraguay **95 A4** 22 30S 55 40W
Pee Dee →, *U.S.A.* **77 J6** 33 22N 79 16W
Peebinga, *Australia* **63 E3** 34 52S 140 57 E
Peebles, *U.K.* **12 F5** 55 40N 3 11W
Peekskill, *U.S.A.* **79 E11** 41 17N 73 55W
Peel, *U.K.* **10 C3** 54 13N 4 40W
Peel →, *Australia* **63 E5** 30 50S 150 29 E
Peel →, *Canada* **68 B6** 67 0N 135 0W
Peel Sound, *Canada* **68 A10** 73 0N 96 0W
Peera Peera Poolanna L.,
Australia **63 D2** 26 30S 138 0 E

Pinglu, *China* **34 E7** 39 31N 112 30 E
Pingluo, *China* **34 E4** 38 52N 106 30 E
Pingquan, *China* **35 D10** 41 1N 118 37 E
Pingrup, *Australia* **61 F2** 33 32S 118 29 E
P'ingtung, *Taiwan* **33 D7** 22 38N 120 30 E
Pingwu, *China* **34 H3** 32 25N 104 30 E
Pingxiang, *China* **32 D5** 22 6N 106 46 E
Pingyao, *China* **34 F7** 37 12N 112 10 E
Pingyi, *China* **35 G9** 35 30N 117 35 E
Pingyin, *China* **34 F9** 36 20N 116 25 E
Pingyuan, *China* **34 F9** 37 10N 116 22 E
Pinhal, *Brazil* **95 A6** 22 10S 46 46W
Pinheiro, *Brazil* **93 D9** 2 31S 45 5W
Pinheiro Machado, *Brazil* **95 C5** 31 34S 53 23W
Pinhel, *Portugal* **19 B2** 40 50N 7 1W
Pini, *Indonesia* **36 D1** 0 10N 98 40 E
Piniós →, *Greece* **21 E10** 39 55N 22 41 E
Pinjarra, *Australia* **61 F2** 32 37S 115 52 E
Pink Mountain, *Canada* **72 B4** 57 3N 122 52W
Pinnacles, *U.S.A.* **84 J5** 36 33N 121 19W
Pinnaroo, *Australia* **63 F3** 35 17S 140 53 E
Pinnes, Ákra, *Greece* **21 D11** 40 5N 24 20 E
Pinon Hills, *U.S.A.* **85 L9** 34 26N 117 39W
Pinos, *Mexico* **86 C4** 22 20N 101 40W
Pinos, Mt., *U.S.A.* **85 L7** 34 49N 119 8W
Pinos Pt., *U.S.A.* **83 H3** 36 38N 121 57W
Pinotepa Nacional, *Mexico* **87 D5** 16 19N 98 3W
Pinrang, *Indonesia* **37 E5** 3 46S 119 41 E
Pins, Pte. aux, *Canada* **78 D3** 42 15N 81 51W
Pinsk, *Belarus* **17 B14** 52 10N 26 1 E
Pintados, *Chile* **92 H5** 20 35S 69 40W
Pinyug, *Russia* **24 B8** 60 5N 48 0 E
Pioche, *U.S.A.* **83 H6** 37 56N 114 27W
Piombino, *Italy* **20 C4** 42 55N 10 32 E
Pioner, Ostrov, *Russia* **27 B10** 79 50N 92 0 E
Piorini, L., *Brazil* **92 D6** 3 15S 62 35W
Piotrków Trybunalski, *Poland* **17 C10** 51 23N 19 43 E
Pīp, *Iran* **45 E9** 26 45N 60 10 E
Pipar, *India* **42 F5** 26 25N 73 31 E
Pipar Road, *India* **42 F5** 26 27N 73 27 E
Piparia, *Mad. P., India* **42 H8** 22 45N 78 23 E
Piparia, *Mad. P., India* **42 J7** 21 49N 77 37 E
Pipestone, *U.S.A.* **80 D6** 44 0N 96 19W
Pipestone →, *Canada* **70 B2** 52 53N 89 23W
Pipestone Cr. →, *Canada* **73 D8** 49 38N 100 15W
Piplan, *Pakistan* **42 C4** 32 17N 71 21 E
Piploda, *India* **42 H6** 23 37N 74 56 E
Pipmuacan, Rés., *Canada* **71 C5** 49 45N 70 30W
Pippingarra, *Australia* **60 D2** 20 27S 118 42 E
Piqua, *U.S.A.* **76 E3** 40 9N 84 15W
Piquiri →, *Brazil* **95 A5** 24 3S 54 14W
Pir Panjal Range, *India* **42 C7** 32 30N 76 50 E
Pīr Sohrāb, *Iran* **45 E9** 25 44N 60 54 E
Piracicaba, *Brazil* **95 A6** 22 45S 47 40W
Piracuruca, *Brazil* **93 D10** 3 50S 41 50W
Piræus = Piraiévs, *Greece* **21 F10** 37 57N 23 42 E
Piraiévs, *Greece* **21 F10** 37 57N 23 42 E
Pirajuí, *Brazil* **95 A6** 21 59S 49 29W
Piram I., *India* **42 J5** 21 36N 72 21 E
Pirané, *Argentina* **94 B4** 25 42S 59 6W
Pirapora, *Brazil* **93 G10** 17 20S 44 56W
Pirawa, *India* **42 G7** 24 10N 76 2 E
Pírgos, *Greece* **21 F9** 37 40N 21 27 E
Piribebuy, *Paraguay* **94 B4** 25 26S 57 2W
Pirimapun, *Indonesia* **37 F9** 6 20S 138 24 E
Pirin Planina, *Bulgaria* **21 D10** 41 40N 23 30 E
Pírineos = Pyrénées, *Europe* **18 E4** 42 45N 0 18 E
Piripiri, *Brazil* **93 D10** 4 15S 41 46W
Pirmasens, *Germany* **16 D4** 49 12N 7 36 E
Pirot, *Serbia, Yug.* **21 C10** 43 9N 22 33 E
Piru, *Indonesia* **37 E7** 3 4S 128 12 E
Piru, *U.S.A.* **85 L8** 34 25N 118 48W
Pisa, *Italy* **20 C4** 43 43N 10 23 E
Pisagua, *Chile* **92 G4** 19 40S 70 15W
Pisco, *Peru* **92 F3** 13 50S 76 12W
Písek, *Czech Rep.* **16 D8** 49 19N 14 10 E
Pishan, *China* **32 C2** 37 30N 78 33 E
Pīshīn, *Iran* **45 E9** 26 6N 61 47 E
Pishin, *Pakistan* **42 D2** 30 35N 67 0 E
Pishin Lora →, *Pakistan* **42 E1** 29 9N 64 5 E
Pising, *Indonesia* **37 F6** 5 8S 121 53 E
Pismo Beach, *U.S.A.* **85 K6** 35 9N 120 38W
Pissis, Cerro, *Argentina* **94 B2** 27 45S 68 48W
Pissouri, *Cyprus* **23 E11** 34 40N 32 42 E
Pistóia, *Italy* **20 C4** 43 55N 10 54 E
Pistol B., *Canada* **73 A10** 62 25N 92 37W
Pisuerga →, *Spain* **19 B3** 41 33N 4 52W
Pit →, *U.S.A.* **82 F2** 40 47N 122 6W
Pitarpunga, L., *Australia* **63 E3** 34 24S 143 30 E
Pitcairn I., *Pac. Oc.* **65 K14** 25 5S 130 5W
Pite älv →, *Sweden* **8 D19** 65 20N 21 25 E
Piteå, *Sweden* **8 D19** 65 20N 21 25 E
Piteşti, *Romania* **17 F13** 44 52N 24 54 E
Pithapuram, *India* **41 L13** 17 10N 82 15 E
Pithara, *Australia* **61 F2** 30 20S 116 35 E
Pithoragarh, *India* **43 E9** 29 35N 80 13 E
Pithoro, *Pakistan* **42 G3** 25 31N 69 23 E
Pitlochry, *U.K.* **12 E5** 56 42N 3 44W
Pitsilia, *Cyprus* **23 E12** 34 55N 33 0 E
Pitt I., *Canada* **72 C3** 53 30N 129 50W
Pittsburg, *Calif., U.S.A.* **84 G5** 38 2N 121 53W
Pittsburg, *Kans., U.S.A.* **81 G7** 37 25N 94 42W
Pittsburg, *Tex., U.S.A.* **81 J7** 33 0N 94 59W
Pittsburgh, *U.S.A.* **78 F5** 40 26N 80 1W
Pittsfield, *Ill., U.S.A.* **80 F9** 39 36N 90 49W
Pittsfield, *Maine, U.S.A.* **77 C11** 44 47N 69 23W
Pittsfield, *Mass., U.S.A.* **79 D11** 42 27N 73 15W
Pittsfield, *N.H., U.S.A.* **79 C13** 43 18N 71 20W
Pittston, *U.S.A.* **79 E9** 41 19N 75 47W
Pittsworth, *Australia* **63 D5** 27 41S 151 37 E
Pituri →, *Australia* **62 C2** 22 35S 138 30 E
Piura, *Peru* **92 E2** 5 15S 80 38W
Pixley, *U.S.A.* **84 K7** 35 58N 119 18W
Pizhou, *China* **34 G9** 34 44N 116 55 E
Placentia, *Canada* **71 C9** 47 20N 54 0W
Placentia B., *Canada* **71 C9** 47 0N 54 40W
Placerville, *U.S.A.* **84 G6** 38 44N 120 48W
Placetas, *Cuba* **88 B4** 22 15N 79 44W
Plainfield, *N.J., U.S.A.* **79 F10** 40 37N 74 25W
Plainfield, *Ohio, U.S.A.* **78 F3** 40 13N 81 43W
Plainfield, *Vt., U.S.A.* **79 B12** 44 17N 72 26W
Plains, *Mont., U.S.A.* **82 C6** 47 28N 114 53W
Plains, *Tex., U.S.A.* **81 J3** 33 11N 102 50W
Plainview, *Nebr., U.S.A.* **80 D6** 42 21N 97 47W
Plainview, *Tex., U.S.A.* **81 H4** 34 11N 101 43W
Plainwell, *U.S.A.* **76 D3** 42 27N 85 38W
Plaistow, *U.S.A.* **79 D13** 42 50N 71 6W
Pláka, Ákra, *Greece* **23 D8** 35 11N 26 19 E
Plana Cays, *Bahamas* **89 B5** 22 38N 73 30W
Planada, *U.S.A.* **84 H6** 37 16N 120 19W
Plano, *U.S.A.* **81 J6** 33 1N 96 42W
Plant City, *U.S.A.* **77 M4** 28 1N 82 7W
Plaquemine, *U.S.A.* **81 K9** 30 17N 91 14W
Plasencia, *Spain* **19 B2** 40 3N 6 8W
Plaster City, *U.S.A.* **85 N11** 32 47N 115 51W
Plaster Rock, *Canada* **71 C6** 46 53N 67 22W
Plastun, *Russia* **30 B8** 44 45N 136 19 E
Plata, Río de la, *S. Amer.* **94 C4** 34 45S 57 30W
Plátani →, *Italy* **20 F5** 37 23N 13 16 E
Plátanos, *Greece* **23 D5** 35 28N 23 33 E
Platte, *U.S.A.* **80 D5** 43 23N 98 51W
Platte →, *Mo., U.S.A.* **80 F7** 39 16N 94 50W
Platte →, *Nebr., U.S.A.* **80 E7** 41 4N 95 53W
Platteville, *U.S.A.* **80 D9** 42 44N 90 29W
Plattsburgh, *U.S.A.* **79 B11** 44 42N 73 28W
Plattsmouth, *U.S.A.* **80 E7** 41 1N 95 53W
Plauen, *Germany* **16 C7** 50 30N 12 8 E
Plavinas, *Latvia* **9 H21** 56 35N 25 46 E
Playa Blanca, *Canary Is.* **22 F6** 28 55N 13 37W
Playa Blanca Sur, *Canary Is.* **22 F6** 28 51N 13 50W
Playa de las Americas, *Canary Is.* **22 F3** 28 5N 16 43W
Playa de Mogán, *Canary Is.* **22 G4** 27 48N 15 47W
Playa del Inglés, *Canary Is.* **22 G4** 27 45N 15 33W
Playa Esmerelda, *Canary Is.* **22 F5** 28 8N 14 16W
Playgreen L., *Canada* **73 C9** 54 0N 98 15W
Pleasant Bay, *Canada* **71 C7** 46 51N 60 48W
Pleasant Hill, *U.S.A.* **84 H4** 37 57N 122 4W
Pleasant Mount, *U.S.A.* **79 E9** 41 44N 75 26W
Pleasanton, *Calif., U.S.A.* **84 H5** 37 39N 121 52W
Pleasanton, *Tex., U.S.A.* **81 L5** 28 58N 98 29W
Pleasantville, *N.J., U.S.A.* **76 F8** 39 24N 74 32W
Pleasantville, *Pa., U.S.A.* **78 E5** 41 35N 79 34W
Plei Ku, *Vietnam* **38 F7** 13 57N 108 0 E
Plenty →, *Australia* **62 C2** 23 25S 136 31 E
Plenty, B. of, *N.Z.* **59 G6** 37 45S 177 0 E
Plentywood, *U.S.A.* **80 A2** 48 47N 104 34W
Plesetsk, *Russia* **24 B7** 62 43N 40 20 E
Plessisville, *Canada* **71 C5** 46 14N 71 47W
Plétipi, L., *Canada* **71 B5** 51 44N 70 6W
Pleven, *Bulgaria* **21 C11** 43 26N 24 37 E
Plevlja, *Montenegro, Yug.* **21 C8** 43 21N 19 21 E
Plevna, *Canada* **78 B8** 44 58N 76 59W
Płock, *Poland* **17 B10** 52 32N 19 40 E
Plöckenstein, *Germany* **16 D7** 48 46N 13 51 E
Ploieşti, *Romania* **17 F14** 44 57N 26 5 E
Plonge, Lac la, *Canada* **73 B7** 55 8N 107 20W
Plovdiv, *Bulgaria* **21 C11** 42 8N 24 44 E
Plum, *U.S.A.* **78 F5** 40 29N 79 47W
Plum I., *U.S.A.* **79 E12** 41 11N 72 12W
Plumas, *U.S.A.* **84 F7** 39 45N 120 4W
Plummer, *U.S.A.* **82 C5** 47 20N 116 53W
Plumtree, *Zimbabwe* **55 G2** 20 27S 27 55 E
Plungė, *Lithuania* **9 J19** 55 53N 21 59 E
Plymouth, *U.K.* **11 G3** 50 22N 4 10W
Plymouth, *Calif., U.S.A.* **84 G6** 38 29N 120 51W
Plymouth, *Ind., U.S.A.* **76 E2** 41 21N 86 19W
Plymouth, *Mass., U.S.A.* **79 E14** 41 57N 70 40W
Plymouth, *N.C., U.S.A.* **77 H7** 35 52N 76 43W
Plymouth, *N.H., U.S.A.* **79 C13** 43 46N 71 41W
Plymouth, *Pa., U.S.A.* **79 E9** 41 14N 75 57W
Plymouth, *Wis., U.S.A.* **76 D2** 43 45N 87 59W
Plynlimon = Pumlumon Fawr, *U.K.* **11 E4** 52 28N 3 46W
Plzeň, *Czech Rep.* **16 D7** 49 45N 13 22 E
Po →, *Italy* **20 B5** 44 57N 12 4 E
Po Hai = Bo Hai, *China* **35 E10** 39 0N 119 0 E
Pobeda, *Russia* **27 C15** 65 12N 146 12 E
Pobedy, Pik, *Kyrgyzstan* **26 E8** 42 0N 79 58 E
Pocahontas, *Ark., U.S.A.* **81 G9** 36 16N 90 58W
Pocahontas, *Iowa, U.S.A.* **80 D7** 42 44N 94 40W
Pocatello, *U.S.A.* **82 E7** 42 52N 112 27W
Pochutla, *Mexico* **87 D5** 15 50N 96 31W
Pocito Casas, *Mexico* **86 B2** 28 32N 111 6W
Pocomoke City, *U.S.A.* **76 F8** 38 5N 75 34W
Poços de Caldas, *Brazil* **95 A6** 21 50S 46 33W
Podgorica, *Montenegro, Yug.* **21 C8** 42 30N 19 19 E
Podilska Vysochyna, *Ukraine* **17 D14** 49 0N 28 0 E
Podolsk, *Russia* **24 C6** 55 25N 37 30 E
Podporozhye, *Russia* **24 B5** 60 55N 34 2 E
Pofadder, *S. Africa* **56 D2** 29 10S 19 22 E
Pogranitšnyi, *Russia* **30 B5** 44 25N 131 24 E
Poh, *Indonesia* **37 E6** 0 46S 122 51 E
P'ohang, *S. Korea* **35 F15** 36 1N 129 23 E
Pohjanmaa, *Finland* **8 E20** 62 58N 22 50 E
Pohnpei, *Micronesia* **64 G7** 6 55N 158 10 E
Pohri, *India* **42 G6** 25 32N 77 22 E
Poinsett, C., *Antarctica* **5 C8** 65 42S 113 18 E
Point Arena, *U.S.A.* **84 G3** 38 55N 123 41W
Point Baker, *U.S.A.* **72 B2** 56 21N 133 37W
Point Edward, *Canada* **70 D3** 43 0N 82 30W
Point Hope, *U.S.A.* **68 B3** 68 21N 166 47W
Point L., *Canada* **68 B8** 65 15N 113 4W
Point Pedro, *Sri Lanka* **40 Q12** 9 50N 80 15 E
Point Pleasant, *N.J., U.S.A.* **79 F10** 40 5N 74 4W
Point Pleasant, *W. Va., U.S.A.* **76 F4** 38 51N 82 8W
Pointe-à-Pitre, *Guadeloupe* **89 C7** 16 10N 61 32W
Pointe-Claire, *Canada* **79 A11** 45 26N 73 50W
Pointe-Gatineau, *Canada* **79 A9** 45 28N 75 42W
Pointe-Noire, *Congo* **52 E2** 4 48S 11 53 E
Poisonbush Ra., *Australia* **60 D3** 22 30S 121 30 E
Poissonnier Pt., *Australia* **60 C2** 19 57S 119 10 E
Poitiers, *France* **18 C4** 46 35N 0 20 E
Poitou, *France* **18 C3** 46 40N 0 10W
Pojoaque, *U.S.A.* **83 J11** 35 54N 106 1W
Pokaran, *India* **40 F7** 27 0N 71 50 E
Pokataroo, *Australia* **63 D4** 29 30S 148 36 E
Pokhara, *Nepal* **43 E10** 28 14N 83 58 E
Poko, *Dem. Rep. of the Congo* **54 B2** 3 7N 26 52 E
Pokrovsk = Engels, *Russia* **25 D8** 51 28N 46 6 E
Pokrovsk, *Russia* **27 C13** 61 29N 129 0 E
Pola = Pula, *Croatia* **16 F7** 44 54N 13 57 E
Polacca, *U.S.A.* **83 J8** 35 50N 110 23W
Polan, *Iran* **45 E9** 25 30N 61 10 E
Poland ■, *Europe* **17 C10** 52 0N 20 0 E
Polar Bear Prov. Park, *Canada* **70 A2** 55 0N 83 45W
Polatsk, *Belarus* **24 C4** 55 30N 28 50 E
Polcura, *Chile* **94 D1** 37 17S 71 43W
Polessk, *Russia* **9 J19** 54 50N 21 8 E
Polesye = Pripet Marshes, *Europe* **17 B15** 52 10N 28 10 E
Polevskoy, *Russia* **24 C11** 56 26N 60 11 E
Pŏlgyo-ri, *S. Korea* **35 G14** 34 51N 127 21 E
Police, *Poland* **16 B8** 53 33N 14 33 E
Polillo Is., *Phil.* **37 B6** 14 56N 122 0 E
Polis, *Cyprus* **23 D11** 35 2N 32 26 E
Políyiros, *Greece* **21 D10** 40 23N 23 25 E
Polk, *U.S.A.* **78 E5** 41 22N 79 56W
Pollachi, *India* **40 P10** 10 35N 77 0 E
Pollença, *Spain* **22 B10** 39 54N 3 1 E
Pollença, B. de, *Spain* **22 B10** 39 53N 3 8 E
Polnovat, *Russia* **26 C7** 63 50N 65 54 E
Polonne, *Ukraine* **17 C14** 50 6N 27 30 E
Polonnoye = Polonne, *Ukraine* **17 C14** 50 6N 27 30 E
Polson, *U.S.A.* **82 C6** 47 41N 114 9W
Poltava, *Ukraine* **25 E5** 49 35N 34 35 E
Põltsamaa, *Estonia* **9 G21** 58 41N 25 58 E
Polunochnoye, *Russia* **26 C7** 60 52N 60 25 E
Põlva, *Estonia* **9 G22** 58 3N 27 3 E
Polyarny, *Russia* **24 A5** 69 8N 33 20 E
Polynesia, *Pac. Oc.* **65 J11** 10 0S 162 0W
Polynésie française = French Polynesia ■, *Pac. Oc.* **65 K13** 20 0S 145 0W
Pomaro, *Mexico* **86 D4** 18 20N 103 18W
Pombal, *Portugal* **19 C1** 39 55N 8 40W
Pómbia, *Greece* **23 E6** 35 0N 24 51 E
Pomene, *Mozam.* **57 C6** 22 53S 35 33 E
Pomeroy, *Ohio, U.S.A.* **76 F4** 39 2N 82 2W
Pomeroy, *Wash., U.S.A.* **82 C5** 46 28N 117 36W
Pomézia, *Italy* **20 D5** 41 40N 12 30 E
Pomona, *Australia* **63 D5** 26 22S 152 52 E
Pomona, *U.S.A.* **85 L9** 34 4N 117 45W
Pomorskie, Pojezierze, *Poland* **17 B9** 53 40N 16 37 E
Pomos, *Cyprus* **23 D11** 35 9N 32 33 E
Pomos, C., *Cyprus* **23 D11** 35 10N 32 33 E
Pompano Beach, *U.S.A.* **77 M5** 26 14N 80 8W
Pompeys Pillar, *U.S.A.* **82 D10** 45 59N 107 57W
Pompton Lakes, *U.S.A.* **79 F10** 41 0N 74 17W
Ponape = Pohnpei, *Micronesia* **64 G7** 6 55N 158 10 E
Ponask L., *Canada* **70 B1** 54 0N 92 41W
Ponca, *U.S.A.* **80 D6** 42 34N 96 43W
Ponca City, *U.S.A.* **81 G6** 36 42N 97 5W
Ponce, *Puerto Rico* **89 C6** 18 1N 66 37W
Ponchatoula, *U.S.A.* **81 K9** 30 26N 90 26W
Poncheville, L., *Canada* **70 B4** 50 10N 76 55W
Pond, *U.S.A.* **85 K7** 35 43N 119 20W
Pond Inlet, *Canada* **69 A12** 72 40N 77 0W
Pondicherry, *India* **40 P11** 11 59N 79 50 E
Ponds, I. of, *Canada* **71 B8** 53 27N 55 52W
Ponferrada, *Spain* **19 A2** 42 32N 6 35W
Ponnani, *India* **40 P9** 10 45N 75 59 E
Ponoka, *Canada* **72 C6** 52 42N 113 40W
Ponorogo, *Indonesia* **37 G14** 7 52S 111 27 E
Ponoy, *Russia* **24 A7** 67 0N 41 13 E
Ponoy →, *Russia* **24 A7** 66 59N 41 17 E
Ponta do Sol, *Madeira* **22 D2** 32 42N 17 7W
Ponta Grossa, *Brazil* **95 B5** 25 7S 50 10W
Ponta Pora, *Brazil* **95 A4** 22 20S 55 35W
Pontarlier, *France* **18 C7** 46 54N 6 20 E
Pontchartrain L., *U.S.A.* **81 K10** 30 5N 90 5W
Ponte do Pungué, *Mozam.* **55 F3** 19 30S 34 33 E
Ponte Nova, *Brazil* **95 A7** 20 25S 42 54W
Ponteix, *Canada* **73 D7** 49 46N 107 29W
Pontevedra, *Spain* **19 A1** 42 26N 8 40W
Pontiac, *Ill., U.S.A.* **80 E10** 40 53N 88 38W
Pontiac, *Mich., U.S.A.* **76 D4** 42 38N 83 18W
Pontian Kecil, *Malaysia* **39 M4** 1 29N 103 23 E
Pontianak, *Indonesia* **36 E3** 0 3S 109 15 E
Pontine Is. = Ponziane, Ísole, *Italy* **20 D5** 40 55N 12 57 E
Pontine Mts. = Kuzey Anadolu Dağları, *Turkey* **25 F6** 41 30N 35 0 E
Pontivy, *France* **18 B2** 48 5N 2 58W
Pontoise, *France* **18 B5** 49 3N 2 5 E
Ponton →, *Canada* **72 B5** 58 27N 116 11W
Pontypool, *Canada* **78 B6** 44 6N 78 38W
Pontypool, *U.K.* **11 F4** 51 42N 3 2W
Ponziane, Ísole, *Italy* **20 D5** 40 55N 12 57 E
Poochera, *Australia* **63 E1** 32 43S 134 51 E
Poole, *U.K.* **11 G6** 50 43N 1 59W
Poole □, *U.K.* **11 G6** 50 43N 1 59W
Poona = Pune, *India* **40 K8** 18 29N 73 57 E
Pooncarie, *Australia* **63 E3** 33 22S 142 31 E
Poopelloe L., *Australia* **63 E3** 31 40S 144 0 E
Poopó, L. de, *Bolivia* **92 G5** 18 30S 67 35W
Popayán, *Colombia* **92 C3** 2 27N 76 36W
Poperinge, *Belgium* **15 D2** 50 51N 2 42 E
Popilta L., *Australia* **63 E3** 33 10S 141 42 E
Popio L., *Australia* **63 E3** 33 10S 141 52 E
Poplar, *U.S.A.* **80 A2** 48 7N 105 12W
Poplar →, *Canada* **73 C9** 53 0N 97 19W
Poplar Bluff, *U.S.A.* **81 G9** 36 46N 90 24W
Poplarville, *U.S.A.* **81 K10** 30 51N 89 32W
Popocatépetl, Volcán, *Mexico* **87 D5** 19 2N 98 38W
Popokabaka, *Dem. Rep. of the Congo* **52 F3** 5 41S 16 40 E
Poprad, *Slovak Rep.* **17 D11** 49 3N 20 18 E
Porali →, *Pakistan* **42 G2** 25 58N 66 26 E
Porbandar, *India* **42 J3** 21 44N 69 43 E
Porcher I., *Canada* **72 C2** 53 50N 130 30W
Porcupine →, *Canada* **73 B8** 59 11N 104 46W
Porcupine →, *U.S.A.* **68 B5** 66 34N 145 19W
Pordenone, *Italy* **20 B5** 45 57N 12 39 E
Pori, *Finland* **9 F19** 61 29N 21 48 E
Porlamar, *Venezuela* **92 A6** 10 57N 63 51W
Poronaysk, *Russia* **27 E15** 49 13N 143 0 E
Poroshiri-Dake, *Japan* **30 C11** 42 41N 142 52 E
Poroto Mts., *Tanzania* **55 D3** 9 0S 33 30 E
Porpoise B., *Antarctica* **5 C9** 66 0S 127 0 E
Porreres, *Spain* **22 B10** 39 31N 3 2 E
Porsangen, *Norway* **8 A21** 70 40N 25 40 E
Porsgrunn, *Norway* **9 G13** 59 10N 9 40 E
Port Alberni, *Canada* **72 D4** 49 14N 124 50W
Port Alfred, *S. Africa* **56 E4** 33 36S 26 55 E
Port Alice, *Canada* **72 C3** 50 20N 127 25W
Port Allegany, *U.S.A.* **78 E6** 41 48N 78 17W
Port Allen, *U.S.A.* **81 K9** 30 27N 91 12W
Port Alma, *Australia* **62 C5** 23 38S 150 53 E
Port Angeles, *U.S.A.* **84 B3** 48 7N 123 27W
Port Antonio, *Jamaica* **88 C4** 18 10N 76 30W
Port Aransas, *U.S.A.* **81 M6** 27 50N 97 4W
Port Arthur = Lüshun, *China* **35 E11** 38 45N 121 15 E
Port Arthur, *Australia* **62 G4** 43 7S 147 50 E
Port Arthur, *U.S.A.* **81 L8** 29 54N 93 56W
Port au Choix, *Canada* **71 B8** 50 43N 57 22W
Port au Port B., *Canada* **71 C8** 48 40N 58 50W
Port-au-Prince, *Haiti* **89 C5** 18 40N 72 20W
Port Augusta, *Australia* **63 E2** 32 30S 137 50 E
Port Austin, *U.S.A.* **78 B2** 44 3N 83 1W
Port Bell, *Uganda* **54 B3** 0 18N 32 35 E
Port Bergé Vaovao, *Madag.* **57 B8** 15 33S 47 40 E
Port Blandford, *Canada* **71 C9** 48 20N 54 10W
Port Bradshaw, *Australia* **62 A2** 12 30S 137 20 E
Port Broughton, *Australia* **63 E2** 33 37S 137 56 E
Port Burwell, *Canada* **78 D4** 42 40N 80 48W
Port Canning, *India* **43 H13** 22 23N 88 40 E
Port-Cartier, *Canada* **71 B6** 50 2N 66 50W
Port Chalmers, *N.Z.* **59 L3** 45 49S 170 30 E
Port Charlotte, *U.S.A.* **77 M4** 26 59N 82 6W
Port Chester, *U.S.A.* **79 F11** 41 0N 73 40W
Port Clements, *Canada* **72 C2** 53 40N 132 10W
Port Clinton, *U.S.A.* **76 E4** 41 31N 82 56W
Port Colborne, *Canada* **78 D5** 42 50N 79 10W
Port Coquitlam, *Canada* **72 D4** 49 15N 122 45W
Port Credit, *Canada* **78 C5** 43 33N 79 35W
Port Curtis, *Australia* **62 C5** 23 57S 151 20 E
Port d'Alcúdia, *Spain* **22 B10** 39 50N 3 7 E
Port Dalhousie, *Canada* **78 C5** 43 13N 79 16W
Port d'Andratx, *Spain* **22 B9** 39 32N 2 23 E
Port Darwin, *Australia* **60 B5** 12 24S 130 45 E
Port Darwin, *Falk. Is.* **96 G5** 51 50S 59 0W
Port Davey, *Australia* **62 G4** 43 16S 145 55 E
Port-de-Paix, *Haiti* **89 C5** 19 50N 72 50W
Port de Pollença, *Spain* **22 B10** 39 54N 3 4 E
Port de Sóller, *Spain* **22 B9** 39 48N 2 42 E
Port Dickson, *Malaysia* **39 L3** 2 30N 101 49 E
Port Douglas, *Australia* **62 B4** 16 30S 145 30 E
Port Dover, *Canada* **78 D4** 42 47N 80 12W
Port Edward, *Canada* **72 C2** 54 12N 130 10W
Port Elgin, *Canada* **78 B3** 44 25N 81 25W
Port Elizabeth, *S. Africa* **56 E4** 33 58S 25 40 E
Port Ellen, *U.K.* **12 F2** 55 38N 6 11W
Port Erin, *U.K.* **10 C3** 54 5N 4 45W
Port Essington, *Australia* **60 B5** 11 15S 132 10 E
Port Etienne = Nouâdhibou, *Mauritania* **50 D2** 20 54N 17 0W
Port Ewen, *U.S.A.* **79 E11** 41 54N 73 59W
Port Fairy, *Australia* **63 F3** 38 22S 142 12 E
Port Gamble, *U.S.A.* **84 C4** 47 51N 122 35W
Port-Gentil, *Gabon* **52 E1** 0 40S 8 50 E
Port Germein, *Australia* **63 E2** 33 1S 138 1 E
Port Gibson, *U.S.A.* **81 K9** 31 58N 90 59W
Port Glasgow, *U.K.* **12 F4** 55 56N 4 41W
Port Harcourt, *Nigeria* **50 H7** 4 40N 7 10 E
Port Hardy, *Canada* **72 C3** 50 41N 127 30W
Port Harrison = Inukjuak, *Canada* **69 C12** 58 25N 78 15W
Port Hawkesbury, *Canada* **71 C7** 45 36N 61 22W
Port Hedland, *Australia* **60 D2** 20 25S 118 35 E
Port Henry, *U.S.A.* **79 B11** 44 3N 73 28W
Port Hood, *Canada* **71 C7** 46 0N 61 32W
Port Hope, *Canada* **78 C6** 43 56N 78 20W
Port Hope, *U.S.A.* **78 C2** 43 57N 82 43W
Port Hope Simpson, *Canada* **71 B8** 52 33N 56 18W
Port Hueneme, *U.S.A.* **85 L7** 34 7N 119 12W
Port Huron, *U.S.A.* **78 D2** 42 58N 82 26W
Port Jefferson, *U.S.A.* **79 F11** 40 57N 73 3W
Port Jervis, *U.S.A.* **79 E10** 41 22N 74 41W
Port Kelang = Pelabuhan Kelang, *Malaysia* **39 L3** 3 0N 101 23 E
Port Kenny, *Australia* **63 E1** 33 10S 134 41 E
Port Lairge = Waterford, *Ireland* **13 D4** 52 15N 7 8W
Port Laoise, *Ireland* **13 C4** 53 2N 7 18W
Port Lavaca, *U.S.A.* **81 L6** 28 37N 96 38W
Port Leyden, *U.S.A.* **79 C9** 43 35N 75 21W
Port Lincoln, *Australia* **63 E2** 34 42S 135 52 E
Port Loko, *S. Leone* **50 G3** 8 48N 12 46W
Port Louis, *Mauritius* **49 H9** 20 10S 57 30 E
Port MacDonnell, *Australia* **63 F3** 38 5S 140 48 E
Port McNeill, *Canada* **72 C3** 50 35N 127 6W
Port Macquarie, *Australia* **63 E5** 31 25S 152 25 E
Port Maria, *Jamaica* **88 C4** 18 25N 76 55W
Port Matilda, *U.S.A.* **78 F6** 40 48N 78 3W
Port Mellon, *Canada* **72 D4** 49 32N 123 31W
Port-Menier, *Canada* **71 C7** 49 51N 64 16W
Port Moody, *Canada* **84 A4** 49 17N 122 51W
Port Morant, *Jamaica* **88 C4** 17 54N 76 19W
Port Moresby, *Papua N. G.* **64 H6** 9 24S 147 8 E
Port Musgrave, *Australia* **62 A3** 11 55S 141 50 E
Port Neches, *U.S.A.* **81 L8** 30 0N 93 59W
Port Nolloth, *S. Africa* **56 D2** 29 17S 16 52 E
Port Nouveau-Québec = Kangiqsualujjuaq, *Canada* **69 C13** 58 30N 65 59W
Port of Spain, *Trin. & Tob.* **89 D7** 10 40N 61 31W
Port Orange, *U.S.A.* **77 L5** 29 9N 80 59W
Port Orchard, *U.S.A.* **84 C4** 47 32N 122 38W
Port Orford, *U.S.A.* **82 E1** 42 45N 124 30W
Port Pegasus, *N.Z.* **59 M1** 47 12S 167 41 E
Port Perry, *Canada* **78 B6** 44 6N 78 56W
Port Phillip B., *Australia* **63 F3** 38 10S 144 50 E
Port Pirie, *Australia* **63 E2** 33 10S 138 1 E
Port Radium = Echo Bay, *Canada* **68 B8** 66 5N 117 55W
Port Renfrew, *Canada* **72 D4** 48 30N 124 20W
Port Roper, *Australia* **62 A2** 14 45S 135 25 E
Port Rowan, *Canada* **78 D4** 42 40N 80 30W
Port Safaga = Bûr Safâga, *Egypt* **44 E2** 26 43N 33 57 E
Port Said = Bûr Sa'îd, *Egypt* **51 B12** 31 16N 32 18 E
Port St. Joe, *U.S.A.* **77 L3** 29 49N 85 18W
Port St. Johns = Umzimvubu, *S. Africa* **57 E4** 31 38S 29 33 E
Port St. Lucie, *U.S.A.* **77 M5** 27 20N 80 20W
Port Sanilac, *U.S.A.* **78 C2** 43 26N 82 33W
Port Severn, *Canada* **78 B5** 44 48N 79 43W
Port Shepstone, *S. Africa* **57 E5** 30 44S 30 28 E
Port Simpson, *Canada* **72 C2** 54 30N 130 20W
Port Stanley = Stanley, *Falk. Is.* **96 G5** 51 40S 59 51W
Port Stanley, *Canada* **78 D3** 42 40N 81 10W
Port Sudan = Bûr Sûdân, *Sudan* **51 E13** 19 32N 37 9 E
Port Sulphur, *U.S.A.* **81 L10** 29 29N 89 42W
Port Talbot, *U.K.* **11 F4** 51 35N 3 47W
Port Townsend, *U.S.A.* **84 B4** 48 7N 122 45W
Port-Vendres, *France* **18 E5** 42 32N 3 8 E
Port Vila, *Vanuatu* **64 J8** 17 45S 168 18 E
Port Vladimir, *Russia* **24 A5** 69 25N 33 6 E
Port Wakefield, *Australia* **63 E2** 34 12S 138 10 E
Port Washington, *U.S.A.* **76 D2** 43 23N 87 53W

Q

R

Rio Hato, Panama 88 E3 8 22N 80 10W
Rio Lagartos, Mexico 87 C7 21 36N 88 10W
Rio Largo, Brazil 93 E11 9 28S 35 50W
Rio Mulatos, Bolivia 92 G5 19 40S 66 50W
Rio Muni □, Eq. Guin. 52 D2 1 30N 10 0 E
Rio Negro, Brazil 95 B6 26 0S 49 55W
Rio Pardo, Brazil 95 C5 30 0S 52 30W
Rio Rancho, U.S.A. 83 J10 35 14N 106 38W
Rio Segundo, Argentina 94 C3 31 40S 63 59W
Rio Tercero, Argentina 94 C3 32 15S 64 8W
Rio Verde, Brazil 93 G8 17 50S 51 0W
Rio Verde, Mexico 87 C5 21 56N 99 59W
Rio Vista, U.S.A. 84 G5 38 10N 121 42W
Riobamba, Ecuador 92 D3 1 50S 78 45W
Riohacha, Colombia 92 A4 11 33N 72 55W
Riosucio, Colombia 92 B3 7 27N 77 7W
Riou L., Canada 73 B7 59 7N 106 25W
Ripley, Canada 78 B3 44 4N 81 35W
Ripley, Calif., U.S.A. 85 M12 33 32N 114 39W
Ripley, N.Y., U.S.A. 78 D5 42 16N 79 43W
Ripley, Tenn., U.S.A. 81 H10 35 45N 89 32W
Ripley, W. Va., U.S.A. 76 F5 38 49N 81 43W
Ripon, U.K. 10 C6 54 9N 1 31W
Ripon, Calif., U.S.A. 84 H5 37 44N 121 7W
Ripon, Wis., U.S.A. 76 D1 43 51N 88 50W
Rishā', W. ar →, Si. Arabia 44 E5 25 33N 44 5 E
Rishiri-Tō, Japan 30 B10 45 11N 141 15 E
Rishon le Ẕiyyon, Israel 47 D3 31 58N 34 48 E
Rison, U.S.A. 81 J8 33 58N 92 11W
Risør, Norway 9 G13 58 43N 9 13 E
Rita Blanca Cr. →, U.S.A. 81 H3 35 40N 102 29W
Ritter, Mt., U.S.A. 84 H7 37 41N 119 12W
Rittman, U.S.A. 78 F3 40 58N 81 47W
Ritzville, U.S.A. 82 C4 47 8N 118 23W
Riva del Garda, Italy 20 B4 45 53N 10 50 E
Rivadavia, Buenos Aires, Argentina 94 D3 35 29S 62 59W
Rivadavia, Mendoza, Argentina 94 C2 33 13S 68 30W
Rivadavia, Salta, Argentina 94 A3 24 5S 62 54W
Rivadavia, Chile 94 B1 29 57S 70 35W
Rivas, Nic. 88 D2 11 30N 85 50W
River Cess, Liberia 50 G4 5 30N 9 32W
River Jordan, Canada 84 B2 48 26N 124 3W
Rivera, Argentina 94 D3 37 12S 63 14W
Rivera, Uruguay 95 C4 31 0S 55 50W
Riverbank, U.S.A. 84 H6 37 44N 120 56W
Riverdale, U.S.A. 84 J7 36 26N 119 52W
Riverhead, U.S.A. 79 F12 40 55N 72 40W
Riverhurst, Canada 73 C7 50 55N 106 50W
Rivers, Canada 73 C8 50 2N 100 14W
Rivers Inlet, Canada 72 C3 51 42N 127 15W
Riversdale, S. Africa 56 E3 34 7S 21 15 E
Riverside, U.S.A. 85 M9 33 59N 117 22W
Riverton, Australia 63 E2 34 10S 138 46 E
Riverton, Canada 73 C9 51 1N 97 0W
Riverton, N.Z. 59 M2 46 21S 168 0 E
Riverton, U.S.A. 82 E9 43 2N 108 23W
Riverton Heights, U.S.A. 84 C4 47 28N 122 17W
Riviera, U.S.A. 85 K12 35 4N 114 35W
Riviera di Levante, Italy 18 D8 44 15N 9 30 E
Riviera di Ponente, Italy 18 D8 44 10N 8 20 E
Rivière-au-Renard, Canada 71 C7 48 59N 64 23W
Rivière-du-Loup, Canada 71 C6 47 50N 69 30W
Rivière-Pentecôte, Canada 71 C6 49 57N 67 1W
Rivière-Pilote, Martinique 89 D7 14 26N 60 53W
Rivière St. Paul, Canada 71 B8 51 28N 57 45W
Rivne, Ukraine 17 C14 50 40N 26 10 E
Rívoli, Italy 18 D7 45 3N 7 31 E
Rivoli B., Australia 63 F3 37 32S 140 3 E
Riyadh = Ar Riyāḍ, Si. Arabia 46 C4 24 41N 46 42 E
Rize, Turkey 25 F7 41 0N 40 30 E
Rizhao, China 35 G10 35 25N 119 30 E
Rizokarpaso, Cyprus 23 D13 35 36N 34 23 E
Rizzuto, C., Italy 20 E7 38 53N 17 5 E
Rjukan, Norway 9 G13 59 54N 8 33 E
Road Town, Br. Virgin Is. 89 C7 18 27N 64 37W
Roan Plateau, U.S.A. 82 G9 39 20N 109 20W
Roanne, France 18 C6 46 3N 4 4 E
Roanoke, Ala., U.S.A. 77 J3 33 9N 85 22W
Roanoke, Va., U.S.A. 76 G6 37 16N 79 56W
Roanoke →, U.S.A. 77 H7 35 57N 76 42W
Roanoke I., U.S.A. 77 H8 35 55N 75 40W
Roanoke Rapids, U.S.A. 77 G7 36 28N 77 40W
Roatán, Honduras 88 C2 16 18N 86 35W
Robāt Sang, Iran 45 C8 35 35N 59 10 E
Robbins I., Australia 62 G4 40 42S 145 0 E
Robe →, Australia 60 D2 21 42S 116 15 E
Robert Lee, U.S.A. 81 K4 31 54N 100 29W
Robertsdale, U.S.A. 78 F6 40 11N 78 6W
Robertsganj, India 43 G10 24 44N 83 4 E
Robertson, S. Africa 56 E2 33 46S 19 50 E
Robertson I., Antarctica 5 C18 65 15S 59 30W
Robertson Ra., Australia 60 D3 23 15S 121 0 E
Robertstown, Australia 63 E2 33 58S 139 5 E
Roberval, Canada 71 C5 48 32N 72 15W
Robeson Chan., Greenland 4 A4 82 0N 61 30W
Robesonia, U.S.A. 79 F8 40 21N 76 8W
Robinson, U.S.A. 76 F2 39 0N 87 44W
Robinson →, Australia 62 B2 16 3S 137 16 E
Robinson Ra., Australia 61 E2 25 40S 119 0 E
Robinvale, Australia 63 E3 34 40S 142 45 E
Roblin, Canada 73 C8 51 14N 101 21W
Roboré, Bolivia 92 G7 18 10S 59 45W
Robson, Canada 72 D5 49 20N 117 41W
Robson, Mt., Canada 72 C5 53 10N 119 10W
Robstown, U.S.A. 81 M6 27 47N 97 40W
Roca, C. da, Portugal 19 C1 38 40N 9 31W
Roca Partida, I., Mexico 86 D2 19 1N 112 2W
Rocas, I., Brazil 93 D12 4 0S 34 1W
Rocha, Uruguay 95 C5 34 30S 54 25W
Rochdale, U.K. 10 D5 53 38N 2 9W
Rochefort, Belgium 15 D5 50 9N 5 12 E
Rochefort, France 18 D3 45 56N 0 57W
Rochelle, U.S.A. 80 E10 41 56N 89 4W
Rocher River, Canada 72 A6 61 23N 112 44W
Rochester, U.K. 11 F8 51 23N 0 31 E
Rochester, Ind., U.S.A. 76 E2 41 4N 86 13W
Rochester, Minn., U.S.A. 80 C8 44 1N 92 28W
Rochester, N.H., U.S.A. 79 C14 43 18N 70 59W
Rochester, N.Y., U.S.A. 78 C7 43 10N 77 37W
Rock →, Canada 72 A3 60 7N 127 7W
Rock Creek, U.S.A. 78 E4 41 40N 80 52W
Rock Falls, U.S.A. 80 E10 41 47N 89 41W
Rock Hill, U.S.A. 77 H5 34 56N 81 1W
Rock Island, U.S.A. 80 E9 41 30N 90 34W
Rock Rapids, U.S.A. 80 D6 43 26N 96 10W
Rock Sound, Bahamas 88 B4 24 54N 76 12W
Rock Springs, Mont., U.S.A. 82 C10 46 49N 106 15W
Rock Springs, Wyo., U.S.A. 82 F9 41 35N 109 14W
Rock Valley, U.S.A. 80 D6 43 12N 96 18W
Rockall, Atl. Oc. 6 D3 57 37N 13 42W
Rockdale, Tex., U.S.A. 81 K6 30 39N 97 0W
Rockdale, Wash., U.S.A. 84 C5 47 22N 121 28W
Rockefeller Plateau, Antarctica 5 E14 80 0S 140 0W
Rockford, U.S.A. 80 D10 42 16N 89 6W
Rockglen, Canada 73 D7 49 11N 105 57W
Rockhampton, Australia 62 C5 23 22S 150 32 E
Rockingham, Australia 61 F2 32 15S 115 38 E
Rockingham, U.S.A. 77 H6 34 57N 79 46W
Rockingham B., Australia 62 B4 18 5S 146 10 E
Rocklake, U.S.A. 80 A5 48 47N 99 15W
Rockland, Canada 79 A9 45 33N 75 17W
Rockland, Idaho, U.S.A. 82 E7 42 34N 112 53W
Rockland, Maine, U.S.A. 77 C11 44 6N 69 7W
Rockland, Mich., U.S.A. 80 B10 46 44N 89 11W
Rocklin, U.S.A. 84 G5 38 48N 121 14W
Rockmart, U.S.A. 77 H3 34 0N 85 3W
Rockport, Mass., U.S.A. 79 D14 42 39N 70 37W
Rockport, Mo., U.S.A. 80 E7 40 25N 95 31W
Rockport, Tex., U.S.A. 81 L6 28 2N 97 3W
Rocksprings, U.S.A. 81 K4 30 1N 100 13W
Rockville, Conn., U.S.A. 79 E12 41 52N 72 28W
Rockville, Md., U.S.A. 76 F7 39 5N 77 9W
Rockwall, U.S.A. 81 J6 32 56N 96 28W
Rockwell City, U.S.A. 80 D7 42 24N 94 38W
Rockwood, Canada 78 C4 43 37N 80 8W
Rockwood, Maine, U.S.A. 77 C11 45 41N 69 45W
Rockwood, Tenn., U.S.A. 77 H3 35 52N 84 41W
Rocky Ford, U.S.A. 80 F3 38 3N 103 43W
Rocky Gully, Australia 61 F2 34 30S 116 57 E
Rocky Harbour, Canada 71 C8 49 36N 57 55W
Rocky Island L., Canada 70 C3 46 55N 83 0W
Rocky Lane, Canada 72 B5 58 31N 116 22W
Rocky Mount, U.S.A. 77 H7 35 57N 77 48W
Rocky Mountain House, Canada 72 C6 52 22N 114 55W
Rocky Mountain Nat. Park, U.S.A. 82 F11 40 25N 105 45W
Rocky Mts., N. Amer. 82 G10 49 0N 115 0W
Rocky Point, Namibia 56 B2 19 3S 12 30 E
Rod, Pakistan 40 E3 28 10N 63 5 E
Rødbyhavn, Denmark 9 J14 54 39N 11 22 E
Roddickton, Canada 71 B8 50 51N 56 8W
Rodez, France 18 D5 44 21N 2 33 E
Rodhopoú, Greece 23 D5 35 34N 23 45 E
Ródhos, Greece 23 C10 36 15N 28 10 E
Rodney, Canada 78 D3 42 34N 81 41W
Rodney, C., N.Z. 59 G5 36 17S 174 50 E
Rodriguez, Ind. Oc. 3 E13 19 45S 63 20 E
Roe →, U.K. 13 A5 55 6N 6 59W
Roebling, U.S.A. 79 F10 40 7N 74 47W
Roebourne, Australia 60 D2 20 44S 117 9 E
Roebuck B., Australia 60 C3 18 5S 122 20 E
Roermond, Neths. 15 C6 51 12N 6 0 E
Roes Welcome Sd., Canada 69 B11 65 0N 87 0W
Roeselare, Belgium 15 D3 50 57N 3 7 E
Rogachev = Ragachow, Belarus 17 B16 53 8N 30 5 E
Rogagua, L., Bolivia 92 F5 13 43S 66 50W
Rogatyn, Ukraine 17 D13 49 24N 24 36 E
Rogdhia, Greece 23 D7 35 22N 25 1 E
Rogers, U.S.A. 81 G7 36 20N 94 7W
Rogers City, U.S.A. 76 C4 45 25N 83 49W
Rogersville, Canada 71 C6 46 44N 65 26W
Roggan →, Canada 70 B4 54 24N 79 25W
Roggan L., Canada 70 B4 54 8N 77 50W
Roggeveldberge, S. Africa 56 E3 32 10S 20 10 E
Rogoaguado, L., Bolivia 92 F5 13 0S 65 30W
Rogue →, U.S.A. 82 E1 42 26N 124 26W
Róhda, Greece 23 A3 39 48N 19 46 E
Rohnert Park, U.S.A. 84 G4 38 16N 122 40W
Rohri, Pakistan 42 F3 27 45N 68 51 E
Rohri Canal, Pakistan 42 F3 26 15N 68 27 E
Rohtak, India 42 E7 28 55N 76 43 E
Roi Et, Thailand 38 D4 16 4N 103 40 E
Roja, Latvia 9 H20 57 29N 22 43 E
Rojas, Argentina 94 C3 34 10S 60 45W
Rojo, C., Mexico 87 C5 21 33N 97 20W
Rokan →, Indonesia 36 D2 2 0N 100 50 E
Rokiškis, Lithuania 9 J21 55 55N 25 35 E
Rolândia, Brazil 95 A5 23 18S 51 23W
Rolla, U.S.A. 81 G9 37 57N 91 46W
Rolleston, Australia 62 C4 24 28S 148 35 E
Rollingstone, Australia 62 B4 19 2S 146 24 E
Roma, Australia 63 D4 26 32S 148 49 E
Roma, Italy 20 D5 41 54N 12 29 E
Roma, Sweden 9 H18 57 32N 18 26 E
Roma, U.S.A. 81 M5 26 25N 99 1W
Romain C., U.S.A. 77 J6 33 0N 79 22W
Romaine, Canada 71 B7 50 13N 60 40W
Romaine →, Canada 71 B7 50 18N 63 47W
Roman, Romania 17 E14 46 57N 26 55 E
Romang, Indonesia 37 F7 7 30S 127 20 E
Români, Egypt 47 E1 30 59N 32 38 E
Romania ■, Europe 17 F12 46 0N 25 0 E
Romano, Cayo, Cuba 88 B4 22 0N 77 30W
Romanovka = Basarabeasca, Moldova 17 E15 46 21N 28 58 E
Romans-sur-Isère, France 18 D6 45 3N 5 3 E
Romblon, Phil. 37 B6 12 33N 122 17 E
Rome = Roma, Italy 20 D5 41 54N 12 29 E
Rome, Ga., U.S.A. 77 H3 34 15N 85 10W
Rome, N.Y., U.S.A. 79 C9 43 13N 75 27W
Rome, Pa., U.S.A. 79 E8 41 51N 76 21W
Romney, U.S.A. 76 F6 39 21N 78 45W
Romney Marsh, U.K. 11 F8 51 2N 0 54 E
Rømø, Denmark 9 J13 55 10N 8 30 E
Romorantin-Lanthenay, France 18 C4 47 21N 1 45 E
Romsdalen, Norway 9 E12 62 25N 7 52 E
Romsey, U.K. 11 G6 51 0N 1 29W
Ron, Vietnam 38 D6 17 53N 106 27 E
Rona, U.K. 12 D3 57 34N 5 59W
Ronan, U.S.A. 82 C6 47 32N 114 6W
Roncador, Cayos, Colombia 88 D3 13 32N 80 4W
Roncador, Serra do, Brazil 93 F8 12 30S 52 30W
Ronda, Spain 19 D3 36 46N 5 12W
Rondane, Norway 9 F13 61 57N 9 50 E
Rondônia □, Brazil 92 F6 11 0S 63 0W
Rondonópolis, Brazil 93 G8 16 28S 54 38W
Rong, Koh, Cambodia 39 G4 10 45N 103 15 E
Ronge, L. la, Canada 73 B7 55 6N 105 17W
Rønne, Denmark 9 J16 55 6N 14 43 E
Ronne Ice Shelf, Antarctica 5 D18 78 0S 60 0W
Ronsard, C., Australia 61 D1 24 46S 113 10 E
Ronse, Belgium 15 D3 50 45N 3 35 E
Roodepoort, S. Africa 57 D4 26 11S 27 54 E
Roof Butte, U.S.A. 83 H9 36 28N 109 5W
Rooiboklaagte →, Namibia 56 C3 20 50S 21 0 E
Roorkee, India 42 E7 29 52N 77 59 E
Roosendaal, Neths. 15 C4 51 32N 4 29 E
Roosevelt, U.S.A. 82 F8 40 18N 109 59W
Roosevelt →, Brazil 92 E6 7 35S 60 20W
Roosevelt, Mt., Canada 72 B3 58 26N 125 20W
Roosevelt I., Antarctica 5 D12 79 30S 162 0W
Roper →, Australia 62 A2 14 43S 135 27 E
Roper Bar, Australia 62 A1 14 44S 134 44 E
Roque Pérez, Argentina 94 D4 35 25S 59 24W
Roquetas de Mar, Spain 19 D4 36 46N 2 36W
Roraima □, Brazil 92 C6 2 0N 61 30W
Roraima, Mt., Venezuela 92 B6 5 10N 60 40W
Røros, Norway 9 E14 62 35N 11 23 E
Rosa, Zambia 55 D3 9 33S 31 15 E
Rosa, L., Bahamas 89 B5 21 0N 73 30W
Rosa, Monte, Europe 18 D7 45 57N 7 53 E
Rosalia, U.S.A. 82 C5 47 14N 117 22W
Rosamond, U.S.A. 85 L8 34 52N 118 10W
Rosario, Argentina 94 C3 33 0S 60 40W
Rosário, Brazil 93 D10 3 0S 44 15W
Rosario, Baja Calif., Mexico 86 B1 30 0N 115 50W
Rosario, Sinaloa, Mexico 86 C3 23 0N 105 52W
Rosario, Paraguay 94 A4 24 30S 57 35W
Rosario de la Frontera, Argentina 94 B3 25 50S 65 0W
Rosario de Lerma, Argentina 94 A2 24 59S 65 35W
Rosario del Tala, Argentina 94 C4 32 20S 59 10W
Rosário do Sul, Brazil 95 C5 30 15S 54 55W
Rosarito, Mexico 85 N9 32 18N 117 4W
Roscoe, U.S.A. 79 E10 41 56N 74 55W
Roscommon, Ireland 13 C3 53 38N 8 11W
Roscommon □, Ireland 13 C3 53 49N 8 23W
Roscrea, Ireland 13 D4 52 57N 7 49W
Rose →, Australia 62 A2 14 16S 135 45 E
Rose Blanche, Canada 71 C8 47 38N 58 45W
Rose Pt., Canada 72 C2 54 11N 131 39W
Rose Valley, Canada 73 C8 52 19N 103 49W
Roseau, Domin. 89 C7 15 20N 61 24W
Roseau, U.S.A. 80 A7 48 51N 95 46W
Rosebery, Australia 62 G4 41 46S 145 33 E
Rosebud, S. Dak., U.S.A. 80 D4 43 14N 100 51W
Rosebud, Tex., U.S.A. 81 K6 31 4N 96 59W
Roseburg, U.S.A. 82 E2 43 13N 123 20W
Rosedale, U.S.A. 81 J9 33 51N 91 2W
Roseland, U.S.A. 84 G4 38 25N 122 43W
Rosemary, Canada 72 C6 50 46N 112 5W
Rosenberg, U.S.A. 81 L7 29 34N 95 49W
Rosenheim, Germany 16 E7 47 51N 12 7 E
Roses, G. de, Spain 19 A7 42 10N 3 15 E
Rosetown, Canada 73 C7 51 35N 107 59W
Roseville, Calif., U.S.A. 84 G5 38 45N 121 17W
Roseville, Mich., U.S.A. 78 D2 42 30N 82 56W
Rosewood, Australia 63 D5 27 38S 152 36 E
Roshkhvār, Iran 45 C8 34 58N 59 37 E
Rosignano Maríttimo, Italy 20 C4 43 24N 10 28 E
Rosignol, Guyana 92 B7 6 15N 57 30W
Roşiori de Vede, Romania 17 F13 44 9N 25 0 E
Roskilde, Denmark 9 J15 55 38N 12 3 E
Roslavl, Russia 24 D5 53 57N 32 55 E
Rosmead, S. Africa 56 E4 31 29S 25 8 E
Ross, Australia 62 G4 42 2S 147 30 E
Ross, N.Z. 59 K3 42 53S 170 49 E
Ross I., Antarctica 5 D11 77 30S 168 0 E
Ross Ice Shelf, Antarctica 5 E12 80 0S 180 0 E
Ross L., U.S.A. 82 B3 48 44N 121 4W
Ross-on-Wye, U.K. 11 F5 51 54N 2 34W
Ross River, Australia 62 C1 23 44S 134 30 E
Ross River, Canada 72 A2 62 30N 131 30W
Ross Sea, Antarctica 5 D11 74 0S 178 0 E
Rossall Pt., U.K. 10 D4 53 55N 3 3W
Rossan Pt., Ireland 13 B3 54 42N 8 47W
Rossano, Italy 20 E7 39 36N 16 39 E
Rossburn, Canada 73 C8 50 40N 100 49W
Rosseau, Canada 78 A5 45 16N 79 39W
Rosseau L., Canada 78 A5 45 10N 79 35W
Rosses, The, Ireland 13 A3 55 2N 8 20W
Rossignol, L., Canada 70 B5 52 43N 73 40W
Rossignol Res., Canada 71 D6 44 12N 65 10W
Rossland, Canada 72 D5 49 6N 117 50W
Rosslare, Ireland 13 D5 52 17N 6 24W
Rosso, Mauritania 50 E2 16 40N 15 45W
Rossosh, Russia 25 D6 50 15N 39 28 E
Røssvatnet, Norway 8 D16 65 45N 14 5 E
Røst, Norway 8 C15 67 32N 12 0 E
Rosthern, Canada 73 C7 52 40N 106 20W
Rostock, Germany 16 A7 54 5N 12 8 E
Rostov, Don, Russia 25 E6 47 15N 39 45 E
Rostov, Yaroslavl, Russia 24 C6 57 14N 39 25 E
Roswell, Ga., U.S.A. 77 H3 34 2N 84 22W
Roswell, N. Mex., U.S.A. 81 J2 33 24N 104 32W
Rotan, U.S.A. 81 J4 32 51N 100 28W
Rother →, U.K. 11 G8 50 59N 0 45 E
Rotherham, U.K. 10 D6 53 26N 1 20W
Rothes, U.K. 12 D5 57 32N 3 13W
Rothesay, Canada 71 C6 45 23N 66 0W
Rothesay, U.K. 12 F3 55 50N 5 3W
Roti, Indonesia 37 F6 10 50S 123 0 E
Roto, Australia 63 E4 33 0S 145 30 E
Rotondo, Mte., France 18 E8 42 14N 9 8 E
Rotoroa, L., N.Z. 59 J4 41 55S 172 39 E
Rotorua, N.Z. 59 H6 38 9S 176 16 E
Rotorua, L., N.Z. 59 H6 38 5S 176 18 E
Rotterdam, Neths. 15 C4 51 55N 4 30 E
Rotterdam, U.S.A. 79 D10 42 48N 74 1W
Rottnest I., Australia 61 F2 32 0S 115 27 E
Rottumeroog, Neths. 15 A6 53 33N 6 34 E
Rottweil, Germany 16 D5 48 9N 8 37 E
Rotuma, Fiji 64 J9 12 25S 177 5 E
Roubaix, France 18 A5 50 40N 3 10 E
Rouen, France 18 B4 49 27N 1 4 E
Rouleau, Canada 73 C8 50 10N 104 56W
Round Mountain, U.S.A. 82 G5 38 43N 117 4W
Round Mt., Australia 63 E5 30 26S 152 16 E
Round Rock, U.S.A. 81 K6 30 31N 97 41W
Roundup, U.S.A. 82 C9 46 27N 108 33W
Rousay, U.K. 12 B5 59 10N 3 2W
Rouses Point, U.S.A. 79 B11 44 59N 73 22W
Rouseville, U.S.A. 78 E5 41 28N 79 42W
Roussillon, France 18 E5 42 30N 2 35 E
Rouxville, S. Africa 56 E4 30 25S 26 50 E
Rouyn-Noranda, Canada 70 C4 48 20N 79 0W
Rovaniemi, Finland 8 C21 66 29N 25 41 E
Rovereto, Italy 20 B4 45 53N 11 3 E
Rovigo, Italy 20 B4 45 4N 11 47 E
Rovinj, Croatia 16 F7 45 5N 13 40 E
Rovno = Rivne, Ukraine 17 C14 50 40N 26 10 E
Rovuma = Ruvuma →, Tanzania 55 E5 10 29S 40 28 E
Row'ān, Iran 45 C6 35 8N 48 51 E
Rowena, Australia 63 D4 29 48S 148 55 E
Rowley Shoals, Australia 60 C2 17 30S 119 0 E
Roxas, Phil. 37 B6 11 36N 122 49 E
Roxboro, U.S.A. 77 G6 36 24N 78 59W
Roxburgh, N.Z. 59 L2 45 33S 169 19 E
Roxbury, U.S.A. 78 F7 40 6N 77 39W
Roy, Mont., U.S.A. 82 C9 47 20N 108 58W
Roy, N. Mex., U.S.A. 81 H2 35 57N 104 12W
Roy, Utah, U.S.A. 82 F7 41 10N 112 2W
Royal Canal, Ireland 13 C4 53 30N 7 13W
Royal Leamington Spa, U.K. 11 E6 52 18N 1 31W
Royal Tunbridge Wells, U.K. 11 F8 51 7N 0 16 E
Royale, Isle, U.S.A. 80 B10 48 0N 88 54W
Royan, France 18 D3 45 37N 1 2W
Royston, U.K. 11 E7 52 3N 0 0W
Rozdilna, Ukraine 17 E16 46 50N 30 2 E
Rozhyshche, Ukraine 17 C13 50 54N 25 15 E
Rtishchevo, Russia 24 C7 52 18N 43 46 E
Ruacaná, Namibia 56 B1 17 27S 14 21 E
Ruahine Ra., N.Z. 59 H6 39 55S 176 2 E
Ruapehu, N.Z. 59 H5 39 17S 175 35 E
Ruapuke I., N.Z. 59 M2 46 46S 168 31 E
Ruâq, W. →, Egypt 47 F2 30 0N 33 49 E
Rub' al Khālī, Si. Arabia 46 D4 19 0N 48 0 E
Rubeho Mts., Tanzania 54 D4 6 50S 36 25 E
Rubh a' Mhail, U.K. 12 F2 55 56N 6 8W
Rubha Hunish, U.K. 12 D2 57 42N 6 20W
Rubha Robhanais = Lewis, Butt of, U.K. 12 C2 58 31N 6 16W
Rubicon →, U.S.A. 84 G5 38 53N 121 4W
Rubio, Venezuela 92 B4 7 43N 72 22W
Rubtsovsk, Russia 26 D9 51 30N 81 10 E
Ruby L., U.S.A. 82 F6 40 10N 115 28W
Ruby Mts., U.S.A. 82 F6 40 30N 115 20W
Rubyvale, Australia 62 C4 23 25S 147 42 E
Rūd Sar, Iran 45 B6 37 8N 50 18 E
Rudall, Australia 63 E2 33 43S 136 17 E
Rudall →, Australia 60 D3 22 34S 122 13 E
Rudewa, Tanzania 55 E3 10 7S 34 40 E
Rudnyy, Kazakstan 26 D7 52 57N 63 7 E
Rudolfa, Ostrov, Russia 26 A6 81 45N 58 30 E
Rudyard, U.S.A. 76 B3 46 14N 84 36W
Ruenya →, Africa 55 F3 16 24S 33 48 E
Rufiji →, Tanzania 54 D4 7 50S 39 15 E
Rufino, Argentina 94 C3 34 20S 62 50W
Rufunsa, Zambia 55 F2 15 4S 29 34 E
Rugby, U.K. 11 E6 52 23N 1 16W
Rugby, U.S.A. 80 A5 48 22N 100 0W
Rügen, Germany 16 A7 54 22N 13 24 E
Ruhengeri, Rwanda 54 C2 1 30S 29 36 E
Ruhnu, Estonia 9 H20 57 48N 23 15 E
Ruhr →, Germany 16 C4 51 27N 6 43 E
Ruhuhu →, Tanzania 55 E3 10 31S 34 34 E
Ruidoso, U.S.A. 83 K11 33 20N 105 41W
Ruivo, Pico, Madeira 22 D3 32 45N 16 56W
Rujm Tal'at al Jamā'ah, Jordan 47 E4 30 24N 35 30 E
Ruk, Pakistan 42 F3 27 50N 68 42 E
Rukhla, Pakistan 42 C4 32 27N 71 57 E
Ruki →, Dem. Rep. of the Congo 52 E3 0 5N 18 17 E
Rukwa □, Tanzania 54 D3 7 0S 31 30 E
Rukwa, L., Tanzania 54 D3 8 0S 32 20 E
Rulhieres, C., Australia 60 B4 13 56S 127 22 E
Rum = Rhum, U.K. 12 E2 57 0N 6 20W
Rum Cay, Bahamas 89 B5 23 40N 74 58W
Rum Jungle, Australia 60 B5 13 0S 130 59 E
Rumāḥ, Si. Arabia 44 E5 25 29N 47 10 E
Rumania = Romania ■, Europe 17 F12 46 0N 25 0 E
Rumaylah, Iraq 44 D5 30 47N 47 37 E
Rumbêk, Sudan 51 G11 6 54N 29 37 E
Rumford, U.S.A. 77 C10 44 33N 70 33W
Rumia, Poland 17 A10 54 37N 18 25 E
Rumoi, Japan 30 C10 43 56N 141 39 E
Rumonge, Burundi 54 C2 3 59S 29 26 E
Rumson, U.S.A. 79 F11 40 23N 74 0W
Rumuruti, Kenya 54 B4 0 17N 36 32 E
Runan, China 34 H8 33 0N 114 30 E
Runanga, N.Z. 59 K3 42 25S 171 15 E
Runaway, C., N.Z. 59 G6 37 32S 177 59 E
Runcorn, U.K. 10 D5 53 21N 2 44W
Rundu, Namibia 56 B2 17 52S 19 43 E
Rungwa, Tanzania 54 D3 6 55S 33 32 E
Rungwa →, Tanzania 54 D3 7 36S 31 50 E
Rungwe, Tanzania 55 D3 9 11S 33 32 E
Rungwe, Mt., Tanzania 52 F6 9 8S 33 40 E
Runton Ra., Australia 60 D3 23 31S 123 6 E
Ruoqiang, China 32 C3 38 55N 88 10 E
Rupa, India 41 F18 27 15N 92 21 E
Rupar, India 42 D7 31 2N 76 38 E
Rupat, Indonesia 36 D2 1 45N 101 40 E
Rupen →, India 42 H4 23 28N 71 31 E
Rupert, U.S.A. 82 E7 42 37N 113 41W
Rupert →, Canada 70 B4 51 29N 78 45W
Rupert B., Canada 70 B4 51 35N 79 0W
Rupert House = Waskaganish, Canada 70 B4 51 30N 78 40W
Rupsa, India 43 J12 21 37N 87 1 E
Rurrenabaque, Bolivia 92 F5 14 30S 67 32W
Rusambo, Zimbabwe 55 F3 16 30S 32 4 E
Rusape, Zimbabwe 55 F3 18 35S 32 8 E
Ruschuk = Ruse, Bulgaria 21 C12 43 48N 25 59 E
Ruse, Bulgaria 21 C12 43 48N 25 59 E
Rush, Ireland 13 C5 53 31N 6 6W
Rushan, China 35 F11 36 56N 121 30 E
Rushden, U.K. 11 E7 52 18N 0 35W
Rushmore, Mt., U.S.A. 80 D3 43 53N 103 28W
Rushville, Ill., U.S.A. 80 E9 40 7N 90 34W
Rushville, Ind., U.S.A. 76 F3 39 37N 85 27W
Rushville, Nebr., U.S.A. 80 D3 42 43N 102 28W
Russas, Brazil 93 D11 4 55S 37 50W
Russell, Canada 73 C8 50 50N 101 20W
Russell, Kans., U.S.A. 80 F5 38 54N 98 52W

S

Sálakhos, *Greece* **23 C9** 36 17N 27 57 E
Salālah, *Oman* **46 D5** 16 56N 53 59 E
Salamanca, *Chile* **94 C1** 31 46S 70 59W
Salamanca, *Spain* **19 B3** 40 58N 5 39W
Salamanca, *U.S.A.* **78 D6** 42 10N 78 43W
Salāmatābād, *Iran* **44 C5** 35 39N 47 50 E
Salamis, *Cyprus* **23 D12** 35 11N 33 54 E
Salamís, *Greece* **21 F10** 37 56N 23 30 E
Salar de Atacama, *Chile* **94 A2** 23 30S 68 25W
Salar de Uyuni, *Bolivia* **92 H5** 20 30S 67 45W
Salatiga, *Indonesia* **37 G14** 7 19S 110 30 E
Salavat, *Russia* **24 D10** 53 21N 55 55 E
Salaverry, *Peru* **92 E3** 8 15S 79 0W
Salawati, *Indonesia* **37 E8** 1 7S 130 52 E
Salaya, *India* **42 H3** 22 19N 69 35 E
Salayar, *Indonesia* **37 F6** 6 7S 120 30 E
Salcombe, *U.K.* **11 G4** 50 14N 3 47W
Saldanha, *S. Africa* **56 E2** 33 0S 17 58 E
Saldanha B., *S. Africa* **56 E2** 33 6S 18 0 E
Saldus, *Latvia* **9 H20** 56 38N 22 30 E
Sale, *Australia* **63 F4** 38 6S 147 6 E
Salé, *Morocco* **50 B4** 34 3N 6 48W
Sale, *U.K.* **10 D5** 53 26N 2 19W
Salekhard, *Russia* **26 C7** 66 30N 66 35 E
Salem, *India* **40 P11** 11 40N 78 11 E
Salem, *Ill., U.S.A.* **76 F1** 38 38N 88 57W
Salem, *Ind., U.S.A.* **76 F2** 38 36N 86 6W
Salem, *Mass., U.S.A.* **79 D14** 42 31N 70 53W
Salem, *Mo., U.S.A.* **81 G9** 37 39N 91 32W
Salem, *N.H., U.S.A.* **79 D13** 42 45N 71 12W
Salem, *N.J., U.S.A.* **76 F8** 39 34N 75 28W
Salem, *N.Y., U.S.A.* **79 C11** 43 10N 73 20W
Salem, *Ohio, U.S.A.* **78 F4** 40 54N 80 52W
Salem, *Oreg., U.S.A.* **82 D2** 44 56N 123 2W
Salem, *S. Dak., U.S.A.* **80 D6** 43 44N 97 23W
Salem, *Va., U.S.A.* **76 G5** 37 18N 80 3W
Salerno, *Italy* **20 D6** 40 41N 14 47 E
Salford, *U.K.* **10 D5** 53 30N 2 18W
Salgótarján, *Hungary* **17 D10** 48 5N 19 47 E
Salgueiro, *Brazil* **93 E11** 8 4S 39 6W
Salibabu, *Indonesia* **37 D7** 3 51N 126 40 E
Salida, *U.S.A.* **74 C5** 38 32N 106 0W
Salihli, *Turkey* **21 E13** 38 28N 28 8 E
Salihorsk, *Belarus* **17 B14** 52 51N 27 27 E
Salima, *Malawi* **53 G6** 13 47S 34 28 E
Salina, *Italy* **20 E6** 38 34N 14 50 E
Salina, *Kans., U.S.A.* **80 F6** 38 50N 97 37W
Salina, *Utah, U.S.A.* **83 G8** 38 58N 111 51W
Salina Cruz, *Mexico* **87 D5** 16 10N 95 10W
Salinas, *Brazil* **93 G10** 16 10S 42 10W
Salinas, *Chile* **94 A2** 23 31S 69 29W
Salinas, *Ecuador* **92 D2** 2 10S 80 58W
Salinas, *U.S.A.* **84 J5** 36 40N 121 39W
Salinas →, *Guatemala* **87 D6** 16 28N 90 31W
Salinas →, *U.S.A.* **84 J5** 36 45N 121 48W
Salinas, B. de, *Nic.* **88 D2** 11 4N 85 45W
Salinas, Pampa de las, *Argentina* **94 C2** 31 58S 66 42W
Salinas Ambargasta, *Argentina* **94 B3** 29 0S 65 0W
Salinas de Hidalgo, *Mexico* **86 C4** 22 30N 101 40W
Salinas Grandes, *Argentina* **94 C3** 30 0S 65 0W
Saline →, *Ark., U.S.A.* **81 J8** 33 10N 92 8W
Saline →, *Kans., U.S.A.* **80 F6** 38 52N 97 30W
Salines, C. de ses, *Spain* **22 B10** 39 16N 3 4 E
Salinópolis, *Brazil* **93 D9** 0 40S 47 20W
Salisbury = Harare, *Zimbabwe* **55 F3** 17 43S 31 2 E
Salisbury, *U.K.* **11 F6** 51 4N 1 47W
Salisbury, *Md., U.S.A.* **76 F8** 38 22N 75 36W
Salisbury, *N.C., U.S.A.* **77 H5** 35 40N 80 29W
Salisbury I., *Canada* **69 B12** 63 30N 77 0W
Salisbury Plain, *U.K.* **11 F6** 51 14N 1 55W
Şalkhad, *Syria* **47 C5** 32 29N 36 43 E
Salla, *Finland* **8 C23** 66 50N 28 49 E
Salliq, *Canada* **69 B11** 64 8N 83 10W
Sallisaw, *U.S.A.* **81 H7** 35 28N 94 47W
Salluit, *Canada* **69 B12** 62 14N 75 38W
Salmās, *Iran* **44 B5** 38 11N 44 47 E
Salmo, *Canada* **72 D5** 49 10N 117 20W
Salmon, *U.S.A.* **82 D7** 45 11N 113 54W
Salmon →, *Canada* **72 C4** 54 3N 122 40W
Salmon →, *U.S.A.* **82 D5** 45 51N 116 47W
Salmon Arm, *Canada* **72 C5** 50 40N 119 15W
Salmon Gums, *Australia* **61 F3** 32 59S 121 38 E
Salmon River Mts., *U.S.A.* **82 D6** 45 0N 114 30W
Salo, *Finland* **9 F20** 60 22N 23 10 E
Salome, *U.S.A.* **85 M13** 33 47N 113 37W
Salon, *India* **43 F9** 26 2N 81 27 E
Salon-de-Provence, *France* **18 E6** 43 39N 5 6 E
Salonica = Thessaloníki, *Greece* **21 D10** 40 38N 22 58 E
Salonta, *Romania* **17 E11** 46 49N 21 42 E
Salpausselkä, *Finland* **9 F22** 61 0N 27 0 E
Salsacate, *Argentina* **94 C2** 31 20S 65 5W
Salsk, *Russia* **25 E7** 46 28N 41 30 E
Salso →, *Italy* **20 F5** 37 6N 13 57 E
Salt →, *Canada* **72 B6** 60 0N 112 25W
Salt →, *U.S.A.* **83 K7** 33 23N 112 19W
Salt Lake City, *U.S.A.* **82 F8** 40 45N 111 53W
Salt Range, *Pakistan* **42 C5** 32 30N 72 25 E
Salta, *Argentina* **94 A2** 24 57S 65 25W
Salta □, *Argentina* **94 A2** 24 48S 65 30W
Saltash, *U.K.* **11 G3** 50 24N 4 14W
Saltburn by the Sea, *U.K.* **10 C7** 54 35N 0 58W
Saltcoats, *U.K.* **12 F4** 55 38N 4 47W
Saltee Is., *Ireland* **13 D5** 52 7N 6 37W
Saltfjellet, *Norway* **8 C16** 66 40N 15 15 E
Saltfjorden, *Norway* **8 C16** 67 15N 14 10 E
Saltillo, *Mexico* **86 B4** 25 25N 101 0W
Salto, *Argentina* **94 C3** 34 20S 60 15W
Salto, *Uruguay* **94 C4** 31 27S 57 50W
Salto →, *Italy* **20 C5** 42 26N 12 25 E
Salto del Guaíra, *Paraguay* **95 A5** 24 3S 54 17W
Salton City, *U.S.A.* **85 M11** 33 29N 115 51W
Salton Sea, *U.S.A.* **85 M11** 33 15N 115 45W
Saltsburg, *U.S.A.* **78 F5** 40 29N 79 27W
Saluda →, *U.S.A.* **77 J5** 34 1N 81 4W
Salûm, *Egypt* **51 B11** 31 31N 25 7 E
Salur, *India* **41 K13** 18 27N 83 18 E
Salvador, *Brazil* **93 F11** 13 0S 38 30W
Salvador, *Canada* **73 C7** 52 10N 109 32W
Salvador, L., *U.S.A.* **81 L9** 29 43N 90 15W
Salween →, *Burma* **41 L20** 16 31N 97 37 E
Salyan, *Azerbaijan* **25 G8** 39 33N 48 59 E
Salzach →, *Austria* **16 D7** 48 12N 12 56 E
Salzburg, *Austria* **16 E7** 47 48N 13 2 E
Salzgitter, *Germany* **16 B6** 52 9N 10 19 E
Salzwedel, *Germany* **16 B6** 52 52N 11 10 E
Sam, *India* **42 F4** 26 50N 70 31 E
Sam Neua, *Laos* **38 B5** 20 29N 104 5 E
Sam Ngao, *Thailand* **38 D2** 17 18N 99 0 E
Sam Rayburn Reservoir, *U.S.A.* **81 K7** 31 4N 94 5W
Sam Son, *Vietnam* **38 C5** 19 44N 105 54 E
Sam Teu, *Laos* **38 C5** 19 59N 104 38 E
Sama de Langreo = Langreo, *Spain* **19 A3** 43 18N 5 40W
Samagaltay, *Russia* **27 D10** 50 36N 95 3 E
Samales Group, *Phil.* **37 C6** 6 0N 122 0 E
Samana, *India* **42 D7** 30 10N 76 13 E
Samana Cay, *Bahamas* **89 B5** 23 3N 73 45W
Samanga, *Tanzania* **55 D4** 8 20S 39 13 E
Samangān □, *Afghan.* **40 B5** 36 15N 68 3 E
Samangwa, *Dem. Rep. of the Congo* **54 C1** 4 23S 24 10 E
Samani, *Japan* **30 C11** 42 7N 142 56 E
Samar, *Phil.* **37 B7** 12 0N 125 0 E
Samara, *Russia* **24 D9** 53 8N 50 6 E
Samaria = Shōmrōn, *West Bank* **47 C4** 32 15N 35 13 E
Samariá, *Greece* **23 D5** 35 17N 23 58 E
Samarinda, *Indonesia* **36 E5** 0 30S 117 9 E
Samarkand = Samarqand, *Uzbekistan* **26 F7** 39 40N 66 55 E
Samarqand, *Uzbekistan* **26 F7** 39 40N 66 55 E
Sāmarrā, *Iraq* **44 C4** 34 12N 43 52 E
Samastipur, *India* **43 G11** 25 50N 85 50 E
Samba, *Dem. Rep. of the Congo* **54 C2** 4 38S 26 22 E
Samba, *India* **43 C6** 32 32N 75 10 E
Sambalpur, *India* **41 J14** 21 28N 84 4 E
Sambar, Tanjung, *Indonesia* **36 E4** 2 59S 110 19 E
Sambas, *Indonesia* **36 D3** 1 20N 109 20 E
Sambava, *Madag.* **57 A9** 14 16S 50 10 E
Sambawizi, *Zimbabwe* **55 F2** 18 24S 26 13 E
Sambhal, *India* **43 E8** 28 35N 78 37 E
Sambhar, *India* **42 F6** 26 52N 75 6 E
Sambhar L., *India* **42 F6** 26 55N 75 12 E
Sambiase, *Italy* **20 E7** 38 58N 16 17 E
Sambir, *Ukraine* **17 D12** 49 30N 23 10 E
Sambor, *Cambodia* **38 F6** 12 46N 106 0 E
Samborombón, B., *Argentina* **94 D4** 36 5S 57 20W
Samch'ŏk, *S. Korea* **35 F15** 37 30N 129 10 E
Samch'onp'o, *S. Korea* **35 G15** 35 0N 128 6 E
Same, *Tanzania* **54 C4** 4 2S 37 38 E
Samfya, *Zambia* **55 E2** 11 22S 29 31 E
Samnah, *Si. Arabia* **44 E3** 25 10N 37 15 E
Samo Alto, *Chile* **94 C1** 30 22S 71 0W
Samoa ■, *Pac. Oc.* **59 B13** 14 0S 172 0W
Samokov, *Bulgaria* **21 C10** 42 18N 23 35 E
Sámos, *Greece* **21 F12** 37 45N 26 50 E
Samothráki = Mathráki, *Greece* **23 A3** 39 48N 19 31 E
Samothráki, *Greece* **21 D11** 40 28N 25 28 E
Sampacho, *Argentina* **94 C3** 33 20S 64 50W
Sampang, *Indonesia* **37 G15** 7 11S 113 13 E
Sampit, *Indonesia* **36 E4** 2 34S 113 0 E
Sampit, Teluk, *Indonesia* **36 E4** 3 5S 113 3 E
Samrong, *Cambodia* **38 E4** 14 15N 103 30 E
Samrong, *Thailand* **38 E3** 15 10N 100 40 E
Samsø, *Denmark* **9 J14** 55 50N 10 35 E
Samsun, *Turkey* **25 F6** 41 15N 36 22 E
Samui, Ko, *Thailand* **39 H3** 9 30N 100 0 E
Samusole, *Dem. Rep. of the Congo* **55 E1** 10 2S 24 0 E
Samut Prakan, *Thailand* **38 F3** 13 32N 100 40 E
Samut Songkhram →, *Thailand* **36 B1** 13 24N 100 1 E
Samwari, *Pakistan* **42 E2** 28 30N 66 46 E
San, *Mali* **50 F5** 13 15N 4 57W
San →, *Cambodia* **38 F5** 13 32N 105 57 E
San →, *Poland* **17 C11** 50 45N 21 51 E
San Agustin, C., *Phil.* **37 C7** 6 20N 126 13 E
San Agustín de Valle Fértil, *Argentina* **94 C2** 30 35S 67 30W
San Ambrosio, *Pac. Oc.* **90 F3** 26 28S 79 53W
San Andreas, *U.S.A.* **84 G6** 38 12N 120 41W
San Andrés, I. de, *Caribbean* **88 D3** 12 42N 81 46W
San Andres Mts., *U.S.A.* **83 K10** 33 0N 106 30W
San Andrés Tuxtla, *Mexico* **87 D5** 18 30N 95 20W
San Angelo, *U.S.A.* **81 K4** 31 28N 100 26W
San Anselmo, *U.S.A.* **84 H4** 37 59N 122 34W
San Antonio, *Belize* **87 D7** 16 15N 89 2W
San Antonio, *Chile* **94 C1** 33 40S 71 40W
San Antonio, *N. Mex., U.S.A.* **83 K10** 33 55N 106 52W
San Antonio, *Tex., U.S.A.* **81 L5** 29 25N 98 30W
San Antonio →, *U.S.A.* **81 L6** 28 30N 96 54W
San Antonio, C., *Argentina* **94 D4** 36 15S 56 40W
San Antonio, C., *Cuba* **88 B3** 21 50N 84 57W
San Antonio, Mt., *U.S.A.* **85 L9** 34 17N 117 38W
San Antonio de los Baños, *Cuba* **88 B3** 22 54N 82 31W
San Antonio de los Cobres, *Argentina* **94 A2** 24 10S 66 17W
San Antonio Oeste, *Argentina* **96 E4** 40 40S 65 0W
San Ardo, *U.S.A.* **84 J6** 36 1N 120 54W
San Augustín, *Canary Is.* **22 G4** 27 47N 15 32W
San Augustine, *U.S.A.* **81 K7** 31 30N 94 7W
San Bartolomé, *Canary Is.* **22 F6** 28 59N 13 37W
San Bartolomé de Tirajana, *Canary Is.* **22 G4** 27 54N 15 34W
San Benedetto del Tronto, *Italy* **20 C5** 42 57N 13 53 E
San Benedicto, I., *Mexico* **86 D2** 19 18N 110 49W
San Benito, *U.S.A.* **81 M6** 26 8N 97 38W
San Benito →, *U.S.A.* **84 J5** 36 53N 121 34W
San Benito Mt., *U.S.A.* **84 J6** 36 22N 120 37W
San Bernardino, *U.S.A.* **85 L9** 34 7N 117 19W
San Bernardino Mts., *U.S.A.* **85 L10** 34 10N 116 45W
San Bernardino Str., *Phil.* **37 B6** 13 0N 125 0 E
San Bernardo, *Chile* **94 C1** 33 40S 70 50W
San Bernardo, I. de, *Colombia* **92 B3** 9 45N 75 50W
San Blas, *Mexico* **86 B3** 26 4N 108 46W
San Blas, Arch. de, *Panama* **88 E4** 9 50N 78 31W
San Blas, C., *U.S.A.* **77 L3** 29 40N 85 21W
San Borja, *Bolivia* **92 F5** 14 50S 66 52W
San Buenaventura, *Mexico* **86 B4** 27 5N 101 32W
San Carlos = Sant Carles, *Spain* **22 B8** 39 3N 1 34 E
San Carlos, *Argentina* **94 C2** 33 50S 69 0W
San Carlos, *Chile* **94 D1** 36 10S 72 0W
San Carlos, *Baja Calif. S., Mexico* **86 C2** 24 47N 112 6W
San Carlos, *Coahuila, Mexico* **86 B4** 29 0N 100 54W
San Carlos, *Nic.* **88 D3** 11 12N 84 50W
San Carlos, *Phil.* **37 B6** 10 29N 123 25 E
San Carlos, *Uruguay* **95 C5** 34 46S 54 58W
San Carlos, *U.S.A.* **83 K8** 33 21N 110 27W
San Carlos, *Venezuela* **92 B5** 9 40N 68 36W
San Carlos de Bariloche, *Argentina* **96 E2** 41 10S 71 25W
San Carlos de Bolívar, *Argentina* **96 D4** 36 15S 61 6W
San Carlos del Zulia, *Venezuela* **92 B4** 9 1N 71 55W
San Carlos L., *U.S.A.* **83 K8** 33 11N 110 32W
San Clemente, *Chile* **94 D1** 35 30S 71 29W
San Clemente, *U.S.A.* **85 M9** 33 26N 117 37W
San Clemente I., *U.S.A.* **85 N8** 32 53N 118 29W
San Cristóbal = Es Migjorn Gran, *Spain* **22 B11** 39 57N 4 3 E
San Cristóbal, *Argentina* **94 C3** 30 20S 61 10W
San Cristóbal, *Dom. Rep.* **89 C5** 18 25N 70 6W
San Cristóbal, *Venezuela* **92 B4** 7 48N 72 14W
San Cristóbal de la Casas, *Mexico* **87 D6** 16 50N 92 33W
San Diego, *Calif., U.S.A.* **85 N9** 32 43N 117 9W
San Diego, *Tex., U.S.A.* **81 M5** 27 46N 98 14W
San Diego, C., *Argentina* **96 G3** 54 40S 65 10W
San Diego de la Unión, *Mexico* **86 C4** 21 28N 100 52W
San Dimitri, Ras, *Malta* **23 C1** 36 4N 14 11 E
San Dimitri Point = San Dimitri, Ras, *Malta* **23 C1** 36 4N 14 11 E
San Estanislao, *Paraguay* **94 A4** 24 39S 56 26W
San Felipe, *Chile* **94 C1** 32 43S 70 42W
San Felipe, *Mexico* **86 A2** 31 0N 114 52W
San Felipe, *Venezuela* **92 A5** 10 20N 68 44W
San Felipe →, *U.S.A.* **85 M11** 33 12N 115 49W
San Félix, *Chile* **94 B1** 28 56S 70 28W
San Félix, *Pac. Oc.* **90 F2** 26 23S 80 0W
San Fernando = Sant Ferran, *Spain* **22 C7** 38 42N 1 28 E
San Fernando, *Chile* **94 C1** 34 30S 71 0W
San Fernando, *Baja Calif., Mexico* **86 B1** 29 55N 115 10W
San Fernando, *Tamaulipas, Mexico* **87 C5** 24 51N 98 10W
San Fernando, *La Union, Phil.* **37 A6** 16 40N 120 23 E
San Fernando, *Pampanga, Phil.* **37 A6** 15 5N 120 37 E
San Fernando, *Spain* **19 D2** 36 28N 6 17W
San Fernando, *Trin. & Tob.* **89 D7** 10 20N 61 30W
San Fernando, *U.S.A.* **85 L8** 34 17N 118 26W
San Fernando de Apure, *Venezuela* **92 B5** 7 54N 67 15W
San Fernando de Atabapo, *Venezuela* **92 C5** 4 3N 67 42W
San Francisco, *Argentina* **94 C3** 31 30S 62 5W
San Francisco, *U.S.A.* **84 H4** 37 47N 122 25W
San Francisco →, *U.S.A.* **83 K9** 32 59N 109 22W
San Francisco, Paso de, *S. Amer.* **94 B2** 27 0S 68 0W
San Francisco de Macorís, *Dom. Rep.* **89 C5** 19 19N 70 15W
San Francisco del Monte de Oro, *Argentina* **94 C2** 32 36S 66 8W
San Francisco del Oro, *Mexico* **86 B3** 26 52N 105 50W
San Francisco Javier = Sant Francesc de Formentera, *Spain* **22 C7** 38 42N 1 26 E
San Francisco Solano, Pta., *Colombia* **90 C3** 6 18N 77 29W
San Gabriel, *Chile* **94 C1** 33 47S 70 15W
San Gabriel Mts., *U.S.A.* **85 L9** 34 20N 118 0W
San Gorgonio Mt., *U.S.A.* **85 L10** 34 7N 116 51W
San Gottardo, P. del, *Switz.* **18 C8** 46 33N 8 33 E
San Gregorio, *Uruguay* **95 C4** 32 37S 55 40W
San Gregorio, *U.S.A.* **84 H4** 37 20N 122 23W
San Ignacio, *Belize* **87 D7** 17 10N 89 0W
San Ignacio, *Bolivia* **92 G6** 16 20S 60 55W
San Ignacio, *Mexico* **86 B2** 27 27N 113 0W
San Ignacio, *Paraguay* **88 C2** 26 52S 57 3W
San Ignacio, L., *Mexico* **86 B2** 26 50N 113 11W
San Ildefonso, C., *Phil.* **37 A6** 16 0N 122 1 E
San Isidro, *Argentina* **94 C4** 34 29S 58 31W
San Jacinto, *U.S.A.* **85 M10** 33 47N 116 57W
San Jaime = Sant Jaume, *Spain* **22 B11** 39 54N 4 4 E
San Javier, *Misiones, Argentina* **95 B4** 27 55S 55 5W
San Javier, *Santa Fe, Argentina* **94 C4** 30 40S 59 55W
San Javier, *Bolivia* **92 G6** 16 18S 62 30W
San Javier, *Chile* **94 D1** 35 40S 71 45W
San Jeronimo Taviche, *Mexico* **87 D5** 16 38N 96 32W
San Joaquin, *U.S.A.* **84 J6** 36 36N 120 11W
San Joaquin →, *U.S.A.* **84 G5** 38 4N 121 51W
San Joaquin Valley, *U.S.A.* **84 J6** 37 20N 121 0W
San Jon, *U.S.A.* **81 H3** 35 6N 103 20W
San Jordi = Sant Jordi, *Spain* **22 B9** 39 33N 2 46 E
San Jorge, *Argentina* **94 C3** 31 54S 61 50W
San Jorge, B. de, *Mexico* **86 A2** 31 20N 113 20W
San Jorge, G., *Argentina* **96 F3** 46 0S 66 0W
San José = San Josep, *Spain* **22 C7** 38 55N 1 18 E
San José, *Costa Rica* **88 E3** 9 55N 84 2W
San José, *Guatemala* **88 D1** 14 0N 90 50W
San José, *Mexico* **86 C2** 25 0N 110 50W
San Jose, *Mind. Occ., Phil.* **37 B6** 12 27N 121 4 E
San Jose, *Nueva Ecija, Phil.* **37 A6** 15 45N 120 55 E
San Jose, *U.S.A.* **84 H5** 37 20N 121 53W
San Jose →, *U.S.A.* **83 J10** 34 25N 106 45W
San Jose de Buenavista, *Phil.* **37 B6** 10 45N 121 56 E
San José de Chiquitos, *Bolivia* **92 G6** 17 53S 60 50W
San José de Feliciano, *Argentina* **94 C4** 30 26S 58 46W
San José de Jáchal, *Argentina* **94 C2** 30 15S 68 46W
San José de Mayo, *Uruguay* **94 C4** 34 27S 56 40W
San José del Cabo, *Mexico* **86 C3** 23 0N 109 40W
San José del Guaviare, *Colombia* **92 C4** 2 35N 72 38W
San Josep, *Spain* **22 C7** 38 55N 1 18 E
San Juan, *Argentina* **94 C2** 31 30S 68 30W
San Juan, *Mexico* **86 C4** 21 20N 102 50W
San Juan, *Puerto Rico* **89 C6** 18 28N 66 7W
San Juan □, *Argentina* **94 C2** 31 9S 69 0W
San Juan →, *Argentina* **94 C2** 32 20S 67 25W
San Juan →, *Nic.* **88 D3** 10 56N 83 42W
San Juan →, *U.S.A.* **83 H8** 37 16N 110 26W
San Juan Bautista = Sant Joan Baptista, *Spain* **22 B8** 39 5N 1 31 E
San Juan Bautista, *Paraguay* **94 B4** 26 37S 57 6W
San Juan Bautista, *U.S.A.* **84 J5** 36 51N 121 32W
San Juan Bautista Valle Nacional, *Mexico* **87 D5** 17 47N 96 19W
San Juan Capistrano, *U.S.A.* **85 M9** 33 30N 117 40W
San Juan Cr. →, *U.S.A.* **84 J5** 35 40N 120 22W
San Juan de Guadalupe, *Mexico* **86 C4** 24 38N 102 44W
San Juan de la Costa, *Mexico* **86 C2** 24 23N 110 45W
San Juan de los Morros, *Venezuela* **92 B5** 9 55N 67 21W
San Juan del Norte, *Nic.* **88 D3** 10 58N 83 40W
San Juan del Norte, B. de, *Nic.* **88 D3** 11 0N 83 40W
San Juan del Río, *Mexico* **87 C5** 20 25N 100 0W
San Juan del Sur, *Nic.* **88 D2** 11 20N 85 51W
San Juan I., *U.S.A.* **84 B3** 48 32N 123 5W
San Juan Mts., *U.S.A.* **83 H10** 37 30N 107 0W
San Justo, *Argentina* **94 C3** 30 47S 60 30W
San Kamphaeng, *Thailand* **38 C2** 18 45N 99 8 E
San Lázaro, C., *Mexico* **86 C2** 24 50N 112 18W
San Lázaro, Sa., *Mexico* **86 C3** 23 25N 110 0W
San Leandro, *U.S.A.* **84 H4** 37 44N 122 9W
San Lorenzo = Sant Llorenç des Cardassar, *Spain* **22 B10** 39 37N 3 17 E
San Lorenzo, *Argentina* **94 C3** 32 45S 60 45W
San Lorenzo, *Ecuador* **92 C3** 1 15N 78 50W
San Lorenzo, *Paraguay* **94 B4** 25 20S 57 32W
San Lorenzo →, *Mexico* **86 C3** 24 15N 107 24W
San Lorenzo, I., *Mexico* **86 B2** 28 35N 112 50W
San Lorenzo, Mte., *Argentina* **96 F2** 47 40S 72 20W
San Lucas, *Bolivia* **92 H5** 20 5S 65 7W
San Lucas, *Baja Calif. S., Mexico* **86 C3** 22 53N 109 54W
San Lucas, *Baja Calif. S., Mexico* **86 B2** 27 10N 112 14W
San Lucas, *U.S.A.* **84 J5** 36 8N 121 1W
San Lucas, C., *Mexico* **86 C3** 22 50N 110 0W
San Luis, *Argentina* **94 C2** 33 20S 66 20W
San Luis, *Cuba* **88 B3** 22 17N 83 46W
San Luis, *Guatemala* **88 C2** 16 14N 89 27W
San Luis, *Ariz., U.S.A.* **83 K6** 32 29N 114 47W
San Luis, *Colo., U.S.A.* **83 H11** 37 12N 105 25W
San Luis □, *Argentina* **94 C2** 34 0S 66 0W
San Luis, I., *Mexico* **86 B2** 29 58N 114 26W
San Luis, Sierra de, *Argentina* **94 C2** 32 30S 66 10W
San Luis de la Paz, *Mexico* **86 C4** 21 19N 100 32W
San Luis Obispo, *U.S.A.* **85 K6** 35 17N 120 40W
San Luis Potosí, *Mexico* **86 C4** 22 9N 100 59W
San Luis Potosí □, *Mexico* **86 C4** 22 10N 101 0W
San Luis Reservoir, *U.S.A.* **84 H5** 37 4N 121 5W
San Luis Río Colorado, *Mexico* **86 A2** 32 29N 114 58W
San Manuel, *U.S.A.* **83 K8** 32 36N 110 38W
San Marcos, *Guatemala* **88 D1** 14 59N 91 52W
San Marcos, *Mexico* **86 B2** 27 13N 112 6W
San Marcos, *Calif., U.S.A.* **85 M9** 33 9N 117 10W
San Marcos, *Tex., U.S.A.* **81 L6** 29 53N 97 56W
San Marino, *San Marino* **16 G7** 43 55N 12 30 E
San Marino ■, *Europe* **20 C5** 43 56N 12 25 E
San Martín, *Argentina* **94 C2** 33 5S 68 28W
San Martín →, *Bolivia* **92 F6** 13 8S 63 43W
San Martín, L., *Argentina* **96 F2** 48 50S 72 50W
San Martín de los Andes, *Argentina* **96 E2** 40 10S 71 20W
San Mateo = Sant Mateu, *Spain* **22 B7** 39 3N 1 23 E
San Mateo, *U.S.A.* **84 H4** 37 34N 122 19W
San Matías, *Bolivia* **92 G7** 16 25S 58 20W
San Matías, G., *Argentina* **96 E4** 41 30S 64 0W
San Miguel = Sant Miguel, *Spain* **22 B7** 39 3N 1 26 E
San Miguel, *El Salv.* **88 D2** 13 30N 88 12W
San Miguel, *Panama* **88 E4** 8 27N 78 55W
San Miguel, *U.S.A.* **84 K6** 35 45N 120 42W
San Miguel →, *Bolivia* **92 F6** 13 52S 63 56W
San Miguel de Tucumán, *Argentina* **94 B2** 26 50S 65 20W
San Miguel del Monte, *Argentina* **94 D4** 35 23S 58 50W
San Miguel I., *U.S.A.* **85 L6** 34 2N 120 23W
San Nicolás, *Canary Is.* **22 G4** 27 58N 15 47W
San Nicolás de los Arroyas, *Argentina* **94 C3** 33 25S 60 10W
San Nicolas I., *U.S.A.* **85 M7** 33 15N 119 30W
San Onofre, *U.S.A.* **85 M9** 33 22N 117 34W
San Pablo, *Bolivia* **94 A2** 21 43S 66 38W
San Pablo, *U.S.A.* **84 H4** 37 58N 122 21W
San Pedro, *Buenos Aires, Argentina* **94 C4** 33 40S 59 40W
San Pedro, *Misiones, Argentina* **95 B5** 26 30S 54 10W
San Pedro, *Chile* **94 C1** 33 54S 71 28W
San Pédro, *Ivory C.* **50 H4** 4 50N 6 33W
San Pedro, *Mexico* **86 C2** 23 55N 110 17W
San Pedro □, *Paraguay* **94 A4** 24 0S 57 0W
San Pedro →, *Chihuahua, Mexico* **86 B3** 28 20N 106 10W
San Pedro →, *Nayarit, Mexico* **86 C3** 21 45N 105 30W
San Pedro →, *U.S.A.* **83 K8** 32 59N 110 47W
San Pedro, Pta., *Chile* **94 B1** 25 30S 70 38W
San Pedro Channel, *U.S.A.* **85 M8** 33 30N 118 25W
San Pedro de Atacama, *Chile* **94 A2** 22 55S 68 15W
San Pedro de Jujuy, *Argentina* **94 A3** 24 12S 64 55W
San Pedro de las Colonias, *Mexico* **86 B4** 25 50N 102 59W
San Pedro de Macorís, *Dom. Rep.* **89 C6** 18 30N 69 18W
San Pedro del Norte, *Nic.* **88 D3** 13 4N 84 33W
San Pedro del Paraná, *Paraguay* **94 B4** 26 43S 56 13W
San Pedro Mártir, Sierra, *Mexico* **86 A1** 31 0N 115 30W
San Pedro Mixtepec, *Mexico* **87 D5** 16 2N 97 7W
San Pedro Ocampo = Melchor Ocampo, *Mexico* **86 C4** 24 52N 101 40W

Sarvar, India 42 F6 26 4N 75 0 E
Sarvestān, Iran 45 D7 29 20N 53 10 E
Sary-Tash, Kyrgyzstan 26 F8 39 44N 73 15 E
Saryshagan, Kazakstan 26 E8 46 12N 73 38 E
Sasan Gir, India 42 J4 21 10N 70 36 E
Sasaram, India 43 G11 24 57N 84 5 E
Sasebo, Japan 31 H4 33 10N 129 43 E
Saser, India 43 B7 34 50N 77 50 E
Saskatchewan □, Canada 73 C7 54 40N 106 0W
Saskatchewan →, Canada 73 C8 53 37N 100 40W
Saskatoon, Canada 73 C7 52 10N 106 38W
Saskylakh, Russia 27 B12 71 55N 114 1 E
Sasolburg, S. Africa 57 D4 26 46S 27 49 E
Sasovo, Russia 24 D7 54 25N 41 55 E
Sassandra, Ivory C. 50 H4 4 55N 6 8W
Sassandra →, Ivory C. 50 H4 4 58N 6 5W
Sássari, Italy 20 D3 40 43N 8 34 E
Sassnitz, Germany 16 A7 54 29N 13 39 E
Sassuolo, Italy 20 B4 44 33N 10 47 E
Sasumua Dam, Kenya 54 C4 0 45S 36 40 E
Sasyk, Ozero, Ukraine 17 F15 45 45N 29 20 E
Sata-Misaki, Japan 31 J5 31 0N 130 40 E
Satadougou, Mali 50 F3 12 25N 11 25W
Satakunta, Finland 9 F20 61 45N 23 0 E
Satara, India 40 L8 17 44N 73 58 E
Satara, S. Africa 57 C5 24 29S 31 47 E
Satbarwa, India 43 H11 23 55N 84 16 E
Satevó, Mexico 86 B3 27 57N 106 7W
Satilla →, U.S.A. 77 K5 30 59N 81 29W
Satka, Russia 24 C10 55 3N 59 1 E
Satmala Hills, India 40 J9 20 15N 74 40 E
Satna, India 43 G9 24 35N 80 50 E
Sátoraljaújhely, Hungary 17 D11 48 25N 21 41 E
Satpura Ra., India 40 J10 21 25N 76 10 E
Satsuna-Shotō, Japan 31 K5 30 0N 130 0 E
Sattahip, Thailand 38 F3 12 41N 100 54 E
Satu Mare, Romania 17 E12 47 46N 22 55 E
Satui, Indonesia 36 E5 3 50S 115 27 E
Satun, Thailand 39 J3 6 43N 100 2 E
Saturnina →, Brazil 92 F7 12 15S 58 10W
Sauce, Argentina 94 C4 30 5S 58 46W
Sauceda, Mexico 86 B4 25 55N 101 18W
Saucillo, Mexico 86 B3 28 1N 105 17W
Sauda, Norway 9 G12 59 40N 6 20 E
Sauðarkrókur, Iceland 8 D4 65 45N 19 40W
Saudi Arabia ■, Asia 46 B3 26 0N 44 0 E
Sauerland, Germany 16 C4 51 12N 7 59 E
Saugeen →, Canada 78 B3 44 30N 81 22W
Saugerties, U.S.A. 79 D11 42 5N 73 57W
Saugus, U.S.A. 85 L8 34 25N 118 32W
Sauk Centre, U.S.A. 80 C7 45 44N 94 57W
Sauk Rapids, U.S.A. 80 C7 45 35N 94 10W
Sault Ste. Marie, Canada 70 C3 46 30N 84 20W
Sault Ste. Marie, U.S.A. 69 D11 46 30N 84 21W
Saumlaki, Indonesia 37 F8 7 55S 131 20 E
Saumur, France 18 C3 47 15N 0 5W
Saunders, C., N.Z. 59 L3 45 53S 170 45 E
Saunders I., Antarctica 5 B1 57 48S 26 28W
Saunders Point, Australia 61 E4 27 52S 125 38 E
Saurimo, Angola 52 F4 9 40S 20 12 E
Sausalito, U.S.A. 84 H4 37 51N 122 29W
Savá, Honduras 88 C2 15 32N 86 15W
Sava →, Serbia, Yug. 21 B9 44 50N 20 26 E
Savage, U.S.A. 80 B2 47 27N 104 21W
Savage I. = Niue, Cook Is. 65 J11 19 2S 169 54W
Savage River, Australia 62 G4 41 31S 145 14 E
Savai'i, Samoa 59 A12 13 28S 172 24W
Savalou, Benin 50 G6 7 57N 1 58 E
Savane, Mozam. 55 F4 19 37S 35 8 E
Savanna, U.S.A. 80 D9 42 5N 90 8W
Savanna-la-Mar, Jamaica 88 C4 18 10N 78 10W
Savannah, Ga., U.S.A. 77 J5 32 5N 81 6W
Savannah, Mo., U.S.A. 80 F7 39 56N 94 50W
Savannah, Tenn., U.S.A. 77 H1 35 14N 88 15W
Savannah →, U.S.A. 77 J5 32 2N 80 53W
Savannakhet, Laos 38 D5 16 30N 104 49 E
Savant L., Canada 70 B1 50 16N 90 44W
Savant Lake, Canada 70 B1 50 14N 90 40W
Save →, Mozam. 57 C5 21 16S 34 0 E
Sāveh, Iran 45 C6 35 2N 50 20 E
Savelugu, Ghana 50 G5 9 38N 0 54W
Savo, Finland 8 E22 62 45N 27 30 E
Savoie □, France 18 D7 45 26N 6 25 E
Savona, Italy 18 D8 44 17N 8 30 E
Savona, U.S.A. 78 D7 42 17N 77 13W
Savonlinna, Finland 24 B4 61 52N 28 53 E
Savoy = Savoie □, France 18 D7 45 26N 6 25 E
Savur, Turkey 44 B4 37 34N 40 53 E
Sawahlunto, Indonesia 36 E2 0 40S 100 52 E
Sawai, Indonesia 37 E7 3 0S 129 5 E
Sawai Madhopur, India 42 G7 26 0N 76 25 E
Sawang Daen Din, Thailand 38 D4 17 28N 103 28 E
Sawankhalok, Thailand 38 D2 17 19N 99 50 E
Sawara, Japan 31 G10 35 55N 140 30 E
Sawatch Range, U.S.A. 83 G10 38 30N 106 30W
Sawel Mt., U.K. 13 B4 54 50N 7 2W
Sawi, Thailand 39 G2 10 14N 99 5 E
Sawmills, Zimbabwe 55 F2 19 30S 28 2 E
Sawtooth Range, U.S.A. 82 E6 44 3N 114 58W
Sawu, Indonesia 37 F6 10 35S 121 50 E
Sawu Sea, Indonesia 37 F6 9 30S 121 50 E
Saxby →, Australia 62 B3 18 25S 140 53 E
Saxmundham, U.K. 11 E9 52 13N 1 30 E
Saxony = Sachsen □, Germany 16 C7 50 55N 13 10 E
Saxony, Lower = Niedersachsen □, Germany 16 B5 52 50N 9 0 E
Saxton, U.S.A. 78 F6 40 13N 78 15W
Sayabec, Canada 71 C6 48 35N 67 41W
Sayaboury, Laos 38 C3 19 15N 101 45 E
Sayán, Peru 92 F3 11 8S 77 12W
Sayan, Vostochnyy, Russia 27 D10 54 0N 96 0 E
Sayan, Zapadnyy, Russia 27 D10 52 30N 94 0 E
Saydā, Lebanon 47 B4 33 35N 35 25 E
Sayhandulaan = Oldziyt, Mongolia 34 B5 44 40N 109 1 E
Sayḥūt, Yemen 46 D5 15 12N 51 10 E
Saylac = Zeila, Somali Rep. 46 E3 11 21N 43 30 E
Saynshand, Mongolia 33 B6 44 55N 110 11 E
Sayre, Okla., U.S.A. 81 H5 35 18N 99 38W
Sayre, Pa., U.S.A. 79 E8 41 59N 76 32W
Sayreville, U.S.A. 79 F10 40 28N 74 22W
Sayula, Mexico 86 D4 19 50N 103 40W
Sayward, Canada 72 C3 50 21N 125 55W
Sazanit, Albania 21 D8 40 30N 19 20 E
Sázava →, Czech Rep. 16 D8 49 53N 14 24 E
Sazin, Pakistan 43 B5 35 35N 73 30 E
Scafell Pike, U.K. 10 C4 54 27N 3 14W
Scalloway, U.K. 12 A7 60 9N 1 17W
Scalpay, U.K. 12 D3 57 18N 6 0W
Scandia, Canada 72 C6 50 20N 112 0W
Scandicci, Italy 20 C4 43 45N 11 11 E
Scandinavia, Europe 8 E16 64 0N 12 0 E
Scapa Flow, U.K. 12 C5 58 53N 3 3W
Scappoose, U.S.A. 84 E4 45 45N 122 53W
Scarba, U.K. 12 E3 56 11N 5 43W
Scarborough, Trin. & Tob. 89 D7 11 11N 60 42W
Scarborough, U.K. 10 C7 54 17N 0 24W
Scariff I., Ireland 13 E1 51 44N 10 15W
Scarp, U.K. 12 C1 58 1N 7 8W
Scebeli, Wabi →, Somali Rep. 46 G3 2 0N 44 0 E
Schaffhausen, Switz. 18 C8 47 42N 8 39 E
Schagen, Neths. 15 B4 52 49N 4 48 E
Schaghticoke, U.S.A. 79 D11 42 54N 73 35W
Schefferville, Canada 71 B6 54 48N 66 50W
Schelde →, Belgium 15 C4 51 15N 4 16 E
Schell Creek Ra., U.S.A. 82 G6 39 15N 114 30W
Schellsburg, U.S.A. 78 F6 40 3N 78 39W
Schenectady, U.S.A. 79 D11 42 49N 73 57W
Schenevus, U.S.A. 79 D10 42 33N 74 50W
Schiedam, Neths. 15 C4 51 55N 4 25 E
Schiermonnikoog, Neths. 15 A6 53 30N 6 15 E
Schio, Italy 20 B4 45 43N 11 21 E
Schleswig, Germany 16 A5 54 31N 9 34 E
Schleswig-Holstein □, Germany 16 A5 54 30N 9 30 E
Schoharie, U.S.A. 79 D10 42 40N 74 19W
Schoharie →, U.S.A. 79 D10 42 57N 74 18W
Scholls, U.S.A. 84 E4 45 24N 122 56W
Schouten I., Australia 62 G4 42 20S 148 20 E
Schouten Is. = Supiori, Indonesia 37 E9 1 0S 136 0 E
Schouwen, Neths. 15 C3 51 43N 3 45 E
Schreiber, Canada 70 C2 48 45N 87 20W
Schroffenstein, Namibia 56 D2 27 11S 18 42 E
Schroon Lake, U.S.A. 79 C11 43 50N 73 46W
Schuler, Canada 73 C6 50 20N 110 6W
Schumacher, Canada 70 C3 48 30N 81 16W
Schurz, U.S.A. 82 G4 38 57N 118 49W
Schuyler, U.S.A. 80 E6 41 27N 97 4W
Schuylerville, U.S.A. 79 C11 43 6N 73 35W
Schuylkill →, U.S.A. 79 G9 39 53N 75 12W
Schuylkill Haven, U.S.A. 79 F8 40 37N 76 11W
Schwäbische Alb, Germany 16 D5 48 20N 9 30 E
Schwaner, Pegunungan, Indonesia 36 E4 1 0S 112 30 E
Schwarzrand, Namibia 56 D2 25 37S 16 50 E
Schwarzwald, Germany 16 D5 48 30N 8 20 E
Schwedt, Germany 16 B8 53 3N 14 16 E
Schweinfurt, Germany 16 C6 50 3N 10 14 E
Schweizer-Reneke, S. Africa 56 D4 27 11S 25 18 E
Schwenningen = Villingen-Schwenningen, Germany 16 D5 48 3N 8 26 E
Schwerin, Germany 16 B6 53 36N 11 22 E
Schwyz, Switz. 18 C8 47 2N 8 39 E
Sciacca, Italy 20 F5 37 31N 13 3 E
Scilla, Italy 20 E6 38 15N 15 43 E
Scilly, Isles of, U.K. 11 H1 49 56N 6 22W
Scioto →, U.S.A. 76 F4 38 44N 83 1W
Scituate, U.S.A. 79 D14 42 12N 70 44W
Scobey, U.S.A. 80 A2 48 47N 105 25W
Scone, Australia 63 E5 32 5S 150 52 E
Scoresbysund = Ittoqqortoormiit, Greenland 4 B6 70 20N 23 0W
Scotia, Calif., U.S.A. 82 F1 40 29N 124 6W
Scotia, N.Y., U.S.A. 79 D11 42 50N 73 58W
Scotia Sea, Antarctica 5 B18 56 5S 56 0W
Scotland, Canada 78 C4 43 1N 80 22W
Scotland □, U.K. 12 E5 57 0N 4 0W
Scott, C., Australia 60 B4 13 30S 129 49 E
Scott City, U.S.A. 80 F4 38 29N 100 54W
Scott Glacier, Antarctica 5 C8 66 15S 100 5 E
Scott I., Antarctica 5 C11 67 0S 179 0 E
Scott Is., Canada 72 C3 50 48N 128 40W
Scott L., Canada 73 B7 59 55N 106 18W
Scott Reef, Australia 60 B3 14 0S 121 50 E
Scottburgh, S. Africa 57 E5 30 15S 30 47 E
Scottdale, U.S.A. 78 F5 40 6N 79 35W
Scottish Borders □, U.K. 12 F6 55 35N 2 50W
Scottsbluff, U.S.A. 80 E3 41 52N 103 40W
Scottsboro, U.S.A. 77 H3 34 40N 86 2W
Scottsburg, U.S.A. 76 F3 38 41N 85 47W
Scottsdale, Australia 62 G4 41 9S 147 31 E
Scottsdale, U.S.A. 83 K7 33 29N 111 56W
Scottsville, Ky., U.S.A. 77 G2 36 45N 86 11W
Scottsville, N.Y., U.S.A. 78 C7 43 2N 77 47W
Scottville, U.S.A. 76 D2 43 58N 86 17W
Scranton, U.S.A. 79 E9 41 25N 75 40W
Scugog, L., Canada 78 B6 44 10N 78 55W
Scunthorpe, U.K. 10 D7 53 36N 0 39W
Scutari = Shkodër, Albania 21 C8 42 4N 19 32 E
Seabrook, L., Australia 61 F2 30 55S 119 40 E
Seaford, U.K. 11 G8 50 47N 0 7 E
Seaford, U.S.A. 76 F8 38 39N 75 37W
Seaforth, Australia 62 C4 20 55S 148 57 E
Seaforth, Canada 78 C3 43 35N 81 25W
Seaforth, L., U.K. 12 D2 57 52N 6 36W
Seagraves, U.S.A. 81 J3 32 57N 102 34W
Seaham, U.K. 10 C6 54 50N 1 20W
Seal →, Canada 73 B10 59 4N 94 48W
Seal L., Canada 71 B7 54 20N 61 30W
Sealy, U.S.A. 81 L6 29 47N 96 9W
Searchlight, U.S.A. 85 K12 35 28N 114 55W
Searcy, U.S.A. 81 H9 35 15N 91 44W
Searles L., U.S.A. 85 K9 35 44N 117 21W
Seascale, U.K. 10 C4 54 24N 3 29W
Seaside, Calif., U.S.A. 84 J5 36 37N 121 50W
Seaside, Oreg., U.S.A. 84 E3 46 0N 123 56W
Seaspray, Australia 63 F4 38 25S 147 15 E
Seattle, U.S.A. 84 C4 47 36N 122 20W
Seaview Ra., Australia 62 B4 18 40S 145 45 E
Sebago L., U.S.A. 79 C14 43 52N 70 34W
Sebago Lake, U.S.A. 79 C14 43 51N 70 34W
Sebastián Vizcaíno, B., Mexico 86 B2 28 0N 114 30W
Sebastopol = Sevastopol, Ukraine 25 F5 44 35N 33 30 E
Sebastopol, U.S.A. 84 G4 38 24N 122 49W
Sebewaing, U.S.A. 76 D4 43 44N 83 27W
Sebha = Sabhah, Libya 51 C8 27 9N 14 29 E
Şebinkarahisar, Turkey 25 F6 40 22N 38 28 E
Sebring, Fla., U.S.A. 77 M5 27 30N 81 27W
Sebring, Ohio, U.S.A. 78 F3 40 55N 81 2W
Sebringville, Canada 78 C3 43 24N 81 4W
Sebta = Ceuta, N. Afr. 19 E3 35 52N 5 18W
Sebuku, Indonesia 36 E5 3 30S 116 25 E
Sebuku, Teluk, Malaysia 36 D5 4 0N 118 10 E
Sechelt, Canada 72 D4 49 25N 123 42W
Sechura, Desierto de, Peru 92 E2 6 0S 80 30W
Secretary I., N.Z. 59 L1 45 15S 166 56 E
Secunderabad, India 40 L11 17 28N 78 30 E
Security-Widefield, U.S.A. 80 F2 38 45N 104 45W
Sedalia, U.S.A. 80 F8 38 42N 93 14W
Sedan, France 18 B6 49 43N 4 57 E
Sedan, U.S.A. 81 G6 37 8N 96 11W
Seddon, N.Z. 59 J5 41 40S 174 7 E
Seddonville, N.Z. 59 J4 41 33S 172 1 E
Sedé Boqér, Israel 47 E3 30 52N 34 47 E
Sedeh, Fārs, Iran 45 D7 30 45N 52 11 E
Sedeh, Khorāsān, Iran 45 C8 33 20N 59 14 E
Sederot, Israel 47 D3 31 32N 34 37 E
Sédhiou, Senegal 50 F2 12 44N 15 30W
Sedley, Canada 73 C8 50 10N 104 0W
Sedona, U.S.A. 83 J8 34 52N 111 46W
Sedova, Pik, Russia 26 B6 73 29N 54 58 E
Sedro Woolley, U.S.A. 84 B4 48 30N 122 14W
Seeheim, Namibia 56 D2 26 50S 17 45 E
Seeis, Namibia 56 C2 22 29S 17 39 E
Seekoei →, S. Africa 56 E4 30 18S 25 1 E
Seeley's Bay, Canada 79 B8 44 29N 76 14W
Seferihisar, Turkey 21 E12 38 10N 26 50 E
Seg-ozero, Russia 24 B5 63 20N 33 46 E
Segamat, Malaysia 39 L4 2 30N 102 50 E
Segesta, Italy 20 F5 37 56N 12 50 E
Seget, Indonesia 37 E8 1 24S 130 58 E
Segezha, Russia 24 B5 63 44N 34 19 E
Ségou, Mali 50 F4 13 30N 6 16W
Segovia = Coco →, Cent. Amer. 88 D3 15 0N 83 8W
Segovia, Spain 19 B3 40 57N 4 10W
Segre →, Spain 19 B6 41 40N 0 43 E
Séguéla, Ivory C. 50 G4 7 55N 6 40W
Seguin, U.S.A. 81 L6 29 34N 97 58W
Segundo →, Argentina 94 C3 30 53S 62 44W
Segura →, Spain 19 C5 38 3N 0 44W
Seh Konj, Kūh-e, Iran 45 D8 30 6N 57 30 E
Seh Qal'eh, Iran 45 C8 33 40N 58 24 E
Sehitwa, Botswana 56 C3 20 30S 22 30 E
Sehore, India 42 H7 23 10N 77 5 E
Sehwan, Pakistan 42 F2 26 28N 67 53 E
Seil, U.K. 12 E3 56 18N 5 38W
Seiland, Norway 8 A20 70 25N 23 15 E
Seiling, U.S.A. 81 G5 36 9N 98 56W
Seinäjoki, Finland 9 E20 62 40N 22 51 E
Seine →, France 18 B4 49 26N 0 26 E
Seistan = Sīstān, Asia 45 D9 30 50N 61 0 E
Seistan, Daryācheh-ye = Sīstān, Daryācheh-ye, Iran 45 D9 31 0N 61 0 E
Sekayu, Indonesia 36 E2 2 51S 103 51 E
Seke, Tanzania 54 C3 3 20S 33 31 E
Sekenke, Tanzania 54 C3 4 18S 34 11 E
Sekondi-Takoradi, Ghana 50 H5 4 58N 1 45W
Sekuma, Botswana 56 C3 24 36S 23 50 E
Selah, U.S.A. 82 C3 46 39N 120 32W
Selama, Malaysia 39 K3 5 12N 100 42 E
Selaru, Indonesia 37 F8 8 9S 131 0 E
Selby, U.K. 10 D6 53 47N 1 5W
Selby, U.S.A. 80 C4 45 31N 100 2W
Selçuk, Turkey 21 F12 37 56N 27 22 E
Selden, U.S.A. 80 F4 39 33N 100 34W
Sele →, Italy 20 D6 40 29N 14 56 E
Selebi-Pikwe, Botswana 57 C4 21 58S 27 48 E
Selemdzha →, Russia 27 D13 51 42N 128 53 E
Selenga = Selenge Mörön →, Asia 32 A5 52 16N 106 16 E
Selenge Mörön →, Asia 32 A5 52 16N 106 16 E
Seletan, Tanjung, Indonesia 36 E4 4 10S 114 40 E
Sélibabi, Mauritania 50 E3 15 10N 12 15W
Seligman, U.S.A. 83 J7 35 20N 112 53W
Selîma, El Wâhât el, Sudan 51 D11 21 22N 29 19 E
Selinda Spillway →, Botswana 56 B3 18 35S 23 10 E
Selinsgrove, U.S.A. 78 F8 40 48N 76 52W
Selkirk, Canada 73 C9 50 10N 96 55W
Selkirk, U.K. 12 F6 55 33N 2 50W
Selkirk I., Canada 73 C9 53 20N 99 6W
Selkirk Mts., Canada 68 C8 51 15N 117 40W
Selliá, Greece 23 D6 35 12N 24 23 E
Sells, U.S.A. 83 L8 31 55N 111 53W
Selma, Ala., U.S.A. 77 J2 32 25N 87 1W
Selma, Calif., U.S.A. 84 J7 36 34N 119 37W
Selma, N.C., U.S.A. 77 H6 35 32N 78 17W
Selmer, U.S.A. 77 H1 35 10N 88 36W
Selowandoma Falls, Zimbabwe 55 G3 21 15S 31 50 E
Selpele, Indonesia 37 E8 0 1S 130 5 E
Selsey Bill, U.K. 11 G7 50 43N 0 47W
Seltso, Russia 24 D5 53 22N 34 4 E
Selu, Indonesia 37 F8 7 32S 130 55 E
Selva, Argentina 94 B3 29 50S 62 0W
Selvas, Brazil 92 E5 6 30S 67 0W
Selwyn L., Canada 73 B8 60 0N 104 30W
Selwyn Mts., Canada 68 B6 63 0N 130 0W
Selwyn Ra., Australia 62 C3 21 10S 140 0 E
Seman →, Albania 21 D8 40 47N 19 30 E
Semarang, Indonesia 36 F4 7 0S 110 26 E
Sembabule, Uganda 54 C3 0 4S 31 25 E
Semeru, Indonesia 37 H15 8 4S 112 55 E
Semey, Kazakstan 26 D9 50 30N 80 10 E
Seminoe Reservoir, U.S.A. 82 F10 42 9N 106 55W
Seminole, Okla., U.S.A. 81 H6 35 14N 96 41W
Seminole, Tex., U.S.A. 81 J3 32 43N 102 39W
Seminole Draw →, U.S.A. 81 J3 32 27N 102 20W
Semipalatinsk = Semey, Kazakstan 26 D9 50 30N 80 10 E
Semirara Is., Phil. 37 B6 12 0N 121 20 E
Semitau, Indonesia 36 D4 0 29N 111 57 E
Semiyarka, Kazakstan 26 D8 50 55N 78 23 E
Semiyarskoye = Semiyarka, Kazakstan 26 D8 50 55N 78 23 E
Semmering P., Austria 16 E8 47 41N 15 45 E
Semnān, Iran 45 C7 35 40N 53 23 E
Semnān □, Iran 45 C7 36 0N 54 0 E
Semporna, Malaysia 37 D5 4 30N 118 33 E
Semuda, Indonesia 36 E4 2 51S 112 58 E
Sen →, Cambodia 36 B3 13 45N 105 12 E
Senā, Iran 45 D6 28 27N 51 36 E
Sena, Mozam. 55 F4 17 25S 35 0 E
Sena Madureira, Brazil 92 E5 9 5S 68 45W
Senador Pompeu, Brazil 93 E11 5 40S 39 20W
Senanga, Zambia 53 H4 16 7S 23 16 E
Senatobia, U.S.A. 81 H10 34 37N 89 58W
Sencelles, Spain 22 B9 39 39N 2 54 E
Sendai, Kagoshima, Japan 31 J5 31 50N 130 20 E
Sendai, Miyagi, Japan 30 E10 38 15N 140 53 E
Sendai-Wan, Japan 30 E10 38 15N 141 0 E
Sendhwa, India 42 J6 21 41N 75 6 E
Seneca, U.S.A. 77 H4 34 41N 82 57W
Seneca Falls, U.S.A. 79 D8 42 55N 76 48W
Seneca L., U.S.A. 78 D8 42 40N 76 54W
Senecaville L., U.S.A. 78 G3 39 55N 81 25W
Senegal ■, W. Afr. 50 F3 14 30N 14 30W
Sénégal →, W. Afr. 50 E2 15 48N 16 32W
Senegambia, Africa 48 E2 12 45N 12 0W
Senekal, S. Africa 57 D4 28 20S 27 36 E
Senga Hill, Zambia 55 D3 9 19S 31 11 E
Senge Khambab = Indus →, Pakistan 42 G2 24 20N 67 47 E
Sengua →, Zimbabwe 55 F2 17 7S 28 5 E
Senhor-do-Bonfim, Brazil 93 F10 10 30S 40 10W
Senigállia, Italy 20 C5 43 43N 13 13 E
Senj, Croatia 16 F8 45 0N 14 58 E
Senja, Norway 8 B17 69 25N 17 30 E
Senkaku-Shotō, Japan 31 L1 25 45N 124 0 E
Senlis, France 18 B5 49 13N 2 35 E
Senmonorom, Cambodia 38 F6 12 27N 107 12 E
Senneterre, Canada 70 C4 48 25N 77 15W
Seno, Laos 38 D5 16 35N 104 50 E
Sens, France 18 B5 48 11N 3 15 E
Senta, Serbia, Yug. 21 B9 45 55N 20 3 E
Sentani, Indonesia 37 E10 2 36S 140 37 E
Sentery = Lubao, Dem. Rep. of the Congo 54 D2 5 17S 25 42 E
Sentinel, U.S.A. 83 K7 32 52N 113 13W
Seo de Urgel = La Seu d'Urgell, Spain 19 A6 42 22N 1 23 E
Seohara, India 43 E8 29 15N 78 33 E
Seonath →, India 43 J10 21 44N 82 28 E
Seondha, India 43 F8 26 9N 78 48 E
Seoni, India 43 H8 22 5N 79 30 E
Seoni Malwa, India 42 H8 22 27N 77 28 E
Seoul = Sŏul, S. Korea 35 F14 37 31N 126 58 E
Sepīdān, Iran 45 D7 30 20N 52 5 E
Sepo-ri, N. Korea 35 E14 38 57N 127 25 E
Sepone, Laos 38 D6 16 45N 106 13 E
Sept-Îles, Canada 71 B6 50 13N 66 22W
Sequim, U.S.A. 84 B3 48 5N 123 6W
Sequoia Nat. Park, U.S.A. 84 J8 36 30N 118 30W
Seraing, Belgium 15 D5 50 35N 5 32 E
Seraja, Indonesia 39 L7 2 41N 108 35 E
Serakhis →, Cyprus 23 D11 35 13N 32 55 E
Seram, Indonesia 37 E7 3 10S 129 0 E
Seram Sea, Indonesia 37 E7 2 30S 128 30 E
Seranantsara, Madag. 57 B8 18 30S 49 5 E
Serang, Indonesia 37 G12 6 8S 106 10 E
Serasan, Indonesia 39 L7 2 29N 109 4 E
Serbia □, Yugoslavia 21 C9 43 30N 21 0 E
Serdobsk, Russia 24 D7 52 28N 44 10 E
Seremban, Malaysia 39 L3 2 43N 101 53 E
Serengeti Plain, Tanzania 54 C4 2 40S 35 0 E
Serenje, Zambia 55 E3 13 14S 30 15 E
Sereth = Siret →, Romania 17 F14 45 24N 28 1 E
Sergino, Russia 26 C7 62 25N 65 12 E
Sergipe □, Brazil 93 F11 10 30S 37 30W
Sergiyev Posad, Russia 24 C6 56 20N 38 10 E
Seria, Brunei 36 D4 4 37N 114 23 E
Serian, Malaysia 36 D4 1 10N 110 31 E
Seribu, Kepulauan, Indonesia 36 F3 5 36S 106 33 E
Sérifos, Greece 21 F11 37 9N 24 30 E
Sérigny →, Canada 71 A6 56 47N 66 0W
Seringapatam Reef, Australia 60 B3 13 38S 122 5 E
Sermata, Indonesia 37 F7 8 15S 128 50 E
Serov, Russia 24 C11 59 29N 60 35 E
Serowe, Botswana 56 C4 22 25S 26 43 E
Serpentine Lakes, Australia 61 E4 28 30S 129 10 E
Serpukhov, Russia 24 D6 54 55N 37 28 E
Serra do Navio, Brazil 93 C8 0 59N 52 3W
Sérrai, Greece 21 D10 41 5N 23 31 E
Serrezuela, Argentina 94 C2 30 40S 65 20W
Serrinha, Brazil 93 F11 11 39S 39 0W
Sertanópolis, Brazil 95 A5 23 4S 51 2W
Serua, Indonesia 37 F8 6 18S 130 1 E
Serui, Indonesia 37 E9 1 53S 136 10 E
Serule, Botswana 56 C4 21 57S 27 20 E
Ses Salines, Spain 22 B10 39 21N 3 3 E
Sese Is., Uganda 54 C3 0 20S 32 20 E
Sesepe, Indonesia 37 E7 1 30S 127 59 E
Sesfontein, Namibia 56 B1 19 7S 13 39 E
Sesheke, Zambia 56 B3 17 29S 24 13 E
S'Espalmador, Spain 22 C7 38 47N 1 26 E
S'Espardell, Spain 22 C7 38 48N 1 29 E
S'Estanyol, Spain 22 B9 39 22N 2 54 E
Setana, Japan 30 C9 42 26N 139 51 E
Sète, France 18 E5 43 25N 3 42 E
Sete Lagôas, Brazil 93 G10 19 27S 44 16W
Sétif, Algeria 50 A7 36 9N 5 26 E
Seto, Japan 31 G8 35 14N 137 6 E
Setonaikai, Japan 31 G6 34 20N 133 30 E
Settat, Morocco 50 B4 33 0N 7 40W
Setting L., Canada 73 C9 55 0N 98 38W
Settle, U.K. 10 C5 54 5N 2 16W
Settlement Pt., Bahamas 77 M6 26 40N 79 0W
Settlers, S. Africa 57 C4 25 2S 28 30 E
Setúbal, Portugal 19 C1 38 30N 8 58W
Setúbal, B. de, Portugal 19 C1 38 40N 8 56W
Seul, Lac, Canada 70 B1 50 20N 92 30W
Sevan, Ozero = Sevana Lich, Armenia 25 F8 40 30N 45 20 E
Sevana Lich, Armenia 25 F8 40 30N 45 20 E
Sevastopol, Ukraine 25 F5 44 35N 33 30 E
Seven Sisters, Canada 72 C3 54 56N 128 10W
Severn →, Canada 70 A2 56 2N 87 36W
Severn →, U.K. 11 F5 51 35N 2 40W
Severn L., Canada 70 B1 53 54N 90 48W
Severnaya Zemlya, Russia 27 B10 79 0N 100 0 E
Severnyye Uvaly, Russia 24 C8 60 0N 50 0 E
Severo-Kurilsk, Russia 27 D16 50 40N 156 8 E
Severo-Yeniseyskiy, Russia 27 C10 60 22N 93 1 E
Severodvinsk, Russia 24 B6 64 27N 39 58 E
Severomorsk, Russia 24 A5 69 5N 33 27 E
Severouralsk, Russia 24 B10 60 9N 59 57 E
Sevier, U.S.A. 83 G7 38 39N 112 11W
Sevier →, U.S.A. 83 G7 39 4N 113 6W
Sevier Desert, U.S.A. 82 G7 39 40N 112 45W

Sierra Blanca, *U.S.A.* **83 L11** 31 11N 105 22W
Sierra Blanca Peak, *U.S.A.* **83 K11** 33 23N 105 49W
Sierra City, *U.S.A.* **84 F6** 39 34N 120 38W
Sierra Colorada, *Argentina* **96 E3** 40 35S 67 50W
Sierra Gorda, *Chile* **94 A2** 22 50S 69 15W
Sierra Leone ■, *W. Afr.* **50 G3** 9 0N 12 0W
Sierra Madre, *Mexico* **87 D6** 16 0N 93 0W
Sierra Mojada, *Mexico* **86 B4** 27 19N 103 42W
Sierra Nevada, *Spain* **19 D4** 37 3N 3 15W
Sierra Nevada, *U.S.A.* **84 H8** 39 0N 120 30W
Sierra Vista, *U.S.A.* **83 L8** 31 33N 110 18W
Sierraville, *U.S.A.* **84 F6** 39 36N 120 22W
Sifnos, *Greece* **21 F11** 37 0N 24 45 E
Sifton, *Canada* **73 C8** 51 21N 100 8W
Sifton Pass, *Canada* **72 B3** 57 52N 126 15W
Sighetu-Marmaţiei, *Romania* **17 E12** 47 57N 23 52 E
Sighişoara, *Romania* **17 E13** 46 12N 24 50 E
Sigli, *Indonesia* **36 C1** 5 25N 96 0 E
Siglufjörður, *Iceland* **8 C4** 66 12N 18 55W
Signal, *U.S.A.* **85 L13** 34 30N 113 38W
Signal Pk., *U.S.A.* **85 M12** 33 20N 114 2W
Sigsig, *Ecuador* **92 D3** 3 0S 78 50W
Sigüenza, *Spain* **19 B4** 41 3N 2 40W
Siguiri, *Guinea* **50 F4** 11 31N 9 10W
Sigulda, *Latvia* **9 H21** 57 10N 24 55 E
Sihanoukville = Kampong Saom, *Cambodia* **39 G4** 10 38N 103 30 E
Sihora, *India* **43 H9** 23 29N 80 6 E
Siikajoki →, *Finland* **8 D21** 64 50N 24 43 E
Siilinjärvi, *Finland* **8 E22** 63 4N 27 39 E
Sijarira Ra. = Chizarira, *Zimbabwe* **55 F2** 17 36S 27 45 E
Sika, *India* **42 H3** 22 26N 69 47 E
Sikao, *Thailand* **39 J2** 7 34N 99 21 E
Sikar, *India* **42 F6** 27 33N 75 10 E
Sikasso, *Mali* **50 F4** 11 18N 5 35W
Sikeston, *U.S.A.* **81 G10** 36 53N 89 35W
Sikhote Alin, Khrebet, *Russia* **27 E14** 45 0N 136 0 E
Sikhote Alin Ra. = Sikhote Alin, Khrebet, *Russia* **27 E14** 45 0N 136 0 E
Síkinos, *Greece* **21 F11** 36 40N 25 8 E
Sikkani Chief →, *Canada* **72 B4** 57 47N 122 15W
Sikkim □, *India* **41 F16** 27 50N 88 30 E
Sikotu-Ko, *Japan* **30 C10** 42 45N 141 25 E
Sil →, *Spain* **19 A2** 42 27N 7 43W
Silacayoapan, *Mexico* **87 D5** 17 30N 98 9W
Silawad, *India* **42 J6** 21 54N 74 54 E
Silchar, *India* **41 G18** 24 49N 92 48 E
Siler City, *U.S.A.* **77 H6** 35 44N 79 28W
Silesia = Śląsk, *Poland* **16 C9** 51 0N 16 30 E
Silgarhi Doti, *Nepal* **43 E9** 29 15N 81 0 E
Silghat, *India* **41 F18** 26 35N 93 0 E
Silifke, *Turkey* **25 G5** 36 22N 33 58 E
Siliguri = Shiliguri, *India* **41 F16** 26 45N 88 25 E
Siling Co, *China* **32 C3** 31 50N 89 20 E
Silistra, *Bulgaria* **21 B12** 44 6N 27 19 E
Silivri, *Turkey* **21 D13** 41 4N 28 14 E
Siljan, *Sweden* **9 F16** 60 55N 14 45 E
Silkeborg, *Denmark* **9 H13** 56 10N 9 32 E
Silkwood, *Australia* **62 B4** 17 45S 146 2 E
Sillajhuay, Cordillera, *Chile* **92 G5** 19 46S 68 40W
Sillamäe, *Estonia* **9 G22** 59 24N 27 45 E
Silloth, *U.K.* **10 C4** 54 52N 3 23W
Siloam Springs, *U.S.A.* **81 G7** 36 11N 94 32W
Silsbee, *U.S.A.* **81 K7** 30 21N 94 11W
Šilutė, *Lithuania* **9 J19** 55 21N 21 33 E
Silva Porto = Kuito, *Angola* **53 G3** 12 22S 16 55 E
Silvani, *India* **43 H8** 23 18N 78 25 E
Silver City, *U.S.A.* **83 K9** 32 46N 108 17W
Silver Cr. →, *U.S.A.* **82 E4** 43 16N 119 13W
Silver Creek, *U.S.A.* **78 D5** 42 33N 79 10W
Silver L., *U.S.A.* **84 G6** 38 39N 120 6W
Silver Lake, *Calif., U.S.A.* **85 K10** 35 21N 116 7W
Silver Lake, *Oreg., U.S.A.* **82 E3** 43 8N 121 3W
Silverton, *Colo., U.S.A.* **83 H10** 37 49N 107 40W
Silverton, *Tex., U.S.A.* **81 H4** 34 28N 101 19W
Silvies →, *U.S.A.* **82 E4** 43 34N 119 2W
Simaltala, *India* **43 G12** 24 43N 86 33 E
Simanggang = Bandar Sri Aman, *Malaysia* **36 D4** 1 15N 111 32 E
Simard, L., *Canada* **70 C4** 47 40N 78 40W
Simav, *Turkey* **21 E13** 39 4N 28 58 E
Simba, *Tanzania* **54 C4** 2 10S 37 36 E
Simbirsk, *Russia* **24 D8** 54 20N 48 25 E
Simbo, *Tanzania* **54 C2** 4 51S 29 41 E
Simcoe, *Canada* **78 D4** 42 50N 80 20W
Simcoe, L., *Canada* **78 B5** 44 25N 79 20W
Simdega, *India* **43 H11** 22 37N 84 31 E
Simeria, *Romania* **17 F12** 45 51N 23 1 E
Simeulue, *Indonesia* **36 D1** 2 45N 95 45 E
Simferopol, *Ukraine* **25 F5** 44 55N 34 3 E
Sími, *Greece* **21 F12** 36 35N 27 50 E
Simi Valley, *U.S.A.* **85 L8** 34 16N 118 47W
Simikot, *Nepal* **43 E9** 30 0N 81 50 E
Simla, *India* **42 D7** 31 2N 77 9 E
Simmie, *Canada* **73 D7** 49 56N 108 6W
Simmler, *U.S.A.* **85 K7** 35 21N 119 59W
Simojoki →, *Finland* **8 D21** 65 35N 25 1 E
Simojovel, *Mexico* **87 D6** 17 12N 92 38W
Simonette →, *Canada* **72 B5** 55 9N 118 15W
Simonstown, *S. Africa* **56 E2** 34 14S 18 26 E
Simplonpass, *Switz.* **18 C8** 46 15N 8 3 E
Simpson Desert, *Australia* **62 D2** 25 0S 137 0 E
Simpson Pen., *Canada* **69 B11** 68 34N 88 45W
Simpungdong, *N. Korea* **35 D15** 40 56N 129 29 E
Simrishamn, *Sweden* **9 J16** 55 33N 14 22 E
Simsbury, *U.S.A.* **79 E12** 41 53N 72 48W
Simushir, Ostrov, *Russia* **27 E16** 46 50N 152 30 E
Sin Cowe I., *S. China Sea* **36 C4** 9 53N 114 19 E
Sinabang, *Indonesia* **36 D1** 2 30N 96 24 E
Sinadogo, *Somali Rep.* **46 F4** 5 50N 47 0 E
Sinai = Es Sînâ', *Egypt* **47 F3** 29 0N 34 0 E
Sinai, Mt. = Mûsa, Gebel, *Egypt* **44 D2** 28 33N 33 59 E
Sinai Peninsula, *Egypt* **47 F3** 29 30N 34 0 E
Sinaloa □, *Mexico* **86 C3** 25 0N 107 30W
Sinaloa de Leyva, *Mexico* **86 B3** 25 50N 108 20W
Sinarádhes, *Greece* **23 A3** 39 34N 19 51 E
Sincelejo, *Colombia* **92 B3** 9 18N 75 24W
Sinch'ang, *N. Korea* **35 D15** 40 7N 128 28 E
Sinchang-ni, *N. Korea* **35 E14** 39 24N 126 8 E
Sinclair, *U.S.A.* **82 F10** 41 47N 107 7W
Sinclair Mills, *Canada* **72 C4** 54 5N 121 40W
Sinclair's B., *U.K.* **12 C5** 58 31N 3 5W
Sinclairville, *U.S.A.* **78 D5** 42 16N 79 16W
Sincorá, Serra do, *Brazil* **93 F10** 13 30S 41 0W
Sind, *Pakistan* **42 G3** 26 0N 68 30 E
Sind □, *Pakistan* **42 G3** 26 0N 69 0 E
Sind →, *Jammu & Kashmir, India* **43 B6** 34 18N 74 45 E
Sind →, *Mad. P., India* **43 F8** 26 26N 79 13 E
Sind Sagar Doab, *Pakistan* **42 D4** 32 0N 71 30 E
Sindangan, *Phil.* **37 C6** 8 10N 123 5 E
Sindangbarang, *Indonesia* **37 G12** 7 27S 107 1 E
Sinde, *Zambia* **55 F2** 17 28S 25 51 E
Sindh = Sind □, *Pakistan* **42 G3** 26 0N 69 0 E
Sindri, *India* **43 H12** 23 45N 86 42 E
Sines, *Portugal* **19 D1** 37 56N 8 51W
Sines, C. de, *Portugal* **19 D1** 37 58N 8 53W
Sineu, *Spain* **22 B10** 39 38N 3 1 E
Sing Buri, *Thailand* **38 E3** 14 53N 100 25 E
Singa, *Sudan* **51 F12** 13 10N 33 57 E
Singapore ■, *Asia* **39 M4** 1 17N 103 51 E
Singapore, Straits of, *Asia* **39 M5** 1 15N 104 0 E
Singaraja, *Indonesia* **36 F5** 8 7S 115 6 E
Singida, *Tanzania* **54 C3** 4 49S 34 48 E
Singida □, *Tanzania* **54 D3** 6 0S 34 30 E
Singitikós Kólpos, *Greece* **21 D11** 40 6N 24 0 E
Singkaling Hkamti, *Burma* **41 G19** 26 0N 95 39 E
Singkang, *Indonesia* **37 E6** 4 8S 120 1 E
Singkawang, *Indonesia* **36 D3** 1 0N 108 57 E
Singkep, *Indonesia* **36 E2** 0 30S 104 25 E
Singleton, *Australia* **63 E5** 32 33S 151 0 E
Singleton, Mt., *N. Terr., Australia* **60 D5** 22 0S 130 46 E
Singleton, Mt., *W. Austral., Australia* **61 E2** 29 27S 117 15 E
Singoli, *India* **42 G6** 25 0N 75 22 E
Singora = Songkhla, *Thailand* **39 J3** 7 13N 100 37 E
Singosan, *N. Korea* **35 E14** 38 52N 127 25 E
Sinhung, *N. Korea* **35 D14** 40 11N 127 34 E
Sinjai, *Indonesia* **37 F6** 5 7S 120 20 E
Sinjār, *Iraq* **44 B4** 36 19N 41 52 E
Sinkat, *Sudan* **51 E13** 18 55N 36 49 E
Sinkiang Uighur = Xinjiang Uygur Zizhiqu □, *China* **32 C3** 42 0N 86 0 E
Sinmak, *N. Korea* **35 E14** 38 25N 126 14 E
Sinnamary, *Fr. Guiana* **93 B8** 5 25N 53 0W
Sinni →, *Italy* **20 D7** 40 8N 16 41 E
Sinop, *Turkey* **25 F6** 42 1N 35 11 E
Sinor, *India* **42 J5** 21 55N 73 20 E
Sinp'o, *N. Korea* **35 E15** 40 0N 128 13 E
Sinsk, *Russia* **27 C13** 61 8N 126 48 E
Sintang, *Indonesia* **36 D4** 0 5N 111 35 E
Sinton, *U.S.A.* **81 L6** 28 2N 97 31W
Sintra, *Portugal* **19 C1** 38 47N 9 25W
Sinŭiju, *N. Korea* **35 D13** 40 5N 124 24 E
Siocon, *Phil.* **37 C6** 7 40N 122 10 E
Siófok, *Hungary* **17 E10** 46 54N 18 3 E
Sion, *Switz.* **18 C7** 46 14N 7 20 E
Sion Mills, *U.K.* **13 B4** 54 48N 7 29W
Sioux City, *U.S.A.* **80 D6** 42 30N 96 24W
Sioux Falls, *U.S.A.* **80 D6** 43 33N 96 44W
Sioux Lookout, *Canada* **70 B1** 50 10N 91 50W
Sioux Narrows, *Canada* **73 D10** 49 25N 94 10W
Siping, *China* **35 C13** 43 8N 124 21 E
Sipiwesk L., *Canada* **73 B9** 55 5N 97 35W
Sipra →, *India* **42 H6** 23 55N 75 28 E
Sipura, *Indonesia* **36 E1** 2 18S 99 40 E
Siquia →, *Nic.* **88 D3** 12 10N 84 20W
Siquijor, *Phil.* **37 C6** 9 12N 123 35 E
Siquirres, *Costa Rica* **88 D3** 10 6N 83 30W
Şīr Banī Yās, *U.A.E.* **45 E7** 24 19N 52 37 E
Sir Edward Pellew Group, *Australia* **62 B2** 15 40S 137 10 E
Sir Graham Moore Is., *Australia* **60 B4** 13 53S 126 34 E
Sir James MacBrien, Mt., *Canada* **68 B7** 62 8N 127 40W
Sira →, *Norway* **9 G12** 58 23N 6 34 E
Siracusa, *Italy* **20 F6** 37 4N 15 17 E
Sirajganj, *Bangla.* **43 G13** 24 25N 89 47 E
Sirathu, *India* **43 G9** 25 39N 81 19 E
Sīrdān, *Iran* **45 B6** 36 39N 49 12 E
Sirdaryo = Syrdarya →, *Kazakstan* **26 E7** 46 3N 61 0 E
Siren, *U.S.A.* **80 C8** 45 47N 92 24W
Sirer, *Spain* **22 C7** 38 56N 1 22 E
Siret →, *Romania* **17 F14** 45 24N 28 1 E
Sirghāyā, *Syria* **47 B5** 33 51N 36 8 E
Sirmaur, *India* **43 G9** 24 51N 81 23 E
Sirohi, *India* **42 G5** 24 52N 72 53 E
Sironj, *India* **42 G7** 24 5N 77 39 E
Síros, *Greece* **21 F11** 37 28N 24 57 E
Sirretta Pk., *U.S.A.* **85 K8** 35 56N 118 19W
Sirri, *Iran* **45 E7** 25 55N 54 32 E
Sirsa, *India* **42 E6** 29 33N 75 4 E
Sirsa →, *India* **43 F8** 26 51N 79 4 E
Sisak, *Croatia* **16 F9** 45 30N 16 21 E
Sisaket, *Thailand* **38 E5** 15 8N 104 23 E
Sishen, *S. Africa* **56 D3** 27 47S 22 59 E
Sishui, *Henan, China* **34 G7** 34 48N 113 15 E
Sishui, *Shandong, China* **35 G9** 35 42N 117 18 E
Sisipuk L., *Canada* **73 B8** 55 45N 101 50W
Sisophon, *Cambodia* **38 F4** 13 38N 102 59 E
Sisseton, *U.S.A.* **80 C6** 45 40N 97 3W
Sīstān, *Asia* **45 D9** 30 50N 61 0 E
Sīstān, Daryācheh-ye, *Iran* **45 D9** 31 0N 61 0 E
Sīstān va Balūchestān □, *Iran* **45 E9** 27 0N 62 0 E
Sisters, *U.S.A.* **82 D3** 44 18N 121 33W
Siswa Bazar, *India* **43 F10** 27 9N 83 46 E
Sitamarhi, *India* **43 F11** 26 37N 85 30 E
Sitampiky, *Madag.* **57 B8** 16 41S 46 6 E
Sitapur, *India* **43 F9** 27 38N 80 45 E
Siteki, *Swaziland* **57 D5** 26 32S 31 58 E
Sitges, *Spain* **19 B6** 41 17N 1 47 E
Sitía, *Greece* **23 D8** 35 13N 26 6 E
Sitka, *U.S.A.* **72 B1** 57 3N 135 20W
Sitoti, *Botswana* **56 C3** 23 15S 23 40 E
Sittang Myit →, *Burma* **41 L20** 17 20N 96 45 E
Sittard, *Neths.* **15 C5** 51 0N 5 52 E
Sittingbourne, *U.K.* **11 F8** 51 21N 0 45 E
Sittoung = Sittang Myit →, *Burma* **41 L20** 17 20N 96 45 E
Sittwe, *Burma* **41 J18** 20 18N 92 45 E
Situbondo, *Indonesia* **37 G16** 7 45S 114 0 E
Siuna, *Nic.* **88 D3** 13 37N 84 45W
Siuri, *India* **43 H12** 23 50N 87 34 E
Sīvand, *Iran* **45 D7** 30 5N 52 55 E
Sivas, *Turkey* **25 G6** 39 43N 36 58 E
Siverek, *Turkey* **44 B3** 37 50N 39 19 E
Sivomaskinskiy, *Russia* **24 A11** 66 40N 62 35 E
Sivrihisar, *Turkey* **25 G5** 39 30N 31 35 E
Sîwa, *Egypt* **51 C11** 29 11N 25 31 E
Sîwa, El Wâhât es, *Egypt* **48 D6** 29 10N 25 30 E
Siwa Oasis = Sîwa, El Wâhât es, *Egypt* **48 D6** 29 10N 25 30 E
Siwalik Range, *Nepal* **43 F10** 28 0N 83 0 E
Siwan, *India* **43 F11** 26 13N 84 21 E
Siwana, *India* **42 G5** 25 38N 72 25 E
Sixmilebridge, *Ireland* **13 D3** 52 44N 8 46W
Sixth Cataract, *Sudan* **51 E12** 16 20N 32 42 E
Siziwang Qi, *China* **34 D6** 41 25N 111 40 E
Sjælland, *Denmark* **9 J14** 55 30N 11 30 E
Sjumen = Shumen, *Bulgaria* **21 C12** 43 18N 26 55 E
Skadarsko Jezero, *Montenegro, Yug.* **21 C8** 42 10N 19 20 E
Skaftafell, *Iceland* **8 D5** 64 1N 17 0W
Skagafjörður, *Iceland* **8 D4** 65 54N 19 35W
Skagastølstindane, *Norway* **9 F12** 61 28N 7 52 E
Skagaströnd, *Iceland* **8 D3** 65 50N 20 19W
Skagen, *Denmark* **9 H14** 57 43N 10 35 E
Skagerrak, *Denmark* **9 H13** 57 30N 9 0 E
Skagit →, *U.S.A.* **84 B4** 48 23N 122 22W
Skagway, *U.S.A.* **68 C6** 59 28N 135 19W
Skala-Podilska, *Ukraine* **17 D14** 48 50N 26 15 E
Skala Podolskaya = Skala-Podilska, *Ukraine* **17 D14** 48 50N 26 15 E
Skalat, *Ukraine* **17 D13** 49 23N 25 55 E
Skåne, *Sweden* **9 J15** 55 59N 13 30 E
Skaneateles, *U.S.A.* **79 D8** 42 57N 76 26W
Skaneateles L., *U.S.A.* **79 D8** 42 51N 76 22W
Skara, *Sweden* **9 G15** 58 25N 13 30 E
Skardu, *Pakistan* **43 B6** 35 20N 75 44 E
Skarżysko-Kamienna, *Poland* **17 C11** 51 7N 20 52 E
Skeena →, *Canada* **72 C2** 54 9N 130 5W
Skeena Mts., *Canada* **72 B3** 56 40N 128 30W
Skegness, *U.K.* **10 D8** 53 9N 0 20 E
Skeldon, *Guyana* **92 B7** 5 55N 57 20W
Skellefte älv →, *Sweden* **8 D19** 64 45N 21 10 E
Skellefteå, *Sweden* **8 D19** 64 45N 20 50 E
Skelleftehamn, *Sweden* **8 D19** 64 40N 21 9 E
Skerries, The, *U.K.* **10 D3** 53 25N 4 36W
Ski, *Norway* **9 G14** 59 43N 10 52 E
Skíathos, *Greece* **21 E10** 39 12N 23 30 E
Skibbereen, *Ireland* **13 E2** 51 33N 9 16W
Skiddaw, *U.K.* **10 C4** 54 39N 3 9W
Skidegate, *Canada* **72 C2** 53 15N 132 1W
Skien, *Norway* **9 G13** 59 12N 9 35 E
Skierniewice, *Poland* **17 C11** 51 58N 20 10 E
Skikda, *Algeria* **50 A7** 36 50N 6 58 E
Skilloura, *Cyprus* **23 D12** 35 14N 33 10 E
Skipton, *U.K.* **10 D5** 53 58N 2 3W
Skirmish Pt., *Australia* **62 A1** 11 59S 134 17 E
Skíros, *Greece* **21 E11** 38 55N 24 34 E
Skive, *Denmark* **9 H13** 56 33N 9 2 E
Skjálfandafljót →, *Iceland* **8 D5** 65 59N 17 25W
Skjálfandi, *Iceland* **8 C5** 66 5N 17 30W
Skoghall, *Sweden* **9 G15** 59 20N 13 30 E
Skole, *Ukraine* **17 D12** 49 3N 23 30 E
Skópelos, *Greece* **21 E10** 39 9N 23 47 E
Skopi, *Greece* **23 D8** 35 11N 26 2 E
Skopje, *Macedonia* **21 C9** 42 1N 21 26 E
Skövde, *Sweden* **9 G15** 58 24N 13 50 E
Skovorodino, *Russia* **27 D13** 54 0N 124 0 E
Skowhegan, *U.S.A.* **77 C11** 44 46N 69 43W
Skull, *Ireland* **13 E2** 51 32N 9 34W
Skunk →, *U.S.A.* **80 E9** 40 42N 91 7W
Skuodas, *Lithuania* **9 H19** 56 16N 21 33 E
Skvyra, *Ukraine* **17 D15** 49 44N 29 40 E
Skye, *U.K.* **12 D2** 57 15N 6 10W
Skykomish, *U.S.A.* **82 C3** 47 42N 121 22W
Skyros = Skíros, *Greece* **21 E11** 38 55N 24 34 E
Slættaratindur, *Færoe Is.* **8 E9** 62 18N 7 1W
Slagelse, *Denmark* **9 J14** 55 23N 11 19 E
Slamet, *Indonesia* **37 G13** 7 16S 109 8 E
Slaney →, *Ireland* **13 D5** 52 26N 6 33W
Slangberge, *S. Africa* **56 E3** 31 32S 20 48 E
Śląsk, *Poland* **16 C9** 51 0N 16 30 E
Slate Is., *Canada* **70 C2** 48 40N 87 0W
Slatina, *Romania* **17 F13** 44 28N 24 22 E
Slatington, *U.S.A.* **79 F9** 40 45N 75 37W
Slaton, *U.S.A.* **81 J4** 33 26N 101 39W
Slave →, *Canada* **72 A6** 61 18N 113 39W
Slave Coast, *W. Afr.* **50 G6** 6 0N 2 30 E
Slave Lake, *Canada* **72 B6** 55 17N 114 43W
Slave Pt., *Canada* **72 A5** 61 11N 115 56W
Slavgorod, *Russia* **26 D8** 53 1N 78 37 E
Slavonski Brod, *Croatia* **21 B8** 45 11N 18 1 E
Slavuta, *Ukraine* **17 C14** 50 15N 27 2 E
Slavyanka, *Russia* **30 C5** 42 53N 131 21 E
Slavyansk = Slovyansk, *Ukraine* **25 E6** 48 55N 37 36 E
Slawharad, *Belarus* **17 B16** 53 27N 31 0 E
Sleaford, *U.K.* **10 D7** 53 0N 0 24W
Sleaford B., *Australia* **63 E2** 34 55S 135 45 E
Sleat, Sd. of, *U.K.* **12 D3** 57 5N 5 47W
Sleeper Is., *Canada* **69 C11** 58 30N 81 0W
Sleepy Eye, *U.S.A.* **80 C7** 44 18N 94 43W
Slemon L., *Canada* **72 A5** 63 13N 116 4W
Slide Mt., *U.S.A.* **79 E10** 42 0N 74 25W
Slidell, *U.S.A.* **81 K10** 30 17N 89 47W
Sliema, *Malta* **23 D2** 35 55N 14 30 E
Slieve Aughty, *Ireland* **13 C3** 53 4N 8 30W
Slieve Bloom, *Ireland* **13 C4** 53 4N 7 40W
Slieve Donard, *U.K.* **13 B6** 54 11N 5 55W
Slieve Gamph, *Ireland* **13 B3** 54 6N 9 0W
Slieve Gullion, *U.K.* **13 B5** 54 7N 6 26W
Slieve Mish, *Ireland* **13 D2** 52 12N 9 50W
Slievenamon, *Ireland* **13 D4** 52 25N 7 34W
Sligeach = Sligo, *Ireland* **13 B3** 54 16N 8 28W
Sligo, *Ireland* **13 B3** 54 16N 8 28W
Sligo, *U.S.A.* **78 E5** 41 6N 79 29W
Sligo □, *Ireland* **13 B3** 54 8N 8 42W
Sligo B., *Ireland* **13 B3** 54 18N 8 40W
Slippery Rock, *U.S.A.* **78 E4** 41 3N 80 3W
Slite, *Sweden* **9 H18** 57 42N 18 48 E
Sliven, *Bulgaria* **21 C12** 42 42N 26 19 E
Sloan, *U.S.A.* **85 K11** 35 57N 115 13W
Sloansville, *U.S.A.* **79 D10** 42 45N 74 22W
Slobodskoy, *Russia* **24 C9** 58 40N 50 6 E
Slobozia, *Romania* **17 F14** 44 34N 27 23 E
Slocan, *Canada* **72 D5** 49 48N 117 28W
Slonim, *Belarus* **17 B13** 53 4N 25 19 E
Slough, *U.K.* **11 F7** 51 30N 0 36W
Slough □, *U.K.* **11 F7** 51 30N 0 36W
Sloughhouse, *U.S.A.* **84 G5** 38 26N 121 12W
Slovak Rep. ■, *Europe* **17 D10** 48 30N 20 0 E
Slovakia = Slovak Rep. ■, *Europe* **17 D10** 48 30N 20 0 E
Slovakian Ore Mts. = Slovenské Rudohorie, *Slovak Rep.* **17 D10** 48 45N 20 0 E
Slovenia ■, *Europe* **16 F8** 45 58N 14 30 E
Slovenija = Slovenia ■, *Europe* **16 F8** 45 58N 14 30 E
Slovenské Rudohorie, *Slovak Rep.* **17 D10** 48 45N 20 0 E
Slovyansk, *Ukraine* **25 E6** 48 55N 37 36 E
Sluch →, *Ukraine* **17 C14** 51 37N 26 38 E
Sluis, *Neths.* **15 C3** 51 18N 3 23 E
Słupsk, *Poland* **17 A9** 54 30N 17 3 E
Slurry, *S. Africa* **56 D4** 25 49S 25 42 E
Slutsk, *Belarus* **17 B14** 53 2N 27 31 E
Slyne Hd., *Ireland* **13 C1** 53 25N 10 10W
Slyudyanka, *Russia* **27 D11** 51 40N 103 40 E
Småland, *Sweden* **9 H16** 57 15N 15 25 E
Smalltree L., *Canada* **73 A8** 61 0N 105 0W
Smallwood Res., *Canada* **71 B7** 54 0N 64 0W
Smarhon, *Belarus* **17 A14** 54 20N 26 24 E
Smartt Syndicate Dam, *S. Africa* **56 E3** 30 45S 23 10 E
Smartville, *U.S.A.* **84 F5** 39 13N 121 18W
Smeaton, *Canada* **73 C8** 53 30N 104 49W
Smederevo, *Serbia, Yug.* **21 B9** 44 40N 20 57 E
Smerwick Harbour, *Ireland* **13 D1** 52 12N 10 23W
Smethport, *U.S.A.* **78 E6** 41 49N 78 27W
Smidovich, *Russia* **27 E14** 48 36N 133 49 E
Smith, *Canada* **72 B6** 55 10N 114 0W
Smith Center, *U.S.A.* **80 F5** 39 47N 98 47W
Smith Sund, *Greenland* **4 B4** 78 30N 74 0W
Smithburne →, *Australia* **62 B3** 17 3S 140 57 E
Smithers, *Canada* **72 C3** 54 45N 127 10W
Smithfield, *S. Africa* **57 E4** 30 9S 26 30 E
Smithfield, *N.C., U.S.A.* **77 H6** 35 31N 78 21W
Smithfield, *Utah, U.S.A.* **82 F8** 41 50N 111 50W
Smiths Falls, *Canada* **79 B9** 44 55N 76 0W
Smithton, *Australia* **62 G4** 40 53S 145 6 E
Smithville, *Canada* **78 C5** 43 6N 79 33W
Smithville, *U.S.A.* **81 K6** 30 1N 97 10W
Smoky →, *Canada* **72 B5** 56 10N 117 21W
Smoky Bay, *Australia* **63 E1** 32 22S 134 13 E
Smoky Hill →, *U.S.A.* **80 F6** 39 4N 96 48W
Smoky Hills, *U.S.A.* **80 F5** 39 15N 99 30W
Smoky Lake, *Canada* **72 C6** 54 10N 112 30W
Smøla, *Norway* **8 E13** 63 23N 8 3 E
Smolensk, *Russia* **24 D5** 54 45N 32 5 E
Smolikas, Óros, *Greece* **21 D9** 40 9N 20 58 E
Smolyan, *Bulgaria* **21 D11** 41 36N 24 38 E
Smooth Rock Falls, *Canada* **70 C3** 49 17N 81 37W
Smoothstone L., *Canada* **73 C7** 54 40N 106 50W
Smorgon = Smarhon, *Belarus* **17 A14** 54 20N 26 24 E
Smyrna = İzmir, *Turkey* **21 E12** 38 25N 27 8 E
Smyrna, *U.S.A.* **76 F8** 39 18N 75 36W
Snæfell, *Iceland* **8 D6** 64 48N 15 34W
Snaefell, *U.K.* **10 C3** 54 16N 4 27W
Snæfellsjökull, *Iceland* **8 D2** 64 49N 23 46W
Snake →, *U.S.A.* **82 C4** 46 12N 119 2W
Snake I., *Australia* **63 F4** 38 47S 146 33 E
Snake Range, *U.S.A.* **82 G6** 39 0N 114 20W
Snake River Plain, *U.S.A.* **82 E7** 42 50N 114 0W
Snåsavatnet, *Norway* **8 D14** 64 12N 12 0 E
Sneek, *Neths.* **15 A5** 53 2N 5 40 E
Sneeuberge, *S. Africa* **56 E3** 31 46S 24 20 E
Snelling, *U.S.A.* **84 H6** 37 31N 120 26W
Sněžka, *Europe* **16 C8** 50 41N 15 50 E
Snizort, L., *U.K.* **12 D2** 57 33N 6 28W
Snøhetta, *Norway* **9 E13** 62 19N 9 16 E
Snohomish, *U.S.A.* **84 C4** 47 55N 122 6W
Snoul, *Cambodia* **39 F6** 12 4N 106 26 E
Snow Hill, *U.S.A.* **76 F8** 38 11N 75 24W
Snow Lake, *Canada* **73 C8** 54 52N 100 3W
Snow Mt., *Calif., U.S.A.* **84 F4** 39 23N 122 45W
Snow Mt., *Maine, U.S.A.* **79 A14** 45 18N 70 48W
Snow Shoe, *U.S.A.* **78 E7** 41 2N 77 57W
Snowbird L., *Canada* **73 A8** 60 45N 103 0W
Snowdon, *U.K.* **10 D3** 53 4N 4 5W
Snowdrift →, *Canada* **73 A6** 62 24N 110 44W
Snowflake, *U.S.A.* **83 J8** 34 30N 110 5W
Snowshoe Pk., *U.S.A.* **82 B6** 48 13N 115 41W
Snowtown, *Australia* **63 E2** 33 46S 138 14 E
Snowville, *U.S.A.* **82 F7** 41 58N 112 43W
Snowy →, *Australia* **63 F4** 37 46S 148 30 E
Snowy Mt., *U.S.A.* **79 C10** 43 42N 74 23W
Snowy Mts., *Australia* **63 F4** 36 30S 148 20 E
Snug Corner, *Bahamas* **89 B5** 22 33N 73 52W
Snyatyn, *Ukraine* **17 D13** 48 27N 25 38 E
Snyder, *Okla., U.S.A.* **81 H5** 34 40N 98 57W
Snyder, *Tex., U.S.A.* **81 J4** 32 44N 100 55W
Soahanina, *Madag.* **57 B7** 18 42S 44 13 E
Soalala, *Madag.* **57 B8** 16 6S 45 20 E
Soaloka, *Madag.* **57 B8** 18 32S 45 15 E
Soamanonga, *Madag.* **57 C7** 23 52S 44 47 E
Soan →, *Pakistan* **42 C4** 33 1N 71 44 E
Soanierana-Ivongo, *Madag.* **57 B8** 16 55S 49 35 E
Soanindraniny, *Madag.* **57 B8** 19 54S 47 14 E
Soavina, *Madag.* **57 B8** 20 23S 46 56 E
Soavinandriana, *Madag.* **57 B8** 19 9S 46 45 E
Sobat, Nahr →, *Sudan* **51 G12** 9 22N 31 33 E
Sobhapur, *India* **42 H8** 22 47N 78 17 E
Sobradinho, Reprêsa de, *Brazil* **93 E10** 9 30S 42 0 E
Sobral, *Brazil* **93 D10** 3 50S 40 20W
Soc Giang, *Vietnam* **38 A6** 22 54N 106 1 E
Soc Trang, *Vietnam* **39 H5** 9 37N 105 50 E
Socastee, *U.S.A.* **77 J6** 33 41N 79 1W
Soch'e = Shache, *China* **32 C2** 38 20N 77 10 E
Sochi, *Russia* **25 F6** 43 35N 39 40 E
Société, Is. de la, *Pac. Oc.* **65 J12** 17 0S 151 0W
Society Is. = Société, Is. de la, *Pac. Oc.* **65 J12** 17 0S 151 0W
Socompa, Portezuelo de, *Chile* **94 A2** 24 27S 68 18W
Socorro, *N. Mex., U.S.A.* **83 J10** 34 4N 106 54W
Socorro, *Tex., U.S.A.* **83 L10** 31 39N 106 18W
Socorro, I., *Mexico* **86 D2** 18 45N 110 58W
Socotra, *Yemen* **46 E5** 12 30N 54 0 E
Soda L., *U.S.A.* **83 J5** 35 10N 116 4W
Soda Plains, *India* **43 B8** 35 30N 79 0 E
Soda Springs, *U.S.A.* **82 E8** 42 39N 111 36W
Sodankylä, *Finland* **8 C22** 67 29N 26 40 E
Soddy-Daisy, *U.S.A.* **77 H3** 35 17N 85 10W
Söderhamn, *Sweden* **9 F17** 61 18N 17 10 E

T

Tubuai Is., Pac. Oc. 65 K13 25 0S 150 0W
Tuc Trung, Vietnam 39 G6 11 1N 107 12 E
Tucacas, Venezuela 92 A5 10 48N 68 19W
Tuchodi →, Canada 72 B4 58 17N 123 42W
Tuckanarra, Australia 61 E2 27 7S 118 5 E
Tucson, U.S.A. 83 K8 32 13N 110 58W
Tucumán □, Argentina 94 B2 26 48S 66 2W
Tucumcari, U.S.A. 81 H3 35 10N 103 44W
Tucupita, Venezuela 92 B6 9 2N 62 3W
Tucuruí, Brazil 93 D9 3 42S 49 44W
Tucuruí, Reprêsa de, Brazil 93 D9 4 0S 49 30W
Tudela, Spain 19 A5 42 4N 1 39W
Tudmur, Syria 44 C3 34 36N 38 15 E
Tudor, L., Canada 71 A6 55 50N 65 25W
Tugela →, S. Africa 57 D5 29 14S 31 30 E
Tuguegarao, Phil. 37 A6 17 35N 121 42 E
Tugur, Russia 27 D14 53 44N 136 45 E
Tui, Spain 19 A1 42 3N 8 39W
Tuineje, Canary Is. 22 F5 28 19N 14 3W
Tukangbesi, Kepulauan, Indonesia 37 F6 6 0S 124 0 E
Tukarak I., Canada 70 A4 56 15N 78 45W
Tukayyid, Iraq 44 D5 29 47N 45 36 E
Tuktoyaktuk, Canada 68 B6 69 27N 133 2W
Tukums, Latvia 9 H20 56 58N 23 10 E
Tukuyu, Tanzania 55 D3 9 17S 33 35 E
Tula, Hidalgo, Mexico 87 C5 20 5N 99 20W
Tula, Tamaulipas, Mexico 87 C5 23 0N 99 40W
Tula, Russia 24 D6 54 13N 37 38 E
Tulancingo, Mexico 87 C5 20 5N 99 22W
Tulare, U.S.A. 84 J7 36 13N 119 21W
Tulare Lake Bed, U.S.A. 84 K7 36 0N 119 48W
Tularosa, U.S.A. 83 K10 33 5N 106 1W
Tulbagh, S. Africa 56 E2 33 16S 19 6 E
Tulcán, Ecuador 92 C3 0 48N 77 43W
Tulcea, Romania 17 F15 45 13N 28 46 E
Tulchyn, Ukraine 17 D15 48 41N 28 49 E
Tūleh, Iran 45 C7 34 35N 52 33 E
Tulemalu L., Canada 73 A9 62 58N 99 25W
Tuli, Zimbabwe 55 G2 21 58S 29 13 E
Tulia, U.S.A. 81 H4 34 32N 101 46W
Tulita, Canada 68 B7 64 57N 125 30W
Ṭūlkarm, West Bank 47 C4 32 19N 35 2 E
Tulla, Ireland 13 D3 52 53N 8 46W
Tullahoma, U.S.A. 77 H2 35 22N 86 13W
Tullamore, Australia 63 E4 32 39S 147 36 E
Tullamore, Ireland 13 C4 53 16N 7 31W
Tulle, France 18 D4 45 16N 1 46 E
Tullow, Ireland 13 D5 52 49N 6 45W
Tully, Australia 62 B4 17 56S 145 55 E
Tully, U.S.A. 79 D8 42 48N 76 7W
Tulsa, U.S.A. 81 G7 36 10N 95 55W
Tulsequah, Canada 72 B2 58 39N 133 35W
Tulua, Colombia 92 C3 4 6N 76 11W
Tulun, Russia 27 D11 54 32N 100 35 E
Tulungagung, Indonesia 37 H14 8 5S 111 54 E
Tuma →, Nic. 88 D3 13 6N 84 35W
Tumaco, Colombia 92 C3 1 50N 78 45W
Tumatumari, Guyana 92 B7 5 20N 58 55W
Tumba, Sweden 9 G17 59 12N 17 48 E
Tumba, L., Dem. Rep. of the Congo 52 E3 0 50S 18 0 E
Tumbarumba, Australia 63 F4 35 44S 148 0 E
Tumbaya, Argentina 94 A2 23 50S 65 26W
Tumbes, Peru 92 D2 3 37S 80 27W
Tumbwe, Dem. Rep. of the Congo 55 E2 11 25S 27 15 E
Tumby Bay, Australia 63 E2 34 21S 136 8 E
Tumd Youqi, China 34 D6 40 30N 110 30 E
Tumen, China 35 C15 43 0N 129 50 E
Tumen Jiang →, China 35 C16 42 20N 130 35 E
Tumeremo, Venezuela 92 B6 7 18N 61 30W
Tumkur, India 40 N10 13 18N 77 6 E
Tump, Pakistan 40 F3 26 7N 62 16 E
Tumpat, Malaysia 39 J4 6 11N 102 10 E
Tumu, Ghana 50 F5 10 56N 1 56W
Tumucumaque, Serra, Brazil 93 C8 2 0N 55 0W
Tumut, Australia 63 F4 35 16S 148 13 E
Tumwater, U.S.A. 84 C4 47 1N 122 54W
Tuna, India 42 H4 22 59N 70 5 E
Tunas de Zaza, Cuba 88 B4 21 39N 79 34W
Tunbridge Wells = Royal Tunbridge Wells, U.K. 11 F8 51 7N 0 16 E
Tuncurry, Australia 63 E5 32 17S 152 29 E
Tundla, India 42 F8 27 12N 78 17 E
Tunduru, Tanzania 55 E4 11 8S 37 25 E
Tundzha →, Bulgaria 21 C11 41 40N 26 35 E
Tungabhadra →, India 40 M11 15 57N 78 15 E
Tungla, Nic. 88 D3 13 24N 84 21W
Tungsten, Canada 72 A3 61 57N 128 16W
Tunguska, Nizhnyaya →, Russia 27 C9 65 48N 88 4 E
Tunguska, Podkamennaya →, Russia 27 C10 61 50N 90 13 E
Tunica, U.S.A. 81 H9 34 41N 90 23W
Tunis, Tunisia 50 A7 36 50N 10 11 E
Tunisia ■, Africa 50 B6 33 30N 9 10 E
Tunja, Colombia 92 B4 5 33N 73 25W
Tunkhannock, U.S.A. 79 E9 41 32N 75 57W
Tunliu, China 34 F7 36 13N 112 52 E
Tunnsjøen, Norway 8 D15 64 45N 13 25 E
Tunungayualok I., Canada 71 A7 56 0N 61 0W
Tununirusiq = Arctic Bay, Canada 69 A11 73 1N 85 7W
Tunuyán, Argentina 94 C2 33 35S 69 0W
Tunuyán →, Argentina 94 C2 33 33S 67 30W
Tuolumne, U.S.A. 84 H6 37 58N 120 15W
Tuolumne →, U.S.A. 84 H5 37 36N 121 13W
Tūp Āghāj, Iran 44 B5 36 3N 47 50 E
Tupã, Brazil 95 A5 21 57S 50 28W
Tupelo, U.S.A. 77 H1 34 16N 88 43W
Tupinambaranas, Brazil 92 D7 3 0S 58 0W
Tupiza, Bolivia 94 A2 21 30S 65 40W
Tupman, U.S.A. 85 K7 35 18N 119 21W
Tupper, Canada 72 B4 55 32N 120 1W
Tupper Lake, U.S.A. 79 B10 44 14N 74 28W
Tupungato, Cerro, S. Amer. 94 C2 33 15S 69 50W
Tuquan, China 35 B11 45 18N 121 38 E
Túquerres, Colombia 92 C3 1 5N 77 37W
Tura, Russia 27 C11 64 20N 100 17 E
Turabah, Si. Arabia 46 C3 28 20N 43 15 E
Tūrān, Iran 45 C8 35 39N 56 42 E
Turan, Russia 27 D10 51 55N 95 0 E
Ṭurayf, Si. Arabia 44 D3 31 41N 38 39 E
Turda, Romania 17 E12 46 34N 23 47 E
Turek, Poland 17 B10 52 3N 18 30 E
Turen, Venezuela 92 B5 9 17N 69 6W
Turfan = Turpan, China 32 B3 43 58N 89 10 E
Turfan Depression = Turpan Hami, China 28 E12 42 40N 89 25 E
Turgeon →, Canada 70 C4 50 0N 78 56W
Tŭrgovishte, Bulgaria 21 C12 43 17N 26 38 E
Turgutlu, Turkey 21 E12 38 30N 27 43 E
Turgwe →, Zimbabwe 57 C5 21 31S 32 15 E
Turia →, Spain 19 C5 39 27N 0 19W
Turiaçu, Brazil 93 D9 1 40S 45 19W
Turiaçu →, Brazil 93 D9 1 36S 45 19W
Turin = Torino, Italy 18 D7 45 3N 7 40 E
Turkana, L., Africa 54 B4 3 30N 36 5 E
Turkestan = Türkistan, Kazakstan 26 E7 43 17N 68 16 E
Turkey ■, Eurasia 25 G6 39 0N 36 0 E
Turkey Creek, Australia 60 C4 17 2S 128 12 E
Türkistan, Kazakstan 26 E7 43 17N 68 16 E
Türkmenbashi, Turkmenistan 25 G9 40 5N 53 5 E
Turkmenistan ■, Asia 26 F6 39 0N 59 0 E
Turks & Caicos Is. ■, W. Indies 89 B5 21 20N 71 20W
Turks Island Passage, W. Indies 89 B5 21 30N 71 30W
Turku, Finland 9 F20 60 30N 22 19 E
Turkwel →, Kenya 54 B4 3 6N 36 6 E
Turlock, U.S.A. 84 H6 37 30N 120 51W
Turnagain →, Canada 72 B3 59 12N 127 35W
Turnagain, C., N.Z. 59 J6 40 28S 176 38 E
Turneffe Is., Belize 87 D7 17 20N 87 50W
Turner, U.S.A. 82 B9 48 51N 108 24W
Turner Pt., Australia 62 A1 11 47S 133 32 E
Turner Valley, Canada 72 C6 50 40N 114 17W
Turners Falls, U.S.A. 79 D12 42 36N 72 33W
Turnhout, Belgium 15 C4 51 19N 4 57 E
Turnor L., Canada 73 B7 56 35N 108 35W
Tŭrnovo = Veliko Tŭrnovo, Bulgaria 21 C11 43 5N 25 41 E
Turnu Măgurele, Romania 17 G13 43 46N 24 56 E
Turnu Roşu, P., Romania 17 F13 45 33N 24 17 E
Turpan, China 32 B3 43 58N 89 10 E
Turpan Hami, China 28 E12 42 40N 89 25 E
Turriff, U.K. 12 D6 57 32N 2 27W
Tursāq, Iraq 44 C5 33 27N 45 47 E
Turtle Head I., Australia 62 A3 10 56S 142 37 E
Turtle L., Canada 73 C7 53 36N 108 38W
Turtle Lake, U.S.A. 80 B4 47 31N 100 53W
Turtleford, Canada 73 C7 53 23N 108 57W
Turukhansk, Russia 27 C9 65 21N 88 5 E
Tuscaloosa, U.S.A. 77 J2 33 12N 87 34W
Tuscany = Toscana □, Italy 20 C4 43 25N 11 0 E
Tuscarawas →, U.S.A. 78 F3 40 24N 81 25W
Tuscarora Mt., U.S.A. 78 F7 40 55N 77 55W
Tuscola, Ill., U.S.A. 76 F1 39 48N 88 17W
Tuscola, Tex., U.S.A. 81 J5 32 12N 99 48W
Tuscumbia, U.S.A. 77 H2 34 44N 87 42W
Tuskegee, U.S.A. 77 J3 32 25N 85 42W
Tustin, U.S.A. 85 M9 33 44N 117 49W
Tuticorin, India 40 Q11 8 50N 78 12 E
Tutóia, Brazil 93 D10 2 45S 42 20W
Tutong, Brunei 36 D4 4 47N 114 40 E
Tutrakan, Bulgaria 21 B12 44 2N 26 40 E
Tuttle Creek L., U.S.A. 80 F6 39 22N 96 40W
Tuttlingen, Germany 16 E5 47 58N 8 48 E
Tutuala, E. Timor 37 F7 8 25S 127 15 E
Tutuila, Amer. Samoa 59 B13 14 19S 170 50W
Tutume, Botswana 53 J5 20 30S 27 5 E
Tututepec, Mexico 87 D5 16 9N 97 38W
Tuva □, Russia 27 D10 51 30N 95 0 E
Tuvalu ■, Pac. Oc. 64 H9 8 0S 178 0 E
Tuxpan, Mexico 87 C5 20 58N 97 23W
Tuxtla Gutiérrez, Mexico 87 D6 16 50N 93 10W
Tuy = Tui, Spain 19 A1 42 3N 8 39W
Tuy An, Vietnam 38 F7 13 17N 109 16 E
Tuy Duc, Vietnam 39 F6 12 15N 107 27 E
Tuy Hoa, Vietnam 38 F7 13 5N 109 10 E
Tuy Phong, Vietnam 39 G7 11 14N 108 43 E
Tuya L., Canada 72 B2 59 7N 130 35W
Tuyen Hoa, Vietnam 38 D6 17 50N 106 10 E
Tuyen Quang, Vietnam 38 B5 21 50N 105 10 E
Tūysarkān, Iran 45 C6 34 33N 48 27 E
Tuz Gölü, Turkey 25 G5 38 42N 33 18 E
Ṭūz Khurmātū, Iraq 44 C5 34 56N 44 38 E
Tuzla, Bos.-H. 21 B8 44 34N 18 41 E
Tver, Russia 24 C6 56 55N 35 55 E
Twain, U.S.A. 84 E5 40 1N 121 3W
Twain Harte, U.S.A. 84 G6 38 2N 120 14W
Tweed, Canada 78 B7 44 29N 77 19W
Tweed →, U.K. 12 F6 55 45N 2 0W
Tweed Heads, Australia 63 D5 28 10S 153 31 E
Tweedsmuir Prov. Park, Canada 72 C3 53 0N 126 20W
Twentynine Palms, U.S.A. 85 L10 34 8N 116 3W
Twillingate, Canada 71 C9 49 42N 54 45W
Twin Bridges, U.S.A. 82 D7 45 33N 112 20W
Twin Falls, Canada 71 B7 53 30N 64 32W
Twin Falls, U.S.A. 82 E6 42 34N 114 28W
Twin Valley, U.S.A. 80 B6 47 16N 96 16W
Twinsburg, U.S.A. 78 E3 41 18N 81 26W
Twitchell Reservoir, U.S.A. 85 L6 34 59N 120 19W
Two Harbors, U.S.A. 80 B9 47 2N 91 40W
Two Hills, Canada 72 C6 53 43N 111 52W
Two Rivers, U.S.A. 76 C2 44 9N 87 34W
Two Rocks, Australia 61 F2 31 30S 115 35 E
Twofold B., Australia 63 F4 37 8S 149 59 E
Tyachiv, Ukraine 17 D12 48 1N 23 35 E
Tychy, Poland 17 C10 50 9N 18 59 E
Tyler, Minn., U.S.A. 80 C6 44 18N 96 8W
Tyler, Tex., U.S.A. 81 J7 32 21N 95 18W
Tynda, Russia 27 D13 55 10N 124 43 E
Tyndall, U.S.A. 80 D6 43 0N 97 50W
Tyne →, U.K. 10 C6 54 59N 1 32W
Tyne & Wear □, U.K. 10 B6 55 6N 1 17W
Tynemouth, U.K. 10 B6 55 1N 1 26W
Tyre = Sūr, Lebanon 47 B4 33 19N 35 16 E
Tyrifjorden, Norway 9 F14 60 2N 10 8 E
Tyrol = Tirol □, Austria 16 E6 47 3N 10 43 E
Tyrone, U.S.A. 78 F6 40 40N 78 14W
Tyrone □, U.K. 13 B4 54 38N 7 11W
Tyrrell →, Australia 63 F3 35 26S 142 51 E
Tyrrell, L., Australia 63 F3 35 20S 142 50 E
Tyrrell L., Canada 73 A7 63 7N 105 27W
Tyrrhenian Sea, Medit. S. 20 E5 40 0N 12 30 E
Tysfjorden, Norway 8 B17 68 7N 16 25 E
Tyulgan, Russia 24 D10 52 22N 56 12 E
Tyumen, Russia 26 D7 57 11N 65 29 E
Tywi →, U.K. 11 F3 51 48N 4 21W
Tywyn, U.K. 11 E3 52 35N 4 5W
Tzaneen, S. Africa 57 C5 23 47S 30 9 E
Tzermiádhes, Greece 23 D7 35 12N 25 29 E
Tzukong = Zigong, China 32 D5 29 15N 104 48 E

U

U Taphao, Thailand 38 F3 12 35N 101 0 E
U.S.A. = United States of America ■, N. Amer. 74 C7 37 0N 96 0W
Uatumã →, Brazil 92 D7 2 26S 57 37W
Uaupés, Brazil 92 D5 0 8S 67 5W
Uaupés →, Brazil 92 C5 0 2N 67 16W
Uaxactún, Guatemala 88 C2 17 25N 89 29W
Ubá, Brazil 95 A7 21 8S 43 0W
Ubaitaba, Brazil 93 F11 14 18S 39 20W
Ubangi = Oubangi →, Dem. Rep. of the Congo 52 E3 0 30S 17 50 E
Ubauro, Pakistan 42 E3 28 15N 69 45 E
Ubayyiḍ, W. al →, Iraq 44 C4 32 34N 43 48 E
Ube, Japan 31 H5 33 56N 131 15 E
Úbeda, Spain 19 C4 38 3N 3 23W
Uberaba, Brazil 93 G9 19 50S 47 55W
Uberlândia, Brazil 93 G9 19 0S 48 20W
Ubolratna Res., Thailand 38 D4 16 45N 102 30 E
Ubombo, S. Africa 57 D5 27 31S 32 4 E
Ubon Ratchathani, Thailand 38 E5 15 15N 104 50 E
Ubondo, Dem. Rep. of the Congo 54 C2 0 55S 25 42 E
Ubort →, Belarus 17 B15 52 6N 28 30 E
Ubundu, Dem. Rep. of the Congo 54 C2 0 22S 25 30 E
Ucayali →, Peru 92 D4 4 30S 73 30W
Uchab, Namibia 56 B2 19 47S 17 42 E
Uchiura-Wan, Japan 30 C10 42 25N 140 40 E
Uchquduq, Uzbekistan 26 E7 41 50N 62 50 E
Uchur →, Russia 27 D14 58 48N 130 35 E
Ucluelet, Canada 72 D3 48 57N 125 32W
Uda →, Russia 27 D14 54 42N 135 14 E
Udagamandalam, India 40 P10 11 30N 76 44 E
Udainagar, India 42 H7 22 33N 76 13 E
Udaipur, India 42 G5 24 36N 73 44 E
Udaipur Garhi, Nepal 43 F12 27 0N 86 35 E
Udala, India 43 J12 21 35N 86 34 E
Uddevalla, Sweden 9 G14 58 21N 11 55 E
Uddjaur, Sweden 8 D17 65 56N 17 49 E
Uden, Neths. 15 C5 51 40N 5 37 E
Udgir, India 40 K10 18 25N 77 5 E
Udhampur, India 43 C6 33 0N 75 5 E
Údine, Italy 20 A5 46 3N 13 14 E
Udmurtia □, Russia 24 C9 57 30N 52 30 E
Udon Thani, Thailand 38 D4 17 29N 102 46 E
Udupi, India 40 N9 13 25N 74 42 E
Udzungwa Range, Tanzania 55 D4 9 30S 35 10 E
Ueda, Japan 31 F9 36 24N 138 16 E
Uedineniya, Os., Russia 4 B12 78 0N 85 0 E
Uele →, Dem. Rep. of the Congo 52 D4 3 45N 24 45 E
Uelen, Russia 27 C19 66 10N 170 0W
Uelzen, Germany 16 B6 52 57N 10 32 E
Ufa, Russia 24 D10 54 45N 55 55 E
Ufa →, Russia 24 D10 54 40N 56 0 E
Ugab →, Namibia 56 C1 20 55S 13 30 E
Ugalla →, Tanzania 54 D3 5 8S 30 42 E
Uganda ■, Africa 54 B3 2 0N 32 0 E
Ugie, S. Africa 57 E4 31 10S 28 13 E
Uglegorsk, Russia 27 E15 49 5N 142 2 E
Ugljan, Croatia 16 F8 44 12N 15 10 E
Uhlenhorst, Namibia 56 C2 23 45S 17 55 E
Uhrichsville, U.S.A. 78 F3 40 24N 81 21W
Uibhist a Deas = South Uist, U.K. 12 D1 57 20N 7 15W
Uibhist a Tuath = North Uist, U.K. 12 D1 57 40N 7 15W
Uig, U.K. 12 D2 57 35N 6 21W
Uíge, Angola 52 F2 7 30S 14 40 E
Uijŏngbu, S. Korea 35 F14 37 48N 127 0 E
Ŭiju, N. Korea 35 D13 40 15N 124 35 E
Uinta Mts., U.S.A. 82 F8 40 45N 110 30W
Uis, Namibia 56 B2 21 8S 14 49 E
Uitenhage, S. Africa 56 E4 33 40S 25 28 E
Uithuizen, Neths. 15 A6 53 24N 6 41 E
Ujh →, India 42 C6 32 10N 75 18 E
Ujhani, India 43 F8 28 0N 79 6 E
Uji-guntō, Japan 31 J4 31 15N 129 25 E
Ujjain, India 42 H6 23 9N 75 43 E
Ujung Pandang, Indonesia 37 F5 5 10S 119 20 E
Uka, Russia 27 D17 57 50N 162 0 E
Ukara I., Tanzania 54 C3 1 50S 33 0 E
Uke-Shima, Japan 31 K4 28 2N 129 14 E
Ukerewe I., Tanzania 54 C3 2 0S 33 0 E
Ukhrul, India 41 G19 25 10N 94 25 E
Ukhta, Russia 24 B9 63 34N 53 41 E
Ukiah, U.S.A. 84 F3 39 9N 123 13W
Ukki Fort, India 43 C7 33 28N 76 54 E
Ukmergė, Lithuania 9 J21 55 15N 24 45 E
Ukraine ■, Europe 25 E5 49 0N 32 0 E
Ukwi, Botswana 56 C3 23 29S 20 30 E
Ulaan-Uul, Mongolia 34 B6 44 13N 111 10 E
Ulaanbaatar, Mongolia 27 E11 47 55N 106 53 E
Ulaangom, Mongolia 32 A4 50 5N 92 10 E
Ulaanjirem, Mongolia 34 B3 45 5N 105 30 E
Ulamba, Dem. Rep. of the Congo 55 D1 9 3S 23 38 E
Ulan Bator = Ulaanbaatar, Mongolia 27 E11 47 55N 106 53 E
Ulan Ude, Russia 27 D11 51 45N 107 40 E
Ulaya, Morogoro, Tanzania 54 D4 7 3S 36 55 E
Ulaya, Tabora, Tanzania 54 C3 4 25S 33 30 E
Ulcinj, Montenegro, Yug. 21 D8 41 58N 19 10 E
Ulco, S. Africa 56 D3 28 21S 24 15 E
Ulefoss, Norway 9 G13 59 17N 9 16 E
Ulhasnagar, India 40 K8 19 15N 73 10 E
Uliastay = Ulyasutay, Mongolia 32 B4 47 56N 97 28 E
Ulladulla, Australia 63 F5 35 21S 150 29 E
Ullapool, U.K. 12 D3 57 54N 5 9W
Ullswater, U.K. 10 C5 54 34N 2 52W
Ullŭng-do, S. Korea 31 F5 37 30N 130 30 E
Ulm, Germany 16 D5 48 23N 9 58 E
Ulmarra, Australia 63 D5 29 37S 153 4 E
Ulonguè, Mozam. 55 E3 14 37S 34 19 E
Ulricehamn, Sweden 9 H15 57 46N 13 26 E
Ulsan, S. Korea 35 G15 35 20N 129 15 E
Ulsta, U.K. 12 A7 60 30N 1 9W
Ulster □, U.K. 13 B5 54 35N 6 30W
Ulubat Gölü, Turkey 21 D13 40 9N 28 35 E
Uludağ, Turkey 21 D13 40 4N 29 13 E
Uluguru Mts., Tanzania 54 D4 7 15S 37 40 E
Ulungur He →, China 32 B3 47 1N 87 24 E
Uluru = Ayers Rock, Australia 61 E5 25 23S 131 5 E
Ulutau, Kazakstan 26 E7 48 39N 67 1 E
Ulva, U.K. 12 E2 56 29N 6 13W
Ulverston, U.K. 10 C4 54 13N 3 5W
Ulverstone, Australia 62 G4 41 11S 146 11 E
Ulya, Russia 27 D15 59 10N 142 0 E
Ulyanovsk = Simbirsk, Russia 24 D8 54 20N 48 25 E
Ulyasutay, Mongolia 32 B4 47 56N 97 28 E
Ulysses, U.S.A. 81 G4 37 35N 101 22W
Umala, Bolivia 92 G5 17 25S 68 5W
Uman, Ukraine 17 D16 48 40N 30 12 E
Umaria, India 41 H12 23 35N 80 50 E
Umarkot, Pakistan 40 G6 25 15N 69 40 E
Umarpada, India 42 J5 21 27N 73 30 E
Umatilla, U.S.A. 82 D4 45 55N 119 21W
Umba, Russia 24 A5 66 42N 34 11 E
Umbagog L., U.S.A. 79 B13 44 46N 71 3W
Umbakumba, Australia 62 A2 13 47S 136 50 E
Umbrella Mts., N.Z. 59 L2 45 35S 169 5 E
Ume älv →, Sweden 8 E19 63 45N 20 20 E
Umeå, Sweden 8 E19 63 45N 20 20 E
Umera, Indonesia 37 E7 0 12S 129 37 E
Umfuli →, Zimbabwe 55 F2 17 30S 29 23 E
Umgusa, Zimbabwe 55 F2 19 29S 27 52 E
Umkomaas, S. Africa 57 E5 30 13S 30 48 E
Umlazi, S. Africa 53 L6 29 59S 30 54 E
Umm ad Daraj, J., Jordan 47 C4 32 18N 35 48 E
Umm al Qaywayn, U.A.E. 45 E7 25 30N 55 35 E
Umm al Qittayn, Jordan 47 C5 32 18N 36 40 E
Umm Bāb, Qatar 45 E6 25 12N 50 48 E
Umm el Fahm, Israel 47 C4 32 31N 35 9 E
Umm Keddada, Sudan 51 F11 13 33N 26 35 E
Umm Lajj, Si. Arabia 44 E3 25 0N 37 23 E
Umm Ruwaba, Sudan 51 F12 12 50N 31 20 E
Umnak I., U.S.A. 68 C3 53 15N 168 20W
Umniati →, Zimbabwe 55 F2 16 49S 28 45 E
Umpqua →, U.S.A. 82 E1 43 40N 124 12W
Umreth, India 42 H5 22 41N 73 4 E
Umtata, S. Africa 57 E4 31 36S 28 49 E
Umuarama, Brazil 95 A5 23 45S 53 20W
Umvukwe Ra., Zimbabwe 55 F3 16 45S 30 45 E
Umzimvubu, S. Africa 57 E4 31 38S 29 33 E
Umzingwane →, Zimbabwe 55 G2 22 12S 29 56 E
Umzinto, S. Africa 57 E5 30 15S 30 45 E
Una, India 42 J4 20 46N 71 8 E
Una →, Bos.-H. 16 F9 45 0N 16 20 E
Unadilla, U.S.A. 79 D9 42 20N 75 19W
Unalakleet, U.S.A. 68 B3 63 52N 160 47W
Unalaska, U.S.A. 68 C3 53 53N 166 32W
Unalaska I., U.S.A. 68 C3 53 35N 166 50W
'Unayzah, Si. Arabia 44 E4 26 6N 43 58 E
'Unāzah, J., Asia 44 C3 32 12N 39 18 E
Uncía, Bolivia 92 G5 18 25S 66 40W
Uncompahgre Peak, U.S.A. 83 G10 38 4N 107 28W
Uncompahgre Plateau, U.S.A. 83 G9 38 20N 108 15W
Underbool, Australia 63 F3 35 10S 141 51 E
Ungarie, Australia 63 E4 33 38S 146 56 E
Ungarra, Australia 63 E2 34 12S 136 2 E
Ungava, Pén. d', Canada 69 C12 60 0N 74 0W
Ungava B., Canada 69 C13 59 30N 67 30W
Ungeny = Ungheni, Moldova 17 E14 47 11N 27 51 E
Unggi, N. Korea 35 C16 42 16N 130 28 E
Ungheni, Moldova 17 E14 47 11N 27 51 E
União da Vitória, Brazil 95 B5 26 13S 51 5W
Unimak I., U.S.A. 68 C3 54 45N 164 0W
Union, Miss., U.S.A. 81 J10 32 34N 89 7W
Union, Mo., U.S.A. 80 F9 38 27N 91 0W
Union, S.C., U.S.A. 77 H5 34 43N 81 37W
Union City, Calif., U.S.A. 84 H4 37 36N 122 1W
Union City, N.J., U.S.A. 79 F10 40 45N 74 2W
Union City, Pa., U.S.A. 78 E5 41 54N 79 51W
Union City, Tenn., U.S.A. 81 G10 36 26N 89 3W
Union Gap, U.S.A. 82 C3 46 33N 120 28W
Union Springs, U.S.A. 77 J3 32 9N 85 43W
Uniondale, S. Africa 56 E3 33 39S 23 7 E
Uniontown, U.S.A. 76 F6 39 54N 79 44W
Unionville, U.S.A. 80 E8 40 29N 93 1W
United Arab Emirates ■, Asia 46 C5 23 50N 54 0 E
United Kingdom ■, Europe 7 E5 53 0N 2 0W
United States of America ■, N. Amer. 74 C7 37 0N 96 0W
Unity, Canada 73 C7 52 30N 109 5W
University Park, U.S.A. 83 K10 32 17N 106 45W
Unjha, India 42 H5 23 46N 72 24 E
Unnao, India 43 F9 26 35N 80 30 E
Unsengedsi →, Zimbabwe 55 F3 15 43S 31 14 E
Unst, U.K. 12 A8 60 44N 0 53W
Unuk →, Canada 72 B2 56 5N 131 3W
Uozu, Japan 31 F8 36 48N 137 24 E
Upata, Venezuela 92 B6 8 1N 62 24W
Upemba, L., Dem. Rep. of the Congo 55 D2 8 30S 26 20 E
Upernavik, Greenland 4 B5 72 49N 56 20W
Upington, S. Africa 56 D3 28 25S 21 15 E
Upleta, India 42 J4 21 46N 70 16 E
'Upolu, Samoa 59 A13 13 58S 172 0W
Upper Alkali L., U.S.A. 82 F3 41 47N 120 8W
Upper Arrow L., Canada 72 C5 50 30N 117 50W
Upper Foster L., Canada 73 B7 56 47N 105 20W
Upper Hutt, N.Z. 59 J5 41 8S 175 5 E
Upper Klamath L., U.S.A. 82 E3 42 25N 121 55W
Upper Lake, U.S.A. 84 F4 39 10N 122 54W
Upper Musquodoboit, Canada 71 C7 45 10N 62 58W
Upper Red L., U.S.A. 80 A7 48 8N 94 45W
Upper Sandusky, U.S.A. 76 E4 40 50N 83 17W
Upper Volta = Burkina Faso ■, Africa 50 F5 12 0N 1 0W
Uppland, Sweden 9 F17 59 59N 17 48 E
Uppsala, Sweden 9 G17 59 53N 17 38 E
Upshi, India 43 C7 33 48N 77 52 E
Upstart, C., Australia 62 B4 19 41S 147 45 E
Upton, U.S.A. 80 C2 44 6N 104 38W
Ur, Iraq 44 D5 30 55N 46 25 E
Urad Qianqi, China 34 D5 40 40N 108 30 E
Urakawa, Japan 30 C11 42 9N 142 47 E

Ural = Zhayyq →, *Kazakstan* **25 E9** 47 0N 51 48 E
Ural, *Australia* **63 E4** 33 21S 146 12 E
Ural Mts. = Uralskie Gory, *Eurasia* **24 C10** 60 0N 59 0 E
Uralla, *Australia* **63 E5** 30 37S 151 29 E
Uralsk = Oral, *Kazakstan* **25 D9** 51 20N 51 20 E
Uralskie Gory, *Eurasia* **24 C10** 60 0N 59 0 E
Urambo, *Tanzania* **54 D3** 5 4S 32 0 E
Urandangi, *Australia* **62 C2** 21 32S 138 14 E
Uranium City, *Canada* **73 B7** 59 34N 108 37W
Uraricoera →, *Brazil* **92 C6** 3 2N 60 30W
Urawa, *Japan* **31 G9** 35 50N 139 40 E
Uray, *Russia* **26 C7** 60 5N 65 15 E
'Uray'irah, *Si. Arabia* **45 E6** 25 57N 48 53 E
Urbana, *Ill., U.S.A.* **76 E1** 40 7N 88 12W
Urbana, *Ohio, U.S.A.* **76 E4** 40 7N 83 45W
Urbino, *Italy* **20 C5** 43 43N 12 38 E
Urbión, Picos de, *Spain* **19 A4** 42 1N 2 52W
Urcos, *Peru* **92 F4** 13 40S 71 38W
Urdinarrain, *Argentina* **94 C4** 32 37S 58 52W
Urdzhar, *Kazakstan* **26 E9** 47 5N 81 38 E
Ure →, *U.K.* **10 C6** 54 5N 1 20W
Ures, *Mexico* **86 B2** 29 30N 110 30W
Urfa = Sanliurfa, *Turkey* **25 G6** 37 12N 38 50 E
Urganch, *Uzbekistan* **26 E7** 41 40N 60 41 E
Urgench = Urganch, *Uzbekistan* **26 E7** 41 40N 60 41 E
Ürgüp, *Turkey* **44 B2** 38 38N 34 56 E
Uri, *India* **43 B6** 34 8N 74 2 E
Uribia, *Colombia* **92 A4** 11 43N 72 16W
Uriondo, *Bolivia* **94 A3** 21 41S 64 41W
Urique, *Mexico* **86 B3** 27 13N 107 55W
Urique →, *Mexico* **86 B3** 26 29N 107 58W
Urk, *Neths.* **15 B5** 52 39N 5 36 E
Urla, *Turkey* **21 E12** 38 20N 26 47 E
Urmia = Orūmīyeh, *Iran* **44 B5** 37 40N 45 0 E
Urmia, L. = Orūmīyeh, Daryācheh-ye, *Iran* **44 B5** 37 50N 45 30 E
Uroševac, *Kosovo, Yug.* **21 C9** 42 23N 21 10 E
Uruaçu, *Brazil* **93 F9** 14 30S 49 10W
Uruapan, *Mexico* **86 D4** 19 30N 102 0W
Urubamba →, *Peru* **92 F4** 10 43S 73 48W
Uruçara, *Brazil* **92 D7** 2 32S 57 45W
Uruçuí, *Brazil* **93 E10** 7 20S 44 28W
Uruguai →, *Brazil* **95 B5** 26 0S 53 30W
Uruguaiana, *Brazil* **94 B4** 29 50S 57 0W
Uruguay ■, *S. Amer.* **94 C4** 32 30S 56 30W
Uruguay →, *S. Amer.* **94 C4** 34 12S 58 18W
Urumchi = Ürümqi, *China* **26 E9** 43 45N 87 45 E
Ürümqi, *China* **26 E9** 43 45N 87 45 E
Urup, Ostrov, *Russia* **27 E16** 46 0N 151 0 E
Usa →, *Russia* **24 A10** 66 16N 59 49 E
Uşak, *Turkey* **25 G4** 38 43N 29 28 E
Usakos, *Namibia* **56 C2** 21 54S 15 31 E
Usedom, *Germany* **16 B8** 53 55N 14 2 E
Useless Loop, *Australia* **61 E1** 26 8S 113 23 E
Ush-Tobe, *Kazakstan* **26 E8** 45 16N 78 0 E
Ushakova, Ostrov, *Russia* **4 A12** 82 0N 80 0 E
Ushant = Ouessant, Î. d', *France* **18 B1** 48 28N 5 6W
Ushashi, *Tanzania* **54 C3** 1 59S 33 57 E
Ushibuka, *Japan* **31 H5** 32 11N 130 1 E
Ushuaia, *Argentina* **96 G3** 54 50S 68 23W
Ushumun, *Russia* **27 D13** 52 47N 126 32 E
Usk, *Canada* **72 C3** 54 38N 128 26W
Usk →, *U.K.* **11 F5** 51 33N 2 58W
Uska, *India* **43 F10** 27 12N 83 7 E
Usman, *Russia* **24 D6** 52 5N 39 48 E
Usoke, *Tanzania* **54 D3** 5 8S 32 24 E
Usolye Sibirskoye, *Russia* **27 D11** 52 48N 103 40 E
Uspallata, P. de, *Argentina* **94 C2** 32 37S 69 22W
Uspenskiy, *Kazakstan* **26 E8** 48 41N 72 43 E
Ussuri →, *Asia* **30 A7** 48 27N 135 0 E
Ussuriysk, *Russia* **27 E14** 43 48N 131 59 E
Ussurka, *Russia* **30 B6** 45 12N 133 31 E
Ust-Aldan = Batamay, *Russia* **27 C13** 63 30N 129 15 E
Ust-Amginskoye = Khandyga, *Russia* **27 C14** 62 42N 135 35 E
Ust-Bolsheretsk, *Russia* **27 D16** 52 50N 156 15 E
Ust-Chaun, *Russia* **27 C18** 68 47N 170 30 E
Ust-Ilimpeya = Yukta, *Russia* **27 C11** 63 26N 105 42 E
Ust-Ilimsk, *Russia* **27 D11** 58 3N 102 39 E
Ust-Ishim, *Russia* **26 D8** 57 45N 71 10 E
Ust-Kamchatsk, *Russia* **27 D17** 56 10N 162 28 E
Ust-Kamenogorsk = Öskemen, *Kazakstan* **26 E9** 50 0N 82 36 E
Ust-Khayryuzovo, *Russia* **27 D16** 57 15N 156 45 E
Ust-Kut, *Russia* **27 D11** 56 50N 105 42 E
Ust-Kuyga, *Russia* **27 B14** 70 1N 135 43 E
Ust-Maya, *Russia* **27 C14** 60 30N 134 28 E
Ust-Mil, *Russia* **27 D14** 59 40N 133 11 E
Ust-Nera, *Russia* **27 C15** 64 35N 143 15 E
Ust-Nyukzha, *Russia* **27 D13** 56 34N 121 37 E
Ust-Olenek, *Russia* **27 B12** 73 0N 120 5 E
Ust-Omchug, *Russia* **27 C15** 61 9N 149 38 E
Ust-Port, *Russia* **26 C9** 69 40N 84 26 E
Ust-Tsilma, *Russia* **24 A9** 65 28N 52 11 E
Ust Urt = Ustyurt Plateau, *Asia* **26 E6** 44 0N 55 0 E
Ust-Usa, *Russia* **24 A10** 66 2N 56 57 E
Ust-Vorkuta, *Russia* **24 A11** 67 24N 64 0 E
Ústí nad Labem, *Czech Rep.* **16 C8** 50 41N 14 3 E
Ustica, *Italy* **20 E5** 38 42N 13 11 E
Ustinov = Izhevsk, *Russia* **24 C9** 56 51N 53 14 E
Ustyurt Plateau, *Asia* **26 E6** 44 0N 55 0 E
Usu, *China* **32 B3** 44 27N 84 40 E
Usuki, *Japan* **31 H5** 33 8N 131 49 E
Usulután, *El Salv.* **88 D2** 13 25N 88 28W
Usumacinta →, *Mexico* **87 D6** 17 0N 91 0W
Usumbura = Bujumbura, *Burundi* **54 C2** 3 16S 29 18 E
Usure, *Tanzania* **54 C3** 4 40S 34 22 E
Usutuo →, *Mozam.* **57 D5** 26 48S 32 7 E
Uta, *Indonesia* **37 E9** 4 33S 136 0 E
Utah □, *U.S.A.* **82 G8** 39 20N 111 30W
Utah L., *U.S.A.* **82 F8** 40 10N 111 58W
Utarni, *India* **42 F4** 26 5N 71 58 E
Utatlan, *Guatemala* **88 C1** 15 2N 91 11W
Ute Creek →, *U.S.A.* **81 H3** 35 21N 103 50W
Utena, *Lithuania* **9 J21** 55 27N 25 40 E
Utete, *Tanzania* **54 D4** 8 0S 38 45 E
Uthai Thani, *Thailand* **38 E3** 15 22N 100 3 E
Uthal, *Pakistan* **42 G2** 25 44N 66 40 E
Utiariti, *Brazil* **92 F7** 13 0S 58 10W
Utica, *N.Y., U.S.A.* **79 C9** 43 6N 75 14W
Utica, *Ohio, U.S.A.* **78 F2** 40 14N 82 27W
Utikuma L., *Canada* **72 B5** 55 50N 115 30W
Utopia, *Australia* **62 C1** 22 14S 134 33 E
Utraula, *India* **43 F10** 27 19N 82 25 E
Utrecht, *Neths.* **15 B5** 52 5N 5 8 E
Utrecht, *S. Africa* **57 D5** 27 38S 30 20 E
Utrecht □, *Neths.* **15 B5** 52 6N 5 7 E
Utrera, *Spain* **19 D3** 37 12N 5 48W
Utsjoki, *Finland* **8 B22** 69 51N 26 59 E
Utsunomiya, *Japan* **31 F9** 36 30N 139 50 E
Uttar Pradesh □, *India* **43 F9** 27 0N 80 0 E
Uttaradit, *Thailand* **38 D3** 17 36N 100 5 E
Uttaranchal □, *India* **43 D8** 30 0N 79 30 E
Uttoxeter, *U.K.* **10 E6** 52 54N 1 52W
Uummannarsuaq = Nunap Isua, *Greenland* **69 C15** 59 48N 43 55W
Uusikaarlepyy, *Finland* **8 E20** 63 32N 22 31 E
Uusikaupunki, *Finland* **9 F19** 60 47N 21 25 E
Uva, *Russia* **24 C9** 56 59N 52 13 E
Uvalde, *U.S.A.* **81 L5** 29 13N 99 47W
Uvat, *Russia* **26 D7** 59 5N 68 50 E
Uvinza, *Tanzania* **54 D3** 5 5S 30 24 E
Uvira, *Dem. Rep. of the Congo* **54 C2** 3 22S 29 3 E
Uvs Nuur, *Mongolia* **32 A4** 50 20N 92 30 E
'Uwairidh, Ḥarrat al, *Si. Arabia* **44 E3** 26 50N 38 0 E
Uwajima, *Japan* **31 H6** 33 10N 132 35 E
Uweinat, Jebel, *Sudan* **51 D10** 21 54N 24 58 E
Uxbridge, *Canada* **78 B5** 44 6N 79 7W
Uxin Qi, *China* **34 E5** 38 50N 109 5 E
Uxmal, *Mexico* **87 C7** 20 22N 89 46W
Üydzin, *Mongolia* **34 B4** 44 9N 107 0 E
Uyo, *Nigeria* **50 G7** 5 1N 7 53 E
Uyûn Mûsa, *Egypt* **47 F1** 29 53N 32 40 E
Uyuni, *Bolivia* **92 H5** 20 28S 66 47W
Uzbekistan ■, *Asia* **26 E7** 41 30N 65 0 E
Uzen, *Kazakstan* **25 F9** 43 29N 52 54 E
Uzen, Mal →, *Kazakstan* **25 E8** 49 4N 49 44 E
Uzerche, *France* **18 D4** 45 25N 1 34 E
Uzh →, *Ukraine* **17 C16** 51 15N 30 12 E
Uzhgorod = Uzhhorod, *Ukraine* **17 D12** 48 36N 22 18 E
Uzhhorod, *Ukraine* **17 D12** 48 36N 22 18 E
Užice, *Serbia, Yug.* **21 C8** 43 55N 19 50 E
Uzunköprü, *Turkey* **21 D12** 41 16N 26 43 E

V

Vaal →, *S. Africa* **56 D3** 29 4S 23 38 E
Vaal Dam, *S. Africa* **57 D4** 27 0S 28 14 E
Vaalwater, *S. Africa* **57 C4** 24 15S 28 8 E
Vaasa, *Finland* **8 E19** 63 6N 21 38 E
Vác, *Hungary* **17 E10** 47 49N 19 10 E
Vacaria, *Brazil* **95 B5** 28 31S 50 52W
Vacaville, *U.S.A.* **84 G5** 38 21N 121 59W
Vach = Vakh →, *Russia* **26 C8** 60 45N 76 45 E
Vache, Î. à, *Haiti* **89 C5** 18 2N 73 35W
Vadnagar, *India* **42 H5** 23 47N 72 40 E
Vadodara, *India* **42 H5** 22 20N 73 10 E
Vadsø, *Norway* **8 A23** 70 3N 29 50 E
Vaduz, *Liech.* **18 C8** 47 8N 9 31 E
Værøy, *Norway* **8 C15** 67 40N 12 40 E
Vágar, *Færoe Is.* **8 E9** 62 5N 7 15W
Vågsfjorden, *Norway* **8 B17** 68 50N 16 50 E
Váh →, *Slovak Rep.* **17 D9** 47 43N 18 7 E
Vahsel B., *Antarctica* **5 D1** 75 0S 35 0W
Váï, *Greece* **23 D8** 35 15N 26 18 E
Vaigach, *Russia* **26 B6** 70 10N 59 0 E
Vail, *U.S.A.* **74 C5** 39 40N 106 20W
Vaisali →, *India* **43 F8** 26 28N 78 53 E
Vakh →, *Russia* **26 C8** 60 45N 76 45 E
Val-d'Or, *Canada* **70 C4** 48 7N 77 47W
Val Marie, *Canada* **73 D7** 49 15N 107 45W
Valahia, *Romania* **17 F13** 44 35N 25 0 E
Valandovo, *Macedonia* **21 D10** 41 19N 22 34 E
Valcheta, *Argentina* **96 E3** 40 40S 66 8W
Valdayskaya Vozvyshennost, *Russia* **24 C5** 57 0N 33 30 E
Valdepeñas, *Spain* **19 C4** 38 43N 3 25W
Valdés, Pen., *Argentina* **96 E4** 42 30S 63 45W
Valdez, *U.S.A.* **68 B5** 61 7N 146 16W
Valdivia, *Chile* **96 D2** 39 50S 73 14W
Valdosta, *U.S.A.* **77 K4** 30 50N 83 17W
Valdres, *Norway* **9 F13** 61 5N 9 5 E
Vale, *U.S.A.* **82 E5** 43 59N 117 15W
Vale of Glamorgan □, *U.K.* **11 F4** 51 28N 3 25W
Valemount, *Canada* **72 C5** 52 50N 119 15W
Valença, *Brazil* **93 F11** 13 20S 39 5W
Valença do Piauí, *Brazil* **93 E10** 6 20S 41 45W
Valence, *France* **18 D6** 44 57N 4 54 E
Valencia, *Spain* **19 C5** 39 27N 0 23W
Valencia, *U.S.A.* **83 J10** 34 48N 106 43W
Valencia, *Venezuela* **92 A5** 10 11N 68 0W
Valencia □, *Spain* **19 C5** 39 20N 0 40W
Valencia, G. de, *Spain* **19 C6** 39 30N 0 20 E
Valencia de Alcántara, *Spain* **19 C2** 39 25N 7 14W
Valencia I., *Ireland* **13 E1** 51 54N 10 22W
Valenciennes, *France* **18 A5** 50 20N 3 34 E
Valentim, Sa. do, *Brazil* **93 E10** 6 0S 43 30W
Valentin, *Russia* **30 C7** 43 8N 134 17 E
Valentine, *U.S.A.* **81 K2** 30 35N 104 30W
Valera, *Venezuela* **92 B4** 9 19N 70 37W
Valga, *Estonia* **9 H22** 57 47N 26 2 E
Valier, *U.S.A.* **82 B7** 48 18N 112 16W
Valjevo, *Serbia, Yug.* **21 B8** 44 18N 19 53 E
Valka, *Latvia* **9 H21** 57 42N 25 57 E
Valkeakoski, *Finland* **9 F20** 61 16N 24 2 E
Valkenswaard, *Neths.* **15 C5** 51 21N 5 29 E
Vall de Uxó = La Vall d'Uixó, *Spain* **19 C5** 39 49N 0 15W
Valladolid, *Mexico* **87 C7** 20 40N 88 11W
Valladolid, *Spain* **19 B3** 41 38N 4 43W
Valldemossa, *Spain* **22 B9** 39 43N 2 37 E
Valle de la Pascua, *Venezuela* **92 B5** 9 13N 66 0W
Valle de las Palmas, *Mexico* **85 N10** 32 20N 116 43W
Valle de Santiago, *Mexico* **86 C4** 20 25N 101 15W
Valle de Suchil, *Mexico* **86 C4** 23 38N 103 55W
Valle de Zaragoza, *Mexico* **86 B3** 27 28N 105 49W
Valle Fértil, Sierra del, *Argentina* **94 C2** 30 20S 68 0W
Valle Hermoso, *Mexico* **87 B5** 25 35N 97 40W
Valledupar, *Colombia* **92 A4** 10 29N 73 15W
Vallehermoso, *Canary Is.* **22 F2** 28 10N 17 15W
Vallejo, *U.S.A.* **84 G4** 38 7N 122 14W
Vallenar, *Chile* **94 B1** 28 30S 70 50W
Valletta, *Malta* **23 D2** 35 54N 14 31 E
Valley Center, *U.S.A.* **85 M9** 33 13N 117 2W
Valley City, *U.S.A.* **80 B6** 46 55N 98 0W
Valley Falls, *Oreg., U.S.A.* **82 E3** 42 29N 120 17W
Valley Falls, *R.I., U.S.A.* **79 E13** 41 54N 71 24W
Valley Springs, *U.S.A.* **84 G6** 38 12N 120 50W
Valley View, *U.S.A.* **79 F8** 40 39N 76 33W
Valley Wells, *U.S.A.* **85 K11** 35 27N 115 46W
Valleyview, *Canada* **72 B5** 55 5N 117 17W
Vallimanca, Arroyo, *Argentina* **94 D4** 35 40S 59 10W
Valls, *Spain* **19 B6** 41 18N 1 15 E
Valmiera, *Latvia* **9 H21** 57 37N 25 29 E
Valognes, *France* **18 B3** 49 30N 1 28W
Valona = Vlorë, *Albania* **21 D8** 40 32N 19 28 E
Valozhyn, *Belarus* **17 A14** 54 3N 26 30 E
Valparaíso, *Chile* **94 C1** 33 2S 71 40W
Valparaíso, *Mexico* **86 C4** 22 50N 103 32W
Valparaiso, *U.S.A.* **76 E2** 41 28N 87 4W
Valparaíso □, *Chile* **94 C1** 33 2S 71 40W
Vals →, *S. Africa* **56 D4** 27 23S 26 30 E
Vals, Tanjung, *Indonesia* **37 F9** 8 26S 137 25 E
Valsad, *India* **40 J8** 20 40N 72 58 E
Valverde, *Canary Is.* **22 G2** 27 48N 17 55W
Valverde del Camino, *Spain* **19 D2** 37 35N 6 47W
Vammala, *Finland* **9 F20** 61 20N 22 54 E
Vámos, *Greece* **23 D6** 35 24N 24 13 E
Van, *Turkey* **25 G7** 38 30N 43 20 E
Van, L. = Van Gölü, *Turkey* **25 G7** 38 30N 43 0 E
Van Alstyne, *U.S.A.* **81 J6** 33 25N 96 35W
Van Blommestein Meer, *Surinam* **93 C7** 4 45N 55 5W
Van Buren, *Canada* **71 C6** 47 10N 67 55W
Van Buren, *Ark., U.S.A.* **81 H7** 35 26N 94 21W
Van Buren, *Maine, U.S.A.* **77 B11** 47 10N 67 58W
Van Buren, *Mo., U.S.A.* **81 G9** 37 0N 91 1W
Van Canh, *Vietnam* **38 F7** 13 37N 109 0 E
Van Diemen, C., *N. Terr., Australia* **60 B5** 11 9S 130 24 E
Van Diemen, C., *Queens., Australia* **62 B2** 16 30S 139 46 E
Van Diemen G., *Australia* **60 B5** 11 45S 132 0 E
Van Gölü, *Turkey* **25 G7** 38 30N 43 0 E
Van Horn, *U.S.A.* **81 K2** 31 3N 104 50W
Van Ninh, *Vietnam* **38 F7** 12 42N 109 14 E
Van Rees, Pegunungan, *Indonesia* **37 E9** 2 35S 138 15 E
Van Wert, *U.S.A.* **76 E3** 40 52N 84 35W
Van Yen, *Vietnam* **38 B5** 21 4N 104 42 E
Vanadzor, *Armenia* **25 F7** 40 48N 44 30 E
Vanavara, *Russia* **27 C11** 60 22N 102 16 E
Vancouver, *Canada* **72 D4** 49 15N 123 10W
Vancouver, *U.S.A.* **84 E4** 45 38N 122 40W
Vancouver, C., *Australia* **61 G2** 35 2S 118 11 E
Vancouver I., *Canada* **72 D3** 49 50N 126 0W
Vandalia, *Ill., U.S.A.* **80 F10** 38 58N 89 6W
Vandalia, *Mo., U.S.A.* **80 F9** 39 19N 91 29W
Vandenburg, *U.S.A.* **85 L6** 34 35N 120 33W
Vanderbijlpark, *S. Africa* **57 D4** 26 42S 27 54 E
Vandergrift, *U.S.A.* **78 F5** 40 36N 79 34W
Vanderhoof, *Canada* **72 C4** 54 0N 124 0W
Vanderkloof Dam, *S. Africa* **56 E3** 30 4S 24 40 E
Vanderlin I., *Australia* **62 B2** 15 44S 137 2 E
Vänern, *Sweden* **9 G15** 58 47N 13 30 E
Vänersborg, *Sweden* **9 G15** 58 26N 12 19 E
Vang Vieng, *Laos* **38 C4** 18 58N 102 32 E
Vanga, *Kenya* **54 C4** 4 35S 39 12 E
Vangaindrano, *Madag.* **57 C8** 23 21S 47 36 E
Vanguard, *Canada* **73 D7** 49 55N 107 20W
Vanino, *Russia* **27 E15** 48 50N 140 5 E
Vanna, *Norway* **8 A18** 70 6N 19 50 E
Vännäs, *Sweden* **8 E18** 63 58N 19 48 E
Vannes, *France* **18 C2** 47 40N 2 47W
Vanrhynsdorp, *S. Africa* **56 E2** 31 36S 18 44 E
Vansbro, *Sweden* **9 F16** 60 32N 14 15 E
Vansittart B., *Australia* **60 B4** 14 3S 126 17 E
Vantaa, *Finland* **9 F21** 60 18N 24 58 E
Vanua Balavu, *Fiji* **59 C9** 17 40S 178 57W
Vanua Levu, *Fiji* **59 C8** 16 33S 179 15 E
Vanuatu ■, *Pac. Oc.* **64 J8** 15 0S 168 0 E
Vanwyksvlei, *S. Africa* **56 E3** 30 18S 21 49 E
Vanzylsrus, *S. Africa* **56 D3** 26 52S 22 4 E
Vapnyarka, *Ukraine* **17 D15** 48 32N 28 45 E
Varanasi, *India* **43 G10** 25 22N 83 0 E
Varangerfjorden, *Norway* **8 A23** 70 3N 29 25 E
Varangerhalvøya, *Norway* **8 A23** 70 25N 29 30 E
Varaždin, *Croatia* **16 E9** 46 20N 16 20 E
Varberg, *Sweden* **9 H15** 57 6N 12 20 E
Vardak □, *Afghan.* **40 B6** 34 0N 68 0 E
Vardar = Axiós →, *Greece* **21 D10** 40 57N 22 35 E
Varde, *Denmark* **9 J13** 55 38N 8 29 E
Vardø, *Norway* **8 A24** 70 23N 31 5 E
Varella, Mui, *Vietnam* **38 F7** 12 54N 109 26 E
Varėna, *Lithuania* **9 J21** 54 12N 24 30 E
Varese, *Italy* **18 D8** 45 48N 8 50 E
Varginha, *Brazil* **95 A6** 21 33S 45 25W
Varillas, *Chile* **94 A1** 24 0S 70 10W
Varkaus, *Finland* **9 E22** 62 19N 27 50 E
Varna, *Bulgaria* **21 C12** 43 13N 27 56 E
Värnamo, *Sweden* **9 H16** 57 10N 14 3 E
Vars, *Canada* **79 A9** 45 21N 75 21W
Varysburg, *U.S.A.* **78 D6** 42 46N 78 19W
Varzaneh, *Iran* **45 C7** 32 25N 52 40 E
Vasa Barris →, *Brazil* **93 F11** 11 10S 37 10W
Vascongadas = País Vasco □, *Spain* **19 A4** 42 50N 2 45W
Vasht = Khāsh, *Iran* **40 E2** 28 15N 61 15 E
Vasilevichi, *Belarus* **17 B15** 52 15N 29 50 E
Vasilkov = Vasylkiv, *Ukraine* **17 C16** 50 7N 30 15 E
Vaslui, *Romania* **17 E14** 46 38N 27 42 E
Vassar, *Canada* **73 D9** 49 10N 95 55W
Vassar, *U.S.A.* **76 D4** 43 22N 83 35W
Västerås, *Sweden* **9 G17** 59 37N 16 38 E
Västerbotten, *Sweden* **8 D18** 64 36N 20 4 E
Västerdalälven →, *Sweden* **9 F16** 60 30N 14 7 E
Västervik, *Sweden* **9 H17** 57 43N 16 33 E
Västmanland, *Sweden* **9 G16** 59 45N 16 20 E
Vasto, *Italy* **20 C6** 42 8N 14 40 E
Vasylkiv, *Ukraine* **17 C16** 50 7N 30 15 E
Vatersay, *U.K.* **12 E1** 56 55N 7 32W
Vatican City ■, *Europe* **20 D5** 41 54N 12 27 E
Vatili, *Cyprus* **23 D12** 35 6N 33 40 E
Vatnajökull, *Iceland* **8 D5** 64 30N 16 48W
Vatoa, *Fiji* **59 D9** 19 50S 178 13W
Vatólakkos, *Greece* **23 D5** 35 27N 23 53 E
Vatoloha, *Madag.* **57 B8** 17 52S 47 48 E
Vatomandry, *Madag.* **57 B8** 19 20S 48 59 E
Vatra-Dornei, *Romania* **17 E13** 47 22N 25 22 E
Vatrak →, *India* **42 H5** 23 9N 73 2 E
Vättern, *Sweden* **9 G16** 58 25N 14 30 E
Vaughn, *Mont., U.S.A.* **82 C8** 47 33N 111 33W
Vaughn, *N. Mex., U.S.A.* **83 J11** 34 36N 105 13W
Vaujours L., *Canada* **70 A5** 55 27N 74 15W
Vaupés = Uaupés →, *Brazil* **92 C5** 0 2N 67 16W
Vaupes □, *Colombia* **92 C4** 1 0N 71 0W
Vauxhall, *Canada* **72 C6** 50 5N 112 9W
Vav, *India* **42 G4** 24 22N 71 31 E
Vavatenina, *Madag.* **57 B8** 17 28S 49 12 E
Vava'u, *Tonga* **59 D12** 18 36S 174 0W
Vawkavysk, *Belarus* **17 B13** 53 9N 24 30 E
Växjö, *Sweden* **9 H16** 56 52N 14 50 E
Vaygach, Ostrov, *Russia* **26 C6** 70 0N 60 0 E
Váyia, Ákra, *Greece* **23 C10** 36 15N 28 11 E
Vechte →, *Neths.* **15 B6** 52 34N 6 6 E
Vedea →, *Romania* **17 G13** 43 42N 25 41 E
Vedia, *Argentina* **94 C3** 34 30S 61 31W
Veendam, *Neths.* **15 A6** 53 5N 6 52 E
Veenendaal, *Neths.* **15 B5** 52 2N 5 34 E
Vefsna →, *Norway* **8 D15** 65 48N 13 10 E
Vega, *Norway* **8 D14** 65 40N 11 55 E
Vega, *U.S.A.* **81 H3** 35 15N 102 26W
Vegreville, *Canada* **72 C6** 53 30N 112 5W
Vejer de la Frontera, *Spain* **19 D3** 36 15N 5 59W
Vejle, *Denmark* **9 J13** 55 43N 9 30 E
Velas, C., *Costa Rica* **88 D2** 10 21N 85 52W
Velasco, Sierra de, *Argentina* **94 B2** 29 20S 67 10W
Velddrif, *S. Africa* **56 E2** 32 42S 18 11 E
Velebit Planina, *Croatia* **16 F8** 44 50N 15 20 E
Veles, *Macedonia* **21 D9** 41 46N 21 47 E
Vélez-Málaga, *Spain* **19 D3** 36 48N 4 5W
Vélez Rubio, *Spain* **19 D4** 37 41N 2 5W
Velhas →, *Brazil* **93 G10** 17 13S 44 49W
Velika Kapela, *Croatia* **16 F8** 45 10N 15 5 E
Velikaya →, *Russia* **24 C4** 57 48N 28 10 E
Velikaya Kema, *Russia* **30 B8** 45 30N 137 12 E
Veliki Ustyug, *Russia* **24 B8** 60 47N 46 20 E
Velikiye Luki, *Russia* **24 C5** 56 25N 30 32 E
Veliko Tŭrnovo, *Bulgaria* **21 C11** 43 5N 25 41 E
Velikonda Range, *India* **40 M11** 14 45N 79 10 E
Velletri, *Italy* **20 D5** 41 41N 12 47 E
Vellore, *India* **40 N11** 12 57N 79 10 E
Velsk, *Russia* **24 B7** 61 10N 42 5 E
Velva, *U.S.A.* **80 A4** 48 4N 100 56W
Venado Tuerto, *Argentina* **94 C3** 33 50S 62 0W
Vendée □, *France* **18 C3** 46 50N 1 35W
Vendôme, *France* **18 C4** 47 47N 1 3 E
Venézia, *Italy* **20 B5** 45 27N 12 21 E
Venézia, G. di, *Italy* **20 B5** 45 15N 13 0 E
Venezuela ■, *S. Amer.* **92 B5** 8 0N 66 0W
Venezuela, G. de, *Venezuela* **92 A4** 11 30N 71 0W
Vengurla, *India* **40 M8** 15 53N 73 45 E
Venice = Venézia, *Italy* **20 B5** 45 27N 12 21 E
Venice, *U.S.A.* **77 M4** 27 6N 82 27W
Venkatapuram, *India* **41 K12** 18 20N 80 30 E
Venlo, *Neths.* **15 C6** 51 22N 6 11 E
Vennesla, *Norway* **9 G12** 58 15N 7 59 E
Venray, *Neths.* **15 C6** 51 31N 6 0 E
Ventana, Punta de la, *Mexico* **86 C3** 24 4N 109 48W
Ventana, Sa. de la, *Argentina* **94 D3** 38 0S 62 30W
Ventersburg, *S. Africa* **56 D4** 28 7S 27 9 E
Venterstad, *S. Africa* **56 E4** 30 47S 25 48 E
Ventnor, *U.K.* **11 G6** 50 36N 1 12W
Ventoténe, *Italy* **20 D5** 40 47N 13 25 E
Ventoux, Mt., *France* **18 D6** 44 10N 5 17 E
Ventspils, *Latvia* **9 H19** 57 25N 21 32 E
Ventuarí →, *Venezuela* **92 C5** 3 58N 67 2W
Ventucopa, *U.S.A.* **85 L7** 34 50N 119 29W
Ventura, *U.S.A.* **85 L7** 34 17N 119 18W
Venus B., *Australia* **63 F4** 38 40S 145 42 E
Vera, *Argentina* **94 B3** 29 30S 60 20W
Vera, *Spain* **19 D5** 37 15N 1 51W
Veracruz, *Mexico* **87 D5** 19 10N 96 10W
Veracruz □, *Mexico* **87 D5** 19 0N 96 15W
Veraval, *India* **42 J4** 20 53N 70 27 E
Verbánia, *Italy* **18 D8** 45 56N 8 33 E
Vercelli, *Italy* **18 D8** 45 19N 8 25 E
Verdalsøra, *Norway* **8 E14** 63 48N 11 30 E
Verde →, *Argentina* **96 E3** 41 56S 65 5W
Verde →, *Goiás, Brazil* **93 G8** 18 1S 50 14W
Verde →, *Mato Grosso do Sul, Brazil* **93 H8** 21 25S 52 20W
Verde →, *Chihuahua, Mexico* **86 B3** 26 29N 107 58W
Verde →, *Oaxaca, Mexico* **87 D5** 15 59N 97 50W
Verde →, *Veracruz, Mexico* **86 C4** 21 10N 102 50W
Verde →, *Paraguay* **94 A4** 23 9S 57 37W
Verde →, *U.S.A.* **74 D4** 33 33N 111 40W
Verde, Cay, *Bahamas* **88 B4** 23 0N 75 5W
Verden, *Germany* **16 B5** 52 55N 9 14 E
Verdi, *U.S.A.* **84 F7** 39 31N 119 59W
Verdun, *France* **18 B6** 49 9N 5 24 E
Vereeniging, *S. Africa* **57 D4** 26 38S 27 57 E
Verga, C., *Guinea* **50 F3** 10 30N 14 10W
Vergara, *Uruguay* **95 C5** 32 56S 53 57W
Vergemont Cr. →, *Australia* **62 C3** 24 16S 143 16 E
Vergennes, *U.S.A.* **79 B11** 44 10N 73 15W
Verín, *Spain* **19 B2** 41 57N 7 27W
Verkhnevilyuysk, *Russia* **27 C13** 63 27N 120 18 E
Verkhniy Baskunchak, *Russia* **25 E8** 48 14N 46 44 E
Verkhoyansk, *Russia* **27 C14** 67 35N 133 25 E
Verkhoyansk Ra. = Verkhoyanskiy Khrebet, *Russia* **27 C13** 66 0N 129 0 E
Verkhoyanskiy Khrebet, *Russia* **27 C13** 66 0N 129 0 E
Vermilion, *Canada* **73 C6** 53 20N 110 50W
Vermilion, *U.S.A.* **78 E2** 41 25N 82 22W
Vermilion →, *Alta., Canada* **73 C6** 53 22N 110 51W
Vermilion →, *Qué., Canada* **70 C5** 47 38N 72 56W
Vermilion, B., *U.S.A.* **81 L9** 29 45N 91 55W
Vermilion Bay, *Canada* **73 D10** 49 51N 93 34W
Vermilion L., *U.S.A.* **80 B8** 47 53N 92 26W
Vermillion, *U.S.A.* **80 D6** 42 47N 96 56W
Vermont □, *U.S.A.* **79 C12** 44 0N 73 0W
Vernal, *U.S.A.* **82 F9** 40 27N 109 32W
Vernalis, *U.S.A.* **84 H5** 37 36N 121 17W
Verner, *Canada* **70 C3** 46 25N 80 8W
Verneukpan, *S. Africa* **56 E3** 30 0S 21 0 E
Vernon, *Canada* **72 C5** 50 20N 119 15W
Vernon, *U.S.A.* **81 H5** 34 9N 99 17W
Vernonia, *U.S.A.* **84 E3** 45 52N 123 11W
Vero Beach, *U.S.A.* **77 M5** 27 38N 80 24W

Véroia, Greece 21 D10 40 34N 22 12 E
Verona, Canada 79 B8 44 29N 76 42W
Verona, Italy 20 B4 45 27N 10 59 E
Verona, U.S.A. 80 D10 42 59N 89 32W
Versailles, France 18 B5 48 48N 2 8 E
Vert, C., Senegal 50 F2 14 45N 17 30W
Verulam, S. Africa 57 D5 29 38S 31 2 E
Verviers, Belgium 15 D5 50 37N 5 52 E
Veselovskoye Vdkhr., Russia 25 E7 46 58N 41 25 E
Vesoul, France 18 C7 47 40N 6 11 E
Vesterålen, Norway 8 B16 68 45N 15 0 E
Vestfjorden, Norway 8 C15 67 55N 14 0 E
Vestmannaeyjar, Iceland 8 E3 63 27N 20 15W
Vestspitsbergen, Svalbard 4 B8 78 40N 17 0 E
Vestvågøy, Norway 8 B15 68 18N 13 50 E
Vesuvio, Italy 20 D6 40 49N 14 26 E
Vesuvius, Mt. = Vesuvio, Italy 20 D6 40 49N 14 26 E
Veszprém, Hungary 17 E9 47 8N 17 57 E
Vetlanda, Sweden 9 H16 57 24N 15 3 E
Vetlugu →, Russia 24 C8 56 36N 46 4 E
Vettore, Mte., Italy 20 C5 42 49N 13 16 E
Veurne, Belgium 15 C2 51 5N 2 40 E
Veys, Iran 45 D6 31 30N 49 0 E
Vezhen, Bulgaria 21 C11 42 50N 24 20 E
Vi Thanh, Vietnam 39 H5 9 42N 105 26 E
Viacha, Bolivia 92 G5 16 39S 68 18W
Viamão, Brazil 95 C5 30 5S 51 0W
Viana, Brazil 93 D10 3 13S 44 55W
Viana do Alentejo, Portugal 19 C2 38 17N 7 59W
Viana do Castelo, Portugal 19 B1 41 42N 8 50W
Vianden, Lux. 15 E6 49 56N 6 12 E
Viangchan = Vientiane, Laos 38 D4 17 58N 102 36 E
Vianópolis, Brazil 93 G9 16 40S 48 35W
Viaréggio, Italy 20 C4 43 52N 10 14 E
Vibo Valéntia, Italy 20 E7 38 40N 16 6 E
Viborg, Denmark 9 H13 56 27N 9 23 E
Vic, Spain 19 B7 41 58N 2 19 E
Vicenza, Italy 20 B4 45 33N 11 33 E
Vich = Vic, Spain 19 B7 41 58N 2 19 E
Vichada →, Colombia 92 C5 4 55N 67 50W
Vichy, France 18 C5 46 9N 3 26 E
Vicksburg, Ariz., U.S.A. 85 M13 33 45N 113 45W
Vicksburg, Miss., U.S.A. 81 J9 32 21N 90 53W
Victor, India 42 J4 21 0N 71 30 E
Victor, U.S.A. 78 D7 42 58N 77 24W
Victor Harbor, Australia 63 F2 35 30S 138 37 E
Victoria = Labuan, Malaysia 36 C5 5 20N 115 14 E
Victoria, Argentina 94 C3 32 40S 60 10W
Victoria, Canada 72 D4 48 30N 123 25W
Victoria, Chile 96 D2 38 13S 72 20W
Victoria, Malta 23 C1 36 3N 14 14 E
Victoria, Kans., U.S.A. 80 F5 38 52N 99 9W
Victoria, Tex., U.S.A. 81 L6 28 48N 97 0W
Victoria □, Australia 63 F3 37 0S 144 0 E
Victoria →, Australia 60 C4 15 10S 129 40 E
Victoria, Grand L., Canada 70 C4 47 31N 77 30W
Victoria, L., Africa 54 C3 1 0S 33 0 E
Victoria, L., Australia 63 E3 33 57S 141 15 E
Victoria, Mt., Burma 41 J18 21 15N 93 55 E
Victoria Beach, Canada 73 C9 50 40N 96 35W
Victoria de Durango = Durango, Mexico 86 C4 24 3N 104 39W
Victoria de las Tunas, Cuba 88 B4 20 58N 76 59W
Victoria Falls, Zimbabwe 55 F2 17 58S 25 52 E
Victoria Harbour, Canada 78 B5 44 45N 79 45W
Victoria I., Canada 68 A8 71 0N 111 0W
Victoria L., Canada 71 C8 48 20N 57 27W
Victoria Ld., Antarctica 5 D11 75 0S 160 0 E
Victoria Nile →, Uganda 54 B3 2 14N 31 26 E
Victoria River, Australia 60 C5 16 25S 131 0 E
Victoria Str., Canada 68 B9 69 30N 100 0W
Victoria West, S. Africa 56 E3 31 25S 23 4 E
Victoriaville, Canada 71 C5 46 4N 71 56W
Victorica, Argentina 94 D2 36 20S 65 30W
Victorville, U.S.A. 85 L9 34 32N 117 18W
Vicuña, Chile 94 C1 30 0S 70 50W
Vicuña Mackenna, Argentina 94 C3 33 53S 64 25W
Vidal, U.S.A. 85 L12 34 7N 114 31W
Vidal Junction, U.S.A. 85 L12 34 11N 114 34W
Vidalia, U.S.A. 77 J4 32 13N 82 25W
Vidho, Greece 23 A3 39 38N 19 55 E
Vidin, Bulgaria 21 C10 43 59N 22 50 E
Vidisha, India 42 H7 23 28N 77 53 E
Vidzy, Belarus 9 J22 55 23N 26 37 E
Viedma, Argentina 96 E4 40 50S 63 0W
Viedma, L., Argentina 96 F2 49 30S 72 30W
Vielsalm, Belgium 15 D5 50 17N 5 54 E
Vieng Pou Kha, Laos 38 B3 20 41N 101 4 E
Vienna = Wien, Austria 16 D9 48 12N 16 22 E
Vienna, Ill., U.S.A. 81 G10 37 25N 88 54W
Vienna, Mo., U.S.A. 80 F9 38 11N 91 57W
Vienne, France 18 D6 45 31N 4 53 E
Vienne →, France 18 C4 47 13N 0 5 E
Vientiane, Laos 38 D4 17 58N 102 36 E
Vientos, Paso de los, Caribbean 89 C5 20 0N 74 0W
Vierzon, France 18 C5 47 13N 2 5 E
Vietnam ■, Asia 38 C6 19 0N 106 0 E
Vigan, Phil. 37 A6 17 35N 120 28 E
Vigévano, Italy 18 D8 45 19N 8 51 E
Vigia, Brazil 93 D9 0 50S 48 5W
Vigía Chico, Mexico 87 D7 19 46N 87 35W
Víglas, Ákra, Greece 23 D9 35 54N 27 51 E
Vigo, Spain 19 A1 42 12N 8 41W
Vihowa, Pakistan 42 D4 31 8N 70 30 E
Vihowa →, Pakistan 42 D4 31 8N 70 41 E
Vijayawada, India 41 L12 16 31N 80 39 E
Vijosë →, Albania 21 D8 40 37N 19 24 E
Vík, Iceland 8 E4 63 25N 19 1W
Vikeke = Viqueque, E. Timor 37 F7 8 52S 126 23 E
Viking, Canada 72 C6 53 7N 111 50W
Vikna, Norway 8 D14 64 55N 10 58 E
Vila da Maganja, Mozam. 55 F4 17 18S 37 30 E
Vila de João Belo = Xai-Xai, Mozam. 57 D5 25 6S 33 31 E
Vila do Bispo, Portugal 19 D1 37 5N 8 53W
Vila Franca de Xira, Portugal 19 C1 38 57N 8 59W
Vila Gamito, Mozam. 55 E3 14 12S 33 0 E
Vila Gomes da Costa, Mozam. 57 C5 24 20S 33 37 E
Vila Machado, Mozam. 55 F3 19 15S 34 14 E
Vila Mouzinho, Mozam. 55 E3 14 48S 34 25 E
Vila Nova de Gaia, Portugal 19 B1 41 8N 8 37W
Vila Real, Portugal 19 B2 41 17N 7 48W
Vila-real de los Infantes, Spain 19 C5 39 55N 0 3W
Vila Real de Santo António, Portugal 19 D2 37 10N 7 28W
Vila Vasco da Gama, Mozam. 55 E3 14 54S 32 14 E
Vila Velha, Brazil 95 A7 20 20S 40 17W
Vilagarcía de Arousa, Spain 19 A1 42 34N 8 46W
Vilaine →, France 18 C2 47 30N 2 27W
Vilanandro, Tanjona, Madag. 57 B7 16 11S 44 27 E
Vilanculos, Mozam. 57 C6 22 1S 35 17 E
Vilanova i la Geltrú, Spain 19 B6 41 13N 1 40 E
Vileyka, Belarus 17 A14 54 30N 26 53 E
Vilhelmina, Sweden 8 D17 64 35N 16 39 E
Vilhena, Brazil 92 F6 12 40S 60 5W
Viliga, Russia 27 C16 61 36N 156 56 E
Viliya →, Lithuania 9 J21 55 8N 24 16 E
Viljandi, Estonia 9 G21 58 28N 25 30 E
Vilkitskogo, Proliv, Russia 27 B11 78 0N 103 0 E
Vilkovo = Vylkove, Ukraine 17 F15 45 28N 29 32 E
Villa Abecia, Bolivia 94 A2 21 0S 68 18W
Villa Ahumada, Mexico 86 A3 30 38N 106 30W
Villa Ana, Argentina 94 B4 28 28S 59 40W
Villa Ángela, Argentina 94 B3 27 34S 60 45W
Villa Bella, Bolivia 92 F5 10 25S 65 22W
Villa Bens = Tarfaya, Morocco 50 C3 27 55N 12 55W
Villa Cañás, Argentina 94 C3 34 0S 61 35W
Villa Cisneros = Dakhla, W. Sahara 50 D2 23 50N 15 53W
Villa Colón, Argentina 94 C2 31 38S 68 20W
Villa Constitución, Argentina 94 C3 33 15S 60 20W
Villa de María, Argentina 94 B3 29 55S 63 43W
Villa Dolores, Argentina 94 C2 31 58S 65 15W
Villa Frontera, Mexico 86 B4 26 56N 101 27W
Villa Guillermina, Argentina 94 B4 28 15S 59 29W
Villa Hayes, Paraguay 94 B4 25 5S 57 20W
Villa Iris, Argentina 94 D3 38 12S 63 12W
Villa Juárez, Mexico 86 B4 27 37N 100 44W
Villa María, Argentina 94 C3 32 20S 63 10W
Villa Mazán, Argentina 94 B2 28 40S 66 30W
Villa Montes, Bolivia 94 A3 21 10S 63 30W
Villa Ocampo, Argentina 94 B4 28 30S 59 20W
Villa Ocampo, Mexico 86 B3 26 29N 105 30W
Villa Ojo de Agua, Argentina 94 B3 29 30S 63 44W
Villa San José, Argentina 94 C4 32 12S 58 15W
Villa San Martín, Argentina 94 B3 28 15S 64 9W
Villa Unión, Mexico 86 C3 23 12N 106 14W
Villacarlos, Spain 22 B11 39 53N 4 17 E
Villacarrillo, Spain 19 C4 38 7N 3 3W
Villach, Austria 16 E7 46 37N 13 51 E
Villafranca de los Caballeros, Spain 22 B10 39 34N 3 25 E
Villagrán, Mexico 87 C5 24 29N 99 29W
Villaguay, Argentina 94 C4 32 0S 59 0W
Villahermosa, Mexico 87 D6 17 59N 92 55W
Villajoyosa, Spain 19 C5 38 30N 0 12W
Villalba, Spain 19 A2 43 26N 7 40W
Villanueva, U.S.A. 81 H2 35 16N 105 22W
Villanueva de la Serena, Spain 19 C3 38 59N 5 50W
Villanueva y Geltrú = Vilanova i la Geltrú, Spain 19 B6 41 13N 1 40 E
Villarreal = Vila-real de los Infantes, Spain 19 C5 39 55N 0 3W
Villarrica, Chile 96 D2 39 15S 72 15W
Villarrica, Paraguay 94 B4 25 40S 56 30W
Villarrobledo, Spain 19 C4 39 18N 2 36W
Villavicencio, Argentina 94 C2 32 28S 69 0W
Villavicencio, Colombia 92 C4 4 9N 73 37W
Villaviciosa, Spain 19 A3 43 32N 5 27W
Villazón, Bolivia 94 A2 22 0S 65 35W
Ville-Marie, Canada 70 C4 47 20N 79 30W
Ville Platte, U.S.A. 81 K8 30 41N 92 17W
Villena, Spain 19 C5 38 39N 0 52W
Villeneuve-d'Ascq, France 18 A5 50 38N 3 9 E
Villeneuve-sur-Lot, France 18 D4 44 24N 0 42 E
Villiers, S. Africa 57 D4 27 2S 28 36 E
Villingen-Schwenningen, Germany 16 D5 48 3N 8 26 E
Vilna, Canada 72 C6 54 7N 111 55W
Vilnius, Lithuania 9 J21 54 38N 25 19 E
Vilvoorde, Belgium 15 D4 50 56N 4 26 E
Vilyuy →, Russia 27 C13 64 24N 126 26 E
Vilyuysk, Russia 27 C13 63 40N 121 35 E
Viña del Mar, Chile 94 C1 33 0S 71 30W
Vinarós, Spain 19 B6 40 30N 0 27 E
Vincennes, U.S.A. 76 F2 38 41N 87 32W
Vincent, U.S.A. 85 L8 34 33N 118 11W
Vinchina, Argentina 94 B2 28 45S 68 15W
Vindelälven →, Sweden 8 E18 63 55N 19 50 E
Vindeln, Sweden 8 D18 64 12N 19 43 E
Vindhya Ra., India 42 H7 22 50N 77 0 E
Vineland, U.S.A. 76 F8 39 29N 75 2W
Vinh, Vietnam 38 C5 18 45N 105 38 E
Vinh Linh, Vietnam 38 D6 17 4N 107 2 E
Vinh Long, Vietnam 39 G5 10 16N 105 57 E
Vinh Yen, Vietnam 38 B5 21 21N 105 35 E
Vinita, U.S.A. 81 G7 36 39N 95 9W
Vinkovci, Croatia 21 B8 45 19N 18 48 E
Vinnitsa = Vinnytsya, Ukraine 17 D15 49 15N 28 30 E
Vinnytsya, Ukraine 17 D15 49 15N 28 30 E
Vinton, Calif., U.S.A. 84 F6 39 48N 120 10W
Vinton, Iowa, U.S.A. 80 D8 42 10N 92 1W
Vinton, La., U.S.A. 81 K8 30 11N 93 35W
Viqueque, E. Timor 37 F7 8 52S 126 23 E
Virac, Phil. 37 B6 13 30N 124 20 E
Virachei, Cambodia 38 F6 13 59N 106 49 E
Virago Sd., Canada 72 C2 54 0N 132 30W
Viramgam, India 42 H5 23 5N 72 0 E
Viranşehir, Turkey 44 B3 37 13N 39 45 E
Virawah, Pakistan 42 G4 24 31N 70 46 E
Virden, Canada 73 D8 49 50N 100 56W
Vire, France 18 B3 48 50N 0 53W
Virgenes, C., Argentina 96 G3 52 19S 68 21W
Virgin →, U.S.A. 83 H6 36 28N 114 21W
Virgin Gorda, Br. Virgin Is. 89 C7 18 30N 64 26W
Virgin Is. (British) ■, W. Indies 89 C7 18 30N 64 30W
Virgin Is. (U.S.) ■, W. Indies 89 C7 18 20N 65 0W
Virginia, S. Africa 56 D4 28 8S 26 55 E
Virginia, U.S.A. 80 B8 47 31N 92 32W
Virginia □, U.S.A. 76 G7 37 30N 78 45W
Virginia Beach, U.S.A. 76 G8 36 51N 75 59W
Virginia City, Mont., U.S.A. 82 D8 45 18N 111 56W
Virginia City, Nev., U.S.A. 84 F7 39 19N 119 39W
Virginia Falls, Canada 72 A3 61 38N 125 42W
Virginiatown, Canada 70 C4 48 9N 79 36W
Viroqua, U.S.A. 80 D9 43 34N 90 53W
Virovitica, Croatia 20 B7 45 51N 17 21 E
Virpur, India 42 J4 21 51N 70 42 E
Virton, Belgium 15 E5 49 35N 5 32 E
Virudunagar, India 40 Q10 9 30N 77 58 E
Vis, Croatia 20 C7 43 4N 16 10 E
Visalia, U.S.A. 84 J7 36 20N 119 18W
Visayan Sea, Phil. 37 B6 11 30N 123 30 E
Visby, Sweden 9 H18 57 37N 18 18 E
Viscount Melville Sd., Canada 4 B2 74 10N 108 0W
Visé, Belgium 15 D5 50 44N 5 41 E
Višegrad, Bos.-H. 21 C8 43 47N 19 17 E
Viseu, Brazil 93 D9 1 10S 46 5W
Viseu, Portugal 19 B2 40 40N 7 55W
Vishakhapatnam, India 41 L13 17 45N 83 20 E
Visnagar, India 42 H5 23 45N 72 32 E
Viso, Mte., Italy 18 D7 44 38N 7 5 E
Visokoi I., Antarctica 5 B1 56 43S 27 15W
Vista, U.S.A. 85 M9 33 12N 117 14W
Vistula = Wisła →, Poland 17 A10 54 22N 18 55 E
Vitebsk = Vitsyebsk, Belarus 24 C5 55 10N 30 15 E
Viterbo, Italy 20 C5 42 25N 12 6 E
Viti Levu, Fiji 59 C7 17 30S 177 30 E
Vitigudino, Spain 19 B2 41 1N 6 26W
Vitim, Russia 27 D12 59 28N 112 35 E
Vitim →, Russia 27 D12 59 26N 112 34 E
Vitória, Brazil 93 H10 20 20S 40 22W
Vitória da Conquista, Brazil 93 F10 14 51S 40 51W
Vitória de São Antão, Brazil 93 E11 8 10S 35 20W
Vitoria-Gasteiz, Spain 19 A4 42 50N 2 41W
Vitsyebsk, Belarus 24 C5 55 10N 30 15 E
Vittória, Italy 20 F6 36 57N 14 32 E
Vittório Véneto, Italy 20 B5 45 59N 12 18 E
Viveiro, Spain 19 A2 43 39N 7 38W
Vivian, U.S.A. 81 J8 32 53N 93 59W
Vizcaíno, Desierto de, Mexico 86 B2 27 40N 113 50W
Vizcaíno, Sierra, Mexico 86 B2 27 30N 114 0W
Vize, Turkey 21 D12 41 34N 27 45 E
Vizianagaram, India 41 K13 18 6N 83 30 E
Vlaardingen, Neths. 15 C4 51 55N 4 21 E
Vladikavkaz, Russia 25 F7 43 0N 44 35 E
Vladimir, Russia 24 C7 56 15N 40 30 E
Vladimir Volynskiy = Volodymyr-Volynskyy, Ukraine 17 C13 50 50N 24 18 E
Vladivostok, Russia 27 E14 43 10N 131 53 E
Vlieland, Neths. 15 A4 53 16N 4 55 E
Vlissingen, Neths. 15 C3 51 26N 3 34 E
Vlorë, Albania 21 D8 40 32N 19 28 E
Vltava →, Czech Rep. 16 D8 50 21N 14 30 E
Vo Dat, Vietnam 39 G6 11 9N 107 31 E
Voe, U.K. 12 A7 60 21N 1 16W
Vogelkop = Doberai, Jazirah, Indonesia 37 E8 1 25S 133 0 E
Vogelsberg, Germany 16 C5 50 31N 9 12 E
Voghera, Italy 18 D8 44 59N 9 1 E
Vohibinany, Madag. 57 B8 18 49S 49 4 E
Vohilava, Madag. 57 C8 21 4S 48 0 E
Vohimarina = Iharana, Madag. 57 A9 13 25S 50 0 E
Vohimena, Tanjon' i, Madag. 57 D8 25 36S 45 8 E
Vohipeno, Madag. 57 C8 22 22S 47 51 E
Voi, Kenya 54 C4 3 25S 38 32 E
Voiron, France 18 D6 45 22N 5 35 E
Voisey B., Canada 71 A7 56 15N 61 50W
Vojmsjön, Sweden 8 D17 64 55N 16 40 E
Vojvodina □, Serbia, Yug. 21 B9 45 20N 20 0 E
Volborg, U.S.A. 80 C2 45 51N 105 41W
Volcano Is. = Kazan-Rettō, Pac. Oc. 64 E6 25 0N 141 0 E
Volda, Norway 9 E12 62 9N 6 5 E
Volga →, Russia 25 E8 46 0N 48 30 E
Volga Hts. = Privolzhskaya Vozvyshennost, Russia 25 D8 51 0N 46 0 E
Volgodonsk, Russia 25 E7 47 33N 42 5 E
Volgograd, Russia 25 E7 48 40N 44 25 E
Volgogradskoye Vdkhr., Russia 25 D8 50 0N 45 20 E
Volkhov →, Russia 24 B5 60 8N 32 20 E
Volkovysk = Vawkavysk, Belarus 17 B13 53 9N 24 30 E
Volksrust, S. Africa 57 D4 27 24S 29 53 E
Volochanka, Russia 27 B10 71 0N 94 28 E
Volodymyr-Volynskyy, Ukraine 17 C13 50 50N 24 18 E
Vologda, Russia 24 C6 59 10N 39 45 E
Vólos, Greece 21 E10 39 24N 22 59 E
Volovets, Ukraine 17 D12 48 43N 23 11 E
Volozhin = Valozhyn, Belarus 17 A14 54 3N 26 30 E
Volsk, Russia 24 D8 52 5N 47 22 E
Volta →, Ghana 48 F4 5 46N 0 41 E
Volta, L., Ghana 50 G6 7 30N 0 0W
Volta Redonda, Brazil 95 A7 22 31S 44 5W
Voltaire, C., Australia 60 B4 14 16S 125 35 E
Volterra, Italy 20 C4 43 24N 10 51 E
Volturno →, Italy 20 D5 41 1N 13 55 E
Volzhskiy, Russia 25 E7 48 56N 44 46 E
Vondrozo, Madag. 57 C8 22 49S 47 20 E
Vopnafjörður, Iceland 8 D6 65 45N 14 50W
Vóriai Sporádhes, Greece 21 E10 39 15N 23 30 E
Vorkuta, Russia 24 A11 67 48N 64 20 E
Vormsi, Estonia 9 G20 59 1N 23 13 E
Voronezh, Russia 25 D6 51 40N 39 10 E
Voroshilovgrad = Luhansk, Ukraine 25 E6 48 38N 39 15 E
Voroshilovsk = Alchevsk, Ukraine 25 E6 48 30N 38 45 E
Võrts Järv, Estonia 9 G22 58 16N 26 3 E
Võru, Estonia 9 H22 57 48N 26 54 E
Vosges, France 18 B7 48 20N 7 10 E
Voss, Norway 9 F12 60 38N 6 26 E
Vostok I., Kiribati 65 J12 10 5S 152 23W
Votkinsk, Russia 24 C9 57 0N 53 55 E
Votkinskoye Vdkhr., Russia 24 C10 57 22N 55 12 E
Votsuri-Shima, Japan 31 M1 25 45N 123 29 E
Vouga →, Portugal 19 B1 40 41N 8 40W
Voúxa, Ákra, Greece 23 D5 35 37N 23 32 E
Vozhe, Ozero, Russia 24 B6 60 45N 39 0 E
Voznesensk, Ukraine 25 E5 47 35N 31 21 E
Voznesenye, Russia 24 B6 61 0N 35 28 E
Vrangelya, Ostrov, Russia 27 B19 71 0N 180 0 E
Vranje, Serbia, Yug. 21 C9 42 34N 21 54 E
Vratsa, Bulgaria 21 C10 43 15N 23 30 E
Vrbas →, Bos.-H. 20 B7 45 8N 17 29 E
Vrede, S. Africa 57 D4 27 24S 29 6 E
Vredefort, S. Africa 56 D4 27 0S 27 22 E
Vredenburg, S. Africa 56 E2 32 56S 18 0 E
Vredendal, S. Africa 56 E2 31 41S 18 35 E
Vrindavan, India 42 F7 27 37N 77 40 E
Vrises, Greece 23 D6 35 23N 24 13 E
Vršac, Serbia, Yug. 21 B9 45 8N 21 20 E
Vryburg, S. Africa 56 D3 26 55S 24 45 E
Vryheid, S. Africa 57 D5 27 45S 30 47 E
Vu Liet, Vietnam 38 C5 18 43N 105 23 E
Vukovar, Croatia 21 B8 45 21N 18 59 E
Vulcan, Canada 72 C6 50 25N 113 15W
Vulcan, Romania 17 F12 45 23N 23 17 E
Vulcaneşti, Moldova 17 F15 45 41N 28 18 E
Vulcano, Italy 20 E6 38 24N 14 58 E
Vulkaneshty = Vulcaneşti, Moldova 17 F15 45 41N 28 18 E
Vunduzi →, Mozam. 55 F3 18 56S 34 1 E
Vung Tau, Vietnam 39 G6 10 21N 107 4 E
Vyatka = Kirov, Russia 24 C8 58 35N 49 40 E
Vyatka →, Russia 24 C9 55 37N 51 28 E
Vyatskiye Polyany, Russia 24 C9 56 14N 51 5 E
Vyazemskiy, Russia 27 E14 47 32N 134 45 E
Vyazma, Russia 24 C5 55 10N 34 15 E
Vyborg, Russia 24 B4 60 43N 28 47 E
Vychegda →, Russia 24 B8 61 18N 46 36 E
Vychodné Beskydy, Europe 17 D11 49 20N 22 0 E
Vyg-ozero, Russia 24 B5 63 47N 34 29 E
Vylkove, Ukraine 17 F15 45 28N 29 32 E
Vynohradiv, Ukraine 17 D12 48 9N 23 2 E
Vyrnwy, L., U.K. 10 E4 52 48N 3 31W
Vyshniy Volochek, Russia 24 C5 57 30N 34 30 E
Vyshzha = imeni 26 Bakinskikh Komissarov, Turkmenistan 45 B7 39 22N 54 10 E
Vyškov, Czech Rep. 17 D9 49 17N 17 0 E
Vytegra, Russia 24 B6 61 0N 36 27 E

W

W.A.C. Bennett Dam, Canada 72 B4 56 2N 122 6W
Waal →, Neths. 15 C5 51 37N 5 0 E
Waalwijk, Neths. 15 C5 51 42N 5 4 E
Wabana, Canada 71 C9 47 40N 53 0W
Wabasca →, Canada 72 B5 58 22N 115 20W
Wabasca-Desmarais, Canada 72 B6 55 57N 113 56W
Wabash, U.S.A. 76 E3 40 48N 85 49W
Wabash →, U.S.A. 76 G1 37 48N 88 2W
Wabigoon L., Canada 73 D10 49 44N 92 44W
Wabowden, Canada 73 C9 54 55N 98 38W
Wabuk Pt., Canada 70 A2 55 20N 85 5W
Wabush, Canada 71 B6 52 55N 66 52W
Waco, U.S.A. 81 K6 31 33N 97 9W
Waconichi, L., Canada 70 B5 50 8N 74 0W
Wad Hamid, Sudan 51 E12 16 30N 32 45 E
Wad Medanî, Sudan 51 F12 14 28N 33 30 E
Wad Thana, Pakistan 42 F2 27 22N 66 23 E
Wadai, Africa 48 E5 12 0N 19 0 E
Wadayama, Japan 31 G7 35 19N 134 52 E
Waddeneilanden, Neths. 15 A5 53 20N 5 10 E
Waddenzee, Neths. 15 A5 53 6N 5 10 E
Waddington, U.S.A. 79 B9 44 52N 75 12W
Waddington, Mt., Canada 72 C3 51 23N 125 15W
Waddy Pt., Australia 63 C5 24 58S 153 21 E
Wadebridge, U.K. 11 G3 50 31N 4 51W
Wadena, Canada 73 C8 51 57N 103 47W
Wadena, U.S.A. 80 B7 46 26N 95 8W
Wadeye, Australia 60 B4 14 28S 129 52 E
Wadhams, Canada 72 C3 51 30N 127 30W
Wādī as Sīr, Jordan 47 D4 31 56N 35 49 E
Wadi Halfa, Sudan 51 D12 21 53N 31 19 E
Wadsworth, Nev., U.S.A. 82 G4 39 38N 119 17W
Wadsworth, Ohio, U.S.A. 78 E3 41 2N 81 44W
Waegwan, S. Korea 35 G15 35 59N 128 23 E
Wafangdian, China 35 E11 39 38N 121 58 E
Wafrah, Si. Arabia 44 D5 28 33N 47 56 E
Wageningen, Neths. 15 C5 51 58N 5 40 E
Wager B., Canada 69 B11 65 26N 88 40W
Wagga Wagga, Australia 63 F4 35 7S 147 24 E
Waghete, Indonesia 37 E9 4 10S 135 50 E
Wagin, Australia 61 F2 33 17S 117 25 E
Wagner, U.S.A. 80 D5 43 5N 98 18W
Wagon Mound, U.S.A. 81 G2 36 1N 104 42W
Wagoner, U.S.A. 81 H7 35 58N 95 22W
Wah, Pakistan 42 C5 33 45N 72 40 E
Wahai, Indonesia 37 E7 2 48S 129 35 E
Wahiawa, U.S.A. 74 H15 21 30N 158 2W
Wâḥid, Egypt 47 E1 30 48N 32 21 E
Wahnai, Afghan. 42 C1 32 40N 65 50 E
Wahoo, U.S.A. 80 E6 41 13N 96 37W
Wahpeton, U.S.A. 80 B6 46 16N 96 36W
Waiau →, N.Z. 59 K4 42 47S 173 22 E
Waibeem, Indonesia 37 E8 0 30S 132 59 E
Waigeo, Indonesia 37 E8 0 20S 130 40 E
Waihi, N.Z. 59 G5 37 23S 175 52 E
Waihou →, N.Z. 59 G5 37 15S 175 40 E
Waika, Dem. Rep. of the Congo 54 C2 2 22S 25 42 E
Waikabubak, Indonesia 37 F5 9 45S 119 25 E
Waikari, N.Z. 59 K4 42 58S 172 41 E
Waikato →, N.Z. 59 G5 37 23S 174 43 E
Waikerie, Australia 63 E3 34 9S 140 0 E
Waikokopu, N.Z. 59 H6 39 3S 177 52 E
Waikouaiti, N.Z. 59 L3 45 36S 170 41 E
Wailuku, U.S.A. 74 H16 20 53N 156 30W
Waimakariri →, N.Z. 59 K4 43 24S 172 42 E
Waimate, N.Z. 59 L3 44 45S 171 3 E
Wainganga →, India 40 K11 18 50N 79 55 E
Waingapu, Indonesia 37 F6 9 35S 120 11 E
Waini →, Guyana 92 B7 8 20N 59 50W
Wainwright, Canada 73 C6 52 50N 110 50W
Waiouru, N.Z. 59 H5 39 28S 175 41 E
Waipara, N.Z. 59 K4 43 3S 172 46 E
Waipawa, N.Z. 59 H6 39 56S 176 38 E
Waipiro, N.Z. 59 H7 38 2S 178 22 E
Waipu, N.Z. 59 F5 35 59S 174 29 E
Waipukurau, N.Z. 59 J6 40 1S 176 33 E
Wairakei, N.Z. 59 H6 38 37S 176 6 E
Wairarapa, L., N.Z. 59 J5 41 14S 175 15 E
Wairoa, N.Z. 59 H6 39 3S 177 25 E
Waitaki →, N.Z. 59 L3 44 56S 171 7 E
Waitara, N.Z. 59 H5 38 59S 174 15 E
Waitsburg, U.S.A. 82 C5 46 16N 118 9W
Waiuku, N.Z. 59 G5 37 15S 174 45 E
Wajima, Japan 31 F8 37 30N 137 0 E

Wajir, *Kenya* **54 B5** 1 42N 40 5 E
Wakasa, *Japan* **31 G7** 35 20N 134 24 E
Wakasa-Wan, *Japan* **31 G7** 35 40N 135 30 E
Wakatipu, L., *N.Z.* **59 L2** 45 5S 168 33 E
Wakaw, *Canada* **73 C7** 52 39N 105 44W
Wakayama, *Japan* **31 G7** 34 15N 135 15 E
Wakayama □, *Japan* **31 H7** 33 50N 135 30 E
Wake Forest, *U.S.A.* **77 H6** 35 59N 78 30W
Wake I., *Pac. Oc.* **64 F8** 19 18N 166 36 E
WaKeeney, *U.S.A.* **80 F5** 39 1N 99 53W
Wakefield, *N.Z.* **59 J4** 41 24S 173 5 E
Wakefield, *U.K.* **10 D6** 53 41N 1 29W
Wakefield, *Mass., U.S.A.* **79 D13** 42 30N 71 4W
Wakefield, *Mich., U.S.A.* **80 B10** 46 29N 89 56W
Wakkanai, *Japan* **30 B10** 45 28N 141 35 E
Wakkerstroom, *S. Africa* **57 D5** 27 24S 30 10 E
Wakool, *Australia* **63 F3** 35 28S 144 23 E
Wakool →, *Australia* **63 F3** 35 5S 143 33 E
Wakre, *Indonesia* **37 E8** 0 19S 131 5 E
Wakuach, L., *Canada* **71 A6** 55 34N 67 32W
Walamba, *Zambia* **55 E2** 13 30S 28 42 E
Wałbrzych, *Poland* **16 C9** 50 45N 16 18 E
Walbury Hill, *U.K.* **11 F6** 51 21N 1 28W
Walcha, *Australia* **63 E5** 30 55S 151 31 E
Walcheren, *Neths.* **15 C3** 51 30N 3 35 E
Walcott, *U.S.A.* **82 F10** 41 46N 106 51W
Wałcz, *Poland* **16 B9** 53 17N 16 27 E
Waldburg Ra., *Australia* **61 D2** 24 40S 117 35 E
Walden, *Colo., U.S.A.* **82 F10** 40 44N 106 17W
Walden, *N.Y., U.S.A.* **79 E10** 41 34N 74 11W
Waldport, *U.S.A.* **82 D1** 44 26N 124 4W
Waldron, *U.S.A.* **81 H7** 34 54N 94 5W
Walebing, *Australia* **61 F2** 30 41S 116 13 E
Wales □, *U.K.* **11 E3** 52 19N 4 43W
Walgett, *Australia* **63 E4** 30 0S 148 5 E
Walgreen Coast, *Antarctica* **5 D15** 75 15S 105 0W
Walker, *U.S.A.* **80 B7** 47 6N 94 35W
Walker, L., *Canada* **71 B6** 50 20N 67 11W
Walker L., *Canada* **73 C9** 54 42N 95 57W
Walker L., *U.S.A.* **82 G4** 38 42N 118 43W
Walkerston, *Australia* **62 C4** 21 11S 149 8 E
Walkerton, *Canada* **78 B3** 44 10N 81 10W
Wall, *U.S.A.* **80 D3** 44 0N 102 8W
Walla Walla, *U.S.A.* **82 C4** 46 4N 118 20W
Wallace, *Idaho, U.S.A.* **82 C6** 47 28N 115 56W
Wallace, *N.C., U.S.A.* **77 H7** 34 44N 77 59W
Wallaceburg, *Canada* **78 D2** 42 34N 82 23W
Wallachia = Valahia, *Romania* **17 F13** 44 35N 25 0 E
Wallal, *Australia* **63 D4** 26 32S 146 7 E
Wallam Cr. →, *Australia* **63 D4** 28 40S 147 20 E
Wallambin, L., *Australia* **61 F2** 30 57S 117 35 E
Wallangarra, *Australia* **63 D5** 28 56S 151 58 E
Wallaroo, *Australia* **63 E2** 33 56S 137 39 E
Wallenpaupack, L., *U.S.A.* **79 E9** 41 25N 75 15W
Wallingford, *U.S.A.* **79 E12** 41 27N 72 50W
Wallis & Futuna, Is., *Pac. Oc.* **64 J10** 13 18S 176 10W
Wallowa, *U.S.A.* **82 D5** 45 34N 117 32W
Wallowa Mts., *U.S.A.* **82 D5** 45 20N 117 30W
Walls, *U.K.* **12 A7** 60 14N 1 33W
Wallula, *U.S.A.* **82 C4** 46 5N 118 54W
Wallumbilla, *Australia* **63 D4** 26 33S 149 9 E
Walmsley, L., *Canada* **73 A7** 63 25N 108 36W
Walney, I. of, *U.K.* **10 C4** 54 6N 3 15W
Walnut Creek, *U.S.A.* **84 H4** 37 54N 122 4W
Walnut Ridge, *U.S.A.* **81 G9** 36 4N 90 57W
Walpole, *Australia* **61 F2** 34 58S 116 44 E
Walpole, *U.S.A.* **79 D13** 42 9N 71 15W
Walsall, *U.K.* **11 E6** 52 35N 1 58W
Walsenburg, *U.S.A.* **81 G2** 37 38N 104 47W
Walsh, *U.S.A.* **81 G3** 37 23N 102 17W
Walsh →, *Australia* **62 B3** 16 31S 143 42 E
Walterboro, *U.S.A.* **77 J5** 32 55N 80 40W
Walters, *U.S.A.* **81 H5** 34 22N 98 19W
Waltham, *U.S.A.* **79 D13** 42 23N 71 14W
Waltman, *U.S.A.* **82 E10** 43 4N 107 12W
Walton, *U.S.A.* **79 D9** 42 10N 75 8W
Walton-on-the-Naze, *U.K.* **11 F9** 51 51N 1 17 E
Walvis Bay, *Namibia* **56 C1** 23 0S 14 28 E
Walvisbaai = Walvis Bay, *Namibia* **56 C1** 23 0S 14 28 E
Wamba, *Dem. Rep. of the Congo* **54 B2** 2 10N 27 57 E
Wamba, *Kenya* **54 B4** 0 58N 37 19 E
Wamego, *U.S.A.* **80 F6** 39 12N 96 18W
Wamena, *Indonesia* **37 E9** 4 4S 138 57 E
Wamsutter, *U.S.A.* **82 F9** 41 40N 107 58W
Wamulan, *Indonesia* **37 E7** 3 27S 126 7 E
Wan Xian, *China* **34 E8** 38 47N 115 7 E
Wana, *Pakistan* **42 C3** 32 20N 69 32 E
Wanaaring, *Australia* **63 D3** 29 38S 144 9 E
Wanaka, *N.Z.* **59 L2** 44 42S 169 9 E
Wanaka, L., *N.Z.* **59 L2** 44 33S 169 7 E
Wanapitei L., *Canada* **70 C3** 46 45N 80 40W
Wandel Sea = McKinley Sea, *Arctic* **4 A7** 82 0N 0 0W
Wanderer, *Zimbabwe* **55 F3** 19 36S 30 1 E
Wandhari, *Pakistan* **42 F2** 27 42N 66 48 E
Wandoan, *Australia* **63 D4** 26 5S 149 55 E
Wanfu, *China* **35 D12** 40 8N 122 38 E
Wang →, *Thailand* **38 D2** 17 8N 99 2 E
Wang Noi, *Thailand* **38 E3** 14 13N 100 44 E
Wang Saphung, *Thailand* **38 D3** 17 18N 101 46 E
Wang Thong, *Thailand* **38 D3** 16 50N 100 26 E
Wanga, *Dem. Rep. of the Congo* **54 B2** 2 58N 29 12 E
Wangal, *Indonesia* **37 F8** 6 8S 134 9 E
Wanganella, *Australia* **63 F3** 35 6S 144 49 E
Wanganui, *N.Z.* **59 H5** 39 56S 175 3 E
Wangaratta, *Australia* **63 F4** 36 21S 146 19 E
Wangary, *Australia* **63 E2** 34 35S 135 29 E
Wangdu, *China* **34 E8** 38 40N 115 7 E
Wangerooge, *Germany* **16 B4** 53 47N 7 54 E
Wangi, *Kenya* **54 C5** 1 58S 40 58 E
Wangiwangi, *Indonesia* **37 F6** 5 22S 123 37 E
Wangqing, *China* **35 C15** 43 12N 129 42 E
Wankaner, *India* **42 H4** 22 35N 71 0 E
Wanless, *Canada* **73 C8** 54 11N 101 21W
Wanning, *China* **38 C8** 18 48N 110 22 E
Wanon Niwat, *Thailand* **38 D4** 17 38N 103 46 E
Wanquan, *China* **34 D8** 40 50N 114 40 E
Wanrong, *China* **34 G6** 35 25N 110 50 E
Wantage, *U.K.* **11 F6** 51 35N 1 25W
Wapakoneta, *U.S.A.* **76 E3** 40 34N 84 12W
Wapato, *U.S.A.* **82 C3** 46 27N 120 25W
Wapawekka L., *Canada* **73 C8** 54 55N 104 40W
Wapikopa L., *Canada* **70 B2** 52 56N 87 53W
Wapiti →, *Canada* **72 B5** 55 5N 118 18W
Wappingers Falls, *U.S.A.* **79 E11** 41 36N 73 55W
Wapsipinicon →, *U.S.A.* **80 E9** 41 44N 90 19W
Warangal, *India* **40 L11** 17 58N 79 35 E
Waraseoni, *India* **43 J9** 21 45N 80 2 E
Waratah, *Australia* **62 G4** 41 30S 145 30 E
Waratah B., *Australia* **63 F4** 38 54S 146 5 E
Warburton, *Vic., Australia* **63 F4** 37 47S 145 42 E
Warburton, *W. Austral., Australia* **61 E4** 26 8S 126 35 E
Warburton Ra., *Australia* **61 E4** 25 55S 126 28 E
Ward, *N.Z.* **59 J5** 41 49S 174 11 E
Ward →, *Australia* **63 D4** 26 28S 146 6 E
Ward Mt., *U.S.A.* **84 H8** 37 12N 118 54W
Warden, *S. Africa* **57 D4** 27 50S 29 0 E
Wardha, *India* **40 J11** 20 45N 78 39 E
Wardha →, *India* **40 K11** 19 57N 79 11 E
Ware, *Canada* **72 B3** 57 26N 125 41W
Ware, *U.S.A.* **79 D12** 42 16N 72 14W
Waregem, *Belgium* **15 D3** 50 53N 3 27 E
Wareham, *U.S.A.* **79 E14** 41 46N 70 43W
Waremme, *Belgium* **15 D5** 50 43N 5 15 E
Warialda, *Australia* **63 D5** 29 29S 150 33 E
Wariap, *Indonesia* **37 E8** 1 30S 134 5 E
Warin Chamrap, *Thailand* **38 E5** 15 12N 104 53 E
Warkopi, *Indonesia* **37 E8** 1 12S 134 9 E
Warm Springs, *U.S.A.* **83 G5** 38 10N 116 20W
Warman, *Canada* **73 C7** 52 19N 106 30W
Warmbad, *Namibia* **56 D2** 28 25S 18 42 E
Warmbad, *S. Africa* **57 C4** 24 51S 28 19 E
Warminster, *U.K.* **11 F5** 51 12N 2 10W
Warminster, *U.S.A.* **79 F9** 40 12N 75 6W
Warner Mts., *U.S.A.* **82 F3** 41 40N 120 15W
Warner Robins, *U.S.A.* **77 J4** 32 37N 83 36W
Waroona, *Australia* **61 F2** 32 50S 115 58 E
Warracknabeal, *Australia* **63 F3** 36 9S 142 26 E
Warragul, *Australia* **63 F4** 38 10S 145 58 E
Warrego →, *Australia* **63 E4** 30 24S 145 21 E
Warrego Ra., *Australia* **62 C4** 24 58S 146 0 E
Warren, *Australia* **63 E4** 31 42S 147 51 E
Warren, *Ark., U.S.A.* **81 J8** 33 37N 92 4W
Warren, *Mich., U.S.A.* **76 D4** 42 30N 83 0W
Warren, *Minn., U.S.A.* **80 A6** 48 12N 96 46W
Warren, *Ohio, U.S.A.* **78 E4** 41 14N 80 49W
Warren, *Pa., U.S.A.* **78 E5** 41 51N 79 9W
Warrenpoint, *U.K.* **13 B5** 54 6N 6 15W
Warrensburg, *Mo., U.S.A.* **80 F8** 38 46N 93 44W
Warrensburg, *N.Y., U.S.A.* **79 C11** 43 29N 73 46W
Warrenton, *S. Africa* **56 D3** 28 9S 24 47 E
Warrenton, *U.S.A.* **84 D3** 46 10N 123 56W
Warri, *Nigeria* **50 G7** 5 30N 5 41 E
Warrina, *Australia* **63 D2** 28 12S 135 50 E
Warrington, *U.K.* **10 D5** 53 24N 2 35W
Warrington, *U.S.A.* **77 K2** 30 23N 87 17W
Warrington □, *U.K.* **10 D5** 53 24N 2 35W
Warrnambool, *Australia* **63 F3** 38 25S 142 30 E
Warroad, *U.S.A.* **80 A7** 48 54N 95 19W
Warruwi, *Australia* **62 A1** 11 36S 133 20 E
Warsa, *Indonesia* **37 E9** 0 47S 135 55 E
Warsak Dam, *Pakistan* **42 B4** 34 11N 71 19 E
Warsaw = Warszawa, *Poland* **17 B11** 52 13N 21 0 E
Warsaw, *Ind., U.S.A.* **76 E3** 41 14N 85 51W
Warsaw, *N.Y., U.S.A.* **78 D6** 42 45N 78 8W
Warsaw, *Ohio, U.S.A.* **78 F3** 40 20N 82 0W
Warszawa, *Poland* **17 B11** 52 13N 21 0 E
Warta →, *Poland* **16 B8** 52 35N 14 39 E
Warthe = Warta →, *Poland* **16 B8** 52 35N 14 39 E
Waru, *Indonesia* **37 E8** 3 30S 130 36 E
Warwick, *Australia* **63 D5** 28 10S 152 1 E
Warwick, *U.K.* **11 E6** 52 18N 1 35W
Warwick, *N.Y., U.S.A.* **79 E10** 41 16N 74 22W
Warwick, *R.I., U.S.A.* **79 E13** 41 42N 71 28W
Warwickshire □, *U.K.* **11 E6** 52 14N 1 38W
Wasaga Beach, *Canada* **78 B4** 44 31N 80 1W
Wasagaming, *Canada* **73 C9** 50 39N 99 58W
Wasatch Ra., *U.S.A.* **82 F8** 40 30N 111 15W
Wasbank, *S. Africa* **57 D5** 28 15S 30 9 E
Wasco, *Calif., U.S.A.* **85 K7** 35 36N 119 20W
Wasco, *Oreg., U.S.A.* **82 D3** 45 36N 120 42W
Waseca, *U.S.A.* **80 C8** 44 5N 93 30W
Wasekamio L., *Canada* **73 B7** 56 45N 108 45W
Wash, The, *U.K.* **10 E8** 52 58N 0 20 E
Washago, *Canada* **78 B5** 44 45N 79 20W
Washburn, *N. Dak., U.S.A.* **80 B4** 47 17N 101 2W
Washburn, *Wis., U.S.A.* **80 B9** 46 40N 90 54W
Washim, *India* **40 J10** 20 3N 77 0 E
Washington, *U.K.* **10 C6** 54 55N 1 30W
Washington, *D.C., U.S.A.* **76 F7** 38 54N 77 2W
Washington, *Ga., U.S.A.* **77 J4** 33 44N 82 44W
Washington, *Ind., U.S.A.* **76 F2** 38 40N 87 10W
Washington, *Iowa, U.S.A.* **80 E9** 41 18N 91 42W
Washington, *Mo., U.S.A.* **80 F9** 38 33N 91 1W
Washington, *N.C., U.S.A.* **77 H7** 35 33N 77 3W
Washington, *N.J., U.S.A.* **79 F10** 40 46N 74 59W
Washington, *Pa., U.S.A.* **78 F4** 40 10N 80 15W
Washington, *Utah, U.S.A.* **83 H7** 37 8N 113 31W
Washington □, *U.S.A.* **82 C3** 47 30N 120 30W
Washington, Mt., *U.S.A.* **79 B13** 44 16N 71 18W
Washington Court House, *U.S.A.* **76 F4** 39 32N 83 26W
Washington I., *U.S.A.* **76 C2** 45 23N 86 54W
Washougal, *U.S.A.* **84 E4** 45 35N 122 21W
Wasian, *Indonesia* **37 E8** 1 47S 133 19 E
Wasilla, *U.S.A.* **68 B5** 61 35N 149 26W
Wasior, *Indonesia* **37 E8** 2 43S 134 30 E
Waskaganish, *Canada* **70 B4** 51 30N 78 40W
Waskaiowaka, L., *Canada* **73 B9** 56 33N 96 23W
Waskesiu Lake, *Canada* **73 C7** 53 55N 106 5W
Wasserkuppe, *Germany* **16 C5** 50 29N 9 55 E
Waswanipi, *Canada* **70 C4** 49 40N 76 29W
Waswanipi, L., *Canada* **70 C4** 49 35N 76 40W
Watampone, *Indonesia* **37 E6** 4 29S 120 25 E
Water Park Pt., *Australia* **62 C5** 22 56S 150 47 E
Water Valley, *U.S.A.* **81 H10** 34 10N 89 38W
Waterberge, *S. Africa* **57 C4** 24 10S 28 0 E
Waterbury, *Conn., U.S.A.* **79 E11** 41 33N 73 3W
Waterbury, *Vt., U.S.A.* **79 B12** 44 20N 72 46W
Waterbury L., *Canada* **73 B8** 58 10N 104 22W
Waterdown, *Canada* **78 C5** 43 20N 79 53W
Waterford, *Canada* **78 D4** 42 56N 80 17W
Waterford, *Ireland* **13 D4** 52 15N 7 8W
Waterford, *Calif., U.S.A.* **84 H6** 37 38N 120 46W
Waterford, *Pa., U.S.A.* **78 E5** 41 57N 79 59W
Waterford □, *Ireland* **13 D4** 52 10N 7 40W
Waterford Harbour, *Ireland* **13 D5** 52 8N 6 58W
Waterhen L., *Canada* **73 C9** 52 10N 99 40W
Waterloo, *Belgium* **15 D4** 50 43N 4 25 E
Waterloo, *Ont., Canada* **78 C4** 43 30N 80 32W
Waterloo, *Qué., Canada* **79 A12** 45 22N 72 32W
Waterloo, *Ill., U.S.A.* **80 F9** 38 20N 90 9W
Waterloo, *Iowa, U.S.A.* **80 D8** 42 30N 92 21W
Waterloo, *N.Y., U.S.A.* **78 D8** 42 54N 76 52W
Watersmeet, *U.S.A.* **80 B10** 46 16N 89 11W
Waterton Lakes Nat. Park, *U.S.A.* **82 B7** 48 45N 115 0W
Watertown, *Conn., U.S.A.* **79 E11** 41 36N 73 7W
Watertown, *N.Y., U.S.A.* **79 C9** 43 59N 75 55W
Watertown, *S. Dak., U.S.A.* **80 C6** 44 54N 97 7W
Watertown, *Wis., U.S.A.* **80 D10** 43 12N 88 43W
Waterval-Boven, *S. Africa* **57 D5** 25 40S 30 18 E
Waterville, *Canada* **79 A13** 45 16N 71 54W
Waterville, *Maine, U.S.A.* **77 C11** 44 33N 69 38W
Waterville, *N.Y., U.S.A.* **79 D9** 42 56N 75 23W
Waterville, *Pa., U.S.A.* **78 E7** 41 19N 77 21W
Waterville, *Wash., U.S.A.* **82 C3** 47 39N 120 4W
Watervliet, *U.S.A.* **79 D11** 42 44N 73 42W
Wates, *Indonesia* **37 G14** 7 51S 110 10 E
Watford, *Canada* **78 D3** 42 57N 81 53W
Watford, *U.K.* **11 F7** 51 40N 0 24W
Watford City, *U.S.A.* **80 B3** 47 48N 103 17W
Wathaman →, *Canada* **73 B8** 57 16N 102 59W
Wathaman L., *Canada* **73 B8** 56 58N 103 44W
Watheroo, *Australia* **61 F2** 30 15S 116 0 E
Wating, *China* **34 G4** 35 40N 106 38 E
Watkins Glen, *U.S.A.* **78 D8** 42 23N 76 52W
Watling I. = San Salvador I., *Bahamas* **89 B5** 24 0N 74 40W
Watonga, *U.S.A.* **81 H5** 35 51N 98 25W
Watrous, *Canada* **73 C7** 51 40N 105 25W
Watrous, *U.S.A.* **81 H2** 35 48N 104 59W
Watsa, *Dem. Rep. of the Congo* **54 B2** 3 4N 29 30 E
Watseka, *U.S.A.* **76 E2** 40 47N 87 44W
Watson, *Australia* **61 F5** 30 29S 131 31 E
Watson, *Canada* **73 C8** 52 10N 104 30W
Watson Lake, *Canada* **72 A3** 60 6N 128 49W
Watsontown, *U.S.A.* **78 E8** 41 5N 76 52W
Watsonville, *U.S.A.* **84 J5** 36 55N 121 45W
Wattiwarriganna Cr. →, *Australia* **63 D2** 28 57S 136 10 E
Watuata = Batuata, *Indonesia* **37 F6** 6 12S 122 42 E
Watubela, Kepulauan, *Indonesia* **37 E8** 4 28S 131 35 E
Watubela Is. = Watubela, Kepulauan, *Indonesia* **37 E8** 4 28S 131 35 E
Wau = Wâw, *Sudan* **51 G11** 7 45N 28 1 E
Waubamik, *Canada* **78 A4** 45 27N 80 1W
Waubay, *U.S.A.* **80 C6** 45 20N 97 18W
Wauchope, *N.S.W., Australia* **63 E5** 31 28S 152 45 E
Wauchope, *N. Terr., Australia* **62 C1** 20 36S 134 15 E
Wauchula, *U.S.A.* **77 M5** 27 33N 81 49W
Waukarlycarly, L., *Australia* **60 D3** 21 18S 121 56 E
Waukegan, *U.S.A.* **76 D2** 42 22N 87 50W
Waukesha, *U.S.A.* **76 D1** 43 1N 88 14W
Waukon, *U.S.A.* **80 D9** 43 16N 91 29W
Waupaca, *U.S.A.* **80 C10** 44 21N 89 5W
Waupun, *U.S.A.* **80 D10** 43 38N 88 44W
Waurika, *U.S.A.* **81 H6** 34 10N 98 0W
Wausau, *U.S.A.* **80 C10** 44 58N 89 38W
Wautoma, *U.S.A.* **80 C10** 44 4N 89 18W
Wauwatosa, *U.S.A.* **76 D2** 43 3N 88 0W
Waveney →, *U.K.* **11 E9** 52 35N 1 39 E
Waverley, *N.Z.* **59 H5** 39 46S 174 37 E
Waverly, *Iowa, U.S.A.* **80 D8** 42 44N 92 29W
Waverly, *N.Y., U.S.A.* **79 E8** 42 1N 76 32W
Wavre, *Belgium* **15 D4** 50 43N 4 38 E
Wâw, *Sudan* **51 G11** 7 45N 28 1 E
Wāw al Kabir, *Libya* **51 C9** 25 20N 16 43 E
Wawa, *Canada* **70 C3** 47 59N 84 47W
Wawanesa, *Canada* **73 D9** 49 36N 99 40W
Wawona, *U.S.A.* **84 H7** 37 32N 119 39W
Waxahachie, *U.S.A.* **81 J6** 32 24N 96 51W
Way, L., *Australia* **61 E3** 26 45S 120 16 E
Waycross, *U.S.A.* **77 K4** 31 13N 82 21W
Wayland, *U.S.A.* **78 D7** 42 34N 77 35W
Wayne, *Nebr., U.S.A.* **80 D6** 42 14N 97 1W
Wayne, *W. Va., U.S.A.* **76 F4** 38 13N 82 27W
Waynesboro, *Ga., U.S.A.* **77 J4** 33 6N 82 1W
Waynesboro, *Miss., U.S.A.* **77 K1** 31 40N 88 39W
Waynesboro, *Pa., U.S.A.* **76 F7** 39 45N 77 35W
Waynesboro, *Va., U.S.A.* **76 F6** 38 4N 78 53W
Waynesburg, *U.S.A.* **76 F5** 39 54N 80 11W
Waynesville, *U.S.A.* **77 H4** 35 28N 82 58W
Waynoka, *U.S.A.* **81 G5** 36 35N 98 53W
Wazirabad, *Pakistan* **42 C6** 32 30N 74 8 E
We, *Indonesia* **36 C1** 5 51N 95 18 E
Weald, The, *U.K.* **11 F8** 51 4N 0 20 E
Wear →, *U.K.* **10 C6** 54 55N 1 23W
Weatherford, *Okla., U.S.A.* **81 H5** 35 32N 98 43W
Weatherford, *Tex., U.S.A.* **81 J6** 32 46N 97 48W
Weaverville, *U.S.A.* **82 F2** 40 44N 122 56W
Webb City, *U.S.A.* **81 G7** 37 9N 94 28W
Webequie, *Canada* **70 B2** 52 59N 87 21W
Webster, *Mass., U.S.A.* **79 D13** 42 3N 71 53W
Webster, *N.Y., U.S.A.* **78 C7** 43 13N 77 26W
Webster, *S. Dak., U.S.A.* **80 C6** 45 20N 97 31W
Webster City, *U.S.A.* **80 D8** 42 28N 93 49W
Webster Springs, *U.S.A.* **76 F5** 38 29N 80 25W
Weda, *Indonesia* **37 D7** 0 21N 127 50 E
Weda, Teluk, *Indonesia* **37 D7** 0 20N 128 0 E
Weddell I., *Falk. Is.* **96 G4** 51 50S 61 0W
Weddell Sea, *Antarctica* **5 D1** 72 30S 40 0W
Wedderburn, *Australia* **63 F3** 36 26S 143 33 E
Wedgeport, *Canada* **71 D6** 43 44N 65 59W
Wedza, *Zimbabwe* **55 F3** 18 40S 31 33 E
Wee Waa, *Australia* **63 E4** 30 11S 149 26 E
Weed, *U.S.A.* **82 F2** 41 25N 122 23W
Weed Heights, *U.S.A.* **84 G7** 38 59N 119 13W
Weedsport, *U.S.A.* **79 C8** 43 3N 76 35W
Weedville, *U.S.A.* **78 E6** 41 17N 78 30W
Weenen, *S. Africa* **57 D5** 28 48S 30 7 E
Weert, *Neths.* **15 C5** 51 15N 5 43 E
Wei He →, *Hebei, China* **34 F8** 36 10N 115 45 E
Wei He →, *Shaanxi, China* **34 G6** 34 38N 110 15 E
Weichang, *China* **35 D9** 41 58N 117 49 E
Weichuan, *China* **34 G7** 34 20N 113 59 E
Weiden, *Germany* **16 D7** 49 41N 12 10 E
Weifang, *China* **35 F10** 36 44N 119 7 E
Weihai, *China* **35 F12** 37 30N 122 6 E
Weimar, *Germany* **16 C6** 50 58N 11 19 E
Weinan, *China* **34 G5** 34 31N 109 29 E
Weipa, *Australia* **62 A3** 12 40S 141 50 E
Weir →, *Australia* **63 D4** 28 20S 149 50 E
Weir →, *Canada* **73 B10** 56 54N 93 21W
Weir River, *Canada* **73 B10** 56 49N 94 6W
Weirton, *U.S.A.* **78 F4** 40 24N 80 35W
Weiser, *U.S.A.* **82 D5** 44 10N 117 0W
Weishan, *China* **35 G9** 34 47N 117 5 E
Weiyuan, *China* **34 G3** 35 7N 104 10 E
Wejherowo, *Poland* **17 A10** 54 35N 18 12 E
Wekusko L., *Canada* **73 C9** 54 40N 99 50W
Welch, *U.S.A.* **76 G5** 37 26N 81 35W
Welkom, *S. Africa* **56 D4** 28 0S 26 46 E
Welland, *Canada* **78 D5** 43 0N 79 15W
Welland →, *U.K.* **11 E7** 52 51N 0 5W
Wellesley Is., *Australia* **62 B2** 16 42S 139 30 E
Wellingborough, *U.K.* **11 E7** 52 19N 0 41W
Wellington, *Australia* **63 E4** 32 35S 148 59 E
Wellington, *Canada* **78 C7** 43 57N 77 20W
Wellington, *N.Z.* **59 J5** 41 19S 174 46 E
Wellington, *S. Africa* **56 E2** 33 38S 19 1 E
Wellington, *Somst., U.K.* **11 G4** 50 58N 3 13W
Wellington, *Telford & Wrekin, U.K.* **11 E5** 52 42N 2 30W
Wellington, *Colo., U.S.A.* **80 E2** 40 42N 105 0W
Wellington, *Kans., U.S.A.* **81 G6** 37 16N 97 24W
Wellington, *Nev., U.S.A.* **84 G7** 38 45N 119 23W
Wellington, *Ohio, U.S.A.* **78 E2** 41 10N 82 13W
Wellington, *Tex., U.S.A.* **81 H4** 34 51N 100 13W
Wellington, I., *Chile* **96 F2** 49 30S 75 0W
Wellington, L., *Australia* **63 F4** 38 6S 147 20 E
Wells, *U.K.* **11 F5** 51 13N 2 39W
Wells, *Maine, U.S.A.* **79 C14** 43 20N 70 35W
Wells, *N.Y., U.S.A.* **79 C10** 43 24N 74 17W
Wells, *Nev., U.S.A.* **82 F6** 41 7N 114 58W
Wells, L., *Australia* **61 E3** 26 44S 123 15 E
Wells, Mt., *Australia* **60 C4** 17 25S 127 8 E
Wells Gray Prov. Park, *Canada* **72 C4** 52 30N 120 15W
Wells-next-the-Sea, *U.K.* **10 E8** 52 57N 0 51 E
Wells River, *U.S.A.* **79 B12** 44 9N 72 4W
Wellsboro, *U.S.A.* **78 E7** 41 45N 77 18W
Wellsburg, *U.S.A.* **78 F4** 40 16N 80 37W
Wellsville, *N.Y., U.S.A.* **78 D7** 42 7N 77 57W
Wellsville, *Ohio, U.S.A.* **78 F4** 40 36N 80 39W
Wellsville, *Utah, U.S.A.* **82 F8** 41 38N 111 56W
Wellton, *U.S.A.* **83 K6** 32 40N 114 8W
Wels, *Austria* **16 D8** 48 9N 14 1 E
Welshpool, *U.K.* **11 E4** 52 39N 3 8W
Welwyn Garden City, *U.K.* **11 F7** 51 48N 0 12W
Wem, *U.K.* **10 E5** 52 52N 2 44W
Wembere →, *Tanzania* **54 C3** 4 10S 34 15 E
Wemindji, *Canada* **70 B4** 53 0N 78 49W
Wen Xian, *China* **34 G7** 34 55N 113 5 E
Wenatchee, *U.S.A.* **82 C3** 47 25N 120 19W
Wenchang, *China* **38 C8** 19 38N 110 42 E
Wenchi, *Ghana* **50 G5** 7 46N 2 8W
Wenchow = Wenzhou, *China* **33 D7** 28 0N 120 38 E
Wenden, *U.S.A.* **85 M13** 33 49N 113 33W
Wendeng, *China* **35 F12** 37 15N 122 5 E
Wendesi, *Indonesia* **37 E8** 2 30S 134 17 E
Wendover, *U.S.A.* **82 F6** 40 44N 114 2W
Wenlock →, *Australia* **62 A3** 12 2S 141 55 E
Wenshan, *China* **32 D5** 23 20N 104 18 E
Wenshang, *China* **34 G9** 35 45N 116 30 E
Wenshui, *China* **34 F7** 37 26N 112 1 E
Wensleydale, *U.K.* **10 C6** 54 17N 2 0W
Wensu, *China* **32 B3** 41 15N 80 10 E
Wensum →, *U.K.* **10 E8** 52 40N 1 15 E
Wentworth, *Australia* **63 E3** 34 2S 141 54 E
Wentzel L., *Canada* **72 B6** 59 2N 114 28W
Wenut, *Indonesia* **37 E8** 3 11S 133 19 E
Wenxi, *China* **34 G6** 35 20N 111 10 E
Wenxian, *China* **34 H3** 32 43N 104 36 E
Wenzhou, *China* **33 D7** 28 0N 120 38 E
Weott, *U.S.A.* **82 F2** 40 20N 123 55W
Wepener, *S. Africa* **56 D4** 29 42S 27 3 E
Werda, *Botswana* **56 D3** 25 24S 23 15 E
Weri, *Indonesia* **37 E8** 3 10S 132 38 E
Werra →, *Germany* **16 C5** 51 24N 9 39 E
Werrimull, *Australia* **63 E3** 34 25S 141 38 E
Werris Creek, *Australia* **63 E5** 31 18S 150 38 E
Weser →, *Germany* **16 B5** 53 36N 8 28 E
Wesiri, *Indonesia* **37 F7** 7 30S 126 30 E
Weslemkoon L., *Canada* **78 A7** 45 2N 77 25W
Wesleyville, *Canada* **71 C9** 49 8N 53 36W
Wesleyville, *U.S.A.* **78 D4** 42 9N 80 0W
Wessel, C., *Australia* **62 A2** 10 59S 136 46 E
Wessel Is., *Australia* **62 A2** 11 10S 136 45 E
Wessington Springs, *U.S.A.* **80 C5** 44 5N 98 34W
West, *U.S.A.* **81 K6** 31 48N 97 6W
West →, *U.S.A.* **79 D12** 42 52N 72 33W
West Baines →, *Australia* **60 C4** 15 38S 129 59 E
West Bank □, *Asia* **47 C4** 32 6N 35 13 E
West Bend, *U.S.A.* **76 D1** 43 25N 88 11W
West Bengal □, *India* **43 H13** 23 0N 88 0 E
West Berkshire □, *U.K.* **11 F6** 51 25N 1 17W
West Beskids = Západné Beskydy, *Europe* **17 D10** 49 30N 19 0 E
West Branch, *U.S.A.* **76 C3** 44 17N 84 14W
West Branch Susquehanna →, *U.S.A.* **79 F8** 40 53N 76 48W
West Bromwich, *U.K.* **11 E6** 52 32N 1 59W
West Burra, *U.K.* **12 A7** 60 5N 1 21W
West Canada Cr. →, *U.S.A.* **79 C10** 43 1N 74 58W
West Cape Howe, *Australia* **61 G2** 35 8S 117 36 E
West Chazy, *U.S.A.* **79 B11** 44 49N 73 28W
West Chester, *U.S.A.* **79 G9** 39 58N 75 36W
West Columbia, *U.S.A.* **81 L7** 29 9N 95 39W
West Covina, *U.S.A.* **85 L9** 34 4N 117 54W
West Des Moines, *U.S.A.* **80 E8** 41 35N 93 43W
West Dunbartonshire □, *U.K.* **12 F4** 55 59N 4 30W
West End, *Bahamas* **88 A4** 26 41N 78 58W
West Falkland, *Falk. Is.* **96 G5** 51 40S 60 0W
West Fargo, *U.S.A.* **80 B6** 46 52N 96 54W
West Farmington, *U.S.A.* **78 E4** 41 23N 80 58W
West Fjord = Vestfjorden, *Norway* **8 C15** 67 55N 14 0 E
West Fork Trinity →, *U.S.A.* **81 J6** 32 48N 96 54W
West Frankfort, *U.S.A.* **80 G10** 37 54N 88 55W
West Hartford, *U.S.A.* **79 E12** 41 45N 72 44W
West Haven, *U.S.A.* **79 E12** 41 17N 72 57W
West Hazleton, *U.S.A.* **79 F9** 40 58N 76 0W
West Helena, *U.S.A.* **81 H9** 34 33N 90 38W

West Hurley, *U.S.A.* **79 E10** 41 59N 74 7W
West Ice Shelf, *Antarctica* **5 C7** 67 0S 85 0 E
West Indies, *Cent. Amer.* **89 D7** 15 0N 65 0W
West Jordan, *U.S.A.* **82 F8** 40 36N 111 56W
West Lorne, *Canada* **78 D3** 42 36N 81 36W
West Lothian □, *U.K.* **12 F5** 55 54N 3 36W
West Lunga →, *Zambia* **55 E1** 13 6S 24 39 E
West Memphis, *U.S.A.* **81 H9** 35 9N 90 11W
West Midlands □, *U.K.* **11 E6** 52 26N 2 0W
West Mifflin, *U.S.A.* **78 F5** 40 22N 79 52W
West Milton, *U.S.A.* **78 E8** 41 1N 76 50W
West Monroe, *U.S.A.* **81 J8** 32 31N 92 9W
West Newton, *U.S.A.* **78 F5** 40 14N 79 46W
West Nicholson, *Zimbabwe* **55 G2** 21 2S 29 20 E
West Palm Beach, *U.S.A.* **77 M5** 26 43N 80 3W
West Plains, *U.S.A.* **81 G9** 36 44N 91 51W
West Point, *N.Y., U.S.A.* **79 E11** 41 24N 73 58W
West Point, *Nebr., U.S.A.* **80 E6** 41 51N 96 43W
West Point, *Va., U.S.A.* **76 G7** 37 32N 76 48W
West Pt. = Ouest, Pte. de l', *Canada* **71 C7** 49 52N 64 40W
West Pt., *Australia* **63 F2** 35 1S 135 56 E
West Road →, *Canada* **72 C4** 53 18N 122 53W
West Rutland, *U.S.A.* **79 C11** 43 38N 73 5W
West Schelde = Westerschelde →, *Neths.* **15 C3** 51 25N 3 25 E
West Seneca, *U.S.A.* **78 D6** 42 51N 78 48W
West Siberian Plain, *Russia* **28 C11** 62 0N 75 0 E
West Sussex □, *U.K.* **11 G7** 50 55N 0 30W
West-Terschelling, *Neths.* **15 A5** 53 22N 5 13 E
West Valley City, *U.S.A.* **82 F8** 40 42N 111 57W
West Virginia □, *U.S.A.* **76 F5** 38 45N 80 30W
West-Vlaanderen □, *Belgium* **15 D2** 51 0N 3 0 E
West Walker →, *U.S.A.* **84 G7** 38 54N 119 9W
West Wyalong, *Australia* **63 E4** 33 56S 147 10 E
West Yellowstone, *U.S.A.* **82 D8** 44 40N 111 6W
West Yorkshire □, *U.K.* **10 D6** 53 45N 1 40W
Westall Pt., *Australia* **63 E1** 32 55S 134 4 E
Westbrook, *U.S.A.* **77 D10** 43 41N 70 22W
Westbury, *Australia* **62 G4** 41 30S 146 51 E
Westby, *U.S.A.* **80 A2** 48 52N 104 3W
Westend, *U.S.A.* **85 K9** 35 42N 117 24W
Westerland, *Germany* **9 J13** 54 54N 8 17 E
Westerly, *U.S.A.* **79 E13** 41 22N 71 50W
Western □, *Kenya* **54 B3** 0 30N 34 30 E
Western □, *Zambia* **55 F1** 15 0S 24 4 E
Western Australia □, *Australia* **61 E2** 25 0S 118 0 E
Western Cape □, *S. Africa* **56 E3** 34 0S 20 0 E
Western Dvina = Daugava →, *Latvia* **9 H21** 57 4N 24 3 E
Western Ghats, *India* **40 N9** 14 0N 75 0 E
Western Isles □, *U.K.* **12 D1** 57 30N 7 10W
Western Sahara ■, *Africa* **50 D3** 25 0N 13 0W
Western Samoa = Samoa ■, *Pac. Oc.* **59 B13** 14 0S 172 0W
Westernport, *U.S.A.* **76 F6** 39 29N 79 3W
Westerschelde →, *Neths.* **15 C3** 51 25N 3 25 E
Westerwald, *Germany* **16 C4** 50 38N 7 56 E
Westfield, *Mass., U.S.A.* **79 D12** 42 7N 72 45W
Westfield, *N.Y., U.S.A.* **78 D5** 42 20N 79 35W
Westfield, *Pa., U.S.A.* **78 E7** 41 55N 77 32W
Westhill, *U.K.* **12 D6** 57 9N 2 19W
Westhope, *U.S.A.* **80 A4** 48 55N 101 1W
Westland Bight, *N.Z.* **59 K3** 42 55S 170 5 E
Westlock, *Canada* **72 C6** 54 9N 113 55W
Westmar, *Australia* **63 D4** 27 55S 149 44 E
Westmeath □, *Ireland* **13 C4** 53 33N 7 34W
Westminster, *U.S.A.* **76 F7** 39 34N 76 59W
Westmont, *U.S.A.* **78 F6** 40 19N 78 58W
Westmorland, *U.S.A.* **85 M11** 33 2N 115 37W
Weston, *Oreg., U.S.A.* **82 D4** 45 49N 118 26W
Weston, *W. Va., U.S.A.* **76 F5** 39 2N 80 28W
Weston I., *Canada* **70 B4** 52 33N 79 36W
Weston-super-Mare, *U.K.* **11 F5** 51 21N 2 58W
Westover, *U.S.A.* **78 F6** 40 45N 78 40W
Westport, *Canada* **79 B8** 44 40N 76 25W
Westport, *Ireland* **13 C2** 53 48N 9 31W
Westport, *N.Z.* **59 J3** 41 46S 171 37 E
Westport, *N.Y., U.S.A.* **79 B11** 44 11N 73 26W
Westport, *Oreg., U.S.A.* **84 D3** 46 8N 123 23W
Westport, *Wash., U.S.A.* **84 D2** 46 53N 124 6W
Westray, *Canada* **73 C8** 53 36N 101 24W
Westray, *U.K.* **12 B5** 59 18N 3 0W
Westree, *Canada* **70 C3** 47 26N 81 34W
Westville, *U.S.A.* **84 F6** 39 8N 120 42W
Westwood, *U.S.A.* **82 F3** 40 18N 121 0W
Wetar, *Indonesia* **37 F7** 7 48S 126 30 E
Wetaskiwin, *Canada* **72 C6** 52 55N 113 24W
Wete, *Tanzania* **52 F7** 5 4S 39 43 E
Wetherby, *U.K.* **10 D6** 53 56N 1 23W
Wethersfield, *U.S.A.* **79 E12** 41 42N 72 40W
Wetteren, *Belgium* **15 D3** 51 0N 3 53 E
Wetzlar, *Germany* **16 C5** 50 32N 8 31 E
Wewoka, *U.S.A.* **81 H6** 35 9N 96 30W
Wexford, *Ireland* **13 D5** 52 20N 6 28W
Wexford □, *Ireland* **13 D5** 52 20N 6 25W
Wexford Harbour, *Ireland* **13 D5** 52 20N 6 25W
Weyburn, *Canada* **73 D8** 49 40N 103 50W
Weymouth, *Canada* **71 D6** 44 30N 66 1W
Weymouth, *U.K.* **11 G5** 50 37N 2 28W
Weymouth, *U.S.A.* **79 D14** 42 13N 70 58W
Weymouth, C., *Australia* **62 A3** 12 37S 143 27 E
Wha Ti, *Canada* **68 B8** 63 8N 117 16W
Whakatane, *N.Z.* **59 G6** 37 57S 177 1 E
Whale →, *Canada* **71 A6** 58 15N 67 40W
Whale Cove, *Canada* **73 A10** 62 11N 92 36W
Whales, B. of, *Antarctica* **5 D12** 78 0S 165 0W
Whalsay, *U.K.* **12 A8** 60 22N 0 59W
Whangamomona, *N.Z.* **59 H5** 39 8S 174 44 E
Whangarei, *N.Z.* **59 F5** 35 43S 174 21 E
Whangarei Harb., *N.Z.* **59 F5** 35 45S 174 28 E
Wharfe →, *U.K.* **10 D6** 53 51N 1 9W
Wharfedale, *U.K.* **10 C5** 54 6N 2 1W
Wharton, *N.J., U.S.A.* **79 F10** 40 54N 74 35W
Wharton, *Pa., U.S.A.* **78 E6** 41 31N 78 1W
Wharton, *Tex., U.S.A.* **81 L6** 29 19N 96 6W
Wheatland, *Calif., U.S.A.* **84 F5** 39 1N 121 25W
Wheatland, *Wyo., U.S.A.* **80 D2** 42 3N 104 58W
Wheatley, *Canada* **78 D2** 42 6N 82 27W
Wheaton, *Md., U.S.A.* **76 F7** 39 3N 77 3W
Wheaton, *Minn., U.S.A.* **80 C6** 45 48N 96 30W
Wheelbarrow Pk., *U.S.A.* **84 H10** 37 26N 116 5W
Wheeler, *Oreg., U.S.A.* **82 D2** 45 41N 123 53W
Wheeler, *Tex., U.S.A.* **81 H4** 35 27N 100 16W
Wheeler →, *Canada* **71 A6** 57 2N 67 13W
Wheeler L., *U.S.A.* **77 H2** 34 48N 87 23W
Wheeler Pk., *N. Mex., U.S.A.* **83 H11** 36 34N 105 25W
Wheeler Pk., *Nev., U.S.A.* **83 G6** 38 57N 114 15W
Wheeler Ridge, *U.S.A.* **85 L8** 35 0N 118 57W
Wheeling, *U.S.A.* **78 F4** 40 4N 80 43W
Whernside, *U.K.* **10 C5** 54 14N 2 24W
Whiskey Jack L., *Canada* **73 B8** 58 23N 101 55W
Whistleduck Cr. →, *Australia* **62 C2** 20 15S 135 18 E
Whistler, *Canada* **72 C4** 50 7N 122 58W
Whitby, *Canada* **78 C6** 43 52N 78 56W
Whitby, *U.K.* **10 C7** 54 29N 0 37W
White →, *Ark., U.S.A.* **81 J9** 33 57N 91 5W
White →, *Ind., U.S.A.* **76 F2** 38 25N 87 45W
White →, *S. Dak., U.S.A.* **80 D5** 43 42N 99 27W
White →, *Tex., U.S.A.* **81 J4** 33 14N 100 56W
White →, *Utah, U.S.A.* **82 F9** 40 4N 109 41W
White →, *Vt., U.S.A.* **79 C12** 43 37N 72 20W
White →, *Wash., U.S.A.* **84 C4** 47 12N 122 15W
White, L., *Australia* **60 D4** 21 9S 128 56 E
White B., *Canada* **71 C8** 50 0N 56 35W
White Bird, *U.S.A.* **82 D5** 45 46N 116 18W
White Butte, *U.S.A.* **80 B3** 46 23N 103 18W
White City, *U.S.A.* **82 E2** 42 26N 122 51W
White Cliffs, *Australia* **63 E3** 30 50S 143 10 E
White Hall, *U.S.A.* **80 F9** 39 26N 90 24W
White Haven, *U.S.A.* **79 E9** 41 4N 75 47W
White Horse, Vale of, *U.K.* **11 F6** 51 37N 1 30W
White I., *N.Z.* **59 G6** 37 30S 177 13 E
White L., *Canada* **79 A8** 45 18N 76 31W
White L., *U.S.A.* **81 L8** 29 44N 92 30W
White Mountain Peak, *U.S.A.* **83 G4** 37 38N 118 15W
White Mts., *Calif., U.S.A.* **84 H8** 37 30N 118 15W
White Mts., *N.H., U.S.A.* **79 B13** 44 15N 71 15W
White Nile = Nîl el Abyad →, *Sudan* **51 E12** 15 38N 32 31 E
White Otter L., *Canada* **70 C1** 49 5N 91 55W
White Pass, *U.S.A.* **84 D5** 46 38N 121 24W
White Plains, *U.S.A.* **79 E11** 41 2N 73 46W
White River, *Canada* **70 C2** 48 35N 85 20W
White River, *S. Africa* **57 D5** 25 20S 31 0 E
White River, *U.S.A.* **80 D4** 43 34N 100 45W
White Rock, *Canada* **84 A4** 49 2N 122 48W
White Russia = Belarus ■, *Europe* **17 B14** 53 30N 27 0 E
White Sea = Beloye More, *Russia* **24 A6** 66 30N 38 0 E
White Sulphur Springs, *Mont., U.S.A.* **82 C8** 46 33N 110 54W
White Sulphur Springs, *W. Va., U.S.A.* **76 G5** 37 48N 80 18W
White Swan, *U.S.A.* **84 D6** 46 23N 120 44W
Whitecliffs, *N.Z.* **59 K3** 43 26S 171 55 E
Whitecourt, *Canada* **72 C5** 54 10N 115 45W
Whiteface Mt., *U.S.A.* **79 B11** 44 22N 73 54W
Whitefield, *U.S.A.* **79 B13** 44 23N 71 37W
Whitefish, *U.S.A.* **82 B6** 48 25N 114 20W
Whitefish L., *Canada* **73 A7** 62 41N 106 48W
Whitefish Point, *U.S.A.* **76 B3** 46 45N 84 59W
Whitegull, L., *Canada* **71 A7** 55 27N 64 17W
Whitehall, *Mich., U.S.A.* **76 D2** 43 24N 86 21W
Whitehall, *Mont., U.S.A.* **82 D7** 45 52N 112 6W
Whitehall, *N.Y., U.S.A.* **79 C11** 43 33N 73 24W
Whitehall, *Wis., U.S.A.* **80 C9** 44 22N 91 19W
Whitehaven, *U.K.* **10 C4** 54 33N 3 35W
Whitehorse, *Canada* **72 A1** 60 43N 135 3W
Whitemark, *Australia* **62 G4** 40 7S 148 3 E
Whiteriver, *U.S.A.* **83 K9** 33 50N 109 58W
Whitesand →, *Canada* **72 A5** 60 9N 115 45W
Whitesands, *S. Africa* **56 E3** 34 23S 20 50 E
Whitesboro, *N.Y., U.S.A.* **79 C9** 43 7N 75 18W
Whitesboro, *Tex., U.S.A.* **81 J6** 33 39N 96 54W
Whiteshell Prov. Park, *Canada* **73 D9** 50 0N 95 40W
Whitesville, *U.S.A.* **78 D7** 42 2N 77 46W
Whiteville, *U.S.A.* **77 H6** 34 20N 78 42W
Whitewater, *U.S.A.* **76 D1** 42 50N 88 44W
Whitewater Baldy, *U.S.A.* **83 K9** 33 20N 108 39W
Whitewater L., *Canada* **70 B2** 50 50N 89 10W
Whitewood, *Australia* **62 C3** 21 28S 143 30 E
Whitewood, *Canada* **73 C8** 50 20N 102 20W
Whithorn, *U.K.* **12 G4** 54 44N 4 26W
Whitianga, *N.Z.* **59 G5** 36 47S 175 41 E
Whitman, *U.S.A.* **79 D14** 42 5N 70 56W
Whitney, *Canada* **78 A6** 45 31N 78 14W
Whitney, Mt., *U.S.A.* **84 J8** 36 35N 118 18W
Whitney Point, *U.S.A.* **79 D9** 42 20N 75 58W
Whitstable, *U.K.* **11 F9** 51 21N 1 3 E
Whitsunday I., *Australia* **62 C4** 20 15S 149 4 E
Whittier, *U.S.A.* **85 M8** 33 58N 118 3W
Whittlesea, *Australia* **63 F4** 37 27S 145 9 E
Wholdaia L., *Canada* **73 A8** 60 43N 104 20W
Whyalla, *Australia* **63 E2** 33 2S 137 30 E
Wiarton, *Canada* **78 B3** 44 40N 81 10W
Wiay, *U.K.* **12 D1** 57 24N 7 13W
Wibaux, *U.S.A.* **80 B2** 46 59N 104 11W
Wichian Buri, *Thailand* **38 E3** 15 39N 101 7 E
Wichita, *U.S.A.* **81 G6** 37 42N 97 20W
Wichita Falls, *U.S.A.* **81 J5** 33 54N 98 30W
Wick, *U.K.* **12 C5** 58 26N 3 5W
Wicked Pt., *Canada* **78 C7** 43 52N 77 15W
Wickenburg, *U.S.A.* **83 K7** 33 58N 112 44W
Wickepin, *Australia* **61 F2** 32 50S 117 30 E
Wickham, *Australia* **60 D2** 20 42S 117 11 E
Wickham, C., *Australia* **62 F3** 39 35S 143 57 E
Wickliffe, *U.S.A.* **78 E3** 41 36N 81 28W
Wicklow, *Ireland* **13 D5** 52 59N 6 3W
Wicklow □, *Ireland* **13 D5** 52 57N 6 25W
Wicklow Hd., *Ireland* **13 D6** 52 58N 6 0W
Wicklow Mts., *Ireland* **13 C5** 52 58N 6 26W
Widgeegoara Cr. →, *Australia* **63 D4** 28 51S 146 34 E
Widgiemooltha, *Australia* **61 F3** 31 30S 121 34 E
Widnes, *U.K.* **10 D5** 53 23N 2 45W
Wieluń, *Poland* **17 C10** 51 15N 18 34 E
Wlen, *Austria* **16 D9** 48 12N 16 22 E
Wiener Neustadt, *Austria* **16 E9** 47 49N 16 16 E
Wiesbaden, *Germany* **16 C5** 50 4N 8 14 E
Wigan, *U.K.* **10 D5** 53 33N 2 38W
Wiggins, *Colo., U.S.A.* **80 E2** 40 14N 104 4W
Wiggins, *Miss., U.S.A.* **81 K10** 30 51N 89 8W
Wight, I. of □, *U.K.* **11 G6** 50 40N 1 20W
Wigston, *U.K.* **11 E6** 52 35N 1 6W
Wigton, *U.K.* **10 C4** 54 50N 3 10W
Wigtown, *U.K.* **12 G4** 54 53N 4 27W
Wigtown B., *U.K.* **12 G4** 54 46N 4 15W
Wilber, *U.S.A.* **80 E6** 40 29N 96 58W
Wilberforce, *Canada* **78 A6** 45 2N 78 13W
Wilberforce, C., *Australia* **62 A2** 11 54S 136 35 E
Wilburton, *U.S.A.* **81 H7** 34 55N 95 19W
Wilcannia, *Australia* **63 E3** 31 30S 143 26 E
Wilcox, *U.S.A.* **78 E6** 41 35N 78 41W
Wildrose, *U.S.A.* **85 J9** 36 14N 117 11W
Wildspitze, *Austria* **16 E6** 46 53N 10 53 E
Wilge →, *S. Africa* **57 D4** 27 3S 28 20 E
Wilhelm II Coast, *Antarctica* **5 C7** 68 0S 90 0 E
Wilhelmshaven, *Germany* **16 B5** 53 31N 8 7 E
Wilhelmstal, *Namibia* **56 C2** 21 58S 16 21 E
Wilkes-Barre, *U.S.A.* **79 E9** 41 15N 75 53W
Wilkie, *Canada* **73 C7** 52 27N 108 42W
Wilkinsburg, *U.S.A.* **78 F5** 40 26N 79 53W
Wilkinson Lakes, *Australia* **61 E5** 29 40S 132 39 E
Willandra Creek →, *Australia* **63 E4** 33 22S 145 52 E
Willapa B., *U.S.A.* **82 C2** 46 40N 124 0W
Willapa Hills, *U.S.A.* **84 D3** 46 35N 123 25W
Willard, *N.Y., U.S.A.* **78 D8** 42 40N 76 50W
Willard, *Ohio, U.S.A.* **78 E2** 41 3N 82 44W
Willcox, *U.S.A.* **83 K9** 32 15N 109 50W
Willemstad, *Neth. Ant.* **89 D6** 12 5N 69 0W
Willet, *U.S.A.* **79 D9** 42 28N 75 55W
William →, *Canada* **73 B7** 59 8N 109 19W
William 'Bill' Dannely Res., *U.S.A.* **77 J2** 32 10N 87 10W
William Creek, *Australia* **63 D2** 28 58S 136 22 E
Williams, *Australia* **61 F2** 33 2S 116 52 E
Williams, *Ariz., U.S.A.* **83 J7** 35 15N 112 11W
Williams, *Calif., U.S.A.* **84 F4** 39 9N 122 9W
Williams Harbour, *Canada* **71 B8** 52 33N 55 47W
Williams Lake, *Canada* **72 C4** 52 10N 122 10W
Williamsburg, *Ky., U.S.A.* **77 G3** 36 44N 84 10W
Williamsburg, *Pa., U.S.A.* **78 F6** 40 28N 78 12W
Williamsburg, *Va., U.S.A.* **76 G7** 37 17N 76 44W
Williamson, *N.Y., U.S.A.* **78 C7** 43 14N 77 11W
Williamson, *W. Va., U.S.A.* **76 G4** 37 41N 82 17W
Williamsport, *U.S.A.* **78 E7** 41 15N 77 0W
Williamston, *U.S.A.* **77 H7** 35 51N 77 4W
Williamstown, *Australia* **63 F3** 37 51S 144 52 E
Williamstown, *Ky., U.S.A.* **76 F3** 38 38N 84 34W
Williamstown, *Mass., U.S.A.* **79 D11** 42 41N 73 12W
Williamstown, *N.Y., U.S.A.* **79 C9** 43 26N 75 53W
Willimantic, *U.S.A.* **79 E12** 41 43N 72 13W
Willingboro, *U.S.A.* **76 E8** 40 3N 74 54W
Willis Group, *Australia* **62 B5** 16 18S 150 0 E
Williston, *S. Africa* **56 E3** 31 20S 20 53 E
Williston, *Fla., U.S.A.* **77 L4** 29 23N 82 27W
Williston, *N. Dak., U.S.A.* **80 A3** 48 9N 103 37W
Williston L., *Canada* **72 B4** 56 0N 124 0W
Willits, *U.S.A.* **82 G2** 39 25N 123 21W
Willmar, *U.S.A.* **80 C7** 45 7N 95 3W
Willoughby, *U.S.A.* **78 E3** 41 39N 81 24W
Willow Bunch, *Canada* **73 D7** 49 20N 105 35W
Willow L., *Canada* **72 A5** 62 10N 119 8W
Willow Wall, The, *China* **35 C12** 42 10N 122 0 E
Willowick, *U.S.A.* **78 E3** 41 38N 81 28W
Willowlake →, *Canada* **72 A4** 62 42N 123 8W
Willowmore, *S. Africa* **56 E3** 33 15S 23 30 E
Willows, *U.S.A.* **84 F4** 39 31N 122 12W
Willowvale = Gatyana, *S. Africa* **57 E4** 32 16S 28 31 E
Wills, L., *Australia* **60 D4** 21 25S 128 51 E
Wills Cr. →, *Australia* **62 C3** 22 43S 140 2 E
Willsboro, *U.S.A.* **79 B11** 44 21N 73 24W
Willunga, *Australia* **63 F2** 35 15S 138 30 E
Wilmette, *U.S.A.* **76 D2** 42 5N 87 42W
Wilmington, *Australia* **63 E2** 32 39S 138 7 E
Wilmington, *Del., U.S.A.* **76 F8** 39 45N 75 33W
Wilmington, *N.C., U.S.A.* **77 H7** 34 14N 77 55W
Wilmington, *Ohio, U.S.A.* **76 F4** 39 27N 83 50W
Wilmington, *Vt., U.S.A.* **79 D12** 42 52N 72 52W
Wilmslow, *U.K.* **10 D5** 53 19N 2 13W
Wilpena Cr. →, *Australia* **63 E2** 31 25S 139 29 E
Wilsall, *U.S.A.* **82 D8** 45 59N 110 38W
Wilson, *N.C., U.S.A.* **77 H7** 35 44N 77 55W
Wilson, *N.Y., U.S.A.* **78 C6** 43 19N 78 50W
Wilson, *Pa., U.S.A.* **79 F9** 40 41N 75 15W
Wilson →, *Australia* **60 C4** 16 48S 128 16 E
Wilson Bluff, *Australia* **61 F4** 31 41S 129 0 E
Wilson Inlet, *Australia* **61 G2** 35 0S 117 22 E
Wilsons Promontory, *Australia* **63 F4** 38 55S 146 25 E
Wilton, *U.S.A.* **80 B4** 47 10N 100 47W
Wilton →, *Australia* **62 A1** 14 45S 134 33 E
Wiltshire □, *U.K.* **11 F6** 51 18N 1 53W
Wiltz, *Lux.* **15 E5** 49 57N 5 55 E
Wiluna, *Australia* **61 E3** 26 36S 120 14 E
Wimborne Minster, *U.K.* **11 G6** 50 48N 1 59W
Wimmera →, *Australia* **63 F3** 36 8S 141 56 E
Winam G., *Kenya* **54 C3** 0 20S 34 15 E
Winburg, *S. Africa* **56 D4** 28 30S 27 2 E
Winchendon, *U.S.A.* **79 D12** 42 41N 72 3W
Winchester, *U.K.* **11 F6** 51 4N 1 18W
Winchester, *Conn., U.S.A.* **79 E11** 41 53N 73 9W
Winchester, *Idaho, U.S.A.* **82 C5** 46 14N 116 38W
Winchester, *Ind., U.S.A.* **76 E3** 40 10N 84 59W
Winchester, *Ky., U.S.A.* **76 G3** 38 0N 84 11W
Winchester, *N.H., U.S.A.* **79 D12** 42 46N 72 23W
Winchester, *Nev., U.S.A.* **85 J11** 36 6N 115 10W
Winchester, *Tenn., U.S.A.* **77 H2** 35 11N 86 7W
Winchester, *Va., U.S.A.* **76 F6** 39 11N 78 10W
Wind →, *U.S.A.* **82 E9** 43 12N 108 12W
Wind River Range, *U.S.A.* **82 E9** 43 0N 109 30W
Windau = Ventspils, *Latvia* **9 H19** 57 25N 21 32 E
Windber, *U.S.A.* **78 F6** 40 14N 78 50W
Winder, *U.S.A.* **77 J4** 34 0N 83 45W
Windermere, *U.K.* **10 C5** 54 23N 2 55W
Windhoek, *Namibia* **56 C2** 22 35S 17 4 E
Windom, *U.S.A.* **80 D7** 43 52N 95 7W
Windorah, *Australia* **62 D3** 25 24S 142 36 E
Window Rock, *U.S.A.* **83 J9** 35 41N 109 3W
Windrush →, *U.K.* **11 F6** 51 43N 1 24W
Windsor, *Australia* **63 E5** 33 37S 150 50 E
Windsor, *N.S., Canada* **71 D7** 44 59N 64 5W
Windsor, *Ont., Canada* **78 D2** 42 18N 83 0W
Windsor, *U.K.* **11 F7** 51 29N 0 36W
Windsor, *Colo., U.S.A.* **80 E2** 40 29N 104 54W
Windsor, *Conn., U.S.A.* **79 E12** 41 50N 72 39W
Windsor, *Mo., U.S.A.* **80 F8** 38 32N 93 31W
Windsor, *N.Y., U.S.A.* **79 D9** 42 5N 75 37W
Windsor, *Vt., U.S.A.* **79 C12** 43 29N 72 24W
Windsor & Maidenhead □, *U.K.* **11 F7** 51 29N 0 40W
Windsorton, *S. Africa* **56 D3** 28 16S 24 44 E
Windward Is., *W. Indies* **89 D7** 13 0N 61 0W
Windward Passage = Vientos, Paso de los, *Caribbean* **89 C5** 20 0N 74 0W
Winefred L., *Canada* **73 B6** 55 30N 110 30W
Winfield, *U.S.A.* **81 G6** 37 15N 96 59W
Wingate Mts., *Australia* **60 B5** 14 25S 130 40 E
Wingham, *Australia* **63 E5** 31 48S 152 22 E
Wingham, *Canada* **78 C3** 43 55N 81 20W
Winisk, *Canada* **70 A2** 55 20N 85 15W
Winisk →, *Canada* **70 A2** 55 17N 85 5W
Winisk L., *Canada* **70 B2** 52 55N 87 22W
Wink, *U.S.A.* **81 K3** 31 45N 103 9W
Winkler, *Canada* **73 D9** 49 10N 97 56W
Winlock, *U.S.A.* **84 D4** 46 30N 122 56W
Winnebago, L., *U.S.A.* **76 D1** 44 0N 88 26W
Winnecke Cr. →, *Australia* **60 C5** 18 35S 131 34 E
Winnemucca, *U.S.A.* **82 F5** 40 58N 117 44W
Winnemucca L., *U.S.A.* **82 F4** 40 7N 119 21W
Winnett, *U.S.A.* **82 C9** 47 0N 108 21W
Winnfield, *U.S.A.* **81 K8** 31 56N 92 38W
Winnibigoshish, L., *U.S.A.* **80 B7** 47 27N 94 13W
Winnipeg, *Canada* **73 D9** 49 54N 97 9W
Winnipeg →, *Canada* **73 C9** 50 38N 96 19W
Winnipeg, L., *Canada* **73 C9** 52 0N 97 0W
Winnipeg Beach, *Canada* **73 C9** 50 30N 96 58W
Winnipegosis, *Canada* **73 C9** 51 39N 99 55W
Winnipegosis L., *Canada* **73 C9** 52 30N 100 0W
Winnipesaukee, L., *U.S.A.* **79 C13** 43 38N 71 21W
Winnisquam L., *U.S.A.* **79 C13** 43 33N 71 31W
Winnsboro, *La., U.S.A.* **81 J9** 32 10N 91 43W
Winnsboro, *S.C., U.S.A.* **77 H5** 34 23N 81 5W
Winnsboro, *Tex., U.S.A.* **81 J7** 32 58N 95 17W
Winokapau, L., *Canada* **71 B7** 53 15N 62 50W
Winona, *Minn., U.S.A.* **80 C9** 44 3N 91 39W
Winona, *Miss., U.S.A.* **81 J10** 33 29N 89 44W
Winooski, *U.S.A.* **79 B11** 44 29N 73 11W
Winooski →, *U.S.A.* **79 B11** 44 32N 73 17W
Winschoten, *Neths.* **15 A7** 53 9N 7 3 E
Winsford, *U.K.* **10 D5** 53 12N 2 31W
Winslow, *Ariz., U.S.A.* **83 J8** 35 2N 110 42W
Winslow, *Wash., U.S.A.* **84 C4** 47 38N 122 31W
Winsted, *U.S.A.* **79 E11** 41 55N 73 4W
Winston-Salem, *U.S.A.* **77 G5** 36 6N 80 15W
Winter Garden, *U.S.A.* **77 L5** 28 34N 81 35W
Winter Haven, *U.S.A.* **77 M5** 28 1N 81 44W
Winter Park, *U.S.A.* **77 L5** 28 36N 81 20W
Winterhaven, *U.S.A.* **85 N12** 32 47N 114 39W
Winters, *U.S.A.* **84 G5** 38 32N 121 58W
Wintersville, *U.S.A.* **78 F4** 40 23N 80 42W
Winterswijk, *Neths.* **15 C6** 51 58N 6 43 E
Winterthur, *Switz.* **18 C8** 47 30N 8 44 E
Winthrop, *U.S.A.* **82 B3** 48 28N 120 10W
Winton, *Australia* **62 C3** 22 24S 143 3 E
Winton, *N.Z.* **59 M2** 46 8S 168 20 E
Wirrulla, *Australia* **63 E1** 32 24S 134 31 E
Wisbech, *U.K.* **11 E8** 52 41N 0 9 E
Wisconsin □, *U.S.A.* **80 C10** 44 45N 89 30W
Wisconsin →, *U.S.A.* **80 D9** 43 0N 91 15W
Wisconsin Rapids, *U.S.A.* **80 C10** 44 23N 89 49W
Wisdom, *U.S.A.* **82 D7** 45 37N 113 27W
Wishaw, *U.K.* **12 F5** 55 46N 3 54W
Wishek, *U.S.A.* **80 B5** 46 16N 99 33W
Wisła →, *Poland* **17 A10** 54 22N 18 55 E
Wismar, *Germany* **16 B6** 53 54N 11 29 E
Wisner, *U.S.A.* **80 E6** 41 59N 96 55W
Witbank, *S. Africa* **57 D4** 25 51S 29 14 E
Witdraai, *S. Africa* **56 D3** 26 58S 20 48 E
Witham, *U.K.* **11 F8** 51 48N 0 40 E
Witham →, *U.K.* **10 E7** 52 59N 0 2W
Withernsea, *U.K.* **10 D8** 53 44N 0 1 E
Witney, *U.K.* **11 F6** 51 48N 1 28W
Witnossob →, *Namibia* **56 D3** 23 55S 18 45 E
Wittenberge, *Germany* **16 B6** 53 0N 11 45 E
Wittenoom, *Australia* **60 D2** 22 15S 118 20 E
Witvlei, *Namibia* **56 C2** 22 23S 18 32 E
Wkra →, *Poland* **17 B11** 52 27N 20 44 E
Wlingi, *Indonesia* **37 H15** 8 5S 112 25 E
Włocławek, *Poland* **17 B10** 52 40N 19 3 E
Włodawa, *Poland* **17 C12** 51 33N 23 31 E
Woburn, *U.S.A.* **79 D13** 42 29N 71 9W
Wodian, *China* **34 H7** 32 50N 112 35 E
Wodonga = Albury-Wodonga, *Australia* **63 F4** 36 3S 146 56 E
Wokam, *Indonesia* **37 F8** 5 45S 134 28 E
Woking, *U.K.* **11 F7** 51 19N 0 34W
Wokingham □, *U.K.* **11 F7** 51 25N 0 51W
Wolf →, *Canada* **72 A2** 60 17N 132 33W
Wolf Creek, *U.S.A.* **82 C7** 47 0N 112 4W
Wolf L., *Canada* **72 A2** 60 24N 131 40W
Wolf Point, *U.S.A.* **80 A2** 48 5N 105 39W
Wolfe I., *Canada* **79 B8** 44 7N 76 20W
Wolfeboro, *U.S.A.* **79 C13** 43 35N 71 13W
Wolfsberg, *Austria* **16 E8** 46 50N 14 52 E
Wolfsburg, *Germany* **16 B6** 52 25N 10 48 E
Wolin, *Poland* **16 B8** 53 50N 14 37 E
Wollaston, Is., *Chile* **96 H3** 55 40S 67 30W
Wollaston L., *Canada* **73 B8** 58 7N 103 10W
Wollaston Lake, *Canada* **73 B8** 58 3N 103 33W
Wollaston Pen., *Canada* **68 B8** 69 30N 115 0W
Wollongong, *Australia* **63 E5** 34 25S 150 54 E
Wolmaransstad, *S. Africa* **56 D4** 27 12S 25 59 E
Wolseley, *S. Africa* **56 E2** 33 26S 19 7 E
Wolsey, *U.S.A.* **80 C5** 44 24N 98 28W
Wolstenholme, C., *Canada* **66 C12** 62 35N 77 30W
Wolvega, *Neths.* **15 B6** 52 52N 6 0 E
Wolverhampton, *U.K.* **11 E5** 52 35N 2 7W
Wondai, *Australia* **63 D5** 26 20S 151 49 E
Wongalarroo L., *Australia* **63 E3** 31 32S 144 0 E
Wongan Hills, *Australia* **61 F2** 30 51S 116 37 E
Wŏnju, *S. Korea* **35 F14** 37 22N 127 58 E
Wonosari, *Indonesia* **37 G14** 7 58S 110 36 E
Wonosobo, *Indonesia* **37 G13** 7 22S 109 54 E
Wonowon, *Canada* **72 B4** 56 44N 121 48W
Wŏnsan, *N. Korea* **35 E14** 39 11N 127 27 E
Wonthaggi, *Australia* **63 F4** 38 37S 145 37 E
Wood Buffalo Nat. Park, *Canada* **72 B6** 59 0N 113 41W
Wood Is., *Australia* **60 C3** 16 24S 123 19 E
Wood L., *Canada* **73 B8** 55 17N 103 17W
Woodah I., *Australia* **62 A2** 13 27S 136 10 E
Woodbourne, *U.S.A.* **79 E10** 41 46N 74 36W
Woodbridge, *Canada* **78 C5** 43 47N 79 36W
Woodbridge, *U.K.* **11 E9** 52 6N 1 20 E
Woodburn, *U.S.A.* **82 D2** 45 9N 122 51W
Woodenbong, *Australia* **63 D5** 28 24S 152 39 E

Woodend, *Australia* 63 F3 37 20S 144 33 E
Woodford, *Australia* 63 D5 26 58S 152 47 E
Woodfords, *U.S.A.* 84 G7 38 47N 119 50W
Woodlake, *U.S.A.* 84 J7 36 25N 119 6W
Woodland, *Calif., U.S.A.* 84 G5 38 41N 121 46W
Woodland, *Maine, U.S.A.* 77 C12 45 9N 67 25W
Woodland, *Pa., U.S.A.* 78 F6 40 59N 78 21W
Woodland, *Wash., U.S.A.* 84 E4 45 54N 122 45W
Woodland Caribou Prov. Park, *Canada* 73 C10 51 0N 94 45W
Woodridge, *Canada* 73 D9 49 20N 96 9W
Woodroffe, Mt., *Australia* 61 E5 26 20S 131 45 E
Woods, L., *Australia* 62 B1 17 50S 133 30 E
Woods, L. of the, *Canada* 73 D10 49 15N 94 45W
Woodstock, *Australia* 62 B4 19 35S 146 50 E
Woodstock, *N.B., Canada* 71 C6 46 11N 67 37W
Woodstock, *Ont., Canada* 78 C4 43 10N 80 45W
Woodstock, *U.K.* 11 F6 51 51N 1 20W
Woodstock, *Ill., U.S.A.* 80 D10 42 19N 88 27W
Woodstock, *Vt., U.S.A.* 79 C12 43 37N 72 31W
Woodsville, *U.S.A.* 79 B13 44 9N 72 2W
Woodville, *N.Z.* 59 J5 40 20S 175 53 E
Woodville, *Miss., U.S.A.* 81 K9 31 6N 91 18W
Woodville, *Tex., U.S.A.* 81 K7 30 47N 94 25W
Woodward, *U.S.A.* 81 G5 36 26N 99 24W
Woody, *U.S.A.* 85 K8 35 42N 118 50W
Woody →, *Canada* 73 C8 52 31N 100 51W
Woolamai, C., *Australia* 63 F4 38 30S 145 23 E
Wooler, *U.K.* 10 B5 55 33N 2 1W
Woolgoolga, *Australia* 63 E5 30 6S 153 11 E
Woomera, *Australia* 63 E2 31 5S 136 50 E
Woonsocket, *R.I., U.S.A.* 79 E13 42 0N 71 31W
Woonsocket, *S. Dak., U.S.A.* 80 C5 44 3N 98 17W
Wooramel →, *Australia* 61 E1 25 47S 114 10 E
Wooramel Roadhouse, *Australia* 61 E1 25 45S 114 17 E
Wooster, *U.S.A.* 78 F3 40 48N 81 56W
Worcester, *S. Africa* 56 E2 33 39S 19 27 E
Worcester, *U.K.* 11 E5 52 11N 2 12W
Worcester, *Mass., U.S.A.* 79 D13 42 16N 71 48W
Worcester, *N.Y., U.S.A.* 79 D10 42 36N 74 45W
Worcestershire □, *U.K.* 11 E5 52 13N 2 10W
Workington, *U.K.* 10 C4 54 39N 3 33W
Worksop, *U.K.* 10 D6 53 18N 1 7W
Workum, *Neths.* 15 B5 52 59N 5 26 E
Worland, *U.S.A.* 82 D10 44 1N 107 57W
Worms, *Germany* 16 D5 49 37N 8 21 E
Worsley, *Canada* 72 B5 56 31N 119 8W
Wortham, *U.S.A.* 81 K6 31 47N 96 28W
Worthing, *U.K.* 11 G7 50 49N 0 21W
Worthington, *Minn., U.S.A.* 80 D7 43 37N 95 36W
Worthington, *Pa., U.S.A.* 78 F5 40 50N 79 38W
Wosi, *Indonesia* 37 E7 0 15S 128 0 E
Wou-han = Wuhan, *China* 33 C6 30 31N 114 18 E
Wousi = Wuxi, *China* 33 C7 31 33N 120 18 E
Wowoni, *Indonesia* 37 E6 4 5S 123 5 E
Wrangel I. = Vrangelya, Ostrov, *Russia* 27 B19 71 0N 180 0 E
Wrangell, *U.S.A.* 72 B2 56 28N 132 23W
Wrangell Mts., *U.S.A.* 68 B5 61 30N 142 0W
Wrath, C., *U.K.* 12 C3 58 38N 5 1W
Wray, *U.S.A.* 80 E3 40 5N 102 13W
Wrekin, The, *U.K.* 11 E5 52 41N 2 32W
Wrens, *U.S.A.* 77 J4 33 12N 82 23W
Wrexham, *U.K.* 10 D4 53 3N 3 0W
Wrexham □, *U.K.* 10 D5 53 1N 2 58W
Wright, *U.S.A.* 80 D2 43 47N 105 30W
Wright Pt., *Canada* 78 C3 43 48N 81 44W
Wrightson Mt., *U.S.A.* 83 L8 31 42N 110 51W
Wrightwood, *U.S.A.* 85 L9 34 21N 117 38W
Wrigley, *Canada* 68 B7 63 16N 123 37W
Wrocław, *Poland* 17 C9 51 5N 17 5 E
Września, *Poland* 17 B9 52 21N 17 36 E
Wu Jiang →, *China* 32 D5 29 40N 107 20 E
Wu'an, *China* 34 F8 36 40N 114 15 E
Wubin, *Australia* 61 F2 30 6S 116 37 E
Wubu, *China* 34 F6 37 28N 110 42 E
Wuchang, *China* 35 B14 44 55N 127 5 E
Wucheng, *China* 34 F9 37 12N 116 20 E
Wuchuan, *China* 34 D6 41 5N 111 28 E
Wudi, *China* 35 F9 37 40N 117 35 E
Wuding He →, *China* 34 F6 37 2N 110 23 E
Wudinna, *Australia* 63 E2 33 0S 135 22 E
Wudu, *China* 34 H3 33 22N 104 54 E
Wuhan, *China* 33 C6 30 31N 114 18 E
Wuhe, *China* 35 H9 33 10N 117 50 E
Wuhsi = Wuxi, *China* 33 C7 31 33N 120 18 E
Wuhu, *China* 33 C6 31 22N 118 21 E
Wukari, *Nigeria* 50 G7 7 51N 9 42 E
Wulajie, *China* 35 B14 44 6N 126 33 E
Wulanbulang, *China* 34 D6 41 5N 110 55 E
Wular L., *India* 43 B6 34 20N 74 30 E
Wulian, *China* 35 G10 35 40N 119 12 E
Wuliaru, *Indonesia* 37 F8 7 27S 131 0 E
Wuluk'omushih Ling, *China* 32 C3 36 25N 87 25 E
Wulumuchi = Ürümqi, *China* 26 E9 43 45N 87 45 E
Wundowie, *Australia* 61 F2 31 47S 116 23 E
Wunnummin L., *Canada* 70 B2 52 55N 89 10W
Wuntho, *Burma* 41 H19 23 55N 95 45 E
Wuppertal, *Germany* 16 C4 51 16N 7 12 E
Wuppertal, *S. Africa* 56 E2 32 13S 19 12 E
Wuqing, *China* 35 E9 39 23N 117 4 E
Wurtsboro, *U.S.A.* 79 E10 41 35N 74 29W
Würzburg, *Germany* 16 D5 49 46N 9 55 E
Wushan, *China* 34 G3 34 43N 104 53 E
Wusuli Jiang = Ussuri →, *Asia* 30 A7 48 27N 135 0 E
Wutai, *China* 34 E7 38 40N 113 12 E
Wuting = Huimin, *China* 35 F9 37 27N 117 28 E
Wutonghaolai, *China* 35 C11 42 50N 120 5 E
Wutongqiao, *China* 32 D5 29 22N 103 50 E
Wuwei, *China* 32 C5 37 57N 102 34 E
Wuxi, *China* 33 C7 31 33N 120 18 E
Wuxiang, *China* 34 F7 36 49N 112 50 E
Wuyang, *China* 34 H7 33 25N 113 35 E
Wuyi, *China* 34 F8 37 46N 115 56 E
Wuyi Shan, *China* 33 D6 27 0N 117 0 E
Wuyuan, *China* 34 D5 41 2N 108 20 E
Wuzhai, *China* 34 E6 38 54N 111 48 E
Wuzhi Shan, *China* 38 C7 18 45N 109 45 E
Wuzhong, *China* 34 E4 38 2N 106 12 E
Wuzhou, *China* 33 D6 23 30N 111 18 E
Wyaaba Cr. →, *Australia* 62 B3 16 27S 141 35 E
Wyalkatchem, *Australia* 61 F2 31 8S 117 22 E
Wyalusing, *U.S.A.* 79 E8 41 40N 76 16W
Wyandotte, *U.S.A.* 76 D4 42 12N 83 9W
Wyandra, *Australia* 63 D4 27 12S 145 56 E
Wyangala, L., *Australia* 63 E4 33 54S 149 0 E
Wyara, L., *Australia* 63 D3 28 42S 144 14 E
Wycheproof, *Australia* 63 F3 36 5S 143 17 E
Wye →, *U.K.* 11 F5 51 38N 2 40W
Wyemandoo, *Australia* 61 E2 28 28S 118 29 E
Wymondham, *U.K.* 11 E9 52 35N 1 7 E
Wymore, *U.S.A.* 80 E6 40 7N 96 40W
Wyndham, *Australia* 60 C4 15 33S 128 3 E
Wyndham, *N.Z.* 59 M2 46 20S 168 51 E
Wynne, *U.S.A.* 81 H9 35 14N 90 47W
Wynyard, *Australia* 62 G4 41 5S 145 44 E
Wynyard, *Canada* 73 C8 51 45N 104 10W
Wyola L., *Australia* 61 E5 29 8S 130 17 E
Wyoming, *Canada* 78 D2 42 57N 82 7W
Wyoming □, *U.S.A.* 82 E10 43 0N 107 30W
Wyomissing, *U.S.A.* 79 F9 40 20N 75 59W
Wyong, *Australia* 63 E5 33 14S 151 24 E
Wytheville, *U.S.A.* 76 G5 36 57N 81 5W

X

Xaçmaz, *Azerbaijan* 25 F8 41 31N 48 42 E
Xai-Xai, *Mozam.* 57 D5 25 6S 33 31 E
Xainza, *China* 32 C3 30 58N 88 35 E
Xangongo, *Angola* 56 B2 16 45S 15 5 E
Xankändi, *Azerbaijan* 25 G8 39 52N 46 49 E
Xánthi, *Greece* 21 D11 41 10N 24 58 E
Xanxerê, *Brazil* 95 B5 26 53S 52 23W
Xapuri, *Brazil* 92 F5 10 35S 68 35W
Xar Moron He →, *China* 35 C11 43 25N 120 35 E
Xàtiva, *Spain* 19 C5 38 59N 0 32W
Xau, L., *Botswana* 56 C3 21 15S 24 44 E
Xavantina, *Brazil* 95 A5 21 15S 52 48W
Xenia, *U.S.A.* 76 F4 39 41N 83 56W
Xeropotamos →, *Cyprus* 23 E11 34 42N 32 33 E
Xhora, *S. Africa* 57 E4 31 55S 28 38 E
Xhumo, *Botswana* 56 C3 21 7S 24 35 E
Xi Jiang →, *China* 33 D6 22 5N 113 20 E
Xi Xian, *China* 34 F6 36 41N 110 58 E
Xia Xian, *China* 34 G6 35 8N 111 12 E
Xiachengzi, *China* 35 B16 44 40N 130 18 E
Xiaguan, *China* 32 D5 25 32N 100 16 E
Xiajin, *China* 34 F9 36 56N 116 0 E
Xiamen, *China* 33 D6 24 25N 118 4 E
Xi'an, *China* 34 G5 34 15N 109 0 E
Xian Xian, *China* 34 E9 38 12N 116 6 E
Xiang Jiang →, *China* 33 D6 28 55N 112 50 E
Xiangcheng, *Henan, China* 34 H8 33 29N 114 52 E
Xiangcheng, *Henan, China* 34 H7 33 50N 113 27 E
Xiangfan, *China* 33 C6 32 2N 112 8 E
Xianggang = Hong Kong □, *China* 33 D6 22 11N 114 14 E
Xianghuang Qi, *China* 34 C7 42 2N 113 50 E
Xiangning, *China* 34 G6 35 58N 110 50 E
Xiangquan, *China* 34 F7 36 30N 113 1 E
Xiangquan He = Sutlej →, *Pakistan* 42 E4 29 23N 71 3 E
Xiangshui, *China* 35 G10 34 12N 119 33 E
Xiangtan, *China* 33 D6 27 51N 112 54 E
Xianyang, *China* 34 G5 34 20N 108 40 E
Xiao Hinggan Ling, *China* 33 B7 49 0N 127 0 E
Xiao Xian, *China* 34 G9 34 15N 116 55 E
Xiaoyi, *China* 34 F6 37 8N 111 48 E
Xiawa, *China* 35 C11 42 35N 120 38 E
Xiayi, *China* 34 G9 34 15N 116 10 E
Xichang, *China* 32 D5 27 51N 102 19 E
Xichuan, *China* 34 H6 33 0N 111 30 E
Xieng Khouang, *Laos* 38 C4 19 17N 103 25 E
Xifei He →, *China* 34 H9 32 45N 116 40 E
Xifeng, *Gansu, China* 34 G4 35 40N 107 40 E
Xifeng, *Liaoning, China* 35 C13 42 42N 124 45 E
Xifengzhen = Xifeng, *China* 34 G4 35 40N 107 40 E
Xigazê, *China* 32 D3 29 5N 88 45 E
Xihe, *China* 34 G3 34 2N 105 20 E
Xihua, *China* 34 H8 33 45N 114 30 E
Xiliao He →, *China* 35 C12 43 32N 123 35 E
Ximana, *Mozam.* 55 F3 19 24S 33 58 E
Xin Xian = Xinzhou, *China* 34 E7 38 22N 112 46 E
Xinavane, *Mozam.* 57 D5 25 2S 32 47 E
Xinbin, *China* 35 D13 41 40N 125 2 E
Xing Xian, *China* 34 E6 38 27N 111 7 E
Xing'an, *China* 33 D6 25 38N 110 40 E
Xingcheng, *China* 35 D11 40 40N 120 45 E
Xinghe, *China* 34 D7 40 55N 113 55 E
Xinghua, *China* 35 H10 32 58N 119 48 E
Xinglong, *China* 35 D9 40 25N 117 30 E
Xingping, *China* 34 G5 34 20N 108 28 E
Xingtai, *China* 34 F8 37 3N 114 32 E
Xingu →, *Brazil* 93 D8 1 30S 51 53W
Xingyang, *China* 34 G7 34 45N 112 52 E
Xinhe, *China* 34 F8 37 30N 115 15 E
Xining, *China* 32 C5 36 34N 101 40 E
Xinjiang, *China* 34 G6 35 34N 111 11 E
Xinjiang Uygur Zizhiqu □, *China* 32 C3 42 0N 86 0 E
Xinjin = Pulandian, *China* 35 E11 39 25N 121 58 E
Xinkai He →, *China* 35 C12 43 32N 123 35 E
Xinle, *China* 34 E8 38 25N 114 40 E
Xinlitun, *China* 35 D12 42 0N 122 8 E
Xinmin, *China* 35 D12 41 59N 122 50 E
Xintai, *China* 35 G9 35 55N 117 45 E
Xinxiang, *China* 34 G7 35 18N 113 50 E
Xinzhan, *China* 35 C14 43 50N 127 18 E
Xinzheng, *China* 34 G7 34 20N 113 45 E
Xinzhou, *China* 34 E7 38 22N 112 46 E
Xiongyuecheng, *China* 35 D12 40 12N 122 5 E
Xiping, *Henan, China* 34 H8 33 22N 114 5 E
Xiping, *Henan, China* 34 H6 33 25N 111 8 E
Xique-Xique, *Brazil* 93 F10 10 50S 42 40W
Xisha Qundao = Paracel Is., *S. China Sea* 36 A4 15 50N 112 0 E
Xiuyan, *China* 35 D12 40 18N 123 11 E
Xixabangma Feng, *China* 41 E14 28 20N 85 40 E
Xixia, *China* 34 H6 33 25N 111 29 E
Xixiang, *China* 34 H4 33 0N 107 44 E
Xiyang, *China* 34 F7 37 38N 113 38 E
Xizang Zizhiqu □, *China* 32 C3 32 0N 88 0 E
Xlendi, *Malta* 23 C1 36 1N 14 12 E
Xuan Loc, *Vietnam* 39 G6 10 56N 107 14 E
Xuanhua, *China* 34 D8 40 40N 115 2 E
Xuchang, *China* 34 G7 34 2N 113 48 E
Xun Xian, *China* 34 G8 35 42N 114 33 E
Xunyang, *China* 34 H5 32 48N 109 22 E
Xunyi, *China* 34 G5 35 8N 108 20 E
Xúquer →, *Spain* 19 C5 39 5N 0 10W
Xushui, *China* 34 E8 39 2N 115 40 E
Xuyen Moc, *Vietnam* 39 G6 10 34N 107 25 E
Xuzhou, *China* 35 G9 34 18N 117 10 E
Xylophagou, *Cyprus* 23 E12 34 54N 33 51 E

Y

Ya Xian, *China* 38 C7 18 14N 109 29 E
Yaamba, *Australia* 62 C5 23 8S 150 22 E
Yaapeet, *Australia* 63 F3 35 45S 142 3 E
Yablonovy Ra. = Yablonovyy Khrebet, *Russia* 27 D12 53 0N 114 0 E
Yablonovyy Khrebet, *Russia* 27 D12 53 0N 114 0 E
Yabrai Shan, *China* 34 E2 39 40N 103 0 E
Yabrūd, *Syria* 47 B5 33 58N 36 39 E
Yacheng, *China* 33 E5 18 22N 109 6 E
Yacuiba, *Bolivia* 94 A3 22 0S 63 43W
Yacuma →, *Bolivia* 92 F5 13 38S 65 23W
Yadgir, *India* 40 L10 16 45N 77 5 E
Yadkin →, *U.S.A.* 77 H5 35 29N 80 9W
Yaeyama-Rettō, *Japan* 31 M1 24 30N 123 40 E
Yagodnoye, *Russia* 27 C15 62 33N 149 40 E
Yahila, *Dem. Rep. of the Congo* 54 B1 0 13N 24 28 E
Yahk, *Canada* 72 D5 49 6N 116 10W
Yahuma, *Dem. Rep. of the Congo* 52 D4 1 0N 23 10 E
Yaita, *Japan* 31 F9 36 48N 139 56 E
Yaiza, *Canary Is.* 22 F6 28 57N 13 46W
Yakima, *U.S.A.* 82 C3 46 36N 120 31W
Yakima →, *U.S.A.* 82 C3 47 0N 120 30W
Yakobi I., *U.S.A.* 72 B1 58 0N 136 30W
Yakovlevka, *Russia* 30 B6 44 26N 133 28 E
Yaku-Shima, *Japan* 31 J5 30 20N 130 30 E
Yakumo, *Japan* 30 C10 42 15N 140 16 E
Yakutat, *U.S.A.* 68 C6 59 33N 139 44W
Yakutia = Sakha □, *Russia* 27 C13 66 0N 130 0 E
Yakutsk, *Russia* 27 C13 62 5N 129 50 E
Yala, *Thailand* 39 J3 6 33N 101 18 E
Yale, *U.S.A.* 78 C2 43 8N 82 48W
Yalgoo, *Australia* 61 E2 28 16S 116 39 E
Yalinga, *C.A.R.* 52 C4 6 33N 23 10 E
Yalkubul, Punta, *Mexico* 87 C7 21 32N 88 37W
Yalleroi, *Australia* 62 C4 24 3S 145 42 E
Yalobusha →, *U.S.A.* 81 J9 33 33N 90 10W
Yalong Jiang →, *China* 32 D5 26 40N 101 55 E
Yalova, *Turkey* 21 D13 40 41N 29 15 E
Yalta, *Ukraine* 25 F5 44 30N 34 10 E
Yalu Jiang →, *China* 35 E13 40 0N 124 22 E
Yam Ha Melah = Dead Sea, *Asia* 47 D4 31 30N 35 30 E
Yam Kinneret, *Israel* 47 C4 32 45N 35 35 E
Yamada, *Japan* 31 H5 33 33N 130 49 E
Yamagata, *Japan* 30 E10 38 15N 140 15 E
Yamagata □, *Japan* 30 E10 38 30N 140 0 E
Yamaguchi, *Japan* 31 G5 34 10N 131 32 E
Yamaguchi □, *Japan* 31 G5 34 20N 131 40 E
Yamal, Poluostrov, *Russia* 26 B8 71 0N 70 0 E
Yamal Pen. = Yamal, Poluostrov, *Russia* 26 B8 71 0N 70 0 E
Yamanashi □, *Japan* 31 G9 35 40N 138 40 E
Yamantau, Gora, *Russia* 24 D10 54 15N 58 6 E
Yamba, *Australia* 63 D5 29 26S 153 23 E
Yambarran Ra., *Australia* 60 C5 15 10S 130 25 E
Yâmbiô, *Sudan* 51 H11 4 35N 28 16 E
Yambol, *Bulgaria* 21 C12 42 30N 26 30 E
Yamdena, *Indonesia* 37 F8 7 45S 131 20 E
Yame, *Japan* 31 H5 33 13N 130 35 E
Yamethin, *Burma* 41 J20 20 29N 96 18 E
Yamma-Yamma, L., *Australia* 63 D3 26 16S 141 20 E
Yamoussoukro, *Ivory C.* 50 G4 6 49N 5 17W
Yampa →, *U.S.A.* 82 F9 40 32N 108 59W
Yampi Sd., *Australia* 60 C3 16 8S 123 38 E
Yampil, *Moldova* 17 D15 48 15N 28 15 E
Yampol = Yampil, *Moldova* 17 D15 48 15N 28 15 E
Yamuna →, *India* 43 G9 25 30N 81 53 E
Yamunanagar, *India* 42 D7 30 7N 77 17 E
Yamzho Yumco, *China* 32 D4 28 48N 90 35 E
Yana →, *Russia* 27 B14 71 30N 136 0 E
Yanagawa, *Japan* 31 H5 33 10N 130 24 E
Yanai, *Japan* 31 H6 33 58N 132 7 E
Yan'an, *China* 34 F5 36 35N 109 26 E
Yanaul, *Russia* 24 C10 56 25N 55 0 E
Yanbu 'al Baḥr, *Si. Arabia* 46 C2 24 0N 38 5 E
Yanchang, *China* 34 F6 36 43N 110 1 E
Yancheng, *Henan, China* 34 H8 33 35N 114 0 E
Yancheng, *Jiangsu, China* 35 H11 33 23N 120 8 E
Yanchep Beach, *Australia* 61 F2 31 33S 115 37 E
Yanchi, *China* 34 F4 37 48N 107 20 E
Yanchuan, *China* 34 F6 36 51N 110 10 E
Yanco Cr. →, *Australia* 63 F4 35 14S 145 35 E
Yandoon, *Burma* 41 L19 17 0N 95 40 E
Yang Xian, *China* 34 H4 33 15N 107 30 E
Yangambi, *Dem. Rep. of the Congo* 54 B1 0 47N 24 24 E
Yangcheng, *China* 34 G7 35 28N 112 22 E
Yangch'ü = Taiyuan, *China* 34 F7 37 52N 112 33 E
Yanggao, *China* 34 D7 40 21N 113 55 E
Yanggu, *China* 34 F8 36 8N 115 43 E
Yangliuqing, *China* 35 E9 39 2N 117 5 E
Yangon = Rangoon, *Burma* 41 L20 16 45N 96 20 E
Yangpingguan, *China* 34 H4 32 58N 106 5 E
Yangquan, *China* 34 F7 37 58N 113 31 E
Yangtse = Chang Jiang →, *China* 33 C7 31 48N 121 10 E
Yangtze Kiang = Chang Jiang →, *China* 33 C7 31 48N 121 10 E
Yangyang, *S. Korea* 35 E15 38 4N 128 38 E
Yangyuan, *China* 34 D8 40 1N 114 10 E
Yangzhou, *China* 33 C6 32 21N 119 26 E
Yanji, *China* 35 C15 42 59N 129 30 E
Yankton, *U.S.A.* 80 D6 42 53N 97 23W
Yanonge, *Dem. Rep. of the Congo* 54 B1 0 35N 24 38 E
Yanqi, *China* 32 B3 42 5N 86 35 E
Yanqing, *China* 34 D8 40 30N 115 58 E
Yanshan, *China* 35 E9 38 4N 117 22 E
Yanshou, *China* 35 B15 45 28N 128 22 E
Yantabulla, *Australia* 63 D4 29 21S 145 0 E
Yantai, *China* 35 F11 37 34N 121 22 E
Yanzhou, *China* 34 G9 35 35N 116 49 E
Yao Xian, *China* 34 G5 34 55N 108 59 E
Yao Yai, Ko, *Thailand* 39 J2 8 0N 98 35 E
Yaoundé, *Cameroon* 52 D2 3 50N 11 35 E
Yaowan, *China* 35 G10 34 15N 118 3 E
Yap I., *Pac. Oc.* 64 G5 9 30N 138 10 E
Yapen, *Indonesia* 37 E9 1 50S 136 0 E
Yapen, Selat, *Indonesia* 37 E9 1 20S 136 10 E
Yapero, *Indonesia* 37 E9 4 59S 137 11 E
Yappar →, *Australia* 62 B3 18 22S 141 16 E
Yaqui →, *Mexico* 86 B2 27 37N 110 39W
Yar-Sale, *Russia* 26 C8 66 50N 70 50 E
Yaraka, *Australia* 62 C3 24 53S 144 3 E
Yaransk, *Russia* 24 C8 57 22N 47 49 E
Yare →, *U.K.* 11 E9 52 35N 1 38 E
Yaremcha, *Ukraine* 17 D13 48 27N 24 33 E
Yarensk, *Russia* 24 B8 62 11N 49 15 E
Yarí →, *Colombia* 92 D4 0 20S 72 20W
Yarkand = Shache, *China* 32 C2 38 20N 77 10 E
Yarker, *Canada* 79 B8 44 23N 76 46W
Yarkhun →, *Pakistan* 43 A5 36 17N 72 30 E
Yarmouth, *Canada* 71 D6 43 50N 66 7W
Yarmūk →, *Syria* 47 C4 32 42N 35 40 E
Yaroslavl, *Russia* 24 C6 57 35N 39 55 E
Yarqa, W. →, *Egypt* 47 F2 30 0N 33 49 E
Yarra Yarra Lakes, *Australia* 61 E2 29 40S 115 45 E
Yarram, *Australia* 63 F4 38 29S 146 39 E
Yarraman, *Australia* 63 D5 26 50S 152 0 E
Yarras, *Australia* 63 E5 31 25S 152 20 E
Yartsevo, *Russia* 27 C10 60 20N 90 0 E
Yarumal, *Colombia* 92 B3 6 58N 75 24W
Yasawa Group, *Fiji* 59 C7 17 0S 177 23 E
Yaselda, *Belarus* 17 B14 52 7N 26 28 E
Yasin, *Pakistan* 43 A5 36 24N 73 23 E
Yasinski, L., *Canada* 70 B4 53 16N 77 35W
Yasinya, *Ukraine* 17 D13 48 16N 24 21 E
Yasothon, *Thailand* 38 E5 15 50N 104 10 E
Yass, *Australia* 63 E4 34 49S 148 54 E
Yāsūj, *Iran* 45 D6 30 31N 51 31 E
Yatağan, *Turkey* 21 F13 37 20N 28 10 E
Yates Center, *U.S.A.* 81 G7 37 53N 95 44W
Yathkyed L., *Canada* 73 A9 62 40N 98 0W
Yatsushiro, *Japan* 31 H5 32 30N 130 40 E
Yatta Plateau, *Kenya* 54 C4 2 0S 38 0 E
Yavari →, *Peru* 92 D4 4 21S 70 2W
Yávaros, *Mexico* 86 B3 26 42N 109 31W
Yavatmal, *India* 40 J11 20 20N 78 15 E
Yavne, *Israel* 47 D3 31 52N 34 45 E
Yavoriv, *Ukraine* 17 D12 49 55N 23 20 E
Yavorov = Yavoriv, *Ukraine* 17 D12 49 55N 23 20 E
Yawatahama, *Japan* 31 H6 33 27N 132 24 E
Yazd, *Iran* 45 D7 31 55N 54 27 E
Yazd □, *Iran* 45 D7 32 0N 55 0 E
Yazd-e Khvāst, *Iran* 45 D7 31 31N 52 7 E
Yazman, *Pakistan* 42 E4 29 8N 71 45 E
Yazoo →, *U.S.A.* 81 J9 32 22N 90 54W
Yazoo City, *U.S.A.* 81 J9 32 51N 90 25W
Yding Skovhøj, *Denmark* 9 J13 55 59N 9 46 E
Ye Xian = Laizhou, *China* 35 F10 37 8N 119 57 E
Ye Xian, *China* 34 H7 33 35N 113 25 E
Yebyu, *Burma* 38 E2 14 15N 98 13 E
Yechŏn, *S. Korea* 35 F15 36 39N 128 27 E
Yecla, *Spain* 19 C5 38 35N 1 5W
Yécora, *Mexico* 86 B3 28 20N 108 58W
Yedintsy = Edineţ, *Moldova* 17 D14 48 9N 27 18 E
Yegros, *Paraguay* 94 B4 26 20S 56 25W
Yehuda, Midbar, *Israel* 47 D4 31 35N 35 15 E
Yei, *Sudan* 51 H12 4 9N 30 40 E
Yekaterinburg, *Russia* 26 D7 56 50N 60 30 E
Yekaterinodar = Krasnodar, *Russia* 25 E6 45 5N 39 0 E
Yelarbon, *Australia* 63 D5 28 33S 150 38 E
Yelets, *Russia* 24 D6 52 40N 38 30 E
Yelizavetgrad = Kirovohrad, *Ukraine* 25 E5 48 35N 32 20 E
Yell, *U.K.* 12 A7 60 35N 1 5W
Yell Sd., *U.K.* 12 A7 60 33N 1 15W
Yellow Sea, *China* 35 G12 35 0N 123 0 E
Yellowhead Pass, *Canada* 72 C5 52 53N 118 25W
Yellowknife, *Canada* 72 A6 62 27N 114 29W
Yellowknife →, *Canada* 72 A6 62 31N 114 19W
Yellowstone →, *U.S.A.* 80 B3 47 59N 103 59W
Yellowstone L., *U.S.A.* 82 D8 44 27N 110 22W
Yellowstone Nat. Park, *U.S.A.* 82 D9 44 40N 110 30W
Yelsk, *Belarus* 17 C15 51 50N 29 10 E
Yemen ■, *Asia* 46 E3 15 0N 44 0 E
Yen Bai, *Vietnam* 38 B5 21 42N 104 52 E
Yenangyaung, *Burma* 41 J19 20 30N 95 0 E
Yenbo = Yanbu 'al Baḥr, *Si. Arabia* 46 C2 24 0N 38 5 E
Yenda, *Australia* 63 E4 34 13S 146 14 E
Yenice, *Turkey* 21 E12 39 55N 27 17 E
Yenisey →, *Russia* 26 B9 71 50N 82 40 E
Yeniseysk, *Russia* 27 D10 58 27N 92 13 E
Yeniseyskiy Zaliv, *Russia* 26 B9 72 20N 81 0 E
Yennádhi, *Greece* 23 C9 36 2N 27 56 E
Yenyuka, *Russia* 27 D13 57 57N 121 15 E
Yeo →, *U.K.* 11 G5 51 2N 2 49W
Yeo, L., *Australia* 61 E3 28 0S 124 30 E
Yeo I., *Canada* 78 A3 45 24N 81 48W
Yeola, *India* 40 J9 20 2N 74 30 E
Yeoryioúpolis, *Greece* 23 D6 35 20N 24 15 E
Yeovil, *U.K.* 11 G5 50 57N 2 38W
Yeppoon, *Australia* 62 C5 23 5S 150 47 E
Yerbent, *Turkmenistan* 26 F6 39 30N 58 50 E
Yerbogachen, *Russia* 27 C11 61 16N 108 0 E
Yerevan, *Armenia* 25 F7 40 10N 44 31 E
Yerington, *U.S.A.* 82 G4 38 59N 119 10W
Yermak, *Kazakstan* 26 D8 52 2N 76 55 E
Yermo, *U.S.A.* 85 L10 34 54N 116 50W
Yerólakkos, *Cyprus* 23 D12 35 11N 33 15 E
Yeropol, *Russia* 27 C17 65 15N 168 40 E
Yeropótamos →, *Greece* 23 D6 35 3N 24 50 E
Yeroskipos, *Cyprus* 23 E11 34 46N 32 28 E
Yershov, *Russia* 25 D8 51 23N 48 27 E
Yerushalayim = Jerusalem, *Israel* 47 D4 31 47N 35 10 E
Yes Tor, *U.K.* 11 G4 50 41N 4 0W
Yesan, *S. Korea* 35 F14 36 41N 126 51 E
Yeso, *U.S.A.* 81 H2 34 26N 104 37W
Yessey, *Russia* 27 C11 68 29N 102 10 E
Yetman, *Australia* 63 D5 28 56S 150 48 E

Z